Child Development

Its Nature and Course

Child Development

Its Nature and Course

Third Edition

L. ALAN SROUFE
University of Minnesota

ROBERT G. COOPER
San Jose State University

GANIE B. DeHART
State University of New York at Geneseo

MARY E. MARSHALL

Advisory Editor
URIE BRONFENBRENNER
Cornell University

McGRAW-HILL, INC.
New York St. Louis San Francisco Auckland Bogotá Caracas
Lisbon London Madrid Mexico City Milan Montreal
New Delhi San Juan Singapore Sydney Tokyo Toronto

CHILD DEVELOPMENT
Its Nature and Course

Credits and Acknowledgments appear on pages
655–659, and on this page by reference.

This book is printed on acid-free paper.

3 4 5 6 7 8 9 0   DOW   DOW   9 0 9 8

ISBN 0-07-060570-X

This book was set in New Baskerville
by The Clarinda Company.
The editors were Cecilia Gardner, Jane Vaicunas, and
James R. Belser; the designer was Joan E. O'Connor;
the production supervisor was Louise Karam.
The photo editor was Inge King.
R. R. Donnelley & Sons Company was printer and
binder.

Cover photo: © Jeffry W. Myers, Stock/Boston

Library of Congress Cataloging-in-Publication Data

Sroufe, L. Alan.
  Child development: its nature and course / L. Alan Sroufe, Robert
G. Cooper, Ganie B. DeHart; Mary E. Marshall [reviser]; advisory
editor, Urie Bronfenbrenner.—3rd ed.
     p.   cm.
  Includes bibliographical references and indexes.
  ISBN 0-07-060570-X
  1. Child development.   2. Child psychology.   3. Adolescence.
I. Cooper, Robert G.   II. DeHart, Ganie,   III. Title
HQ767.9.S725   1996
305.23′ 1—dc20   95-12636

About the Authors

L. Alan Sroufe is William Harris Professor of Child Psychology at the Institute of Child Development, University of Minnesota (and professor of psychiatry, University of Minnesota Medical School). He has taught undergraduate child psychology classes for 27 years and is internationally recognized as an expert on attachment, emotional development, and developmental psychopathology, having published three books and more than 90 articles on these and related topics in psychology, child development, and psychiatry journals. Dr. Sroufe graduated with highest honors from Whittier College in 1963 and received his Ph.D. from the University of Wisconsin in 1967. From 1984 to 1985, he was a fellow at the Center for Advanced Study in the Behavioral Sciences at Stanford. He has been consulting editor or associate editor for numerous journals, including *Developmental Psychology, Infant Behavior and Development, Child Development, Development and Psychopathology,* and *Psychiatry.*

Robert G. Cooper is professor of psychology at San Jose State University. He has taught undergraduate and graduate classes in developmental psychology and cognitive development for two decades. His professional career has focused on issues in the development of cognitive skills that are particularly relevant in educational settings. His major research in the area of cognitive development, which has been supported by NIMH and NIE, concerns the development of mathematical concepts. Dr. Cooper graduated cum laude from Pomona College in 1968 and received his Ph.D. from the University of Minnesota in 1973. He has published numerous articles, contributed chapters to several books, and has been a consulting editor for numerous journals, including *Developmental Psychology, Cognitive Development,* and *Child Development.*

Ganie B. DeHart is assistant professor of psychology at the State University of New York at Geneseo. She has taught undergraduate courses in child and adolescent development, atypical development, applied developmental psychology, and cross-cultural psychology. Her research interests lie at the intersection of language, cognitive, and social development, especially the roles played by family and school as contexts for children's development. Her publications and conference presentations are in the areas of preschool language development and sibling interaction. Dr. DeHart graduated summa cum laude from Brigham Young University in 1972, received an M.S. in education of exceptional children from The Johns Hopkins University in 1980, and received a Ph.D. from the Institute of Child Development at the University of Minnesota in 1990.

To June
LAS

To Don Faust,
my teacher and friend
RGC

and
To Jim
GBD

Contents in Brief

Contents

Advisor's Foreword

URIE BRONFENBRENNER

This is an unusual developmental text, for it accomplishes that rare, dual feat of translating science into life, and life into science. The achievement is no accident. As the authors note in their preface, their work represents the fulfillment of a dream to produce a new kind of textbook in child development—one that would illuminate contemporary knowledge in developmental science by making it manifest in human lives.

And that is exactly what this book has done. It is first and foremost an excellent textbook—solid in its science, comprehensive in its coverage, and remarkably balanced in its treatment of controversial issues. But the book's most distinctive feature is the way in which these riches are conveyed. For this textbook also tells a story—three stories, in fact. It begins with the anticipated birth of three rather different children in three rather different families, each living in three rather different everyday worlds. The authors then trace the psychological development of the three children, and also their parents, as the families move through time and space.

This view of development as a process of progressive interaction between an active, growing organism and its environment constitutes the second hallmark of this somewhat unusual text. When this volume was first conceived, the aim was to produce a textbook that would reflect the significant advances taking place in research on human development. These advances are the result of a convergence in theory and research design that involves a threefold focus: 1) a view of the child as a dynamic agent that not only responds to but actively interprets, shapes, and even creates its own environment and development; 2) an expansion of the research process beyond the laboratory into the real-life settings, and broader social contexts, in which children live and grow; 3) a conception of development as the progressive reorganization of psychological functioning in which cognitive, emotional, and social processes are treated not as separate domains but as interrelated aspects of a complex living being in an equally complex world.

In preparing the new edition of their outstanding text, the authors have accomplished a difficult feat—surpassing the already excellent. Moreover, they have done so not merely in the conventional way of updating research. Rather, in keeping with the exciting developmental principles that inform the book as a whole, they have aspired to, and achieved, a new level of integration that keeps pace with current dynamic trends in both science and society. Beyond the new facts, the book introduces the reader to new ways of thinking in such areas as prenatal development, linguistics, psychopathology, cognition, issues of gender, peer relationships, and cultural differences—in each instance pointing up implications for policy, practice, and—especially—everyday life. The result is to enhance still further the distinctive quality that has won the respect and affection of both teachers and students—a text that combines the best in science with the best in story-telling.

Preface

Several years ago at a meeting of the Society for Research in Child Development, a group of developmental psychologists was convened to discuss the kind of textbook that was needed for the child development course. Despite the diversity of perspectives represented by the group (Urie Bronfenbrenner, Shirley Feldman, Tiffany Field, Marion Gindes, Scott Paris, and Alan Sroufe), there was notable agreement that certain key developmental ideas were not well represented in existing texts. In particular, the systematic and integrated nature of development, the mutual influences of child and context, and the way previous development influences current development seemed not to be fully conveyed. It was felt that these ideas were well established in the field but had proved difficult to build into a textbook. Facts often are easier to present than principles, and facets of development are easier to convey than the nature of development itself.

Beyond the belief that a child development text organized around coherent principles could and should be written, the working group believed that instructors shouldn't have to choose either a text that was authoritative *or* a text that was readable and engaging. A multifaceted view of development and a solid treatment of research and theory can be presented effectively to undergraduates by organizing material around a core set of themes within a chronological format and by presenting the material in a way that captivates the students. To do so, this text introduces three families and follows them throughout the book. These families, which are fictionalized composites of research case histories, serve as a device to illustrate graphically the role of context, the systematic interplay between child and environment, and the coherence of development. The families provide a way of showing how various influences come together to determine both normative development and individual development. They let us bring life to the complex facts, research findings, and theories about child development. They also help students develop a clear understanding of the concepts of causality, continuity, and change.

The book is organized around principles and themes of development, which are reinforced continually in different ways. The developmental principles under consideration are order, continuity, and directionality. The major themes highlighted are the role of context, the issue of continuity versus change, the interplay between social/experiential and cognitive and/or maturational aspects of development, and the contrast between individual and normative development. These principles and themes provide a framework for the presentation of the facts and theories of developmental psychology and a means of unifying the disparate aspects of development.

FEATURES OF THIS BOOK

This thematic orientation inspired a number of features in the book. First we adopted a chronological format. This seemed to be the most suitable way to illustrate the orderly, organic, and integrated nature of development and to underscore our other themes and principles. Like other chronological texts, this one has cognitive and social/emotional chapters within units that cover particular developmental periods. There also are several unique chapters.

In Part One, there is a distinctive chapter (2) on contexts, which not only brings together information about the various levels and kinds of influence on the developing child (e.g., the roles of biological factors, family influence, and culture) but sets the stage for considering the interaction of child and environment throughout the text. There is a separate two-chapter section on toddlerhood (Part Three), which spans the transition from infancy to childhood. The last chapter (15), on developmental psychopathology, focuses on abnormal behavior as developmental deviation. Not only is this chapter fascinating to students, it is also a vehicle for reinforcing the relationships among the major themes in the text and for once again relating material on normative development, individual development, and context to the experiences of the three families. Preceding each chronological unit is a vignette about our three families; these vignettes introduce the basic issues for each developmental period and carry themes forward from section to section. Each unit concludes with an epilogue, in which cognitive and social aspects are interwoven and in which the family stories and the research are brought together.

FAMILY VIGNETTES

Our family vignettes begin with the conception of three children, each in a different set of circumstances. One child is born into a white working-class family where there are two daughters and a son is strongly desired. The second child is born to a teenager abandoned by her boyfriend, and rejected by her own single mother. The third child is an unplanned but welcome addition to an inner-city, extended black family. The families represent a moderate degree of diversity; for example, none of the children is handicapped and none of the families is from a third world culture. With such a strategy we thought we could illustrate the subtlety as well as the dramatic influence of context and yet keep the stories maximally relevant to students.

Although the family stories are fictionalized, they are drawn from our experience studying hundreds of families longitudinally and conducting research with countless subjects from early infancy through childhood. Our black family was the result of further collaboration with Diana Slaughter and her students at Northwestern University, who developed the characters, scenes, and dialogue as part of a graduate seminar entitled "Developmental Tasks of the Black Child in Urban America." Our families are abstractions from real families grappling with the range of developmental and life issues. Their life stories are drawn from and are consistent with developmental research. The capacities of the children and the issues they are facing at each age are those reported in the literature. Likewise, the contextual influences on individual lives are based on research; for example, the son in one of our families reacts differently than his sisters to their parents' marital breakup—a pattern suggested by the literature on gender differences in the impact of divorce.

As a teaching device the family vignettes serve several purposes. Reading these engaging stories, students will begin to understand major developmental issues, themes, and achievements for a given period. The stories also help make connections between developmental periods, both in normative terms and in terms of individual children.

Perhaps the major content contribution of the vignettes is to convey a systems perspective to students. The concept of a system is hard to explain, but it can be illustrated. The stories will give students a feel for the direct and indirect influence of context on children, the influences of each child's particular developmental history, and the roles of the children in creating their own environments. Child, family, and larger environment adapt to each other in an ongoing process. The text chapters underscore these ideas through the more traditional research and theory presentation, but students will see the workings of systems in the family stories.

Once students have read the vignettes, the content chapters on research and theory will be both more understandable and more relevant to them. The research questions and methods will make sense, and students will be able to see more coherence in the total body of research. The goal is for our questions to be their questions; that is, the presentation of the families should raise the very questions that contemporary researchers are pursuing.

EPILOGUES

The family vignettes were written to convey important themes and critical issues. Then the cognitive and social/emotional chapters in each unit present contemporary research in the context of those themes and issues. Finally, integrative unit summaries, called "Epilogues," explicitly tie together this material. The epilogues summarize major achievements of the period across domains, review key themes, and apply research findings to the three families' experiences. Not only does an integrated picture of the child emerge, in a way that students will remember, but cutting-edge issues in the field are also made understandable. The themes of continuity and change and the interplay between child and environment are reworked throughout the book.

ABOUT THE THIRD EDITION

We believe that a new edition should be a new edition. While you will find the same thematic structure in this new edition and the same emphasis on going beyond isolated facts about children's capacities to an understanding of the nature of development itself, you will also find that every chapter has been revised to reflect current research and emerging trends.

Since the publication of the second edition there has been an outpouring of research on cultural and subcultural diversity in development, early cognitive skills in infants and preschoolers, and the child's theory of mind. There has also been an explosion of information in the areas of prenatal teratogens, peer relationships in middle childhood, parent–adolescent relationships, gender concept development, and gender differences in development. In addition, important efforts are under way both to apply major research findings in cognitive development (e.g., new work on memory and scripts) to issues in social development and to understand the social context of cognitive development. There is also very new work on the interaction of postnatal brain development and experience and the consequences of this interaction for emotional regulation. Emotional development itself is a very active area of current research. You will find all these new developments amply covered in this edition, along with other changes which reflect extensive surveying of both students and faculty.

This edition also features material on applications of research in the form of a series of new boxes, which appear in Chapters 4–14. Our box material has been carefully selected to underscore important research themes and to illustrate how research findings may be applied to pressing societal issues, such as infants in institutions and intergang conflict.

We hope you will find that this new edition gives you what you expect from a contemporary child development textbook, but also something more. When you look at theoretical coverage you will find information-processing perspectives as well as Piaget's views; cognitive social learning theory and Bowlby's attachment theory as well as traditional learning and psychoanalytic theories. You will find traditional topics such as sex-role development and conservation along with newer topics such as inner working models, scaffolding, and scripts. You will find very contemporary material on day care, stress, family conflict, and prenatal teratogens such as AIDS. But beyond this, we hope you will find that we have told a coherent story of the unfolding of development.

A number of people helped make this a high-quality third edition. Mary Marshall helped us with the entire revision. As usual, she did an outstanding job. We would also like to acknowledge the superb efforts of Sherry-Muret Wagstaff and Susan Berry, Department of Pediatrics, University of Minnesota Medical School, who made major contributions to Chapter 3.

In addition, we would like to thank the members of the McGraw-Hill team who were consistently supportive and responsive. First and foremost, we are grateful to Jane Vaicunas, who was not only our editor but our advocate, and to Cecilia Gardner, developmental editor, who worked closely with us every step of the way. Your support was invaluable. We also thank the other members of the McGraw-Hill team who gave us at all times fully competent, professional assistance: Beth Kaufman, associate editor; James Belser, editing supervisor; Inge King, our talented photo researcher; and Suzanne Thibodeau, director of editing and development, who consulted with us throughout the project. It was great to be a part of this team.

SUPPLEMENTS

A complete supplements package is available to instructors and students using *Child Development*, 3d edition. Each component of the package has been thoroughly revised and updated.

Study Guide by Ganie DeHart, State University of New York at Geneseo. For each chapter of the text, the Study Guide provides learning objectives, a chapter summary, review questions, self-tests, and essay questions with suggested answers. A special *How to Study preface* outlines how students can integrate the Study Guide into an overall study program.

Instructor's Manual by Dana Gross, St. Olaf College. This outstanding Instructor's Manual includes learning objectives, chapter summaries, suggested lecture topics with related references, discussion topics and activities, and an updated, comprehensive film and video list.

Test Bank by Thomas Moye, Coe College. The Test Bank includes a balanced mix of factual and conceptual multiple-choice items. Computerized versions of the Test Bank are available for IBM-compatible and Macintosh PCs.

The supplements package for *Child Development* also includes an impressive set of four-color overhead transparencies and special videos.

REVIEWERS

Finally, we wish to thank the thoughtful reviewers who helped us improve the chapters in this edition:

Martha A. Arterberry, *Gettysburg College*
Julia M. Braungart-Rieker, *University of Notre Dame*
Brenda Bryant, *University of California, Davis*
William S. Cassel, *Boise State University*
Lawrence Clark, *Southeast Missouri State University*
David Conner, *Northeast Missouri State University*
Eric De Vos, *Saginaw Valley State University*
Joan Downs, *Governor's State University*
Paul M. Fromson, *Elon College*
Harvey Ginsburg, *Southwest Texas State University*
Virginia A. Marchman, *University of Wisconsin, Madison*
Ella Mauriello, *Salem State College*
Richard Metzger, *University of Tennessee, Chattanooga*
Mary Mindess, *Lesley College*
John J. Mitchell, *University of Alberta*
Catherine Murray, *St. Joseph's University*
Dennis R. Papini, *Western Illinois University*
Colin Pitblado, *Teikyo Post University*
Suzanne Prescott, *Governor's State University*
Andrew G. Renouf, *University of Pittsburgh*
Jane A. Rysberg, *California State University, Chico*
Connie Schimmel, *Millsaps College*
Laura R. Thompson, *Midlands Technical College*
David Uttal, *Northwestern University*
Ruth L. Wynn, *Syracuse University*

L. Alan Sroufe
Robert G. Cooper
Ganie B. DeHart

Child Development

Its Nature

and Course

Chapter 1

The Nature of Development

This book is about an important part of human development, the period from conception through adolescence. These are the years when a remarkable transformation takes place. A single fertilized egg cell, smaller than the period at the end of this sentence, grows first into a human infant, and then, through successive phases of childhood, into a young adult. How this fascinating set of changes occurs is what you are about to study. You will learn about the unfolding of many general human capacities, such as the abilities to speak and reason, to feel a variety of emotions, and to form enduring interpersonal relationships. You will also learn about the origins of individual differences in intellectual abilities, emotional responses, and styles of social interaction.

Like other psychology textbooks, this one seeks not only to describe human behavior but also to explain it. In doing so, we adopt a *developmental perspective*, a view that enables you to see how particular behaviors emerge in children, how they change in predictable ways over time, and what forms they are apt to take in the future. As a result, such behaviors begin to make more sense. We see them not as isolated happenings, but rather as part of a developmental sequence. For instance, when you know that a 1-year-old will soon acquire language, the child's pointing and gesturing become more meaningful. Pointing, gesturing, and speaking are linked to one another in the progressive development of communication. Thus, knowing the developmental phase that the child will soon enter provides a perspective for understanding where the child is right now. Similarly, knowing a child's individual developmental history also makes current behavior more understandable.

In this chapter we introduce you to the concept of development and explore some of the major ideas about how development occurs. We begin by looking at several characteristics of development: qualitative change, behavioral reorganization, and an orderly, cumulative, directional nature. We also explain the difference between normative and individual development. Next, we present a framework for understanding the factors that shape the course of development. Here we consider the interplay of genetic potentials, past development, and current environmental conditions. Then we discuss some theories proposed to explain why children behave and think differently at different ages, and why different children the same age do not all act the same. Finally, we discuss the methods that developmental psychologists use to study children and to collect data that can be used to understand the developmental process.

THE CONCEPT OF DEVELOPMENT

WHAT DOES DEVELOPMENT ENTAIL?

The mother of 6-month-old Mikey puts one end of a cloth in her mouth and dangles the other end in front of her baby, shaking her head from side to side. Mikey grows still and watches the cloth intently, a fixed expression on his face. Soberly, he reaches for it and pulls it away from his mother. Still without a smile, he puts part of the cloth in his own mouth and begins to explore it with his tongue.

In the same situation another child, 10-month-old Meryl, behaves quite dif-

4

ferently. She watches with rapt attention as her mother dangles the cloth. Glancing back and forth between the cloth and her mother's face, she smiles and starts to laugh. Gleefully, she grabs the cloth away. Then, laughing even harder, she tries to stuff the cloth back into her mother's mouth.

What explains the remarkable difference between these two babies? You might think that Meryl, through practicing this game, has learned skills for playing it that Mikey doesn't yet have. Certainly learning plays some role here, but if you were to play the game over and over with a 6-month-old, the practice would lead to boredom, not laughter. So perhaps the different reactions stem from individual differences in temperament. Maybe Meryl has a sunny disposition and would have laughed at the game at age 6 months, whereas Mikey is a serious child who would not laugh even if older. Although this explanation seems plausible when you look at only two children, it is not adequate. If you were to repeat the experiment with many babies of different dispositions, both boys and girls, you would find that Mikey and Meryl are typical of their ages. It is almost impossible to get *any* 6-month-old to laugh using this procedure, whereas most 10-month-olds will at least smile. Yet 6-month-olds already have many of the major capacities needed to respond that 10-month-olds do. They recognize their mother as distinct from other people; they laugh in certain situations, such as being tickled; and they have the physical coordination to replace the cloth in their mother's mouth. Nevertheless, their reactions differ sharply from those of 10-month-olds. We are still left with the question of why.

A developmental perspective can provide an explanation (e.g., Glick, 1992; Kitchener, 1983). Developmental psychologists look at how the child at one age unfolds through a series of transformations, or **qualitative changes,** to become the child at a later age. Six- and 10-month-old babies are qualitatively different. Compared with Mikey, 10-month-old Meryl is vastly more capable; she is in a different league. Mikey does not even seem aware of the connection between the cloth and his mother. It is as if his mother recedes into the background as the cloth captures his attention. He pulls the cloth out of her mouth just as he would pull on any other object to get it. He sees no game in this at all. Meryl, in contrast, can consider both the cloth and her mother at the same time, and she responds to the relationship between them. She can remember her mother without the cloth and recognize that her mother with the cloth is discrepant from what her mother is usually like. She also knows that she can recreate the incongruity by stuffing the cloth back in her mother's mouth. She laughs because she remembers each previous state and anticipates the outcome of her actions. Far more than Mikey, she has a sense of past and future. She also understands that people and objects have permanence. They are not really altered by simple changes in appearance. Mother without the cloth is still there in mother with the cloth.

The 6-month-old, of course, is busy acquiring the experiences that, with further maturation, will allow the 10-month-old's capacities to emerge. Links exist between the two ages. A 6-month-old can also "remember" and "anticipate," but these capabilities are primitive compared with those of a 10-month-old. Although both 6-month-olds and 10-month-olds are active learners, 10-month-olds can learn things of greater complexity because of their greater ability to process information and their generally greater understanding of the world.

Closely related to the concept of qualitative change is the concept of **behavioral reorganization.** Meryl not only has more capacities than 6-month-old Mikey, she also has a new way of *organizing* her thoughts and actions, of using

A 10-month old can enjoy a game of putting a cloth in his mother's mouth because he understands the relation between the cloth and his mother, and he anticipates the outcome of his actions.

Qualitative change: A developmental change involving a transformation, rather than simply an increase of a physical or cognitive ability.

Behavioral reorganization: A developing child's qualitatively new way of fitting together, or organizing, and using his or her capabilities.

her capabilities and fitting them together. It is because she can coordinate her memories, actions, and anticipations that she laughs at the game. The successive reorganization of thoughts and actions that occurs as children mature allows them to engage in increasingly complex behaviors.

The concepts of qualitative change and behavioral reorganization, both central to development, may become clearer if you think about how they apply to other areas of life. Consider an accounting company in which all work has traditionally been done using hand-held calculators. For a while the firm grows simply by adding new accountants, each of whom does the same thing (*quantitative* change). But then computers are installed. This new technology produces dramatic *qualitative* change. Not only is the firm able to handle vastly more accounts, but tasks are now performed in very different ways. Specialization occurs: some employees work on writing computer programs; others focus on inputting data; still others concentrate on interpreting the output. A more elaborate organizational hierarchy evolves. Knowledge from the old system is used in the new one, but it is now part of a totally *different organization*. So it seems to be with human development.

Qualitative change and behavioral reorganization are evident throughout development. Consider the parents who repeatedly tell their 8-year-old not to leave the tap water running because it wastes a valuable resource. The message at this age often seems to fall on deaf ears. But, to the parents' surprise, the same child comes home from school a few years later and begins to lecture them on the necessity of water conservation with all the fervor of an evangelist. This new ability to grasp the significance of an issue is part of a fundamentally new perspective on the world and the future. Eight-year-olds may learn concrete rules like "turn off the water tap," but adolescents have a broader sense of the human community and a far greater capacity to project their lives into the future. Nevertheless, 8-year-olds are learning many things about the world that allow these later, more abstract understandings to emerge. At each age the capacities and experiences of the younger child prepare the way for the development of new, more complex abilities.

Putting together all the concepts we have mentioned in this section, we can summarize what development entails: **development** involves age-related, qualitative changes and behavioral reorganizations that are orderly, cumulative, and directional (Gottlieb, 1991; Waters and Sroufe, 1983). By *orderly* we mean that the changes follow a logical sequence, with each one paving the way for future changes and making sense in the light of what went before. By *cumulative* we mean that any given phase includes all that went before it as well as something more (just as baking a mixture of flour, sugar, eggs, baking powder and salt retains these ingredients in the final product but also creates something more—cake). And by *directional* we mean that development always moves toward greater complexity. These orderly, cumulative, and directional changes and reorganizations are a central focus of this book.

NORMATIVE AND INDIVIDUAL DEVELOPMENT

Part of what you will be studying as you read this book is **normative development,** the general changes and reorganizations in behavior that virtually all children share as they grow older. (*Normative* means typical or average.) Describing, understanding, and explaining normative changes are major concerns of developmental psychologists. To many developmentalists, however, **individual devel-**

Development:
The process of orderly, cumulative, directional, and age-related behavioral reorganizations and qualitative changes in a person.

Normative development:
The general changes and reorganization in behavior that virtually all children share as they grow older.

Individual development:
The variations around the average, or normative, course of development seen in individual persons; the individual differences in personality and expertise that each person aquires.

Each child is unique and will reach developmental milestones at his or her own rate. Children may be advanced in some areas, somewhat delayed in others. Some children may be more adventuresome, others more cautious.

opment is equally important. Individual development refers to the fact that each individual develops in some ways differently from every other.

Individual differences in development are of two kinds. One kind involves individual variations around the normative course of developing various abilities. If you were to chart the progress of 100 children from birth through adolescence, you would find many differences in when and how they reach developmental milestones, such as walking, talking, counting to 10, playing cooperatively with another child, and so forth. This is why we can state only *average* ages at which various abilities emerge. For instance, when we say that 22-month-olds recognize their reflections in a mirror, we give that age only as an average one. Sometimes this ability emerges later, even in normal healthy children, while occasionally it can be seen as early as 15 months. There is always a range of variation in human development. Children with the chromosomal defect that causes Down syndrome do not smile at the cloth-in-the-mouth game until their second year and do not recognize themselves in a mirror until about age 2½ years (Mans, Cicchetti, and Sroufe, 1978). They progress toward these achievements in the same way as other children, only at a slower pace. In sum, this first aspect of individual differences refers to variations with regard to the common human developmental achievements.

A second kind of individual development involves different developmental pathways. Progress along these different paths produces differences in *personality,* such as being outgoing rather than shy or preferring high-risk activities to low-risk ones, as well as differences in skills and knowledge, or *expertise*. These individual differences tend to be stable and continuous. For example, an exuberant and confident 2-year-old is less likely to end up hesitant and withdrawn three years later than is a 2-year-old with a more negative developmental history (Arend, Grove, and Sroufe, 1979). Even when dramatic changes in individual personality do take place, logical reasons can generally be found. Just as normative development is coherent and predictable, so too is individual development.

Developmental psychologists have offered a variety of explanations for this continuity of individual differences. Some have focused on inborn characteristics. Others have looked at specific experiences, such as the kind of child-rearing techniques the parents use. Still others have focused on overall characteristics of the child's environment, such as the family's income level. Finally, many developmentalists have recently begun to focus on the differences in developmental pathways among different cultures. The effects of these different contexts on development are the focus of Chapter 2, and they form one of the central themes of this text: the course of development is constrained by the contexts within which it occurs.

A FRAMEWORK FOR UNDERSTANDING DEVELOPMENT

A fundamental challenge facing developmentalists is to explain how and why developmental changes come about. From the broadest perspective, development depends on three factors: (1) developmental potentials provided by the organism's genes; (2) the organism's developmental history; and (3) current environmental conditions. The first two factors may be thought of as existing "in the organism." Every human child carries a set of genes that contains the basic guidelines for the unfolding of development (see Chapters 2 and 3). But which genes are "turned on," or are in operation, depends on the particular point in development a child has reached, that is, on the changes that have gone before. Moreover, the unfolding also depends on current environmental support. Current support includes all of the nutrients, inputs, circumstances, and challenges the developing organism encounters. Somehow, all three influences—genetic potentials, past development, and current environmental circumstances—account for the dramatic process we call development, whereby from just two cells evolves an individual who is capable of reading and understanding this textbook. Understanding how genes, past development, and current environmental conditions interact to produce developmental changes is a major task for the field of developmental psychology.

ORIGINS OF THE FRAMEWORK: EVOLUTIONARY THEORY

Important clues concerning how this interaction works are found in the evolutionary theory of Charles Darwin (1809–1882). Darwin, who is considered the father of the theory of evolution, was one of the most influential scientists to ponder developmental influences. Although his theory of evolution is not a theory of child development, it *is* a theory of the development and adaptation of species. As such, it is a useful starting point for thinking about how development of any kind takes place.

Darwin was a naturalist who wanted a scientific explanation for the diversity of living things on earth and for their ability to exist in all kinds of environments. His careful observations of plants and animals led to one of the most important insights in all of science: the idea that any given species is *equipped for survival and reproduction* in its particular environment. For example, lizards on two different islands have different colors that precisely match the colors of the local rocks and vegetation. Darwin wondered how these adaptations came about. His answer was the concept of **natural selection,** the process by which individuals with traits that help them survive in a particular setting are most likely to live long enough to reproduce and pass those advantageous traits on to their young. As a result, the advantageous traits become increasingly common

Natural selection: The process by which individuals with traits that help them survive in a particular setting are most likely to live long enough to reproduce and pass those advantageous traits on to their young.

Charles Darwin with his eldest son.

in each generation, until eventually the traits are very widespread. Suppose, for example, that when sea currents carry lizards to a new island most of them are too dark to blend in with the sandy soil there and they are easily spotted by predators. Among the lizards that survive the longest are many that are slightly lighter in color. These lizards pass the genes for lighter color on to their young. In the next generation, therefore, lighter-colored lizards increase in number. So it goes, generation after generation, until eventually the lizards on this island are predominantly light-colored—a survival advantage in this particular setting. If this process of adaptation to a new environment occurs regarding other characteristics too, a new subspecies of lizard could evolve. Because the earth has so many different environments, and because there is also substantial genetic diversity, natural selection has been able to produce a huge number of species. We call this development of species *evolution*.

The details of Darwin's theory have been criticized, especially assumptions that evolutionary change must always be so gradual and that there has been a single line of evolution from the lowest life form to humans (Gould, 1989). Nonetheless, his view that the evolution of species is based on an interaction of genes and environment is widely accepted today. You can see how our three-factor model of human development derives from it. Darwin argued that species development depends, on the one hand, on what already exists (the organism's evolutionary history and its set of genes) and, on the other hand, on the potentially changing environment in which the organism lives. Similarly, human development, in our model, is also the product of genes, developmental history, and current environmental conditions.

Evolutionary theory is important to the study of child development in other ways as well. It helps to focus attention on the genetically based inclinations and

Each animal has unique adaptive capacities. The cheetah is blessed with great speed. The porcupine has a particular protective device. The katydid blends well with the vegetation that surrounds it.

abilities that have helped our species survive. These include a group-living nature and propensity to form social ties, an ability to create complex systems of communication, a motivation to explore and discover, and an exceptional capacity to learn, reason, and solve problems. These are key areas to consider in the study of child development. At the same time, successful development depends on how good the "fit" is between a child's inclinations and his or her particular environment. A baby may have a built-in propensity to form relationships with others, but others must be regularly available to the infant in order for strong social bonds to develop. Similarly, a child may have a built-in motivation to explore and discover, but if few things are available to look at or handle, the motivation will go largely unused. This suggests the importance of assessing the adequacy of a child's environment. The environment must be responsive to and supportive of the child's predispositions and capacities.

OTHER VIEWS ON HEREDITY AND ENVIRONMENT

Even before Darwin's groundbreaking work, people speculated on the roles of heredity and environment in shaping human development. They were not concerned with the evolution of the human species, but rather with how individuals develop as they do. For example, the old saying "As the twig is bent, the tree's inclined" suggests that early environmental forces are critical, while the saying "The apple never falls far from the tree" stresses genetic traits inherited from parents.

Two views from recent centuries have been quite influential. Seventeenth-century English philosopher John Locke saw the human infant as a *tabula rasa,* a totally blank slate to be written on by life's experiences. Children, in Locke's view, are neither good nor bad by nature. They become what they become because of their environments. If parents raise their children properly, according to Locke, the children will develop into responsible members of society. Today, traces of Locke's ideas can be seen in theories that stress the importance of rewards, punishments, and other learning experiences in shaping the way children act.

Shortly after Locke died, a French philosopher was born whose ideas helped establish a different point of view. Jean Jacques Rousseau believed that human development unfolds naturally in very positive ways as long as society allows it to do so. Parents, Rousseau argued, need not shape their children forcibly. They merely have to let human development take its natural course. In this century, Rousseau's idea of a natural unfolding of development has appealed to those who focus on inherited potentials in children and to those who stress general patterns of development that virtually all children share (so-called normative patterns). Arnold Gesell, who during the 1920s and 1930s conducted research at Yale University on children's physical and motor development, is probably the best known of those who have focused on normative patterns. Gesell's view was that these patterns unfold naturally with maturation. A current outgrowth of Rousseau's thinking is seen in the work of those who stress the child's natural tendency to comply with the wishes of parents who have raised them in a nurturant way (e.g., Ainsworth, Bell, and Stayton, 1974).

Discussion of how heredity and environment influence development continues to this day. While some researchers focus more on heredity (e.g., Plomin, 1989; Scarr and McCartney, 1983), and others more on environment (e.g., Wachs, 1991), all agree that both work together in guiding how people develop (Wachs and Plomin, 1991). There are countless examples of this constant interaction of heredity and environment. For instance, having a biological parent who has suffered clinical depression predicts depression in children to a modest degree, even when the children were raised in adoptive homes. This suggests a genetic influence. However, the number of foster care placements before permanent adoption also predicts depression. This suggests an environmental influence. Most important, the two influences together predict depression far better than either alone (Cadoret et al., 1990). Environmental influences, in other words, work hand in hand with genetic ones. Both genes and environment are always involved in development.

Rousseau believed that "primitive peoples," living in the "natural state," are intrinsically good. It is civilization, he thought, that brings out undesirable characteristics in people.

Identical twins, especially those reared apart, have been of great interest to researchers seeking to understand the role of genetic inheritance in individual development and behavior. The physiological responses of such individuals, for example, are often quite similar.

Similarities and differences between siblings also illustrate the complex interplay between heredity and environment. Identical twins, even those reared apart, are more similar than fraternal twins or non-twin siblings in such characteristics as verbal ability and shyness (Plomin, 1989; Waller et al., 1990). This suggests the importance of genetic factors, since identical twins have all their genes in common (see Chapter 3). However, other siblings share on average half their genes, yet they are as different in social and emotional characteristics as unrelated children (Hoffman, 1991; Plomin and Daniels, 1987). This finding suggests an important role for environment. Perhaps the presence of a sibling (an environmental factor) leads children to assert their individuality and develop distinct personalities; or families with more than one child may treat the children very differently, exaggerating their differences; or both. Even identical twins are treated differently by parents, and such differential treatment seems to influence later behavior. In one study, the identical twin who reported having been treated more critically by the parents in childhood was more often unhappy and depressed as an adult (Baker and Daniels, 1990).

Our own view of heredity and environment is that it is not fruitful to try to determine which is more important. Each is essential. Without genetic guidelines there can be no development, and without environmental support, development cannot proceed either. To illustrate the critical influence of both genes and environment, plus the influence of past development, consider this example from the prenatal period. What happens if at an early stage in the development of a chick embryo, a piece of tissue is surgically removed from the base of a bud that will grow into a leg and placed at the tip of a bud that will grow into a wing? The transplanted tissue goes on to develop into a normal-looking wing tip. Apparently, chemical signals in the wing bud tell the genes in the transplanted leg bud tissue to direct that tissue's development into wing instead of leg. But if this same procedure is done much later in the embryo's development, the leg tissue will not be incorporated normally into the wing. It is now too late for the new context to alter the course of development. Chemical signals in the leg bud have already triggered genes there to start the tissue differentiating into part of a thigh. What if the transplant is done at an intermediate stage, when the tissue is already "committed" to becoming leg, but not yet fully committed to becoming thigh? Amazingly, the result is a clawlike structure at the end of the wing! In other words, at this stage the tissue carries instructions to become leg tissue but no final instructions to become thigh. The new context can induce the tissue to become a tip, but only the tip of a leg. What develops depends on genes, environment, and past development. The genetic makeup ensures that the tissue will become part of a chicken. (It can never become a fin, for example.) Genes and developmental history combine to determine that it will be a chick *leg* part. The current context induces it to be a tip. The tissue becomes the tip of a chicken leg, a claw.

Although this experiment was done with chick embryos for ethical reasons, the same principles apply to both prenatal and postnatal human development. In Chapter 4 you will discover that the development of *binocular vision* (that is, the brain's integration of information received from two eyes) depends on appropriate visual experience occurring at the appropriate time. If it does not occur at the correct time, the part of the brain that would have been used to interpret binocular vision is put to other uses. In fact, brain development itself mirrors the general developmental picture presented in this book. Genetic information constrains how the brain develops, but much of its ultimate organization is a consequence of experience. Furthermore, brain development does not occur just by the addition of new parts or functions as the brain matures; rather, an increasingly complex organization of functions emerges with development (Schore, 1994).

Examples such as these lead us to conclude that neither genes nor environment can be considered more important. Changes in a group of cells, the emergence of walking, the personality a child displays, and countless other developmental changes are all joint products of heredity, past development, and current environment.

THEORETICAL PERSPECTIVES ON DEVELOPMENT

Although the interaction of heredity and environment, past as well as present, provides a general framework for understanding development, it does not give a total picture of how development unfolds. Researchers want to know exactly how this interaction takes place. Over the years they have developed a number of theoretical perspectives. Each puts the factors involved in development into a different context, thus providing a different focus on developmental changes. In the following sections we introduce you to five major theoretical perspectives in the field of child development. But first we explain what scientists mean by a *theoretical perspective*. It is a perspective founded on a certain theory, but what is a theory?

THE NATURE OF THEORIES

A **theory** is an organized set of ideas about how things operate. It is an attempt to summarize current observations in light of past observations and to predict future ones. Individual observations take on meaning by being interpreted on the basis of some theory.

Theory:
An organized set of ideas about how things operate, intended to provide a framework for interpreting facts and findings and to guide scientific research.

Different theories provide different perspectives. Suppose that Father's Day is coming up and a mother takes her two sons shopping. The 3-year-old picks out a shiny toy truck for his father, while the 6-year-old selects a baseball cap. Both children see Father's Day as a special occasion and want the best for their dad, but the 6-year-old's choice is far more likely to be used by the father. Why do they make such different choices?

According to the theories of the Swiss psychologist Jean Piaget, the 6-year-old's choice is evidence of a developmental decline in egocentrism—that is, a movement away from viewing the world only from one's own perspective. Piaget theorized that children become less egocentric with age: 6-year-olds are fundamentally less egocentric than 3-year-olds, who in turn are vastly less egocentric than 1-year-olds.

In contrast, part of Sigmund Freud's psychoanalytic theory holds that, beginning at around age 4, children strive to be like, or identify with, the parent of the same sex. This identification is an indirect way for children to feel they have power in the world. Viewed through Freudian theory, a 6-year-old boy who picks a cap for his father and a similar cap for himself is doing so partly because of identification with his father.

Other theories would bring still other interpretations to bear on the boys' actions. For example, some would stress that the 6-year-old has learned cultural stereotypes about gender-appropriate behavior. This is why he selects a baseball cap for his father, not an apron, as he might for his mother. (Likewise, the younger child picks out a truck, not a doll.)

Note that each of these approaches attempts to explain a particular change in terms of more general characteristics or processes of development. One of the important functions of theories is to provide concepts that organize specific facts in terms of general explanatory principles. This makes it possible to apply our knowledge to a range of new situations.

In addition to providing a framework for interpreting facts and findings, a theory can also guide scientific research. Researchers could explore an infinite number of questions about human development. Theories help them decide which questions are important to ask and, to some extent, how to ask them. For example, if you hold the theory that much of individual behavior is determined by heredity, you would give high priority to contrasting people with similar and dissimilar genetic makeups (identical twins versus unrelated individuals, for instance). If, however, you think that early experience is a major determinant of behavior, you would conduct studies contrasting people with different childhood histories. A researcher with an interactionist perspective might try to examine both genetic and environmental variation in the same study.

A theory is evaluated in several ways. First, it must be sensible and consistent. It must not contain assumptions that are incompatible with one another or known to be false. Second, it must organize, integrate, and make understandable the body of research findings on a topic. It must help us interpret and make sense of what we know. Third, it must provide a useful guide to further research. We must be able to derive statements from the theory that are open to proof or disproof. In other words, the theory must be specific enough to be testable. Of course, the validity, or usefulness, of a theory in the behavioral sciences usually cannot be decided by one or two critical tests. Rather, an ongoing check of research findings is needed.

The capacity for empathic response develops notably in the preschool and early school years. Four-year-olds commonly look on in concern when another child is injured. Such concern is even more obvious at about age 6.

FIVE MAJOR THEORIES OF DEVELOPMENT

Consider this scene in a day-care center playground. A boy who is climbing the ladder of a slide slips and falls, cutting his lip. His cries draw others' attention. One 2-year-old playing nearby becomes upset himself and starts crying also. Another 2-year-old tries offering the injured child her teddy bear and continues to do so even though he shows no interest in the toy. With a clear expression of concern on his face, a 5-year-old calls a teacher and stands by while she tends to the boy. Another 5-year-old might walk away or even tease the injured child, something a 2-year-old would be unlikely to do.

The reactions of these children may be explained in different ways, and different theories focus on different aspects of the situation. Some theories focus on individual differences among children who are the same age. Why, for example, do some 5-year-olds show empathy, while others do not? Other theories focus on general age-related changes. Why do 5-year-olds act so differently from 2-year-olds in this instance? Theories also differ in that some stress cognitive aspects of the children's reactions (how they think about and understand the situation), while others stress social and emotional aspects. Some recent theories attempt to combine both viewpoints, seeing them as interrelated.

In the sections that follow we introduce you to five major theories of child development, showing how different theories lead to different explanations. The first two theories share a focus on **cognitive development**—the development of the child's memory, thinking, use of language, and other mental skills. The other three theories share a focus on **social and emotional development**—the development of the child's feelings and relationships with others. This same order (cognitive development first, then social and emotional development) is also used in later chapters of this book. This is because researchers who study social and emotional development often build on the ideas and work of those who study cognitive development. More specific and detailed discussions of particular theories are found in later chapters.

Cognitive developmental theory:
A theory that attempts to explain developmental change in a person's memory, thinking, use of language, and other mental skills.

Social and emotional developmental theory:
A theory that attempts to explain developmental change in a person's feelings and relationships with others.

THEORIES STRESSING COGNITIVE DEVELOPMENT

Information-processing theory:
A theory that seeks to explain human cognition by drawing an analogy between a person's thought processes and the workings of a computer; that is, the brain, the central processing unit, receives information from the environment and processes it, making comparisons and adjustments on the basis of information already stored in the memory.

Declarative knowledge:
Knowledge of things and events that is stored in memory.

Procedural knowledge:
Knowledge of how to do things that is stored in memory.

INFORMATION-PROCESSING THEORY **Information-processing theory** seeks to understand human thought processes by comparing them to the workings of a computer. Like a computer, a person receives input (information from the environment) and processes it by making comparisons and adjustments, drawing on information already stored in memory.

Developmentalists who take an information-processing perspective are particularly interested in age-related changes in memory and problem-solving skills (Kail, 1991; Siegler, 1986). They would explain the different responses of 2- and 5-year-olds to a hurt playmate in terms of the amount of experience the children have in solving problems, their skills in using memory to store and retrieve information, and the ease and flexibility with which they apply past experiences to new situations.

Consider all that is involved, mentally speaking, in helping the hurt child. First, the helper must match stored knowledge of things and events (called **declarative knowledge**) with aspects of the current situation in order to determine if the current situation requires help. For instance, the child must match the injured boy's cries with knowledge that a child who is hurt and upset often begins crying. He or she must also match the bleeding lip with knowledge that a cut is painful and can be a serious matter. The 5-year-old's greater experience facilitates these matches. He therefore makes a quicker, more accurate judgment that some kind of help is needed. Some 2-year-olds, in contrast, might not even recognize that the situation requires help. For example, they might incorrectly associate the other child's crying with failure to get a particular toy that he wants.

In addition to deciding whether help is needed, the helper must determine what kind of assistance is best. To do so, the child must sort through memories of possible responses he or she has used in the past or has seen others using and decide which one is likely to have the quickest and most successful results. Since a 5-year-old has a much broader store of knowledge about possible responses to someone who is hurt, he or she is more likely to find a good solution. A 2-year-old might be unable to think of any solution at all (and therefore start to cry himself), or the child might try an ineffective solution (offering a teddy). A broader store of knowledge about possible solutions also makes a 5-year-old more flexible in responding than a 2-year-old. For instance, if a teacher were not nearby to call for assistance, a 5-year-old would probably be able to think of some alternative solution, such as going inside to find an adult. In contrast, a 2-year-old who thought of the solution of calling her own mother to help might not know how to modify this strategy upon realizing that her own mother was not around.

Once the child has decided what to do to help, the choice must be carried out. This involves searching through memory to recall the right actions—which is part of **procedural knowledge**, or knowledge of how to do things. Just as a 5-year-old's declarative knowledge is usually more elaborate than a 2-year-old's, so is a 5-year-old's procedural knowledge usually more complete. A 5-year-old, for example, would probably have a better idea of how best to get a teacher's attention in an emergency and how to convey the problem to her than a 2-year-old would.

Thus, according to information-processing theory, the 5-year-old's greater effectiveness in this situation stems from two things. One is a larger base of information than that of a 2-year-old. A 5-year-old simply has more knowledge stored in memory, more knowledge of both the meaning of events and how to do things. The other advantage is that a 5-year-old can use information more effectively than a 2-year-old can. He or she can retrieve it more quickly, make more appropriate comparisons using it, draw conclusions more rapidly, and so forth. These two factors together give the 5-year-old an information-processing edge in recognizing and solving problems.

In recent years some information-processing theorists have begun to emphasize specific domains of knowledge, such as learning to count or learning word meanings. In our example the specific domain concerns understanding and responding to an injury. Areas in which a child has highly developed knowledge or skills are described as **areas of expertise.** Different individuals develop different areas of expertise, and one of the reasons for these differences is variations in domain-specific cognitive skills.

Areas of expertise: Specific areas in which a person has highly developed knowledge or skills

Information-processing theorists see development in terms of gradual improvements in attention, memory, and thinking that lead to greater skill in interpreting events and a wider range of problem-solving strategies. By analyzing the steps that children take (or fail to take) in performing a mental task, these researchers seek to chart and explain cognitive changes that occur with age. Although most information-processing theorists are interested in universal patterns of development, the perspective can also be applied to understanding individual differences among children of the same age. Educational psychologists in particular have begun to use it in this way. We will describe information-processing theory in more detail in Chapter 9, where we discuss memory and attention in preschoolers.

PIAGET'S THEORY OF COGNITIVE DEVELOPMENT   The Swiss developmental psychologist Jean Piaget (1896–1980) formulated an influential theory of cognitive development. Piaget began developing his theory 40 years before the emergence of information-processing theory, but since he continued to modify his theory up to the year of his death, its most recent form includes some insights from information-processing theory as well as some responses to it.

Jean Piaget

Like information-processing theorists, Piaget was mainly interested in normative cognitive development—that is, in changes in thinking that occur with age among all children. But unlike information-processing theorists, Piaget argued that as children grow older they undergo major qualitative changes in how they understand and learn about the world. Older children do not just have more skills and information than younger ones. Their thinking is also organized in fundamentally different ways. Just as Darwin proposed that biological adaptation leads to the emergence of new species, Piaget proposed that adaptation over the course of development leads to the emergence of new kinds of thinking.

These major shifts in thinking are believed to take place at the approximate ages of 2 years, 7 years, and 11 years. These ages mark the end of one major developmental period and the beginning of another. Piaget argued that all normal children go through the same major periods of development, in the same order, and at about the same ages. Within each major period, moreover, he proposed a series of stages that involve smaller qualitative changes in thinking. Children also pass through these stages in the same order, according to Piaget. He claimed that passage through the stages and the major periods cannot be greatly accelerated through training. Knowledge and skills acquired through training would simply not be enough to boost a child to a higher cognitive level. The knowledge and skills have to be organized within a new, broader cognitive structure before the next step in cognitive development can take place. This is why educators who apply Piaget's theory argue that instruction must be carefully designed to be appropriate to a child's current way of understanding and learning about the world.

To illustrate Piaget's theory, consider again the 2-year-olds and the 5-year-olds on the playground when the boy gets hurt on the slide. The 2-year-olds are just entering the second major period of cognitive development in Piaget's theory, whereas the 5-year-olds have been in this period for several years. The new way of thinking that characterizes the period is the ability to think *representationally*—that is, to use mental symbols to stand for or represent the self, other people, objects, and events. When this ability first develops, children use it in an immature, egocentric way. They mentally represent things from their *own* perspective and have a hard time thinking about how other people might be experiencing or representing the world. This does not mean that 2-year-olds are self-centered in the sense of putting their own interests first. Rather, they simply don't understand that other people have other points of view. The 2-year-old on the playground who offers her *own* teddy to the boy doesn't yet grasp that for him the teddy isn't a much-loved, comforting object as it is for her.

Five-year-olds, in contrast, are beginning to understand that the views of other people are sometimes different from their own. In a limited way they can think about what the hurt child is experiencing and what might relieve his distress. (They can also figure out what might make the child feel worse; helping and teasing draw on the same cognitive capacity.) In Piaget's view, therefore, 5-year-olds do not simply have more mental skills than 2-year-olds; they think in a different way from children three years younger. Still, 5-year-olds have a long way to go before they think like adults, or even like older children. Their notions of cause and effect are hazy. For instance, a 5-year-old might scold the slide for hurting his playmate, something that a typical 9-year-old would never do.

Piaget's theory and more contemporary views derived from it have had a major impact on developmental psychology. We will refer to them throughout this book. Using a Piagetian approach involving qualitatively different stages of thinking allows us to predict the kinds of problems that a child of a certain age can solve, as well as the kinds of errors that the child will make. In Chapter 5, where we describe the development of thinking during infancy, we will say more about Piaget's perspective and the mechanisms he proposed to explain cognitive development.

THEORIES STRESSING SOCIAL AND EMOTIONAL DEVELOPMENT

Social learning theory:
A developmental theory that borrows heavily from behavioral models in emphasizing the importance of gradual modification of behavior through positive and negative reinforcement, especially through the observation of the social consequences of particular acts.

Behaviorism:
A theoretical perspective that stresses the role of experience in shaping and modifying behavior.

Modeling:
The imitation by children of behavior they have observed.

SOCIAL LEARNING THEORY **Social learning theory** is an outgrowth of another perspective called **behaviorism,** which stresses the role of experience in shaping behavior. An especially important part of experience, according to these views, are the *consequences* of our actions. We tend to repeat behaviors that have resulted in rewards or have allowed us to avoid unpleasant consequences. We tend to discontinue behaviors that do not have one of these two outcomes. In addition, social learning theorists believe that a great deal of learning comes about through *observation* of others. Through a process known as **modeling** we often imitate behaviors that we have seen others do, especially if we observe them to have positive consequences. Notice that social learning theorists stress human learning in a social context (through observation and interaction with others). This stress is what gives social learning theory its name.

Like information-processing theorists, social learning theorists see development as a gradual, cumulative process. However, unlike both information-processing theorists and Piaget, their focus is on social *behavior* rather than on thinking. Additionally, social learning theorists are more interested in explaining differences among children the same age than in explaining differences among children of different ages.

Returning to our example of the children on the playground, social learning theorists would argue that the 5-year-old who helped the hurt boy had probably seen other people behaving helpfully and may have been praised for helping other children himself. As a result, he had acquired the notion that helping is called for in this situation, and perhaps the expectation that praise comes to those who help. In contrast, a 5-year-old girl who teases the injured child may have learned that a good way to get attention from her parents is to get her baby brother upset. Such attention may not be as rewarding as praise, but it is better than being ignored. A 5-year-old who walks away may have been ignored or even hit by children he has tried to help, so he associates helping with punishment. Alternatively, he may not have been exposed to frequent models of helping behavior. Or he may have little experience with this particular situation (for instance, he may be an only child who just entered day care). The 2-year-olds' responses may also be explained in terms of their inexperience.

In general, social learning theory is more useful in explaining specific social and emotional responses in children than it is in explaining universal patterns of behavioral change with age. In later chapters we will apply social learning theory to the issue of why some children, in certain situations, respond differently from their peers.

PSYCHOANALYTIC VIEWS **Psychoanalytic theories** refer to perspectives on human development that derive from the ideas of the Viennese physician, Sigmund Freud (1856–1939). After treating a number of emotionally disturbed patients, Freud concluded that abnormal behavior results from inadequate expression of innate drives—intense urges based in human biology, such as the need for sex or the expression of aggression.

Out of his ideas about the causes of emotional problems Freud developed a general theory of psychological development from infancy to adulthood. He argued that at birth a person's mind consists only of a reservoir of primitive drives and instincts, called the **id.** Then, over the first few years of life, the **ego,** or self, emerges. The ego's major role, as Freud saw it, is to find safe and appropriate ways for instinctual drives to be expressed. Thus, the child develops the ability to delay the gratification of impulses in order to meet society's demands, particularly demands conveyed by parents. At first it is fear of punishment that encourages this new self-control. But, beginning in the late preschool years, the child develops a **superego,** or conscience. Now the child has made the parents' rules and values part of the self. He or she feels guilty for misbehavior and tries to be "good" even when adults are not around.

Returning again to our playground example, Freud would argue that the 5-year-old who helps shows a major increase in the ability to control impulses. For instance, he does not become angry with the hurt boy for crying loudly and blocking access to the slide. Instead, he puts aside his own immediate desires

Sigmund Freud

Psychoanalytic theory:
Any theory of development that leans heavily on Freudian or neo-Freudian explanations of behavioral disorders and neurosis.

Id:
Freud's word for the part of a person's mind that consists of a reservoir of primitive drives and instincts.

Ego:
Freud's word for the self, or I, the part of the mind whose major role is to find safe and appropriate ways for instinctual drives to be gratified.

Superego:
Freud's word for conscience; the part of the mind that has internalized the rules and values governing "good" behavior.

and looks for help. This response is partly due to maturation of the ego. The boy's ego is now well developed enough to know that anger would not be a very good reaction since it would probably bring a teacher's rebuke. But at the same time, the 5-year-old is also developing a superego; he is internalizing his parents' rules and values and acquiring a conscience. He now feels it is "wrong" to ignore a hurt child, and he might even feel guilty if he did so. Another 5-year-old who does ignore the injured playmate and seems to feel no guilt would be said to be less far along in development of a superego.

Freud also proposed a theory of individual personality development, a theory of how adults come to have different styles of social and emotional behavior. In Freud's early writing, personality was viewed as unfolding during childhood in a series of five stages (see Table 1.1). In each stage the child's primary motivation is to gratify the drive for sensual pleasure in a particular part of the body. Freud considered these stages part of normal development. All children, he claimed, go through them in the same order, at about the same ages. Presumably, adult personality is a result of how much the gratification of drives is restricted or indulged in particular stages. Both undergratification and overgratification can lead to anxiety and **fixation,** in which a person who has failed to resolve the major issues of a stage goes on reliving them over and over in symbolic ways. For example, a baby who is harshly weaned from the breast may become anxious that this major source of oral gratification has been withheld, and so continue to focus on "oral issues" later in life. Such a person may become preoccupied with getting care from others, or may begin drinking heavily to counter feelings of loneliness. Because the earlier oral conflict is buried in the person's subconscious, he or she is unaware of the reasons for these behaviors.

With its great emphasis on the satisfaction of innate drives for sensual pleasure, Freud's original theory has little direct influence on developmental psychology today. Modern psychoanalytic thinkers have proposed broader sets of developmental issues and conflicts that people face from infancy through the various stages of adulthood. Modern psychoanalytic thinkers (and even Freud in his later writings) also put more emphasis on ego development, or development of the self, and they see people as far more actively involved in determining the course of their own development. Still, certain of Freud's core ideas have been incorporated into modern psychoanalytical perspectives. Freud's view that emotions have a critical impact on a person's thinking, his notion that early relationships are vitally important to human development, his belief that past conflicts can be pushed out of conscious awareness but still affect a person's life, and his idea that the same events can have different meanings to different people depending on their developmental histories are all part of Freud's legacy to modern psychology (Emde, 1992).

The writings of Erik Erikson (1902–1994) are an example of a modern approach to social and emotional development that stems in part from Freud's legacy. Like Freud, Erikson (1963) assigned a critical role to feelings and social relationships, especially those that develop early in life. Also like Freud, Erikson proposed a series of qualitatively distinct stages through which people pass in a certain order. But unlike Freud, Erikson did not believe that a person can become fixated at a certain stage. Instead, each of his stages involves a certain developmental issue that everyone resolves in some way, although some people do so more satisfactorily than others. Erikson's issues are also much broader than Freud's. For example, while Erikson saw feeding as an important arena for infant–parent interaction, he believed that the quality of care a baby receives

Fixation:
According to Freud's psychoanalytic theory, the failure to resolve the major issues of one of the five psychosexual stages of development, as a result of which the person symbolically relives those issues over and over.

Erik Erikson

TABLE 1.1
A COMPARISON OF FREUD'S PSYCHOSEXUAL STAGES WITH ERIKSON'S BROADER PSYCHOSOCIAL STAGES

Age	Freud's Psychosexual Stages	Erikson's Psychosocial Stages	Erikson's Developmental Issues
Birth to 1 year	Oral	Basic trust vs. mistrust	Infants learn to trust others to satisfy their needs and therefore develop feelings of self-worth. Infants receiving inconsistent care may grow to mistrust the people in their world.
1 to 3 years	Anal	Autonomy vs. shame and doubt	Children learn to be self-sufficient by mastering tasks such as feeding and dressing themselves, and they begin to separate from their parents. They also learn to conform to social rules. Children who do not develop autonomy may doubt their abilities and their capacity to act on the world and develop feelings of shame.
3 to 6 years	Phallic	Initiative vs. guilt	Expanding on the autonomy developed in the previous stage, children initiate pretend play with peers and accept responsibilities such as helping with household chores. Sometimes these activities create conflicts with other family members, and these conflicts create guilt. Excessive guilt will inhibit initiative; children can resolve the crisis by learning to balance initiative against the demands of others (e.g., parents).
7 to 11 years	Latency	Industry vs. inferiority	Children must master increasingly difficult skills, particularly social interaction with peers and academic performance. Children whose industry enables them to succeed in these areas develop a sense of mastery and self-assurance. Children who do not experience mastery of particular skills feel inferior and shun new activities.
12 to 18 years	Genital	Identity vs. role confusion	Adolescents build on all earlier experiences to develop a sense of self-identity, particularly in relation to their society. Failure to reach this goal may cause confusion in identity, the choice of an occupation, and the roles they perform as adults.
Young adulthood		Intimacy vs. isolation	Young adults strive to form strong friendships and to achieve love and companionship with another person. Individuals who do not develop a strong identity in adolescence may now have difficulty forming friendships and intimate relationships and experience isolation and loneliness.
Adulthood		Generativity vs. stagnation	Generativity includes responsibilities such as raising and caring for children and productivity in one's work. Adults who cannot perform these tasks become stagnant.
Maturity/ Old age		Ego integrity vs. despair	Older adults achieve ego integrity if they can look back on their lives and view life as productive and satisfying. If they view life as a disappointment, despair results.

entails much more than feeding and oral gratification alone. Playing, rocking, comforting, changing, and bathing are also opportunities for the baby to learn about the responsiveness and dependability of parents. To Erikson it is the overall quality of care that determines whether the child will develop *basic trust* or *mistrust*. And whatever the developmental outcome, the child does not become fixated, but moves forward to later developmental issues.

Erikson's eight psychosocial stages are summarized in Table 1.1, along with Freud's five psychosexual stages. (Erikson's stages are called psycho*social* because relationships with others play a prominent role in all of them; Freud's stages are called psycho*sexual* because they revolve around the gratification of basic drives for sensual pleasure). The issues that define each of Erikson's eight stages have provided an important organizing scheme for describing human social and emotional development. We will discuss the first five of those issues at various points in this book.

BOWLBY'S ADAPTATIONAL THEORY The English psychiatrist John Bowlby (1908–1990) sought to bring together social, emotional, and cognitive aspects of development in his **adaptational theory.** Of all the theorists we discuss here, Bowlby is the most heavily indebted to Darwin's theory of evolution as the basis for explaining social behavior. But, like Erikson, Bowlby was strongly influenced by Freud's psychoanalytic views on individual development, especially the importance of early relationships. Finally, his is a cognitive theory in which acquisition of mental structures fundamentally changes the child's engagement with the world and in which the child is viewed as actively processing information to guide social behavior.

> **Adaptational theory:** The developmental theory formulated by John Bowlby, which integrates evolutionary, psychoanalytic, and cognitive models.

Bowlby began with the idea that human babies are predisposed to behave in ways that promote closeness with their caregivers. This is part of our evolutionary heritage, an adaptation we share with our primate relatives. Much as baby monkeys cling to their mother's fur to avoid separation, human babies cry, call, and crawl after their caregivers until they achieve proximity. The tendency to form early attachments is biologically built-in, and for virtually all children it unfolds through a sequence of stages culminating in "goal-corrected" partnerships with parents (see Chapter 6).

To the idea that babies are predisposed to form attachments to their caregivers, Bowlby added the psychoanalytic notion that the quality of infant-adult attachment is heavily influenced by the quality of care the baby experiences. Thus, while both the tendency to form attachments and the stages of their development are universal, the security of those attachments can vary greatly. Bowlby argued that the infant who experiences responsive care will develop a belief that he or she can influence the environment and obtain care from others when it is needed. In time, securely attached children believe more generally that they can prevail even in the face of stress or adversity. In contrast, infants who do not receive responsive care and who are not secure in their attachments may be dependent and doubtful of their own abilities, and may also become socially isolated or aggressive. This would include infants and toddlers who are pushed toward independence too early.

Bowlby's theory therefore has an important role for cognition and learning. Through hours of interaction with caregivers, infants develop generalized expectations about the caregivers' responses and the infant's own role in producing those responses. Bowlby called these expectations **internal working models** and argued that once formed they guide future social relationships. By participating in a responsive relationship, the infant learns not only that the caregiver is available and responsive but also that this is the way that relationships work. Such broader patterns of beliefs will be applied in many different contexts. In this sense, Bowlby's theory has much in common with Piaget's structural theory of cognitive development.

> **Internal working model:** An infant's set of generalized expectations about the caregiver's responses and about the infant's own role in producing those responses.

Bowlby's theory would explain the different reactions to the injured child in the school yard in terms of differences in attachment history. The boy who comes to the injured child's aid has probably experienced empathic and

John Bowlby and Mary Ainsworth, who developed a procedure for investigating Bowlby's theory, discuss attachment research.

responsive care. Children who have experienced such a nurturing relationship not only learn to expect and receive care but also learn more generally that when one partner in a relationship is needy, the other responds. In addition, they have inner confidence in their own ability to try to solve problems. In contrast, a 5-year-old who responds with hostility to the injured boy has probably experienced hostility, rejection, and lack of emotional responsiveness himself. We will describe Bowlby's ideas more fully in several later chapters.

WHY SO MANY THEORIES?

We have described only a few of the theories of human development. There are many others, some of which we will discuss later in this book. Why so many different theories? Why hasn't developmental psychology produced a single theory, accepted by all?

One answer is that different theories focus on different aspects of development. Piaget, for example, focused on cognitive development, while Erikson focused on social and emotional development. Piaget's theory is not an alternative to Erikson's. They each concentrate on different things. Moreover, even theories that look at the same general area of development may still focus on different factors *within* that area. For instance, Bowlby's adaptational theory looks at prior relationships with caregivers and the expectations derived from them in trying to understand why one child is less empathic and caring than another. Social learning theory, in contrast, is more concerned with the particular behaviors a certain aggressive child displays, how he or she came to learn them (by observing aggressive models and seeing aggression rewarded), and the specific situations that tend to elicit these aggressive responses. Thus, Bowlby's theory and social learning theory differ in part because each is looking at different pieces of a large and complex puzzle.

A second reason why there is no single, universally accepted theory in developmental psychology is that we do not yet have enough information to formulate such an all-encompassing theory and demonstrate its validity. Often the findings that researchers make can be interpreted in different ways. We are still working to find out which interpretations are best. One goal of developmental psychology is to describe the course of development, but another equally important goal is to refine existing theories, resolve disputes between theories, and generate new theories that are more accurate and comprehensive in scope.

As developmentalists pursue this second goal, the theories they propose often turn out to have more and more in common. For example, modern social learning theory stresses the general beliefs that people acquire through their observations of others and their histories of rewards and punishments. These include beliefs about one's own ability to be effective, what Albert Bandura (1985) refers to as *self-efficacy*. Self-efficacy, in turn, is very similar to Bowlby's notion of a person's expectations about the self. So the question is not whether people have ideas about themselves that influence their behavior. Both theories agree that they do. Instead, the question is whether these attitudes about the self are specific to particular situations and derive from particular learning experiences (as social learning theory contends), or whether they derive from the general quality of early relationships (as adaptational theory holds). The answers to such questions can come only from additional research.

MAJOR ISSUES IN DEVELOPMENT

If you think about the five theories we have presented, you may notice several issues about which they disagree. First, they disagree as to whether development is best viewed as a gradual, cumulative process or as a process that occurs in a series of qualitatively distinct stages. This is sometimes referred to as the *continuity versus discontinuity issue*. Second, the theories disagree as to whether early experiences have a decisive impact on future development, or whether current behavior largely reflects current experiences. This is sometimes called the *stability versus change issue*. Do we remain in some fundamental ways the person our early experiences made us, or are we open to becoming quite different in new circumstances? In the following sections we will explore where our five theoretical perspectives stand on these two major issues.

STAGES OR GRADUAL DEVELOPMENT?

The question of whether development occurs gradually or in stages comes up most often in relation to normative development, the general patterns of change that all children experience. General patterns of cognitive change, in particular, have been the subject of this debate. Information-processing theorists believe that cognitive development is the result of gradual improvement in attention, memory, and problem-solving skills. Their position is based on research that shows that younger children can perform certain cognitive tasks almost as well as older children if they are helped to break down the tasks into simpler steps, or if they are taught the required skills before testing. In contrast, Piaget's theory holds that cognitive development consists not merely of quantitative changes in attention, memory, and problem-solving skills, but also of qualitative changes in how children think and understand the world. Older children approach problems and understand things in ways that younger children simply cannot. This position is based on research showing that training children on advanced tasks is only modestly successful and that younger children consistently make the same mistakes on problems that older children see as easy and obvious. When asked to explain their answers, younger children's responses suggest that they think in ways fundamentally different from the way older children think. Moreover, they approach problems in different ways. For example, research suggests that not only do younger children have less memory capacity than older children, they may not realize that there are a variety of ways to remember things (such as rehearsal or grouping things) or even that memory is an important element of problem solving.

Contemporary developmentalists who build on Piaget's perspective have mixed opinions on the issue of developmental stages. Some, such as Robbie Case (1985), agree with the information-processing theorists. They, too, attempt to show how apparently stagelike changes are actually based on more gradual underlying developments. But other developmentalists who build on Piaget's work continue to argue in favor of developmental stages. They say that qualitatively distinct transitions take place at certain points in cognitive development (e.g., Campbell and Bickhard, 1986; Karmiloff-Smith, 1991).

Cognitive development is not the only area in which the issue of developmental stages has arisen. Stage theories have been debated concerning moral development and the development of peer relationships. And it should be remembered that the psychoanalytic theories of Freud and Erikson are stage theories. In later chapters of this book you will notice that we sometimes describe development in terms of acquiring new and different behaviors, thinking skills, or understandings of oneself or of social relationships. Other times we describe development in terms of modifications to and extensions of existing skills or behaviors, which occur gradually. We believe that both gradual and stage transitions are part of development.

EARLY EXPERIENCES VERSUS CURRENT EXPERIENCES

The question of which is more important, early experiences or current experiences, most often arises in discussions of social and emotional development. Social learning theorists attach little importance to the age at which experiences occur. They see a child's style of responding to other people as resulting from the total, accumulated history of reactions to the child's behavior. In fact, many view current experiences as more important than previous ones because the child is, after all, acting in the present. Jerome Kagan (1984) draws an analogy between experience and tape recordings. Each experience (the child's behavior plus any positive or negative consequences it brings) is recorded in memory. However, the "record button" in the child's mind is always turned on. If current experiences echo past experiences, the tape will remain essentially unchanged. But if current behavior leads to different consequences, the old tape will be erased and a new message recorded. In support of this view, research has shown that a person's style of responding can change over time if relevant circumstances change. Moreover, the same person may behave differently in different situations (one way with family members, for example, and another way with peers) if each situation involves different consequences.

But other theorists assign greater importance to early experiences. Erikson, for example, holds that each stage of psychosocial development is influenced by the previous one. For instance, how well a toddler negotiates the issue of a new-found capacity for independence is influenced by the degree to which that child as a baby developed basic trust through close relationships with adults. Lacking the emotional security of basic trust makes it harder to act independently during the toddler years. Similarly, it is easier for a young adult to form a satisfying intimate relationship with someone if earlier, as an adolescent, that

FIGURE 1.1 BOWLBY'S
MODEL OF
DEVELOPMENTAL
PATHWAYS

Change always remains possible, but "choices" at each point are constrained by directions previously taken. The person following path A and the person following path B may wind up being quite similar in their pattern of adaptation despite different directions taken in early life. The people on paths C and D are quite different and perhaps atypical because of extreme directions continually taken. [Adapted from Waddington (1957) in Bowlby (1973).]

person had achieved a coherent sense of himself or herself as a person. This is not to say that how well an earlier developmental issue is resolved affects a person indelibly for life. There is always opportunity for change given new experiences. For example, a satisfying intimate relationship in young adulthood may help a formerly mistrustful child become more trusting as an adult. Nevertheless, early experiences, in Erikson's view, generally have a powerful influence on later behavior.

Bowlby's adaptational theory gives importance to the influence of current experiences, while still granting a special role to early experiences, as Erikson does. In Bowlby's view, development proceeds within the framework of previous patterns of adaptation. New situations are faced and interpreted in light of previously formed expectations about the self and others. Fundamental change remains possible, however, for subsequent adaptations are a product both of development up to that point and of new circumstances. Bowlby summarized this perspective using a model of a branching developmental tree, which he adopted from C. H. Waddington (1957) and which is illustrated in Figure 1.1. In this model, early experience does not irrevocably determine what a child will become. The child who has traveled path A, for instance, might have taken several different routes at certain points in development. Early choices, however, do limit the alternatives available at later stages. (The path-A child may branch left or right midway through development, but may not suddenly switch to path D.)

In Bowlby's theory, as in Piaget's, children are not passive recipients of environmental influences; they are not lumps of clay that can be shaped this way or that. Instead, children are active participants in their own development. In part, they create their own environments through the choices they make. This position is based on research that shows considerable predictability and continuity in behavior from early to later development. Even when patterns of behavior change, further development or new situations may bring out earlier behavior patterns (Sroufe, Egeland, and Kreutzer, 1990).

RESEARCH METHODS FOR STUDYING DEVELOPMENT

Developmentalists use many research methods to gather information. Some, such as the laboratory experiment, are modeled after methods used in the physical sciences. Others, such as observing people in natural settings, are more similar to procedures used in the biological sciences, in which description and classification are of major importance. Still others, such as certain methods for interviewing children, are unique to developmental psychology. Each method for studying development has its strengths and weaknesses. None is more or less "scientific" than the others. A method's power and meaningfulness depend on how that method is used. Basically, the choice of method depends on the question being asked. Some questions are best approached with one procedure, other questions with entirely different techniques. And many issues must be studied with a combination of methods before they are fully understood.

THE EXPERIMENT

Suppose you wanted to answer the question: Do newborn babies have a preference for looking at human faces? You might start by watching some newborns in their homes to find out what they look at. If you kept track of the time they spent looking at faces, you would probably conclude that faces must be interesting to them. But how would you know whether human faces are more interesting than other things to newborns? And just what is it about a face that captures a baby's interest—a particular facial feature, or the face as a whole? Or maybe it is the sound of a person's voice that makes the baby look at the face from which the sound comes. In the baby's home, separating all these different factors would be difficult. That is why psychologists usually study such issues in a laboratory. There they can use sophisticated equipment to determine precisely where a baby is looking. Also, by systematically controlling the stimuli presented (a normal human face, a scrambled face, a black-and-white checkerboard pattern, and so forth), they can find out what best captures the child's attention.

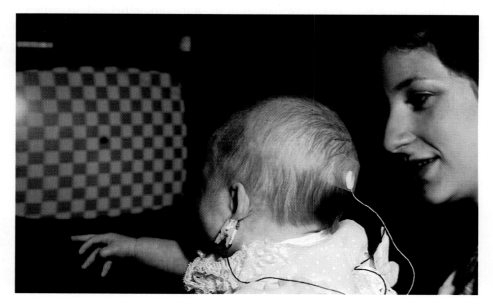

In the laboratory, researchers can control what the infant experiences and can also use technical apparatus to ensure precise measurement. Here, an infant's brain waves are being recorded while different visual displays are presented.

Suppose laboratory research showed not only that newborns look at faces, but that they tend to focus particularly on the hairline (Maurer and Salapatek, 1976). What is it about hairlines that holds infants' interest? One possible answer is the color contrast (lighter versus darker) between the forehead and the hair. To test this possibility, or **hypothesis** as it is called, an experiment is required. An **experiment** is a study in which researchers control conditions so as to rule out all other influences except the one being investigated. In this case, they would randomly assign a number of babies to one of two groups. The random assignment "shuffles" the children, so to speak, thus minimizing the chances that infants with some unusual visual preference inadvertently all end up in the same group. The researchers would then show one group of babies a picture of a face with a sharp light-dark contrast at the hairline and the other group of babies exactly the same face with the light-dark contrast removed. If the first group looks longer at the face, and at the hairline in particular, the researchers would have evidence that light-dark contrasts are indeed appealing to newborns. Note that in a laboratory experiment researchers can be very systematic in exploring possibilities and ruling out alternatives. They can also be very precise in setting up the conditions for each group tested. Control and precision are the chief advantages of the laboratory experiment.

Laboratory experiments also have disadvantages, however. For one thing, their results may not always apply to everyday settings. People may behave differently in a laboratory than they do in natural settings, either because the lab is strange and intimidating to them or because they want to "look good" to the experimenter. For example, Daryl Bem and David Funder (1978) found that children's ability to delay gratification in a laboratory (to refrain from touching an attractive toy at the request of the experimenter) did not predict their ability to control impulses at school. Instead, delay of gratification in the lab predicted obedience, lack of curiosity, and submissiveness to adults in everyday situations. Thus, laboratory findings may not always mean what they seem to mean at first. Psychologists call this the issue of **ecological validity:** findings inside the laboratory may or may not generalize to the outside world.

Moreover, when laboratory findings do generalize to everyday settings, researchers must still be cautious in drawing implications. If an experiment reveals that a certain stimulus can cause a certain response, one cannot conclude that this cause-and-effect relationship is common in the everyday world. For example, psychologist John Watson (1928) once induced a fear of rats in a young boy named Albert by repeatedly making a loud noise near the child's ear while a laboratory rat was presented. Does this mean that most people who fear rats do so because they associate rats with some intrinsically frightening stimulus? Not likely. Surely many people are afraid of rats without ever having had such an experience.

Another limitation of laboratory experiments is that many questions of interest to developmentalists are not open to experimentation. This is especially true in the area of social development. For instance, researchers cannot assign children to abusive conditions just to observe the results, even though they are very interested in the effects of child abuse. Purposely exposing children to pain and anguish is ethically unthinkable. For the same reason, Watson's study of little Albert would not be done today. Nor can researchers create certain everyday events (the birth of a brother or sister, the decision of a mother to work outside the home) within the confines of a laboratory. This doesn't mean that these important issues can't be studied scientifically, however. It just means that other research methods must be used.

NATURALISTIC OBSERVATION

An alternative to conducting laboratory experiments is to observe behavior in everyday settings as it occurs naturally. This approach to research has a long history. In the last century it was used by Charles Darwin, and in this century it has been central to a field of study called **ethology.** Ethology seeks to understand animal behavior through careful observation of species in their natural habitats. One example is Jane Goodall's study of chimpanzee social behavior. The information about free-ranging chimps that she collected through years of observation in East African forests could never have been obtained by studying chimps in a laboratory.

Much research on human development also uses the technique of **naturalistic observation.** Researchers go to homes, schools, and playgrounds to watch and record the everyday behavior of children and adults. At times they try to simulate natural settings in their own research rooms. For instance, they might create an attractive playroom, bring in a group of children to play, and observe or videotape the children through a one-way window so as not to interfere with what they say and do.

Naturalistic observation can also be used to make group comparisons. For example, a researcher could compare the amount of conflict in families with young adolescents versus the amount of conflict in families with younger or older children. The families might be observed in their own homes—say, at the dinner table—and the researcher could record the number of disagreements, negative personal comments, and other signs of discord.

In all the various settings where naturalistic observations take place, researchers are precise and systematic in recording what they see. They count the frequencies of particular behaviors, note sequences as they occur, and rate

Ethology:
A field of study relying on observation of behavior in natural habitats, rather than in the laboratory, in order to develop generalizations about patterns of behavior and their functions.

Naturalistic observation:
A method of collecting data in which researchers carefully observe and record naturally occuring behavior in everyday settings.

Observation in natural circumstances has the advantage that one can claim with more confidence to be studying the way children usually behave.

the people observed for qualitative factors such as mood or level of enthusiasm. Sophisticated automated devices are also available for keeping records. This careful recording of data distinguishes the trained psychologist from the casual observer. The psychologist does not just watch and try to remember but is constantly keeping an account, usually in quantitative form (the number of times a child pushes another or offers to share a toy, the number of times a child asks an adult for assistance or the adult gives assistance when it is not requested).

Naturalistic observation has the advantage of describing human behavior in real-life situations, rather than behavior under conditions an experimenter controls. Naturalistic observation is therefore very useful for studying many socially relevant issues. Its major disadvantage is that it cannot tell us why a certain behavior occurs. Suppose researchers observe greater conflict in families with young teenagers and wonder whether the presence of the young teenagers might be the cause. They have no way of knowing through observation alone whether this hypothesis is right. The fact that two factors are often found together does not necessarily mean that one *causes* the other. For example, a study in England once showed that the number of storks in an area was **positively correlated** with the number of human births there—that is, the more storks, the more births. This does not mean that storks bring babies, however. Instead, some third factor, related to both the others, must be at work. As it turns out, that factor is population density. Heavily industrialized urban areas have a large number of big chimneys where storks like to nest, and these areas also have large populations and consequently many babies. In the same way, some factor other than the presence of young teenagers could be causing conflict in families that include young teens. Naturalistic observation doesn't provide a way of ruling out other possible factors. To rule out at least some of them, researchers could conduct what is called a natural experiment.

Positive correlation:
A statistical relationship in which the incidence of a particular phenomenon is directly related to the incidence of some other phenomenon.

THE NATURAL EXPERIMENT

Natural experiment:
An observational method, used when a laboratory study is not feasible, in which researchers compare groups of people whose circumstances differ naturally along the critical dimensions.

A **natural experiment** is called for when it is not possible to assign people to groups randomly, as is done in a laboratory experiment. For instance, researchers cannot take a large number of families and randomly give half of them a young teenager and the other half a preteen or an older teen. Instead, they must make do with the families that nature provides. To minimize the chances that some factor other than the age of the children is influencing family conflict, the researchers could try to select families that are similar in many ways. For example, they could choose families in which the parents are similar in income, marital satisfaction, job-related pressures, and so forth. If among these similar families those with young teenagers still turned out to have the most conflict, the researchers would have an indication that their hypothesis might be right. Confidence in the hypothesis would grow if the degree of family conflict increased as preteens moved into early adolescence and decreased again in the *same* families as young teenagers became older teens. The more similar the families in the study were in ways other than the ages of their children, the stronger the evidence in support of the hypothesis would be.

COMBINING OBSERVATION AND EXPERIMENTATION

To understand some aspects of development, researchers often go back and forth between observational and experimental approaches. Suppose observation suggests that family conflict is to some degree caused by parents' failure to appreciate teenagers' growing competence and desire for independence (e.g., Collins, 1990). It would be possible to do an experiment in which one group of parents was informed about these changes in adolescents and the signs that the changes were taking place, while another group of parents was not so informed. If, in family interaction, the informed group showed less conflict than the non-informed group, we would have evidence that the hypothesis derived from observation was right.

Consider another example of the complementary use of observational and experimental approaches. On the basis of observation, animal researchers hypothesized that the tendency of babies to cling to their mothers is a genetically based behavior that helps protect the young. Staying close to the mother is not just learned because the mother provides food. It is a built-in behavior related to the security the mother gives. Psychologist Harry Harlow conducted an experiment to test this hypothesis. He found that baby monkeys separated from their real mothers will cling to a soft terrycloth "surrogate mother" that does not dispense food in preference to a wire "surrogate mother" that does dispense food (Harlow and Harlow, 1966). Harlow's experiment showed that feeding by a mother is not necessary to the formation of a baby's attachment. Other researchers built on this finding, again using observation. By observing interactions between infants and their mothers, they began to clarify how mother-infant attachments develop in natural settings. Thus, through a combination of these two techniques—observation and experimentation—our understanding of this important topic has grown.

STUDYING CHANGE OVER TIME

In addition to observation and experimentation, developmentalists have methods to address special problems in research. One is the problem of measuring the degree to which a certain potentially influential factor affects people over a relatively long period of time. Consider early day care, for example. Developmentalists want to know whether entering full-time day care as a very young baby in any way affects the quality of a child's development, not only during infancy but at later points in development as well. To answer this question, researchers would have to conduct a natural experiment, but that natural experiment would have to have a long time span. It would have to assess how day-care versus home-reared children fare from infancy through, perhaps, early adolescence. How do developmentalists go about making such assessments? How do they approach the problem of studying change over time?

One way is to study the same people over the designated time period. This is called a **longitudinal study.** In the case of studying the effects of early day care, the researchers would select one group of babies whose parents had placed them in day care by the age of, say, 3 months and another group of babies whose parents raised them at home for the first year and a half. They would try to choose families that were similar in characteristics such as socioeconomic background, current marital status and satisfaction, and general attitudes toward child rearing. In this way, they could be confident that the choice of day care or home care would be the major difference between the two groups. Periodically the researchers would interview the parents and assess the children's emotional adjustment, social skills, and cognitive growth. Each assessment would allow them to compare how the two groups developed. If they wanted to

Longitudinal study:
A study of the same group of subjects over a number of weeks, months, or years.

Cross-sectional study:
A study in which researchers compare groups of people of different ages at the same time.

follow these children through early adolescence, this study would take them about 14 years.

A way to speed up the investigation would be to conduct a **cross-sectional study,** in which groups of people of different ages are studied at the same time. In this case, the researchers would select a sample of children who ranged in age from 1 to 14 years. Half the children would have been placed in day care by the age of 3 months, while the other half would have been raised at home during infancy. Again, the researchers would try to match the families in terms of other influential factors, such as the parents' socioeconomic background and social support. Then they would assess and compare children looked after in day care versus children reared at home in the 1-year-old group, the 2-year-old group, and the 3-year-old group, and so forth.

Longitudinal and cross-sectional studies are two ways of studying change over time. Each has advantages and disadvantages. Cross-sectional studies can be done more quickly and cheaply, which can be very important when findings have crucial implications for child-rearing practices. Cross-sectional studies, however, are somewhat limited in what they can reveal. Although they show what children of different ages are like, they are not good at showing the *process* of development. That is, they do not reveal the path from one developmental phase to the next. Also, because cross-sectional findings are statistics about groups examined at a single point in time, they reveal nothing about individual change. The study of physical growth provides a good example. If you were to plot the average height of 1-year-olds, 2-year-olds, 3-year-olds, and so on, the resulting curve would be smooth and steady. Such a curve, however, is not a good indicator of an individual child's growth from year to year. Individual children grow at different rates and have growth spurts at different ages, but all this unevenness is "averaged out" in a group curve. Individual differences in physical growth can be discovered only by studying the same children over time.

Accelerated longitudinal design:
A type of longitudinal study in which researchers study several different age groupings simultaneously and follow them over a specified period of time.

Developmentalists thus rely on a combination of cross-sectional and longitudinal methods. Sometimes they even combine the two in the same study. For example, in what is called an **accelerated longitudinal design,** researchers begin studying several age groups simultaneously and then follow each group over a period of time. If you started with, say, groups of 1-, 4-, 7-, and 10-year-olds and followed each of them for four years, you would have covered a developmental span of 14 years in a much shorter time frame. You would also be able to demonstrate that observed changes were developmental changes and not merely due to some peculiar factor in your original groups if you could show that your new 4-year-olds (the infants three years later) were comparable to the original 4-year-old group. And you could show that individual performance at each age was predicted by performance at the earlier age.

THE THEMES OF THIS BOOK

In this chapter we have introduced a number of the important themes in this book. The first concerns the nature of development. Development is characterized by both *change* and *continuity*. Change is sometimes minor and gradual, at other times fundamental and dramatic. But even in the case of major qualitative changes, there are logical connections between past and present. What was there previously is the foundation for what emerges next.

The second theme introduced in this chapter is the interplay between *individ-*

ual development and *normative development*. Children are more similar to each other than they are different from one another. Each child goes through the same major developmental phases, on roughly the same timetable. In other words, most children follow the norms of human development. Yet each child is also a unique individual, in some ways different from every other. This is because each child has his or her own genetic makeup and history of experiences. Individual development, like normative development, unfolds in a coherent manner, with continuity between past and present. The individual patterns of behavior that a particular child currently displays are an outgrowth of that child's previous patterns of behavior.

A third theme concerns the critical role of *developmental context*. The particular set of circumstances in which children find themselves influence both the timing of normative developmental changes and the unique patterns of behavior that each individual evolves. In trying to understand human development, we must consider the total developmental context, which includes biological makeup, the sociocultural context, personal experiences, and prior development.

A fourth and final theme is the *integrated nature of development*. Although this book has separate chapters on cognitive development and social development, that division isn't meant to imply that these two areas are unrelated. Developmental changes in children's thinking are always closely related to developmental changes in how children interact with other people, and interacting with others frequently triggers changes in how children think. We will continually point out how each aspect of development influences other aspects, often in a mutual, back-and-forth way.

To help illustrate these major themes, we present three family case histories that focus primarily on the lives of three individual children. These stories are based on composites of actual research cases. Although the stories are fictionalized, they are drawn from the authors' extensive research experience, at times in consultation with ethnic minority psychologists. A new chapter in these case histories appears at the beginning of each part of the book. We also use the cases to illustrate specific points raised within the text.

When you first meet these families at the beginning of Part One, the future mother is either pregnant or considering having a child. Each family lives in different circumstances. Throughout the book, as the three children develop from infants to adolescents, their family situations change as they go through good times and bad. You will see how changing life circumstances influence children and how individual children respond to various challenges. By getting to know these families, by seeing in a tangible way how individuals unfold within a context, we believe that you will be better able to understand the theories and findings of developmental psychology presented in this book.

At the end of each part, in sections we call "Epilogues," we tie the content of the chapters to the lives of the children we are following. We think this structure will not only help you better remember the material you are learning; it will also give you a more lifelike and holistic picture of the developing child. Although the facts and theories of child development are interesting in themselves, we believe that they can be even more fascinating when connected to the lives of three developing children.

CHAPTER SUMMARY

1. A developmental perspective is a way of understanding children's behavior. It includes the idea that children undergo **qualitative change** in their thoughts, feelings, and actions as they grow older. Developmental change is *orderly, cumulative,* and *directional.*

2. Developmentalists are interested in both normative and individual development. **Normative development** refers to the general age-related changes in behavior that virtually all children share. **Individual development** refers to the individual pace of normative development as well as to individual differences in personality and expertise that each person evolves.

3. An important framework for understanding development is Charles Darwin's theory of evolution. According to Darwin, humans evolved in a particular way because of the history of pressures and opportunities in their environments, and because of consequent progressive changes in the mix of genes that the human population carries. This process is known as **natural selection** because traits that are well adapted to the current environment are being selected through a natural process. A contribution of evolutionary theory to the study of human development has been to identify the adaptive significance of various human behaviors. Both the general course of human development and the particular requirements for the adequate development of children derive from our evolutionary heritage.

4. Three factors—genes, developmental history, and current environmental conditions—combine to shape the course of development. All contemporary researchers agree that it is important to consider genes and environment in interaction. Genetic influences can unfold only within an environmental context, and environmental influences need a base of genetic potentialities to work on. What current potentials are drawn upon and how circumstances are engaged and interpreted are also influenced by past history. The major issue today is exactly how the various factors that are involved in development interact with one another. In addition, contemporary developmentalists are keenly aware of the importance of considering the individual's sociocultural context in assessing the effects of developmental history and of current environmental conditions.

5. Observations about children take on meaning by being interpreted on the basis of theories. A **theory** is an organized set of assumptions about how things operate. It is an attempt to account for current observations and to predict future ones. Theories give direction to scientific research.

6. Some theories presented in this book emphasize cognitive development. One of these, **information-processing theory,** focuses on memory abilities and skills for solving problems. This theory sees developmental change as gradual. Piaget's **theory of cognitive development** focuses on major qualitative changes in the way children think. According to Piaget, all children go through the same stages as their thought becomes progressively less egocentric and less tied to immediate experience.

7. Other theories in this book emphasize social and emotional development. An important goal of all these theories is to explain how individual differences in behavior come about. **Social learning theory** has historically emphasized gradual changes in behavior through reinforcement and opportunities to observe other people. Sigmund Freud's **psychoanalytic theory,** and later views partly derived from it, such as Erik Erikson's theory, emphasize the power of early emotional experiences to influence later behavior. Finally, John Bowlby's **adaptational theory** combines psychoanalytic theory with cognitive theories and Darwin's ideas about evolution. Bowlby's approach emphasizes the quality of the child's earliest attachment relationships.

8. Researchers use a number of methods to study human development. In an **experiment** they deliberately control conditions in an effort to rule out all other influences on behavior except the one being studied. Control in investigating cause and effect is the chief advantage of a laboratory experiment. Another research method is **naturalistic observation,** in which behavior is systematically observed and recorded as it occurs in everyday settings. A third method is the **natural experiment,** used when a laboratory study is not feasible. In a natural experiment researchers compare groups of people whose circumstances differ naturally along the critical dimensions. To observe change over time, developmentalists may use a **longitudinal study,** in which the same group of people is followed over a certain period. Alternatively, they may conduct a **cross-sectional study,** comparing groups of people of different ages at the same time. In an **accelerated longitudinal design** researchers combine these two methods by studying several age groups at the same time and following them across overlapping periods.

9. This book has several themes: development is characterized by both change and continuity; individual development occurs within a framework of normative developmental patterns; context plays a critical role in development; and different aspects of development constantly influence one another.

PART ONE

Beginnings

JOHN AND DELORES WILLIAMS

"Three twenty-two . . . four seventy . . . sixty-eight cents . . . Your total is two hundred thirty-nine dollars and fifty-seven cents," the supermarket cashier said, staring blankly at Delores Williams from behind strands of dyed blond hair. Delores looked at her husband John in disbelief. "Two hundred and thirty-nine dollars," she repeated, as if to make sure that he had heard. How could they have spent so much money on food for the family? Granted, 11-year-old John, Jr., ate like a horse. "Be sure to get some broccoli for dinner," John's mother, Momma Jo, had teased, knowing that JJ hated broccoli. "Then there'll be something left for the rest of us to eat." But 8-year-old Teresa didn't eat like JJ; she hardly ate anything at all. And John's youngest sister Denise skipped a lot of meals. She was always running off to her part-time job or to one of her college courses. So how did they need $239 worth of groceries for a week? It didn't seem possible.

"Let me see that receipt," Delores demanded, as they walked toward the curb. "There's gotta be somethin' wrong. I only have twenty dollars left over to last the rest of the week! What's gonna happen when we have to start buyin' diapers and formula? Do you know how much those things cost? How are we gonna *pay* for this baby? What a mistake this whole thing is!"

"A mistake?" John stopped the shopping cart abruptly. "Come on now, DeeDee. This is our *child* you're talkin' about. We're gonna manage. Why, look how my momma managed when my poppa died. Black teachers in Mississippi didn't make nothin' in those days. But she worked hard and she did it. She saved enough to move us here to Chicago and things got better."

DeeDee looked at him doubtfully. She didn't want to struggle like John's mother had struggled. Already she felt tired. Too tired even to try. Her voice grew quiet, discouraged.

"I guess I'm worried too about whether the baby's gonna be all right. I'm *thirty-six*. What am I doin' pregnant again?"

"Honey," John said, more gently now, "we've been over and over this. You'll get the test next month and it'll tell us everything's OK. But even if there's somethin' wrong, it don't matter. We made this baby together and together we're gonna love him, and raise him, and *pay* for him. We've just got to take things one step at a time. So stop talkin' this 'It ain't no good, it ain't gonna work' stuff. You've been playin' those tunes for weeks now. Get rid of them and start playin' some new ones."

DeeDee looked at John and started to smile faintly, but a sudden squeal of brakes made her turn around quickly. Already a small crowd was gathering around a young woman who lay on the parking lot pavement. Pale and dazed, she was trying to prop herself up, but her ankle was oddly twisted. Her arms and legs looked frail and thin next to her obviously pregnant belly. "The baby," she said. "My God, the baby!"

DeeDee stared. The thought of losing a baby struck her suddenly. Of having a child slip away before you can even see it and hold it. Of course she wanted this baby. It was part of her already, part of both her and John. She wanted it more than anything else in the world.

The driver of the car was bending over the injured woman. "Lady, are you all right? I was just backing up. I was watching where I was going. I swear to God I was. But you fell right into the car. Are you OK? Is someone calling a doctor? For God's sake, let's get an ambulance here!"

DeeDee felt an urge to go to the woman, to try to comfort her. But what would this white woman think of a strange black woman stepping out of the crowd? DeeDee didn't care. She walked over and knelt beside her.

"You'll be OK," she said gently. "You didn't fall very hard. I think it's just your ankle. Why don't you lie back on my sweater here and try to relax. Someone's gone to call an ambulance."

The woman's head sank into the green softness of DeeDee's sweater. "Thanks," she answered gratefully, the fear starting to fade from her face. "It's just . . . This is my first baby."

"I know," said DeeDee. Her voice was almost a whisper. "You don't have to explain to me. I'm pregnant too."

The woman looked at DeeDee and smiled. She reached out her hand and lightly touched DeeDee's wrist. And though DeeDee knew it wasn't possible at such an early stage, she had the sense that she could feel the new life inside her.

FRANK AND CHRISTINE GORDON

"Hey! Way to go! Strike that turkey out! What an arm that guy has," Frank Gordon exclaimed to his wife's brothers-in-law as he rose from his chair before the TV set to reach for another beer. Like everyone else in Pawtucket, Rhode Island, he was an avid Red Sox fan.

"Hey, Paula. Game's over. Let's get goin'," Dan shouted to his wife five minutes later.

"Yeah, we're gonna shove off too," Chuck added. "I gotta be on the job early tomorrow."

The three men sauntered into the kitchen, leaving behind them a chaos of pizza cartons, beer cans, and potato chip bags. Their wives were seated around the small kitchen table, laughing and talking over mugs of coffee.

"You'd think you girls never got to see each other, the way you three go on," Frank commented, as he tossed Dan and Chuck their jackets. Paula, Sarah, and Christine rose reluctantly from the table and carried their mugs to the sink. Then Paula and Sarah went into the back bedroom, each to collect a sleeping child.

"See ya soon, Chrissie," they said to their sister, as they picked their way carefully down the dimly lit back steps. As usual, Dan and Chuck were already in their cars, revving the engines, anxious to be off.

Usually on a weeknight after a ball game Frank would head for the bedroom, leaving Christine to clean up. But tonight he hung around. "You're lookin' good, Chrissie," he said, catching hold of her arm as she passed by. "You could get in trouble lookin' like that."

"I don't know that I want to get in trouble," Christine answered, with an uneasy laugh, knowing exactly what Frank had in mind. "You know I'm not so sure about having another baby just yet."

"What's not to be sure about? We have two girls; we want a boy. You've said so yourself. It's as simple as that."

"Yeah. Well, I know. But . . . Well, I've been kind of thinking about getting a job at the dress shop where Paula works."

"Oh, jeeze, here we go again. Look, Chrissie, I'm not gonna get into another big thing about this. I don't want

you workin' and that's that. You belong here at home with the kids. I can support this family just fine."

"That's not really it, Frank," Christine replied. "I was watching this program on TV this morning, you know? And they were talking about how important it is for a woman to have a sense of really doing something, you know? Accomplishing something . . ."

"So selling dresses to a bunch of broads is accomplishing something and raising your own kids isn't? Is that what you're tryin' to tell me? I swear I can't figure you out. What more do you want for accomplishment? You've got two daughters, a decent apartment, a bunch of fancy gadgets in the kitchen. What's this job of yours gonna get us that we don't already have? Tell me that. I'll tell you what it's *not* gonna get us. It's not gonna get us a son."

"Well, I don't know," Christine answered. "You know, I just think it's something we have to talk about more."

"So we're talkin' about it now. What more do you want?"

Christine wondered what more she did want. It wasn't really something she could put her finger on. Just a vague idea about someday maybe having her own dress shop. Everyone said she had a real flair for clothes. But when she tried to picture getting from her life as it was now to the running of her own business, the whole thing seemed impossible. If I had really wanted to be a businesswoman, Christine thought, I wouldn't have been so quick to marry Frank right after high school.

Christine looked at her wedding picture on top of the TV. A thin, pretty girl of 19 looked back from beneath a lacy white veil. Beside her was Frank, with an air of self-assurance even at 24. The happiest day of her life, she had thought back then. Frank was so handsome he made her the envy of all her friends. Christine's father, Mike, had encouraged the match. He said that Frank was the first "real man" Christine had dated. "He's not like some of those college wimps you've brought home lately," he told her. "You'd be crazy not to hang onto that guy." And hang on Christine did. She built her life around Frank—around his strength, his decisiveness, his self-confidence. He made this once-shy girl feel like the most desirable woman on earth.

"You know what more I want?" Christine said, staring down at the carpet and slowly looking up. "I want us to feel real close. Remember? Like we used to?"

"Hey. We're married. Seven years. How could we be closer?"

"Well, there's having another baby together, I guess," Christine answered. "Raising a little all-star for the Red Sox. What more in life could you accomplish, huh?"

"Now you're thinkin' right!" Frank said, failing to notice the lingering note of doubt in her voice.

"You're doing great, Chrissie," said the large, gray-haired nurse with the ruddy complexion and clear blue eyes. "I didn't have this easy a time until my fifth baby."

Christine's lips and mouth felt too dry from her breathing exercises to respond with more than just a faint smile. But the nurse was right. This delivery was incredibly easy compared to her other two. She felt enormous pressure with each contraction, but not the excruciating pain that had accompanied Becky's and Janie's births. In fact, the whole pregnancy had been easy. Despite her large size in the last trimester, she had felt wonderful. "Sit down. Take it easy," other people would tell her, and Christine would wonder why. She felt like repainting the whole apartment, not sitting around with her feet up.

"It must be a boy," she said to the nurse, after a particularly strong contraction. "Just like his father. Can't wait to get going." She looked over at Frank, who stood by the door, looking nervous and ill-at-ease.

"We'll find out soon," the doctor said. "I can see the head crowning. Push *hard* this time, Christine. Push!"

The details of what happened next were difficult for Christine to remember later. She became totally absorbed in the act of pushing her new baby into the world. With her eyes intently focused on a small spot of sunlight on the ceiling, the voices around her seemed at a distance, muffled and indistinct. A final push, and she felt the baby emerging. Joy flooded her body, like the rush of some intoxicating drug. Then she heard Frank's voice, loud and excited: "What is it? What is it?"

"What a beautiful baby," the nurse said, as she took the baby from the doctor.

"But is it a boy? Tell me, is it a *boy*?"

KAREN POLONIUS

When the bell rang announcing the end of class, 16-year-old Karen Polonius quickly gathered up her belongings and was the first person out the door. She practically ran down the corridor to her locker, whirled the combination, and tugged open the door. Reaching into the jumble of school books and discarded candy wrappers, she grabbed what she needed for her homework assignments and rushed out the side exit. The number 6 bus was at the corner, just ready to pull away. Karen jumped on. Now she relaxed a little. Sliding into a seat, she unwrapped a stick of gum and gazed aimlessly out the window. All too soon she reached her stop. She got off and walked the two short blocks east. Here she was. There was no more putting it off. Taking a deep breath, she pushed open the glass door and stepped inside the building. The sign overhead read: FRESNO FAMILY PLANNING CLINIC.

Karen sat down and began nervously poking through a stack of magazines, waiting to be called. So what if she felt a little queasy in the mornings and her period was six weeks late. It might just be because she was frightened. Jeff did use condoms, after all. Except for just once or twice. But that couldn't be enough to get her pregnant, could it?

Karen felt numb as she sat in Dr. Rich's office, listening to his sympathetic voice. "As I see it, Karen, you have several choices. You can go through with the pregnancy and give up the baby for adoption . . ." This can't be happening, Karen thought. It's *got* to be a mistake. Or maybe it's an April Fool's joke. That's it! Today's April first. Dr. Rich's voice droned on: "At this early stage there would be little risk to you in removing the products of conception, but going this route would of course depend on your personal beliefs . . ." What did he mean "the products of conception"? Does he mean the baby? He *must* mean the baby.

The trip home was a blur for Karen. All she could remember clearly was fumbling in her bag for her keys as she stood on the doorstep in the late afternoon shadows. Thank God her mother wasn't home from work yet. She could go upstairs and try to get herself together.

"Maybe Mom won't even notice anything's the matter," Karen said to herself as she flopped onto her bed. Mom was always preoccupied these days trying to sell those dumb houses to those stupid people. Well, maybe she shouldn't knock it. It hadn't been easy for Mom since the divorce. Dad was almost always late with the support payments, and sometimes he didn't send them at all. "What did I tell you? Men are no damn good. They only think of themselves," Karen's mother would say when the end of the month came and went and no check had arrived in the mail. "I hope Mom's not right," Karen prayed, as she picked up the phone to call Jeff.

Karen wasn't sure how Jeff would react when she broke the news to him. But she wasn't prepared for what happened. Jeff, usually so cool and easygoing, panicked. And Karen's mention of possible marriage only made things worse.

"Married? Are you *crazy*? I'm not ready to get married. I don't know about you, but *I'm* going to college. And what about law school, huh? I'm not gonna ruin my life!" There was an icy silence. "I'm telling you, Karen," Jeff finally said, barely containing his anger, "if you keep trying to push this fatherhood thing on me, I'll swear it's not my kid."

So much for Mr. Wonderful, Karen thought bitterly, as she ripped the pictures of Jeff off her bedroom wall. Mom *was* right. Men are no damn good. But what was she going to do now? Have an abortion? No, she couldn't destroy her own baby. But what then? Adoption? Could she really give away a part of herself?

It took Karen two weeks to summon the courage to tell her mother what the problem was. By then she had decided: She was going to keep the baby.

Karen's mother was incredulous. She just stood there with the potato peeler poised in midair, as if she couldn't believe what she was hearing. Then she got angry. "How could you do such a dumb thing? Didn't I tell you to be careful when you went out with that guy? Well, you can't keep the baby. That's all there is to it. The idea's *ridiculous!*"

Karen exploded. She was sick and tired of people telling her she was crazy or ridiculous. "Damn it, Mom! It's *my* body and *my* baby. I have the right. For once in my life I'm gonna make a decision without other people telling me what to do. Make love! Have an abortion! I've had it with all of you. I'm gonna love this baby and this baby's gonna love me. And nobody's ever gonna hurt my baby the way they've hurt me!"

Karen was crying now and nearly hysterical. She ran out the back door, with her mother calling behind her. "Karen, come back here! Come back!"

Karen lay on her bed, the early autumn sunlight streaming through the window and forming geometric patterns on the folds of the blue-flowered sheets. Only one thought occupied her mind this morning: How in the world was she going to get up? It was as if she had no stomach muscles any longer, nothing with which to pull herself into a sitting position. She decided to dangle her legs over the side of the mattress and slide out of bed. She edged her way to the side of the bed, holding her pregnant belly, as if carrying the baby in her hands. Suddenly, a small foot sharply kicked her left palm. Karen pulled her hand back quickly. She didn't like it when the baby kicked so hard. The sensation of her own flesh rippling and bulging was disturbing to her.

Karen lay still for a minute, until the baby finally stopped moving. She was just about to resume her shuffle to the side of the bed, when an intense pain gripped her abdomen. It encircled her like a large belt being pulled tighter and tighter. Karen gasped and struggled to sit up. The baby wasn't due for another two weeks. What was happening to her? The pain grew worse, until it seemed to envelop her whole body. Karen began to panic. This wasn't the way it was *supposed* to happen. Everyone had told her that labor would start slowly, giving her time to get in control. This sudden, agonizing pain was not what she expected. As Karen lay gripped by the strong contraction, she felt a warm wet-ness slowly soaking the mattress beneath her. Oh, no, she thought. My water must have broken! How could this all be happening so fast? And then out loud she began screaming: "Mom! *Mom!*"

THREE CHILDREN IN CONTEXT

One baby has already entered the world, and two more are soon to be born. These three children will encounter different circumstances that will help to shape their lives. John and DeeDee's child will face economic struggles and the challenges of being black, growing up in an inner city. This child, however, will also have a very supportive family, with strong ties of love and commitment. Although DeeDee voices much concern about paying for another child, she feels deep down that the baby is a cherished addition to her life.

Christine Gordon is more ambivalent about having another baby. Nevertheless, she finally agrees to become pregnant, largely in the hope of giving Frank the son he wants. Christine hopes that a son will renew feelings of closeness in her marriage. This child will enter a family-centered environment, where traditional sex roles are accepted as the "natural order" of things.

Karen Polonius, in contrast, does not even have a chance to try out the traditional role of wife. Her baby will be born to a mother who herself is still in many ways a child. Inexperienced at motherhood and lacking emotional support from others, Karen faces a difficult time ahead.

How the course of development is influenced by life circumstances is a major theme of this book. The fictional characters you have just met face different situations, which in turn will affect their children. All, of course, have certain things in common: they are English-speaking, live in the urban United States, and are of moderate means. Despite this common ground, however, enough differences exist among these families for each to raise a child who is in many ways different from the others. By reading about the lives of these three children, we hope you can better appreciate the family's influence on development.

We also hope you will better appreciate the two-way interaction between child and environment. While children are affected by the circumstances around them, they also influence those circumstances. Thus, as a child's individual style emerges over time, that style has an impact on those who are important in the child's world. Lives unfold amid a constant interplay of person and environment. You will witness this process in the lives of our three children.

Chapter 2

The Contexts of Development

If you want a seed to develop into a normal, healthy plant, you must give it appropriate soil, light, and moisture. The quality of these environmental factors, along with characteristics of the seed itself, will determine how it grows and matures. All living things develop in an environment—a *context*—and the nature of that context influences the course of development. This is as true of humans as it is of other species. Human development, both physical and psychological, requires an appropriate context for its unfolding. If that context is abnormal, development may be, too.

Evidence for this comes from the occasional discovery of a child who has been isolated from human contact for years. One such child, a boy of about 12, was found in a forest in Aveyron, France, in 1799. Newspapers called him "the wild boy of Aveyron" because his behavior was more like an animal's than a human's. Authorities surmised that he had been abandoned years before by impoverished parents, a practice not uncommon at the time. A doctor took an interest in the boy's case and tried to "civilize" him. But despite intense efforts, Victor, as the doctor called him, remained abnormal in all respects, without social skills and unable to use language.

A similar, more recent case is that of a girl named Genie. From the time she was a year old, her emotionally unstable father imprisoned her in a small room, harnessed in a sitting position during the day and often bound in a cagelike crib at night. By the time she was discovered at age 13, Genie was physically deformed and underdeveloped from being kept so confined. She was also seriously retarded in every area of human functioning. In time Genie made some progress in physical and intellectual development, including modest use of language, but she remained severely handicapped in establishing social relationships (Curtiss, 1977; Ruch and Shirley, 1985; Rymer, 1993).

Because no one knows what Victor and Genie were like at birth, it is not clear to what extent their deficiencies were caused by their early isolation or why the later attempts to help them had such limited success. We do not know whether they remained abnormal because of inborn defects, such as mental retardation, or because of irreversible damage from their early environmental deprivation. Still, their cases provide support for the idea that human contact is essential for normal development.

Early environmental deprivation need not be as extreme as this to have harmful effects on development. In the past, orphaned infants were sometimes raised in barren institutions, with almost no physical or social stimulation. They were fed and kept clean, but most of the time they were left alone, with little to look at or touch. No one talked to them, played with them, or gave them loving attention. Lacking the physical and social stimulation that human infants need, these children soon became apathetic, unresponsive, and withdrawn (Karen, 1994; Spitz, 1945). In North America and western Europe today, orphanages are uncommon, and babies who spend time in institutions, such as hospitals, are seldom so neglected. Even so, children separated from their parents before age 4 and reared in institutions still show long-term negative effects, especially in their relationships with peers and in their later parenting skills (Rutter, 1988). Current researchers believe that the effects of early institutionalization depend on the type of stimulation and care provided, the appropriateness of that care and stimulation to the age and individual nature of the child, and the

This picture is from a movie about the real-life case of Victor, "the Wild Boy of Aveyron." When found in a forest at about age 12, Victor had no language and scrambled around on all fours. Even after five years of instruction in human ways, he remained abnormal in all respects.

availability of opportunities for normal give-and-take between infant and caregiver (Provence, 1989).

Most people do not suffer early environmental deprivation, but we are all partly the product of the contexts in which we develop. You can see this by comparing people raised in different **cultures**—that is, in the context of different systems of beliefs, values, and guidelines for behavior. These elements of culture help to shape the behavior of the people who share them. As a result, people raised in different cultures tend to show different patterns of personality characteristics, cognitive skills, and social relationships (Harkness, 1992; Rogoff and Morelli, 1989; Whiting and Edwards, 1988).

Culture:
A system of beliefs, values, and guidelines for behavior.

For example, the social organization and expectations of traditional Japanese culture are quite different from those of North American culture. Conformity to the group rather than individual assertiveness is the principal guide to behavior. Respect and agreeableness are highly valued, as are emotional maturity, self-control, and courtesy (Hess et al., 1980). Family bonds are very tight and relationships are closely dependent. Newborns are viewed as initially *independent* (not bound to the group), and making them *dependent* (and part of the group) is considered an urgent task (Caudill and Weinstein, 1969; Doi, 1981). Traditional Japanese mothers *never* part from their young children, even to go shopping (Takahashi, 1986). Many fathers devote long hours to their jobs, leaving mothers to take full responsibility for children and household tasks (Nakagawa et al., 1992). Thus, Japanese culture fosters certain personal and social characteristics that are quite different from those fostered by North American culture (Stevenson, Azuma, and Hakuta, 1986).

Even within the same general culture, variations in living circumstances have an impact on development. The three families we introduced at the beginning of Part One come from different economic circumstances, ethnic groups, and communities. While all three families are influenced by the dominant North

The cultural context has a great influence on development. Japanese infants, for example, are seldom separated from their mothers. Coats are even available with specially designed hoods in which women can carry their babies

American culture, they come from cultural backgrounds that differ in some respects. Other factors in their lives, such as relationships among family members, are continually changing, and these also affect the environment in which their children are raised. In addition, the children born into these three families will each have a unique set of genes, which will further contribute to developmental differences among them. Thus, each of the three children in the vignettes that open each unit of this book will grow up with a different set of contextual influences, and as a result their developmental paths will differ in many ways.

AN OVERVIEW OF DEVELOPMENTAL CONTEXTS

When we say that human development takes place in context, we are actually referring to a set of contexts. The contexts for development include human evolutionary history; the culture into which a child is born; the particular period in history during which the child lives; the community the child is part of; the child's home, family, peer group, and school; and the surrounding socioeconomic climate. All of these influence development—usually in complex, interlocking ways. For instance, many common features of modern North American culture, such as television sets, two working parents, out-of-home child care, and formal schooling, do not go together just by coincidence; they are part of the same societal pattern, and their influences supplement one another.

Urie Bronfenbrenner (1979, 1989) of Cornell University has suggested a way of conceptualizing developmental contexts that helps to clarify how they are related to each other and how they influence development. He proposes a model of concentric rings, with each ring influencing all the rings inside it. As you can see in Figure 2.1, the child is at the center of the rings, bringing to development a particular *biological makeup*. Surrounding the child is the first ring, the *immediate environment*. It contains all the settings, the people, and the physical objects with which the child has direct contact. For almost all North American children, this includes home, family, toys, playgrounds, peers, classrooms, and teachers.

The immediate environment, however, does not exist in a vacuum. It is embedded in a broader *social and economic context*. For instance, the materials present in a classroom and the curriculum taught there are shaped by both a school board and the community's economic circumstances. Indirectly, therefore, these other factors influence the child. Similarly, while a child may have no direct contact with a parent's boss, the boss may affect the parent's behavior at home, which in turn affects the child. These broader, indirect social and economic influences make up the second ring in Figure 2.1.

The third ring in Figure 2.1 is the *cultural context*. It consists of all the beliefs, attitudes, values, and guidelines for behavior that people in a particular society tend to share. For example, most adults in our society believe that babies need a great deal of individual attention and that they should ideally receive much of their care from their mothers. This belief is part of our culture and affects how babies are cared for. The value that most Americans place on democracy, independence, and economic success is also part of our culture and influences what children are taught, both at home and at school. Culture, in fact, is the main source of people's ideas about what is "good" and "right."

The rest of this chapter is devoted to looking at each of the rings in Bronfenbrenner's model. We will examine the impact of these developmental contexts throughout the book as we look at the major periods of child development.

THE BIOLOGICAL CONTEXT

The first developmental context we will consider is the child's biological makeup, which lies at the center of Bronfenbrenner's model. It includes three components: (1) the evolutionary heritage shared by all humans; (2) the child's individual genetic inheritance; and (3) the results of interactions between genes and the environment.

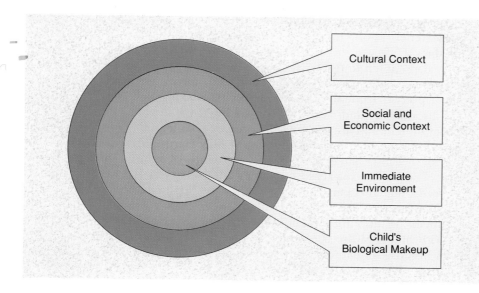

FIGURE 2.1 THE CHILD'S DEVELOPMENTAL CONTEXTS
Urie Bronfenbrenner has suggested that a child's development is influenced not only by his or her biological heritage but also by the immediate environment and the larger circumstances in which he or she is brought up.

Cultural Context

Social and Economic Context

Immediate Environment

Child's Biological Makeup

THE HUMAN EVOLUTIONARY HERITAGE

Children do not enter the world as totally blank slates or neutral creatures that have to be taught all "human" behaviors. Instead, they come equipped with a rich evolutionary heritage that greatly affects how they act. This heritage consists of some traits shared by all mammals; others shared by all primates (the order of animals that includes humans, apes, and monkeys); and still others characteristic of humans alone. For example, human infants, like other mammals, are born with the ability to suck and obtain physical nourishment from their mothers. Like other primates, they also have an inherited tendency to seek social stimulation and to form strong attachments to caregivers. In addition, they have a built-in tendency to detect and attend to speech sounds, something unique to members of the human species. Our evolutionary heritage also includes a rather precise timetable for many developmental milestones, from reaching for and grasping nearby objects to showing the emotion of fear. This timetable applies to babies in widely varying circumstances, a fact that suggests a strong influence of heredity (Suomi, 1977).

A basic "biological given" of primates, including humans, is the strong motivation to investigate novel aspects of the environment and to manipulate objects and solve problems.

Perhaps the most basic of all human biological givens is a strong disposition to act on the environment, rather than being passive. From the beginning, human infants examine and manipulate things around them. This tendency is characteristic of all mammals, but it is most pronounced in the higher primates, with their strong inquisitiveness and inclination to solve problems (Suomi, 1977; White, 1959). For example, monkeys and chimpanzees will work hard to solve a problem, such as unfastening a latch, just for a chance to watch other animals through a window (Butler, 1953). Human children, too, solve problems just for the fun of it. The satisfaction humans get from discovery has helped our species survive by encouraging exploration and invention (Breger, 1974; Harter, 1980).

Closely related to humans' curiosity is their innate propensity for learning. For instance, by the age of 4, children around the world can speak their native language quite fluently. Young children, it seems, have a built-in "readiness" to acquire this complex skill (Lenneberg, 1967). Our nearest animal relatives, the chimpanzees, have great difficulty learning even the rudiments of symbolic communication (Petitto, 1991).

Of course, the ease with which humans learn depends on what they are learning. Researchers at one time were dismayed by the difficulty of "training" newborn babies. However, the trouble stemmed largely from the particular behaviors they had chosen to teach. Newborns can quickly learn to adjust the rate of their sucking (DeCasper and Fifer, 1980) or to turn their heads from side to side in a precise sequence (Papoušek, 1969). Sucking and head turning are related to nursing and are vital for survival. Babies are born with these responses built in and are biologically "prepared" to learn various ways of using them. As children mature, what they can readily learn undergoes change. The facility for learning language emerges at about 18 months of age; certain abstract concepts are mastered only after adolescence. What we can learn, in other words, depends partly on our level of development. Still, a basic facility for learning is part of our biological inheritance.

As humans, we also inherit a predisposition to be social, to interact and form bonds with others of our species. This social predisposition is essential to our survival. Because human children take years to become self-sufficient, forming ties to others helps ensure that they get the care they need. It is therefore not surprising that babies come equipped with behaviors that tend to elicit caregiving responses from adults. Looking and listening, smiling and cooing, crying, clinging, and following are all biologically based behaviors that help establish early social relationships. Throughout development the human social predisposition can be seen again and again. The preschooler who seeks out peers to play with, the adolescent who forms a romantic attachment, the adult who raises children, are all acting in accordance with their biological makeup.

INDIVIDUAL GENETIC CHARACTERISTICS

We have been discussing biological influences at the species level—the level of inherited predispositions that all humans share. Such predispositions derive from our evolutionary history, as do the general sequences of developmental change that all humans have in common (Charlesworth, 1992; McDonald, 1988). This is not to say that everyone has exactly the same set of genetic traits. Individual differences in physical and mental traits have allowed our species to meet environmental challenges over hundreds of thousands of years. In fact, the evolution of a species can't occur without individual differences. As environmental conditions change, individuals with genetic traits suited to the new conditions survive, while those lacking such traits do not.

Except for identical twins (see Chapter 3), each child has a different individual genetic makeup and thus a somewhat different biological context for development. Such individual differences have both direct and indirect influences on development. Consider the genetic defect that produces Down syndrome. It has direct effects by impairing mental and physical development. But it also has indirect effects because people have certain expectations of what a child with Down syndrome can do, which in turn affect the child's education, living situation, and job opportunities. Similarly, some researchers believe that genes directly influence certain aspects of behavior, such as activity level and wariness (Goldsmith, 1983; Plomin, 1989; Thomas and Chess, 1977). If this is true, these genes would also indirectly influence development through the reactions of other people to the behaviors the genes produce in children (Chipuer et al., 1993; Scarr and McCartney, 1983).

INTERACTIONS BETWEEN GENES AND THE ENVIRONMENT

Even biological characteristics do not stem solely from genetic inheritance. At birth, a child's biological makeup already includes characteristics produced partly by the influence of environmental factors. Maternal health, nutrition, and drug or alcohol use during pregnancy can all influence the child's physical makeup. (We will consider these influences in more detail in Chapter 3.) After birth, the child's biological makeup continues to be influenced by a wide range of environmental factors—for example, nutrition, illnesses, and exposure to lead. In fact, everything the child experiences can have an impact on further biological development. The child's developing brain and central nervous system are particularly susceptible to the effects of experience and the environment—and these, in turn, have a powerful influence on further development and behavior.

As we noted in Chapter 1, many developmentalists are interested in how genes and environment interact to produce behavior. A major question concerns the degree to which genes *constrain*, or put limits on, the environment's influence on particular traits. C. H. Waddington (1966) used the term **canaliza-**

Canalization:
The extent to which environmental influences on particular traits are constrained by genes.

tion to refer to these genetic constraints. In his view, some behaviors are strongly canalized, or "channeled," from the beginning. For example, babies begin to babble, producing consonant-vowel combinations that resemble speech, at about 4 to 6 months of age, regardless of culture or social context. Even with a great deal of environmental variation, this behavior follows its genetically determined course. Other characteristics, such as skill in social interaction, are thought to be much more open to environmental influences.

For some capacities, canalization is relatively weak early in life, and the constraints become more rigid with age. The process is analogous to what happens when water runs down a sandy hillside. At first, the water establishes broad paths, or channels. If water continues to pour down in the same direction, some of the grooves deepen. Eventually, the channels become so deep that rather massive environmental change is needed to reroute them. Some human characteristics develop this way. For example, children may be born with genetic tendencies to be more or less irritable, active, or wary, but initially such tendencies are not firmly established. Genes simply provide broad dispositions for behavior, which may be either intensified or diminished over time, depending on the child's environment. Such behavior is susceptible to environmental input at first, but it becomes difficult to change later.

For other capacities, strong genetic canalization exists early, but later there is increased openness to environmental influences. For example, institutionalization during the first four months of life has little lasting effect on children, which suggests that development during this period is strongly canalized. But institutionalization from 4 to 12 months has a dramatic impact on social and emotional development, indicating that the older infant is more vulnerable to environmental factors. Robert McCall (1981) has proposed that cognitive development also follows such a course. Until the age of 2 years, he argues, cognitive development is strongly canalized by the child's biological makeup. The range of behavior across children is narrow, and widely differing environments have relatively little impact. After age 2, however, developmental pathways diverge. Genetically determined tendencies have a decreasing impact on behavior, and children become more susceptible to variations in experience.

Over time, experience has an impact on the child's biological makeup, just as biological development gives rise to new behaviors and produces new experiences for the child. Gilbert Gottlieb (1991) has suggested that experience plays a role in the canalization of development described above. It is not simply that genes are preprogrammed to gain or lose influence over time, but also that experience changes the biological nature of the child and the way in which genes are expressed. Brain maturation underlies the emergence of many behaviors, such as the increasing perceptual abilities of early infancy and the acquisition of language in the second year of life. However, it is also clear that experience, made possible by new behavioral capacities, in turn actually promotes the further development of brain structures and connections (Schore, 1994).

THE CHILD'S IMMEDIATE ENVIRONMENT

Ultimately, all the contextual factors that influence a child operate through the people, places, and things with which the child has direct contact—that is to say, through the child's immediate environment. The people in the immediate environment are especially important, both because they interact directly with the

Young children especially enjoy objects and playthings that invite action. They will often carry out the same action over and over simply for the reward of doing it.

The child's development is influenced not just by parents but by the entire family system. In some cases this involves an extended family, including grandparents and other relatives.

child and because they are largely responsible for the child's physical surroundings. Parents, for example, not only play with their children but also choose their playthings. The way in which they do each of these things can affect the children's development. While no particular set of toys is required for optimal development, availability of objects that are responsive to a child's actions (such as "busy boxes" or home computers) has been found to be related to the pace of cognitive development (Bradley et al., 1989; Gross, 1990; Lepper and Gurtner, 1989).

In the following sections we will look at several parts of the typical North American child's immediate environment. First and foremost is the family, but also important are day care, peer groups, neighborhoods, and schools.

THE FAMILY CONTEXT

The family is a dominant part of a child's immediate environment. Family members interact directly with the child every day, stimulating language development and other cognitive skills. Family members provide children with their first opportunities to form social relationships. The emotional quality of these relationships can have far-reaching effects, influencing a child's curiosity, problem-solving attitude, and interactions with peers. Family members also provide models for behavior. Children imitate the people around them, especially the people they love and admire (Bandura, 1986). Parents and older siblings model not only specific behaviors, but also general roles. Much of a child's understanding of what it is to be male or female, mother or father, husband or wife, comes from the family (Parsons and Bales, 1955; Sroufe and Fleeson, 1986). Finally, the ways in which families are structured and the tasks children are given to do foster the development of particular characteristics. For example, children in many cultures develop the capacity to nurture by helping to care for younger siblings (Whiting and Edwards, 1988).

THE FAMILY AS A SYSTEM

For many years researchers who studied the family's influence on children focused almost exclusively on the role of the mother, because she traditionally had the major *direct* impact on young children. The importance of maternal care is also a cornerstone of psychoanalytic theory, which became quite influential earlier in this century. Insofar as it underscored children's psychological need for a warm, emotionally supportive environment, this stress on the mother-child relationship was beneficial. But developmentalists came to realize that such a focus was too narrow (Thomas and Chess, 1982; Parke and Stearns, 1993). In some cultures, the mother is not the only caregiver, even for very young children (Tronick et al., 1992). In many African-American families, grandmothers play an important role in child rearing (Pearson et al., 1990). Across cultures, the roles of fathers and siblings had been neglected in the earlier research. The traditional view of the family's influence on children had to be expanded to include other family members besides the mother.

Even the influence of mothers on children had to be examined more broadly. Mothers never care for children in isolation. The quality of their caregiving is influenced, both directly and indirectly, by other family members. Today, the developmental influences of fathers and siblings are topics of active study, as is the broader family support system that includes grandparents and other members of extended families (Bengtson and Robertson, 1985; Clingempeel et al., 1992; Hartup, 1989; Pearson et al., 1990). Also of great interest is the child's own role in shaping family interactions. Modern developmentalists do not see the family as a set of separate relationships existing side by side. Instead, they see the family as a complex, interconnected system (Belsky and Isabella, 1987; Minuchin, 1985; Sroufe and Fleeson, 1988).

At the simplest level, the idea of a system implies that each family member's behavior depends in part on the behavior of the others. What a mother does, for instance, depends in part on what her husband and children do, just as a child's behavior is partly determined by the behavior of parents and siblings. Notice that influences between family members always move in two directions, not just one. While characteristics of parents help to shape the behavior of their children, characteristics of the children in turn influence the parents' behavior. These **bidirectional effects** (Bell, 1968) can be seen very clearly in the development of sex-typed behavior in children. Many American parents behave differently toward their sons than toward their daughters. Toddler girls get their hair tied in ribbons; toddler boys get tossed in the air. These different styles of caregiving encourage children to act in sex-typed ways, which in turn reinforce the parents' beliefs and child-rearing practices. Developmentalists also call this two-way stream of influence **reciprocal determinism** (Bandura, 1985).

Arnold Sameroff has introduced a **transactional model** to describe the ongoing bidirectional effects between parents and children, taking into account the family's social and economic context as well (Sameroff and Fiese, 1989; Sameroff and Chandler, 1975). A newborn baby enters the family system with certain innate tendencies. The parents, because of their own circumstances and characteristics, respond to the baby in particular ways. The baby's behavior then gradually changes, partly because of the parents' influences, partly because of maturation. These changes in the baby's behavior in turn elicit new responses from the parents, which further influence the child, and so on, in an ongoing cycle.

Sameroff's transactional model can help to answer some otherwise puzzling

Bidirectional effects/reciprocal determinism: Two-way processes by which child and parent influence each other's development.

Transactional model: Sameroff's model describing ongoing two-way influences between children and environmental context.

These siblings are playing cooperatively together, with the older sister assuming a role of authority. Researchers are interested in the consequences of such sibling relationships and in how they are influenced by other relationships in the family system.

questions, such as why certain moderately premature infants have developmental problems. The answer does not lie solely with the babies, for in general such infants develop quite well (Cohen and Beckwith, 1979; Greenberg and Crnic, 1988). Moreover, those who later encounter developmental problems are physically indistinguishable at birth from those who do not. It seems that the premature babies who have trouble are mainly those in very low-income homes (Sameroff and Chandler, 1975). Sameroff's transactional model can help us understand what goes wrong in these cases. A premature infant requires special care and poses special challenges for parents. These demands can be overtaxing for parents already burdened with the many stresses of poverty. Thus, the baby's condition at birth interacts with the parents' psychological state, which itself is shaped by their economic and social circumstances. In some cases the parents become less effective caregivers, and the baby fails to thrive.

Note that it is the transaction between *particular* actors in a *particular* context that gives rise to the outcome. In middle-class families, which do not suffer the extra burdens of poverty, moderate prematurity in an infant does *not* predict negative outcomes. Studies have found that middle-class mothers of premature babies generally provide more intensive and supportive care than do middle-class mothers of full-term infants. Premature babies in these families generally catch up with full-term babies developmentally by about age 2 (Cohen and Beckwith, 1979; Greenberg and Crnic, 1988). Apparently, premature infants, with their special needs, tend to elicit sensitive care from caregivers who have adequate social support and are not unduly stressed.

CHARACTERISTICS OF FAMILY SYSTEMS

Family systems are complex, partly because they are made up of many subsystems (relationships between siblings, between parents and children, between mother and father, and so forth), all of which are joined together in a coherent, interlocking network. The various relationships in a family system fit together like pieces of the same jigsaw puzzle. For example, qualities of siblings' relationships are predictable from qualities of mother-child relationships (Dunn and Kendrick, 1982a; Hetherington, 1988; Robb and Mangelsdorf, 1987). Similarly, one parent's relationship with a particular child is connected with all other relationships in the family. If a mother is seductive toward her son, her relationship with her daughter is often hostile (Sroufe et al., 1985), and her relationship with her husband is often emotionally distant (Sroufe and Fleeson, 1988). Rather than saying that the mother-son relationship causes the mother-father distance, or that the mother-father distance causes seductiveness toward the son, we would prefer to emphasize that the network of relationships within the family is a coherent one. Close, supportive relationships between spouses generally are not found in families in which one parent is emotionally overinvolved with an opposite-gender child, and vice versa. Thus, the idea of the family as a system means more than that each individual member affects the other members. It also means that each family member is affected fundamentally by the organization of the *whole* (Sroufe and Fleeson, 1988).

In addition to being a complex and coherent network of relationships, a family is a dynamic, *open* system, subject to change as well as continuity. One way in which family systems change is by adding or losing members. For instance, family relationships change fundamentally when a new child is born (Cowan and Cowan, 1992). Before the birth, a family system already exists, and the child is fitted into that system more or less smoothly. How the child fits into the existing family system can even be influenced by such factors as whether the parents wanted a boy or a girl (Stattin and Klackenberg-Larson, 1991). Consider the Gordon family that we introduced in the story preceding this chapter. Wanting a son is Frank and Christine's primary reason for having a third child. A place in the system is already prepared for the child. If the baby *does* turn out to be a boy, he will immediately have a role of sizable importance—he will make the family "complete." But if the baby turns out to be a girl, Frank may actively show his disappointment toward both the child and his wife, and Christine may feel she has failed by not producing a boy. Or, if she has a son and the wished-for closeness with Frank doesn't result, Christine may become angry at her husband. The wishes, expectations, and needs of the Gordons will influence how they react to the baby and to each other after the baby's birth. The arrival of the new baby will alter the family system, with effects on all the individuals and relationships within it.

Family systems also change as circumstances change, as crises are faced, and as members enter new developmental phases (Conger et al., 1990; Hill, 1970). Developmentalists are particularly interested in how a child's development influences and is influenced by the overall development of the family. The Gordons' hoped-for son may initially be *given* the role of holding the family together, but as he grows older, he may actively *seek out* this role, particularly if the relationship between his mother and father worsens. As they develop, children become active participants in defining and maintaining the family system. Individual development and family development are always closely linked.

Another feature of family systems is that they are subject to cyclical influences that can be repeated across generations. For example, parents' level of marital harmony is related to their children's personality development (Emery, 1982; Patterson and Dishion, 1988; Rutter, 1988). Children's personalities in turn predict their future marital satisfaction and harmony (Cowan, Cowan, and Hemming, 1986; Stolnick, 1981). Family harmony or discord, in other words, tends to perpetuate itself. In one study such cycles of influence were demonstrated across four generations (Elder, Caspi, and Downey, 1986). The same seems to be true of harsh parenting practices (Simons et al., 1991): when the parents of one generation are harsh, their children tend to be harsh when they become parents. Fortunately, this cycle can be broken if a child from such a background manages to establish a solid, supportive marital relationship in adulthood.

FATHERS IN THE FAMILY SYSTEM

Developmentalists have become increasingly interested in fathers' influences on children, which can be either direct or indirect (Hewlett, 1992; Lamb, 1986; Parke and Stearns, 1993). Studies of the *direct* effects of fathers on children's development have revealed that children are involved with their fathers and emotionally attached to them even in infancy (Cohen and Campos, 1974; Lamb, 1981; Parke and Stearns, 1993). Such involvement intensifies during the toddler period, especially for boys. In later chapters you will read about the influences of fathers on sex-role learning, cognitive development, achievement motivation, and personality development.

Fathers are commonly quite involved with their toddlers, often engaging them in play.

Fathers also have important *indirect* influences through their impact on the behavior of mothers or siblings. There is evidence that when a father and mother are together, they tend to show more positive emotion toward their children than either does separately (Parke and Stearns, 1993). Apparently, the mere presence of a partner can affect parent-child interactions. In general, marital harmony is associated with nurturant parenting and good child adjustment (Belsky, 1984; Cowan and Cowan, 1992; Easterbrooks and Emde, 1988; Hetherington, 1988). So a father who maintains a positive, supportive relationship with his wife is indirectly benefitting his children. For example, when the father of an infant provides strong emotional support for the mother, her care of their infant is more effective (Belsky and Isabella, 1987; Rutter, 1988). Even women who were troubled as children can become nurturant mothers if they marry supportive men (Caspi and Elder, 1988; Quinton, Rutter, and Liddle, 1984).

A study by Byron Egeland and his colleagues (Erickson, Egeland, and Sroufe, 1985) provides further evidence for the positive effects that fathers can have on children. Actually, not all the men involved in this study were biological fathers. Some were merely involved on a steady basis with the child's mother, perhaps living with her, perhaps not. Most of the families in the study had low incomes. Egeland assessed the children from birth through school age to see how well they fared in their social and emotional development. Some children functioned well at all ages; others did poorly at all ages; still others started out functioning poorly but ended up functioning well. Egeland wondered why some children made this positive turnaround. He and his colleagues found one major difference between children whose functioning improved over time and children who showed consistently poor development. The difference was that the mothers of improving children were more likely to have formed a stable partnership during the intervening years. The fact that these two factors are related does not necessarily mean that one caused the other. A child's improved behavior could have been due to other situational changes that just happened to coincide with the mother's formation of a stable relationship. The presence of the new "stepfather" could have had a direct and positive influence on the child. Or the mother's partner could have had an *indirect* effect on her parenting by giving her emotional support. This last possibility is the one that Egeland thinks is most likely.

Both older and younger siblings learn a great deal from each other about nurturance, responsibility, sharing, leadership, and conflict resolution.

Birth-order effects:
Systematic differences in children's behavior depending on whether they are first-born, second-born, third-born, and so on.

SIBLINGS IN THE FAMILY SYSTEM

Within the family system siblings, too, have both direct and indirect effects. Older siblings' direct effects on younger children include serving as companions, teachers, and models. In one study that compared girls with and without older siblings, those with older brothers were found to be more competitive, while those with older sisters were more "feminine" (Clarke-Stewart, 1977). Apparently, when an older sibling is present, a younger child may learn directly from that sibling's behavior. Older children also learn directly from the experience of having a younger sibling as they take on a new role in the family and learn to interpret the younger child's behavior (Mendelson, 1990). At the same time, siblings indirectly influence one another's development through the impact they have on their parents' behavior (Dunn, 1988).

Some researchers believe that sibling influences are responsible for what are called **birth order effects**—systematic differences in children's behavior depending on whether they are first-born, second-born, third-born, and so on (Ernst and Angst, 1983; Zajonc and Markus, 1975). For example, second-born children tend to be less motivated to achieve in school than first-borns, but they are also more sociable and outgoing (Clarke-Stewart, 1977). Many factors may contribute to such differences, but all arise from direct or indirect sibling influences. For instance, parents' attention necessarily is divided when a second child is born, so the second-born may get less parental stimulation and encouragement. The parents may also have a more relaxed attitude toward a second child. In addition, the second-born has a live-in peer to interact with from the start, a situation that could promote a more sociable nature.

Sibling influences are not the same across all families, not even in families matched by the age and sex of their children. One reason is that the influence of siblings is mediated by other aspects of family functioning. For example, the impact of a younger sibling on a first-born depends on how the family system was previously working, how the parents prepared the older child for the baby's arrival, and how the family adjusts to developmental changes in each child (Dunn, 1988; Howe, 1991; Kreppner, 1988).

You will learn about other sibling influences in later chapters. The important point for now is that many of these influences, and the reasons for them, could never be discovered if researchers failed to view the family as a system. Sibling relationships clearly affect children's development. Parents' treatment of each of their children influences the children's relationships with each other, and the sibling relationships in turn have an impact on the parents' behavior. Each relationship touches every other (Hetherington, 1988), and much is missed when any one relationship is viewed in isolation.

IMMEDIATE CONTEXTS OUTSIDE THE FAMILY

As children grow older, they increasingly find themselves in settings outside the family. Four of these have major roles in development: (1) day care; (2) the peer group; (3) the neighborhood; and (4) the school. We will say a great deal about the influences of these settings in later chapters. Here we simply provide an introduction and raise some of the questions that researchers have tried to answer.

THE DAY-CARE SETTING

As the proportion of single parents steadily rises, and as more mothers seek work outside the home, the use of day care is increasing in the United States. By

1991, there were about 10 million American children under the age of 5 with employed mothers (U.S. Bureau of the Census, 1994). As shown in Figure 2.2, the majority of these children were not enrolled in formal day-care centers or preschools. Twenty percent were cared for by their father at home while their mother worked. Nearly a quarter were cared for by a grandparent or other relative. A comparable number were cared for by a nonrelative—either an individual babysitter or a **family day-care** provider, who cares for several children at a time. Most of the remainder simply accompanied their mothers to work.

Since the use of day care in the United States is so widespread and is growing so rapidly, developmentalists are interested in its impact. Many important questions have not yet been answered. The effects of day care on cognitive development appear to be minimal but positive, with early day care a particularly positive factor in the cognitive development of low-income children (Baydar and Brooks-Gunn, 1991; Caughy, DiPietro, and Strobino, 1994; Fein and Fox, 1990). But what are the short-term and long-term effects on children's social and emotional growth? How does day care affect parent-child relationships, especially in infancy? Does the developmental impact differ depending on the age at which day care begins? Does it differ depending on the social class from which a child comes or the type of day care used? These are some of the issues addressed in subsequent chapters, particularly Chapter 6.

Family day care:
A day-care setting in which a group of children are cared for in the home of a nonrelative.

THE PEER GROUP

As a setting for human development, the peer group is second in importance only to the family (Hartup, 1992). And the peer group's influence increases at each developmental period. By adolescence, peers exert a heavy influence on dress, tastes, and activities (Sprinthall and Collins, 1995). The importance of peers grows as children spend more time with them as they get older. By age 11, peers occupy about as much of the average child's time as do adults (Barker and Wright, 1955; Hartup, 1992); thereafter, the balance tips in favor of peers. Teenagers spend seemingly endless hours with their special friends and often view activities with parents as an intrusion. What are children learning in all

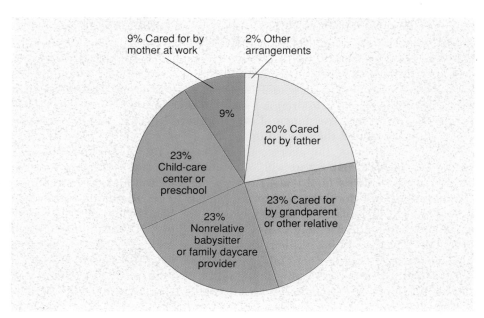

FIGURE 2.2 CHILD CARE ARRANGEMENTS FOR U.S. CHILDREN UNDER 5 WITH EMPLOYED MOTHERS, 1991
Relatively few children of employed mothers attend formal day-care centers or preschools. One reason may be that there are not enough such facilities in this country to meet the need. In any case, the impact of the various alternatives to in-home care by the mother is of great interest to developmental psychologists. (Source: U.S. Bureau of the Census, 1994.)

Ten million U.S. children under the age of 5 now spend some time being cared for by someone other than their parents. Most of these children are in informal day-care arrangements in homes, as shown here.

those hours spent with peers? What skills, values, and expectations do peers convey to one another?

One thing the peer group teaches is how to interact in equal-status, or *symmetrical*, relationships. (In fact, the term *peer* means equal.) Relationships between children and adults are inherently *unequal*. However warm and caring the interactions may be, the adult always retains the power to tell the child what to do. This is not so within a group of same-age peers. Here no child holds any formal authority over the others. As a result, the peer group is a critical setting for practicing and understanding concepts such as fairness, reciprocity, and cooperation. It is also a major setting in which children learn to manage interpersonal aggression (Hartup, 1992).

Another powerful learning experience provided by the peer group is reinforcement of the values, beliefs, and behavior standards that are part of the child's culture. Consider our culture's sex-role standards, the different behaviors expected of girls and of boys. Although parents initially convey them to children, peers are their most dogmatic enforcers. This is particularly true in boys' peer groups, in which a preference for "feminine" toys or pastimes meets with derision even among preschoolers (Langlois and Downs, 1980). There are probably several reasons children are such cultural hard-liners, as we'll discuss in Chapter 10. In any case, much of the process of learning to follow society's rules takes place within the peer group.

We will first examine the peer group in Chapter 10, which deals with early childhood. In later chapters we will follow the peer group's influence into the elementary and high school years. In the process we will answer some important questions: why do some children find it easy to get along with peers while others are socially isolated or actively rejected by them? When do true friendships between children emerge, and what underlies this development? When do children begin to think of their peer groups as having boundaries—of their own friends as "we" and other children as "they"? What promotes this sense of peer solidarity? How conforming are children to their peer groups, and why does conformity seem to intensify during middle childhood and early adolescence? To what extent do the norms and values of adolescent peer groups conflict with those of parents and other adults? Research findings regarding these questions are of great interest to many who study child development.

THE NEIGHBORHOOD

Every family lives in a particular neighborhood with physical and social characteristics that can affect children's development. The type and condition of housing, yards, streets, sidewalks, recreational facilities, and businesses in a neighborhood have an impact on children's activities and developmental opportunities. Even more important, children are also influenced by the other people who live in the neighborhood and by their activities, values, beliefs, and resources. All these factors are obviously affected by the larger social and economic context, which we will discuss shortly. However, there is evidence that the neighborhood itself exerts an influence on children's development that is separate from family influences, on the one hand, and from general social and economic influences, on the other (Burton, in press; Aber, 1994; Brooks-Gunn et al., 1993).

Most of the research on neighborhoods has focused on the impact of various factors associated with community poverty (as opposed to family poverty) on children's development. Having affluent neighbors is associated with positive developmental outcomes in both early childhood and adolescence, regardless of a child's own family income level (Brooks-Gunn et al., 1993). Conversely, adolescents who live in neighborhoods where there are few affluent residents with high-status jobs are at heightened risk for pregnancy and dropping out of school (Crane, 1991). These research results suggest that neighborhoods have their effects on children and adolescents by means of *collective socialization,* in which adults in a neighborhood provide role models and monitoring for local children, rather than by means of *behavioral contagion,* in which negative peer influences spread problem behaviors. The social networks that form in neighborhoods can provide both support and access to resources such as jobs for adolescents. Affluent neighbors may decrease adolescents' risk for certain negative outcomes because they are able to help in practical ways (by providing job leads, for example), as well as in less tangible ways (Aber, 1994).

THE SCHOOL

The school is often thought of as the child's workplace. By age 6 or 7, children in North America spend six hours a day, five days a week, in school. Children in Japan and Western Europe spend even more time in the classroom. The school is thus a potentially powerful influence on development.

School activities vary with a child's age. In North America, nursery schools are often flexibly structured, with an emphasis on social activities. More formal instruction usually begins in the early elementary school years, when most children are cognitively ready for it (White, 1965). Generally, children do not begin to have different teachers for different subjects until middle school. The practice of having one central teacher each year rests on the belief that such a relationship is important for preadolescents, who are more emotionally dependent on adults than older children. Having a central teacher also eases the transition to middle or junior high school (Linney and Seidman, 1989).

Children learn much more at school than the information in their textbooks. Like the peer group, the school is a great instructor in cultural norms and values. For example, studies show that American elementary school teachers respond to their students in ways that reinforce traditional sex roles (American Association of University Women, 1992; Sadker and Sadker, 1994). American schools are also strong conveyors of such mainstream values as neatness, discipline, punctuality, competition, hard work, and material success.

As for the impact of schools on cognitive, social, and emotional development, there is some evidence that how a school is run and how teachers interact with students can affect how positive the school experience is for children (Linney and Seidman, 1989; Rutter, 1983a; Stevenson and Lee, 1990). Characteristics associated with effective schools include strong leadership, teacher participation in decision making, an orderly but not oppressive atmosphere, high expectations, and monitoring of student performance. There is also evidence that cooperative learning experiences, in which students work together in groups rather than competing as individuals, improve both academic performance and social relations, especially race relations (Linney and Seidman, 1989; Slavin, 1987). We will examine these issues further in Chapter 11.

THE SOCIAL AND ECONOMIC CONTEXT

While the family, the day-care setting, the peer group, and the school are major environments in which children develop, all are embedded in a broader social and economic context (the second ring in Figure 2.1). This context includes the community in which a child's immediate environments exist, as well as social institutions such as local and national governments, health-care systems, and religious organizations. It also includes social and economic conditions in the community and in the larger society, such as birth and marriage rates, average family size, crime rates, employment patterns, income levels, and inflation rates. The social and economic context can directly affect children, as when youngsters in low-income inner-city neighborhoods feel the effects of unsafe housing, poor health care, high crime rates, and general overcrowding. At the same time, the social and economic context indirectly affects children by influencing their parents' behavior. If parents are stressed by the hardships of poverty or job loss, the quality of their child care may diminish.

You will see the impact of differences in social and economic context in many parts of this book, especially in the stories of our three families. Later in this chapter, we will discuss the special hardships that a context of extreme poverty and social disadvantage brings. But first we look at changes that most American families have experienced as a result of widely shared changes in social and economic context.

FAMILY CHANGES CAUSED BY SOCIAL AND ECONOMIC FACTORS

A popular TV show of the 1950s, tellingly called *Father Knows Best*, always began with the businessman father arriving at his house in the suburbs after a hard day's work. "Margaret, I'm home!" he would call out, as he opened the front door. In the kitchen his homemaker wife, who had spent the day tending the house and children, was making dinner. Wiping her hands on her clean apron, she would rush to the door to greet the family breadwinner.

Few American families fit this traditional pattern today. Social and economic forces have changed the way most families live. In any single year, only about 60 percent of U.S. children are living with both biological parents (U.S. Bureau of

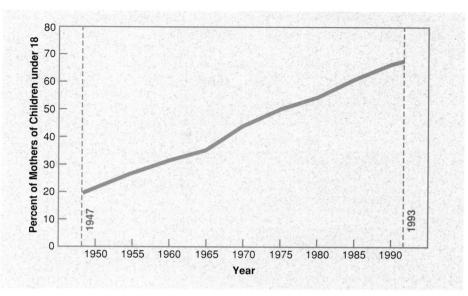

FIGURE 2.3 EMPLOYED MARRIED MOTHERS OF CHILDREN UNDER 18 YEARS, 1947–1993
The proportion of mothers in the work force who are also raising children has more than tripled in 45 years. Researchers are investigating the impact of this change. (Sources: Norton and Glick, 1986; U.S. Bureau of the Census, 1994.)

the Census, 1994). More than 10 percent are living in families with stepparents. In addition, the majority of married women are now working outside the home. This is partly due to changing values and aspirations that have led many women to pursue careers and partly due to economic circumstances that make it hard for families to manage on only one salary. As Figure 2.3 shows, in the years between 1947 and 1985, the proportion of employed married mothers grew from 20 to 60 percent (Norton and Glick, 1986); by 1993 it was approaching 70 percent (U.S. Bureau of the Census, 1994). (Employment rates are even higher for divorced, widowed, and separated mothers.) Even among women with very young children (under age 3), nearly half now have full- or part-time jobs.

Another change in American families that has had a significant effect on child development is an increase in single-parent families. Between 1970 and 1993, the number of single parents with children under 18 in their home doubled (see Figure 2.4). Twenty-seven percent of all children in the United States (17.9 million) live with one parent only (24 percent with the mother; 3 percent with the father) (U.S. Bureau of the Census, 1994). It is estimated that more than 50 percent will spend at least part of their childhood in a single-parent household (Select Committee, 1989). The rise of single-parent families is due both to a high divorce rate and to a growing tendency for unmarried mothers to keep their babies.

To analyze the developmental consequences of these dramatic changes, we begin by considering the impact of mothers' employment on families and children. Then we look at the effects of single-parent families—both those created by teenage pregnancy and those created by divorce. Finally, we consider some other kinds of nontraditional families.

MATERNAL EMPLOYMENT AND ITS EFFECTS

The effects of a mother's employment depend on a host of factors, including the child's age, the amount of time the mother spends at work, the quality of shared time remaining (are both parents exhausted when they get home?), the quality of substitute care, the strength of the parent-child relationship, and, per-

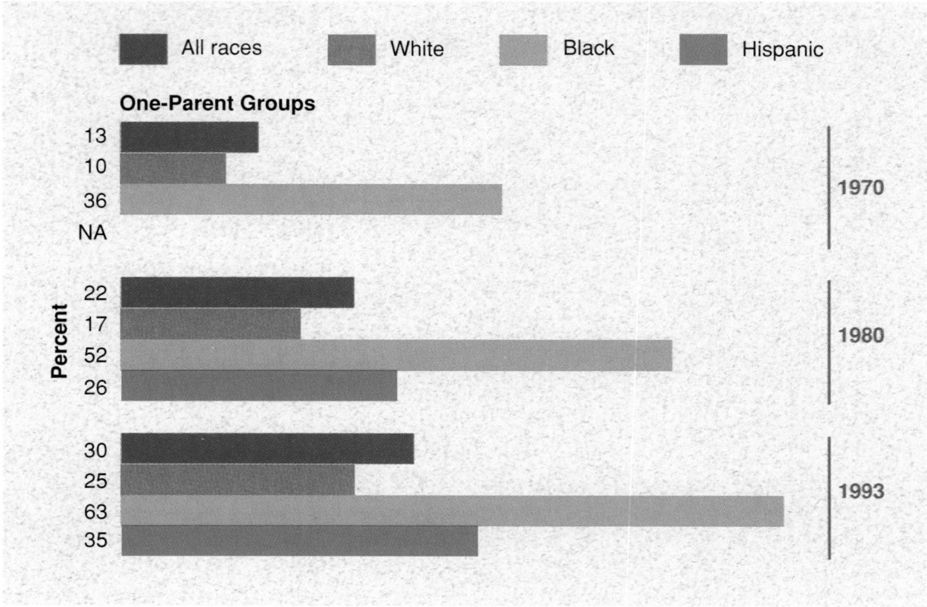

FIGURE 2.4 SINGLE-PARENT FAMILIES, 1970–1993

The proportion of single-parent families has doubled since 1970, and is especially high for black families. The average income level is dramatically lower in such households than in two-parent families. (Source: U.S. Bureau of the Census, 1994.)

haps most significant, the meaning of the woman's employment to both herself and her husband (Hoffman, 1989; Newberger, Melnicoe, and Newberger, 1986). Investigating this last factor, Marion Yarrow found that child development outcomes are related to the mother's satisfaction with her employment status, *whether or not she is working*. Mothers who are unhappy with their situation—especially dissatisfied *nonworking* mothers—have more problems with child rearing than do those who are satisfied. These women enjoy their children less, are less confident as parents, and have more difficulty controlling their children (Yarrow et al., 1962). More recent studies have supported this finding (Benn, 1986; Crockenberg and Litman, 1991; Hock and DeMeis, 1990; Hoffman, 1989). Rita Benn (1986), for example, found that working mothers' feelings about their employment influenced the quality of attachment between them and their infants.

The impact of maternal employment also depends on the father's reaction to the situation. When a father is displeased about his wife's working, he may have more negative feelings toward his children and his parental responsibilities (Crouter et al., 1987). Fathers in two-income families typically perform more household and child-rearing chores than do fathers in one-income families; this increased involvement may be beneficial for the children and may reduce the mother's stress, but it also seems to be related to increased marital discord.

Overall, however, there are few differences between two-parent families in which the mother is employed and those in which she stays home. The differences that do exist appear to be related to family members' satisfaction with the situation and to the degree of social support available to the mother (Hoffman, 1989).

SINGLE PARENTING AND ITS EFFECTS

UNMARRIED MOTHERS   In the last 25 years, the rate of births to unmarried American women has increased greatly. In 1970, 11 percent of all births in the

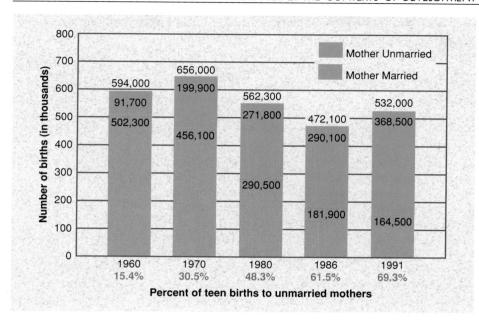

FIGURE 2.5 BIRTHS TO MOTHERS YOUNGER THAN 20 BY MARITAL STATUS, U.S., 1960–1991 *After peaking in 1970, the number of births to teens declined until the mid-1980s, but has recently risen again. The proportion of teenage mothers who are unmarried has risen steadily since 1960. (Source: U.S. Bureau of the Census, 1994.)*

United States were to unwed mothers; by 1991, this figure had risen to 28 percent. About one-third of unmarried mothers in 1991 were teenagers. The total number of births to teenage mothers (married and unmarried) actually declined from 1970 to 1986, but it has been rising since 1987 (see Figure 2.5). In addition, the percentage of teenage mothers who are *unmarried* has more than doubled since 1970 (U.S. Bureau of the Census, 1994).

Children of unmarried teenage mothers often have developmental problems, such as cognitive lags or behavior problems in preschool (Furstenberg, Brooks-Gunn, and Chase-Lansdale, 1989; Musick, 1993). Since these mothers frequently have limited education and very low incomes, the stresses of being poor (not single parenting as such) may be largely responsible for the troubles the children experience. One way to assess the contribution of poverty in these cases is to compare the children of low-income single mothers with the children of low-income two-parent families. Such comparisons reveal few obvious differences in the early years of life (Egeland and Brunnquell, 1979). Poverty, it appears, is a critical factor.

Developmental problems are not inevitable for children of teenage mothers. In cultural settings in which becoming a mother during the teenage years is the norm and in which families provide strong social support, negative impacts on the children of adolescent mothers seem to be minimal (Garcia Coll, in press). In the United States, three factors beyond economic circumstances seem to be critical. Children born to teenagers seem to do best if their mothers finish high school, receive adequate social and emotional support from others, and have reached a high enough level of cognitive development to be able to practice good parenting skills (Furstenberg et al., 1989; Musick, 1993; Sandven and Resnick, 1990; Sommer et al., 1993).

DIVORCED PARENTS   Developmentalists are also concerned about the consequences of being raised by divorced parents. Children may experience certain negative effects if their parents divorce. School-age boys, for instance, tend to show a short-term decline in school achievement and to become more demanding and less obedient toward the parent who has been awarded custody of them (Emery, 1988; Hetherington, 1988). The consequences of divorce and remarriage are diverse and complex, however. Some children prosper, others have sustained developmental problems, and still others show delayed effects during adolescence. These variable outcomes seem to be related to the child's age, sex, and personality, to the quality of home life and parenting, and to the resources available to both parents and child (Hetherington et al., 1989; Hetherington and Clingempeel, 1992).

An important question is whether the reactions observed in children of divorce are caused by the divorce itself or by the parents' conflict (Block, Block, and Gjerde, 1986). Apparently, both factors can play a part. Research has shown that divorce that ends parental conflict is generally better for children than a conflict-ridden marriage, but divorce in which the parents' animosities continue is usually worse for children than a marriage with conflict. Ongoing contact with the noncustodial parent (usually the father) generally reduces the negative consequences of divorce, provided there is no serious conflict between the parents (Hetherington, 1988). These two factors—reduced conflict and continued contact with both parents—seem to be more influential than the particular custody arrangement following a divorce. There are no major differences in the effects of joint custody versus sole custody (usually with the mother), as long as the arrangement leads to reduced quarreling and bitterness (Kline et al., 1989). Adolescents seem to adjust best to a divorce if they can avoid feeling caught between their parents; this outcome is most likely with low conflict and high cooperation between parents (Buchanan, Maccoby, and Dornbusch, 1991).

Divorce can also have a negative impact on children if the parent who has custody is under stress because of a sharp decline in income. Unfortunately, this situation very often arises. In 1992, the median family income for two-parent families was $42,064; for families with no father present, it was only $17,221 (U.S. Bureau of the Census, 1994). The consequences of divorce will be discussed further in Chapters 12 and 14.

Families in the United States are more varied today than ever. Many couples, both heterosexual and homosexual, become parents by adopting children from other countries.

OTHER NONTRADITIONAL FAMILIES

Not all nontraditional families are headed by an unmarried teenage mother or by a divorced parent. The family context for today's children includes adult career women who choose to become mothers outside of marriage, single adoptive parents, and families in which one or both parents are homosexual. Research on such nontraditional families is just beginning, but some important findings are already known. For example, research shows that homosexual parents are as involved with their children as heterosexual parents are, and they report no more problems with their children than do other parents. Moreover, being reared by homosexual parents produces no obvious differences in gender identity, sex-role behavior, or sexual orientation, and it does not appear to put a child at risk for psychological problems (Bailey et al., 1995; Bigner and Jacobsen, 1989; Flaks et al., 1995; Harris and Turner, 1986; Patterson, in press). Other factors, such as social support, parental adjustment, and attitudes toward child rearing appear to be more important than a parent's sexual orientation per se.

SOCIAL CLASS, POVERTY, STRESS, AND THE FAMILY

Another important aspect of the social and economic context is **social class,** or the grouping of people within a society on the basis of their income, occupation, and education. Developmentalists have long been interested in how social class affects child rearing because they assume that living conditions, opportunities, and educational background influence values, attitudes, and expectations regarding children. Researchers have indeed found many differences in child-rearing practices between working-class and middle-class parents. For example, working-class parents in general use more physical means of discipline and emphasize obedience, whereas middle-class parents are more likely to reason with their children and encourage self-expression (McLoyd, 1990).

> **Social class:**
> The grouping of people within a society on the basis of their income, occupation, and education.

These findings do not imply, however, that the techniques favored by middle-class parents are necessarily superior. Both styles of parenting have potential drawbacks. Reasoning, when carried to extremes, can induce much guilt in children, just as physical discipline can become physical abuse. Moreover, different socioeconomic settings may demand different styles of parenting. For middle-class families, a parenting style that is firm and consistent but allows children considerable input in family rule- and decision-making seems to produce the best results (Baumrind, 1989). In poor, inner-city neighborhoods, a parenting style featuring strict rules and an emphasis on obedience may protect children from the dangers of the environment (Musick, 1994). In less threatening settings, parents may be more free to focus on issues such as self-expression because day-to-day life is less dangerous for their children.

In any case, excellent and poor-quality child care cut across class lines (Egeland and Sroufe, 1981). When poor-quality care does occur in low-income families, it is not caused by social class in itself, any more than the simple fact that a mother works means that her children will be cared for inadequately. Instead, poor-quality child care is usually the result of a whole set of circumstances that often accompany economic disadvantage.

The United States is the world's wealthiest nation, yet nearly 14 million American children lived in poverty in 1992, and the number is growing (see Figure 2.6) (U.S. Bureau of the Census, 1994). This figure includes one in five children in the United States overall; the rate is twice as high for African-American

FIGURE 2.6
PERCENTAGES OF
CHILDREN AND ELDERLY
LIVING IN POVERTY,
1960–1992

These figures show that poverty among children has increased in the last two decades, after falling noticeably during the 1960s. Meanwhile, poverty among the elderly continues to decline. Such data have been used to argue that social programs can be effective. Programs to reduce poverty were begun in 1960, but those specifically addressed to children were cut back in the 1970s and 1980s. (Sources: U.S. Bureau of the Census, 1994; Select Committee, 1989. Figures for children under 6 not available prior to 1970.)

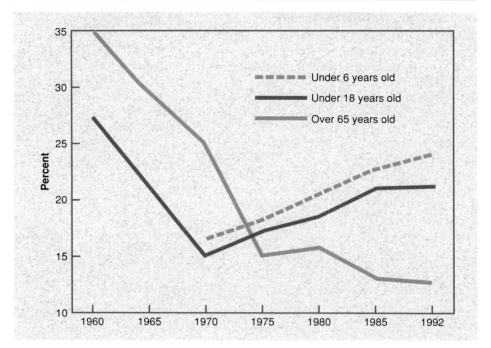

and Hispanic children. As we've said, children in single-parent homes are at high risk for poverty; more than half the children in single-parent American homes are poor (Smeeding and Torrey, 1988). Moreover, single mothers with young children are the most rapidly growing segment of the homeless population (Bassuk and Rosenberg, 1990). At some time during the year, at least 200,000 children in the United States are without a permanent home (Select Committee, 1989).

The factors that often accompany poverty can have serious consequences for child development. Children who grow up in poverty suffer more frequent, persistent, and severe health problems than do children who grow up in better financial circumstances. Often these problems begin before birth (McLoyd, 1990). Many infants born into poverty are of low birth weight, which is associated with a wide range of preventable physical and mental disabilities. They are more likely to be irritable or sickly and to die suddenly before their first birthday. In part because they often live in unsafe environments, children raised in poverty have a much higher rate of accidents than do other children. During middle childhood they generally receive poorer health care and poorer nutrition, and they miss school more often because of illness. They are twice as likely as other children to have impaired vision, impaired hearing, and iron deficiency anemia, and 5 to 10 times as likely to have elevated levels of lead in their blood, which can impair brain function (Baumeister, 1987; Garcia Coll, 1990; Kopp and Kaler, 1989; Lozoff, 1989; Newberger, Melnicoe, and Newberger, 1986).

Moreover, poor families usually experience much more stress than middle-class families do (Egeland, Breitenbucher, and Rosenberg, 1980; McLoyd, 1990). In addition to financial uncertainty, they are more likely to be exposed to a continuous string of negative events (such as job loss, eviction, illness, and

This child's drawing, with its references to drugs and injury, reflects the impact of the high levels of violence to which many poor inner-city children are exposed.

criminal assault) and to chronic problems (such as substandard, overcrowded housing and dangerous neighborhoods). These many sources of stress can adversely affect parenting and child development (Belsky, 1984; Halpern, 1990; Patterson and Dishion, 1988; Pianta, Egeland, and Sroufe, 1990; Werner and Smith, 1989). Parents who are experiencing hard economic times are more likely to be depressed, irritable, and distracted than parents who are financially secure. They may become punitive and erratic, issuing orders backed by threats, insults, and physical punishment (McLoyd, 1990; Radke-Yarrow, Richters, and Wilson, 1988). When stress is coupled with the social isolation often associated with being poor, it can take an even higher toll on the quality of child care (Egeland and Brunnquell, 1979; Gottlieb, 1980; Pianta, Egeland, and Sroufe, 1990; Rutter, 1988; Salzinger, Kaplan, and Artemyeff, 1983).

Levels of stress in the family have been shown to change with changing economic circumstances. Studies during economic recessions reveal that job loss and its hardships are associated with conflict and violence in families, including child abuse (Belsky, 1980; Garbarino, 1981; Margolis, 1982; McLoyd, 1990). Glen Elder and his colleagues (e.g., Elder, Caspi, and Burton, 1987) examined the consequences of paternal unemployment and loss of income for families during the Great Depression of the 1930s. The effects they found included changes in family relationships (with mothers assuming more responsibility), increased irritability and conflict between parents, and less consistent discipline of children. Similar consequences were seen in many farm families during the recession in the rural United States in the 1980s (Conger et al., 1990, 1994). Whether a father's job loss and other economic strains have a negative impact on children depends on the father's behavior and disposition, as well as on the degree of emotional support offered by his wife (McLoyd, 1989; Simons et al., 1992). Children whose fathers become irritable and punitive often develop social and emotional problems. But strong support and encouragement from the mother and other adults can buffer children against these effects.

Another factor associated with poverty that affects child development is the level of violence to which children are exposed. Children in inner cities are surrounded by violence in their schools and on the streets. Half have witnessed acts of violence firsthand. In one study, 24 percent of urban teenagers had witnessed a murder; 72 percent knew someone who had been shot; and 20 percent had had their own lives threatened (Zinsmeister, 1990). At the same time, substantiated cases of abuse and neglect of children in the home continue to increase (820,000 cases in 1991, up 2 percent from 1990) (U.S. Bureau of the Census, 1994). Although abuse occurs in families at all socioeconomic levels, families living in poverty are at particularly high risk (Hashima and Amato, 1994).

Homelessness carries a particularly strong set of risks for children. Compared to children living in poverty but having homes, homeless children suffer from more health problems and are less likely to receive proper immunizations (Wright, 1990). Homeless women are less likely than other impoverished women to receive prenatal care, and rates of low birth weight and infant mortality are higher for their babies (Chavkin et al., 1987). Homeless children experience even greater life stress than other poor children, including more disruption of school and friendships, and they show higher rates of behavior problems (Masten et al., 1993).

Psychologists and social policy makers are especially concerned about the effects of poverty on the "black underclass," the growing numbers of unemployed, welfare-dependent African Americans trapped in inner-city ghettos (Wilson, 1989). Many of the industries that formerly provided employment for the black working class (automobile, textiles, rubber, steel, meat packing) have shut their plants. New industries that might employ these displaced workers have located in the suburbs. The jobs that have remained in the city usually either require advanced education or pay less than a living wage. Consequently, unemployment rates for inner-city blacks have soared. At the same time, middle-class professional blacks have left the inner city for more comfortable neighborhoods. As a result of this exodus, many churches, neighborhood associations, schools, and businesses have either cut back services or closed their doors. Thus, many young people growing up in the inner city lack not only job opportunities but also role models for a successful working life and institutions that could offer them encouragement and guidance (McLoyd, 1990).

Although Hispanic Americans are almost as likely as African Americans to be poor, not all inner-city Hispanic neighborhoods have undergone the profound changes that many black neighborhoods have (Moore, 1989). Working- and middle-class families have not left the *barrio* (urban Spanish-speaking neighborhood) in large numbers, and most social institutions there remain strong. Moreover, local Hispanic-owned businesses and low-skill industries (textiles, apparel, furniture manufacturing) provide the barrio with a wage-based, rather than welfare-based, economy. Similarly, extended kin networks, family businesses, and cultural institutions have enabled recent Asian immigrants to avoid permanent poverty and social isolation (Tharp, 1989).

Climbing out of poverty is difficult for anyone, however. At its worst, poverty can become a self-perpetuating cycle (Baumeister, 1987; Gephart and Pearson, 1988; McLoyd, 1990). Compared with middle-class children, children raised in poverty are more likely to have behavioral, emotional, and cognitive deficits

(Duncan, Brooks-Gunn, and Klebanov, 1994). They are more apt to drop out of school, to be labeled learning disabled, and to spend time in a correctional institution as teenagers (McLoyd, 1990). Being raised in poverty also increases the risk of serious mental disorders, such as schizophrenia (Wolkind and Rutter, 1985). All these outcomes put the children of poverty at an extreme disadvantage in the job market. Lack of good jobs, in turn, ensures continued poverty, and the cycle repeats itself. The stress associated with poverty negatively influences parenting, and inadequately nurtured children grow up less able to cope with stress (Patterson and Dishion, 1988). Of course, some families do a good job of rearing their children under the worst of conditions. "But . . . most parents who live in poverty don't beat the odds; they reflect the odds" (Halpern, 1990, p. 14). Anyone concerned about the development of healthy children must also be concerned about the developmental problems caused by poverty.

THE CULTURAL CONTEXT

In a nursery school in Beijing, China, a teacher is showing a group of 3-year-olds a mechanical Ping-Pong game. The toy consists of a miniature table with a net and two mechanical "players" who stiffly swing their paddles. The teacher explains how the new toy works and then places it on the ground so the children can see it in action. A sea of little bodies quickly surrounds the toy. Thirty pairs of eyes intently watch the performance, but not a single child moves. Those in the front do not even stretch out an arm to hold or finger the toy. The children squat quietly in a tightly packed circle, staring in delighted fascination. At the back of the circle a teacher is holding a Western child, the son of a diplomat stationed in Beijing. She lets the boy down, and without hesitation he breaks through the ranks and lunges for the toy. The teacher quickly scoops him up, while the Chinese children look on (Kessen, 1975).

These differences in behavior between Chinese and Western children are largely a reflection of two different cultures—two different sets of values, beliefs, and guidelines for behavior (Stevenson and Lee, 1990). (The term *culture* is sometimes also used to refer to groups of people who share a common set of values, beliefs, and guidelines for behavior.) The cultural context is represented by the third ring in Figure 2.1. Family, peer groups, schools, and communities always exist within a culture and are greatly influenced by it. These influences, in turn, affect the developing child.

CULTURAL INFLUENCES

Children born in every culture share the same human biological inheritance and the same fundamental need for care. Thus, adults in every culture face the same major tasks in rearing children. First, they must provide infants with the basic nurturance needed for development. Second, they must prepare children to function as adults in their particular social worlds. The latter task involves passing along to children the rules and values of the culture, a process known as **socialization.** Cultures differ from each other in the ways the tasks of nurturance and socialization are carried out; in the *specific* rules and values that are passed along; and in the final outcome of socialization—that is, the behaviors, beliefs, values, and worldview that children in each culture adopt.

Socialization:
The process by which the rules and values of a culture are passed along to children.

Different cultures have different expectations for children and provide different contexts for their education and development. While Chinese children will be exuberant at recess, they are expected to pay close attention during lessons. Fewer requirements of this type are placed on North American preschoolers.

Socialization occurs not only through explicit instruction but also through the day-to-day experiences of childhood. The values that are important in a particular culture are often reflected in the structure of the settings in which children spend their time. In turn, these differences in structure result in different developmental outcomes. To Western eyes, for example, a Chinese nursery school seems spartan because there are few toys and little play equipment. Chinese nursery school teachers initiate and organize most of the daily activities, while the children listen, follow instructions, take turns, and share. This classroom structure very efficiently teaches the important Chinese values of self-control, obedience, and group cooperation. In contrast, North Americans tend to consider self-expression and individuality important. Accordingly, a typical North American nursery school provides a wide array of toys and equipment that children can use in their own ways. Teachers organize some activities, but much of the time is given to free play in which children choose and structure their own activities, with teachers monitoring (Tobin, Wu, and Davidson, 1989).

As another example of how the daily experiences of children implicitly convey cultural beliefs and values, consider the educational practices common in Japan (Stevenson and Lee, 1990). Japanese culture places a high value on formal education. From an early age, Japanese children are expected to devote themselves to learning. They spend many more hours in the classroom and doing homework than North American youngsters do. In addition, many Japanese children attend special schools, called *juku*, after regular school hours to receive extra tutoring for exams or enrichment courses in subjects such as calligraphy. Because Japanese parents believe that achievement depends on effort, they are rarely satisfied with their children's academic achievement, and keep urging them to work harder. North American parents, in contrast, tend to believe that academic success depends on innate ability as much as on effort, and most assume that their children are doing about as well as they can. On international tests of math and science, Japanese students score much higher than North American students do. However, Japanese-American students who have been reared in this country score about the same as other American students (Stevenson, 1990). This strongly suggests that the differences in academic achievement are the result of cultural influences and not genetic differences.

Laboratory studies also illustrate the impact of culture. Some years ago, Millard Madsen at UCLA developed a series of two-person games that could be used to study children's inclinations to cooperate or compete (Kagan and Madsen, 1972; Madsen, 1971). In one game, four hands were needed to open a box. Only if the two players worked together, pushing all four latches at the same time, would either of them get a prize. In another game, the players moved toward a goal by putting marks in circles. Sometimes the first child to reach the goal won a prize. Other times both children received a prize when either reached the goal. In another variation, one of the players was prohibited from winning a prize, but could still make the other player lose. Madsen found dramatic differences in behavior between urban Anglo-American and rural Mexican children. The Anglo-American children, especially older ones, were far more competitive. They even clung to a competitive strategy when it had no benefit for them. The rural Mexican children, in contrast, avoided competition at all costs, even when a competitive strategy would have benefited *both* players. Madsen's point is not that one playing style is better than the other, but that different cultural values lead to distinctly different behaviors.

Anthropologists who specialize in the study of cultural diversity believe that such differences are generally *adaptive.* By adaptive, they mean that the values adults instill tend to produce the kinds of children best able to perform the activities required in their particular culture. Beatrice and John Whiting (1975) demonstrated this in a study of children living in six different cultures: the United States, India, Kenya, Mexico, Okinawa, and the Philippines. Children in the nonindustrialized cultures were given tasks important to the well-being of their families, such as caring for younger siblings and tending goats while their mothers worked in the fields. These children showed nurturant and responsible

When children are given tasks important for community survival, responsible behavior is promoted.

behavior, traits suited to the roles they performed. If they failed to tend the goat, the family would have no milk.

In contrast, children in the industrialized cultures were more egoistic and self-centered. Apparently, the economic efficiency of industrialized cultures reduces the need for children to contribute to their family's survival, so a self-centered orientation can be tolerated in them (Munroe and Munroe, 1975). In fact, some would argue that egoism is actually an asset in cultures that depend on a desire for personal profit to motivate economic growth.

The notion of cultural adaptiveness also implies that the same child-rearing practice may have different meanings and therefore produce different outcomes in two different cultures. For example, in the United States, most people would hold that having children share a bed with their parents, especially past infancy, is a form of maltreatment. Indeed, this practice is often associated with negative consequences in our culture. But in many parts of the world, including Japan, India, and the highlands of Guatemala, children routinely sleep with parents or other adult relatives without harm. Members of these cultures would view the American practice of forcing infants to sleep alone in separate rooms as abhorrent and abusive (Morelli et al., 1992). The entire cultural context must be considered before the meaning and impact of a particular practice can be determined (Shweder, in press).

While we believe that children born in all cultures around the world share some basic human characteristics and needs, being reared in different cultures nonetheless leads to profound differences in experience and outcomes. Identical twins reared from birth in dramatically different cultures would have some characteristics in common, but so great is the impact of culture that they would undoubtedly differ greatly from each other by the time they reached adulthood.

CULTURAL CHANGE AND CHILD DEVELOPMENT

There once was a culture in which the most important goal in raising children was to establish strong parental control. Training the child to be obedient began in the first year. To avoid "spoiling" a baby, only the infant's physical needs were met. Babies' bids for attention were strongly discouraged, and sentimental treatment was avoided. Infants were never picked up when they cried and were fed on a strict schedule, not when they indicated they were hungry.

Where in the world did such harsh practices exist? You may be surprised to learn that this is a description, not of some remote, primitive culture, but of our own society's child-rearing customs in the 1920s and 1930s. (See Newsom and Newsom, 1974; Truby-King, 1937; Watson, 1928.) Until quite recently, children in Western societies were viewed as miniature adults and were pressured toward assuming adult responsibility as soon as possible. People did not believe children needed an extended period of nurturant caregiving. This outlook originated many centuries ago, perhaps because of the harshness of life in earlier times. Even as late as the eighteenth century, death at birth or during childhood was common, and many infants of poor families were abandoned because their parents could not support them. (Remember the case of Victor, described at the beginning of this chapter.) In eighteenth-century Paris, one out of every three babies was abandoned (Piers, 1978). Children admitted to foundling homes usually died. Out of 10,272 babies admitted to one Dublin institution between 1775 and 1800, only 45 survived (Kessen, 1965).

This grim prognosis has gradually changed as technological progress has steadily raised both the average standard of living and our ability to combat disease. Today, many parents in the wealthier nations of the world can afford the luxury of devoting themselves to their children's emotional welfare. In poorer countries, the physical survival of children remains the primary concern, and parents must still bend much of their effort to ensuring that their children survive infancy (LeVine, 1988).

Undoubtedly, cultural change will continue to affect parenting and child development. In some societies, cultural changes are happening very rapidly. For instance, far-reaching change is taking place in China, where a family-centered culture is being transformed into a state-centered one. Imagine the consequences of establishing universal preschool education in a society where young children have traditionally been cared for at home. Imagine the effects of a one-child-per-family policy in a culture that for centuries has considered large families a blessing. One result of the one-child policy has been for both families and the government to devote increased resources to the care and education of these single children, to ensure their optimal development. Chinese researchers and officials have been concerned that such concentrated attention might produce a generation of "little emperors"—children whose sense of privilege and individualism may not be well suited to the collective orientation of Chinese society. Research aimed at determining whether such concern is justified has produced mixed results (Falbo and Poston, 1993; Jiao, Ji, and Jing, 1986).

SUBCULTURES

We have been talking about societies as if all their members shared a single culture. However, this is seldom the case, especially in complex, industrialized societies. Many societies have a number of **subcultures**—that is, groups whose beliefs, values, and guidelines for behavior differ in some ways from those of the dominant culture. North American societies consist of a wide variety of subcul-

Subculture:
A group whose beliefs, values, and guidelines for behavior differ in some ways from those of the dominant culture.

Different subcultures may have different ways of teaching children. Here, a Navajo child watches her mother weave. The Navajo believe that it is important to understand the task as a whole, rather than to dissect it into its parts, which is the common approach in dominant North American culture.

tures, including Native American tribes; African Americans, Latinos, Asian Americans, and Europeans from a variety of national backgrounds; and many different religious groups. Like the larger culture, particular subcultures have a major influence on child development (Harrison et al., 1990).

Sometimes the beliefs, values, and guidelines for behavior that are part of a child's subculture clash with those of the larger culture. Consider how social relations and communications are structured in a typical North American classroom (Tharp, 1989). Material is usually presented to the class as a whole, after which students are given time to practice on their own and receive some individual instruction. Communication follows a "switchboard" format, with the teacher asking rapid-fire questions, students answering quickly, and the teacher pronouncing the answer right or wrong before moving on to the next point. The emphasis is on individual achievement, and cooperation on homework or tests is considered cheating.

This format is well suited to children from most white, middle-class families, where the dominant cultural values of individual achievement and competition are stressed, but it is not equally suited to children from other backgrounds. For example, in traditional Hawaiian culture, older siblings care for younger siblings in small *companion bands,* in which cooperation and mutual help are valued. This cultural pattern prepares children for group problem solving, but not for whole-class or individual instruction. In many Native American communities, children are taught skills holistically; boning a fish or weaving a rug would be taught as a complete process, rather than in the step-by-step manner practiced in school. Children accustomed to this style of learning may find the typical classroom approach to such topics as arithmetic skills unnatural and confusing. Moreover, the oral traditions of some subcultures clash with the communication style of the typical classroom. For example, the black oral tradition includes *challenge games,* in which children are encouraged to take on adult roles and issue commands and reprimands. In class, this verbal game playing is often viewed as rude or impertinent (Heath, 1989).

Thus, how well a child fares in the typical North American classroom greatly depends on the norms and values that the child has absorbed. If those norms and values are compatible with those of the dominant culture, academic success is more likely. The success of many recent Asian immigrants rests in part on subcultural values that emphasize education, expectations of academic success, and a belief that children have a moral obligation to do well for the family (Stevenson, 1990). There is now considerable evidence that when educators take subcultural differences into account, academic achievement increases (Tharp, 1989). We consider cultural compatibility in education practices in Chapter 11.

You will see the impact of subcultural differences in our three family stories. For example, as black Americans living in an urban center, members of the Williams family are influenced by certain subcultural norms, including reliance on an extended family (Harrison et al., 1990; McLoyd, 1990; Wilson, 1989). The Williamses' lives provide a good example of how subcultural influences continually interact with broader cultural forces.

DEVELOPMENT AS CONTEXT

No discussion of developmental contexts would be complete without a mention of development itself as a context for further development. Development provides a context in two ways. First, it gives each person a developmental history, which influences the course of future development. This idea is central to Erik Erikson's theory, discussed in Chapter 1. According to Erikson, the way a child negotiates the issues of a particular developmental period depends in part on development during earlier periods. For example, toddlers must learn to strike a balance between their emerging sense of autonomy and capacity for self-assertion, on the one hand, and the limits that their parents impose, on the other. But a toddler's tendency to comply with parents' demands is forecast by the nature of the *infant*-parent relationship (Dodge, Bates, and Pettit, 1990; Londerville and Main, 1981; Matas, Arend, and Sroufe, 1978). In other words, part of the context for development in the toddler period is development in the preceding period, infancy. Similarly, children enter preschool with differing orientations toward their peers and teachers, and with differing expectations about their own capacities to master new situations. These differences, which are rooted in each child's developmental history, become part of the context for development in the preschool years.

Second, development provides a context for future development because children change physically and intellectually as they mature. The transformations in physical and cognitive capacities that occur with maturation have a dramatic influence on how children interact with their environments. Because of physical maturation, the toddler is much more mobile than the infant, much more able to "get into things." This new mobility encourages parents to impose new demands, and the child's world consequently changes. At the same time, the toddler begins to understand and use language as a result of neurological and cognitive maturation. This opens up a whole new way of dealing with the world, which greatly affects future development, as we will discuss in Chapter 7.

CONTEXTS IN INTERACTION

This chapter's central message has been that human development always occurs within a set of contexts: the biological context, the child's immediate environment, the broader social and economic context, the cultural context, and the context of the child's own developmental level and history. None of these contexts exists in isolation. None exerts its influence apart from the others. All are constantly interacting, helping to shape how the child develops.

As an example of how contexts interact, consider maternal employment in the United States, discussed earlier in this chapter. As attitudes toward mothers working outside the home have become more favorable (a change in the cultural context), and as economic pressures on families have increased (a change in the social and economic context), the number of employed women with young children has grown dramatically. This change has altered the physical surroundings in which many young children spend their time and the people with whom they have regular contact (a change in the child's immediate environment). In turn, as the number of two-earner families has increased, maternal employment has become even more socially acceptable—a further alteration of the cultural context in which children are reared in our society. Thus, change in one developmental context goes hand in hand with changes in others, and all affect child development in an interconnected way.

Another important point to remember in thinking about developmental contexts is that certain environmental factors tend to go together (Gephart and Pearson, 1988; Masten et al, 1990). Economic advantage, job satisfaction, adequate food and housing, a stable home life, and social support often accompany one another, as do high crime rates, ineffective schools, unemployment, and family disorganization (McLoyd, 1990).

Remember, too, that all the environmental influences we have discussed in this chapter are funneled to some extent through the family. For instance, children are not *directly* affected by their parents' social isolation or job stress. Instead, these factors have an *indirect* influence by affecting the quality of care the children receive at home (Crouter and McHale, 1993; Flanagan and Eccles, 1993). Not even the influences of day care, the school, and the peer group are removed from the family. It is parents who arrange for day care, select schools for their children, and promote or fail to promote peer relationships (Parke et al., 1992). In short, the significance that various developmental contexts have for a child is always affected by the child's family. Biological, socioeconomic, and cultural factors provide both the challenges parents face and the resources they may draw on for the task of child rearing.

CHAPTER SUMMARY

1. Optimal development greatly depends on favorable developmental contexts. One of these contexts is the child's *biological makeup,* which consists of: (1) the evolutionary heritage shared by all human beings, including a strong disposition to explore and master the environment, an innate propensity for learning, and a built-in tendency to be social; (2) the child's individual genetic inheritance; and (3) characteristics that result from interactions between genes and the environment.

2. Another important developmental context is a child's *immediate environment,* which contains all the settings, people, and objects that touch the child's life. The family is a dominant part of a child's immediate environment. Family members stimulate cognitive development, model various roles and behaviors, provide opportunities for early social relationships, and filter other developmental influences. The family is an interconnected system in which each member's behavior depends in part on the behaviors of the others.

3. The child's immediate environment also includes settings outside the family. One such setting is day care, which a growing number of American children are experiencing. Another is the peer group, a child's circle of same-age companions. In peer groups children learn about such concepts as fairness, reciprocity, and cooperation, as well as about society's norms and values. Neighborhoods constitute another setting that influences children's development, probably through a process of collective socialization. Schools are also conveyors of social norms and values. Because American children spend so much time in classrooms, their schools, like their peer groups, can have a powerful influence on their development.

4. A child's immediate environment is influenced by the broader *social and economic context* in which it is embedded. For instance, the general social and economic climate in the modern-day United States has encouraged some dramatic changes in the average family setting. Compared with families 40 years ago, contemporary families are much more likely to include just one parent and to include a mother who works outside the home. Developmentalists have found that the impact of these trends is complex and depends on individual circumstances.

5. The social and economic context has an especially important influence for children living in poverty. Poor nutrition and medical care are likely to cause them health problems both before and after birth. Impoverished households are also likely to experience high levels of stress due to overcrowding, financial uncertainty, and generally unstable life circumstances. This stress, coupled with isolation and lack of social support, can adversely affect parenting and child development.

6. A child's *cultural context* consists of all the beliefs, values, and guidelines for behavior that people in a particular society tend to share. Since any **culture** is always changing, researchers are concerned about how such changes may affect child development. Researchers are also interested in the effects of **subcultures**—groups of people within the larger society whose beliefs, values, and guidelines for behavior differ from those of the dominant culture.

7. Even development itself provides a context for future development. It gives each person a developmental history, which in turn affects how that person deals with new demands and challenges. Development also entails the process of maturation, which changes children both physically and intellec-

tually. These changes then have a dramatic influence on how children interact with their environments and continue to develop.

8. All the contexts of development interact with one another. None exerts its influence apart from the others. Certain environmental factors tend to go together, such as level of economic advantage, adequacy of food and housing, stability of home life, and degree of social support. All the environmental factors that children experience are funneled to some extent through the family.

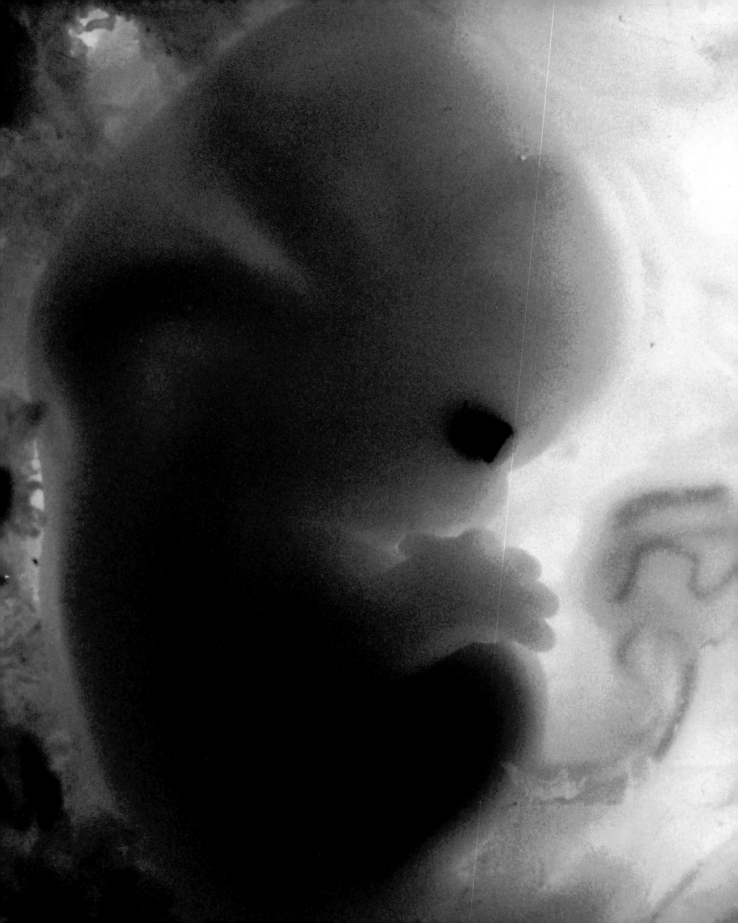

Chapter 3

Heredity and Prenatal Development

Ｉf you stand outside a maternity-ward nursery, you are likely to find adults searching for family resemblances in their newborns. "Those big eyes are just like her mother's," someone might observe, or "He has his father's dimpled chin." Many such family resemblances are the product of genes, the chemical guidelines for development that each of us inherits from our parents. In this chapter you will learn how genes express themselves and how they interact with environmental influences. A major theme of this chapter is that *genes are only one part of a complex developmental system.* Genes guide development, but they function in an environmental context. We stress the role of context and the importance of a systems view throughout this book. That view is especially apparent when we consider the period prior to birth, which is called the *prenatal period.*

Differentiation:
A developmental process in which structures and functions become increasingly specialized.

Another important theme of this chapter is that *development involves **differentiation,** the process by which parts of an organism progressively take on specialized forms and functions.* Differentiation always moves in the direction of greater refinement, complexity, and specialization. For instance, every human begins life as a single cell, which at first divides to produce cells that are similar to itself. Soon, however, as further divisions create more new cells, the cells begin to take on specialized forms and functions. Ultimately, the body will consist of such diverse cell types as red blood cells, muscle cells, nerve cells, and skin cells. Just as the one-celled creatures that first appeared on this planet differentiated into many species over millions of generations, so the initial cell that begins a human life differentiates through successive generations of cell division to produce all the parts of the body.

Human development entails more than differentiation alone. As cells differentiate, they also undergo *reorganization.* Cells migrate to form various tissues, and tissue cells reorganize further to build organs that have intricate structures.

Many similarities between parents and children are genetic, but the environmental context always plays an important role, too.

Along the way, the developing organism undergoes *qualitative change.* The embryo at five weeks is fundamentally different than it was at two weeks; at eight weeks it is fundamentally different than it was at five weeks. Not only have new parts been added, but the developing human has achieved new levels of organization and functioning. The fact that *development repeatedly entails qualitative change and reorganization* is a third theme of this chapter.

A fourth and final theme is that during prenatal development *new structures and capacities emerge in an orderly manner from those that existed before.* The pictures of human embryos in this chapter show that each stage is a logical outgrowth of the previous one. This orderliness of development is not confined to the prenatal period. As you learned in Chapter 1, human development at all points in the life cycle is orderly, cumulative, and directional.

This chapter traces the development of a human being from conception through birth, with special attention to qualitative changes produced by the interaction of genes and environment. We begin with a look at the set of genes that each of us inherited from our parents. As you will see, genes interact not only with their cellular environments but also with one another. Next, we turn to the events leading up to conception, when sperm penetrates egg and a new organism is formed. From there we take up the major stages of prenatal development, in which a single-celled organism is transformed over time into a baby ready to be born. We look in detail at some environmental influences that can disrupt prenatal development, such as exposure to certain drugs and diseases. We also examine genetic abnormalities that can cause developmental problems, and we explore the latest methods of diagnosing and treating them. Finally, we look at the birth of a baby, some of the problems that can arise at this time, and some of the trends in childbirth that have occurred in recent decades.

GENES AND HEREDITY

Every cell in your body contains the complete set of genetic instructions that have helped to guide your development from a single fertilized egg. These genetic instructions have led to your human characteristics (such as hands instead of hooves or fins), as well as your unique combination of variable traits (such as eye color and blood type). Your genetic instructions are stored in threadlike structures known as **chromosomes,** which are located in the *nucleus,* or central region, of each of your cells. Chromosomes are composed mainly of long molecules of *DNA (deoxyribonucleic acid),* which have a twisted, double-helix structure that resembles a spiral staircase (see Figure 3.1). This structure gives DNA molecules the remarkable capacity to "unzip" down the middle and produce exact copies of themselves. Both the original and the copies contain blueprints for assembling the proteins that give each cell its particular structure and enable it to carry out its work. Proteins are the major building blocks of all living things. A **gene** is simply a segment of DNA that contains the code for producing a particular protein, thereby contributing to the process of development. A single chromosome may have as many as 20,000 genes.

WHAT YOU INHERITED FROM YOUR PARENTS

Your life began with one cell—a fertilized egg—containing one set of 46 chromosomes. Copies of these original 46 chromosomes are today found in each of

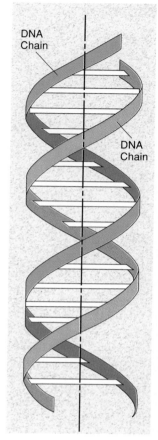

FIGURE 3.1 DNA, THE DOUBLE HELIX
DNA has a twisted, double-helix structure that consists of two long strands of molecules, (like the railing of two spiral staircases) connected by several short strands (resembling steps).

Chromosome:
Threadlike structures in which the organism's genetic instructions are stored, composed of DNA and located in the nucleus of each cell.

Gene:
A segment of DNA that contains the code for producing a particular protein.

the billions of cells that make up your body, with the exception of your egg or sperm cells. Your 46 chromosomes consist of 23 pairs; the 2 chromosomes in a pair are called **homologues.** Homologous chromosomes resemble each other in size, shape, and the type of genes they contain. One member of each pair of homologues (23 chromosomes in all) came from your mother, carried in the egg from which you were conceived. The other member of each pair (again 23 in number) came from your father, carried in one of his sperm.

But how did your mother's egg and your father's sperm come to have only 23 chromosomes, when all the other cells in their bodies have 46? The answer lies in a special kind of cell division that gives rise to eggs and sperm. During this process, called **meiosis,** the number of chromosomes in egg and sperm cells is reduced to only 23 each, so that when an egg is fertilized (united with a sperm), it will have the 46 chromosomes needed for normal development.

Some traits are due to genes located on the X chromosome. These traits, such as baldness and hemophilia, are referred to as sex-linked traits *because they appear mainly in males.*

Homologues:
Two chromosomes that form one of the 23 pairs of human chromosomes and resemble each other in size, shape, and the type of genes they carry.

Meiosis:
The process of cell division by which egg and sperm cells are formed.

FIGURE 3.2 MEIOSIS
In the process of meiosis the cells produced have the number of chromosomes reduced by half, so that when a sperm cell combines with an egg cell there will be only the normal complement of 46 chromosomes. (Source: Adapted from Hall, Perlmutter, and Lamb, 1982, p. 81; Larsen, 1993, p. 6.)

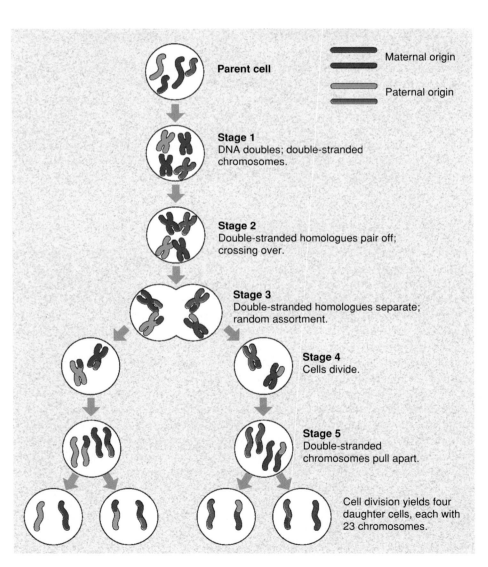

Maternal origin

Paternal origin

Parent cell

Stage 1
DNA doubles; double-stranded chromosomes.

Stage 2
Double-stranded homologues pair off; crossing over.

Stage 3
Double-stranded homologues separate; random assortment.

Stage 4
Cells divide.

Stage 5
Double-stranded chromosomes pull apart.

Cell division yields four daughter cells, each with 23 chromosomes.

The steps involved in meiosis are shown in Figure 3.2. First, the DNA in the cells from which eggs or sperm are produced (called *germ cells*) duplicates itself, resulting in *double-stranded* chromosomes. Next, the homologous chromosomes arrange themselves in pairs; in each pair, one homologue originated from the person's mother, the other from the person's father. The homologous chromosomes then separate and move to opposite ends of the cell in preparation for cell division. When the cell divides, each of the two "daughter" cells receives 23 double-stranded chromosomes. These two cells in turn divide and the double-stranded chromosomes split, yielding four cells, each with a single set of 23 chromosomes. In males, all four of these cells go on to become mature sperm; in females, only one goes on to become a mature egg. But in both cases, the mature reproductive cell, or **gamete,** has half the normal number of chromosomes. Think what would happen without this important halving process. An egg and a sperm would each contain 46 chromosomes, like all other cells. The fertilized egg would then contain 92 chromosomes, double the correct number.

Gamete:
A mature reproductive cell (egg or sperm).

Thanks to meiosis, then, children inherit the correct number of chromosomes needed for normal development. Also thanks to meiosis, children inherit a unique mix of genes, a genetic combination that no one else has ever possessed (except in the case of identical twins). To understand how so many different genetic combinations are possible, you must know a little more about what takes place during meiosis.

Early in meiosis, when the homologous chromosomes in the germ cells arrange themselves in pairs, the homologues connect at various points along their length and may exchange several corresponding segments—a process known as **crossing over** (see Figure 3.3). By corresponding segments, we mean segments containing genes that code for the same characteristic, such as eye color. Since there are often several alternative forms of any given gene, crossing over creates new genetic combinations within chromosomes. For example, a chromosome that originally contained genes that produce blue eyes may give up those genes to its homologous chromosome in exchange for genes that produce brown or green eyes. Many such exchanges make for a substantial shuffling of genes.

Crossing over:
An exchange of corresponding segments of genetic material between homologous chromosomes during meiosis.

Further shuffling of genes occurs during the stage of meiosis when the homologous chromosomes separate and move to opposite ends of the germ cell in preparation for cell division. This "sorting" of homologues occurs without regard to their original sources. Purely by chance, some of the chromosomes that move to each end of the cell originally came from the person's mother, while others originally came from the person's father. Because of this reshuffling, each of the new reproductive cells contains a **random assortment** of chromosomes from the mother's and father's sides.

Random assortment:
The shuffling of chromosomes from the mother and the father that occurs during meiosis when homologues separate in preparation for cell division.

By itself, the random assortment of chromosomes during meiosis allows a man or woman to produce 8 *million* different chromosome combinations (all of the possible combinations from 23 chromosome pairs, or 2^{23}). Because of crossing over, the variability in an individual's egg or sperm cells is actually even greater than this. The chance that a couple would produce two identical children is thus less than 1 in 64 *trillion*. Except for identical twins, who develop from one fertilized egg that separates into two separate units, children of the same parents are never genetically exactly alike. On average, siblings share 50 percent of their genetic material; exactly which traits they have in common is a matter of chance.

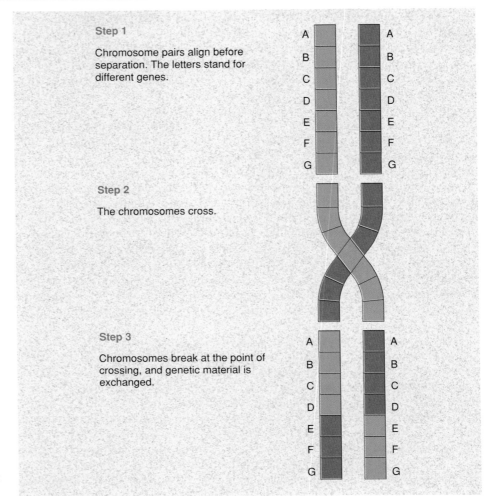

Step 1

Chromosome pairs align before separation. The letters stand for different genes.

Step 2

The chromosomes cross.

Step 3

Chromosomes break at the point of crossing, and genetic material is exchanged.

FIGURE 3.3
CROSSING OVER
Variety in human offspring is greatly increased because during meiotic cell division chromosomes cross over, exchanging genetic material. (Source: Adapted from Shaffer, 1985, p. 81.)

HOW GENES INFLUENCE DEVELOPMENT

Genes do not control development the way a computer program controls a computer. Instead, development is the result of an interplay between genes and the environment. Just as children's behavior is influenced by their surroundings, genes are influenced by their environments. In the normal course of development, genes are activated or inactivated by chemical signals in their most immediate environment, the cell. At the same time, the cell is affected by a host of environmental factors (from nutrients to drugs to viruses that enter the bloodstream). Thus, the presence or absence of vital ingredients in the cell, or the introduction of harmful substances, can influence how a gene is expressed. In addition, genes are influenced by the organism's developmental history, the cumulative effects of all the changes that have taken place so far. The development of gender in the prenatal period illustrates all of these points.

THE INTERACTION OF GENES AND ENVIRONMENT: THE CASE OF PHYSICAL GENDER DEVELOPMENT

The development of human gender begins at the moment of conception, when sperm fuses with egg. The new individual's gender is shaped by just one pair of chromosomes, the **sex chromosomes,** which scientists label number 23. If this twenty-third pair consists of two long chromosomes, called **X chromosomes,** the stage has been set for the development of a female. If it consists of one X chromosome plus a much shorter **Y chromosome,** the development of a male has been set into motion. Note that in males, with their XY pattern, the twenty-third pair of chromosomes is not completely homologous. The X and Y chromosomes are alike for only part of their lengths.

Since females carry only X chromosomes, they can pass on only an X to their children via the eggs they produce. In contrast, men, with their XY chromosome pattern, produce both X-carrying and Y-carrying sperm. Consequently, a child's sex is determined by whether the father's sperm contained an X or a Y chromosome. Whichever type of sperm fertilizes the egg sets gender development in motion. It is thought that a particular gene or set of genes, typically located on the Y chromosome, plays a major role in sex determination; the search continues for the precise gene or genes involved.

The moment of conception is just the beginning of this developmental process. An XX or an XY chromosome pattern determines only whether an embryo will develop testes or ovaries—a development that does not take place until several weeks after conception. Thus, sexual differentiation is an example of how the action of genes is sometimes delayed until a critical period in development (Plomin, 1990). A **critical period** is a limited time during which some part of a developing organism is susceptible to influences that can bring about specific and permanent changes. The critical period for sexual differentiation begins in the seventh week after conception. For the first six weeks, the primitive **gonad** (sex gland) tissues look exactly the same in males as in females. Then, in the seventh week, the presence of a Y chromosome triggers part of this tissue to begin differentiating into testes, the male sex glands. If no Y is present, the gonad tissues start differentiating into ovaries, or female sex glands, in another week or so. From here on, gender development in the embryo is shaped by **hormones** (chemicals produced in the body that regulate physiological processes).

Once testes are partially formed, they begin to secrete male sex hormones called *androgens.* Androgens cause certain primitive structures to differentiate into the male reproductive tract and induce the formation of a penis. At the same time, the testes secrete another hormone that causes atrophy of structures with the potential to become parts of the female reproductive system. In XX embryos, female sex hormones need not be present in order for female sex organs to develop. All that is needed is the *absence* of male hormones.

Several lines of evidence show that the presence or absence of androgens is the key factor in physical gender development (Larsen, 1993). One involves studies in which scientists have manipulated prenatal hormones in animals. If androgens are withheld at the critical point in development, genetically male embryos will develop female-looking genitals. Conversely, if genetically female embryos are given large doses of androgens, these genetic females will develop male-looking genitals. Another line of evidence involves studies of human embryos that were accidentally exposed to too much or too little androgen in the critical prenatal period. For instance, XX embryos are sometimes exposed to abnormally high levels of androgens, either because their mothers receive hormone treatments without knowing they are pregnant or because their mothers' adrenal glands secrete excessive amounts of androgens. These genetically female embryos often develop male-looking genitals. Conversely, genetically male embryos sometimes develop female-looking genitals because the cells

Sex chromosomes:
In humans, the twenty-third pair of chromosomes, which determine genetic gender. Females normally have two **X chromosomes,** males one X chromosome and one **Y chromosome.**

Critical period:
A limited time during which some part of a developing organism is susceptible to influences that can bring about specific and permanent changes.

Gonads:
The sex glands: the ovaries and testes.

Hormone:
A chemical produced in the body that regulates physiological processes.

of their bodies for some reason are insensitive to androgens and react as if no androgens were present (Money and Ehrhardt, 1972).

The key point here is that genes and environment interact to guide development. Thus, if you ask whether the genes in a fertilized egg are sufficient to produce a male or a female, the answer would have to be no. Genes contain information for guiding development, but how that information is actually used depends on the environment in which the genes operate. For instance, the presence of a Y chromosome in certain cells of the embryo causes those cells to develop into testes. But note the great importance of the cells' *location*. Not all the embryo's cells differentiate into testes, even though all of them contain a Y chromosome. The particular environment in which the Y chromosome operates is critical. Genes are part of a developmental system that also includes the environmental context.

HOW GENES AFFECT ONE ANOTHER

Genes interact not only with the environment but also with one another. A simple example can be seen in the development of blood type (Plomin, 1990). Each person inherits two genes that code for blood type, one from each parent. These genes come in several different forms; such alternate forms of genes for the same trait are called **alleles.** In the case of blood type, the alleles are A, B, and O.

What blood type an individual has depends on the combination of alleles he or she inherits and how they interact with one another. If a person inherits the same allele from both parents—that is, if he or she has the combination AA, BB, or OO—that person is said to be *homozygous* for this trait. A homozygous person will always display whatever characteristic the two identical genes code for. For example, a person with the combination OO will have type O blood. A different outcome occurs in people who are *heterozygous*—that is, who carry two different alleles for a single trait. Sometimes one allele dominates the other. For instance, people who inherit one allele for type A blood and one for type O will have blood type A because the A allele is *dominant* and the O allele is *recessive*. Similarly, a person with a B and O combination will have type B blood because the B allele is also dominant over the O. But if a person inherits one A allele and one B, neither allele overrides the other; the two are said to be *codominant*. Both will be expressed, and the person will have blood type AB.

The example of blood type shows that you cannot always tell a person's **genotype** (genetic makeup) simply by looking at his or her **phenotype** (observable traits). Dominant alleles mask the presence of recessive alleles. In the case of blood types, there are actually six possible genotypes (AA, AO, BB, BO, AB, and OO), but only four phenotypes (A, B, AB, and O) because the recessive O gene can be masked by a dominant A or B.

Some recessive genetic traits are called **sex-linked traits** because they are carried on one of the sex chromosomes, the X, and are commonly expressed only in males. Examples are red-green color blindness and hemophilia. Males are vulnerable to these traits because they have only one X chromosome, inherited from their mothers. If a male's X chromosome happens to carry a gene for one of these traits, he will invariably exhibit the trait. His smaller Y chromosome doesn't carry the gene at all, so there can be no dominant allele to cancel out the recessive allele's effects. Females, who have two X chromosomes, will not exhibit the trait unless they inherit it from *both* parents, which occurs very rarely

Allele:
One of several alternate forms of a particular gene.

Genotype:
A person's genetic makeup.

Phenotype:
A person's observable traits.

Sex-linked traits:
Recessive genetic traits that are carried on the X chromosome and are commonly expressed only in males.

for most sex-linked traits. If a woman inherits the trait from *either* parent, however, she will be a carrier of the trait and can pass it on to her sons.

So far we have been discussing traits that are governed by a single gene or by a single pair of alleles. Actually, such traits are not very common (Plomin, 1990). Many human characteristics are influenced by numerous gene pairs, often on different chromosomes. Such characteristics are **polygenic.** Examples include height, weight, skin color, and intelligence. In fact, any trait for which people show a large range of variation (in contrast to an "either/or" characteristic) is probably polygenic. We will explore two important polygenic characteristics later in this book when we discuss the development of intelligence (Chapter 11) and the mental disorder schizophrenia (Chapter 15).

Polygenic:
Influenced by multiple gene pairs.

SUMMING UP THE INFLUENCE OF GENES

It is important to remember that relatively few traits are directly determined by genes acting alone (as is the case for blood type). Rather, the outcome depends on interactions of genes and environment at particular times in development. Consider, for example, *phenylketonuria (PKU)*, a genetic disorder in which phenylalanine (a naturally occurring substance found in many foods) builds up within a child's body, causing permanent brain damage and mental retardation. This disorder occurs in children who inherit a particular recessive gene from both parents. Fortunately, the outcome for babies with the genes for PKU can be influenced by environmental intervention. Children who test positive for PKU at birth can be put on a low-phenylalanine diet. If the diet is started in the first 6 weeks of life, these children suffer few harmful effects; in most cases, they will later display the normal range of intelligence. Children who start the special diet later, however, usually have IQs below 70.

This is a clear example of both the critical period concept (the infant's first six weeks in this case) and how genes interact with environment to produce developmental outcomes. The important point to remember is that genes always act within a context that influences how they are expressed.

CONCEPTION

For thousands of years, people have understood the link between sexual intercourse and conception, but only recently have they come to understand exactly what takes place when a new life begins. Up until the eighteenth century, it was believed that inside either the egg or the sperm was a miniature person, called a *homunculus,* already fully formed. All that was needed was something to trigger the growth of this tiny person. Some believed that the sperm was the trigger for a homunculus inside the egg. Today, of course, we know that there is no homunculus. Instead, both sperm and egg contain genes that help guide the complex developmental process that results in a new human being. In this section we will explore the joining of sperm and egg that initiates this process.

EVENTS LEADING UP TO CONCEPTION

Like many other aspects of development, conception depends on appropriate timing of a chain of events. In most women an egg cell, or **ovum**, ripens in one of the ovaries over a period of about 28 days. When the ovum is ready for fertil-

Ovum:
An egg cell.

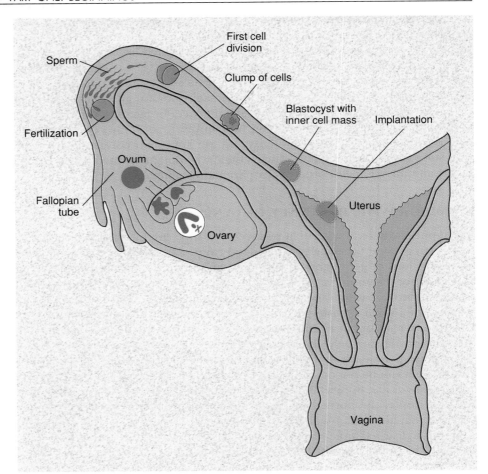

FIGURE 3.4
FERTILIZATION

Fertilization normally occurs at the upper end of the fallopian tube. The fertilized egg begins the process of cell division even as it is traveling to the uterus. In normal pregnancies this clump of cells will then become implanted in the uterine wall. (Source: Adapted from Hall, Perlmutter, and Lamb, 1982, p. 80.)

Ovulation:
Release of an ovum into one of the fallopian tubes, the passages that lead into the uterus.

Zygote:
The cell resulting from the union of a sperm cell with an ovum.

Dizygotic twins:
"Fraternal" twins, the result of the fertilization of two ova by two different sperm.

ization (penetration by a sperm cell), **ovulation** occurs and the ovum is released into one of the fallopian tubes, the passages that lead from each ovary to the uterus. The journey down the fallopian tube, as shown in Figure 3.4, takes several days. If the ovum is not fertilized by a sperm within the first 24 hours, it disintegrates upon reaching the uterus. However, if sexual intercourse has occurred at the appropriate time, the ovum will meet thousands of sperm, sometimes as many as a million. From several hundred million sperm ejaculated into the vagina, these are the ones that just happened to find their way into the correct fallopian tube. If one of these sperm penetrates the ovum's outer membrane, a tiny single-celled organism called a **zygote** is produced. Once an ovum has been penetrated, a biochemical change occurs that prevents other sperm from entering.

Occasionally a woman's ovaries release more than one ovum at a time. The use of modern fertility drugs has made this increasingly common. If two ova are fertilized by two different sperm, the result is **dizygotic** ("two zygote") **twins,** also called fraternal twins. Since different ova and sperm produce each twin in a dizygotic pair, these children are no more similar genetically than any other two siblings.

Sometimes a single fertilized egg splits into two separate units very early in its development, and identical twins are formed. Since twins produced in this manner are the product of only one ovum and one sperm, they are called **monozygotic** ("one zygote") **twins** and are genetically identical. Monozygotic twins are of great interest to researchers studying the interaction of genes and environment.

Monozygotic twins: "Identical" twins, the result of the division of a single fertilized egg into two separate units during its early cell division.

INFERTILITY

Some couples are *infertile,* that is, unable to conceive a child. Female infertility may be caused by failure to ovulate, blockage of the fallopian tubes, or cervical mucus with a chemical makeup that kills or impairs sperm. Male infertility is most frequently caused by low numbers of sperm per ejaculation or by sperm with low activity and a low survival rate. Blocked fallopian tubes can be treated by surgery, and ovulation can often be induced by hormone treatments. If the cause of infertility is a low sperm count, a physician may pool the sperm from several ejaculations and insert them into the uterus with a syringe—a procedure known as *artificial insemination*. If neither husband nor wife is sterile but they still cannot conceive, they can try *in vitro fertilization*. In this procedure, doctors extract one or more mature eggs from the woman's ovaries and collect sperm from her husband. Each ovum is then fertilized in the laboratory, and if cell division begins, the growing mass of cells is placed in the woman's uterus, which has been readied by hormone treatments.

Conceiving a child requires the perfect timing of interconnected systems. Problems or obstacles at any one point can lead to infertility. But as complex as human conception is, the next nine months of prenatal development are even more so. The more we learn about the intricate process of transforming a single fertilized egg into a complete human being, the more miraculous the birth of each baby seems.

PRENATAL DEVELOPMENT

The prenatal period—from conception to birth approximately 38 weeks later—is a time of tremendous differentiation and rapid growth. Starting from a single fertilized egg, cells divide, migrate, and interact to take on specialized forms and functions. Out of all this cellular activity emerges a human fetus and its life-support system. As you read the following sections, notice the way increasingly complex structures develop out of initially limited resources. This is characteristic of all human development: the simpler capacities present at one stage pave the way for fundamental reorganizations and the emergence of new, more complex patterns. Notice also how prenatal development follows a predetermined schedule, with different structures and capabilities emerging at specific times. In this way prenatal development is similar to later development, in which qualitative changes in children unfold according to relatively predictable timetables.

THE STAGES OF PRENATAL DEVELOPMENT

Prenatal development is often divided into three major periods: the germinal, the embryonic, and the fetal. Although the boundaries separating these periods are somewhat fuzzy, the developing organism is qualitatively different in each

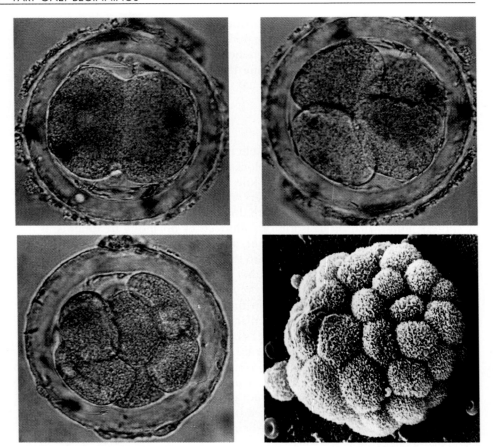

Within 36 hours of fertilization the first cell division occurs. Then cell divisions continue at shorter intervals until, by the end of the first week, more than a hundred cells have formed in a cluster. This hollow, ball-like structure is called the blastocyst.

Mitosis:
The process of cell division by which the body grows and repairs itself, in which the genetic material from the parent cell is duplicated in each daughter cell.

Blastocyst:
The hollow, ball-like structure into which a zygote develops in the first week following conception.

Inner cell mass:
A group of cells at one end of the blastocyst that develop into the embryo.

Trophoblast:
The cells in the blastocyst that form the basis of the embryo's life-support system.

Embryo:
The term applied to the developing organism during weeks 3 through 8 of prenatal development.

Organogenesis:
The formation of organs and other major body structures.

one. During the *germinal period* a tiny, self-contained cluster of cells becomes implanted in the lining of the mother's uterus. During the *embryonic period,* the major organs and body parts develop, the heart begins to beat, and blood flows through microscopic vessels. Finally, during the *fetal period,* the organism greatly increases in size and becomes a moving, sleeping, waking, "breathing" being.

THE GERMINAL PERIOD: CONCEPTION THROUGH WEEK 2
The germinal period begins at the moment of conception, when a zygote is formed. For more than a day, the zygote remains a single cell, tumbling slowly down the fallopian tube. About 30 hours after fertilization, the zygote's single cell divides in two, in a process called **mitosis.** During mitosis, the chromosomes in the parent cell duplicate themselves. Then the original and duplicate chromosomes line up along the cell's center and separate from one another, each moving to opposite sides. Finally, the original cell divides down the middle, producing two "daughter" cells that are exact replicas of the original (see Figure 3.5). Mitotic cell division is repeated again and again throughout an organism's life. It is the basic process by which the body grows and maintains itself.

About 60 hours after conception, mitosis occurs again, and the two cells of the zygote each divide, making four cells, all still structurally alike. Cell divisions continue at shorter intervals, until by the end of a week there are more than a hundred cells clustered together in a hollow ball-like structure called a **blastocyst.** By this time an amazing process has already started; cells in the blastocyst have begun to differentiate, to take on specialized forms and functions. A group of cells at one end of the blastocyst, the **inner cell mass,** will develop into the embryo. The rest of the blastocyst, known as the **trophoblast,** will form the basis of the embryo's life-support system. This early cell differentiation is an example of qualitative change. The zygote is now a fundamentally different organism than it was just a week before.

While the cells of the blastocyst are dividing and differentiating, another essential process is taking place: implantation of the zygote in the lining of the mother's uterus. About the sixth day after fertilization, the blastocyst makes contact with the uterine lining. Hormone secretions have stimulated the lining to become rich with blood, preparing it to nourish the fertilized egg. The trophoblast rapidly grows tendril-like extensions that burrow into the uterine wall. By the end of the second week, the organism is firmly attached to the uterus, drawing nutrients and oxygen from its blood vessels.

THE EMBRYONIC PERIOD: WEEKS 3 THROUGH 8

Once the zygote is firmly implanted, it is called an **embryo.** The embryonic period, from the end of the second week after conception to the end of the eighth, is a time of rapid cell division and differentiation. It is the period when all the vital organs and other major body structures are formed—a process called **organogenesis** (Larsen, 1993). Table 3.1 lists some of the major develop-

TABLE 3.1
DEVELOPMENTAL MILESTONES OF THE EMBRYO

Time After Conception	Physical Changes
12–13 days	Implantation is complete.
14 days	Mature placenta begins to develop.
3 weeks (15–20 days)	Development of endoderm, mesoderm, and ectoderm. Embryo becomes attached to wall of uterus by short, thick umbilical cord. Placenta develops rapidly.
4 weeks (21–28 days)	Eyes begin to form. Heart starts beating. Crown-rump length is 5 mm (less than ¼ in.); growth rate is about 1 mm per day. Vascular system (blood vessels) develops. Placenta maternal-infant circulation begins to function.
5 weeks	Arm and leg buds form.
7 weeks	Facial structures fuse (otherwise, facial defects).
8 weeks	Crown-rump length is 3 cm (slightly more than 1 in.). Major development of organs is completed. Most external features recognizable at birth are present.

SOURCE: Rosenblith and Sims-Knight, 1985, p. 24.

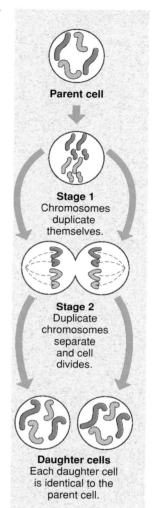

Parent cell

Stage 1
Chromosomes duplicate themselves.

Stage 2
Duplicate chromosomes separate and cell divides.

Daughter cells
Each daughter cell is identical to the parent cell.

FIGURE 3.5 MITOSIS
Mitosis is the process of cell duplication that produces two identical daughter cells. The basic mechanism for growth and maintenance of body tissues, it begins with each chromosome in the cell duplicating itself, followed by cell division. In this way each of the new cells contains all of the genetic information of the previous cell. (Source: Adapted from Shaffer, 1985, p. 84.)

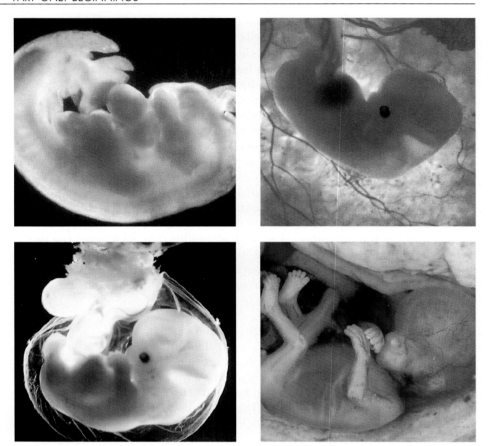

These photographs show a developing human embryo at (A) 4 to 5 weeks after conception, (B) 5 to 6 weeks, (C) 7 weeks, and (D) 8 weeks. At 8 weeks the embryo is an inch long, compared to 1/4 inch in the fourth week. Notice the dramatic increase in complexity of organization in just one month of pregnancy, from the fourth to the eighth week.

Placenta:
A mass of tissue that supplies oxygen and nutrients to the embryo and carries away waste products.

Umbilical cord:
A cord containing blood vessels that connects the embryo with the placenta.

mental landmarks during the embryonic period, and the photographs above show what an embryo looks like at different ages. Let's examine in detail what occurs during these important prenatal weeks, beginning with development of the embryo's life-support system.

THE EMBRYO'S LIFE-SUPPORT SYSTEM   The support system for the developing embryo consists of three major parts: the placenta, the umbilical cord, and the fluid-filled amniotic sac. The **placenta** is a mass of tissue that forms partly from cells of the uterine lining and partly from cells of the trophoblast. Separate sets of blood vessels link the placenta to the embryo, via the **umbilical cord,** and to the mother, via the uterine wall. In the placenta, oxygen and nutrients are transferred from the mother to the embryo, and waste products are transferred from the embryo to the mother. Because the mother and the embryo have completely separate blood supplies, these transfers occur through the cell membranes of the placenta. Oxygen and carbon dioxide molecules are small enough to pass through these cell membranes, but blood cells are too large. The cell membranes also offer protection against some substances that could be harmful to the embryo. Most bacteria, for instance, are too large to pass through them. However, the placenta does not offer absolute protection against harmful substances. Some viruses, as well as molecules of alcohol and many other drugs, are small enough to pass through, with effects that we will discuss later in the chapter.

Another major part of the embryo's life-support system is the fluid-filled **amniotic sac,** which provides a closed, protective environment within which the embryo develops. Foreign substances cannot come in contact with the embryo except by way of the placenta and the umbilical cord. The amniotic fluid also cushions the embryo against bumps and jostling. Recall the minor parking lot accident that DeeDee Williams witnessed in the story at the beginning of this part of the book. Because of the protection of the amniotic fluid, the pregnant woman's fetus was probably unharmed. Amniotic fluid also helps to minimize temperature changes as the mother experiences warm and cold environments.

EMBRYONIC CELL DIFFERENTIATION   While the placenta, umbilical cord, and amniotic sac are developing, the embryo itself is also undergoing major changes (Larsen, 1993). During the third week after conception (the first week of the embryonic period), the new organism becomes oval in shape and then indented. This indentation is the beginning of what will become the mouth and digestive tract. Cells on the surface of the embryo migrate to this indentation and then move inward to form a central layer between two other layers. By the end of the week, three layers of differentiated tissues have formed: the endo-derm, the mesoderm, and the ectoderm. *Endoderm* cells will develop into inter-nal organs such as the stomach, liver, and lungs; *mesoderm* cells will become the muscles, skeleton, and blood; and *ectoderm* cells will form the central nervous system, sensory organs, and skin.

The movements of cells that give rise to differentiated layers set the stage for important interactions among tissues that eventually shape the various parts of the body. These critical tissue interactions, which trigger developmental changes, are called **embryonic inductions.** Scientists believe they are caused by chemical substances that spread from one tissue to the other. Embryonic induc-tions provide another example of how the environmental context (in this case, the placement of cells) plays an indispensable role in carrying out an organ-ism's genetic potential (Oski et al., 1994).

In the first embryonic induction, cells of the mesoderm induce overlying ectoderm tissue to begin further differentiation into a structure that will even-tually become the brain and spinal cord. This differentiation occurs because some genes in the ectoderm are "turned on" and others are "turned off," caus-ing the cells containing those genes to change structure and function. Scientists know it is the mesoderm that induces these changes, and not the ectoderm itself, because of studies with animal embryos. In those studies, transplanting mesoderm tissue from one embryo to another at the same stage of develop-ment triggered formation of a second brain and spinal cord on the host embryo.

Another embryonic induction controls the formation of the lens of the eye. The lens develops wherever a certain outgrowth of the forebrain comes in con-tact with the embryo's outer surface. Animal studies show that if this outgrowth is transplanted so that it contacts, say, the embryo's back instead of the front of its head, a lens will proceed to form in this odd location.

Timing is often a crucial factor in gene-environment interactions during the embryonic period. Suppose, for example, that the outgrowth of the forebrain that induces formation of an eye lens is transplanted from the head of a younger animal embryo to the back of an older one. The older embryo is well beyond the stage at which the lenses of the eyes normally form. Will this older embryo go on to acquire yet another lens? No, it will not. The cells on the sur-

Amniotic sac: The fluid-filled sac that surrounds and protects the embryo and the fetus.

Embryonic induction: A chemical interaction between the cells of different tissues that triggers developmental changes.

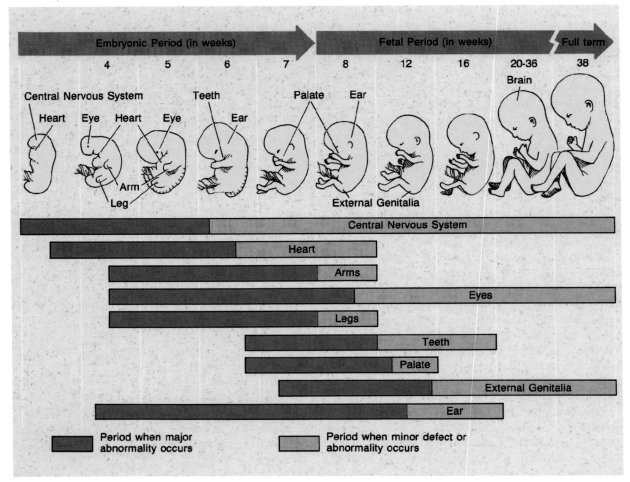

FIGURE 3.6 CRITICAL PERIODS IN THE DEVELOPMENT OF VARIOUS ORGANS, SYSTEMS, AND BODY PARTS

Each organ, system, and part has its own critical timetable and, as we shall see, is most susceptible to disruption during that time. (Source: Adapted from Moore, 1974, p. 96.)

face of the older embryo's back are now committed to being skin, and induction of a new lens is no longer possible. The time *prior* to this commitment is another example of a critical period—in this case, a critical period during which the embryo's ectoderm tissue can be induced to develop in one of several directions. After this period, the cells involved have started to take on particular forms and functions and cannot reverse their development.

THE TIMETABLE FOR EMBRYONIC DEVELOPMENT   Figure 3.6 shows the critical periods for the emergence of some of the body parts in the human embryo and fetus. As you can see, embryonic developments occur in a very predictable order, according to a strict timetable (Larsen, 1993). By the end of the third week after conception, the central nervous system has started to form, and the beginnings of the eyes can be seen. By the fourth week, the heart and digestive system are appearing, and by the fifth week, limb buds that will become arms and legs are visible. Finally, in the sixth through the eighth weeks, fingers and toes start to emerge and the bones begin to harden. This sequence reveals two principles of prenatal growth: (1) development proceeds from the head downward **(cephalocaudal development)**; and (2) development proceeds from the center of the body outward to the extremities **(proximodistal development).**

This predictable sequence and timing of embryonic development can be observed in newborns with certain combinations of problems. For example, infants with malformed outer ears also often have kidney defects, not because the outer ears and the kidneys have any direct connection, but because they are formed at the same time prenatally (Oski et al., 1994). If something goes wrong during a critical period and an organ becomes malformed, that defect can be corrected only through surgery. The developmental process cannot be redone at some later stage. When a critical period is over, the tissues involved have completed their differentiation, and the embryo has become a qualitatively different organism.

The embryonic period is a time when many crucial changes take place, making the unborn child most vulnerable to developmental errors. Yet it is also a time when the mother may not yet realize she is pregnant. If she neglects her own health now, or ingests the wrong substances, the development of her child may be severely compromised, as you will see later in this chapter.

THE FETAL PERIOD: WEEK 9 TO BIRTH

From the ninth week until the thirty-eighth week after conception, when birth usually occurs, the developing organism is called a **fetus.** The fetal period differs from the embryonic period in several fundamental ways. While the embryonic period is the time when most of the major body parts are formed, the fetal period is the time when those parts grow rapidly and become refined in structure (Larsen, 1993). Table 3.2 shows that growth in body length reaches its maximum rate early in the fetal period and then tapers off, whereas weight gains are greatest as the time of delivery approaches. Refinements in body parts occur throughout the fetal period, with each change taking place on a predictable schedule. For example, in the fourth month the pads on the fingers and toes form; in the fifth month eyebrows and eyelashes grow; and in the seventh month the male testes usually descend into the scrotum. These refinements are very important, but they differ fundamentally from the laying down of basic structures that occurred during the embryonic period.

Another major difference between the embryonic and fetal periods is the greater responsiveness of the fetus compared to that of the embryo. During the embryonic period, the developing organism merely floats in the amniotic fluid, moored by its umbilical cord. By the tenth week after conception, however, the nervous system is mature enough so that the fetus will flex its entire trunk if any part of its body is touched. Such a global reaction occurs even if the stimulation is directed to a specific body part. Gradually, fetal movements become less global and more specialized. After the eighteenth week, when various parts of the body are touched, the responses are very specific. Touching the sole of the foot now produces a leg withdrawal, not movement of the entire body, as occurred early in the fetal period. The fetus has achieved a fundamentally more advanced way of responding, which is thought to be due to the development of higher brain centers responsible for coordinating motor acts (Hofer, 1981). Notice how these qualitative changes in behavior are directly linked to qualitative changes in the structure of the nervous system. Development, as you will see throughout this book, always involves changes in both structure *and* function (Gottlieb, 1991).

Fetal movements, of course, do not occur only in response to external stimu-

Cephalocaudal development: The principle that development proceeds from the head downward.

Proximodistal development: The principle that development proceeds from the center of the body outward.

Fetus: The term applied to the developing organism during weeks 9 through 38 of prenatal development.

TABLE 3.2
LENGTH AND WEIGHT GAINS DURING PRENATAL DEVELOPMENT

Week	Length	Weight
8	1 in.	$\frac{1}{30}$ oz.
12	3 in.	1 oz.
16	6 in.	4 oz.
20	10 in.	1 lb.
24	12 in.	2 lb.
28	15 in.	3 lb.
32	17 in.	4 ½ lb.
36	18 in.	7 ½ lb.

The period from the end of the first trimester until just before the birth is usually the most enjoyable part of pregnancy. The period of morning sickness has passed, and yet the woman is not experiencing the back-aches and other discomfort of carrying the nearly full-grown fetus.

lation. By the twelfth week the fetus spontaneously moves its arms and legs, swallows, and "breathes" (inhales and exhales amniotic fluid). Still later, as the nervous system becomes increasingly refined, more precise limb and finger movements are possible.

The fetal period is also the time when behaviors become increasingly regular and integrated. The fetus develops a relatively regular sleep-wake cycle, usually adopting the same position for sleep. If the mother moves into a position that causes the fetus discomfort, it will move around until it finds a more comfortable position. At 7 months some fetuses regularly suck their thumbs or hands while they are sleeping. Their eyelids, which previously were fused shut, now separate and allow them to open and close their eyes. By the eighth month, fetuses are responsive to moderately loud sounds; they can hear and react to some of what goes on outside the womb. All these changes are evidence that an initially passive organism is gradually being transformed into an active, adapting baby.

THE MOTHER'S EXPERIENCE OF PREGNANCY

From the mother's point of view, the development of her baby is usually gauged in terms of the progress of her pregnancy. Obstetricians divide pregnancy into three 3-month periods called *trimesters,* which correspond to changes in the mother's experiences. Fatigue and drowsiness are common during the first trimester. The woman may also experience swelling of the breasts, frequent urination, and, in many cases, morning sickness. But the intensity of these symptoms varies from woman to woman (Cunningham, et al., 1993). Especially if she did not expect to get pregnant, a woman can easily misinterpret or overlook the early signs of pregnancy. Even cessation of the menstrual cycle can sometimes be overlooked, especially by women with irregular periods. In addition, some pregnant women experience intermittent vaginal bleeding, or "spotting," in the first trimester, which they may interpret as an unusually light period. If a woman is taking medications or using alcohol or illegal drugs, failure to recognize pregnancy can have serious consequences for the developing child, as we will discuss shortly.

The second trimester is often the most enjoyable for the mother. Her fatigue and nausea usually disappear. The first fetal movements, called *quickening,* can usually be felt around the end of the fourth month. Soon the fetus's initial fluttering movements change into substantial movements of the body and limbs. The mother now has the extraordinary experience of feeling new life inside her. Her bulging abdomen becomes apparent, but she is not yet so large as to feel awkward or burdened.

Physically, the third trimester can be trying for the mother. The increase in size of the fetus and uterus puts pressure on her other organs. Fetal kicking can now extend for long periods, sometimes causing discomfort or keeping the mother awake at night. Some women report that by the ninth month they felt as if they had been pregnant forever; others recall late pregnancy as one of the happiest times in their lives.

ENVIRONMENTAL EFFECTS ON PRENATAL DEVELOPMENT

Given the enormous complexity of creating a human being, it seems amazing that the process can ever take place without error. In the delivery room parents commonly count the fingers and toes of their newborn to make sure everything is there. In most cases, the baby is fine. But sadly, some infants are born with abnormalities. Any abnormality that is present at birth is called a **congenital defect,** or **birth defect.**

Congenital defects can arise from aberrations in the prenatal environment, in the infant's genes, or in both. About 3 percent of congenital defects are due solely to environmental factors, and about 25 percent are purely genetic in origin. Nearly 25 percent are caused by a combination of genetic and environmental factors (called *multifactorial inheritance*). For over 40 percent of all birth defects, the cause is unknown (Oski et al., 1994).

Substances in the environment that can cause abnormalities during prenatal development are called **teratogens,** and the study of their effects is called *teratology*. Teratology reveals the critical role that environment plays in development. Teratogens usually cause abnormalities by preventing or modifying normal cell division and differentiation. Thus, teratogens generally pose the greatest danger during the critical periods of the embryonic stage, when the major body parts are forming. Because later development consists primarily of refinements of existing structures, teratogens tend to do less damage during the fetal period. This is not to say that the fetus is immune to environmental hazards. The central nervous system, for example, grows and differentiates rapidly throughout gestation and thus can be damaged at any point in the prenatal period. All prenatal development is important, so teratogens should be avoided throughout pregnancy (Hoyme, 1990). In the following sections we'll take a look at some of the most common teratogens and other environmental factors that can contribute to birth defects.

DRUGS

Most people realize that illegal drugs, such as heroin and cocaine, are harmful to an embryo or fetus. Fewer, however, are aware of the hazards of legal drugs, like alcohol and tobacco, and fewer still are wary of over-the-counter medications. However, all these types of drugs have been implicated as teratogens. Because there are so many drugs whose effects are not yet known, women are often advised to avoid all drugs during pregnancy except those that have been proven safe.

THALIDOMIDE   Thalidomide is the classic example of a teratogen. This sedative was sold over the counter in Europe and Canada in the early 1960s as a remedy for morning sickness, a common symptom of early pregnancy. The drug was kept off the market in the United States because Frances Kelsey, a physician at the Food and Drug Administration, wanted more evidence of its safety than the animal studies that had been conducted. As it turned out, what was safe for developing rats was not at all safe for human embryos. Women who took thalidomide during the first 2 months of pregnancy gave birth to babies with a variety of severe malformations. The particular defect depended on exactly when the drug had been taken. For example, if it was taken about 3 weeks after conception, the baby was likely to be born without ears. If it was taken about 4 weeks after conception, the child was likely to have deformed legs, or even no legs at all. However, if it was first taken later than the eighth week of pregnancy, after the major body parts had formed, no birth defects were likely (Apgar and Beck, 1974; Newman, 1986). Sadly, birth defects from thalidomide are not entirely a thing of the past. Thalidomide has turned out to

Congenital (birth) defect: Any abnormality that is present at birth.

Teratogen: A substance in the environment that can cause abnormalities during prenatal development.

In Brazil and other countries with a high incidence of leprosy, thalidomide is readily available and subject to misuse. This baby was born without arms or legs after his mother took thalidomide while she was pregnant.

be an effective treatment for leprosy, and in Brazil there have been new reports of birth defects caused by its use for that purpose (Gorman, 1994).

The thalidomide episode teaches several lessons. First, drugs that are safe for some animals may not be safe for humans. Second, prolonged use of a drug is not required for it to have a negative effect on development. Some women who used thalidomide for only 1 or 2 days still gave birth to babies with deformities (Taussig, 1962). This was possible because developmental change occurs rapidly during the embryonic period, and once tissues have differentiated incorrectly there is no turning back. Third, the case of thalidomide shows how precise the timetable for prenatal development is. Dramatically different but predictable abnormalities occurred in each of the early weeks of pregnancy. Finally, the thalidomide tragedy underscores the fact that teratogens are particularly hazardous during the critical embryonic period, when all the basic body parts are forming and the developing embryo is highly sensitive to chemical changes in the cellular environment.

ALCOHOL   The odds of having a healthy baby are reduced if the mother drinks alcohol during pregnancy. Heavy drinkers have an estimated 1 in 6 chance of a stillbirth and a 1 in 2 chance of delivering a child with a birth defect (Little et al., 1990). Alcohol consumption is particularly hazardous if the pregnant woman is a binge drinker (regularly having more than five drinks at a time) or if she drinks heavily early in pregnancy (Streissguth, Sampson, and Barr, 1989).

About one-third of all babies born to heavy drinkers have a constellation of problems called *fetal alcohol syndrome* (Hoyme, 1990). In the United States, fetal alcohol syndrome is seen about once in every 1000 births (Coplan, 1993). Babies with the syndrome show three major features: (1) poor growth; (2) a distinctive pattern of unusual facial characteristics; and (3) evidence of central nervous system problems, such as mental retardation, irritability, and hyperactivity. These problems cannot be corrected after birth. For example, even with an adequate diet, these children remain small and thin for their age in early childhood. In adolescence and adulthood, their unusual facial features become less pronounced, but their cognitive impairment remains.

A flattened nose, an underdeveloped upper lip, and widely spaced eyes are three common physical symptoms of fetal alcohol syndrome. Mental retardation and behavioral abnormalities also result.

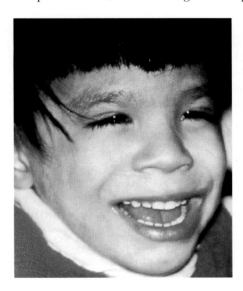

Even babies whose mothers drank only moderately during pregnancy have a higher than average chance of behavioral disorders from birth through the early school years. These effects include irritability and reduced information-processing speed in infancy, motor difficulties in the preschool years, and problems with arithmetic and reading skills at 7 years of age (Jacobson et al., 1993; Streissguth, Sampson, and Barr, 1989).

Researchers are still debating the effects of occasional, moderate drinking *late* in pregnancy. Since the brain is developing and vulnerable to the effects of alcohol right up to the time of birth, many doctors recommend that women abstain from alcohol throughout pregnancy. But others argue that such advice may unnecessarily frighten women who have had only a drink or two during their pregnancy. It may also lead heavy drinkers not to bother trying to restrain themselves because they believe irreparable damage has already been done.

TOBACCO   The harmful effects of smoking on a fetus have been under investigation for more than 40 years. Pregnant women who smoke are more likely than nonsmokers to deliver prematurely and to have babies with low birth weights; the more they smoke, the greater the risk (Rush and Callahan, 1989). We will discuss the dangers of prematurity and low birth weight later in the chapter.

It is not yet clear whether smoking directly causes prematurity and low birth weight. One study found a higher than average number of underweight babies born to mothers who began smoking only *after* giving birth. Perhaps there is some third factor associated with both smoking and poor weight gain in a fetus, such as low income or lack of education (Kavale and Karge, 1986). However, a recent study in which factors such as mother's diet, age, and education were statistically controlled showed that smoking 10 or more cigarettes per day during pregnancy had a small but significant impact on children's intellectual performance at age 4 (Olds et al., 1994).

In any case, smoking is known to have certain effects on the body that could cause problems in prenatal development. For instance, smoking raises carbon monoxide levels in the blood, which decreases the amount of life-sustaining oxygen the blood can carry to the fetus. The nicotine in cigarette smoke causes constriction of tiny blood vessels, including those in the placenta, further reducing oxygen to the fetus. Not surprisingly, a rise in fetal heart rate, resulting from low oxygen levels in the blood, can be observed after a pregnant woman has smoked two cigarettes in 10 minutes (Rush and Callahan, 1989).

HEROIN AND METHADONE   The narcotic drugs heroin and methadone (used to wean addicts from heroin) pass through the placenta to the embryo or fetus. Children of chronic users are born addicted. After birth these babies go through classic symptoms of drug withdrawal, including breathing difficulties, vomiting, tremors, and convulsions (Brown and Zuckerman, 1991). To minimize these negative effects, addicted newborns are usually put on maintenance doses of narcotics, which are then withdrawn slowly.

Even after withdrawal from drugs, however, these children have problems (Zuckerman and Bresnahan, 1991). As infants they tend to be hypersensitive. A loud noise, a change in position, even being held and talked to causes them to cry inconsolably. Because their nervous systems are so easily overloaded, they tend to avoid stimulation and therefore miss normal opportunities to explore and learn from their environment. Over time, this hypersensitivity can translate into learning difficulties and poor relationships with parents, who find these children unrewarding. As they grow older, children born addicted to narcotics often show such behavioral problems as hyperactivity and short attention spans. Although there is no evidence that heroin causes physical deformities, babies born to addicted mothers are often underweight at birth, with smaller than usual head circumference, and they remain small for their age throughout childhood. However, since mothers who use narcotics often provide poor post-natal environments for their children, it is not clear whether prenatal exposure to the drugs is the sole cause of these problems (Brown and Zuckerman, 1991).

COCAINE   The use of cocaine—especially in the extremely potent and rela-tively inexpensive form of crack—increased dramatically in the 1980s. By the early 1990s, cocaine was reported to be the most common illicit drug used by women of childbearing age in the United States (Hawley and Disney, 1992). Women who use cocaine during pregnancy have a much higher than average risk of miscarriage, stillbirth due to premature separation of the placenta from the uterine wall, and premature delivery (Handler et al., 1991). Their babies tend to be small for their gestational age and to have smaller than average-size heads. Babies exposed to cocaine prenatally have also shown a variety of con-genital deformities, particularly of the limbs and urinary tract. However, no consistent pattern of deformities has been identified (Brown and Zuckerman, 1991).

Newborns who have been exposed to cocaine show a variety of behavioral effects. Some are unusually excitable, while others show a depressed pattern of responding to their environment (Lester et al., 1991). They often spend the majority of their time either sleeping or crying and seem hypersensitive to stim-ulation, making smooth interaction with caregivers difficult (Hawley and Dis-ney, 1992).

Researchers are not yet certain how these effects are produced. One strong possibility is that cocaine interrupts the blood supply to embryonic and fetal tis-sues. However, it has been difficult to isolate the effects of cocaine because most women who use cocaine also use other drugs, receive little or no prenatal care, and have poor nutrition and overall health.

While the long-term effects of prenatal cocaine exposure are not yet known, preliminary reports suggest that it can lead to disorganized play and difficulty establishing social relationships in toddlerhood (Rodning, Beckwith, and Howard, 1991). These effects are especially likely when the drug exposure is combined with other prenatal risks and social disruption.

HORMONES   Both male and female hormones can cause birth defects if they are taken during pregnancy (Cunningham, 1993). As already mentioned, girls whose mothers receive androgens early in pregnancy can develop masculine-looking genitals. However, the most widespread problem caused by hormone treatments resulted from use of the drug diethylstilbestrol (DES), which is a synthetic *estrogen,* or female hormone. From the 1940s through the 1960s, DES was often prescribed to prevent miscarriages. Since millions of normal-looking babies were born to women who took DES, it appeared to be perfectly safe. However, when these children became adults, problems began to appear, such as high rates of genital-tract cancers in women and abnormalities of the testes in men. Such incidents show that teratogens can sometimes have effects that do not become apparent for years.

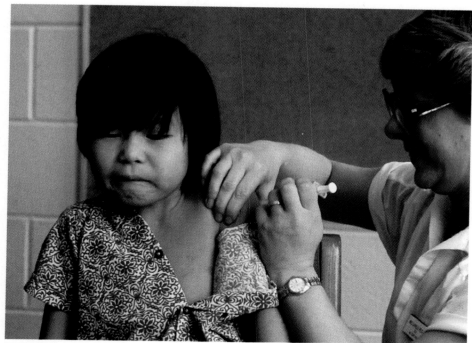

Immunization can prevent some diseases from harming the development of future offspring.

DISEASES

Many viruses can pass through the placenta, and some can have serious consequences for the embryo or fetus. For instance, children whose mothers had rubella (German measles) early in pregnancy have a high incidence of blindness, deafness, mental retardation, and heart defects. Birth defects from rubella have declined dramatically since the rubella vaccine became available in 1969; they could be eliminated if all women in their childbearing years were immunized. How dangerous rubella is to an unborn child depends on the point in prenatal development at which exposure to the virus occurs. If a pregnant woman gets rubella during the third or fourth week after conception, the probability of birth defects is 60 percent. That rate drops to 25 percent in the second month of pregnancy and to 8 percent in the third month (Oski et al., 1994). Again we see evidence of a strict timetable for development and of greater vulnerability during the critical period when basic structures are forming.

Rubella causes some of the same birth defects as thalidomide. Often quite different teratogens have identical effects if they are present at the same critical time in development. This makes sense when you consider that a certain set of changes is occurring in the embryo at any given point, so anything that disrupts those changes is likely to cause similar abnormalities. By the same token, if two women are exposed to the same teratogen but at different times in pregnancy, the effects will probably differ.

The *human immunodeficiency virus (HIV)*, the virus that causes AIDS, also poses a threat to unborn babies, but for a different reason than rubella. In the case of HIV, the danger is of infection with the virus, rather than of congenital abnormalities. HIV can cross the placenta and infect the fetus; it can also be passed to a baby by exposure to an infected mother's blood during delivery or to her milk through breast feeding. A woman may carry the virus for up to 11 years without developing symptoms, so she may not know that she is HIV-positive when she becomes pregnant.

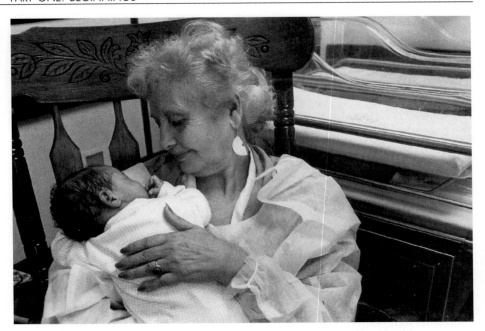

New programs for the increasing number of infants born with HIV are being developed. While such infants may need a great deal of care, the ingredients of that care are familiar. As this volunteer knows, like all other babies, "They need to be held."

Worldwide, an estimated 3 million women, most of them of childbearing age, were infected with HIV by the end of 1992. In the United States, women of childbearing age are the fastest growing HIV-infected group. In most of the world, women become infected mainly through heterosexual contact; in the United States, about half of the cases are associated with intravenous drug use and about one-third with sexual contact (Boyer, 1993). Obviously, the increasing prevalence of HIV infection among women poses a growing risk to unborn children.

Not all babies born to HIV-positive mothers are infected with the virus. In the United States, about 20 to 30 percent of infected mothers transmit the disease to their babies; in some areas of Africa, the rate of transmission is closer to 50 percent (Wara et al., 1993). Doctors are now searching for ways to reduce this risk of infection. One recent study suggests that giving HIV-positive pregnant women AZT (a drug commonly used to treat AIDS) may cut the rate of HIV transmission from mother to unborn child in half (Connor et al., 1994).

By the end of 1992, about one million children worldwide had been infected with HIV before or at the time of birth. In the United States, HIV-related illnesses are among the top 10 causes of death for small children. In New York City, they are the leading cause of death for Hispanic children aged 1 to 4 and the second leading cause of death for African-American children in that age group (Annunziato and Frenkel, 1993).

Babies infected with HIV by their mothers may develop problems related to the disease soon after birth, or they may remain free of symptoms for years. The first sign of HIV infection is often failure to grow, followed by a variety of repeated and serious infections, such as pneumonia. Brain development is usually affected, resulting in problems in motor and cognitive development. Learning disorders are common among children infected with HIV, but it is not clear whether these are due to the virus or to other risk factors such as maternal drug use during pregnancy and chaotic family situations (Church, 1993).

The outlook for children with HIV is not bright. Up to 50 percent of those who show signs of infection in the first year of life die by age 3, although some are still alive at age 10 (Annunziato and Frenkel, 1993). Improved diagnosis and treatment methods are constantly lengthening the life span of HIV-infected babies.

Many other diseases are known to have harmful effects on prenatal development. Some, such as diabetes, affect the unborn child indirectly, through their impact on the mother's body chemistry. Others, such as influenza and mumps, can have direct effects on the development of the embryo or fetus. Still others, such as herpes and syphilis, can be directly transmitted from mother to child before or during delivery.

MATERNAL STRESS

Because emotional stress is so subjective, it is hard to study its effects on prenatal development. Some researchers have used negative life events (such as divorce or loss of a job) to estimate levels of stress, while others have used more direct measures of pregnant women's physiological states. Studies using both of these yardsticks suggest a link between high levels of stress during pregnancy and such conditions as prematurity, low birth weight, and newborn irritability (Lobel et al., 1990; Molitor et al., 1984). While it is difficult to rule out all other possible explanations for these findings, high stress in pregnant women seems to be implicated as a potentially harmful influence on prenatal development (Bower, 1990; Lobel et al., 1990).

One way in which high maternal stress may adversely affect an embryo or fetus is by stimulating production of the hormone adrenaline, which alters blood flow. Excessive, prolonged stress may therefore reduce the availability of oxygen and nutrients to an unborn child. In addition, stress may cause general changes in the mother's body chemistry, producing substances that can cross the placenta.

The effects of excessive and prolonged stress should not be interpreted to mean that *any* stress during pregnancy is potentially harmful. Periodic stress by no means causes frequent prenatal harm. If it did, far more children would be born with developmental problems. Thus, mild, occasional stress is of little concern to developmental researchers or prospective parents.

MATERNAL NUTRITION

Good nutrition both before and during pregnancy is important to producing a healthy baby. As with other influences on prenatal development, the presence or absence of particular nutrients may have different effects at different times. This was shown in a study of babies conceived and born during a famine in Holland toward the end of World War II. The famine greatly reduced the population's fertility rate and increased infant mortality. Moreover, if a woman was malnourished during her last three months of pregnancy, the time when the fetus normally gains the most weight, her baby was likely to be born small and thin (Stein et al., 1975).

Some researchers claim that poor maternal nutrition (particularly protein deficiency) in the last few months of pregnancy irreversibly lowers the number of brain cells a baby is born with. Several studies of children born to malnour-

Adequate calories and a balanced diet for the pregnant woman can contribute to the healthy development of the fetus.

ished mothers seem to support this contention, but all these studies have flaws. The clearest evidence comes from studies of rats raised in controlled conditions. Those that experienced significant prenatal malnutrition did have fewer brain cells and also had learning deficits (Winick, 1975). But it may be unwise to generalize from rats to people. Some researchers remain unconvinced that nutrition directly affects nerve-cell development in humans. In the Dutch study mentioned earlier, no IQ differences were found between children born during the wartime famine and children born afterward. But there is no way of knowing whether the fetuses who managed to survive the famine would normally have been more robust and intelligent than their peers. This problem is common in interpreting natural experiments; alternative explanations are often difficult to rule out. We believe that prenatal nutrition does directly affect neurological development, which, because of its complexity, is often sensitive to disruption.

The need for specific vitamins and minerals during pregnancy is another widely researched topic. Calcium, for instance, is essential to the formation of bones and teeth. If the mother's diet is deficient in calcium, some of it will be drawn from her own bones to partially meet the fetus's needs. In general, however, the fetus cannot take nutritional stores from the mother's body to compensate for deficiencies in her diet. Consequently, doctors often recommend vitamin and mineral supplements for pregnant women. But excessive vitamin intake, particularly of fat-soluble vitamins that the body can store, is also a danger. Both deficiencies and excesses of some vitamins can cause birth defects. Therefore, pregnant women should ask their doctors what nutritional supplements they should take.

MATERNAL AGE

If we examine the rates of miscarriage, stillbirths, and infant deaths in the United States as a function of maternal age, an interesting pattern emerges. The rates are highest for teenagers and for women over 35. There are several possible reasons why teenagers have generally less successful pregnancies than women in their 20s and early 30s. Teenagers' reproductive organs are not yet fully mature and may have more trouble supporting a fetus. In addition, because teenage mothers are often single and poor, they are less likely to receive good prenatal care and nutrition, as we mentioned in Chapter 2.

The potential reproductive difficulties of older-than-average mothers are different from those of teenagers. After about age 30, the walls of the uterus become thinner, making successful implantation of a fertilized egg less likely. In addition, since all of a woman's ova are present in immature form from the time she is born, the older woman's egg cells have been exposed over more years to drugs, diseases, and radiation. Such exposure may make many eggs defective and unable to produce a viable fetus. As a result of these changes, women in their 30s often take longer to conceive, and some are unable to conceive without medical intervention. After about age 40, declines in fertility are even greater. However, women in their 30s and early 40s who are able to become pregnant and sustain the pregnancy have almost as good a chance of bearing a normal, healthy baby as do younger women. In fact, one study of 500,000 women showed no association between the mother's age and the vast majority of birth defects (Baird et al., 1991). Only birth defects caused by chromosomal abnormalities, such as Down syndrome, are clearly linked to maternal age.

The number of previous pregnancies a woman has had also can influence the success of childbearing. First pregnancies are more likely than subsequent ones to end in miscarriage, low birth weight, or malformations, mainly because teenagers account for a higher percentage of first pregnancies than of later pregnancies. After four pregnancies the incidence of problems again rises (Institute of Medicine, 1985). Maternal age is a factor here, but reproductive fatigue may also be a cause. Women who have had more than four pregnancies are likely to have had them in rapid succession, without enough recovery time in between.

GENETIC DEFECTS

Developmental problems can also arise due to genetic defects. Some genetic defects involve inheritance of a single gene for some disorder. These **single-gene disorders** are also called **Mendelian disorders** because they follow the basic principles of genetic inheritance described by Gregor Mendel more than a hundred years ago. Most single-gene disorders are the result of inheriting a recessive allele from each parent, as in the case of PKU (discussed earlier). Other examples of disorders caused by recessive genes are sickle-cell anemia (a painful and potentially fatal blood disorder found primarily in people whose ancestors came from West Africa and some areas around the Mediterranean Sea) and Tay-Sachs disease (a steady deterioration of the nervous system leading to death before age 2, primarily found in Eastern European Jews and their descendants).

Single-gene (Mendelian) disorder:
Any disorder produced by inheritance of a single gene.

A few single-gene disorders are caused by inheritance of a dominant allele. One such disorder is *Huntington disease,* a fatal neurological disorder that often does not appear until after age 40. Because the gene for Huntington disease is a dominant allele, those who carry it inevitably develop and die from the disorder, in many cases after they have produced children. Each child of a person who develops Huntington disease has a 50 percent chance of inheriting the disorder.

Other genetic defects involve **chromosomal abnormalities,** which occur when errors in meiosis produce sperm or egg cells with incorrect numbers of chromosomes or with damaged chromosomes. Over 90 percent of all fertilized eggs with chromosomal abnormalities are ultimately miscarried. But about 1 in every 160 newborns has some sort of chromosomal abnormality (Thompson et al., 1991). Some chromosomal abnormalities cause no particular developmental problems; others produce a predictable set of physical abnormalities.

Chromosomal abnormality:
Any genetic defect that occurs when errors in meiosis produce sperm or egg cells with incorrect numbers of chromosomes or with damaged chromosomes.

The best-known example of a chromosomal abnormality is *Down syndrome,* which involves the pair of chromosomes that scientists label number 21. If the twenty-first chromosome pair fails to separate during meiosis, when reproductive cells are formed, the resulting egg or sperm will contain two twenty-first chromosomes. When this egg or sperm joins another reproductive cell at conception, the result is a zygote with three twenty-first chromosomes instead of the usual two (which is why Down syndrome is also called *tri*somy 21). About 75 percent of trisomy 21 conceptions result in miscarriage. Those babies who survive suffer multiple problems. Their physical development is abnormal in a number of ways. They are usually short, with stubby fingers, a broad face, and rather flat facial features. Many also have heart or digestive-system defects and die by early adulthood. Down syndrome is the most common genetic cause of moderate mental retardation (Thompson et al., 1991). Despite this, Down syndrome chil-

Almond-shaped eyes, a broad, flattened face, and poor muscle tone are prominent features of Down syndrome. The children are variously retarded, with a small subset approaching normal intelligence.

dren show the same sequences of development as normal children, only delayed (Beeghly and Cicchetti, 1990). With supportive environments many can achieve near normal functioning, particularly if a carefully designed intervention program starts in infancy (Cicchetti and Beeghly, 1990b). But there is no environmental cure for Down syndrome, as there is for PKU. All the damage occurs during the prenatal period, and it cannot be reversed.

Down syndrome is relatively rare, affecting about 1 in every 800 births. But the frequency increases with the age of the mother (and perhaps with the age of the father too). For women aged 20 to 24, the rate is 1 in 1,400 births, whereas for women over 45 the rate is 1 in 25 (Thompson et al., 1991). Scientists believe that this higher incidence in older women is caused by damage to egg cells over time, due to exposure to harmful environmental factors.

Another type of chromosomal abnormality occurs when a baby receives an abnormal number of sex chromosomes, again due to an error in meiosis when the mother's egg or the father's sperm was produced. These *sex chromosome abnormalities* are among the most common genetic disorders, occurring about once in every 500 births (Thompson et al., 1991). For example, males may receive an extra X chromosome (a condition known as *Klinefelter syndrome*) or an extra Y chromosome *(XYY syndrome)*. Females may also have an extra X chromosome *(trisomy X)*, or they may have only one X chromosome *(Turner syndrome)*. Most sex chromosome abnormalities do not cause serious developmental problems, but some of these abnormalities result in infertility (Klinefelter and Turner syndromes), some in educational problems (Klinefelter syndrome and trisomy X), and some in reduced IQ (XYY syndrome).

DETECTION AND TREATMENT OF FETAL DISORDERS

Ultrasound:
A technique that produces a computer image of a fetus by bouncing sound waves off it.

Thanks to new technology, some fetal disorders can now be detected relatively early in pregnancy. **Ultrasound,** a technique that produces a computer image of the fetus by bouncing sound waves off it, allows physicians to detect structural abnormalities as small as a cleft palate. In combination with other tests, ultrasound has made it possible to diagnose more than 20 types of heart defects and heart rhythm disturbances before birth (Chervenak, Isaacson, and Mahoney, 1986). Because it is not invasive and carries little or no risk to the mother or fetus, ultrasound has begun to replace other techniques for identifying a wide variety of disorders. Ultrasound can also be used to monitor growth of the fetus and to guide instruments safely to permit the extraction of samples of amniotic fluid, fetal blood, and other tissue for diagnostic analysis.

Early detection of genetic disorders requires other procedures. In **amniocentesis,** a needle is inserted through the mother's abdomen to withdraw a sample of the amniotic fluid that surrounds the developing fetus (Cunningham, et al., 1993). Cells that the fetus has shed into the fluid can then be analyzed for chromosomal abnormalities; one of the first disorders to be detected by this method was Down syndrome. Amniocentesis is usually done 16 to 18 weeks after the pregnant woman's last menstrual period. However, recent research suggests that amniocentesis is safe and reliable when done even earlier in pregnancy— 11 to 14 weeks after the woman's last period (Shulman, et al., 1994).

Neural tube defects, such as absence of part of the brain or failure of the spine to close, can also be detected through amniocentesis, because the fetus with these deficits leaks excess amounts of a substance called *alpha-fetoprotein* into the surrounding fluid. The mother's blood can also be tested for levels of this fetal protein. While high levels of alpha-fetoprotein indicate neural tube defects, low levels indicate the need to test further for Down syndrome.

In another diagnostic technique, called **chorionic villus sampling (CVS),** cells are suctioned from the developing placenta via a small tube passed through the vagina and cervix or through the abdominal wall (Cunningham, et al., 1993). These cells are then analyzed to determine the fetus's genetic makeup. CVS can be performed earlier than conventional amniocentesis—usually 8 to 12 weeks after the mother's last menstrual period. However, it is a more difficult procedure and is not as widely available as amniocentesis.

The burgeoning field of fetal diagnosis has made it possible to treat some disorders prenatally, with transfusions, drug therapy, and even surgery. But fetal diagnosis also has created difficult moral and emotional dilemmas, both for parents and for society as a whole. In the past, there was no way of predicting congenital abnormalities. If a child was born with severe physical deformities or mental retardation, no one was to blame. But today we know how to detect many serious disorders prenatally, and such knowledge brings responsibility. What should prospective parents do if they discover that their fetus has a serious disorder? What should society allow them to do? The controversy surrounding abortion shows that there are no simple answers to these questions.

Another approach to preventing birth defects is for parents who are at high risk for producing children with a genetic disorder to receive genetic testing and counseling before they attempt a pregnancy. Because of the expense and the generally low incidence of most genetic defects, such testing is not necessary for everyone. But it can be worthwhile for couples with a family history of genetic disorders. Consider a Jewish couple of Eastern European descent worried about having a child with Tay-Sachs disease. If tests show that they both carry the recessive gene for this disorder, they know that there is a 25 percent chance that any child of theirs will have the fatal illness. But if only one of them is a carrier of the gene, *none* of their children will have Tay-Sachs. The many healthy, happy babies born to parents like these are testimony to the benefits of genetic testing and counseling.

Amniocentesis: Withdrawal of amniotic fluid through a needle inserted into the mother's abdomen for the purpose of testing for chromosomal abnormalities.

Chorionic villus sampling: A technique for analyzing the fetus's genetic makeup in which cells are suctioned from the developing placenta through a small tube passed through the vagina and cervix or through the abdominal wall.

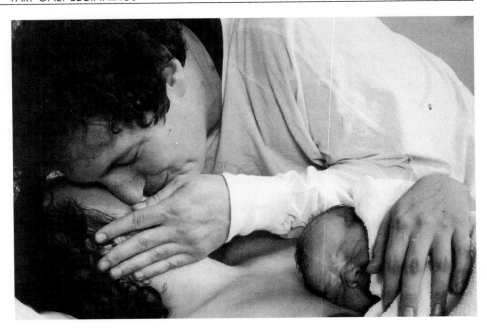

Often, the birth of an infant is an unparalleled joy for parents.

BIRTH

After nine months of gestation, human infants are ready to be born. In most cases the process is routine, as it has been for thousands of years. The fetus prepares for birth by moving into a head-down position, and the mother's uterus responds with contractions, which help move the baby through the birth canal, or vagina. Although most pregnant women have some anxiety about childbirth, that anxiety can be decreased by classes that inform first-time mothers about what to expect (Crowe and von Baeyer, 1989).

THE STAGES OF LABOR

Childbirth is also referred to as *labor* because of the work it entails. There are three stages of labor. During the first stage, regular, strong contractions begin 15 to 20 minutes apart and become stronger and more frequent as labor proceeds. This stage continues until the cervix becomes fully opened, or *dilated,* a process that may take just one hour or last more than a day. For normal, head-first deliveries, the second stage of labor begins with *crowning,* when the crown of the infant's head pushes through the cervix into the vagina. Now contractions are about a minute apart and last about 45 seconds. As the head and shoulders emerge, the head usually turns to the side. Once the shoulders are clear, the rest of the body slips out quickly. The second stage of labor usually lasts between 30 minutes and 2 hours. The final stage of labor begins when the baby is born. The uterus continues contracting, and the *afterbirth,* which includes the placenta and other membranes, is delivered.

BIRTH COMPLICATIONS

Not all pregnancies and deliveries are routine. One major concern in birthing is the maintenance of a steady supply of oxygen to the infant. A long disruption in the oxygen supply, called **anoxia,** can cause damage to the infant's brain. Anoxia can occur in two basic ways. First, the umbilical cord may become pinched during delivery, constricting blood flow through it and cutting off the oxygen supply to the baby. This is most common in a *breech birth,* in which the infant is delivered in a bottom- or feet-first position. Such births often take longer than head-first births, and in the final stages of delivery the cord may become tangled or pinched. Second, anoxia can occur if the baby fails to begin breathing immediately after birth.

Doctors can quickly gauge the condition of a newborn by looking at the results of a set of standard tests routinely given at 1 and 5 minutes after birth. These tests include the Apgar scale shown in Table 3.3. The baby's score on the Apgar is the sum of the ratings for heart rate, respiration, reflexes, muscle tone, and skin color. A score below 5 is cause for concern and requires immediate medical treatment.

Anoxia:
A disruption in the baby's oxygen supply during or just after birth.

LOW BIRTH WEIGHT AND PREMATURITY

The question of how old or how large a fetus must be before it is able to survive outside of the womb cannot be answered precisely. Babies as young as 23 weeks and as small as 13 ounces have managed to survive, but this is very unusual. Up to the average full-term birth weight of 7½ pounds, the heavier a fetus is, the greater its chances of survival. Since the most rapid weight gain occurs late in prenatal development (when it reaches a peak of over 2 ounces a day), staying in the womb for the full 38 weeks is highly advantageous. Any baby born less

TABLE 3.3
THE APGAR SCALE

Sign	Criterion*	Score
Heart rate (beats/minute)	100 or more	2
	Less than 100	1
	Not detectable	0
Respiratory effort	Lusty crying and breathing	2
	Any shallowness, irregularity	1
	Not breathing	0
Reflex irritability	Vigorous response to stimulation (e.g., sneezing or coughing in response to stimulation of nostrils), urination, defecation	2
	Weak response	1
	No response	0
Muscle tone	Resilient, limbs spontaneously flexed and resistant to applied force	2
	Limpness, lack of resistance	1
	Complete flaccidity	0
Skin color	Pink all over	2
	Partially pink	1
	Bluish or yellowish	0

*Observations made at 60 seconds after birth.
SOURCE: Apgar et al., 1958.

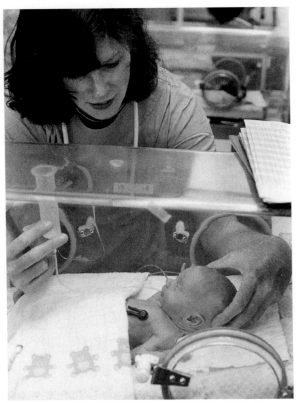

Technological advances increase the possibility that extremely premature and low birth weight infants will survive. However, such babies are at increased risk for a variety of developmental problems.

Premature:
Referring to a baby born less than 35 weeks after conception.

than 35 weeks after conception (37 weeks after the mother's last menstrual period) is considered **premature;** any baby weighing under 5½ pounds at birth is considered of low birth weight.

Low birth weight can be due to premature delivery, retarded growth while in the womb, or both. Premature babies born after 7 months of normal gestation often suffer no lasting ill effects (Greenberg and Crnic, 1988). However, babies born small for their gestational age, even if they are carried to full term, remain at risk for later difficulties. The explanation for this is that prenatal growth retardation is usually associated with other problems, such as maternal illness, malnutrition, smoking, or drug use.

The problem of low birth weight is relatively common in our society, affecting about 7 percent of babies born in the United States. It is especially common among those living in poverty. Babies who are born too small have an increased incidence of neurological problems, physical abnormalities, and lung ailments compared with babies of ideal weight. Neonatal intensive care units have made dramatic strides in keeping low-birth-weight babies alive and enhancing their developmental outcomes, but the mortality rate for babies who weigh less than 5½ pounds at birth is still twice that for normal-size newborns. Most infants weighing less than 1½ pounds at birth do not survive. Extremely low-birth-weight babies who do survive have an increased long-term risk for impairments in cognitive, sensory, and motor abilities (Institute of Medicine, 1985). Early intervention programs can reduce the cognitive deficits associated with low birth weight, but they are most effective for infants who weigh 4.4 pounds or more at birth (Infant Health and Development Program, 1990).

TRENDS IN CHILDBIRTH

Although the biological process of labor and delivery is the same the world over, beliefs and practices surrounding childbirth vary widely. In Western societies, generations of babies have been delivered by physicians in hospital rooms. To some extent, this medical approach to childbirth has changed in the last 20 years. Providing hospital birthing centers with a homelike atmosphere, using nurse midwives, allowing fathers to be present in the delivery room, and permitting mothers to room in with the newborn are all part of the trend toward more natural childbirth.

One of the most popular approaches to childbirth today is the *Lamaze method.* Lamaze uses several strategies to lessen the mother's fear and pain and make birth a more positive experience, including prior education about the birth process, participation of both parents in the pregnancy and delivery, and use of special breathing techniques during labor. A major advantage of natural childbirth methods such as Lamaze is a decreased reliance on painkilling drugs during labor.

Drugs commonly used during childbirth include *anesthetics* (which either block sensory signals or induce complete unconsciousness), *analgesics* (which reduce pain), and *sedatives* (which reduce anxiety). These drugs can affect the baby in two ways. First, they tend to lower the mother's blood pressure and the oxygen content of her blood, which in turn lowers the amount of oxygen supplied to the child. Second, most of these drugs rapidly cross the placenta and can directly affect the infant both during and after birth. The current trend, therefore, is to limit and carefully monitor the use of drugs during labor and delivery. *General* anesthetics, which cause complete unconsciousness, are now rarely used during childbirth. *Regional* and *local* anesthetics, which deaden sensations only in specific parts of the body, are preferred because they have less effect on the baby and allow the mother to participate actively in the delivery (Cunningham, et al., 1993).

At the same time that natural childbirth has gained in popularity, modern-day obstetrics has seen an increase in deliveries by **cesarean section**—that is, by surgical incision in the abdomen and uterus of the mother. Cesarean deliveries are used when heart-rate monitors indicate fetal distress, when the mother's pelvis is too small for the baby's head to pass through, or when vaginal delivery is otherwise not going well. There is, however, clear indication that the procedure is overused in the United States. The frequency of cesarean delivery in the United States increased steadily from 5 percent in 1965 to 23 percent in the mid-1980s and remained at this level into the 1990s (Entwisle and Alexander, 1987; Centers for Disease Control, 1993). However, there is no evidence that this procedure has reduced infant mortality or birth-related damage to the nervous system. Cesarean section carries with it the risks of any major surgery and can compromise the mother's ability to deliver vaginally in future births. It also increases the risk of postdelivery complications (for example, urinary tract infections) and lengthens hospital stays. Current government guidelines set a goal of 15 percent cesarean deliveries. This official goal, combined with insurance company pressures, may now be bringing the rate down.

Cesarean section: Delivery of a baby by surgical incision in the abdomen and uterus of the mother.

PRENATAL DEVELOPMENT IN CONTEXT

A major theme of this book is that development can be fully understood only by examining the context in which it occurs. That theme is very apparent in this chapter. Prenatal development unfolds partly in a hereditary context: a set of genes that each individual inherits from his or her parents. Those genes are guidelines for constructing a new human being—a person in many ways like all human beings, in other ways unique. Prenatal development also unfolds in an environmental context: a set of hormones, nutrients, and other substances that help shape the way the genes are expressed. Sometimes these substances are a product of the developing organism itself. Other times they come from outside the womb via the placenta and the mother's bloodstream. Moreover, it is not just present events that create the environmental context. Past developmental changes also play a role. For instance, when an embryo develops masculine genitals under the influence of male hormones, that embryo's current environment is influenced by a critical past event—either the formation of androgen-producing glands or an influx of androgens from some other source. Past development, in other words, is part of the context for present development.

The enormous importance of the environmental context in prenatal development can be seen by considering a paradox. At the moment of fertilization the new organism receives all the genetic material it will ever have. As development proceeds, these genes are duplicated each time a cell divides, and each new cell receives an identical set. Thus it would seem that the genetic information in the initial fertilized egg must be sufficient to guide all of development. After all, in those rare cases in which the initial fertilized cell forms two separate units after duplication, identical twins result, not two half-children. Yet if this information is truly sufficient, how can we explain the remarkable differentiation of cells that occurs? How does one cell "know" to use only certain of its genes to function as a blood cell, while another cell "knows" to use other genes to function as part of a muscle or nerve?

The answer is that some genes are activated and others are deactivated in response to environmental signals, many of which stem from interactions with other cells. Recall from Chapter 1 that the same tissue from a young chick embryo could become part of a thigh, a claw, or a wing tip, depending on its location and the timing of its placement. This same process of influence by surrounding cells is what leads some cells on the surface of the new embryo to migrate into the core to form the human nervous system. You have seen the importance of this interaction of genes and the environment throughout this chapter, and you will see it again in all later sections of this book. Development is never simply the product of some initial genetic blueprint. Previous development and current circumstances always influence it too. This is the hallmark of all development, whether at the level of the cell, the embryo, the fetus, the newborn, the child, or the adult.

The environmental context that shapes development always has several layers, like Bronfenbrenner's concentric rings of influence (discussed in Chapter 2). During the prenatal period, some of the substances that influence development come from the developing organism itself, while others come from the mother's body via the placenta. But the environmental context of prenatal development does not stop there. The mother herself is embedded in a physical, social, and cultural environment that can greatly affect her body and the fate of her developing child.

CHAPTER SUMMARY

1. Prenatal development includes several important processes that occur in other developmental periods too. One is an interaction of genes and environment in shaping the characteristics a person shows. Another is the process of **differentiation,** in this case the differentiation of cells and tissues in the body. As cells differentiate, they also undergo reorganization, giving rise to qualitative change.

2. **Genes** are segments of **DNA** located on structures called **chromosomes.** Every cell in the human body, except reproductive cells, contains 23 *pairs* of chromosomes, or 46 in all.

3. Human cells multiply through a process of cellular division called **mitosis,** whereby chromosomes create duplicates of themselves before dividing to form daughter cells. A special kind of cell division, known as **meiosis,** occurs in the formation of reproductive cells. During meiosis, reproductive cells divide so that the sperm or egg that is formed contains only 23 *single* chromosomes. Later, upon fertilization, two sets of single chromosomes from the egg and sperm unite to form a **zygote** having the normal 23 pairs of chromosomes. Meiosis also creates a great variety of gene combinations, partly because of **crossing over,** a process in which chromosome pairs exchange some genes, and partly because of the **random assortment** of chromosomes when they separate to form daughter cells.

4. Gender development is a good example of how genes operate in a particular environmental context. The presence of a **Y chromosome** results in primitive **gonad** tissue differentiating into testes. If the embryo has two **X chromosomes** and no Y chromosome is present, the same tissue differentiates into ovaries. Subsequently, hormones—a part of the embryo's internal environment—influence the further development of physical gender.

5. In addition to interacting with the environment, genes also interact with one another. Alternate forms of a gene for the same trait are called **alleles.** Sometimes one allele is dominant and the other recessive. In other cases, no single allele dominates, and codominant alleles determine how a characteristic is expressed. An individual's **phenotype** (observable characteristics) may not reveal all the genetic information present in his or her **genotype** (all the genes he or she inherited).

6. The 38 weeks of prenatal development can be divided into three major periods. During the germinal period (from conception through week 2), the **zygote** begins the process of cell division and differentiation and becomes implanted in the uter-

ine lining. During the embryonic period (from week 3 through week 8) a life-support system for the embryo develops, and the embryo acquires all its major body parts according to a strict timetable. Finally, during the fetal period (from week 9 to birth), the fetus grows rapidly in size and weight, its structures become refined, and it becomes increasingly active and responsive to its environment. The developing organism is qualitatively different at each of the three periods of prenatal development. During each period, it acquires not only new structures, but also new levels of organization and functioning.

7. The developmental changes that occur within an embryo are often triggered by interactions among tissues, called **embryonic inductions.** These interactions are an example of the vital role the environment (in this case, the cell's location) plays in the overall developmental system.

8. **Congenital defects,** or **birth defects,** can be caused by environmental factors, by genetic defects, or by multifactorial inheritance, a combination of the two. A **teratogen** is any substance in the environment that can cause prenatal developmental abnormalities. Common teratogens include drugs, hormones, and viruses. Teratogens can prevent or modify normal cell division and differentiation. Since most of this differentiation goes on during the embryonic period, embryos are especially vulnerable to the effects of teratogens.

9. Some genetic defects are caused by **single-gene disorders** that follow the basic principles of genetic inheritance described by Mendel. Others are the result of **chromosomal abnormalities,** which occur when errors in meiosis produce sperm or egg cells with incorrect numbers of chromosomes or with damaged chromosomes.

10. Fetuses at risk for congenital defects can be screened by using **ultrasound** in combination with **amniocentesis** or **chorionic villus sampling.** These procedures are used to detect a variety of abnormalities.

11. Prenatal development and birth illustrate all the rings of contextual influence in Bronfenbrenner's model. The developing fetus is influenced by inherited genes and by maternal nutrition, stress, illnesses, and drug taking. The well-being of the newborn is also affected by socioeconomic circumstances surrounding the pregnancy and by technological advances and changing childbirth practices at the cultural and societal levels.

PART TWO

Infancy

PART TWO

Three Children as Infants

MALCOLM WILLIAMS

"Let me hold him first, Momma," Teresa pleaded the moment her mother and father walked through the apartment door. "I get to hold him first 'cause I'm a girl, so I'm next to be a momma."

"What about me, girl?" laughed 21-year-old Denise, as she and the other members of the Williams household crowded around DeeDee and the tiny baby she cradled in her arms. "Are you sayin' that this boy's aunt is never gonna find herself a man?"

"My Lord. Look at that red hair!" Momma Jo exclaimed. "Where'd he get that from? Where on earth? And his eyes are so wide open, like he's takin' in everything. I never have seen a brand-new baby lookin' 'round like he does. Hi, sugar. Hi. I'm your gran'ma. Can I have a kiss?" Momma Jo moved the pale-blue blanket aside for a better look. As she bent closer, the baby's face puckered and he began to cry with the same piercing wails that had announced his birth 3 days earlier. "That cry is just grand," Momma Jo declared, clasping her hands together. "Just grand!"

"Sounds like I'd better keep my earphones handy," laughed 12-year-old John, Jr. His sister Teresa was speechless. She watched in fascination as the baby wriggled forcefully and turned a glowing shade of dark auburn.

"So what'll we name him?" DeeDee asked. "We've got to decide soon. Is it gonna be Muhammad, the great Ali, or Malcolm, the great leader? What do you think, Momma Jo?"

"Well, I sure don't like some pagan name like Muhammad. I prefer Malachi from the Old Testament. The prophet who foresaw the judgment day."

"Oh, Momma Jo. No one's named Malachi anymore. Other kids would tease him."

"Then name him Malcolm if that's your pleasure."

"What do the rest of you think?" asked DeeDee.

"Malcolm, 'cause he's red, like Malcolm X was," John, Jr., said with a grin.

"Yeah. Malcolm's okay," added Teresa thoughtfully.

"John, what's your pleasure?" DeeDee asked, passing the baby to him.

"My pleasure is Malcolm Muhammad Williams. The kid's a class-A fighter and he needs a name to cover him right."

"Then Malcolm M. Williams it is," said DeeDee smiling, and the others nodded in agreement.

"You're one helluva kid, man," John whispered proudly into little Malcolm's ear.

In the weeks that followed DeeDee was amazed at Malcolm's energy and alertness. By 10 weeks he seemed to fix his large brown eyes on everything that came into his view. The family responded to those inquisitive eyes by talking to Malcolm often and bringing him a variety of everyday objects to look at—a bright-green piece of crinkly paper, an orange feather from a feather duster, a shiny silver lid from a frying pan that reflected light on Malcolm. They enjoyed the eagerness with which he inspected new things and the delight he showed. At mealtime Malcolm ate at the table with the rest of the family, passed from person to person as he sucked hungrily on a bottle. Even awkward positions in the arms of Teresa never seemed to disturb him. He intently studied every face that smiled and talked above his.

By the middle of his fourth month Malcolm's height and weight were above the ninety-eighth percentile on the pediatrician's chart. Although his fiery coloring had become subdued to a rich, clear brown, his activity level remained as high as ever. As he lay on his back on a blanket spread on the living room floor, his little arms would cycle round and round and his feet would kick vigorously. He could turn himself from back to stomach in an instant. On his belly he pushed and pulled his legs so hard that he looked like a frog swimming.

"Motor Man, I'm gonna call you," John, Jr., said one evening, catching hold of Malcolm's furiously kicking feet. "How's the little Motor Man?" Malcolm froze for an instant, then brought a fist up to his mouth. He began to suck on all five fingers so intently that the whole family started to laugh. Malcolm gurgled with pleasure and began kicking again.

The next week a freezing rain enveloped Chicago for days. Although it seemed that spring would never come as ice covered the windows, DeeDee knew that Monday would be the first of March and her 4-month maternity leave would be over. When she was still pregnant she had thought this time would go by slowly, but life with Malcolm was like a fairground ride. He made her feel younger and more energetic than she had felt in years. The idea of going back to her job at the phone company seemed dull in comparison. But the family needed the money. There was no question she had to work.

"When people call in tomorrow complainin' about their phone service, I'm gonna tell them just what I really think," DeeDee told the family at the dinner table Sunday night. "Honey, I'm gonna say, of *course* we're slow in gettin' your bill corrected. This is the *phone* company you're talkin' to, darlin'. What did you expect? Now if you want to see *fast,* you should come 'round to my house and see my boy Malcolm in action. . ." At that moment Malcolm screeched in glee and beat the air with his fists. Everyone roared with laughter.

The following morning DeeDee's spirits were far less buoyant. Momma Jo carried Malcolm down to the front steps of the apartment so that she could wave his little hand goodbye as DeeDee left for work.

"Come on now, honey," John said to her gently, as she looked out the window of the car. "It's nothin' to cry about. He knows you're his momma. He's not gonna love you any less."

"I know," DeeDee answered. "I never thought that for a minute. It's just that I miss him so much already. Can you believe that? And I guess, too, I see that boy pushin'

and shovin' his way into the future so fast that I'm afraid I'm gonna miss it all if I'm gone too much. Do you know what I mean?"

"I know exactly what you mean," John said, covering her hand with his.

MIKEY GORDON

"Ahh-ba-ba-ba-ba-ba-ba.   Ahh-ba-ba-ba-ba-ba-ba. Eeeeeeeeh! Eeeeeeeeh! Yo-yo-yo-yo. Jo-jo-jo. Ahhuuup! Ahhuuup!" THUD! Silence.

Christine Gordon opened her eyes. The orange numerals on the digital clock radio read 5:45 a.m. What's he up to now? she wondered. Why doesn't he say something just to let me know he's all right?

"You'd better get in there, Christine. He may have fallen out of his crib." It was Frank's voice, still groggy with sleep. He, too, had been listening to Mikey's predawn chatter.

Christine climbed out of bed and shuffled toward the door, stumbling over the family dog still asleep on the floor. She went down the hall to Mikey's room, pushed open the door, and turned on the light. There he was at the foot of the crib, flinging things over the side. The thud must have been the sound of his half-empty bottle hitting a nearby wall. As usual, the crib was a shambles. Mikey had pulled the blanket and sheet completely off the mattress, dumping them in one corner. "Yi!" he said turning to Christine and giving her his warmest eight-toothed smile. Her 13-month-old son, Michael Francis Gordon, was ready to start a new day.

Frank had been ecstatic when Mikey was born. He hung a king-sized bed sheet on the highway overpass that the construction company he worked for was building. Written on it in huge blue letters were the words: IT'S A BOY!!! The next day a reporter from News Watch 10 stopped by to interview Frank at the end of his shift. "I just want everyone to know," Frank explained, beaming into the TV camera, "that a new World Series pitcher for the Red Sox has just been born. You should see the hands on him already! What a kid!"

Now, 13 months later, on a warm August morning, Christine picked up the future baseball star to change his soggy diaper. This task completed, the two of them went down to the kitchen to get breakfast started. As Christine began to measure coffee into the coffeemaker, Mikey stood tugging at her nightgown, chanting "joos, joos."

Through the kitchen wall Christine could hear the toilet flushing in the bathroom. They'd have to do something about that plumbing. Noisiest plumbing she'd ever heard. Oh, well. She shouldn't complain. At least they had a house of their own now, which was what Frank had always wanted. Those nights last winter back in the old apartment had been the final straw. Mikey had been sleeping in their room because there was no space with the girls. His presence had begun to put a real crimp in their sex life.

"Do you think he can hear us?" Christine would whisper when they started making love.

"For Christ's sake, what does it matter? He's only five months old! How the hell will he know what we're doing?"

"That's just it. He may think something terrible is going on. I read that . . ."

"Nuts to what you read! I'm not gonna let some Sigfried Freud crap turn me into a monk. If it bothers you so much, why don't you let him sleep in the living room?"

"Keep your voice down! You'll wake him. There, now you've done it!" And by the time Christine had nursed Mikey a little and rocked him back to sleep, Frank had also drifted off—with an angry scowl creased into his face.

So a bigger place was a must or they'd end up in divorce court. It was then that Frank had heard through his boss about a deal on a run-down three-bedroom house. Somehow they had managed to scrape together the down payment. The place had loose shingles, peeling paint, a leaky roof, and a worn-out furnace. But at least it was a start, and Frank could do the fix-up work himself.

By 6:30, with sunlight pouring through the open windows, the Gordon family had assembled at the kitchen table. Mikey sat loftily in his highchair, banging his feet against the footrest and pressing little nuggets of Cocoa Puffs into his mouth. The sugar-coated cereal stuck to his wet fingers, making the job of feeding himself easier. "Remember it's Wednesday," Christine said to Frank as she passed a spoonful of scrambled eggs in Mikey's direction. "I need the car to make a delivery to the store."

"I know, I know." Frank answered irritably. He hated to be reminded that Christine now had a job of sorts. It was such an odd kind of job that he didn't really have much reason to object to it at first. It had started the Christmas Christine was pregnant with Mikey, when she had made a pair of matching dresses for Janie and Becky. They were red, hand-smocked, and had wide white collars with little green Christmas trees appliquéd on them. Everyone had oohed and aahed over them on Christmas day. Christine's sister Paula had taken pictures and shown them to her boss at the dress shop. That had gotten the ball rolling. The woman wanted Christine to make some girls' dresses to sell on consignment at the store. It seemed harmless enough to Frank at the time— just a little extra sewing to help keep Christine busy until the baby was born. How was he to know the things she made would become such a hit? Within a few months, the store had turned a large storage closet into a special area to display Christine's clothes. Frank felt as if he had somehow been tricked into going along with something he never wanted. If it wasn't for the extra money and the fact that she did all the sewing at home, he would *make* her quit. He looked at her with growing annoyance across the kitchen table. As if on cue to break the tension, Mikey strained forward pointing at Christine's toast and demanding "beh, beh!"

"Hey, I think he said bread!" Frank exclaimed, momentarily forgetting his annoyance. And for the next 5 minutes he kept pointing to the toast that Christine had placed in Mikey's outstretched fingers, repeating "bread, bread," over and over. Mikey grinned and slapped the tray of his highchair in unrestrained delight.

That evening, as Christine sat at her sewing machine in a corner of the living room, Janie and Becky sprawled on the floor beside her, collecting leftover pieces of fabric for doll clothes. "That blue one's *mine*," Becky said, pulling a turquoise scrap out of Janie's pile. "No, it's not. Mommy gave it to *me*. Mommy, make her give it back!"

"Quiet, you two," Frank demanded. "Chrissie, will ya quiet things down over there? I'm tryin' to watch this program. Us men can't get any peace around here, can we Mikey?" Frank added, addressing the little boy beside him. Father and son had become real buddies since Mikey had started to walk and talk. "Jeeze. Now we've got another damn commercial!"

Mikey moved onto his father's lap and sat facing him. "Dee!" he said looking up with bright, eager eyes. "Wanna bounce, huh?" Frank smiled, his irritation fading. Soon father and son were engrossed in a game they had invented. Frank would hold Mikey on his lap and bounce him vigorously. Then, still supporting Mikey by the arms, he would suddenly spread his knees apart and let the baby drop between them. As Mikey squealed with laughter, Frank would hoist him back up and start all over again.

Now's as good a time as any, Christine thought as she walked over to the living room sofa. "Something happened at the store today," she started, trying to sound casual. "The owner, you know, Helen? She'd like to expand the kids' clothes a bit, in addition to my stuff, you know. And she asked me to go on a buying trip to Boston with her. Help her pick things out. Just for a day. What do you think?"

"I think it's a rotten idea! What do ya need to do that for? You got plenty to keep you busy here. And who's gonna take care of the kids? Tell me that."

"That's no problem," Christine answered quickly. "I'd have my mom come over for the day. And Helen's going to pay me, you know. A hundred dollars! Can you believe it? I nearly fainted."

"A hundred bucks, huh?" Frank muttered with grudging interest. "When does she want you to go?"

"Next Thursday. She's got the schedule all set up. What do you say? OK?"

"I'll never hear the end of it if I say no," Frank grumbled. "Yeah, go ahead. A hundred bucks. Why not?"

MERYL POLONIUS

"We'll be back with our third game of the day right after this!" the host of the TV quiz show announced with a huge artificial smile. I really should rinse out those sheets Meryl threw up on, Karen thought with a sigh, as she sat slumped in the worn tweed armchair. Then, after Meryl's nap, I can take everything down to the laundromat.

In an effort to shake herself out of her lethargy, Karen slid to the floor beside her daughter, Meryl. The baby was busily stacking brightly colored rings onto a plastic post. She performed this task slowly and soberly, as if diligently trying to master it. It's easy to love her at times like this when she's not fussing or screaming, Karen thought. Watching the child's tiny fingers clumsily handling a small blue ring, Karen felt a warm glow.

Bored with the rings, Meryl looked around and eyed the laundry basket. Soon she was crawling toward it. "Oh no, you don't," Karen warned as she scooped her off the floor. "You'll tip it over and I'll have to pick everything up." Meryl immediately began to cry and wriggled to escape from Karen's arms. "Someone's tired," Karen declared. "It's time for your nap." Meryl cried even louder as they headed toward the bedroom. "Let's go look for teddy," Karen said, trying to soothe her daughter. I'll bet teddy's already asleep. Shhh. You don't want to wake him, do you?" Meryl's cries turned into piercing screams. "Hey, come on," Karen pleaded, as she put Meryl into her crib. "Be good and go to sleep, and when you wake up I'll give you a cookie." Meryl's face was now a deep crimson as she screamed and pulled at a crib rail.

"Tough," muttered Karen, closing the bedroom door behind her. "You're just going to have to cry it out." Meryl's screams grated on Karen as she sat back down in front of the TV. But at least things were a lot better than they had been a year ago. Those first few months of Meryl's life had been really terrible. A small baby at birth, weighing just 6 pounds, Meryl was a fitful sleeper and a poor eater from the start. Often she would take only an ounce or so of formula and then spit it up.

Karen had tried breast-feeding at the urging of Meryl's pediatrician, but nursing was difficult for her and the baby remained colicky. Finally, Karen found a formula that Meryl could tolerate. This was a definite improvement. Nevertheless, Meryl continued to cry often and for long periods.

The strain got to Karen and to her mother. It seemed to Karen that her mother was constantly harping at her, telling her what she was doing wrong. One day at the Fresno Teen Mother Project, while waiting to talk with her counselor, Karen began pouring out her gripes to another girl named Kay. "Hey, that's really tough," Kay had said sympathetically. "But you don't have to take that crap from your mom. I'm lookin' for someone to share my apartment. Why don't you and Meryl move in with me and Ashley?"

"Yeah, what'll I do for money?" Karen asked, with a short laugh. "I've got *nothing*."

"You can collect from welfare, dummy," Kay answered. "That's what I do."

So Karen had moved into Kay's apartment above a shoe-repair shop. Her mother had been furious. "You're going to live *where*?" she asked Karen. "On West End Avenue near the freeway? That neighborhood's terrible! And going on welfare to boot. I can't *believe* it. You're doing this just to spite me!" When the counselor at the Teen Mother Project tactfully suggested that living apart might help mother and daughter bridge the gap between them, Karen's mother threw up her hands and walked out of the room. The next day, Karen moved clothes, toys, crib, and highchair into her new home. She felt apprehensive as she climbed the steep stairs leading up from the alley, but Kay's enthusiasm put her at ease. "Here," Kay smiled, "let me take that." And she dragged Karen's heavy suitcase into the shabby bedroom that Karen and Meryl would share.

Karen soon discovered that life with Kay and her young daughter Ashley was far from ideal. About a week after Karen had settled in, Kay's brother arrived, asking if he could stay for a day or two. That day or two dragged on into weeks and soon the apartment was overrun with his friends. As if Meryl wasn't fitful enough, all the disruption was making her unbearable. Karen was contemplating going back to her mother's when Kay got a call one night. It was Eric, Kay's on-again-off-again boyfriend and the father of Ashley. He was in Texas, working on construction and making all kinds of money, he said. He wanted Kay and Ashley to come down for a visit. "Maybe this time we can work things out," he had told Kay over the phone. Two days later, when the bus fare from Eric arrived, Kay was off to Dallas. The same day Kay's brother moved to his new girlfriend's apartment, leaving Karen and Meryl alone.

Karen was determined to make up for the strain that the last few months had put on Meryl. She took the few dollars she had saved from her monthly check and bought Meryl a new toy. It was Oscar the Grouch from *Sesame Street* in his battered garbage can. When you pressed a bulb attached to the side, the scowling Oscar would pop up like a jack-in-the-box. Karen couldn't wait to unwrap the toy when she got it home. She placed it in front of Meryl, who began to inspect it quietly. Then Karen pressed the bulb and Oscar leaped up, the lid of the garbage can perched on top of his head. Meryl startled, her lower lip protruded, and she began to cry. "Come on, honey. It's Oscar the Grouch," Karen said. "I got this nice new toy just for you." Meryl turned her head away as Karen pushed the toy toward her. "Don't you *like* it?" Karen asked, moving around to stay in front of Meryl's averted face. In exasperation she made the puppet pop up one more time. Meryl wailed louder.

As the weeks rolled by and Kay didn't return, the loneliness began to get to Karen. Some afternoons at Meryl's nap time, when she just wouldn't stop crying, Karen would have a sudden urge to walk out the door. She could picture herself walking down the street, the sun warm and inviting, with the cries of her baby growing fainter and fainter behind her. Karen was horrified at these fantasies. She loved Meryl; she knew she did. But sometimes it all just seemed too much. Karen often wished that she could talk to her mother the way daughters were supposed to be able to. But whenever she tried, they always ended up fighting. Even Karen's old friends from high school seemed to have deserted her. The few who hadn't gone off to college were busy working and having fun. Sitting around in a dumpy apartment with a cranky baby wasn't their idea of a good time. If it wasn't for the counselor at the Teen Mother Project, Karen didn't know what she would do.

That night as Karen sat in the living room, listening to the traffic in the street below, tears welled up in her eyes. "Damn you, Jeff," she whispered, "Damn you!" and pressing Meryl's teddy bear to her face, she cried as if her heart would break.

Chapter 4

First Adaptations

Chapter 4

First Adaptations

Karen Polonius watched as Dr. Bryant gave newborn Meryl her first physical exam. Meryl squirmed on the examining table at the touch of Dr. Bryant's cold stethoscope. Her tiny face crumpled into a scowl, and she flailed her thin little arms and legs.

"She may be small, Karen," Dr. Bryant said, "but she's very alert."

"She is?" Karen answered doubtfully. To her, Meryl looked totally helpless and unaware of what was going on.

"Sure," said Dr. Bryant, smiling. "Watch." And she began to talk to Meryl in gentle, soothing tones. "Hi there, little one. Hi, sweetie. Going to show your mom how smart you are, hmmm?" Meryl immediately quieted and looked up.

"She hears you," whispered Karen.

Then Dr. Bryant slowly moved a bright orange ball across Meryl's field of vision. Meryl's eyes followed it.

"She sees it!" Karen exclaimed.

"Now you try," said Dr. Bryant, encouraging Karen to move her head slowly back and forth while she talked to the baby.

"She sees me!" Karen smiled, looking up at the doctor. "Does she know I'm a person? Does she know I'm her mom?"

"Not yet," Dr. Bryant answered kindly, "but she will. In a few months she'll have learned a lot about people, and she'll know you from all others."

Meryl faces developmental tasks similar to those we all face: she must learn about the world in which she lives and form relationships with the people in it. Compared with adults, however, Meryl faces these tasks at a disadvantage. While adults have extensive past experience to draw on, newborns do not. Meryl must learn from scratch that objects exist, that different objects have different properties (which sometimes change), and that actions she performs on objects have consequences. In addition, she must learn that people are very special objects that possess their own wishes and feelings and that engage in actions independent of hers. In the process, Meryl must come to the realization that she, too, is a person.

How do newborns make these discoveries with no prior knowledge of the world? Fortunately, they come equipped with certain built-in capacities that help them to tackle the task. At birth they have a set of useful **reflexes** (automatic reactions to particular stimuli, such as sucking when something is placed in the mouth), as well as an impressive learning ability. Their perceptual abilities improve rapidly, and they become able to make increasingly refined movements of their bodies. All these capacities make possible their first adaptations—their first efforts to adjust to and understand the world.

A child's early competencies, which are the building blocks of more complex behaviors, have a number of characteristics:

1. *Very early competencies depend on abilities that are **prewired**—*that is, built into the nervous system at birth. Rapid changes and refinements in these earliest competencies often depend on both experience and maturation of the central nervous system.
2. *Infants' competencies often meet **survival needs.*** For example, the sucking reflex secures nourishment, the gagging reflex prevents choking, and the crying reflex elicits care.
3. *From the very beginning, infants' competencies involve **organized sequences of actions that***

Reflex:
An automatic response to a particular stimulus.

serve some purpose. For instance, when Meryl reflexively turned her head and eyes in the direction of Dr. Bryant's voice, this coordinated series of movements served the purpose of helping her locate the source of a sound. Such organized sequences are very simple in newborns, but they become more elaborate with further development. When Meryl is some months older, for example, she will conduct more complex and intentional searches to find where a sound is coming from.

4. *Infants' competencies involve **selective responses.*** For instance, newborns do not look with equal attention at everything around them. Instead, they tend to look at things that are fairly large and have sharp color contrast, such as a pair of eyes or the border between a person's hair and forehead. This early "selective looking" is an automatic action and does not involve a conscious or intentional focusing of attention. Nevertheless, it gives the baby opportunities to learn about the distinguishing features of human faces.

5. *Early competencies allow infants to detect the **relationship between an action and its consequences.*** For example, a newborn may detect the connection between placing the thumb in the mouth and the good feelings it generates. (A thumb in the eye, in contrast, does not feel good.) The connection between an action and its consequences is called a **contingency.**

Contingency: The relationship between an event and its consequences.

This chapter focuses on the capacities that infants possess for interacting with the world. In particular, it looks at what babies are able to do and their skills for obtaining information about their environments. First, we describe the states that newborns experience: from sleep to various wakeful states (quiet, active, fussy, crying). These states are the framework within which a baby experiences the world. As you will see, the amount of time spent in each state changes during infancy. Next, we examine some reflexes present in newborns. Sometimes these serve as building blocks for more elaborate later behaviors. In the third section we look at infant motor skills (skills involving voluntary movements) and their relationship to earlier reflexes. Then we discuss early sensory capacities and developmental changes in perceptual abilities. Here we give particular attention to vision and hearing. In a box later in the chapter we look in depth

The seemingly simple act of turning in the direction of a sound demonstrates the organized nature of young infants' behavior.

at the consequences of early visual and hearing disabilities and at some of the attempts to ameliorate these problems. Finally, we examine infants' learning capabilities, which provide one of the means by which changes come about.

As you read about these earliest capacities in children and how they change over time, think about how they allow interaction with the world, including other people, from the moment of birth. Also think about how limitations on infants' abilities restrict what they are able to perceive and learn. For example, as you read about the limitations on early visual capacities, imagine how hard it would be for a newborn like Meryl to actually *see* the difference between her mother and some other woman.

This chapter has two major themes. One focuses on development as a process and emphasizes the complementary roles played by genetics and experience. The other focuses on how the skills that are inborn or that emerge in the first weeks of life relate to skills that develop later in the first year.

The first of the two themes provides one way to look at the nature-nurture question. In this chapter particularly, the emphasis is on how heredity and the environment work jointly to guide the course of development. We are not concerned here with quantifying the contributions of genetics and environment to particular developmental skills. Early development provides a good place to examine the nature-nurture issue because infant skills and behaviors are relatively limited (and thus easy to assess) and because their initial state is relatively untouched by experience. Infants raised in different environments or cultures and infants with specific disabilities offer a variation in experience that allows developmentalists to assess how such variations affect development.

Another way to look at the complementary roles of heredity and environment is to see how they each contribute to the development of the brain, particularly the **cerebral cortex,** the brain's thin outer layer. The cerebral cortex is the master control center for many abilities, including voluntary movement, perception, communication, problem solving, and thought. At birth a baby's brain has almost all the **neurons** (or nerve cells) it will ever have, but many neurons in the cortex don't yet function efficiently.

After birth, the cortex develops in several ways. It undergoes a small increase in its number of cells, accompanied by a rapid increase in cell size and interconnectedness (see Figure 4.1). Fatty *myelin sheaths* begin to form around cell fibers

Cerebral cortex:
The thin outer layer of the brain, in which most higher-level mental processes are localized. Also called the *neocortex* because it is the most recently evolved part of the brain.

Neuron:
The specialized cells that are the basic building blocks of the nervous system (nerve cells).

FIGURE 4.1 CEREBRAL CORTEX NEURONS, 1–15 MONTHS
During the first 15 months of life, the interconnections among neurons in the cerebral cortex multiply rapidly. (Source: Conel, 1939–1963.)

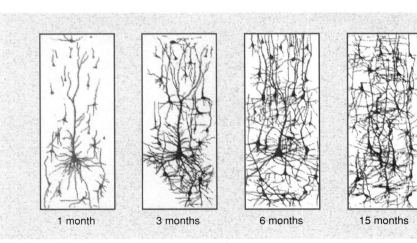

1 month   3 months   6 months   15 months

to help speed the conduction of messages in the brain (a process called *myelination*). This rapid development of the cortex in the first months after birth partly explains many of the changes that take place in infant competencies. But this development, especially the increase in interconnections among neurons, also depends on the experiences that infants have (Schore, 1994). Two clear examples discussed in this chapter are control over leg movements and development of binocular vision. Experience is an important ingredient in the developing organization of the nervous system. At the same time that the developing nervous system is fostering and constraining infants' capacities, the nervous system itself is being fostered and constrained by experiences.

The second theme of this chapter emphasizes that infants' initial skills, and the experiences they allow infants to have, provide the seeds for the development of the more complex and flexible skills seen by the end of the first year. The sensory systems, behavior systems, and learning skills with which newborns enter the world are limited, but their very limitations are useful for guiding infants to the kinds of experiences that foster the development of complex skills. For example, the hearing system of newborns is quite immature, but it seems to be specially tuned to pay attention to the human voice, an important factor in developing language skills. Similarly, their limited visual capabilities lead them to look initially at large parts of nearby objects, such as the outline of the human face, and to ignore much of the detail that they are not yet prepared to understand. The movements of their arms and legs, which seem to be at least partially dependent on reflexes, lead them to repeat the movement patterns that they need if they are to acquire effective voluntary control of their movements.

INFANT STATES

Infants enter many different states during a typical day. In the scene that opened this chapter, newborn Meryl started to become fussy while undergoing the physical exam, but then became alert and quiet while listening to Dr. Bryant's voice and watching the orange ball. These two states are qualitatively different, as any observer can see. One frequently used classification system identifies six infant states: two kinds of sleep (quiet sleep and active sleep); two kinds of wakefulness (awake-and-quiet and awake-and-active); and two states of distress (fussing and crying) (Brazelton, 1973; Prechtl and Beintema, 1964).

States and the transitions between them are important in the study of infants' capabilities, because babies respond to their environments very differently depending on their current state. For example, a bell sounded next to a newborn may elicit an eye movement or head turn in the direction of the sound if the baby is in an awake-and-quiet state, but not if the baby is in an active-sleep or fussing state. During the first few months of life, infants become increasingly easy to study, in part because they gain increasing control over their states, and the states themselves become more stable and predictable.

SLEEP STATES

States of sleep consume a great deal of a newborn's time. The average newborn spends more than 16 hours sleeping each day (Berg and Berg, 1979, 1987; Thoman and Whitney, 1989). Time spent sleeping decreases rapidly during infancy and childhood, and then declines more gradually until it reaches a little

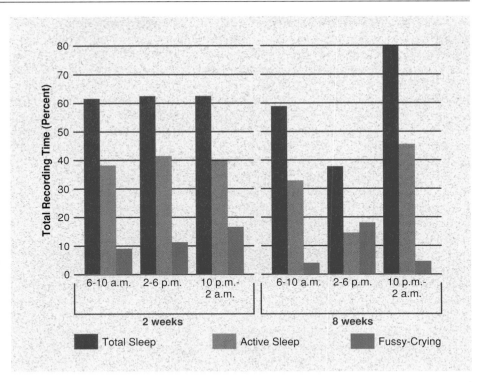

FIGURE 4.2 CHANGES IN INFANTS' SLEEP-WAKE CYCLE

At 2 weeks of age infants do not follow the conventional sleep-wake cycle of sleeping more at night and being awake more during the day. By the time they reach 8 weeks of age, infants in middle-class American families have increased the percentage of time they spend sleeping between 10 p.m. and 2 a.m. and have decreased the percentage of time they spend sleeping between 2 p.m. and 6 p.m. (Source: Sostek and Anders, 1981.)

more than 6 hours a day in old age (Roffwarg, Muzio, and Dement, 1966). Newborns distribute their sleeping and waking time equally between day and night, which creates difficulties for parents, who usually have their sleep-wake times organized in larger blocks. Although it will be weeks, months, or even years before a child sleeps through the night consistently, most middle-class American babies show signs of starting to acquire the conventional day-night pattern by 8 weeks of age (Sostek and Anders, 1981). As Figure 4.2 shows, compared with the typical 2-week-old, the typical American 8-week-old spends less time sleeping in the late afternoon and more time sleeping in the early part of the night.

Although this shift may be based partly on brain maturation, how infants are cared for also seems to play a part. In the United States, parents invest considerable effort in getting their babies to sleep through the night. They often try to keep them awake in the late afternoon, and they may feed them more than usual before putting them to bed in the evening. In societies that are not so concerned about infants sleeping through the night, the newborn pattern of short sleep cycles distributed around the clock tends to last much longer than it does in our society. Infant caregiving practices tend to accommodate to this pattern rather than trying to change it. In one African tribe, researchers found that it was customary for babies to sleep with the mother and to nurse as much as they wanted when they awakened during the night (Super and Harkness, 1972). This caregiving practice could be accommodated because a mother's daytime activities were less rigidly scheduled than they are in our society.

As we mentioned earlier, there are actually two kinds of infant sleep states. One is a quiet sleep in which babies lie completely still, breathing slowly and regularly. The other is an active sleep, in which they stir often, move their arms and legs, crinkle up their faces, breathe faster and more irregularly than in quiet sleep, and sometimes show rapid movements of their eyes behind closed eyelids. Infant active sleep is in some ways like adult REM sleep, in which rapid eye movements (REMs) also occur (Roffwarg, Muzio, and Dement, 1966). Newborns spend 50 percent of their sleep time in active sleep, as opposed to the roughly 20 percent of sleep time that adults spend in REM. Newborns' active and quiet sleep states are intermixed irregularly, unlike adults' stages of sleep, which occur in quite regular sequences. (Adult REM, for example, usually starts about 90 minutes into the sleep cycle, and then repeats at approximately 90-minute intervals.) In addition, the brain-wave patterns characteristic of the different stages of adult sleep are not present in newborns (Spitz, Emde, and Metcalf, 1970). These differences between newborn and adult sleep quickly diminish, however. By 3 months of age, babies generally start sleep with a non-REM period, just as adults do, and they also show the brain-wave patterns typical of adult sleep.

DISTRESSED STATES

Unlike sleep states, which occupy so much of a newborn's time, the crying state occupies relatively little of it. Newborns usually spend less than 10 percent of their time crying (Korner et al., 1981). In the first two months after birth, the average infant engages in full-blown crying only about 2 percent of the time. Another 10 percent is spent fussing (Wolff, 1987).

Three distinct crying patterns have been reported: *hungry cries,* which start with a whimper and become louder and more sustained; *upset cries,* which are louder and often begin more suddenly; and *pain cries,* which start with a high-pitched, high-intensity wail followed by loud crying. Most adults can distinguish among these types of cries (Barr, Desilets, and Rotman, 1991). Even inexperienced mothers respond more rapidly to the pain cry than to either of the other two (Wolff, 1969). Experience, however, does help to sharpen an adult's ability to perceive a cry's meaning. For instance, experienced nurses who work in hospital nurseries are better able to discriminate among different types of cries than are less experienced nurses (Wasz-Hockert et al., 1968). Experience with a particular baby also helps adults to interpret what that child's cries mean. That is why a mother is better at distinguishing among the cries of her own baby than of a baby she doesn't know (Wiesenfeld, Malatesta, and DeLoach, 1981).

While caregivers often soothe crying infants, the babies also have a built-in capacity to soothe themselves. Sucking is often part of this process. Allowing infants to suck on a pacifier is one effective soothing technique (Field and Goldson, 1984). Techniques with more caregiver involvement include voice stimulation, rocking, holding closely, and swaddling. Not all techniques are effective with all babies, and babies differ in the ease with which they can be soothed by others or by themselves (Bates, 1980).

CHANGES IN STATES

During the first few months after birth, an infant's state changes often, and parents are frequently involved in the transitions from one state to another. For instance, parents rock their newborns to sleep, rouse them to alertness for a feeding, soothe them out of fussiness or crying, and so forth. By age 5 months, however, an infants's state no longer changes so often, and transitions between states are more predictable (Sostek and Anders, 1981). Now parents' involvement with their infants focuses much more on the babies' behavior during both awake states. This change occurs more rapidly and smoothly for some babies than for others, and how rapidly and smoothly it happens can help to predict some of a child's future characteristics. Individual differences in the speed and smoothness of this development are affected by both biological makeup and environmental influences, but we do not yet know the degree to which each of these factors contributes.

REFLEXES IN THE NEWBORN

As stated earlier, a *reflex* is an automatic or built-in reaction elicited by particular *stimuli*. Blinking your eye when an object is poked at it is one example of a reflex that you have had since birth. A newborn displays many other reflexes, some of which disappear as the baby grows older and others of which are eventually incorporated into more complex voluntary movements. Examples of infant reflexes are given in Table 4.1.

These reflexes enable young babies to make organized and sometimes adap-

TABLE 4.1
EXAMPLES OF INFANT REFLEXES

Reflex	Description	Developmental Pattern
Blink	To a flash of light or a puff of air, an infant closes both eyes.	Permanent.
Babinski	When the side of an infant's foot is stroked from the heel toward the toes, the toes fan out and the foot twists inward.	Disappears around 1 year.
Babkin	When an infant is lying supine, pressure applied to the palms of both hands causes the head to turn straight ahead, the mouth to open, and the eyes to close.	Disappears around 3 months.
Grasping	Pressure on an infant's palms produced by an object like a parent's finger causes the fingers to curl with a strong enough grasp to support the infant's own weight.	Weakens after 3 months and disappears by 1 year.
Moro	This reflex pattern, which involves extending the arms and then bringing them rapidly toward the midline while closing the fingers in a grasping action, can be triggered by several kinds of startling stimuli, such as a sudden loud noise or holding the infant horizontally face-up and then rapidly lowering the baby about 6 inches.	Disappears around 5 months.
Rooting	When an infant's cheek is stroked lightly, the infant turns the head in the direction of the stroked cheek and opens the mouth to suck the object that stroked the cheek.	Disappears around 4 months.
Stepping	When an infant is held above a surface and then lowered until the feet touch the surface, the infant will make stepping movements like walking.	Disappears around 3 months.
Sucking	When an object such as a nipple or a finger is inserted into an infant's mouth, rhythmic sucking occurs.	Changes into voluntary sucking by 2 months.
Tonic Neck	An infant placed on the back tends to turn the head to one side and extend the arm and leg on that side while flexing the limbs on the other side (like a fencing position).	Disappears around 4 months.

tive responses to their environments before they have a chance to learn. For example, the fact that newborns reflexively suck when an object is placed in the mouth allows them to obtain nourishment before they learn the connection between a nipple and food. Certain other reflexes found in newborns have less obvious functions. Some seem to provide initial responses that learning later modifies, thus allowing more rapid acquisition of important new behaviors. Examples include the grasping and stepping reflexes. Still other reflexes may be a legacy of our evolutionary past. For instance, when a newborn's head or body is allowed to drop backward, the **Moro reflex** occurs: the arms fling out and then come back toward the body's midline, with the hands curling in as if to grasp something. Might the Moro reflex be the response of an animal trying to grasp its mother or the limb of a tree to keep from falling? If so, it was crucial to our early ancestors' survival.

When young infants are placed on their backs, they assume a characteristic position with head turned to one side, the arm and leg on that side extended, and the arm and leg on the opposite side flexed.

SURVIVAL REFLEXES

Some of the reflexes present at birth—such as blinking, sneezing, and gagging—clearly aid survival by helping an infant deal with threats to the body. But because these reflexes remain throughout a person's life, they are not of great interest to developmentalists. Developmentalists are more concerned with survival reflexes that are present at birth but disappear as the infant acquires more advanced skills.

For example, when you stroke a newborn's cheek or touch a corner of the child's mouth, the baby responds by turning the head toward the side that was touched, in an apparent attempt to find something to suck. This is called the **rooting reflex.** When an object enters a newborn's mouth, the **sucking reflex** is activated. Both these reflexes have obvious survival value to newborn mammals, who drink milk and must suck to get food. These reflexes begin to change in minor ways in the first week or two of life, as an infant becomes more skilled at nursing. In fact, infants learn to suck differently depending on whether they are breast- or bottle-fed. This shows that the organization of behavior that reflexes provide is not totally rigid; it can be modified by experience. Despite these modifications, the behaviors remain reflexive for a time; for example, sucking continues to be the response to any object placed in the mouth. Between 2 and 4 months of age, however, a major developmental change occurs: both these reflexes disappear and give way to voluntary eating behaviors. It is important for the sucking reflex to disappear if babies are to begin eating solid foods. If infants continued to suck automatically every time food entered their mouths, they would never learn to chew.

Moro reflex:
The reaction of a newborn to the situation in which his or her head is allowed to drop back: the arms fling out and then come back toward the body's midline, with the hands curling in as if to grasp something.

Rooting reflex:
The infant's response to a touch on the cheek or a corner of the mouth by turning the head toward the side that was touched.

Sucking reflex:
The automatic sucking engaged in by an infant whenever the mouth captures any object.

OTHER REFLEXES

Some reflexes that are present at birth and disappear as the baby grows older have no apparent survival value. However, the behaviors displayed in these reflexes later become part of more sophisticated voluntary actions. One example is the **grasping reflex.** If you stimulate the palm of a newborn's hand, the baby responds by automatically curling the fingers inward as if to grasp. When an adult uses the index fingers to stimulate a newborn's palms, the infant will grasp each finger so firmly that the adult can actually lift the baby up. Since a newborn's grasp is reflexive, the child cannot voluntarily let go, although fatigue will eventually set in and weaken the grip. By the end of the third

Grasping reflex:
The newborn's response to a stimulation of the palm of the hand by automatically curling the fingers inward.

Newborns appear to be able to walk when supported, but the behavior is purely a reflex that usually disappears before true walking occurs.

Stepping reflex:
The reflexive, rhythmic stepping motion that resembles walking and that is elicited when the infant is held upright and lowered until the feet touch a surface.

month, the grasping reflex declines and the baby develops a more voluntary grasp, usually elicited by seeing an object or hearing one in the dark (Clifton et al., 1993). For instance, when Meryl is 4 or 5 months old, the sight of a bright orange ball would probably cause her to reach out and try to grasp it. This voluntary grasp, which becomes more adept with age, is a very important capability. It allows older infants to secure and manipulate objects they wish to explore.

Another example of a behavior that is a reflex for infants and that reappears later as a component of a skilled behavior is the **stepping reflex.** The pediatrician who examined Meryl could have elicited this reflex by holding her upright and then lowering her toward the table until her feet touched the surface. Meryl would have responded to the touch on the bottom of her feet by reflexively moving them in a rhythmic stepping motion that resembles walking. The stepping reflex usually disappears when a baby is around 3 months old. Then, a number of months later, the same movements reappear, this time under voluntary control, as the child learns to walk.

Developmentalists have been fascinated by reflexive movements that are eventually incorporated into more complex, voluntary actions. Some have suggested that early in development the grasping and stepping reflexes are probably controlled by lower brain centers (e.g., Zelazo, 1983). As the baby grows older, higher brain regions take control and allow the reflexes to be stopped. Voluntary control via these higher brain regions then enables the formerly reflexive actions to be integrated into more complex behaviors. This transfer of control from lower to higher brain centers may be related to the development of neurons in the cerebral cortex—both the laying down of a myelin sheath around their fibers and the proliferation of connections among them. The fact that several reflexes disappear or are modified at around 3 or 4 months of age supports the idea that brain maturation is involved. But the process is probably even more complex than that. Why, for instance, does practicing certain reflexes (such as the stepping reflex) both slow the disappearance of that reflex and speed up the emergence of voluntary actions that involve the same movements? A transfer of control to higher brain centers as neurons there mature can't be the complete answer to this question. A fuller understanding of the process is needed.

INFANT MOTOR SKILLS

When Mikey was born, Christine knew from experience that she had to keep his fingernails well trimmed. If his nails were allowed to grow too long, he could easily scratch his face as he moved his arms and hands around in the poorly coordinated manner of newborns. By the time Mikey was 1 year old, his motor skills had improved dramatically. Now he could sit unsupported, crawl rapidly wherever he wished, pull himself up into a standing position, and take a few tentative steps while hanging on to furniture. His movements were much more deliberate and coordinated than the random flailing of his arms and legs when he was a newborn. Guided by sight, he could reach for and grasp an object, pick it up for inspection, and move it from hand to hand. Figure 4.3 summarizes some of the major milestones in motor development during a child's first two years, giving the average age at which each occurs. Both Jean Piaget (1952) and Arnold Gesell (1946) argued that perceptual and motor development were the

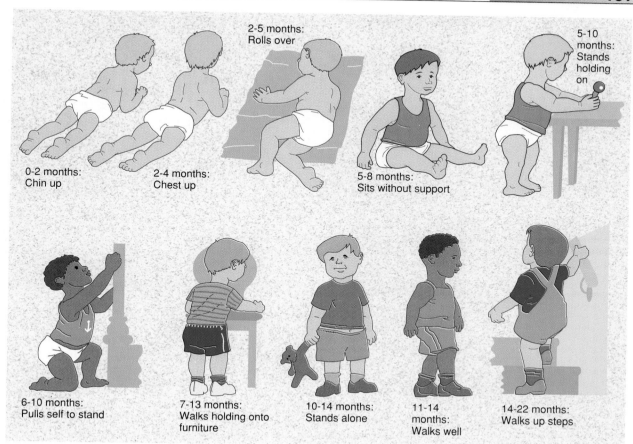

FIGURE 4.3

MILESTONES IN MOTOR DEVELOPMENT

Normal children vary considerably in the ages at which they achieve major motor milestones. (Source: Frankenburg and Dodds, 1967.)

foundations of all mental life. Without the abilities to perceive the world and actively explore it, a child is severely handicapped in acquiring knowledge.

MOTOR SKILLS AND PHYSICAL GROWTH

Infant motor skills develop in the context of dramatic physical growth. During the first year after birth, babies on average triple in weight and grow 10 inches in length. Bones, which were soft and pliable at birth, become harder and more rigid. Muscle mass increases, allowing greater muscle strength. Body proportions change. At the end of the first year the head still appears large relative to the rest of the body, but not as out of proportion as in newborns. The trunk is also long relative to the arms and legs. Just as during the prenatal period, different parts of the body are growing at different times and rates.

Rapid physical growth provides a challenge for the development of motor skills: infants must learn to control their movements using a body that is changing in size. For example, babies must learn to reach for objects with an arm that is growing in length. In the discussion that follows we will focus mainly on the initial acquisition of motor skills. But keep in mind that, throughout development, the motor system must recalibrate to adapt to physical changes.

Babies gradually become more accurate and coordinated in their attempts to reach for and grasp objects as these behaviors change from reflexes to voluntary actions.

SOME PRINCIPLES OF MOTOR-SKILL DEVELOPMENT

We will look at four major principles involved in the development of motor skills: differentiation, cephalocaudal development, proximodistal development, and the joint role of maturation and experience.

The first of these principles, *differentiation,* comes into play when with development global, poorly defined skills turn into a set of precise skills, each adapted to a specific function. Consider an infant's reactions when his or her mouth and nose are covered by an adult's hand (Bühler, 1930). The newborn reacts reflexively with the whole body: arms and legs go into random motion, the body twists, the infant wails. The result of such a global reaction may, of course, be the withdrawal of the hand, and is therefore adaptive. Some weeks later, in the same situation, the baby will respond with relatively more arm movements, mostly directed toward the center of the body. The child thus increases the chances of inadvertently batting away the hand. But not until age 6 months does the infant precisely push the hand away using a directed swipe, perhaps with only one arm. A month or two later, the baby may even block the hand from covering the nose and mouth by using a specific anticipatory movement.

The second and third principles in the development of motor skills, cephalocaudal development and proximodistal development, were both introduced in Chapter 3 when we discussed prenatal growth. *Cephalocaudal development* means that control over motor movements tends to progress from head to tail, which in humans means the end of the spinal column. (Unlike most other primates, we no longer have tails.) For instance, during infancy refined sucking and eye movements emerge first and refined walking movements last. *Proximodistal development* means that control over motor movements tends to progress from the center of the body out to the extremities. For example, a baby shows refined control of head movements before arm movements, and of arm movements before hand movements. These patterns seem to be caused by differences in the rates at which the relevant muscles develop and the brain areas that control those muscles mature.

The fourth principle we will consider is that the development of motor skills is influenced, not just by biological maturation, but also by experience. In the early part of this century there was great interest in charting the course of motor skill development, which was viewed as consisting of an inevitable sequence of milestones. It was also widely believed that the course of this development was governed by maturation of the central nervous system. Modern developmentalists have modified this view. They argue that the biological constraints on development are "softer" than had been believed. While the gross outlines of neural pathways may be biological givens, and while there are physical limits to what the human body can potentially do, these biological constraints only establish *general* behavioral tendencies. Experience is essential for these general tendencies to unfold and become refined, and in fact is necessary to support and guide the developing organization of the central nervous system. This view is supported not only by evidence that practice influences the rate of motor skill development, but also by the fact that there are individual differences in how babies accomplish the same task (Thelen et al., 1993).

Rather than discussing all the motor skills that emerge during infancy, we will focus in the following sections on a few representative ones: controlled eye movements, reaching and grasping, and walking.

CONTROLLED EYE MOVEMENTS

Your eye movements are so automatic that you probably don't think of them as a motor skill. However, controlled eye movements are one of the earliest motor skills to develop. Without them, Mikey could look only at whatever happened to be in his line of sight. He could not study the different parts of an object one after another, follow people visually as they moved about, or keep his eyes fixed on something despite movements of his own head and body. In short, if infants lacked control over their eye movements, their ability to learn about the world would be severely limited.

Even newborns show some controlled eye movements. When they have no stimulus to look at, they move their eyes more often and farther than normal, as if searching for something to see (Salapatek and Kessen, 1966). As the weeks pass, babies become more effective at controlling where they look. For instance, when 1-month-old babies look at a person's face, they tend to focus on border areas of high contrast. If a new stimulus appears off to one side, the baby may move his or her eyes to look at the new object. This tendency is more pronounced, and the eye shifts are more accurate, by the time the child is 2 months old (Aslin and Salapatek, 1975). It is important that this system be well organized early in order to allow the baby to explore the world visually. Nevertheless, control over eye movements continues to improve until at least 7 years of age (Zaporozhets, 1965).

Researchers have studied the age at which babies become able to "track" a moving object using **pursuit eye movements.** These are the smooth, continuous movements of the eyes used to follow a person or object in motion. In contrast, **saccadic eye movements** are the rapid, jerky eye movements used to shift one's gaze quickly to something new. When an object suddenly starts to move, your eyes move saccadically to catch up with it. Then you follow the object using smooth, continuous pursuit eye movements. If a newborn is presented with a moving object, the eyes tend to move in the appropriate direction, but neither accurately nor smoothly. At 2 months of age, smooth pursuit eye movements are

Pursuit eye movements: The smooth, continuous eye motions used to track a moving object.

Saccadic eye movements: The rapid, jerky eye movements that occur when the gaze is shifted to a new object.

common, but these movements can usually be applied only to slowly moving objects (Dayton and Jones, 1964). This is probably why adults tend to move their heads slowly from side to side when talking to very young infants: very young babies simply cannot follow rapid side-to-side or up-and-down motions. The ability to follow more-rapidly moving objects develops during the period between 2 and 4 months of age (Aslin, 1981).

Visual tracking skills are also needed in situations in which infants themselves are in motion. To keep their eyes fixed on stationary objects while they are being carried around, babies must move either their eyes or their entire heads to compensate for their own movement through space. Even in the first months of life, infants make compensatory eye movements when they feel their bodies being moved (Evitar, Evitar, and Naray, 1974). By 16 weeks, infants' compensatory head movements have developed almost to adult levels, but their ability to keep their eyes on target is still far below adult standards (Daniel and Lee, 1990).

REACHING AND GRASPING

Reaching and grasping are examples of behaviors that appear early in an infant's life, decline or disappear with development, and then reappear in more advanced forms (Bower, 1974). T. G. R. Bower claims that "all the components of reaching and grasping can be elicited in fetuses at a postconception age of 14 to 16 weeks" (1974, pp. 149–150), and that reaching—or a reaching reflex— can be elicited relatively easily from infants in the first month after birth. Between 1 and about 4 months, however, infants show a decline in reaching, unless they are given continual practice at it. Then intentional reaching emerges and gradually becomes more refined. By age 15 months, children commonly reach for things smoothly and accurately.

Until recently it was widely believed that the earliest accurate intentional reaching was visually guided and emerged between 3 and 5 months of age (Piaget, 1952; White, Castle, and Held, 1964). Visually guided intentional reaching requires that infants simultaneously see both the object they are reaching for and their own hand so that they can adjust their hand movements appropriately. It was assumed that early experience with visually guided reaching "taught" the motor system, so to speak, so that later in development children could reach for objects without visually monitoring their hands. But we now know that extensive experience with visually guided reaching is not essential for intentional, *non*-visually guided reaching to occur. At about 15 weeks of age, the same time that visually guided reaching begins, babies will reach for a glowing object in the dark (where they can't see their hands); they will also reach for an object that is totally obscured by darkness but makes an interesting sound (Clifton et al., 1993).

This does not mean, however, that a baby's brain is programmed to produce certain trajectories of arm and hand movements. Esther Thelen and her colleagues (Thelen et al., 1993), who have studied the early development of reaching in detail, conclude that reaching is refined through active exploration of the environment and the pursuit of particular goals. Refined reaching, in other words, does not just emerge automatically as a baby matures. It is also a product of intentional efforts, practice, and experience.

Effective reaching, of course, depends on an object being within arm's length, or on moving the rest of the body so as to put the object within reaching distance. This means that reaching must ultimately be integrated into a more complex system of body movements. Young infants have been found to reach more for nearby objects than for distant ones (Gordon and Yonas, 1976), which shows that they perceive the relative distance of things, a topic we will return to later. Five-month-old babies who can sit up and lean forward will lean and try to reach objects that are beyond arm's length, whereas babies who have not yet developed the leaning skill do not try to reach in this situation (Yonas and Hartman, 1993). Similarly, a study of 8- to 10-month-olds found that they simply reach for objects that are within arm's length, but they simultaneously lean and reach for objects that are beyond this distance (McKenzie et al., 1993). By 8 months, then, reaching and leaning have become part of an integrated system. The babies do not try to reach first, fail to get the object they want, and then lean to get it. They lean and reach *simultaneously* if an object is not close at hand.

The development of grasping follows a similar course to the development of reaching. It too begins with a reflexive behavior that declines and is replaced by a voluntary one. Then, with further maturation, practice, and experience, voluntary grasping becomes increasingly refined. The newborn's strong grasping reflex has declined enough for babies to pick up objects voluntarily by 3 to 4 months of age. They still use a whole-hand grasp, however, making it hard to pick up things that don't fit in the hand. And until about 6 months of age they still have difficulty letting go of objects voluntarily. By 8 months infants are able to use the thumb in opposition to the fingers, but the fingers act primarily in unison. It is not until around 1 year of age that infants are finally able to oppose the thumb and forefinger, allowing them to grasp very small things easily. Figure 4.4 illustrates some important developments in grasping during the first year after birth.

We have seen that a number of initially reflexive behaviors seem to gradually become voluntary as control of them shifts from lower brain centers to the cerebral cortex. To bring these actions under voluntary control, the infant apparently must first acquire the ability to stop them. As this ability develops, the early, automatic forms of the behaviors gradually disappear. Then the child is ready to put the actions back together in a purposeful way, as in reaching for and grasping objects the infant wants. The same general description applies to eye movements. The eye movements of infants develop from being controlled by the nature of the stimuli to being under the infants' voluntary control

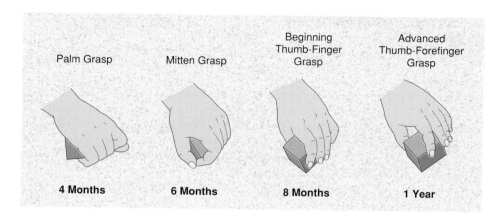

Palm Grasp   Mitten Grasp   Beginning Thumb-Finger Grasp   Advanced Thumb-Forefinger Grasp

4 Months   6 Months   8 Months   1 Year

FIGURE 4.4 DEVELOPMENT OF GRASPING DURING THE FIRST YEAR

depending on what they want to look at. You will see this pattern again in the next section, on the development of walking. Some of the components of walking are built in, but voluntary walking is delayed until such time as maturation and the appropriate experiences prepare the infant for its emergence.

WALKING

By 7 months of age Malcolm Williams had learned to slide along the floor on his stomach, propelled by his legs. His family was suddenly faced with all the challenges presented by a baby who could go almost anywhere he wanted. Nothing was safe any longer. Infants this age often acquire different methods of getting around. Some push themselves by their legs; others pull their bodies along with their arms; still others sit upright and scoot across the floor on their bottoms. Later, many babies learn to creep on their hands and knees. Before their first birthday they can usually hoist themselves into a standing position and "cruise"—that is, walk along while holding onto things. Most babies take their first solo steps shortly after the age of 1, although the age at which walking begins varies greatly. Malcolm walked early; Mikey at an average age; Meryl somewhat late. The age at which a baby starts walking and the pattern of development of prior abilities, such as crawling, are unrelated to later intelligence. Thus, parents should not be concerned about early walkers who never crawled or, unless the delay is extreme, about late walkers.

The motor movements of walking are apparent in the stepping reflex, which is present at birth and then starts to decline at around 2 months. As in the case of reaching, some developmentalists argue that the decline of the reflex is related to the development of inhibitory connections in the brain, which bring the reflexive activity under useful control. It may also be that as babies get heavier they simply don't have the leg strength to make stepping movements. Thelen (1986) has shown that the stepping reflex can continue to be elicited even in 7-month-olds if they are supported over a treadmill. This indicates that the reflex's normal disappearance involves more than just the development of inhibition.

Thelen argues that walking depends on the ability to integrate many systems. Consider balance, for instance. Studies of balance in infants show that even 5-month-olds begin to make appropriate movements to remain upright when sitting, although not always successfully (Woollacott, 1987). After further refinement, this balancing system will later be necessary for walking.

Thelen (1981) has also illustrated the role of early rhythmic, repetitive movements in the transition from the stepping reflex to real walking. As infants develop, their initial random and often jerky movements give way to smoother, more controlled ones. For example, all normal infants show stereotypic leg movements, such as kicking like a frog, when they are excited. These movements, mentioned in our story about Malcolm Williams, begin to appear around 1 month of age and peak at 5 to 6 months. After that, they decline. Stereotypic leg movements are not reflexes, since a wide variety of stimuli can elicit them, but they are not really voluntary actions either. Often, infants lying on their backs reach a certain level of excitement and then begin to kick repetitively. Evolution may have provided these coordinated movements to allow the infant to practice what will be voluntary and useful movements later. No other reason for this behavior is apparent. Babies simply do it as part of being excited. Interestingly, infants do not learn to control their leg movements until after the rhythmic, repetitive patterns have appeared (Rovee-Collier and Gekoski, 1979). Thus, these rhythmic patterns seem to be an important way station between reflexes and learned motor behaviors.

Although we don't yet know exactly what determines when a baby finally starts to walk, we do know that the onset of walking depends partly on maturation of the muscles and nervous system and partly on practice. To investigate the role of practice, researchers have studied babies who differ in their opportunities to walk. For instance, many years ago Wayne Dennis and M. C. Dennis (1940) studied Hopi Indian babies who spent much of their first year bound to cradle boards. The babies were unbound from the boards to have their clothes changed, but otherwise they had little chance to move their legs. Toward the end of their first year, the Hopi infants were given the same freedom of movement that babies in a control group had had since birth. Surprisingly, children in *both* groups learned to walk at about the same age. This and other early studies suggested that physical maturation exerts a greater influence over the onset of walking than does a child's total amount of practice moving the legs.

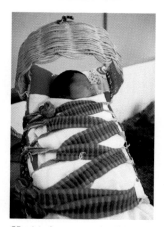

Hopi infants restrained in cradleboards learn to walk at about the same age as infants who have not been so confined.

More recent studies have shown the need for some refinement of this conclusion. The Hopi babies were given complete freedom of movement toward the end of their first year. If their movement had continued to be restricted, their walking might well have been delayed. Consider the Ache people of Paraguay, who live in a rain forest that presents numerous dangers. Ache mothers carry their babies around for much of the day and keep young children within arm's reach for several years. The children do not walk well until 2 years of age (Kaplan and Dove, 1987). Apparently, prolonged restriction of movement can affect the development of walking.

Conversely, certain kinds of practice can speed up the development of walking, at least to some degree. For example, the Kipsigis people of Kenya begin to teach their babies to sit up, stand, and walk starting between their second and third month (Super, 1976). Kipsigis children start walking about 3 weeks earlier on average than American children do, although they aren't generally more advanced in acquiring motor skills for which they haven't received any training. This suggests that practice specific to walking can make a difference in getting children to take their first steps.

Some insights into the nature of this practice come from an interesting experiment in which researchers regularly exercised the stepping reflex in a group of young babies (André-Thomas and Dargassies, 1952). This practice had two effects. First, the stepping reflex did not decline as rapidly in these children as it usually does. Second, these babies walked somewhat sooner than did a control group of infants whose stepping reflex was not exercised. Both findings are consistent with the theory that reflexes are the raw materials out of which more advanced skills are built. But even with all their early practice, the experimental babies did not walk a great deal sooner than others. Maturation still plays the major role in the onset of walking. We do not recommend that parents exercise the stepping reflex in their infants. The time spent in this effort could be better used interacting with the baby in other ways.

SENSING AND PERCEIVING THE WORLD

When John and DeeDee Williams brought Malcolm home from the hospital, all the members of the family, talking and smiling, clustered around to see him. How did the newborn perceive all this commotion? Could he see distinct faces peering into his? Could he hear different voices and distinguish speech from laughter? Could he smell soap on Momma Jo's hands as she touched his cheek?

SENSORY SYSTEMS IN THE NEWBORN

For years people have wondered how newborns like Malcolm experience the world. Since they respond reflexively to a variety of stimuli, their sensory systems must be working to some extent. But exactly what do babies experience when they see, hear, taste, smell, and touch things around them? And what causes them to direct their senses to one thing or another?

VISION

Visual acuity:
The degree to which one can perceive fineness of detail.

The pictures below illustrate how a mother's face may look to an infant of 1, 2, and 3 months of age. These pictures are created by computer and are based on estimates of the average baby's **visual acuity,** the fineness of detail he or she is able to see. Even an adult with "perfect" eyesight has somewhat limited visual acuity. You can demonstrate this to yourself by looking at any of the normal black-and-white photos in this book. Inspection under a magnifying glass shows that the photo is made up of a great many tiny dots, but without magnification you can't see the dots because your visual acuity isn't great enough. Because young infants have substantially less visual acuity than normal adults, they see much less fine detail. In fact, newborns have such poor acuity that they meet the criterion for being legally blind. Still, they are able to use their limited visual abilities effectively to experience the world from the very beginning. Over the next 6 months, moreover, their visual acuity rapidly improves.

DETERMINING HOW CLEARLY BABIES SEE   How do researchers determine an infant's visual acuity, since babies cannot *say* how clearly they see? One method takes advantage of a baby's motivation to try to look at things. If you place a solid gray card next to a card with broad black and white stripes, even a newborn looks longer at the striped card with its contrasting features. This *preferential looking* technique, which was developed decades ago by R. L. Fantz (1961), enables researchers to tell when a baby can see the difference between two stimuli. When researchers make the stripes progressively narrower and closer together, at some point babies no longer show a preference for the striped card. Presumably this is the point at which the limits of the infants' visual acuity make the striped card look like the uniformly gray card.

The pictures below simulate what infants of different ages may see when looking at a person from a distance of about 6 inches. Poor acuity in younger infants can be partly overcome by allowing them to view from a closer distance.

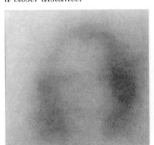   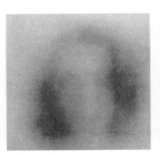      

1 month   2 months   3 months   Adult

Studies using preferential looking and a variety of other behavioral measures of visual acuity produce very similar results. Translating these results into the ratios used to describe adult acuity, M. S. Banks and P. Salapatek (1983) estimate that at 2 weeks of age a baby's acuity is about 20/300: the child sees at 20 feet what an adult with normal vision can see at 300 feet. Five months later, a baby's visual acuity has usually improved to about 20/100.

Infant visual acuity has also been studied by examining the electrical activity that occurs in a baby's brain in response to visual stimuli—activity known as *visual evoked potentials*. When a new visual stimulus is presented, a characteristic pattern of electrical activity appears in the brain. This makes it possible to tell when a baby can detect the difference between two stimuli. Studies measuring brain activity tend to give somewhat higher estimates of infants' visual acuity than those based on behavioral measures, but they show the same general pattern of development (Atkinson and Braddick, 1989; Norcia and Tyler, 1985).

The reasons for young infants' limited acuity are not yet well understood. Researchers once thought that it was partly due to the fact that the lenses of infants' eyes didn't **accommodate**—that is, didn't adjust their focus in response to an object's distance. But more recent studies show that infants' eyes *do* focus in response to their distance from an object, even though this accommodation does not reach an adult level until 4 months of age (Banks, 1980; Brookman, 1980). Interestingly, for younger babies the limitations on visual acuity probably limit accommodation, not the other way around (Banks and Salapatek, 1983). Low acuity reduces the ability to detect when accommodation is needed because it prevents the baby from seeing fine detail. This suggests that if you want a young baby to see an object clearly, you should hold it relatively close to his or her face. The details of the object will then appear larger, making it easier for the infant to tell if it is out of focus and accommodate to its distance.

Young babies' limited visual acuity is also not the result of some other deficiency in the eyes themselves. The optical quality of an infant's eyes is quite good and allows a sharp image to be focused on the retina, the light-sensitive surface at the back of the eye. Thus, the limitation on acuity in infants probably lies somewhere in the system that changes this image into neural signals, transmits them to the brain, and then analyzes the information. The exact nature of the limitation, however, is not yet well understood.

Despite their limited visual acuity, young babies are still motivated to try to see things clearly. This was demonstrated in a study in which researchers showed a series of slides to babies 1 to 3 months old and allowed them to control the focus of the projector (Kalnins and Bruner, 1973). The researchers cleverly did this by taking advantage of the sucking reflex. Although this reflex is automatic—that is, an infant will suck on any object placed in the mouth—the *rate* of sucking is under voluntary control. So the researchers connected the focusing mechanism of the projector to a device that measured the babies' rate of sucking on a pacifier. When the babies sucked rapidly, the picture came into focus; when their sucking slowed, the picture blurred. The infants quickly adjusted their rate of sucking and "worked hard" to keep the slides clear. (In addition to showing that babies are motivated to see things clearly, this study demonstrates *contingency learning*. These infants detected a contingency, or association, between their own rate of sucking and the clarity of the slides. This kind of learning will be discussed in the last section of this chapter.)

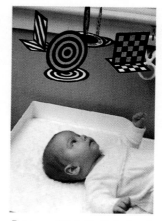

Because of their limited visual acuity, young infants pay particular attention to bold patterns with high contrast.

Accommodate:
To change the focus of the eye in response to looking at objects at different distances. (In Chapter 5 you will see that Piaget used this term for a different concept.)

What causes infants' visual acuity to improve gradually with age? Does this just happen automatically with maturation? Although the visual system may be genetically predisposed to make the connections among brain cells that ultimately produce high visual acuity, appropriate visual experience also seems necessary to foster this development. Studies of cats, whose visual systems are very much like humans', show that visual experience with patterned stimuli is needed to produce the developments that lead to normal acuity. If kittens are raised in the dark, or see only diffuse light, they do not develop normal acuity. This result has been related to the development of acuity in infants with visual defects (Held, 1978). (The box on p. 157 provides more information on the role of visual experience in the development of vision.)

CAN INFANTS SEE COLORS?   Determining whether young infants see colors is difficult because of the need to distinguish between color (determined by the wavelength of light) and brightness (determined by the light's intensity). When you see the difference between a red car and a blue one on a color television set, you are doing so on the basis of color. When you see a difference between the same two cars on a black-and-white set, you are doing so on the basis of brightness. Thus, when you show two different colors to a baby and the child looks longer at one than the other, you have to make sure that this visual preference is based on color, not relative brightness.

By using two different colors of the same intensity, researchers have been able to show that babies as young as 2 months can discriminate on the basis of color alone (Bornstein, 1978; Teller and Bornstein, 1987). Even infants as young as 2 weeks have been found to have some ability to discriminate colors judging from visual evoked potentials in their brains (Allen, Banks, and Norcia, 1993). Marc Bornstein (1978, 1981) has argued that by 3 to 4 months, babies possess all of an adult's color vision abilities.

How babies acquire adult color vision is still being studied. Any limitations that may exist in a newborn's color vision system could arise in a number of different areas. For instance, there might be initial immaturity in the receptors that change colored light into neural signals, in the pathways that transmit this information to the brain, or in the brain cells that analyze the incoming data. New information about the development of color vision during the first 6 months after birth could help provide insights into how the underlying mechanisms develop in a baby's central nervous system.

HEARING

It has long been known that pregnant women often feel the fetus move seconds after there is a loud noise (Forbes and Forbes, 1927). Studies measuring fetal heart rate have shown this sensitivity to sound in fetuses 26 to 28 weeks old (Kisilevsky, Muir, and Low, 1992). Infants who are born prematurely but are otherwise normal have the ability to hear (Aslin, Pisoni, and Jusczyk, 1983), as do all normal full-term newborns. In fact, hearing prior to birth is sufficiently well developed that newborns in one study showed some memory of the sound characteristics of stories that their mothers had read out loud twice a day for 6 weeks prior to their scheduled delivery (DeCasper and Spence, 1986). It was not the content of the stories that they remembered; rather, it was probably something about the pacing or rhythm of the prose. This may be evidence that infants' hearing is particularly tuned to pick up characteristics of the human voice.

TABLE 4.2
SOME COMMON SOUND LEVELS IN DECIBELS

Sound	dB
Barely audible sound (threshold)	1
Leaves rustling	20
Quiet residential community	40
Average speaking voice	60
Loud voices	80
Subway	100
Rock band	120
Jet engine at takeoff	140

To measure the sensitivity of a baby's hearing, researchers monitor eye blinks, changes in heart rate, and changes in the brain's electrical activity as sounds are presented. They have found that in order for young infants to hear a noise, it must be 10 to 20 decibels louder than it has to be for adults to be able to hear it (Hecox and Deegan, 1985; Schulman-Galambos and Galambos, 1979). To give you some idea of how much louder that is, Table 4.2 lists the approximate decibel levels of some familiar sounds. Adults can just detect a 1-decibel sound in otherwise quiet conditions. For a sound to be just detectable to a baby (especially a low-pitched sound), it must be substantially louder (Sinnott, Pisoni, and Aslin, 1984). Of course, a child's sensitivity to sound gradually improves with age, but it may take 12 to 13 years to become equal to an adult's (Maurer and Maurer, 1988). A baby's ability to detect the direction of a sound is also present very early and improves with age. By the time a child is only 18 months old this skill has reached an adult level of accuracy (Morrongiello and Rocca, 1990).

As with improvements in visual acuity, researchers have wondered how improvements in hearing ability happen. Do they occur automatically with maturation, or is auditory experience also needed? Apparently, experience does play a part. Just as it is essential to have stimuli to look at in order to develop normal visual acuity, so it is important to have sounds to listen to in order to develop normal hearing.

Another topic of interest to researchers who study the development of babies' hearing is the infants' ability to discriminate among sounds. How different must two sounds be for a baby to notice the difference between them? A widely used way of answering this question takes advantage of the infant's tendency to get accustomed to stimuli. When you perceive something new in your environment, you focus your attention on it, but if the stimulus is repeated over and over it loses its ability to hold your attention. This phenomenon, called **habituation,** is true of a baby too. Habituation is the basis for a very powerful research tool in the study of infants. In studies of hearing, researchers repeatedly present one sound over and over until the baby apparently loses interest in it. Then they change the sound. If the baby responds with renewed attention, they conclude that the child has detected the change. Using this method, investigators have found that 6-month-olds can distinguish between sounds that differ in loudness by as little as 10 decibels, perhaps even less (Aslin, Pisoni, and Jusczyk, 1983; Moffitt, 1973). By the time they are 5 to 8 months old, babies are also quite good at detecting small changes in pitch (Olsho et al., 1982). Infants are sensitive to a broad range of pitches and hear higher frequencies than adults do.

Habituation:
The decrease in attention that occurs when the same stimulus is presented repeatedly.

Infants' engagement with the world around them is based partly on their steadily improving hearing abilities. By 6 months of age infants are quite sensitive to changes in loudness and pitch.

When babies begin eating solid food, parents quickly learn about their infants' taste preferences, which are based on both taste and smell.

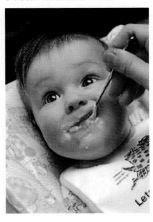

This may be one reason that adults learn to talk in high-pitched "baby talk" to infants.

Young infants are also especially good at discriminating among speech sounds, even better than they are at discriminating among pitches. This ability may well be tied to the importance of language in humans. Peter Eimas and his colleagues (Eimas, Siqueland, and Jusczyk, 1971) found that even babies 1 month old can discriminate between the syllables /ba/ and /pa/. Moreover, they discriminate among sounds that fall between /ba/ and /pa/ in the same way that adults do. Eimas used a computer to generate a continuum of sounds between /ba/ and /pa/. When this continuum is presented to adults, they do not hear it as consisting of a large number of different sounds. Instead, they perceive sounds closer to /ba/ as all sounding just like /ba/, and sounds closer to /pa/ as all sounding just like /pa/. This phenomenon of perceiving stimuli that actually vary along a continuum as belonging instead to an unchanging category is called *categorical perception* (Liberman et al., 1957). Infants, too, display categorical perception when listening to sounds between /ba/ and /pa/. For a part of this sound range, they show no discrimination. Then, at the same point where adults make the distinction between /ba/ and /pa/, infants make a distinction too. Other research has demonstrated categorical perception in babies regarding other speech sounds (Eimas, 1985). This suggests that the basic sensory system needed to learn language is probably genetically given, even though speech perception changes with development and also depends partly on experience (Eimas, 1985).

SMELL AND TASTE

Young infants are very sensitive to odors. When various odors are placed on cotton swabs and held beneath a baby's nose, the child's facial expressions and body movements indicate reactions similar to those of adults. For instance, infants respond positively to the odor of a banana, somewhat negatively to fishy odors, and very negatively to the odor of rotten eggs (Steiner, 1977). Babies are also capable of making very fine discriminations among odors, as shown in habituation studies involving very similar smells (Alberts, 1981; Engen and Lipsitt, 1965). In one such study, newborns discriminated between a perfume used by their mothers and another perfume (Schleidt and Genzel, 1990). In another study, they actually discriminated between the smell of their own mothers' breast pads and those of other women (MacFarlane, 1975).

As for taste, researchers have found that even young infants can discriminate among sweet, bitter, and salty tastes (Ganchrow, Steiner, and Daher, 1983). Newborns can also discriminate between the sweetness of a fairly weak sugar solution and the taste of plain water (Engen, Lipsitt, and Peck, 1974). This ability to detect sweetness, coupled with the fact that mother's milk is sweet, helps explain the early development in humans of a preference for sweetness.

The fact that young infants can discriminate among tastes does not necessarily mean that their sensory system for taste is fully mature. From studying the tongues of premature and full-term babies, researchers know that receptors for taste—the taste buds—are present throughout the mouth prior to birth, and that they become more localized on the tongue around the normal time of delivery. But, as in the case of vision, there seems to be a difference in maturity between the newborn's sensory receptors and the newborn's nervous system. Although the taste buds are relatively mature at birth, the nervous system initially processes taste information in an inefficient way. Nervous system development related to taste is quite rapid, however, so the initial immaturity does not last long.

ORGANIZATION OF INFANT SENSORY BEHAVIOR

Newborns use their sensory capacities in an organized way. Not only do they look at and listen to things, they also appear to be guided by "rules" in exploring the world (Haith, 1980). When awake and alert, babies visually scan their environment rather than simply staring straight ahead. If they hear a sound, they direct their gaze toward it. If no sound attracts them, they scan with their eyes until they find an edge (a border of light-dark contrast). Having found an edge, they scan the zone of the edge for some time, passing back and forth over it.

As babies grow older, this pattern of visual scanning changes. For example, they begin to look at the internal features of a stimulus rather than its borders. Their sensory behavior remains organized, however. The organization of sensory behavior guarantees that infants will attend to and learn a great deal about people, since people are a rich source of the kinds of auditory and visual stimulation that attract babies' attention.

DEVELOPMENT OF PERCEPTUAL ABILITIES

Perception is the process by which the brain interprets information from the senses, giving it order and meaning. The fact that Malcolm can see lines and colors (two sensory capabilities) does not mean that he *interprets* them as you and I do (a perceptual skill). For instance, when Malcolm looks at the faces of his family clustered around him, can he tell that some are closer and others farther away? Or when DeeDee turns her back to him, does Malcolm know he is

Perception:
The process by which the brain interprets information from the senses, giving it order and meaning.

still viewing the same head as before, just from a different angle? These questions focus on visual perception in infants.

DEPTH AND DISTANCE PERCEPTION

When can a baby estimate how far away something is? Eleanor Gibson and Richard Walk (1960) provided a partial answer through a clever experiment that used the apparatus shown in Figure 4.5. It consists of a sheet of thick glass, one side of which has a checkerboard surface directly underneath it (the "shallow" side), and the other side of which has a similar surface several feet below (the "deep" side), which gives the illusion of a cliff. Gibson and Walk observed whether babies old enough to crawl would venture over the visual cliff. They found that the babies preferred the shallow side, a preference that increased with age. Apparently, babies 6 or 7 months and older (when crawling usually begins) can perceive depth.

Joseph Campos and his colleagues (Campos et al., 1978) tested even younger babies for depth perception using Gibson and Walk's apparatus. They placed the infants facedown on each side while measuring their physiological responses, such as heart rate. Babies only 2 months old could distinguish a difference between the sides. However, *fear* of the deep side did not emerge until a child could crawl. Thus, direct experience with edges, drops, and distances probably contributes to a fear of heights in humans (Campos, Bertenthal, and Caplovitz, 1982).

Psychologists have long been interested in exactly how people are able to perceive depth. After all, the images of things projected onto the eye's retina are in two dimensions only. What makes our brains register them not as flat, but as three-dimensional? Visual cues that enable depth perception can be divided into three types: binocular cues (*binocular* means involving two eyes), static monocular cues (*monocular* means available to one eye alone), and kinetic cues (*kinetic* means involving movement), that are also monocular (Yonas and Granrud, 1985). Developmentalists want to know when children begin to use

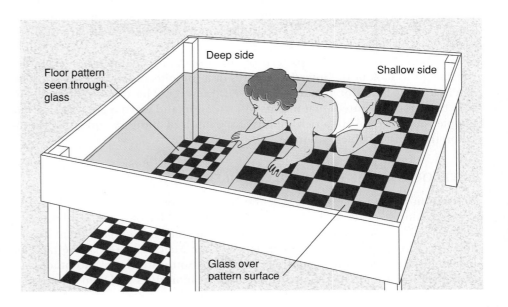

FIGURE 4.5 VISUAL CLIFF EXPERIMENT
By the time infants can crawl, they are reluctant to cross to the "deep" side of this apparatus.

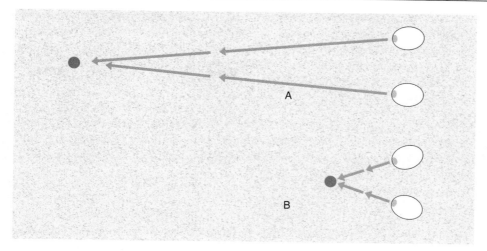

FIGURE 4.6
INFORMATION ABOUT
DISTANCE FROM
CONVERGENCE
*(A) When viewing a distant
object, the eyes look almost
straight ahead. (B) When
viewing a nearby object, the
eyes rotate inward, toward the
nose.*

each of these types of cues and ultimately organize them to obtain an adultlike perception of depth.

Binocular depth cues result from the fact that visual information reaches the brain from two eyes rather than one. One binocular depth cue is **convergence,** which occurs when the eyes turn inward to focus on a near object. Figure 4.6 (A) shows two eyes "pointing" toward a distant object. Notice that the center of each eye is facing almost straight ahead. Now look at Figure 4.6 (B), which shows two eyes focused on a nearer object. You can see that each eye must point inward to accomplish this. The closer an object is, the more the eyes must angle inward if both are to see "front-on." Your brain uses the degree of convergence to help estimate distance.

Richard Aslin (1977) measured infants' degree of convergence as they watched objects that were moved closer and farther away. He found that 1-month-old babies converged and diverged their eyes in the appropriate directions, but that they were not good at locating the precise angle for a given distance. In contrast, 2- to 3-month-old babies were fairly accurate in the angles at which they converged their eyes. By age 5 months, infants are able to use convergence as an effective cue for determining distance when they reach for something (Von Hofsten, 1977).

Another binocular depth cue, called **retinal disparity,** arises because the eyes are set apart from each other and view the world from slightly different angles. Infants show signs of sensitivity to retinal disparity by age 3 months (Atkinson and Braddick, 1989), and by 5 months retinal disparity becomes an efficient depth cue for detecting an approaching object and for guiding reaching (Gordon and Yonas, 1976; Yonas and Granrud, 1985). Since the degree of retinal disparity is affected by changes in the distance between the eyes, children must recalibrate this depth cue as they grow older and larger (Banks, 1987).

A sensitive period exists during which experiences have greater influence on the development of the ability to use binocular depth cues than experiences that occur at other times. Evidence for this comes from studying children who were born with their eyes misaligned. These children are often called cross-eyed or walleyed, but the medical term for their condition is *strabismus*. Children with strabismus get little practice coordinating their eyes in a normal way. If the condition is not corrected, these children do not receive the visual experience

Binocular depth cue:
A visual clue about depth and distance resulting from the fact that visual information reaches the brain from two eyes.

Convergence:
In visual perception, the change in the inward-turning angle of the eyes to look at objects at different distances; a binocular depth cue.

Retinal disparity:
A binocular depth cue that arises from the fact that the eyes are set apart in the face and so perceive objects from different angles.

needed to produce connections among neurons that respond to binocular information. The result is deficient binocular depth perception. Fortunately, surgeons can correct the condition by adjusting the length of the eye muscles. Richard Aslin and Martin Banks (1978) wondered if the timing of this operation affected the later quality of binocular depth perception. They discovered that an index of the binocular vision of people who had the operation in early infancy was comparable to that of people born without strabismus. However, when the surgery was performed after 1 year of age, sensitivity to binocular information declined substantially. Apparently, a sensitive period for the development of binocular depth perception occurs sometime during a baby's first year.

The example of children with strabismus shows that the development of binocular depth perception requires both maturation of an appropriate neural system *and* appropriate visual experience. In children with uncorrected strabismus, appropriate connections within the brain are never made because the children lack the visual experience needed to guide this developmental process. Moreover, it is not just that visual experience shapes brain development. The reverse is also true. Infants who are born lacking the brain cells that respond to binocular information later develop strabismus despite having normal eye muscles. This is because their visual system does not "tell" them when their eyes are properly aligned (Atkinson and Braddick, 1989). Brain development and visual experience, in short, are interconnected in a circular way.

Yet people who lack normal binocular vision still have some ability to judge depth. Indeed, some have managed to pilot airplanes and play professional baseball. Obviously, depth cues must also be available through each eye independently. These are called **monocular depth cues.**

One monocular depth cue is **linear perspective**—the seeming convergence of parallel lines as they extend away from the viewer, thus giving the impression of increasing distance. Because of linear perspective, a picture of a rectangular window viewed from an angle will be trapezoidal in shape, not rectangular. When people look at a trapezoidal window (see Figure 4.7), their perception of it depends on whether they look at it with one eye or two. When viewed with two eyes, it appears as what it is—an abnormal window in the shape of a trapezoid. When viewed with only one eye, however, it appears to be a normal rectangular window that is slanting away from the viewer (Ames, 1951). This depth effect occurs because one-eyed viewers use linear perspective to interpret what they see.

Albert Yonas and his colleagues investigated when babies begin to use linear perspective as a depth cue by letting infants look at a trapezoidal window with a patch over one eye (Yonas, Cleaves, and Pettersen, 1978). They found that 5-month-olds reached equally often toward each side of the window, but 7-month-olds reached more often toward the "closer" side. This finding suggests that infants begin to use linear perspective as a depth cue sometime between 5 and 7 months of age.

Yonas and his colleagues have investigated the onset of a number of other monocular depth cues. One is **interposition**—the partial overlap of objects that makes ones that are partly covered appear to be farther away (see Figure 4.8). Another is **shading**—the fact that objects that have depth cast shadows in one direction when they are protruding forward and in another direction when they are concave. Babies become sensitive to these depth cues between 5 and 7 months of age, the same age at which they become sensitive to linear perspec-

Monocular depth cue:
A visual clue about depth and distance that is available through each eye independently of the other.

Linear perspective:
A monocular depth cue that allows the viewer to perceive distance on the basis of the fact that parallel lines seem to converge as they extend away from the viewer, indicating increasing distance.

Interposition:
A monocular depth cue that relies on the fact that when objects partially overlap, the ones covered appear to be farther away.

Shading:
A monocular depth cue relying on the fact that objects with depth cast shadows in different directions depending on whether they are protruding or concave.

FIGURE 4.7
TRAPEZOIDAL WINDOW
When subjects in an experiment look at this window with both eyes open, they see it as a trapezoid. When they look at it with one eye closed, it appears rectangular and slanted because of linear perspective. Infants become sensitive to linear perspective by 7 months.

tive (Yonas and Owsley, 1987). The simultaneous onset of the use of several monocular depth cues suggests that neural maturation plays a significant role in their development.

Information about depth and distance is also carried in the motion of objects, known as **kinetic depth cues.** One such cue is the apparent expansion in size of approaching objects. Yonas and his colleagues have shown that 3-month-old babies consistently blink and often move their heads backward in response to a rapidly expanding shape projected on a screen in front of them. And they respond this way more frequently to shapes that appear to be about to collide with them than to shapes that appear to be making a near miss. One-month-olds do not make this distinction between apparently dangerous and nondangerous approaching objects, though they do blink more often in response to shapes that are expanding than to shapes that are contracting (Yonas et al., 1980).

Just as the image of an approaching object gets larger, its sound also gets louder. When do babies start to integrate these visual and auditory cues to distance? In a study designed to answer this question, babies were shown a drum-beating clown, panda, or Santa Claus that approached, receded, or remained stationary (Morrongiello and Fenwick, 1991). At the same time, they heard drumbeats that grew louder, grew softer, or remained the same. Seven-month-olds looked at the two moving toys when there was a change in the loudness of the drumbeats, but they didn't look consistently at the approaching toy when they heard increases in loudness, nor consistently at the receding toy when they heard decreases in loudness. In contrast, 9-month-olds looked consistently at the appropriate object for each sound condition, pairing the approaching object with sounds that increased in loudness, the receding object with sounds that decreased in loudness, and the stationary object with sounds that remained the same. Apparently, they had developed the ability to integrate auditory and visual information about distance.

Kinetic depth cue:
A visual clue to depth and distance involving movements of objects, such as the apparent expansion in size of approaching objects.

FIGURE 4.8
INFORMATION FOR DISTANCE FROM INTERPOSITION
Most adults perceive the square on the left to be in front of the square on the right. By 7 months most infants seem to make the same judgment.

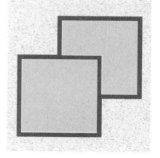

SIZE AND SHAPE CONSTANCY

As Christine Gordon walks toward Mikey to lift him out of his crib, he sees her image growing larger and larger. Does Mikey think his mother is growing in size? When Christine hands Mikey a bottle and he tips it up to drink, does he think that the bottle changes shape as he views it from a different angle? At the age of 13 months, Mikey makes neither of these mistakes. He possesses perceptual skills called size and shape constancy. **Size constancy** is the perception of an object as being constant in size, even though its image on the retina actually grows larger or smaller as the object is viewed from different distances. Similarly, **shape constancy** is the perception of an object as having a constant shape, even though its image on the retina actually changes shape when the object is viewed from different angles. Both these processes are crucial to perceiving the world as relatively stable.

In a study designed to determine when infants first develop these abilities, researchers repeatedly showed one group of babies a square displayed at different angles but never directly perpendicular to a child's line of sight (Caron, Caron, and Carlson, 1979). As a result, the image the infants saw was always trapezoidal, not truly square. After they habituated and lost interest in this stimulus, the researchers presented them with a real trapezoid displayed head-on. Infants as young as 4 months showed a preference for looking at this new stimulus, meaning that they could distinguish it from a square held at an angle. In other words, they exhibited shape constancy.

The evidence suggests that both shape and size constancy emerge at around 3 months of age (Banks and Salapatek, 1983; Day, 1987). However, researchers are still investigating whether these constancies exist at earlier ages. For example, Slater (1989) has concluded that even newborns exhibit shape constancy. As with less complex visual skills, it may be that very young infants have some poorly developed tendencies toward shape and size constancy that become efficient and stable by 3 to 5 months. We know for certain that sometime during the first half year babies begin to perceive objects around them as relatively stable and unchanging, which is an important step in organizing their physical world. Understanding that the world consists of *particular* objects and people begins with the perception of constancies.

PERCEPTION OF FACES

Recognition of faces requires several perceptual skills. It requires the ability to discriminate one object from another and the ability to treat different views or versions of an object as the same. Infants can discriminate simple shapes in the first month of life, but they cannot discriminate a square with a circle in it from one with a triangle in it (Bushnell, 1979; Milewski, 1978). This suggests that they rely heavily on outline shape in perceiving objects. However, 1-month-olds are able to distinguish between two compound figures if the inside figure flashes or moves (Bushnell, 1979), or if it is more salient than the outside figure (such as a bull's-eye surrounded by a circle) (Ganon and Swartz, 1980).

The ability to distinguish between the internal features of two compound figures is important to face recognition. To perceive differences among faces, an infant must pay attention to the internal features of those faces, such as eyes, nose, and mouth. Where infants look on a face tells us something about the information they are taking in. As we discussed earlier, when 1-month-olds look at faces, they scan only a small portion of the face and tend to look at the outer

Size constancy:
The ability to perceive an object viewed from different distances as being constant in size even though its image on the retina is growing larger or smaller.

Shape constancy:
The ability to perceive the shape of an object as constant, even though its image on the retina changes shape when the object is viewed from different angles.

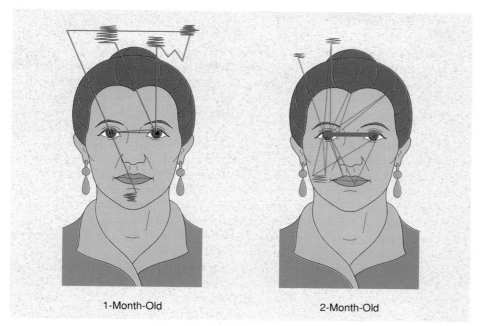

1-Month-Old   2-Month-Old

FIGURE 4.9
DEVELOPMENT OF
INFANT SCANNING
PATTERNS
*One-month-olds do not look at
faces as much as 2-month-olds
do. When they do look, they
tend to concentrate on the
outer edges of the face. Two-
month-olds look more at
internal features, particularly
the eyes. (Source: Maurer and
Salapatek, 1976.)*

edges, whereas 2-month-olds scan within the face and spend time looking at internal features (Maurer and Salapatek, 1976; see Figure 4.9). Newborns prefer to look at abstract high-contrast patterns, whereas 2- to 3-month-olds prefer to look at facelike patterns (Dannemiller and Stephens, 1988; Kliener and Banks, 1987).

By the age of 3 months an infant can recognize photographs of his or her mother and prefers to look at pictures of her rather than a stranger (Barrera and Maurer, 1981). One study suggests that infants prefer looking at their own mothers' actual face after just two days of life (see Slater, 1989), although there is some uncertainty about what this preference is based on. By 5 months infants can remember and distinguish among the faces of strangers (Olson and Sherman, 1983), a task that requires them to make some very subtle distinctions. Even as adults, we have trouble discriminating among the faces of members of racial and ethnic groups with whom we have had little or no contact. This phenomenon illustrates that at least part of infants' improving skills for perceiving faces must be a consequence of the experience of looking at faces.

A surprising finding is that infants show a preference for faces that adults judge to be more attractive faces. Curtis Samuels and Richard Ewy (1985) demonstrated this preference in 3- and 6-month-olds using black-and-white slides of faces as stimuli. Judith Langlois and her colleagues (Langlois et al., 1987) demonstrated the same preference in 2- and 3-month-olds using color slides. Later they showed that the preference generalizes across faces of different genders, races, and ages (Langlois et al., 1991). It is not yet clear what specific characteristics of faces influence infants' preferences. These results have led developmentalists to reexamine what they had presumed were learned cultural stereotypes, since infants—long before they could acquire cultural standards of attractiveness—begin to show a preference for the same kinds of faces that adults find attractive.

INFANT LEARNING

After Malcolm was born, the members of his family took charge of most of what happened to him. Where he lay, what he saw, what he heard, and what he felt were largely controlled by other people. But within 6 months this situation had changed substantially. Malcolm was now able to do many things for himself. He could turn over, sit up, grasp objects and put them in his mouth; he was even starting to crawl. By the time he was 1, he had acquired many other skills, including taking his first steps and saying a few single words.

Modern developmental psychologists view such dramatic changes in behavior as the joint outcome of genetic control and learning. By this they mean that the changes are based on a biological unfolding as well as on experience—on both nature and nurture. Some changes may appear more dependent on learning, others on genetic control. But both factors are needed to produce the dramatic transformations that occur in a baby's first year. Since both are necessary, it is more productive to try to understand how they work together.

In examining the interaction of learning and genetic control, developmentalists ask questions such as: When do infants start learning? What limitations are there on the things they can learn? Does the way infants learn and unlearn, remember and forget, change as they grow older? The answers to these questions are not just of scientific interest; they are also of very practical interest to parents. Does reading to a baby improve the child's later reading skills? What kinds of toys are best for infants? Will a baby remember an injury, illness, or other trauma that happened early in life? Research into infants' learning capabilities can help shed light on such concerns. In the following sections we'll look at several different kinds of learning, beginning with the basic process of habituation.

HABITUATION AND DISHABITUATION

Orienting response:
The initial response, involving both behavioral and physiological changes, to a stimulus when the stimulus is first presented.

Dishabituation:
The eliciting of an orienting response to a new stimulus after a subject has become habituated to a previous stimulus.

Habituation is one of the first signs that newborns are able to retain information about their environments. As described in our discussion of infant hearing, *habituation* is the decrease in attention that occurs when the same stimulus is presented repeatedly. For example, when the pediatrician first spoke to Meryl, she ceased her other behaviors and attended to the doctor's voice. This reaction, called an **orienting response,** includes certain physiological changes that casual observers wouldn't notice, such as a change in heart rate and a slight dilation of the pupils. Researchers, however, have measured these changes in the laboratory and have found that when the same stimulus is presented over and over, the orienting response disappears and the baby resumes other activities. The novelty of the stimulus has apparently worn off. We know that such a decline in responding is due to learning and not merely to fatigue, because presentation of a new stimulus again elicits the orienting response. The response to a new stimulus after decreased interest in an old stimulus is often called **dishabituation.** (The technical definition of *dishabituation* is the return of the orienting response to the original stimulus after an intervening new stimulus.) The crucial feature of dishabituation is that it allows developmentalists to determine when infants can detect that two stimuli are different and, conversely, when infants believe that the stimuli are the same despite superficial differences (such as a face presented straight on versus a face presented at a slight angle).

The same processes of orientation, gradual habituation, and dishabituation also occur in adults. Imagine that you are lying in bed alone in a strange house. As the wind begins to blow, a tree outside the window makes a groaning noise. Initially you are startled and attend carefully to the sound. But soon you become used to it and simply ignore it. Then a door somewhere in the house begins to creak. Again, you find yourself orienting to the new sound. The return of the orienting response is an indication that you have noticed a change. Noticing such a change requires two things. First, you must learn enough about the first stimulus to realize it is the same from one presentation to another. Second, you must make some kind of comparison between the first and second stimulus and recognize the second one as new.

In our discussions of infant hearing, we saw how habituation and dishabituation enable researchers to study infants' ability to tell the difference between two or more sounds. Research using habituation provides insight into what kinds of stimuli babies can distinguish, how many repetitions are required for a memory to form, and how long a memory will endure once it has been formed.

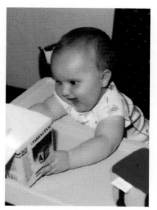

New objects in the environment usually elicit a response of interest from infants.

ASSOCIATIVE LEARNING

Psychologists have spent a great deal of time studying **associative learning**—how infants learn that certain events tend to go together or be associated. Researchers have wondered at what point in development infants are able to learn associations. Two kinds of associative learning they have explored extensively are *classical conditioning* and *instrumental conditioning*.

Associative learning: Learning that certain stimuli or events tend to go together or to be associated with one another.

CLASSICAL CONDITIONING

Classical conditioning is a learning process in which a new stimulus becomes capable of eliciting an established reflex response through association with an old stimulus. The early Russian psychologist Ivan Pavlov (1849–1936) produced the salivation reflex in dogs by giving them food and at the same time ringing a bell. Eventually, the sound of the bell alone caused the dogs to salivate. Pavlov thus conditioned the dogs to salivate in response to a stimulus that would not normally produce that reaction.

Classical conditioning: A learning process in which a new stimulus, through association with an old stimulus, becomes capable of eliciting an established reflex response.

From the 1930s through the 1950s many researchers (e.g., Wickens and Wickens, 1940) attempted classical conditioning with newborns and infants under 3 months of age. Although they failed to convincingly demonstrate classical conditioning, many of these studies did demonstrate changes in behavior produced by experience, and thus some kind of learning. More recent studies of classical conditioning in newborns have met with greater success. One has even shown some retention of a conditioned eyeblink over a 10-day period within the first month of life (Lipsitt, 1990). However, the difficulty of demonstrating classical conditioning in newborns suggests that it is not a very likely explanation for very early changes in behavior. Along with a variety of other abilities we have discussed, the disposition toward classical conditioning does not become well established until around 3 months of age.

Moreover, classical conditioning by itself cannot explain the emergence of any *new* behavior. The response that is to be conditioned must always be one that the person already performs when the unconditioned stimulus is present. Classical conditioning simply causes an old response to be elicited in a new situation. A famous example of the classical conditioning of an older infant is John

B. Watson's work with an 11-month-old named Albert. In an experiment that would not pass ethical muster today, Watson (1928) conditioned Albert to fear a white rat (the conditioned stimulus) by pairing presentation of the rat with a sudden loud noise (the unconditioned stimulus). Note, however, that Albert already possessed a fear reaction. All Watson did was to make the initially neutral rat into an effective elicitor of fear. Thus, classical conditioning may play a role in certain aspects of emotional development, especially during infancy, but it cannot account for the crucial emergence of new behaviors and skills.

INSTRUMENTAL CONDITIONING

When Mikey Gordon uttered "beh" while pointing at a piece of bread, his father immediately showered him with praise and encouragement for saying a new word. Frank's positive reaction to Mikey's efforts at speech is a form of **reinforcement** because it increases the likelihood that Mikey will say "beh" again in a similar situation.

Positive reinforcement and **negative reinforcement** are important to the type of learning called **operant** or **instrumental conditioning,** in which behaviors are influenced by the consequences that they have (or seem to have). If those consequences include pleasant stimulation, such as a hug from a parent, the child is said to be positively reinforced (or rewarded) and is likely to do the same thing again. Similarly, when a behavior—crying, for example—is followed by the removal of an unpleasant stimulus, such as a wet diaper, that behavior is said to be negatively reinforced and is more likely to occur again. Both positive and negative reinforcement *increase* the likelihood of a particular behavior. Note that punishment, the presentation of a negative stimulus, such as a spanking after a behavior, is not called negative reinforcement because it is intended to *decrease* the likelihood of the behavior.

In older children and adults, behaviors that are operantly, or instrumentally, conditioned are generally ones over which the person exerts strictly voluntary control. In newborns, however, researchers condition behaviors with an underlying reflexive component. Examples are sucking on a nipple (related to the sucking reflex) and turning the head from side to side (related to the rooting reflex).

Sucking rates of 3-day-old infants have been instrumentally conditioned. Newborns automatically suck in a "burst-pause" pattern: a succession of rapid sucks is followed by a period during which little sucking occurs. Andrew DeCasper and William Fifer (1980) measured the average interval of time between a baby's bursts of sucking on a nipple to establish what is called the **base rate.** Then the researchers rewarded 50 percent of the babies every time the interval between their sucking bursts was *longer* than average, and rewarded the other 50 percent every time their interval was *shorter* than average. The reward they used as reinforcement was simply the sound of the child's mother speaking. As expected, the sucking rate of the first group of babies decreased, while that of the second group increased. This experiment demonstrates not only instrumental conditioning, but also the fact that a human voice can be reinforcing for an infant only 3 days old.

Instrumental conditioning is of particular interest to psychologists because it provides one possible means by which new behaviors may be acquired. Consider again Mikey Gordon learning to say "bread." When he utters something that vaguely resembles this word, his father provides reinforcement in the form of smiles and attention. Mikey may respond by saying "beh" again. Over time,

Reinforcement:
Any event or development following an action or response that makes it more likely that the individual will respond in a similar way to a similar stimulus in the future.

Positive reinforcement:
The presentation of a pleasant stimulus (that is, a reward) following an action or response so as to increase the likelihood that the action or response will be repeated.

Negative reinforcement:
The withdrawal of an unpleasant stimulus following an action or response so as to increase the likelihood that the action or response will be repeated.

Operant or instrumental conditioning:
Learning in which behaviors are influenced by the consequences they have or seem to have (that is, by positive or negative reinforcement).

Base rate:
The frequency of a behavior exhibited during a standard observation period prior to experimental manipulation.

Frank may become more selective in his reinforcement. He may require that Mikey say something closer to the real word before giving him praise. If Mikey were to utter the sound "breh," for instance, his father might grin and exclaim, "Atta boy!" In time, Mikey will say the word "bread." Reinforcing gradually closer approximations of some target behavior is an example of a process called **shaping.**

Systematic shaping can sometimes result in quite remarkable feats. For example, Hanus Papoušek (1967b) has produced complex sequences of behavior in babies only a few weeks old. When the infants turned their heads in one direction, they were rewarded with a taste of sugar solution. Soon they were turning their heads repeatedly in that direction. Next the babies were rewarded only after two head turns, and again they learned the pattern. Eventually they were required to—and did—perform even longer chains of responses, such as two head turns to the right, then two to the left!

It is apparently much easier to instrumentally condition newborns than to classically condition them. The difficulty of classically conditioning a newborn and the relative ease of doing so by age 3 months probably reflect a difference in maturation of the baby's brain. The ease of instrumental conditioning, even in newborns, suggests that human infants come preadapted to respond to contingencies—a point to which we will return.

IMITATIVE LEARNING

Imagine how difficult it would be for Mikey Gordon to learn to talk if shaping were the only learning technique available to him. His parents would have to wait until he happened to make some sounds that remotely resembled an English word. Then they would have to reinforce him immediately and continue offering reinforcement every time he came closer to the correct pattern. This laborious process would have to be repeated for every word Mikey learned. Although this is the only way totally deaf children can learn to use spoken language, children with normal hearing face a far easier task. They are motivated to attend to and imitate speech sounds, even when they don't understand what those sounds mean. This **imitative learning** helps explain why Mikey will acquire speech so rapidly in his early years.

Psychologists have proposed that imitation is a powerful mechanism for learning (e.g., Bandura, 1977). It is a much faster way of acquiring new skills than shaping. But in order to imitate a new behavior, children must be able to reproduce the behavior and remember it for future use. For example, if Mikey is to imitate a word his father says, he must first be able to translate the sounds he hears into a set of movements of his own lips and tongue. Second, Mikey must be able to store some memory of these movements for future use. Both these abilities are needed for the imitation to be successful. Jean Piaget (1962) argued that these abilities develop gradually during a child's first two years.

In general agreement with Piaget's view, Ina Uzgiris has observed a four-step sequence in the development of imitation (Uzgiris, 1972; Uzgiris and Hunt, 1975). During the first step, in the first six months of life, infants are able to match the behaviors of other people, or reproduce their own behaviors, based on similarity of perceptual consequences, such as sound. Imitation at this step is limited to behaviors the infant has already produced spontaneously. For example, if a young infant makes a cooing sound and an adult imitates it, the infant will often make the sound again.

Shaping:
A process whereby some target behavior is achieved by reinforcing gradually closer approximations of it.

Imitative learning:
A way of learning new behaviors by modeling (copying) others' behaviors.

During the second step, which begins at around 6 months, babies try to imitate behaviors that they see or hear but that they have never attempted before. Frequently they manage only a partial imitation, or they fail altogether. For example, during the second half of their first year, babies begin to imitate some of the characteristics of the language they hear, so that their babbling begins to sound more like normal speech, but it is not yet composed of words that are understandable.

During the third step, which begins at around 12 months, babies become much better at imitating unfamiliar behaviors. Their imitation of language leads to some intelligible words, and other kinds of imitation become increasingly common. A 15-month-old may watch a preschooler stacking blocks and then try to produce a similar tower. Such imitations are often coupled with frequent checking of the other child's behavior for assurance that the imitation is right.

During the fourth and final step, at around 18 months, children's imitations, even of novel behaviors, become very accurate and require little checking for accuracy. Children this age become adept at imitating actions even when they cannot directly monitor their own success, as when they imitate the facial expressions of others (Abravanel and Gingold, 1985).

Although psychologists still hotly debate what underlies the development of imitation, most agree that these four basic steps occur. Most also acknowledge that imitation is an extremely powerful and enduring form of learning.

Many issues about the development of imitation are still unsettled. One is how the baby's early imitative abilities change into the much more elaborate ones of later infancy and toddlerhood. Piaget argued that the answer resides in the development of the child's underlying cognitive capacities. According to Piaget, young infants possess very limited capacities for thought. Over the first two years, however, their cognitive capacities systematically develop. This regular development, in turn, affects many behaviors, including imitation.

Jerome Bruner agrees with Piaget's basic viewpoint that infant cognitive development involves a gradual removal of earlier limitations. But unlike Piaget, Bruner conceptualizes the emergence of imitation as the development and organization of skills (Bruner, 1970, 1981). Thus, Bruner would attribute a child's early imitative failures to limits on organization—that is, limits on skills for putting together past behaviors into a pattern that we would call imitation. Piaget, in contrast, would attribute the same early failures to the inability to remember the behavior of a model or to mentally translate such a memory into a required set of actions.

Regardless of their differences, Piaget and Bruner share the view that imitation develops gradually. The ability to imitate facial expressions, for example, is generally thought to emerge quite late in the process (the fourth step in our earlier description). Such imitation requires children to "match" an expression while they are unable to see their own face, and Piaget would have argued that very young babies are not cognitively ready for this. On this point, a study by Andrew Meltzoff and M. Keith Moore (1977) has become controversial. These researchers had adults display facial gestures to infants only 12 to 21 days old. The gestures included sticking out the tongue and opening the mouth wide. The babies often seemed to imitate the adults. Some researchers have replicated this finding; others have been unable to do so (Harris, 1983; Olson and Sherman, 1983; Slater, 1989; Kaitz et al., 1990). It seems that newborn "imitation" is another reflexive behavior that gives way later to more purposive voluntary behavior.

Adults often try to elicit imitation from infants and toddlers, and sometimes they are successful.

One criticism of the Meltzoff and Moore study is that the infant behaviors they observed may not have been true imitation. Some activities you might try with a young infant are suggested in a paper by Sandra W. Jacobson (1979). Suppose that, rather than sticking your tongue out, you make a circle with your thumb and fingers and push a pencil through it in the baby's direction. Don't be surprised if the baby responds by sticking out his or her tongue. Many actions may elicit this reflexive response. As another experiment, try interlocking your fingers in front of the baby's face. The child will not be able to duplicate this gesture, because the behaviors that you can elicit from young infants are limited to ones they already do spontaneously. Imitation as a means of learning *new* behaviors must await further development. In fact, more than a year must pass before the baby will be able to imitate new behaviors quickly and without error. This speed and accuracy are what give imitation its special importance as a learning mechanism.

THE CONCEPT OF PREPAREDNESS

The example of trying to get a baby to imitate interlocking fingers stresses something important about infant learning. Some things are relatively easy for young infants to learn; some things are difficult. Notice how many of the learning studies we have discussed rely on behaviors such as mouth movements and head turning. These behaviors have two things in common: (1) they can be elicited reflexively; (2) and they have obvious survival value. For the newborn, being able to turn the head toward the nipple and to suck appropriately are matters of vital importance. Behaviors that babies do not spontaneously engage in are usually very difficult to instill. Thus, the answer to the question of

Preparedness:
The genetic predisposition to learn certain behaviors.

whether newborns can learn is more complicated than a simple yes or no. It depends partly on what is to be learned and how. Heredity seems to have endowed infants with a predisposition to acquire some behaviors but not others. The genetic predisposition to learn certain behaviors is called **preparedness** (Seligman, 1970).

Many developmentalists argue that some of a baby's early social behaviors are prepared responses. Examples are smiling back when an adult smiles and cooing when an adult speaks. These responses are easy for young babies; they seem biologically inclined to learn to perform them in social contexts. Other easily learned behaviors emerge in later infancy. For example, in the baby's second 6 months he or she readily babbles the sounds of the language spoken in the home. Think how complex a process it is to distinguish and reproduce speech sounds. Evolution must have prepared human babies to acquire this skill quite early. Thus, the concept of preparedness provides one way to think about the limitations on infant learning. Babies learn most easily those behaviors they are prepared to learn; they learn other behaviors more slowly or not at all.

An important aspect of prepared learning is a predisposition to analyze the connection between certain behaviors and their consequences. For example, humans (as well as other animals) are prepared to analyze the connection between the taste and smell of what they eat and any subsequent feelings of nausea (Garcia and Koelling, 1966). For this reason you readily develop an aversion to whatever food you ate just before you got sick. Note that you don't acquire a similar aversion to the people you were with or the color of the shirt you were wearing. Your brain is programmed to focus on the food-nausea connection, not the others. Babies, too, are prepared to learn certain contingencies between their own actions and the consequences produced. Instrumental conditioning of infants is often very easy when the association to be learned is one that they're *prepared* to discover.

The idea of learning contingencies adds an important dimension to our understanding of infant learning. During the first year of life, a major task that babies face is learning how to control their environment (Rovee-Collier, 1993). By learning the connections between their own behaviors and subsequent reinforcements, infants gradually discover the things they can do to get what they want. In the process, the helpless newborn who merely responds reflexively to stimuli is transformed into an agent who quite actively controls many aspects of his or her world.

Preadapted:
A term referring to infants' bias to select and attend to certain kinds of perceptual stimuli, including the stimuli provided by a caregiver in a social context.

We saw earlier that, in addition to having a variety of sensory capacities, babies direct their attention in an organized way. They are biased, or **preadapted,** to select and attend to certain kinds of stimuli, such as light-dark contrasts and the sound of a human voice. Infants are also preadapted to detect contingencies—connections between their actions and changes in the environment. These capacities will serve them well as they explore the properties of objects and deepen their understanding of the physical world. This preadaptation also represents an important foundation for developing social relationships. Other people, and caregivers in particular, are the most complex, contingently responsive objects in the infant's world. Infants are biased to attend to and direct behavior toward others, who likewise are disposed to respond to an infant's behavior. This sets up a primary contingency relationship that further motivates the infant's engagement.

Many babies are born each year with impaired hearing or vision caused by either genetic defects or factors in the prenatal environment (such as exposure to the rubella, or German measles, virus.) About 1 in 1,000 are born with severe loss of hearing (Downs, 1986). Serious visual impairments occur at similar rates of incidence. The more severe the sensory deficit, the more challenging adaptation to it is. For instance, learning to speak is only slightly more difficult for children with mild hearing loss, but it is very difficult for those with severe loss of hearing, and for the profoundly deaf it is impossible to learn fully functional language.

Today doctors try to treat many sensory disorders early, based on the finding that later treatment (in middle childhood, adolescence, or adulthood) is often less effective or not effective at all. This finding has led to speculation that sensitive or critical periods are involved in the development of vision and hearing, during which time normal sensory inputs must be experienced (Ruben and Nelson, 1993). Evidence for this belief has come from studies showing that when baby animals are deprived of certain sensory stimulation, they do not develop a normally functioning sensory system and cannot recover one even if later given normal sensory input. Similarly, abnormal sensory input received at this time (such as blurred visual images or unclear sounds) can also cause development of the sensory system to go awry.

Several factors could explain these developmental patterns. Perhaps there is atrophy (wasting away) of the parts of the nervous system that aren't being stimulated. Or maybe these same parts are recruited for other nervous system uses, and this recruitment cannot be reversed. In addition, when a sensory system is stimulated but the messages received through it are degraded (due to a poorly focused eye, for example), the incoming data may be so confusing that a child learns to ignore them; he or she may then find it hard to redirect attention to them if normal sensory stimulation is later restored.

Virtually all experts agree that enhanced auditory stimulation should begin as early as possible in hearing-impaired babies to try to prevent abnormal development of basic auditory connections in the brain (Shannon, 1989). These children are fitted with powerful hearing aids. (The technique of cochlear implants, in which an artificial sensing apparatus is surgically implanted, is not appropriate for children younger than 2 years, and then only for those with profound loss of hearing. Infants with up to 110-decibel hearing loss can benefit from early enhanced auditory stimulation via a hearing aid (Broakroyd et al., 1986). A 110-decibel hearing loss means that noise that sounds very loud to someone with normal hearing is just barely detectable to the person with the hearing defect. The hearing aid is used even if the baby shows no signs of hearing the amplified sounds, because in some cases the child develops responsiveness to sound later.

Just as early stimulation is important to many aspects of hearing, so it is important to many aspects of vision. In the text of this chapter we mention the importance of early stimulation to the development of binocular depth perception. Lack of appropriate early visual stimulation can also cause a condition called *amblyopia*, or poor acuity despite a well-focused image on the retina. Permanent amblyopia can be caused by abnormalities in a baby's eye that are not corrected early. These abnormalities include opacities that prevent light from passing through some areas of the cornea (the normally transparent window that covers the eyeball) and extreme refractive errors (errors in the way in which light is bent to focus it on the retina). Opacities in the cornea can now be corrected with corneal implants, and extreme refractive errors can be corrected with glasses. However, if these conditions are left *uncorrected* until later childhood or beyond, normal vision can no longer be restored (Loed, 1989; King, 1993).

Amblyopia in one eye is frequently caused by strabismus, or misalignment of the eyes. Because information from the two eyes doesn't correspond, input from one of them is suppressed in the nervous system. This suppression seems to prevent the eye from developing normal acuity. The treatment is to place a patch over the "good" eye to force the other eye to develop normally (Ruben and Nelson, 1993). This treatment must be monitored carefully or else amblyopia can also arise in the patched eye due to insufficient stimulation. When properly carried out, however, and begun early enough, this treatment usually leads to normal vision in both eyes.

For developmentalists, it is fascinating to see how important early experience is to maintaining and refining sensory systems, even though their basic structure is specified by genes. Conditions that limit sensory input early in life impair the development of normal vision and hearing, often permanently. Appropriate early experience may in fact be critical to the normal development of a wide range of other human capabilities on which the impact of early experience is harder to measure.

CHAPTER SUMMARY

1. Newborns come equipped with certain built-in capacities that help them to survive and adapt to their new environments. These capacities include reflexes, motor skills, perceptual abilities, and learning abilities. Development of these capacities is a process in which genetics and experience work together. Moreover, early very limited skills and experiences provide the basis for development of more complex skills throughout the first year.

2. Developmentalists divide the infant's rest-activity cycle into several states. One system divides it into six states: quiet sleep, active sleep, awake and quiet, awake and active, fussing, and crying. The state an infant is in determines how the environment is perceived and acted upon.

3. A **reflex** is an automatic, or built-in, reaction elicited by particular stimuli. Some reflexes found in newborns enable them to respond adaptively to their environments before they have a chance to learn. Examples of newborn reflexes with clear survival value are the **rooting reflex** and the **sucking reflex,** which allow the baby to nurse. Examples of newborn reflexes that are later incorporated into more complex voluntary actions are the **grasping reflex** and the **stepping reflex.**

4. During their first 2 years children show remarkable development of motor skills. Global actions become more refined and specific in the process of **differentiation,** and reflexes are integrated into more elaborate behaviors. One of the earliest skills that emerges is control over eye movements. By the middle of the first year, babies intentionally reach for and grasp objects, and soon after the age of 1, most start to walk. Psychologists believe that an important part of motor development during the first year is the inhibition of early reflex systems, followed by increasingly refined voluntary control over movements.

5. Newborns come equipped with a range of sensory capabilities, and they are biased to detect certain kinds of stimuli. Although their **visual acuity** (the amount of detail they see) is not as good as that of normal adults, they can see and they do visually inspect their surroundings. Visual acuity gradually improves in the first year. Newborns are particularly attracted to objects, such as the human face, that have light-dark contrasts, and they are quite good at following slowly moving objects with their eyes. They can also hear sounds, especially human speech sounds, can discriminate one from another, and will turn toward the source of a sound. Likewise, newborns discriminate a variety of odors and at least some of the four basic tastes.

6. Developmentalists have also studied **perception** in infants—the process by which a baby's brain interprets information from the senses, giving it order and meaning. Adultlike depth perception appears to emerge gradually as a baby becomes increasingly effective at using various depth cues. Infants can interpret **binocular depth cues,** which depend on both eyes working together, from about 3 months of age, and **monocular depth cues,** which are available to each eye independently, at about 5 months of age. In the first 6 months they also start to use **kinetic depth cues** from objects in motion. As the infant begins to crawl, good depth perception has an obvious protective advantage. Around 3 months of age infants are also showing an awareness of **size** and **shape constancy,** which enables them to ignore moment-to-moment alterations in the size or shape of visual images if those alterations are caused by changes in either distance or viewing angle. The ability to perceive objects and people as constant clearly is essential for learning about them.

7. One of the first signs that infants are capable of learning is a process called **habituation.** Habituation is a decrease in attention when the same stimulus is repeatedly presented. At first an individual shows an **orienting response** to the stimulus and becomes more alert, but his or her interest gradually drops as the stimulus becomes familiar. If a new stimulus is presented, the person may show signs of **dishabituation** by paying increased attention. Habituation shows that infants are able to retain information about their environments—that is, that they are able to remember enough about a stimulus to recognize it as being the same from one presentation to another.

8. In **associative learning,** infants learn that certain events tend to go together or tend to be associated. One kind of associative learning is **classical conditioning,** a process whereby a new stimulus, through association with an old one, becomes able to elicit an established reflex response. It is apparently difficult to classically condition newborns, but the process becomes easier after about 3 months of age. Classical conditioning, by itself, cannot explain the emergence of any *new* behaviors.

9. Another form of associative learning is operant, or **instrumental conditioning,** whereby a person's be-

haviors are influenced by their consequences. When the consequences are pleasant, the behavior is said to be **positively reinforced** (or rewarded) and the person is likely to perform the same behavior again. **Negative reinforcement** encourages specific behaviors by *removing* unpleasant stimuli. Research has shown that even newborns can be instrumentally conditioned. Moreover, systematic reinforcement can be used to gradually **shape** a sequence of responses that an infant has never before displayed.

10. **Imitative learning** is a way of rapidly acquiring new behaviors. The ability to imitate others quickly and without error develops gradually over the first 18 months of life. Psychologists still debate what underlies this important advancement.

11. Heredity seems to have endowed babies with a predisposition to acquire certain behaviors. This genetic predisposition is called **preparedness.** Part of prepared learning is a predisposition to notice **contingencies**—especially the relationship between one's own behaviors and the consequences they seem to have. Contingency learning helps babies gain control over their environments and encourages responsiveness from others, which further promotes infants' engagement with the world.

Chapter 5

Infant Cognitive Development

One day when Mikey Gordon was 7 months old he crawled over to a stack of pictures his sister Becky had drawn. Reaching out his hand he grasped the top one, wrinkling the corner as he pulled it toward himself. The thick paper made a pleasant rustling sound. Mikey dropped the first picture and reached for another, wrinkling it with two hands and then shaking it. The paper rustled and flapped. Mikey smiled and reached for a third. As he held the third picture his hands pulled slightly apart, and the paper responded by tearing down the middle with a wonderful ripping noise. Mikey dropped one half and put the other in his mouth, feeling it grow soft and moist as he stroked it with his tongue. Just as he was reaching for a brightly colored drawing of a little girl jumping rope, Becky walked into the room. "Mikey, no!" she screamed, as she ran to rescue her artwork. "Look what you've done to my drawings! You're bad! I'm gonna tell Mommy!"

Why did Mikey destroy Becky's pictures? Was he really being bad, as Becky said? In this chapter you will discover that this explanation is highly unlikely. The mind of a 7-month-old does not grasp the concepts of "*my* drawings" or "bad." Mikey cannot yet understand language, nor can he imagine how Becky must feel about what he has done. This example makes a very important point: how children perceive and interpret what they experience depends on their level of cognitive development. Mikey is incapable of feeling shame and remorse because his understanding of the world is as yet too limited. But he may be able to grasp the distressed tone of Becky's voice, something that 6 months ago he would not have been able to do.

In this chapter we will examine how a baby's understanding of the world develops. We might say that we are going to explore the changing intelligence of infants. In psychology, however, the term **intelligence** is usually used to talk about individual differences in thinking skills. This chapter is concerned primarily with changes in thinking skills that are common to all normal infants. We call these skills **cognitive abilities.**

You will encounter several major themes in this chapter. One is the *orderly nature* of cognitive development. In part this orderliness arises from the process by which previous capacities pave the way for new ones. Inborn reflexes are building blocks for early voluntary actions, which in turn provide the foundation for later capabilities. The orderliness of cognitive development also results from maturation of certain general capacities that are important for all areas of development. These include the ability to coordinate actions and the capacity to store and retrieve information efficiently from memory.

A second theme of this chapter is that infants are *active participants* in their own development. They engage the environment with every means they have, practicing their skills and in the process encountering problems beyond their current capacities. On the basis of feedback from these encounters and the continuing maturation of their brains, infants evolve more advanced and serviceable abilities. While at first they seem to apply their new abilities automatically, when some object or event triggers them, in time infants become *intentional planners,* deliberately trying out actions and investigating their consequences. This deliberate exploration of actions and consequences moves the child's understanding forward at an ever-increasing pace.

Intelligence:
Individual differences in thinking and reasoning skills.

Cognitive abilities:
Thinking skills common to all normal individuals in an age group.

During infancy, behavior changes from reflexive single acts to organized sequences of goal-directed behaviors.

A third theme of this chapter is that infant cognitive development is marked by both *advances and limitations.* One major advance is a basic understanding of *causality,* especially the understanding that one's own actions can produce particular effects. Seven-month-old Mikey, for example, noticed the interesting sound he produced by wrinkling a piece of paper, so he repeated this action and observed the effect again, apparently for the simple pleasure of mastery. A second major cognitive advance of infancy is an understanding of *means and ends.* Before they are 1 year old, babies realize that sometimes doing one thing will enable them to do another (removing an obstacle, for example, will enable them to get to a toy). A third achievement of profound significance is an understanding of *object permanence.* Infants learn not only that objects exist outside their own observations, but also that objects may change their locations even if those changes aren't seen. This knowledge reflects a fourth major cognitive advance of infancy: the ability to store and recall information from *memory.*

Still, the cognitive abilities of infants have limitations. Advances are tempered by constraints on what and how babies know. For instance, babies know the world primarily through action—that is, by actually doing things rather than just by thinking about them. In fact, some developmentalists define infancy as the period prior to the development of *symbolic thought,* the capacity to let one thing stand for or represent another. In their view, an inability to engage in symbolic thought makes it impossible for infants to understand many things that older children can. This is true no matter how much teaching the babies' parents provide. Other developmentalists dispute the claim that infants lack symbolic thought. They focus instead on other limitations that prevent babies from *using* symbolic thinking capacities. In all cases, however, there is a recognition of limitations. All developmentalists agree that a baby's thinking is significantly constrained in some respects, despite the fact that children make great cognitive strides in the first 2 years of life.

In this chapter we begin with a six-stage description of infant cognitive development proposed by Jean Piaget. We include this description both to provide an overview of some of the changes in infants' cognitive capabilities and to show how important Piaget's ideas have been as a starting point for more recent theories and research. We then turn to two important cognitive advances of infancy. The first is an understanding that objects are permanent—that is, that objects do not cease to exist when they are out of sight. In our discussion of the concept of object permanence we use Piaget's perspective as a framework and then consider other, more recent viewpoints. The second major cognitive advance of infancy we discuss is that of the steady improvement of memory. In particular, we explore recent research showing how a baby's memory becomes more complex and long-lasting with age. In our next major section, we review Piaget's explanation of how infant cognitive development unfolds, and then present various challenges and alternatives to it. Finally, we look at individual differences in infant cognitive development. Recent findings suggest that babies the same age often perform at different levels on various cognitive tasks. Moreover, performance on these tasks can sometimes help predict a child's future IQ. This does not mean that intelligence is biologically set, however. Experience always plays a major role in the development of cognitive abilities.

THE COURSE OF INFANT COGNITIVE DEVELOPMENT: PIAGET'S STAGES

Sensorimotor period:
According to Piaget, that period, during the first 2 years of the child's life, in which the child's awareness of the world is limited to what he or she knows through sensory awareness and motor acts.

Piaget called infancy the **sensorimotor period,** because he viewed the child's awareness of the world as limited to what he or she knows through sensory awareness and motor acts. Piaget subdivided the period into six stages (see Table 5.1). His initial description of these stages was drawn from observing his own three children as infants (Piaget, 1962). Although findings from later experiments caused him to change some of his ideas, Piaget's book on infancy, *The Origins of Intelligence,* still demonstrates how much can be learned from careful observation of individual children.

As you read about the six stages of infant cognitive development that Piaget proposed, remember three things: First, Piaget was describing the most

TABLE 5.1
PIAGET'S STAGES OF SENSORIMOTOR DEVELOPMENT

0–1 month	Stage 1: Reflexes	Minor refinement of inborn behavior patterns
1–4 months	Stage 2: Primary circular reactions	Development of simple repeated actions centered on infant's own body
4–8 months	Stage 3: Secondary circular reactions	Development of repeated actions involving external objects
8–12 months	Stage 4: Coordination of schemes	Coordination of separate actions into goal-directed sequences of behaviors
12–18 months	Stage 5: Tertiary circular reactions	Variation of repeated actions through trial-and-error experimentation
18–24 months	Stage 6: Beginnings of representational thought	Emergence of mental schemes, as seen in deferred imitation

advanced level of performance that can be seen at each stage; early in any stage a baby is only beginning to attain these accomplishments. Second, the age ranges given are only approximate; different babies enter and complete each stage at different paces. What is important in stage theories is the *sequence* of stages, not their precise timing. Third, Piaget's stage description is only one of several explanations of infant cognitive development. As you read this section and the beginning of the next section, try to think of alternative explanations for the changes Piaget observed. In constructing these alternatives, you might consider the learning mechanisms you read about in Chapter 4, which become increasingly flexible and powerful during the first year; you might think about concepts like increasing memory capacity; or you might make use of concepts like maturation and refinement of inborn skills. Later in the chapter, we will take a look at some of the alternatives to Piaget's explanation that other theorists have proposed.

STAGE 1: REFLEXES (BIRTH TO 1 MONTH)

Piaget proposed that in the first month of life a baby's capabilities are limited to genetically programmed reflexes. Development during this stage consists of minor refinements of these reflexes; no truly new behaviors emerge. Piaget used the term *reflex* in a much broader sense than most American psychologists. To him a reflex was any built-in behavior pattern. It did not have to be an automatic response to one particular stimulus. For instance, the *active looking* that Malcolm engaged in when he came home from the hospital Piaget would consider a reflex, because these eye movements are a built-in response to many kinds of visual stimuli. In addition to eye movements, other behaviors that Piaget considered reflexes include sucking, grasping, and larger movements of the arms and hands. All of these are refined during the first month after birth. Piaget was particularly interested in these early reflexes because they provide the building blocks for later development. The research on early learning that you read about in Chapter 4 is consistent with this principle of Piaget's theory.

STAGE 2: PRIMARY CIRCULAR REACTIONS (1 TO 4 MONTHS)

One evening when John Williams was putting 2-month-old Malcolm to bed, he took a minute to sit and watch his son as he lay on his back in his crib. Malcolm was moving his arms in a seemingly random but rhythmic up-and-down pattern. As his semi-clenched right hand brushed against his face, he turned his head to the right and his arm movements became smaller. The next time the hand brushed against his face, he opened his mouth and captured it. After sucking for a while he released the hand, moved it up and down again, and then recaptured it with his mouth. Over and over Malcolm repeated this sequence. John Williams was observing what Piaget called a primary circular reaction.

A **circular reaction** is a behavior that produces an interesting event (initially by chance) and so is repeated. The reaction is circular in the sense that the end of one sequence triggers the start of another. A **primary circular reaction** like Malcolm's is one that involves only a person's own body, not an external object or event. You are engaging in a primary circular reaction when you discover that pressing on the outside corner of one of your eyes produces double vision and you repeatedly press and release to observe this interesting phenomenon.

Thumb sucking frequently is learned as a primary circular reaction, just as

Circular reaction: A sequence in which a behavior produces an interesting event (initially by chance) and so is repeated. The end of one sequence triggers the start of another.

Primary circular reaction: A sequence, involving a person's own body (rather than an external object), in which a behavior accidentally produces an interesting event and so is repeated.

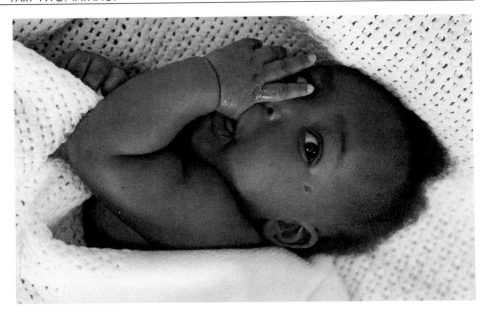

Repeatedly moving the hand to the mouth so a thumb, fingers, or fist can be sucked is a common example of a primary circular reaction.

Malcolm learned to suck his whole hand. As a young baby's hands and arms move randomly, a thumb often comes in contact with the mouth. This stimulation may trigger the sucking reflex. You might think that once the thumb is inside the mouth the child would go on sucking until he or she grew tired. Often, however, this is not what happens. Piaget noticed that infants frequently pull the thumb out and attempt to repeat the actions that led to sucking on it. The babies seem to be trying to gain control over behaviors that originally occurred by accident. This is an early example of infants being active participants in their own cognitive development. Babies don't just passively take in information about the world around them. Instead, their own activities help generate and select information that is useful for development. Piaget believed that this active role for infants was a central component of the developmental process, and most contemporary developmentalists agree with him.

You may wonder why we say that thumb sucking is often learned as a primary circular reaction when babies younger than stage 2 sometimes suck their thumbs. In fact, this behavior has even been observed in fetuses. At this early point in development, however, thumb sucking is probably a purely reflexive response to the accidental presence of a thumb near the mouth. It has not yet become a primary circular reaction. This is not to say that infants younger than one month are totally incapable of performing such reactions. The limitations on behavior that Piaget believed were present before stage 2 are not absolute. Many of the capabilities observable in infants between 1 and 4 months of age are also present at birth, but are very hard to detect.

The inborn behaviors characteristic of babies in stage 1 are the foundation of the primary circular reactions that typically develop during stage 2. For one thing, inborn behaviors (such as moving the arms and sucking) determine which kinds of events are likely to happen by accident. In addition, when babies do something that produces an interesting sensory experience, they are intrinsically motivated to try to repeat the behavior. Malcolm does not consciously think about the connection between capturing the fist in his mouth and the pleasant sensation of sucking on it. For him, repeating this behavior is automatic, not intentional. It is simply the nature of babies to try to repeat an action that causes an interesting consequence. Piaget's stage 2 marks the emergence of new behaviors as a result of this intrinsic motivation.

STAGE 3: SECONDARY CIRCULAR REACTIONS (4 TO 8 MONTHS)

At breakfast one day 6-month-old Meryl accidentally knocked a spoon off her high-chair tray. The spoon clattered to the floor, and Karen gave her a clean one. Moments later Meryl knocked the new spoon to the floor. This was not an attempt by Meryl to annoy Karen. Rather, Meryl was simply engaging in what Piaget called a secondary circular reaction.

In a **secondary circular reaction,** infants actively experience the effects their behaviors have on *external* objects. As with a primary circular reaction, the interesting sensory consequence is at first produced by accident. But the baby then repeats the behavior, causing the consequence again.

An experiment that Piaget conducted on his infant son, Laurent, shows both the skills and limitations of babies at this stage. Piaget tied a string from Laurent's wrist to a rattle suspended above his crib. If Laurent moved his arm vigorously enough, the rattle would make a noise. Just by randomly moving his limbs, Laurent soon caused the rattling sound. At this point he stopped, listened, and then moved his whole body so the sound occurred again. Repeating this secondary circular reaction, Laurent gradually adapted his movements until he moved only the appropriate arm. The next day Piaget again tied the string from Laurent's wrist to the rattle, but Laurent did not spontaneously start to move the arm again. Only when his father first shook the rattle for him did Laurent revive the previous day's circular reaction. On the third day Piaget tied the string to Laurent's *other* wrist. Again Piaget had to reinstate the circular reaction by first shaking the rattle himself. Only then did Laurent begin moving his arm, and he moved the one that *didn't* have the string. When no sound resulted, Laurent moved his body more extensively until he finally heard the rattle. As Laurent repeated the circular reaction, his movements again adapted until he eventually moved only the arm connected to the rattle.

We can say that Laurent understood the connection between moving his arm and the resulting sound, but this understanding was quite limited. Even when the wrist to which the string was tied was in clear view, Laurent moved the other arm. He did not grasp the fact that the arm pulled the string, which in turn shook the rattle. Instead, he merely learned a connection between a particular behavior—moving his arm—and a particular sensory consequence—hearing the rattle.

According to Piaget, during the first year of life babies learn many such pairings between their own behaviors and sensory consequences. Another example can be seen in the early form of imitation that emerges during stage 3. When 6-month-old Malcolm coos, for instance, DeeDee may coo back, causing the baby to coo in return. Here Malcolm is learning a connection between making a certain sound and having his mother repeat it. According to Piaget, such circular reactions are limited to behaviors that Malcolm can already perform and that he can actually hear or see himself produce. Malcolm is not yet capable of consciously mimicking another person and thus acquiring *new* behaviors through imitation.

Secondary circular reaction: A sequence involving the child and an external object or objects in which a behavior accidentally produces an interesting event and so is repeated.

STAGE 4: COORDINATION OF SCHEMES
(8 TO 12 MONTHS)

When Meryl was 7 months old, she would become very frustrated if she wanted a toy and some other object was blocking the way. Karen thought it was strange that Meryl should make such a fuss when she could grasp the unwanted object and put it to one side. Karen decided the reason must be Meryl's "cranky" nature. Then, a couple of months later, when Meryl was 9 months old, she started crawling over to inspect the television plug. To distract Meryl, Karen quickly placed a large toy dog directly in front of the socket. To her surprise, this tactic failed completely. With a sweep of her arm, Meryl knocked the dog out of the way and reached for the cord.

Goal-directed chain: A behavioral sequence in which the individual does something not for its own sake but as a means of accomplishing something else.

This kind of action—in which a baby performs a behavior in order to do something else—clearly indicates Piaget's stage 4 thinking. In stage 4, infants begin to put actions together into **goal-directed chains** of behavior. In other words, they sometimes do a thing not for its own sake but as a means of accomplishing something else. Meryl knocks the toy dog out of the way *in order* to get to the electrical cord. Notice that this action required her to first anticipate the results of hitting the dog. The ability to anticipate future consequences is a major cognitive leap forward, even though it is still limited to well-learned motor actions. Piaget claimed that this kind of behavior is the first clear sign of purposefulness in infants. Meryl intends to grasp the plug, and she knows that if she hits the dog it will no longer be in the way. Thus, by coordinating her hitting, reaching, and grasping strategies, she gets what she wants.

Piaget also argued that infants at stage 4 understand their own behavior well enough to be able to imitate actions that they seldom perform spontaneously. For instance, Piaget's 9-month-old daughter Jacqueline gradually learned how to imitate her father as he bent and straightened his index finger, something that she rarely did on her own (Piaget, 1962).

STAGE 5: TERTIARY CIRCULAR REACTIONS (12 TO 18 MONTHS)

Thirteen-month-old Mikey is standing at the top of the stairs, his way blocked by a wooden safety gate. As he peers over the gate with a rubber ball in one hand, the ball accidentally drops and bounces all the way down. Mikey watches intently as the ball rolls on and hits the front door. He then picks up his blue stuffed dog and drops it over the gate, watching to see what happens. The dog lands on the top step, somersaults down another, and stops when it hits the third, nose draped over the edge. Christine comes out of the bedroom just in time to see Mikey forcefully hurling a shoe over the gate.

Tertiary circular reaction: A sequence involving the child and an external object or objects in which a behavior accidentally produces an interesting event, leading the child to experiment with variations of the behavior.

Mikey's behavior illustrates what Piaget called a **tertiary circular reaction.** As with primary and secondary circular reactions, a tertiary (or third-order) circular reaction begins when some action accidentally leads to an interesting sensory consequence. But rather than just repeating the same behavior, the infant at this stage "experiments." Thus Mikey tries dropping other objects over the gate and launching them in a variety of ways. These purposeful, trial-and-error variations allow him to discover new cause-and-effect relationships rapidly. His understanding of the world and strategies for acting on it greatly expand as a result.

As you would expect, infants at stage 5 get into everything. They actively explore each new object, trying to discover its potential for responding. This exploration affords many opportunities to learn new means of reaching goals.

The active exploration of stage 5 babies may also explain why children around 18 months of age rapidly begin to acquire simple tool-using skills (Flavell, 1985). For instance, at a little over 18 months, Mikey spontaneously began using a stick to "help dig" his mother's flower garden. According to Piaget, the active trial-and-error approach of stage 5 infants readily enables them to learn to imitate behaviors they have never before performed.

STAGE 6: BEGINNINGS OF REPRESENTATIONAL THOUGHT (18 TO 24 MONTHS)

[Piaget's 1½-year-old daughter] Jacqueline had a visit from a little boy of 18 months whom she used to see from time to time, and who, in the course of the afternoon, got into a terrible temper. He screamed as he tried to get out of a playpen and pushed it backward, stamping his feet. Jacqueline stood watching him in amazement, never having witnessed such a scene before. The next day, she herself screamed in her playpen and tried to move it, stamping her foot lightly several times in succession. (Piaget, 1962 b, p. 63)

This example of **deferred** (or delayed) **imitation** illustrates one of the new capabilities that mark stage 6 intelligence. Jacqueline watched another toddler throw a temper tantrum. A day later, without ever having tried out these tantrum behaviors beforehand, she performed a good imitation of them. Apparently, she had stored in memory a representation of screaming, pushing, and stamping. The ability to form mental representations like this one is a very important cognitive advance.

Piaget described stage 6 as the start of the transition from sensorimotor to **symbolic** or **representational thought,** the term Piaget used to describe the ability to make one thing stand for something else. In this case, Jacqueline created some kind of memory trace of a tantrum that stood for or represented the actual behaviors. Stage 6 children also start to solve problems "in their heads," without having to go through the physical actions involved. Their symbolic thought is still quite limited, however, in that it is confined to behaviors that the child *could* act out. Nevertheless, the ability to have actions "in mind" without performing them is a great cognitive leap forward.

Deferred imitation—reproducing behavior observed in the past—demonstrates the child's growing abilities of mental representation.

Deferred imitation:
The ability of the child to retain in memory a representation of an observed behavior and to imitate that behavior after time has elapsed.

Symbolic or representational thought:
In Piaget's theory, the ability to conceptualize one thing as standing for another; for example, to have an action "in mind" without performing it.

DEVELOPING THE CONCEPT OF OBJECTS

Developing the concept of objects is a major task of infancy. When you look around, you do not simply see patterns of light. You see books, chairs, pencils, and other objects. You know that these objects have a durability that goes beyond their colors or the shadows they cast (both of which disappear in the absence of light), and that also goes beyond your own perception (which depends on you being there). Such a realization is central to your whole understanding of the world, including your knowledge that you are distinct from other people.

Some of Piaget's most fascinating ideas concerned the concept of objects. He argued that newborns have no such concept. He believed that this concept, like other knowledge, is "actively constructed" over time. Although a majority of developmentalists still endorse this view, it has been criticized. Even if Piaget's general claims are true, the particulars of his description of how the object con-

Object permanence:
The understanding that
objects continue to exist
even when they are out of
sight.

cept develops have undergone substantial revision. In the next section we focus on one aspect of the concept of objects: **object permanence,** or the understanding that objects continue to exist even when they are out of sight. We examine the emergence of the object permanence concept, first from Piaget's perspective, and then in light of more recent findings.

PIAGET'S VIEW OF THE DEVELOPMENT OF OBJECT PERMANENCE

STAGES 1 AND 2
In stages 1 and 2 of the sensorimotor period, infants become able to track moving objects with their eyes and reach for them if they are close enough. However, if an object the baby is watching moves behind something else, the child loses interest in it and gazes off in another direction as if the object has ceased to exist. A similar reaction happens when an object is partially covered. For example, suppose a stage 2 infant is hungry and looking at a bottle. Then, while the infant is still looking, you cover the nipple end of the bottle with a cloth so the infant can see only the bottom half. Frequently, a baby this young will quickly lose interest and begin looking at other things. It is as if the child cannot imagine the "missing" part and no longer perceives the object as familiar.

STAGE 3
In the third sensorimotor stage (approximately 4 to 8 months) an infant will reach for an object that is partially covered. But if an object is totally covered while the infant is watching and the child is prevented from reaching for it immediately, the infant will no longer try to reach for it. Apparently, babies this age need at least some perceptual cues to remind them that an object still exists. You saw a related cognitive limitation in Piaget's son Laurent at stage 3. The day after playing with the rattle connected to his wrist by a string, Laurent at first did not remember how to make the interesting sound. However, once his father shook the rattle, this minimal cue revived the whole secondary circular reaction. In order to remember objects and how behaviors affect them, stage 3 infants still depend on current perceptual information, although a partial view of something is now enough to elicit a concept of the whole.

During stages 1 and 2 of the sensorimotor period, infants almost immediately lose interest in objects that become hidden from view. By stage 3, a longer period of hiding is required before the infant loses interest, and seeing only a small part of the object reactivates search behavior.

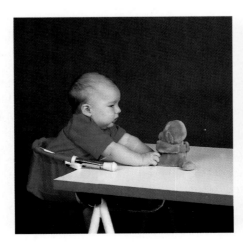

FIGURE 5.1
ASSESSMENT OF OBJECT PERMANENCE

In the top sequence (A), the stage 4 infant searches wherever the object was previously found. If the object is repeatedly hidden under the cloth on the infant's left, the infant immediately searches under the cloth and finds the object. When the object is hidden under the cloth on the right, the stage 4 infant still searches on the left. In the bottom sequence (B), the stage 5 infant searches wherever the object disappeared from sight. When the object is put under the cloth in the adult's closed hand, the infant searches in the adult's hand.

STAGE 4

In the fourth sensorimotor stage infants will search for hidden objects. If you cover a toy with a pillow, for instance, the child will remove the pillow to get the toy. This behavior shows that the stage 4 baby can combine sensorimotor schemes into goal-directed actions. It also shows that the baby understands that an object can be recovered after searching.

You might conclude that infants now possess an adultlike concept of object permanence, but studies show that the child's understanding of object permanence is still "flawed" (e.g., Gratch, 1975). For example, suppose you repeatedly hide a rattle under a cloth, each time letting the child retrieve the toy. This game is so interesting for an 8- to 10-month-old baby that he or she will play it for a long time. Now, while the infant is still watching, you put the rattle beneath a different cloth. Surprisingly, the infant will continue to look for the toy underneath the first cloth, where it has always been before. Failing to find the rattle there, the baby will search randomly, perhaps finally discovering it under the second cloth where he or she *saw* you put it. (Sequence A in Figure 5.1 illustrates the search behavior of stage 4 infants.)

Many researchers believe that the continued searching by the stage 4 infant indicates that the child knows the object is permanent and must be somewhere (Siegler, 1986). But looking under the first cloth shows an incomplete understanding of the constraints that govern where an object can be found. Piaget believed that infants in stage 4 connect the reappearance of the object with one of their own motor behaviors (lifting a certain cloth), so they repeat this behavior in the expectation that it will bring the object back. For them the object does not yet have a permanence independent of their own activity.

STAGE 5

In the fifth sensorimotor stage (approximately 12 to 18 months) infants no longer make the stage 4 error. Instead, they search for a hidden object wherever it last disappeared from sight. (Sequence B in Figure 5.1 illustrates the search behavior of stage 5 infants.) Once again it may seem that the baby has attained an adultlike understanding, but the following procedure reveals otherwise. In this sequence, you show the baby a small toy until the child's attention is captured; then you close your hand around it, place your hand under a cloth, leave the toy there, and withdraw your still-closed hand. Where do you think the child will search for the toy? At this stage the infant looks first in your hand, which is where the toy disappeared from view. When the object isn't there, the child often becomes upset and stops searching or may begin searching at random. The child may or may not move the cloth and find the toy. Apparently, a baby of this age cannot make inferences about what may happen to an object while it is out of sight.

STAGE 6

In the sixth and final sensorimotor stage children at last acquire a mature understanding of object permanence. They can now imagine movements of an object that they do not actually see. As a result, if you perform the stage 5 experiment with them, they will immediately search under the cloth after failing to find the toy in your hand. This ability to imagine the object leaving your hand while it was under the cloth is another example of early representational thought. Just as Jacqueline could form a mental representation of a temper tantrum, stage 6 babies can also form mental representations of movements and actions.

RECENT RESEARCH ON INFANTS' UNDERSTANDING OF OBJECTS

Researchers have continued to be very interested in how and when infants develop an understanding of objects. The object concept is, after all, central to a general understanding of the world. Some investigators have taken the approach of trying to replicate Piaget's studies. They have found that even though many children reach the various milestones in developing the object concept at somewhat earlier ages than Piaget recorded, babies do pass through the sequences of behavior that Piaget observed (e.g., Corman and Escalona, 1969; Kramer, Hill, and Cohen, 1975; Uzgiris and Hunt, 1975).

Other researchers, however, have questioned Piaget's interpretation of his findings. They contend that babies substantially younger than Piaget's stage 4 (8 to 12 months) may understand that objects are permanent but simply lack the skills either to determine where an object is or to carry out an effective search (Bower, 1977; Harris, 1983, 1989). Thus, younger infants may in fact "know" more about objects than they appear to in Piaget's experiments. Researchers have therefore devised other tests of the object concept that do not require the baby to search for and locate something. One test involves the perception of partially hidden objects.

THE PERCEPTION OF PARTIALLY HIDDEN OBJECTS

Philip Kellman and Elizabeth Spelke (1983) have demonstrated that when an object is partially hidden from view, babies can infer the existence of the whole object earlier than Piaget reported. These researchers presented 3½- to 4½-month-old infants with the display shown in the top part of Figure 5.2. During the first phase of the experiment the babies watched a rod moving back and forth behind a wood block, with the central segment of the rod always hidden. Then the babies were shown one of the two displays in the bottom part of Figure 5.2. The experimenters reasoned that the babies would spend more time looking at whichever stimulus was *un*familiar to them. Thus, if the babies had interpreted the original display to be a single rod behind a wood block, the single rod would be familiar, and they would look at it for *less* time. This is exactly what happened. Additional research has shown that it is the fact that the two visible pieces of the rod move in unison that leads the infants to perceive them as part of the same partially hidden whole (Kellman, Spelke, and Short, 1986).

Researchers have wondered if even younger babies can infer whole objects from visible pieces that move as one. One study found that this ability is absent in newborns (Slater et al., 1990). This suggests that the ability is an acquired one, as Piaget argued. But apparently it is acquired earlier than Piaget thought.

OTHER TESTS OF OBJECT PERMANENCE AND WHAT THEY SHOW

There is also evidence that by 5 months of age babies have some understanding that an object still exists even though they can no longer see it (Harris, 1989), but tests other than Piaget's must be used to reveal this understanding. In one study (Hood and Willatts, 1986), an object was presented to either the left or the right side of 5-month-olds. The babies were prevented from reaching for it until after the lights were turned out. Even though the babies could no longer see the object, they reached more often to the correct side, indicating an understanding that the object was still there.

Renée Baillargeon has conducted a series of experiments that suggests an even more sophisticated understanding of objects and object permanence in babies 5 to 7 months old (Baillargeon, 1987; Baillargeon, Spelke, and Wasserman, 1985). In one experiment, a screen was pivoted forward and backward 180 degrees while babies watched. Then a block that interfered with the screen's backward movement was placed behind the screen. On "trick" trials, the block was surreptitiously removed and the screen was allowed to move freely. When the screen moved through the space that should have been occupied by the block, the babies looked longer, suggesting that they detected something unusual. Baillargeon believes that the infants assume the block is still there, even though they can't see it. If so, they not only understand that objects continue to exist when they can't be seen, they also grasp that one object can block the movement of another, even when the blocking object is hidden from view.

In a follow-up study Baillargeon (1991) used the same procedure with babies ages 4½ to 6½ months. She found that the 6½-month-olds retained a good idea of the size and location of the hidden block. They showed expectations that the backward-moving screen would stop at a certain point. The 4½-month-olds, in contrast, showed no accurate expectations about where the screen would stop. Baillargeon concluded that the general concept of object permanence (the simple idea that something hidden is still there) seems to develop before the ability to mentally represent a hidden object's size and location.

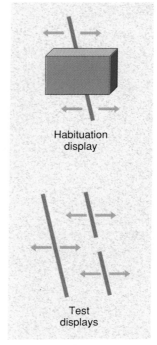

Habituation display

Test displays

FIGURE 5.2 TESTING INFANTS' PERCEPTION OF PARTIALLY OBSCURED OBJECTS

In Kellman and Spelke's experiment, 3½- to 4½-month-olds who had been habituated to the top display looked longer at the test display on the bottom right, suggesting that this was a novel stimulus to them and that they had perceived the habituation display as a single rod moving back and forth behind the block. (Source: Kellman and Spelke, 1983.)

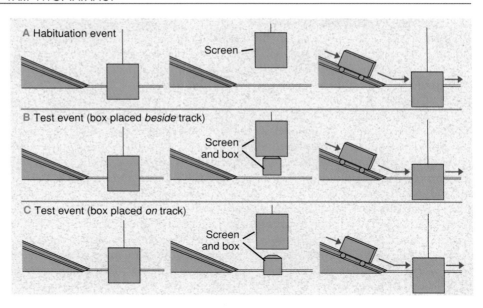

FIGURE 5.3 TESTING INFANTS' ASSUMPTIONS ABOUT HIDDEN OBJECTS *Baillargeon found that 6- to 8-month-olds who had been habituated to the event shown in A looked longer at test event C than at test event B, suggesting that they understood that the car should not be able to roll through the box placed on the track. (Source: Baillargeon, 1986.)*

In another test of the object permanence concept that doesn't require babies to search for something, Baillargeon (1986) showed babies 6 to 8 months old a toy car that rolled down a track, disappeared behind a screen, and then reappeared, as shown in row A of Figure 5.3. After the infants had viewed this event several times and showed signs of habituation to it, the screen was removed and a box was placed either beside the track or on it, as shown in rows B and C of Figure 5.3. Then the screen was replaced so as to hide the box. If the box had been placed *on* the track, it was removed without the infants' knowledge. Again the car rolled down the track, disappeared behind the screen, and reappeared. When this happened, infants who had seen the box placed *on* the track looked longer at the scene than did those who had seen the box placed *beside* the track. The longer looking seemed to indicate surprise that the car's progress was not blocked by the box. Apparently, the babies knew not only that the car and the box continued to exist behind the screen, but also that the car should not be able to travel through space that the box occupied.

Baillargeon has tried this same experiment on even younger babies (Baillargeon and DeVos, 1991). In a study of 4-month-olds she found that the girls in the sample were surprised when the car rolled "through" the box, but the boys were not. This gender difference could easily happen if girls are slightly developmentally advanced relative to boys and if 4 months is about the age when the necessary understanding of object permanence is acquired. Evidence from other sources does suggest that female infants may be slightly developmentally advanced over boys, so Baillargeon did an additional study to determine if 4 months is about the age at which this understanding is acquired. She tested a new group of 4-month-old girls, and compared them with a group of 3½-month-old girls. The 4-month-olds again detected the surprising event, but the babies half a month younger did not (Baillargeon and DeVos, 1991).

To summarize, recent research on the development of the object permanence concept suggests that Piaget was fairly accurate about the *sequence* in which this understanding is acquired, but he underestimated the *rate* of acquisition. It now appears that an understanding of object permanence emerges sometime between 3 and 5 months of age, several months sooner than Piaget believed. This earlier estimate results from research methods that catch more subtle signs of understanding than Piaget's did. In contrast to Piaget, Baillargeon's techniques and those of other infancy researchers who use habituation or familiarization do not require that all, or even most, infants in an age group exhibit an understanding of the concept being tested. It is sufficient that a substantial minority of infants within an age group do so for this understanding to be attributed to the age group. In addition to using techniques that have a lower criterion for attributing object permanence, Baillargeon's studies require less active responses from babies than Piaget's did, and they make fewer demands on memory. In Baillargeon's procedures a baby must remember a hidden object for at most only a few seconds. As you will see, memory powers of very limited duration may be one of the central constraints on young infants' grasp of object permanence in everyday life. Thus, Baillargeon's more sensitive measures allow skills to be detected when they are still emerging. But in most situations outside the laboratory, these skills are not yet well enough developed to be useful and apparent.

EXPLAINING INFANTS' SEARCH BEHAVIOR

Not only was Piaget's timetable for the development of object permanence apparently too conservative, but some of his ideas about why infants make certain object-related errors have not proved correct. For instance, Piaget speculated that the stage 4 infant mistakenly looks for a hidden object in its previous location because the child connects the act of searching there with the object's reappearance. Looking under the first cloth brought the object back before—why not another time? But research shows that this explanation can't be entirely correct. For one thing, stage 4 babies do not always search in the previous location when a hiding place has been changed. They do so only about 50 percent of the time (Butterworth, 1974, 1975, 1977). Additionally, if you let stage 4 infants search *immediately* after an object is hidden, they go to the right location 100 percent of the time (Gratch et al., 1974). The longer you make a baby wait, the more likely he or she will be to make an error (Baillargeon, DeVos, and Graber, 1989; Harris, 1989; Wellman, Cross, and Bartsch, 1986). And the older the baby, the longer the wait has to be before he or she makes a mistake (Diamond, 1985, 1988). Why would delay be a factor if the baby thought that searching in the old hiding place was what made the object reappear? Finally, when a baby watches an object being hidden in a new location, and there are six possible hiding places to choose from, any errors the child makes are usually near the correct location (Bjork and Cummings, 1984). It seems again that the infant is not just repeating a previously successful response. Instead, he or she is *trying* to remember the right location, but sometimes cannot.

To understand this explanation of the common "stage 4 error," try to put yourself in the baby's place. Where would you search for an object if you had forgotten where it was? Just as an adult who has lost his keys or eyeglasses might look where he has found them in the past, a reasonable approach for an infant might be to look for a desired object where it had previously been found. Perhaps stage 4 babies are doing just that when they search in the old location. If so, we need to know why they so quickly forget seeing the object put in the new hiding place. This question is about the limitations of a baby's memory, a topic we will explore shortly.

INFANTS' UNDERSTANDING OF OTHER OBJECT PROPERTIES

By the end of their first year, infants also show a remarkable understanding of properties of objects other than their permanence. In one study (Baillargeon and Hanko-Summers, 1990), babies between the ages of 7½ and 9½ months were shown two objects on top of each other to see if they understood the concept of one object supporting another and could gauge when the upper object should fall. Some of the arrangements were rigged to look as if they should fall, but they did not. When these rigged arrangements were very simple, infants looked at them longer than at arrangements that looked normal. However, if the rigged arrangements were a little more complex, the infants showed no preference for looking at them. Apparently, just as with their early understanding of object permanence, babies at this age seem to have a rudimentary grasp of the concepts of support and balance regarding objects, but they can apply these concepts only in simple situations.

Researchers have tested infants for a grasp of other object properties too. One is the causal link between one object hitting another and the movement of the second object. In one study, 6- and 10-month-olds were shown videotapes of different sequences involving objects. In one, an object was immediately launched when hit by another object; in a second, the launching of an object was delayed after it was hit; in a third, an object was launched even though another object didn't make contact with it; and in a fourth, a single object simply moved along (Oakes and Cohen, 1990). Judging from how they habituated and dishabituated, the 10-month-olds could discriminate sequences in which a causal link occurred from those in which it did not. The 6-month-olds, in contrast, seemed to become habituated to the presence of particular objects, not to the occurence of a causal connection between one object's movements and another's. Thus, knowledge about an object's relationship to other objects seems to develop in the second half-year, at roughly the same time as other aspects of the object concept.

MEMORY DEVELOPMENT IN INFANCY

Several years ago, while on a vacation, one of the authors of this book and his family were involved in an automobile accident. The author's son, then less than a year old, was taken to a hospital by ambulance to have minor injuries treated. Two years later the family was driving through the same town where the accident had occurred. The little boy, now 3 years old, looked around and spontaneously asked: "Are we going to see the ambulance now?" Did he remember the accident from 2 years earlier, when he had known the meaning of only a few words ("ambulance" certainly not among them)? And if babies *can* form lasting memories of things that happen to them, why do most adults recall almost nothing about their infancies (a phenomenon known as **infantile amnesia**)?

Infantile amnesia: Adults' inability to recall events from their infancies.

Different theorists have different views of memory development in infancy. Some see it as only one of many significant cognitive changes, while others see it as the key to understanding all cognitive development in this period. We will examine both these views shortly. But first we'll give you an overview of how memory capabilities change during the first year of life. We will explore two important aspects of memory: (1) *what* can be remembered; and (2) *how long* it can be remembered. Of course, these skills are quite limited initially. The memory skills we observe in very young infants are similar to those of many other

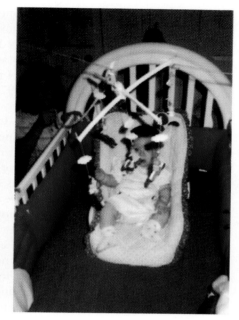

In the picture on the left, a 3-month-old infant's kicking is being reinforced by the movement of the mobile, which is attached to her ankle with a ribbon. When she is later placed in the crib again (right), she begins kicking at the sight of the mobile, this time moved by experimenter sitting beside her.

animal species, and the skills we see at 1 year of age are like those reported in higher primates (Klein, 1987). However, this is just the beginning of memory development; later chapters of this book will show how dramatically human memory skills continue to develop.

MEMORY IN THE FIRST HALF-YEAR

Even newborns have some memory capabilities. They readily habituate to novel sights and sounds, indicating that they must remember enough about a stimulus to recognize it as familiar (Kiselevsky and Muir, 1984; Slater, Morison, and Rose, 1984). But newborns learn most easily those things they are *prepared* to learn. Their brains are predisposed to retain certain kinds of information—often information related to survival and mastering the environment.

Even though newborns are capable of learning, researchers have not been able to show that they can remember learned information over a 24-hour period (Rosenblith and Sims-Knight, 1985). Such relatively long-term learning has been demonstrated in infants only a few weeks old, however. For instance, experiments in which infants less than 1 month old were conditioned to turn their heads upon hearing a certain sound suggest that this kind of learning is retained for more than a day (Papouŝek, 1959, 1967a). Another study demonstrated similar long-term memory for a word that had been repeated 60 times a day for 13 days (Ungerer, Brody, and Zelazo, 1978). Still, the extensive training needed to demonstrate memory over a 24-hour period in very young infants makes it seem unlikely that they retain much information about their experiences in the first month of life.

We know more about the memory capabilities of slightly older infants. In an interesting set of studies Caroline Rovee-Collier and her colleagues (e.g., Rovee-Collier, 1989, 1993; Rovee-Collier and Hayne, 1987) explored the long-term memories of 2- to 4-month-olds. In one study, babies learned to kick their legs in order to move a mobile that was attached to one leg by a ribbon. Six to 8 days later, these infants showed that they remembered what they had previously learned by starting to kick when they were placed in the experimental setting. After a 2-week interval, however, they no longer spontaneously started to kick (Sullivan, Rovee-Collier, and Tynes, 1979). Does this mean that after 14 days the memory had totally faded?

A second study suggests otherwise. In this experiment the researchers found that the babies' memory of the connection between kicking and moving the mobile could be reactivated if they were shown the mobile the day before testing (Rovee-Collier, 1979; Rovee-Collier et al., 1980). This finding differs somewhat from Piaget's observations of his son Laurent when a string was tied from one of Laurent's arms to a rattle above his crib. Just seeing the rattle again a day later, suspended above his crib, was not enough to get Laurent to resume moving his arm. Piaget had to shake the rattle for Laurent to remember this connection. But note that in both these experiments the babies' memories could be triggered by some perceptual reminder. In Laurent's case it was the sound of the rattle (probably its most salient feature); in Rovee-Collier's experiment it was the sight of the mobile's interesting shapes or colors. Apparently, although young babies do form long-term memories, they may have trouble retrieving them without clear-cut cues. This kind of memory is called **cued recall,** because the sight of the mobile or the sound of the rattle cues, or triggers, the memory of the appropriate behavior.

Cued recall is consistent with Piaget's view that babies' memories are sensorimotor in nature, not true representations. But the fact that young infants can retrieve a piece of information when cued by some related perceptual experience shows that they are making progress from **recognition memory** (in which they simply perceive a particular stimulus as familiar) toward **recall memory** (in which they pull information out of memory storage for current use).

Compared with older children, however, young babies have definite limitations in their ability to engage in cued recall. One such limitation may have to do with the small number of potential retrieval cues they can store. In summarizing the results of many studies, Robert Kail (1990) has suggested that younger babies may simply store fewer pieces of information about the events they experience, that may later serve as memory cues. In the case of Rovee-Collier's initial experiment, for instance, forgetting after a 2-week interval may have been due to the fact that the babies had stored only one or two features of the mobile. When these few features were forgotten, the contingency was forgotten too.

Another limitation on young babies' memories was revealed in a study of 6-month-olds which showed that babies sometimes link what they learn to irrelevant features of the environment, features that may be absent in a new situation and therefore can't serve as memory cues (Boller and Rovee-Collier, 1992). As in earlier studies, the babies in this one learned to kick their legs to move a mobile above a crib. Surprisingly, the color and design of the crib liner affected their later success at recalling the connection between their leg movements and the movement of the mobile. If they learned the connection while they were surrounded by a liner of one color and design, and later were tested in a crib with a different liner, they did not generalize what they had learned to the new context. Thus, the learning of young infants may be limited not only because they encode into memory fewer features of the environment, but also because

Cued recall:
A type of memory in which a familiar stimulus triggers, or cues, recall of stored information.

Recognition memory:
A type of memory in which a particular stimulus is simply perceived as familiar.

Recall memory:
The ability to retrieve information from memory storage in the absence of any obvious cue

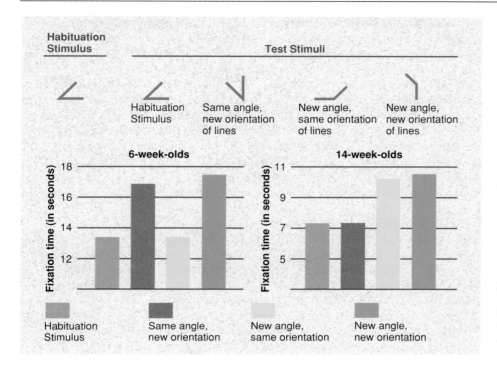

FIGURE 5.4 INFANT MEMORY FOR ANGLES *Cohen and Younger habituated 6- and 14-week-olds to various angles, such as the habituation stimulus on the left. After habituation, a variety of test stimuli were presented to the infants to see which ones they thought were different, as indicated by longer looking times. (Source: Adapted from Cohen and Younger, 1984.)*

they associate *all* those features (even irrelevant ones) with the information they are learning. This makes recall in young infants much more dependent on the total context in which the information was originally acquired. As the babies move from one context to another, they may be unable to recall and apply previously learned skills.

A third limitation on young babies' memories is their difficulty in storing information about the relationships between things, even very simple things like the angles formed by two straight lines. Cohen and Younger (1984) investigated infants' memories for angles (see Figure 5.4). They found that although 14-week-olds could remember angles, 6-week-olds could not. The younger babies evidently could remember only single features of an angle—that is, each individual line. You may think that knowledge about infants' memories for angles isn't crucial to understanding their memory development. However, studies using these simple stimuli provide information that helps us understand why very young infants might have difficulty remembering more relevant stimuli. If they remember each feature independently rather than in relationship to other features, they cannot remember complex patterns, such as human faces. Studies that directly explore babies' memories for faces generally support this view. These studies suggest that, before 3 months of age, babies don't seem to organize and store concepts of particular people (Olson and Sherman, 1983).

MEMORY IN THE SECOND HALF-YEAR

By the second half-year, in contrast, babies *do* store concepts of particular people and many other things, and they can retain those memories for relatively long periods of time. In one study babies almost 1 year old were tested with a variety of devices, such as a rattle inside a box. These children remembered the characteristics of the devices 2 years later, when they were almost 3 (Myers, Clifton, and Clarkson, 1987). Other studies have demonstrated that 1-year-olds can retain event or at least action on an object representation over an 8-month interval (Bauer, Hertsgaaral, and Dun, 1994; Bauer, 1995). The long-term memory skills that emerge in the second half-year are the basis of the strong emotional bonds that children develop with their parents. Babies this age frequently smile, gurgle, and coo when their mother or father approaches and cry when the parent departs. Undoubtedly, they must have formed a set of enduring memories about these important people. By the end of the first year, most babies also start to say their first words. Being able to use a word correctly from day to day and week to week also shows long-term memory.

THE ABILITY TO REMEMBER USING CATEGORIES

Suppose one day an infant is fed from a bottle with a pale, translucent nipple rather than the light brown nipple the child has used before. Will the infant notice this difference? Probably not. To most babies, this "new" bottle will not seem novel because the nipple's color is not significant to them. This example illustrates an important facet of human memory. People do not store precisely detailed memories of everything they see. Instead, they filter what they see through general categories they have formed and remember things partly as instances of those categories. Researchers wonder when infants begin to categorize the world. When do they start to remember two or more distinguishable objects as broadly similar?

In an experiment designed to help answer this question, Joseph Fagan (1979) habituated one group of 7-month-olds to pictures of different male faces and a second group to a picture of only one male face. Later, babies in the first group showed renewed interest when a *female* face was presented, but *not* a different male face. Apparently, at age 7 months, they were able to learn the category "male faces" and had grown tired of seeing repeated examples of it. In contrast, babies in the second group showed renewed interest in either of the new pictures—either a picture of a female face or a picture of a different male one. This experiment shows that for 7-month-olds to perceive and remember a category such as male faces, they must be presented with more than one instance of it.

Leslie Cohen and his colleagues (e.g., Cohen and Strauss, 1979; Husaim and Cohen, 1982; Younger and Cohen, 1986) have extensively studied the categories infants use to store information about fictitious animals. In one study

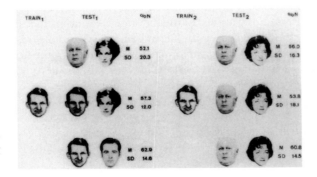

Joseph Fagan used pictures of male and female faces to study infants' ability to perceive and remember categories.

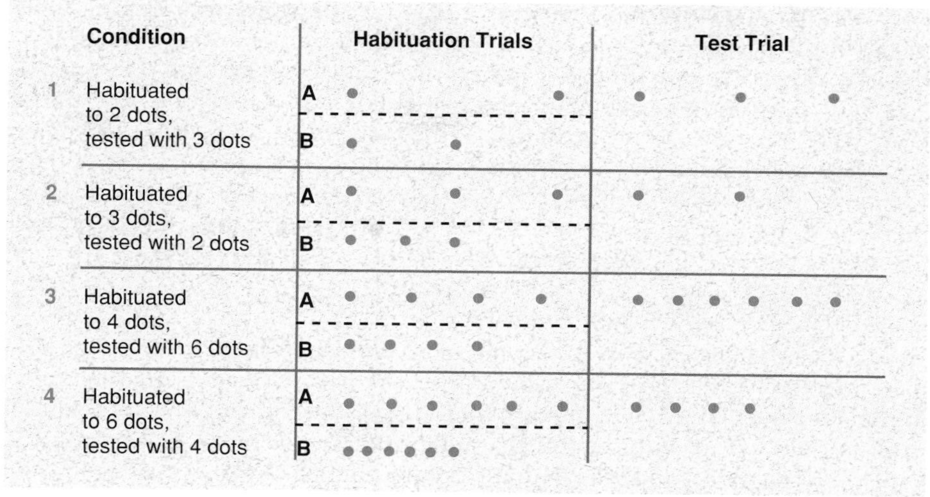

Condition	Habituation Trials		Test Trial

1 Habituated to 2 dots, tested with 3 dots

2 Habituated to 3 dots, tested with 2 dots

3 Habituated to 4 dots, tested with 6 dots

4 Habituated to 6 dots, tested with 4 dots

FIGURE 5.5 INFANT MEMORY FOR NUMERICAL INFORMATION
In Starkey and Cooper's experiment, 6- to 8-month-olds increased their looking times on test trials in conditions 1 and 2 but not in conditions 3 and 4. They could discriminate numerosities less than four but not greater. (Source: Starkey and Cooper, 1980.)

they created pictures of fictitious animals that varied in type of body, type of tail, and type of feet. Certain features, such as type of feet, went with certain other features, such as type of body. That is, the animals could be categorized according to how their various features were combined. When 4-month-olds were shown these pictures they did not learn the categories, but 10-month-olds did. Seven-month-olds could also learn categories, but only when the three types of features were perfectly correlated with one another—that is, when no variation existed within a category. Thus, the ability to use categories to store information in memory begins by at least 7 months of age and is fairly well developed by 10 months. Apparently, 10-month-olds combine information across specific examples of a category, so that what they remember about the category is a "typical example" of it, rather than the set of specific examples they saw (Younger, 1985, 1992). Babies younger than 10 months old can do this, too, if the stimuli involved are very simple (Younger and Gotlieb, 1988).

THE ABILITY TO REMEMBER HOW MANY

Researchers have also been intrigued by the question of when infants start to process numbers of objects into memory. The ability to notice "how many" is called **numerosity perception.** Prentice Starkey and Robert Cooper (1980) tested 6- to 8-month-olds for their perception of numerosity by using habituation. They showed one group of babies drawings of three dots each, with the arrangement of the dots varying from picture to picture. Other babies saw varying arrangements of two, four, or six dots (see Figure 5.5). After the babies' interest declined, the researchers changed the number of dots. Infants who had habituated to sets of three dots showed renewed attention when presented with two dots, and those who had habituated to two dots showed renewed attention to three. But switching from four dots to six or from six to four did *not* prompt renewed attention, even in 8-month-olds. Apparently, 6- to 8-month-old babies can perceive and remember very small numbers of objects, a skill that may emerge before 2 months of age (Antell and Keating, 1983). Perceiving and remembering larger numbers of objects, however, seems to depend on further cognitive advances.

Researchers have wondered exactly what babies store in memory when they

Numerosity perception: The ability to notice how many objects are present in a small grouping.

perceive that a picture has a certain number of dots. Do they store a visual image of the particular group of items, or a more abstract notion of how many things are there? In one study researchers presented 6- to 8-month-olds with two arrays of objects side by side, one array containing two objects, the other three. When the babies heard two drumbeats, they tended to look at the two-object set; when they heard three drumbeats, they tended to look at the set of three (Starkey, Spelke, and Gelman, 1983). This finding suggests that what babies remember and match in such studies is a surprisingly abstract concept of "how many," not just the physical characteristics of the stimuli seen or heard.

THE ABILITY TO ENGAGE IN RECALL

In the second half-year babies become increasingly effective at recalling information—that is, at actively retrieving it from memory storage, not just at knowing that it's familiar when it's presented to them. Recent studies have begun to explore the kinds of information that older infants can recall. In one study 9- and 14-month-olds saw adults demonstrate a number of actions with different objects, such as pushing a button to produce a beeping sound. One day later, when the objects were presented to the infants, both age groups reproduced the actions they had seen; that is, they recalled the appropriate behaviors and performed them (Meltzoff, 1988a, 1988b). This, of course, was cued recall, since the presence of the objects cued the infants' recall of the previously seen actions.

The cued recall of 14-month-olds is superior to that of 9-month-olds, however. Compared to 9-month-olds, 14-month-olds can learn more rapidly, can acquire a much wider variety of actions, can learn more things simply by watching other people do them, and can generalize what they have learned to a broader range of contexts. The older infants are also able to retain information longer. When the babies in the experiment just described were tested again a week later, only the 14-month-olds recalled the appropriate responses. The 9-month-olds had apparently forgotten them, or could no longer retrieve what they had previously learned.

Although all normal infants experience substantial improvements in recall ability during the first year of life, babies differ in the complexity of the information they can remember at any given age. Several investigators have reported significant relationships between measures of memory development during the first year and later measures of IQ, a topic that we will return to later (DiLalla et al., 1990; Fagan, 1984; Rose and Wallace, 1985). These results indicate the central role that an infant's memory plays in cognitive development (Kail, 1990).

EXPLAINING COGNITIVE DEVELOPMENT

How do we explain the remarkable cognitive changes that occur during infancy? How can we best conceptualize exactly what is changing in babies, and what spurs these changes? Equally important, what is the nature of the cognitive limitations that constrain how fast infant cognitive development can unfold? As we said earlier, different developmentalists have different answers to these questions. In this section we turn to the major theories of cognitive development. We begin with Piaget's theory, and then explore alternatives to it.

PIAGET'S THEORY

Piaget proposed the first comprehensive theory of cognitive development. The sensorimotor period he described is just one segment in his larger theory, which we discussed briefly in Chapter 1. One of Piaget's enduring contributions to developmental psychology is the view that cognitive development is not just the passive acquisition of new facts. To Piaget, cognitive development proceeds as the child *actively constructs* a system for understanding the world. Piaget also believed that children's understanding of the world at any given stage is limited by their current cognitive structures. As they pass through the various stages of development, their cognitive structures become increasingly abstract and sophisticated.

ASSUMPTIONS ABOUT THE NATURE OF INFANTS

At the start of this chapter you saw 7-month-old Mikey Gordon learning about the world by perceiving the effects of his own actions. He grasped a sheet of paper and watched it wrinkle, thus learning that this object is flexible. He shook the paper and heard it rustle, thus learning that it makes a faint, pleasant sound. Mikey's knowledge was growing through the interplay of perceptual skills and motor actions. This interplay is the cornerstone of Piaget's sensorimotor period of development, which spans the first 2 years of life. In Piaget's view this interplay provides the opportunities for cognitive growth at this age.

During the sensorimotor period, Piaget contended, a child's knowledge of the world is limited to what he or she knows through sensory awareness and motor actions (hence the term *sensorimotor*). Mikey's thinking at this age does not include language or abstract concepts. What he knows and remembers is directly tied to what he can see, hear, feel, taste, and do. Although not all developmentalists agree with Piaget's explanation of cognitive skills in infancy, most do agree on the general nature of the limitations he saw. However much the infant's understanding of the world progresses, it is still based largely on action, not reflection.

Even so, a great deal of cognitive development occurs in the first two years of life. At birth Mikey had only his inborn reflexes. When the side of his face was gently stroked, he automatically turned his head. When an object came in contact with his mouth, he automatically sucked. Specific stimuli triggered specific responses, with no conscious intention on Mikey's part. When we see Mikey 7 months later, the contrast is dramatic. He is purposefully reaching for and inspecting Becky's drawings, trying out motor actions and observing the results. This is a good example of Piaget's view that infants are busy, active learners trying to understand their worlds. At first, of course, the discoveries babies make occur by accident as they look around, move their limbs, manipulate parts of their bodies, and suck on what they can put into their mouths. Later, discoveries become more intentional. Older infants deliberately try out actions and investigate their consequences. At all stages, however, children are active participants in the processes that lead to more mature cognitive skills.

When Piaget said that infants are active participants in their own cognitive development, he used the term *active* to refer to both motor activity *and* mental activity. Infants do not wait for things to happen to them; they act on objects around them in whatever ways they can and then perceive the results. At the same time, infants are mentally constructing an understanding of the world. To accomplish this, they do not just passively absorb bits of information. Instead, they actively put together a rudimentary interpretation of how things work.

PROCESSES OF CHANGE

When Meryl was 6 months old, Karen offered her a sip of milk from a cup for the first time. As the rim touched her lips, Meryl started sucking to draw the milk out. The liquid spilled down both sides of her chin. With practice, however, Meryl soon learned how to use her lips and tongue to drink successfully from a cup. In time she much preferred drinking from a cup to drinking from a bottle. Piaget would have said that Meryl's responses show two key mechanisms of development: adaptation and equilibration. In Piaget's view, these two mechanisms account for developmental changes at every age.

To Piaget, **adaptation** is the process by which a person changes in order to function more effectively in a certain situation. This process is analogous to evolutionary adaptation, which we discussed in Chapter 1. In evolutionary adaptation, the traits of a species change in ways that improve its members' chances of survival. Piaget, of course, was talking about *individual* change, not change in an entire species. But like the evolutionists, he was interested in how behavior can be modified to meet the challenges a person faces. You saw an example of Piaget's concept of adaptation when Meryl altered her style of drinking to get milk from a cup. Without this change in her behavior, she would continue to function poorly in this situation.

Meryl adapts not only in her actions but also in her underlying thinking. For example, during her first year she will acquire an understanding of object permanence. Without this knowledge, her search for objects would be very inefficient; with it she will function much better in her environment. From Piaget's perspective Meryl's thinking is adapting to the demands and realities of the world in which she lives.

But the fact that a skill or concept is useful does not mean it can always be acquired through adaptation. Adaptation involves modifying some capability a person *already* has in order to make it more effective. Thus Meryl adapts her sucking behaviors in learning to drink from a cup, and she adapts her new-found understanding that objects are permanent to include a sense of where to look if an object suddenly disappears behind something else. Because certain capacities must be present if more advanced skills are to emerge, there are many things that infants cannot learn. For instance, Mikey cannot yet learn to draw pictures like Becky's because he simply does not possess the prerequisite skills for this task. Just as evolution can occur only through change in existing genes, adaptation in a child can take place only by modifying what the youngster already knows and can do.

You can more fully understand how adaptation works by considering its two subprocesses: assimilation and accommodation. **Assimilation** is the process of applying an existing capability to various situations that may be appropriate to it. For instance, when Karen was given an assortment of baby-bottle nipples to take home with newborn Meryl from the hospital, Meryl easily *assimilated* their slightly different sizes and shapes to her sucking reflex. The same basic sucking movements worked for all of them. **Accommodation,** in contrast, is the process of making modifications in an existing strategy or skill in order to continue dealing successfully with the world. For example, when Meryl encountered different kinds of objects (hands, toys, blankets, and so on), she learned that her

Babies apply their sucking scheme to a variety of new objects (assimilation). At the same time, they adjust their sucking bahavior to suit the shape and size of the various objects they put in their mouths (accommodation).

Adaptation:
In Piaget's theory, the process involving assimilation and accommodation by which a person changes in order to function more effectively in a given situation. In evolutionary theory, the changes in traits of a species that improve its members' chances of survival.

Assimilation:
In Piaget's theory, the process of applying an existing motor or mental scheme to various situations that may be appropriate to it.

Accommodation:
In Piaget's theory, the ongoing process of modifying an existing strategy or skill in order to make it better fit the continually changing circumstances in one's environment.

sucking strategy had to be modified to suit (or *accommodate*) them. Through accommodation Meryl gradually refined her innate sucking reflex into different sucking patterns suited to different objects. Still later, when confronted with the challenge of learning to drink from a cup, Meryl had to accommodate again, modifying the movements of her lips and tongue so that the liquid wouldn't spill. This skill now acquired, she is adapted for drinking from a cup.

As these examples show, adaptation is the joint product of assimilation and accommodation; the two occur together. During the first 2 years of life, assimilation and accommodation modify inborn capabilities into a variety of sensory and motor skills that the child can apply in many different situations. Piaget believed that these skills reflect underlying cognitive (or mental) structures that provide a strategy for coordinating sensory and motor information. He called these underlying cognitive structures **schemes.** An infant's cognitive structures include sucking schemes, grasping schemes, and looking schemes. In later periods of development, assimilation and accommodation enlarge and refine the child's concepts about the world. The cognitive structures that develop are then applied to mental representations (ideas and thoughts), rather than to sensory and motor information. Piaget frequently referred to these more abstract schemes as *operations.*

Scheme:
In Piaget's theory, a cognitive structure for coordinating sensory and motor information that can be applied to a variety of situations.

Schemes initially develop from reflexes, which provide a very limited range of behaviors. As infants interact with their environments, their early schemes become adapted to more and more situations. Stage 4 babies become able to combine schemes to create even more elaborate organizations of behavior. In Piaget's view, development through the six sensorimotor stages entails development of more complex and effectively adapted schemes, with each successive stage representing a different and more advanced level. The schemes of the sensorimotor period are important in Piaget's theory, not only because they make up the cognitive abilities of infancy, but also because they provide the basis for abilities in later periods. Just as reflexes provide the starting point for sensorimotor schemes, sensorimotor schemes provide the starting point for mental representations, which are important in the next major period of development.

You may wonder what keeps a child moving forward through the various stages of cognitive development. Piaget's answer was a mechanism called **equilibration,** a self-regulatory process that leads the child toward increasingly effective adaptations. When children are functioning adaptively in their environments, they are in a state of *equilibrium* because their behavior matches the demands of their situations. Sometimes, however, children encounter situations that demand skills somewhat beyond their current level of development. The result is a state of *disequilibrium.* You saw an example of this when Meryl sucked on the rim of her cup and the milk ran down her chin. Her behavior was inappropriate to the challenge she faced. Piaget argued that the natural response to a state of disequilibrium is to try to bring things back into equilibrium by making one's behavior match the new demands. This is accomplished through the processes of assimilation and accommodation. For example, Meryl continued to swallow the milk that made it into her mouth, just as she had done when drinking from a bottle (assimilation), but she also gradually adjusted the movements of her tongue and lips to keep the milk from spilling (accommodation). Ideally, each change involved in equilibration decreases the size of any subsequent changes needed.

Equilibration:
In Piaget's theory, the self-regulatory process that leads the child toward increasingly effective adaptations.

Learning to feed themselves requires babies to coordinate a series of actions to produce a desired outcome.

CHALLENGES TO PIAGET'S THEORY

You have already learned that there are aspects of Piaget's theory that now seem incorrect or incomplete. For instance, Piaget believed that babies don't engage in secondary circular reactions (repeatedly experiencing the effect that one of their actions has on an external object) until 4 months of age. Yet in one of Rovee-Collier's experiments, babies only 2 months old learned to kick their feet repeatedly to make a mobile move. How can this behavior be explained? Perhaps by connecting the infant's leg to the mobile with a ribbon, Rovee-Collier had made the mobile an extension of the child's body, so the learning in effect involved a *primary* circular reaction, not a secondary one. Alternatively, Piaget may simply have been wrong about when secondary circular reactions emerge. Maybe by observing only his own children, he missed the earliest appearance of this new skill. Developmentalists testing many infants with more sensitive measures of performance find a variety of skills at earlier ages than Piaget reported. Development of the object concept is another example. As we've already stated, the major milestones in this concept's development don't always occur at the ages Piaget noted, and they may not even always follow the sequences he described.

To rectify these and other problems with Piaget's theory, some contemporary developmentalists have proposed modifications to it. A few have offered alternative general theories of infant cognitive development. Among these are the theories of Kurt Fischer (1980) and Robbie Case (1985). Since both Fischer and Case retain Piaget's goal of describing the general course of development, their theories are sometimes called *neo-Piagetian* (*neo* meaning new). However, there are significant differences between Piaget's theory and these two newer ones in how they describe specific developmental changes and the mechanisms they propose for explaining development.

Fischer characterizes cognitive development as the acquisition of increasingly complex *skills*, rather than the construction of increasingly complex *schemes*. He sees skills as acquired in the context of particular experiences, so they may or may not be generalized to other situations. Skills, in other words, are more specific to particular domains than schemes are.

Case's theory is based on the idea that cognitive development results from increases in available memory capacity that allow the child to deal with increasingly complex information and to perform increasingly complex tasks. A central concept in his theory is **executive processing space,** which is "the maximum number of independent schemes a child can activate at any one time" (Case, 1985, p. 289). In the course of development, a child's amount of executive processing space increases as mental activities become more efficient, partly because of biological maturation and partly because well-practiced activities become increasingly automatic.

Along with the theories of Fischer and Case, challenges to Piaget's ideas can be found in the research of other developmental psychologists working from a variety of theoretical perspectives. This research has raised four major issues. First, infants' development does not always seem to fit the broad, unvarying, qualitatively distinct stages that Piaget proposed. Second, many of the cognitive limitations that babies display seem to result more from constraints on their capacity to process information than from the kinds of cognitive structures they have (Piaget's view). Third, babies may have a broader range of innate abilities and knowledge than Piaget thought. And lastly, the social context may have an

Executive processing space:
In Case's theory, "the maximum number of independent schemes a child can activate at any one time"; analogous to *working memory.*

even more powerful influence on infant development than Piaget acknowledged. In the next sections we will examine each of these issues in some detail.

REASSESSING THE CONCEPT OF STAGES

For each of the six sensorimotor stages Piaget proposed, he offered detailed
descriptions of how infants in that particular age range function when confronted with various tasks. Understanding the nature of objects is just one of
these tasks. In addition, Piaget investigated such tasks as imitating others,
understanding cause and effect, and understanding spatial relationships. He
implied that if an infant is at a particular stage with respect to understanding
objects, he or she should be at the same stage for other major tasks. Piaget
believed that certain general cognitive advances characterize each stage, so
these general advances should enable simultaneous progress in a number of different areas. Was Piaget correct in this assumption?

When Ina Uzgiris and J. McVicker Hunt (1975) tested a large number of
infants at different stages of sensorimotor development, they found a great deal
of inconsistency in what each baby had achieved. For instance, an infant might
be at stage 4 in understanding objects, but at stage 3 or 5 for other cognitive
tasks. No single ability seemed to develop in all infants first. One baby might be
most advanced in imitative skills, another in understanding cause and effect, a
third in understanding object permanence. Some researchers view this inconsistency as a major problem with Piaget's theory (Fischer, 1980; Gelman and Baillargeon, 1983). If it is a problem, at least Piaget was aware of it. He used the
term **décalage** to refer to the lack of simultaneous development in different
areas. Piaget has been criticized because he never adequately explained why
décalage occurs.

The phenomenon of décalage has led many researchers, including Kurt Fischer, to see cognitive development partly as the acquisition of *separate* skills and
understandings. Fischer (1980) argues that development entails both *general*
cognitive advances and constraints, like those Piaget described, and advances
and constraints that are related to *specific* areas. As a result, a baby's progress in
mastering any particular cognitive task is to some degree independent of the
child's progress in mastering other tasks. A baby's understanding of objects, for
instance, may be a level or two ahead of that child's grasp of cause and effect.
However, particular cognitive skills are not *entirely* independent of each other.
There is never a lag of more than a level or two in the development of different
skills.

Robert McCall and his colleagues have also studied the development of skills
during infancy, and their findings support Fischer's views (McCall, 1979). Like
Fischer, McCall uses the word *skill* to describe what babies develop, because he
analyzes their development in terms of what they can accomplish with their
behaviors. McCall believes that skills during the first 2 months of life are controlled by the baby's state. For example, when infants are in either of the two
awake states (awake and active or awake and quiet), they reflexively look at
high-contrast stimuli, visually track slow-moving objects, and become more alert
if they hear a new sound. Next, in the period from 2 to 7 months, infants
acquire skills that produce direct perceptual consequences—for example, shaking a rattle that makes a sound. The period from 7 to 13 months brings goal-oriented skills, such as pulling up a blanket to retrieve an object underneath it.
Finally, in the period after 13 months, representational skills, such as linking a
name with an object, develop. McCall found that at the beginning of each

Décalage:
The word used by Piaget to
describe the fact that the
child's ability to perform
cognitive tasks does not
seem to appear strictly
according to stages; that is,
an infant might be at stage
4 in ability to perform one
task but at another stage in
ability to perform a
different task.

period, not all the skills expected to emerge do so immediately. Instead, particular skills take time to develop, and babies differ as to which skills they acquire first (McCall, Eichorn, and Hogarty, 1977). According to McCall, development from one stage to the next occurs when some important new capacity is acquired. The new capacity allows infants to overcome previous obstacles, but specific experience is still needed for the development of particular skills.

REASSESSING INFANTS' COGNITIVE CONSTRAINTS

Piaget believed that infants' cognitive development was constrained by the sensorimotor nature of their cognitive structures. In his view, there are limits to what babies can learn and do because they cannot mentally represent things. Not all developmentalists agree with Piaget, however. Another possibility, raised in the theories of both Case and Fischer, is that constraints on cognitive development are caused at least in part by limits on information-processing capacity.

A number of concepts help describe the capacity to process information. One is **attention span,** a concept first proposed by James Mark Baldwin over a hundred years ago. Attention span refers to the number of items that a person can consider (hold in mind) at any one time (Case, 1985). The neo-Piagetian Juan Pascual-Leone (1970, 1976) proposed a related concept, **mental power,** often called "M-power" or "M-space." Pascual-Leone analyzed some of the skills that Piaget had studied in terms of the amount of mental power, or M-space, they require. Both these concepts are similar to Case's notion of executive processing space, discussed above. In this book we use the term **working memory** to refer to information-processing capacity, so as not to be tied to any one theory. To find a hidden toy, imitate another person, or apply a familiar strategy to a new situation, an infant must use working memory to remember things, initiate actions, and control what he or she does. If a baby's working memory becomes temporarily "filled" before a task is finished, the child faces a kind of information overload that stymies further progress.

Fischer has described various levels of cognitive development in terms of the information-processing capacity associated with each one (Fischer and Lazerson, 1984). At level 1, infants do not have enough capacity to manage more than one action at a time. As their processing capacity expands, however, they gradually advance, first to combining two related actions, then to coordinating several actions into a more complex system, and finally to forming single mental representations of actions. According to Fischer, when an infant initially reaches a new level of cognitive development, he or she remains there for some time, perhaps because performing the new abilities at first requires the entire capacity of working memory. But as working memory grows or as new abilities become more practiced and automatic, space is freed in working memory, allowing for further advances.

Researchers are gathering more and more information about the dramatic changes that occur in the brain during the first year of life, and Fischer (1987) has speculated about the connection between these changes and the development of cognitive abilities. Brain maturation might provide greater overall information-processing capacity; or experience and learning may cause changes in the brain that are associated with the development of specific skills. Case has suggested that with repeated practice, a child may start to perform a new skill as one large "chunk" of behavior rather than as a series of related but separate tasks. As a result, performing that skill no longer exceeds the capacity of working memory, and the child readily masters it (Case, 1985; Shatz, 1978). The skill

Attention span:
Baldwin's term for the limit on the number of mental elements that can be considered at any one time; analogous to *working memory.*

Mental power:
Pascual-Leone's term for the information-processing capacity of the infant or child; analogous to *working memory.*

Working memory:
The information-processing capacity available at any one time for the performance of a given cognitive task.

Older infants show great inter-est in exploring objects. Devel-opmentalists disagree about what babies this age know about objects—and, in partic-ular, about what categories of knowledge might be innate.

then becomes a building block for acquiring other abilities because the child can use it and still have room left over in working memory.

Working-memory theories of constraints on cognitive development seem plausible, but they have not been widely accepted. One reason is that researchers have not been able to measure either the capacity of working memory in infants or infants' ability to "chunk" pieces of information. Instead, information-processing theorists are simply hypothesizing changes in the size of or demands placed on working memory to account for the diminishing cognitive limitations that can be observed as babies grow older. More research is needed to test whether the capacity of an infant's working memory does in fact increase over time.

REASSESSING INFANTS' INBORN ABILITIES

We have seen that Piaget assumed that babies come equipped with only a set of reflexive behaviors and a tendency to actively engage the world. All other cognitive capacities, he argued, develop gradually over childhood. This view, that infants have relatively few inborn abilities, has been challenged by some contemporary developmentalists, known as **neo-nativists.** The neo-nativists have reintroduced into developmental psychology the idea that babies may have a relatively broad range of innate abilities and knowledge.

For example, Elizabeth Spelke (1985, 1988) argues that infants are born with a primitive object concept, and Frank Keil (1989) believes that an understanding of both objects and causation may be innate. Based on a review of studies on infants' cognitive skills, Jean Mandler (1990) has concluded that babies are much more competent, and more competent at earlier ages, than Piaget proposed. Among the studies challenging Piaget's notion that infants come equipped with only a set of reflexes are those described earlier in this chapter that deal with infants' early understanding of objects and numerosity. It appears that babies also have primitive understandings of some fairly complex concepts. New research techniques have allowed developmentalists to detect these previ-

Neo-nativist:
A developmental theorist who believes, in contrast to Piaget, in the existence of a wide range of sophisticated innate abilities yet who also stresses the importance of experience and the sequential acquisition of skills.

ously unsuspected abilities. The existence of very early competencies supports the view that certain skills and understandings are innate.

REASSESSING THE INFLUENCE OF SOCIAL CONTEXT ON DEVELOPMENT

Piaget argued that the role of the environment was to provide an overall context in which children could expore. This active exploration led naturally to cognitive growth. Neo-Piagetians and information-processing theorists frequently see the environment as providing more specific pieces of information or contexts for practicing more specific skills. However, many developmentalists, inspired by the work of Russian psychologist Lev Vygotsky, see both these views as far too limited in accounting for the influence of the environment. Consider the following observation:

> The young child is often thought of as a little scientist exploring the world and discovering the principles of its operation. We often forget that while the scientist is working on the border of human knowledge and finding out things that nobody yet knows, the child is finding out precisely what everybody knows. (Newman, 1982, cited in Rogoff, 1990)

When adults know what children should or must know, they may deliberately structure the environment to foster this learning. Formal schooling in middle childhood shows this kind of help most clearly (see Chapter 11), but there are many examples during infancy. The box on p. 194 mentions school-like training programs that seek to accelerate cognitive performance. Such programs illustrate two important features of social context. First, because the social context exists within a culture, it tends to emphasize development in areas that are culturally valued, which for much of the United States includes accelerated academic performance. Second, with help from adults, infants can learn to perform a variety of tasks at an earlier age than is typical.

You can see this phenomenon in media reports of infants or young children who are able to perform some challenging skill. According to *The Guinness Book of World Records,* Parks Bonifay learned to water-ski before the age of 8 months. We can be fairly sure that Parks did not acquire this skill simply by virtue of being raised in an environment in which water and water skis were available for him to explore freely. Rather, we would expect that this accomplishment resulted from a large amount of instructional effort by the adults around him. Further, we would expect to find that waterskiing and athletic prowess in general are highly valued in his family's subculture.

Piagetians have argued that such direct training is not really "development" because it consists only of isolated skills that are not part of an integrated system for doing, thinking, and understanding. In some cases the Piagetians may be correct, but there are other cases in which a skill taught early in life becomes an important component in later development. One example comes from a program at the University of California at Los Angeles that teaches older infants and young children to use computers to overcome disabilities due to cerebral palsy, Down syndrome, and a variety of other conditions. The computers help provide learning experiences that would be difficult for these children to have in a more "natural" environment. But the children must first be provided with an interface they can use and then be taught to interact with the computer. This direct training provides them with tools that allow for continued development in a number of important cognitive domains. From a Vygotskian perspective, a crucial characteristic of this program is that these children are taught skills by adults and then the children incorporate these skills into a system that fosters additional development.

The Vygotskian perspective makes several important observations that contribute to our understanding of cognitive development. First, infants frequently are more like guided tourists than like explorers as they develop cognitively. Second, infants in some cases can learn more rapidly from adults and in other cases are *only* able to learn things with substantial support from adults. Third, the skills that children learn from adults are almost always highly valued within those adults' social context or culture.

INDIVIDUAL DIFFERENCES IN INFANT COGNITIVE SKILLS

One day when Malcolm was 6 months old he reacted with genuine surprise when his brother J J made a finger puppet disappear up his sleeve. Malcolm's eyes widened and he strained forward in his seat, his brow slowly furrowing into a puzzled look. In contrast, when Meryl was 6 months old, Karen never noticed her reacting with obvious surprise to disappearing objects.

Research confirms that babies the same age often respond differently when presented with a given cognitive task. There are several possible explanations for these differences in performance. One is that babies differ in the states they are typically in. For instance, because Meryl is often fussy, she may frequently fail to notice or attend to disappearing things. If this is the case, how long and with what facial expression she stares at the space where an object disappeared may not be a good measure of her grasp of the situation. (Notice that this explanation attributes differences in performance to a factor that is irrelevant to the child's cognitive level. Differences in mood affect how easy it is to tell what the baby thinks and knows.)

Although most developmentalists acknowledge that explanations like this do have some validity, they also believe that there can be genuine differences in cognitive skills among babies the same age. For decades they have tried to find ways to measure these differences. The results are a number of tests of cognitive skills for infants and toddlers. These include the Bayley Scales of Infant Development, the Gesell Developmental Schedule, and the Cattell Intelligence Tests for Infants and Young Children. Table 5.2 shows some of the items contained in the Bayley Scales. Notice that the items designed to assess younger babies measure attention and sensorimotor coordination, while those designed to assess older infants and toddlers include yardsticks that are more cognitive in nature.

Developmentalists have wondered if a baby's performance on tests of infant cognitive skills is predictive of that child's performance on cognitive tests in later periods of development. In a longitudinal study that took many years to complete, Nancy Bayley (1949) attempted to find out by testing a group of children from age 3 months to 18 years. She found that test scores at different ages did not reliably correlate with one another until after a child was 4 years old. Many other researchers made similar findings. Measures of cognitive ability in infancy and toddlerhood were not very predictive of later IQ (e.g., Honzik, 1983). Many developmentalists took this to mean that individual differences in cognitive skills during infancy were not stable and therefore were probably not important in trying to understand how to optimize cognitive development.

Recently, however, a large number of studies have found that there *are* stable

TABLE 5.2
SELECT ITEMS FROM BAYLEY SCALES OF INFANT DEVELOPMENT

TO SCORE: CHECK P (PASS) OR F (FAIL). IF OTHER, MARK O (OMIT),
R (REFUSED), OR RPT (REPORTED BY MOTHER).

Item No.	Age Placement and Range (Months)	Item Title	SCORE			Notes
			P	F	Other	
1	0.1	Responds to sound of bell				
2	0.7 (.3–2)	Eyes follow moving person				
3	1.6 (.5–4)	Turns eyes to light				
4	1.9 (1–4)	Blinks at shadow of hand				
5	2.4 (1–5)	Reacts to disappearance of face				
6	3.1 (1–5)	Reaches for dangling ring				
7	3.8 (2–6)	Inspects own hands				
8	4.1 (2–6)	Reaches for cube				
9	4.4 (2–6)	Eye-hand coordination in reaching				
10	5.4 (3–12)	Smiles at mirror image				
11	5.8 (4–11)	Lifts cups with handle				
12	7.1 (5–10)	Pulls string adaptively: secures ring				
13	8.1	Uncovers toy				
14	9.1 (6–14)	Responds to verbal request				
15	10.4 (7–15)	Attempts to imitate scribble				
16	12.0 (8–18)	Turns pages of book				
17	12.5 (9–18)	Imitates words (Record words used)				
18	14.2 (10–23)	Says 2 words (Note words)				
19	16.7 (13–21)	Builds tower of 3 cubes				

differences in infant cognitive skills that *do* predict cognitive differences in later developmental periods. For instance, Robert McCall and Michael Carriger (1993) reviewed the results of 23 studies that measured infants' performance on memory tasks and then gave IQ tests to the same children when they were older. (Although IQ tests have limitations, as we will discuss in Chapter 11, they are the most commonly used assessment of individual differences in cognitive skills among older children and adults.) McCall and Carriger found across-age correlations of around .40; others have argued that the real correlation is closer to .25. Either figure suggests a low-to-moderate predictability of later IQ from early cognitive performance. Figure 5.6 illustrates the relationship between infant and later assessments that yields a correlation of around .40. In general, children who score higher on the infant tests also score higher on the later tests, but there is also a fairly large number of exceptions. Some children who score high in infancy score average or below average later. Others who score low or average as infants later perform well above average.

These results make two important points. First, although there is some predictability from infancy to later childhood, there is no indication that cognitive ability is biologically fixed early in development. On the contrary, the data suggest that experiences are always critical for the development of cognitive skills. Second, the magnitude of the correlation between infant tests and later perfor-

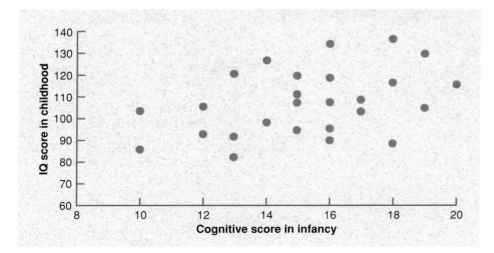

FIGURE 5.6

Illustrative data that exhibit a correlation of .40 between a cognitive measure in infancy and an IQ measure in childhood. Note that although higher cognitive scores in infancy are predictive of higher IQ scores in childhood, there is so much variability that you could not accurately predict a single child's IQ score by knowing the cognitive score that child achieved in infancy.

mance helps developmentalists understand the origin of individual differences in cognitive skills, but the correlation is too low to be useful in making judgments about the intellectual skills of individual infants. In fact, infants vary a great deal from day to day in performance on the tasks used on these tests, providing further evidence that caution is needed in drawing conclusions about the cognitive abilities of individual children from such test results.

You may wonder why the earlier tests of infants' cognitive skills were poor predictors of later IQ, whereas the newer tests are somewhat better. It may be that the earlier tests were measuring abilities different from those measured by IQ tests for older children and adults (Bornstein and Sigman, 1986; Fagan and McGrath, 1981). The newer tests, in contrast, may be measuring cognitive processing skills more like those assessed on traditional IQ tests. John Colombo (1993) believes that two variables measured on the newer infant tests are particularly important for good predictability of future IQ: speed of information processing and capacity of working memory. Colombo argues that individual differences in these two variables may be influenced by both heredity and experience. Interestingly, one of them, capacity of working memory, has also been used to explain developmental changes in cognitive skills.

ADVANCES AND LIMITATIONS: AN OVERVIEW

As babies grow older, their cognitive capacities change dramatically. From initially being limited to a set of inborn abilities, they develop an increasingly refined understanding of the world and an ever greater purposefulness to their behavior. These developmental trends are very important both in their own right and as preparation for the verbal world of the toddler.

Infants take an active role in influencing their own development. Through their efforts at mastery and the "mistakes" they make in the process, they learn to adapt their actions to better suit environmental demands. What babies learn is also influenced by the concepts they form to help make sense of their experiences. These concepts result from the infants' daily interactions with objects and other people.

Sometimes, influenced by current "experts," parents present their infants with special types of stimulation in hopes that they can dramatically advance their cognitive development. Thus, we hear of parents reading to a baby every night even *before* he or she is born, or buying flash cards of letters, words, or numbers to get a toddler started on the basics of reading and math.

Parents who take up the latest fad in infant stimulation are usually making two important errors in reasoning. *First,* they are assuming that if a certain kind of stimulation is good at one age, it must be good at other ages, and more of it is better than less. But what helps to foster optimal development in an older child is not necessarily helpful to the development of a younger one. Although flash cards may help a second grader master addition and subtraction, they have little value for a youngster who is only 12 months old. Parents of infants can do more to foster optimal cognitive development by devoting their time to normal interactions with their babies, such as talking to them often, responding to their vocalizations, and playing simple games like peekaboo.

Second, parents who adopt the latest fads in infant stimulation make the mistake of assuming that acceleration of some aspect of cognitive development will ultimately lead to higher levels of academic performance and a higher overall IQ. This, too, is a fallacy. Earlier does not necessarily mean better in the long run. The person who was taught to read at age 4 is not likely to be a better reader at age 21 than the person who started reading at the more typical age of 6.

WHEN STIMULATION PROGRAMS ARE IMPORTANT

Special programs for stimulating infants do have their place, however. Babies who are born prematurely are among those who can benefit from them. These infants are deprived of the tactile and motion stimulation they would normally experience in the uterus during the last weeks of gestation. In addition, prematurity is often associated with poverty and maternal stress, factors that can place babies at risk for developmental problems after birth.

Successful programs for premature infants provide stimulation suited to the age of the child. In the earliest weeks after birth, they are given tactile stimulation, including handling, rocking, and even the use of water beds. Such stimulation has been found to help prevent the motor and perceptual problems that can occur in preterm infants, and also to promote weight gain (Korner, 1989). The most likely explanation is that such stimulation promotes central nervous system develop-

ment, much the same way early visual and auditory stimulation promotes normal development of certain brain functions. (See box on p. 157.)

Longer-term programs, beginning after hospital discharge, typically provide more varied forms of stimulation for premature babies as well as support for their parents. In one program, for instance, families were visited weekly in their homes during the first year of the child's life, and the parents were helped to engage the baby in games and activities that fostered cognitive, language, and social development (Brooks-Gunn et al., 1993). In the second and third years, these visits occurred twice a month, the children attended a child development center daily, and a parents' support group met six times a year. Compared with children in a control group who received only routine pediatric care and referral services, the youngsters in this treatment program experienced cognitive benefits. At 24 months, they scored significantly higher on the Bayley Scales of Infant Development, and at 36 months they scored higher on the Wechsler Intelligence Scales for preschoolers. There had been no cognitive differences between the two groups at 12 months, confirming that all the children were similar at the outset and suggesting that the success of such programs accrues over time. This program also had an important social benefit in that it promoted a more effective parent-child collaboration (Spiker et al., 1993).

WHY INFANT STIMULATION IS EFFECTIVE

The various theoretical perspectives discussed in this chapter guide researchers in their decisions about the kinds of activities to include in programs for preterm infants and other babies at developmental risk. From a Piagetian perspective, the optimal environment for cognitive development is one that gives the infant opportunities to explore the world in ways appropriate to his or her current level of functioning. From an information-processing perspective, development in large part consists of elaborating an organized set of procedures and knowledge. Stimulation programs should provide specific experiences that fit into the knowledge structure that already exists. From a Vygotskian perspective, the child should not only be having appropriately stimulating experiences, but should also be developing an interaction system with caregivers that will support later social transmission of knowledge. The program described here, as well as other successful ones (e.g., Campbell and Ramey, 1991), does all of this by simultaneously providing stimulating, child-appropriate experiences and fostering social interaction between the child and adults.

Despite the great cognitive advances that take place during infancy, significant cognitive limitations remain. Babies cannot learn many of the things older children can, no matter how much training adults give them. Developmentalists may dispute the reasons for these cognitive constraints, but none deny that they exist. Discovering how such constraints affect a baby's view of the world remains a challenging task for developmentalists.

CHAPTER SUMMARY

1. Piaget identified six stages in what he called the **sensorimotor period** of cognitive development. He argued that these stages are invariant; all children go through them in the same order, even though their rates of progress may differ. In stage 1 (birth to 1 month), cognitive development is limited to minor refinements of the baby's inborn reflexes. In stage 2 (1 to 4 months), primary circular reactions emerge. A circular reaction involves a behavior that accidentally produces an observable event, which in turn leads to repetition of the behavior. A primary circular reaction is one that involves only a person's own body, rather than an external object. In stage 3 (4 to 8 months), secondary circular reactions emerge; now infants investigate the effects their actions have on external objects. In stage 4 (8 to 12 months), babies begin to coordinate their actions into goal-directed chains of behavior—the first clear sign of purposefulness in infants. In stage 5 (12 to 18 months), tertiary circular reactions appear, in which babies intentionally vary a behavior that produces an interesting consequence so as to further explore cause-and-effect connections. Finally, in stage 6 (18 to 24 months), symbolic, or representational, thought begins to emerge. Children now have mental images that stand for actual behaviors, people, and things.

2. Some studies of early cognitive development have focused on how babies come to understand that objects still exist even though they disappear from sight. This is called the concept of **object permanence.** Piaget argued that this concept emerges in stage 4 of the sensorimotor period, when babies begin to search for things that become hidden from view. Such searching indicates that they know the objects still exist somewhere. However, not until stage 6 do infants have a mature understanding of objects. At this stage they can imagine an object moving even though they do not see it move. Contemporary research suggests that while Piaget was correct in his general description of how the object concept develops, his timetable for its development may have been too conservative, and he may have been wrong in some of his ideas about

why babies make certain "mistakes" with regard to objects.

3. The study of early cognitive development has also focused on memory development. We know that even newborns must have some kind of memory, because they are able to habituate to stimuli. Still not clear is how long their memories last. Studies suggest that when babies forget things previously learned, the problem sometimes lies in lack of appropriate cues to help retrieve the memories. By the second half-year, there are many indications that babies are forming long-term memories. At this stage they also start to remember things in categories, and they reliably perceive and remember small numerosities. These are both important advances toward a more mature understanding of the world.

4. Piaget proposed the first comprehensive theory of cognitive development. Key assumptions in his theory are: (1) that children are actively involved in constructing their understandings of the world; and (2) that cognitive abilities at any stage are limited by the type of cognitive structures a child has developed. Infants' understandings of the world are limited to what they can know through perceptual skills and motor actions. In Piaget's view, cognitive development occurs because of two key processes: adaptation and equilibration. **Adaptation** is the process by which a person changes an existing way of thinking or behaving in order to function more effectively in a given situation. Adaptation involves two subprocesses: **assimilation** and **accommodation.** When children assimilate, they apply an existing capability to new circumstances. When children accommodate, they modify a strategy to meet new demands. **Assimilation** and **accommodation** together gradually transform inborn behaviors into sensorimotor **schemes,** or underlying cognitive structures, that can be applied to a variety of situations. **Equilibration** is the overall self-regulatory process that leads toward increasingly effective adaptations.

5. Critics of Piaget agree with his view of the infant as an active learner and with his emphasis on the role

of perceiving and doing in a baby's opportunities for cognitive growth. Disagreements center on his concept of broad, invariant developmental stages; his characterization of the constraints on infant cognitive development; his assumptions about inborn abilities; and his insufficient attention to social context and socially transmitted knowledge.

6. One difficulty with Piaget's concept of developmental stages is that a child's development does not always proceed evenly in all areas. Piaget acknowledged the existence of this phenomenon, which he called *décalage,* but he never adequately explained it. This unevenness in infants' development has led Kurt Fischer and other researchers to argue that cognitive development consists of the acquisition of relatively specific skills in addition to broad abilities.

7. Piaget believed that infants' cognitive development is constrained primarily by the sensorimotor nature of their cognitive structures. Other researchers, including Robbie Case, have suggested that it may be constrained by limitations on information-processing capacity. In particular, Case stresses the role of **executive processing space** in cognitive limitations. A similar concept, widely used in psychology, is **working memory.**

8. Piaget believed that infants' inborn capacities consist simply of reflexes and a predisposition toward active engagement with the world. In contrast, Bruner and the **neo-nativists** attribute a number of more sophisticated abilities to newborns, including a form of mental representation, intentional behavior, and a primitive understanding of objects and causality.

9. Piaget emphasized the role of the infant as junior scientist, growing cognitively by actively exploring the world and constructing an understanding of it from the ground up. In contrast, developmentalists in the Vygotskian tradition emphasize the role played by others in transmitting—or helping the child discover—knowledge that is already available to older members of the society. They explain that the skills and information that are valued by a group are usually those for which the greatest efforts at social transmission are made.

10. Babies the same age sometimes differ in how well they perform on cognitive tasks. Researchers have tried to develop tests to measure these differences in infants' cognitive abilities. Performance on the first tests was not predictive of a child's later IQ. But more recent assessments of infants' cognitive skills, particularly those that include measures of information-processing speed and working-memory capacity, are better at predicting future performance on traditional intelligence tests. This is not to say that cognitive abilities are biologically fixed at birth. Experience always plays a critical role in the development of cognitive skills. Additionally, these tests are still too unreliable to provide good information about individual children.

11. In summarizing cognitive development in the first 2 years of life, three general themes stand out. First, a baby's present abilities pave the way for future accomplishments. The reflexive skills of the newborn, for instance, provide the building blocks for later, more advanced abilities. Second, all infants are active participants in their own development. By seeking out new experiences and trying to master their environment, they give themselves opportunities to grow cognitively. Third, infant cognitive development is marked by both advances and limitations. Although children acquire numerous abilities during their first 2 years, many things remain beyond their understanding.

Chapter 6

Infant Social and Emotional Development

Chapter 6

Infant Social and Emotional Development

One day when Mikey Gordon was 4 months old, he woke up early from his morning nap. Cooing contentedly to himself, he began kicking his legs. The toys on his crib gym jangled, and he kicked some more. Then he waved his arms and batted a bright red ring, gurgling happily as it bobbed in response. Christine arrived and stood by the crib, smiling down at the baby. Mikey's face brightened. He broke into a broad grin and kicked his feet harder.

Eight months later, Uncle Dan was showing 12-month-old Mikey a new mechanical toy. When he released it, it made a loud clacking noise. Frightened, Mikey turned away and scurried to Christine, raising his arms to be picked up. In her arms he looked at the toy again and began smiling and pointing at it.

This chapter is about the beginnings of emotion and the emergence of a child's attachment relationships with caregivers, usually the parents. Such relationships are the culmination of all cognitive, social, and emotional development in the first year of life. To become a social partner, a baby must be attracted to social encounters; human faces and voices must engage the child's interest. With development, the infant must learn to sustain attention, to follow complex changes in another person's voice and face. In addition, the infant must learn to tolerate the excitement caused by social stimulation. Soon the baby begins to go beyond reacting to others; the coordinated turn-taking of more advanced social interaction emerges. When 6-month-old Mikey smiles and kicks his feet, his father or mother touches and talks to him. Mikey chortles and kicks again, and his parent smiles and touches him some more.

For Mikey to form a true attachment to Christine, as distinct from other people, he must learn to differentiate her from others. He must do more than simply recognize his mother; he must understand that she is a specific, "constant" person. This understanding is related to the concept of object permanence we discussed in Chapter 5, a concept that emerges in the second half-year. By the time Mikey is 8 or 10 months old he will show his understanding that Christine is a specific, constant person by becoming distressed when she temporarily leaves him with someone unfamiliar. He will know that his mother still exists even when out of sight, and when distressed he will want her *specifically*. Given his involvement with Frank, Mikey will show many similar reactions with him.

As you learned in Chapter 5, the second half-year is also the time babies develop both expectations and purposefulness. The 8-month-old is surprised when an object "magically" vanishes, angry when an intended action is thwarted, and joyous when a goal is achieved. Events and feelings are now intimately connected; perception, cognition, and emotion are all integrated (Sroufe, in press). Experiences are categorized partly by the emotions associated with them. For example, a 10-month-old may react negatively to a doctor *immediately* upon sight, evaluating the doctor in terms of the feelings she or he has generated in the past.

Attachments between infants and caregivers develop in the context of this differentiating emotional and social world. By the end of the first year, an infant feels secure in the presence of his or her caregivers, turns to them purposefully when distressed (as 12-month-old Mikey did when frightened by the new mechanical toy), and organizes play and exploration around them. The caregivers take center stage in the child's world and provide the basis for many of the baby's expectations about whether or not the environment is responsive.

In this chapter we trace the infant's emerging capacity for social relations from the very first weeks of life. How does a newborn, with only primitive reflexes, develop into an active social partner who can anticipate another's actions, respond to social overtures, and even purposefully direct social give-and-take? The answer lies in a developmental process that we will explore in the chapter's first major section. In the second major section we consider social and emotional development in the second half-year. We examine how infants acquire specific attachments to their principal caregivers, and how such relationships affect their growing capacities for emotional expression and regulation. In the third major section we discuss individual differences in social and emotional development. What determines the particular quality of an infant's attachment relationships and the child's particular style of reacting to things? Finally, we turn to the overall importance of early care. Here we discuss whether early experience has a special significance for a child's development.

Six-month-old infants will laugh in response to vigorous stimulation.

DEVELOPMENT IN THE FIRST HALF-YEAR

For decades researchers have been probing the competencies of the newborn. This subject has produced two extreme views: one historical, the other more recent. The historical view is closely associated with the nineteenth-century psychologist William James. James believed that human infants are born with no perceptual or social skills whatsoever. Their world is meaningless and chaotic, a "blooming, buzzing confusion." Directly opposing this outlook is the more recent view that newborns are socially quite advanced, able to imitate complex behaviors, to infer another person's perspective, and to feel disappointment when social expectations aren't met (Meltzoff and Moore, 1989; Trevarthan, 1977). This view sees even very young infants as possessing desires, expectations, purpose, and even will.

From a developmental perspective neither of these views is satisfactory. The first is at odds with much contemporary research. As discussed in Chapter 4, newborns have many competencies; their world is not a meaningless confusion. The second view, while a useful antidote to the first, also runs counter to some important current findings. For instance, the cortex of a baby's brain, which is used for thinking and reasoning, is not fully functional at birth (see Figure 4.1, p. 124). Interconnections among cortical neurons are not well established, so it is hard to imagine how a baby could possess expectations and purpose (Collins and Depue, 1992; Nelson, 1994). Moreover, we need not assume that newborns are socially competent in order to account for some of the things they soon become able to do. All we need to assume is that their simpler capacities prepare or "preadapt" them to become part of a social system under normal caregiving circumstances.

A caregiver's response to the newborn's cry begins a pattern of communication that will be refined over time.

THE NEWBORN AS PREADAPTED TO SOCIAL EXCHANGES

In the modern developmental perspective, newborns are seen as coming equipped with certain predispositions that enable them to participate in early social exchanges, provided that they are part of a responsive caregiving system (Ainsworth and Bell, 1974; Fogel, 1993; Sander, 1975). These predispositions are what we mean when we say that the newborn is *preadapted* to becoming social. But note that a certain developmental context is needed for this social potential to unfold, much as the turning on of genes in certain cells depended on surrounding cells during prenatal development (see Chapter 3). If caregivers provide the baby with appropriate stimulation and are responsive to the child's inborn reactions, then—and only then—will coordinated social exchanges be possible, exchanges that will ultimately lead to genuine social partnerships (Schore, 1994).

One predisposition of newborns that sets the stage for early social exchanges is a built-in ability to "signal" psychological and physiological needs in ways that adults can interpret and are likely to respond to. These early signals often take the form of the newborn's lusty cries. Babies cry whenever their nervous systems are overly excited, whether that overexcitement is due to hunger, cold, pain, or simply too much stimulation (a loud noise, for example, or even excessive touching and patting). Note that newborns' cries are as purely reflexive as a shiver when you are cold. Young babies do not cry to be defiant or "get their way." A newborn's cry is not intentional. Nevertheless, this cry becomes the precursor of a true social signal when caring adults respond by administering to the baby's needs. This is a subtle but important point: a newborn's behaviors serve the function of social communication only to the extent that others treat those behaviors as communications (Fogel, 1993).

Another predisposition of newborns that helps to make early social exchanges possible is the capacity to detect contingencies in the environment (discussed in Chapter 4). Infants notice events caused by their behaviors and repeat the behaviors over and over (Dunham and Dunham, 1990; Papoušek et al., 1986). Significantly, the events they produce are often reactions in their caregivers, such as getting mother to smile and talk by looking at her. A sensitivity to these contingencies preadapts infants to become part of a social system (Brazelton and Cramer, 1990).

Closely related to the newborn's inclination to detect and respond to contingencies is a built-in inclination to be attracted to social stimuli. For instance, as discussed in Chapter 4, the newborn's visual system is designed in such a way that the baby is naturally attentive to light/dark contrasts and to movement (Salapatek and Banks, 1967; Schore, 1994). Since adult faces have several light/dark contrasts and adults tend to smile and nod when looking at a baby, a newborn is innately drawn to faces. This attraction does not occur because the baby recognizes the social significance of faces, but simply because the child's visual system is especially sensitive to the kind of stimulation that faces provide. The newborn's inspection of faces is further encouraged by the fact that caregivers tend to hold their heads about 8 inches away from a baby when interacting face-to-face. This close distance is ideal for a newborn's limited visual acuity.

In a strikingly parallel way, newborns are also predisposed to respond to human speech. Babies discriminate among different speech sounds at a very early age, and they can hear quite well in the pitch range of human voices, including the squeaky baby-talk voice that many parents use (Fogel, 1993; Moffitt, 1971). In addition, newborns have built-in coordination between their hearing and their head movements. They turn automatically in the direction of a voice and look at the face of the person who is speaking.

A final predisposition that helps the newborn become part of a social system is the baby's tendency to "fall in step" with the caregiver's behavior (Fogel, 1993). Consider a study in which babies soon to be given up for adoption were cared for 24 hours a day by one of two nurses, Nurse A or Nurse B (Sander, 1975). Compared with Nurse B, Nurse A did not respond as quickly to her babies' cries of distress, but when she did respond her caretaking was less hurried and less perfunctory. Nurse B's behavior was somewhat abrupt and fragmented. Within 10 days, the infants in Nurse A's charge were more regular in their sleeping and eating patterns than those cared for by Nurse B. The behavior of Nurse A's babies, in other words, seemed to mirror her own easygoing style. Even more striking, when the infants were suddenly switched from one nurse to the other, they showed marked disruptions in sleeping and eating. Apparently, babies have a built-in inclination to adapt to the kind of care they receive.

What we observe in a newborn baby, then, is a range of tendencies and abilities that prepare the child to enter the social world very rapidly. Yet if you ask whether the newborn is innately social, the answer would have to be no—not in the sense of being able to have organized, intentional interaction with other people. The newborn, however, is exquisitely attuned to *becoming* social, provided that responsive social partners are available. The development of this true social give-and-take is the subject we turn to next.

THE ORIGINS OF RECIPROCITY

Over the first few months of life, developmental changes take place that set the stage for the emergence of true social interactions involving mutual exchanges, or **reciprocity,** between the partners. One of the developmental changes underlying reciprocity is the baby's ability to stay alert for increasingly long periods, during which he or she actively engages the environment. At the same time, the infant becomes able to control attention, coordinate looking and reaching, and turn toward or away from stimulation *voluntarily*. Coupled with this is the baby's

Reciprocity: True social interactions involving mutual exchanges between infant and caregiver.

By 6 months of age, infants can coordinate their looking and reaching, leading to more complex interaction with their caregivers.

ability to punctuate attentive looking with smiles, coos, and actions. Parents take advantage of these newfound capacities to build longer and more complex chains of interaction with their infants. Consider this example of John Williams interacting with Malcolm when he is 4 months old:

> Hi there, big fella. Whatcha lookin' at? Can you look at me? That's right. Hey! Your ol' man's gonna get ya. Yes he is. (Brief pause.) He's gonna get ya and gobble ya right up. What do you think of that? Come on. Come on, you little tiger. Let me see those gums. Hmmm? (Pause.) Yeah, that's right . . . that's right. (Malcolm smiles broadly and bobs his head. His father responds in kind.) Well, now, are ya gonna say somethin'? Are ya? (Another pause during which John nods his head and widens his eyes.) Come on! (He pauses again, and Malcolm starts cycling his arms and kicking his feet.) Come oooon! (Longer pause. Then Malcolm gurgles happily.) Yeah, that right! (John's smile broadens and he laughs.)

Social learning theorists would emphasize the mutual reinforcement experienced at the end of this sequence: both father and son have derived pleasure from it. But researchers have also pointed out the importance of the broader learning context. Notice how John stages, or "frames," this interaction (Fogel, 1993; Stern, 1985). First he waits for a time when Malcolm seems receptive. Then he creates a proper climate for the baby to respond by beginning with gentle vocal and visual stimulation. Next he builds Malcolm's interest by varying the stimulation and gradually increasing its intensity. He takes cues from Malcolm about the timing of his words and actions. Equally important, John pauses often and waits for Malcolm's responses, thus creating opportunities for Malcolm to take his turn in the shared "dialogue," and for John to reinforce Malcolm's vocal behavior. Detailed observational studies have shown how exchanges between caregivers and infants become more varied and complex through such interactions over time (Papoušek et al., 1986).

T. Berry Brazelton, who has studied parent-infant dialogues extensively, sees the caregiver as providing a "holding" framework for the baby. She or he holds the infant with hands, eyes, voice, smile, and with changes from one form of stimulation to another. "All these holding experiences are opportunities for the infant to learn how to contain himself, how to control motor responses, how to attend for longer and longer periods. They amount to a kind of learning about organization of behavior in order to attend" (Brazelton, Kowslowski, and Main, 1974). Such shared emotional experiences may also provide the foundation for later empathy and moral development (Damon, 1988).

Again, note that infants can play their part and share in the joyful outcome only if caregivers appropriately guide the interaction (Brazelton and Cramer, 1990; Fogel, 1993; Hayes, 1984). In our example, John must allow the level of tension to rise and fall in its natural course until the joy spills over. He cannot *force* interactions on Malcolm when he is unreceptive. If Malcolm temporarily looks away to slow the pace of the stimulation, John cannot pursue him or else Malcolm is likely to cry. John must wait for Malcolm to indicate his readiness to continue (see Figure 6.1).

The parent's role in such interactions is clearly quite complex. The parent must draw forth and enhance the infant's attention and involvement, pacing and modifying the stimulation in coordination with signs from the child. Daniel Stern (1985) and Mary Ainsworth call this process "attunement." It is part of a more general style of behavior known as **sensitive care** (Ainsworth et al., 1978). Sensitive care involves being aware of a baby's feelings and needs and respond-

Sensitive care:
A caregiving style in which the caregiver fits his or her own behavior to the perceived wants and needs of the infant.

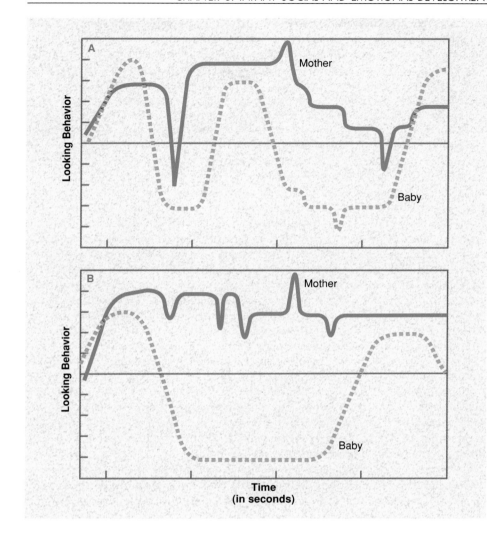

FIGURE 6.1 SENSITIVE AND INSENSITIVE INTERACTIONS
These figures show the reactions of two different mothers to their babies' efforts to pace the interaction by turning away. The dashed line shows the baby's looking behavior. When the dashed line is below the horizontal center line, the baby is looking away from the mother. The solid line shows the mother's behaviors (talking, touching, making faces, etc.). The mother in part (A) shows a pattern of sensitive care, reducing her stimulation when the baby looks away; he soon looks back to her and she stimulates again. The mother in part (B) keeps stimulating her baby, which seems to keep him away for a long time. (Source: Adapted from Brazelton, Koslowski, and Main, 1974.)

ing to them promptly and effectively. Sensitive caregivers do not overstimulate an infant by continuing stimulation when the child is not ready for it; nor are they chronically unresponsive to the baby. Sensitive care is something that can be learned in the natural course of tending to a baby. Through hours of interaction most parents become able to read the moods and signals of their infant and modify their own behavior accordingly. At its best, this coordinated interaction has the grace of a dance in which each partner's movements cue the other's (Fogel, 1993).

The beginnings of this intricate coordinated interaction can be seen in the first few weeks (Fogel, 1993). Consider the feeding of a newborn. As we mentioned in Chapter 4, a newborn's sucking is organized into a burst-pause pattern: a succession of rapid sucks is followed by a period during which little or no sucking occurs. Lower brain regions control this pattern; the baby does not intentionally produce it. Yet caregivers often interpret the pause as a cue to respond by stroking, cuddling, or talking to the infant (Kaye and Wells, 1980). In this way, a kind of turn-taking emerges. The baby sucks, then pauses; next the caregiver talks and moves; then the baby starts sucking again. The caregiver is behaving as if the baby's pauses were intended to elicit some response, but in fact, this is only a pseudo-dialogue (Hayes, 1984). The caregiver is single-handedly orchestrating the pattern by coordinating his or her behavior to the baby's sucking reflex. Through such coordination, however, the infant is probably learning to associate burst-pause sucking cycles with caregiver behavior. More generally, the child is being initiated into the turn-taking that is characteristic of human communication.

Soon the baby's involvement in social encounters becomes more complex (Papoušek et al., 1986). By age 3 or 4 months, infants have acquired many behaviors that can be used in interactions—everything from smiles and other facial expressions to a rich range of coos, gurgles, and sounds. Even more important, babies this age have very mature control over their head movements, so they have substantial influence over the type of stimulation they pay attention to and over its pacing. When social overtures are dull and repetitive and the child's arousal level falls too low, he or she will typically search for something more interesting to look at. Conversely, when social overtures become too arousing, a baby will typically turn away as if to reduce the stimulation temporarily, or perhaps to process it. Ideally, the caregiver is sensitive to such cues from the infant for more, less, or different stimulation. The baby, in short, has a "voice" in how the interaction unfolds, and very early develops primitive expectations about the course of interactions (Stern, 1985).

Reciprocity is learned gradually, with each advancement setting the stage for another one. The process is analogous to teaching Ping-Pong to a child (Sroufe and Ward, 1984). First you simply hit the ball right to the child's paddle so it can bounce back without much active involvement on the part of the child. The child's shots may go anywhere, and it is up to you to keep the ball moving and to maintain the appearance of a game. Next, you encourage the child to start to swing the paddle and gradually to learn how to aim the ball. Social learning theorists refer to this gradual teaching process as *shaping*. In time, the youngster becomes a full participant in the give-and-take. So it goes with the development of reciprocity. Over the first year of life, the infant gradually becomes a fuller partner in social interactions.

BECOMING AN ACTIVE PARTICIPANT: THE EXAMPLE OF SOCIAL SMILING

The emergence of reciprocity that we have been describing is typical of how social skills emerge in a baby's earliest months. In the beginning an infant does not consciously seek out social interaction. The child is merely attracted to certain patterns of stimulation. From these rudimentary beginnings the child gradually develops into a purposeful, social being. This development is made possible not only by maturation of the baby's brain but also by the caregiver's responses to the baby (Schore, 1994). The newborn's behavior normally prompts adults to provide stimulation that leads the infant toward more focused and organized interaction. Since this interaction is pleasurable for both the infant and the caregiver, it tends to be repeated. Gradually, the caregiver provides richer stimulation and encourages more participation from the baby. Ultimately, in a spiraling fashion, genuine social partnerships develop as the behavior of each member of the pair fits with that of the other.

An excellent example of this developmental process can be seen in the emergence of a baby's social smiling. Imagine Christine in the hospital soon after Mikey is born. She has just finished nursing him, and as he drifts off to sleep the corners of his mouth twist up in a tiny smile. Christine is elated. She is sure that Mikey is "telling" her that he is warm, full, and content. Like Christine, many parents attribute to very young infants emotions such as joy, anger, fear, and surprise (Emde, 1985). Such feelings on Christine's part are natural and play an important role in the developing relationship with the infant.

Technically, however, Christine's interpretation is not correct. Newborns' smiles do not really indicate pleasure; they are due merely to spontaneous discharges in lower brain regions. Researchers draw this conclusion partly because newborns smile almost solely during sleep (Emde, Gaensbauer, and Harmon, 1976). If their smiles were a sign of pleasure, they would occur when wide awake as well. Other evidence comes from the study of premature infants and those born without a cerebral cortex (the part of the brain that controls higher mental activities). The newborn smile is more common in these babies than it is in normal children. This suggests the involvement of lower brain regions, as does the fact that in normal babies the newborn sleep smile disappears as the cortex matures.

You may wonder what happens in lower brain regions during sleep to cause a newborn to smile. The answer seems to be a temporary rise above, followed by a drop below, some critical threshold of arousal, leading the facial muscles to relax into a little smile (see Figure 6.2). In keeping with this theory, a newborn who is sleeping lightly will tend to smile some 5 to 8 seconds after you gently shake a rattle. It takes time for the newborn's arousal level to rise slightly and then fall, bringing on the smile. Also, if you gently shake a sleeping baby toward wakefulness, you will get a series of little smiles. Finally, if you startle a sleeping newborn, causing the arousal level to shoot up, no sleep smiles occur for quite some time. All this suggests that arousal fluctuations around some low threshold are what cause the newborn's smiles (Sroufe, 1995).

Newborn sleep smile. Note that the mouth is closed and that there is no crinkling of the skin beside the eyes.

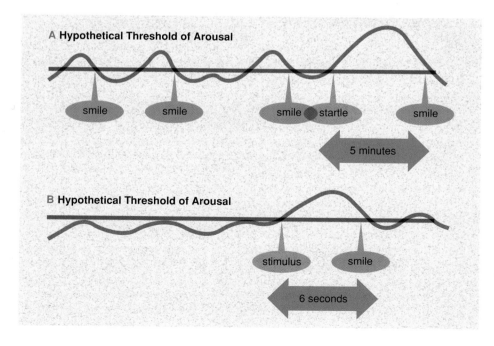

FIGURE 6.2
HYPOTHETICAL THRESHOLD OF AROUSAL
The newborn's smiles during sleep are due to fluctuations in central nervous system arousal or excitation. These may occur spontaneously, as is shown in part (A), when the infant's depth of sleep changes. Notice that following a startle reaction, it is some time before the excitation falls below the arousal threshold (the green line) and the smile recurs. Sleep smiles may also occur following stimulation, as shown in part (B). Here a rattle is shaken, and 6 seconds later a smile occurs.

Even though Christine is technically wrong in the meaning she gives to Mikey's first smiles, she is correctly anticipating what is to come. These winsome little expressions strike a chord within her, drawing her closer to the baby. Just as infants are preadapted to interact with adults, adults are preadapted to interact with infants. Over the next few weeks Mikey will begin to smile when he is awake, as Christine talks to him, nuzzles him, and gently claps his hands together. She will spend quite a bit of time engaged with him, partly because his smiling and cooing are so rewarding to her (Stern, 1985). Like most parents, she will interpret her baby's behavior as more advanced and "intelligent" than it really is. For instance, at 5 weeks, when Mikey grins and coos as Christine chirps at him, she assumes it is because he has a special liking for her voice. In fact, *any* gentle stimulation (music boxes, bells tinkling on his crib) can produce the proper degree of excitation to elicit a smile (Sroufe, 1995). Soon, however, Christine's voice *will* be special to Mikey.

At 8 to 10 weeks, Mikey begins to smile when Christine's face appears above his looking down into his crib. He is not smiling because he visually "knows" her, as Christine might think. At this age Mikey's smiles are not reserved for his mother. He smiles when the kicking of his feet makes his mobile turn, when his sister repeatedly presents him with the same stuffed bear, and when *any* face appears before him (Shultz and Zigler, 1970; Sroufe, 1995). These smiles are due to a form of visual mastery called **recognitory assimilation** (Piaget, 1952; Zelazo, 1972). With effort, Mikey is making sense of some familiar object; he is recognizing it as something he has seen before. In Piaget's terms, he is assimilating an event to an established scheme. The effort causes tension, which is broken by recognition, and the smile follows. Again you see fluctuations in arousal leading to a smile, but here those fluctuations are due to cognitive effort and assimilation. Turning mobiles, dangling clown dolls, and human faces can all be assimilated with effort at age 10 weeks, so all produce smiles. Since these smiles are related to the meaning of the events for Mikey, it is appropriate to say that he is now smiling in pleasure. The mastery of recognition, in other words, is an enjoyable experience for him.

Christine's natural feeling of being special to Mikey serves to encourage further interaction. By age 3 months Mikey can discriminate familiar from unfamiliar faces and prefers to look at familiar ones. Then, by age 4 or 5 months, he not only can discriminate Christine's face from other people's but also reacts specifically to her face. At this point he stops smiling at strangers (Sroufe, 1995). His smiles are reserved for people he knows. Now his mother's and father's faces really are special to him. His parents' responses to this specialness, stimulated by Mikey's truly social smiles, promote his ongoing development.

In summary, Mikey's social development is a product of the interplay between him and his parents. Partly on the basis of Mikey's responses when his parents talk to and play with him, Christine and Frank experience meaning in these interactions. That meaning prompts them to continue their attentions toward Mikey and to elaborate the stimulation they provide him. In time, with cognitive maturation, Mikey comes to share in the meaning of the social exchanges. By 10 weeks he feels pleasure in interacting with his parents; by 4 or 5 months he visually recognizes Christine and Frank as distinct from other people. Gradually he comes to participate reciprocally in the games they play, even initiating them. Thus, what were at first merely built-in reactions to the stimulation his parents provided have led to remarkable social behavior by the end of Mikey's first 6 months.

Recognitory assimilation: A form of visual mastery in which the infant reacts to stimuli that are similar to stimuli he or she has previously encountered.

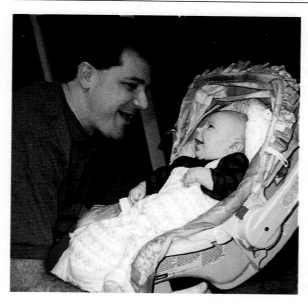

This 3-month-old, attracted by his father's voice and recognizing his face, smiles broadly.

DEVELOPMENT IN THE SECOND HALF-YEAR

As extraordinary as development is in the first 6 months, it is equally rapid and far-reaching in the second 6. Cognitively, the second half-year is a period during which the baby is increasingly able to differentiate among persons. More and more, the child is recognizing people as separate, independent entities who act and can be acted upon. At the same time, the infant is developing the capacity for intentional behavior and with it a rudimentary sense of self (Emde, 1989; Sroufe, 1990; Stern, 1985). These advances have important implications for the emergence of many sophisticated emotions, such as anger, fear, sadness, and joy, as well as for the capacity to regulate and control emotions.

Also in the second half-year of life, the baby's social behavior becomes increasingly organized around the principal caregivers, with a purposefulness not seen in earlier months. Ten-month-old Malcolm greets his mother joyfully and purposefully seeks her out when he is distressed. These behaviors indicate that he has formed a specific attachment to her, a special closeness and sense of security in her presence. This specific attachment, which also occurs with fathers and other regular caregivers (such as Malcolm's grandmother), is one of the major developmental landmarks of infancy.

Developments in the second half-year are so dramatic that they can be considered qualitative advances, not just quantitative ones. Remember from Chapter 1 the enormous difference that exists between the 6-month-old and the 10-month-old when confronted with the sight of mother with a cloth dangling from her mouth. The older baby is a fundamentally different child from the younger one. This difference was demonstrated in a classic study on the effects of hospitalization during infancy (Schaffer and Callender, 1959). Babies older than 7 months protested being hospitalized, were negative toward the hospital staff, and needed a period of readjustment after returning home, during which they showed much insecurity centered on their mothers. Apparently, disruption in the relationship with the mother was the core of the problem. Babies younger than 7 months, in contrast, had none of these adverse reactions. They had not yet undergone the critical emotional changes that occur during the second half-year. In the section that follows we'll take a look at some of these changes.

EMOTIONAL DEVELOPMENT

There are two aspects of emotional development. The first is the *emergence of the various emotions,* such as joy, fear, anger, and sorrow. Some researchers have argued that all these emotions are present in the earliest weeks of life, because young infants sometimes show the culturally universal facial expressions associated with them (e.g., Izard and Malatesta, 1987). However, in the early months negative emotional expressions are not easily distinguished from each other and are more reasonably viewed as differing in intensity rather than as reflecting specific different emotions (Matias and Conn, 1992; Oster et al., 1992). For example, as newborns become more and more distressed, their body movements and facial changes suggest "anger," but such reactions are quite distinct from anger reactions in the second half-year, which may be immediate and are focused on an obstacle blocking a goal. Thus converging evidence suggests that basic emotions emerge over the course of infancy.

The second aspect of emotional development (which is closely related to the first) is *emotional regulation,* the capacity to control and modulate emotion. Gradually babies acquire the ability to deliberately attend to or ignore stimulation and to otherwise modify their reactions to the environment. Many of the early techniques they use require cooperation from the caregiver, as when Mikey signaled his mother to pick him up when he was frightened by Uncle Dan's new toy. In time, however, children gain considerable control over their own emotional lives.

THE EMERGENCE OF EMOTIONS

Emotion:
A subjective relationship between a person and an event, characterized by a particular feeling state.

If we define **emotions** as states of feeling that arise when a person psychologically processes certain kinds of events, then by age 3 months infants certainly experience emotion. We saw emotion when 10-week-old Mikey smiled after effortful recognition of a human face. No longer does Mikey smile merely because of physical stimulation, such as being jostled. Now he smiles because of his success at imposing a primitive form of meaning on the world. The accompanying state of feeling is the genuine emotion of pleasure.

Emotional reactions in the second half-year are both more frequent than, and fundamentally different from, those in the first half-year (Lewis and Michaelson, 1989; Papoušek et al., 1986; Sroufe, 1995). Reactions in the first half-year often require some time to build up (Bronson and Pankey, 1977; Sroufe, 1995). Three-month-old Meryl may smile at a toy clown, but only after several presentations of it. Five-month-old Malcolm may become intensely distressed when he cannot reach a toy in front of his infant seat, but only after looking at it and straining to reach it for some time. In the second half-year, in contrast, emotional reactions may be immediate (Camras et al., 1992), and they are in response to the particular meaning of an event (Sroufe, 1995). By this time infants can recall past experiences, anticipate outcomes, and behave intentionally.

Laughing while pulling a cloth from the caregiver's mouth and stuffing it back in is not based simply on recognition of the caregiver and the cloth, but on the anticipated consequences of an action. Such an immediate positive emo-

Surprise, like fear and anger, is one of many emotional reactions that emerge in the second half year. Shown here is an example of the classic surprise expression, first seen at this time.

tional reaction may be called *joy*. Likewise, an 8- to 10-month-old may immediately become upset when pursuing a ball that has rolled beneath a couch or show negative reactions upon seeing an adult in a white lab coat following a trip to the doctor for shots. Such reactions are examples of genuine *anger* and *fear*, in contrast to the proto-emotions of the first half-year. Genuine *surprise*, too, is apparent in the second half-year. It is elicited when something unexpected happens, as when a toy suddenly disappears through a trapdoor in a high chair tray (Hiatt, Campos, and Emde, 1979). All the classic facial expressions of emotions, which are fleeting and irregular in the first half-year, appear quite regularly by the end of infancy (Izard and Malatesta, 1987; Oster et al., 1992).

EMOTIONAL REACTIONS TO THE UNFAMILIAR

As infants come to know objects and people in their world and to have expectations about them, they experience some events as novel or unfamiliar. By the end of the first year, reactions to the unfamiliar are quite varied and complex. A widely studied topic is reactions to unfamiliar adults. While at 3 months of age babies smile at all faces rather indiscriminately, by 5 months they begin to smile preferentially at caregivers. If a stranger locks a 5-month-old in a fixed stare, the baby often peruses the stranger soberly and then starts crying after 30 seconds or so (Bronson and Pankey, 1977). A few months later (usually between ages 7 and 10 months), babies begin to react negatively to strangers even without prolonged inspection of them (see Figure 6.3). This **stranger distress** usually continues for 2 or 3 months, sometimes extending into the second year (Emde, Gaensbauer, and Harmon, 1976; Waters, Matas, and Sroufe, 1975). The degree of stranger distress varies greatly from baby to baby. At its most intense, it has all the earmarks of real fear, with wary looks followed by turning away, pulling

Stranger distress:
The negative reaction to strangers which babies begin to exhibit at about 5 months of age and which increases in intensity between the ages of 7 and 10 months; it continues for 2 or 3 months and sometimes extends into the second year.

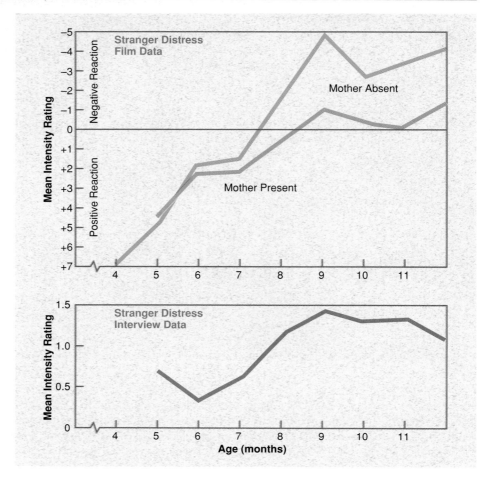

FIGURE 6.3 THE ONSET OF STRANGER DISTRESS

Several studies have demonstrated a notable increase in wariness toward strangers in the second half year. This developmental trend is illustrated here in both filmed reactions of infants and maternal reports from interviews. (Source: Data from Emde, Gaensbauer, and Harmon, 1976.)

away, and occasional whimpering and crying. Significantly, at this same age, infants first show fear in other situations, such as high places or impending collisions (Hruska and Yonas, 1971; Schwartz, Campos, and Baisel, 1973; Sroufe, 1995).

Research shows that this distress reaction toward strangers does not just reflect a wariness toward unfamiliar things in general. A 10-month-old's mother can do something highly novel, like cover her face with a mask in the infant's presence and then approach the child, and the result will usually be squeals of delight. Yet if a stranger dons a mask and approaches, the baby typically gets upset; and if, after this, the mother approaches with the *same* mask, the infant also becomes distressed (Sroufe et al., 1974). All these events are novel, so it is not novelty alone that elicits a negative reaction. In fact, mother putting on a mask after a stranger does so should be *less* novel than when mother put on the mask first. Clearly, novel events can be either frightening or delightful, depending on how secure the baby feels in the context.

The context also influences reactions to strangers without masks. In a standard stranger-response study, a stranger greets an infant from the doorway of a room, then gradually approaches and picks the baby up. Although babies may smile at the stranger from a distance, they become alarmed when the stranger walks over and tries to lift them (Water, Matas, and Sroufe, 1975). The more rapidly the stranger approaches and the more intrusively he or she behaves, the more likely the baby is to become distressed. Familiar surroundings, however, can greatly reduce stranger distress. Babies show less fear of strangers in the home than in a laboratory, and less when the caregiver is close by. Stranger distress is even reduced when the newcomer uses familiar formats to interact with the infant, such as playing with a favorite toy in the same way the caregiver does (Gunnar, 1980; Sroufe, 1977), or when the infant is allowed to have control over the stranger's approach (Mangelsdorf et al., 1991). Moreover, if the caregiver shows a worried expression, infants cry more and smile less at strangers (Boccia and Campos, 1989).

In summary, by late in the first year infant emotional reactions are based on the specific meaning of events, not their mere occurrence. By about age 10 months infants are capable of making rudimentary *evaluations* of strangers and other novel events, a kind of appraisal of the threat posed (Kagan et al., 1978). These evaluations depend on the stranger's behavior and the context in which it occurs (Sroufe, 1977). Particularly important aspects of the context are the child's sense of security (is the caregiver present?) and the options left open to the baby (can the child crawl or turn away?). On the basis of such factors and previous experience with strangers, the infant categorizes the present event as liked or disliked. This explains why a baby who is wary on the first approach of a stranger becomes upset even more quickly on the person's second approach. The child can now rapidly evaluate this particular interaction as unpleasant. If novelty were the cause of distress, the infant should be less frightened the second time the stranger approaches. Such complex behavior is congruent with evidence that by this time pathways have been established between the cortex (the reasoning part of the brain) and emotional areas of the limbic system (Schore, 1994).

THE BEGINNINGS OF EMOTIONAL REGULATION AND COPING

The infant's capacity to cope with or manage emotionally arousing situations also expands dramatically in the second half-year (Bridges and Grolnick, 1995). Newborns have built-in coping mechanisms, such as sleeping deeply following surgery or falling asleep in the face of repeated noxious stimulation (Tennes et al., 1972). But such global reactions are involuntary and remove the infant entirely from interaction with the environment. By 4 or 5 months, infants can, for example, turn away from the source of stimulation. But again, this response is fairly global and not well controlled by the baby. A 5-month-old has difficulty turning away from a staring stranger, for instance. Instead, the baby is drawn back to the stranger's face, becoming locked in to the stare, and ultimately crying. Crying is a coping technique, for it may elicit help; but it, too, essentially terminates contact with the environment.

By 10 months, in contrast, the infant is capable of more subtle, flexible, and serviceable techniques (Gunnar et al., 1989a). A remarkable example can be seen in the stranger-approach procedure (Waters, Matas, and Sroufe, 1975). As a stranger approaches, many 10-month-old infants show a pattern of brief glances down and away, followed by looking again. As shown in Figure 6.4, these gaze aversions are precisely coordinated with heart rate acceleration, an index of emotional arousal. As the infant watches the approaching stranger, the heart rate speeds up. Then the infant glances away, and the heart rate slows again. The infant is then relaxed enough to look at the stranger once more, and so

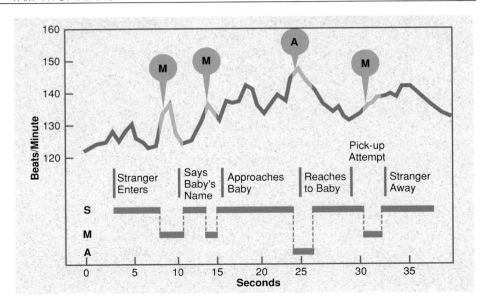

FIGURE 6.4 HEART RATE AND VISUAL REGARD
Visual-regard behavior and continuous heart rate (2-beat averages) in a standard stranger approach situation for a 10-month-old male previously rated "wary" when the stranger reached for and tried to pick up the infant. S denotes "looks at stranger"; A denotes "looks away"; and M denotes "looks to mother." Markers above indicate onset and direction of looks away from the stranger. (Source: Waters, Matas, and Sroufe, 1975.)

the pattern continues. Infants who show this pattern typically do not cry and are more accepting of the stranger on a second approach. Infants who cry or turn completely away typically are more upset on a second approach.

Another important coping technique that emerges during the second half-year is purposeful signaling to the caregiver (calling, gesturing, emitting distress signals) or moving to the caregiver when threatened. Unlike crying, these techniques help the infant maintain organized behavior and stay in contact with the environment (Tronick, 1989). They also pave the way for the toddler's signaling and "referencing" at a distance, topics we will discuss in Chapter 8. In general, regulation of emotion in infancy is often *dyadic regulation*—that is, accomplished by caregiver and infant together (Bridges and Grolnick, 1995). This use of the caregiver as a way of coping with novelty or threat is a hallmark of attachment, our next topic.

THE FORMATION OF ATTACHMENTS

Attachment:
The enduring emotional tie between infant and caregiver that is established through repeated interaction over time.

Attachment is an enduring emotional tie between an infant and a caregiver (Bowlby, 1969/1982). The attachment relationship has special emotional qualities, which are evident not only in the baby's distress on being separated from the caregiver and joyous greeting on being reunited, but also in the security the child seems to derive just from being in the caregiver's presence. By age 12 months, babies want to be picked up *specifically* by the caregiver, they seek the caregiver out when they are upset, and they are happier exploring new surroundings when the caregiver is nearby (Ainsworth et al., 1978; Tracy, Lamb, and Ainsworth, 1976).

HALLMARKS OF ATTACHMENT

Separation distress:
A hallmark of attachment in which infants cry when their principal caregiver temporarily leaves them.

The development of attachment follows a regular course across diverse cultures. One sign that attachment is emerging is **separation distress.** In the second half-year, at about the same time infants show negative reactions to strangers, they

This infant's exuberant greeting of his arriving father reveals important mental and emotional development.

also cry when their caregivers temporarily leave them. These reactions occur somewhat earlier in cultures such as that of the Ganda people of East Africa, in which mothers remain in constant contact with their infants (Ainsworth, 1967). However, they are seen by the end of the first year in all cultures (e.g., Kagan, Kearsley, and Zelazo, 1978).

At about this same time **greeting reactions** emerge. As soon as Christine appears in the doorway, Mikey smiles, squeals, bounces up and down, and stretches out his arms (Vaughn, 1978). He does not look, ponder his mother, and wait for some social signal. The joyous response is immediate. Apparently, Christine has become linked in Mikey's mind with special, very positive feelings. Things in his world are acquiring emotional significance, just as they do for adults.

A final hallmark of attachment is **secure-base behavior.** Year-old infants show a pattern of exploration centered on the caregiver. They explore more confidently when the caregiver is present, and they monitor the caregiver's accessibility, checking back from a distance. They will retreat to their "secure base"—the caregiver—when threatened, then venture forth again when reassured.

THE BASES OF ATTACHMENT

The attachment relationship develops over the first year and continues to evolve during toddlerhood and beyond. Like any other relationship, it is the product of countless hours of interaction during which the caregiver and infant learn to coordinate their behavior. Attachment, in other words, develops over time. Attachment is distinct from **bonding,** the parent's tie to the newborn, which some argue can occur only in the first hours after birth (Klaus and Kennell, 1976). The need for immediate bonding has been called into question by numerous studies that have failed to demonstrate the critical importance of immediate contact between parents and newborns. For example, even prema-

Greeting reactions:
A hallmark of attachment in which the infant shows pleasure when the caregiver appears, often by smiling, bouncing, and extending the arms.

Secure-base behavior:
A hallmark of attachment in which the infant uses the caregiver as a base for exploration.

Bonding:
The parent's initial emotional tie to the newborn.

ture infants initially separated from their biological mothers at birth can still develop normal attachment later in infancy (Easterbrooks, 1989; Rode et al., 1981). Early contact between parents and infants can be important because it starts a relationship process, but it is not absolutely critical.

Since attachment is the product of repeated interaction with a caregiver, it does not have to be the biological parent to whom a baby becomes attached. When infants are adopted early in the first year, they are just as likely as other infants to develop healthy attachment relationships in their adoptive families (Nordhaus and Solnit, 1990; Singer et al., 1985). Moreover, infants can, and often do, become attached to more than one person. For instance, infants in Israeli kibbutzim, who are largely tended by communal nurses but who spend time each evening with their parents, become attached to both their parents and the substitute caregivers (Sagi et al., 1994). In our own society babies typically become attached to both fathers and mothers, though frequently they show a preference for the mother during times of threat (Cohen and Campos, 1974; Cox et al., 1992). This preference is probably the result of the greater involvement that mothers usually have with infants. If someone other than the mother is the principal caregiver, in terms not only of time but also of emotional commitment, that person is likely to become the child's main attachment figure.

One study took advantage of social policies in Sweden to study infant attachment to mothers and fathers (Lamb et al., 1982). Swedish law permits either a mother or a father to take up to 12 months of paid leave to stay home with a new baby. The investigators were interested in cases in which the primary daytime caregiver was the father. They found, as have others, that these infants were attached to both mother and father, although they did not investigate which relationship was stronger. But they also found that very few fathers chose to become the daytime caregiver. In fact, to get an adequate sample of such "nontraditional" fathers, the researchers required only that the father stay home with the baby for 3 months, rather than all 12. Moreover, during evening observations, with both parents present, they found that mothers did the bulk of the feeding and nurturance, even when the father was the principal daytime caregiver.

For an infant to have several attachment figures ordered into a hierarchy on the basis of each relationship's strength makes a great deal of sense. From a learning perspective, it makes sense that if an infant interacts regularly with two (or more) people, he or she will become attached to both. The attachment will be strongest to the person who has the greatest involvement with the child. From an evolutionary perspective, a hierarchy of attachment figures seems essential. When threatened by a predator in past millennia, the human infant could not debate where to flee. The baby had to seek protection immediately, and having a primary attachment figure to go to helped ensure that protection would be found. Yet should this primary attachment figure die or be otherwise unavailable, the infant must have the capacity for other attachments.

Developmental psychologists have debated the processes underlying attachment formation. Many theories have been proposed. In early psychoanalytic theory and traditional learning theory, infants were viewed as becoming attached to the mother because she is associated with feeding and need reduction. Modern theorists such as Erikson and Bowlby place more emphasis on the interaction between caregiver and child. Bowlby (1969/1982) has argued that the tendency to become attached has been built into humans and other primates through natural selection. All that is required for an attachment to form is that an adult be present to engage the infant. The formation of attachment is independent of feeding or the reduction of needs.

A classic set of studies by Harry Harlow and his colleagues at the University of Wisconsin supports the view that association with feeding is not the basis of attachment (e.g., Arling and Harlow, 1967; Harlow and Harlow, 1966). Harlow separated baby rhesus monkeys from their mothers and raised them with various kinds of surrogate (substitute) mothers. In one study, each baby was raised with two surrogate "mothers," one made of stiff, bare wire, the other covered with soft terry cloth. Only the wire mother was equipped with a bottle for feeding. From the perspective of associative learning, the infant monkeys would be expected to become attached to the wire mother, because this surrogate was associated with food. But the babies clearly preferred the terry cloth mother. They spent more time with the terry cloth mother and quickly ran to it when distressed. Apparently, for the development of an attachment, the ability to cling to the terry cloth mother and derive security from it was more important than feeding. Human infants, too, do not become attached to their parents simply because the parents feed them. Rather, they become attached because the parents engage them in interaction.

Although all human infants become attached, not all attachments are the same. In the next section we will consider differences in the security of infants' attachments, as well as other individual differences during infancy.

EXPLAINING INDIVIDUAL DIFFERENCES IN EARLY SOCIAL AND EMOTIONAL DEVELOPMENT

Observers are often impressed with the dramatic differences among babies. Some are easily aroused, cry often, and are difficult to settle. Others are quite placid, rarely becoming upset. Some are confident when encountering new

Individual differences in infant behaviors are obvious. By age 12 months, such differences are somewhat stable and consistent across situations. Explaining such differences is an active concern of researchers.

experiences, especially in the presence of attachment figures. Others are timid and hesitant in the face of anything novel. Even infants in the newborn nursery differ in how much they sleep and cry and in how quickly they soothe themselves or may be soothed by others.

Researchers ask a number of questions about such individual differences during infancy: How consistent are the differences? Do differences in newborns predict differences in 12-month-olds? What are the implications of individual differences in infancy for later development? Do they continue to be part of the child's personality? Finally, how are such differences to be explained?

Current efforts to answer these questions center on two major approaches. One, based in Erikson's psychosocial theory and Bowlby's attachment theory, emphasizes the quality of care the infant receives and the context surrounding that care. This approach contends that, because of differences in the quality of child-caregiver interaction, the attachments that babies form can vary greatly in security, and these differences in the security of attachment affect how babies behave. The other approach to explaining individual differences among infants emphasizes the baby's inborn temperament, based on genetic makeup and other biological influences, especially those surrounding pregnancy and birth. While these approaches have led to two distinct lines of research, they are not necessarily in conflict with each other. Rather, they are two different perspectives on the same phenomenon. Moreover, a great deal of recent effort has been aimed at harmonizing or integrating the two views.

THE ATTACHMENT FRAMEWORK

In all but the most extreme cases, infants become attached to a caregiver. Mentally retarded infants become attached, though at a later age (Cicchetti and Beeghly, 1989). Blind infants and physically disabled infants become attached, though there are some differences in the behaviors they use to express attachment (Fraiberg and Friedman, 1964; Marvin and Pianta, 1992). Even abused infants become attached (Carlson et al., 1989). Only if there is no opportunity for ongoing interaction with a specific caregiver will there be a failure to attach, as in the case of some institutionalized infants (Smirnova, 1990; Dubrovina and Ruzska, 1990).

Noting the universality of attachment, John Bowlby sought to identify individual differences in the quality or particular nature of attachments. Such differences could be seen in Harlow's studies of monkeys raised with surrogate mothers. When some of these monkeys later had their own babies, they proved to be rejecting and punitive parents. Still, their infants were clearly attached to them. The attachments had an anxious quality, however, with the infants constantly trying to cling to the mother.

Bowlby hypothesized that the quality of a baby's attachment is based on the quality of care the infant receives. When infants have experienced sensitive care, they are confident in the responsiveness of the caregiver. Being able to count on the caregiver's presence and comfort gives the infant a base for exploring the environment and a ready resource in case of threat or distress. Having had repeated experiences in which the caregiver responds to signals, is available for communication, and alleviates stress, the baby comes to expect that such care will always be available. This confidence in the caregiver's availability is what Erikson means by *trust* and what Bowlby refers to as *secure attachment*. Secure attachment relationships cannot develop if care is unavailable or

TABLE 6.1
PATTERNS OF ATTACHMENT

Secure Attachment
   A. Caregiver is a secure base for exploration
      1. Readily separate to explore toys
      2. Affective sharing of play
      3. Affiliative to stranger in caregiver's presence
      4. Readily comforted when distressed (promoting a return to play)
   B. Active in seeking contact or interaction upon reunion
      1. If distressed
         (a) Immediately seek and maintain contact
         (b) Contact is effective in terminating distress
      2. If not distressed
         (a) Active greeting behavior (happy to see caregiver)
         (b) Strong initiation of interaction
Anxious-resistant Attachment
   A. Poverty of exploration
      1. Difficulty separating to explore, may need contact even prior to separation
      2. Wary of novel situations and people
   B. Difficulty settling upon reunion
      1. May mix contact seeking with contact resistance (hitting, kicking, squirming, rejecting toys)
      2. May simply continue to cry and fuss
      3. May show striking passivity
Anxious-Avoidant Attachment
   A. Independent exploration
      1. Readily separate to explore during preseparation
      2. Little affective sharing
      3. Affiliative to stranger, when caregiver absent (little preference)
   B. Active avoidance upon reunion
      1. Turning away, looking away, moving away, ignoring
      2. May mix avoidance with proximity
      3. Avoidance more extreme on second reunion
      4. No avoidance of stranger

SOURCE: Adapted from Ainsworth, Blehar, Waters, and Wall, 1978.

hit-or-miss, or if the adult actively rejects the infant's bids for attention and care. In such cases the infant will probably develop an insecure or anxious attachment.

To test Bowlby's hypothesis, researchers needed a means of measuring both security of attachment and sensitivity of care, so they could examine links between the two. While this is a difficult task, it has been the focus of much effort.

PATTERNS OF ATTACHMENT

Mary Ainsworth, a psychologist at the University of Virginia, pioneered in the study of qualitative differences in attachment (Ainsworth et al., 1978). On the basis of observations in both the home and the laboratory, she identified a pattern of attachment that she called *secure* and several patterns that she called *anxious* (see Table 6.1). To identify patterns of attachment, Ainsworth devised a laboratory procedure known as the *Strange Situation*. In this procedure, the baby and the caregiver (always the mother in Ainsworth's experiments) enter a playroom, which the baby is free to explore. Then, in a series of steps, the baby is exposed to a strange adult with and without the mother present, is left alone briefly, and is reunited with the mother. The baby's behavior in the Strange Situation is thought to reveal the sort of attachment that he or she has to the caregiver.

Most infants (around 70 percent) form a **secure attachment.** These children show a good balance between play and exploration on the one hand and a desire for proximity to the caregiver on the other. In Ainsworth's laboratory experiments, they separated readily from the mother to explore. When a minor source of stress was introduced (the appearance of a stranger), they were usually not unduly wary. But when distinctly threatened and upset (following a brief separation from the mother), they quickly and effectively sought the mother out and remained with her until reassured. Usually this comforting was smooth and rapid; before long the child was crawling or toddling off contentedly to explore the world again. Throughout, the child's responses to the mother were emotionally positive, not tinged with anger. In play, securely attached infants smile at the mother and share discoveries and delights with her.

In contrast, infants with an **anxious attachment** are unable to use the caregiver as a secure base for exploration. Such a lack of security is shown in different ways. One pattern is **anxious-resistant attachment.** Children who exhibit this pattern seek a great deal of contact with the caregiver. In fact, in Ainsworth's Strange Situation, they were reluctant to separate from the mother despite an array of attractive toys. When they finally did venture forth on their own, even a minor stress often sent them scurrying back to the mother. Typically, they were quite upset if the mother temporarily left them. Yet ironically, they couldn't be readily comforted by her when she returned. Many just continued crying and fussing despite the mother's efforts to reduce their distress. Most important, they tended to mix bids for physical closeness with *resistance* to such contact. One moment they were raising their arms and asking to be picked up, the next moment they were twisting and squirming, pushing away, or kicking out in anger. Their ambivalent approach to the mother greatly interfered with their ability to become settled and begin exploring the environment again. They behaved as though they could not get what they needed from the mother.

Anxious-avoidant attachment is a quite different pattern but is equally distinct from secure attachment. Children who exhibited this pattern in Ainsworth's Strange Situation readily separated from the mother and began examining the toys. Typically they were not wary upon the arrival of a stranger, nor did they usually cry when their mother first left the room. What was striking about these children was their response when the mother returned. They actively *avoided* her, turning away, increasing their distance, or studiously ignoring her. Infants normally display this pattern following a separation from the caregiver that lasts for several weeks (Heinicke and Westheimer, 1966), but not one that lasts just 3 minutes. Significantly, avoidance of the mother was even more pronounced following a second separation, during which many of the babies clearly became upset. Yet when the mother returned, they still didn't seek her out, nor did they respond to contact with her. The more the stress of the situation increased, the more they avoided interaction with the mother. Like resistance to the mother, avoidance of her also greatly interferes with the ability to become settled and return to active play and exploration.

Secure attachment:
The type of relationship between infant and principal caregiver in which the infant is able to rely on the emotional and physical availability of the caregiver and the caregiver's sensitive response to his or her needs, and so can use the caregiver as a secure base from which to explore; contrasted with *anxious attachment*.

Anxious attachment:
A type of relationship between infant and principal caregiver in which the infant is not able to rely on the emotional and physical availability of the caregiver and so is not able to use the caregiver as a secure base from which to explore; contrasted with *secure attachment*.

Anxious-resistant attachment:
A subtype of anxious attachment in which the infant is reluctant to be separated from the caregiver but at the same time exhibits ambivalence toward the caregiver.

Anxious-avoidant attachment:
A subtype of anxious attachment in which infants readily separate from the caregiver but, when the caregiver returns after a short separation, either ignore the caregiver or show other signs of active avoidance.

Since Ainsworth's pioneering work, Mary Main at the University of California at Berkeley has introduced another category of anxious attachment, **disorganized-disoriented attachment.** In the Strange Situation, infants with this kind of attachment show contradictory features of several patterns or appear dazed and disoriented. Their movements may be incomplete or very slow, or they may become motionless. They may appear depressed. Main has argued that these infants have no consistent way of relating to the caregiver when they are stressed, presumably because of some persistent threat or incoherence in the caregiver's behavior (Main, 1994; Main and Hesse, 1990).

Expressions of attachment behavior in the Strange Situation vary from culture to culture (Levine and Miller, 1990; Main, 1990). For example, most infants in traditional Japanese families become extremely upset in the Strange Situation (Takahashi, 1990). This does not mean that these infants all have anxious-resistant attachments, however. Rather, these infants have almost no experience with separation, and Ainsworth's procedure is not appropriate for them.

Sensitive care involves responding promptly and effectively to crying and to more subtle signals that infants exhibit.

Disorganized-disoriented attachment:
A subtype of anxious attachment in which infants show contradictory features of several patterns of anxious attachment or become dazed and disoriented in an experimental situation in which the caregiver briefly leaves them with a stranger.

QUALITY OF CARE AND SECURITY OF ATTACHMENT

To assess the effects of the quality of care on the quality of attachment, researchers have used two approaches. One is to identify groups of parents who clearly neglect or maltreat their infants and compare the attachments that their children form with those of children whose parents don't maltreat them. Such studies have routinely found more anxious attachments in the maltreated groups (Carlson et al., 1989; Egeland and Sroufe, 1981). For example, extreme poverty and physical neglect have been found to be associated with an increase in anxious-resistant attachment, while anxious-avoidant attachment is predicted by physical abuse and "emotional unavailability," a pattern in which the caregiver is emotionally unresponsive to the infant (Egeland and Sroufe, 1981). For the group defined as experiencing emotionally unavailable care, all had anxious-avoidant attachments by age 18 months, a striking result. Several studies have also shown maltreatment to be strongly related to Main's disorganized-disoriented pattern of anxious attachment (Carlson et al., 1989; Lyons-Ruth et al., 1990).

The other approach to assessing the effects of the quality of care on attachment is to look at the details of parent-infant interaction when the baby is still very young and record the frequency of certain kinds of behaviors or make ratings of the degree to which parents are sensitive and responsive to the infant's moods and signals. Then, when the baby is older, the researchers assess the security of attachment. Numerous studies of this type have found that sensitive care is associated with secure attachment to mothers (Ainsworth et al., 1978; Bates et al., 1985; Kiser et al., 1986; Belsky and Isabella, 1987; Egeland and Farber, 1984; Grossman et al., 1985) and to fathers (Main and Weston, 1981; Cox et al., 1992). In these studies, researchers observed parent-child interactions in the home for several days when the baby was 4 to 6 months old (sometimes at other ages too). On the basis of these observations they rated the parent's degree of sensitivity as a caregiver. Later, when the infant was 1 year old, the researchers assessed the quality of the child's attachment to the parent in the Strange Situation. The caregiver's rated sensitivity or intrusiveness in the early months of the baby's life predicted later secure or anxious attachment, but the infant's early behavior did not (Ainsworth et al., 1978; Egeland and Farber, 1984).

Studies of this kind also reveal that particular types of insensitive care are associated with particular types of anxious attachment. Anxious-avoidant attachment tends to be associated with a caregiver who is either indifferent and emotionally unavailable or who actively rejects the baby when the child seeks physical closeness (Isabella, 1993; Bohlin et al., 1990). Anxious-resistant attachment tends to be associated with inconsistent care (Sroufe, 1988), with exaggerated behaviors on the part of the mother and ineffective soothing (overstimulation), or, in an Israeli kibbutz sample, with infants who sleep away from the mother at night (Sagi et al., 1994).

Since sensitive care involves responding promptly to the baby's cries and other signals, you might think that rewarding crying with attention and comforting would encourage the baby to cry more often. In fact, however, when caregivers promptly and effectively respond to their infant's cries, the babies actually cry *less* by the end of the first year and are generally securely attached (Ainsworth and Bell, 1974). These children do not learn to be "crybabies" through reinforcement. Instead, a broader learning seems to occur. Infants who have sensitive caregivers apparently learn that their signals will receive quick and appropriate responses and that adults can be counted on to help. By age 12 months they are so confident of prompt responses that they don't need to signal alarm at the slightest stress. They know that if ever serious distress arises, comfort will be quickly provided.

It should be pointed out that sensitive care does not mean perfect care. Parents need not always attend to the infant immediately or always do the right thing. And picking up the infant all the time, even when the baby doesn't want it, can be intrusive. Care only needs to be "good enough" (Winnicott, 1965). In most cases infant care is adequately sensitive, and the majority of babies are securely attached.

THE CONTEXT OF CAREGIVING

If the development of secure attachment depends on the kind of care the baby receives, then factors that influence the quality of caregiving should be related to attachment. Three such factors have been investigated: (1) the amount of stress in the caregiver's life; (2) the social support available to the caregiver; and (3) the caregiver's own developmental history. Studies of these topics underscore the inappropriateness of simply blaming parents when attachment goes awry. To blame parents is to fail to view caregiving in its broader social and psychological context.

LIFE STRESS AND SOCIAL SUPPORT   Stress and support are closely related. It is easier to cope with ongoing problems and everyday hassles when others are available to help and give emotional support. Those who must care for infants without help and support from others also tend to experience more financial pressure and more stresses of other kinds. Many studies have linked the quality of infant-parent attachment to the amounts of stress and social support in caregivers' lives, as measured through interviews with caregivers (Crockenberg, 1981; Cox et al., 1989; Easterbrooks, 1989; Egeland et al., 1980; Howes and Markman, 1989; Jacobson and Frye, 1991; Lyons-Ruth et al., 1990; Vaughn et al., 1979). If support increases or stress decreases, the quality of the child's relationship with the caregiver can improve, sometimes becoming secure when it had originally been anxious (Erickson, Egeland, and Sroufe, 1985; Vaughn et al., 1979).

PARENTS' DEVELOPMENTAL HISTORY   Several studies have now related caregivers' descriptions of their own childhoods to the quality of the infant-caregiver attachment (Ainsworth and Eichberg, 1991; Cox et al., 1992; Fonagy et al., 1991; Main, in press; Ricks, 1985; Ward and Carlson, 1995). Many of these studies have used the Adult Attachment Interview, developed by Mary Main. From the ease with which adults talk about attachment-related feelings, and from inconsistencies among their statements, the degree to which they experienced responsive care and the degree to which they have resolved any feelings of being mistreated are inferred. Such reports may be obtained even before the parents' own child is born. From these reports it is possible to predict the quality of the baby's later attachment.

Of course, studies based on people's recall of their childhood experiences have some limitations. The difficulties a mother is experiencing today may lead her both to have problems with her infant and to report her own developmental history negatively. Main notes that her Adult Attachment Interview captures the adult's "current state of mind" concerning attachment and does not necessarily reflect the adult's actual early attachment relationship. Some adults whose early lives were quite negative nonetheless achieve a substantial degree of understanding and emotional freedom regarding attachment.

Other clues to a link between parents' developmental histories and the security of attachment in their own infants come from animal studies. While such studies are only suggestive for humans, they allow researchers to look at parenting across generations in a short period of time. Lynn Fairbanks (1989) studied mothering among Vervet monkeys and found that the amount of physical contact a female monkey received from her mother when she was an infant predicted the amount of contact she later gave her own baby. Moreover, this similarity in behavior was not due to genetic similarity between the mother and daughter, nor to observational learning on the part of the daughter. The amount of contact received predicted the amount of contact given better than the average amount of contact the monkey's mother gave to *all* her offspring (a measure of her genetic inclination to give physical contact) or the amount of contact she was currently giving to younger siblings of her daughter (which could serve as a model for the daughter to observe and imitate).

INFANT ATTACHMENT AND LATER DEVELOPMENT

Individual differences in security of attachment are thought to be important because of their implications for later development. The crux of Bowlby's theory is that different patterns of attachment reflect differences in infants' expectations, or **internal working models,** of the social world. An infant who has experienced reliable, responsive care, and who is secure in his or her attachment, has begun to develop a model of the caregiver as available and, at the same time, of the self as worthy of care and effective in obtaining it. According to Bowlby, these attitudes and representations are carried forward and influence later experience, coloring the child's perceptions and interpretations of events, as well as influencing the kinds of experiences that the child seeks or avoids.

Research tends to support Bowlby's theory that the quality of attachment helps to shape a child's internal working model of the social world. Attachment classifications in infancy have been shown to be related to attachment behavior in the home (Ainsworth et al., 1978; Vaughn and Waters, 1989), to be stable in typical samples (Main and Weston, 1981; Waters, 1978), and to predict how well children will function later. Curiosity, enthusiasm in solving problems, high self-esteem, and positive relations with teachers and peers have all been found to be strongly linked to the quality of early attachments (see Chapters 8, 10, 12, and 14).

Internal working model: A set of generalized expectations of the caregiver as either available and responsive or not responsive, and representations of the self as worthy or not worthy of care, that is carried forward from infancy into childhood.

In summary, attachment theorists focus on the organization of an infant's behavior with respect to the principal caregiver who becomes an attachment figure. The quality of this attachment relationship is the result of the history of interaction with the caregiver. That interaction, in turn, is influenced by the overall context of care, which includes such things as the amounts of stress and social support the caregiver experiences, as well as the characteristics of the particular child. As a result of the infant-caregiver interaction, a secure or insecure relationship develops. That relationship then provides a framework for later development and is reflected in the child's degree of self-confidence, sociability, and capacity to cope with challenges.

THE TEMPERAMENT FRAMEWORK

Temperament:
The individual mix of primary behavioral characteristics, such as activity level, moods, and emotional responsiveness, that is exhibited by a person.

The second approach to explaining individual differences in babies' behavior focuses less on attachment than on the idea of inborn temperament. **Temperament** refers to a variety of behavioral characteristics, such as general activity level, quality of mood, and reactivity to new situations (e.g., Bates, 1989). Temperament researchers generally assume that individual differences in such characteristics are genetically or biologically rooted, although they acknowledge that they can be influenced by environment as well (Bates, 1989; Goldsmith et al., 1987). Using combinations of such characteristics, Alexander Thomas and Stella Chess (1977) categorized some babies as "easy" and others as "difficult." While earlier temperament research tended to focus on very specific descriptive features of behavior, such as amount of activity and amount of crying (see Table 6.2), more recent efforts have broadened the concept of temperament to include such things as a tendency to express certain emotions (joy or fear, for example), an ability to adapt to new situations, and a capacity to regulate one's own behavior (Bridges and Grolnick, 1995; Goldsmith et al., 1987; Rothbart, 1989).

One of the central issues in temperament research concerns the stability or consistency of behavior over time. If stable characteristics exist in infancy, perhaps these are the roots of later personality. Stability from very early in infancy would be especially important, since it would suggest that such differences are inborn. In addition, stable infant characteristics might be shown to influence the infant-caregiver relationship, with significant implications for development.

THE STABILITY OF TEMPERAMENT

Are differences in fussiness and irritability among newborns stable? If so, do such characteristics lead to caregiving problems?

Early research relied heavily on parents' reports as measures of a baby's temperament (Thomas and Chess, 1977). These studies and many that followed did indeed find various aspects of temperament to be stable over time. However, the studies were criticized for two reasons. First, they did not begin in the newborn period, so it was not clear that truly inborn factors were being measured. Second, parents' reports may have been biased (Bates, 1989). Early studies found little agreement between parents' reports and data obtained by other observers (Vaughn et al., 1987). Moreover, in one study questionnaires were given to parents even before the unborn infant was moving in the uterus (Zeanah et al., 1988). These parents' prenatal "descriptions" (really, expectations about what the baby would be like) correlated with their descriptions of the infant months later. This finding suggests that parents' expectations play at least some role in their reports about a baby's temperament.

More recent research, using other approaches to measuring infant tempera-

TABLE 6.2
INFANT TEMPERAMENT CHARACTERISTICS OF THOMAS AND CHESS (1977)

Characteristic	Description
1. Activity	General degree of mobility as reflected in the frequency and tempo of movement, locomotion, and other activity; from highly active to inactive.
2. Rhythmicity	Extent to which sleeping, resting, eating, elimination, and other body functions are regular and predictable; from regular to irregular.
3. Approach-withdrawal	Type of first reaction a child has when encountering a new situation such as a different person, place, toy, and so on; from approach to withdrawal.
4. Adaptability	Extent to which initial withdrawal response to a new situation becomes modified over time; from adaptable to nonadaptable.
5. Intensity	Typical intensity of the child's reaction to internal states or environmental situations; from intense to mild.
6. Threshold	Strength of the stimulus needed to cause the child to respond; from high threshold to low threshold.
7. Mood	Typical behavior patterns related to a general quality of mood; from pleasant to unpleasant.
8. Distractibility	Difficulty or ease with which the child's ongoing activities can be interrupted; from high to low.
9. Persistence of attention	Extent to which the child remains engaged in an activity or returns to the activity after interruption; from high to low.

ment, has been much more compelling (Rothbart, 1989; Matheny, 1989; Matheny et al., 1985). By devising questionnaires in which parents' judgments are more objective, and by combining parents' reports with those of other observers and with laboratory tests, researchers have been able to show that there are clear differences in temperament among infants. The question is whether these differences remain stable over time.

A number of researchers have tried to answer this question by conducting comprehensive assessments of newborn behavior as well as assessments at later stages of development. From this research we know that, by the end of an infant's first year, measurements of such things as the frequency of negative and positive emotions and the strength of the child's reactions to sensory stimulation are quite stable and predict well to later ages (Emde et al., 1992; Matheny, 1989; Rothbart, 1989). These results are clear and impressive. In contrast, predictions from the newborn period are not so reliable, although a few studies do find some consistency between temperament in the newborn and in the older infant (Korner et al., 1991; Worobey and Lewis, 1989). Assessments of temperament made by parents and other observers bear out this difference, too; there is much more agreement about older babies' and toddlers' temperaments than about those of babies only a few months old (St. James-Roberts and Wolke, 1988; Johnson and Rosen, 1990; Worobey and Blajda, 1989). Also, predictions from temperament in early infancy to the preschool years and beyond are not very powerful; but this matter is still the subject of much research.

THE BIOLOGY OF TEMPERAMENT

Researchers have wondered whether differences in infant temperament reflect underlying biological differences. For example, it has been found that infants who are wary in new situations have higher or more variable heart rates and blood pressure than less wary infants do (Fox, 1989; Kagan, 1992). Associations also have been found between hormone levels and a baby's emotional responses. When Megan Gunnar and her colleagues (1989b) measured infants' excretion of cortisol (a hormone linked to stress), they found that higher levels of cortisol were related to parents' reports that the baby was less adaptable and more emotionally negative, as well as to greater amounts of crying in the Strange Situation 3 months later. Thus, there seem to be at least some biological factors related to the temperament differences observed in babies.

THE GENETICS OF TEMPERAMENT

These differences in temperament, however, are not necessarily genetic in origin—that is, caused largely by genes that the child has inherited from parents. Demonstrating a genetic component to temperament would lend support to the view that some of the biological differences related to temperament are at least partly inborn. Many studies show more *concordance,* or similarity, in temperament between identical (or monozygotic) twins than between fraternal (or dizygotic) twins (Emde et al., 1992; Goldsmith, 1989; Loehlin et al., 1982; Matheny, 1989). Since identical twins are more closely related genetically (they developed from the same fertilized egg and have all their genes in common), this research suggests a genetic component to temperament. However, fraternal twins often show very little similarity in temperament, and this is perplexing, since these twins, on average, share half their genes. Also, the similarity in temperament that identical twins display may be due *not* to genetic factors but rather to similar treatment by parents and others. This possibility is strengthened by the fact that the difference in concordance between identical and fraternal twins increases with age, with the identical twins becoming more and more similar in temperament.

An adoption study, in which twins are reared in different homes, can help demonstrate genetic influences. Identical twins who are raised apart experience at least somewhat different environments, so similarities in temperament between them can be seen as more likely due to genetic similarity. One such study, the Colorado Adoption Study (Plomin, 1989), found evidence for a genetic component to such personality dimensions as inhibition and negative emotions; identical twins raised apart showed some similarity in these characteristics. However, the concordance between identical twins was much smaller than in studies where the twins are raised together, so environment also seems to be an important influence. Interestingly, concordances between identical twins raised apart still increase with age, suggesting that genetic factors may become more prominent after early infancy (Plomin et al., 1993).

In summary, by the end of infancy, various dimensions of behavior, often referred to as temperament, become stable, with some children being more irritable, more sociable, or more emotionally reactive than others. By this age, too, there is agreement among parents and other observers in their descriptions of particular children. However, with the exception of premature infants, there is little evidence for stability of behavior beginning in the newborn period (Korner et al., 1991). There is also some evidence that physiological factors are related to temperament differences. But such correlations do not demonstrate that physiological differences are inborn and *cause* differences in behavior. For example, babies who are often fretful may show strong cortisol reactions or markedly variable heart rates not because these physiological changes produce their fretfulness, but rather because these are ways in which the fretfulness is expressed. They may show cortisol or heart rate responses simply *because* they are so fretful.

Research with monkeys reveals the complexity of understanding temperament. First, some characteristics, such as reactivity to stimulation, have a genetic component, while other characteristics (the tendency to be nurturant) are more based on experience (Suomi, 1995). Second, temperament and even brain physiology may be shaped and altered by experience (Schore, 1994). Gary Kraemer (1992) describes a process whereby the infant's capacity to stay physiologically regulated is entrained by the caregiver. Sorting out how much of temperament is inborn and how much is due to the environment may not be the most important question (Gunnar, 1991).

TEMPERAMENT AND ATTACHMENT

Attachment and temperament researchers are describing two different things. Attachment researchers are studying the quality, or effectiveness, of the infant-caregiver relationship. Temperament researchers, in contrast, are studying differences in the frequency or intensity of individual infants' behaviors in various contexts. It is important to understand both aspects of development and to consider how they might be related (Stevenson-Hinde, 1990).

For a time during the 1980s, efforts were made to explain attachment differences on the basis of temperament differences (Goldsmith, 1989; Kagan, 1984). One argument was that differences seen in the Strange Situation were simply differences in infants' tendencies to cry and so forth, and that relationship differences were not being tapped. Anxious-resistant infants were just temperamentally irritable, and anxious-avoidant infants were aloof. But it was discovered that often an infant behaved differently toward each of his or her parents in the Strange Situation (e.g., Cox et al., 1992; Fox et al., 1991), that how a baby behaved and was classified in these studies changed with changes in level of parental stress (e.g., Vaughn et al., 1979), and that traditional measures of temperament were not related to the quality of attachment (Bates et al., 1985; Bohlin et al., 1990; Egeland and Farber, 1984; Vaughn et al., 1989). Moreover, measures of heart rate and cortisol reactions showed that anxious-avoidant infants were not detached, but physiologically aroused (Spangler and Grossman, 1993). Thus, differences in Strange Situation behavior cannot be explained by infant temperament alone (Sroufe, 1985). It seems equally unlikely that differences in care and the resulting quality of attachment can account for all variations in children's temperaments, especially given the findings of twin adoption studies. Quality of attachment and temperament, as we have said, are two different aspects of development.

To reiterate, *quality of attachment* refers to the overall organization of behavior with respect to a particular partner, while *temperament* refers to certain styles of behavior regardless of partner. Thus, securely attached infants can have very different temperaments. Some are cuddly, cry a great deal, and are very active.

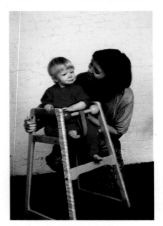

By 12 months infants have a unique and individual style. This mother describes her baby as very determined and curious. Researchers believe such individual differences are a complex product of temperament and experiences in attachment relationships.

Others cry little, are placid, and rarely want physical contact. But regardless of their differences in temperament, all securely attached infants have in common an effective relationship with a caregiver that serves exploration. Securely attached infants seek the contact with the caregiver that they need, however little or much it may be, and that contact is effective in alleviating distress and helping them become settled enough to return to play. Anxiously attached infants, too, may have different temperaments, which may affect how their insecurity toward the caregiver is expressed. Thus, an insecurely attached infant's doubtfulness about parent availability is probably due to the quality of care he or she has experienced, but the infant's tendency to be outwardly angry or more passively distressed may be due to temperament (Belsky and Rovine, 1987).

Not surprisingly, then, temperament is related to certain behaviors in the Strange Situation, but not to security of attachment itself. For example, Brian Vaughn and his colleagues found that a widely used temperament questionnaire predicted how much infants would cry during the separation episodes of the Strange Situation (Vaughn et al., 1989). However, the temperament questionnaire did not predict how much an infant would cry when reunited with the caregiver (which attachment researchers believe is more reflective of the quality of the infant-caregiver relationship), nor did it predict whether the relationship was classified as secure or anxious. Similarly, Megan Gunnar, in the research described earlier on differences in hormone excretion, found that cortisol reactions at 9 months predicted later crying in the Strange Situation but not anxious-resistant attachment. Thus, the baby's tendency to get upset may have some basis in temperament, but how well an infant copes with that upset in the context of the attachment relationship seems to be based on experience.

This is not to say that the two features of development are completely unrelated. One way to look at the role of temperament in attachment formation is in defining caregiver sensitivity, which predicts secure attachment (Sroufe, 1988). For a temperamentally placid baby, frequent stimulation may represent sensitive care, whereas for an easily over-aroused infant, frequent, intense stimulation may be insensitive. Here temperament helps to define the nature of sensitive care, which in turn is what fosters secure attachment.

Temperament and attachment may be related in other ways as well. In some cases, the particular moods and styles of the infant are at odds with the wishes or tendencies of a particular caregiver. The idea that the preferences or capacities of the caregiver and the tendencies of the infant may clash is referred to as the *match-mismatch hypothesis*. There is some support for this idea. For instance, neither a measure of an infant's proneness to distress nor a measure of a caregiver's need for control predicts anxious attachment, but the two measures taken together do (Mangelsdorf et al., 1990). Here it seems that a parent with a high need to control situations may have difficulty being sensitive to the needs of a baby who is easily upset.

A third way in which temperament and attachment may be related is for early differences in infants to feed into the quality of care that parents provide and thereby affect the quality of attachment that develops. For instance, two studies have shown that newborn irritability predicts anxious attachment in low-income families, with increased anxious-resistant attachment found in the United States (Susman et al., 1994) and more anxious-avoidant attachment found in a Dutch sample (van den Boom, 1989). The cultural differences make clear that these cannot be direct temperament effects. The measures of anxious attachment are not just tapping a tendency toward irritability; rather, the effects must be due to the influence of a baby's temperament on caregiving. Significantly, in middle-class samples, no overall effect of infant irritability is found. Presumably, the social support typically available to such caregivers allows them to compensate for the infants' early difficulties (Crockenberg, 1981).

Finally, temperament can be related to attachment when an infant's characteristics are so difficult and demanding that they tax many caregivers' ability to cope, regardless of their personalities. For example, extremely premature infants with serious health problems are more likely to show anxious-resistant attachment (Plunkett et al., 1986), while prenatally drug-exposed infants are more likely to show anxious-avoidant or disorganized-disoriented attachment, or both (Rodning et al., 1989). These effects may occur because some of these infants cry very often and are difficult to soothe, and because such difficulties are extremely stressful for many parents.

In conclusion, it is useful to think about the development of attachment in terms of an interacting system of infant, caregiver, and the larger environment. Trying to decide whether quality of care or infant temperament is the most important factor in an infant's development is misguided. Infant irritability may predict caregiver insensitivity, but early caregiver insensitivity predicts later irritability even better (Engfer, 1988). A baby's temperament is also predicted by the parents' degree of marital satisfaction and self-confidence (Belsky et al., 1991; Teti and Gelfand, 1991), and newborn irritability is predicted by the mother's stress and anxiety during pregnancy (Molitor et al., 1984). Thus, the two influences—quality of care and infant temperament—influence one another in a circular way. The total context of development is more important than either the caregiver's behavior or the baby's temperament alone. If Karen Polonius is ambivalent about being a mother, and Meryl is cranky as a newborn, interaction between the two will tend to intensify these traits. As long as Karen's situation does not improve, Meryl is likely to become a truly difficult child, even though in different circumstances her initial irritability might have been only temporary (Egeland and Sroufe, 1981; van den Boom, 1989). This is the transactional model in operation: the various parts of the system all affect one another. Positive temperament and security of attachment, while uncorrelated in early infancy, do converge by the preschool years (Vaughn et al., 1992).

THE IMPORTANCE OF EARLY CARE

One of the most fundamental issues in all of developmental psychology concerns the special importance of early experience. If development simply reflects the tally of all experiences, or if new experiences supplant prior ones, then there is no unique role for early care (Kagan, 1984). If, on the other hand, early experience establishes basic patterns of social responsiveness and emotional regulation, then early experience is of unique and fundamental importance.

THE SENSITIVE PERIOD HYPOTHESIS

The idea that certain kinds of experience may be especially important during a particular period of life is known as the **sensitive period hypothesis.** For example, many developmentalists believe that the quality of primary attachments formed in infancy sets the stage for later relationships. This is not to say that

Sensitive period hypothesis: In theories about the importance of early care, the idea that although patterns of social relatedness that form early in a child's life are profoundly important for later normal development they are not irreversible; that is, the early years represent a highly significant, or sensitive, period for the development of social relatedness rather than a critical period.

Infant monkeys separated from their parents in the early months of life are often quite wary and hesitant to explore. Here, a 6-month-old clings to a familiar peer rather than engaging in play.

attachments can form only in infancy or that later relationships will always be identical to early ones. These ideas, referred to as the "critical period hypothesis," are no longer given credence. In contrast, there is ample support for the sensitive period hypothesis.

The most convincing studies of the power of early experience have been with monkeys. Monkeys reared with peers but without parents in the early months of life show abnormal behavior, such as marked fearfulness and clinging (Suomi, 1977). Monkeys isolated from all other monkeys for 6 months are social "misfits," and monkeys isolated from all social contact for the first full year are completely unable to relate to others (Suomi and Harlow, 1971). Moreover, isolation for the first 6 months (equivalent to more than a year in human terms) has more profound effects than isolation in the second 6 months (Sackett, 1968). The social handicaps of monkeys isolated for their first half-year are very difficult to overcome, requiring special rehabilitation efforts (Suomi et al., 1972). And even prolonged rehabilitation cannot erase the damaging effects. Monkeys that were isolated as babies but appear to be functioning normally after years in supportive groups, revert to their earlier disturbed behavior when placed in cages reminiscent of those from their infancy. As reported by Stephen Suomi and his colleagues, they show remarkable "signature stereotypes"—that is, very individual and peculiar mannerisms that they had shown as deprived infants (Novak et al., 1992).

All the evidence suggests that humans, too, are adversely affected by inadequate care in infancy. In fact, because of the greater complexity of their social and emotional development, human children may be even more vulnerable to early deprivation. Recent studies in England that followed up children institutionalized early in life found that as adolescents they had difficulty establishing close contact with peers and later encountered problems in parenting (Rutter et al., 1990). The earlier and longer the institutionalization, the more profound the effects (Rutter, 1988). Studies of children raised in Eastern European and Russian orphanages also show the very negative consequences of early institutional rearing. For example, children in overcrowded Romanian orphanages typically are both physically and socially deprived. As many as 20 children may be cared for by one nurse, and the care is perfunctory and oriented only to the children's basic physical needs. There is no playing with the children and almost no face-to-face interaction. As a result, the children are listless and emotionless and have numerous physical problems (Johnson et al., 1992). Children from less physically depriving but still socially sterile Russian institutions at first seemed in some ways precocious. They could dress themselves early and showed skill in handling objects. However, later they were quite needy of adult contact and were aggressive with other children (Dubrovina and Ruzska, 1990; Smirnova, 1990). The box on p. 237 describes some ways in which institutional care of infants might be improved.

CULTURAL DIVERSITY AND CULTURAL VARIATION

A consideration of cultures throughout the world also suggests that there is a universal understanding of the importance of infancy. There is great diversity among cultures in terms of styles of living, child-rearing goals, and particular patterns of behavior. Yet caregivers in all cultures recognize the importance of providing consistent, responsive care for young infants (Bornstein et al., 1992; Fernald and Morikawa, 1993; Richman, Miller, and Levine, 1992). For example, Japanese mothers direct their baby's looking more to themselves than to objects, while U.S. mothers do the reverse (also labeling the objects); but in both cultures mothers encourage a baby to explore, imitate the child's vocalizations, and respond to the infant's distress with nurturance (Bornstein et al., 1992). Mothers in Boston and in the Gusii tribe of Kenya both respond promptly to a baby who is upset, although the Gusii are more physically responsive and the U.S. mothers more verbally responsive, a pattern related to education level across cultures (Richman et al., 1992).

The existence of other relationships for a child doesn't seem to weaken the cultural belief that early nurturing care from the mother is important. Among the Efe foragers in Zaire, for example, children have many relationships with kin, and by age 3 they spend 60 percent of their time with older children. Still, up to age 2 they are primarily with their mothers, especially during the first 8 months (Tronick et al., 1992). In many cultures, mothers carry their infants at all times during waking hours and sleep with them at night (Morelli et al., 1992). Even when such constant physical proximity is not the case, as in the United States, caregivers typically respond promptly to infant distress. The universal recognition of the need for such responsive, consistent care in infancy suggests that it is vital for human adaptation.

ENHANCING THE QUALITY OF EARLY CARE

The idea that early care is of special importance has inspired efforts to work with families in which infant development is going awry or seems likely to be problematic. In addition to being of great practical value in improving children's lives, such early intervention is of theoretical importance because any long-term effects it produces support the sensitive period hypothesis. At the same time, successful interventions that start after the earliest months show that infants remain open to change.

Successful early interventions generally have had two things in common.

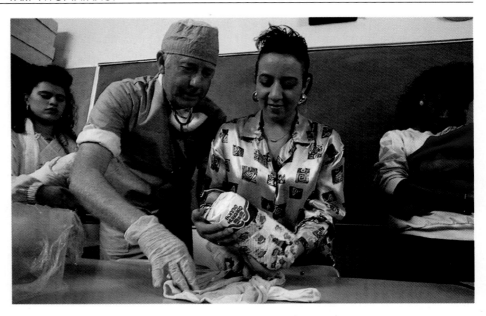

In an effort to prevent early pregnancy, a sex education course at Mission High School in San Francisco requires each student to tend a 5 pound sack of flour as if it were a baby. This means consistent attention and gentle handling, and making arrangements for the "baby" when the parent has other activities. Such an experience gives young people an idea of the level of commitment involved in being a parent.

First, they have begun by identifying groups of babies whose development was clearly going awry. Second, they have been comprehensive in scope and focused on creating more responsive caregiving. Interventions with broad populations defined as being at risk for problems (due to poverty, for example) have not consistently produced positive results (e.g., Egeland and Erickson, 1993; Olds et al., 1986).

Several successful intervention projects have focused on infants with a condition known among health-care professionals as *non-organic failure to thrive syndrome.* These babies show either a decline in growth, or growth below the third percentile on standard age charts. No physical cause for the problem can be found; it seems to stem from parental indifference or neglect (Drotar, 1991; Evans et al., 1972; Steele, 1986). Often a cycle develops: an anxious or depressed caregiver produces a child who feeds poorly; the caregiver then misinterprets the feeding difficulty and gives up on a feeding too soon, leaving the infant hungry and angry (Skuse, 1985). Many of these infants have delays in motor development, as well as skin disorders. Often they smile and vocalize little and avoid eye contact. In general, they are withdrawn and apathetic.

To be successful, interventions for failure to thrive must improve the quality of the caregiver-child relationship rather than just getting parents to feed the baby adequately (Drotar, 1991; Mira and Cairns, 1981; Ramey et al., 1979). For example, in a study by Craig Ramey and his colleagues (1979), intervention efforts were focused specifically on parent-infant interaction. The babies in the study were all given nutritional rehabilitation, but parents in the experimental group were also given a 1-hour tutoring session each day by a specialist in child development. Among other things, the specialist trained the parents to respond positively when the baby was able to perform certain behaviors. At the end of the study, all the infants showed adequate weight gain, but only those in the experimental group also vocalized more and were better able to master new tasks.

Other important intervention experiments have identified infants at birth who are at risk for developmental problems. One large-scale study focused on low-birth-weight, premature infants (Gross, 1990; Spiker et al., 1993). Families in the treatment group were given comprehensive services, and the children were followed from birth to age 3 years. Services for the intervention group included home visits, child attendance at a child development center, and parent group meetings. At 2 and 3 years of age, children in the intervention group showed cognitive gains and significantly fewer behavior problems than those in a nontreatment control group. These improvements were found primarily in families with less education, so the intervention may have helped some parents with relatively little knowledge of child development to become better informed about age-appropriate behaviors, or to learn more effective techniques for managing their children's behavior. Alternatively, the intervention may have directly altered the children's behavior (rather than affecting the child by changing the parent), or it may have done some of both.

Some studies have focused specifically on enhancing the quality of attachment between infant and caregiver. For 50 low-income mothers of highly irritable newborns, van den Boom (1989) provided extensive guidance aimed specifically at teaching the components of responsive care: perceiving and interpreting infant signals correctly; selecting an appropriate response; and implementing the response effectively. Compared with a control group of 50 comparable cases, caregivers who had experienced this intervention were indeed more responsive in the second half-year and a dramatically greater number of their infants were securely attached (68 percent compared to 22 percent).

In another study, Alicia Lieberman and her colleagues (1991) began with a low-income group of Hispanic mothers and their 12-month-old infants who were already anxiously attached. For one subgroup, staff members provided emotional support and were responsive to each mother's own inner conflicts, with the aim of enhancing her empathy for the child's developmental needs and experiences. One year later, in a laboratory session, the researchers assessed mother-child interaction and the child's socioemotional functioning in relation to the mother. Compared with the anxiously attached control group, children in the intervention group were rated significantly lower in avoidance, resistance, and anger toward the mother and higher in partnership with her.

Through studies such as these, researchers have learned much about the essential components of effective intervention. Interventions must focus not just on the infant, but also on the caregiver and the interaction between the two (Seitz and Provence, 1990). Services must be both extensive and available early in the infant-parent relationship (Egeland and Erickson, 1993; Olds et al., 1986).

DAY CARE IN INFANCY

Nonparental care of infants, commonly referred to as day care, has attracted a great deal of attention partly because of the sensitive period hypothesis. What impact does day care have on babies? Does it matter when such care begins? And how important is the quality of the care given? With most U.S. infants now experiencing day care of some kind, it has become an important part of the overall care provided to young children in our society (Sroufe, 1990).

Day care has always generated controversy among child development researchers, partly because of its social and political overtones, including its repercussions for women's rights. When the use of day care began to increase rapidly in the 1970s, concern was expressed that it might actually prevent

Whether out-of-home care for infants has consequences for parent–child relationships or other aspects of development is still being actively investigated. Important factors seem to be the timing of day-care entry, amount of time per week, and the quality of the day care.

attachment to parents by reducing opportunities for parent-child interaction. This concern has proven to be groundless. Children in day care still become attached to their mothers or other primary caregivers, and in general these attachments remain more important than attachments to the substitute caregivers (Sagi et al., 1994; Sroufe, 1990). Infants or toddlers seldom grieve when they change day-care providers, but they do grieve when they lose a parent. As long as the parent is the child's primary caregiver outside of working hours, she or he will become the child's central attachment figure.

Researchers also now agree that even full-time day care for toddlers and preschool-aged children has no demonstrable negative effects (Clarke-Stewart, 1989). In fact, there is substantial evidence that good-quality day care can be beneficial, promoting both cognitive and social development. Many early studies were carried out at high-quality university-based centers, and they produced no hint of developmental difficulties in the children involved.

Debate continues, however, over the issue of day care for infants under 12 months of age, with strong arguments on both sides (Belsky, in press; Clarke-Stewart, 1989; Fein and Fox, 1990; Scarr et al., 1990). The issue is complex and difficult to study, for a number of reasons. It is hard to measure how well infants are developing emotionally, hard to separate the effects of day care from other factors that may be associated with it (such as financial problems in the family), and often hard to determine how best to interpret findings when different interpretations are possible. Our review of the research leads to the conclusion that both the timing and the quality of day care are important. But even then, the issue is not fully settled (Sroufe, 1990).

Controversy centers on the quite consistent finding that babies who begin full-time day care (more than 20 hours a week) *before* 12 months of age are more likely to develop an anxious-avoidant attachment to the mother than are babies raised at home or placed in part-time day care, or babies who begin full-time day care *after* age 12 months (Barglow et al., 1987; Belsky, 1990; Belsky, in press; Schwartz, 1983; Vaughn et al., 1980). These studies now have involved hundreds of children, and the result holds for those in day-care centers *and* those in family day-care homes, for those from middle-class households *and* those of lower socioeconomic status. A study by Brian Vaughn and Byron Egeland (1980) is representative. They studied three groups of babies from economically disadvantaged homes: those who started full-time day care early (before 12 months of age), those who started it later (between 12 and 18 months), and those who were not placed in day care by 18 months. When the quality of attachment was assessed at age 12 months, 47 percent of those already in day care were classified as anxiously attached. Of these, *all* displayed the anxious-avoidant pattern, which is associated with a parent who is physically or emotionally inaccessible. This is a striking finding. In contrast, only 28 percent and 18 percent, respectively, of children in the other two groups were classified as having anxious-avoidant attachments. Assessment of the children and their mothers in terms of socioeconomic status, stress level, personality, and other factors at the beginning of the study suggested that preexisting differences among the groups did not account for these results. Instead, early out-of-home care seems to be the factor underlying the increase in anxious-avoidant attachments.

Day care, however, cannot be seen as a direct cause of anxious-avoidant attachment. After all, most babies become securely attached, even those who start day care early. For this reason Jay Belsky (in press) concludes that early full-time day care is a *risk factor* for anxious attachment—a contributor or marker rather than a cause (see Chapter 15).

An increase in anxious attachment, and anxious-avoidant attachment in particular, among early-day-care infants makes sense in terms of the sensitive period hypothesis. The first year is presumably a sensitive period for the formation of attachment, and anxious-avoidant attachment is linked to the caregiver's emotional unavailability during this time. From this perspective it would also follow that any lasting negative consequences of entering early full-time day care would more likely be due to the impact on the developing parent-child relationship than to any trauma to the infant caused by the care arrangement.

Critics of these studies have argued that attachment differences between home-raised and early-day-care infants may not be important (Clarke-Stewart, 1989; Scarr et al., 1990). One argument is that any negative effects may not be long-lasting. However, follow-up studies have revealed persistent differences among those experiencing early full-time day care, especially problems with aggression (Belsky, 1990; Belsky, in press; Haskins, 1985). Another argument is that early-day-care infants classified as anxious-avoidant in the Strange Situation may simply not be stressed by the procedure because they are more independent as a result of their greater experience with being away from their primary caregiver. However, studies have shown that early avoidance is associated with later dependency (see Chapter 10), not independence, so this argument is weak as well. Moreover, Belsky and Braungart (1991) have shown that day-care infants classified as anxious-avoidant are just as stressed by the Strange Situation as are non-day-care infants.

A more persuasive argument is that the increase in anxious-avoidant attachment among early-day-care infants is caused not by early day care itself, but by poor-quality early care. Numerous studies have confirmed the importance of the quality of substitute care (Andersson, 1992; Burchinal et al., 1989; Howes,

1990; Vandell, in press). The study by Carolee Howes (1990) though not a study of attachment, is especially revealing because she systematically examined both age of entry into day care and quality of care. She found that low-quality day care was related to noncompliance, negative emotions, and hostility during various phases of the preschool period. She also found that entry into poor-quality day care before 12 months of age added to these negative outcomes. Early, good-quality day care, however, did not have such negative effects. Jay Belsky (in press), who has criticized early day care, has also concluded that it is the combination of early and low-quality day care that puts infants at risk.

Given the current status of the evidence on the timing and quality of day care, we would favor more child care options for parents of young infants, so that full-time day care is not their only choice. Many countries, such as Sweden, are far in advance of the United States in providing leave from work for the parents of young children. Beyond this, good-quality day care must become widely available. At present, the millions of poor in this country do not have access to it (Children's Defense Fund, 1994).

THE SPECIAL IMPACT OF EARLY EXPERIENCE

Since all development is important, it makes no sense to say that one period is more important than another. Yet there is a way in which early experience has special significance. An analogy is building a house. All parts of the house are, of course, important. Without a frame there can be no roof, and without a roof any structure will soon deteriorate. But the entire building depends on, and begins with, a solid foundation. Similarly, basic expectations about oneself and the social world are laid out during infancy. Such expectations may guide later encounters with the world, coloring the experiences children seek and how they interpret them.

Psychoanalytically oriented researchers also argue that early experience is important because it cannot be readily brought to consciousness and examined, and therefore any ill effects from it may not be easily corrected (e.g., Bowlby, 1973). It is unlikely that the monkeys studied by Novak and colleagues (1992) remembered their early social deprivation, or that Fairbanks' (1989) monkeys remembered how they were mothered. Rather, patterns of behavioral and emotional regulation laid down in infancy were not erased by intervening experience but remained available when cued by an appropriate context.

Early experience, of course, does not determine the rest of development, and genuine change can always occur. For at least some children whose early care is inadequate, the course of later development ultimately is normal (Egeland 1994; Erickson et al., 1985; Rutter, 1988; Werner and Smith, 1992). Research suggests that such *resiliency* in development is not due to an inherent invulnerability of some children but rather, like troubled behavior itself, reflects processes of development. In part it has to do with the timing of changes in experience, the qualities of later experiences, or both. It is sometimes the case that, where there is a return to healthy development, the early experience itself was not so bad, or the child had some positive experiences to draw on. The important point to remember is that if early deprivation is not extreme and prolonged, later change remains possible.

APPLYING RESEARCH FINDINGS HELPING INFANTS IN INSTITUTIONS TO DEVELOP NORMALLY

In recent years there has been concern about the growing number of babies whose parents cannot care for them but who are hard to place in foster homes. These include infants born drug addicted and the more than 1 million babies worldwide believed to be infected with HIV, the virus that causes AIDS (Annunziato and Frenkel, 1993). There has been discussion of caring for such infants in institutions, but past experience in the United States, and more recent experience in Eastern Europe, shows that raising infants in traditional orphanages can have devastating results (Provence, 1989; Johnson et al., 1992).

For instance, videotapes made in the "best" Romanian orphanages (where conditions are sanitary and the children's nutritional needs are met) document the profound consequences of emotional deprivation. Without attentive, emotionally involved caregivers, babies are apathetic and disengaged from their surroundings; they appear to clinical observers to be depressed. Often they don't even show wariness when it would be expected. If they display positive emotion, it is like that of a much younger child. An 18-month-old, for example, might smile at the face of a stranger in the manner of a normal 2- or 3-month-old. These children's social relations are also abnormal, with social give-and-take notably absent. The infants treat others more like objects than people. They also show unusual mannerisms, such as rocking themselves.

Research suggests that impersonal care is the critical cause of these symptoms. Institutional settings with a more homelike atmosphere, where a baby gets individualized care from the same caregiver, compromise development far less. A classic study by Harriet Rheingold (1956) showed dramatic results with even a modest change in care from the regimented patterns of traditional orphanages. She provided eight institutionalized 6-month-olds with responsive social interaction, while a control group of infants received only the routine institutional care, which was only physically adequate. After 8 weeks of treatment, the experimental group was much more socially responsive. These babies smiled and vocalized more in interactions with adults than the control infants did.

More extensive changes could probably avoid many of the negative consequences of raising infants in institutions. The major goals would be to provide recurrent social interaction and emotional involvement with one caregiver (or a small number of caregivers); to assure continuity in care; and to provide interesting sensory experiences for the child to explore on a daily basis. Some specific changes to accomplish these objectives (based on Provence, 1989) are listed in the accompanying table. Institutionalization of infants is to be avoided if at all possible and should never be considered a routine procedure. But if such settings are developed for certain extreme situations, proper conditions of care must be ensured.

RECOMMENDED CHANGES FROM TRADITIONAL INSTITUTIONAL CARE TO INDIVIDUALIZED CARE

Traditional Institutional Care	Individualized Care
Feeding with propped bottle	Holding with eye-to-eye contact while feeding
Left in crib except for daily bath and dressing	Given floor freedom and interaction with adults on demand
Toys suspended from crib	Interactive play with adults as well as crib toys
An 8-to-1 ratio of infants to caregivers for 8-hour day (a ratio of 32 to 1 at night)	One-on-one contact frequently throughout the day (regular night staff as well)
Confined to the nursery	Varied experiences in and away from the institution

CHAPTER SUMMARY

1. Newborn infants are equipped with certain predispositions that enable them to become participants in early social exchanges, provided that their caregiving system is responsive. These predispositions include the ability to express their needs to adults, the tendency to be attracted to and actively seek social stimuli, and the inclination to "fall in step" with the caregiver's behavior.

2. **Reciprocity** in social interaction, involving truly mutual exchanges, develops gradually. At first the caregiver must orchestrate social dialogues, pacing and modifying the stimulation in coordination with signs from the child. This process of *attunement* is part of a more general style of behavior known as **sensitive care.** Sensitive care involves being aware of a baby's needs and feelings and responding to them promptly and effectively. In time, the baby's involvement in social encounters becomes more complex. In the second half-year, infants become able to anticipate others' actions and deliberately seek them out. They are now partners in social give-and-take.

3. Developments in the second half-year of life are so dramatic that they can be considered qualitative, not just quantitative. Among these developments is the emergence of quite complex **emotions,** such as joy, anger, fear, and surprise. Another reaction appearing at this age is **stranger distress.** Babies in the second half-year also express **separation distress** when the principal caregiver temporarily leaves them, as well as joyous greetings when the caregiver returns. These emotional reactions indicate that the caregiver has become linked to special, very positive feelings.

4. **Attachment** is an enduring emotional tie between infant and caregiver that develops out of many weeks of interaction. Babies apparently form an attachment to whomever is consistently available to them. John Bowlby has proposed that a strong inclination to become attached evolved in our early ancestors because infants who displayed such a tendency had a survival advantage.

5. Currently, there are two major approaches to explaining individual differences in infant social and emotional behavior. One, the *attachment framework,* focuses on the security and confidence of infants with respect to their caregivers. The other, the *temperament framework,* emphasizes dimensions of behavior, such as how active, hesitant, or irritable an infant is. These two views together yield a fuller picture of individual differences among infants.

6. Attachment researchers have focused on the link between the quality of care in early infancy and later **secure** or **anxious attachment.** When care is emotionally unresponsive or parents are rejecting, an increase in **anxious-avoidant attachment** has been found. When care is haphazard or inconsistent, an increase in **anxious-resistant attachment** has been found. When the caregiver's behavior is threatening or incoherent, **disorganized-disoriented attachment** is more likely to occur. However, most infants experience adequate care and have secure attachments. Inadequate care is often related to high stress or low social support for caregivers.

7. **Temperament** researchers often assume that differences in behavioral style are largely determined by inborn factors. Therefore, they have sought to show that such differences appear early and are highly stable over time. Research does show that, by the end of the first year, differences in behavior are rather consistent across situations and stable over time. However, it is more difficult to get agreement among observers about a baby's temperament in the early weeks of life, and there is often little stability from the newborn period to later months or years.

8. It is likely that both differences in temperament and differences in care influence the way infants behave. Recent studies have tried to combine the temperament and attachment frameworks. Quality of care may determine the infant's degree of confidence in the caregiver; differences in temperament may determine how this confidence or lack of confidence is expressed.

9. According to the **sensitive period hypothesis,** early care is of special importance for healthy emotional development. One way to test this hypothesis is to conduct early intervention research, in which caregivers of infants at risk for developmental problems are given special support in rearing their babies. The development of these infants is then compared to that of children whose caregivers did not receive such help. Several such studies have been conducted, with some positive results.

PART TWO

EPILOGUE

Infancy

Development during the first year of life is rapid and dramatic. The weak and uncoordinated newborn who interacts with the world largely through preprogrammed reflexes becomes, 12 months later, a child who can voluntarily reach for, inspect, and manipulate objects, while at the same time skillfully navigating by creeping or even walking. Cognitively, too, 12-month-olds have made remarkable progress. They have a good grasp of object permanence and can recognize and even categorize many things, categorization skills being directly linked to their improving memory abilities. Twelve-month-olds also have expectations and intentions regarding the environment, plus a growing understanding of how actions and events are related to each other. In addition, they show many quite complex emotions, such as joy of mastery, surprise when something unexpected happens, and anger if a goal is blocked. They are now able to engage in true social give-and-take, and they have formed the close relationships with caregivers known as *attachments*.

All these advancements are closely interconnected. There are remarkable parallels between descriptions of cognitive, emotional, and social development in infancy (see the table on p. 241). Infant emotional reactions expand dramatically in the second half-year. Infants show emotions that require anticipation (e.g., surprise) and emotions that require recall and comparison of a past event with a present circumstance (e.g., fear). Such changes in emotion draw upon advances in memory development and in the capacity to coordinate schemes that emerge in the second half-year. In addition, emotional reactions are influenced by context—what has happened just previously, who is present, the familiarity of surroundings, and so forth—and not just by the event. In this change, as in changes in cognitive development described in Chapter 5, we see that infants in the second half-year now respond to more than just their immediate perceptual experience.

Likewise, advances in social relationships and advances in cognitive development are closely connected. The beginning of social relationships is intimately tied to the cognitive ability to detect contingencies (such as the link between the child's own crying and a parent's responses). At the same time, interactions with caregivers provide a wealth of new opportunities to learn about contingencies. To take another example, consider attachment. Although it is viewed as an aspect of social and emotional development, it is based on the cognitive abilities to distinguish among people, to form expectations based on past interactions, and to understand that a caregiver continues to exist even when out of sight. Concurrently, social exchanges with the caregiver provide the infant with many chances to develop and practice these important cognitive skills. These examples point to the integrated nature of development. Cognitive, social, and emotional growth all proceed together.

Research on brain development during infancy also reveals qualitative changes in structures and functioning. One such change occurs over the first 3 months, when the cortex, or outermost layer of the brain, becomes functional. This development promotes a shift from reflexive to more deliberate control of behavior. A second major change occurs at about 10 months, with maturation of the frontal lobes of the cortex and the establishment of connections between the higher brain

STAGES (IN MONTHS) OF COGNITIVE DEVELOPMENT AND RELATED CHANGES IN THE EMOTIONAL AND SOCIAL DOMAINS

Cognitive Development (Piaget)	Emotional Development (Sroufe)	Social Development (Sander)
0–1 Use of reflexes Minimal generalization/accommodation of inborn behaviors	**0–1 Absolute stimulus barrier** Built-in protection	**0–3 Initial regulation** Sleeping, feeding, quieting, arousal fluctuations Beginning preferential responsiveness to caregiver
1–4 Primary circular reaction First acquired adaptations (centered on body) Anticipation based on visual cues Beginning coordination of schemes	**1–3 Turning toward** Orientation to external world Relative vulnerability to stimulation Beginning social smiles	
4–6 Secondary circular reaction Behavior directed toward external world (sensorimotor "classes" and recognition) Beginning goal orientation (procedures for making interesting sights last, deferred circular reactions)	**3–6 Reactions to familiar and unfamiliar** Pleasurable assimilation, failure to assimilate, disappointment, frustration Pleasure as an excitatory process (laughter, social responsivity) Active stimulus barrier (investment and divestment of emotion)	**4–6 Reciprocal exchange** Caregiver and child coordinate feeding, caretaking activities Affective, vocal, and motor play
	7–9 Active participation Joy at being a cause (mastery, initiation of social games) Failure of intended acts (experience of interruption); anger, surprise Differentiation of emotional reactions (initial hesitancy, positive and negative social responses)	**7–9 Initiative** Early directed activity (infant initiates social exchange, preferred activities) Experience of success or interference in achieving goals
8–12 Coordination of secondary schemes and application to new situations Objectification of the world (interest in object qualities and relations, search for hidden objects) True intentionality (means-ends differentiation, tool-using) Imitation of novel responses Beginning appreciation of causal relations (others seen as agents, anticipation of consequences)	**9–12 Attachment** Emotionally toned schemes (specific emotional bond, categorical reactions) Integration and coordination of emotional reactions (context-mediated responses, including evaluation and beginning coping functions) Greeting reactions Fear, anxiety	**10–13 Focalization** Caregiver's availability and responsivity tested (demands focused on caregiver) Exploration from secure base Reciprocity dependent on contextual information
12–18 Tertiary circular reaction Pursuit of novelty (active experimentation to provoke new effects) Trial and error problem solving (invention of new means) Physical causality spatialized and detached from child's actions	**12–18 Practicing** Caregiver as secure base for exploration Elation in mastery Emotion as part of context (moods, stored or delayed feelings) Control of emotional expression	**14–20 Self-assertion** Broadened initiative Success and gratification achieved apart from caregiver
18–24 Invention of new means through mental combination Symbolic representation (language, deferred imitation, symbolic play) Problem-solving without overt action (novel combinations of schemes)	**18–36 Emergence of self-concept** Sense of self as actor (active coping, positive self-evaluation, shame) Sense of separateness (affection, ambivalence, conflict of wills, defiance)	

and subcortical areas related to emotion and memory. This development supports qualitative changes in both cognitive and social behavior. Given these changes in the brain, it is not surprising that a 10-month-old's behavior is so qualitatively different from a 6-month-old's, as you saw in our example of mothers playing the "towel-in-the-mouth" game with their babies at the beginning of Chapter 1. At the same time, development of these brain structures is dependent on cognitive and social stimulation in the previous months (Schore, 1994).

THREE INFANTS

You have seen three infants begin developmental journeys toward becoming both unique individuals and members of a common human community. In many ways these children started life with the same endowments. Each had essentially the same biological equipment—the same inborn sensory and motor capabilities, the same innate inclination to seek and respond to social stimuli. None was retarded, seriously ill, or otherwise significantly impaired. All presented their parents with the task of raising a normal, healthy baby. Over the course of their first year, each went through the same set of developmental sequences, though at somewhat different rates. Each came to recognize the basic properties of objects and to form attachments around which their social, emotional, and cognitive worlds became organized. Each experienced good enough care so as not to suffer failure-to-thrive syndrome or some other severe developmental problem.

Yet despite these shared characteristics and experiences, we also see in these three children the beginnings of three distinct individuals. Malcolm, for instance, is ahead of the others in physical maturation. He is a strong, robust baby who starts to "do for himself" early. Meryl, in contrast, is a rather cranky, difficult infant, easily irritated. Her feeding problems and persistent colic pose special challenges. Mikey, like Malcolm, is good-natured and exuberant, although his activity level is not as high as Malcolm's. Such differences in children's habitual styles of responding can best be understood using the concept of *adaptation*, the process whereby the child and the social environment constantly adjust to one another. Let's look at our three children's caregiving environments and then examine how child and environment interact and mutually adapt.

THREE CAREGIVING ENVIRONMENTS

Just as our three children have basic biological traits in common, so their parents face common caregiving tasks. All the parents must meet their baby's physical needs while providing an environment with enough regularity so that the child's cycles of feeding, sleeping, and interacting with the world can become reasonably organized and stable. The parents must also provide appropriate social stimulation and be adequately responsive to their infants. To a large extent, they must shape their own behavior to that of the baby, so the child's capacity to adapt is not overtaxed. In the process, the child will learn that it is possible to have an impact on the environment.

Although all the parents in our stories face these common tasks, how they perform them is greatly influenced by the contexts in which they live. John and DeeDee Williams, for example, are embedded in a network of caring relationships among the many members of their household. In raising Malcolm they are supported by their two older children, as well as by John's sister, Denise, and his mother, Momma Jo. Thus, Malcolm's early development is taking place in a system of social, psychological, and economic support that is difficult for a parent operating alone to match. In facing the challenges of urban minority-group life, Malcolm is surrounded by a buffering circle of warmth, love, and nurturance.

Mikey's situation has some of these same elements. Both parents are clearly very attached to him. Frank prizes the "all-boy" son he so wanted, and Christine is a competent, responsive mother who offers Mikey a rich social environment. Christine and Frank, too, have some emotional support from Christine's mother and sisters in raising the new baby. Moreover, Mikey's own sisters, who have been well nurtured themselves, occasionally help in the care of their brother.

But one important difference distinguishes Mikey's home environment from Malcolm's: in the Gordon household the seeds of serious conflict exist between husband and wife. Frank is intolerant of Christine's desire to have a life beyond that of wife and mother. Christine, although still generally accepting Frank's wishes, is beginning to realize that her talents are appreciated outside the home. She is vulnerable to feeling that her goals are being unfairly blocked by Frank. Some signs point to Mikey becoming a buffer between his parents, as when his demands at the breakfast table ("beh!

beh!") distract Frank from an argument with Christine. Despite these undercurrents of tension, however, Mikey is developing nicely as an infant.

Meryl's situation contrasts sharply with those of Malcolm and Mikey. An unplanned child, she was born to a mother who was not well prepared to respond to a baby's needs. Karen is not only young and financially dependent, she is also socially isolated—cut off from Meryl's father and her former high school friends, and alienated from her mother, who might have been her one reliable resource. Kay, who is Karen's one new friend, turns out to have a chaotic household and leads an unpredictable life. When she leaves for Dallas, Karen is completely alone except for weekly counseling at the Teen Mother Project. Because of her own unmet needs for care and nurturance, Karen, not surprisingly, has trouble adequately nurturing Meryl. Karen is torn between her strong desire to be a good mother and her feeling of being totally overwhelmed by the task.

THE INTERPLAY BETWEEN CHILD AND ENVIRONMENT

Child and environment constantly interact, each adapting to the other to achieve a temporary fit. The adjustments that are made then serve as a starting point for a new round of interactions and adaptations. A good example can be seen in Frank Gordon's early interactions with Mikey. Frank responds to his normal, healthy son as if he were the most robust, athletic infant ever born. In so doing he draws Mikey's behavior toward more and more exuberance and a greater tolerance for rough-and-tumble play. As Mikey increasingly shows these "masculine" qualities, Frank's expectations about the child are confirmed and he is further encouraged to treat the baby like a "real boy." In this way, father and son interact to create the kind of child Frank so much desires. Notice how both Mikey's characteristics and Frank's behavior are involved here. The fact that Mikey is a boy and his ability to tolerate Frank's level of stimulation are important, but Frank's reaction to Mikey is critical too. Were Frank very low-keyed or uninvolved with his son, Mikey would develop differently.

Similar interactions and adaptations are taking place in our other two households. Malcolm, for instance, enters the world as a loud and lively infant. Rather than being viewed as irritants, these characteristics are cherished in his family. Upon hearing Malcolm's lusty wails, Momma Jo calls them "just grand!" and John Williams

tells his son he is "one helluva kid." In this context Malcolm becomes a sociable, good-natured, "easy" baby, which further promotes positive responses from the members of his family. Not all infants with Malcolm's characteristics would develop this way. Without the easygoing acceptance found in Malcolm's home, what becomes sociability and exuberance could instead have become hyperactivity and a demanding nature.

Meryl and Karen provide a final example of the interaction between infant and caregiving environment. Meryl was a fretful, colicky newborn who cried a great deal. Did these characteristics cause Karen's insecurity in her role as a mother, or did Karen's insecurities, including her stress and anxiety during pregnancy, give rise to Meryl's behavior and physical distress? Clearly it is difficult to say, because the various factors are interrelated. Meryl's difficulties lower the confidence of an already insecure mother, and Karen's doubts and anxieties perpetuate and worsen Meryl's fussiness. In this case, there is a poor match between the particular infant's needs and the particular caregiver's competencies. Mother and child become locked in a negative caregiving cycle that is unlikely to be broken easily. Meryl is a prime candidate for developing the anxious-resistant pattern of attachment associated with inconsistent care.

These, then, are the initial adaptations of our three fictionalized children and their caregiving environments, all based on composites of cases in our research. They will be carried forward to become part of the developmental context during the toddler period. Meryl, Mikey, and Malcolm now have individual styles of behavior that will affect how others respond to them. Likewise, the expectations of the people close to these children have increasingly crystallized, a development that in turn will further influence the kind of care that family members provide.

Many questions remain, however. Is Meryl destined to be a difficult and troubled preschooler? Under what circumstances might she evolve a more positive adaptation? If circumstances dramatically improve for Meryl, will she still be vulnerable in certain ways? Might Mikey, too, have certain vulnerabilities, and how could they manifest themselves in later periods of development? How will the very active Malcolm fare when he enters school, where strict demands for orderliness and quiet will be imposed on him? What special challenges will he face as a black child in a densely populated urban setting? We will address these and other questions in the following units of this book.

PART THREE Toddlerhood

PART THREE

Three Children as Toddlers

MALCOLM WILLIAMS

A gust of breeze rippled the water in the wading pool, sending a large leaf floating slowly across the surface. The little boy leaned over the edge and stretched out his arm. He could almost touch the leaf with his fingers. He reached a little farther, then a little farther.

"Malcolm M. Williams, you get yourself away from that water this instant or you're gonna be one sorry chil'!"

Two-year-old Malcolm turned and looked in Momma Jo's direction. Glancing back at the water, he started to reach for the leaf one more time, but then stopped himself. Momma Jo's tone meant business. He knew better than to defy her when she sounded like that.

"That boy's just like his father was at his age," Momma Jo commented to an elderly woman she often sat with in the park. "You turn your back for just one second and there he's gone and got himself into a pile of mischief. Yes," she laughed softly, "a pile of mischief!" and she gazed lovingly at her grandson, who was now intent upon catching a small gray poodle with a rhinestone collar.

"Doggie, doggie, doggie," Malcolm crowed gleefully, as he ran back and forth, his arms outstretched.

Momma Jo stood up and buttoned her coat against the growing chill. "Well, we best be goin'," she told her friend reluctantly. "It's gettin' dark so early these days. Winter's almost on us, that's for sure. Malcolm, honey! We're leavin' now. You let that dog be." And taking Malcolm firmly by the hand, Momma Jo started toward the park exit.

"Happy to you! Happy to you!" Malcolm sang to himself as they walked along.

"It's not your birthday anymore, honey," Momma Jo explained to Malcolm with a smile. "That was last week. Now you have to wait a whole year more for another birthday. Then you'll be three."

"Malcky two!" the little boy said proudly with an energetic hop as they stopped at the corner of First Street and Delany. Momma Jo now had a choice to make. If she went down Delany past the excavation site for the new post office, she could cut a few blocks off her normal route. But Delany Street was deserted and filled with boarded-up buildings. It was not a safe place after dark. What could anyone want with an old woman and a baby, Momma Jo thought, deciding to risk the short walk down Delany after all. "We'll be home quicker this way," she said to Malcolm, reaching down to make sure the hood of his coat was securely tied beneath his chin. "We're real late already. Your momma's gonna worry."

"Who that?" Malcolm asked, pointing a mittened hand at four teenage boys leaning against the construction site fence. "No one we know, honey," Momma Jo answered. "Come on now, Malcolm, we're gonna walk on the other side of the street." But the four boys crossed with them, two in front and two behind. Quickly they made a circle around Momma Jo and Malcolm.

"Where ya hurryin' to, momma?" one of the four asked.

"Just let us by," Momma Jo said. "We don't want any trouble."

"No trouble, momma," the ringleader answered. "We just wanna know what you got in that bag of yours?"

"Take the bag and just let us be," Momma Jo pleaded, the tension mounting in her voice.

Malcolm looked up at Momma Jo and then at the four strangers. "Go 'way," he said quietly at first; then, louder, "Go 'way."

The four boys looked at Malcolm and started laughing. "You heard what the man said," the ringleader hooted. "He said, go 'way!" The other three laughed louder. "Are we gonna go 'way like the little man says?"

Momma Jo put an arm protectively around Malcolm, but his attention was drawn elsewhere. "Look!" he said in his babyish voice, and his mittened hand shot up. Everyone turned to see a blue and white police car cruising slowly down the street. The four boys scattered.

"Everything all right here?" one of the policemen asked as the car stopped beside Momma Jo and Malcolm.

"It is now, officer," Momma Jo answered. "But we sure would appreciate an escort to the corner in case those four young hoodlums decide to come back."

"I'll do better than that," the policeman said. "Hop in and we'll drive you home."

"I still can't believe you were walkin' there!" John Williams said to his mother after dinner that night. "You read about things happenin' there all the time. Where was your head, Momma?"

"They're safe," said DeeDee, as she cleared the dishes off the table. "That's all that matters. So let's just forget it now."

"If I had been there I would have showed them," 14-year-old JJ remarked, punching the air with his fists. "I ain't afraid of no gang turkeys."

"That's enough of that talk," his father snapped back. "Those dudes are nothin' to mess with, you hear me? You could get yourself hurt bad, boy. Hurt real bad."

"Hurt. Band-Aid. Kiss it better," Malcolm added knowledgeably. And despite himself, John smiled.

Later that night, as DeeDee was getting Malcolm into his pajamas, she stopped and held him by the shoulders. "I know it may be hard for you to understand," she said, "but I want you to know I'm real proud of you for stickin' up for your gran'ma today."

"Malcky go p'lice car!" Malcolm answered, still brimming over with excitement.

"I know, baby, I know," DeeDee said and hugged her little boy close.

MIKEY GORDON

"Where's my little all-star?" Frank Gordon called out as he swung open the back door and stepped into the kitchen. Twenty-five-month-old Mikey, grinning from ear

to ear, ran to greet his father and be scooped up into his arms. "There's my tough guy," Frank said, grinning back at Mikey as he held him at arm's length above his head. Mikey laughed and crowed gleefully: "Daddy home!"

"How was your day?" Christine asked as she washed some tomatoes at the kitchen sink. But Frank was too involved to answer. Mikey had run off to the living room and Frank ran after him. "Here I come!" yelled Frank, and when he caught Mikey he picked him up and tossed him in the air. Mikey squealed with delight.

"Be careful now," Christine called from the kitchen. "You don't want him to bump his mouth again."

"Women!" Christine could hear Frank saying to Mikey. "They don't understand us men, do they, Tiger?"

"No!" said Mikey emphatically with a shake of his head, even though he had no idea what he was agreeing to.

"Anything good happen today?" Frank asked Christine as he came back into the kitchen to get himself a beer. Christine knew exactly what this question meant. Frank wanted to know if anything special had happened with Mikey that day.

"Well, when I wasn't looking he figured out how to open up the vacuum cleaner and take the bag out. Then he wanted to see what was in it, so he ripped the bag open and dumped all the dirt on the floor. When I turned around there he was with the empty bag upside down on his head! 'Party hat,' he kept saying. He must have been remembering Janie's birthday, you know, with those big paper hats I made for the kids. Anyway, it was a real mess to clean up!"

Frank chuckled and shook his head. "What a kid," he said.

Later that night, when she had washed and dried the dishes, Christine tried to lead Mikey upstairs to bed. "No!" said Mikey, pulling his hand away and holding it tightly against his chest.

"Maybe he's not tired," Frank remarked from his seat in front of the TV.

"Frank, he's exhausted," Christine shot back. "But you get him so worked up in the evening he can't get to sleep."

"Yeah, yeah, it's always *my* fault," Frank answered irritably.

By now Christine had Mikey in her arms and was at the foot of the stairs. "No!" he said squirming to get down. "I do it!"

"Okay, sweetie. You do it yourself." And Christine watched with amusement as Mikey determinedly climbed the stairs alone, cautioning himself as he gripped the balusters: "Careful. Hold on."

"Well, he's all settled in," Christine announced to Frank as she came back downstairs after reading Mikey a story. She flopped down beside Frank on the sofa, slid off her shoes, and put her feet up on the table. "The girls are ready for bed, too. I told them they could play one more tape and then lights out."

"Quiet," said Frank. "This is a good program."

"You know," said Christine, "I wouldn't mind if just once in a while we could talk at night instead of you shushing me up so you can watch the damn TV."

"I talked before and what'd it get me? A lousy put-down, that's what."

"All I said was that Mikey was tired, and he was."

"It's the *way* you said it," Frank answered, hitting the off button on the TV remote. "OK. What is it? I know you got somethin' to say. So just say it. Let's get it over with so I can get some peace around here."

"That's right," Christine answered, standing up and looking angrily at her husband. "Yeah, I've got something to tell you. I've been thinking about this a long time now, wondering if I should. But tonight you make me mad enough to be really sure. Helen's opening a new shop just for kids' clothes and she wants *me* to help her manage it. And I'm gonna say yes whether you like it or not! What do you think of that?"

"Oh great! What is this? The new independence? The modern woman crap? It's those damn buying trips I've let you go on. Give you an inch and you want a mile!"

"I *know* I can do it," Christine answered defiantly. "I've got it all figured out. Five mornings a week in the shop, and the rest at home where I can still do my sewing. I've even looked into day care for Mikey."

"Dump Mikey in day care?" Frank shouted, the veins on his neck standing out. "Now you've gone too far, Chrissie! What the hell kind of mother are you?"

"I'm a good mother! This isn't just any old day-care center. It's run by experts on kids. People who teach at Brown."

"Screw experts! I don't want any eggheads messin' with my kid. They'll turn him into a pansy just like themselves!"

"Oh, Frank, that's ridiculous! I could bring in nearly $20,000 a year between this new job and my sewing. And we could really use the money around here, the way you've been doing lately!"

As soon as the words were out of her mouth Christine was sorry. It was true that Frank's hours had been cut back at work, but that wasn't his fault. The construction business was slow all over the state. What a stupid, unfair thing to say, she thought. She was just about to tell him she was sorry when suddenly she felt her head snap sideways. With his large, powerful hand Frank had struck her across the face. Christine was stunned. It was not so much the pain, which was bad enough, but the shock that paralyzed her. Frank had never in his life even so much as raised a finger to her.

"Chrissie," Frank said. "God, I didn't mean to. It just happened. When you said that . . . Look, we'll work this out, OK? Chrissie?"

Mikey came down to breakfast full of smiles as usual. Although at first he had protested being left at day care in the mornings, he now looked forward to going. As he had for the last week and a half, he toted with him an old Raggedy Ann doll that had once belonged to Becky. Mikey was oblivious to the doll's shabby condition. He loved it passionately, perhaps because of the little red heart on its chest. Mikey parked the doll beside his bowl of cereal and began to eat noisily. His father seethed across the table. Finally, he reached out and picked up the toy.

"Mikey," Frank said, "You're a big boy now, and big boys don't play with dolls. Only girls and sissies do. You don't want to be a sissy, do you?" Mikey didn't understand what his father was talking about. All he knew was that his favorite toy had just been taken from him. He let out a loud wail.

"Frank," Christine protested, "he's only two."

"Stay out of this, Chrissie," Frank snapped back. "It's that damn day care center and I'm not gonna let it happen. I'm gonna put a stop to it right now."

Then more gently he said to Mikey: "Don't cry, Mikey. We'll go to the toy store and get you a great big red fire engine. The kind with lights that flash and a siren that goes off when you press a button. Would you like that, huh?"

Mikey stopped crying and wiped his face. For a few days he asked his mother where "Rang-ety" had gone. But soon he forgot all about the doll with the little red heart on its chest.

MERYL POLONIUS

A barrage of large raindrops spattered against the windows. Water overflowed from the gutters and gushed noisily onto the back steps. Sitting warm and dry on the kitchen floor, 15-month-old Meryl Polonius was oblivious to the weather that beat upon the house. For what seemed to her mother like the hundredth time, she was carefully inspecting the contents of the kitchen cabinets. Whenever she took out a pot or other utensil she would hold it up and exclaim: "Eh! Eh!" Besides something that sounded like "muh" (used to refer to her mother as well as her grandmother), "eh" was Meryl's only other word. But she used it very expressively. "Eh?" she asked while pointing to some newfound object, obviously wanting to know what this strange and wonderful thing was. "Eh!" she demanded while holding up a set of sticky fingers, clearly wanting someone to hurry and clean this mess off.

Karen sat at the kitchen table, aimlessly twirling a lock of hair around her index finger. She pored over the Sunday want ads, a red felt-tip pen in her hand. "Let's see. 'ASSEMBLY LINE—light packaging—full-time days.' Forget that. 'CLERICAL—word processing and data entry.' Computers? Are you kidding? 'DELIVERY PERSON—must have own truck or van.' Fat chance. 'RECEPTIONIST—good typing skills essential.' Ha! I can't even type my name without a mistake."

In the midst of this dreary round of pessimism, the kitchen door opened and Karen's mother, Margaret, burst in. "What weather!" she said to Karen, pushing the wet hair back from her face.

"Did you sell the house?" asked Karen, looking up from the paper.

"No. The snooty woman didn't like the color of the tile in the bathroom. And the husband saw that the chimney was leaking a little. 'What doesn't leak in monsoons like this?' I tried to tell him. But his mind was made up."

"Tough luck," said Karen and turned back to her job search.

Karen had moved back in with her mother about a month before, just in time for Christmas. Living alone had become unbearable for her. The counselor at the Teen Mother Project had helped to get Karen and her mother back together. At the second of three sessions they had together, Margaret Polonius poured out her feelings of guilt over Karen's pregnancy. "I feel I failed you as a mother," she told Karen with tears in her eyes. "I wasn't much older than you when I got pregnant and had to marry your father. I of all people should have been able to guide you better. I'm sorry, honey, if I let you down." Karen had cried out of sheer relief that someone in the world really cared about her. She and her mother still disagreed on many subjects, but at least they could talk to one another now without the old battles starting up again.

"See any interesting prospects?" Karen's mother asked, bending over her daughter's shoulder to see what she had circled in the paper. "Look at all these listings. There's got to be something here. Don't be *too* fussy, you know. It doesn't have to be the greatest job to start with. Just something to get you out of the house a little and meeting new people."

"I'm not being fussy!" Karen snapped. "It's just that I'm not qualified for anything. What do I know except housework and babies. Ha! That's it. I'll get a part-time job as a nursemaid!"

"What about these waitress jobs?" Margaret Polonius pressed on, ignoring both her daughter's sarcasm and the loud clanging of metal in the background as Meryl banged the lids of two pots together. "Here. 'WAITRESSES—immediate openings—full- or part-time—apply in person—The Green Door.' That's a nice place. What's wrong with that?"

"But I'm not *experienced*, Mom. That's what's wrong. They want only experienced people."

"How do you know that if you don't try? You're bright and attractive. If I had a restaurant you'd be just the kind of girl I'd want to hire."

Karen rolled her eyes. "Mom. Look. It says *immediate*. I'm not ready immediately. I don't have a sitter lined up for Meryl. And she's so cranky and difficult sometimes it's gonna be hard to find anyone who wants the job."

"Well, I may have the answer to that," Karen's mother said, cutting off her daughter's last excuse. "Arlene Springer down at the office told me about this wonderful woman on Cragmont Street who takes care of children in her home. She's raised five children of her own, and one of them's a doctor. How much more qualified could she be? Just do me one favor, Karen, and apply at The Green Door. I think it could be perfect for you."

The following January was another rainy one in Fresno. Continual rain and local flooding kept traffic moving slowly. It was almost 5:00 p.m. when Karen finally arrived at Mrs. Jaspers' house to pick up Meryl. Usually she arrived by 4:30, right after her 11 to 4 shift at The Green Door. But today she had had to stop at the store, and the lines at the checkout counters had been long. Meryl was sitting on the floor in front of the television when Mrs. Jaspers opened the door and let Karen in.

"Ready to go home?" Karen asked Meryl, picking up her little yellow raincoat.

"No!" said Meryl and kept staring at the TV.

At first Mrs. Jaspers had been hesitant about accepting Meryl into her family day care. With Meryl's long list of allergies and shyness with other children, Mrs. Jaspers thought that this little girl might be too much of a problem. In the beginning Meryl *was* a problem. All day she would follow Mrs. Jaspers around, whining and pouting when urged to play with the other children. At home, Meryl's tantrums, which were bad enough already, became even worse. Her behavior toward Karen was oddly ambivalent. Sometimes she would show a great deal of anger; other times she would cling and demand to sit on Karen's lap.

In time, however, Meryl settled down at Mrs. Jaspers' house and became more interested in playing with the toys. Recently she had begun to play a make-believe game in which a family of stuffed bears acted out everyday activities. "Bye-Bye. Go work now. Don't cry, baby. Mommy be back." Most of her other favorite pastimes were quiet, solitary activities, like stringing large wooden beads. When she was finished she would take her creation to Mrs. Jaspers, requesting "Tie it, pwease," and then wear it around her neck for the rest of the day. Outdoors Meryl's behavior was equally reserved. When Mrs. Jaspers installed a seesaw, Meryl was the only child who refused to try it out, although she quietly watched the other children from a safe distance. When Mrs. Jaspers tried to coax her on, Meryl retreated to the sandbox, where she took up the more secure activity of spooning sand into little plastic cups. But despite her reserve, Meryl had adapted to day care. She no longer gave Mrs. Jaspers any trouble to speak of. Her whining and uncooperativeness tended to surface only when it was time to go home.

"No?" asked Karen of Meryl as she stood holding out one arm of the yellow raincoat. "You don't want to come home with me? Don't you want to have your dinner? I know I'm a little late, but I got held up at the store.

What if we have ice cream for dessert—then will you come home with me?"

"No, I won't!" answered Meryl.

Karen glanced over at Mrs. Jaspers, who was busily picking up toys. Meryl didn't say "no" to her as often as she did to Karen. A few weeks before Karen had asked Mrs. Jaspers why she thought that was. Mrs. Jaspers had smiled that motherly smile and put an arm around Karen's shoulders. "Children need to learn to mind, dear," she said kindly. "They know when you don't mean it. You just love her and mean what you say, and Meryl will be just fine." It sounded so simple. But for Karen it didn't come easily.

"Please, Meryl, come on," Karen tried again, doing her best to sound firm. "We can have ice cream."

"Chocowat?" Meryl finally asked after considering the offer for several seconds. And when her mother nodded assent she stood up so Karen could put on her coat. At least this time there wasn't a tantrum.

Chapter 7

Toddler Language and Thinking

Chapter 7

Toddler Language and Thinking

Meryl was 16 months old before she finally said her first recognizable word. When Karen went into Meryl's room to get her up from her nap, Meryl announced with a serious look: "Mama." Karen was elated. "Mama! Yes, mama! I'm your mama!" she told Meryl, picking her up and giving her a hug that made the little girl squirm. Minutes later Karen was on the phone, sharing the news with her mother at work.

To parents, children's first words are among the most exciting events in their development. Language opens up new, much more efficient ways to communicate. The parents can now *hear* some of what the child is thinking; they can ask a question or give an instruction and get a verbal response. Emerging language is one example of a general capacity for **symbolic representation**—that is, the use of ideas, images, sounds, or some other symbol to stand for objects and events.

The capacity for symbolic representation appears during a major transition period—the transition from infancy to childhood. This transition is called the *toddler period* because it coincides with the time that children learn to walk. The toddler period begins at roughly 12 months of age and extends to about age 30 months.

Because language is such an important accomplishment of the toddler period, it will be the primary focus of this chapter. (Many of the other important aspects of toddler cognition have already been discussed in Chapter 5.) **Language** is an abstract, rule-governed system of arbitrary symbols that can be combined in countless ways to communicate information. Language is not simply synonymous with speech. People who are totally deaf and unable to speak but who can use sign language possess a genuine language. Their hand signs are symbols that allow them to express any idea they wish. Conversely, a parrot that can mimic the words of its trainer is not displaying true language. To the parrot, words are just sounds to be imitated; they do not symbolize anything.

This chapter begins with a look at the various components of human language to give you some idea of all a toddler needs to learn when mastering language. Next we examine the course of early language learning, including mastery of sound patterns, word meanings, grammar, and the social use of language. We then consider the relative contributions of the child and the environment to the process of language development. Finally, we discuss two nonlinguistic aspects of toddler cognitive development that are related to the emergence of symbolic representation—the development of gestures and early pretend play.

Symbolic representation: The use of ideas, images, or other symbols to stand for objects or events.

Language: An abstract, rule-governed system of arbitrary symbols that can be combined in countless ways to communicate information.

THE COMPONENTS OF LANGUAGE

When 2½-year-old Meryl hands Mrs. Jaspers a string of beads and requests "Tie it, pwease," her simple spoken words reflect a major accomplishment. They show that Meryl is mastering the many conventions of language—conventions for combining sounds into meaningful words, and words into meaningful sentences. Meryl knows, for example, that the sound combination /tai/ means to fasten two pieces of string together. She also knows that, for her sentence to

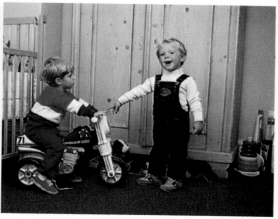

Children's ability to communicate becomes more flexible and precise with the emergence of language. Young infants must rely on crying to make their needs known, but toddlers are able to use language to communicate more specific desires.

make sense, the object "it" must *follow* the verb, not precede it. Meryl, of course, does not think of speech in terms of such rules, but she follows the rules of English nonetheless. She is also starting to follow conventions regarding how an English sentence should be worded in a given social context, such as the convention that "please" should be part of a request, especially one directed to an adult. All this Meryl has mastered in the single year since she spoke her first word. To better understand the magnitude of the task that the language-learning toddler faces, let's look more closely at the various components of language.

SOUNDS, STRUCTURE, MEANING, AND CONVERSATIONAL RULES

All languages can be broken down into five major subsystems: phonology, semantics, morphology, syntax, and pragmatics. Becoming a competent speaker of a language requires learning all five.

Phonology is the set of sounds used in a language, the rules for combining those sounds to make words, and the use of stress and intonation in spoken sentences. Every language has its own set of **phonemes**—speech sounds that contrast with one another and can change the meaning of a word. For example, in English the sound of the /b/ in *bat* is a different phoneme from the sound of the /p/ in *pat,* which is why you immediately recognize these two words as different. Other languages include phonemes not used in English, such as the tongue-trilled /r/ in Spanish, the German /ch/ sounds, and the clicking sounds used in some African languages.

Semantics consists of the meanings of words and sentences. A sentence might be perfectly correct grammatically but nevertheless be confusing because it breaks semantic rules. For instance, if a preschooler told you "My daddy is having a baby," you would ask for clarification, even though the child's grammar is flawless, because the meaning of the word *daddy* is inconsistent with the meaning of the phrase *having a baby.*

Morphology is the system of rules for combining units of meaning to form words or to modify word meanings. The smallest meaningful units in a language are called **morphemes.** Many words are single morphemes, such as *child, language,* and *speak.* Other words consist of several morphemes strung together. The word *unspeakable,* for example, has three morphemes: the prefix *un-* (meaning not), the root word *speak,* and the suffix *-able* (meaning capable of

Phonology:
The set of sounds used in a language, the rules for combining those sounds to make words, and the use of stress and intonation in spoken sentences.

Phonemes:
Speech sounds that contrast with one another in a particular language and can change the meaning of a word.

Semantics:
The meanings of words and sentences.

Morphology:
The system of rules for combining morphemes to form words or to modify word meanings.

Morphemes:
The smallest meaningful units in a language.

being done). Because each of these is a meaningful unit, it is considered a separate morpheme.

Syntax:
The way in which words are organized into phrases and sentences.

Syntax refers to the way in which words are organized into phrases and sentences. Following the rules of syntax allows you to form grammatical sentences and convey the meaning you intend. "The boy kissed the girl" and "The girl kissed the boy" are both grammatical sentences, but they mean different things because of a single change in word order. On the other hand, "Kissed the girl the boy" does not follow the usual rules of English syntax and so is hard to interpret.

Pragmatics:
The set of rules governing conversation and the social use of language.

Pragmatics is the set of rules governing conversation and the social use of language. It includes knowing how to use language to accomplish social goals. For example, there are various ways to make requests in English. If you wanted someone to open a window, you could say "Open the window!" or "Would you please open the window?" or "Can you open the window?" or even "It's hot in here." Native speakers of English implicitly know that all of these sentences can be requests and that they vary in politeness and directness. Pragmatics also includes knowing how to adjust language to fit different social situations. How you talk to your best friends differs substantially from how you talk to your professors, even when you are conveying the same basic information. Similarly, if you were explaining how to play a game to a 5-year-old, your choice of words and sentence structure would be quite different from those you would use in speaking to an adult. In each case your language is guided by rules of pragmatics.

PRODUCTIVE AND RECEPTIVE SKILLS

Another way to view what children master when they learn their native language is in terms of the mental skills required. Actually, children need two sets of skills to be able to communicate effectively: *productive skills*, which are used to put ideas into words, and *receptive skills*, which are used to understand what other people say.

One reason toddlers love to be read to is that their receptive language skills—their ability to understand what they hear—tends to exceed their skill at producing language themselves.

Many parents feel that their infants can grasp much of what they are told before they are able to talk. Although parents tend to overestimate this ability in babies, they are basically correct that receptive skills emerge sooner than productive ones (Golinkoff, Hirsh-Pasek, Cauley, and Gordon, 1987). This can be seen in every aspect of language development, including phonology (Palermo, 1978). Consider Meryl, who as a toddler could not pronounce the phoneme /l/. Her *l*'s came out sounding like *w*'s. One day Karen teasingly said to Meryl, "Wet's go!" Meryl responded "No. Not wet's. Say *wet*'s." Although she still mispronounced the sound of /l/, she could hear the difference between a correct and an incorrect pronunciation by someone else. Her receptive phonology was more advanced than her productive phonology. In a similar manner, young children seem to understand words that are not yet in their active vocabularies, and they also seem to understand sentences that are much longer and more complex than the ones they themselves speak.

MAJOR TASKS IN EARLY LANGUAGE LEARNING

Compared with Meryl, Malcolm was an early talker. Even when just a baby of 8 or 9 months, he was constantly babbling strings of nonsense syllables that sounded startlingly like real speech. "Ah-ma-ka?" he might ask of DeeDee, his voice rising to frame a question as he jangled a set of car keys in the air above his head. And when DeeDee would laugh and answer that those were indeed for the car, he would bob his head smiling as if he understood: "Ah-ka-ba-ba! Ah-ka-ba!"

To follow the progress of children like Malcolm and Meryl in their efforts to communicate with speech, we can look at each of the areas of language introduced in the previous section. First we examine how children master the sound patterns of their native language (phonology) and how they learn the meanings of individual words (semantics). Then we see how they develop sets of rules about the structure of language—rules for modifying word meanings (morphology) and for organizing words into sentences (syntax). Finally, we consider how children learn to use words and sentences in socially appropriate ways (pragmatics).

LEARNING THE SOUND PATTERNS OF A LANGUAGE

One difficult aspect of learning a language is mastering its sound patterns. Think about your own past experiences listening to foreign languages. The sounds probably seemed blurred together, with no pauses between them. You may have wondered how anyone could make sense of such rapid speech. Now imagine the task confronting children who do not even know that words exist. Somehow, just by hearing others talk, they learn to recognize and produce the various phonemes of their language. Ultimately, they break down the stream of speech sounds they hear into words, and they begin to produce recognizable words themselves.

Much progress toward mastering the sounds of a language occurs in the first year of life, even before a baby actually begins to produce words. During this time, dramatic changes in babies' vocalizations take place, culminating in the ability to produce speech sounds. This early period of **prelinguistic vocalization** can be divided into five stages (Menn and Stoel-Gammon, 1993).

Prelinguistic vocalization: Sounds produced by infants during the first year of life, before they begin to speak.

Crying:
Reflexive vocalization that occurs automatically whenever an infant is overly aroused.

Cooing:
Prelinguistic vocalizations that consist largely of vowel sounds and express pleasure and contentment.

Vocal play:
Prelinguistic vocalizations that vary greatly in pitch and loudness, including occasional simple syllables.

Canonical babbling:
Prelinguistic vocalizations consisting of strings of syllables that sound increasingly like speech.

Conversational babbling or jargon:
Prelinguistic vocalizations in which infants use adultlike stress and intonation.

Protowords:
Vocalizations that seem to have consistent meanings for a child and are used in attempts to communicate, but do not closely resemble adult words.

In the first stage, the baby's only means of vocal communication is **crying.** Crying is a reflexive vocalization that occurs automatically whenever an infant is overly aroused. As you learned in Chapter 4, however, babies' cries vary somewhat depending on the nature of their discomfort. A cry of pain, for instance, is noticeably different from a hunger cry.

The second stage of prelinguistic vocalization begins at around 2 months of age. Now the baby starts to make sounds that express pleasure and contentment. This behavior is called **cooing** because it involves many vowel sounds, especially /u/, and very few consonant sounds. Babies also begin to laugh and chuckle during the cooing stage.

At about four months of age, babies enter the third stage, **vocal play.** During this stage, they seem to be trying out the range of their vocal abilities, and they produce sounds that vary greatly in pitch and loudness. They also begin to utter occasional simple syllables consisting of consonant-vowel combinations (*ba, ga, ma,* and so forth).

The fourth stage, **canonical babbling,** begins at about 6 months of age. During this stage, babies' vocalizations sound increasingly like speech. Instead of isolated syllables, they begin to produce strings of syllables. At first, these strings consist mostly of one syllable repeated over and over (for example, *ma-ma-ma-ma-ma*). Later, strings of different vowel and consonant combinations become more common, with babies producing utterances like "Ma-ga-bi-gu-gi," or Malcolm's "Ah-ka-ba-ba."

During the canonical babbling stage, children are not yet imitating the particular phonemes of their native language. When Meryl, Malcolm, and Mikey were beginning to babble, they not only made sounds corresponding to English phonemes, they also made some sounds that are phonemes in other languages. Infants around the world initially babble similar sounds, despite being exposed to very different languages. Moreover, they do not seem to produce *all* the phonemes found in human speech, and the most frequently and infrequently produced sounds are fairly similar across languages (Locke, 1983). This suggests that the early development of speech sounds is constrained more by infants' physical limitations than by their environments. Linguistic input from the environment begins to become important during this stage, though. Deaf infants engage in vocal play very similar to that of babies who can hear, but they are slow to produce the clear consonant-vowel syllables of canonical babbling (Oller and Eilers, 1988).

By 10 months or so, most infants progress to the fifth stage, **conversational babbling** or **jargon,** in which they begin to use adult-like stress and intonation, as Malcolm did when "asking" DeeDee about the car keys. Because of its patterns of stress and intonation, jargon sounds quite like conversational speech. It seems to include clear questions and statements, but without identifiable words. During this stage, there begin to be differences in how often babies produce particular sounds, depending upon the language they are acquiring (Boysson-Bardies and Vihman, 1991).

Between 10 and 12 months, most children start to make the transition from babbling to true speech. A few **protowords** may appear—vocalizations that seem to have consistent meanings for a child and are used in attempts to communicate, but do not closely resemble adult words. Meryl's "eh" and "muh" are examples of protowords. Children's protowords and their first real words are constructed from a limited set of speech sounds appropriate to their native lan-

Toddlers' first words are often names of familiar objects or persons. The naming of the object is frequently accompanied by pointing, an earlier and much less differentiated form of communication.

guage. These are usually the same speech sounds that became predominant during the conversational babbling stage.

Interestingly, there is great similarity across languages in children's early pronunciation errors, suggesting continuing physical constraints on children's sound production. For example, English-speaking children frequently substitute a /t/ sound for a /k/ sound, as in saying "tat" for "cat." The same error has been observed in children learning such disparate languages as German and Hindi (Locke, 1983).

The developmental sequence involved in acquiring speech sounds during the first year of life suggests that two things are needed to prepare children to begin speaking. First, they must gain control over their speech apparatus—the mouth, lips, tongue, and vocal cords. This control enables them to produce speech sounds intentionally. The process is aided considerably by such physical changes as the emergence of teeth and the development of the muscles in the tongue. Second, children must learn the phonemes of their particular native language. They must pay close attention to the speech sounds they hear and begin to imitate them. Only when they can recognize and produce at least a small repertoire of appropriate speech sounds are they ready to combine sounds to make words.

LEARNING WORDS AND THEIR MEANINGS

FIRST WORDS

Most children say their first clearly identifiable words around their first birthday, although there is great individual variation in the age at which first words are spoken. In general, children's first words refer to familiar persons ("mama"), body parts ("nose," "feet"), animals ("doggie"), and objects ("shoe," "ball"). Many children's early vocabularies are dominated by words referring to the objects and people that they regularly interact with (Bates, Bretherton, and Snyder, 1988; Dromi, 1987; Nelson, 1973). But first words may also express feelings ("naughty," "goodboy"), movement ("up," "down," "allgone," "byebye"), and social commands that the child uses as a unit and does not break down into their component words ("gimmefive!"). For example, as Meryl watches a car disappear down the street, she might comment "bye" or "allgone." Notice that although "allgone" is two words for adults, many young toddlers treat it as one. Another common topic during the single-word phase is expression of the concept *no*. Young toddlers often develop several ways of expressing this concept. In addition to the traditional "no," they might say "me" or "mine," meaning "No, *me* do it" or "No, that's *mine*."

Children differ in the purposes for which they use their first words. Some initially use words mainly to *refer to objects and events;* their first words are mostly nouns, plus some verbs and adjectives. This is called a **referential style** of word use. Other children initially use words mainly to *express social routines;* their first words are primarily pronouns, such as "me" or "mine," and formulas, such as "stopit." This is called an **expressive style** of word use. These differences in how first words are used are related to other aspects of children's social and cognitive development (Bates et al., 1988; Goldfield and Snow, 1993; Nelson, 1981). For example, expressive children are more likely to be second-born and to come from less educated families than referential children are (Nelson, 1973). Mothers of referential children tend to encourage labeling by asking their children many questions. In contrast, mothers of expressive children tend to use language more as a means of directing their children's behavior (Lieven, 1978; Olsen-Fulero, 1982). Referential children initially tend to acquire words faster than expressive children do, though the two groups speak equally grammatically (Clark, 1983).

VOCABULARY GROWTH

Children's vocabularies grow quite quickly after they begin to speak, although the exact rate of growth is not certain. An early study suggested that the average **productive vocabulary**—the number of words a child can actually use when speaking—is 1222 for a 3½-year-old and 2526 for a 6-year-old (Smith, 1926). More recent work suggests that the productive vocabulary of the average 6-year-old may be much larger—as high as 8000 to 14,000 words (Carey, 1978).

Despite such different estimates of the rate of vocabulary growth, all studies show the same general pattern. New words are usually acquired rather slowly during early toddlerhood, but in most children the rate of vocabulary growth increases dramatically at about 18 months of age, as shown in Figure 7.1. This sudden increase in word acquisition is known as the **vocabulary spurt.** Referential children, who are learning mostly nouns, show a more obvious vocabulary spurt than do expressive children, who are adding roughly equal proportions of nouns and other kinds of words to their vocabularies (Goldfield and Reznick, 1990).

Children's **receptive vocabularies** (the words they can understand, even if they don't use them) are considerably larger than their productive vocabularies. A truly remarkable growth in receptive vocabulary occurs between the ages of 1 and 6. One estimate is that by the time children are 6, the rate of new additions to their receptive vocabularies is an amazing 22 words a day (Miller, 1981).

PROCESSES OF WORD LEARNING

Interestingly, children start to say words even before they really grasp the concept of words or names. These earliest words tend to be bound to the particular contexts in which they are learned (Barrett, 1986; Nelson, 1983, 1985). It is not

---

Referential style:
A language pattern in which the child initially uses words primarily to refer to objects and events.

Expressive style:
A language pattern in which the child initially uses words primarily to express social routines.

Productive vocabulary:
The words a child can actually use when speaking.

Vocabulary spurt:
The sudden increase in word acquisition that occurs at about 18 months of age.

Receptive vocabulary:
The words a child can understand, even if he or she does not use them.

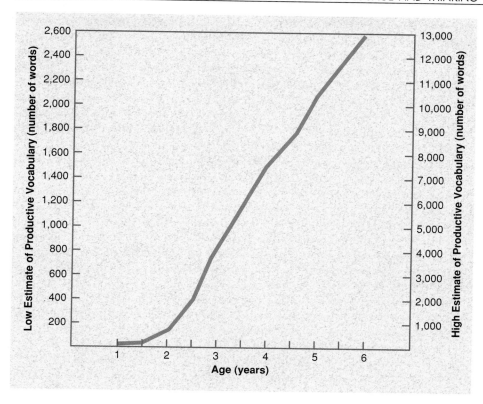

FIGURE 7.1 ESTIMATES OF VOCABULARY GROWTH AS A FUNCTION OF AGE
This figure illustrates the slow initial growth of productive vocabulary, followed by spurts in growth at about 18 months and 2½ years of age. The two scales indicate the uncertainty about the size of toddlers' and preschoolers' vocabularies. (Source: Based on Carey, 1978; Miller, 1981; and Smith, 1926.)

until around the time of the vocabulary spurt that children start to use words to refer to *categories* of objects, people, and events, rather than limiting their use to particular instances and contexts. In fact, many of the earliest words children speak actually disappear from their vocabularies once word learning begins in earnest (Dromi, 1987). This suggests that these earliest words were not part of a true linguistic system. A milestone in language development comes when the child finally discovers that everything has a name (Gopnik and Meltzoff, 1987; Nelson, 1985). Now vocabulary building is speeded up as the toddler begins to ask incessantly, "What that?"

The task of word learning is all the more complex because most of the words that children learn are not often spoken separately. Usually the child must pick out the critical group of sounds from a longer string of sounds the adult is making. When DeeDee says to Malcolm, "Look at the ball *roll*," Malcolm must extract the new word "roll" from his mother's flow of speech. Sometimes toddlers make a mistake in deciding the location of word boundaries, and they produce a sentence like "Readit the book." In this case, the child has incorrectly concluded that the verb is "readit," rather than "read." Such mistakes are called **segmentation errors.** Segmentation errors are fairly common, especially where unstressed syllables come at the boundaries between words (Gleitman and Wanner, 1982), but children usually correct them quickly.

Once toddlers have identified a certain string of sounds as a word, they must figure out what that word means. Children as young as 2 years old seem to be able to use the context—both linguistic and nonlinguistic—in which an unfamiliar word appears to make a quick and reasonably accurate guess as to its

Segmentation error: A mistake in detecting boundaries between words in a sentence.

These three objects might provide toddlers with opportunities for both overextension and underextension of the word ball.

Fast mapping:
A process in which a young child uses context cues to make a quick and reasonably accurate guess about the meaning of an unfamiliar word.

Lexical contrast:
Children's assumption that no two words have the same meaning.

Underextension:
A language error in which the meaning a child attaches to a word is too restricted.

Overextension:
A language error in which the meaning a child attaches to a word is too broad.

meaning (Carey, 1978). This process is known as **fast mapping.** In a study by Tracy Heibeck and Ellen Markman (1987), 2-, 3-, and 4-year-olds received brief exposure to unfamiliar terms for colors ("chartreuse," "amaranth," "maroon"), shapes ("oval," "hexagon," "trapezoid"), and textures ("coarse," "fibrous," "granular"). In each case, the experimenter used the unfamiliar term in contrast to a familiar one, such as "blue," "round," or "fuzzy" ("Bring me the chartreuse one. Not the blue one, the chartreuse one.") When the children were tested a few minutes later, even the 2-year-olds showed comprehension of the unfamiliar terms, especially the ones that referred to shapes.

Fast mapping can work only if children have some built-in assumptions about the most likely meanings of unfamiliar words. Suppose DeeDee points to a large red ball and says the word "ball." How is Malcolm to figure out that "ball" is the name of the thing itself, not one of its qualities ("red," "round," "large"), or even one of DeeDee's actions ("look," "point")? Some theorists suggest that children have a built-in tendency to perceive objects from a very early age (Gibson and Spelke, 1983) and to assume that unfamiliar words are names for objects rather than for attributes or actions (Huttenlocher and Smiley, 1987; Markman and Hutchinson, 1984).

But what if DeeDee holds up the red ball and says, "Look, Malcolm, it's red"? How can Malcolm figure out that "red" is not just another word meaning "ball"? Several researchers propose that children have a built-in tendency to assume that no two words have the same meaning. Thus, they tend to assume that unfamiliar words do not refer to things for which they already have labels (Barrett, 1986; Clark, 1988, 1990; Markman, 1987). This assumption is known as **lexical contrast** (*lexical* means "pertaining to words"). When Malcolm hears "red" spoken in reference to this ball, he assumes that it must contrast in meaning with the word "ball," which he already knows. He therefore explores features for which he does not yet have labels as possible meanings for "red." When he hears "red" also applied to his toy fire truck, his overalls, and his new winter coat, he concludes that "red" must be the name for this particular color.

ERRORS IN EARLY WORD LEARNING

Once toddlers have properly isolated a word, they very seldom assign entirely the wrong meaning to it. Malcolm, for example, is not very likely to decide that "red" means any round object that bounces and scream "Red!" when his brother comes home with a new basketball. Such errors are not very frequent in toddlers' productive language, the words they actually speak. They may be more common in their receptive understanding of what others are saying.

The semantic errors that toddlers make are usually errors of under- and overextension. **Underextensions** occur when a word is used correctly but in too restricted a way. Suppose Mikey is given a toy dump truck and told that this is a "truck." He then starts to use the word to refer to toy trucks only, not to full-sized trucks he sees on the road. Mikey has an underextended concept of truck. The meaning he attaches to the word does not extend to all instances of trucks. In **overextensions,** toddlers make the opposite mistake. Because their definition of a certain word is not sufficiently restricted, they sometimes use it when it doesn't really apply. If Mikey initially uses "truck" to refer to *any* wheeled vehicle—cars, trains, even wagons—he is using the word too broadly; he is overextending its meaning.

Underextensions are much less obvious than overextensions are. When children overextend the meaning of a word, they use it in clearly inappropriate ways, such as calling a squirrel "kitty." When they underextend the meaning of a word, they simply fail to use it where it could have been used. But by carefully observing toddlers over time, we can see that they do sometimes underextend word meanings. For instance, one little boy at age 8 months responded to the word "shoes" by crawling to the shoes in a particular closet (Reich, 1976). Gradually he generalized the meaning of this word to shoes in another closet, then to shoes left outside closets, and finally to shoes on people's feet. A similar pattern can be seen in a little girl who at first applied the word "car" only to cars moving on the street outside her living room window (Bloom, 1973). Six months passed before she extended the meaning to encompass cars in other situations.

Overextensions are very common in most toddlers' speech. The word "ball," for example, is frequently applied to a range of relatively small, rounded objects, such as apples, melons, and eggs. Most overextensions of nouns refer to objects broadly similar in appearance, especially those similar in shape (Clarke, 1983). Children may overextend the same word in a variety of ways. One little boy used the word "Nunu" (the name of the family dog) to refer not only to all dogs but also to other animals and birds, to furry slippers and coats, and even to black olives in a salad, which resembled the dog's nose (de Villiers and de Villiers, 1979). Toddlers also overextend verbs and other parts of speech. One toddler initially used the word "out" to refer to opening or closing a door. Later the child generalized the meaning of "out" to peeling fruit, shelling peas, and undoing shoelaces (Clark, 1973, 1983).

One study of language development in six children found that the rate of overextensions was very high in the initial stages of building a vocabulary (Kuczaj, 1982). Then, as the toddlers learned more words, the rate of overextensions dropped dramatically. This pattern makes a great deal of sense. The more words children know, the higher the likelihood they will know the right word to use in a given context.

When children do overextend the use of a word, does it mean that they are totally unaware of the boundaries of that word's meaning? Not necessarily. Put yourself in Mikey's place when he wants to call attention to a bus that just went by. If he knows the word "truck" but not the word "bus," might he not decide to use "truck" instead of nothing at all? This example suggests that toddlers may

Suppose Meryl has the words "cheese," "truck," "toast," "mama," "kitty," "dada," "blankie," "go," and "milk" in her vocabulary. How would she label the objects shown here? Quite likely she would call the first "truck," the second "toast," and the third "cheese." While such labels are wrong, they represent smart mistakes; she has chosen the best word available. She would label none of these objects "kitty" or "blankie."

sometimes *knowingly* produce overextensions. They use a word in a wrong context not because they're unaware that the word doesn't quite fit, but because that word is the one in their vocabulary with the closest meaning to what they want to say.

Studies of *receptive overextension* show that toddlers have more knowledge of word meanings than their rate of *productive overextensions* suggests. For example, even though Mikey called a bus a "truck," he could probably pick out the correct objects from a set of toys if asked by an adult "Where's the bus? Where's the truck?" (Clark, 1983). This implies that Mikey does have the concept of bus, even though he doesn't know the word "bus" as well as he knows "truck." He uses "truck" when he can't remember "bus" because a truck and a bus have some features in common.

To summarize, there are several reasons why toddlers produce under- and overextensions of words. Apparently, when words are first learned, they tend to be used only in the specific contexts in which they were originally encountered, resulting in underextensions (Bowerman, 1981; Carey, 1978). Later children begin to explore the limits of word meanings. Does "ball" mean all roundish objects? Does "truck" mean anything with wheels? Overextensions occur at this point. At the same time, however, a toddler may knowingly overextend a word because it is the closest one available in his or her vocabulary. In these cases the child is searching for the right word, and is very responsive to corrective feedback from adults ("No, that's not a truck; that's a bus"). Receiving feedback following errors of overextension is probably one of the most effective ways in which children learn new words (Merriman, 1986). Finally, as children's vocabularies grow, the rate of overextensions declines.

LEARNING MORPHOLOGICAL RULES

Grammatical morpheme: A unit of language that carries little meaning by itself, but that changes the meaning of words or sentences in a systematic way.

The words that children first learn are usually single morphemes: "Mommy," "Daddy," "milk," "doggie," "go," "more," "cookie," "sock." Each is a unit of language that represents a single object, action, or quality. As language development proceeds, however, children gradually begin to add grammatical morphemes to the words they speak. **Grammatical morphemes** are units of language that carry little meaning by themselves, but that change the meaning of words and sentences in systematic ways. They include prefixes, suffixes, auxiliary verbs, articles, and certain prepositions. For instance, the sound of /s/

Toddlers' early sentences often require considerable interpretation.

added to the end of a noun such as *sock* changes its meaning from singular to plural. The suffix *-s,* therefore, is a grammatical morpheme.

Roger Brown (1973) studied the learning of grammatical morphemes in three children whom he called Eve, Adam, and Sarah. He found that they acquired these morphemes in a consistent order, although their speed of acquisition varied considerably. The same pattern appeared in a cross-sectional study of a large number of children (de Villiers and de Villiers, 1978). First, children master the grammatical morphemes indicating plural nouns, along with the suffix *-ing* to form the present participle of a verb (as in *going* or *running*). Somewhat later, children acquire the suffix *-ed* to form the past tense of verbs (as in *jumped*), as well as the suffix *-s* to form the third person singular (as in *she sits*). Among the last grammatical morphemes to be mastered are those that form contractions of the verb "to be" (the *'s* in *it's big,* for example, or the *'re* in *they're playing*).

The order in which toddlers acquire grammatical morphemes has nothing to do with how often they hear each of these morphemes in the language spoken to them. Contrary to what you might expect, the most frequently heard morphemes are not acquired first (Brown, 1973). Instead, three other factors seem to govern the order of acquisition.

First, *grammatical* or *structural complexity* plays a role. Roger Brown (1973) suggests that morphemes that produce the simplest change in structure are learned first. For example, the plural suffix *-s,* one of the first grammatical morphemes mastered, involves simply adding an */s/* sound to the end of a noun.

Second, *semantic complexity* helps to determine the order in which morphemes are acquired (Brown, 1973). The *-ing* that forms the present participle, another morpheme acquired early, adds to the verb the quite simple idea of ongoing action. In contrast, appending an *-s* to a verb to form the third person singular (as in "she sit*s*") is more semantically complex even though it appears structurally simple. This is so because it adds several ideas: (1) that we are talking about someone else; (2) that only one person or object is referred to ("he," "she," or "it," not "they"); and (3) that the action takes place in the present.

Finally, the *phonological characteristics* of a morpheme—how it sounds—also seem to influence how early it is acquired. For example, Turkish children acquire some grammatical morphemes earlier than children learning other languages do, probably because Turkish grammatical morphemes are mostly full syllables, and many are word endings that are pronounced with considerable stress (Slobin, 1982). This may make them easier to notice.

The acquisition of grammatical morphemes is of particular interest to developmentalists because it shows that language learning involves discerning rules. For instance, children do not learn the plural forms of nouns word by word, as if each one were an entirely new entity. Instead, they learn a general rule about forming plurals: add the suffix *-s* or *-es* and the noun becomes "more than one." In an interesting study, Jean Berko (1958) showed how children apply morphological rules even to words they have never heard before. For example, she taught children that the name of an unusual birdlike creature was a *wug*. Then she showed them a picture of two of these creatures and said: "Here are two ____." The children's task was to fill in the blank. Those who had acquired the rule of adding *-s* to form the plural readily answered "wugs." Berko's study shows the great *productivity* of language—the fact that it allows almost unlimited output because it is governed by general rules. As a result, we can take even an unfamiliar word and modify its meaning in ways that others will understand.

Potential stumbling blocks for toddlers are the exceptions to morphological rules. Most nouns can be made plural by adding *-s* or *-es,* but in some cases this rule does not apply (*mouse/mice,* for example, or *foot/feet*). Similarly, although the usual way to form the past tense of a verb is to add the suffix *-ed,* irregular verbs don't follow this convention (*go/went, come/came*). You might think that children would learn the regular forms first and only afterward tackle the exceptions. This, however, is not the pattern researchers have observed (Marcus et al., 1992). Instead, the correct irregular past tenses and plurals often appear early in a child's speech, with the child correctly saying "came," "did," "mice," "feet," and so forth. Shortly thereafter an odd thing happens. The child starts to impose regular forms on irregular nouns and verbs so that "mice" becomes "mouses," "feet" becomes "foots," "came" becomes "comed," and "did" becomes "doed." These errors are called **overregularizations.** Overregularizations appear at about the same time that the child begins to use regular past tenses and plurals reliably. Apparently, the child has learned the *-ed* and *-s* rules and has started to apply them indiscriminately. Overregularizations do not completely replace the correct irregular forms, however. In fact, most children overregularize verbs only occasionally. By early school age, children are using correct forms almost 100 percent of the time (Cazden, 1968), although school-age children still occasionally produce incorrect irregular forms, such as "I *brang* my lunch."

Overregularization is an example of what developmentalists call a *growth error.* When overregularization appears, there is an increase in the number of mistakes a child makes in forming past tenses and plurals, which on the surface might seem like a setback in language development. However, the mistakes are due not to regression or loss of ability, but rather to the emergence of a more advanced way of thinking. Even though children who overregularize temporarily make more mistakes, they are in fact making progress toward understanding the morphological rules of their language.

Overregularization provides important insights into the cognitive processes that underlie language learning. When learning something complex, such as a language, children seem to search automatically for regularities and rules. To find these regularities, however, they must first learn a number of examples from which the rules can be drawn. At this early stage they learn both regular and irregular forms of plurals and past tenses, each one as a separate entity. Then, from this pool of known examples, they filter out the irregular ones and zero in on the patterns used in the majority of cases. With the rules figured out, they begin to apply them in other cases (including irregular nouns and verbs). Gradually, children develop an understanding of which verbs and nouns are exceptions to the rules, and overregularizations fade out.

This learning process is clearly very complex, as anyone knows who has ever tried to master the irregular forms in a second language. Yet preschoolers seem to accomplish it with little effort, just from hearing language being spoken. Long before adulthood morphological rules and most exceptions to them seem second nature to us, even though we may still be caught off guard when asked what the plural of *moose* is or whether the past tense of *fly* is ever *flied.* (It is, in the sentence "The batter flied out.") Our hesitation in answering such questions reminds us what a remarkable achievement it is for young children to master morphological rules.

Overregularization:
A language error in which a child applies the rules for regular past tense and plurals to irregular verbs and nouns.

LEARNING TO FORM SENTENCES

We noted earlier that *syntax* is a language's rules for organizing words into phrases and sentences. In any system of syntax, individual words belong to particular **form classes,** such as nouns, verbs, and adjectives. In English, for instance, *dog* and *justice* are classified as nouns, *sit* and *believe* as verbs, *lazy* and *purple* as adjectives, and so forth. Syntactic rules specify how words that belong to various form classes can be combined to make phrases, clauses, and sentences.

One set of syntactic rules governs how phrases are formed. For example, an article and a noun make up a noun phrase, such as "the boy" or "a dog." Other syntactic rules limit the ways in which phrases can be put together to make sentences. For example, "A dog bit the boy" and "The boy bit a dog" are acceptable sentences in English, but "Bit the boy a dog" is not.

Form classes, phrases, and sentences are all highly abstract categories. Children cannot learn syntactic rules simply on the basis of noticing how specific words, like *dog* or *boy,* are used in sentences and then figuring out a rule for each individual word. Instead, children somehow extract and use rules involving these abstract categories from the particular, concrete examples of speech they hear. This is *not* to say that young children are consciously aware that they are learning and using grammatical rules. It will be years before they are cognitively advanced enough to understand and talk explicitly about grammatical categories and rules.

A very important feature of syntactic rules is their productivity. Just as morphological rules allow for tremendous output in forming and modifying words, so syntactic rules allow for countless possible sentences just by placing different words in various roles. Once children are able to use the rules of syntax, their ability to create new and meaningful sentences becomes virtually unlimited.

Form class:
A category of words in a language that can fill similar syntactic roles in forming phrases and sentences.

THE ONE-WORD STAGE

When children first start saying recognizable words, they use only one word at a time. To an adult, a single word is often just a label for an object, action, or quality. To a toddler, however, a single word can be an attempt to communicate much more. For example, when Meryl says the word "mama," she may be simply labeling her mother, or she may be trying to express some idea related to Karen that an older child would express with a phrase or sentence (de Villiers and de Villiers, 1978). Your interpretation of Meryl's meaning would probably depend on the context in which she says the word. If she says "mama" when Karen enters the room, she might be trying to communicate "Here is mama." If she says "mama" after Karen leaves the house, she might be trying to tell someone "I want my mama." Or if she says "mama" while holding up Karen's purse, she might be trying to express the idea "This belongs to mama." A word that conveys such extended meaning is called a **holophrase.** Of course, when a toddler says a single word, it is not always obvious whether that word is meant just as a label for something or whether it is intended to communicate a more complex meaning. To tell the difference, listeners must often pay attention not only to the context but also to the child's gestures, facial expression, and tone of voice.

Holophrase:
A single word that conveys the meaning of a phrase or sentence.

FIRST SENTENCES

Usually at around 18 to 24 months of age, toddlers start to put two words together. At the beginning of this phase, they may not really be saying two-word sentences. Often they appear to be expressing two separate ideas, one after the other. For example, psychologist Lois Bloom's daughter Allison said "daddy, car" on one occasion when her father left in the car. On another similar occasion, she said "car, daddy" (Bloom, 1973). In both cases, she paused between one word and the other, as if she were conveying two related, but separate thoughts ("There goes *daddy*. Daddy is in the *car*."). Such a pause between words is not characteristic of true sentences. And since Allison spoke these two words in both possible orders, it appears that word order was unimportant to what she wanted to say. In true English sentences, in contrast, word order *is* important. Thus, the words that toddlers initially speak in close succession may not be genuine sentences. Instead, they may be a kind of transitional step from earlier one-word statements.

When toddlers do start to produce true two-word sentences, those sentences are usually composed of nouns, verbs, and adjectives. Few articles, conjunctions, or prepositions, such as *the, and,* or *of,* appear, even though these words are common in adult speech. Nor do toddlers initially inflect words with suffixes or prefixes to alter their meanings (adding -*s* to make a noun plural, or -*ed* to put a verb in the past tense). They also ignore most auxiliary verbs, such as *can, may,* or *would*. When 22-month-old Meryl wants to express the idea "I can see the teddy bear," she says simply: "See teddy." The child in this phase seems to be omitting the words that are not essential to conveying the central meaning of the sentence. This style of talking is called **telegraphic speech** because it sounds somewhat like the terse wording of a telegram. Interestingly, young toddlers use telegraphic speech even when adults specifically model longer sentences for them (Brown and Fraser, 1963). When Karen repeatedly encouraged Meryl to say "I love my grandma," Meryl's words came out simply "Love gama." It was as if saying more than two words to express a single idea exceeded her current cognitive capacities.

Although a child's earliest sentences are telegraphic, they are not arbitrary groupings of words. Most two-word sentences seem to express a relatively small set of basic meanings, as illustrated in Table 7.1. These categories of meanings expressed at the two-word stage are remarkably similar across languages (Slobin, 1970). Notice, however, that, out of context, children's two-word utterances are nearly as ambiguous as their one-word utterances were. Adults must still rely heavily on context, gestures, facial expressions, and intonation to interpret what a child means. For example, when Malcolm was 19 months old and his father came home from work, he usually greeted him with a broad smile, outstretched arms, and a joyous "Daddy home!" Clearly, this was meant as a happy announcement that his father had returned. On another occasion, when Momma Jo let Malcolm talk to his father on the phone, he said sternly, "Daddy *home*!" with stress on the second word. Here his meaning seemed to be the command "Daddy, come home *now*!"

FURTHER SYNTACTIC DEVELOPMENT

After children have passed through the two-word stage, their knowledge of syntax increases rapidly. Their sentences grow longer and become more grammatically complex. Roger Brown has divided early syntactic development into five stages based on the increasing length of children's utterances (Brown, 1973). Stage I (average utterance length 1.0 to 2.0 morphemes) corresponds roughly to the two-word stage that we have just described. During that stage, children

Telegraphic speech:
A toddler speech style in which words not essential to the meaning of a sentence are omitted.

TABLE 7.1
CATEGORIES OF MEANINGS EXPRESSED IN THE TWO-WORD STAGE

Category of Meaning	Description
Identification	Utterances such as "See doggy" and "That car" are elaborations on pointing, which emerged in the preverbal stage, and naming, which began in the one-word stage.
Location	In addition to pointing, children may use words such as *here* and *there* to signal location—as in "Doggy here" or "Teddy down." To say that something is in, on, or under something else, children juxtapose words, omitting the preposition—as in "Ball [under] chair" or "Lady [at] home."
Recurrence	One of the first things that children do with words is call attention to, and request, repetition—as in "More cookie" or "Tickle again."
Nonexistence	Children who pay attention to the repetition of experiences also notice when an activity ceases or an object disappears. Utterances such as "Ball allgone" and "Nomore milk" are common at this stage.
Negation	At about age 2, children discover that they can use words to contradict adults (pointing to a picture of a cow and saying, "Not horsie") and to reject adults' plans (saying "No milk" when offered milk to drink).
Possession	In the one-word stage children may point to an object and name the owner; in the two-word stage they can signal possession by juxtaposing words—as in "Baby chair" or "Daddy coat."
Agent, object, action	Two-word sentences indicate that children know that agents act on objects. But children at this stage cannot express three-term relationships. Thus, "Daddy throw ball" may be expressed as "Daddy throw" (agent-action), "Throw ball" (action-object), or "Daddy ball" (agent-object). Children may also talk of the recipient of an action by using similar constructions—saying, "Cookie me" or simply "Give me" instead of "Give me a cookie."
Attribution	Children begin to modify nouns by stating their attributes as in "Red ball" or "Little dog." Some two-word sentences indicate that children know the functions as well as the attributes of some objects—for example, "Go car."
Question	Children can turn types of sentences described here into questions by speaking them with a rising intonation. They may also know question words, such as *where,* to combine with others—as in "Where kitty?" or "What that?"

SOURCE: Adapted from Brown, 1973. From Wortman and Loftus, 1988.

begin to express simple semantic and syntactic relationships. This is followed by Stage II (average utterance length 2.0 to 2.5 morphemes), during which children acquire the basic grammatical morphemes, such as the suffix -s to form the plural. In Stage III (average utterance length 2.5 to 3.0 morphemes), variations on simple sentences appear, including questions ("Can I go?" "Where's Mommy?") and negation ("You can't come." "It's not here."). At Stage IV (average utterance length 3.0 to 3.5 morphemes), children begin to embed one sentence in another, producing various kinds of subordinate clauses ("I see what you made." "I want you to do it."). By Stage V (average utterance length 3.5 to 4.0 morphemes), children are able to join two simple sentences in various ways to form compound sentences ("I had cake and Daddy had ice cream."). Most children pass through Brown's five stages by the time they reach age 3½.

LEARNING TO USE LANGUAGE SOCIALLY

At the same time that children are acquiring the sound system, vocabulary, morphology, and grammar of their native language, they are also learning pragmatics—that is, how to use the language socially. In other words, they are acquiring not only linguistic competence but also **communicative competence.** Linguistic competence involves syntactically and semantically correct use of a language. Communicative competence involves the ability to carry on conversations, to recognize and repair breakdowns in communication, and to use language in a socially appropriate way in a particular culture.

Some of the skills involved in communicative competence begin to appear in infancy, long before children speak their first words. As you learned in Chapter 6, caregivers respond to infants' vocalizations, facial expressions, and gestures from very early on as if they were attempts at intentional communication. With the caregiver's assistance, infants develop skills that will be needed later on in conversation, such as turn-taking. The principle of taking turns with a conversational partner is well established by 1 year of age. Thereafter, the child simply develops more skill at making *relevant* responses to what conversational partners say (Warren and McCloskey, 1993).

By late in the first year of life, infants' vocalizations and gestures show clear communicative intent. For example, many babies point or use protowords to request objects that are out of reach. With communicative intent comes the possibility of communication failure, and children must learn how to recognize when they are not being understood and how to make conversational repairs. Roberta Golinkoff (1986) studied communication failures between preverbal 11- to 18-month-olds and their mothers, often involving the mother's failure to understand the baby's request. In such cases, the baby would typically show frustration but would also attempt a conversational repair by repeating or altering the request—all by means of gesture, vocalization, facial expression, and behavior, since these babies were not yet using language fluently.

Pragmatic skills continue to develop after true language appears. For instance, 2-year-olds will attempt to repair breakdowns in understanding during conversations with adults, thereby demonstrating an ability to tell whether they are successfully communicating (Anselmi, Tomasello, and Acunzo, 1986). They do this by responding appropriately to adults' requests for clarification, as in the following example:

Communicative competence: The ability to carry on conversations, to recognize and repair breakdowns in communication, and to use language in a socially appropriate way in a particular culture.

    Child: Hide it.
    Mother: What?
    Child: Hide it behind my . . .
    Mother: You gonna hide it behind your back?
    Child: Yeah.
    (Tomasello, Conti-Ramsden, and Ewert, 1990, p. 123)

Although this child is successfully clarifying an assertion of fact ("I will hide it behind my back"), it is even more common for toddlers to successfully clarify a request that has not been fulfilled:

    Child: You do that. (Holding a toy that rolls on wheels.)
    Father: You want me to do it?
    Child: Yes, you do it. (Father pushes toy, as child watches with a smile.)
    (Shatz and O'Reilly, 1990, p. 137)

Thus, toddlers' clarification ability may depend more on their desire to make sure their goals are met than on a real understanding of other people's communication needs (Shatz and O'Reilly, 1990).

Another aspect of pragmatic development is learning the social routines and conventions for communication and language use in one's native culture. The particular routines and conventions to be taught vary, but across a wide range of cultures caregivers provide considerable pragmatic instruction to young children. This instruction begins in infancy, before children have even begun to use language, with the teaching of communicative routines. Examples common across many Western cultures include playing peekaboo and teaching a baby to wave bye-bye. In Italy, for instance, babies are taught to wave *ciao* (New, 1988).

Once children begin to speak, adults teach them verbal routines. For example, mothers in the Kaluli culture of New Guinea use an imitation routine to teach infants how to speak appropriately and how to use language for various social purposes. They model what they want their language-learning children to say, ending these utterances with the word *elema*, which means "say it" (Schieffelin, 1990).

As children's language development proceeds, parents continue to provide instruction in pragmatic routines. In middle-class American culture, these include greetings and leave-takings *(hi, how are you?, bye-bye, see you soon)*, politeness formulas *(please, thank you)*, appropriate forms of address *(ma'am, sir, Mrs., Mr.)*, and specific-occasion routines, such as what to say when trick-or-treating (Becker, 1994; Greif and Gleason, 1980; Gleason and Weintraub, 1978). Parents also instruct children in qualitative aspects of speech, such as loudness ("Use your indoor voice"), tone of voice ("Don't talk to your sister like that!"), and clarity ("I can't understand you when you mumble"). Pragmatic instruction can be either direct or indirect, with prompting ("What's the magic word?") a particularly common strategy in middle-class American families (Becker, 1994; Gleason, Perlman, and Greif, 1984).

In Japan, politeness formulas are more elaborate and numerous than in the United States, and Japanese mothers place even more emphasis on teaching them to toddlers than American mothers do (Clancy, 1986). To accomplish this, they use direct instruction, model the correct forms for children, point out politeness formulas used by other people and by storybook characters, and

Japanese culture places a high value on sensitivity to the feelings of others. Accordingly, Japanese toddlers receive even more instruction in the use of polite language than American children do.

show great insistence in correcting their children when they do not use a needed expression. A common Japanese strategy for correcting children's insufficiently polite speech is to appeal to general rules for behavior, often pointing out that others will feel hurt or angry if the child does not speak politely.

THE CHILD AND THE ENVIRONMENT IN LANGUAGE DEVELOPMENT

In the brief year and a half of the toddler period, most children progress from speaking a few isolated words to using a great many words in properly structured sentences. How are they able to accomplish the complex task of learning a language in such a short period of time? A long-standing debate exists between environmentalist and nativist theories of language acquisition. **Environmentalist theories** center on factors in the child's environment that support language acquisition, including the language the child hears, the structure of the child's social interactions, and characteristics of the physical environment. **Nativist theories,** in contrast, center on inborn, biologically based factors within the child that make language acquisition possible.

The most famous debate between environmentalist and nativist theorists took place between psychologist B.F. Skinner and linguist Noam Chomsky in the late 1950s. In his book *Verbal Behavior* (1957), Skinner argued that parents and others instrumentally condition children to talk. When the baby begins to babble, the parents smile, pay attention, and talk to the child in response. Their attention reinforces the infant for babbling, and babbling becomes more frequent. The increased frequency of babbling raises the probability that the baby will, just by chance, say things that sound like words. When the parents hear these wordlike sounds, they reinforce them in preference to nonword sounds. The child responds by repeating what sound to the parents like words, and so "words" enter the baby's repertoire of verbal behaviors. Skinner argued that the

Environmentalist theories: Theories that stress environmental factors in language acquisition.

Nativist theories: Theories that stress inborn, biologically based factors in language acquisition.

grammar of a language is acquired through similar reinforcement. Parents reinforce grammatically correct statements and reject or show confusion over incorrect ones. As a result, the child learns proper grammar.

At first glance, Skinner's account of language acquisition seems reasonable—and not very different from many people's assumptions about how language is learned. There are problems with Skinner's explanation, however. For one thing, parents do not actually provide much reinforcement and feedback for children's learning of grammar. Examining how parents respond to their young children's speech, Brown and Hanlon (1970) found that they are much more likely to correct statements that are untrue than statements that are grammatically incorrect. For instance, when Malcolm says "Me sit doggie chair," while placing a new toy elephant on top of the sofa, DeeDee is apt to ignore his rough-edged grammar but tell him gently, "That's an elephant, honey, not a dog." This response is typical of most parents (Hirsh-Pasek, Treiman, and Schneiderman, 1984; Morgan and Travis, 1989). It is inaccuracy of a remark, not improper grammar, that tends to prompt a correction. Despite this pattern of reinforcement, most children learn to use correct grammar anyway—even though they don't always use it to tell the truth.

In a review of Skinner's book, Chomsky (1957) offered a strong critique of Skinner's arguments. Chomsky contended that you could not pack into an entire lifetime all the reinforcement episodes needed to learn language through instrumental conditioning. Children speak an extraordinarily large number of sentences, and each of these could not have been learned separately through reinforcement. Even if you add imitation as a learning mechanism, you can still explain only how children learn to repeat the things they have heard. But children do not simply repeat other people's sentences. One of the most important features of language, Chomsky pointed out, is that words can be combined to say things that we have never heard anyone else say. In principle, there is no limit to the novel sentences we can form.

So compelling was Chomsky's critique of Skinner's book that most developmentalists strongly agreed with his reasoning. This is not to say that they dismissed reinforcement and imitation as irrelevant to language learning. Reinforcement and imitation remain useful principles for explaining how some of the details of language are learned (Speidel and Nelson, 1989; Whitehurst, 1982). Certainly, babies learn the sounds of their native language by imitating the speech they hear. Moreover, specific words must be learned by imitation, because the connection between a certain string of sounds and a certain meaning is entirely a matter of convention. Reinforcement and imitation alone, however, do not fully explain language acquisition.

As an alternative to Skinner's reinforcement approach, Chomsky (1957) argued that all languages share certain structural characteristics, presumably because languages and the human mind evolved together. Our early ancestors fashioned language as they did because of certain innate capacities of the brain that led them to perceive and understand their world in certain ways. The same innate capacities allow very young children to extract the rules of any language that they hear spoken, especially the language's syntax. Chomsky called these innate capacities the **language acquisition device,** or **LAD.** He maintained that part of the brain is specially adapted for language learning. When a toddler is merely exposed to language, the LAD automatically focuses on the rules that govern it.

But just as there were limitations to Skinner's explanation of language acqui-

Language acquisition device (LAD): Chomsky's term for innate capacities of the human brain that make language acquisition possible.

sition, so there are limitations to Chomsky's. Chomsky focuses on the question of how children acquire syntax and has little interest in the development of other aspects of linguistic and communicative competence. In addition, because of his emphasis on innate capacities, he ignores the social contexts in which language acquisition occurs.

Today, virtually no researchers hold a purely nativist or a purely environmentalist position on language acquisition. Instead, as in other nature-nurture issues, debate focuses on the relative contributions of inborn and environmental factors. Even researchers who are strongly oriented toward the role of the environment admit that *something* must be built into the child's brain for language learning to be possible. And even the most nativist researchers acknowledge that environmental input is essential for language acquisition to occur. What is at issue is exactly what is built into the child biologically and exactly what kind of information is provided by the environment.

WHAT THE CHILD BRINGS TO LANGUAGE ACQUISITION

There is plenty of evidence that, as a species, humans are biologically predisposed to learn language. For one thing, language is learned so rapidly and with so little explicit teaching that it is clear the process must have a biological basis. For another, there is considerable similarity in the general processes of language acquisition across cultures, despite variations in linguistic structure and socialization practices (Slobin, 1985).

One indication of the biological underpinnings of language acquisition is the fact that there appears to be a critical period during which language can be learned with relative ease (Lenneberg, 1967). It is difficult to show that a critical period does exist, however, because it is rare to find a child who can serve as a test case—a child who has received no linguistic input early in life. An exception would be a severely neglected child like Victor or Genie, whom we discussed in Chapter 2. The difficulties these children had learning language in their adolescent years lend some support to the critical period hypothesis, although we have no way of knowing whether they were born with cognitive impairments. Another, less problematic test case is the deaf child with hearing parents who does not begin to learn sign language until after early childhood. Research by Elissa Newport (1982, 1988) suggests that the earlier deaf children begin to acquire sign language, the greater their ultimate fluency.

Research on second language acquisition has produced similar findings. Jacqueline Johnson and Elissa Newport (1989) demonstrated that knowledge of English grammar among a group of Chinese- and Korean-speaking adults depended on the age at which they had first been exposed to English. Those who started to learn English before age 7 seemed to understand English grammar as well as native speakers of English. As the age of first exposure to English increased beyond age 7, however, their ultimate level of competence in English grammar decreased. (The box on pp. 284 discusses childhood bilingualism in more detail.)

Another indication that language acquisition has a biological basis is the fact that it is *species-specific*—that is, an ability that all humans share as a result of their common genetic inheritance, but that is not found in members of other species. Although many other species of animals (from honeybees to vervet monkeys to dolphins) have impressive communication abilities, none of their communication systems is as abstract, flexible, or productive as human language. Many attempts to teach chimpanzees to use sign language and other symbolic communication systems show that, while chimps probably have some symbolic abilities, they are not able to use rules of syntax to combine words into a wide variety of meaningful sentences (Lieberman, 1984; Premack, 1986). They may, however, be able to *understand* simple syntax and to grasp the meaning of novel sentences made up of familiar words (Savage-Rumbaugh et al., 1993). Thus, their receptive language skills may surpass their productive ones, but they still don't come close to having the language ability of humans.

Scientists have wondered exactly how the human brain is prewired for language learning. Their answers include possible inborn *strategies* for interpreting language input (Slobin, 1985; Peters, 1985). These are not strategies consciously used by language-learning children, but rather descriptions of the way their nervous systems operate. They include strategies for perceiving and storing linguistic information, as well as strategies for organizing that information into patterns and grammatical principles. For instance, children may have a built-in predisposition to pay attention to perceptually salient stretches of speech, including stressed syllables and the beginnings and ends of words. This would help them to zero in on many grammatical morphemes used by adults ("Look, Mikey. There are two truck*s*!").

Along with having built-in strategies for interpreting language, the human brain may come equipped with certain *constraints* on the conclusions that can be drawn about language structure. It is hard to imagine how children could correctly work out all the rules (and exceptions) in any language without such constraints. The range of possible rules that could be generated from the input children receive is simply too broad. As a result, a growing number of theorists have proposed that language learning must be governed by constraints that limit in advance what kinds of rules can be generated.

For instance, children's learning of syntax may be constrained by a predisposition to detect fairly broad syntactic categories common to all languages, such as nouns, verbs, subjects, objects, and grammatical phrases (Pinker, 1987). Although an infant's brain would not be specifically prewired to recognize *English* nouns, for example, the general concept of nouns could be built in, along with a range of possible rules for nouns.

Another built-in constraint that might assist in learning syntax is an assumption that words contain morphemes that mark certain grammatical characteristics, such as number, tense, and case (Newport, 1988). How these characteristics are marked would vary from language to language, but children would be predisposed to look for some sort of morphology. Newport has found evidence that this particular constraint may be associated with a critical period early in life, when language learning normally takes place. This evidence comes from the study of people who have learned American Sign Language (ASL) at various ages. Those who learn ASL as children are more likely to break it down into morphemes and make the same sorts of overregularization errors observed in children learning spoken languages. In contrast, those who learn ASL later in life, after the critical period for language acquisition, tend to learn signs in a more holistic fashion and not to recognize many morphological markings.

Researchers have also proposed built-in constraints that may help in the learning of words (Behrend, 1990; Markman, 1987). Two that we have already mentioned are inborn assumptions that unfamiliar words are the names for objects and that new words mean something different from words already known.

The ability to combine words into sentences seems to be related to other combinatorial abilities, such as block building.

General cognitive abilities and constraints wired into the human brain may contribute to language learning as well. For example, human infants seem to have an inborn ability to perceive objects, motion, and other characteristics of the world, rather than perceiving a disorganized stream of sensory information. This ability gives them an early knowledge of things, qualities, and actions to which word labels can be attached. In a similar manner, general symbolic representation and memory abilities can also aid language learning. This has been suggested by several studies showing correlations between toddlers' language development and various cognitive skills. For example, Cecilia Shore (1986) found that 2-year-olds' ability to put two or more words together is related to their block-building, memory, and symbolic-play abilities. Similarly, the ability to string words together into well-formed sentences is linked to an improved capacity to remember sequences of things, which occurs between the ages of 1 and 3. Alison Gopnik and Andrew Meltzoff (1987) have found as well that the vocabulary spurt that occurs at about age 18 months is specifically connected to the development of mature object permanence and to the ability to sort objects into two categories.

In summary, human infants clearly come equipped with a general predisposition to learn language. They may also have a range of more specific built-in strategies, constraints, and abilities that make language acquisition possible. In all likelihood, children bring a number of inborn factors, both linguistic and cognitive, to the task of acquiring language.

A CLOSER LOOK AT THE CHILD'S LANGUAGE ENVIRONMENT

Built-in strategies, constraints, and abilities are not the whole story of how children acquire language. Environment also plays a part. Without exposure to language, after all, children cannot even begin to learn to speak. Moreover, the nature of the language environment seems to make a difference. For instance, the more a mother talks to her baby in the child's first year of life, the larger the child's vocabulary is likely to be at 17 months of age (Clarke-Stewart, 1973). Greater exposure to language apparently speeds language learning. But what about the type of speech to which young children are exposed and the structure of their interactions with adults? Can these aspects of the language environment facilitate language learning by making linguistic rules and meanings easier to decipher?

To answer this question, we must first take a look at exactly how adults talk to young children. A number of researchers have argued that adults modify their speech to toddlers in ways that make it easier for children to acquire language (e.g., Ferguson, 1964; Snow, 1972; Kemler-Nelson et al., 1989). These speech modifications are known as **child-directed speech (CDS),** or **motherese,** even though many fathers and other adults use them also (Gleason, 1975). The following conversation between a mother and her 19-month-old daughter provides a typical example of middle-class American CDS:

Child-directed speech (CDS) or motherese: The modifications adults make in their speech when talking to young children.

Mother:	What should I draw first?
Child:	Bi goggie.
Mother:	A big doggie. All right. Is that big?
Child:	Oggie bi. Bi gog.
Mother:	What's this? What's this part of the doggie? Is that a big enough doggie?
Child:	Bi goggie.

Mother: Well, I did make a big doggie. Look.
  Child: Bi goggie.
Mother: You make a big doggie. Make a kitty.
  Child: Kiki.
(Genishi and Dyson, 1984, p. 45)

There are several differences between CDS and adult-directed speech. For one thing, CDS is grammatically simpler and includes fewer grammatical errors (Molfese, Molfese, and Carrell, 1982). CDS is also spoken in a higher than normal pitch, its intonations are more exaggerated, and it has fewer lapses in fluency (Fernald et al., 1989; Garnica, 1974). In CDS the boundaries between phrases and clauses are more clearly marked by such devices as pauses and intonation (Fernald, 1984; Morgan, 1986; Ratner, 1985). As to content, CDS tends to focus on objects and events discussed in the present tense, using concrete nouns. The adult frequently comments on what the child is doing or on what is going on around the child. CDS also tends to be quite redundant (Molfese, Molfese, and Carrell, 1982). The mother above, for instance, finds many different ways to repeat the words "big" and "doggie." Notice, too, how this mother often asks her daughter questions about their joint project: "What should I draw?" "Is this a big enough doggie?" "What part of the doggie is this?" Such frequent questioning about objects and events is typical of CDS (Snow, 1977).

Fathers' speech to young children has been observed to differ from mothers', at least in families in which the mother is the primary caregiver and the father a secondary caregiver. Fathers who are secondary caregivers ask for more labels and explanations ("What's this?" "What does it do?"), and they use more advanced vocabulary words, such as *aggravating*. They also ask for more repetitions and clarifications from the child (Masur and Gleason, 1980). One reason for this is that communication breakdowns are more frequent in children's conversations with secondary-caregiver fathers. These fathers are more likely than mothers to ignore children's utterances, and when they don't understand something their child says, they most often respond with a nonspecific request for clarification ("What?"). Mothers, in contrast, more often make a specific request for clarification ("Put it where?") (Tomasello, Conti-Ramsden, and Ewert, 1990). These differences most likely arise because secondary-caregiver fathers spend much less time with their children than primary-caregiver mothers do. They are therefore less familiar with their children's speech and routines—and probably less "tuned in" to their communication needs. However, these fathers make a distinctive contribution to children's linguistic environments by readying them for the broader social world, in which clarity is important and in which not all speakers structure the conversation and adjust their speech as much as mothers do (Mannle and Tomasello, 1987).

Siblings and other older children also adjust their speech to toddlers in many of the ways adults do. When asked to describe the rules of a game to a child younger than themselves, 4-year-olds reduce the complexity of their sentences, speak more slowly, and repeat more often than when they describe the rules to an adult (Shatz and Gelman, 1973). Even 2- and 3-year-olds use shorter sentences and more repetition when talking to their infant siblings than when talking to their mothers (Dunn and Kendrick, 1982c). However, siblings' speech to toddlers also differs from adults' speech in some ways. Siblings' speech adjustments to infants and toddlers are less sensitive than are those made by adults. Siblings ask fewer questions, issue more directives, and put less emphasis on try-

When siblings are talking to toddlers, they make many of the same speech adjustments that adults do.

ing to get the younger child to talk (DeHart, 1990; Hoff-Ginsberg and Krueger, 1991; Tomasello and Mannle, 1985).

Now let's return to the question of whether CDS facilitates language learning, as some researchers have proposed. Studies have not found a relationship between the use of CDS and the *overall* rate of language acquisition (Newport, Gleitman, and Gleitman, 1977). However, certain *particular* characteristics of mothers' speech do seem to support the development of related syntactic structures in their children (Hoff-Ginsberg, 1986, 1990). For example, mothers who ask many questions, which often make auxiliary verbs especially salient, have children who use high numbers of auxiliary verbs. The language *model* provided by CDS is probably not its most important feature, however. Instead, its effects on children's language development are more likely due to the chances it gives them for active participation in conversations (Hoff-Ginsberg, 1986, 1990).

Cross-cultural research on how adults talk to children also sheds some light on the role of CDS in language acquisition. Although there are many similarities in the features of CDS across languages (Fernald et al., 1989), there are also some differences. For example, English speakers exaggerate their pitch and intonation more when addressing young children than speakers of most other languages do. In some cultures, CDS is limited or nonexistent. The Kaluli people of New Guinea believe it is important for infants to hear what they call "hard speech"—the language spoken by adults. They do not use "baby talk" with infants and young children because they do not believe it is good to teach children childish forms of language. Preverbal Kaluli babies are not believed to be capable of communicating on their own. Rather than speaking *to* their babies in a special way, Kaluli mothers often speak *for* their babies in dialogues with other people. The mother holds her baby facing away from her, moves the baby as if he or she were conversing, and speaks for the baby in a special, high-pitched voice. This style of interaction is quite different from the middle-class American practice of face-to-face "conversations" with preverbal infants. Despite these differences from the way American mothers interact with their babies,

Kaluli babies develop language according to a timetable comparable to that of American babies (Schieffelin, 1990).

Thus, CDS by itself does not explain children's language acquisition. It does simplify and structure the linguistic input children receive, which may be useful in syntactic development. In addition, the concrete, present-oriented nature of adult-child conversations may help children make connections between words and the things they refer to. The frequent questions and clear turn-taking provide opportunities for linguistic practice and the learning of conversational skills. Jerome Bruner (1983) has suggested that the ways in which adults structure children's language environments should be considered a *language acquisition support system (LASS)*—a complement to Chomsky's LAD. We have already seen how biology and environment interact in children's acquisition of the sound system of their language; similar interactions are probably also present in semantic and syntactic development.

Some researchers have argued that CDS serves a primarily attentional or affective function in mother-child interaction—that is, mothers use it to capture their babies' attention and to communicate with them emotionally, but it has little or no direct impact on children's syntactic development (Newport, Gleitman, and Gleitman, 1977). It is true that infants as young as 4 months old attend more to CDS than to adult-directed speech and show a preference for listening to CDS (Fernald, 1985). Both English- and German-speaking mothers vary their pitch and intonation in consistent ways to engage their babies in interaction and to soothe distressed infants (Papoušek, Papoušek, and Bornstein, 1985; Stern, Spieker, and MacKain, 1982). Brown (1977) has suggested that CDS arises from parents' desires both to communicate with their infants, which leads to simplification, and to express affection toward them. In all likelihood, CDS serves more than one function in early parent-child relationships and in children's early language development.

NONLINGUISTIC ASPECTS OF SYMBOLIC REPRESENTATION

In Piaget's view, the principal cognitive development of toddlerhood is the emergence of symbolic thought—that is, the ability to let one thing stand for another that is not physically present. Symbols can be purely mental representations, or they can be words, objects, or actions. When Mikey forms a mental image of a piece of candy, he is using a symbol to represent an object that he wants. When Malcolm tells his grandmother "Daddy go work," he is using words as symbols for something that has already happened. When Meryl takes a paper plate and pretends it's a steering wheel, she is using the plate and her actions as symbols for the real act of driving.

Implicit in Piaget's notion of symbols is the ability to manipulate symbols intentionally, thus creating new ideas and thoughts. In the case of linguistic symbols, the child becomes able to combine words into sentences. This deliberate manipulation of symbols enables the child to say anything imaginable. In Piaget's view, a toddler's first words are not really symbols, because they refer only to objects or events in the here and now. Not until a child begins to talk about things that are not currently present does he or she use language symbolically as Piaget defined the term. This point in language development usually occurs between 18 and 24 months of age—the age range that marks the last of Piaget's six sensorimotor stages, as we discussed in Chapter 5.

According to Piaget, the general symbolic abilities that emerge during toddlerhood are a developmental outgrowth of sensorimotor activities. In particular, Piaget emphasized the role of imitation in the development of a toddler's use of symbols. Consider the following observation he made of his daughter Jacqueline:

> At 15 months Jacqueline was playing with a clown with long feet and happened to catch the feet in the low neck of her dress. She had difficulty in getting them out, but as soon as she had done so she tried to put them back in the same position . . . . As she did not succeed she put her hand in front of her, bent her forefinger at a right angle to reproduce the shape of the clown's feet, described exactly the same trajectory as the clown, and thus succeeded in putting her finger into the neck of her dress. She looked at the motionless finger for a moment, then pulled at her dress, without of course being able to see what she was doing. Then satisfied, she removed her finger and went on to something else. (Piaget, 1962, p. 65)

Notice how Jacqueline is imitating with the action of her finger the previous action of the clown's feet. This is not yet mature symbolic representation, but it is the forerunner of it and helps to show the origins of this important new ability.

By the end of the sensorimotor period, Piaget contended, the child's imitations become more abbreviated. For example, rather than going through the whole process of imitating the clown's feet getting caught in her dress, Jacqueline at 20 months might simply flex her finger slightly to stand for the shape of the feet. She is now able to employ a symbol that bears a much less obvious relationship to the thing being symbolized. Still later she will use words ("feet caught") to represent the incident with purely verbal symbols. Piaget maintained that the meaning of any symbol lies in the child's current schemes for interacting with the thing symbolized. Symbols, in other words, do not represent things in themselves. Instead, they represent the child's present understanding of things.

The development of language is a dramatic indication of the toddler's emerging capacity for the use of symbols. But language, as our examples have shown, is not the only way in which toddlers exercise representational skills. Two other manifestations of symbolic representation are pretend play and the use of gestures. Both become increasingly important during the toddler period.

TODDLERS' PRETEND PLAY

Toddlers' emerging representational ability is especially obvious in their play. Several investigators have separately demonstrated an orderly sequence in the development of symbolic play during the toddler period (Belsky and Most, 1981; McCune-Nicolich, 1981). Initially, symbolic representation is seen in behaviors directed to the self. A 16-month-old may, for example, pretend to drink from a toy cup. Later, toddlers will direct such acts to others (as in pretending to feed a doll). Before the end of the second year, they can combine a series of such acts around a theme (such as building a "fence" with blocks around pretend animals).

As representational skills develop, toddlers are also able to use less and less realistic objects as symbols in their play (Fein, 1981). Between 14 and 19 months, children's pretend play with *replica objects* (dolls, toy horses, toy cars)

By the time they are 2 years old, most children are using substitute objects in pretend play—for example, using a block to represent a telephone.

increases sharply, but their use of *substitute objects* (using a pillow to represent a baby, for instance, or a block to represent a car) is still rare. Between 19 and 24 months, the use of substitute objects greatly increases, and by 24 months most children can manage to use one substitute object in a pretend scenario (using a block to feed a baby doll, for example). A *double substitution* (using a block as a bottle *and* a pillow as the baby) is more troublesome. Still, the 2-year-old is clearly no longer restricted to understanding the world solely through direct perception and action.

The social context has a definite effect on children's ability to engage in pretend play. Toddlers show more advanced forms of pretend play when they are pretending with other people than when they are pretending by themselves, particularly when the play partner is an older sibling or a parent. For example, children as young as 24 months have been observed to take on such complementary roles as mother and baby, teacher and pupil, and airplane pilot and passenger in play with their older brothers and sisters (Dunn and Dale, 1984). This more sophisticated play results partly from direction by the more skilled partner, but participation in these scenarios nevertheless requires the toddler to have some understanding of pretense and the partner's intentions. Another reason siblings elicit advanced forms of pretend play from toddlers is that they provide an opportunity for repeated enactment of the same scenario. The familiarity of both the sibling and the particular game of pretend makes possible fairly sophisticated role playing.

TODDLERS' USE OF GESTURES

A second area in which emerging representational skills can be observed during toddlerhood is the use of gestures (Acredolo and Goodwyn, 1990; Petitto, 1992; Volterra and Erting, 1990). Simple *communicative gestures,* such as pointing, normally emerge at around 9 months. These early gestures are sometimes accompanied by vocalizations, as when a baby points at a toy she cannot reach and whimpers. *Conventional social gestures* (such as waving bye-bye, nodding for

Gestures that represent a desired action are commonly used by toddlers. This little girl is holding up both arms in a request to be picked up.

"yes," and shaking the head for "no") usually appear between 9 and 12 months. But although these early gestures communicate meaning, they do not directly represent or symbolize an action or object. That is, there is no resemblance between the gesture and what it communicates.

By about 13 months, a new type of gesture emerges that appears to be more directly representational. These *instrumental gestures* include empty-handed gestures that reproduce a portion of an action, such as the classic begging gesture with an outstretched hand or holding up both arms to be picked up. They also include gestures with objects, as when an infant puts an empty cup to her lips to represent drinking. Finally, between 12 and 18 months, children begin to produce *symbolic gestures* that directly represent an action or object. For example, they might move their hands as if screwing the lid on a jar, or sniff to represent a flower.

Studies reveal that symbolic gestures most often develop in the context of interactive routines between child and parent, or in the course of the child's own interactions with objects (Acredolo and Goodwyn, 1985, 1988; Volterra, 1981). For example, Acredolo's daughter took the raised-arms gesture used in the common parent-infant game of "So Big!" and applied it to objects that were big in comparison to other, similar objects. Early symbolic gestures usually reflect the function of an object rather than its physical form. For example, the child might use a bouncing motion to represent a ball rather than indicating its round shape. Acredolo and Goodwyn (1988) found that toddlers tend to use symbolic gestures as requests earlier than they use them to label objects. They also found that some children combine symbolic gestures to make quite complicated requests. For instance, one little girl got her mother to let the dog out by panting and moving her hand as if turning a doorknob.

Another gestural advance during the toddler period is the ability to coordinate divergent gestural and visual signals. For example, 12-month-olds have trouble following an adult's pointing gesture if the adult is not looking and pointing in the same direction, but 17-month-olds can follow the direction of a point even when the adult is looking elsewhere. Similarly, 12-month-olds tend to look in the direction of an object they are pointing at, but 18-month-olds can look at a conversational partner even while pointing at something else. The emergence of this ability to coordinate divergent signals seems to correspond roughly to the emergence of true words in children (Masur, 1990).

As the ability to use gestures advances, the total frequency of a child's gestures first rises and then falls. From about 10 months of age to 18 months, children gradually use more and more gestures. After 18 months the frequency of gestures declines, until it levels off at around 24 months of age. The early increase in gesturing seems to parallel the beginnings of word learning, while the later decline occurs at about the same time as the vocabulary spurt. Some researchers suggest that, as vocabulary size increases, language begins to replace gesturing as the child's main channel of communication (Lock et al., 1990). But note that the early increase in gesturing *at the same time* as early word learning implies that gesturing is not just a precursor to language. Gesturing and language are apparently two separate systems that develop side by side.

The study of deaf children also reveals the parallel development of gesturing and language. Deaf children who are acquiring sign language produce gestures that are very similar to those produced by children who can hear. Deaf children's gestures are not more complex, despite their experience with manual signing (Petitto, 1992). In addition, they seem to keep their linguistic signs and their gestures distinct; they do not mix or confuse them. Here again we see that gestures are more than just precursors to language. Gestures form a communication system that remains separate even after language has emerged. However, the fact that *symbolic* gestures appear at around the same time as children's first words suggests that both reflect the toddler's emerging symbolic abilities.

THE TODDLER PERIOD: AN OVERVIEW

In this chapter we have looked at the representational skills that begin to emerge in toddlerhood—skills that involve using ideas, images, sounds, and other symbols to stand for, or represent, objects and events. The infant who knew the world through *physical* actions has grown into the toddler who is capable of *mental* actions. Just as the infant actively explored objects by grasping them, manipulating them, and combining them, so the toddler actively manipulates symbolic elements, such as words, thereby learning about both the symbols themselves and the rules for interrelating them.

These representational abilities build upon the emerging long-term memory skills discussed in Chapter 5 (Bauer, 1995). Storage of past experience and the ability to compare past and present are the foundation for symbolic representation. At the same time, of course, emerging representational abilities dramatically enhance memory. Symbolic representation is an efficient way of summarizing experience for storage and retrieval.

The representational skills that emerge during toddlerhood provide the foundation for more elaborate social interactions, for pretend play, for dreams and nightmares, and for new kinds of problem solving. Representational skills allow toddlers to be dramatically more flexible in their behavior and to engage in much more planning of their actions than they could do as infants. These skills also enable children to think about the world in new, more complex ways. Consider a form of fantasy play that Mikey Gordon invented when he was about 2½. He pretended that the living room couch was his boat, the rug was the ocean, the coffee table was an island, and an umbrella was his fishing pole. Once when his sister Janie walked through the room, he complained to her crossly: "No walk water!" As we have seen, the ability to engage in make-believe play grows dramatically between the ages of 1 and 3. Developmental psychologist John Flavell (1985) believes that make-believe play marks the beginning of an important awareness in the child: the awareness of a distinction between appearance and reality.

Although many cognitive advances take place during the toddler period, toddlers' thinking is still constrained by a lack of logic in using their new mental skills and by limited memory abilities. Advances in logic and memory will take place during the preschool period that follows. Also during the preschool period, the important ability to distinguish between what is real and what is not will expand rapidly.

Most Americans think of *bilingualism*—the ability to speak two languages—as relatively rare, but in most parts of the world, it is common. From a worldwide perspective, *monolingualism*—speaking only one language—is the exception to the rule (Snow, 1993). Even in the United States, bilingualism is becoming increasingly prevalent, due to recent waves of immigration from Asia and Latin America. Nationally, about 16 percent of the school-age population speaks a language other than English at home. In some states, including New York, California, Texas, New Mexico, and Hawaii, the percentage is much higher (U.S. Bureau of the Census, 1994).

What is language development like for *native bilinguals*—that is, children who grow up learning two languages simultaneously? In the earliest stages of language development, children who are exposed to two languages at home don't seem to realize that the languages are two separate systems. Until they are about 18 months old, they tend to learn isolated words from each language. After that, they begin to recognize that words in one language can be translated into the other (Taeschner, 1983). From an early age, native bilinguals often mix their two languages or switch back and forth between them. However, the mixing is not random and does not indicate a lack of understanding of the boundaries between the two languages. Language mixing most often occurs when a child knows a word in only one of the languages or when a concept is closely tied to the child's experiences with one language but not the other (Snow, 1993). Children who are exposed to two languages at home do not remain bilingual unless they continue to have opportunities to use both languages. If they are living in a country where only one of their two languages is regularly spoken, they often begin to lose proficiency in the other language once they start school.

What effect does bilingualism have on children's linguistic and cognitive development? Native bilinguals tend to develop *metalinguistic awareness,* the ability to think about language as an arbitrary system, at an earlier age than children who speak only one language (Hakuta and Diaz, 1985). There is also some evidence for greater cognitive flexibility in bilingual children than in monolingual children (Peal and Lambert, 1962). The only negative effect that has been found is a tendency for preschool bilingual children to show slower than average vocabulary growth in both languages (Snow, 1993). However, a recent study of first graders who were bilingual in English and Spanish showed that a significant proportion of the words they knew in the two languages did not overlap and that single-language tests underestimated the total size of their vocabularies (Umbel et al., 1992).

In contrast to native bilinguals, some children learn one language at home and later learn a second in school. The outcomes for these children depend on the situation in which they become bilingual. Foreign language instruction in elementary schools, in which children receive limited exposure to a second language, is typically not very successful (Snow, 1993). In fact, elementary school children are slower than adolescents or adults at learning a second language by means of standard classroom instruction. Children are most likely to become truly bilingual if they participate in a *language immersion curriculum,* in which the second language is used for routine classroom interactions and instruction in subjects other than the language itself. French immersion classes for English-speaking children have been common in Canadian schools for some time, and this approach is becoming more widely used in the United States, both for teaching immigrant children English and for teaching English-speaking children second languages.

The distinction between *additive bilingualism* and *subtractive bilingualism* has important implications for teaching children second languages. Additive bilingualism involves learning a second language while maintaining proficiency in the first one; subtractive bilingualism involves learning a second language but losing proficiency in the first one. Most educators agree that bilingual education programs should be designed to foster additive rather than subtractive bilingualism. One approach that seems to accomplish that goal is the *two-way immersion program* (Sleek, 1994). In this type of program, children who are native English speakers and children who are native speakers of another language, such as Spanish, are in classes together. For half of the day, instruction is in English; for the other half, it is in the second language. In this setting, both English speakers and non-English speakers stand the greatest chance of becoming truly bilingual.

CHAPTER SUMMARY

1. Toddlerhood is the period from roughly 12 to 30 months of age. Its major cognitive developments include learning to talk and to use symbols to think about and interact with the world.

2. The components of language include **phonology,** the set of sounds used in a particular language; **semantics,** the meanings of words and sentences; **morphology,** the rules for combining units of meaning in words; **syntax,** the rules for organizing words into phrases and sentences; and **pragmatics,** the rules for the social use of language. Children must develop two sets of skills to use language: *productive skills* for putting ideas into words and *receptive skills* for understanding what other people say. In general, toddlers' receptive skills are more advanced than their productive skills.

3. In the first year of life, children's vocalizations change dramatically, culminating in the ability to produce true speech. At first, babies' vocalizations consist only of reflexive **crying,** but soon they move on to **cooing,** producing vowel-like sounds of pleasure. This stage is followed by **vocal play,** when babies produce a range of sounds varying widely in pitch and volume. The next stage is **canonical babbling,** when infants produce strings of syllables that sound increasingly speechlike. Finally, children produce **conversational babbling.** At this stage, adultlike stress and intonation patterns appear, the range of sounds resembles that of the child's native language, and a few **protowords** emerge.

4. Although toddlers' first words often label many of the same everyday concepts (simple nouns, verbs, and adjectives), children also show differences in the purposes for which they use their first words. Some have a tendency to use words to refer to objects and events (a **referential style** of word use), while others tend to use words mainly to express social routines (called an **expressive style**). Once children begin to produce recognizable words, their vocabularies grow rapidly, with their receptive vocabulary outpacing their productive vocabulary.

5. To learn words, toddlers must first separate them out from the stream of speech they hear and then assign meanings to them. Through the process of **fast mapping,** young children are able to use context to arrive at a quick guess about a word's meaning. This process may be aided by built-in assumptions that words refer to objects and that new words have different meanings than words already known. Children's early word-learning errors consist mainly of **underextensions** and **overextensions** of word meanings.

6. As language develops in the toddler period, children begin to learn **grammatical morphemes,** which include prefixes and suffixes that change the meaning of words, as well as auxiliary verbs, articles, and some prepositions. Studies suggest that children learn the structurally and semantically simplest grammatical morphemes first. More complex grammatical morphemes and exceptions are mastered somewhat later. The acquisition of grammatical morphemes demonstrates that children are learning linguistic rules.

7. Children use their first words singly, often to convey what an adult would say with a phrase or sentence. A word used to express such broader meaning is called a **holophrase.** Around 18 to 24 months of age toddlers start to construct two-word sentences. Because such sentences consist only of the words necessary to convey the essential meaning, this type of speech is called **telegraphic speech.** After children pass through the two-word stage, the grammatical complexity of their speech increases rapidly.

8. A long-standing debate among child language researchers pits **environmentalist** against **nativist** explanations of language acquisition. According to the nativist perspective, children have some built-in predispositions for language learning, but the exact nature of those predispositions is not yet known. Some possibilities include strategies for attending to and analyzing linguistic information, constraints on semantic and syntactic categories, and general cognitive abilities. But these built-in predispositions, by themselves, are not enough to foster language acquisition. A language environment is also essential, and qualities of that environment can affect how language is learned.

9. Adults tend to modify their speech toward toddlers in ways that may make it easier for children to learn language. These speech modifications, including simple sentence structure, repetition of key words, and a focus on present objects and events, are known as **child-directed speech (CDS),** or **motherese.** Researchers are still debating the function of CDS in toddlers' language learning.

10. The newly emerging symbolic capacities of toddlerhood pave the way for more complex social interactions, for make-believe play, and for new kinds of problem solving. These symbolic capacities can also be observed in the increasingly sophisticated gestures that toddlers use.

Chapter 8

Toddler Social and Emotional Development

As twelve-month-old Mikey Gordon sits playing with toys a few feet away from his mother, his attention is suddenly captured by a large wooden puzzle piece. It is a bright orange carrot with a cluster of emerald green leaves. Mikey grasps the wooden carrot with widened eyes. Then, in a smooth motion, as though automatically, he turns and extends the piece toward his mother. "Ya-ka!" he says with a broad smile. "Yes, sweetie, that's a carrot," Christine answers, smiling in return. "Do you like carrots?" "Ya-ka!" Mikey repeats happily.

A little more than a year later Mikey is with his mother at the university child study laboratory. Mikey has been presented with a series of problems to solve. The final problem is difficult. It requires him to weigh down a long board in order to lift candy through a hole in a Plexiglas box and hold the candy up long enough so he can get it (see photo on p. 304). Mikey attacks the problem eagerly, but it is beyond his cognitive abilities. He promptly calls upon Christine for help. She gives him clues and leads him step-by-step to see that he must weigh down the board with a large wooden block. Mikey cooperates with her suggestions and is ecstatic when he gets the candy. "I take it out!" he exclaims proudly.

Mikey has undergone dazzling development in just a little more than a year. At age 2, he is not only able to talk and solve quite challenging problems; he is also able to interact with others on a much more mature level. Mikey's new social and emotional capacities and the changes that underlie them are a major subject of this chapter. We will also explore how the quality of the parent-child relationship that formed during infancy paves the way for the kinds of adaptations the child makes during toddlerhood, which extends roughly from age 1 to age 2½ years.

Developmentalists have increasingly recognized the importance of the toddler period. In the first 12 months, the regulation of excitement, emotions, and behavior is orchestrated by caregivers, though the infant plays an ever more active role. In the later preschool period, children are expected to begin to regulate and control themselves. The toddler period is the *transition* during which control is transferred to the child.

Toddlerhood is a period of other major developments as well. Important cognitive changes occur, especially the emergence of language and other forms of symbolic thought. There also are dramatic changes in the parent-child relationship. During toddlerhood, children move from almost complete dependence on their parents toward greater self-reliance. As toddlers become motivated to exert their own will, parents must learn to impose control when needed while still fostering independence and growth. Since this is also the period when children first develop a rudimentary sense of self, the way in which parents handle the issue of autonomy at this time can greatly influence children's self-esteem and ultimately their capacity for flexible self-control.

In addition to moving toward greater self-reliance, toddlers start to acquire the rules, standards, and values of their society. As we saw in Chapter 2, this important process is often called **socialization** (Maccoby, 1992). At first, socialization simply involves responding to the expectations that parents and others in authority hold. In time, however, the child begins to *internalize* these standards—to incorporate them into the self. This second phase in the socialization process takes place in the preschool years and beyond, but it builds upon experiences in the toddler period (Damon, 1988; Emde, 1992). Learning the rules

Socialization:
The acquisition by the child of the rules, standards, and values of society.

within the family (or within the day-care setting) paves the way for a more general respect for social order.

As children become more mobile, especially when they start to walk, and as their learning of language opens up new means of communication, most parents in Western societies greatly increase the demands they impose. Children can now "get into things" and can understand the word *no*, so parents start establishing some rules. It has been reported that young toddlers (11 to 17 months) experience one prohibition from an adult every 9 minutes on average (Power and Chapieski, 1986). At the same time, weaning from the breast or bottle is accomplished, and not long thereafter toilet training begins. In other words, during the toddler period, parents begin to expect a fair degree of compliance with social norms.

To summarize, toddlers in Western culture face two important tasks: (1) to move from near-total dependence on their parents toward greater self-reliance; and (2) to begin complying with social rules and expectations. Although children around the world must confront these same two tasks, societies vary in how the tasks are presented and in how rapidly they are carried out (Rogoff et al., 1993). In some cultures, such as the Ilocos Barrio people of the Philippines (Whiting and Edwards, 1988), or the Samoan society studied by Margaret Mead (1928), children are indulged fully until weaning and then rapidly socialized. In our own society, the demands parents make regarding independence and compliance change gradually. Nevertheless, by the age of about 5, children are expected to do many things for themselves, to be able to exert considerable control over their impulses, and to have a sense of appropriate and inappropriate behavior.

In this chapter you will learn much more about the major developments of toddlerhood. We begin with a closer look at the process of socialization, exploring two views of how it comes about. To provide a more detailed idea of what children this age are like, we then examine the major ways in which toddlers differ from infants. Here we cover toddlers' greater autonomy from parents and greater competence in social interaction, their broader range of emotions, including emotional responses when social rules are broken, and their more sophisticated understanding of the self and others. Next we turn to parent-child relations during toddlerhood, focusing on the role that parents play in encouraging the child's development. This leads to a discussion of individual adaptations, the roots of personality in toddlers. What causes one toddler to be eager and cooperative, while another is persistently prone to tantrums? This section provides some answers. Finally, we address the issue of parental neglect and abuse of toddlers. Although abuse can be directed at children of any age, toddlers are particularly vulnerable to it.

The more mobile toddler can "get into things."

TWO VIEWS OF SOCIALIZATION

Traditionally, socialization has been thought of as a process in which rules and values are imposed on an unwilling child by parents and other adults—a kind of "socialization from the outside." Early forms of both psychoanalytic and social learning theories adopted such a view. More recently, however, many developmentalists have argued in favor of a perspective that might be called "socialization from the inside." For example, Barbara Rogoff (1990) uses the term **appropriation** to convey the idea that children naturally take on the rules and values

Appropriation:
The term used by Barbara Rogoff to refer to the natural process by which children take on the rules and values of their culture as part of their participation in relationships with caregivers.

of their culture as part of their participation in relationships with caregivers. Let's look more closely at the origins of these two different views.

SOCIALIZATION FROM THE OUTSIDE

Sublimation:
The term used by Freud for the blocking and redirection of biological drives and impulses.

In his early thinking, Freud considered the infant a seething mass of biological drives and impulses. Society's job was to curb these innate impulses and channel them in acceptable directions. If parents blocked the expression of biological drives to a moderate degree, the child would learn to redirect this energy toward more socially desirable goals. The end result would be compliance with the parents' wishes in order to maintain their love and nurturance. Freud called this blocking and redirecting of biological drives **sublimation.** As long as the child was not excessively thwarted and overwhelmed by anxiety or anger, Freud believed, sublimation was a positive process.

Early social learning theory shared Freud's view that as children grow older, social rules and values are actively imposed on them. Some early social learning theorists suggested that children comply with these standards in order to maintain closeness with the parents, who have been associated with reducing hunger and meeting other basic needs. The most common theme in the traditional social learning view, however, is the direct teaching of acceptable behavior by means of selective rewards and punishments. Children, this perspective argues, are rewarded when they act "good" and punished when they act "bad." As a result, they come to behave properly.

Contemporary social learning theorists put less emphasis on the direct and purposeful teaching of appropriate behavior than their predecessors did (Bandura, 1995; Mischel and Mischel, 1983). Instead, they underscore the importance of imitation and vicarious rewards and punishments that a child observes (those the child sees *others* experiencing). In this view, children come to behave appropriately just by being exposed to desirable behavior in others whom they love or respect and by seeing those people socially rewarded for adhering to norms and values. Meryl Polonius, for instance, may observe her mother, Karen, comforting a neighbor's child who has fallen and hurt himself. When the child's mother appears on the scene, she thanks Karen profusely. From these observations Meryl learns a set of actions that can be used with others in distress. She also learns that kindness is the "right" response in such a situation and that being kind may result in gratitude and praise. Note how modern social learning theorists emphasize the various cognitions (the ideas and understandings) that Meryl acquires. They believe that once Meryl knows the behaviors considered appropriate in this situation she will naturally tend to adopt them. Meryl, like all children, wants to be socially competent, and learning society's rules is one way of acquiring such competence. Here you can see how modern social learning theory is leaning increasingly toward the view of socialization from within.

SOCIALIZATION FROM THE INSIDE

Mary Ainsworth has argued persuasively that socialization emanates from inside children (Ainsworth, Bell, and Stayton, 1974). She believes that in the natural course of events children *want* to comply with their parents' requests and expectations (see also Waters et al., 1990). This desire stems from our evolution as a group-living species. It is also encouraged by the social context in which children are embedded from birth.

Take Malcolm Williams, for example. Early in life he has become a participant in smoothly operating relationships with his caregivers. His behavior has become organized around DeeDee, John, and Momma Jo, who represent bases of security for him. Upon becoming a toddler, Malcolm naturally wants to maintain these close and harmonious relationships. There is no reason to assume that he will routinely resist the adults in his family or that they will have to force his compliance through punishment or threat of withholding love. Malcolm *enjoys* pleasing them and participating in partnerships with them. They have been reliable and responsive to him, so it makes sense that he wants to be responsive to them.

Ainsworth's research shows that most children do behave in this way. Children whose caregivers are consistently responsive to them are found to be compliant as early as 12 months of age and tend to be secure in their attachments (Ainsworth, Bell, and Stayton, 1974). This tendency is also seen at age 2 years (Frankel and Bates, 1990; Londerville and Main, 1981; Matas, Arend, and Sroufe, 1978). Toddlers who persistently resist their caregivers are primarily those whose caregivers have been unresponsive to them and who have developed anxious attachments.

Most toddlers are of course negativistic at times. Even those who have secure relationships with their parents will periodically oppose parental wishes and demand their own way, at times with great intensity. For this reason the toddler period is often called the "terrible twos." As Erik Erikson (1963) has argued, some negativism is a natural and inevitable outcome of the toddler's expanding capabilities coupled with the movement toward greater self-reliance. When Mikey refuses to let Christine help him up the stairs, he is showing a normal desire to exercise his newfound skills and autonomy. Ainsworth's point is simply that a motivation toward cooperation and compliance is as natural in toddlers as this thrust toward independence. Toddlers generally are oppositional when the adult request is counter to their own goals, not when they are seeking assistance from a parent (Matas, Arend, and Sroufe, 1978; Schneider-Rosen and Wenz-Gross, 1990; Rheingold, 1983). When a toddler seems dedicated to thwarting the parents, when he or she consistently opposes or ignores most parental requests, a problem in the parent-child relationship is likely. This is not simply something in the toddler's nature. Later in this chapter you will read about several studies that demonstrate this point. But first let's arrive at a better picture of toddlerhood by looking at some major developments in this important period.

Toddlers learn not just because parents make them do things but also because they want to cooperate with parents. They enjoy doing things with and helping their parents.

MAJOR DEVELOPMENTS IN THE TODDLER PERIOD

In addition to starting to comply with social rules and expectations, there are several other important social and emotional developments in toddlerhood. One is greater independence from parents and greater self-reliance; another is greater sociability and more mature forms of social interaction; a third is greater awareness of the self and other people; and a fourth is a broader range of emotional responses. As you read about these important developments in the toddler period, notice how each helps to fundamentally change the nature of the child's social relationships.

MOVING TOWARD INDEPENDENCE

Toddlers will tolerate being a considerable distance from caregivers when it is they who initiate the separation.

Executive competence: The term used by Charles Wenar for the child's feeling that he or she is an autonomous force in the world, with the ability to manipulate objects and influence the outcome of events.

One of the most obvious developmental changes in the toddler period is a decline in physical closeness to and contact with caregivers. Mobile toddlers readily separate from their caregivers to play and to explore. The distance toddlers venture from parents can be quite substantial when they are the ones who initiate the separation (Rheingold and Eckerman, 1971). Occasionally, in the course of other activities, the toddler will return to the caregiver before going off again. But more often the child will merely show a toy or vocalize across a distance, as in our opening example of Mikey at 1 year of age. Whereas Mikey as a young infant needed *physical* contact to support his explorations, he is now relying more on *psychological* contact (Sroufe, 1995). Psychological contact can be maintained by interactions that do not involve physical touching. Examples are exchanges of words, smiles, and looks. Note that Mikey's secure attachment to his parents, in toddlerhood as well as infancy, supports his explorations and mastery of the environment. But much more than in infancy, he is now able to draw support from cues across a distance, and this ability in turn makes it possible for him to be more independent (Emde, 1992).

Several studies have illustrated this important development. In one, researchers placed a screen between mothers and their toddlers as the children played in a room full of toys (Carr, Dabbs, and Carr, 1975). These children tended to play less than toddlers who were not blocked from seeing their mothers. It was as if in losing visual contact with their mothers they had lost a significant support for their explorations. The same children tended to compensate for the screen by chattering away to their mothers, thus maintaining vocal contact with them. Interestingly, when the screen was taken away, these toddlers did not actually look at their mothers very often. The mere possibility of visual contact was sufficient support at this age. The critical factor is that the toddler knows the parent is available *if needed*.

Compared with infants, toddlers also show less distress when caregivers briefly leave them in a laboratory setting, and they settle down quickly when the caregiver returns (Sroufe and Waters, 1977). Apparently, by age 18 months, most children have acquired the expectation that contact with the caregiver will alleviate distress, and so they are comforted quickly. Moreover, when a caregiver prepares a toddler for separation by interacting more beforehand or by explaining the departure, the child is much less distressed (Lollis, 1990). Such efforts to reduce separation distress have little impact on infants.

At the same time that toddlers are becoming more comfortable with separations from their caregivers, they are also actively experimenting with mastery over objects. Recall the incident in which 13-month-old Mikey is exploring the effects of throwing objects over a gate and down the stairs. We pointed out how Mikey is not just repeating an action; he is actively experimenting with cause and effect. Through active experimentation Mikey is learning to integrate his various capabilities in new and purposeful ways. He is learning that it is fun to explore and manipulate objects and that the possibilities for exploration are endless. Mikey's motivation to discover is fed by these experiences. Perhaps most important of all, he is learning that "I" can do things, that "I" can be in charge. Charles Wenar (1976) calls this **executive competence.** As toddlers like Mikey begin to understand that they can use things for their own ends, they start to develop a sense of personal agency, of knowing that they are autonomous forces in the world. This emerging sense of personal agency, coupled with an attraction toward objects, helps promote independence in toddlers.

Executive competence does not apply only to objects. Toddlers are quite capable of using adults, especially caregivers, as props for problem solving and mastery (Matas et al., 1978). They look to them for help as well as for information, as Mikey does with Christine to solve the lever problem in our chapter opening. An analysis of the coping strategies used by toddlers in challenging situations showed that most of them involve turning to the caregiver for support and assistance (Parritz, 1989).

THE GROWTH OF SOCIABILITY

Supported by rapid cognitive advances, children become more sociable and more competent in their interactions with adults and other children during the toddler period (Caplan et al., 1991; Dunn and Munn, 1986; Eckerman et al., 1989; Howes, 1988; Mueller and C. Cooper, 1986). Compared with infants, toddlers have a greatly expanded capacity to observe and interpret other people's actions, to imitate others, and to maintain sequences of social interaction. They are also keenly interested in interacting with others, especially with peers (Mueller and C. Cooper, 1986).

SHARING EXPERIENCES

One characteristic behavior of toddlers is their constant communication about objects they discover in an effort to share them with others. Toddlers persistently point at things, talk about them, and bring them to others for inspection (Emde, 1992). Such behavior is important both because it illustrates the general sociability of the toddler and because it reveals an increased social awareness and rudimentary ability to take another person's perspective. When Malcolm deliberately seeks out Momma Jo to show her some newfound treasure, he must understand that just because *he* sees the object, he cannot assume that she sees it too, unless her attention is directed to it. Increased social awareness is also illustrated by the fact that toddlers smile much more often when another person is attentive to them than when another person isn't looking. This shows that they recognize that communication requires a receptive partner (Scanlon-Jones and Raag, 1989).

Related to a frequent sharing of discoveries is the toddler's frequent sharing of emotions, called **affective sharing** (Emde, 1992; Waters, Wippman, and Sroufe, 1979). When Mikey turns, smiles exuberantly, and extends the wooden puzzle piece toward his mother, exclaiming happily "Ya-ka!," he is doing more than merely calling attention to an object; he is also sharing his pleasure. While toddlers show things to a variety of people, automatic displays of newfound objects accompanied by happy smiles and vocalizations are directed almost exclusively to attachment figures.

Affective sharing: The toddler's sharing of emotional experiences.

SOCIAL REFERENCING

Another development in toddlers is the ability to use a caregiver's facial expressions or tone of voice as a cue for how to deal with a novel situation. This "reading" of another person to guide one's own behavior is called **social referencing** (e.g., Boccia and Campos, 1989; Emde, 1992). In a typical study of social referencing, 12-month-olds were enticed across a low table to the edge of a thick sheet of glass raised a foot above the floor (Sorce, Emde, and Klinnert, 1981).

Social referencing: The use of unspoken cues from another person, such as facial expression and tone of voice, to guide one's own behavior.

Sharing of affect is one way that toddlers continue to feel close to caregivers as they become more independent.

As the child peered over the edge of this variation of the "visual cliff" (see Figure 4.5), the mother was instructed either to smile broadly at the child or to show exaggerated fear. Whereas most of the children whose mothers smiled crossed over the glass, none of the children whose mothers showed fear were willing to take this risk. The youngsters apparently took their cues about the safety of the glass from their mothers' facial expressions.

Research shows that the toddler looks to the caregiver as a social reference largely in ambiguous situations, in which the right response is not clear (Rosen, Adamson, and Bakeman, 1992). In one experiment, for example, Megan Gunnar showed children ages 12 to 13 months a pleasant, an ambiguous, or a frightening toy. She asked each child's mother either to smile (suggesting the situation was positive) or to adopt a neutral face. As expected, a mother's smile encouraged play with the ambiguous toy, but it had no effect on behavior toward the other two playthings. The children consistently avoided the frightening toy regardless of a smile from the mother, and they generally approached the pleasant toy even if the mother looked neutral (Gunnar and Stone, 1984).

You can see the role of ambiguity in social referencing in our story of Malcolm. When he and Momma Jo are accosted by the group of boys, Malcolm doesn't know what to make of the situation at first. He therefore takes his cues from Momma Jo's face and voice to interpret the encounter as a negative one. This responsiveness to caregivers' emotional signals increases rapidly between the ages of 1 and 2 years (Emde, 1992).

INTERACTION BETWEEN TODDLERS

Part of moving out into the social world is the toddler's increased interest in interacting with other young children. In the period between 15 and 24 months, children develop the ability to behave in a complementary manner with a peer. This allows the emergence of games between toddlers (Eckerman et al., 1989). Often these games are rooted in imitation (Brownell, 1990; Eckerman and Stein, 1990; Eckerman et al., 1989). One toddler does something, and the other repeats the action; and so it goes back and forth, much to the delight of each child. There is much more complexity and positive emotion in interactions between toddlers than in interactions between infants (Brownell, 1990). Moreover, 2-year-olds clearly distinguish among playmates, preferring certain ones over others (Howes, 1988).

Most of the interactions between young toddlers are centered on objects (both children playing with the same set of blocks, for example) (Bronson, 1981). But rarely do two young toddlers who are playing with the same object focus on the same theme (one may be using the blocks to build a tower, while the other is building an unrelated road). At three years of age, shared themes among playmates become somewhat more prominent (Howes, 1988), and social pretend play, in contrast to solitary pretend play, emerges (Howes et al., 1989). Social pretend play involves children acting out interrelated roles, such as doctor and patient or teacher and student. These new developments reflect the fact that 3-year-olds are much more capable of coordinated play than 2-year-olds are (Eckerman et al., 1990; Howes, 1988).

Rapid advances in peer interactions continue to take place during the preschool and middle childhood years. In the preschool period children start to differentiate friends from playmates, showing more reciprocity and more positive emotions with friends (Howes, 1988). They also start to develop a concept of "friend." At the same time, they begin to understand that other people, their peers included, have "rights" as well as intentions (Smetana, 1989). Because of these social advances that occur later in the preschool years, we don't use the terms *friendship* or *peer relationship* until after the toddler period. Still, the foundations for peer relationships and friendships among peers are laid out in toddler interactions and the caregiver-infant interactions that preceded them.

AWARENESS OF THE SELF AND OTHERS

Although a person's self-concept and sense of identity evolve throughout life, knowledge of one's own existence as a separate individual begins in the toddler

Toddlers are very interested in one another and like playing in the same area. This play is often "parallel," however. They rarely develop themes together or coordinate play.

period. Children at this age become aware that their own behaviors and intentions are distinct from those of others. In this sense, we can say that awareness of self emerges during toddlerhood. This development goes hand in hand with a more mature understanding of other people's selves.

AWARENESS OF SELF

Several lines of research suggest the existence of self-awareness in toddlers. First, self-awareness can be inferred from what we know about cognitive development. If toddlers can form mental representations of objects, they should be able to represent themselves mentally as people and actors. A good deal of evidence suggests that representational skills unfold rapidly during a child's second and third years (e.g., Cicchetti and Beeghly, 1990a; Ungerer et al., 1981).

Self-awareness in toddlers is also revealed by studies of children's reactions to their images in a mirror. Using a procedure introduced by Gordon Gallup in research with chimpanzees, children were shown their faces in a mirror (Amsterdam, 1972). Then, unobtrusively, a dab of rouge was placed on each child's face and the child was shown the mirror again. If the child reached directly to the spot of rouge, not in the reflection but on his or her own face, the child was assumed to know that he or she was the person in the mirror. This reaction was common by about 20 months of age and sometimes appeared by 18 months or even a little earlier. Subsequent researchers have confirmed these findings. In one study, three-quarters of the children between the ages of 21 and 24 months touched their rouge-marked noses when looking into a mirror, thus showing self-recognition. In contrast, only one-quarter of the children ages 15 to 18 months and none of the children ages 9 to 12 months responded in this way (Lewis and Brooks, 1978).

Self-recognition seems to be closely tied to general cognitive development. The age at which a child with Down syndrome starts touching his or her rouge-marked nose when it is revealed in a mirror is directly related to the child's degree of mental retardation. The more severe the retardation, the more delayed the youngster is in showing this sign of self-awareness (Mans, Cicchetti and Sroufe, 1978).

The final indication of self-awareness in toddlers is the addition of "I" to their vocabularies, coupled with clear examples of self-assertion and will (e.g., Breger, 1974). "No! I do it!" Mikey says emphatically, squirming to get down from Christine's arms and climb the stairs by himself. During the toddler period children have a heightened awareness of their own intentions and often are determined to direct their own activity (Sander, 1975).

UNDERSTANDING OF OTHERS

Closely related to the emergence of a sense of self is a changing understanding of others. Dennie Wolf (1982) has suggested three major steps in the development of this understanding. In the first step, when children are about age 1, they recognize that others can do things they cannot, but they do not yet grasp that others are agents in their own right. Wolf gives the example of a mother initiating a game of peek-a-boo by covering her face with her hands. Her 1-year-old son responds by covering his own face, and when he lifts his hands away, he is surprised to find that his mother's face is still covered. It is as if he has blurred the distinction between the two sets of hands and the two faces.

During their second year children reach step 2 in their understanding of others. Now they grasp the boundaries between their own actions and other people's, and this allows them to engage in genuine turn-taking. To some extent, however, their grasp of the concept "other" is still limited. Rather than waiting for mother to remove her hands from her face, the toddler at this age may pull her hands away for her. It seems as if the child does not yet have a mature grasp of the two independent roles involved in this game.

By the end of the second year step 3 emerges: a genuine understanding that people are independent agents. At this stage, children come to realize that each actor in a social exchange is playing a role separate from the others. Now toddlers can finally play a real game of hide-and-seek. At a younger age they are likely to jump out of hiding before they are found, as if the distinction between hider and seeker is blurred in their minds. By age 2, waiting to be found may still be difficult for them, but at least they run in the opposite direction when the seeker comes near. This action implies that they recognize the separateness of people's roles, intentions, and aims.

This child knows it is herself in the mirror.

This new recognition underlies the battles of will that tend to arise during toddlerhood. It also underlies the compromises arrived at when parents set limits. In our story, Mikey goes to bed when his mother tells him, but he insists on climbing the stairs by himself. Here he understands that his mother and he have independent wishes. As a result, their social interactions are more sophisticated.

A more advanced understanding of others affects interactions with peers as well. For example, during the second year, toddlers come to understand the "possession" rule: the idea that if someone else already has possession of an object that person has some claim on it. As a result, 24-month-olds try less often to take an object from a peer than do 18-month-olds, and they are more likely to negotiate over the object (Brownell and Brown, 1985). Twenty-four-month-olds are also more likely to relinquish an object when a peer who was playing with it earlier tries to take it away. Such changes in interaction follow from a growing understanding that other people have rights. At the same time, the increased self-assertion of other toddlers helps promote this understanding.

EMOTIONAL CHANGES

All the developments discussed so far are related to changes in the emotional capacities of a toddler. A more mature awareness of other people, for example, is related to a new sensitivity to the feelings that others have, just as a growing awareness of the self is related to the emergence of new emotions that require self-consciousness (such as shame). The emotional developments of toddlerhood also make possible a new level of relating to other people. They play a key role in the child's beginning acceptance of social rules and standards.

FEELINGS, SOCIAL SENSITIVITY, AND THE BEGINNINGS OF MORALITY

Even by the middle of the second year, toddlers show a sensitivity to social demands—understanding, for example, that certain activities are forbidden (Kochanska, 1993). They may stop the behavior, hesitate, start and then stop or, at times, engage in the behavior while looking at the caregiver. The beginnings of behavioral control, which are consequent to the dawning awareness of standards for behavior, is considered a hallmark of the toddler period.

Such changes are guided by feelings available to toddlers at this time. For example, they show an awareness of things not being as they should be (Emde et al., 1991; Stipek et al., 1992). This awareness is revealed in expressions of

"Do it myself."

Deviation anxiety:
The negative feelings that
toddlers experience when
they are doing, or are
about to do, something
forbidden.

uncertainty or distress regarding a flawed object, or distress when an external standard is violated or cannot be met (as when they cannot do something they are told to do). Moreover, they begin to be sensitive to others who are in pain, for the first time approaching those who are distressed (Zahn-Waxler et al., 1992). This is an early sign of empathy.

At this stage, however, these emotional reactions remain quite primitive. They are usually undifferentiated—that is, similar regardless of the particular situation. The reaction that occurs when a parental rule is violated is the same as that which occurs when a performance standard is not met (as when the peas persistently roll off the fork and onto the floor). These reactions have been interpreted as reflecting a generalized response to adult disapproval. They are best characterized as generalized arousal, often with a strong quality of uncertainty (Kochanska, 1993), and may be combinations of interest, upset, and amusement (e.g., Dunn et al., 1985).

By the end of the second year toddlers are responsive to negative emotional signals from others (Emde, 1992). They also react with specific negative feelings to their own transgressions, showing distress or **deviation anxiety** when they are doing, or are about to do, something forbidden (Kochanska, 1993). In experiments involving staged mishaps (juice spilled on a new shirt, a doll breaking while being played with), toddlers show a variety of negative emotions along with verbalized concern and even attempts at reparation (Cole et al., 1992). In more naturalistic research situations, they also show spontaneous self-corrections when they catch themselves doing something "bad," self-corrections that are often mediated by language (Londerville and Main, 1981). They might, for example, say "No, can't" and get back down from a counter they had been told not to climb on. The standards involved in such situations are always externally imposed by adults, and the toddler's adherence to them almost always requires an adult presence. Still, awareness that there are standards and sensitivity to the reactions of others represent the early beginnings of what Robert Emde calls a "moral self" (Emde et al., 1991).

CHANGING EMOTIONS AND NEW EMOTIONS

During the toddler period some previously existing emotions are fundamentally changed. One reason is that high levels of emotional arousal are now less likely to make a child behave in a disorganized way. This means that the toddler is more tolerant of intense emotions. For example, a 1-year-old who became very frightened by a large barking dog might simply cry and become immobile, but an equally frightened 2-year-old might retain the presence of mind to turn and run away. Glee as well as fear can now be experienced at levels that would have been totally disorganizing earlier. As a result, the toddler becomes able to initiate and sustain raucous games. Mikey, for instance, can laugh uproariously while getting Frank to chase him, yet he is still able to keep running and decide on places to flee.

Another factor underlying a fundamental change in existing emotions during the toddler period is the child's increasingly mature ability to differentiate the self and others. Mikey is aware not only that Christine is a separate person (as he knew at age 10 months), but also that he too is separate. This awareness gives him new ways of expressing both anger and joy toward his caregivers. Now he may deliberately oppose Christine when he becomes angry, expressing *defiance* of her as a way of asserting his independent will. He may also run up and hug her even when he isn't upset, thereby showing *his* affection as a separate person toward *her* as a separate person. This is the prototype of love.

Important new emotions also arise during the toddler period, emotions that were totally absent in infancy. These include **shame** and what may be termed **positive self-evaluation,** a forerunner of pride. Shame is the sense of the self as exposed and vulnerable, the "bad" self (Erikson, 1963). It is the toddler's new understanding of the self that makes shame possible. But because the sense of self at this age is still quite fragile, a toddler who is punished (even for some very specific misdeed) is vulnerable to feeling that the entire self is dissolving. This is especially true when the punishment is harsh or degrading. By the same token, a toddler is capable of feeling an all-encompassing sense of pleasure with the self, a cockiness that is qualitatively different from anything he or she displayed as a baby. When Momma Jo extolls 2-year-old Malcolm for putting on his own socks, his whole self seems to swell with joy. (Later in the preschool period, when children begin to experience such emotional reactions in response to meeting standards they themselves have set, we see more genuine pride.)

Michael Lewis calls the new emotions that emerge during the toddler period and the preschool years the **self-conscious emotions,** or the "secondary emotions," to distinguish them from the qualitatively different "fundamental emotions" of infancy (such as joy, fear, anger, and surprise) (e.g., Lewis 1992; Lewis et al., 1992). Unlike the fundamental emotions, the self-conscious emotions require some objective sense of self (including a sense of the self as an agent or "doer" of things), as well as some understanding of standards for behavior. Lewis has found, for example, that toddlers who can recognize themselves in a mirror are much more likely to show embarrassment than those who can't yet recognize their mirror image. Emotions such as embarrassment and shame, Lewis argues, clearly indicate an emerging sense of self, and at the same time they are critical for consolidating the self that is emerging. Experiencing connections between one's own actions and the feelings to which they give rise is central to a sense of self.

Shame:
An emotion in which the self feels "bad," exposed, and vulnerable.

Positive self-evaluation:
An emotion in toddlers that is the forerunner of pride.

Self-conscious emotions:
The term used by Michael Lewis for the new emotions of toddlers and preschoolers which (unlike joy, fear, and the other "fundamental" emotions of infancy) require some objective sense of self and some understanding of standards for behavior.

By the end of the toddler period the child knows enough about different roles that he or she can play more complicated games.

Lewis also maintains that, in contrast to the fundamental emotions of infancy, the self-conscious emotions manifest themselves in an array of postural, bodily, and verbal reactions rather than solely in a stereotyped facial expression. Shame, for example, is expressed not just with a sheepish smile but also with lowered head and eyes, a "collapsed" or hunched body, and a tense, still posture.

PARENT-TODDLER RELATIONS

All the developmental changes we have outlined dramatically influence the parent-child relationship. On the one hand, they offer parents new sources of pleasure and new avenues for communication with the child. On the other hand, they create new demands and challenges for caregivers. In this section, we look at the parents' role in the parent-toddler relationship. This sets the stage for our subsequent discussion of how the personalities and self-concepts of individual children begin to take shape in the toddler period.

THE PARENTS' TASKS

One of the parents' tasks during the toddler period is to adjust their own behavior in keeping with the child's current capacities and limitations. Parents can do this by participating in the toddler's efforts to communicate with language, as well as in the child's sharing of joy and excitement when discovering new things. Frank and Christine do this automatically in their interactions with Mikey. They respond even to his nonsense words as if they conveyed real meaning; they express delight when Mikey shows them the simplest of objects. At the same time, they allow Mikey to try things on his own and push his capacities to the limit, always being available to help if he exceeds his resources. You can see this in how Christine handles the stair-climbing incident and in the way she helps Mikey solve the lever problem. The parents' task is to create an arena in which the child has space and support to develop. Jerome Bruner has called what the parents provide "scaffolding" (see Chapter 9). We use the term **guided self-regulation,** because during the toddler period children are capable of regulating themselves—but only with the guidance of caregivers (Sroufe, 1995).

Guided self-regulation: The ability of toddlers to regulate their own behavior within guidelines provided by caregivers.

Another parental task during the toddler period is to set appropriate limits for the child. A dramatic increase in the number of instructions from both parents occurs when the child is between 12 and 18 months old (Fagot and Kavanaugh, 1993). One way parents set limits is through commands, comments, and questions, making use of the child's growing comprehension of language (Damon, 1988). Toddlers have countless verbal experiences that help them learn to behave appropriately. When a father asks, "Is that toothpaste *supposed* to be on the mirror?" and pauses to allow the child to answer, the child learns more than where the toothpaste goes. He or she also learns that there are constraints on behavior and that there are right and wrong things to do. As social learning theorists emphasize, toddlers also learn a great deal about limits by watching parents praise, reprimand, and correct siblings (Dunn and Munn, 1986). Most developmentalists believe that providing toddlers with limits is just as important as providing them with encouragement to master new skills. Their reasoning is this: if toddlers can be confident that their parents will impose limits when needed, they can explore their capacities freely, testing how far they will reach. The limits reassure the toddler that parents will not let their impulses go too far. The limits therefore provide a kind of safety zone in which development can take place.

Notice that what is important here is the parents' *general* approach toward the child, not specific child-rearing practices. For instance, there is no evidence that the specific age at which a child is weaned or toilet trained has a major impact on development (Hetherington and Brackbill, 1963; Maccoby, 1992); however, there *is* evidence that the general quality of care, in particular the consistency with which parents set limits and provide guidance, does make a difference in how well a child fares (Arend, Gove, and Sroufe, 1979; Baumrind, 1967; Crockenberg and Litman, 1990; Erikson, Egeland, and Sroufe, 1985; Frankel and Bates, 1990; Matas, Arend, and Sroufe 1978). In one study, for instance, researchers found that a combination of control and supportive guidance produced a maximum of child compliance without compromising assertiveness (Crockenberg and Litman, 1990). Negative control alone led to defiance. The combination of support *and* control is referred to by Diana Baumrind (1967) as "authoritative" parenting. It will be discussed further in Chapters 10 and 12.

Involvement of fathers often increases during the toddler period, and interactions commonly center around play.

CHANGES IN CAREGIVING DURING THE TODDLER PERIOD

Throughout the world the care of children often changes dramatically during the toddler period (Tronick et al., 1992; Whiting and Edwards, 1988). In some societies when a child becomes mobile and stops nursing (often when a new baby is born), siblings, sometimes quite young themselves, take on much of the responsibility for the toddler's care and supervision. This practice is followed, for example, by the Efe (pigmy) foragers of central Africa (Tronick et al., 1992). In other societies, such as the Gusii of East Africa, all adult kin, or even all adults in the community, assume a role in socializing children after infancy (Whiting and Edwards, 1988).

Even in Western industrialized societies marked changes in caregiving occur during toddlerhood. One change that has been studied extensively is the father's increasing involvement with the child. Fathers are much less involved with infants than mothers are, but this often changes somewhat during the toddler period, especially for boys (Lamb, 1981; Parke and Stearns, 1992). Fathers' behavior during interaction with toddlers is often quite different from that of mothers. Fathers are less often involved in care and nurturance and more often involved in play (Lamb, 1981). The playful style of fathers, which we illustrated with our description of Frank's interaction with Mikey, is well suited to the child's general orientation at this age. Since a major task for the toddler is to evolve new ways of relating to parents, ways that are more in keeping with growing independence, the father's input may be very helpful now. At the same time, the father's increased involvement with and emotional support of the toddler may ease the beginnings of psychological separation from the mother. Thus, having two caregivers with somewhat different styles of interaction can have certain advantages for a young child.

INDIVIDUAL ADAPTATIONS: THE ROOTS OF PERSONALITY

As toddlers acquire more self-awareness and begin to experience a broader range of emotions, their developmental paths may diverge even more than was

Both parents and toddlers are pleased by the toddler's first steps. This new ability promotes the child's advancing independence. It also leads to new challenges for child and parents.

Pattern of adaptation:
The overall style of responding to others and to the environment displayed by each individual child.

Separation-individuation process:
According to Margaret Mahler, the child's psychological separation from the caregiver coupled with a growing sense of self.

the case in infancy. Some develop very positive attitudes and expectations about the self, while others view the self quite negatively. Some show proficiency at handling their emotions, while others tend to be overwhelmed by them. Such individual differences affect how others respond to individual children and how the children themselves respond to others, as well as to opportunities and challenges. These individual styles of responding, or **patterns of adaptation,** form the roots of personality.

BECOMING A SEPARATE PERSON

An important starting point for the development of individual adaptations in toddlerhood is what Margaret Mahler called the **separation-individuation process** (Mahler et al., 1975). This term refers to the child's psychological separation from the caregiver, coupled with a growing awareness of being an individual. Mahler describes the way in which early closeness with the caregiver supports the toddler's first ventures into the surrounding world, which in turn bring an inevitable sense of separateness. As children move away from the caregiver and experience doing things on their own, they increasingly realize that they are independent, that their actions are separate from the caregiver's. The way the connection with the caregiver supports this progress toward greater autonomy and a sense of self has been beautifully described by the philosopher Søren Kierkegaard:

> The loving mother teaches her child to walk alone. She is far enough from him so that she cannot actually support him but she holds out her arms to him. She imitates his movements, and if he totters, she swiftly bends as if to seize him, so that the child might believe that he is not walking alone. . . . Her face beckons like a reward, an encouragement. Thus, the child walks alone with his eyes fixed on his mother's face, not on the difficulties in his way. He supports himself by the arms that do not hold him and constantly strives toward the refuge in his mother's embrace, little suspecting that at the very same moment he is emphasizing his need of her, he is proving that he can do without her, because he is walking alone. (1938, p. 85).

But the separation-individuation process does not proceed with equal smoothness for every child. In Erik Erikson's theory a major factor affecting how smoothly it unfolds is the way in which parents impose limits on the child. According to Erikson, when a toddler's sense of self begins to emerge and the child confronts parental limits, there is the potential either to develop a positive sense of independence and competence or to feel shamed by parents and experience profound self-doubt (1963). Thus, the defining issue for this stage in Erikson's theory is "autonomy versus shame and doubt."

Another factor affecting how smoothly separation-individuation proceeds is the degree of basic trust the child has developed. When basic trust is strong, the toddler can seek autonomy and still feel secure. Louis Sander (1975) has described this way of reconciling toddlers' striving toward independence with their continuing need for closeness to and security from parents. He points out that toddlers do not exclusively try to achieve self-reliance. Instead, their strivings toward autonomy are balanced by bids for a continuing emotional partnership with the caregiver. The success of these bids has important psychological consequences. If toddlers know they can reclaim the former closeness with the caregiver—if they have confidence that the attachment relationship is secure and that care remains available—they will feel free to explore their capacities to the fullest (Schore, 1994). Such confidence is a product of each child's history of interactions with the caregiver. The parent's reliability during infancy breeds a basic trust, which later enables the toddler to make initiatives toward independence. As Erikson argues, trust supports autonomy during this period of development.

You have seen this developmental process going well with both Mikey and Malcolm. These toddlers have been able to become more autonomous while still maintaining psychological contact with their caregivers. Even when they do things against their parents' wishes and temporarily annoy them, they remain confident that closeness with the parents can be reclaimed. Their bids for independence do not threaten their strong emotional ties to their parents. Because their early attachment relationships were secure, they are certain of their parents' continued availability, readily reassured by them in times of stress, and accepting of the limits they have set. Like other toddlers who have had these positive experiences, Mikey and Malcolm are confident, eager, resourceful, and secure.

A more negative outcome is illustrated in our story of Meryl and can be seen in other toddlers who have experienced less secure relationships with their caregivers. When children are unduly anxious about the caregiver's availability, when autonomy is forced upon them too early, or when their bids for independence are viewed negatively, self-reliance is compromised (Matas, Arend, and Sroufe, 1978; Sroufe, Fox, and Pancake, 1983). This compromising of self-reliance can take many forms, including timidity and continued preoccupation with the caregiver, unremitting power struggles, persistent angry interactions, lack of emotional interest in mastery, and general emotional detachment. We have described some of these reactions in Meryl.

RESEARCH ON THE ROLE OF PARENT-CHILD RELATIONSHIPS

THE ATTACHMENT HISTORY

A number of studies support the view of toddler social and emotional development that we have just described (Clarke-Stewart, 1973; Frankel & Bates, 1990;

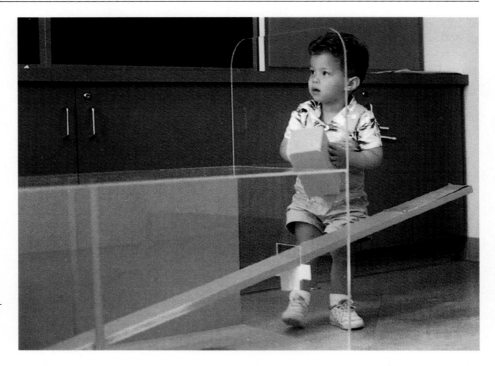

This child is working hard to solve this problem. He seems more interested in the problem itself than in the reward the experimenter has provided. For humans, there seems to be something intrinsically rewarding in making discoveries, solving problems, and mastering the environment.

Londerville and Main, 1981; Matas, Arend, and Sroufe, 1978). These studies show a clear association between the quality of the infant-caregiver relationship and how well the child later functions as a toddler.

In one study (Matas, Arend, and Sroufe, 1978) children whose attachment to their mothers had been assessed at ages 12 and 18 months were seen again at age 2 years. The researchers presented the children with a series of four problems that required the use of simple tools. The first two problems were relatively easy; one involved using a long stick to push a lure from inside a tube, for example. The final two problems were more difficult. The last was the one we described Mikey solving at the beginning of this chapter: holding down the end of a board with a large wooden block to get candy out of a deep box. This problem is beyond the capacity of almost all 2-year-olds, but in this study each child's mother was present as a potential resource. The researchers looked at the quality of each toddler's problem solving, including his or her emotional responses, enthusiasm, and ability to face challenges without quickly becoming frustrated. They also looked at the child's persistence and flexibility regarding the task, and at the ability to call upon and accept the mother's help when needed. At the same time, the researchers examined the timing and clarity of the mother's clues and the degree of emotional support she provided.

The findings were striking. Two-year-olds who had been securely attached as infants (confident in their caregiver's availability) were as a group more enthusiastic in approaching the problems, showed more positive emotions and less frustration, were more persistent and flexible, and cooperated more with their mother to reach a solution. These differences were not related to earlier measures of temperament.

In contrast, many of the children who had experienced an insecure attachment during infancy showed a variety of maladaptive responses. Some were intermittently clingy and dependent or whiny and prone to tantrums, quickly becoming frustrated or embroiled in conflict with their mother while the problem to be solved faded into the background. This reaction was most common in children like Meryl with a history of anxious-resistant attachment. Other anxiously attached toddlers showed no enthusiasm or pleasure and little involvement in the problems. They either ignored or refused to act on their mother's suggestions, or they expressed rejection of her indirectly. (For instance, when a mother said "Get the block," the child did get it but put it on the floor instead of on the board.) Such reactions were most common in children with a history of anxious-avoidant attachment.

Some toddlers are quite hesitant in the face of novel situations, while other toddlers are quite outgoing. Researchers actively debate the origins of such differences.

THE ROLE OF ONGOING PARENTAL SUPPORT

It would not be appropriate to say that the quality of the infant-caregiver attachment *caused* the differences observed among the toddlers' behavior in this study. More is involved in explaining toddlers' adaptations than the attachment aspect of the child's developmental history. Parental support and stimulation *during* the toddler period itself promotes positive functioning (Frankel and Bates, 1990; Holden and West, 1989; Silverman and Ragusa, 1990; Wachs et al., 1993). When caregivers are emotionally available and provide consistent and clear guidance, their toddlers tend to be more eager, persistent, and resourceful.

Additionally, the simple fact of consistency in parental behavior across a child's early years (Pianta et al., 1989) makes it difficult to separate the impact of early parenting from that of later parenting. Caregivers whose children were securely attached as infants were more likely to be supportive of their toddlers in the problem-solving situation just described (Gove, 1983). They tended to adjust their behavior depending on the particular demands of the situation and the child's needs. They allowed their toddlers to proceed on their own until they approached the limits of their resources. Then they calmly increased the number of clues they offered and eventually gave direct assistance if the child signaled a need for it. In this way the parents anticipated frustration and took steps to prevent it. Research has shown that such anticipatory behavior is more effective with toddlers than waiting for full-blown problems to arise (Holden and West, 1989; Spiker et al., 1993).

In sharp contrast to this pattern, caregivers of children with a history of anxious-avoidant attachment failed to increase the amount of help they offered as their toddlers struggled to solve the problems in the study. Most remained rather uninvolved throughout the child's efforts, despite the increasing difficulty of the problems. The caregivers of children with a history of anxious-resistant attachment did increase the amount of help they gave, but that help became less and less appropriate and clear. Both caregiver and child became more frustrated and ineffective as the pressure of the situation mounted.

This failure to provide clear guidelines was very different from the actions of caregivers whose toddlers had been securely attached as infants. Such caregivers generally tend to be very clear in the help they give their children. In a parallel way, they are very clear in establishing limits, and they are firm in maintaining those limits once they are set. Such differences in caregiver behavior during the toddler period are predictive of the child's later functioning (Arend et al., 1979; Erickson, Egeland, and Sroufe, 1985; Spiker et al., 1993).

HOW CHILDREN AFFECT THEIR OWN ADAPTATIONS

Some researchers believe that from the beginning a child's inborn tendencies heavily influence how the parents behave toward him or her (e.g., Scarr, 1992). In extreme cases this clearly happens. Such cases include children who were seriously ill and premature at birth (Plunkett et al., 1986); those whose mothers abused drugs during pregnancy and so gave birth to babies with drug addictions and other problems (Rodning et al., 1989); or those who developed a chronic illness in their first year of life (Goldberg et al., in press). As toddlers such children often show signs of maladaptation, such as lethargy and irritability. Presumably the serious developmental problems these children had as infants negatively affected the behavior of their caregivers, which in turn affected the child's behavior even after the original problems had been treated.

What about children *without* serious developmental problems? To what extent do *their* characteristics affect their adaptations? Developmentalists are still debating this question. Research has established that during the toddler period various temperament characteristics (such as activity level, intensity of emotional responses, and degree of boldness or inhibition) become more stable as well as more consistent across situations (Matheny, 1989; Robinson et al., 1992; Rothbart, 1986; Ruff et al., 1990; Silverman and Ragusa, 1990). By the toddler period there is more agreement between parents and other observers in describing a particular child. Brian Vaughn and his colleagues have suggested several interpretations for this finding (1992). The child's behavior may simply be more clear, and parents may have become better at describing their children. Alternatively, the children may actually be shaped over time toward conforming to parental descriptions.

The characteristics displayed in the toddler period also tend to be fairly enduring; they predict similar behaviors at later ages. For example, toddlers who tend to smile often and express many positive emotions, or those who frequently whine and behave irritably, or those who are very timid and inhibited, tend to show these same characteristics in the preschool and middle childhood years (Robinson et al., 1992; Rothbart, 1986, 1989).

It is also the case that during the toddler period a child's behavior becomes more coherent overall (Vaughn et al., 1992). For instance, security of attachment and temperament characteristics, which are not related in infancy, are related by age 3 years. By this we mean that a securely attached older toddler tends to have many positive aspects of temperament, whereas the opposite tends to be true of an anxiously attached older toddler.

It may be that the attachment relationship has influenced the child's stabilizing temperament, that temperamental differences influence attachment security at later ages, or both.

The clear and coherent differences in temperament that emerge among toddlers are an important part of the developmental picture. Children with different temperament characteristics may respond differently to the same situation, a phenomenon called **organismic specificity** (Wachs and Gruen, 1982). A toddler with a high activity level, for instance, may squirm vigorously when his mother tries to get him to sit in her lap and look at a book she is reading, whereas a more placid toddler may sit contentedly and listen to several stories read in the same way (Gandour, 1989). Such differences in toddlers' responses

Organismic specificity: The phenomenon whereby children with different characteristics of temperament respond differently to the same situation.

Some toddlers are surrounded by an extended family, which may include parents, siblings, grandparents, aunts, uncles, and cousins.

can affect how caregivers perceive them and behave toward them. When toddlers are agreeable and compliant, caregivers tend to impose fewer limits, discipline less often, and more often give positive support. These adult responses, in turn, encourage further compliance and agreeableness in the child. Toddlers perceived as "difficult," in contrast, may receive more harsh discipline from parents (Elder et al., 1986) and more negative responses in general (Lee and Bates, 1985; Wittmer and Honig, 1988). These responses may tend to foster the very "difficultness" to which they were reactions. Thus, whatever triggered the process to begin with—be it the parents' behavior or the inborn characteristics of the child—there is a clear potential for positive or negative cycles by the toddler period.

Negative cycles can take several forms. In one, toddlers who need more support and consistent handling (perhaps because of their attachment histories) tend to be those who are harder to care for and whose parents have more difficulty being consistent. As a result, the parents' responses tend to perpetuate the difficult aspects of these children. In another type of negative cycle, toddlers are rather detached from their parents, and at the same time the parents are emotionally distant, making cooperative partnerships increasingly unlikely.

We have illustrated the first of these negative cycles in our description of the relationship between Karen and Meryl. Meryl frequently resists her mother's wishes, throwing tantrums when Karen tries to insist, perhaps in part because of Karen's inconsistency. So Karen often backs down and lets Meryl have her way, just to keep the peace. Here Meryl's behavior is clearly affecting her mother's behavior, and the reverse is also true. By vacillating and failing to set firm limits, Karen is inadvertently promoting Meryl's difficult behavior. And by being difficult, Meryl makes it hard for Karen to be consistent. This is what is meant by reciprocal determinism or the transactional model we introduced in Chapter 2 (Bandura, 1986; Sameroff and Chandler, 1975). The child is influencing the parent at the same time the parent is influencing the child.

INDIVIDUAL ADAPTATIONS AND THE BROADER DEVELOPMENTAL CONTEXT

The transactional model helps to show that a parent is not solely responsible for the relationship that evolves with a child. Once a parent has started to respond to an infant in a certain way, the child's reactions often work to maintain the parent's style of caregiving. In addition, parent and child do not exist in a vacuum. They are surrounded by a larger social environment that includes other adults and children in the family, as well as people and institutions with which the family comes in contact. This larger social environment can impose pressures and challenges or offer various kinds of support. Developmentalists increasingly stress the need to view child-caregiver interactions as partly a product of this broader social context (e.g., National Research Council, 1993).

Developmentalists are becoming especially interested in how the quality of care children receive is influenced by the quality of relationships between adults in the family, the amount of stress the family experiences, and the various forms of social support available to parents (Belsky, 1988). These factors interact, often aggravating or lessening one another's effects. For instance, the loss of a job or a serious illness may produce enough stress to tax a parent's capacity to emotionally support a child. However, if the parent has supportive relationships with other adults, that stress may be easier to cope with and its negative effects greatly reduced. Particularly important is the quality of parental relationships. For example, research shows that when a father is supportive of a mother, she is more affectionate and responsive toward their child (Belsky and Isabella, 1987; Easterbrooks and Emde, 1988). Without such psychological backing by the marital partner or someone else, a caregiver tends to take less pleasure in parenting and is more susceptible to its stresses.

The potential effects of stress on the quality of child care is illustrated in a study by Byron Egeland and his colleagues (Vaughn et al., 1979). These researchers found that the quality of a child's attachment to the mother sometimes changes during the toddler period. A relationship classified as anxious when the child was 12 months of age might be classified as secure 6 months later, and vice versa. Significantly, a switch from an insecure to a secure attachment was linked to a reduction in the disruptive life changes and stress that the caregiver was experiencing. This finding suggests that when parents have greater stability in their lives, they are better able to provide for the emotional needs of a child. It also suggests that a pattern of anxious attachment may be changed if circumstances change for the better. As is true at every phase of life, patterns of adaptation depend on current situations as well as developmental history.

PARENTAL ABUSE AND NEGLECT OF TODDLERS

More than 1 million cases of physical battering, sexual abuse, and gross neglect of children are reported in the United States each year (Krugman and Davidson, 1990; National Research Council, 1993). Although parents may mistreat a child of any age, abused and neglected children are most likely to be under the age of 3. This is partly because toddlers can be very challenging, with their frequent efforts to assert their independence (often in ways that inconvenience or frustrate adults) and their tendency during explorations to "get into things" they shouldn't. An adult can easily misinterpret a toddler's behavior as intentionally contrary or naughty, and some may conclude that increasingly severe punishment is needed to "set the child right." Others, overwhelmed by the parenting task, may have given up early and neglect their child. Toddlers, for their part, have not yet learned how to avoid mistreatment or to meet their own needs, so they are particularly vulnerable to abuse or neglect.

PROBLEMS RELATED TO CHILD MALTREATMENT

Demonstrating consequences of maltreatment is sometimes difficult because other factors associated with it, such as poverty and family stress, may also influence children. Still, certain of its correlates are quite well established (Cicchetti and Carlson, 1989; National Research Council, 1993). These include aggression, social withdrawal, and other difficulties with peers (Cicchetti and Olson, 1990; Dodge, Bates, and Pettit, 1990; Pianta, Egeland, and Erickson, 1989; National Research Council, 1993). Problems of low self-esteem and difficulty maintaining a coherent sense of self, as well as problems describing one's own feelings and actions, have been found (Coster et al., 1989; National Research Council, 1993), as have emotional disturbances ranging from lack of ability to experience pleasure to uncontrollable anger. In addition, there may be serious problems of apathy in the face of challenges, or difficulties in balancing the desire to explore with the need to feel secure. Such problems may persist into later childhood and even adulthood. In adulthood, the most widely reported outcomes of having been maltreated as a child are aggression and parenting problems (Egeland, Jacobvitz, and Sroufe, 1988; National Research Council, 1993).

One reason the correlates of maltreatment are so varied is that it takes many forms (Egeland and Sroufe, 1981). *Physical neglect* (failure to meet the child's basic needs for food, warmth, cleanliness, and medical attention) tends to be related to devastating health consequences, a lack of competence in dealing with the world of objects, and major problems of achievement in school (Eckenrode et al., 1993; Egeland, 1988; National Research Council, 1993).

Physical abuse (deliberately causing the child physical injury) often promotes behavioral and emotional problems, including avoidant and disorganized attachment relationships (Egeland and Sroufe, 1981; Cicchetti and Olson, 1990), lack of social sensitivity and aggressiveness with peers (Dodge et al., in press; National Research Council, 1993; Pianta, Egeland, and Erickson, 1989), and blunted emotions (Cicchetti and Carlson, 1989). A study by Ken Dodge and his colleagues (in press) is especially important because it shows that physical abuse predicts later aggressiveness, even after differences in children's temperaments and family characteristics (such as income and marital stability) are taken into account. These researchers, like others (e.g., Elicker et al., 1992), have concluded that abuse leads to aggression by influencing both children's perceptions of other people (whom they tend to see as potentially hostile and threatening) and their social competency, which leads to failure in strategies for problem solving.

Emotional unavailability, which is often a result of depression in the parent, can be a particularly devastating form of maltreatment (Pianta, Egeland, and Erickson, 1989; National Research Council, 1993). Over time, children who experience a chronic lack of parental involvement and emotional responsiveness show a marked decline in functioning, eventually becoming apathetic, devoid of joy or pleasure, and easily frustrated and upset (Egeland and Sroufe, 1981).

Verbal abuse is a pattern in which caregivers continually criticize their children, yell at them, or subject them to demeaning comments. It has been associated with problems of self-esteem and school adjustment in children (Egeland, 1988; National Research Council, 1993).

Sexual abuse of toddlers has been identified, but has been much more widely studied in older children and adolescents. A pattern of seductive care, where the parent uses sensuality to control the child, has been related to later hyperactivity and attention problems in children (Jacobvitz and Sroufe, 1987).

SEARCHING FOR CAUSES OF MALTREATMENT

While maltreatment of children is generally associated with parents who are poor, young, lacking in education, and unprepared for raising a child, it certainly is not confined to people with these characteristics (National Research Council, 1993; Trickett et al., 1991). The problem crosses all ethnic, social class, age, and religious lines. Some abusing parents appear to outsiders to be devoted mothers or fathers. Most want to do well by their children but are unable to. The question is, why?

CHARACTERISTICS OF THE CHILD

In the past some researchers have proposed that abused children may have certain inherent characteristics that elicit mistreatment from adults (Segal and Yahres, 1978). Prematurity, physical defects, and infant irritability and fussiness have all been suggested as causes of abuse (e.g., Frodi, 1984). However, these suggestions were based on investigations made *after* cases of child abuse were reported. In such studies, people's perceptions and memories might easily become distorted in order to help explain the known outcome. Sometimes, too, the consequences of abuse can be confused with its causes.

Much more dependable are the findings of prospective studies, those in which assessments of the children are made *before* abuse occurs. Such studies do not find a correlation between prematurity, early infant irritability, or any other measures of infant temperament and later child abuse (Brunnquell, Crichton, and Egeland, 1981; Pianta, Egeland, and Erickson, 1989). Moreover, only a very modest relationship has been found to exist between complications of pregnancy or childbirth and a woman's subsequent mistreatment of her child. This modest relationship may not be one of cause and effect. Abusive mothers generally receive inadequate prenatal care, thus increasing the risk of childbearing complications. And some of the same factors that could prompt a woman to neglect her health during pregnancy could also prompt her to abuse her child after he or she is born.

It remains possible that late-emerging temperament characteristics play some role in child abuse, and might explain why one child in a family and not another is maltreated. But by the toddler period, temperament is difficult to sort out from experience; moreover, it is a fact that parents treat their children differently from the beginning (depending, for example, on whether they are boys or girls, their first- or second-born, and so on).

To date, then, the evidence is scant that certain inherent characteristics of children are major causes of child abuse. In some cases, an infant who is ill and difficult to care for may add to the pressures on an already overstressed parent, with the end result being mistreatment. But here the cause of the mistreatment is the cumulative stress on the parent, not the child's nature. Of course, a maltreated infant or toddler may well become a difficult child, so the cycle of stress and maltreatment is perpetuated (Lee and Bates, 1985). But the child's contribution in this case is a learned set of behaviors, the product of a history of mistreatment. (For a further discussion of whether abused children in some way elicit maltreatment, see the box on pp. 313–314.)

CHARACTERISTICS OF THE PARENT

If child abuse cannot be explained by inherent characteristics of the children involved, perhaps it can be explained by mental disturbance in the parents. Although this line of inquiry seems reasonable, it turns out not to be very productive. The vast majority of abusing parents suffer no psychotic disorder, and there is *no single personality trait* (such as extreme hostility) that abusive parents share. However, *a broad set of adult characteristics* is associated with child maltreatment (National Research Council, 1993; Pianta, Egeland, and Erickson, 1989). These include low self-esteem, poor impulse control, doubts about personal power, negative emotions, and antisocial behavior.

Perhaps more important than the personality makeup of abusing parents are their thoughts and feelings about their child and child rearing. In one large-scale study, researchers interviewed and tested new mothers, most of whom were single, both before they gave birth to their first baby and again during the child's infancy (Pianta, Egeland, and Erickson, 1989). They found that those who later became abusers differed from nonabusers in two ways. First, they were less able to cope with the ambivalence and stress inherent in a first pregnancy. Second, they had significantly less understanding of what is involved in caring for a baby. When the inevitable difficulties of raising an infant arose, these mothers became more stressed and doubtful about their parenting abilities. Often they suspected that the baby was being deliberately contrary. Thus, the stage was set for these unprepared mothers to start a pattern of child abuse. Similar factors probably also help to trigger a father's abuse of his children (National Research Council, 1993).

Further encouraging a downward spiral into child abuse is a parent's own experience of being maltreated. Mothers and fathers who were abused themselves as children are, as a group, dramatically more likely to abuse their own children than are parents who were not abused. Apparently, the experience of abuse provides models of hostile and neglectful ways of dealing with stress. In their study of new mothers, Byron Egeland and his colleagues found that 30 percent of those with childhood histories of abuse maltreated their own child sometime during the child's early years. This percentage of abusers was far higher than the percentage in a nonabused comparison group from the same general population (Egeland, Jacobvitz, and Sroufe, 1988).

Still, not all parents who were maltreated themselves abuse their own children. In the same study, 30 percent of the mothers were observed to provide fully adequate care. Three key differences were found in the women who overcame their history of abuse: (1) many of them had compensated for their abusive parent by forming a stable, supportive relationship with some other adult during childhood; (2) many of them had undergone extensive psychotherapy; and (3) all of them were currently involved in a stable partnership. Apparently, a troubled past need not impair current parenting ability if a person has a chance to experience positive relationships and adequate social support.

TABLE 8.1
THE CONTEXT OF CHILD ABUSE AND NEGLECT

Factors That Increase the Risk of Abuse	Factors That Decrease the Risk of Abuse
Long-term vulnerability factors	*Long-term protective factors*
1. Poverty and ongoing stress	1. Nurturant care by someone in
2. Parental history of abuse	childhood
3. Unfulfilled relationship needs	2. Good relationship with spouse
4. Lack of understanding of the child as a complex individual	3. Awareness of one's own inner needs
Current challenges	*Short-term buffers*
1. Relationship instability	1. Reduction in stress
2. Violence, alcoholism, or drug abuse in the home	2. Separation from abusive partner
3. Lack of social support	3. Child entry into school
4. Job loss or other acute stressers	4. Crisis counseling

SOURCE: Adapted from Belsky, 1988; Cicchetti and Olson, 1990.

THE ENVIRONMENTAL CONTEXT

Because parents are the caretakers of children and the more mature members of a family, they must bear the responsibility for child abuse. Nonetheless, given the data on how a history of maltreatment and current high levels of stress can contribute to the abuse of children, it is shortsighted simply to blame the parents when abuse occurs. Child abuse takes place within a context (Belsky, 1988; Cicchetti and Olson, 1990; see Table 8.1). While it is found at every socioeconomic level, its likelihood increases with poverty, social isolation, and lack of education. Within low-income families, the greater the stress experienced (frequent household moves, job loss, serious illness, and so forth), the greater the chances that the parents will mistreat their children (National Research Council, 1993).

Another part of the child abuse context in the United States is the level of violence our culture tolerates. Many of the heroes in our books and movies use violence of one form or another to right wrongs and to teach people lessons. This cultural acceptance of violence as a solution to certain problems is a likely contributor to child abuse (National Research Council, 1993). In the traditional culture of Japan and many Native American societies that placed great stress on harmony and personal restraint, the physical abuse of children was virtually unknown.

In many traditional societies, moreover, the nuclear family was not isolated, as it sometimes is in the United States today; rather, it was part of an extended kin network. Research shows that the high degree of social support a close-knit network of kin provides can help prevent child abuse (Cicchetti and Olson, 1990). This helps explain why poor neighborhoods differ greatly in their incidence of child abuse. In poor neighborhoods where the incidence is low, there is much interaction among families and social institutions, adults are present in the home when children return from school, and there is community pride and involvement. Social support for the principal caregiver is extremely important. In the large-scale study we mentioned earlier, less than half the mothers who mistreated their children had adequate social support, as opposed to virtually all the mothers who provided adequate care (Pianta, Egeland, and Erickson, 1989). Even a mother who herself was mistreated as a child is unlikely to abuse her own children if she gets enough support from others (Crockenberg, 1986; Egeland, Jacobvitz, and Sroufe, 1988). For example, Susan Crockenberg (1986) found that mothers who had been mistreated as children were not angry and punitive toward their 2-year-olds if they had high levels of support from their husbands or other significant persons in their lives.

THE IMPORTANCE OF THE TODDLER PERIOD

Like all developmental periods, toddlerhood has special significance in the development of a child. During this period, a primitive sense of self emerges, and the foundations of self-esteem, the patterns of emotional expression and emotional regulation, and perhaps even the roots of morality are laid down.

Current views of socialization suggest an openness (or vulnerability) on the part of the toddler to family and cultural influences. By participating in relationships with the people around them, toddlers begin to take in, or appropriate, the major patterns of thought, feeling, and behavior that exist in their world. If the caregiving environment is supportive, the child comes to view relationships as supportive and to evolve a sense of self-worth. He or she is prepared to become an empathic, responsive member of the community. If, however, the toddler experiences abusive, neglectful, or rejecting caregiving, the seeds of low self-esteem are sown, and social relationships may come to be viewed as worthless or exploitative.

But development is not fixed in the first 2½ years of life. As you will learn in later chapters, there are many opportunities for positive change in child development as family circumstances improve and as the child is influenced by a broader social world. Nonetheless, early experiences remain very important influences.

APPLYING RESEARCH FINDINGS DO ABUSED CHILDREN CAUSE THE MALTREATMENT?

Some children are highly aggressive and provocative, especially by middle childhood or adolescence. They may deliberately break rules and blatantly defy adults. They often inspire rejection by other children and anger from teachers (Sroufe and Fleeson, 1988). Some observers have suggested that perhaps this negative child behavior is responsible for the frequently reported association between aggression and harsh parental treatment. Segal and Yahres (1978), for example, argue that it is aggression that causes child abuse, not abuse that causes child aggressiveness. In support of this view, they point to the fact that toddlers who are treated very harshly by parents and placed in foster homes are often

treated harshly by their new caregivers, too, as if there is something about these children that demands severe discipline from caregivers. We believe that this conclusion is incorrect.

Is it possible to determine whether caregiving experiences lead to the child's problem behavior or difficult children draw forth harsh treatment? A simple correlation at one point in time cannot answer the question. Harsh parenting and child aggression would be seen in the same families whichever was the cause. Moreover, each would support the other. Harsh treatment would lead to further problem behavior, and problem behavior would lead to further harsh treatment, in what Gerald

Patterson calls *coercive cycles* (Patterson and Dishion, 1988).

Only prospective, longitudinal studies can resolve this issue. The child and parents must be assessed in an ongoing way, beginning very early in the child's life. Such studies show that harsh parental discipline *precedes* negative child behavior, rather than the other way around (Egeland, 1994; Egeland, Sroufe, and Erickson, 1983). Neither premature birth nor measures of infant temperament predict maltreatment, and parenting practices predict child aggressiveness well before the child is even capable of such behavior. One recent study found that parental violence toward a child predicted later aggression in the child that could not be attributed to his or her initial levels of aggression (Strassberg et al., 1994). In this study, even spanking was found to be related to more frequent aggressive reactions in a child, although the rate of aggression was elevated much more when the parents' punishment practice took the form of violent physical abuse. (See the graphs in Figure 8.A.)

Another line of evidence that children can internalize a coercive relationship system comes from the finding that violence on the part of a child's father toward his or her mother predicts behavior problems, including aggression, in the child (Dodds, 1995). This is true even after such other factors as violence against the child,

poverty, and general life stress are taken into account. Clearly, the child cannot be held responsible for the father's abuse of the mother. It is much more likely that the father's abusive behavior is influencing the child's behavior. Apparently, a coercive relationship system is part of such children's developmental context, a way of life they learn.

Why, then, are children who are abused at home frequently punished by teachers or abused again in later foster placements? A key concept from this chapter, appropriation, helps provide an explanation. Children *appropriate,* or take into themselves, aspects of the relationship systems that surround them. When they are part of a coercive system, they develop expectations and attitudes about themselves and others that are in keeping with such a system. In part, this means that they learn the role of victim, including provocative behaviors. They also develop a basic understanding about how relationships work: when someone is vulnerable, others attack. Connection between people occurs through confrontation. When you are upset, you will be punished. These attitudes and learned behaviors are carried forward into new relationships. Thus, it is true that abused children often are provocative and otherwise difficult. But this does not mean that they caused their own maltreatment in the first place.

FIGURE 8.A RELATIONSHIP BETWEEN PARENTAL PUNISHMENT PRACTICES AND CHILD AGGRESSION
(Source: Strassberg et al., 1994, pp. 453–454.)

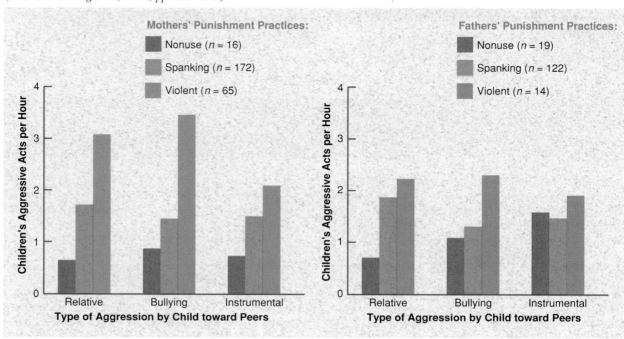

CHAPTER SUMMARY

1. Dramatic social and emotional developments occur during the toddler period. One is the beginnings of **socialization,** the process by which children come to learn the rules, standards, and values of their society. Although socialization has traditionally been viewed as the imposition of rules and standards on an unwilling child, psychologists increasingly see children as actively seeking to comply with parents' requests as well as with their own understandings of proper behavior. In a process that has been called **appropriation,** children naturally take on their culture's rules and values.

2. Compared with infants, who require physical contact with caregivers in order to feel closeness with them, toddlers are able to maintain psychological closeness. This psychological closeness involves interactions with the caregiver across a distance, including exchanges of looks, words, smiles, and positive emotions, called **affective sharing.** Toddlers are thus freed for more active exploration of their physical and social worlds. In the process, they learn that they can do things by themselves, that they can be in charge. This awareness of their own capacities, called **executive competence,** encourages more independence. This in turn encourages a sense of being an autonomous force in the world.

3. Along with the toddler's psychological separation from the caregiver and greater autonomy comes an increase in sociability. Toddlers are constantly communicating with other people about the things that they discover; they want to share with others their excitement and pleasure in discovery. At the same time, toddlers become more sophisticated in their social interactions. For example, they become capable of **social referencing**—using a caregiver's facial expressions or tone of voice as a cue for how to deal with a novel and ambiguous situation. Toddlers also have a growing interest in interacting with peers, and they become able to behave toward other toddlers in a complementary fashion. These early peer interactions set the stage for later peer relationships.

4. During toddlerhood children become aware that their own behaviors are distinct from those of others—that is, they develop self-awareness. Awareness of the self goes hand in hand with a more mature understanding of other people's selves. Toddlers increasingly realize that other people are independent agents.

5. Another hallmark of the toddler period is a set of important emotional changes. Children this age begin to show sensitivity to the rules and expectations of adults, guided by feelings of uncertainty and discomfort that the violation of rules arouses in them (called **deviation anxiety**). Toddlers are also able to tolerate more intense emotions than infants are, and they begin to experience **self-conscious emotions,** such as **positive self-evaluation** (a forerunner of pride), embarrassment, and **shame**—emotions that require some objective sense of self.

6. The role of the caregiver during the toddler period is to support the child's movements toward independence while remaining ready to step in when the child's capacities are exceeded. The caregiver provides a framework for the child's **guided self-regulation.** Parents of toddlers must also set and maintain reasonable limits on their children's behavior. Such limits help to give toddlers a sense of security in acting on their newfound independence.

7. An individual's **pattern of adaptation,** or unique style of responding to others and the environment, forms the roots of personality. As toddlers become aware of their own separateness and autonomy (a process called **separation-individuation**), they may grow anxious about leaving the former closeness with the caregiver. If they know they can reclaim that closeness, if they have confidence that the attachment relationship is secure, they will feel free to explore their capacities to the fullest. In contrast, if toddlers are anxious about the caregiver's availability, their self-reliance is likely to be compromised.

8. Many factors are required to explain child abuse. Longitudinal studies discredit the idea that some children by nature draw forth abuse from otherwise nurturant parents. There is also no support for the idea that most abusive parents are mentally disturbed or simply hostile people. Instead, child abuse is more accurately viewed as a pattern of care that develops when parents who are subject to unusual stress, including the stress of child rearing, lack the knowledge and social support needed to cope effectively with it.

9. Toddlerhood is a very important period of development. During this time the child begins to acquire views of the self and of social relationships. These views, which are heavily influenced by the quality of care the toddler has experienced, can affect the child's future social and emotional development.

PART THREE | Toddlerhood

EPILOGUE

Development in the toddler period builds upon the achievements of infancy. For example, toward the end of the first year of life, advances in memory enable infants to recall past experiences and anticipate outcomes. When 10-month-old Mikey spotted a jar of seashells his sister Becky had collected, he remembered the interesting sound he had recently made by shaking this object. So he grasped and shook the jar again, anticipating the result. But note that *seeing* the jar was necessary to trigger this recollection in Mikey. At 10 months of age, he was not yet able to imagine the jar if it was not physically present. The ability to imagine—to *represent things mentally*—is an extremely important development that emerges in the toddler period. Like all the major developmental changes of toddlerhood, it builds upon foundations (in this case memory capabilities) established in infancy.

MILESTONES IN TODDLER DEVELOPMENT

The emergence of representational skills is one of the milestones of toddler development. It is supported by development of the brain's left hemisphere, which includes regions for language comprehension and speech. The ability to use words (strings of sounds) to stand for things that are not actually present is one of the most obvious representational skills that emerges in the toddler period. Another underlies the ability to infer things not actually experienced with the senses. If Becky has a seashell in her hand and moments later it has disappeared, Mikey as a toddler can infer that Becky must have put the shell somewhere. This is because he has stored a mental image of the shell and knows that the real shell still exists. The ability to store mental images of things also allows toddlers to imitate other people's actions long after they have seen them performed. In addition, representational skills enable toddlers to engage in symbolic play, letting one object stand for another, as when Mikey uses a block of wood as a toy car.

With representational skills comes an awareness of the self as an agent and an object. Children now understand that it is "I" who shakes this object, "I" to whom Mommy talks, "I" who wants to find the thing that has been hidden away. This emerging awareness of self is accompanied by a growing understanding of others as independent agents with their own wishes and intentions. Mikey, for instance, now recognizes that his intentions (such as a desire to continue playing) may be different from or even in conflict with those of his mother (who may want to put him to bed). Language helps Mikey to communicate about this clash of intentions, to exert his own autonomy, and to find compromises (such as complying with his mother's wishes but going "by myself").

Representational skills also promote the beginnings of self-control in children. Malcolm starts to reach again for the leaf in the water, but he remembers Momma Jo's no-nonsense tone, and he stops himself. This is a common capacity in toddlers (Emde et al., 1985; Maccoby, 1980). Recent research indicates that brain mechanisms related to it (such as the ability to balance excitement and inhibition) are in place by the toddler period (Schore, 1994).

New emotions arise as well during the toddler period. Recognizing the self as a separate, autonomous person, the toddler is now capable of having negative feelings about the self, of experiencing shame and vulnerability. By the same token, the toddler is also capable of positive self-evaluations. When DeeDee hugs Malcolm and praises his actions following the incident with the teenage boys, we can imagine Malcolm's feeling of being positively valued. This is the forerunner of genuine pride. Differentiation of the self from others likewise enables toddlers to experience new interpersonal emotions, such as affection. While love pats of parents and dolls are rare at age 12 months, they are common at 18 months of age (Sroufe, 1979a).

Just as a toddler's growing autonomy helps to foster new emotions, it also helps to bring about major changes in the parent-child relationship. Parents in our culture expect a toddler to show increasing self-reliance. At the same time, they expect the child to begin complying with the rules and limits that they set. The process of taking in or "appropriating" these rules on the child's part is an important foundation for moral development.

As an increasingly active participant in the parent-child relationship, the toddler exerts a stronger force than the infant in determining that relationship's course. Although personality is certainly not fully formed in toddlerhood, children this age are less malleable than they were as babies. Toddlers have rather definite expectations about their parents' availability and actions, and these expectations in turn affect children's customary ways of responding.

Change in the parent-child relationship is always possible, of course. Parents who were unresponsive or inconsistent toward their children as infants can make a concerted effort to turn the relationship around. These efforts at first may be somewhat puzzling to a toddler who doubts the parent's new availability and questions the new firmness. Such a toddler is likely to be whiny and negative, having learned in the past that only through such behavior can the desired response from the caregiver be achieved. It takes time and resolve to change the negative patterns of adaptation that have become established over the previous months. In the end, however, even "difficult" toddlers generally respond to reassuring firmness from their parents. We may be seeing the beginning of such a change in Meryl, helped along by the model of loving firmness that Mrs. Jaspers provides. Let's look more closely at Meryl's development in toddlerhood, as well as that of Mikey and Malcolm.

THREE CHILDREN AS TODDLERS

All three of our children show normal development in terms of the major toddler milestones that we have just reviewed. All are walking, talking, and becoming more autonomous in their thought and behavior. Although Meryl is progressing more slowly than the other two, she is well within the normal range. Each child, however, is also developing an individual style consistent with his or her past. Despite dramatic changes as they grow older, all three are building on foundations laid down in the prior developmental period.

You can see this clearly in Mikey, whose development is proceeding well. He is an easygoing toddler who has taken day care in stride. Given his history of secure attachment, his mother's continuing nurturance and availability, and the high-quality day-care program in which he is enrolled, this is not surprising. An additional ingredient in Mikey's positive adjustment is his father's strong interest in and involvement with him. Frank is proud of Mikey's "boyish" behavior; he enjoys being with his son, playing their physically active games together. The differences in Frank's and Christine's styles of interacting with Mikey are typical of mother-father differences revealed by research. We also see in Frank the beginnings of a serious concern about gender-"appropriate" behavior. This is a common paternal influence in the socialization of boys. We will return to it when we discuss the preschool child.

But as well as things are going for Mikey, there is also growing trouble in the Gordon family. Partly because of the stress of Frank's reduced hours at work, partly because of their sharply differing views about women working outside the home, Christine and Frank are experiencing conflict. They also show less unity regarding parenting than many other couples do. What one thinks is good for Mikey, the other often opposes. Most troublesome of all, they frequently center their arguments on Mikey. How this will affect Mikey's future development bears watching.

Like Mikey, Malcolm is developing well. As you might have expected of this robust baby, he has become a live wire of a toddler. He is exuberant, energetic, and into everything. The members of his family continue to view his liveliness very positively. Momma Jo delights in telling friends what a "pile of mischief" Malcolm gets into. For her, as for DeeDee and John, Malcolm is a source of great joy and pride. In a family with fewer social and psychological resources, Malcolm's style of responding might not be valued so highly. Notice, too, how the Williams' network of mutual caring and support more than makes up for the stresses they face as a moderate-income, urban, minority-group family. Malcolm reaps the benefits of this rich social network. DeeDee, John, Momma Jo, Denise, Teresa, and John, Jr., are all actively involved with him and contribute to his ongoing feelings of security and acceptance.

Things are not going as well for Meryl as they are for Malcolm and Mikey. Meryl is in many ways a difficult toddler. She is lagging in terms of achieving self-reliance; she is easily stressed and unusually needy of adult contact; she can be whiny and negative, and she is prone to tantrums. In addition to being difficult, Meryl shows signs of being what Alexander Thomas and Stella Chess (1977) call a "slow to warm up" child. This means that she is timid and hesitant in new situations, as when she refuses to try out the new seesaw at Mrs. Jaspers' house. It was predictable that entering day care would be difficult for Meryl and a challenge to the relationship between Meryl and Karen.

There are, however, some seeds of positive change for Meryl. Karen seems to be settling into a happier and more stable life. The détente with her own mother has been a big help. Karen can now draw on her mother's emotional support, counsel, and day-to-day assistance in caring for Meryl. Mrs. Jaspers is also a model from whom she can learn. Karen clearly cares about Meryl and wants to be a good mother, as evidenced by her attentiveness to Mrs. Jaspers' suggestions and the way she keeps trying despite her struggles with Meryl.

There are also seeds of positive change in Meryl herself. We see her actively trying to cope with her anxieties through play. With the stuffed bears she works through her concerns about Karen's availability, thus creating feelings of mastery that may counteract vulnerable feelings. Such active mastery is made possible by the representational skills that Meryl has developed. It is also supported by the increased stability in her life and the improved quality of care she is receiving. Perhaps these seeds of positive change will take root in Meryl's preschool years.

PART FOUR | Early Childhood

PART FOUR

Three Children in Early Childhood

MALCOLM WILLIAMS

"C'mon, Motor Man. You want this horse? You jump for it!" John, Jr., told his little brother. Malcolm reached an arm as high as he could and jumped with all his might, but the toy horse remained tantalizingly just out of his reach. "Now, how you ever gonna make the pros with jumps like that, man?" JJ kept on teasing. "Let's see a real jump." This time Malcolm jumped so hard he fell over backward as he landed. "Gimme!" he yelled. "Gimme it!"

"You give that horse to your brother right now!" said Momma Jo, as she strode into the room. "What are you tryin' to do, makin' him jump and fall all over the place? He's only four years old. Treat him like your brother, not your dog!"

"We were just havin' fun," JJ protested. "He didn't hurt himself none."

"I'm four *and a half*," chimed in Malcolm. "And I'm gonna be the greatest basketball player ever!"

"Hey, Motor Man," said JJ, pretending to dribble a ball in front of Malcolm. Malcolm raised both arms and waved them frantically in a childish imitation of a guard blocking a shot. As Momma Jo looked on in a mixture of exasperation and amusement, the front door opened and John Williams walked in. "Daddy!" yelled Malcolm, running over to his father. "Hey, my man!" John Williams answered, holding out his hand for Malcolm to give him five. "What's happenin'?"

"We're playin' basketball," said Malcolm. "An' I'm the best!"

"Oh, yeah?" his father smiled. "I bet you are."

At dinner that night Malcolm was in high spirits. With great excitement he told the family about a model airplane he had seen flying in the park. "An' the plane goed straight up!" he exclaimed, his hand illustrating a steep upward climb. "An' then it goed round an' round an' round." Malcolm's whole body circled around to help make the point. "But how'd the plane know to do that, Daddy? Was there a little aminal inside it?"

"No, Malcolm. There was nobody inside it. It's called remote control. The man with the plane had a box and when he pressed a button it sent out signals, and the signals told the plane what to do."

"Yeah," said JJ, "remote control. That's what Momma Jo's gonna get for you, Motor Man, to help slow you down some." The whole family laughed.

"You know," DeeDee said to John as they sat in the living room later, "we've gotta decide where to send Malcolm to school next year. If we're gonna send him to St. Dominic's with Teresa, Sister Carmen told me we should get the application in by next month."

"They're strict at St. Dom's," John answered, "and that would be good for Malcolm. I've always said that. And the tuition there isn't *that* high. If we can afford it for Teresa, we can find a way to manage for Malcolm, too. So let's just go with St. Dom's and not worry about it any longer. Why don't you pick up an application tomorrow when you drop Teresa off?"

"Hold still now, Malcolm, while I take your picture," DeeDee said, smiling. "You look so fine and grown up in your new school clothes."

"I gotta go to the bathroom, Momma," Malcolm complained, hopping from one foot to the other.

"This'll just take a second, honey. Stop holding yourself, Malcolm. You can go to the bathroom in a minute. There. That's better. Now you can run along. Teresa? Hurry up, sugar, or we're gonna be late!"

An hour later DeeDee stood with 22 other mothers in the large, sunny kindergarten room. "The mommas have to go now," she told Malcolm, placing a hand on each of his shoulders. "You be good and *mind* your teacher. Bye-bye, honey. You can tell me all about it tonight." And with that DeeDee turned and walked quickly out the door. Malcolm, in his new navy blue shorts and spotless white shirt, was left alone, wide-eyed with wonder, for his first day at school.

It didn't take Malcolm long to adjust to school life. Every morning he was eager to be off. He loved having so many other children to play with. His "best friend in the whole world" was a large, good-humored, red-headed boy with a face full of freckles. His name was Patrick Coleman, nicknamed Pug. As soon as Mrs. Hennessy, their teacher, announced outdoor play, Malcolm and Pug would race to the door so they could claim the two blue tricycles kept in the schoolyard. On one particular Wednesday late in October Malcolm and Pug rushed out the door and climbed on the bikes as usual. Pug pedaled furiously down the path, but before Malcolm could get started April Kaid stepped out in front of him.

"I wanna ride," she said. "It's my turn. Let me ride."

"I was here first!" Malcolm answered. "Get outa my way! It's my bike."

"No, it's not!" said April, gripping the handlebar with both hands."

"Get outa my way," Malcolm repeated, trying to pry her fingers off the bike. Finally, when April refused to let go, Malcolm made a fist and punched her in the chest. She wailed and ran to the teacher.

"What does she *mean*, 'a little hyperactive'?" John Williams asked indignantly as DeeDee told him about her meeting with Mrs. Hennessy.

"'Hyperactive,' indeed!" Momma Jo added. "That child's just full of pep, that's all. What he needs is a firm hand from a good teacher."

"Now, Momma Jo," DeeDee answered. "Mrs. Hennessy *is* a good teacher. She said that Malcolm is a real smart boy and the other children like him. He just has to work harder at controlling himself sometimes. He's got so much energy inside him, he gets impatient when he doesn't get his way. But he's gotta learn he just can't go hittin' other kids."

"Well, look who's here," said John as Malcolm burst through the door ahead of his brother JJ. "Just the man we're talkin' about."

"Uh-oh, Motor Man. You're in for it now," JJ cautioned, walking off toward the kitchen, sniffing the aroma of chicken in the oven, his basketball tucked under one arm.

"I went to see your teacher today," DeeDee said to Malcolm, "and she told me you hit a little girl."

"Yucky April Kaid!" Malcolm answered. "She wouldn't let go of my bike! I just wanted to get her away. I didn't mean to hurt her."

"It wasn't *your* bike, boy," Malcolm's father cut in sharply. "It belongs to the whole class. And even if it *was* your bike, you still shouldn't have hit her. Men don't hit women, you hear me? Your momma had to leave work to go talk to your teacher. I don't want that ever happenin' again!"

"OK, Daddy," said Malcolm, starting to sniffle as tears welled up in his eyes.

"Now you just dry up, boy," John Williams admonished. "I mean dry up right now."

"Malcolm," DeeDee added, "you've gotta learn to share. You can't always get what you want and do what you want. Do you understand me?" Malcolm nodded slowly as he wiped his eyes with his hands. "OK," his mother concluded. "Now go wash up for supper."

MIKEY GORDON

The boys stood back, gazing at their masterpiece. "Wow!" said Mikey in admiration. "That's tall!" The tower of blocks was indeed impressive. It stood as tall as the boys could reach. Some oddly angled pieces formed the base, making one wonder why the whole thing didn't topple over.

"I'm gonna put this purple one on the very top," Justin Davis announced, picking up a large pyramid-shaped block.

"No!" said Bryan Packer, pushing Justin's hand away. "I'm gonna put this green one there."

"I thought of it first!" Justin answered angrily, pushing Bryan back.

"Hey, I got it! Let's make a space station at the top!" Mikey suggested.

"Yeah! That's neat!" the other two agreed, forgetting their momentary tussle. "Go get the rocket ship!"

Once again 4-year-old Mikey Gordon had warded off a fight among his playmates at preschool. Mikey always seemed eager to avoid unpleasant incidents. He was successful at defusing trouble so often that his teachers fondly called him "the little peacemaker." Mikey was one of the most popular children in his class. A friendly, competent little boy with an infectious giggle, he was also very intelligent. Even at 3 he could complete puzzles that some 5-year-olds had trouble with.

"Mikey," called out Sue, one of the preschool teachers. "Your mom's here. Time to go home."

"Gotta go," said Mikey to his friends, as he ran toward the door where his mother was waiting. Then stopping abruptly, he darted to his cubby to get a drawing he had done. "Look, Mom," he said proudly, running back to Christine. "Look how good I wrote my name on this!"

"Late as usual," Frank Gordon grumbled, sliding into his customary place at the head of the dinner table. "Pretty soon you're gonna be starving us 'til midnight."

"I'm sorry, Frank," Christine answered, trying to placate him. "But it's not *that* late. It's not even six o'clock."

"Yeah, but it's later and later every night. We're hungry, aren't we kids?"

Three pairs of eyes kept staring down at the table. No one said a word.

"Well, *I'm* hungry," Frank persisted irritably, rising slightly from his chair so he could reach the large platter of pork chops.

"Janie, pass Daddy the biscuits, please, honey, and the butter. He should get them first."

"Yeah, I guess I'll have some of those," Frank remarked unenthusiastically. "But they're not as good as the ones you used to make from scratch. You kids remember when Mommy used to have time to bake good things for us?"

"I like *these* biscuits," piped up Mikey. "They're yummy!" As if to prove it, he placed an extra-large glob of butter in the steamy center of the biscuit he had just broken open.

"Thank you, Mikey," Christine answered. "Why don't you tell Daddy about the tower you built at school today?"

"Yeah!" said Mikey. "It was neat! It was so high it almost hit the ceiling! An' you know what? When I was runnin' Justin grabbed my back pocket and ripped it almost off! Wanna see?" And he stood up to display the torn pocket flapping on the back of his jeans.

"You're gonna have to wait a long time for Mommy to fix *that*," Frank commented. "I've been waiting months for her just to sew a few lousy buttons back on my shirt. But she doesn't have time these days. She can find time to sew for a bunch of strangers but not for us!"

Mikey's face fell as he climbed back onto his chair. He began to fidget with a bone on his plate. Across from him his sisters ate silently, eyes cast downward. As Mikey hit the end of the bone with his finger, it flipped up and fell to the floor.

"Whoops," said Mikey. And he climbed back down from his chair to look for the bone. Seconds later his face appeared above the edge of the table. Clenching the bone between his teeth he began to growl like a dog.

"Mikey," Christine laughed. "You silly boy!"

The girls looked up and started to giggle at Mikey's clowning. Even Frank stopped his griping and helped himself to another biscuit. Mikey got back up on his chair. Temporarily, at least, the tension had eased.

"A man's got to feel like he's the provider, Chrissie. It's only natural. Your father was just the same way. You made your bed when you decided to take that job of yours. Now you've got to lie in it."

"But, Mom," Christine said, the phone propped between her ear and shoulder as she washed the dishes, "I've got *my* life too. It shouldn't always be what Frank wants."

"If you ask me, your life is with Frank and the children. This job is only a sideline. Think of what's really important to you and work harder at being a good wife."

"I've gotta go now, Mom. Frank's coming. I'll talk to you later."

"So your mom sided with me again," Frank said smugly as he sauntered into the kitchen for a beer.

"Oh, shut up," Christine answered, defeated. It seemed the more gingerly she treated Frank, the more belligerent he became, as if efforts to appease him made him feel he had a right to criticize and complain. So she had made up her mind not to be so deferential to him. Often now she just said what she thought.

"That's a hell of a way to talk to your husband," Frank shot back. "What's eatin' you?"

"Nothing. Just leave me alone, will you? I'm tired."

"You wouldn't be half so tired if you quit that stupid job of yours," Frank continued, spotting his opening.

"Look. Not tonight, OK? I'm not gonna be dragged into another argument with you."

"I'm not arguing," Frank answered. "I'm just tellin' ya what's what."

"Well, I wouldn't be half so tired," Christine snapped, "if you'd take one-tenth the effort you put into griping and put it into helping me around here!"

"Why should I help?" Frank persisted, popping open his beer. "It's your damn job to take care of the house and kids."

"Oh, so you don't live here too!" Christine shouted. "You don't dirty the clothes, or eat the food, or mess up the floors, or anything else, huh?"

At the top of the stairs Mikey sat listening to his parents' voices growing louder and louder. He hugged his legs tightly with both arms and rested his chin on one wrist. This was a scene he had heard countless times before.

"What are you doing, Mikey?" Christine asked the next day as she was making dinner. As he often did, he was playing with trucks on the kitchen floor, but this time the trucks were crashing into each other.

"The trucks just ran over a boy," Mikey answered.

Christine was disturbed. "That's an awful story, Mikey," she said. "Where are the little boy's mommy and daddy? They wouldn't let that happen."

"They was drivin' the trucks," Mikey explained, "an' the boy felled out by accident."

Then he continued the make-believe drama: "Oh no! He got his leg broken! Here comes the ambilenz." He brought a white truck to a screeching halt, opened and closed its doors, and drove it off again quickly. "They take him to the hospital. They fix it!"

Christine just stood there looking at Mikey, not knowing what to say.

MERYL POLONIUS

"Mommy, pick me up! I want to see what you doing."

"Not now, Meryl," Karen answered as she peeled carrots at the kitchen sink. "Why don't you go play with your new toy farm."

"Nooo!" whined Meryl, tugging the leg of Karen's pants. "I don't waaant to. Pick me up!"

"I'm peeling the carrots, Meryl, and I can't keep doing it if I'm holding you. Now go and play."

"No!" said Meryl, hanging on Karen's pants now. "I want to seeee!"

"Now *stop* it, Meryl," Karen snapped, losing her temper. "Don't be such a pest!"

Meryl's face puckered and she ran to the kitchen table. Placing her head on one of the chairs, she began sobbing.

"Oh, Meryl. I'm sorry," Karen relented. "Come here, honey. It's OK. Mommy's sorry."

But Meryl was not to be appeased. "No!" she shouted, clenching her hands into two tight fists. "I won't!"

Before Karen could answer, the back door swung open and Joe Turner walked in. "Hi," he said, smiling at Karen, and then to Meryl: "What's the matter, honey?"

"Go 'way!" Meryl pouted as Joe approached her. Then, turning her back, she started sucking her thumb.

"Don't ask me how my day was," Karen said, returning Joe's affectionate kiss. "This is the high point."

Karen and Joe had been living together for nearly a month now. Seven months before, right after Meryl turned 3, another waitress at The Green Door had introduced them. Joe worked as a reporter for the local paper and was 7 years older than Karen. At first she had not been very interested in him. There was something soft and vague-looking about Joe Turner. As far as looks were concerned, he was certainly no Jeff. Even at 26 his hair was thinning, and Karen suspected he would soon have a fair-sized bald patch. But there was also something about Joe that made Karen feel warm and comfortable. With him she didn't have to pretend to be anyone other than exactly who she was. In time she grew to love Joe for making her feel so special, and for his genuine affection for Meryl.

"Do you think Meryl will ever get over these awful tantrums?" Karen asked doubtfully after mother and daughter had staged yet another battle of wills, this time over whether Meryl would brush her teeth before bed.

"Sure she will. Do you think ten years from now you're going to have a teenager who stamps her feet and pouts?"

"Yes," laughed Karen. "That's *exactly* what I'm afraid I'm going to have! Don't joke about it! Seriously now, is there anything you think I could do to get the whining and tantrums to stop? I must be doing *something* wrong."

"Well, I'm no expert on kids," Joe answered, "but you might try not waffling quite so much." You go back and forth a lot. First you tell her she can't have something, then you give it to her anyway. Next you tell her she can't sit on your lap, then you pick her up when she pouts. She's not gonna die if she doesn't get her way all the time, you know."

"I know," agreed Karen. "It's just that when she gets upset I think I must have done the wrong thing, so I turn around and do the opposite. I know it doesn't help. Mrs. Jaspers told me that, too. She said I just have to mean what I say more."

"I think she's probably right," said Joe.

In the weeks that followed Joe not only advised Karen about dealing with Meryl, he also showed her. One day when Karen was in the living room, she overheard Joe and Meryl in the kitchen. "I want another cookie!" Meryl demanded in her close-to-tantrum wail. "No," Joe said firmly, "one is all you get until dinner. Now, why don't you come over here and help me put this silverware away. Do you think you can put everything in the right places? Sure you can. Get the stool so you can see what you're doing." In a voice that sounded as sweet as an angel's Meryl answered, "Here I come!" Why is it so easy for him and so hard for me? Karen wondered.

"I think it's partly because she doesn't know any different with me," Joe said later. "Give it time, and keep meaning what you say, just like Mrs. Jaspers said. Things will settle down."

And in time they did. After about 4 months of the new living arrangements, Meryl had become far more cheerful and cooperative. Karen thought Joe was the major reason. He read Meryl stories and played with her a lot. Counting games became one of their favorite activities together. "Two bears and two more. How many does *that* make?" Joe would ask Meryl, as he lined up an assortment of teddy bears on the living room couch. "Now point to each one carefully as you count them."

"One . . . two . . . three . . . four," Meryl would

answer. "Four bears. And that other one in your hand is five!"

To Meryl these enjoyable pastimes were much more interesting than pouting and clinging. As the whining and tantrums declined, Karen became more confident in dealing with Meryl. This helped to break the negative cycle they had been tangled in before. The improvements helped make Meryl's fourth birthday a real celebration for them all.

"I have a surprise for you, sweetie," Karen said to Meryl, as she put her to bed after a party with ice cream and cake. "Joe and Mommy are getting married. That means we're going to have another party—just like a birthday party, only without the balloons and candles. And you'll get a new dress to wear. What do you think of that?"

"Oh, boy!" said Meryl. "Can I have flowers?"

"Of course," smiled Karen. "We'll get you flowers to wear in your hair."

"You know," said Joe as he and Karen walked arm in arm to the living room, "after we're married I'd like to adopt Meryl. I feel like her father already, and adoption would make it all legal."

"Adopt her! Oh, Joe, that'd be wonderful," Karen answered. "It'll make Meryl so happy! You know, I often wonder when she's going to start asking about Jeff and why *he* didn't want to be her daddy. I'm even afraid that someday she may want to look for him."

"Let's not worry about Jeff now," Joe said softly. "Right now I just want Meryl to know that I love her very much."

Meryl Polonius Turner stood shy and hesitant in the roomful of kindergarten children. She looked down at her unscuffed new shoes and began wriggling her toes.

"Would you like to come play in the store, Meryl?" Mrs. Schultz asked in a kind, encouraging voice.

Meryl walked slowly toward the teacher without saying a word and stood in the doorway of the large cardboard structure. Inside were shelves stocked with brightly colored boxes, just like in a real supermarket. To one side was a counter with a toy cash register and even a toy conveyor belt to move the groceries along. Two little girls toting bright red shopping baskets were busily inspecting the wares. One had on a long string of beads, the other a pair of large purple sunglasses. Meryl smiled slightly and glanced up at Mrs. Schultz.

"We need someone to work at the checkout counter, Meryl. Would you like to do that?"

Meryl walked quietly behind the counter. She pressed one of the buttons on the cash register and the drawer flew open, revealing a tray crammed full of make-believe money. Meryl's smile grew bigger. She had never seen such a wonderful play store in her life.

One of the shoppers approached Meryl with her "purchases." "Do you have any coupons?" Meryl asked shyly, just as she had heard checkout clerks asking her mother.

The shopper looked disappointed. "No," she said, adjusting the sunglasses on her nose. "I just have money."

"Don't worry," said Meryl. "We *give* coupons." And ripping some strips of paper from a brown bag, she handed them to the shopper.

"Thank you," said the shopper, smiling happily at Meryl. "My name is Amy."

From that morning on, Meryl and Amy were the best of playmates.

Chapter 9

Cognitive Development in Early Childhood

Chapter 9

Cognitive Development in Early Childhood

"Mommy, who was born first, you or me?

"Daddy, when you were little, were you a little boy or a little girl?"

"Why do they put a pit in every cherry? We have to throw the pit away anyway."

"When the sun sets into the sea, why isn't there any steam?"

These are questions actually asked by preschool children in the former Soviet Union (Chukovsky, 1941/1971). In every country, preschoolers—children between the ages of 2 ½ and 5—ask exactly the same kinds of questions as they strive to understand their world. Some of the strange and humorous things about preschoolers' ideas stem from a simple lack of information. We might imagine intelligent aliens from another planet making some of these same errors just because they didn't yet have all the relevant facts. However, young children's thinking also differs in basic ways from the thinking of adults, and this is what makes it so interesting. A preschooler's thinking is particularly fascinating because it possesses both mature and immature qualities. It is sufficiently different from the thinking of an adult so that we notice its magical elements. Yet it is similar enough to adult thinking to enable the construction of complex ideas and to allow us to observe developmental continuities. A major goal of this chapter is to explore both the cognitive skills and the cognitive limitations of preschoolers, pointing out the mature and the immature aspects of their thinking.

As you explore preschoolers' cognitive abilities, think about how they differ in fundamental ways from the cognitive abilities of infants and toddlers. As infants, children understand the world by perceiving it and acting on it. They know things by seeing, hearing, touching, tasting, and doing. Then, in toddlerhood, they begin to acquire representational thought, the ability to use symbols

Preschoolers want to know "why?" Such everyday processes as the ripening of tomatoes are mysterious and fascinating to them.

to stand for objects, people, and events. Representational thought, which emerges in the context of learning a vocabulary and developing concepts, allows a more intellectual kind of knowledge. Children can now imagine the consequences of an action without actually carrying it out, and they can combine symbols to express more complex ideas, as when they put several words together into simple sentences. Next, preschoolers try to understand the world at an even more advanced level. They attempt to explain how things work and why events take place. When Malcolm strives to grasp the workings of a remote-controlled model plane, he is functioning in a way that no toddler can. His idea that a small animal might be piloting the plane seems far-fetched to us, but it shows a remarkable advance over the ability he had as a toddler to imagine and to think about causes.

Despite the cognitive differences between a preschooler and a younger child, all the preschooler's new skills emerged from the more limited abilities possessed at younger ages. For instance, Malcolm's ability to think of an explanation for how a remote-controlled airplane works was constructed upon his ability to perceive causality which he began to acquire as a baby (recall our discussion in Chapter 5). New skills, in other words, do not just emerge out of nowhere. They are built upon abilities the child already has. This is the theme of *logical connections between past and present development* that we introduced in Chapter 1.

As you read this chapter, you will encounter some other themes you have met before. One is that children during the preschool years continue to be *active participants in their own development.* By this we mean not only that they actively explore the world, but also that they actively construct an understanding of it. Preschoolers progress from observing and describing events to trying to explain them. An important part of this active construction of understandings is a continued search for general patterns and rules. Just as toddlers search for patterns in forming early concepts, so preschoolers search for patterns in trying to master new cognitive challenges. For instance, Malcolm has identified a general pattern when he says the airplane "goed." Although this is not the way adults form the past tense of the verb *to go*, Malcolm's error can be thought of as a "smart" mistake. It shows that he is using a general pattern found in English to understand how language works and to impose order on it.

Another familiar theme reflected in this chapter is the *continual interplay between a child's developing capacities and the environment in which that child grows.* Preschoolers' advancing cognitive skills allow them to engage the environment in new ways and to draw forth new types of social interaction. At the same time, both adults and peers provide young children with continual feedback about their efforts at dealing with the world. For example, when Meryl gets a positive response from Amy as she acts the part of a clerk in the kindergarten store, she is learning that she dealt with this new situation in an appropriate way, which in turn helps to refine her general ability to engage in imaginary play with other children.

Finally, this chapter contains the familiar theme of *cognitive limitations.* Despite their many cognitive advances, young children still have significant limitations to their thinking. One limitation is their difficulty integrating several pieces of information. For example, when asked which of two cars is going faster, 4-year-old Mikey is likely to consider only which car is currently ahead, even if the car that is behind has been rapidly narrowing the gap. This tendency

Centration:
The tendency, characteristic of preschoolers, to focus on only one piece of information at a time.

Appearance–reality problem:
The tendency, characteristic of young preschoolers, to equate superficial appearance with reality.

Egocentrism:
The failure to differentiate the perspective of others from one's own point of view.

to consider only one piece of information when multiple pieces are relevant is called **centration.** A second limitation in young children's thinking is their difficulty distinguishing between appearance and reality. For instance, when 3-year-olds look at a white object, look at it again through a blue filter, then remove the filter, and so forth, they think that the object is really changing color, not just appearing to change (Flavell, 1985). This tendency to define reality by surface appearance is called the **appearance-reality problem.** A third cognitive limitation in early childhood is difficulty with tasks that require memory-enhancing strategies. Meryl is beginning to understand the value of such strategies when she holds on to her sweater after her mother tells her not to forget it as they are preparing to leave the house. But preschoolers do not usually know about memory-enhancing strategies, and even when they do they don't often use them.

We must be cautious when discussing young children's cognitive limitations, however. In the past some researchers believed that preschoolers totally lacked certain cognitive capabilities, only to find out later that these abilities may be present to some extent by the middle of the preschool period. Whether young children display certain skills depends in part on the difficulty of the tasks they are given. For example, Jean Piaget once found that 4-year-olds who were allowed to inspect all sides of a large model of a mountain range could not pick out a picture of the model that showed it as viewed by a person sitting on the side opposite the one the child was currently facing. On the basis of this and other studies, Piaget argued that preschoolers' thought is characterized by **egocentrism:** they see the world from their own viewpoint and are unable to take the perspective of another person. Today we know that egocentrism is not absolute in young children. When given relatively simple perspective-taking tasks, they *can* adopt another person's viewpoint in a limited way. For example, if researchers show preschoolers a block that is red on one side and white on the other, the children can often correctly identify the color viewed by a person looking at the opposite side. This perspective-taking ability unfolds gradually during the preschool years and is applied in an increasing number of contexts. Thus, understanding preschool cognitive development requires attention both to how new skills are gained and to how existing skills become more widely used.

This chapter explores preschoolers' cognitive abilities and limitations in three major sections. The first examines general characteristics of preschoolers' thought. We begin by exploring how young children reason and how they try to explain the causes of things. Here you will learn that a young child's understandings are often quite different from an adult's. This first major section also examines some conceptual tools that are very valuable in learning about and dealing with the world. Two examples are the ability to group things into categories and the ability to arrange things in a logical progression. Researchers have made some interesting findings regarding the extent to which preschoolers possess such abilities. Our second major section turns to the topic of preschoolers' attention and memory capabilities. Here we explore cognitive skills from an information-processing perspective. Finally, in the third major section, we take up the subject of social cognition—children's knowledge about and understanding of the social world. You will learn that the cognitive advances of preschoolers go hand in hand with more mature social relations; each one promotes the other.

GENERAL CHARACTERISTICS OF PRESCHOOLERS' THOUGHT

REASONING ABOUT CAUSES

Jean Piaget was very interested in how children's reasoning changes as they grow older. In his early work he used interviews to explore this topic. He asked children questions, such as why clouds move, and searched for developmental trends in their answers. Here are examples of children's responses at four different developmental levels which are characteristically seen in the age range of 3 to 10 years.

Level 1

Adult: What makes clouds move?
Child: When we move along they move along too.
Adult: Can you make them move?
Child: Yes.
Adult: When I walk and you are still, do they move?
Child: Yes.
Adult: And at night, when everyone is asleep, do they move?
Child: Yes.
Adult: But you tell me that they move when somebody walks.
Child: They always move. The cats, when they walk, and then the dogs, they make
        the clouds move.
(Piaget, 1930/1969a, p. 62)

Level 2

Adult: What makes the clouds move along?
Child: God does.
Adult: How?
Child: He pushes them.
(Piaget, 1930/1969a, p. 63)

Level 3

Adult: What makes the clouds move along?
Child: It's the sun.
Adult: How?
Child: With its rays. It pushes the clouds.
(Piaget, 1930/1969a, p. 65)

Level 4

Adult: What makes the clouds move along?
Child: Because they have a current.
Adult: What is this current?
Child: It's in the clouds.
(Piaget, 1930/1969a, p. 72)

At the first level, which is characteristic of preschoolers, the child reports that when we move along the clouds move along too. Where did he or she get such a strange idea? To understand, stop and think about how objects appear in relation to us as we walk along. Nearby objects appear closer as we approach them, and then they recede into the distance after we pass them. This is not true of things that are very far away, however, such as the sun and moon in the sky. They never seem to get any closer or farther away. For instance, if you start out

Although preschoolers have some understanding of the differences between animate and inanimate objects, their understanding is still incomplete and prone to errors.

on a walk and the sun is directly overhead, it will still be in virtually the same position an hour later, during which time you could have walked 3 miles. The same is true of clouds far in the distance. Young children often notice this phenomenon and interpret it to mean that the sun, moon, and clouds must be moving with them. As one Soviet preschooler on a trip to the mountains described the moon's behavior: "The moon flew along as we went on the train. She wanted to see the Caucasus too!" (Chukovsky, 1941/1971, p. 20).

Notice how the child is using observations to construct an understanding of the world. The child can be said to be actively constructing his or her own reality. We adults do not perceive the sun, moon, and clouds to be moving with us because our understanding of reality differs from that of preschoolers. Notice, too, that for a child at this level, reality is defined by the superficial appearance of things. The moon *appears* to be keeping up with the fast-moving train, and so it must be moving too. This focus on appearance is one of the cognitive limitations of early childhood.

As children grow older, their interpretations of things change, and with these changes come different understandings of the world. At causal reasoning level 2 in Piaget's research, the child often appeals to an all-powerful force that controls objects and events. This omnipotent force may be called God, or perhaps Mommy or Daddy. At reasoning level 3 the child begins appealing to causes in nature to explain natural phenomena. At this stage, however, those causes may be quite improbable (the rays of the sun pushing clouds along, for instance). Finally, at level 4, the child is approaching an adult explanation, even though that explanation is still incomplete.

Although Piaget did not find mature reasoning about causes until well into middle childhood, other researchers have shown that the level of reasoning is influenced by the complexity and familiarity of the problems posed. Preschool children can quickly learn the cause-and-effect relationships that operate in very simple systems. For example, children as young as 3 can learn that putting a marble down one chute causes a Snoopy doll to appear, while putting it down another chute does not, and 5-year-olds can give reasonable explanations as to why this difference occurs (Bullock and Gelman, 1979). What's more, if young children are asked for explanations of things they are familiar with (such as how a bicycle works), their responses are more mature than when they are asked about unfamiliar things (Berzonsky, 1971). Such findings show that preschoolers have the skills to give good explanations if the things to be explained are simple and familiar.

Such findings also suggest a reason why preschoolers sometimes explain things in ways that adults find fanciful. The thing to be explained may be too complex and too unfamiliar for a young child to give a reasonably accurate explanation of it. In addition, preschoolers do not yet understand what a "good" explanation is, so when they don't know the reason for something they may invent one that seems far-fetched to adults. Young children, in other words, lack an abstract idea of what constitutes a plausible cause. Acquiring various understandings of specific causes during the preschool period gives them the foundation for developing this more mature and abstract concept.

UNDERSTANDING QUANTITATIVE TOOLS

As an adult you understand many things about quantities. You know, for example, that when a tall glass of water is poured into a flat dish, the amount of water does not diminish even though it becomes very shallow. Psychologists say you understand conservation of liquid volume—the fact that the quantity of a liquid remains the same despite changes in the liquid's shape. You also possess a number of other quantitative tools—that is, tools for gauging the amount of something that is present. These include concepts of number and measurement as well as your ability to count. As you will see, quantitative tools only begin to develop during the preschool period. What's more, centration and the appearance-reality problem place limits on preschoolers' knowledge about quantities. We will begin by examining a limitation that may surprise you: preschoolers' inability to understand concepts of conservation.

CONCEPTS OF CONSERVATION

Concepts of **conservation** all include the general idea that the amount of something remains the same (is conserved) despite changes in its form, shape, or appearance. You probably know of Einstein's famous equation, $E = mc^2$. It is a formula about the conservation of mass and energy which says that while mass and energy can be transformed from one to the other, their total amount is fixed, or conserved. A transformation from mass to energy, or vice versa, produces neither an increase nor a decrease in the total. Although to physicists this idea seems intuitive and obvious, many adults find it difficult to grasp. In the same way, other concepts of conservation that seem obvious to adults are not at all obvious to preschoolers.

One such concept is the *conservation of liquid volume*, which we have already mentioned. This is the idea that the total amount of a liquid remains the same despite changes in shape when it is poured into different containers. Other concepts of conservation not obvious to preschoolers include: *conservation of number*, the idea that the number of items in a group remains the same despite repositioning of those items; *conservation of mass*, the notion that the quantity of matter in an object remains the same despite changes in the object's shape (rolling a large ball of clay into a thin snake does not reduce its mass); and *conservation of length*, the idea that the length of something remains the same

Conservation:
The idea that the amount of something remains the same despite changes in its form, shape, or appearance.

regardless of whether it is straight, bent, or twisted (a coiled-up string pulled out full length does not grow any longer). A mature understanding of these concepts of conservation usually doesn't emerge until middle childhood, as we'll discuss in Chapter 11. Moreover, children do not grasp all of the concepts at once. Some are learned well before others. It is as if the child approaches each concept as a new problem.

Approaching each concept as a new problem makes some sense when you consider that whether or not a quantity is conserved after a transformation depends in part on the particular transformation made. For instance, if you cut out 16 1-inch squares of paper and assembled them into different patterns, the area of those patterns would always be 16 square inches; area would be conserved. However, if you tied together the ends of a 22-inch piece of string and pulled the string into different shapes, the area within the string would vary greatly; it would *not* be conserved. If the string formed a circle, the area inside it would be 38.5 square inches. If the string formed a rectangle 1 by 10 inches, the area inside it would be only 10 square inches. With such seeming inconsistencies, it's no wonder that it takes time for children to master concepts of conservation.

CONSERVATION OF LIQUID VOLUME: AN EXAMPLE   One of the first concepts of conservation that children acquire is the concept of conservation of liquid volume, which we will use as an example. Piaget investigated how this concept develops by presenting children of different ages with two glasses of equal size and shape filled with identical amounts of water (see Figure 9.1 A). He then asked each child which glass had more water, *a* or *b*, or whether the two had the same amount. Most children said that the two had the same, although for some, small adjustments had to be made before they declared the amounts to be equal. Next, while the child observed, Piaget poured the water from glass *b* into another glass *c*, which was wider and shorter than the other two glasses (see Figure 9.1 B). The child was then asked if glass *a* had more water, if *c* had more, or if they both had the same. Young preschoolers almost invariably answered that *a* had more. When asked why, they pointed out that the water in glass *a* rose to a higher level. This experiment shows that young children do not seem to grasp that a volume of water remains the same regardless of the size and shape of the container into which it is poured.

In addition, this experiment illustrates two limitations on preschoolers'

FIGURE 9.1
CONSERVATION OF
LIQUID VOLUME
When glasses a *and* b *are filled to equal heights, preschoolers judge that they have equal amounts of water. However, when the water in glass* c, *which is shorter and wider, they judge glass* c *to have less water than glass* a. *This is an example of preschoolers' failure to conserve.*

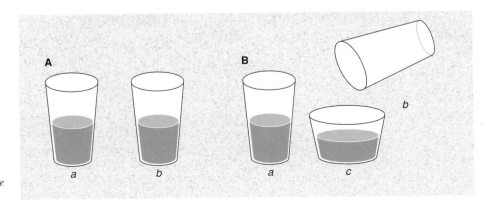

thought that we mentioned earlier. First, the children are misled by the appearance of the liquid in the tall, narrow glass compared to the short, wide glass. By mistaking superficial appearance for reality, they manifest the appearance-reality problem. Second, by focusing on only one aspect of the stimulus, the height to which the water has risen, they show their tendency toward centration.

Studies using Piaget's method reveal that children gradually overcome these limitations and develop more mature reasoning. As they do so, they pass through several stages. In what Piaget called stage 1 of acquiring a conservation concept (which includes virtually all 3-year-olds and most 4-year-olds), children are "nonconservers." They consistently judge the amount of a liquid by the height to which it rises. But note that although stage 1 children fail to distinguish between appearance and reality and have a tendency to centrate on only one aspect of the liquid, they *are* using a consistent rule to judge the amount: higher is more. This rule is wrong from an adult's point of view, but nonconservers are perfectly happy with it and consistently apply it. Certain that their answers are correct, they have no motivation to change their thinking.

In what Piaget called stage 2 of acquiring a conservation concept, children enter a transitional period, which for conservation of liquid volume is typical of 5- to 6-year-olds. Now youngsters are less decisive in answering questions about which container has more. They may first say that the taller one has more water, but then wonder if the second container doesn't have more because it is wider. They may also begin to notice that if the "low" water is poured back into its original container, the two amounts of water are once again equal. Thus, children in stage 2 seem to be displaying two underlying changes. First, they seem aware that their answers may be wrong, and they are motivated to find a consistent and correct basis for responding. Second, their uncertainty seems to stem from the ability to bring new information to bear on the problem. Centration no longer limits their focus to a single perceptual dimension. They can now consider more than one dimension, at least sequentially (first height, then width, then back to height again). For this reason they vacillate in making a decision. Stage 2 children are also able to use information about how the water changes over time (when it is poured back into its original container, for example), rather than merely considering how it looks at a particular moment. Here we see the increased information-handling capacity of the 5- to 6-year-old. It allows skills that emerged earlier to be further developed and integrated into more complex problem-solving systems.

In Piaget's stage 3, mature conservation, children answer the experimenter's questions quickly, confidently, and correctly. To them the correct answer seems obvious, and the incorrect answers of younger children seem "dumb." They show no awareness that at a slightly younger age they gave similarly "dumb" answers. Conservation of liquid volume is usually understood at about age 7 and is one of the cognitive markers for the transition into middle childhood.

To further assess stage 3 children's understanding of conservation, the experimenter may challenge them to justify their answer by asking, "How can both have the same when one is so much higher?" To this a stage 3 child might reply: "This one is higher, but it's narrower too; the other is shorter, but wider. So they're both the same." This kind of justification is called **compensation** because the child realizes that two dimensions have been affected, with an increase in one compensated for by a decrease in the other. Depending on how stage 3 children are questioned, they may offer other justifications (Goodnow, 1973). Sometimes they appeal to **reversibility** by pointing out how the effects of

Compensation:
In conservation tasks, the ability to realize that changes in one dimension of something can be compensated for by changes in another dimension.

Reversibility:
In conservation tasks, the realization that if the effects of a transformation can be undone, the essential properties of the transformed object remain unchanged.

Nothing added or subtracted criterion: In conservation tasks, an explanation that focuses on lack of a relevant change in the transformed object.

the transformation can be undone, in this case by pouring the water back into the original container. Other times they focus on an identity ("It's still the same water") or on lack of a relevant change ("You only poured it into a different glass"). This last explanation is called the **nothing added or subtracted criterion** (Peill, 1975). Piaget was very interested in how children explain conservation, but most recent research (particularly on early childhood) has focused on the development of correct conservation judgments, with much less attention paid to explanations.

CAN CONCEPTS OF CONSERVATION BE TAUGHT? American developmentalists have been fascinated by the question of whether concepts of conservation can be taught to young children. In Piaget's view, such efforts would not be very successful, because a child's current stage of mastering conservation depends on an interaction of both physical maturation and experience in the world. Thus, we cannot simply tell a 4-year-old that the water in the containers remains the same and expect the child to grasp the underlying concept. In keeping with Piaget's expectations, the earliest attempts to teach conservation to young children failed (see Flavell, 1963). Subsequent studies, however, have met with more success. For example, Jerome Bruner has shown that when the learning situation is constructed to help children overcome cognitive limitations, many can be taught to "discover" conservation sooner than they normally would.

In one of Bruner's studies (Bruner, Olver, and Greenfield, 1966), the experimenters first presented children with the standard conservation of liquid volume task to find out what they already knew about conservation. Next they modified the standard conservation task: they screened the containers so that the children couldn't *see* the height to which the water rose after it was poured from one container to another. The children had to determine which container had more, or whether they remained the same, without any visual information. Bruner hoped that this technique might help preschoolers overcome the appearance-reality problem. Finally, the researchers conducted a post-test using the standard conservation task again. The post-test allowed them to see if the modified task had significantly changed the children's general level of thinking.

Bruner and his colleagues found that 4-year-olds didn't conserve on either the pretest or the post-test; they consistently said that the higher water was more. On the screened test the 4-year-olds performed randomly: they were right 50 percent of the time and wrong 50 percent. Apparently, they depended on appearance to make their judgments about quantity, and when the look of the water was hidden from view they resorted to hit-or-miss guessing. In contrast, the 6-year-olds, who in the pretest were in Piaget's transitional stage 2, showed dramatically improved performance on the screened task. It was as if, when no longer distracted by contradictory visual information, they were able to consider the underlying concept of conservation. Apparently, they were on the verge of grasping conservation, but they had trouble overcoming the final hurdle of the appearance-reality problem. When that problem was avoided, they could reason more maturely. On the post-test, moreover, these children maintained their improved performance. It seemed they were able to overcome the perception of the water's height once they had a chance to think through the situation with that distraction eliminated.

Other studies, focusing on the development of other conservation concepts, have produced similar results. For instance, older preschoolers who do not yet grasp the concept of conservation of number (the fact that the spacing between objects does not affect how many objects are there) can be helped to do so by being encouraged to use the strategy of counting in order to judge the number of items in each of two rows (Gold, 1978). This strategy helps them to break reliance on the *length* of the row (its appearance). Significantly, though, younger preschoolers who have been helped to improve their performance on conservation of number tasks using this training technique don't retain that improvement on a post-test given several weeks later (Gelman, 1982).

Thus, older preschoolers and very young elementary school children can sometimes be trained to succeed with problems that they wouldn't usually solve until a year or more later. We suspect that in these cases the training procedures are merely speeding development along its normal course. For younger preschoolers, however, such learning is unstable because these children haven't yet acquired a large enough framework of understanding into which they can fit new conservation skills. A grasp of conservation is only one part of an overall cognitive system. As children attempt to solve problems and to understand how things work, their various cognitive abilities need to be coordinated within a framework that creates a consistent view of the world. Cognitive developments, in short, are interdependent, a fact that inhibits early acquisition of just a single skill.

CONCEPTS OF NUMBER

During the preschool years, children make substantial progress in developing a *concept of number*—an awareness of "how many" items are present and of how addition, subtraction, and rearrangement affect this number. A grasp of this concept is necessary in order to solve the typical conservation of number task. In one study, for example, illustrated in Figure 9.2, children were shown a row of doll beds and two rows of dolls (Cooper, 1976). One of the rows of dolls contained the same number of dolls as there were beds, and this row was initially arranged to be the same length as the row of beds (Figure 9.2 A). The child was asked which row of dolls fit into the beds with no dolls or beds left over. After choosing the correct row, the child was instructed to put the dolls in that row into the beds to be sure this answer was right. The experimenter then removed the dolls from the beds and lined them up again so that they formed a row equal in length to the row of beds. Again the child was asked which row of dolls just fit into the row of beds, and again the child answered correctly. Next the experimenter manipulated both rows of dolls, either spreading them both out to become longer or compressing them both to become shorter. As a result, the "wrong" row of dolls was now the same length as the row of beds (Figure 9.2 B). Again the child was asked which row fit into the beds. This time the typical 4-year-old usually answered incorrectly, responding as if equality of length indicated equality of number. The typical child this age, in other words, did not understand that the number of dolls remains the same despite a change in the space between them. He or she solved the problem by focusing solely on length, not on the number of dolls.

Yet preschoolers develop a substantial understanding of *small* numbers before they fully master conservation of number tasks. The 4-year-olds in the study just described made significantly fewer mistakes when fewer dolls were in the rows. With rows containing only 2 or 3 dolls, they made errors only 27 percent of the time, compared to error rates of more than 64 percent when rows of 6 or more dolls were used. Apparently, 4-year-olds have a grasp of small numbers even when they don't yet understand conservation of number.

FIGURE 9.2 NUMBER CONSERVATION
Children were shown the dolls and beds as they appear in part A and were asked which row of dolls fit in the beds with no dolls left over and no beds left over. Both rows of dolls were then spread so they appeared as illustrated in part B and the children were asked the same question.
Preschoolers' inability to conserve number on this task illustrates that their failure on standard two-row conservation tasks is not caused by being misled by the question.

UNDERSTANDING THE EFFECTS OF ADDITION AND SUBTRACTION Other studies have demonstrated that preschoolers not only have a grasp of small numbers, but also have some understanding of the effects that addition and subtraction have on small numbers of things. For instance, Rochele Gelman (1972) presented young children with two plates, each containing toy mice fastened to a Velcro strip. One of the plates had a row of two mice, the other a row of three. The children were told that they were going to play a game in which they had to identify the "winning" plate. Gelman pointed to the plate with three mice and said that it would always be the winner, but she never described the plate in any way. The children had to decide for themselves which characteristic—number of mice or length of the row—made that plate the winner. Next, Gelman covered each plate with a large lid and shuffled them. Each child was then asked to pick the winning plate by lifting the lids and determining if the plate underneath was the winner. Whenever the child identified the plate with three mice as the winner, he or she was given a small prize. After several rounds of shuffling and picking, Gelman surreptitiously changed the plate with three mice, either by moving the mice closer together or farther apart, or by removing one mouse entirely. (Because this change was made without the child's knowledge, this experiment has been dubbed the "magic" study.)

Gelman's findings showed that even 3- and 4-year-olds defined the winning plate by the number of mice, not by the length of the row. Almost no child claimed that a change in the length of the three-mouse row disqualified the plate as a winner. Many failed even to notice such a change. In contrast, almost all the children noticed *removal* of a mouse. Many showed great surprise that one of the mice was missing, exclaiming, "Where is it? Where'd it go?" and searching for the missing mouse. The overwhelming majority doubted that a three-mouse plate with one of its mice missing could still be considered a winner. Over two-thirds emphatically declared that the plate was now a loser. The only way to fix things, they said, would be to add another mouse. Clearly, these children understood something about the effects of addition and subtraction on small numbers.

This understanding has been demonstrated in other studies as well (Cooper, 1991; Starkey, 1987; Starkey and Gelman, 1982). In one of them (Cooper, 1984), children were presented with two groups of objects which initially were equal in number, differed by 1, or differed by 2. The experimenter then either added an object to one of the groups or took an object away. The children were to say if one group now had more or less than the other, and which group that was.

All the children used a rule of some kind to determine their answers, and all showed at least some understanding that addition to a set *increases* its number, while subtraction from it *decreases* the number that was there. The rules used by children of different ages, however, varied in sophistication and effectiveness. The youngest children (2- and 3-year-olds) had a rule that involved ignoring the initial number of items in each group and always saying that a group added to now had more than the other group, or a group subtracted from now had less. Because of its lack of sophistication, this can be called a *primitive rule*. In contrast, most 4- and 5-year-olds used a *qualitative rule*, in which they took into account any initial difference between the two groups, but not the magnitude of that difference. It was as if they encoded the two groups in purely qualitative terms: "less than," "equal to," or "more than." This rule led to errors when the initial arrays differed by more than 1. For instance, if one group initially had 5

Young preschoolers do not understand that changing the spatial arrangement of a group of objects does not change their number. Because the red checkers are spaced farther apart, this child thinks there are more red checkers than black ones.

and another initially had 7, and 1 more was added to the smaller group, a child using this rule would say that the two groups had become equal in number. Finally, most 6- to 7-year-olds had developed a *quantitative rule* in which they took into account the magnitude of the differences between the initial groups—that is, the quantities involved. This enabled them to give consistently correct answers.

The use of these three rules is related to the development of conservation of number. Children who use the primitive rule do not show any grasp of number conservation, while many of those who use the qualitative rule appear to be transitional (at Piaget's stage 2). Among those who use the quantitative rule, all exhibit number conservation; they have reached Piaget's stage 3. This finding lends support to Piaget's belief that children's understanding of number conservation is related to their general understanding of numbers. But Piaget's perspective on this developmental process is probably not completely accurate. Many studies (including the ones just described) show that the acquisition of number concepts begins earlier than Piaget suggested and also extends longer (Gelman and Baillargeon, 1983; Gelman, Meck, and Merkin, 1986).

LEARNING TO COUNT   Learning to count is a skill involving numbers that often begins in the early preschool years. Television programs like *Sesame Street* have helped substantially to improve the counting skills of many young children in the United States. By the end of early childhood, most children can consistently count 5 or 6 objects accurately. Occasionally, younger preschoolers make strange errors in counting, which reveal that their understanding of the process is not the same as an adult's. One young boy, for example, appeared to count correctly the fingers on one hand. However, when the researchers held up his index finger and asked "How many is this?" the child replied, "four." A little probing revealed that he was using the number names as names for each of the fingers: The little finger was "one," the ring finger "two," the middle finger "three," the index finger "four," and the thumb "five."

Gelman and Gallistel (1978, 1973) have identified five principles involved in counting that children eventually master. One is the *one-to-one principle,* the idea that correct counting occurs when each member of a set to be counted is paired with one and only one number name. Two- and 3-year-olds have difficulty with this procedure when counting more than 3 or 4 objects, despite attempts to keep track by pointing as they count. They count some objects more than once (often by saying the sequence of numbers faster than their finger moves), and they skip objects, especially when the objects are not arranged neatly in a row. When Meryl was 3, for example, she would become hopelessly muddled when trying to count the 8 animals pictured in a forest in one of her favorite books. To Karen's surprise, Meryl didn't seem at all aware of her mistakes. She would happily count the animals incorrectly again and again. Then, when Meryl was 4, her verbal counting and simultaneous pointing gradually came into sync, and she was usually able to handle that page of her book with no errors at all.

Another principle involved in learning to count is the *stable-order principle.* This is the idea that correct counting occurs when the number names are listed in a certain (always the same) order as they are paired with objects. For speakers of English the correct order is one, two, three, and so forth, but young children sometimes use idiosyncratic orders. The son of one of the authors of this book consistently left out the number 7 when counting at age 2½, and another researcher has reported the same error by her son (Rosser, 1994). Young children use a stable order for counting smaller numbers (1 to 3), and then expand the range of a consistent order as they move through the preschool years. The rate of expansion is influenced by the counting system used in different cultures. The Oksapmin of Papua New Guinea use a counting system that depends on the names of body parts from the thumb on the right hand (corresponding to English "one") through all the fingers, wrist, forearm, elbow (corresponding to English "eight"), and on across the body to the other hand. Although the concrete reference to the body may help in early learning of number names, it appears to slow the development of more abstract numerical skills (Saxe, 1982). In contrast, the Chinese counting system, which uses a more consistent naming system than English (e.g., "ten-one" rather than "eleven") seems to accelerate the expansion of the counting range and the development of some abstract numerical skills (Miller and Stigler, 1987).

The *cardinal principle* is a third rule in learning how to count. It holds that correct counting results when the counter uses the final word in the counting sequence to describe the total number of objects in the set. For example, if there are four objects in a set, the child would count "one, two, three, *four*" and then say that the total number of objects is four. Researchers disagree about when young children begin to use this principle. Three-year-olds often appear to use it when counting two or three objects, but not for larger numbers. If 3-year-old Mikey counts a set of four blocks and is then asked how many blocks are in the group, he is very likely to count them again. Use of the cardinal principle is more evident at 4 years of age. For instance, when given a conservation of number task, 4-year-olds sometimes seem to miscount intentionally so that the result of their counting is consistent with their judgment that the longer row has more objects. It makes sense to do this only if they are using the cardinal principle. After conducting her own research and reviewing the work of others, Wynn (1990) concluded that children use the cardinal principle after about age 3½.

A fourth principle in learning to count is the *abstraction principle*. This is the idea that any set of objects is potentially countable. Although the abstraction principle has not been the direct focus of any research, young children have been asked to count a variety of different things, including imaginary things, and they always seem to find the task plausible. They are also willing to group together different kinds of things in a set to be counted, such as grouping together and counting animate and inanimate objects. These informal findings suggest that children begin to understand the abstraction principle from quite an early age.

Finally, learning to count involves the *order-irrelevant principle*, the idea that correct counting can occur regardless of the order in which things are counted. When young children are asked to count a set of objects more than once, they frequently count them in a different order, as if they know that the order does not make any difference. By age 5, many children are able to state explicitly that order is irrelevant (Flavell, Miller, and Miller, 1993).

Developmentalists have debated exactly how these five principles involved in counting develop. Rochele Gelman has argued that children grasp them at some level even before they start to count (Gelman and Gallistel, 1978; Gallistel and Gelman, 1990). This is often interpreted to mean that the principles are innate (Rosser, 1994). But others say that counting behaviors and skills develop first, and from them children extract the principles (Fuson, 1988; Siegler,

1991). This debate is part of a larger one concerning how much knowledge must be built into children in order for them to use their experiences effectively to elaborate their knowledge systems. At present the debate remains unresolved. We know, however, that by the end of the preschool period, children understand the five principles involved in counting and apply them appropriately.

CONCEPTS OF MEASUREMENT

Piaget believed that learning about conservation was required to understand measurement. Yet preschoolers show an intuitive grasp of measurement before they correctly solve conservation problems, just as they show an intuitive grasp of number concepts and counting. For example, Kevin Miller (1984) has shown that young children will divide a string in half by grasping it near the center and adjusting that hold until the length of the two segments is equal. Also, preschoolers will form two equal groups of cookies by dividing a large group a pair at a time (Cooper, 1984).

Young children make measurement errors when the appearance of two equal quantities makes them look unequal, as when two strings of equal length are laid down side by side, one straight and the other wavy. But in the absence of misleading perceptual information, preschoolers frequently perform reasonably well on simple measurement tasks. What they are lacking is a systematic understanding of quantity that justifies their measurement activities.

SUMMING UP

We can summarize what we've discussed about quantitative concepts in preschool children with four basic points. First, preschoolers do not usually display an understanding that quantities are conserved despite changes in appearance. Second, when preschoolers fail to demonstrate a grasp of conservation, they tend to focus on only a single aspect of the stimulus. They look at the height of the water in the glass and ignore the narrower width; they look at the length of a row overall and ignore the spacing between objects. To them, the immediate appearance seems to be what counts. Third, teaching can lead to the stable acquisition of a new cognitive skill, but probably only to the extent that training speeds normal development and not before the child has the cognitive framework necessary to integrate that skill. Fourth, failure to understand conservation does not prevent preschoolers from learning a substantial amount about counting, measurement, and small quantities, and about how numbers can be changed through addition and subtraction.

UNDERSTANDING OTHER CONCEPTUAL TOOLS

In addition to quantitative skills and concepts, there are several other conceptual tools that adults take for granted but preschoolers are still in the process of mastering. One is the conceptual tool of **classification,** the ability to group things by shared characteristics, such as size, shape, make, color, or price. You think nothing of classifying along several dimensions simultaneously, as when you group together all the high-priced, midsize, foreign-made cars. Another conceptual tool you take for granted is **seriation,** the ability to arrange things in a logical progression, such as organizing a batch of newspapers from earliest to latest. You also take for granted the conceptual tool of **transitive inference,** the ability to infer the relationship between two objects by knowing their respective

Classification:
The conceptual tool that enables us to group things by shared characteristics, such as size, shape, make, color, or price.

Seriation:
The conceptual tool that enables us to arrange things in a logical progression, such as from oldest to newest.

Transitive inference:
The conceptual tool that enables us to infer the relationship between two objects by knowing their respective relationships to a third.

relationships to a third. When you infer that two children are equal in height because their heads both just reach the top of the same kitchen counter, you are using transitive inference to deduce something. Like quantitative tools, classification, seriation, and transitive inference only begin to develop during the preschool period. In using these tools, preschoolers are hampered by centration and the appearance-reality problem, just as they were hampered in using quantitative concepts and skills.

This preschooler has no trouble sorting blocks by color (or by shape), but sorting them by both color and shape at the same time would be beyond her present abilities.

CLASSIFICATION

When Joe Turner empties the dishwasher and puts the glasses away in one cupboard, the plates in another, and the silverware in a drawer, he is organizing these items into classes. A **class** is any set of objects or events that we think of as having certain features in common and therefore as being the same in certain ways. If Meryl, after watching Joe, takes one of her toy spoons and puts it into the silverware drawer, we can say that she seems to understand the class *silverware*.

When do children first display classification skills? Infants show an implicit form of classification when they treat certain stimuli as the same on the basis of shared characteristics. For instance, if you give bottles of slightly different sizes with different colored nipples to a baby, the child will ignore the perceptual variations and treat the bottles similarly. Although the child is not aware of this implicit classification, he or she is nevertheless showing a primitive form of this skill. In time the child begins to "group" more intentionally. Before they are 2, toddlers can be seen sorting objects on the basis of common properties (Gopnik and Meltzoff, 1987). Meryl as a toddler loved to explore a lower kitchen cupboard and sort the pots from the lids. However, not until the preschool years are children consistently able to make simple classifications when they are asked to do so.

Piaget studied classification in preschoolers by presenting them with different colored shapes and instructing them to sort the things that "go together" into separate groups (Inhelder and Piaget, 1964). In the simplest form of this task there were only two colors (such as red and blue) and only two shapes (such as circles and squares). Piaget found that the youngest preschoolers would sometimes sort correctly along one dimension (shape *or* color). For instance, they might put all the red circles and squares in one pile and all the blue ones in another. It was not unusual for 3-year-olds to start sorting on the basis of color and then to switch suddenly by matching the shape of the last object added to a pile. Older preschoolers were more consistent in their sorting, until by age 5 they were quite consistently correct in classifying along one dimension. Even the 5-year-olds, however, still focused on only a single characteristic (color alone, for example, not both color and shape). A 10-year-old, in contrast, would sort using both dimensions simultaneously, putting all the blue squares in one pile, all the blue circles in another, all the red squares in a third, and all the red circles in a fourth. Piaget saw this difference between preschoolers and older children as another example of the preschoolers' centration.

Later research has shown that this centration is not completely rigid, however. Two-dimensional sorting can be encouraged in preschoolers by giving them experience in classifying objects. In one study, children who had been trained to sort along one dimension showed substantial two-dimensional sorting by age 4 (Watson, Hayes, and Vietze, 1979). But preschoolers seldom spontaneously use two-dimensional sorting to organize objects in their everyday

Class:

Any set of objects or events that we think of as having certain features in common and therefore as being the same in certain ways.

Preschoolers can identify which object in a pair is larger, but they have trouble with problems of transitive interference. They find it hard to keep in mind that the same object can be either small or large, depending on what it is compared to.

worlds. Although training can to some extent overcome centration on a single dimension, young children return to this narrower focus in situations that differ from the training examples.

SERIATION

We noted earlier that *seriation* is the ability to arrange things in a logical series or progression—from smallest to largest, for example, or from oldest to newest. Piaget was interested in children's ability to perform seriation tasks because he believed that this ability indicated an underlying cognitive skill required to appreciate numbers and to measure effectively. Piaget (1952) studied seriation by asking children to arrange a group of sticks in a row from smallest to largest (see Figure 9.3). If the child succeeded in organizing the sticks into an orderly progression, he or she was given another stick of intermediate length to insert at the appropriate place in the series. Piaget discovered that young preschoolers can find the largest or the smallest stick in a group, but they have great difficulty constructing an ordered series of 7 sticks. By age 6 or 7, however, most children can easily construct such a series, and they can also insert an additional stick in the correct place.

Interestingly, when the number of sticks to be put in a series is smaller, such as only 3 or 4, preschool children perform much better (Blevins and Cooper, 1986; Cooper, Leitner, and Moore, 1977). This is because of the way they approach a seriation task. If you were given this task, you would probably start by finding the smallest stick and putting it on the left, finding the next smallest and putting it second, and so on until all the sticks had been arranged. This planned course of action requires that you grasp the nature of a seriated set before you begin to work. Such an overall plan guiding each move is not apparent in the behavior of young children, even when they are organizing only a small number of sticks. Instead, preschoolers seem to arrange the sticks more or less at random and then check to see if the results look right. This trial-and-error strategy involves corrections based on the appearance of the array. Such a strategy works for a small number of sticks, which can be arranged in only a very limited number of ways. But with a larger number, such as 7, there are far more alternatives, and the trial-and-error approach is less likely to succeed.

The preschooler's approach to seriation tasks illustrates some of the cognitive limitations characteristic of this age. Preschoolers cannot conceive of the relationship between members of an ordered set when the set is not visually present. They must see what the array looks like in order to know if it is right. This is the appearance-reality problem in a slightly different form. To a preschooler, what a series *looks* like determines what it is. Some of young children's attempts to order a set of seven sticks also show evidence of centration. The array produced by a preschooler in Figure 9.3 B looks seriated if you focus only on the tops, which is apparently what this child did. It is as if the child could not coordinate information from the two ends simultaneously, and so focused on the tops alone.

TRANSITIVE INFERENCE

We have defined *transitive inference* as a reasoning process for drawing conclusions about the relative characteristics of two objects by knowing their respective relationships to a third object. For example, if you know that A equals B and that B equals C, you can conclude by transitive inference that A and C are also equal. Transitive inference can be used to reason about inequalities as well. If you know that Mikey is taller than Bryan, and Bryan is taller than Justin, you know by transitive inference that Mikey is the tallest of the three.

In Piaget's initial studies of transitive inference, children were unable to solve such problems until middle childhood (Piaget, 1970). Subsequent research has challenged this conclusion, however (Bryant and Trabasso, 1971; Riley and Trabasso, 1974). Tom Trabasso and his colleagues have shown that even 4-year-olds can succeed at these problems if they are given sufficient training to remember the premise conditions (such as that Mikey is taller than Bryan, and Bryan is taller than Justin). To rule out alternative explanations as to why 4-year-olds succeed, Trabasso had to train his young subjects to remember five premise pairs, all involving relationships between pairs of real objects. It takes a long time to get 4-year-olds to master these five pairs, but in the end they can answer questions such as "Who is taller, Mikey or Justin?" even though they have never been directly taught that relationship.

There is still disagreement about exactly what 4-year-olds have learned when they demonstrate such knowledge (Breslow, 1981; Russell, 1981). Some say that when they are taught the premise pairs in a seriated order (from tallest to shortest, for example), they may simply remember the series, and then use their knowledge of the series to answer questions about new relationships, *without* employing transitive inference. For example, a preschooler could reason that Mikey is taller than Justin just on the basis of knowing that Mikey is the tallest. Even so, it is impressive that young children can make correct judgments about relative size based on a mental representation they have formed of a series. This feat shows that they can accomplish an important part of transitive inference.

Despite the accomplishments 4-year-olds made in Trabasso's studies, they clearly face cognitive limitations that older children do not. For instance, preschoolers have a dramatically harder time learning Trabasso's premise pairs than do school-age children. To understand why, consider the series $A > B > C > D > E$. Is C big or little? To answer this question you would probably compare C simultaneously to B and D, concluding that it is small relative to one and big relative to the other. But as you know, performing two comparisons at once is usu-

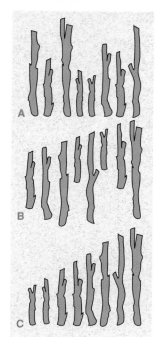

FIGURE 9.3
DEVELOPMENT OF SERIATION
When young preschoolers are asked to order a set of sticks from smallest to largest, they frequently produce a random order such as that shown in A. Older preschoolers sometimes centrate on the top ends of the sticks and produce an arrangement like that in B. Usually between 5 and 7 years of age, children can produce the correct ordering shown in C.

ally beyond the capabilities of a preschooler, partly because of centration. To a 4-year-old, then, the premise pairs in this series may seem confusing and inconsistent. Sometimes a given object is the big one; other times, it is the little one. Coordinating all this information is extremely difficult for a preschooler.

DISTINGUISHING BETWEEN APPEARANCE AND REALITY

Throughout our discussion of the general characteristics of preschoolers' thought we have given many examples in which children are misled by the surface appearance of something. In recent years the development of the ability to distinguish between appearance and reality has become an area of research in its own right. In one of the earliest studies of this topic, children 3 to 6 years old got to know a cat named Maynard, and then researchers put a dog mask over Maynard's head (De Vries, 1969). The children were then asked questions like, "What kind of animal is it now? Would this animal eat dog food or cat food? Does it bark or meow?" Three-year-olds frequently seemed to believe that the mask changed the identity of the animal whereas 5- and 6-year-olds did not.

John Flavell and his colleagues have conducted many studies in which they attempted to rule out other explanations of young preschoolers' errors (e.g., Flavell, Green, and Flavell, 1986, 1990). In these studies, they showed children objects that looked like other objects, such as a sponge that looked like a rock. They also had children view things through colored glass, which made the things appear to change color. They asked the children what the objects looked like and what they really were. Despite great efforts to ensure that the children understood the questions, they found that 3-year-olds consistently interpreted the appearance of an object as reality. The fact that other researchers have usually failed in attempts to train 3-year-olds to make the appearance-reality distinction further strengthens Flavell's findings (Taylor and Hart, 1990).

More recently, however, a number of studies have shown that the limitations of preschoolers in this area are not as pervasive as originally thought. In one series of studies, children were presented with food that they had previously seen contaminated in some way, but that currently looked fine (Siegel and Share, 1990). For example, they watched a cockroach being removed from a glass of juice and were asked if the juice was now all right to drink. Children as young as 2½ years said that it was not drinkable, even though it looked fine. In another study, 3-year-olds were observed to use the word "real" to distinguish between toys and the *real* objects they represent, and the word "really" to differentiate between imaginary events and events that *really* happened (Woolley and Wellman, 1990). Clearly, they show the start of distinguishing between appearance and reality, even though in most situations their view of reality is dominated by appearances. By the end of the preschool years this difficulty is largely overcome. Five- and 6-year-olds still have a lot to learn about reality, but their view of reality is no longer dominated by the way things look at the moment.

PRESCHOOLERS' ATTENTION AND MEMORY ABILITIES

While the cognitive skills discussed so far have been mainly ones that Piaget investigated, the focus in this section will be on topics central to information-processing approaches. These topics include the abilities to select and attend to information, to store it in memory, and to retrieve it.

Sensory register:
That part of memory in which incoming information from one of the five senses is stored very briefly. There is one sensory register for each of the five senses.

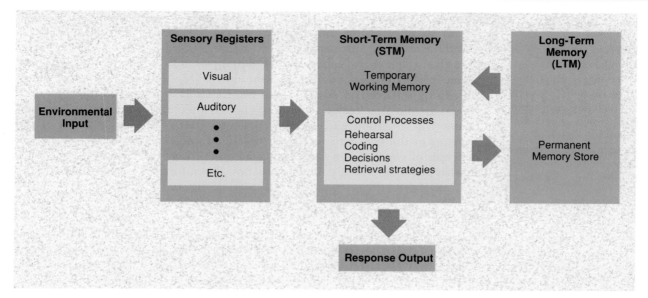

FIGURE 9.4 AN INFORMATION-PROCESSING MODEL
In this model of human information processing, information enters the sensory registers, which have a large capacity. Information here fades in less than 1 second, but before it fades some is transferred to short-term memory, and part of this information is transferred to long-term or permanent memory. (Source: Adapted from Atkinson and Shiffrin, 1968.)

According to many information-processing theorists, the information you input from your environment goes through the various steps of processing shown in Figure 9.4 (Atkinson and Shiffrin, 1968). First it enters a **sensory register** (you have one sensory register for each of your five senses), where it is stored very briefly (less than 1 second for visual information). Whatever information you consciously note moves to **short-term,** or **working, memory,** which is of more limited capacity than a sensory register but holds information longer (usually 10 to 20 seconds). Some of the information in working memory then moves to **long-term memory,** which has a very large capacity and holds information for a very long time. Using memory strategies, (such as rehearsing material, organizing it into categories, or relating it to other things) tends to increase the likelihood that information will be stored in long-term memory.

The information-processing model in Figure 9.4 can be used to help define attention and memory skills. *Attention skills* are the processes that control the transfer of information from a sensory register to working memory, while *memory skills* are the processes that retain information in working memory (short-term storage), transfer it to long-term memory, or both. Attention skills and memory skills may have a central role in cognitive development. Recall from Chapter 5 that some theorists have described cognitive development in terms of increases in the capacity of working memory.

Information-processing theorists are also interested in the factors that underlie improvements in memory skills. Craik and Lockhart (1972) have proposed that a key factor is the "depth" to which new information is processed—that is, the extent to which it is thought about, examined, elaborated on, and linked to other things we know. Deeply processed information is better remembered than information that is processed "shallowly." For example, after showing children a picture of a country scene, a researcher might ask, "Is there any green in the picture?" (a shallow characteristic) or, "Is it spring in the picture?" (a deeper characteristic). Presumably, children asked the second question would remember the picture better, because they were encouraged to think about it in

Short-term, or working, memory:
That part of the memory, with a relatively small storage capacity in which consciously noted information is stored for 10 to 20 seconds.

Long-term memory:
That part of memory which has the largest storage capacity and in which information is stored for a very long time.

more depth. From this perspective, memory skills develop as children learn to attend to information that requires deeper processing. This perspective is called the **levels of processing view.**

In this section we will focus on the development of both attention skills and memory skills in preschoolers. You should realize, however, that information-processing theorists do not see these two topics as unrelated to the topics discussed in the first major section of this chapter. Instead, they believe that changes in attention and memory skills are part of the explanation of the changes in thinking and reasoning described earlier. For example, acquiring concepts of conservation can be explained in terms of developmental changes in what information is attended to and how that information is processed.

Levels of processing view: A model of cognitive processing in which the emphasis is on the "depth" to which new information is processed (that is, the extent to which it is thought about, examined, elaborated on, and linked to other things we know).

DEPLOYING ATTENTION

> In Meryl's kindergarten class the teacher is telling the children about the names of different shapes. Meryl is paying no attention to the teacher but instead is observing a red-tailed hawk that is hunting in a field just outside the window. The teacher notices that Meryl is looking out the window and says gently, "Meryl, pay attention."

Meryl, of course, *has* been paying attention, but to the hawk, not to her teacher. Her problem is one of failing to focus on the "right" thing. Meryl is not alone in experiencing this problem. The tasks of selecting information to attend to, staying focused on it, and ignoring irrelevant stimuli all pose challenges to preschoolers because their attentional systems are not yet fully developed.

In a classic study, Elaine Vurpillot (1968) showed children pairs of houses like those in Figure 9.5 and asked them to determine if the two houses were the same. Half the house pairs were identical, while the other half differed in the way the windows looked. One, three, or five of the six pairs of windows were different. The children's eye movements were filmed as they made their judgments so the researchers could tell what parts of the houses they were looking at. Although the preschoolers in this study frequently made correct judgments, they made more errors than older children because they did not use systematic, organized strategies in their scanning. As a result, they sometimes missed important information—in this case, some of the windows.

In other situations young children scan *more* information than they need to (Miller, 1990). In one study, for instance, children were shown 12 pictures, half of animals and half of household objects. The pictures were arranged on a board with 12 windows, one picture inside each window. The children could view any picture they wanted just by opening that particular window. The researcher asked them to remember only the animal pictures and told them they could open each window as often as they wanted to memorize the picture inside it. The most efficient strategy, after finding the six animal pictures, would be to open only the windows covering those pictures. But preschoolers, unlike older children, did not use this selective behavior. They continued to open all 12 windows during the entire "study" period. As in Vurpillot's study, the preschoolers failed to direct their attention in an organized and effective way.

Although preschoolers seem less advanced than older children in effectively focusing their attention, they have made progress compared with toddlers. For example, when Daniel Anderson and Stephen Levin (1976) observed 2- to 4-year-olds while they were watching the TV program *Sesame Street*, they found that

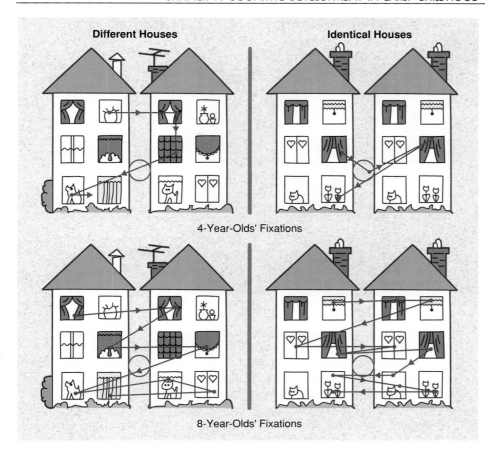

FIGURE 9.5
DEVELOPMENT OF VISUAL ATTENTION
Children were asked if the houses were the same or different. Preschoolers compared only a few of the windows, whereas older children scanned back and forth more systematically. (Source: Vurpillot, 1968.)

the youngest children spent the least amount of time viewing the screen. This was especially true when toys were placed in the same room. The younger children often wandered around, playing with the toys and talking with other people, while the older children were more likely to divide their attention between the television and the toys. Apparently, during the preschool years, children become much more skilled at deploying their attention. It is not until middle childhood, however, that children conceive of attention as a limited resource which must be deployed selectively (Miller, 1985; Miller and Harris, 1990).

PRESCHOOLERS' MEMORY

One Friday evening when Mikey was 3, his parents decided to take the family to the beach the next day. Mikey was very excited but did little planning for the trip. If Christine hadn't made a list of what to take along, Mikey would have forgotten most of his favorite toys. Three years later, when Mikey was 6, another trip to the beach was planned. This time Mikey thought about what he wanted to take with him, and he hoped he wouldn't forget anything. When he saw Christine putting together a number of things to take, he gathered his toys and added them to the pile. Three years later, when Mikey was 9, he would often go to the beach on summer days. At this age, Mikey was much more organized in his efforts to remember. The night before, on his own, he

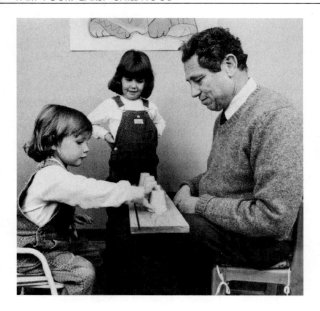

*Preschoolers show good imme-
diate memory for the location
of hidden objects. Here, psychologist Jerome Kagan gives a
simple memory test to a
preschooler.*

would place his kite and fishing gear at the front door to make sure he would
see them on his way out.

    This example illustrates many key features of memory development. Often,
young preschoolers, such as Mikey at age 3, are oblivious to the memory
demands of a situation. Thinking about the need to remember doesn't occur to
them, even though they may be devastated if they forget something important
to them. By the end of the preschool years, children are often aware that a particular task requires remembering, but they are not very good at generating a
plan to facilitate memory. Mikey at age 6, for example, simply copied his
mother's strategy by adding to her "ready to go" pile. Still, although Mikey did-
n't generate his own plan, he at least recognized that his mother's plan was
effective. Finally, by age 9, we see Mikey spontaneously using intentional memory strategies: he puts the things he wants to take in a place where he knows
he'll see them. In this section we'll focus on the aspects of memory development that occur during the preschool years, saving those that occur in middle
childhood for Chapter 11.

ABILITIES AND LIMITATIONS

In their daily activities preschoolers demonstrate both *recognition memory* (the
ability to perceive a particular stimulus as familiar) and *free recall* (the ability to
pull information out of long-term memory for current use). Sometimes
preschoolers' skills at recognition and recall are quite impressive. For example,
at age 3 Mikey could tell you the correct names for a wide variety of construction vehicles and equipment, from backhoe loaders to stone crushers to excava-
tors and road rollers. Malcolm at 5 knew the names of basketball teams that his
mother had trouble recalling. He even knew the names of most of their home
cities. Studies verify that preschoolers can often absorb a tremendous amount
of information. This was shown, for instance, in a study of what preschool children remembered about a trip to an amusement park they had never visited
before (Hamond and Fivush, 1991).

    Yet oddly enough, although preschoolers sometimes display surprising memory capabilities, they usually perform poorly compared with older children and adults when asked to remember things like a set of pictures or numbers (Flavell, Miller, and Miller, 1993). Consider how they do on a digit span test, in which numbers of increasing length are read at a rate of one digit per second, and the person is asked to repeat each number out loud. The longest number that preschoolers can remember averages only four digits, compared with five digits for 6- to 8-year-olds, six digits for 9- to 12-year-olds, and eight digits for college students (Chi, 1978).

There are several possible explanations for this poorer performance of preschoolers compared with older children and adults. One is that they are less familiar with the number names they are asked to remember. Another is that they are less able to use intentional strategies to help themselves remember. Both these explanations seem to have merit. When preschoolers know as much about a topic as older children do, and when the task prevents the use of memory-enhancing strategies, preschoolers sometimes remember as well as older children. For example, in a study in which people were asked to recognize pictures of cartoon characters viewed the previous day, when they had not been told they would be given a memory test, preschoolers remembered just as well as older children and even adults (Chi and Ceci, 1987). It is when people are *instructed* to remember material that older children and adults almost always perform better than preschoolers (Flavell, Miller, and Miller, 1993). No doubt this is partly because the older subjects know better how to go about remembering.

This is not to say that young children never use memory strategies. Sometimes they do, especially when simple strategies are fairly obvious. Consider a study in which researchers hid a toy dog under one of several containers, asked preschoolers to remember where the toy was, and then left the room to observe the children through a one-way mirror (Wellman, Ritter, and Flavell, 1975). Even 3-year-olds sometimes used memory strategies, such as looking fixedly at the correct container, moving it away from the others so it was easy to recognize, or resting their hand on it. Many 3-year-olds also showed use of memory strategies in a study in which the child was asked to find a camera that had recently been used to take his or her picture (Wellman, Sommerville, and Haake, 1979). The child's picture was taken first at location 1, then 2, then 3. Children 3½ years and older were much more likely to begin their search at location 3 than locations 1 or 2. They made use of logical constraints on where the object might be, rather than simply looking in places where they had seen it before.

But preschoolers' occasional active efforts to memorize information or to search systematically for something lost are the exceptions rather than the rule. They depend either on a situation that fosters simple memory-related activities or on guidance from adults. (The susceptibility of young children to adult suggestion has implications for their reliability as witnesses, as the box on pp. 361 explains.)

In most cases, preschoolers perform significantly worse on memory tasks than older children because their memory strategies are still so limited. For example, when 5-year-olds were asked to remember the objects they saw in a set of pictures, they did nothing to help themselves remember, and they performed no better than if they had been asked simply to look at the pictures (Appel et al., 1972). This is true of younger children, too. Most children younger than 5 do not spontaneously rehearse information—that is, they don't go over it several times in their minds to encourage retention (Perlmutter and Myers, 1979). Harriet Waters has proposed that whatever memory strategies preschoolers initially use tend to be limited, context-specific, and inconsistently applied (Waters and Andreassen, 1983). With further development, however, these strategies become more general and more consistent, so memory performance improves.

ENCOURAGING IMPROVED PERFORMANCE

L. S. Vygotsky, a prominent Russian psychologist, proposed a valuable concept that provides a perspective for viewing the memory performance of preschoolers and how it can be improved (Vygotsky, 1978). He focused on the gap between a particular child's current performance and that child's potential performance if given guidance by someone more skilled. Vygotsky called this gap the **zone of proximal development**—*proximal* meaning near the point of origin or near the level of understanding that the child currently has. For example, a preschool child who is asked to remember the pictures in a set may simply look at the pictures and do nothing else. It is not that the child is totally unaware that there are things that can be done to improve memory. It is usually just that he or she doesn't know what to do. However, if an adult helps by suggesting that the child repeatedly go through the set and say the name of each picture several times out loud, the child will exhibit a higher level of competence on the memory task. Vygotsky emphasized the role of more knowledgeable others in helping children make progress within their zones of proximal development by building on skills the youngsters already have.

Zone of proximal development:
Vygotsky's term for the gap between a child's current performance in a particular area and the child's potential performance if given guidance by someone more skilled.

SOCIAL COGNITION

The improvements in memory skills and other aspects of thinking that occur during the preschool years have an impact on a child's understanding of the social world, an understanding that is often referred to as **social cognition.** During the preschool period children start to learn something about how other people think and feel, about what their motives and intentions are, and about what they are likely to do. They also begin to understand that other people's perspectives sometimes differ from their own, which helps them to communicate more effectively with others. Also aiding communication are the general understandings that preschoolers acquire about how various social exchanges are supposed to be carried out. All this new knowledge about the social world enables children to respond more appropriately to other people and to relate to them in more mature ways. More mature social relationships, in turn, provide children with additional knowledge that fosters their cognitive growth. Thus, the development of social cognition is an excellent example of how cognitive and social development are interdependent, constantly influencing one another.

Social cognition:
A child's understanding of the social world.

Social cognition is predicated on having some understanding of the human mind as an agent of thought, feeling, and perception, and as a controller of speech and behavior. We will look at the development of this understanding of the mind before turning to two other important areas of research in the field of social cognition: egocentrism and interpersonal communication.

THE CHILD'S THEORY OF MIND

During the preschool years children are constructing not only an understanding of physical reality but also an understanding of the human mind and such concepts as "knowing," "wanting," "thinking," "remembering," and "intending." These concepts are an important part of a system for explaining why people do what they do. Just as preschoolers are beginning to understand physical causality, so they are also beginning to understand the causes of human behavior. Taken together, this area of development has been called the **child's theory of mind.** The term "theory" may seem excessive when referring to a preschooler's understanding of the mind, but "theory" is really appropriate here. The young child's grasp of the mind goes beyond *empirical knowledge* (knowledge based on experience and observation in the physical world) to include *theoretical knowledge* (explanations based on constructs that cannot be directly observed). This is the essential definition of a theory (Yates et al., 1988).

In developing a theory of mind, children come to understand five *postulates* or fundamental principles, according to developmental psychologist John Flavell (Flavell, Miller, and Miller, 1993). The first postulate is simply that *minds exist*. Babies do not understand the existence of minds, even though they may be able to distinguish things that have minds (living things capable of moving and experiencing the world) from things without minds (inanimate objects) (Wellman and Gelman, 1992). It is not until the toddler period that children start referring to mental states such as feelings and desires. This tells us they have begun to grasp the notion that minds exist. Thus, this important first postulate is established even before the preschool years.

The second postulate in the child's theory of mind is that *minds have connections to the physical world*. That is to say, what people think, feel, know, and want is linked to the objects and events around them. Substantial improvement in this understanding occurs between the ages of 2 and 3. For example, 3-year-olds (but not 2-year-olds) know that if something is hidden in a container, someone who has looked in the container *knows* that it is there, whereas someone who hasn't looked doesn't know (unless that person saw the object being hidden or has been told where it is) (Pratt and Bryant, 1990; Wolley, 1991). But though 3- and 4-year-olds know that what is in the mind has connections to the physical world, their understanding of the nature of those connections is very limited. They still make mistakes in predicting the kind of experiences that are needed to know certain things, and they also make errors in predicting how particular kinds of knowledge will influence behavior (Flavell, Miller, and Miller, 1993).

The third postulate that children come to understand is that *minds are separate and different from the physical world*. For example, 3-year-olds know that the mind can fantasize about things that don't really exist (Wellman and Ester, 1986). They know that if one child has a cookie and another is thinking about a cookie, only one of those cookies can be actually seen and touched. This new understanding of mental events makes children less fearful of imagined ghosts and monsters, although such fears are not entirely gone. Even adults, after all, are often apprehensive after seeing ghosts and monsters in a horror film (Flavell, Miller, and Miller, 1993).

Fourth, children come to understand the postulate that *minds can represent objects and events accurately or inaccurately*. Understanding this idea requires that

Child's theory of mind: An understanding of the human mind that in preschoolers begins to include explanations based on constructs that cannot be directly observed, including the idea that minds actively interpret reality and can sometimes make errors.

children reflect upon mental representations, so it is not usually grasped by 2- and 3-year-olds. Four- and 5-year-olds, however, clearly exhibit some understanding of it. In one study, for example, children heard a story about a child who put some candy in a blue cabinet, and while he was out playing his mother moved it to a green cupboard (Wimmer and Perner, 1983). The children were asked where the boy would look for the candy when he came back. Whereas 3-year-olds predicted the green cupboard (where they knew the candy really was), 4- and 5-year-olds predicted the blue cabinet (where they knew the boy *thought* it was). Apparently, 4- and 5-year-olds are able to reflect upon the accuracy of the boy's beliefs and predict how a false belief will affect his behavior. Notice that the belief-reality distinction involved in this example is very similar to the appearance-reality distinction discussed earlier. The two show similar developmental patterns, although the belief-reality distinction emerges somewhat sooner.

Finally, children come to understand a fifth postulate: that *minds actively interpret reality and emotional experiences.* The beginnings of this understanding are revealed in success on tasks that involve false beliefs, like the one in the study just described. Preschoolers are very limited in this understanding, however. They tend to treat mental representations as passively acquired copies of real events, not as actively constructed *ideas* about reality (Piaget's view of them). Even children as old as 8 believe that everyone who hears the same message, regardless of their ages, will understand it in the same way (Montgomery, 1991). Similarly, it is not until well into middle childhood that children become aware that emotional responses are influenced not just by what happens but also by a person's prior feelings and expectations (Gnepp, 1989; see Chapter 12). Thus, this fifth postulate in the theory of mind is the one the child still has the most to learn about at the end of the preschool period.

Developmental psychologists widely agree that children acquire a theory of mind from their experiences in the world, especially their social experiences. In the next section you will see how social experiences help preschoolers to overcome *egocentrism,* in a process closely linked to developing a more mature theory of mind.

EGOCENTRISM IN PRESCHOOLERS

As stated earlier in this chapter, *egocentrism,* the failure to distinguish the perspectives of others from one's own point of view, is a cognitive limitation that appears at all levels of development (Elkind, 1967, 1978), but it is most easily seen and most often studied during the preschool years. One of the authors of this book once saw a 4-year-old girl put her fingers in her ears and then ask her father, "Can you hear me?" When he responded "no," she raised her voice and asked, "Can you hear me now?" There are two illustrations of egocentrism in this example. First, the little girl apparently believed that because she put her fingers in her own ears she made it hard for her father to hear. She was not differentiating her own perceptual experience from that of her father. Second, when the father answered "no" to the child's first question, she repeated the question, only louder, showing lack of awareness that his "no" meant her father must have heard her. Here the little girl failed to take into account her father's cognitive perspective and realize that in this situation he was only teasing her. This second kind of egocentrism is not overcome until middle childhood. The first kind, in contrast, is gradually conquered during the preschool years.

Because this young preschooler cannot see her mother, she believes that her mother cannot see her.

Other examples of egocentrism abound in the early and middle preschool period. One day when 4-year-old Meryl was excited about a new pair of shoes, she asked Karen if she could call her grandmother to tell her about them. "Look, Grandma," Meryl said into the receiver, as she held up one foot. "Aren't they beautiful?" Four-year-old Mikey did much the same thing one evening as he looked through pictures of airplanes in a new book. "These planes are neat!" he exclaimed to his father, who was sitting at the other end of the sofa. And without bothering to turn the book so that Frank could see it, he asked, "Which do you like best?" These are both examples of perceptual egocentrism—the assumption that other people's perceptions are the same as one's own.

Other forms of egocentrism are equally common in preschoolers. Young children assume, for example, that others have the same knowledge and beliefs that they do. Suppose a young preschooler sees cookies being hidden in a crayon box, and then a second child enters the room (Moses and Flavell, 1990). When asked what the second child thinks is in the box, the first child will answer "cookies," not "crayons" ("crayons" being the most likely guess by someone who doesn't share the first child's knowledge). Apparently young preschoolers can't adopt the other child's perspective. Because the first child *knows* there are cookies in the box, he or she can't imagine another person answering anything else. This egocentrism may be closely connected to the difficulties young children have with the appearance-reality distinction. Preschoolers behave as if the way the world appears to them is reality, and so their own perspective *must* be shared by everyone else.

Another form of egocentrism concerns desires and wishes. It can be seen in a study that John Flavell conducted by asking children ages 3 to 6 to select gifts for various people—their mother, their father, a brother or a sister if they had one, their teacher, and themselves (Flavell et al., 1968). The gifts to choose from included silk stockings, a necktie, a toy truck, a doll, and an adult book. Three-year-olds showed clear egocentrism by often selecting dolls and trucks for their mothers and fathers. They failed to differentiate their own desires from those of adults. If they wanted a doll or a truck, they presumed everyone else wanted one too.

But this study also showed the gradual progress that older preschoolers make in overcoming egocentrism. Unlike the 3-year-olds, the 4-year-olds seemed aware that everyone in the world might not want what they want, although they still had trouble taking an adult's perspective and picking out an appropriate gift. Interestingly, the 4-year-olds were more egocentric in making a gift choice for a teacher than for a parent, perhaps because they knew more about what parents buy for themselves. It was not until age 5 that 50 percent of the children chose appropriate gifts for everyone on the list; and it was not until age 6 that *all* the children chose appropriately. Thus, during the preschool period, children come to realize that others may have desires different from their own, and they begin to take another person's perspective in trying to determine what that person's wishes might be.

Flavell has analyzed the cognitive components needed to overcome egocentrism and to take another's perspective (e.g., Flavell, 1985). First, children must realize that other people have thoughts, viewpoints, and desires that may differ from their own. Flavell calls this a *knowledge of existence*. Second, children must realize that it can be useful to consider another's perspective, that doing so can facilitate social interaction and communication. Flavell calls this an *awareness of need*. Finally, children must become skilled at *social inference*. They must be able to "read" another person's actions and imagine that person's point of view.

The same cognitive components enable children to understand the feelings and emotions of others. Very early signs of sensitivity to other people's feelings are not indications that the child truly comprehends what others feel. For instance, the social referencing of early toddlerhood, in which the child takes cues from the caregiver's face in a novel situation, involves only a primitive awareness of the caregiver's feelings. Not until about age 4 do we have strong evidence that children interpret facial expressions as belonging to general categories, such as "feels good" and "feels bad" (Shantz, 1975). More finely tuned interpretations of other people's feelings take substantially longer to develop. Even adults often have trouble with the inference part of this process. They recognize the existence of other people's feelings and the need to assess them, but they aren't always correct in deducing what those feelings are. In preschoolers, the emerging ability to grasp other people's feelings does not mean that this new skill is regularly used. Its use is still quite limited (Flavell, 1985). We will return to the topic of understanding someone else's feelings when we discuss the development of empathy in Chapter 10.

COMMUNICATION AND THE DECLINE OF EGOCENTRISM

Communicating with others involves more than simply having a vocabulary and knowing how to put words together. It also involves an understanding of how to participate in conversations. How much information do others require to understand your meaning? Which of your ideas must you spell out in detail and which can your listeners infer? How do you know when clarifications are needed? Children start to understand these aspects of communication during the preschool period. One way to conceptualize their progress in this area is to think of it as part of a general decline in egocentrism. When children's speech begins to reflect more than just their own perspectives, they are on the way to being more effective communicators.

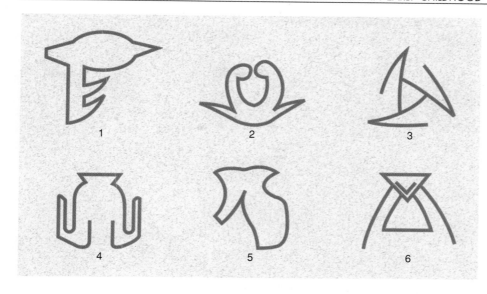

FIGURE 9.6 PICTURES ON BLOCKS IN GLUCKSBERG AND KRAUSS'S COMMUNICATION EXPERIMENT
Preschoolers had great difficulty communicating orally the nature of these abstract designs. When simpler designs are used, preschoolers can communicate much more effectively. (Source: Glucksberg and Krauss, 1967.)

Of course, how egocentric a young child's speech is often depends on the complexity of the communication task. This was demonstrated in a study by Sam Glucksberg and Robert Krauss (1967), who had two children sit on opposite sides of a screen, with identical sets of blocks in front of them. Each block had on it one of the abstract designs shown in Figure 9.6. The children's task was to stack the blocks in exactly the same order without seeing what the other child was doing. One of the children was given the job of describing each block to the other youngster so that this child could pick it out of the pile and add it to his or her stack. Four- and 5-year-olds performed very poorly on this task because they gave so many egocentric and uninformative descriptions: "A curved part of a pipe," the child might say, or simply "The first one." In another study, two children on either side of a screen had identical sets of pictures in front of them. The task again was for the listener to figure out which picture the speaker was describing. Here is a sample conversation between preschoolers:

First child points to a picture in front of him and says: "It's this one."
Second child points to a different picture in front of him and asks: "You mean this one?"
First child answers: "That's right."

These results don't mean that preschoolers can *never* analyze what a listener needs to know to understand their meaning. In more conducive circumstances they *can* convey their ideas to others in ways that are understood. For instance, when the abstract figures on the blocks in Glucksberg and Krauss's study were replaced with simple geometric shapes in different colors (a yellow circle, a blue square, and so forth), preschoolers were much more successful at describing them to another child. In another study, preschoolers spontaneously adapted the amount of detail in their explanations to suit the knowledge of particular listeners. This study involved exposing 4-year-olds to a staged "accident" in which an adult spilled a cup of liquid. When asked a week later why the empty cup was in the room, the children varied their answers depending on

Preschoolers are able to adjust their speech to the level of their partner. For example, they talk in simpler terms and "check in" more often with younger children than with peers or adults.

whether they were speaking to the adult who had knocked the cup over or to another person who knew nothing about the previous accident (Menig-Peterson, 1975). Preschoolers also spontaneously vary their clarifications of something they have said depending upon the age of their listener (Warren-Leubecker and Bohannon, 1983). They clarify one way if talking to an adult and another way if talking to another child, again showing an awareness of the listener's needs.

If preschoolers do have some ability to select their speech in accordance with a listener's needs, why did they perform so poorly in early experiments like that of Glucksberg and Krauss? The answer, as we've suggested, may lie in the difficulty of the task. The figures on the blocks in the Glucksberg and Krauss experiment were abstract and hard to describe. Such a task may use all the cognitive capacity of a young child, leaving nothing for use in determining an appropriate wording. As a result, the child lapses into egocentric wording, which doesn't take into account the listener's needs (Shatz, 1978). This explanation may remind you of some of the theories of cognitive development that were discussed in Chapter 5. Some researchers think that limitations on working memory are the major constraints on a child's ability to master new cognitive skills. When a task exceeds the present capacity of working memory, the child either fails to perform it or performs it very poorly.

The idea that performing a task consumes cognitive resources suggests something important about how children's abilities should be studied. To determine a child's *maximum* skill at a particular task, you should limit all other cognitive demands as much as possible. However, if you want to know how children *typically* perform, you should make sure that they are in an environment with all the demands and distractions usually found in a natural setting. Malcolm, for example, if observed in a laboratory might be able to settle a disagreement with a peer more maturely than he settled the disagreement with April. But in a natural setting like a playground, where many cognitive demands are simultaneously occurring (the argument itself, shouted suggestions from friends, the perceptual distraction of other children at play), resorting to force is a course of action that a 5-year-old might take.

LIMITED COGNITIVE RESOURCES AND COMMUNICATION

As they grow older, children become better at communicating effectively despite environmental distractions. This has been shown in studies of children working together to solve problems (Cooper, 1980; Cooper and Cooper, 1985). In one of them, pairs of preschoolers seated in a quiet room tried to find blocks of equal weight using a balance scale (one with a fulcrum at the center, supporting a pan on either side). Even in this quiet setting, conversation was important for maintaining the children's focus on their task. If they allowed themselves to digress to topics other than the task at hand, their performance suffered significantly. In another study, older children observed in a busy classroom proved better able to tolerate conversational digressions (Cooper, Marquis, and Edwards, 1986). Apparently, preschoolers, when faced with an unfamiliar task, find it hard to simultaneously engage in normal conversation. The demands of communication seem to draw on resources that are needed to master the new skill.

What is it that older children have acquired that makes conversational digressions less distracting to them? One possibility is found in the concept of scripts (Myles-Worsley, Cromer, and Dodd, 1986; Nelson and Gruendel, 1979; Schank and Abelson, 1977). A **script** is an abstract representation of a sequence of actions needed to accomplish some goal. For example, most older children have a mental script of how to use a balance scale to find objects of equal weight: you put an object on one side of the scale, select another that seems about equal in weight, try it out on the opposite side of the scale, and proceed until a balanced match is found. With such a script firmly in mind, it becomes much easier to engage in the appropriate behaviors. Most preschoolers are unfamiliar with balance scales and so lack a script for their use. This is probably one reason why they have trouble performing the block-weighing task while simultaneously carrying on an unrelated conversation.

Script:
An abstract representation of the sequence of actions needed to accomplish some goal.

While most preschoolers lack a "balance scale" script, they do have knowledge of other sequences of behavior they experience in their daily lives, such as eating at a fast-food restaurant, going to a birthday party, or shopping in a supermarket. Here is a conversation between two 4-year-olds that shows they have acquired the basics of a "talking on the phone" script.

Gay:	Hi.
Daniel:	Hi.
Gay:	How are you?
Daniel:	Fine.
Gay:	Who am I speaking to?
Daniel:	This is your daddy. I need to speak to you.
Gay:	All right.
Daniel:	When I come tonight, we're gonna have peanut butter and jelly sandwich, uh, at dinner time.
Gay:	Uhmmm. Where're we going at dinner time?
Daniel:	Nowhere. But we're just gonna have dinner at 11 o'clock.
Gay:	Well, I made a plan of going out tonight.
Daniel:	We're going out.

(Nelson and Gruendel, 1979, p. 76)

Preschoolers quickly learn the format of a birthday party: you arrive, you play games, you have cake and ice cream. This format is an example of a script.

Katherine Nelson, one of the researchers who recorded this conversation, believes that such scripts can be learned either by firsthand experience or by observation of others. Meryl's "going shopping" script, seen in the story that precedes this chapter, was probably acquired by watching her mother and checkout clerks at the supermarket. Notice that a script only occasionally involves *specific* words or actions (such as singing "Happy Birthday"). More often, what is acquired is a *general* idea of the appropriate things to say and do, so learning a script involves something more complex than just memorizing exactly what one did or saw happen.

When young children communicate with adults instead of with peers, a knowledge of scripts is probably less essential. Usually the adult ensures that the dialogue progresses smoothly, that intended meanings are understood, and that confusions are clarified (Ellis and Rogoff, 1986). This is another example of the role of more knowledgeable others within the zone of proximal development. In peer interactions, in contrast, children must monitor and coordinate their own conversations. For preschoolers this can take substantial cognitive effort, so there are limits to the kinds of tasks they can do simultaneously. A shared understanding of the scripts for various activities can greatly facilitate communication.

The learning of such scripts steadily increases across the childhood years and with it the effectiveness of peer communications. Still, there remain substantial individual differences in children's skill at conveying their ideas and feelings to others, as well as in their skill at understanding what others are trying to say. These individual differences, which persist into adulthood, help explain differences in social acceptance or rejection.

AN OVERVIEW OF PRESCHOOL COGNITIVE DEVELOPMENT

Whereas infants know the world only through perception and direct action, toddlers make a major advance by becoming able to represent actions and events mentally. Toddlers can imagine something taking place without actually

In the summer of 1983 a bizarre story of child abuse on a vast scale began to unfold in Manhattan Beach, California. A mother accused a male teacher at the McMartin Preschool of sexually molesting her son. Seven months later authorities had enough evidence to indict not only the originally accused teacher, but six female teachers as well. Over the course of the legal proceedings, which lasted seven years, nearly 400 children who had attended the school were interviewed. The overwhelming majority—369—reported a range of sexual abuses by employees of the school, including genital fondling, oral sex, rape, sodomy, and being photographed nude. There were also reports of satanic rituals and animal mutilations, all said to have gone on while the children were on the premises (Sauer, 1993). Eventually, charges were dropped against five of the female teachers, and the sixth was later found not guilty. In two separate trials, juries became deadlocked on 12 counts of molestation against the male teacher. Many jurors said they found the credibility of the children suspect because of the suggestive ways they had been questioned.

This highly publicized case came down to the issue of the reliability of young children's memories. Were the young witnesses recalling events that had really happened to them, or were they recalling events that interviewers had put into their heads? Asking a leading question just once isn't usually enough to change a young child's memory (Saywitz et al., 1991). However, *repeatedly* asking suggestive questions *can* be influential, especially when the questioning occurs some time after the actual event.

This was shown in a study conducted by Stephen Ceci and his colleagues (Ceci, Leichtman, and White, in press). Preschool children witnessed a gamelike event and were questioned about it one month later by two interviewers, a preschool teacher and an experienced social worker. They were asked to use whatever strategies they thought would elicit accurate reports from the children. Before the questioning began, the interviewers were told some things that *might* have happened during the game, which they had not seen. Half the time this information was true and half the time it was false. Apparently, the interviewers used this information to form hypotheses about what had happened, and their hypotheses, in turn, influenced what they said during their interviews with the children, to the point that they sometimes got children to corroborate false information. When the interviewer was correctly informed at the outset, the children accurately reported 93 percent of the events from the game they had seen. But when the interviewer was incorrectly informed, 34 percent of the 3- and 4-year-olds and 18 percent of the 5- and 6-year-olds claimed to recall one or more pieces of false information.

This study makes two important points. First, adults who have a hypothesis about what a child experienced will sometimes make inadvertent suggestions when asking the child what happened. Reviewing some highly publicized cases, such as the McMartin Preschool case, Ceci found that adults who are interviewing a child often persist in pursuing their suspicions about the child's experiences, even when the child initially denies that the suspicions are correct (Ceci, in press). Second, when an interviewer persists in a line of questioning and repeatedly makes the same suggestions, a young child can be swayed to believe that the interviewer's perspective is accurate, even when it isn't. Older children and adults can be similarly swayed, but they are less susceptible to suggestions than preschoolers are (Ceci and Bruck, 1993).

Research on young children's susceptibility to suggestion has important policy implications. Adults must be extremely careful in how they interview child witnesses. When interviewers believe that the accused is probably guilty, they may convey that belief in their questions, and may eventually get children to corroborate their view, even when it is false. In addition, the more an interviewer persists in suggesting a certain sequence of events, the more credible and less hesitant the child's corroboration of it often becomes (Ceci, Leichtman, and White, in press). Frequently, too, adult interviewers praise young witnesses for reporting events consistent with their own beliefs and reprimand them for sticking to an alternative story. They may also tell young witnesses that other children have already corroborated the interviewer's suspicions, thereby creating additional pressure to go along with the interviewer's view (Ceci and Bruck, 1993). Stricter guidelines for interviewing child witnesses should be established to help prevent this kind of inappropriate questioning.

The susceptibility of preschoolers to repeated suggestions should not be taken to mean that their testimony is always suspect. In the right circumstances, they can give quite reliable testimony. Research shows that young children's testimony is most likely to be accurate when they are asked very specific, concrete questions that do not suggest a certain answer, and when the questions posed concern things that happened to their own bodies, rather than events they merely observed (Goodman, 1991). These findings are in keeping with the cognitive abilities of preschoolers. As you've learned, preschoolers are good at recalling specific events that happened to them, and also at understanding and responding to verbal requests, especially when the requests are clear and concrete

doing it. Preschoolers make additional strides toward mature thinking. First, preschoolers actively seek explanations for things. They understand that there are problems to be solved, which is why they are endlessly asking "why." Second, preschoolers evolve a number of skills for organizing information. They are beginning to understand that their thought processes are something that can be managed. These advances make preschoolers much more cognitively able than toddlers.

Still, preschoolers' repertoire of skills remains quite limited. Often they don't recognize the need for cognitive strategies such as aids for remembering, and they don't select well from the strategies they do have available. They don't seem to have the basic understanding that some ways of organizing information are better than others, especially for attacking particular problems, and they aren't skilled at evaluating the effectiveness of different approaches. Finally, they are still somewhat bound by the appearance of things, and they are prone to errors when appearance and reality are in conflict. All these limitations will be substantially overcome in middle childhood.

CHAPTER SUMMARY

1. Preschoolers provide an excellent example of children as active participants in their own development. Part of this participation involves actively constructing, understandings of things. Preschoolers search for general patterns in what they see and hear, and then they use these patterns as a basis for explaining and organizing their worlds. Preschoolers' thought is still quite immature, however, because of three cognitive limitations. The first is a tendency to equate superficial appearance with reality, called the **appearance-reality problem.** The second is a tendency to focus on only one piece of information at a time, referred to as **centration.** The third is a limited ability to manage their own attention and to direct their memory activities.

2. Preschoolers from different cultures exhibit similar kinds of errors or immaturities when explaining the causes of physical events, such as the movement of clouds. Preschoolers frequently focus on superficial appearance in constructing causes, or they make reference to a powerful being (God or Mommy or Daddy). However, if the event is something with which they are familiar, such as the movement of a bicycle, they sometimes provide more mature explanations. Even when they make errors, preschoolers are still remarkable for their active effort to interpret things and construct explanations.

3. Adults have many implicit understandings about the world, understandings that provide important conceptual tools. Some conceptual tools are quantitative, or related to questions of "how much." Among these tools are **concepts of conservation** (the understanding that certain quantities remain unchanged

despite various transformations carried out on them), as well as concepts of number and measurement. Other conceptual tools that preschoolers have not yet mastered include **classification,** the ability to group things systematically according to shared features; **seriation,** the ability to arrange things in a logical progression; and **transitive inference,** the ability to infer the relationship between two things by knowing their respective relationships to a third thing. The precursors of these skills may be present by 4 years of age, although they do not fully develop until middle childhood.

4. Preschoolers have difficulty paying **selective attention** to stimuli. They scan less systematically and are more distracted by irrelevant information. Improvement in maintaining focused attention is seen during the preschool years. Older preschoolers are just beginning to exhibit more active control over their own attention.

5. Preschoolers do not remember information as well as older children or adults do. One explanation for this limitation is that they are often less familiar with the information to be remembered, and hence find it more difficult. Another is that they usually lack strategies to improve their memories. However, under optimal circumstances, preschoolers show an intent to remember and can engage in activities that increase the likelihood that they will remember. Thus, if adults structure the memory situation properly and provide guidance, preschoolers' performance appears much more mature. This improved memory performance illustrates Vygotsky's concept of the **zone of proximal development,** that area of

performance just barely within the child's potential, which can be realized with proper support.

6. A person's understanding of the social world is often called **social cognition.** Social cognition is based on having some understanding of the human mind as an agent of thought, feeling, and perception, and as a controller of speech and behavior. Young children acquire such an understanding through their social experiences. By the end of the preschool period they have quite a well-developed **theory of mind.**

7. **Egocentrism,** the failure to differentiate the perspective of others from one's own point of view, appears at all developmental levels, but it is particularly pervasive and apparent during the preschool years. Preschoolers show egocentrism when they try to assess other people's perceptions, knowledge, feelings, and wishes. Flavell has identified three cognitive factors needed to overcome egocentric thought. First, children must develop a simple knowledge that other people have motivations and viewpoints different from their own. Second, they must realize that considering another person's perspective can be very useful for effective communica-

tion. Third, children must gradually gain skill at *social inference,* the ability to interpret other people's thoughts and feelings.

8. The preschooler's progress in communicating with others is part of a general decline in egocentrism. During the preschool years children begin to show some ability to adjust their speech in accordance with a listener's needs. Such adjustments require cognitive effort, however, so when performing a task that is very difficult, young children often lapse into egocentric speech. It is as if the difficulty of the task uses all their cognitive resources, leaving nothing for them to use in determining an appropriate form or level of speech.

9. Older children are better able to combine the performance of difficult tasks with effective communication, partly because of the greater number of cognitive scripts they possess. A **script** is an abstract representation of the sequence of actions involved in accomplishing some goal. With a script in mind, it becomes less cognitively demanding to go through the steps in performing a task, so that some cognitive capacity is left for monitoring the effectiveness of one's speech.

Chapter 10

Social and Emotional Development in Early Childhood

Five-year-old Mikey stands in line with 20 other kindergarten children, just ahead of Richie and Jeff, two of his neighborhood friends. Although the three boys are eager to be out on the playground, they wait for the teacher to swing open the large exit door. Then, without any pushing, they walk out quietly, though quickly, with the class. Once outside in the bright October sunshine, however, their self-restraint breaks down. Shouting with glee, they race toward the play equipment. "Hey! It's a boat!" Mikey calls out, pointing to a large climbing apparatus in the center of a sand-filled area. The structure, made of wood, ropes, and old car tires, looks nothing like a boat, but its placement in the middle of the sandlot inspires the boys' imaginations. "C'mon! Let's climb on!" Mikey urges, and the other two scramble up behind him. There they play joyously for a time, taking turns being captain at the "wheel." Just when their excitement has begun to subside, Richie yells in mock alarm: "Oh, no! We're sinkin'! Swim for it!" With that, he jumps into the sand and begins flailing his arms and legs. Laughing and shouting, the others jump off too, and the trio makes its way to "shore."

T his episode, drawn from a detailed observational study of preschool behavior (Sroufe et al., 1984), illustrates much about the social achievements of early childhood. First, Mikey and his friends demonstrate that children between the ages of 2½ and 5 experience a dramatically *expanding world*. Day care, nursery school, and kindergarten take them increasingly away from home and parents. In these new settings young children are propelled by a natural curiosity to explore. No one has to tell Mikey and his friends to play in the sandlot. The motivation and ideas for their activities come from themselves. Notice too how the boys' world is enlarged by their rich interactions with one another. Early childhood is the age when true peer relationships emerge. This capacity for relationships with peers will expand and become more elaborate throughout childhood.

Second, the example of Mikey and his friends illustrates that early childhood is a time of notable developments in *self-control and self-regulation*. In Western societies, it is rare for a large group of toddlers to form a line and wait patiently for a teacher to usher them outdoors. Yet just a few years later children are routinely expected to tolerate minor delays and frustrations. They are also expected to control aggressive impulses, such as pushing, shoving, and hitting. These new expectations have significant effects on children's developing self-concepts. Whether Mikey thinks of himself as capable or incapable, kind or mean, stems in part from how he meets adults' demands for self-regulation.

Third, our opening example shows that during early childhood youngsters begin to *explore adult roles*. Mikey and his friends take turns being captain of a ship, a role they have heard about in stories and seen on television. This exploration of roles takes place during play, especially social fantasy play. Typically preschoolers try out the roles of adults they are close to or see often: mother, father, teacher, grocery store clerk, policeman, and so forth. When children not only mimic adults but also strive to be like them in feelings and values, developmentalists say the children are *identifying* with the grownups.

A fourth social achievement of early childhood, not explicitly illustrated in our opening example, is a growing independence and self-reliance relative to parents, coupled with a greater capacity to be connected to peers. These con-

The preschooler's curiosity is boundless.

trasting trends of *greater independence* and *an expanding connectedness to others* is a theme throughout development (C. Cooper, in press; Shantz and Hobart, 1989). We saw it in infancy when children actively started to create their own effects (thus behaving more independently), while at the same time they developed attachment relationships with their primary caregivers. Now, in the preschool period, children are moving away from total reliance on parents, yet are becoming close to them in a new way through identification, and are becoming more actively involved with peers.

This chapter explores these and other social and emotional changes that occur in early childhood. We begin with a closer look at some of the hallmarks of early childhood development that we just introduced: the child's expanding world, the move toward greater independence, and the emergence of self-control and self-management. We then turn to other areas of development that are important in the preschool years, including young children's sense of self, their peer relationships, their emotions, their play, and the influences of their parents.

A major theme for the entire chapter is the organization and coherence of preschooler behavior. The various emerging capacities we will describe fit together and support one another. For example, the capacity for play supports the capacity for early peer relationships, and vice versa. At the same time, the behavior of individual children becomes increasingly coherent and distinctive; they manifest characteristic styles of responding and pervasive expectations concerning themselves and others. It is no exaggeration to say that by 5 years of age a personality has formed.

SOME HALLMARKS OF EARLY CHILDHOOD SOCIAL AND EMOTIONAL DEVELOPMENT

THE CHILD'S EXPANDING WORLD

One of the major changes of early childhood is expansion of the child's world. Part of this expansion comes through attending school—often a nursery school first, and then kindergarten. Experiences at school and in day care can be extremely important. For example, a young child's general adjustment, competence with peers, and complexity of play have all been found to be related to the quality of day care and relationships with teachers (e.g., Howes and Matheson, 1992; Howes et al., 1994; Pianta and Steinberg, 1992).

Peers also exert an increasing influence during the preschool years. Peer relationships become a central arena for developing and expressing certain new capacities, such as an understanding of fairness and reciprocity (mutual give-and-take). So important are peer relationships that we will devote an entire major section of this chapter to them.

Siblings relationships, too, become increasingly important. Like parents, older siblings can provide a unique framework within which the preschooler's development takes place. For instance, young preschoolers can engage in joint fantasy play with a nurturant older sibling in a way they cannot do with their mothers (Dunn, 1985). They also listen carefully to conversations between their mothers and older siblings, as shown by the fact that their interruptions are much more often relevant to what is being said than are the interruptions of 2-year-olds (Dunn and Shatz, 1989). Thus, some of what children learn from siblings is acquired indirectly by watching and listening to them interacting with others. We will discuss sibling relationships more extensively in Chapter 12.

All these new arenas of development that emerge during the preschool years influence one another. Experiences with preschool teachers, for example, influence peer relationships, as do the skills and understandings developed in relating to siblings. At the same time, successful peer relationships can promote better relationships with siblings (Kramer and Gottman, 1992), and tend to elicit more positive responses from teachers.

MOVING TOWARD GREATER SELF-RELIANCE

Accompanying the preschooler's entry into a broader world is the development of greater self-reliance. All developmental theorists see this as an important achievement. Psychoanalytic theorists emphasize the child's sense of independence, what Erikson (1963) calls **initiative.** Social learning theorists, such as Albert Bandura (1986), emphasize the child's growing **self-efficacy,** or sense of being able to do things. Bandura sees self-efficacy as resulting from repeated experiences of mastery.

Greater self-reliance is supported by a number of capacities that 3- and 4-year-olds possess. First, children this age have motor skills like climbing and manipulating objects that allow them to do many things for themselves. Second, preschoolers have language and other cognitive abilities that enable them to think and plan in ways they could not do as toddlers. These abilities promote the solving of problems that would have baffled the child just a year or two earlier. Third, problem-solving skills are further aided by a growing ability to tolerate delays and frustrations. Compared with toddlers, preschoolers are much better able to stick to a task despite obstacles and setbacks. Finally, an emerging capacity for imagination and fantasy play allows preschoolers to maintain a sense of power in a world generally controlled by adults. This sense of power is an important psychological foundation for strivings toward independence.

Some children, however, have trouble moving toward greater independence. They may hover near teachers or require a great deal of encouragement in order to meet simple challenges (Sroufe, Fox, and Pancake, 1983). For them,

Initiative:
Erik Erikson's term for a child's sense of purposefulness and effectiveness.

Self-efficacy:
A child's sense of being able to do things effectively on his or her own.

Some children need a great deal of support from and contact with their preschool teachers.

infantile dependency is hard to leave behind. We see this problem in Meryl as a 3-year-old when she tries to cling to Karen in everyday situations. Meryl is showing not just **instrumental dependency** (seeking help from adults when trying to do something that is beyond her current capacities); she is also showing **emotional dependency** (frequently demanding physical contact or reassurance from adults) (Sears, Maccoby, and Levin, 1957). Emotionally dependent children need such contact not just when they are upset, but virtually all the time. We will discuss the origins of such problems in a later section.

Instrumental dependency: A child's normal need for adults to help in solving complex problems or performing difficult tasks.

Emotional dependency: A type of overdependency in which the child needs continual reassurance and attention from adults in order to function.

SELF-CONTROL AND SELF-REGULATION

Frank Gordon is organizing a race between 2-year-old Mikey and his playmates Richie and Jeff. The children are to run across the yard, touch the trunk of the big oak tree, and then run back to the starting line. Frank gives the signals "Ready . . . get set . . ." But before he can say, "go," Mikey bolts off toward the oak tree, and the other two boys quickly follow.

It takes Frank five recalls before he can get all three boys to wait until they hear the word "go." Are they just not listening to his instructions, or are they really having trouble following them?

A developmental psychologist could tell the greatly exasperated Frank that the second explanation is correct. The ability to inhibit a physical action until given a signal to proceed is something that emerges gradually during the preschool years (Fuson, 1979). The Soviet psychologist A. R. Luria (1961) studied this ability in children ages 2 through 4. When a green light came on, the children were to press a rubber bulb held in one hand, and when a red light came on, they were not to press. The 2-year-olds made many mistakes, pressing away for red lights as well as for greens. Not until age 4 could most children reliably inhibit a response to the "wrong" color. And it is not just that 4-year-olds understand the instructions better (Miller, Shelton, and Flavell, 1970). The

2-year-olds realize that they are not supposed to press on red, but somehow they just can't stop themselves. The ability to inhibit an action until a "go" signal is given is just one aspect of a larger ability to monitor and direct one's own behavior—that is, to exert some self-control and self-regulation. This larger ability is another major development of the preschool period (Kopp, 1992).

Psychologist Eleanor Maccoby (1980) has listed some other signs of self-control and self-management that emerge by the end of the preschool period. Many of these involve the ability to reflect on one's own actions—that is, to monitor those actions and direct them as needed. Most also involve the abilities to inhibit actions, delay gratification (wait for rewards), tolerate frustration, and adjust behavior to suit situational demands. Maccoby's list includes the following:

1. Older preschoolers are able to weigh future consequences heavily when deciding how to act.
2. Older preschoolers are able to stop and think of possible ways around an obstacle that is blocking a goal.
3. Older preschoolers are better able to control emotions when goal-directed activities are blocked, thus greatly decreasing the likelihood of tantrums.
4. Older preschoolers are better able to concentrate—that is, to block out irrelevant thoughts, sights, and sounds and to focus instead on what is needed to reach a desired objective.
5. Older preschoolers are able to do more than one thing at a time, as long as those things are not incompatible or highly complex.

These abilities are not *fully* developed by the end of the preschool period; further advances will occur later. Nevertheless, the preschool years are a time of great progress in exercising management and control over the self. We will return to the topic of control over the self when we discuss emotional regulation.

THE DEVELOPING SELF

The cognitive advances of the preschool period have a profound effect on the development of a child's sense of self. It is during this time that children start to be able to observe and be aware of themselves as persons (Eder and Mangelsdorf, in press). They know that minds exist, that they have a mind, and that they are a particular person. Partly because of their new capacity for thinking about categories and collections (discussed in Chapter 9), they see themselves as boys or girls—as being like one parent in gender and unlike the other. In this section we will discuss these and other changes in self-understanding that occur during the preschool period.

CHANGES IN SELF-UNDERSTANDING

Late in the toddler period a child becomes able to represent the self mentally—that is, to "know" that he or she exists. But this mental representation involves *immediate* experiences, one at a time (I am eating an apple, I am sitting on the swing, I am walking up the stairs, and so forth) (Fischer, Shaver, and Carnochan, 1990). Not until the preschool period do cognitive advances enable the child to represent a variety of different experiences and *alternate* among them. A preschooler can mentally move back and forth among particular experiences, between particular experiences and more general ones (getting ready for bed last night versus what bedtime is like in general), and between past and present. This ability to represent alternative experiences can also be seen in fantasy play. In the following example, a preschooler, J., is playing with several figures in a doll's house (Wolf, 1990, p. 24):

> "He has to go upstairs, Mommy."
> Then, to the Mommy doll, "Watch, Mommy."
> (J. releases the figure so it falls down the steps.)
> "He fell down, Mommy. He's crying, Mommy. He's a boo boo on his head."
> (J. makes crying sound effects for the figure.)
> "Ouch, ouch, I hurt my head."

This ability to move mentally back and forth among different experiences makes for a much more comprehensive sense of self (Fischer, Shaver and Carnochan, 1990; Wolf, 1990).

Dennie Wolf (1990) has described another capacity that underlies preschoolers' expanding sense of self. Children can now "uncouple" various aspects of experience. They can, for example, pretend and at the same time *observe* themselves pretending. Similarly, they can look at themselves in a mirror and know "that is me," while at the same time being aware that "I am watching myself." This capacity makes the sense of self significantly more mature.

But the preschooler's sense of self is still limited. Children this age have trouble understanding that they are the same person when they feel different in different situations (such as nice in one situation and mean in another) (Fischer, et al., 1990). They cannot coordinate such disparate experiences into a unified sense of self (Eder and Mangelsdorf, in press). Simultaneous understanding of different aspects of the self, understanding the selves of others, and self-reflection must all await later childhood and adolescence.

SELF-CONSTANCY AND SELF-ESTEEM

By internalizing parents' rules, challenging those rules (and feeling guilty), and then once again achieving harmony with parents, preschoolers experience what Louis Sander (1975) calls a sense of **self-constancy.** This is a sense that the self endures despite temporary disruptions in relationships.

To understand the emergence of a sense of self-constancy, picture Malcolm, who has just turned 3. He is eyeing the cords of the window blinds, which he loves to play with but is forbidden to. DeeDee, who is cleaning a nearby closet, glances over at him. Malcolm is aware not only of his own intention to pull on the cords, but also of his mother's knowledge of that intention. Such awareness enables Malcolm to deliberately upset the relationship with DeeDee by doing what he *knows* is counter to her wishes. In this case he reaches for the cords and begins to pull them vigorously, knowing full well that his mother sees his actions as both bad and deliberate (Emde and Buchsbaum, 1990; Kochanska, 1993). "Malcolm!" says DeeDee sharply. "Stop that right now!" This response is just what Malcolm expected. Malcolm also understands that the self who has just done wrong and who is being scolded is the same self who a moment before was in harmony with DeeDee. Equally important, Malcolm knows that he can rein-

Self-constancy:
A sense that the self endures despite temporary disruptions in relationships.

state the former harmony by "making up" with his mother—for example, by saying he is sorry. This is an early form of the concept of "reversibility," discussed in Chapter 9—an understanding that the effects of a transformation can later be undone. A 3-year-old can engage in such advanced thinking only in well-practiced, concrete situations. Nevertheless, the ability to do so is very important. It allows Malcolm to understand the continuity of his self in relation to his mother.

Preschoolers like Malcolm also start to think of themselves as having dispositions—ways of being—that are consistent through time (Eder and Mangelsdorf, in press). Although all children acquire this ability, not all come to think of the self in exactly the same way. Each child develops a particular view of the self based on his or her unique experiences. Among young children, most (but not all) think of the self as good and kind and likeable, and as competent and effective in the world. These positive thoughts and feelings about the self are referred to as **self-esteem** (Coopersmith, 1967). One of our earlier stories about Malcolm suggested that at age 4 he had high self-esteem, or at least a high evaluation of his own physical abilities. ("I'm the best!" he tells his father about his basketball skills.) Such favorable self-evaluations probably stem from a history of positive exchanges with others, especially with caregivers. When adults communicate warmth, empathy, and positive regard for a child, they encourage high self-esteem (Sroufe, 1990). We will say more about the development of positive self attitudes in Chapter 12.

Self-esteem:
The view of the self as good and capable and likable.

GENDER AND THE SELF

Gender is a central organizing theme in development. It plays a key role in the way people define and experience their worlds. In all societies, parents and others treat boys and girls differently and expect different things from them (Whiting and Edwards, 1988). Because of this, children learn cultural stereotypes regarding male and female behaviors and characteristics. This learning begins early and is pervasive. It manifests itself in children's activities, preferences, and social styles (Bem, 1989; Fagot et al., 1992; Lobel and Menashri, 1993; Serbin et al., 1993). Even among preschoolers, gender is so salient that a child's most advanced thinking is often applied to it. Preschoolers label and categorize different activities in terms of gender (Fagot et al., 1992); they remember modeled

In the psychoanalytic view, a child "identifies" with the parent of the same gender, striving to be like him or her. This would be one mechanism promoting the development of sex-typed behavior.

behaviors better when they are "gender-appropriate" (Bauer, 1993); and in general they use gender as a basis for organizing information (Serbin et al., 1993).

Gender is a key aspect of the preschooler's emerging self-concept. Being a boy or a girl is central to the definition of the self. Development of a gender-based self-concept involves three steps. First, children gradually adopt **sex-typed behavior**—actions that conform to cultural expectations regarding what is appropriate for boys or for girls. Second, children simultaneously acquire a **gender-role concept**—a beginning knowledge of the cultural stereotypes regarding males and females. Finally, children develop an emotional commitment to their particular gender. This commitment is part of the process of identification with parents that we will discuss later in this chapter. Right now, let's consider sex-typed behavior and the development of a gender-role concept among preschoolers in more detail.

Sex-typed behavior: Actions that conform to cultural expectations about what is appropriate for boys or for girls.

Gender-role concept: Knowledge of the cultural stereotypes regarding males and females.

CHANGES IN SEX-TYPED BEHAVIOR

The development of sex-typed behavior occurs in a series of phases. By the age of 2, children are already showing gender-related preferences in toys. Boys have learned to play largely with trucks and cars, while girls have learned to gravitate toward soft, cuddly toys (Caldera et al., 1989; Serbin et al., 1993). Such early learning is probably the result of imitation and reinforcement. These early preferences are not absolute, however, as we illustrated in our story of Mikey, who at age 2 became very attached to a Raggedy Ann doll. At this young age, children in all cultures have only a limited understanding of gender-related behaviors. Although they have learned that certain objects go with mommies or daddies (lipsticks versus neckties, for example), they do not yet understand the broader categories of gender, nor do they know that they share a gender with one of their parents.

By age 3 or 4, children know a great deal more about "gender-appropriate" objects and activities, and they also show much more sex-typed behavior (Serbin et al., 1993). Boys in nursery school classes engage in more rough-and-tumble play than girls do, often despite teachers' protests (DiPietro, 1981). Preschool girls around the world show more interest in and nurturance toward babies than do their male peers (Whiting and Edwards, 1988). Preschool girls also prefer to play with one other child at a time, in contrast to boys' preference for group activities (Beneson, 1993).

Studies of how sex-typed behavior is learned in the United States show that it pervades our society. Even when their children are babies, most American parents dress boys and girls in different clothing, decorate their rooms differently, give them different playthings, and interact with them differently (Fagot et al., 1992). Parents encourage sex-typed play beginning in the toddler period by reacting more positively when toddlers play with "gender-appropriate" toys (Caldera et al., 1989). Differential treatment of boys and girls increases during the preschool years (Maccoby, 1990). If children behave in gender-inconsistent ways, parents and peers are often quick to give negative feedback.

Judith Langlois illustrated this by getting preschoolers to play with "gender-inappropriate" toys and then inviting in the mother, father, or peers to watch (Langlois and Downs, 1980). Although mothers were often accepting of the "cross-gender" play, fathers and peers were not. Fathers had the strongest negative reactions, especially to the sight of their sons playing with "feminine" toys. Just as Frank encouraged Mikey to shun girls' toys in our story, so other preschoolers are channeled into sex-typed behaviors.

Sex-typed behavior—that is, behavior the culture prescribes for one gender or the other— becomes very common by the preschool period.

DEVELOPING A GENDER-ROLE CONCEPT

By age 4 or 5, children also start to learn more abstract cultural beliefs about gender differences (Bem, 1989; Serbin et al., 1993); that is, they begin to acquire gender-role concepts. Learning gender-role concepts is based partly on cognitive maturation, and partly on having had countless experiences of being told and shown what is considered appropriate for boys or for girls. From these countless experiences young children begin to abstract more generalized ideas about gender.

Gender-role concepts are well ingrained in adults. In our society, as in many others, males are viewed as more aggressive, competitive, self-confident, and ambitious, while females are seen as more emotional, kind, interpersonally sensitive, and domestic (Ruble, 1988). (A more complete list of gender stereotypes is given in Table 10.1). These gender stereotypes can be summed up by saying that the male role is *instrumental* (men are viewed as geared to getting things done), while the female role is *expressive* (women's lives are seen as revolving around feelings). Preschoolers, of course, have only sketchy understandings of gender stereotypes. Not until middle childhood will they fully incorporate into their beliefs our culture's set of stereotypically "masculine" and "feminine" characteristics (Serbin et al., 1993). Nevertheless, preschoolers do have a well-developed knowledge of concrete aspects of gender roles, such as occupations and activities, and they are becoming aware that males and females are widely viewed as different in their overall styles of behavior.

The marked increase in sex-typed behavior and growing understanding of gender differences that occur during the preschool period help encourage a rather strict gender segregation in the classroom and on the playground (Maccoby, 1990; Serbin et al., 1993). The fact that we see Mikey, Malcolm, and Meryl playing with other children of their own gender is no accident. Children this age know that they are boys or girls, they know that these are categories of people, and they see themselves as members of one category or the other (Levy and

Carter, 1989; Serbin et al., 1993). The preference for interacting with others of one's own gender increases still further during middle childhood.

Striking evidence that a sense of gender emerges during the preschool period comes from studies of children whose genitals were ambiguously formed at birth (Money, 1975). Such children are sometimes assigned to the wrong gender; that is, baby boys are mistakenly identified as girls, and baby girls are mistakenly thought to be boys. If the error is discovered before age 2½ and the child from then on is raised as the biologically correct sex, problems rarely arise. The toddler accepts the new sexual identity with little distress or resistance. However, reassignment to the other sex tends to be very hard for the child if made after toddlerhood. Such children may grow up still thinking of themselves as belonging to their "original" gender. Thus, there seems to be a sensitive period for beginning to develop a sense of gender.

UNDERSTANDING GENDER CONSTANCY

One important aspect of children's developing sense of gender is an understanding of **gender constancy**—the fact that gender is permanent despite changes in age, in dress or hairstyle, or in behavior (Bem, 1989; Emmerich et al., 1977). Three-year-olds know that they are boys or girls, and they know the things usually associated with their gender, but they may still be unsure whether changes in superficial characteristics (such as boys wearing dresses and playing with dolls or girls cutting their hair short and playing with footballs) can produce a change in gender. This uncertainty is related to the appearance-reality distinction discussed in Chapter 9.

Gender constancy: The understanding that gender is permanent despite changes in age, in dress or hairstyle, or in behavior.

TABLE 10.1

SOME CHARACTERISTICS REGARDED AS STEREOTYPICALLY MASCULINE AND FEMININE BY COLLEGE STUDENTS IN THE 1980S

Masculine Characteristics	Feminine Characteristics
Independent	Emotional
Aggressive	Home-oriented
Skilled in business	Kind
Mechanical aptitude	Cries easily
Outspoken	Creative
Acts as a leader	Considerate
Self-confident	Devotes self to others
Takes a stand	Needs approval
Ambitious	Gentle
Not easily influenced	Aware of others' feelings
Dominant	Excitable in a major crisis
Active	Expresses tender feelings
Makes decisions easily	Enjoys art and music
Doesn't give up easily	Tactful
Stands up under pressure	Feelings hurt
Likes math and science	Neat
Competitive	Likes children
Adventurous	Understanding

SOURCE: Ruble, 1983.

The earliest age at which children show an understanding of gender constancy depends on how it is assessed. For example, when researchers made gender-inappropriate changes in hairstyle and dress to a drawing of a boy or a girl, and then asked preschoolers, "If the child did this would he (or she) still be a boy (or a girl)?" very few said that gender remained the same despite these changes in appearance (Emmerich et al., 1977). But it is possible that the children assumed that because these were just drawings, the experimenter could change the figure's gender at will. Sandra Bem (1989) designed a study to see if preschoolers would make the same error regarding real children. She showed them photographs of actual male and female toddlers, first nude with sexual anatomy visible, then dressed in clothing considered appropriate for the other sex. Almost half the 3- to 5-year-olds and more than half the girls knew that the child's gender remained unchanged even when dress changed. Moreover, among those who knew the difference between male and female genitals, 74 percent passed the gender constancy test. Similarly, when preschoolers are asked whether they themselves would change gender if they changed their style of dress, virtually none say yes (Martin and Halverson, 1983).

An understanding of gender constancy is related to the concepts of conservation discussed in Chapters 9 and 11. The child grasps that gender remains the same despite superficial transformations (changes in hairstyle and dress). The fact that a grasp of gender constancy may begin to emerge before an understanding of other conservation concepts suggests the great importance of gender to young children.

EXPLAINING SEX-TYPED BEHAVIOR AND GENDER-ROLE DEVELOPMENT

Social learning theorists explain sex-typed behavior and gender-role development partly in terms of the rewards and punishments that children experience for "appropriate" and "inappropriate" behavior. In contrast, cognitive theorists see gender-role learning as but one example of the child's emerging understanding of collections, categories, scripts, and schemas. When children grasp the categories male and female and learn something about the objects and activities associated with each one, they begin to apply this knowledge to themselves as a member of one category or the other. A third perspective, **gender schema theory,** brings together these two positions (Serbin et al., 1993). It argues that all children form a concept of gender that affects their attitudes and behaviors, but the particular meaning of gender to a given child is based on that child's social learning history.

A fourth perspective on sex-typed behavior and gender-role development is psychoanalytic theory, which emphasizes developmental changes in relationships with parents. In striving to be like the parent of the same gender, a child will adopt that parent's behaviors, attitudes, and values. Note that this theory has cognitive elements because it involves children recognizing a similarity in gender between themselves and one of their parents and then abstracting out the essential features that help define that parent as a man or a woman.

In a variation of psychoanalytic theory, Nancy Chodorow (1989) has argued that boys define their masculinity through contrasting themselves with their mothers, whereas girls define their femininity in terms of similarities with their mothers. Chodorow's theory is based on the Freudian assumption that both boys and girls begin by having the strongest relationship with their mothers. A boy then separates from his mother in terms of identification, emphasizing the differences between them, whereas a girl stresses how she and her mother are

Gender schema theory: The theory that a child's concept of gender is shaped both by emerging abilities to abstract general rules about what is male and female and by direct reinforcement and social modeling.

alike, thus connecting with her mother in new ways. The result, in Chodorow's view, is that boys define themselves in terms of separateness, understand people in terms of their different interests, and show a more emphatic individuation (or sense of being a unique person). Girls, in contrast, define themselves in terms of connectedness, see people in terms of their similarities, and have a stronger capacity for sensing the feelings of others.

SOCIAL DEVELOPMENT: THE NEW WORLD OF PEERS

Peers are of great interest even to toddlers, as we discussed in Chapter 8. Often by age 2 children show the rudiments of social turn-taking (Garvey, 1977; Howes, 1988; Mueller and Lucas, 1975). They speak to or show something to another child, wait for a response, and then repeat the cycle. Most of this early turn-taking, however, centers on objects, and only sometimes do the toddlers really respond to each other's specific intentions (Bronson, 1981). Not until the preschool period, with children's growing mastery of language, do their peer interactions become sustained and highly coordinated (Brownell, 1990; Hartup, 1992).

Two illustrations vividly contrast peer interactions between toddlers and between preschoolers. The first is a "conversation" between two boys, 13 and 15 months of age (Mueller and Lucas, 1975). Bernie, the younger, initiates the exchange by turning and looking at Larry, who has been watching him while mouthing a toy. Bernie then "speaks" to Larry.

Bernie: Da . . . Da.
 Larry: (Laughs very slightly as he continues to look.)
Bernie: Da.
 Larry: (Laughs more heartily this time.)

The same sequence of Bernie saying "da" and Larry responding with laughter is repeated five more times. Then Larry looks away and offers an adult a toy. Bernie pursues him.

Bernie: (Waving both hands and looking directly at Larry.) Da!
 Larry: (Looks back at Bernie and laughs again.)

The sequence of "da" followed by laughter is repeated nine more times. Finally, Bernie turns away abruptly and toddles off. Larry laughs once more in a forced manner and then silently watches Bernie depart. (p. 241)

A second conversation is between a boy and a girl, both 5 years old (Garvey, 1977). The boy is testing the girl's competence, and the girl is rising to the challenge.

Boy: Can you carry this? (Shows girl a toy fish.)
Girl: Yeah, if I weighed 50 pounds.
Boy: You can't even carry it. Can you carry it by the string?
Girl: Yeah. Yes I can. (Lifts fish overhead by string.)
Boy: Can you carry it by the nose?
Girl: Where's the nose?
Boy: That yellow one.
Girl: This? (Carries it by the nose.)
Boy: Can you carry it by its tail?

Girl: Yeah. (Carries it by tail.).
Boy: Can you carry it like this? (Shows how to carry it by fin.)
Girl: (Carries it by fin.) I weigh 50 pounds about, right?
Boy: Right. (p. 59)

Although Bernie and Larry are socially competent for toddlers (perhaps because they are longtime acquaintances), there is a world of difference between their interaction and that of the 5-year-olds. The 5-year-olds can share a fantasy, make up rules for a game, respond to each other's questions, demonstrate novel procedures, and in general coordinate their behaviors in ways far beyond the abilities of any pair of 1-year-olds.

COMPETENCE WITH PEERS

Successful entry into a peer group and effectiveness or competence with peers are complex matters. They cannot be gauged just by measuring the amount of contact that a child has with other children. If a child's contacts are mostly aggressive or consistently asymmetrical (with the child always in the role of follower), even a large number of contacts doesn't imply social competence. Conversely, sometimes playing alone doesn't mean lack of social competence. Playing alone is different from "being alone" (hovering near the group but being unable to join in) (Coplan et al., 1994). Even children rated socially competent by their teachers or who are popular with peers will at times play by themselves in group settings.

A convergence of measures is generally needed to gauge a child's competence with peers. Detailed observational studies show that the child who engages and responds to peers with positive feelings, who is of interest to them and whom they highly regard, who can take the lead as well as follow, and who is able to sustain the give-and-take of peer interaction will be judged by teachers and other observers as having **social competence** (Vaughn and Waters, 1980). These various measures of social competence are usually in agreement, which is

Social competence:
A child's ability to engage and respond to peers with positive feelings, to be of interest to peers and be highly regarded by them, to take the lead as well as follow, and to sustain the give-and-take of peer interaction.

Genuine peer relationships emerge in the preschool period, marked by coordinated play, beginning social preferences, and even early signs of friendship.

not surprising because they tend to foster one another (Black and Hazen, 1990; Howes, 1990; Sroufe et al., 1984). For example, when children engage peers in positive ways, they are better liked, and that popularity can encourage additional positive behaviors that keep attracting peers (Denham and Holt, 1993).

Our chapter-opening example illustrated the socially competent preschooler, especially the positive emotions that such a child expresses toward peers. Mikey conveyed his excitement about seeing the play apparatus in the sandlot through his tone of voice, his body posture, and his facial expression. If he had suggested the boat idea in a flat, matter-of-fact way, the other two boys might have ignored it. But Mikey's enthusiastic "Hey! It's a boat!" brought the other two running. His enthusiasm captured their interest and was contagious. This ability to have fun and to share that fun with others is one reason such a child is popular with peers (Sroufe et al., 1984).

A research technique called **sociometrics** not only reveals socially competent children like Mikey, but also reveals two kinds of children who are socially incompetent (Asher and Parker, 1989). The sociometric technique involves asking children to name others that they especially like or don't like having as play partners. Some children—the socially competent ones—are frequently named as liked. Others—those who are consistently named as disliked—are characterized by the researchers as *rejected* (Rubin et al., 1990). Rejected children are often viewed (by peers, teachers, and other observers) as aggressive or mean. Still other children are rarely named as either liked or disliked. These children—who seem to be of little interest to peers—are characterized by the researchers as *neglected* (Asher and Parker, 1989; Coie, 1985, Rubin et al., 1990). Neglected children tend to be not only ineffective with peers but also dependent on teachers. Generally, however, they are not hostile (Sroufe, 1983). A subgroup of these children, who are submissive and low in assertiveness, are likely to become the chronic victims of aggressive children (Schwartz, Dodge, and Coie, 1993). The distinctions among accepted, rejected, and neglected children are very powerful, predicting later social behavior in important ways, as we'll discuss in Chapter 12 (Asher and Parker, 1989; Hartup, 1992).

Sociometrics:
A research technique in which children's judgments of one another are used to determine popularity.

EARLY FRIENDSHIPS

Preschoolers not only prefer certain other children to play with; interviews and detailed observational studies have shown that they form partnerships with one another that may last for a year or more (Howes, 1988; Park et al., 1993). These early peer relationships may endure partly because adults promote them and partly because the children involved are continually in contact with each other at day care or preschool. Nevertheless, by age 4 or so, children have considerable capacity to maintain friendships through their own efforts (Gottman, 1983; Hartup, 1992).

Young friends behave differently with each other than they do with nonfriends (Hartup, 1992; Hartup and Laursen, 1993). They have more frequent positive exchanges and are more cooperative in problem-solving tasks. When placed in experimental conflict situations—with, for example, each partner being told a different set of rules for a game—friends also disagree with each other more often than mere acquaintances do. However, these conflicts are less heated, result in fairer solutions, and do not cause the children to separate. Preschool friends are clearly motivated to maintain their relationship. Being able to continue a relationship despite conflicts offers important oppor-

Being a peer leader involves more than being the biggest and strongest. Leaders know things that are fun to do, and they have a contagious enthusiasm.

tunities to learn how to be together (Hartup and Laursen, 1993). The sharing that young friends do may also mark the beginnings of learning about justice (Damon, 1988), a topic we will return to when we discuss friendship in Chapter 12.

THE IMPORTANCE OF PEER RELATIONSHIPS

Early relationships with peers are important for several reasons. As we mentioned in Chapter 2, the peer group is a major setting for learning about the concepts of fairness, reciprocity, and cooperation. It is also a critical setting for learning to manage interpersonal aggression (Hartup, 1983), as the episode in which Malcolm hit April illustrated. In peer groups, too, children learn a great deal about cultural norms and values, such as gender roles. Finally, experiences within the peer group—whether positive or negative—can greatly affect a child's self-concept and future dealings with others. Perhaps for this reason, how well a child gets along with peers is one of the strongest predictors of later success. It is related to levels of adjustment, psychological problems, and even school achievement (e.g., Asher and Parker, 1989; Teo et al., in press).

Increased peer interactions can sometimes help children overcome developmental problems. For instance, when socially withdrawn preschoolers were given the opportunity to interact one-on-one with somewhat younger children in a series of special play sessions, they became more outgoing in their regular classrooms (Furman, Rahe, and Hartup, 1979). Having the chance to interact successfully with a peer seemed to enhance both social skills and confidence concerning peer relations. Interacting with a more competent, but tolerant, same-age peer (or even an older sibling) would also be expected to enhance social competence. Another remedial approach, effective to some extent, is directly teaching socially isolated children interaction skills (Mize and Ladd, 1990).

EMOTIONAL DEVELOPMENT

Since different areas of development are all interrelated, it is not surprising that emotional changes during the preschool years are as dramatic as cognitive and social ones. These emotional changes include a growing understanding of emotions and their causes, a rapidly expanding capacity for regulating emotional experiences (part of a general increase in self-regulation), and the further development of what have been called the "self-evaluative" emotions (Eisenberg et al., 1993; Lewis, 1992; Sroufe, in press).

YOUNG CHILDREN'S UNDERSTANDING OF EMOTION

By the preschool period, children have learned a great deal about emotion and emotional expression. For example, their "reading" of positive emotions in natural settings shows close agreement with that of adults, although preschoolers are still not very good at interpreting the range of negative emotions that others may express (Fabes et al., 1994). Preschoolers also have trouble distinguishing what people *really* feel from what they *appear* to feel. This is not surprising, given their struggle with the appearance-reality distinction. Thus, young children have no difficulty distinguishing pictures of happy and sad faces, but they have great difficulty understanding that someone who is sad may "put on" a happy face (for example, to protect someone else's feelings) or that someone who is really happy may not show happiness (e.g., Friend and Davis, 1993).

During the preschool period children acquire a better understanding of the causes of emotions. By age 4 they know that emotions are influenced not only by what happens, but also by what people expect to happen or think happened. For example, 4-year-olds know that a girl may be sad if she *mistakenly* thinks that she isn't going to get a prize she wants (Harris, 1994). But if the girl looks as if she isn't sad, children this age would typically become confused about how she feels. It is not until between the ages of 5 and 8 that children become able to integrate situational cues and visible expressions of emotion to infer how someone else feels.

THE GROWTH OF EMOTIONAL REGULATION

Emotional regulation includes the capacities to control and direct emotional expression, to maintain organized behavior in the presence of strong emotions, and to be guided by emotional experiences. All these capacities expand significantly during the preschool years. Some of them are revealed in the preschooler's increasing ability to tolerate frustration.

TOLERATING FRUSTRATION

An important aspect of emotional regulation is the ability to tolerate frustration—that is, to avoid becoming so upset in a frustrating situation that emotions get out of control and behavior becomes disorganized. This ability begins to appear by about age 2 and expands dramatically throughout the preschool years (Bridges and Grolnick, 1995; Eisenberg et al., 1994; van Lieshout, 1975). When confronting a frustrating situation, such as an attractive toy that is inaccessible,

Emotional regulation:
The capacities to control and direct emotional expression, to maintain organized behavior in the presence of strong emotions, and to be guided by emotional experiences.

Preschoolers have greatly expanded capacities for self-control. They can now tolerate delays before carrying out desired actions. Parents also expect more self-control at this age. The child's changing capacities influence the parents, and the parents' new expectations support the child's new abilities.

Delay of gratification:
The ability to forgo an immediate reward, despite strong desire for it, in order to have a better reward at a later time.

Ego resiliency:
The ability to modify one's degree of self-restraint in adapting to changing circumstances.

Internalization:
The incorporation of standards—in the form of attitudes, values, and beliefs—into the self.

older preschoolers are less angry and tantrum-prone than younger children are. They also stay engaged with the problem despite their frustration, and they make more constructive responses (such as seeking direct help).

This emerging capacity affects relationships with parents. Defiance of parents' requests, and passive noncompliance with them, decline markedly between the ages of 2 and 5 (Kuczynski and Kochanska, 1990). Children are increasingly able to tolerate the frustration of being asked to do something that is counter to their own wishes. They also begin to learn how to negotiate to resolve such a conflict.

Another form of tolerance for frustration is **delay of gratification,** the ability to forgo an immediate reward (such as a small piece of candy), despite strong desire for it, in order to have a better reward later. With support from an adult, preschool children can usually endure the frustration of delaying gratification. The wait may not be easy for them, but most manage to get through it. The ability to delay gratification will expand in the middle childhood years to the point where the child can wait even in the absence of adult help (Mischel et al., 1989).

Researchers are not yet sure why tolerance for frustration improves so noticeably during the preschool years. Children are probably becoming able to suppress their feelings to some extent, so that (outwardly at least) they are not so upset (Maccoby, 1980). At the same time, they seem to be learning strategies that help them limit the buildup of tension that tends to accompany frustration. For instance, in experiments in which attractive toys are locked inside a Plexiglas box, some preschoolers distract themselves by turning to other activities. This strategy redefines the situation as one in which the inaccessible toy is no longer the central focus of attention (e.g., Wolf, 1990). Undoubtedly such strategies help reduce tension and make the situation more bearable.

SHOWING FLEXIBILITY IN EMOTIONAL EXPRESSION

The ability to exert self-control over emotions would be a mixed blessing if children couldn't adjust its level to suit particular situations. Some situations demand a great deal of self-restraint, while others allow children to be as impulsive and expressive as they want. The ability to adapt to these different situations is called **ego resiliency** because the ego, or self, is showing the capacity to be flexible in its control over the expression of impulses and feelings (Block and Block, 1980). Mikey is showing ego resiliency in the scene at the start of this chapter. He is able to line up quietly when the teacher requests, but he also runs, shouts, and plays gleefully during outdoor recess. Like all ego-resilient children, Mikey can be spontaneous and expressive in some settings, reserved and self-disciplined in others (Sroufe, 1983). The behaviors he shows at any given time depend on the particular situation.

INTERNALIZING STANDARDS

Along with the preschooler's growing capacity for controlling the expression of emotion comes a growing awareness of standards for behavior and the use of those standards as guides for words and actions. The incorporation into the self of standards is called **internalization.** At first the standards are held by those responsible for socializing the child, but gradually they become part of the child as well.

Preschoolers can maintain organized behavior in the face of hard problems. They can carry out activities that require several steps and that do not immediately lead to reward.

Once the child has internalized standards, he or she will comply with parents' prohibitions even when the parents aren't present (Kopp et al., 1983). If an experimenter gets a preschool child to do something against a parent's rules, the child will typically show signs of distress and may confess to the parent when the parent returns (Emde and Buchsbaum, 1990). Another indication that internalization of standards is occurring is concern for other people. In their third year children not only respond emotionally to mishaps that they cause or witness but also seek to make reparations—to set things right again (Cole et al., 1992). Thus, internalization is the bridge from control of the child by others to the child's *self*-regulation (Power and Manire, 1992).

Ultimately, internalization is also a cornerstone of moral development. By age 3 or so, according to Robert Emde, the "moral self" arises (Emde et al., 1991). Children begin to understand that some behaviors are right and others are wrong. By age 4 they view "moral transgressions," such as hitting someone or not sharing, as more serious than "conventional transgressions," such as eating ice cream with your fingers. They make such judgments more independently from adults than do younger children (Smetana et al., 1993). It is as if they have internalized not just standards of behavior but also a sense that certain standards entail moral obligations.

Parents encourage this change in preschool children by changing their socialization techniques as the preschool period progresses (Power and Manire, 1992). Instead of direct, at times strong, controls ("No, no! Don't hit!"), they begin to use indirect external controls ("What a good boy to let Bobby play with your new boat!"), and finally, they start to encourage internal self-regulation ("I'm counting on you to divide up those cookies fairly"). Encouraging self-regulation also involves reasoning and persuasion. The parent might explain *why* a certain distribution is fair and just. On the basis of their own studies and a review of others' research, Power and Manire (1992) conclude that when parents provide information about rules and values and underscore that information through their own consistent behavior, young children are more likely to behave responsibly in the parents' absence.

THE SELF-EVALUATIVE EMOTIONS

Internalization of standards affects the emotional experiences of a preschooler. The child can now feel genuine *guilt* and *pride*, two emotions that involve evaluating the self against internalized standards. These emotions are different from the beginnings of pride and shame that a toddler experiences. For example, the guilt reaction of a preschooler occurs not because of what the parents do, or even what they say, but because the child *knows* he or she has done something wrong. The emotion no longer arises only from a fear of being punished; it is also due to an undermining of self-esteem caused by failure to live up to an internalized standard (Kochanska, 1993). The reaction is also more organized than the shame of a toddler (it is not just a global, all-encompassing state of anxiety), and it is more in response to a *particular* behavior. The specificity that characterizes a preschooler's guilt allows the attempts at "making up" that we discussed earlier (Kochanska, 1993; Lewis, 1992).

Likewise, true pride is distinguished from the toddler's joy in mastery because it is based on self-evaluation. Whereas a toddler often shows just as much pleasure when an adult solves a problem as when the child solves it, a preschooler is usually happier when he or she finds the solution (Stipek et al., 1992). The child perceives that he or she has done a good job, and consequently feels proud. Pride reactions are more common and stronger when the problem solved or the task accomplished is difficult than when it is easy (Lewis et al., 1992). This tells us that preschool children evaluate the complexity of what they are trying to do and also have their own standards of performance.

EMOTIONAL DEVELOPMENT, AGGRESSION, AND PROSOCIAL BEHAVIOR

Aggression:
Forceful, negative acts directed against persons or their possessions.

Prosocial behavior:
The act of directing positive feelings and behaviors toward someone else.

Aggression refers to forceful, negative acts directed against persons or their possessions, while **prosocial behavior** is the act of directing positive feelings and behaviors toward someone else. Both types of behavior are closely related to emotional regulation. When Malcolm acts aggressively toward April, hitting her to get possession of the tricycle, he is letting go of self-restraint and acting on impulse. Aggression generally involves relinquishing self-control and spontaneously lashing out, while refraining from aggression involves self-management. Prosocial behavior also involves self-management, but in a different way. In order to be kind or helpful to someone else, you must often make a conscious effort to put aside your own desires and enter into the other person's needs and point of view. This requires a substantial amount of self-regulation. Thus, as the capacities for self-management and emotional regulation unfold in children, we would expect to see changes in both aggression and prosocial behavior, and this is exactly what happens.

DEVELOPMENTAL CHANGES IN AGGRESSION

When 12-month-old Mikey roughly pushes away his mother's hand to get at his favorite toy, he is not really being aggressive. Although his behavior is assertive and purposeful, he does not intend to cause physical or psychological harm. This intent is central to true aggression. Only when Mikey is cognitively advanced enough to appreciate the consequences of his actions can he engage in genuine aggression (Maccoby, 1980). This ability develops sometime during toddlerhood, when representational thought emerges. During toddlerhood we see more angry outbursts in response to constraints that parents impose, as well as more negative behavior directed toward peers. Some of this negative peer interaction is object-centered, as when two children pull on a plaything in order to possess it (Hay, 1984; Howes, 1988). Not until the preschool period, when children better understand the self as an agent and the concept of fairness (when they have a notion of what peers *ought* to do), does true interpersonal aggression become common. The aggression that arises now includes actions that have no other purpose than to cause another person distress (Hartup and Laursen, 1993; Maccoby, 1980). By this age, too, there is consistency in the level of aggression found in individual children, especially boys (Cummings et al., 1989).

During the late preschool and early elementary school years aggressive behavior changes. Children's overall level of aggression declines because of a drop in the use of aggression as a means to get something—so-called **instrumental aggression** (Hartup and Laursen, 1993). Instrumental aggression is what Malcolm engages in when he tries to wrest the tricycle from April's grip. Older children are much less likely to become involved in such a squabble. The reason is that, by the end of the preschool period, children have learned alternative ways to settle disputes over objects.

Although instrumental aggression declines sharply in middle childhood, **hostile aggression**—aggression aimed solely at hurting someone else—does not. Most acts of hostile aggression during middle childhood are concerned with "getting even." Children lash out when they perceive that their rights have been violated or their egos threatened (Maccoby, 1980). Over the elementary school years hostile aggression changes dramatically in form. Older children become much more prone to verbal insults than to hitting. If April calls Malcolm a big bully and Malcolm retaliates by calling her a stupid tattletale, they are engaging in hostile aggression more typical of older children.

THE DEVELOPMENT OF EMPATHY AND ALTRUISM

Two related forms of prosocial behavior are empathy and altruism. **Empathy** (experiencing the emotions of another person) underlies **altruism** (acting unselfishly to aid someone else). When empathy is aroused, children are more willing to be helpful (altruistic) toward others (Strayer and Schroeder, 1989).

Instrumental aggression: The use of aggression as a means to get something.

Hostile aggression: Aggression aimed solely at hurting someone else.

Empathy: The ability to experience the emotions of another person.

Altruism: Acting unselfishly to aid someone else.

Preschoolers have the capacity for both aggression and cooperation.

Both empathy and altruism follow a developmental course parallel to that of aggression, because the same cognitive factors underlie all three. To engage in true aggression, altruism, or empathy, children must understand that they are independent agents responsible for their own actions (Kestenbaum et al., 1989). They must also grasp that their actions can cause feelings in other people that are different from the feelings they themselves are experiencing.

Researchers have suggested that the development of empathy and altruism has three phases (Hoffman, 1979; Zahn-Waxler, et al., 1992). In the first phase, during infancy, the child shows a primitive capacity for empathy by crying when another person is distressed. But the child as yet has little understanding of who is actually upset. On hearing another baby cry, 8-month-olds will often crawl over to their own mother and seek contact with her (Hoffman, 1979). Apparently, the distinction between self and other is not yet clear in the child's mind. At this stage, crying when another person cries is more aptly described as "contagion."

In the second phase, during early toddlerhood, advances in the concepts of self and other enable the child to engage in more purposeful helping behaviors. Children may hug or pat another child who is crying, bring their mother over to the crying youngster, or bring the child a favorite toy. But these actions do not really take into account the needs of the other child. Instead, toddlers do what would be helpful to themselves in that situation: They bring their *own* mother, or their *own* favorite toy.

In phase three, during early childhood, the capacity to take the perspective of others, and with it the capacity to respond to others' needs, increase dramatically (e.g., Radke-Yarrow and Zahn-Waxler, 1984; Zahn-Waxler et al., 1992). Although these capacities are widespread among preschoolers, actual displays of helping are relatively rare in natural settings. The fact that children can experience another person's distress does not guarantee that they will immediately offer comfort or assistance to someone who is upset (Kestenbaum et al., 1989). One reason why they don't may be because they know that adults will often offer help.

How have researchers discovered these various stages in the development of empathy and altruism? The work of Marion Radke-Yarrow deserves special mention because it shows how naturalistic observations and laboratory studies can be used together (e.g., Radke-Yarrow and Zahn-Waxler, 1984). Radke-Yarrow asked 41 mothers to record in detail their children's reactions to distress in others as they occurred in everyday settings. Because of the possibility of bias in the mothers' reports, assistants sometimes observed and recorded the same incidents that the mothers did. In addition, Radke-Yarrow supported all her findings with laboratory experiments.

Not only did Radke-Yarrow's data reveal the developmental phases outlined above, they also suggested that a parent's style of caregiving greatly influences a child's prosocial behavior. In keeping with a social learning perspective, a young child's tendency to feel empathy is related to experience with nurturant caregivers who provide models of empathy and helpfulness toward others. Just telling the child not to hurt other people is apparently not enough. The parent must clearly state the consequences for the victim, explain to the child the principles and expectations regarding kindness, and convey the entire message with intensity of feeling about the issues involved. Not surprisingly, the kind of caring, nurturant parent who provides these types of lessons also tends to foster a secure attachment in young children. In accord with Bowlby's theory, security of attachment in infancy predicts a high level of empathy and prosocial behavior in the preschool years (Kestenbaum et al., 1989). In being part of an empathic caregiving relationship beginning in infancy, children not only learn how to be cared for, but how to care as well. Children with secure histories bring forward a basic responsiveness to others.

THE ROLE OF PLAY IN PRESCHOOL DEVELOPMENT

Play is the province of the child. Once his or her more fundamental needs have been met—that is, whenever the child isn't eating or sleeping or seeking attention from adults—the child will play, often for hours on end. Even emotionally disturbed children play, although the quality of their play is notably affected. The absence of play is considered a sign of extreme abnormality (see Chapter 15). This intrinsic motive to play shows how much of children's behavior lies outside the influence of external reinforcement. No one has to teach children to play; they do so naturally. No one has to reward children for playing; play is its own reward.

Play serves important functions for children. It is a means by which they can be active explorers of their environments, active creators of new experiences, and active participants in their own development. Play is a "laboratory" in which children learn new skills and practice behaviors and concepts that lie at the very edge of their capacities (Lillard, 1993). Play is a child's social workshop, too, an arena for trying out roles alone and with other children, an arena for expanding and preserving a sense of self. For preschoolers, play is also an arena for emotional expression; it is often concerned with important themes and feelings from everyday life (Fischer et al., 1990). We will look more closely at this emotional function of play before turning to some of play's social functions.

PLAY AND MASTERY OF CONFLICT

By the preschool years play becomes the child's foremost tool for dealing with conflict and mastering what is frightening or painful. This was shown in a film that Jeanne Block and her colleagues at Berkeley made during the civil disorders of the 1960s. The sandbox play of children at that time was filled with police and civilians in conflict. We illustrated the importance of play as a vehicle for expressing a young child's current anxieties at the end of our story about Mikey. In Mikey's make-believe drama, which is based on an actual case observation (Rosenberg, 1984), the little boy is caught in the midst of his parents' crashing cars, just as Mikey is caught in the middle of Frank and Christine's persistent clashes. Similarly, another 4-year-old's mother observed her daughter dwelling on a recent fear in her play. The day after she was scared by a large dog, she pretended to be a dog terrorizing a group of dolls. She barked ferociously while crawling on the floor and then reassured the dolls by saying, "It's OK. He won't hurt you." In such ways preschoolers work their anxieties into play and thereby master them. In fact, play often centers on the most frightening of topics, such as being lost or having to fight off "monsters" (George, 1990; Rosenberg, 1984). Apparently, the motive to master fears and conflicts is very powerful.

Play is also an arena for working through ongoing developmental issues. Consider how children resolve the issue that arises when they realize they have less

Through play, children can express and resolve conflicts in a safe setting.

power than their parents. This resolution is often worked out in play (Breger, 1974; Rosenberg, 1984; Wolf, 1990). In play the child can safely turn the tables and become the powerful one. A common game preschoolers initiate with parents is "you be the baby and I'll be the mommy (or daddy)." The child might say: "Now you go right to bed!" (Parent: "Can I read?") "No, you have to go right to sleep!" The power roles are reversed in play, and the parent is charmed, not infuriated.

This use of play to resolve developmental issues helps preschoolers and their parents to get along quite well. Pretending allows the expression of forbidden behaviors and feelings that might not only be punished, but cause the child guilt as well. Remember that a preschooler has started to internalize the parents' values and so is capable of feeling guilty when he or she does wrong. Play opens up an escape valve at this stage of development. In play the child can pretend to be destructive, disobedient, or uncooperative without reprisals from either parents or conscience.

Pretend solutions are usually a healthy outlet for the preschooler. Because they involve active confrontation of a problem, they provide a prototype for more mature solutions in later years. Recognizing a conflict and doing something about it (rather than denying it) is a growth-enhancing response (Breger, 1974). With further development, of course, pretend or play solutions must be left behind. Nevertheless, they represent the beginnings of active mastery of conflict.

A history of parental support and nurturance can help children find these healthy solutions to issues and conflicts. Preschoolers whose parents are nurturant and supportive tend to engage in fantasy play that is more flexible and elaborate, and they are more likely to bring negative themes to successful resolution (Rosenberg, 1984; George, 1990). Mikey, as Rosenberg repeatedly observed in case studies of children with histories of secure attachment, brings the issue of being caught in the midst of parental conflict to a satisfactory close ("He got his leg broken! Here comes the ambilenz. They take him to the hospital. They fixed it!"). Such pretend dramas and their resolutions are an adult's entrée to the child's inner world and an indicator of positive adaptation during the preschool period.

ROLE PLAYING

Another important function of preschoolers' play is providing an opportunity to try out social roles. In play, children can be mommies and daddies, doctors, police officers, or robbers. In play, they can act out their aspirations as well as their fears. Dressing up in grown-up clothes and playing at grown-up jobs are also important parts of identifying with parents and exploring gender roles. When preschool boys and girls play "robbers," with the boys being the robbers and the girls taking flight and hiding, they are working on developmental issues beyond their conscious understanding.

Such fantasy play is normal and healthy for preschoolers. In fact, the more a young child engages in social fantasy play and the more flexible and elaborate that play is, the more likely the child is to be judged socially competent by teachers (Connolly and Doyle, 1985; Rosenberg, 1984). Developmentalists are not yet sure of the reasons for this correlation. Perhaps skill at social fantasy play promotes acceptance among other preschool children. Or perhaps popular preschoolers simply have more opportunities for this kind of play. Whatever the explanation, skill at social fantasy play is an indicator of a preschooler's overall quality of adjustment.

THE PARENTS' ROLE IN EARLY CHILDHOOD DEVELOPMENT

The fact that Mikey is such a competent, well-adjusted preschooler makes sense. He has had supportive, nurturant care from his parents since he was an infant. The development and behavior of preschoolers is related both to their history of earlier care and to the care they receive during the preschool period (e.g., Sroufe, 1988; Youngblade and Belsky, 1992). In the following section, we take a look at some aspects of parenting that are viewed as important at this age.

IMPORTANT ASPECTS OF PARENTING IN THE PRESCHOOL PERIOD

Some of the same basic qualities of parenting remain important during the preschool years. These include parental warmth, emotional responsiveness, and a sharing of positive feelings with the child. For example, preschoolers whose parents are emotionally responsive tend to show empathy for others and to engage in prosocial behavior (Fabes et al., 1994). Similarly, preschoolers whose parents are emotionally responsive, accepting of their child's autonomy, and often share positive feelings tend to be socially competent with peers and cooperative with the parents (Denham et al., 1991; LaFreniere and Dumas, 1992; Kochanska and Aksan, in press). While such correlations do not prove cause and effect, their consistency with infant studies certainly suggests that parental warmth and responsiveness are important.

Certain parental qualities seem to become newly important during the preschool years, largely because the child's needs and abilities are changing. For instance, consistency in the parents' approach to discipline, and agreement between the parents concerning child-rearing practices tend to be more important for preschoolers than for younger children (Block and Block, 1980; LaFre-

Although preschoolers have developed considerable self-reliance, they still depend on adults for support and guidance. Here, the boys' father settles a dispute between them. The preschooler's capacity for guilt is also apparent.

Authoritative parenting: Diana Baumrind's term for a parenting style in which the parents are nurturant, responsive, and supportive, yet set firm limits for their children.

Permissive parenting: Baumrind's term for a parenting style in which parents fail to set firm limits or to require appropriately mature behavior of their children.

Authoritarian parenting: Baumrind's term for a parenting style in which parents are unresponsive to their child's wishes, inflexible, and harsh in controlling behavior.

niere and Dumas, 1992). This is presumably because the expanded cognitive abilities of preschoolers allow them to become confused by such inconsistencies.

As children's abilities and needs change during the preschool period, the developmental tasks they face also change, and with those changes come related changes in the parents' tasks. These new sets of tasks are summarized in Table 10.2. In general, parents must gradually give the child more responsibility, while remaining available to step in and help if his or her resources are exceeded. According to Erik Erikson, the preschool period is a time when children may attempt to do too much as they strive for mastery. If parents frequently ridicule or punish a preschooler's failures, the child may experience pervasive feelings of guilt (Erikson, 1963). Thus, parents must neither push preschoolers too fast nor thwart their efforts. This role is similar to the one parents played when the child was a toddler, but now they are dealing with a much more mature and competent youngster. Parents must also try to display clear roles and values in their own actions and show the flexible self-control they hope to promote in their child.

Some of the characteristics of parents who raise well-adjusted preschoolers are summed up in what Diana Baumrind (1967) calls **authoritative parenting,** a concept we introduced in Chapter 8. Authoritative parents are nurturant, responsive, and supportive, yet they also set firm limits for their children. Their preschoolers typically have a number of positive qualities: they are energetic, emotionally responsive to peers, curious, and self-reliant.

Other parenting styles that Baumrind has identified are not generally associated with such positive characteristics in children. One is **permissive parenting,** in which the parents totally fail to set firm limits or to require appropriately mature behavior. This pattern is associated with children who are impulsive, low in self-control, and lacking in self-reliance. Also associated with problems is **authoritarian parenting.** Authoritarian parents are unresponsive to the child's wishes, and inflexible and harsh in controlling the child's behavior. This pattern is related to apprehension, frustration, and passive hostility in children.

Less successful styles of parenting can themselves be associated with negative situations in the parents' lives, such as high levels of stress or marital conflict. At the same time, such negative family situations can have direct adverse effects on

TABLE 10.2
TASKS FOR PRESCHOOLERS AND THEIR PARENTS

Parents' Tasks	Children's Tasks
Nurturance	Accepting care and developing trust
Training and channeling of physical needs	Complying and controlling self
Teaching and skill training	Learning
Orienting child to family and peers	Developing a general understanding of the social world
Promoting interpersonal skills and control of emotion	Role taking
Guiding formation of goals, plans, and aspirations	Achieving self-regulation
Transmitting cultural values	Developing a sense of right and wrong

SOURCE: Adapted from Clausen, 1968.

children. For instance, preschool children are quite vulnerable to conflict between their parents. Marital conflict has been shown to be related to negative play with peers, anxiety about parents' whereabouts, and an increased level of behavioral problems (Cummings et al., 1989; Katz and Gottman, 1993). The form the marital conflict takes may make a difference. Lynn Katz and John Gottman (1993) have found that mutually hostile patterns of parental interaction are associated with aggression and related problems in children, while a pattern in which the father becomes angry and withdrawn is associated with such problems as anxiety. Divorce may also have a negative impact on a preschool child because the child is now cognitively mature enough to grasp the anger and incompatibility between the parents, but not yet mature enough to understand that the marital breakup is not the child's fault. When Judith Wallerstein and Joan Kelly (1982) interviewed a large number of 3½- to 6-year-olds following their parents' divorce, they found that self-blame was preschoolers' predominant response. Younger children would probably not be capable of such a reaction. In Chapter 12 we will say more about the effects on children of marital conflict and divorce.

IDENTIFICATION WITH PARENTS

The cognitive advances of the preschool period allow children to be influenced not just by how their parents treat them but also by what the parents, in general, are like. Psychoanalytic theory offers a possible explanation for this. It holds that children strive to be *like* their parents, not only in actions but in thoughts and feelings as well. This process is called **identification.** Historically, psychoanalysts have argued that children identify most strongly with the parent of the same sex, and that this is the basis for the child's own sense of gender. Our own more modern view is that relationships with *both* parents, and the parents' relationship with each other, all may influence the preschool child's emerging sense of self.

To better understand the process of identification, consider it from the

Identification: In psychoanalytic theory, the process by which children strive to be like their parents, not only in actions but in thoughts and feelings as well.

In all cultures children of preschool age continue to learn a great deal through direct instruction from adults.

child's point of view—say, from the viewpoint of Mikey Gordon at age 2. In moving away from the great dependency of infancy, Mikey at first sees no boundaries to his newfound abilities. Overflowing with excitement at each new achievement, he feels all-capable and all-powerful. But inevitably clashes of will with his parents bring Mikey face-to-face with limits to his independence. No matter how resistant he might be to his parents' wishes (and children this age are often testimony to the strength of the human spirit), he cannot hold out indefinitely against the overwhelming evidence that his parents are more powerful than he.

What is Mikey to do in this situation? Relinquish his newfound autonomy? Return to his earlier dependency? Surely not. Psychoanalytic theory proposes another solution. Mikey can identify with his parents, incorporating their attributes into his own self. In this way he becomes more like his parents and so more powerful, as they are. Notice how instead of relinquishing his newly formed self, Mikey's sense of self is developing further. He *internalizes* characteristics he perceives in his parents and thus acquires new feelings, beliefs, and values (as well as new standards of behavior, which we discussed earlier). The period that follows—beginning at about age 3 or 3½—is often considered idyllic by parents. The child shows more confidence and security, a new level of cooperativeness, and a closer alignment with the parents.

Of course, identification isn't possible until a child has some ability to *understand* the parents' attitudes and feelings, not just observe their actions. This is why identification doesn't become apparent until the preschool period, when such cognitive ability emerges. It is also no accident that the appearance of identification coincides with the appearance of true interpersonal aggression, true empathy for others, and a marked increase in self-regulation. All of these developmental changes are intimately connected. Self-control, for example, partly involves internalizing parental standards and using them as guides for behavior.

But cognitive readiness to identify with parents and accept their beliefs, rules, and values may not be enough to ensure that this process occurs. There is gen-

There is both change and continuity in the parent–child relationship—change because the child has developed; continuity because the earlier relationship lays the groundwork for the later relationship. For example, the pride in the child's accomplishments shared by parents and child draws upon a history of affection they have shared in other ways.

eral agreement that internalization of the parents' rules and values is also influenced by the quality of the parent-child relationship. A relationship that facilitates internalization probably involves certain cognitive elements, such as clear communication (Grusec and Goodnow, 1994). At the same time, a loving, supportive relationship may provide an important motivational and emotional framework for internalization. For example, Martin Hoffman (1994) suggests that when parents overemphasize their power in teaching rules to children, the children can feel very anxious about prohibitions and fail to internalize them. In contrast, when parents are clear in conveying rules and explain the reasons for them, they generate only moderate anxiety in children and therefore promote genuine acceptance of the rules. Grazyna Kochanska likewise stresses the importance of a base of shared positive feelings between parent and child (e.g., Kochanska and Aksan, in press). Coercive techniques may get a child to comply with the parent's rules, but more positive approaches bring enthusiastic cooperation. Such "committed compliance" leads to true internalization. Now the child complies even when the parent isn't present.

Given that the quality of the parent-child relationship may affect the internalization of rules, it isn't surprising that security of attachment during infancy and toddlerhood is related to a child's openness to socialization and identification with family norms and values during the preschool years. Everett Waters has drawn upon social learning theory, cognitive developmental theory, and Bowlby's attachment theory to explain this connection (Waters et al., 1990). In keeping with our discussion in Chapter 8 of socialization from the inside, Waters argues that securely attached infants are already committed to the family system long before they understand the rules. When the rules are then conveyed to them as preschoolers—through prohibitions, praise, and so forth—their reaction is, "If that's the system, that's for me." In other words, a positive orientation toward socialization and family rules is part of the secure child's attachment relationship. All that is required for internalization of those rules is the cognitive maturity of the preschool years and opportunities to learn the details of the family do's and don'ts.

THE COHERENCE OF BEHAVIOR AND DEVELOPMENT

A major theme of this book is that child behavior and development is coherent, orderly, and logical. There is sense to the way various influences combine to shape the child, to the way each child develops an interrelated set of characteristics, and to the way one phase of development paves the way for the next. While coherence in behavior and development exists from the beginning of life, it becomes even more apparent during the preschool period.

THE COHERENCE OF THE SELF

Coherence can be seen very clearly in the individual characteristics of each preschool child. Clusters of characteristics tend to go together in a logical, meaningful way (Eder and Mangelsdorf, in press). For instance, children who have high self-esteem tend to have flexible self-control, to show more prosocial behavior, and to be better liked by peers (Sroufe, 1983). Those rated as more socially competent by teachers engage in more social play and show more positive feelings toward other children (Howes, 1990). All these positive traits seem to fit logically together. In contrast, children who show hostility do not show much prosocial behavior (Miller and Eisenberg, 1988), nor is prosocial behavior common among children who are highly dependent on their preschool teachers (Sroufe et al., 1983). Once again, the various characteristics make sense together. The child does not display a random assortment of disconnected traits. His or her behavior reflects a logical and coherent underlying self. By the end of the preschool years it is possible to see children as having distinctive personalities.

Parents' behavior helps explain why certain clusters of characteristics tend to be found together in preschoolers, forming logical, coherent patterns. For example, parents who are emotionally supportive of their children, encouraging independent abilities and a capacity for self-control, also support peer relationships, in part by initiating and supporting opportunities for their child to play with other children (Ladd and Hart, 1992; Lieberman, 1977). These aspects of the parents' behavior are logically connected to each other; support in one area is coupled with support in another. Thus, it is not surprising that high self-esteem and self-reliance in preschoolers tend to accompany social competence with peers. Other clusters of characteristics in preschoolers also seem to be logically linked to the kinds of experiences that parents have provided.

THE COHERENCE OF BEHAVIOR OVER TIME

Just as there is logic and coherence to a preschooler's current behavior, so there is logic and coherence to how the child's behavior has developed over time. For instance, preschoolers with a history of secure attachment in infancy—while varying in their social involvement, activity levels, and so forth—tend to show certain positive patterns of behavior (Sroufe, 1983). They have high self-esteem, are popular with peers, and show little negative emotion or hostile aggression. This is not to say that these preschoolers never use force. In fact, they tend to be quite assertive and sometimes display instrumental aggression in struggles over objects (LaFreniere, 1983; Maccoby, 1980). However, preschoolers who have histories of secure attachment do not *seek* to injure other children either in response to frustration or without obvious provocation. Generally, they are empathic toward their peers and, compared with preschoolers with a history of anxious attachment, they have a greater capacity for forming friendships (Pancake, 1985; Kerns, 1994). They also show more self-reliance, more curiosity, greater flexibility, and more positive emotions in interacting with peers (Arend et al., 1979; Sroufe, 1983; Sroufe et al., 1984; Waters et al., 1979).

A very different profile tends to characterize preschoolers with a history of anxious-resistant attachment. These children are unable to sustain the give-and-take of peer interaction and wind up neglected by peers. They have low self-esteem and little capacity for flexible self-management (Sroufe, 1983). They also have a great need for support and contact with teachers, often hovering near them (Sroufe, 1988; Sroufe, Fox, and Pancake, 1983). They show little prosocial behavior toward peers, not because they are hostile but because their immaturity and low tolerance for stress makes them unable to do so. For example, one 4-year-old, on seeing another child with a cut lip, clapped his hand over his own mouth and climbed up on a teacher's lap (Kestenbaum et al., 1989). Such children also are frequent targets of bullying by peers.

Preschoolers with histories of anxious-avoidant attachment show yet another profile. They are often hostile and aggressive toward other children or are emotionally isolated (Sroufe, 1983). Some of these children show aggression that is calculated and without immediate provocation. At times it has a mean quality. For instance, in response to a playmate's remark that she had a stomachache, one little girl jabbed her fist into the other child's stomach. When the playmate complained, "That hurt!" the girl punched her again (Troy and Sroufe, 1987). Lying, blaming others, and behaving defiantly are also common in some of these children. Yet these same antisocial children, as well as the isolated ones, show strong dependency needs. They spend more time than their classmates eliciting guidance, support, and discipline from teachers (Motti, 1986) and more time sitting on the teachers' laps during group activities (Sroufe, Fox, and Pancake, 1988). During group activities or when it's time to go home, their efforts to seek contact with the teacher often have a desperate quality. Yet ironically, when greeted by a teacher or when very upset, they deliberately turn away.

Although this pattern of behavior is complex, its developmental link to anxious-avoidant attachment is coherent and understandable. The hostility toward or isolation from peers, the desperate dependency on adults, coupled with avoidance of adults when contact with them is appropriate, can all be interpreted as reflecting low self-esteem, general mistrust, and unresolved needs for nurturance arising from profound doubts about the availability of care beginning early in life.

EXPLAINING DEVELOPMENTAL COHERENCE

The coherence of a young child's behavior over time is partly due to the fact that many influences on the child continue exerting themselves in much the same ways that they have in the past. Among these consistent influences is the amount of support the child receives from parents. Research shows that there is substantial consistency in the level of parental support over time (Pianta et al., 1989). The child who was nurtured and encouraged but given reasonable limits as a toddler tends to be the child who is treated in a similarly appropriate way as a preschooler.

Another influence on preschool children that helps explain the coherence of their behavior over time is the fact that they are increasingly becoming relatively consistent forces in their own development. By the preschool period, parents and other observers describe particular children as behaving in quite consistent ways (e.g., Vaughn et al., 1993). Moreover, research shows that preschool children have developed consistent expectations about their social worlds (Bretherton, 1990; George, 1990; Main, 1993; Main and Hesse, 1990; Rosenberg, 1984). Some preschoolers routinely expect other people to be responsive to them, while other preschoolers routinely expect the opposite. These consistent expectations and patterns of behavior are powerful influences on current development. They tend to elicit certain reactions from others, and those reactions, in turn, reinforce how the child tends to think and act.

For example, parents, and even adults who are unfamiliar with a particular child show less positive emotions toward that child if he or she is "difficult" than they do toward the child's siblings (Bugental, Blue, and Lewis, 1990). This less positive reaction can, in turn, help maintain the original "difficultness." Similarly, other children do not like aggressive children and frequently reject them as playmates (Asher and Parker, 1989; Sroufe, 1983). This rejection may then encourage further aggression on the part of the disliked children.

Just like parents and peers, preschool teachers can also respond in ways that reinforce the emerging personalities of young children (Motti, 1986; Sroufe and Fleeson, 1988). With children who are well managed, self-reliant, and sociable, teachers are warm and accepting. They hold age-appropriate standards for such youngsters, and expect them to comply with their directives with little external control. At the same time, they directly promote the acceptance of these children by peers (White and Kistner, 1992). These responses, not surprisingly, tend to encourage the very behaviors the children originally displayed.

In contrast, preschool teachers are quite controlling of children who are timid or impulsive (often those with histories of anxious-resistant attachment, like Meryl). They also make allowances for such children, accepting their immature behavior, and are very nurturant toward them, much as one would be with a younger child. Once again, the teachers' responses tend to reinforce the original patterns. With aggressive or hostile children, teachers are controlling and at times even angry. They rarely expect compliance, and they discipline these children often. Since they have no expectations that these children will exert self-control, the children are not encouraged to manage themselves. Thus, although teachers can often have a positive influence on children with troubled histories, the behavior of such children often works against them, eliciting responses from teachers that confirm the children's negative expectations about themselves.

STABILITY AND CHANGE IN INDIVIDUAL BEHAVIOR

Personality may be thought of as a structure that evolves over the early years of life. At its base is the history of responsiveness and care provided during infancy and toddlerhood, a history that gives rise to a certain attachment relationship. The attachment relationship, in turn, strongly predicts certain aspects of a child's behavior during the preschool period. The power of a secure attachment relationship seems to lie in promoting a beginning sense of self-worth and an abiding sense of relatedness or connection to others, which Erikson calls "basic trust."

In subsequent periods, parents build upon this base by supporting the child's independent initiatives, by promoting self-control, and by maintaining a clear parental presence through emotional support and demands for appropriate behavior. The parents, in other words, develop a system for exerting control over the child that doesn't stifle the child's efforts at exploration and autonomy. This *control system* (in addition to the attachment relationship) is another avenue by which parents influence their child's personality development.

The quality of the control system that parents establish predicts different behaviors in children than the quality of the attachment relationship does. For instance, attention and activity problems in elementary school are related to parents' failure to maintain appropriate boundaries between themselves and their child and to support the child's development of self-control and self-management (Carlson et al., 1995). Not surprisingly, measures of the quality of early attachment *combined* with later measures of parental guidance in self-control predict a child's behavior much better than either set of measures does alone (e.g., Sroufe et al., 1990; Teo et al., in press).

When personality is viewed as a developmental structure that is built up over time, it becomes clear that early experiences or early temperament do *not* directly cause the child's behavior in the preschool period. Nor is it the case

Individual differences become even more prominent and stable during the preschool period than they were earlier.

that the child's typical patterns of behavior cannot change. Fundamental change in children is always possible. For instance, since the quality of care a preschooler currently receives affects how well that child functions, improvement in care during the preschool period will have positive consequences for a child's behavior, even for a child who was anxiously attached earlier (Erickson, Egeland, and Sroufe, 1985). As was the case in prior periods of development, the social support available to parents and the level of stress they experience are critical to the quality of the child care they provide. Across various cultural groups, measures of parental stress and social support have been shown to be related to the degree of security a young child feels, the quality of the parent-child relationship, and the child's acceptance by peers (e.g., Jennings et al., 1991; Melson et al., 1993; Nakagawa et al., 1992).

Even though fundamental change in a child is always possible, it can become more difficult as personality increasingly stabilizes. In infancy assessments of the caregiving a child receives or other environmental measures often predict that child's later behavior better than measures of the child's own current behaviors do. By the time the child is a preschooler, however, this is no longer so clearly the case. Assessments of preschoolers (apart from caregivers) predict later behavior quite well, even up to adolescence and early adulthood (Sroufe, Carlson, and Shulman, 1993; Block, 1987). Apparently, developmental history has now become part of the child, and a distinctive personality is emerging and becoming stable. In subsequent periods behavior will become even more stable, with certain patterns like aggressiveness being very difficult to change. For these reasons, researchers have become increasingly interested in early intervention to change maladaptive behaviors. Such interventions are the topic of the box on pp. 398–399.

Since children's basic personality characteristics and the core of their self-esteem emerge by the end of the preschool period, growth-enhancing experiences during early childhood would seem to be quite valuable, an "investment" in the child. This idea has inspired many intervention programs for preschoolers who are at developmental risk, usually because they live in economically disadvantaged environments. Contrary to early expectations, it is not primarily IQ scores that intervention programs affect. Although the programs do tend to boost test scores temporarily, these effects fade within a few years after the program ends. What is of more lasting benefit is the "empowering" of youngsters who participate in quality preschool programs. These children tend to develop a higher level of self-esteem, more positive attitudes toward education, and a stronger belief in themselves as able learners—factors that can continue to affect them even into adulthood. They also, in fact, do better in school.

An excellent example of the long-lasting effects of a preschool intervention program can be seen in the High/Scope Perry Preschool Project. The developers of this very successful program conducted a genuine experiment. They identified 123 young African-American children living in poverty and randomly assigned 58 of them to the program group. The other 65 served as controls. The long-term effects were dramatic, as shown in Figure 10.A, which graphs the major findings at age

27. Compared with subjects in the control group, young adults who had experienced the intervention program as preschoolers were significantly more likely to have at least a twelfth-grade education, to earn a steady income, to stay off welfare, to own their own home, and to keep out of trouble with the law. These positive results translate into important economic benefits for society as a whole. The cost of the program was just a little over $12,000 per child, but society gained back more than $88,000 per participant in terms of savings on the cost of schooling (participants had less need for special education), savings on the costs of welfare and the criminal justice system, savings on settlements for victims of crimes, and more taxes paid on higher incomes (see Figure 10.B).

In order for such long-term benefits to occur, however, the preschool program must be of high quality. The High/Scope Perry Preschool Project was a model of quality early-childhood education. It included 2 years of daily preschool classes in which the children planned their own learning activities in an environment rich with materials and then reported on their experiences to demonstrate and review what they had learned. Such child-initiated learning activities were vital to the program's success because they encouraged the "empowering" of the child we mentioned earlier (Schweinhart, Weikart, and Larner, 1986). The High/Scope Perry Preschool Project also included weekly visits by staff

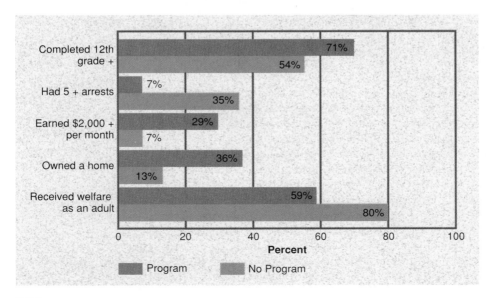

FIGURE 10.A
HIGH/SCOPE PERRY PRESCHOOL PROJECT: MAJOR FINDINGS AT AGE 27
(Source: Schweinhart and Weikart, 1993, p. 54.)

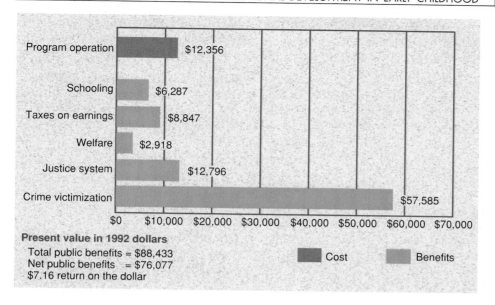

FIGURE 10.B
HIGH/SCOPE PERRY PRESCHOOL PROJECT: PUBLIC COST AND ECONOMIC BENEFIT PER PARTICIPANT
(Source: Schweinhart and Weikart, 1993, p. 55.)

members to the children's homes, which gave parents an opportunity to learn about what their child was doing in the classroom, to witness firsthand their child's progress and skills, and to discover how they could help. In this way, the parents were encouraged to become active participants in supporting their child's development. Active involvement of the parents is central to the long-term success of early-childhood intervention because it can continue long after the preschool program is over. Other factors that contribute to a successful program are a stable staff, a low child-teacher ratio, and a fairly long duration. Preschool intervention programs that lack these key characteristics cannot be expected to yield such a high return on investment (Schweinhart and Weikart, 1993).

CHAPTER SUMMARY

1. Dramatic developments in social and emotional behavior occur during the preschool period. For one thing, children become more self-reliant and begin to explore a much wider world. Included in their broader social environments are peer relationships. Positive peer interactions are important because during childhood much is learned within the peer group.

2. Preschoolers also begin to achieve notable self-regulation. They can inhibit actions, delay gratification, and tolerate frustration much more than toddlers can. Parents begin to expect children at this age to "behave" and obey certain rules even when adults are not there to watch them. Developmentalists are especially interested in children's capacity to modify self-restraint depending on the situation, a capacity called **ego-resiliency.**

3. The child's sense of self undergoes further development during the preschool years. Children acquire an understanding of themselves not only as actors but as directors of action. They also acquire a sense of **self-constancy,** the perception of a stable self that endures despite varied behaviors and varied responses from others. At the same time, children begin to acquire specific thoughts and feelings, either positive or negative, about the self. These self-evaluations are referred to as **self-esteem.**

4. An important part of the preschooler's emerging self-concept concerns gender. There are developmental changes both in the frequency of **sex-typed behaviors** and in the child's **gender-role concept**—that is, the child's understanding of gender categories and the meaning of being male or female. Preschoolers also begin to understand that gender remains permanent despite superficial changes in appearance. This is called a sense of **gender constancy.**

5. Individual differences in **social competence**—the capacity to be effective in the peer group—become notable by the preschool period. Some children engage others in positive ways, form friendships, and are generally popular with peers. Other children are not so effective. Some of these, called *rejected* children, are actively disliked, often because they are aggressive. Others, who are peripheral in the peer group, are *neglected*.

6. Three major changes in emotional development take place during the preschool period. First, children develop a better understanding of emotions and their causes. Second, they evolve a beginning capacity to control and regulate emotional expression; for example, being more able to suppress angry feelings. Third, there are changes in emotions themselves. New emotions emerge, such as guilt and pride.

7. Preschoolers' play differs notably from that of young toddlers in the rich and complex forms of fantasy it involves. This fantasy play is a child's foremost tool for dealing with conflict and mastering what is frightening or painful. Fantasy play also gives preschoolers the chance to try out a large variety of social roles.

8. During the preschool period a major change takes place in children's relationships to their parents. While toddlers often imitate specific actions of their parents, preschoolers go further by identifying with parents. **Identification** involves striving to be like the parents and internalizing their beliefs, values, and standards of behavior. Through identification, preschoolers begin to acquire some of their parents' power and competence.

9. As children undergo these important changes during the preschool years, parents must adjust their own behavior to continue fostering favorable development. Parents must gradually give the child more responsibility, while remaining available to help when the child's resources are exceeded. Parents should also set clear limits on what the child is allowed to do. Warmth and nurturance continue to be important parental characteristics, as is a respect for the child's needs and point of view.

10. By the preschool period, if not before, each child is a coherent individual with characteristic ways of responding to the world. Some children have greater curiosity, more competence with peers, higher self-esteem, greater self-reliance, and more flexible self-management (ego-resiliency) during the preschool years. Others are high-strung and easily frustrated; reticent and overly dependent; hostile and aggressive; or socially withdrawn and lacking in emotional expression. Such emerging patterns of personality are based on both the child's earlier adaptation in response to the history of care received and the child's current experiences.

PART FOUR
EPILOGUE

EARLY CHILDHOOD

Development continues at a very rapid pace during the preschool period, ages 2½ through 5. Preschoolers don't just learn more skills and information; they also undergo qualitative changes in how they think and act. While development always builds on what has gone before, 5-year-olds are fundamentally different people from 2-year-olds. Five-year-olds use language fluently, in contrast to the short, two- or three-word sentences of the toddler. Five-year-olds also reason about the world in ways far beyond the 2-year-old's capacities. Although 5-year-olds' explanations for things often charm us with their magical qualities, the very fact that they are so preoccupied with how things work sets them distinctly apart from children who are only 2. In independence from parents, 5-year-olds are also markedly different from toddlers, who are just discovering their autonomy. Similarly, 5-year-olds exert a degree of self-management absent in children 3 years younger. Five-year-olds are in some ways more similar to adults than to 2-year-olds. For instance, whereas a 5-year-old can easily learn to use a phone to make an emergency call, a 2-year-old cannot be expected to master this skill.

Compared with toddlers, preschoolers have a more advanced ability to represent things mentally. Preschoolers can imagine combinations of things that they have never actually experienced. After spotting some candy on a shelf that is too high to reach, a preschooler might imagine stacking some nearby boxes to form a makeshift set of steps. Representational skills of this sort account for more effective problem solving. The child can "see" the solution without having directly experienced it before or without engaging in a random trial-and-error approach.

Preschoolers' cognitive advances support their social and emotional development. Improvements in language and the ability to take another person's perspective are the basis for rapid advances in peer relationships. Representational skills and imagination make possible fantasy play, which in turn helps the child to resolve conflicts, practice new skills, and try out social roles. Representational skills, along with the ability to categorize things, allow children to conceive of themselves as boys or girls. Representational skills also enable identification with parents, and they contribute to the child's growing ability to delay gratification, inhibit responses, tolerate frustration, and otherwise exert self-control.

Cognitive advances also help promote changes in the parent-child relationship. As a child's language and thinking abilities become more advanced, parents begin to rely more on reasoning to influence behavior. They also expect a preschooler to act more maturely, partly because they believe that the child "knows better" by this age. These expectations help encourage the very behaviors that the parents want.

At the same time that cognitive advances are influencing social and emotional development, the reverse is also taking place. How a preschooler interacts with and feels about other people greatly affects opportunities for cognitive stimulation and growth. For instance, children learn a great deal about the world from peers, so involvement with peers can foster expansion of a child's knowledge. Involvement with peers also affords opportunities to practice language and other cognitive skills.

Different aspects of development are intimately connected. When we see a change in a child's way of thinking and reasoning, we usually see a parallel change in the child's social and emotional life. For example, preschoolers begin acquiring abstract representations of the sequences involved in familiar experiences, such as going to a birthday party. These are called scripts. In a parallel fashion they also develop abstract representations of themselves with others—generalized expectations about how others are likely to respond to them, called internal working models. The various aspects of human development do not proceed in isolation. Each is linked to the others; development is organized and coherent.

STABILITY AND CHANGE IN INDIVIDUAL DEVELOPMENT

Individual development is characterized by a logical coherence and by continuity over time. By the end of the preschool period we see individual adaptations that have evolved from the adaptations that emerged during infancy and toddlerhood. These individual adaptations, or personalities, are intimately related to the caregiving system in which the child has been raised, although temperament also plays a part. By the preschool period, however, temperament and experience, whatever their respective roles, have both become incorporated into the total child.

Continuity in development persists beyond the preschool period. For instance, there is evidence for a link between a child's degree of self-control as a preschooler and his or her self-control between the ages of 7 and 23 (Block, 1987). For girls, the correlation between self-control at age 4 and self-control years later is particularly strong. Researchers have even been able to predict the likelihood of teenage drug abuse from earlier measures of self-control versus impulsiveness. In a similar vein, psychologist Walter Mischel has found that measures of a 5-year-old's ability to delay gratification can be used to predict aspects of behavior at 12 years of age (Mischel et al., 1989).

Complex issues are involved in conducting such longitudinal studies. Often the researchers must look at very different behaviors over time, behaviors appropriate to the child's developmental level and the particular situation (Sroufe, 1988). Nevertheless, as developmental research becomes more conceptually sophisticated, increasing evidence of a marked continuity in individual development is emerging. Children are not chalkboards to be erased and written on anew. Current development unfolds in a logical fashion from what has gone before.

One factor contributing to this developmental continuity over time is stability in the care the child receives. Parents who provide for a child's needs in one developmental period are likely to continue meeting the child's needs in subsequent periods, partly because of continuity in the social support that is available to them. Conversely, parents who have trouble being adequately responsive at one stage of their child's development are likely to continue to have problems with parenting unless their circumstances change. We have repeatedly emphasized the importance of life circumstances for the caregiving system. If stresses on parents diminish, or if their social support is strengthened, the child will probably begin to function better (Crockenberg, 1981; Egeland et al., 1990; Pederson et al., 1977; Vaughn et al., 1979).

Another factor contributing to continuity in children's adaptations is the fact that, increasingly with age, children shape their own environments. This may be partly because certain aspects of behavior (general activity level, for example) are stable by the preschool age and may lead to different kinds of experiences. More important, we believe, is the fact that youngsters develop expectations, and their approach to the world based on those expectations often makes the expectations come true. For instance, imagine two children in a preschool classroom, each asking another child to play (Sroufe, 1988). When the first child is turned down, she is devastated by what she perceives to be a personal rejection. She retreats to a corner, where she sits alone, convinced that nobody likes her. The second child receives a similar refusal, but rather than feeling rejected he simply moves on to another potential playmate, who accepts his invitation, and the two play happily. These children are clearly creating different environments for themselves on the basis of different expectations and outlooks. Both have the cognitive capacity to recognize that their invitation was declined, but the rejection has different meanings to them; they interpret it in different ways. Thus, by the preschool period, children, through their various experiences, have formed expectations about the self and others that greatly influence how they act. These distinctive expectations, which are very general in nature, are central to the child's personality.

How a preschooler's expectations affect the caregiving system is particularly important to maintaining the child's style of thinking and acting. Consider an infant who shows a pattern of anxious-resistant attachment—Meryl, for example. Because of inconsistent care she has developed the expectation that contact with her mother may not always give her comfort in times of stress. As a result, she is anxious in new situations, easily upset, and hard to reassure. Research suggests that such a child is also likely to be whiny, prone to tantrums, and difficult to control, often becoming locked in power struggles with the parent (Gove, 1983).

Meryl as a toddler and young preschooler strongly resisted Karen's efforts to impose limits on her. Such a child requires unusually clear, firm, and consistent handling in order to change her negative expectations; yet, this was precisely what was difficult for the parent to provide in the first place. To break the negative cycle an intervention program may be needed, for parents sometimes need help to believe that they can ultimately master the child's behavior.

Does all this mean that personality is "fixed" by early childhood? No, certainly not. The success of intervention programs underscores the fact that fundamental change in behavior is always possible. It is especially likely during periods of major developmental reorganization, when children acquire new ways of integrating and using the capacities they have. Developmentalists would single out the toddler period, early childhood, adolescence, and early adulthood as periods of notable reorganization. Fundamental change in behavior can occur at any time, however—often spurred, as we said earlier, by changing life circumstances. Meryl again provides a good example. The arrival of Joe Turner makes a real difference in her life. Not only does Meryl respond well to Joe's firm, authoritative parenting, she also benefits from the greater confidence and satisfaction that Joe inspires in Karen as a mother. At the same time, Meryl is fortunate to have a kindergarten teacher who helps create change-producing experiences for her by gently guiding her toward involvement with peers. With this help she is able to make a solid connection in the peer group.

THREE CHILDREN AS PRESCHOOLERS

Despite the fundamental changes that have taken place in Meryl, she is still distinctly different from Malcolm and Mikey, who are also different from each other. Each is developing in his or her own unique way, the product of a certain biology and certain past and present experiences. Let's review the progress each has made during the preschool period.

Mikey is tackling the developmental issues of the preschool period with ease. He is a capable, self-reliant child who shows all the signs of readiness for school. He is interested in cognitive activities and is responsive to his preschool teachers. At the same time, he has moved smoothly into the world of peers, becoming a peer leader who is liked by others.

Even with all these positive developments, however, Mikey may encounter some problems. Because he is such a bright, sensitive, perceptive child, he is vulnerable to internalizing the conflicts between his mother

and father, which are now intensifying. The role of peacemaker we see him playing is not really a new one for Mikey. Earlier, Christine and Frank used Mikey's behavior as an excuse to become distracted from their differences, as happened in an episode at the breakfast table when Mikey was a baby. Now Mikey deliberately distracts them from their arguments with his words and antics. While his awareness of interpersonal tension is impressive in a child this age, it is also worrisome. Mikey is too young to be mediating conflicts between others, especially between his parents. He is essentially assuming responsibility for his parents' needs rather than the other way around. This role reversal is a burden for any child (Minuchin, 1988). Unless the marital conflicts are resolved, Mikey may face difficulties.

Malcolm, the active, precocious toddler, has become a lively and engaging preschooler. He is curious, confident, and full of energy and good humor. His language and thinking skills are well developed when he enters kindergarten. Being very outgoing, Malcolm quickly makes friends at school.

At home Malcolm's social environment continues to be warm and supportive, while still providing him with clear-cut standards of behavior. His mother, father, and grandmother nicely illustrate Baumrind's authoritative parenting: high expectations and firm limits combined with a great deal of love. Their handling of the incident on the playground when Malcolm punched April in their struggle over a tricycle, is a case in point. DeeDee, John, and Momma Jo cherish Malcolm, including his great exuberance. Behavior that to others might seem slightly hyperactive is to them an indication that he is simply full of pep. Yet they do not take Malcolm's physical aggression lightly. They demand of him more self-control and concern for other people. In a family less able to handle Malcolm and less willing to go to bat for him, this incident could have been a negative turning point. But instead, Malcolm's parents take the event in stride and turn it into a valuable learning experience for him. We can imagine Malcolm in the future striving to heed what his parents have said by resolving peer conflicts more peacefully. If the Williams family continues to be this supportive of Malcolm's development, we would expect him to continue to flourish as he enters middle childhood, a time that poses special challenges for urban, minority-group children.

The preschool period for Meryl, as we have said, marks a significant turnaround. She is showing more independence and self-management. When functioning at her best (as in the classroom "store" play when she first meets Amy), she seems every bit as competent as Mikey and Malcolm. This notable improvement is probably due in large part to Meryl's more stable and responsive home environment. In offering Karen his love and support, Joe Turner has helped her to become a more effective parent. Now, potentially stressful situations with Meryl seem more benign to Karen. She can respond to Meryl more firmly and consistently, following the model that Joe provides. Joe has also made a direct contribution to Meryl's improvement by handling her in an affectionate but authoritative way. In these new circumstances, Meryl has become more cooperative, self-reliant, and confident about herself. She is breaking away from the overly passive, weak, and dependent profile often found in children with a history of anxious-resistant attachment.

We cannot say that Meryl is suddenly an entirely different person, however. Her new self shows clear conti-nuities with her past self. While perhaps no longer a "difficult" child, she is still initially hesitant with peers; she is still reluctant to try new things; and transitions continue to be hard for her. Under stress she may revert to her earlier patterns; but, given time, she can adapt well to new situations. As with our two other children, we can be optimistic about Meryl's ultimate adjustment to school.

Our stories are simplified composites of actual cases. The life of any child is more complicated and difficult to understand than the cases we present here. Nevertheless, the coherence in individual development that we describe in each case is supported by an emerging body of research.

PART FIVE

Middle Childhood

PART FIVE

Three Children in Middle Childhood

MALCOLM WILLIAMS

"Here are the arithmetic tests you took yesterday," announced Mrs. Khan to her class of fourth graders. "Four of you scored 90 or above: Gretchen, Andrea, Kevin, and Malcolm." Malcolm felt a glow of pride as the teacher handed him his paper. He sneaked a look at Tammy Wilson, who sat diagonally in front of him. She had been watching Malcolm, but she quickly turned away as soon as he glanced in her direction. She stared down at the paper on her desk and her face broke into a smile. Two large dimples appeared on either side of her mouth. Malcolm quickly turned back to his own paper. He wanted to look at Tammy again but he didn't dare. His friends would tease him to death if they knew he liked her.

The rest of the afternoon dragged endlessly for Malcolm. By 3:02 he was in his coat and hurrying down the stairs, trying as best he could not to break the "no running" rule. Down the corridor, past the cafeteria, turn right by the main bulletin board; the short walk to freedom seemed interminable. Malcolm could feel the cool March air rushing in through the open door. The breeze was like a shot of adrenaline to him. Veering around the other children he raced out the door and down the path, his math test flapping in his grip.

"Hey, Malcolm! Wanna shoot some baskets?" shouted Andy, a neighborhood friend in Mr. Denning's class.

"I gotta get home!" yelled Malcolm over his shoulder, never slowing his pace.

Despite Malcolm's excitement at getting a good grade on the test, doing well in school was not really new for him. Malcolm could be an excellent student when he applied himself. He was nowhere near as diligent as his sister Teresa, but his quick mind and enthusiasm for learning earned the praise of his teachers. "If he would just channel more of that energy into his school work," Mrs. Khan told DeeDee, "Malcolm would routinely be near the top of the class." But channeling his energies into any one thing for long didn't come easily to Malcolm. He was a child with as many interests as there were hours in the day. Collections of everything imaginable cluttered his untidy room. It seemed that every week he was announcing something else he wanted to do when he grew up. All the members of his family took great pleasure in Malcolm's endless plans and projects. They were convinced that this child, with his buoyant high spirits, was a very special one.

"Momma Jo!" called out Malcolm loudly, as he ran up the steps two at a time, still clutching his arithmetic test. "Momma Jo!"

"What is it?" Momma Jo asked. "What's got you so near burstin'?"

"Look!" said Malcolm excitedly, stopping at last to catch his breath, and he extended the precious, now crumpled sheet of paper to his grandmother.

"Well, will you look at that! No wonder you're so proud of yourself!"

"It was one of the best grades in the whole class!" Malcolm added.

"I wouldn't expect any less from such a bright chil' as you," Momma Jo answered. "Now come on here into the kitchen and tell me all about it. Your momma and daddy are gonna be so proud of you when they get home!"

The next two years of Malcolm's life passed quickly. In the sixth grade he was still doing well at school, though concentration remained a problem he constantly had to work on. Malcolm also continued to be popular with his classmates. Because he was filled with enthusiastic schemes for new ways of having fun, other children liked him and often followed his lead. Malcolm's best friends were three other boys from his neighborhood: Andy, Leon, and Curtis. After school "the black pack," as Teresa called them, would usually head for the park. Or, if the weather was bad, they would often congregate in Malcolm's room to play with his model train set. DeeDee marveled at how grown-up the boys were becoming. Beginning this year they had started to ride the bus across town by themselves to browse in their favorite hobby shop.

Given how independent Malcolm normally was, it seemed strange when he began to ask his father if he could catch a ride to school in the morning on John's way to work. Malcolm himself was a little embarrassed by this new arrangement. He didn't want the other kids to think he was a baby, coming to school with his daddy. But at all costs he wanted to avoid tangling with a group of older boys who hung out near the video arcade. They had been hassling him on the way to school for weeks now. Malcolm was not about to tell his parents what the problem was. If his father tried to interfere, it would only make things worse.

One morning when John had dropped him off a block from school, Malcolm spotted an older boy in an alley across the street, throwing something into a trash-can. Normally, Malcolm would have walked on by, not concerned about other people's garbage. But something about the older boy's furtive glances piqued his curiosity. When the older boy had left, Malcolm crossed the street and looked inside the can. There, under a pile of old newspapers, and wrapped in a plastic grocery bag, was a .22-caliber handgun. Malcolm checked the gun and found that it wasn't loaded. He stood there for a minute, his mind racing. Then he stuffed the gun back into the bag and into his backpack.

In the schoolyard he slipped the bag out of his backpack and secretly showed its contents to Andy. "Let 'em mess with me," he said, referring to the boys who hung out near the video arcade. "I know how to take care of myself!"

"What ya got?" asked Derek Sanders as he came up behind Malcolm and Andy and peered over their shoulders. "Hey, Malcolm, you're not supposed to have a gun in school! You're gonna get in trouble!"

"It's just for self-defense, turkey," Malcolm answered. "Everybody has a right to self-defense. It's in the Constitution. C'mon, Andy. Let's go. Derek's being a jerk."

"It's against the *rules*," Derek called out loudly. "You know what Mr. Esquallo told us!"

"Will you slow down, Malcolm. I can't understand what you're saying." John Williams sat on the edge of a desk at the post office, listening into the phone.

"It was just for self-defense, Daddy. Honest it was. To show those gang kids I'm not afraid of them. Only Derek *ratted* on me. He told one of the teachers. I can't believe he did that! No one ever rats. You just don't rat on guys or everyone'll say you're a fink!" Malcolm's voice was high-pitched and very emotional. He sounded on the verge of tears.

"OK, Malcolm, OK. I get the picture. Now put your principal back on the phone. We'll talk more about this when I get to school."

"Do you know how serious what you did was, Malcolm?" DeeDee asked him, as she and John sat at the kitchen table with their son that evening.

"Yes," Malcolm answered, his head hanging, his voice soft and contrite.

"*Why* is bringing a gun to school so bad, no matter what the reason?" DeeDee pressed him.

"'Cause people could get hurt."

"*You* could've gotten hurt—not necessarily by the gun, but by those gang kids who thought you had a *loaded* gun! Do you know that?" DeeDee's face was filled with concern.

"Yes."

"What if that gun had been used in a crime?" John put in sternly. "You're lucky you didn't end up in trouble with the police."

"You're lucky Mr. Esquallo understood the situation and let you off as lightly as he did."

"I don't feel lucky. I hate Derek. I hate all white people. You can't trust 'em."

DeeDee put a hand on Malcolm's shoulder and looked at him for a while. "Let me ask you something," she said softly. "What color were the boys who've been hassling you on the way to school?"

"Black," answered Malcolm, fingering a small hole in the knee of his jeans.

"So you don't put down all black people just because those boys are bad. Why do you put down all white people because of Derek? Anyway," DeeDee added, "Derek may have only been doing what he thought was right. You *did* break an important rule, you know."

"Naah, he didn't think it was right," Malcolm answered scornfully. "He was just tryin' to get me in trouble. He wanted to get back at me 'cause I called him a jerk. He's not so big on followin' the rules, ya know. He cheats on his spelling tests. I've *seen* him do it."

"Well, it's not always easy to live up to what we think is right," answered DeeDee. "Sometimes we all disappoint ourselves that way. White or black, it makes no difference. The important thing is that we learn from our mistakes."

"I guess so," said Malcolm grudgingly, reaching for his glass of milk. "But you know, Momma, when a white guy's a jerk he's the biggest jerk of all."

DeeDee smiled and shook her head. Some lessons are learned in small steps, she thought.

MIKEY GORDON

"Would you read the next page for us please, Mikey." Mrs. Clayton requested.

Mikey swung his gaze back from the window as soon as he heard his name. He looked confused, then embarrassed. "Jimmy . . . ran . . . with the . . . kite," he began hesitantly.

"Mikey, Katie just read that part," Mrs. Clayton corrected gently, as the other children in the reading group started to giggle. "Begin at the top of the next page."

Mikey flushed and fumbled to turn the page. Everyone's eyes were on him. What's wrong with this child? Mrs. Clayton wondered as she showed Mikey where to start. On days like this he hardly seemed the same little boy who eight months ago had been one of the best readers in her second-grade class. Mrs. Clayton was also concerned about Mikey's relationships with his classmates. He no longer seemed the leader he used to be. On the playground he was usually content to follow what the other boys suggested. "I'm a little worried about Mikey," Mrs. Clayton told Christine at a parent-teacher conference toward the end of the school year. "Sometimes he's his old fun-loving self. But other times he seems moody, even a bit lost. Is everything OK at home?"

"Things are fine at home," Christine answered all too quickly. But she knew in her heart that her marriage was going from bad to worse and that Mikey was a barometer of the conflict. Frank now stayed out late two or three nights a week. When he came home he had always

been drinking heavily, and when he was drunk he was surly. Christine treated him gingerly for fear of being struck. But as usual, deferential treatment only seemed to make things worse.

One day in March Frank's boss had called at lunchtime to ask where Frank was. Christine, taken aback, had blurted out some vague story about a possible doctor's appointment. She sensed that Frank's boss knew she was lying. That night, when she asked Frank where he had been, he said it was none of her damn business. "But you'll lose your job!" Christine had shouted.

"That's *my* business," Frank answered. Then he laughed cynically and looked at Christine with contempt. "What the hell's the difference? You don't need my paycheck. You're doing just fine at your high and mighty shop!"

These days Frank and Christine rarely talked except to argue. The best they could do was to try to ignore one another. Mikey, sensing the widening rift between his parents, began to fill the tense silences with hilarious imitations of some of the teachers at his school. He also began praising one parent to the other. When he was with his mother, he would talk excitedly about what he had done with his dad; when he was with his father, he talked in glowing terms about his mom. But even these poignant efforts had no effect on Christine and Frank. The gap between them had become a canyon. There was no bridging it now.

The voices first came to Mikey as if in a dream. His parents were arguing, yelling angrily at each other. The voices grew louder and more filled with heated emotion. Eight-year-old Mikey could feel himself drawn out of sleep. He lay in bed with his eyes wide open. The voices were clearer now, their tone sharper. This wasn't a dream. It was real life. Mikey got out of bed and pulled his door open. There sat his two sisters huddled in their nightgowns at the top of the stairs. Becky and Janie glanced at Mikey and then looked back down the stairs. Mikey walked over and squatted beside them. "They're going to kill each other this time," Becky whispered in her 14-year-old wisdom. "This is really a bad one."

The trouble had started hours earlier, as Frank sat drinking with four of his buddies at the Riverside Tavern. Sam had made a comment about men who couldn't "handle" their wives. The others had laughed and begun ribbing Frank. What was it like being married to such a women's-libber? George wanted to know. When Frank protested, Pete pointed out that Christine had him "well trained." Then Phil began to speculate about all those trips that Christine had been taking to New York. "It's pretty swingin' down there, ya know," he went on relentlessly, "even if most of the guys are really more like girls." By the time Frank left he was very drunk and very humiliated. As soon as he walked through the door he let the anger spill out.

"What do you want me to *do?*" Christine pleaded, knowing that she shouldn't try to reason with him when he was in this condition.

"Be the wife you're supposed to be, damn it! Don't think I don't know what goes on in New York!"

"Frank, that's crazy! I rush back home the same day just to try to keep you happy!"

"Don't call me crazy!" Frank shouted and he pushed her against the wall.

"That's it! I've had it!" Christine shouted back, and she ran to the hall and started up the stairs. As she looked up she was startled to see her three children silently watching, all with strangely calm expressions on their faces. "Get your coats," she instructed sharply. "And be quick about it! We're going to grandma's." Two weeks later Christine filed for divorce.

"So how's it been goin' at home?" Frank Gordon asked his son as the two settled into a booth at Burger King.

"OK, I guess," said Mikey unenthusiastically. It had been almost a year now since the separation. The divorce had been finalized. This had been a difficult time for Christine and the three children. She had rented a small house near her mother's, and everyone despised the cramped quarters. The girls constantly complained that the bedroom they shared was too small even for a pair of ants. There was just no privacy, they said. Christine had given the second bedroom to Mikey, leaving her to sleep on a fold-out couch in the living room. Being so crowded only intensified the stress of a difficult situation.

Then the girls began to complain that their father was always taking Mikey on weekend outings—fishing trips, baseball games, camping excursions—that didn't include them. When Christine insisted that Frank treat the children more fairly, he relented and began asking the girls along. But the girls then said they weren't interested in "a bunch of slimy fish" or living in a tent where you couldn't even plug in your hair dryer. In exasperation Christine let them go their own ways. After all, they were 15 and 13 now and spent most of their free time with their friends. Both were very clothes-conscious; they meticulously painted their nails; and even seventh-grade Janie was starting to wear makeup when she went to parties.

But it was Mikey who gave Christine the greatest worry. Some days he seemed lethargic and depressed. When she tried to talk to him about the divorce, he would pick at his fingernails and mutter one-word responses. His school work also continued to suffer, just as it had before the separation. He had trouble paying attention in class, and many mornings he fought with Christine about going to school at all. Sometimes she gave in and let him stay home. It was only by promising to have him tutored in the summer that Christine prevented Mikey from having to repeat the third grade. Finally, toward the end of the summer, things seemed to be getting a little better. Mikey was happier as he looked forward to a two-week vacation he and his father were going to take in Maine. He smiled more often and spent less time alone in his room. Despite this more cheerful exterior, however, worries lay just beneath the surface. Mikey couldn't shake the idea that somehow *he* was to blame for the divorce. He kept thinking that in some way he had let his parents down. His secret dream was that one day they would get back together.

"Hey, what's up? You're a million miles away." Frank's voice, slightly muffled as he chewed his Whopper, interrupted his son's thoughts. "We're still goin' fishin' this weekend, aren't we?"

"Sure," said Mikey, brightening a little.

"Good. 'Cause there's someone I'm gonna bring along, someone I want you to meet. Her name's Nancy and she works in the office at the construction company. You'll like her. She's OK."

Mikey looked blankly at his father, as if he understood the words but not their meaning.

"Hey, aren't you gonna eat the rest of those fries?" Frank asked, reaching over to help himself to one.

MERYL POLONIUS TURNER

This sumer I got a new bruther. He crys alot. Mom seys all babys cry. Sumtimes I make a fase and he stops crying. Wen he gets biger I will show him my toys. I like haveing a bruther moste of the time.

"Oh, that's *very* good!" Karen exclaimed after reading the story that Meryl had written during her first day in third grade. "And look, you've done a picture of the whole family! There you are holding daddy's hand and here I am holding little Joey. You even drew my fuzzy blue bedroom slippers. Are they really that big and blue?"

"They're pretty big, Mom," Meryl said, considering the picture soberly.

"Well, we'll just have to hang this right up on the refrigerator where everyone can see it."

"You can take down the one with the pussy willows to make room," Meryl suggested. "That one's old and I don't like it very much any more. I can draw a lot better now."

Karen was astounded at how much better Meryl did everything these days. Around the house Meryl was a real little helper. She would stand by, ready to pass the soap and towel, when Karen was giving Joey his bath. She meticulously set the table for dinner, making sure the silverware was neatly aligned. Meryl's second grade teacher had called her "a joy to have in the class." Although Meryl was not the brightest of her pupils, she worked hard, listened carefully, and cooperated well with others. Karen could hardly believe this was the same little girl who used to throw tantrums that could inspire awe in even the most seasoned of parents.

But looking beneath the surface, Karen could see threads from Meryl's past. Meryl was still shy with strangers and hesitant in new situations. Take the time that Joe had tried to teach her to ride a bicycle. Meryl had just turned six and was starting first grade. Other children her age were riding two-wheelers, and Joe thought it was time for Meryl to learn how to ride one too. But she stubbornly refused to give him permission to remove the training wheels from her bike. "I'll fall off!" she insisted. "I *know* I'll fall off!" Joe removed the training wheels anyway and coaxed her to give it a try. He ran alongside until she was riding smoothly and then let go of the bike. Meryl stopped pedaling and slowed to a wobble. "You've got to keep pedaling!" Joe shouted from behind her. "You can't just *sit* there! Pedal!" Meryl slowed to almost a standstill and crashed to the ground. Sobbing, she got up and limped away toward home. "Don't be a quitter, honey," Joe called out after her. Meryl just kept walking. Joe was afraid she might never try riding a bike again.

But Meryl surprised him. She learned to ride a bike her own way. In the weeks that followed she studied other children on their bikes. She watched them pedal, mount and dismount, turn corners, and stop. Then one day shortly before Christmas she suddenly announced to Joe: "I'm ready to ride my bike now." Joe took the bike out again and Meryl gingerly climbed on. "Don't let go this time," she instructed. "You promise?" Joe assured her he would run along right beside her, holding onto the back of the seat until she told him to let go. Within a week she was riding with confidence, as if she had been doing it for years. The following spring she tried roller skating. At first she would inch her way from tree to fence post, clutching at anything that could give her support. But soon she was skating with remarkable skill, even taking the cracks and bumps in stride. It seemed as if every month now she was ready to try something new.

What pleased Karen the most was Meryl's friendship with Amy. The two girls played together every chance they got. Amy would call Meryl on Saturday morning and they would make plans for the weekend:

"Why don't you come over here and we can play in the pool. My Dad's fixing it up today."

"OK. I'll bring my Barbie doll and her beach stuff."

Later that day the two would be back at Meryl's asking if Amy could stay for dinner. Soon they would be calling Amy's mother to ask if Amy could stay overnight. Because both girls had blonde hair, strangers sometimes asked them if they were sisters. "No," Meryl and Amy giggled, putting an arm around each other's shoulder. "We're just *best friends*."

The summer after Meryl finished fourth grade, the Turner family moved into a new house. Meryl was delighted with her new room. She and Amy spent hours picking out a new bedspread and curtains and deciding what color to paint the walls. But Meryl's "most favorite" part of the house was the area under the back deck. It was high enough for a 10-year-old to stand up in but much too low for an adult. Meryl and Amy called it their apartment. They hung old blankets from the deck to form makeshift walls, and they posted a sign that said in large letters: "PRIVATE. KEEP OUT!" When 2-year-old Joey dared to peek in, the girls immediately shooed him away despite his tears and protests. That summer everything seemed perfect to Karen. Two beautiful children, a house of their own—finally, some of the good things in life. Neither she nor Joe realized what a heavy strain a large mortgage could place on their marriage and family.

"Meryl, honey, are you going to stay in *all* Saturday? It's so nice out. Why don't you call Amy and see what she's up to?" The day was truly a beautiful one, particularly warm and sunny for November.

Meryl briefly looked up from the picture she was drawing of a mother dog and her puppies. "Amy's probably over at that dumb Rita Martinez's house," Meryl said jealously. "She's always over there, and Rita can never do anything 'cause she always has to take care of her stupid little brother and help clean the house and stuff. I don't like her much anyway. She's Mexican."

"What has being Mexican got to do with whether you like her?" asked Karen. She tried to think of family conversations that might have triggered this sudden prejudice. All she could remember was something Joe had said about not being able to understand two new Mexican workers at the newspaper loading dock. "If they come to this country they should at least *try* to learn English," he had grumbled. Could remarks like that have influenced Meryl?

Putting a forced smile on her face, Karen returned to the original subject: "Why don't you just ride your bike over to Rita's and see if all three of you can play together?" Karen was worried that Meryl had been spending so much time alone lately. Often she stayed in her room for hours, sprawled on the floor with her crayons spread around her, slowly and carefully drawing. Puppies with their mothers was a frequently repeated theme. But what worried Karen even more was the way her daughter was talking right now. The old negative, insecure Meryl was emerging again.

"I'm busy," answered Meryl, turning back to her drawing and picking up a brown crayon. "And anyway," she added with a touch of bitterness, "who needs *them?*"

Karen knew her daughter too well to think this change had sprung from nowhere. Whenever there were problems that touched on Meryl's life, she tended to withdraw and become more inhibited. This time it must be because things were so tense between Joe and herself. Joe and Karen were finding it hard to make their monthly mortgage payment. Their credit cards were overdrawn. Their bills were piling up. They talked and worried about money almost every day. Even going to the supermarket had become an ordeal for them because they agonized over everything they bought. Did they really *need* that bag of cookies? Joe would ask. Could they get Meryl to eat the no-name brand of peanut butter? Their anxiety was clearly starting to have an effect on Meryl.

One evening about a week later Joe exploded because Karen had splurged on a sirloin steak for dinner.

"I was only trying to do something a little special!" Karen protested, her voice starting to quiver.

"Will you stop whining?" Joe had shouted. "I'm sick and tired of being the only adult around here!"

"Just because you don't show your feelings, don't think that makes you an adult!" Karen shot back.

"Fine! Let's just sell this damn house! I'm fed up with living this way!"

Meryl, who was sitting at the kitchen table, visibly shrank. Later she told her mother she had a stomachache and shut herself in her room. It was then that Karen knew she and Joe somehow had to solve this problem. Gradually they began to talk about it more rationally. They decided that they really loved the house and wanted to keep it. The best solution would be for Karen to find a job. After some thought, Karen settled on the idea of getting a real estate license and going to work with her mother. The idea buoyed her spirits, and she threw herself into studying for the exam. It was a happy day the following April when she took her first clients house hunting.

But the best part for Karen was the change she could see in Meryl. Meryl was thrilled with her mother's new business. She was constantly asking questions about the office, poring over Karen's book of listings, and saying which houses she thought were the prettiest. Meryl's friendship with Amy was also rekindled. The turning point came one Saturday morning when Meryl went over to Rita's to work on a school project that she, Amy, and Rita had been assigned. Meryl had felt nervous when she entered the Martinez's house, but Mrs. Martinez, Rita's warm, outgoing mother, had put her at ease. By the end of the morning the three girls were laughing and talking as they worked together at the kitchen table. From then on, both Amy and Meryl often went to Rita's. They enjoyed helping her with her chores in the large, close-knit Martinez family.

"*Yo ayudo mis amigas,*" Meryl said to Karen one Sunday evening as they cleared away the dinner dishes. "That means 'I help my girl friends' in Spanish. Mrs. Martinez told me. And Rita told me some other Spanish words. *Perro* means dog, and *gato* means cat, and *casa* means house."

"I know some Spanish, too," said Karen, as she smiled and brushed back a lock of Meryl's hair. "*Te amo.* Do you know what that means? It means I love you."

Chapter 11

Cognitive Development in Middle Childhood

Mr. Jones went to a restaurant and ordered a whole pizza for dinner. When the waiter asked if he wanted it cut into six or eight pieces, Mr. Jones said: "You'd better make it six. I could never eat eight!"

"Please stay out of the house today," Susie's mother said. "I have a lot of work to do." "Okay," replied Susie as she walked to the stairs. "Where do you think you're going?" her mother asked. "Well," said Susie, "if I can't stay in the house, I'll just play in my room instead."

Mr. Barley teaches first grade. One day his class was talking about religion, so Mr. Barley asked how many of the children were Catholic. When Bobby didn't raise his hand, the teacher said, "Why, Bobby, I thought you were Catholic too." "Oh no," said Bobby. "I'm not Catholic; I'm American."

These three jokes are taken from a study of children's humor conducted by Paul McGhee (1976). If they don't strike you as hilarious, that is because you are no longer in middle childhood. The typical 8- or 9-year-old finds these jokes very funny. The first one involves a misunderstanding about conservation, a concept we discussed in Chapter 9. Mr. Jones apparently thinks that the amount of pizza increases if it is cut into more slices. The other two jokes involve misunderstandings about classification. Susie is confused over the relationship between the subordinate concept of "room" and the larger concept of "house"; Bobby doesn't realize that he can simultaneously be classified both a Catholic and an American. Each of these errors in reasoning is conquered during middle childhood, which is why children this age find these jokes funny: the punch lines deal with skills that 8- or 9-year-olds have recently acquired. Preschoolers, in contrast, do not find these jokes funny because they don't understand that Mr. Jones, Susie, and Bobby have committed errors in reasoning.

Between the ages of 5 and 8 children become fascinated with telling jokes and riddles. One reason is that they begin to spend more time with their peers, and jokes and riddles are part of what they share in the peer group. Being good at telling jokes and riddles is usually rewarded with social approval, so children are motivated to develop this skill. This is a social learning explanation.

In middle childhood, children become interested in and skilled at telling jokes.

Another explanation is that children this age acquire the cognitive abilities needed to master the format of jokes and riddles and to understand their humor. They take great pleasure in exercising these newfound abilities, so joke and riddle telling blossoms. This is a Piagetian explanation. A third explanation is that between the ages of 5 and 8 all the various skills needed to understand and tell jokes have become practiced and refined enough for the child to integrate them into an effective joke-telling system. This is an information-processing explanation. In searching for the roots of cognitive changes during middle childhood, we will use a combination of all three of these approaches.

Piaget saw the age of 7 as a major cognitive turning point. At around this age, he argued, children make the important transition from preoperational thinking to more advanced concrete operational thought. Many contemporary theorists challenge this view. They see a major developmental reorganization at the age of about 4, rather than several years later (Bickhard, 1978; Fischer and Bullock, 1984). We presented this viewpoint in Chapter 9, when we talked about the early precursors of many concrete operational skills. In this chapter we continue that perspective by examining how the major cognitive developments of middle childhood involve refinements on and more widespread use of skills that existed in primitive form during the preschool years. The picture we present differs from the Piagetian view that middle childhood marks the emergence of an entirely new system of logic.

Among the cognitive changes that occur in middle childhood, several stand out as particularly important. One is that children this age become better at logical, systematic thinking using multiple pieces of information—in other words, they show a marked decline in centration (discussed in Chapter 9). In addition, they become much more capable of perceiving underlying reality despite superficial appearance (Flavell, Miller, and Miller, 1993). This advance helps them to think far more maturely about transformations, such as the ones that occur when pizza is cut into extra slices or when water is poured into a taller, thinner container. The child is now able to understand that no real change in quantity occurs despite these changes in appearance. Finally, elementary school children come to think much more effectively about their own knowledge and processes of thought. This capacity to think about thinking is called **metacognition.** You saw the beginnings of it in Chapter 9, when we discussed the development of the child's theory of mind. During middle childhood metacognitive skills become much more refined and enable the planning of effective problem-solving strategies in many situations.

Metacognition:
The high-level cognitive operation involving reflection on the thought processes through which human beings gain knowledge; the capacity to think about thinking.

Despite these advances, elementary school children still face cognitive limitations. First, they lack the broad base of knowledge that adults possess. This absence of information sometimes makes their reasoning seem immature. For instance, the summer that Mikey turned 10, he and his friends decided that they would build a raft out of pieces of styrofoam held together by large thumbtacks. The raft, of course, fell to pieces as soon as the boys launched it in a nearby stream, much to their disappointment. What the boys lacked was information about appropriate ways to hold structures together against the forces exerted on them.

Second, because elementary school children have only recently acquired some of their thinking skills, they sometimes have trouble using a skill they possess as part of a larger problem-solving system. For instance, when Meryl was 8 she was perfectly capable of taking another person's perspective, but she didn't always do so when playing checkers with Joe. In her struggle to figure out what

Youngsters in middle childhood understand the distinction between appearance and reality. Puzzling appearance–reality distinctions, such as the apparent bending of this straw due to the refraction of light, cause renewed interest and exploration.

move to make next, she often forgot to look upon Joe's moves from *his* viewpoint—namely, as strategies to lure her into making moves that were to *his* advantage. As a result, Meryl fell into Joe's "traps" over and over again.

Finally, elementary school children cannot reason maturely about abstract and hypothetical problems. Their reasoning tends to be confined to the concrete here and now. For example, if Malcolm at age 9 were presented with the hypothetical problem, "What would you do if your train set wouldn't run one day?" he could not construct a comprehensive picture of all the things that *might* be wrong and then systematically set out to test each one, both alone and in various combinations. In the case of a real problem with his train set, Malcolm would make reasonable attempts to solve it, but his efforts would not be organized to address each possibility in a systematic way.

As you read this chapter, you will learn much more about both the cognitive advances and the cognitive limitations of middle childhood. Elementary school children are far more competent than preschoolers are, but their thinking still has many immature aspects. The emergence of adultlike thinking across a broad range of contexts must await adolescence.

In exploring the cognitive world of middle childhood, we begin with an in-depth look at three areas in which major advances are made: concepts of conservation, classification skills, and memory abilities. In each case, you will see how capacities that emerged during the preschool period set the stage for later, more mature accomplishments. Next, we turn to social factors that can facilitate cognitive development during middle childhood. Here we focus on the roles of both peers and adults in promoting cognitive growth. We then discuss individual differences in cognitive functioning, especially as measured by IQ tests. Finally, we consider the significance of culture in intelligence testing and school achievement.

MAJOR COGNITIVE DEVELOPMENTS OF MIDDLE CHILDHOOD

CONSERVATION CONCEPTS

Although preschoolers sometimes show the beginnings of a grasp of concepts of conservation (the fact that quantities remain the same despite superficial transformations to them), they have trouble reasoning about these topics. They

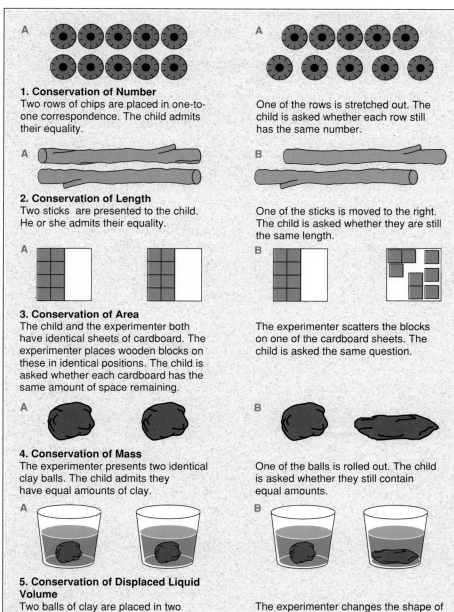

1. Conservation of Number
Two rows of chips are placed in one-to-one correspondence. The child admits their equality.

One of the rows is stretched out. The child is asked whether each row still has the same number.

2. Conservation of Length
Two sticks are presented to the child. He or she admits their equality.

One of the sticks is moved to the right. The child is asked whether they are still the same length.

3. Conservation of Area
The child and the experimenter both have identical sheets of cardboard. The experimenter places wooden blocks on these in identical positions. The child is asked whether each cardboard has the same amount of space remaining.

The experimenter scatters the blocks on one of the cardboard sheets. The child is asked the same question.

4. Conservation of Mass
The experimenter presents two identical clay balls. The child admits they have equal amounts of clay.

One of the balls is rolled out. The child is asked whether they still contain equal amounts.

5. Conservation of Displaced Liquid Volume
Two balls of clay are placed in two identical glasses with an equal amount of water. The child is asked whether they displace equal amounts of water.

The experimenter changes the shape of one of the balls and asks the child the same question.

FIGURE 11.1
ASSESSMENT OF CONSERVATION
Researchers use tasks such as the ones shown here to assess children's understanding of conservation during middle childhood.

are greatly hampered by both centration and the appearance-reality problem. Gradually during middle childhood, however, these earlier limitations are largely overcome. Most elementary school children before age ten exhibit an understanding of conservation of physical quantities such as number, length, liquid volume, area, and mass, and they are able to use this understanding in a variety of circumstances. Figure 11.1 shows how researchers assess children's knowledge of conservation concepts.

Necessary truth:
Knowledge whose validity can be demonstrated without resorting to empirical evidence; a logical necessity.

Contingent truth:
Knowledge that is dependent on empirical observations or on information gathered through the senses.

An understanding of conservation requires children to look beyond the physical characteristics of things and to reason logically about what certain transformations mean (or don't mean). In doing so, they are appealing to **necessary truth,** as opposed to **contingent truth** (Campbell and Bickhard, 1986; Inhelder and Piaget, 1964; Moshman and Timmons, 1982). Contingent truth is dependent (contingent) upon empirical observations. When you look out the window, observe drops of water falling, and conclude that it is raining, you are deducing a contingent truth. In contrast, a necessary truth is based on logical necessity apart from what you observe with your senses. When a twisting line waiting to get into a movie is formed into a longer straight line, you know by logical necessity that your wait to get in will be no greater than it was before, because no more people have been added even though the line is now longer.

In grasping the necessary truth that number is conserved despite a change in spacing, elementary school children are overcoming the appearance-reality problem that constrained them as preschoolers. They are no longer deceived by superficial appearance (the length of a movie line), and can think about the underlying reality. Still, there are limitations to their thinking. During middle childhood, understanding of necessary truth tends to be limited to concrete characteristics, such as the number of people or the volume of a liquid. Children this age find it very hard to grasp the necessary truths of more abstract concepts. You'll see this in a later section, when we talk about classification.

AGE, CULTURE, AND THE EMERGENCE OF CONSERVATION CONCEPTS

Piaget argued that the same skills in logic allow an understanding of *all* the concepts of conservation. In his view, children acquire some of these concepts before others simply because they learn the characteristics of different kinds of quantities at different times. Table 11.1 shows the ages at which 50 percent of American children succeed at different conservation tasks. Because this table is based on a large number of studies, many with different criteria for having attained conservation, a range of ages is shown for each task. In general, these ages are older than those reported in some of the recent studies described in Chapter 9. That is because, in those studies, researchers found ways to elicit the best possible performance preschoolers were capable of.

TABLE 11.1
AGE RANGES WHEN 50 PERCENT OF CHILDREN
PASS TESTS OF CONSERVATION

Task	AGE							
	4	5	6	7	8	9	10	11
Number	▬▬▬▬▬							
Mass			▬▬▬▬▬▬					
Length	▬▬▬▬▬▬▬▬							
Continuous quantity			▬▬▬▬▬					
Area				▬▬▬▬▬▬				
Weight					▬▬▬▬▬			
Displaced liquid volume						▬▬▬▬▬		

SOURCE: Adapted from Gross, 1985.

When researchers assess the ages at which concepts of conservation emerge among children in other Western industrialized societies, they find patterns very similar to those in the United States. This is not the case, however, in traditional societies that lack formal schooling. Here, a lag of one or more years in the development of concepts of conservation is frequently found (Dansen and Heron, 1981). In one early study, for instance, only 50 percent of 10- to 13-year-olds in Senegal correctly solved a conservation of liquid volume problem (Greenfield, 1966). Some studies in traditional societies have even found adults who fail to exhibit an understanding of conservation.

Do these results suggest that people in these societies have major cognitive deficits? No. Developmentalists have gathered considerable evidence in favor of two alternative explanations. One is that the Western researchers conducting studies in traditional societies do not effectively communicate the conservation tasks to their subjects. This was suggested in a study of Nova Scotian children who were tested in English for their understanding of concepts of conservation (Nyiti, 1982). Those who spoke English at school and Micmac (an Algonquin Indian language) at home lagged behind their peers who spoke English both at home and at school. However, when each group was tested in the language they spoke at home, no differences were found. Thus, at least part of the reported delay in the development of conservation concepts in non-Western societies may be due to subtle difficulties in understanding what the Western researchers are asking.

Another explanation is that cultures that lack formal schooling do not provide the opportunities to learn about conservation concepts, or about test-taking, that Western cultures do. As a result, their children are slower in developing these skills. If this theory is right, then providing supplemental learning experiences for non-Western children should help close the gap between them and their Western peers. Research shows that this is often what happens. In one study, for instance, children from non-Western societies were trained to perform cognitive tasks similar to conservation tasks (Dasen, Ngini, and Lavallee, 1979). Then they were given conservation tests. Although the previous training did not entirely eliminate the delay in understanding conservation compared with a group of Western children, it did dramatically reduce it. Apparently, normal youngsters of middle childhood age in all cultures have the cognitive skills needed to rapidly develop an understanding of conservation if given the opportunity to do so. This observation is consistent with the developmental pattern discussed in earlier chapters that when abilities first emerge they are fragile, require substantial cognitive resources, and are used in a limited range of contexts. With additional experience they become more robust, require fewer cognitive resources, and are used in a broader range of contexts. During middle childhood understanding of conservation of physical quantities becomes automatic and is a piece of knowledge that can be used in solving other problems.

AN INFORMATION-PROCESSING APPROACH TO CONSERVATION

Piaget believed that the ability to solve conservation problems resulted from a fundamental shift in children's ability to reason logically. Developmentalists who take an information-processing approach offer other explanations that have to do with changes in the mental procedures that children follow to arrive at their solutions. Information-processing researchers sometimes describe these procedures as a series of rules. Problem-solvers do not *consciously* follow these

At the beginning of middle childhood, children's developing cognitive abilities enhance their understanding of numerical concepts, including their knowledge of number facts (for example, 2 + 3 = 5).

rules; they use them implicitly. But as the rules change, so do the kinds of solutions reached.

Taking an information-processing perspective, Robert Siegler and his colleagues have analyzed children's performance on conservation of number tasks and deduced five rules used at different ages (Siegler, 1981; Siegler and Robinson, 1982). Each rule accounts for a certain pattern of performance, from the immature errors of young preschoolers to the consistently correct responses of children in the middle elementary school years. For example, whereas 3-year-olds seem to follow the rule "The longer one always has more," the rule that many 6-year-olds seem to follow is "Ignore everything else and count." Both the 3-year-olds and the 6-year-olds in this example treat the problem as one that involves a contingent truth; the answer depends on what they *see* about the length of the row or on what they *hear* themselves count. It is not until age 7 and older that children recognize the problem as involving a necessary truth: number cannot change unless something is added or subtracted.

Similar sets of rules could be written to describe children's performance at different ages on other types of conservation tasks. The most mature rule would always entail an understanding of the logical necessity inherent in the problem. The content of less mature rules would vary depending on the particular conservation concept involved, because different physical dimensions and transformations have to be considered. For conservation of liquid volume problems, for example, children have to attend to the height and width of a column of liquid, not to the length of a row and the spacing between objects, as they do in a conservation of number task. A rules approach to solving such problems tends to draw attention to these differences. So it isn't surprising that children at first treat each kind of problem differently and don't develop the various concepts of conservation all at the same time. Only after children understand the logical necessity entailed in two different kinds of conservation problems can they fully appreciate the similarity between them.

SUMMING UP CONSERVATION CONCEPTS

Whether children's performance on conservation problems is explained using a Piagetian or an information-processing framework, several things are clear. First, although some concepts of conservation emerge during the preschool years, it is in middle childhood that youngsters acquire a large set of conservation concepts and use them confidently in measurement and reasoning about concrete quantities. Second, at least within Western cultures, the various concepts of conservation are acquired in a predictable order. Third, once children are able to consistently solve conservation problems, they are soon able to explain their answers in terms that show they understand conservation as a necessary truth. And finally, once children understand conservation, they can think logically about many quantitative issues. For instance, conservation concepts are prerequisites for performing well on many of the arithmetic problems given in elementary school. In general, a close connection exists between the emergence of certain cognitive skills during middle childhood and the age at which societies begin formal schooling of children.

CLASSIFICATION SKILLS

As we discussed in Chapter 9, preschoolers can readily sort things along one dimension, such as separating all the red blocks from the blue ones. But Piaget maintained that not until the concrete operational subperiod, beginning around age 7, can children understand the relationships among categories in a more complex classification system. One such system is **hierarchical classification,** in which items are categorized using a hierarchy of subordinate and superordinate classes. Another is **matrix classification,** in which an item is categorized simultaneously along two independent dimensions, such as shape and color.

HIERARCHICAL CLASSIFICATION

Hierarchical classification is often used to organize bodies of knowledge. Consider how we organize our knowledge of animals (see Figure 11.2). Sam, the Gordon family's pet, is a golden retriever, which is a type of domesticated dog belonging to a category called canines, along with such other species as wolves, jackals, and coyotes. Canines, in turn, are classified as a type of mammal, which is a type of animal. As we move up this hierarchy of classification, each term is broader and more inclusive. Notice, too, that each higher class is composed of all the classes under it in the hierarchy. The concept "domesticated dog," for example, is produced by adding all the various breeds of dog together (golden retriever, poodle, cocker spaniel, and so forth). For this reason, Piaget said that hierarchical classification involves the **addition of classes.** The addition of classes, in Piaget's theory, is a concrete operation.

Researchers use a task called **class inclusion** as the standard test of whether a child understands hierarchical classification. The child is presented with a group of objects—say, six petunias and three begonias. The investigator questions the child to make sure that he or she knows petunias and begonias are both kinds of flowers. The child is then asked, "Are there more petunias or more flowers?" Surprisingly, most 6-year-olds say there are more petunias. They seem to be comparing the two subordinate classes, petunias and begonias. Not until age 8 do most children start to give the correct answer by comparing one of the subordinate classes (petunia) to the superordinate class (flower).

Hierarchical classification: A classification system in which a particular category (e.g., dogs) is defined by the sum of its subordinate categories (e.g., spaniels, setters, retrievers, etc.).

Matrix classification: A classification system in which an item is categorized simultaneously along two independent dimensions, such as shape and color.

Addition of classes: The cumulative process for constructing hierarchical classification systems.

Class inclusion: A task that tests a child's understanding of hierarchical classification—i.e., the ability to differentiate between a subordinate class (such as *petunia*) and a superordinate class (such as *flower*).

FIGURE 11.2
HIERARCHICAL
CLASSIFICATION
This hierarchy is part of the classification system for mammals. Each intersection represents a class (e.g., the class of domesticated dogs, which is composed of the subordinate classes of golden retrievers and all other domesticated dog breeds). An understanding of the relationships between subordinate and superordinate classes develops during middle childhood.

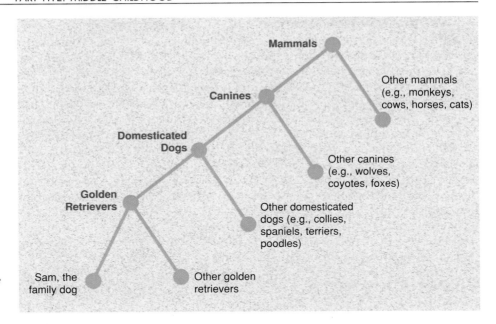

Why do children age six and younger fail at the class-inclusion test? They seem to have trouble thinking about petunias as being simultaneously a member of *two* classes—a subordinate one and a superordinate one. You can think of this as a kind of centration, one of the limitations of preschool thought. Of course, the fact that children under 7 can't usually pass the class-inclusion test doesn't mean they're unable to learn anything about hierarchical classification. By the age of 5 or 6, Mikey certainly knew that Sam was a golden retriever and that a golden retriever is a type of dog. But children this age lack a genuine understanding of a hierarchy's structure and its logical implications.

Typically, such genuine understanding is still absent even when children begin to answer the class-inclusion question correctly. For instance, during the first half of middle childhood, most youngsters don't yet realize that a subclass, by definition, cannot contain more elements than its superordinate class. Ellen Markman (1978) demonstrated this in a study of children age 9 and older. When she asked them the class-inclusion question about objects they could see, most answered correctly. However, when she asked them a *hypothetical* question about classification hierarchies ("Suppose we added 100 more petunias; would there be more petunias or more flowers?"), children younger than 11 often gave the wrong answer. Apparently, not until children are approaching adolescence do they grasp the more abstract, logical structure of classification hierarchies. In the earlier years of middle childhood, a knowledge of hierarchical classes seems to be tied to concrete objects and situations. An 8-year-old knows that there are more flowers than petunias because he or she *sees* that petunias form a smaller group. Such knowledge, in other words, is based on contingent, not necessary, truth.

This is not to minimize the cognitive achievement of early middle childhood. In order to know that there are more flowers than petunias, an 8-year-old must be able to compare the subordinate class "petunia" with the superordinate class "flower." This comparison involves first considering petunias and then mentally constructing the larger group "flowers," using petunias as one of its parts. It also involves the reverse procedure: first considering flowers, then breaking down that group into its component subclasses. This skill exactly parallels the reversible thinking skill we discussed with regard to acquiring concepts of conservation.

Interestingly, when the superordinate term is a naturally occurring collection rather than an abstract class, youngsters in early middle childhood have an easier time thinking about the relationship between levels in the system. Remember from Chapter 9 that a collection is an entity with subparts that seem automatically to go together because of their proximity. *Forest*, for example, is a term that refers to a collection of trees. Markman and her colleagues asked 6- and 7-year-olds the standard class-inclusion question versus a modified version that used a collection for the superordinate class (e.g., Markman and Siebert, 1976). For instance, the child might be shown a picture of a forest with 20 oaks and 10 pines and asked, "Are there more oaks or more trees here?" or an alternative, "Which has more, the oaks or the forest?" Quite often 6- and 7-year-olds were able to answer the second type of question correctly, even though they had failed on the first. Apparently, use of the collective term *forest* helped them to consider different levels simultaneously in this classification system. So, like conservation, class inclusion first appears as a skill in only very specialized circumstances and then, during middle childhood, becomes a more generalized and useful skill for constructing knowledge.

MATRIX CLASSIFICATION

Although hierarchical classification is very useful for organizing some kinds of information, other data are better organized in a matrix system. Suppose you are asked to organize bolts for sale in a hardware store (see Figure 11.3). The bolts come in a range of diameters and lengths. You might arrange them in a set of drawers in which the top horizontal row has bolts one-quarter inch in diameter, the second row has bolts three-eighths inch in diameter, the third row has bolts one-half inch in diameter, and so on, working downward in order of increasing diameter. Similarly, you would put the shortest bolts in the first vertical column of drawers at the left, the next size longer in the second column, and so forth, until the longest bolts were in the column at the far right. In the end you would produce a matrix of diameter times length. The bolts in each cell of the matrix would always be the product of the diameter assigned to that particular row and the length assigned to that column. Piaget's term for the mental operation involved in forming such a matrix was **multiplication of classes:** one classification dimension (diameter) is being multiplied by another (length). Like addition of classes, multiplication of classes is a concrete operation in Piaget's theory.

One way in which researchers study the development of matrix classification is to ask children to sort objects that differ along two or more dimensions. For instance, a child might be given a pile of small and large blocks, some of which are red, others green. The child is asked to put the blocks into separate piles so that all the blocks in each pile "go together." As we said in Chapter 9, preschoolers typically sort along one dimension only (size *or* color), as if centration keeps them from noticing the other dimension. During the transition between the preschool period and middle childhood, children frequently begin by sorting the blocks along one dimension and then subdivide the blocks in each of the two resulting piles along the second dimension. This behavior suggests that they notice both dimensions, and so are no longer centrated, but that they can han-

Multiplication of classes: Piaget's term for the process by which matrix classification takes place through the multiplication of one classification dimension by another.

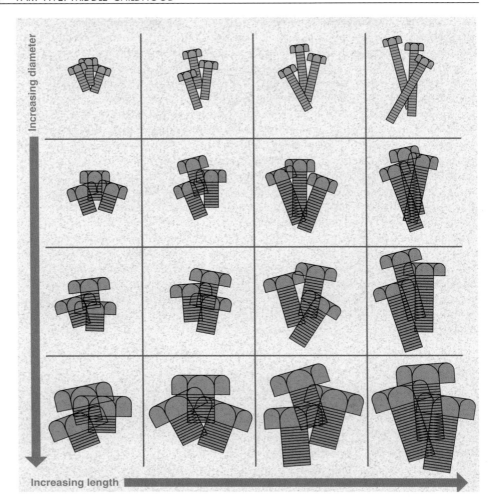

FIGURE 11.3 MATRIX CLASSIFICATION

The bolts for sale in this hardware store have been classified on the basis of both how long they are and how thick they are. As a result, the bolts are organized into a matrix *using the dimensions of bolt length and bolt diameter.*

dle only one dimension at a time. By age 8 or 9, children approach this task much as adults do, sorting along both dimensions simultaneously to produce a classification matrix.

A second way of assessing children's understanding of matrix classification is to ask youngsters to place objects in a matrix that is already partially completed. This task is illustrated in Figure 11.4, which shows a matrix classification system that sorts circles, squares, and triangles of three different colors. A number of studies have confirmed Piaget's findings that preschoolers tend to complete the matrix with an object that is correct along only one of the two dimensions—they choose another red triangle, for example, or another blue square (e.g., Jacobs and Vandeventer, 1968; Overton and Brodzinsky, 1972). In contrast, by age 8, most children find such matrix classification problems easy to solve.

With training, even younger children can solve such problems too (Jacobs and Vandeventer, 1971; Resnick, Siegel, and Kresh, 1971). The children are taught to use a two-step strategy in which they deal first with one dimension and then with the other. This training overcomes the constraints of centration by allowing the children to focus on only one dimension at a time. It also gives them a ready-made approach to the problem. They do not have to formulate their own plan for solving it. But even though 6- and 7-year-olds can learn how to follow the two-step procedure, they don't use it on their own in other situations. This and many other skills that first appear during early childhood aren't used effectively until middle childhood.

A third way to assess children's understanding of matrix classification is to present them with games, such as Twenty Questions, and see what strategies they adopt. In one study, for instance, the child's task was to determine which of 42 pictures the experimenter was thinking of by asking a maximum of 20 yes-or-no questions (Mosher and Hornsby, 1966). (See Figure 11.5.) Two strategies can be used to find the answer. In one, called **hypothesis scanning,** each question is a single, self-contained hypothesis, unrelated to previous questions. The child might ask: "Is it the apple?" If right, the child has won the game, but if wrong, he or she has used up a question and eliminated only one choice. Hypothesis scanning is dominant among 6-year-olds and decreases with age. As children grow older, they become more and more likely to use an approach called **constraint seeking.** Here the player tries, with each consecutive question, to narrow the range of possible alternatives. For example, the child might ask, "Is it bigger than a television?" and when given the answer no, go on to ask, "Is it something you can eat?" If the answer turns out to be yes, the child has eliminated all but four possible choices in the 42-picture game (apple, carrots, fish, and pie). To limit the choices to two, the child might ask next, "Is it something you could grow in a garden?" Notice that this strategy multiplies dimensions of classification (small objects × edible × garden-grown) in order to reduce the alternatives. By age 11 children use this strategy about 80 percent of the time.

Hypothesis scanning:
A strategy for finding the correct answer to a problem by testing unrelated specific hypotheses one at a time.

Constraint seeking:
A strategy for finding the correct answer to a problem in which the player tries, with each consecutive question, to narrow the range of possibilities.

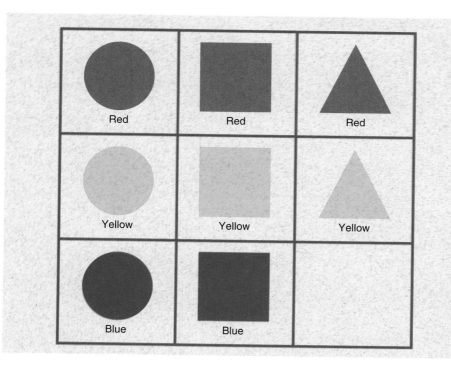

FIGURE 11.4 MATRIX COMPLETION
The objects in this matrix classification scheme are sorted by shape and color. One way to assess a child's understanding of matrix classification is to ask what the shape and color of the missing object should be.

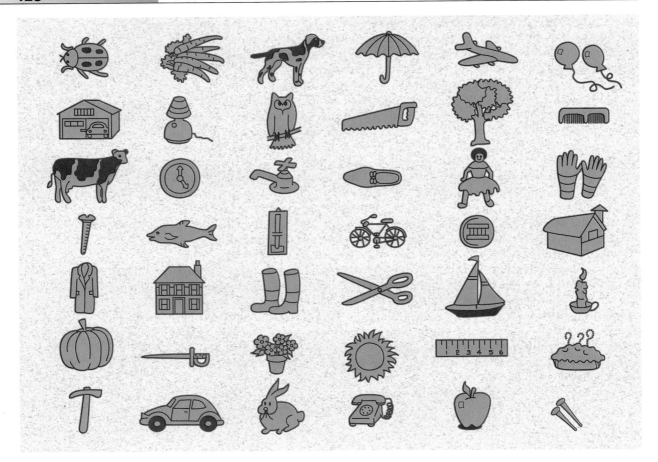

FIGURE 11.5 USING MATRIX CLASSIFICATION TO PLAY TWENTY QUESTIONS

A child is asked to guess which of these pictures the experimenter is thinking of. The child's task is to determine which one by asking yes-no questions. Questions such as "Is it a tool?" are more efficient than "Is it a saw?" for zeroing in on the correct object. Such constraint-seeking questions begin to occur frequently around age 9 and predominates by age 11. (Adapted from Bruner, Olver, and Greenfield, 1966.)

DEVELOPMENTAL PATTERNS: A REVIEW OF CLASSIFICATION SKILLS

We can summarize the development of classification skills in children by reviewing a few key points. First, children begin to classify objects very early in life, but it is not until middle childhood that they make effective use of classification when organizing information. At this point, they start to answer class-inclusion questions correctly and begin to use a constraint-seeking strategy more extensively in games like Twenty Questions. Second—and a major reason why performance on classification tasks improves during middle childhood—children this age largely overcome the limitations imposed by centration. They become able to focus on more than one dimension or level at a time. Finally, although elementary school children make great progress in classification skills, they still do not entirely grasp the logical necessity of classification structures. For them, an understanding of classification is not abstract; it is applied to concrete objects and situations. In other words, it derives from contingent, not necessary, truth.

MEMORY ABILITIES

Recall from Chapter 9 our example of Mikey Gordon trying to remember what to take with him to the beach on a Saturday morning. At age 6 he was not very good at generating a plan to help him remember, but at age 9 he could do so quite well. The night before, on his own, he placed his kite and fishing gear by the front door so he would see them on his way out and remember to take them. Virtually all elementary school children become increasingly better at using their memory capabilities. They also become more aware of the nature of memory and how it works. To explore the major aspects of memory that develop during middle childhood, we will use a framework suggested by John Flavell (1985), who has studied memory development extensively. Flavell's framework includes four factors: basic memory processes, knowledge, memory strategies, and metamemory.

BASIC MEMORY PROCESSES

Basic memory processes are the routine acts of storing and retrieving information. They involve the three kinds of memory systems that we introduced in Chapter 9: sensory storage, short-term (or working) memory, and long-term memory. These systems enable an infant to recognize something as familiar when it is seen again and again. They also enable toddlers to recall their first words, or preschoolers to remember the route to a friend's house.

Increases in both the capacity and the efficiency (or speed) of memory systems have been used to help explain cognitive development. The second of these two factors—increasing memory efficiency or speed—is thought to account for improvements in sensory storage and long-term memory after infancy (Rosser, 1994). Improvements also occur in short-term memory as children grow older. When presented with a string of digits to hold in short-term memory, the average 5-year-old can retain four of them, the average 7-year-old five, the average 9-year-old six, and the average adult seven (Dempster, 1981).

Some believe that this improvement is due to a gradual increase in the *capacity* of short-term memory during the preschool and middle childhood years. Others, however, contend that it is caused by increases in the *efficiency* of processing certain kinds of information. For example, Robbie Case (1985) divides short-term memory into two components: **storage space** (used to store information for short periods of time) and **operating space** (used to perform mental activities on information, such as determining how many items are present or whether two things are similar). The efficiency of these mental activities increases with development. This is probably due in part to practice, which makes the activities more automatic, and in part to neurological changes that affect processing speed (Kail, 1991). Together these mechanisms result in older children requiring less operating space to perform a cognitive activity. When less operating space is needed, more short-term memory space becomes available for temporary information storage.

Not all researchers agree with Case's explanation of the improvements in short-term memory that occur during childhood. That these improvements do take place is not debated, however. Both the amount of information that can be held in short-term memory and the complexity of the cognitive activities that can be carried out there improve gradually from early childhood through the elementary school years.

KNOWLEDGE

Another aspect of memory that changes during middle childhood is the total amount of knowledge that is held in long-term storage. Piaget once called this "memory in the wider sense" (Piaget and Inhelder, 1973). He was referring to the vast networks of accumulated information that people have stored in memory during their lives.

Storage space: Robbie Case's term for the component of short-term memory that is used to store information for short periods of time.

Operating space: Robbie Case's term for the component of short-term memory that is used to perform mental activities on information.

Chess experts of elementary-school age do better than adult chess novices at remembering arrangements of pieces that might occur during a chess game. The children's knowledge of chess enhances their memory abilities.

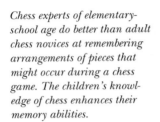

Such knowledge greatly affects what more we are able to learn and remember. In one study that demonstrated this, researchers compared the memory performance of chess masters and amateur chess players (Chase and Simon, 1973). If chess pieces were arranged randomly on the board, the masters were no better at remembering the location of the pieces than the amateurs were. However, if the pieces were arranged in patterns that might occur during an actual game of chess, the masters were much better than the amateurs at recalling the arrangements. Apparently, the chess masters' extensive knowledge of the game gave them an advantage. They were able to remember the arrangements of pieces in terms of layouts they had already stored in memory through their playing experience.

The same results were obtained in a study that used excellent elementary school chess players as the experts and novice adult players as the amateurs (Chi, 1978). The child experts outperformed the adult novices when the arrangements of the pieces on the board made sense in terms of what would be expected in a real game of chess. Knowledge appears to have conferred this memory advantage by providing a framework into which current information could be organized, stored, and retrieved. During the elementary school years children often become quite knowledgeable in a variety of content areas other than games like chess. With this increased knowledge comes the ability to use memory more effectively within the area of expertise.

The organizational framework that knowledge provides also enables children this age to make inferences about new information, and these inferences in turn seem to help them better understand and recall new information. Scott Paris (1975) has studied this process by presenting children with brief stories like this one:

> Linda was playing with her new doll in front of her big red house. Suddenly she heard a strange sound coming from under the porch. It was the flapping of wings. Linda wanted to help so much, but she did not know what to do. She ran inside the house and grabbed a shoe box from the closet. Then Linda looked inside her desk until she found eight sheets of yellow paper. She cut up the paper into little pieces and put them in the bottom of the box. Linda gently picked up the helpless creature and took it with her. Her teacher knew what to do.

Paris then asked the following eight yes-or-no questions:

1. Was Linda's doll new?
2. Did Linda grab a match box?
3. Was the strange sound coming from under the porch?
4. Was Linda playing behind her house?
5. Did Linda like to take care of animals?
6. Did Linda take what she found to the police station?
7. Did Linda find a frog?
8. Did Linda use a pair of scissors?

Questions 1 through 4 can be answered directly from information contained in the paragraph, but questions 5 through 8 require inferences based on general knowledge about what someone's behavior reveals about that person's feelings, about where teachers are normally found, about which animals have wings, and about how paper is usually cut. Paris found that elementary school children automatically make these kinds of inferences in the process of storing and remembering information. He also found that this inference drawing, or **constructive memory** as it is called, is an aid to recall. In one study, the best predictor of how well children would remember information was how well they did on inference questions like 5 through 8 above (Paris and Upton, 1976). Apparently, if children can integrate new information into meaningful structures already stored in memory, they are more likely to make inferences about it and be able to recall it later.

The ability to engage in constructive memory exists in preschoolers to some extent (Paris and Upton, 1976), but it is hard to demonstrate in children this young because of their limited general knowledge and often "illogical" inferences. Not until the elementary school years does constructive memory really come into its own as children make predominantly accurate inferences about things they learn. During this period children also become better able to integrate information gathered through different senses (spoken words and pictures, for example), and they integrate data more rapidly and are less distracted by irrelevant information (Ackerman, 1984; Kail, 1990; Pezdek, 1980; Pezdek and Miceli, 1982). By age 11 the constructive memory processes that children use seem much like those of adults (Kail, 1990). Here we see another example of middle childhood as a time of expanding and refining the cognitive skills that began to emerge in an earlier period of development.

Constructive memory: A cognitive ability involving inference drawing, or the integration of new information into meaningful structures that are already stored in memory, which facilitates retention of the new information.

MNEMONIC STRATEGIES

The increasing use of mnemonic strategies during middle childhood also encourages memory improvements. The term *mnemonic* is derived from the Greek word for memory, so **mnemonic strategies** are simply strategies for facilitating memory. Mikey used a mnemonic strategy when he put the things he wanted to take to the beach right by the front door where he would be sure to see them. Other common mnemonic devices are making a list of things to remember, and **rehearsing** information (repeating it over and over, as you do to keep a telephone number in mind before dialing it). A great many other mnemonic strategies are effective (Kail, 1990). Each is an intentional, goal-oriented behavior designed to improve memory.

Mnemonic strategy: Any cognitive device used to facilitate memory.

Rehearsal: The mnemonic strategy of repeating over and over the information one wants to remember.

During middle childhood, children begin regularly to use mnemonic strategies, such as rehearsal, to memorize information they need to remember later, such as how words are spelled.

In one of the earliest studies of children's use of mnemonic strategies, researchers showed a set of seven pictures to 5-, 7-, and 10-year-olds (Flavell, Beach, and Chinsky, 1966). The experimenters then indicated a subset of pictures that the child was to recall. During the interval between seeing the pictures and the time when the recall test was to start, each child was observed for evidence of rehearsal. The proportion of children using rehearsal increased from only 10 percent among the 5-year-olds, to 60 percent among the 7-year-olds, to 85 percent among the 10-year-olds.

In another study researchers investigated what effect training in rehearsal would have on the memory performance of first graders who didn't yet use rehearsal as a mnemonic strategy (Keeney, Cannizzo, and Flavell, 1967). The children were told to whisper the names of objects to be remembered over and over until it was time for a recall test. Whereas these children previously had not used rehearsal, they now used it in 75 percent of the trials. Moreover, their memory performance improved to the level of first graders who spontaneously rehearsed. At the end of the experiment all the children were told that they didn't have to rehearse any longer if they didn't wish to; they could do whatever they wanted to remember a new set of pictures. Of the 17 children who had been trained to rehearse, 10 reverted to not rehearsing, and their performance declined. We will consider the implications of this last finding in the next section, on metamemory.

Although rehearsal is regularly seen from age 7 or 8 on, there continue to be important developmental changes in its use. When 7- to 10-year-olds are presented with a list of words to remember with a 5-second pause between words, the younger children rehearse almost as much as the older children, but the younger ones often limit their rehearsal to the word just presented, whereas the older ones rehearse some of the previously heard words as well (Kail, 1990; Ornstein, Naus, and Stone, 1977). This tells us that 9- and 10-year-old children have more effective rehearsal strategies than 7- and 8-year-olds do. Still, their strategies are not as flexible as those of older children and adults. For example, when told that they will be given 10 cents for remembering some of the words in a list and only 1 cent for remembering others, they do not rehearse the more valuable words more, as adults do (Cuvo, 1974).

Another mnemonic strategy that children gradually come to use is organization of information when it is stored in memory. In one study of children age 6 to 11, researchers found a large age difference in the use of a simple organizational technique—grouping together by subject various pictures that were to be remembered (Moely et al., 1969). An 11-year-old, for instance, was much more likely than a 6-year-old to separate pictures of animals from pictures of plants and then to store each group as a separate set. The tactics of organizing, classifying, and summarizing data to be learned continue to develop throughout adolescence and into the college years (Brown et al., 1983; Rohwer, 1973; Wellman, 1983).

Robert Kail and John Hagen (1982) have summarized much of what is known about when children begin to use mnemonic strategies as follows: five- and six-year-olds do not spontaneously use mnemonic strategies often. They may feel it is important to remember something, but they seldom turn this motivation into a deliberate effort to improve memory. The period between 7 and 10 years of age seems to be a transitional stage during which mnemonic devices increasingly develop. Exactly when a particular strategy emerges depends on both its nature and the context in which it is used. Finally, beginning at about age 10, children show the first signs of using mnemonic devices consistently and effectively (Kail, 1990; Schneider and Pressley, 1989). This tendency will increase over the next several years, until by adolescence youngsters are quite good at using deliberate strategies to help themselves remember.

METAMEMORY

A fourth aspect of memory that develops during middle childhood is **metamemory,** or knowledge about memory and memory processes. When you think about the need to remember and how to go about remembering, you are using metamemory capabilities. When you know your own strengths and weaknesses in remembering (good at remembering faces, poor at remembering names), you are also using metamemory. In addition, metamemory allows you to monitor your own memory performance. It is what enables you to know when you have learned a certain fact. Like other *metacognitive* skills—the ability to think about thinking—metamemory shows substantial advancement during middle childhood.

John Flavell and his colleagues examined the development of one component of metamemory by asking children of different ages to predict how many pictures they would be able to remember (Flavell, Friedrichs, and Hoyt, 1970). On the first trial each child was shown only one picture. That picture was then covered and the child was asked if he or she could remember it. On each subsequent trial the number of pictures was increased, to a maximum of ten. In the first phase of the experiment, the children were not actually required to remember the pictures, just to say whether they thought they could remember them. In the second phase, actual recall tests were given. Table 11.2 shows both the children's self-predictions and their actual performance. Notice that the preschoolers and kindergarteners were quite poor at remembering, the second graders were better, and the fourth graders were quite good. Notice, too, that the preschoolers and kindergarteners were far off in their predictions of how many pictures they could remember. They overestimated by about twice as many as they actually recalled, whereas the second graders made fairly accurate predictions, and the fourth graders made very accurate ones. Other researchers have similarly found that older children are much better at predicting what they will be able to remember (see Rosser, 1994; Schneider and Pressley, 1989). Apparently, knowledge about one's own memory capabilities increases greatly during middle childhood.

Similar improvements occur in other metamemory skills across the elemen-

Metamemory:
Knowledge about memory and memory processes.

TABLE 11.2
CHILDREN'S PREDICTIONS OF THE NUMBER OF ITEMS THEY COULD REMEMBER AND THEIR ACTUAL PERFORMANCE

	Mean Predicted Memory Span	Mean Actual Memory Span
Preschool	7.21	3.50
Kindergarten	7.97	3.61
Second grade	6.00	4.36
Fourth grade	6.14	5.50

SOURCE: Flavell, Friedrichs, and Hoyt, 1970.

tary school years (Flavell and Wellman, 1977; Waters and Andreassen, 1983; Wellman, 1986). For instance, school-age children become increasingly better at knowing when a particular mnemonic strategy has worked. The fact that first graders who have been trained to use rehearsal often revert to *not* rehearsing when left to remember on their own suggests that they do not yet realize that this strategy improves their memory performance. They lack the metamemory skill of monitoring how well they are doing on a set of memory tasks. Thus, metamemory may be an important factor in using mnemonic devices. Once children realize that mnemonic strategies improve recall, they are more likely to use them (e.g., Fabricius and Hagan, 1984, 1989).

This is true even though, when mnemonic devices are first tried out, they do not improve memory as much as when they are more practiced (Flavell, Miller, and Miller, 1993). Apparently, when a mnemonic device is new to a child, using it consumes so much operating space in short-term memory that little space is left for information storage. Why, then, does the child persist in using the strategy? The same question could be asked about walking. When a child first tries to walk great effort is required, and walking is not as successful a way to get around as crawling. Yet the child continues to try until walking is mastered. For the use of mnemonic strategies, as well as for walking, the keys to persistence may be encouragement from others and the inner motivation to become competent at a new skill.

The fact that the development of metamemory becomes most apparent from the second grade on does not mean that younger children have no metamemory capabilities. Flavell believes that metamemory begins to emerge during the preschool years, but these beginnings are greatly overshadowed by the dramatic progress made later. For instance, even kindergarteners and first graders know that increasing the number of items to be remembered makes a memory task harder; they are aware, in other words, that certain factors can influence memory performance (Kreutzer, Leonard, and Flavell, 1975). Yet these same children are very poor at predicting how much they will remember when presented with increasing amounts of information to recall. It is as if they have trouble making use of the bits of metamemory knowledge they possess.

Among older children, in contrast, metamemory knowledge is much more extensive. When presented with a memory task, many 5- and 6-year-olds can think of only one strategy to help them remember, but older children can think of many more (Kreutzer, Leonard, and Flavell, 1975). In addition, as we mentioned earlier, older children are far more likely to use these memory strategies without prompting from adults. Thus, the developmental patterns for metamemory adds to our picture of middle childhood as a time when cognitive skills that began to emerge earlier are refined, elaborated, and made into more effective practical tools.

SOCIAL INTERACTION AND COGNITIVE DEVELOPMENT

Eight-year-old Mikey and his friends Richie and Jeff are building a fort in the Gordons' backyard out of large cardboard boxes. The boys decide that they want to add a lookout tower on one side. But when they cut out a large hole in the top of one of the boxes, the edges left aren't strong enough to support the tall box they want to put on top. The boys consider the problem, each offering ideas as to how they could make

Working cooperatively with peers fosters cognitive development during middle childhood.

the structure stronger. Just as they are about to try out Jeff's idea, Frank walks by. "That's not gonna work," he advises. "Let me show you what to do." The boys step back and watch intently as Frank sets to work. "Now you see here, you can take this piece and. . . ."

Elementary schoolchildren can learn a great deal from peers as well as from adults. In a peer group like Mikey's, children tend to provide each other with **cooperative learning experiences.** The learners are at approximately the same level of knowledge and skill, and they interact, share ideas, and discover solutions on their own. Adults, in contrast, tend to provide children with **didactic learning experiences.** Here, a knowledgeable teacher who already knows how to solve the problem helps the learner or learners understand what is involved. In the episode above Frank is providing a didactic learning experience for the boys because he is deliberately teaching them something that they don't yet know. In a study of African-American and Latino families it was found that parents with the knowledge to help their children learn mathematics could foster development using didactic teaching. It was also found that parents who lacked such expertise could still foster development by encouraging their children and communicating that they valued achievement in mathematics (Cooper et al., 1995).

Developmentalists have disagreed about whether children learn better in didactic or cooperative situations. This controversy has sparked tremendous interest in the role of peer interaction in cognitive development. As a result, a variety of approaches to cooperative learning and peer tutoring have emerged (see Rogoff, 1990). At present, it appears that the best approach to learning depends on characteristics of both the learners and the teachers, on the nature of the material to be learned, and on the cultural norms for learning and teaching that prevail in a particular setting (Cooper and Cooper, 1991). In this section we'll look at how children can provide both cooperative and didactic learning experiences for other children their age.

Cooperative learning experience: A situation in which learners are at approximately the same level of knowledge and skill, and they interact, share ideas, and discover solutions on their own.

Didactic learning experience: A situation in which a knowledgeable teacher who already knows how to solve the problem helps the learner or learners understand what is involved.

WHAT CHILDREN CAN LEARN FROM OTHER CHILDREN

Research by Frank Murray (1972, 1981) illustrates how peers can provide didactic learning experiences. Murray paired one child who understood conservation with a second child who did not and asked the two to come to a consensus about various conservation questions. Even though the children were similar in age, it was a didactic learning situation because one of the youngsters already knew the correct answers and was deliberately teaching the other. The consensus reached by the two children almost invariably favored conservation; that is to say, the viewpoint of the more advanced child prevailed. And it was not simply a matter of one child's going along with the other out of sheer conformity. Genuine learning had occurred. When the previously nonconserving children were later tested alone, they continued to give correct responses to conservation questions.

Developmentalists are interested in exactly what the teacher provides in a didactic learning situation like this one. One answer involves Jerome Bruner's concept of scaffolding (Bruner, 1975). **Scaffolding** is the support system that others can contribute to advancement within a person's zone of proximal development (which, as we saw in Chapter 9, is Vygotsky's term for the area just beyond the person's current developmental level). In scaffolding, others observe the learner's behaviors and provide guidance, hints, and advice. As the learner advances, the teacher's strategies progressively change to encourage the mastery of increasingly complex understandings (Cazden, 1983).

A teacher need not necessarily be an adult in order to use scaffolding. Fifth graders tutoring second graders have been observed to use it, so we know it is a skill that emerges by middle childhood (Allen, 1976). Of course, the age of a child teacher can be a significant factor in how effective scaffolding is, because the selection of effective scaffolding approaches requires metacognitive awareness of what the learner thinks and understands.

In addition to providing one another with didactic learning experiences, children can learn from their peers in cooperative situations that do not involve a more knowledgeable child intentionally teaching a less knowledgeable one. This was shown in a series of studies by a group of Swiss researchers (Mugny, Perret-Clermont, and Doise, 1981). The researchers allowed children to cooperate on a broad range of tasks over an extended period of time. They found that in order for interaction with a peer to promote cognitive progress, the interaction did not need to be with a more advanced child. In one case, for example, a child who couldn't yet solve number conservation problems, but who understood one-to-one correspondence and could count accurately, interacted with a child who was less advanced in these areas. Through discussing number conservation problems with the less competent child, the more advanced one acquired a grasp of this concept.

Researchers have proposed a number of factors that facilitate cognitive advancement in cooperative learning situations among peers. Three of these are believed to be particularly important (Forman, 1982). First, the children need to work on a concrete task, one that provides a rich source of relevant information. Second, the information available must be somewhat ambiguous; it must be able to support at least two different conclusions. (Here we see something of the cognitive conflict, or disequilibrium, that Piaget believed was important.) And third, the peers must consider reaching a consensus a goal of their interaction. They cannot simply express diverse opinions with no intention of finding an agreed-upon solution. Mikey Gordon and his friends were

Scaffolding:
Jerome Bruner's term for the support system that caregivers, teachers, and peers contribute to the learning process by providing ongoing guidance, hints, feedback, and advice that are developmentally appropriate.

well on their way to effective cooperative learning in our earlier example because all three of these conditions were being met before Frank stepped in.

AGE, INTERACTION, AND LEARNING

As we mentioned in our discussion of scaffolding, children become increasingly effective at teaching one another with age, partly because they become increasingly able to understand what other children are thinking. Catherine Cooper and her colleagues looked at age as a factor in learning from peers in a study of 5- to 12-year-olds at a Montessori school (Cooper, Marquis, and Edwards, 1986). This school particularly encouraged peer interactions as a means of promoting learning. Cooper and her colleagues identified several forms of learning among the children: solitary learning (choosing to work alone), onlooking (learning simply by watching others), parallel-coordinate learning (involving two children working side by side, often briefly exchanging task-relevant information), guidance (a kind of didactic learning because one child is telling another how to accomplish some goal), and collaborative learning (in which the children share in directing their interaction). The researchers concluded that effective didactic and cooperative peer learning emerge early in middle childhood, but improvements occur with age. Because of their increased metacognitive skills, older elementary school children are better able to plan long-term collaborative projects, to engage in more elaborate and extended arguments, to offer more effective teaching approaches, and to progressively adjust the guidance they provide as teachers.

Despite the fact that peer learning is effective in middle childhood, learning among peers is not always *as* effective as learning that occurs when a knowledgeable adult is the teacher. Shari Ellis and Barbara Rogoff (1982) demonstrated this when they studied differences in teaching styles between elementary school children and adults. All the children in this study (both the learners and the child teachers) were 8 or 9 years old, while all the adults were women who had children this age. The learners had to master a relatively complex classification task in which photographs of common objects were sorted into categories.

When peer interaction is encouraged as a legitimate way to learn, both didactic and cooperative peer learning become more elaborate and effective during middle childhood.

Ellis and Rogoff identified three things that the teachers needed to do in order to be successful. First, they had to see that the learners sorted the photos into the appropriate categories. Second, they had to assist the learner in understanding the underlying classification scheme. And third, they had to manage the social interactions between themselves and their learners. Ellis and Rogoff found that the child teachers tended to focus simply on getting their learners to accomplish the sorting task. They concentrated less than the adult teachers did on communicating the underlying classification scheme (even though they understood it). Apparently, the job of coordinating all three tasks was too complex for children this age. They couldn't put together an integrated teaching plan—one that simultaneously demonstrated how to sort, conveyed the underlying categories, and controlled the social give-and-take. As a result, the child teachers were less effective than the adult teachers.

The fact that the participants in this study were relative strangers to one another probably added to the difficulties for the child teachers (Cooper and Cooper, 1984). Peer learning is most effective when the children involved are acquainted and have worked out a smooth system of interaction. Under these conditions, and when the task to be mastered is not too complex, elementary school children can be quite good at helping each other learn.

EXPLAINING THE EFFECTS OF SOCIAL INTERACTION

A number of theorists have addressed the issue of exactly what other people are providing when they help a child master a new skill and thereby make cognitive progress. Vygotsky's theory, as we have said, applies more to didactic learning situations than to cooperative ones. A more knowledgeable teacher provides guidance for a less knowledgeable learner—hints, feedback, what Bruner called scaffolding—within the learner's zone of proximal development. In Vygotsky's theory, a common frame of reference is important to successful scaffolding. The teacher must understand the learner's immature viewpoint in order to plan an effective strategy for conveying the more advanced view.

Piaget also addressed the issue of what interaction with others can do to foster cognitive development in a child. Like Vygotsky, Piaget believed that a common frame of reference is important for effective social interaction. But for Piaget, that common frame of reference results from the similar status of peers who are learning from one another. In Piaget's view, the shared status of peers fosters the detection and resolution of discrepancies between one's own point of view and another person's. If an adult or other "expert" expresses an idea different from a child's own, the new idea will be accepted as correct on the basis of the expert's authority, but it will not be integrated into the rest of the child's knowledge system. Thus, Piaget's perspective, unlike Vygotsky's, applies more to cooperative learning situations than to didactic ones.

Piaget and Vygotsky also viewed the nature of cognitive development differently, which explains their different stances on the role of social interaction in it. For Piaget, cognitive development is constructed by and exists *within the individual*. In contrast, for Vygotsky, cognitive development is part of a social reality; it exists partly in a system that is *shared among people*. For much of this century most developmentalists have agreed with Piaget's perspective on the nature of cognitive development. But recently, without abandoning their belief in the importance of the individual, many developmentalists have also been incorporating Vygotsky's perspective into their thinking. As a result, most developmentalists now see both the didactic and cooperative functions of social interaction as crucial to effective cognitive development.

INDIVIDUAL DIFFERENCES IN INTELLIGENCE

So far in this chapter we have focused on cognitive developments that most children of elementary school age share. In this section we shift our focus to cognitive *differences* among children. We discuss cognitive differences in more depth in this chapter than in earlier ones because a child's level of intellectual competence takes on special importance when he or she enters school. In fact, many theories of intelligence, and most widely used methods of measuring it, have focused on school-related tasks and abilities.

INTELLIGENCE TESTING AND CONCEPTS OF INTELLIGENCE

The first modern intelligence test was developed in France at the beginning of the twentieth century. Administrators of the Paris public school system wanted a way to differentiate normally intelligent children from those requiring special help so that all children could be given education suited to their abilities and needs. The minister of education called upon Alfred Binet, a well-known French psychologist, and his colleague Theodore Simon to develop a reliable test. (Some years later, Jean Piaget received his first exposure to children's cognitive performance when he took a job developing test items for Binet.)

Binet and Simon constructed a large number of potential test items and then evaluated them against a set of criteria. To be included in the test, an item had to predict school performance, and the likelihood that the item would be answered correctly had to increase with the test-taker's age. The types of test items chosen included word definitions, arithmetic problems, verbal reasoning tasks, questions on general information, and tasks requiring an understanding of complex spatial relationships. Within each type of item the questions were placed in order from the easiest to the hardest.

Lewis Terman of Stanford University published an English version of Binet's test in 1916. This test, called the Stanford-Binet, was designed for children between the ages of 3 and 18. Scoring of the test involved the concept of **mental age (MA),** a measure of the level of intellectual development that a particular child had reached. For instance, if a child correctly answered as many questions as the average 12-year-old, that child would be said to have a mental age of 12. Mental age was then divided by the child's chronological age (CA) and multiplied by 100 to produce an **intelligence quotient,** or **IQ** (MA/CA × 100 = IQ). If a child with a mental age of 12 was also 12 years old, that child would be exactly average and would be assigned an IQ of 100 (12/12 × 100 = IQ 100). If this child was only 10, however, mental age would be above chronological age and the child's IQ would be higher than average (12/10 × 100 = IQ 120). By the same token, the IQ of a 14-year-old who had a mental age of 12 would be below average (12/14 × 100 = IQ 86). This simple method of computing IQ scores is no longer used; a more complex calculation has taken its place. Nevertheless, IQ scores are still determined by comparing a person's performance with the performance of others who are the same age.

Notice how Binet's approach entails a *unitary* concept of intelligence. People

Mental age (MA): Applied to a child who has taken an intelligence test, the average age at which children have answered the same number of items correctly as the tested child.

Intelligence quotient (IQ): A measure of a person's intelligence based on a comparison of the person's performance on an IQ test with the performance on the same test of others who are the same age.

This girl has invented a device to turn lights on and off automatically when doors are opened or closed—an example of adaptive problem solving.

Fluid intelligence: A person's ability to solve unfamiliar problems using new information and procedures.

Crystallized intelligence: A person's existing knowledge and well-established problem-solving techniques.

are not thought of as having many different kinds of intelligences. Instead, intelligence is considered to be a *general* cognitive capability that can be measured by a single IQ score. In England during the early part of the twentieth century, an educational psychologist named Charles Spearman (1927) was also sympathetic to the concept of a general intelligence. He labeled this general reasoning ability *g*. In Spearman's view, however, performance on an intellectual task depended not only on *g* but also on knowledge, abilities, and aptitudes *specific* to the particular problem or question at hand. Your performance in a college algebra class, for instance, would be determined in part by your general reasoning ability and in part by your specific aptitude for math.

Many contemporary intelligence tests are based on a combination of Binet's and Spearman's conceptions of intelligence. One example is the widely used Wechsler scales, which include separate tests for ages 4 to 6, for ages 6 to 16, and for adults. The Wechsler scales provide IQ scores that summarize overall performance, so in this regard they use Binet's global approach to intelligence. At the same time, however, the Wechsler scales are made up of verbal subtests (including vocabulary, arithmetic, and general information) and performance subtests (including mazes, block design, and object assembly). This variety of subtests minimizes the contribution to overall performance that any one specialized skill can make. The test-taker also receives a separate subscore for each of the various subtests, a procedure that acknowledges Spearman's stress on specific abilities in addition to general intelligence.

An alternative to the approaches of Binet and Spearman comes from the work of L. L. Thurstone, an American psychologist. Thurstone (1938) rejected the concept of general intelligence. He argued instead that intelligence is composed of seven primary mental abilities: verbal meaning, inductive reasoning, perceptual speed, number facility, spatial relations, memory, and verbal fluency. Thurstone saw these primary mental abilities as relatively independent of one another, with none predominant over the others. From Thurstone's ideas, the Primary Mental Abilities Test was developed. It yields separate scores for each of the seven abilities (although provision is made for calculating an overall score as well). Other researchers have proposed even more components to human intelligence, ranging from 20 (French, 1951) to 120 (Guilford, 1967).

At a minimum, most psychologists today differentiate between two aspects of intelligence known as fluid and crystallized intelligence. **Fluid intelligence** is a person's ability to solve unfamiliar problems using new information and procedures. It is frequently measured by analogy problems, series completion tasks, problems in classification, and so forth. **Crystallized intelligence,** in contrast, consists of a person's existing knowledge and well-established problem-solving techniques. It is assessed by measures of vocabulary size, general information, and reading comprehension (Cattell, 1971; Horn, 1982). The distinction between fluid and crystallized intelligence is particularly important to those who are interested in development throughout the life span. Performance on measures of fluid intelligence generally improves until late adolescence and then slowly declines, but performance on measures of crystallized intelligence continues improving until around the age of 60 (Horn, 1982).

BROADENING THE DEFINITION OF INTELLIGENCE

Although Binet, Spearman, Thurstone, and others differed in the number of specific abilities they thought were involved in intelligence, their approaches emphasized the same *kind* of mental abilities—those useful in school. Other researchers have argued that these abilities do not represent the full range of human intelligence and that intelligence should be defined more broadly. Underlying recent attempts to define intelligence more broadly is the idea that intelligence is what allows us to *adapt* successfully to situations. In this way these newer theories of intelligence have something in common with Piaget's view.

The newer theories address skills for adaptation not just in academic and formal problem-solving settings, but in a wide variety of other contexts as well. In fact, some psychologists believe it is useful to make a distinction between the kind of intelligence that allows a person to perform well in school and on IQ tests, and the kind of intelligence that enables someone to solve problems in everyday settings, personally relevant problems that are often open to many possible solutions. The first can be called **academic intelligence,** the second **practical intelligence.** It is not clear to what extent academic and practical intelligence are related. A high level of one doesn't guarantee a high level of the other (Scribner, 1986; Wagner and Sternberg, 1986). This general point is important to all the newer theories of intelligence that try to broaden how intelligence is defined. Being highly intelligent in one way does not necessarily mean that a person will be highly intelligent in another. This fact is reflected in Howard Gardner's **multiple intelligences theory.**

GARDNER'S THEORY OF MULTIPLE INTELLIGENCES

Gardner (1983) argues that humans have a number of different intellectual competences that he calls intelligences. He defines an intelligence as "an ability or set of abilities that permits an individual to solve problems or fashion products that are of consequence in a particular cultural setting" (Walters and Gardner, 1986, p. 165). Thus, each kind of intelligence allows members of our species to adapt to the many demands and challenges that human societies create. Gardner believes that each kind of human intelligence develops more or less independently from the others, and different ones may draw on different areas of the brain.

On the basis of existing research on human abilities and brain functions, Gardner has proposed seven intellectual competences that appear basic enough, autonomous enough, and universal enough to be considered intelligences, although he cautions that his list should not be considered complete. These seven are: linguistic intelligence (skill in understanding and using language), musical intelligence (skill in the creation of music), logical-mathematical intelligence (skill in logical thinking and reasoning about quantities), spatial intelligence (skill in understanding how patterns and objects are laid out in space), bodily-kinesthetic intelligence (skill in anything that involves complex movement of the body), intrapersonal intelligence (skill in understanding one's own feelings and motives), and interpersonal intelligence (skill in understanding the feelings and behaviors of others). Notice that only three of these intelligences—linguistic, logical-mathematical, and spatial—are addressed in traditional IQ tests.

Gardner makes several points about these seven intelligences. First, a person's level of competence in each depends not only on biological endowment, but also on socialization and education. Someone can be *taught* to be a more competent gymnast or juggler, for example, although innate ability also enters into that person's performance. Second, a person's particular culture determines both how a given competence will be fostered (in one culture a musically gifted child might learn to play the banjo, in another the sitar) and which competences will be most stressed (logical-mathematical intelligence being highly

Academic intelligence: Intellectual capacity as measured by performance on tasks typically encountered in school or on standard IQ tests.

Practical intelligence: Intellectual capacity as reflected in successful performance in natural, everyday, nonschool settings.

Multiple intelligences theory: Howard Gardner's idea that overall intelligence is multifaceted, consisting of at least seven different intellectual competences: linguistic, musical, logical-mathematical, spatial, bodily-kinesthetic, intrapersonal, and interpersonal.

valued in technologically advanced societies like ours). Third, high competence in one area does not imply high competence in others. A child prodigy may show unusual ability in one intellectual domain, while being average or below average in others. There are even individuals (called *idiot savants*) who are extremely retarded in all areas of intellectual functioning except for one small island of remarkably superior skill.

STERNBERG'S TRIARCHIC THEORY

Triarchic theory:
Robert Sternberg's idea that intelligent behavior is governed by three factors: a componential element (various information-processing skills), an experiential element (prior knowledge), and a contextual element (the circumstances in which the behavior takes place).

Psychologist Robert Sternberg (1985) has taken another intriguing approach to broadening the concept of intelligence. Whereas Gardner focuses on recognizing different *types* of intelligence (linguistic, musical, interpersonal, and so forth), Sternberg has analyzed the various factors that contribute to making a particular behavior intelligent or not. Sternberg's approach is called a **triarchic theory** because he sees intelligent behavior as governed by three things.

The first factor in Sternberg's theory is the *componential element* in intelligence. This refers to the many information-processing skills that a person uses in solving problems—skills such as attending to, storing, retrieving, and manipulating information. If a person is highly proficient at using these components of intelligence, he or she will usually do well on traditional IQ tests.

The second factor that governs intelligence, in Sternberg's theory, is the *experiential element*. This refers to prior knowledge that affects how a person goes about tackling a problem. For example, the first time you used a computer to access a library catalog you probably carefully read the printed instructions, cautiously tried out a few examples, and in general proceeded very slowly. Now, however, you can probably use a computerized catalog quite efficiently. You don't stop to read the instructions or take some trial runs. The "intelligent" thing to do has changed with experience. Likewise, throughout development, what is intelligent behavior for a child at a certain age may not be for an older child. Experience changes the choices and actions that are considered intelligent ones.

Finally, Sternberg also sees intelligence as governed by a *contextual element*. This refers to the set of circumstances in which a choice is made or an action is taken. Whereas it is intelligent behavior to check the spark plugs in the context of an engine that won't start, it is not intelligent to check them in the context of an overheated engine. Similarly, the cultural context makes a difference in determining what is intelligent and what is not. For example, traditionally, among certain Indian tribes of the northern Pacific coast of North America, people would periodically hold an event called a *potlatch* in which the host gave away, or sometimes actually destroyed, huge quantities of surplus food and other valuable items (blankets, animal skins, canoes, pieces of copper). To those of us who live in a society where "saving for a rainy day" is considered prudent, this behavior seems the height of folly. But among the tribes who practiced it, potlatching was perfectly intelligent. It was a way of converting surpluses into personal prestige (the host of a potlatch was greatly admired) and of redistributing wealth from those who had plenty to those who did not (the recipients of potlatch gifts included people in economic need). Thus, the intelligence of behavior cannot be assessed outside the cultural context in which it occurs.

To summarize, Sternberg's theory helps us to see that intelligence is more than just the cognitive skills typically measured on standard IQ tests. Intelligent behavior is also governed by experience and by the context in which that behavior takes place. If tests of intelligence fail to take all these factors into account, they will probably not be very good at predicting how intelligently a person will behave in his or her everyday environment.

Despite the value of newer theories of intelligence such as Gardner's and Sternberg's, there are no methods for assessing nonacademic intelligences that are as well established as the standard IQ tests are for measuring academic intelligence. For now, children's IQs are much more likely to be tested than their practical intelligence. Moreover, the research on individual differences in children's intelligence has largely examined differences in their performance on IQ tests. This is why the following section on individual differences in intelligence focuses on IQ differences. Nevertheless, the major points we make regarding differences in IQ probably apply to other aspects of intelligence as well.

EXPLAINING IQ DIFFERENCES

Until recently, virtually all American children at some time in their school careers were given at least one intelligence test. Because of issues of cultural bias and the stigmatizing effect of low scores, IQ tests are no longer universally administered. Of the many students who *are* tested, most score somewhere between 70 and 130, with a few scoring lower or higher. Psychologists have been interested in learning the causes of these IQ differences. This interest has led them to consider the interaction of heredity and environment.

The question of how much heredity and environment each contribute to IQ differences has aroused controversy for decades. The influence of heredity clearly involves *many* genes. No single gene, or small set of genes, makes a person smarter than others. In addition, even the staunchest proponent of a strong role for heredity in intellectual differences acknowledges that the environment also plays an important part. Let's examine some of the evidence for the contributions of both heredity *and* environment.

The evidence for a genetic contribution to IQ differences comes primarily from studies of twins and adopted children. By looking at Table 11.3, you can see that two identical twins are much more similar in IQ than are any other pair of siblings (either fraternal twins or nontwins) or two unrelated individuals. Such data have been used to support the claim that heredity contributes to simi-

TABLE 11.3

IQ SCORE CORRELATIONS FOR INDIVIDUALS WITH GENETIC INHERITANCES AND REARING ENVIRONMENTS OF VARYING SIMILARITY

Number of Samples	Biological Relationship	Condition of Rearing	Median Correlation
34	Monozygotic twins	Same family	.85
3	Monozygotic twins	Separate families	.67
41	Dizygotic twins	Same family	.58
69	Siblings	Same family	.45
2	Siblings	Separate families	.24
11	Unrelated	Same family	.29

SOURCE: Estimated from Figure 1 of Bouchard and McGue, 1981.

larities and differences in IQ. At the same time, however, these figures also show a powerful role for environment. For instance, identical twins, who share identical genes, do not have identical IQs, and the difference in their IQs is likely to be greater if they are raised apart. Clearly, a complex interplay of genes and environment creates IQ differences.

This complex interplay was illustrated in an early study of adopted children (Skodak and Skeels, 1949). The biological mothers had below-average intelligence (their mean IQ was 85.7), while the adoptive parents had above-average intelligence (their mean IQ was about 120). The children were placed in their new homes before 6 months of age, so the rearing environments they experienced were largely those of their adoptive families. The researchers tested the children several times over a period of years. Their mean IQs ranged from 107 to 116. This is 20 to 30 points above the mean IQ of the biological mothers, a very significant difference. However, at age 7 the average correlation between a *particular* child's IQ score and the score of his or her adoptive parents was only .16, as opposed to a .36 correlation between the child's IQ and the biological mother's. This closer resemblance to the IQ of the biological mother tended to increase with age. By the age of 13, the correlation between the child's IQ and that of the adoptive parents had dropped to .04, while the child-biological mother correlation still averaged .38. Apparently, the mean IQ of *all* the children considered as a group was raised as a result of their placement in advantageous environments. However, *individual differences* among the children were more predictable from information about their genetic inheritance. More recent studies have produced essentially the same results (e.g., Honzik, 1983; Scarr and Weinberg, 1983; Ramey and Campbell, 1979; Ramey and Haskins, 1981).

The concept of reaction range can help you understand the interaction of genes and environment that underlies these findings. **Reaction range** refers to the limits within which the effects of genes can vary depending on the particular environment in which a child is raised. Genes, in other words, set outer limits to the traits a person may show, and environment then determines where within those limits the person actually falls. In the case of intelligence, genes can be thought of as setting a lower and an upper limit on potential IQ. If a person is raised in a very stimulating environment, an IQ near the top of the range will likely result; but if the person is raised in a deprived environment, we can expect an IQ near the range's lower end. Since the studies mentioned earlier involved bringing children from relatively poor environments into more advantaged ones, they provide a rough estimate of the size of the IQ reaction range. That range seems to be about 20 to 25 points (Weinberg, 1989).

Recently, psychologist Sandra Scarr (1992) has sparked a controversy by proposing that environmental variations within the typical range of environments in which children are raised have very little effect on IQ. Instead, Scarr has argued, it is only in unusual circumstances, such as extreme deprivation, that the environment has much of an impact on IQ. Scarr's view has triggered strong criticism (Baumrind, 1993; Jackson, 1993), but as yet there are no studies that clearly resolve the issue, nor is there agreement on how to define the "normal" range of rearing environments for children. This controversy highlights our limited understanding of the specific environmental factors that are important to intellectual development and of the ways in which those factors exert their influences.

Even more controversial than Scarr's proposal is the suggestion that there are

Reaction range:
The limits provided by the genes on the effects of the particular environment in which a child is raised.

differences in average IQ among racial, ethnic, and social-class groups that are in part caused by gene pool differences among the groups. Arthur Jensen raised this possibility in an article in the *Harvard Educational Review* in 1969, and it has been raised again by Richard Hernnstein and Charles Murray in their book *The Bell Curve* (1994). Almost all the responses to this book have been highly critical (e.g., Gould, 1994). Herrnstein and Murray recognize that even from within their own perspective their evidence is not conclusive: "The debate about whether and how much genes and environment have to do with ethnic differences remains unresolved" (Herrnstein and Murray, 1994). We expect that, as in the case of Jensen's article, the controversy raised by this book will rage for many years.

THE STABILITY OF IQ

Although it is not clear to what extent small changes in environment can affect a child's IQ, there is little disagreement that enriching a very deprived environment *can* make a difference to performance on IQ tests. But once such changes in IQ have come about, how stable are they? If there is early intervention and no follow-up, the IQ gains produced by the intervention seem to regress (Gray, Ramsey, and Klaus, 1982; Lazer et al., 1982). Although this is disappointing from the standpoint of those who are trying to assist disadvantaged children, it makes sense in terms of the reaction range concept. To maintain a rate of intellectual development toward the top end of the range would seem to require continued environmental support. Just as you would not expect to sustain improved physical growth by giving a malnourished child a balanced diet for just a year, so you cannot expect to sustain improved intellectual growth by providing an intensive but time-limited cognitive intervention. In both cases, dramatic improvements may occur in the short run, but most of the gains will be lost when developmental support ends.

But what about the majority of children who don't experience wide fluctuations in their intellectual environments? Can we expect their IQs to remain rela-

Group IQ tests are part of most children's educational experience in the United States. Individual IQ tests, such as the Stanford-Binet and the Wechsler Intelligence Scale for Children, are administered less frequently.

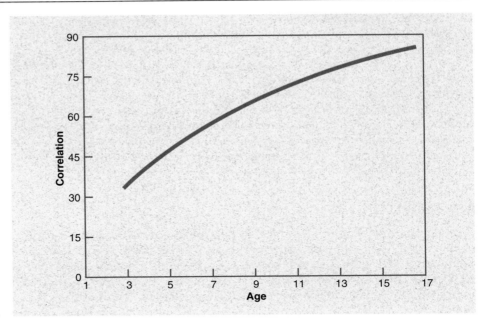

FIGURE 11.6

CORRELATIONS BETWEEN IQ SCORES OBTAINED AT MATURITY AND THOSE OBTAINED AT EARLY AGES

The rising line indicates the increase in stability of IQ scores during childhood and adolescence.

tively stable over time? If their IQs *are* stable, results on childhood IQ tests should be relatively good predictors of adult IQ. And indeed, the ability to predict adult IQ on the basis of a childhood intelligence test generally increases as a child grows older. Figure 11.6 shows that this predictability becomes quite reliable by the elementary school years, suggesting that at this point intelligence tests are measuring relatively stable aspects of cognitive functioning. The stability of what is being measured is probably due to the combined effects of a stable genetic makeup and a relatively stable rearing environment.

HOW MEANINGFUL ARE IQ SCORES?

Ever since IQ scores were introduced, people have debated their value. If one child gets 100 on an IQ test and another gets 120, what exactly does that tell us about these two children? Part of the controversy over IQ scores centers on the issue of cultural bias in the tests. Controversy also arises over the question of just what an IQ score can predict.

THE ISSUE OF CULTURAL BIAS

How well do you think you would perform on Binet's original intelligence test? Since this test was given in French, you would probably do very poorly if you don't speak fluent French. And even if you do, some of the general information questions asked at the turn of the century might be obscure today. Any IQ test is the product of a certain culture, and knowledge of that culture affects how well a test-taker does.

There are also more subtle ways in which cultural background can influence a person's performance on an IQ test. Cultures vary considerably in their definitions of intelligence and in the particular cognitive skills they value (Goodnow, 1976). They also vary in what they consider the right way to perform certain cognitive tasks. For example, if you were asked to sort items into categories, you would probably not think of putting a knife and an orange together, but members of Africa's Kpelle tribe would do so because a knife is used to cut an orange (Glick, 1975). Thus, a person who is not a member of the cultural group for which an intelligence test was designed may answer items on that test incorrectly for reasons that have nothing to do with low intelligence.

The interpersonal setting in which a test is given can also introduce cultural bias. When children are tested by a member of another racial or ethnic group, they may feel uncomfortable and do less well than they would if tested by members of their own group (Nyitii, 1982). Even the interpersonal format of an IQ test—in which a child is asked questions by an adult who already knows the answers to them—is unfamiliar to children from many cultural backgrounds. Consider the following exchange, from a testing session with a 5-year-old lower-middle-class African-American child:

Tester: What is a stove?
Child: You cook. That's what you writing down?
Tester: Yeah. I'm writing down what you say so I can remember it later.
Child: (incredulously) 'Cause you don't know what it's for?
(Miller-Jones, 1989, p. 362)

To overcome the problem of cultural bias, a number of psychologists have tried to develop IQ tests that are either **culture-free** (with no culture-based content) or **culture-fair** (appropriate for all the cultures in which it is used). One attempt at a culture-free test is Raven's Progressive Matrices Test, which requires the use of multiplication of classes to complete a matrix of unfamiliar visual designs. Because the problems on this test are presented visually (not verbally, using language), it was thought that they would be almost free of cultural bias. As it turns out, however, this is not the case. In fact, performance differences between some cultural groups are actually greater for this test than for verbal IQ tests (Sternberg, 1985). Perhaps this is because test-taking experience increases familiarity with solving matrix completion problems, just as it does for solving conservation tasks.

The unsuccessful efforts to develop a culture-free IQ test have led developmentalists to conclude that intelligence is not some inherent cognitive potential independent of a person's environmental experiences. Rather, intelligence *always* exists in some kind of environmental context, and unfamiliarity with a particular context affects how intelligent a person appears. Thus, intelligence tests are an effective means of comparing the abilities of people *within* the same culture or subculture, but for comparisons *across* cultures, IQ tests must be interpreted cautiously.

Culture-free IQ test:
An IQ test entirely free of culture-based content.

Culture-fair IQ test:
An IQ test that is appropriate for all the cultures in which it is used.

WHAT IQ SCORES CAN PREDICT

When we say that IQ tests are good for comparing abilities within the same cultural group, we must qualify that statement even further. In general, IQ tests are fairly good predictors of a person's success in school, at least in the schools created by the culture that developed the tests. In this country the average correlation between IQ score and school grades is about .70, quite a close relationship (McClelland, 1973). This makes sense when you consider that prediction of school performance is the purpose for which IQ tests were originally developed.

As for what else IQ scores are good at predicting, one longitudinal study found a moderate correlation between IQ in childhood and later occupational success (McCall, 1977). Childhood IQ scores may be best at predicting success in occupations that require abstract thought (Ghiselli, 1966). Beyond childhood, however, IQ scores are not very good at predicting job success. The correlation between adult IQ and on-the-job performance is only around .20 (Wigdor and Garner, 1982). This suggests that these tests are poorer measures of practical intelligence than they are of school-related skills.

CULTURE AND SCHOOL ACHIEVEMENT

In most parts of the world, children start formal education somewhere between the ages of 5 and 7, the beginning of middle childhood. By this age, in the course of daily activities, they have already acquired knowledge and skills that should be useful in school. For example, they are fluent speakers of their native language, they understand many things about quantity and number, and they have developed some logical reasoning abilities. Yet the transition to formal education is not always easy. Many children have difficulty applying their informal knowledge of language, number, and logic to more formal classroom tasks, such as learning to read and do math.

Disembedded, or decontextualized, thought: A cognitive skill needed to solve problems that are abstract, self-contained, and removed from any immediate context.

One reason this transition is sometimes difficult is that it involves a shift to **disembedded,** or **decontextualized, thought**—learning to solve problems that are abstract, self-contained, and removed from any immediate context (Donaldson, 1978; Tharp, 1989). Instead of using their informal skills to solve concrete, everyday problems, children in school must learn to deal with problems that seem to have little connection to their lives outside the classroom.

The transition to school is often particularly hard for children who come from cultural backgrounds different from that of the school they attend—for many of the same reasons of cultural bias involved in IQ testing. For instance, the format of social interaction expected at school may be unfamiliar to such children. In one study, Shirley Brice Heath (1983) found that white middle-class preschoolers were accustomed to being asked many questions at home. Up to half the things adults said to them were questions, many of which were *test questions* to which the adult already knew the answers ("What color is that?" "Where's your nose?" "What do cows say?"). Black lower-class preschoolers, in contrast, heard far fewer questions at home, and the questions they were asked served different functions and required different kinds of responses than the white middle-class parents' test questions did. The three most common types of questions they heard were *analogy questions* ("What's that like?"); *story-starter questions* ("Did you see Maggie's dog yesterday?"—to which an appropriate answer would be "What happened to Maggie's dog?"); and *accusation questions* ("What's that all over your face?"). When the black children entered school, their teachers often perceived them to be unresponsive and "slow." Clearly, the white children's experience with test questions allowed them to respond in ways that better matched the expectations of their teachers.

Research with other minority groups, including Polynesian children in Hawaii, Native American children, and East Indian children in England, have revealed similar examples of cultural mismatch between children's usual style of interacting with adults and the style expected in school (Phillips, 1983; Tharp, 1989; Yates, 1987). Such cultural mismatch can affect not only how easily children make the transition to school but also how much they derive from the school experience. Cultural mismatch may help explain why the average achievement test scores for African-American, Latinos, and Native American children are lower than the average scores for whites, and why their dropout and school failure rates are higher (Neisser, 1986; Tharp, 1989; Slaughter-Defoe et al., 1990).

Many attempts are being made to decrease cultural mismatch between children and schools. On a small scale, Heath (1981) was able to convince some teachers to use questioning strategies more familiar to their black pupils, at the same time introducing the black children to the unfamiliar test questions they would continue to encounter in school. On a much larger scale, programs to make the content and format of instruction more compatible with the cultural backgrounds of Hawaiian and Native American children have increased the children's engagement in classroom activities and improved their achievement test scores (Tharp, 1989). All these efforts are based on the belief that how children are taught in school makes a difference to what they derive from their education.

The role that school experiences play in children's achievement may be clearer if we consider a different example of a low-achieving group. Overall, children in the United States do consistently worse than children in many other countries on measures of math and science achievement. For instance, studies comparing the math achievement of American children with that of Japaese and Chinese youngsters show that achievement differences appear as early as first grade and increase in size throughout the elementary school years (Stevenson et al., 1986). No one suggests that American children have learning deficiencies compared with children in these other countries. Instead, researchers and teachers assume that cultural differences in values and classroom practices must be the cause.

Many such differences have been observed in schools in these three countries. Both Japanese and Chinese teachers spend more time on math instruction and assign more homework than American teachers do. Perhaps more important, the *processes* by which math is taught differ. Asian teachers explain math problems in more detail, direct more attention to the principles underlying the problems and less to mechanical computational procedures, and analyze and correct individual students' errors more carefully, thus encouraging them to learn from their failures as well as from their successes (Stigler and Perry, 1990). In addition, Japanese children learn much of their math in cooperative learning settings where they are encouraged to explore a variety of ways to solve a problem rather than focusing on repeated practice of one "correct" strategy (Stevenson, 1993). Such differences in what happens in the classroom could account in large part for the achievement differences that exist between American and Asian students. The box on p. 448 provides more details about research into the differences in math instruction in Japan and the United States.

Differences in mathematical skills among members of different cultures have been the focus of substantial interest and research in recent years. In studies comparing academic performance of students in many different countries, Americans, as a group, are consistently weak in math (Garden, 1987; Husen, 1967). As we mention in this chapter, studies show that Chinese and Japanese youngsters surpass American children in math performance. The gap opens in first grade and widens year by year (Stevenson, 1993; Stevenson, Lee, and Stigler, 1986; Stevenson et al., 1990).

There is also a gap in math performance between boys and girls in our society. In a comprehensive study of gender differences, Maccoby and Jacklin (1974) found that around the age of 12 or 13 the math performance of boys begins to outstrip that of girls, even though throughout the elementary school years boys and girls show similar levels and patterns of mathematical ability. More recent studies have found that the degree of gender differences and the age at which they begin depend on the specific math skills being assessed. There is also evidence that the overall magnitude of these gender differences has been declining (Friedman, 1989; Hyde, Fennema, and Lamon, 1990). Nevertheless, the differences still exist, and they still tend to increase with increasing age (Dossey et al., 1990; Mullis et al., 1991).

Some researchers have tried to discover the respective roles that heredity and environment play in the development of ethnic and gender-based differences in math performance. Although genetic explanations have been proposed (e.g., Lynn, 1982; Herrnstein and Murray, 1994), the evidence for them is not compelling (AAUW, 1992; Stevenson et al., 1985). More important contributing factors seem to be the kind of math instruction that children receive and the attitudes they learn from both peers and adults (AAUW, 1992; Stevenson, 1993; Stevenson et al., 1990; Resnick, 1993).

In examining the classroom differences in how boys and girls are taught, researchers have found that in American schools teachers interact more with boys than with girls, and they give boys more useful feedback on their performance (Sadkers and Sadkers, 1984). At the same time, boys speak up more in class than girls do. These classroom differences disappear, however, when the teaching style is made more "female-friendly"—that is, when the atmosphere is warm and nurturing, with less emphasis on social comparison and competition (AAUW, 1992).

Parents also help to shape gender differences in math performance. For example, most American parents have different attitudes regarding math achievement for their sons and for their daughters. They usually attribute a girl's high achievement in math to good teaching and hard work, whereas they tend to associate a boy's high achievement in math with a natural aptitude for it. For poor math performance, essentially the opposite attributions are made: American parents tend to blame poor math performance on low aptitude in a girl, but on laziness and poor work habits in a boy (Parsons, Adler, and Kaczala, 1982; Holloway and Hess, 1985). In this way, they inadvertently encourage girls who are having trouble with math to give up rather than work harder.

In contrast, in China and Japan, math performance—whether high or low—is attributed to effort and work habits (Stevenson, 1993). This approach tends to build children's confidence that they can do well in math if they really try. There are also differences in what goes on during math instruction in American and in Asian classrooms. For example, Japanese elementary school children spend more time on mathematics than American children do. They also spend a majority of that time in cooperative learning settings in which mastering skills, not outperforming others, is the primary goal. Equally important, Japanese children are expected to learn from their failures as well as from their successes. A mistake is seen as an opportunity to gain further insights into how numbers work, not as a reason to feel defeated or worse at math than peers. At the same time, Japanese children are encouraged to explore a variety of ways to solve a problem, rather than focusing on repeated practice with one "correct" solution strategy. This approach tends to make them more creative mathematical thinkers than their American counterparts, whose learning of math is much more by rote and repetition.

A number of changes in mathematics instruction are currently being tried in an effort to improve the overall math performance of American youngsters and to narrow the gap between boys and girls. The changes aimed at boosting American children's international standing in math incorporate many of the key elements of math instruction used in Japanese schools (Stevenson, 1993). For instance, more classroom time is spent in small, cooperative groups, with more emphasis placed on the group's success than on the performance of individual students. These new programs also stress communication of the value of mathematics and of the benefits of exploring alternative solutions to problems (Resnick, 1993; Slavin, 1990; Shrum, Cheek, and Hunter, 1988). In addition to these new approaches, special short-term interventions for girls have been developed in which girls can explore math and science without having to compete with boys (e.g., Campbell, 1991). Both kinds of programs have had success in meeting their respective goals: to raise overall math performance and to diminish gender differences.

CHAPTER SUMMARY

1. Middle childhood—ages 6 through 12—is a time when cognitive skills that began to emerge in the preschool period become increasingly refined and elaborated, making them much more effective problem-solving tools. Compared with preschoolers, elementary school children are more able to think systematically about multiple pieces of information—that is, they show a marked decline in centration. Youngsters in middle childhood also make strides toward overcoming the appearance-reality problem, and they are able to think more effectively about their own knowledge and thoughts, an ability called **metacognition.** Elementary school children still face some cognitive limitations, however. Their general lack of knowledge and practice in using new skills makes them appear less competent than older children. They also have trouble reasoning maturely about abstract or hypothetical questions.

2. During middle childhood, children's understanding of conservation becomes stronger and more wide-ranging. In particular, they begin to provide explanations of conservation that go beyond the physical characteristics of what they see and instead entail logical reasoning. Such an understanding is based on **necessary truth** rather than **contingent truth.** In contrast to Piaget's stress on fundamental changes in the structure of children's thinking as conservation develops, information-processing theorists describe this development as a set of gradual changes in the rules children use to solve conservation problems.

3. Piaget described two kinds of classification that children become able to understand during the elementary school years: **hierarchical classification,** which involves **addition of classes,** and **matrix classification,** which entails **multiplication of classes.** It is not until age 8 or 9 that children are able to pass the standard **class inclusion** test of hierarchical classification by differentiating between a subclass and its superordinate class. It is at this age, too, that children are first able to solve matrix classification problems by sorting items simultaneously along two or more dimensions (color *and* shape, for example). In both these cases we see the child overcoming centration. An 8- or 9-year-old, however, may not yet grasp the more abstract logic of classification systems. Until about age 11 an understanding of such systems seems to be tied to concrete objects and situations.

4. During the elementary school years children show marked improvement in their ability to remember things. Some of this improvement comes from an expansion of knowledge, for what we know provides mental structures that make it easier to assimilate new information and draw inferences about it during recall tasks. Such inferences are called **constructive memory.** The memory abilities of elementary school children also improve through more spontaneous and effective use of **mnemonic strategies** like rehearsal. Another aspect of remembering that improves during middle childhood is **metamemory,** or knowledge about memory and memory processes. For instance, by the age of about 9, children are much better at predicting how likely they are to remember something and what kinds of memory strategies are likely to aid recall.

5. Children can learn a great deal from other children, as well as from adults, in both **didactic** and **cooperative learning situations.** A more knowledgeable child can often help a less knowledgeable one to make genuine progress in understanding the concept of conservation. Also, interacting with a peer of equal or even lesser competence can sometimes prompt discovery of an underlying principle in a child with prerequisite skills. Piaget believed that an important factor promoting such socially fostered learning is the chance for children to experience conflict between their own ideas and those of peers. In contrast, Vygotsky emphasized the role of others in helping children build on already developed skills within their zone of proximal development. One means of doing this is through **scaffolding,** in which a teacher progressively fits the guidance he or she provides in keeping with the level and progress of the learner's progress. Fifth graders have been observed to use scaffolding in tutoring younger children, one sign of their growing metacognitive skills. Both didactic and cooperative peer learning are apparent early in middle childhood, but the effectiveness of peer teaching increases as children grow older and become better at planning, using more effective teaching strategies, and adjusting their approach to their learner's needs.

6. Various psychologists have had different conceptions of intelligence, from a unitary concept (seeing intelligence as a *general* capacity) to a multifaceted concept (seeing intelligence as made up of many separate and largely independent mental abilities). Some researchers have suggested that a distinction should be made between **academic intelligence** and **practical intelligence.** Howard Gardner has proposed a **theory of multiple intelligences** in which he tries to broaden the definition of intelligence to include more practical cognitive skills, such as those involving music, complex movements of the body, and the ability to understand human feelings and

motives. Another attempt to broaden the definition of intelligence is Robert Sternberg's **triarchic theory,** which analyzes three factors—information-processing skills, experience, and context—that determine whether or not a behavior is intelligent.

7. Researchers agree that individual differences in intelligence are a product of interaction between heredity and environment. The concept of **reaction range** is useful in describing this interaction. It refers to the limits within which the effects of genes can vary depending on environmental influences. Individual differences in intelligence are sometimes measured by **intelligence quotients,** or **IQ** scores. These are determined by comparing a person's performance on a set of cognitive tasks with the performance of others similar in age. Critics have questioned the meaningfulness of IQ scores, given that these tests inevitably have some cultural bias. Others have answered that IQ tests are relatively good predictors of school performance, the purpose for which they were originally created. When comparing children from different cultural backgrounds, however, we must be very cautious in interpreting IQs. These tests should not be taken to be measures of some innate intellectual ability.

8. Although children have already acquired a variety of useful cognitive abilities before they enter school, the transition to school requires them to develop a new set of **decontextualized abilities.** Some children find this difficult. For children from many minority groups, there may be a mismatch between their usual way of interacting with adults and the style of interaction expected in school. Such cultural mismatches often contribute to school achievement problems.

Chapter 12

Social Development in Middle Childhood

Chapter 12

Social and Emotional Development in Middle Childhood

Ten-year-old Malcolm and his buddies Andy, Leon, and Curtis pass Tammy Wilson on the sidewalk with her friends Vanessa and Lorraine. It is as if two powerful force fields have collided. The girls fall silent; the boys get "cool." Vanessa nudges Tammy in the ribs with her elbow. Tammy slaps her arm away and continues looking straight ahead. Lorraine suppresses a giggle. As each group goes in its own direction, Vanessa turns around and yells: "Hey, Malcolm, Tammy likes you!" Tammy covers her face and runs up the street. All three of Malcolm's buddies turn on him:

"Uuuh-ahh, Malcolm, you sweet on her!"

"Yeah! Malcolm got a girlfriend!"

"Why don't you go kiss her, Malcolm!"

Malcolm shoves each of them and shouts defensively, "No way, man! Get outa here." Then, with much laughter, shouting, and playful fighting, the boys proceed to the candy store.

Middle childhood was once considered an uneventful phase of development. Given the whirlwind pace of changes during infancy, toddlerhood, and the preschool period, this view was understandable. The physical growth of school-age children slows to a few inches per year, and their cognitive and social advances no longer seem so dramatic. Freud went so far as to label middle childhood a **latency period.** He believed that children's sexual urges lie relatively dormant at this time, awaiting their great awakening in adolescence. Others took Freud's view to mean that little of importance in social and emotional development happens during the middle childhood years. Partly for this reason, until the last three decades, social and emotional development in middle childhood was one of the least studied topics in all of child psychology.

This lack of attention to the topic was unfortunate. To ignore any period of development creates serious gaps in our knowledge of how children grow. Ignoring middle childhood also hinders our ability to understand how youngsters handle the critical challenges of adolescence, because developmental out-

Latency period:
According to Freud, the period in which the child's sexual urges lie relatively dormant; middle childhood.

Same-set groupings are the major social milieu of middle childhood. In public settings, strict gender segregation is the rule.

comes in adolescence build on earlier outcomes (Blos, 1970). But perhaps most important of all, research into middle childhood has shown very clearly that this is *not* an uneventful time. Critical social and emotional development occurs from ages 6 through 12.

You glimpsed some of these changes in our opening example, which was based on observations made in the Minnesota summer camp study (Sroufe et al., 1993). These school-age children interacted in ways never seen among preschoolers. While the boys and girls stayed in their own groups, as is typical of this age (Huston, Carpenter, and Atwater, 1986; Maccoby, 1990), the beginnings of mutual attraction lay just beneath the surface. In fact, the energy devoted to maintaining a boy-girl separation suggests great curiosity about members of the opposite sex. But for now this curiosity does not take center stage. Middle childhood is a time when other social and emotional issues take precedence.

Erik Erikson (1963) argued that the major issue of middle childhood is the challenge of starting to master many adult skills and the feelings that success or failure foster. Success at meeting this challenge brings what Erikson called a **sense of industry**—that is, a basic belief in one's own competence, coupled with a tendency to initiate activities, to seek out learning experiences, and to work hard to accomplish goals. You saw examples of a sense of industry in our earlier stories of Meryl and Malcolm. These children and their friends felt pride in being able to carry out projects, and they were busy setting new challenges and objectives for themselves. A sense of industry does not derive from the fantasy play of the preschool period (Doyle et al., 1985). Rather, it is concrete achievements in the real world (such as success in school) and effective coping with problems that lead to deep feelings of competence and self-worth. Repeated failure to master new skills, in Erikson's view, leaves a child with feelings of incompetence and inferiority.

What Erikson describes is part of a broader task of middle childhood, pulling together one's history of experience—as a social partner, an initiator, a boy or a girl, a problem solver, and so forth—and integrating these various characteristics into a coherent self-concept. In other words, in middle childhood a self-image with many dimensions becomes consolidated in the child's mind (Harter, 1983; Wolf, 1990). Just as children can consider multiple aspects of a problem with increasing ease in middle childhood, so too can they coordinate multiple characteristics into a more integrated concept of the self.

Middle childhood is not simply a time of turning inward to consolidate an image of the self, however. It is also a period of social expansion. Middle childhood is the age when children first form loyal friendships—peer relations based on mutual trust and support. At the same time, elementary schoolchildren develop a genuine understanding of what it means to be part of a group and adhere to group norms. Meryl and Amy's creation of their own private "apartment" and Malcolm's strong belief that peers shouldn't "rat" on one another reflect these developmental changes.

Children face these central social and emotional tasks of middle childhood in the context of the family. Therefore, parents' styles of discipline, their attitudes toward sex roles, and the existence of marital conflict, separation, and divorce can all have an impact. Before turning to the family as a continuing setting for human development, however, we want to give you a better idea of how children in middle childhood differ socially and emotionally from preschoolers. We begin by stepping inside the mind of school-age children to observe the new ways in which they think about themselves and others. We then look at their

Sense of industry:
In Erikson's theory, the basic belief in one's own competence and ability to master the world, coupled with a tendency to initiate activities and to work hard to accomplish goals.

expanded understanding of peer relationships, as well as their growing understanding of emotions.

THE INNER WORLD OF THE SELF

Psychological self:
A concept of the self that is made up of psychological characteristics, such as mental abilities and customary ways of feeling.

During middle childhood developmental changes lay the groundwork for assembling a more complete, mature, and better-integrated view of the self. This more mature view includes what is called the **psychological self**—a concept of the self that is made up of psychological characteristics, such as mental abilities and customary ways of feeling. To be aware of these psychological characteristics, elementary school children must consider various aspects of their experiences together and see them all as part of the same "inner" self (Wolf, 1990).

THE EMERGENCE OF THE PSYCHOLOGICAL SELF

When psychologist John Broughton (1978) questioned children of different ages about what the self is, he found that preschoolers tend to think of the self not in psychological terms, but as a concrete entity, often synonymous with the brain or the head. Consequently, they tend to think of nonhumans as having "selves" as well. A 4-year-old would say that a dog, and perhaps even a tree, has a self. As one young child charmingly explained self-control over actions: "My mouth told my arm and my arm does what my mouth tells it to do" (Selman, 1980, p. 95). In keeping with this kind of thinking, preschoolers tend to distinguish themselves from others in terms of physical traits. "I'm different from Madeline because I have brown hair," a 5-year-old might explain. Similarly, when preschoolers are asked to list things about themselves, they usually dwell on their physical activities. "I play on the swings," a 4-year-old might say; or "I go to nursery school" (Keller, Ford, and Meachum, 1978).

It is not until middle childhood that the concept of self becomes more psychological. Now children increasingly describe themselves in terms of inner thoughts, feelings, abilities, and attributes (Broughton, 1978; Selman, 1980). Meryl at age 9 described herself this way: "I'm kind, I'm helpful, I love to draw, I'm a good artist, I sometimes feel shy." Underlying such changes in children's self-descriptions are changes in their thinking about the nature of selves in general. This overall view of the self is called a **metatheory of the self.**

Metatheory of the self:
Children's understanding of and ideas about the nature of the self.

A metatheory of the self that involves psychological characteristics requires that children consider multiple situations in order to "know" their own traits, or the traits of others. For example, in concluding that she is kind, 9-year-old Meryl might consider acts of kindness to her friends, to her little brother, to her neighbor's cat, and to Joe's elderly grandmother, and tie them all together as arising from a single characteristic. At the same time, she is aware that her kindness is related to her helpfulness toward others. Such thinking is clearly more mature than the preschooler's focus on specific physical traits.

This is not to say that older children don't sometimes include physical features in their self-descriptions. But when they do it is often because they have compared themselves with others and identified features that stand out as different from those of almost everyone else. (Thus, Meryl might describe herself as having the blondest hair of anyone in her class.) This more sophisticated outlook brings with it a firmer understanding of the self's uniqueness. As one of

Broughton's 10-year-old subjects explained it: "I am one of a kind. . . . There could be a person who looks like me or talks like me, but no one who has every single detail I have. Never a person who thinks exactly like me" (Broughton, 1978, p. 86).

Psychologist Robert Selman (1980) has shown how the emergence of a child's sense of an inner, private self parallels a growing awareness that all people have internal thoughts and feelings that are often hidden from others and sometimes even from themselves. Selman explored this topic by presenting children with dilemmas such as this one:

> Tom has just saved some money to buy Mike Hunter a birthday present. He and his friend Greg go downtown to try to decide what Mike will like. Tom tells Greg that Mike is sad these days because his dog Pepper ran away. They see Mike and decide to try to find out what Mike wants without asking him right off. After talking to Mike for a while the kids realize that Mike is really sad because of his lost dog. When Greg suggests he get a new dog, Mike says he can't just get a new dog and have things be the same. Then Mike leaves to run some errands. As Mike's friends shop some more they see a puppy for sale in the pet store. . . . Tom and Greg discuss whether to get Mike the puppy. . . . What do you think Tom will do? (p. 175)

Selman then presented a number of questions related to the story. Did Mike mean what he said? Can someone say something and not mean it? Did you ever think you'd feel one way and then find out you felt another? How can this happen? Can you ever fool yourself?

Selman found that very young children do not seem to distinguish between people's inner psychological experiences and their external words and actions. Many 5-year-olds conclude that Tom should not buy Mike the puppy because Mike doesn't want another dog. They know this, they say, because Mike told Tom so. In contrast, by about age 8 or 9 an understanding of the internal self has usually emerged. Now children recognize that what people say and do need not conform to what they think and feel. Mike may insist that he doesn't want a puppy, and he may even make himself believe this. Yet underneath it all, his inner, private self could want a new dog very much. Such insights into the private, psychological self show that children make great strides in self-understanding during the elementary school years.

THE DEVELOPMENT OF THE SOCIAL SELF

Another advance in self-understanding that occurs in middle childhood is development of what is often called the **social self** (Damon and Hart, 1988). This is an awareness that "who I am" is often intimately tied to other people around me. During the elementary school years, children's ability to adopt this perspective changes significantly.

Social self: An awareness that one's identity is often intimately tied to other people around one.

One sign of this development is that school-age children begin to describe themselves in terms of the ways they behave in their dealings with others (Benenson and Dweck, 1986). "I am kind," "I am helpful," and "I am sometimes shy" are examples from 9-year-old Meryl's self-description. At the same time, school-age children begin to incorporate social group membership into their self-descriptions (Damon and Hart, 1988). When asked to tell about himself, 10-year-old Mikey's answers include that he is a fifth grader, a Boy Scout, and a member of a Little League team. Such references to social group membership

Both boys and girls engage in group and solitary activities. However, the nature of these activities is often different for boys and girls.

Social comparison:
The tendency to use others as a source of information in evaluating the self.

are very prominent in the self-descriptions of adults, too. Their emergence in middle childhood tells us that youngsters this age are increasingly placing the concept of self within a social context.

Closely linked to the inclination to define the self in terms of relationships with others is the tendency to use others as a source of information in evaluating the self. This is called **social comparison.** The use of social comparison gradually increases during middle childhood. In one set of experiments, children ages 5 to 10 were given feedback about their own and other children's performance on some difficult tasks (Ruble, 1983). The researchers found that youngsters didn't begin to evaluate their own performance in comparison with that of others until age 7 or 8, and not until age 9 or 10 did they consistently and systematically use social comparison in making self-assessments.

The use of social comparison in evaluating the self depends on several things. One is the *decline in centration,* the tendency to focus on only one piece of information at a time (see Chapter 9), that marks the end of the preschool period. Until children are able to consider their own performance *and* someone else's at the same time, it is very hard for them to make social comparisons of any kind. Social comparison is also based on a *normative understanding of ability*—that is, on the capacity to think about ability partly in terms of what "most children" can do. With a normative understanding of ability, a child is naturally inclined to look to others when assessing his or her own skills. Finally, the use of social comparison depends on the *cultural context.* In some cultural settings it is encouraged, in others it is not. Even the purpose for which social comparisons are made can depend on the cultural context. For example, Israeli kibbutzim children, who are socialized to value group cooperation, use social comparison as a guide to how close they are to mastering a task, whereas urban Israeli children use social comparison more as a gauge of who did better (Butler and Ruzany, 1993).

THE DEVELOPING SENSE OF GENDER

The sense of gender, including gender stereotypes, is another aspect of the self that develops during middle childhood (Beal, 1994; Serbin et al., 1993). By the end of elementary school, children know fully the activities, occupations, and personality traits considered appropriate for males and females in their culture. Thus, by this age they have firm notions about what being a boy or a girl means (Beal, 1994).

Knowledge of gender stereotypes has a powerful influence on children's perceptions and memories (Liben and Signorella, 1993). In one study, for instance, children were given stereotyped information about a specific boy and girl and were then shown videos of the two children that contradicted the stereotypes (McAninch et al., 1993). When questioned later they remembered the children as conforming to the stereotypes, not deviating from them. For example, they attributed shy behaviors to the girl in the video that were not in fact shown.

Elementary school children also apply gender stereotypes to themselves. For instance, their preferences for activities tend to conform to traditional gender roles (Serbin et al., 1993). If the children deviate from those traditional preferences, they often criticize themselves (Bussey and Bandura, 1992). Other aspects of their behavior match gender stereotypes too. Elementary school boys, for example, are more adventurous and engage in more risk-taking (Huston et al., 1986), while the girls are more socially aware. The boys are also more assertive in entering groups, whereas the girls are more attentive to new group members (Borja-Alvarez et al., 1991).

Several factors can influence how strict or flexible children are in conforming to gender stereotypes. One is the child's sex. In general, boys are more strongly sex-typed than girls, who tend to show more gender flexibility (Katz and Ksansnak, 1994; Frey and Ruble, 1992). Also, thinking about gender often becomes more flexible with age and cognitive development (Serbin et al., 1993). For instance, as children mature they are more likely to say that hammers and rifles, dishes and brooms might be used by either sex, and that both boys and girls could be adventurous and cruel or weak and gentle. Socialization factors can also influence the flexibility of gender-related thinking. Having a mother of higher socioeconomic status who engages in nontraditional roles is related to more flexibility, as is having important people in one's life who think more flexibly about gender (Katz and Ksansnak, 1994; Serbin et al., 1993).

PERSONAL EFFECTIVENESS AND SELF-MANAGEMENT

A final aspect of the self that develops during the elementary school years is children's belief that they can master and prevail in challenging circumstances, and that their successes come from resources within (Oettingen et al., 1994; Skinner, 1990). Such a belief in personal effectiveness evolves step by step (Benenson and Dweck, 1986). For instance, Susan Harter (1980) has found that while most preschoolers believe their physical and cognitive accomplishments are the result of their own efforts, social success at this age is viewed as a chancier matter. When asked, "How do you find a friend?" a preschooler might answer, "You go up and ring someone's doorbell" or "Maybe a policeman can help you." In contrast, by school age, most children feel that social successes, like physical and cognitive ones, depend on one's own actions. As one 10-year-old girl replied when asked how you get someone to like you: "You talk to them and play with them and be nice to them."

As children develop a sense of personal effectiveness, they tend to perform quite well on tasks requiring self-control (Mischel et al., 1989). For instance, when given the choice of accepting a small reward immediately or waiting for a much larger one later, and when told that certain actions carried out in the meanwhile will shorten the waiting period, school-age children tend to busy themselves with the prescribed behaviors and are able to wait substantial amounts of time. This ability to delay gratification increases markedly between the ages of 5 and 12.

PEER RELATIONSHIPS IN MIDDLE CHILDHOOD

Peer groups become increasingly important in middle childhood, being rivaled only by the family as the child's major developmental setting (Hartup, 1992). The importance of the peer group derives partly from the sheer amount of time that elementary school children spend with peers. By age 11 the time spent with peers usually surpasses the time spent with family (Larsen and Richards, 1991).

But middle childhood peer groups are important for other reasons too. One is the unique learning experiences that peer groups provide (Keller and Edelstein, 1993). Because adult-child relationships are based to some extent on

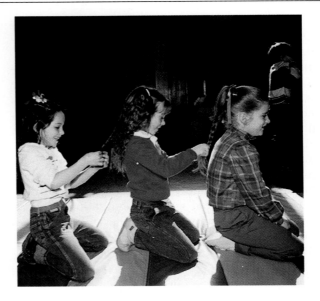

Peer groups provide a major arena for learning about reciprocity, cooperation, and fairness.

power and obedience (the adult has the right to *tell* the child what to do), they are limited in what they can teach the child about such things as reciprocity and cooperation. In the peer group, in contrast, relationships are much more nearly equal (the very word *peer* means equal standing), and they are guided by principles of sharing and fairness. This equality makes the peer group highly conducive to teaching its members about rules and expectations that will guide behaviors with others later in life. Peer relations may be especially important for learning to regulate aggression and for understanding the principles of loyalty and equity, important foundations for moral development (Hartup, 1992; Keller and Edelstein, 1993; Youniss, 1980). When Malcolm and Andy debate how to "get even" with Derek, or when Meryl and Amy discuss how to share a new toy, they are tackling principles that can best be learned within the peer group.

Another reason middle childhood peer groups are important is that they challenge youngsters to develop their interaction skills (Hartup and Sancilio, 1986). Elementary school children must work to make peers grasp what they are thinking and feeling, and they must also struggle to see the points of view that other children hold. Through such efforts toward mutual understanding, children gain in social competence throughout the elementary school years.

ADVANCES THAT ENABLE MORE COMPLEX PEER RELATIONS

A number of advances made during middle childhood enable peer relationships to become significantly more complex. One is the tendency to think of others in terms of their psychological traits (their inner thoughts, feelings, and abilities) rather than merely in terms of what they look like or do (Damon and Hart, 1988; Rogosch and Newcomb, 1989). For example, an elementary schooler might describe another child as friendly or mean, rather than simply saying, "She walks to school with me" or, "He hits people." This advance parallels the development of the psychological self. Because children can now think about others in deeper, more complex ways, they can start to build more mature interpersonal relationships.

Another important advance underlying more mature peer relations is a greater ability to understand the perspective, needs, and feelings of others (Youniss, 1980; Damon and Hart, 1988). For instance, 9-year-old Meryl can understand the feelings and needs of Amy, who one day forgets to bring her lunch to school. When Meryl offers Amy half her own lunch, it is not because she is simply following a rule about sharing. It is because she knows that sharing is the helpful, kind thing to do. She shares to address a need and an inequality, and she shares on a personalized basis (Amy is her best friend). Notice, too, that in addition to enabling more mature peer relations, the capacity to consider the feelings of others enables a marked advance in prosocial behavior.

A third advance related to more mature peer relations is the ability to grasp that different situations can change what is required of people in their dealings with others (Damon and Hart, 1988). For instance, 11-year-old Malcolm knows that when one of his best friends buys a bag of candy, he can help himself to a piece if he wants, as long as he doesn't take more than his fair share. Malcolm understands, however, that helping himself would not be acceptable behavior with a boy he hardly knows. Malcolm also understands that while he and his best friends can laugh, elbow, and playfully shove one another while working on a joint project at home, a joint project at school requires much more restrained behavior. Children this age, in other words, grasp more complex rules regarding interpersonal behavior, and so their relationships with one another become more mature.

A final factor contributing to more mature peer relations is a growing ability to communicate feelings and wishes with words rather than with actions. For instance, when young preschoolers want a toy that another child possesses, they often express their desire for it by trying to wrest the toy away. Elementary schoolers, in contrast, are much less likely to display such instrumental aggression (Hartup, 1983). Instead, they typically try to negotiate or appeal to group norms (such as sharing) in order to get what they want. Similarly, when someone has offended them, elementary school children can communicate their displeasure verbally rather than physically. Compared with preschoolers, they are much more likely to hurl verbal insults intended to cause the offender psychological distress (Maccoby, 1980; Thorne, 1986). This trend makes sense when you consider the developmental changes taking place in their understanding of the self and others. For instance, in order for Derek to be insulted upon being called a jerk, he must want to have an image of himself as competent and well liked. At the same time, only when Malcolm is able to consider Derek's feelings about receiving such an insult will he understand how much the taunt can hurt.

FIVE MAJOR DEVELOPMENTS IN PEER RELATIONS

There are several ways in which peer relations change during middle childhood. Compared with preschoolers, elementary school children expect more from a friend, including loyalty and understanding. They also start to form networks of friends, what we have called peer groups. This requires the additional complexity of coordinating their allegiance to individual friends with their functioning within a group. At the same time, they learn to adhere to peer group norms, including norms about interaction with members of the opposite sex. Let's look at each of these developments.

Close friendships often offer special opportunities for learning and development. By middle childhood children can maintain close friendships while still functioning effectively in groups.

FORMING LOYAL FRIENDSHIPS

Interviewer:	Why is Caleb your friend?
Tony (a preschooler):	Because I like him.
Interviewer:	And why do you like him?
Tony:	Because he's my friend.
Interviewer:	And why is he your friend?
Tony:	(slowly and emphatically, with mild disgust) Because . . . I . . . chosed . . . him . . . for . . . my . . . friend.

(Rubin, 1980)

Interviewer:	Why is Shantel your friend?
Lakisha (age 10):	Shantel tells me things she wouldn't tell anyone else. Like, if she was mad at some of the other kids, she would tell me. And some kids wouldn't do that. I think it's nice that she shares her secrets with me.

(Sroufe, Carlson, and Shulman, 1993)

Although preschoolers routinely label other children their "friends," these relationships lack the reciprocal support and loyalty, the shared intimacy and common interests, of genuine friendships. Not until middle childhood do more mature ideas and expectations about friendship develop (Keller and Edelstein, 1993; Selman, 1980). This is one of the major social accomplishments of the period. By the end of the elementary school years most children are involved in what psychiatrist Harry Stack Sullivan (1953) called "chumships"—very close and personal friendships between two peers, such as that between Meryl and Amy. There is close agreement among various measures of friendship in middle childhood, including teacher assessments, statements made by the children, and direct observation of their interactions (Elicker et al., 1992).

The deepening of peer relationships that occurs in middle childhood is related to various advances in how children think (Hartup, 1992; Keller and Edelstein, 1993; Youniss, 1980). During the elementary school years children come to understand how friends can support one another. No longer do they define a friend simply as "someone I like" or "someone I play with a lot." Friends are now seen as people who help and share with each other, especially in times of need. Remember, too, that middle childhood is the time when

youngsters start to view the self and others in terms of relatively stable dispositions. Consequently, they focus more on the personal traits a friend possesses.
Friends are described as nice, kind, and worthy of trust. This is how one 10-year-
old girl compared her friends with a child who was not her friend:

> *(Why don't you make friends with Bernadette?)* "'Cause we had a fight, a big one." *(Why
> can't you make up?)* "'Cause we're not good friends and I don't like her that much.
> She's not my kind of person. She's not my taste." *(What's your taste?)* "I like nice peo-
> ple. If they're not kind then they're not a friend." (Weinstock, quoted in Damon,
> 1977, p. 158)

Children this age also come to understand that conflict is a part of friendship
and may even strengthen it (Hartup and Laursen, 1994; Selman, 1980). When
asked if an argument could make you stop being friends, 10-year old Lakisha
thought for a while and replied: "No. Actually, you probably would be even better friends because you would understand each other better." Of course, some
less-confident children think that relationships with peers are more fragile, that
other children will not like them very long if they argue with them (Sroufe et
al., 1993). Still, by the end of middle childhood, all children have the capacity
to think about friendship in much more complex ways than they could in the
preschool years. They now recognize that the essence of friendship is mutual
understanding and caring, as well as shared outlooks and interests (Hartup,
1992).

Children behave differently with their friends than with mere acquaintances
(Berndt, Hawkins, and Hoyle, 1986; Hartup, 1992). For instance, in a study in
which pairs of elementary school children were asked to build block towers in
order to win rewards, pairs of friends showed more positive emotion (more
laughing, smiling, exclaiming) than did other pairs (Newcomb, Brady, and
Hartup, 1979). The pairs of friends were also more likely to phrase ideas in
mutual terms ("Let's do it this way," "Let's make sure it's straight"), and they
were more concerned with equity in how rewards were distributed. Similar
findings come from extensive research by John Gottman (1983) at the Univer-

*By middle childhood verbal
hostility replaces physical
hostility as the dominant mode
for expressing anger or
displeasure with a peer.*

sity of Washington. He concludes that children who become friends are better able to find common ground and shared interests, and their relationships are usually characterized by fun, humor, warmth, and harmony.

This is not to say that pairs of friends never argue. In fact, in "closed" situations (Hartup and Laursen, 1994)—in which children must interact and solve a problem presented to them by an experimenter in a certain way—friends show more conflict, and more intense conflict, than nonfriends do. This is presumably because friends have more capacity to stay connected in emotionally arousing situations. Whether cooperating or competing, what most distinguishes friends' interactions is a deeper involvement with each other (Hartup, 1992). Friendships in middle childhood entail a substantial investment of self.

FORMING PEER GROUPS

Friendship network:
The relatively stable cluster of friends with whom an elementary school child interacts; the hallmark of middle childhood.

If beginning peer relationships are the hallmark of the preschool years, **friendship networks** are the hallmark of the middle childhood period (Hartup, 1992). Like conceptions of friendship, conceptions of the peer group also change with age (see Figure 12.1). Preschoolers have very little understanding of groups as such. They have little sense of peer group members sharing a collective identity, only rudimentary feelings of "we" versus "they." By the end of the elementary school years, however, children have a well-defined sense of "groupness" and readily distinguish between those inside and outside their group.

Elementary school children tend to play with relatively stable clusters of friends. These groups are usually smaller for girls, with each girl having one or

FIGURE 12.1 AGE CHANGES IN CHILDREN'S CONCEPTIONS OF THE SELF, FRIENDSHIP, AND THE PEER GROUP
The development of understanding of self and others increases notably during the middle childhood years. (Source: Adapted from Selman, 1980, p. 180.)

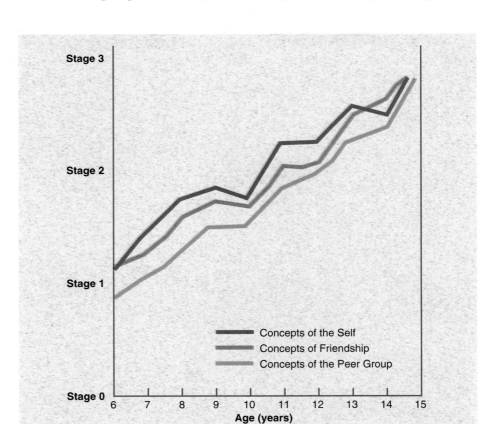

two best friends (Maccoby, 1990). This tendency is in keeping with the stress that school-age girls place on intimacy, sharing of confidences, and mutual support. Meryl and Amy, with their private "apartment," are typical of girls at this age. Boys' peer groups, in contrast, tend to be larger, with an emphasis on loyalty and shared activities. Malcolm and his three buddies—Andy, Leon, and Curtis—provide an accurate snapshot of the kinds of peer groups that school-age boys tend to form.

Boys and girls do different kinds of things in their peer groups (Shulman et al., 1994). Boys often engage in joint building activities, or they make up competitions, such as a skateboard contest. These activities often allow a great deal of individual self-expression and emphasize dominance, in that the boys vie to be the leader or the winner. Also, while there is often considerable physical intimacy in boys' peer groups (playful pushing and wrestling, for example), there is little emotional or verbal intimacy (boys spend little time confiding to each other). In addition, boys are much more likely than girls to participate in team sports, which involve formal rules and coordination of a large number of people. Girls' groups, in contrast, are not only smaller, but often more cohesive, more oriented toward accord and toward verbal and emotional intimacy. Many girls' activities, such as planning a skit, support a great deal of talking, and frequently talking itself *is* the activity. Loyalty may be achieved more quickly in a girls' peer group. One group of girls studied in a summer day camp refused to say whom they liked best in their group because they had made a pact to say they liked one another exactly the same (Shulman et al., 1994).

COORDINATING FRIENDSHIP AND GROUP INTERACTION

Both close friendships and interaction within a group provide children with valuable experiences. Trust and reciprocity are the lessons of close friendships, while cooperation, coordination of activities, and adherence to rules and norms are the primary lessons of the peer group. Both close friendships and acceptance by peer groups are related to feelings of self-worth and lack of loneliness in children (Parker and Asher, 1993), so it is important that they learn to coordinate friendships and group involvement. Observational research has shown that typically these tasks supplement each other (Shulman et al., 1994; Sroufe, Carlson, and Shulman, 1993). Friendships promote integration into a group, and functioning in the group is a rich context for sharing between friends.

Even when two socially competent friends are functioning within a group, the special relationship between them is still apparent in the way they behave toward each other. It is as if an invisible membrane surrounds them, even though they are mingling with other children and some distance from each other. This is not the case for children who are less socially competent (Shulman et al., 1994). Some fail to stay connected with their friend when playing in a group, or the friend leaves them behind. (The membrane around them ruptures.) Other pairs of friends steer clear of peer groups entirely. They form an exclusive relationship, playing apart from others. Apparently the membrane around them is too rigid, allowing no involvement with the outside world.

ADHERING TO PEER GROUP NORMS

If you have ever observed a group of elementary school children scrupulously dividing a large candy bar so that all will receive *precisely* the same amount, you are aware of how concerned children this age are about enforcing **peer group norms,** or rules of conduct. Equity is a very important norm during middle

Peer group norm: An informal rule governing the social conduct of children within a peer group.

Your group helps define who you are and provides standards and feedback for evaluating yourself. It is a context for social comparison.

childhood, perhaps because it helps maintain peer group harmony and cohesiveness (Hartup, 1992). Sometimes, school-age children do divide things unequally, but in that event they often use performance as the basis of the distribution (Graziano, 1984). Thus, Mikey and his Little League teammates might decide that whoever scored the most runs in the game they just won deserves the remaining slice of the pizza they are sharing in celebration. If no one had clearly made a larger contribution to winning, the boys would probably rigidly enforce the equity standard.

Such strict adherence to norms is common in school-age children. You saw one example in our story of Malcolm, who was amazed that Derek could ever break the code of not "ratting" on peers. Another example can be seen in school-age children's often rigid adherence to the rules of a game, as if the rules had sacred status. It is not until adolescence, or even beyond, that a person's conception of rules and norms becomes more flexible.

Sharing is another strictly adhered-to rule in middle childhood. By the age of about 8 or 9, sharing becomes closely tied to fairness and rectifying inequalities. Amy, for example, may say that it's "only fair" to allow Rita to join in some of the bike hikes that she and Meryl take. Such reasoning is seen repeatedly in school-age children. Fairness, equity, and sharing are cardinal principles of their relationships (Hartup, 1992; Youniss, 1980).

Because peer group norms usually agree with the moral values of a child's culture, peer relationships are considered an important arena for promoting moral development (Damon, 1988; Keller and Edelstein, 1993). Although adults are the ones who initially teach children how they are expected to behave, children themselves do much to ensure that those expectations are carried out. Friends and playmates tell each other when they are doing "wrong," and children who refuse to follow the rules are often ostracized. Thus, the peer group is one of the mainstream culture's great watchdogs and enforcers. Partly through peer group vigilance, cultural norms and values become deeply ingrained.

MAINTAINING GENDER BOUNDARIES

One area of socialization in which the peer group's influence stands out is that of maintaining a boundary between the two sexes. Elementary school children are diligent in their efforts to ensure that children do not stray too far across gender lines. Chase games between the sexes may be acceptable, but a boy who tries to enter a girls' game of jump rope is usually shunned as intensely by the girls as he is ridiculed by the boys. Similarly, a girl who hovers near the boys usually gets a negative reaction from both the sexes. Researcher Barrie Thorne (1986) has called these rituals of teasing and ostracism **border work,** because the children are defending the borders of their gender-segregated groups. This is what Malcolm's friends are doing in the scene at the beginning of this chapter. Their teasing keeps Malcolm from showing any reciprocal "liking" for Tammy.

Such self-imposed gender segregation is common in middle childhood—not just in the United States but throughout the world (Beal, 1994; Whiting and Edwards, 1988). In one study at a summer camp in Minnesota, only 6 percent of the observed free time of ethnically diverse 10-year-olds involved a single child interacting exclusively with members of the opposite gender (Sroufe, Bennett, et al., 1993). Even when groups of boys interacted with groups of girls, physical boundaries between the sexes were maintained.

One function that gender segregation may serve is to protect young children from premature sexual contact. Working first on establishing intimacy with peers of their own gender frees them from the added demands of a heterosexual relationship. During adolescence and adulthood intimacy may then be extended to opposite-sex partners.

This is not to say that elementary school children have no contact with members of the opposite sex. A great deal of such contact occurs, but it does so in the context of peer group rules (Elicker et al., 1992; Sroufe et al., 1993). These rules are unwritten, and adults do not teach them (many adults, in fact, seem to have forgotten them), but most children know them well. For example, although children usually consider it inappropriate to interact with children of the opposite sex, especially when a single child is the odd person out in an other-gender group, there *are* exceptions to this norm, such as when a teacher requires such contact. This and other rules of acceptable opposite-sex contact are listed in Table 12.1. In general, school-age children consider it acceptable to

Border work:
Barrie Thorne's term for the rituals of teasing and ostracism with which elementary school children maintain the boundary between their gender-segregated peer groups.

Girls and boys in middle childhood expend much energy trying to show that they don't want to have anything to do with each other. Virtually every 10-year-old, when asked about a recent day camp experience, said the only thing she or he didn't like was "the boys" or "the girls." Despite such protests, it is clear that cross-gender interest runs high.

TABLE 12.1
KNOWING THE RULES: UNDER WHAT CIRCUMSTANCES IS IT PERMISSIBLE TO HAVE CONTACT WITH THE OTHER GENDER IN MIDDLE CHILDHOOD?

RULE:	The contact is accidental.
EXAMPLE:	You're not looking where you're going and you bump into someone of the other gender.
RULE:	The contact is incidental.
EXAMPLE:	You go to get some lemonade and wait while two children of the other gender get some. (There should be no conversation.)
RULE:	The contact involves some clear and necessary purpose.
EXAMPLE:	You may say, "Pass the lemonade" to persons of the other gender at the next table. No interest in them is expressed.
RULE:	An adult compels you to have contact.
EXAMPLE:	A teacher says, "Go get that map from X and Y and bring it to me."
RULE:	You are accompanied by someone of your own gender.
EXAMPLE:	Two girls may talk to two boys though physical closeness with your own partner must be maintained and intimacy with the others is disallowed.
RULE:	The interaction or contact is accompanied by disavowal of any interest in or liking for members of the other gender.
EXAMPLE:	You call members of the other gender ugly or hurl some other insult at them, or (more commonly for boys) you push or throw something at them as you pass by.

SOURCE: Sroufe, Bennett, et al., 1993.

interact with members of the other gender only when they have adequate "cover"—that is, a suitable excuse.

Girls or boys who routinely fail to maintain gender boundaries are less popular with other children and are rated as less socially competent by adult observers. Thus, following peer group rules appears to be a sign of competence and adjustment during middle childhood. It also forecasts successful functioning in mixed-gender peer groups during adolescence (Sroufe et al., 1993).

STATUS AND ACCEPTANCE IN THE PEER GROUP

Not all children are popular with peers. Some unpopular children are *rejected*, or actively disliked, by peers; others are simply *neglected*, or ignored, by them; and still others withdraw on their own from group contact (Cillessen et al., 1993; Crick and Ladd, 1993; Rubin et al., 1993). Some children who are not popular in the group nevertheless have friends, but others are friendless (Parker and Asher, 1993).

Although many unpopular children feel lonely or victimized by peers, not all of them do (Renshaw and Brown, 1993; Schwartz, Dodge, and Coie, 1993). Unpopular children's feelings about their low peer status tend to depend on several factors working together. For example, aggressive children, especially those who exhibit instrumental aggression and bullying, are more likely to be rejected by others (Cillessen et al., 1993; Coie et al., 1991), and the combination of aggression and rejection is strongly associated with maladjustment. Aggressive children who are *not* rejected are better adjusted and less likely to be seen as chronically insensitive (Hymel et al., 1993). Similarly, it is the combination of isolation from the group, friendlessness, and low peer acceptance that is associated with intense loneliness, not one of these factors alone (Renshaw and Brown, 1993).

During the elementary school years a particular child's popularity with peers becomes quite stable (Hartup, 1992; Bukowski, Newcomb, and Hartup, in press). Partly this reflects the growing capacity of children to think of others in terms of enduring traits, and so to form stable expectations about them (Dodge et al., 1986). A child's status among peers is also perpetuated by his or her own behavior. This was suggested in a study in which third and fourth graders were carefully observed on the playground (Ladd, 1983). Rejected children spent more time isolated from others or engaged in negative behavior such as aggression. Neglected children spent more time watching others playing; they merely stood on the sidelines and didn't participate. Popular children spent much of their time in relatively large, heterogeneous play groups that included their friends and other popular youngsters. Thus, how the children acted reinforced their status among peers.

Established patterns of behavior and the peer reactions they bring may carry over into new settings. In one study, for instance, children who were rated high or low in peer acceptance were placed in a new group of youngsters; soon these new peers viewed them the same way their previous peers had (Dodge et al., 1986). Apparently the children continued to behave in ways that encouraged certain peer responses. This can make it hard for unpopular children to change their status among peers. (See Figure 12.2.)

How well an elementary school child functions with peers and is accepted by

FIGURE 12.2 PERCENTAGES OF CHILDREN DISPLAYING INFORMATION-PROCESSING DEFICITS WHEN PROVOKED BY OTHERS

According to Ken Dodge's analysis, upon encountering a provocation, aggressive children show problems at each of five steps in the information-processing sequence: (1) encoding (using cues that are present); (2) interpreting cues correctly; (3) generating response options other than aggression; (4) evaluating the merits of appropriate responses; and (5) enacting a competent response to a provocation. This behavior leads these children to be negatively evaluated by peers. (Source: Dodge et al., 1986, p. 40.)

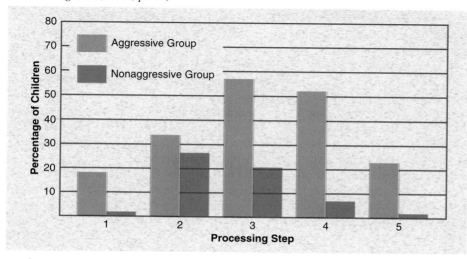

them strongly predicts adjustment in adolescence (Morrison and Masten, 1991; Sroufe, Carlson, and Shulman, 1993), and even mental health in adulthood. For this reason, researchers have tried to find ways to improve the status of unpopular children. One approach has been to change their expectations about how peers will react to them. For example, when researchers assured rejected children that the members of a new group would like them before entering them into that group, the children in the new group did in fact accept them more (Rabiner and Coie, 1989). Another approach has been to change key aspects of how unpopular children behave in the presence of peers. In one study, for instance, aggressive children were trained to perceive other people's intentions more accurately and were thus encouraged not to jump to the conclusion that others were hostile to them (Hudley and Graham, 1993). Compared with aggressive children who had not received the training, the trained youngsters often attributed more appropriate intentions to their peers and seemed to teachers to be less aggressive. However, we do not yet know how long the effects of such interventions last.

EMOTIONAL DEVELOPMENT IN MIDDLE CHILDHOOD

Even though children have experienced all the basic human emotions by the end of the preschool period, emotional development still continues at a rapid pace during middle childhood. During this period, children go beyond experiencing emotions such as guilt and pride to *understanding* these emotions and their causes (Ferguson et al., 1991).

THE CHANGING UNDERSTANDING OF EMOTION

One major advance in understanding emotions that occurs during middle childhood is the ability to consider multiple aspects of an emotion-arousing situation. Elementary school children know, for example, that emotional experience depends not only on what happens to someone at the present time but also on what the person was previously thinking and feeling, including the person's expectations (Gnepp, 1989). Thus, while a preschooler would say that a child expecting a big prize would be happy to receive a small one, an older child would know that this situation is likely to cause disappointment.

School-age children can also take into account the particular situation when determining an appropriate emotional response (Hoffman, 1986; Strayer, 1993). For instance, school-age children say they would be less angry at another child for stealing their cat if they knew that the other child's own cat was lost and the parents had refused to get another one. Similarly, school-age children show a growing understanding that emotions may vary in the same situation depending on the outcome, that different children may experience different emotions in the same circumstances, and that they themselves may experience a different reaction at different times (Gnepp and Klayman, 1992).

Finally, elementary school children know a great deal about "display rules" for emotions (Underwood, Coie, and Herbsman, 1992). They know it is sometimes better not to show your feelings, such as trying hard not to show your disappointment when given a gift you don't like or your anger when a teacher calls on someone else. Because elementary school children become increasingly adept at such *masking* of emotions, it is not always easy to tell exactly what they are feeling.

These changes in emotional understanding seem to be related to increases in true empathy for others. School-age children move beyond simply becoming distressed when someone else is feeling hurt, sad, or angry. Now they are able to feel along with the other person, and they do so more and more as they grow older (Fabes et al., 1993; Strayer, 1993).

EMOTIONAL, SOCIAL, AND COGNITIVE BASES OF MORAL DEVELOPMENT

The advances in children's thinking described in Chapter 11 support a deepening of moral concerns and a greater understanding of moral issues. For instance, as children move away from a focus on their own perspective and centration on only one aspect of a situation, they are increasingly able to consider the feelings of other people—even the feelings of several others simultaneously. Thus, whereas a 4-year-old would say that a boy who pushes another child off a swing feels very happy because he got the swing for himself, an 8-year-old would expect the boy to have mixed feelings and to be aware that the other child may be unhappy (Arsenio and Kramer, 1992). Such consideration for other people's feelings is a major factor in moral growth.

Just as cognitive changes contribute to moral development, so do social and emotional ones. As children strive to adhere to internalized standards in their relationships with peers, feelings of guilt, self-blame, and self-reproach arise when those standards aren't met. These feelings, in turn, prompt children to try to justify their behavior or compensate for what they've done wrong. This leads to deeper understanding of the moral self, as well as to further expansion of it.

Developmentalists stress that cognitive advances, social relationships, and emotions all work together to foster moral development. This was suggested in a set of studies in which European children were presented with a hypothetical choice of either keeping a promise to meet a best friend who needed to talk to them or going to a movie with a new child in the neighborhood who was going to pay for all the treats (e.g., Keller and Edelstein, 1993). Although most 7-year-olds said that a child faced with this moral decision would opt for the movie, 67 percent of 12-year-olds said that the child would choose to keep the promise to the friend. Important changes in thinking, feeling, and interacting with others underlay this difference in choice. While many 7-year-olds said that the child might feel bad (at least a little) for going to the movie, it was because they thought that the friend might be angry or had nice toys that the child wouldn't get to play with. Older children, in contrast, based their decision to opt for meeting the friend on the importance of both the friendship and the promise. They believed not only that a promise should be kept but also that loyalty is part of being a best friend. At the same time, they became able to evaluate and consider the feelings of the two other children. They would think of the friend waiting at home, for example, and this would make them feel bad. Note, however, that the older children's more mature moral thinking is not just the result of cognitive advances that allow them to understand other people's feelings better. They understand other people's feelings better because of their emotional experiences in friendships and their commitment to them. A moral sense, in other words, partly derives from participation in close relationships. Cognitive, social, and emotional development all work together to promote moral growth (Kahn, 1992; Keller and Edelstein, 1993; Smetana, Killen, and Turiel, 1991).

The particular moral principles that children adopt are largely a product of their culture. For example, when young Chinese children are presented with the moral dilemma just described, they use a different reason than young Western children to support the choice of going to the movie: they say the child would go to the movie because it is important to show caring and acceptance toward a new child (Fuix et al., 1994). Such reasoning probably derives from the Chinese concern with interpersonal harmony and the welfare of others. As Chinese children grow older, however, they, like their Western peers, increasingly emphasize the importance of friendship in making this moral decision and say that the child would opt for showing loyalty to the best friend. For Chinese children, a consistency between moral thinking and moral behavior (*doing the same thing that your reasoning tells you is right*) often emerges earlier than in Western children. Even the 7-year-olds were sure they had made the right moral choice, whereas the young European children were uncertain.

CONTEXTS OF DEVELOPMENT IN MIDDLE CHILDHOOD

As in all other periods of development, the changes of middle childhood take place within various environmental contexts. We have already discussed the context of the peer group, but family, school, and after-school care are important contexts too.

THE FAMILY

Within the family, both parents and siblings are powerful influences on the child's behavior. We'll take a look at the parents' influence first, beginning with the nature of the parent-child relationship during middle childhood. Later in the chapter we'll explore the influence of sibling relationships.

PARENT-CHILD RELATIONSHIPS

Relationships with parents change markedly during middle childhood. This is partly due to the child's advancing cognitive abilities. School-age children are more competent and better able to exert self-control, so parents begin to give them more responsibilities, often including participation in household chores (Warton and Goodnow, 1991). At the same time, parents are less inclined to use physical coercion and more likely to use reasoning in order to get their children to do what they should. As in peer relations, there is now more concern for equity and fairness in the parent-child relationship. In general, the parent-child system moves toward more shared responsibility for the child's behavior. Parents no longer explicitly direct the child in a continuous way. The child now has a general knowledge of what he or she should do, and the parents expect the child to follow those internalized guidelines for behavior. Still, the parents' role as *monitors* of behavior remains critically important (Hetherington, 1988; Dishion et al., 1991). The hallmark of effective parenting in this period is keeping track of the child's whereabouts and activities and providing supervision and direction whenever needed. When children deliberately violate rules that parents know they understand, parents believe it is important to assert their power by issuing a reprimand (Dix, Ruble, and Zambarano, 1989).

Parental influences take on new forms in middle childhood. Not only do parents influence the child through behaviors they model and through direct reinforcement (smiles of encouragement, words of praise) as they did in earlier years; now they also influence them through how they supervise and what they expect of the youngster. This can be seen in gender socialization. For example, parents tend to allow boys more freedom to explore and they encourage them to do things on their own (Huston, Carpenter, and Atwater, 1986), whereas parents tend to encourage girls to stay close to home and be more involved in domestic activities (Block, 1979). Similarly, parents expect sons more than daughters to be ambitious, hardworking, achievement-oriented, and assertive, whereas they expect daughters more often than sons to be nurturant, kind, unselfish, and loving. In keeping with these "female" expectations, girls tend to place high value on socially-oriented goals, such as showing concern for other people and being liked in return. When a girl's own achievements jeopardize her social acceptance, she is more likely than a boy to experience anxiety and a drop in her level of performance (Hoffman, 1984).

While parents remain authorities for children, parent–child relations move closer to "co-regulation" in middle childhood.

PARENTING STYLES AND CHILD DEVELOPMENT

Researchers have long been interested in different parenting styles. Many have looked at various characteristics of the parents' behavior, such as warmth versus hostility or restrictiveness versus permissiveness (e.g., Becker, 1964). They have found that certain parental characteristics are closely related to differences in children's behavior. For instance, parenting characterized by warmth, support, and a reasoning approach to discipline has consistently been found to be associated with positive child characteristics, including cooperativeness, effective coping, low levels of behavior problems, strongly internalized norms and values, a sense of personal responsibility, and high levels of moral reasoning (Becker, 1964; Baldwin, Cole, and Baldwin, 1982; Hardy et al., 1993; Radke-Yarrow et al., 1988; Walker and Taylor, 1991). In contrast, absence of parental warmth and a strong reliance on power-assertive discipline (shouting, physical punishment) tend to be associated with aggression and noncompliance in children, as well as with a tendency to project blame for negative outcomes onto other people (Caspi and Elder, 1988; Dishion et al., 1991; Emery, 1989; Weiss et al., 1992).

Such correlations between certain parental behaviors and certain characteristics in children do not prove that the first is causing the second. It may be that the child's characteristics are eliciting a certain style of response in the parents. In other words, the influence may be from child to parent, not the other way around. Some studies that examine sequences of interaction between parents and children have shown that the child does in fact play a role in maintaining negative encounters (e.g., Vuchinich, Bank, and Patterson, 1992). But this is not the whole story. When researchers assess parenting style even before the child is old enough to display stable behavioral characteristics, they find that how the parents act is generally related to how the child acts at a *later* age. For example, one study found that harsh discipline by the parents predicted later aggression by the child, with other potential causes of aggression (temperament, social class, marital violence) statistically controlled for (Weiss, Dodge, Bates, and Pettit, 1992). It has also been found that teaching alternative parenting techniques to parents who discipline harshly can help to improve the behavior of their children (e.g., Patterson and Capaldi, 1991). Such work suggests, although it doesn't prove, that certain characteristics of parents influence children.

Developmentalists have come to realize the importance of looking at clusters of characteristics in parents, not just at isolated traits, because a particular trait may have different effects depending on the other traits that accompany it. For example, parental permissiveness may lead children to be sociable and expressive, on the one hand, or disobedient, irresponsible, and lacking in persistence, on the other (Becker, 1964). It all depends on the other parenting characteristics that go with it. Being relatively permissive with a child in a context where rules are clear, the child is carefully supervised, and nurturance and respect are modeled, has different meaning than being permissive in a context of hostility, ambiguous rules, and lack of attention to the child. The first suggests a pattern of high positive regard; the second suggests a pattern of neglect.

In recent decades researchers have tried to identify clusters of characteristics in parents that are associated with certain outcomes in children. One such effort is Diana Baumrind's work, discussed in Chapter 10 (Baumrind, 1977, 1993). Parents whom Baumrind calls *authoritative* are nurturant and responsive toward their children. When disciplining, they often use reasoning rather than relying mainly on power-assertive techniques. Equally important, they are firm in setting limits and demand maturity of their children, although they take care to respect the child's own point of view. In contrast, parents whom Baumrind calls *authoritarian* are harsh in their discipline and rigid in enforcing rules. Seldom do they try to understand the child's point of view. Very different too are parents whom Baumrind calls *permissive*. They are somewhat nurturant but fail to maintain firm limits and standards.

A follow-up study of Baumrind's Berkeley subjects, conducted when they were 8 and 9, showed that authoritative parenting continued to be associated with positive outcomes in middle childhood (Baumrind, 1977). School-age children raised in authoritative homes tended to score higher in **agency**—the tendency to take initiative, to rise to challenges, and to try to influence events. Interestingly, an added dimension to the parent-child relationship seemed to contribute to the development of agency in daughters, though not in sons. This was an argumentative quality in a girl's interaction with her parents, especially with her father. Baumrind proposes that these argumentative encounters may balance pressures toward conformity and give a girl the extra push she needs to be self-assertive.

Baumrind's three parenting styles are not the only ones that researchers have identified. For instance, Eleanor Maccoby and John Martin (1983) have offered a framework that emphasizes two factors: (1) the frequency of conflict over goals between child and parent; and (2) the degree of balance or fairness in how parent and child tend to resolve their disagreements. The best developmental outcomes, they believe, occur when conflicts over goals are relatively infrequent (the parent is very supportive of the child), and when neither the goals of the parent nor the goals of the child always prevail (the parent sometimes makes demands and other times accedes to the child's wishes and expects the child to do the same). Like Baumrind's authoritative parents, these parents are responsive to their children and willing to negotiate with them, but they also require the children to respect their views.

There are several factors that may encourage harmonious parent-child relationships. Cognitive development for instance, undoubtedly supports the school-age child's ability to comply with parents' wishes in many situations. As

Agency:
The tendency to take initiative, to rise to challenges, and to try to influence events.

Children continue to require "monitoring" in middle childhood, but they are much more able to carry out parental instructions without direct supervision. One reason is that they are better accepting of parental authority. Another is that they are better able to follow through on plans themselves.

children move into middle childhood, they have a greater understanding of the legitimacy of parents' authority (Damon, 1983). They grasp the fact that parents are far more experienced than they are and that parents' decisions are usually intended for their own good.

But more than cognitive advances must be involved in this developmental process, or else all children of school age would be in the kind of relationship with their parents that Maccoby and Martin describe. Other factors must be involved that are found only in certain families. One may be the empathy shown by caring, responsive parents. By observing parents who understand his or her feelings, a child learns not only specific ways to show concern for others but also a complementary set of roles that are characteristic of close relationships (Sroufe and Fleeson, 1988). As a result, the child is more disposed to seek harmony with the parents.

Finally, Maccoby and Martin believe that the nature of parent-child interactions during earlier periods of development is also very important in fostering a positive parent-child relationship during the elementary school years. In their view, a history of parental responsiveness to an infant, coupled with mutual exchanges in which the parents respect the child's needs and feelings, serves as a form of "money in the bank" on which the parents can later draw. That is, later in childhood, when it becomes more necessary to impose controls and refuse some of the child's wishes, the parents can draw on the child's store of confidence in their concern and sensitivity (Maccoby and Martin, 1983). From this situation emerges a pattern of parent-child give-and-take that tends to endure over the years.

The quality of a parent-child relationship, then, may tend to perpetuate itself. One reason for this lies in the expectations that parents and children form about each other. These expectations color the meaning attributed to behavior. For instance, children who early in life have come to expect rejection by their parents may interpret even supportive behavior as a sign of rejection. Some research has shown that the frequency of coercive exchanges between parents and children is predicted by both the child's and the parents' negative expectations (MacKinnon-Lewis et al., 1994). Another reason the quality of a parent-child relationship tends to endure is that certain kinds of behavior often elicit responses that serve to encourage more of the original behavior (Vuchinich et al., 1992). For example, if parents treat a child harshly and the child responds by becoming irritable, that irritability is likely to bring on more punitiveness from the parents. Likewise, a child who expects parental support and responds positively to parental encouragement is likely to inspire more supportive behavior from his or her parents. For these reasons, the quality of the parent-child relationship tends to remain stable over time.

FAMILY VIOLENCE, CONFLICT, AND DIVORCE

Researchers have also been interested in how a climate of violence, conflict, or disruption in a family affects child development. Harsh physical abuse of children has been shown in numerous studies to be related to later negative behavior in the child (e.g., Cicchetti and Carlson, 1989; Egeland, 1994; Emery, 1989). For example, physically abused children studied at a summer camp were found to have lower self-esteem, to withdraw more from peers, and to engage in less prosocial behavior than other children from comparable socioeconomic backgrounds (Kaufman and Cicchetti, 1989). Moreover, even if children aren't physically abused themselves, the existence of violence in the family, especially physical abuse of the mother, is still associated with a variety of child development problems, including aggression and withdrawal (Christopoulos et al., 1987). A recent study has shown that these apparent consequences of family violence hold true even when socioeconomic status, life stress, and direct maltreatment of the child himself or herself are statistically controlled for (Dodds, 1995).

Children are also affected by a climate of conflict in the family (even nonviolent conflict) and by the divorce of their parents or separations from them (Emery, 1982; Grych and Fincham, 1993). Parental divorce typically follows a history of conflict, and often the conflict continues even after the divorce. This conflict is an important part of the impact of divorce on children (Block et al., 1986; Emery, 1982; Kline et al., 1989). Ending the conflict has been shown to moderate the negative consequences of divorce, such as troubled peer relationships and school problems (Hetherington and Clingempeel, 1992; Kline et al., 1989).

While divorce is difficult for children of any age, large-scale follow-up studies show that the impact is greater for younger children (Allison and Furstenberg, 1989). One reason may be that older elementary school children and adolescents are better able to understand disagreements and conflicts between adults and not to blame themselves for them. Also, if divorce occurs when children are older, they may have had a period of conflict-free parenting beforehand.

It was once thought that the consequences of divorce were greater for boys than girls, probably because boys exhibit more obvious and immediate reactions, such as increased aggression and problems of impulse control. But girls exhibit negative reactions, too, just of a different kind (Allison and Furstenberg, 1989). When their parents divorce, girls are more likely to become anxious, inhibited, and withdrawn (Block et al., 1986). Meryl's withdrawal during the period when her parents were having problems illustrates this response. Since such reactions do not disrupt the home or classroom, they are more likely to be ignored or even overlooked. This does not mean that girls are less troubled by divorce, however. Girls miss their fathers, just as boys do. In fact, girls may react more negatively than boys to remarriage by the mother (Hetherington and Clingempeel, 1992). Also, the negative impact of divorce on a girl may be delayed longer than it is for a boy, sometimes not becoming apparent until adolescence (see Chapter 14).

Still, there are some ways in which divorce can have a special impact on boys. Since children of divorce are typically placed in the custody of the mother, boys may miss the role modeling, sex-role socialization, and disciplinary functions that a father often provides. They may also respond more negatively than girls to living with the opposite-sex parent (Zaslow, 1989). Fortunately, the negative effects of a father's absence in the home can be reduced if the mother is not overly anxious and restrictive toward her son, and if she approves of the father as a role model for him (Hetherington, 1988; Hetherington and Clingempeel, 1992).

Researchers are now studying the long-term effects of divorce on children. They have found that many of these children develop well. Factors that promote good outcomes include ongoing contact with both parents, an end to parental conflict, cooperation between the parents concerning child care, the emotional well-being of the custodial parent, and the quality of relationships within the stepfamily if one is created (Hetherington, 1988; Hetherington and Clingempeel, 1992; Pearson and Thoennes, 1990). A good relationship with the custodial parent seems to be of special importance, no doubt because the child spends so much time with this parent. Thus, in our story of Mikey, the fact that he has a good relationship with Christine at the time of his parents' breakup should help him through this developmental crisis.

The recent findings concerning the long-term effects of divorce call into question the traditional assumption that parents should always try to stay together "for the children's sake." When divorce puts an end to severe marital conflict and helps make parental cooperation possible, the children involved usually fare better than those in conflict-ridden two-parent homes. However, if parental conflict continues after divorce, children are likely to suffer even more developmental problems than they would from marital conflict alone. The best advice to divorcing parents, then, is to reduce their levels of mutual hostility as much and as quickly as they can. In addition, if each parent maintains a warm and close relationship with the children, good adjustment is even more likely (Hetherington, 1988). The meaning that children attach to divorce is also a critical factor. When a child feels abandoned by one parent and blamed by the other, negative consequences are likely. We can see this in Mikey, who feels strongly that he is responsible for his parents' breakup because he failed as a mediator between them. Such children need help in understanding that they are not responsible and that both parents will continue to care for and be involved with them.

SIBLING RELATIONSHIPS

Sibling relationships may have a special place in the network of influences affecting child development. Because relationships among siblings continue throughout life and are often deeply emotional, they are in some ways similar to parent-child relationships. By the end of middle childhood, youngsters rate alliances with both parents and siblings as more enduring and reliable than those formed with people outside the family (Buhrmester and Furman, 1990). But siblings are far closer to each other in status than parents and children are, so in this respect relationships among siblings are more similar to those among peers. There are differences between pairs of peers and pairs of siblings, however. First, there is usually a greater age disparity between siblings than between friends, which tends to give one of the siblings more power and privileges than the other. Second, sibling relationships often cross gender boundaries, whereas in middle childhood peer friendships rarely do.

EMOTIONAL QUALITIES OF SIBLING RELATIONSHIPS Sibling relationships are quite complex, often involving both positive and negative feelings. Conflict and rivalry among siblings for their parents' attention and approval is common, especially when both children are boys, or when at least the older one is male (Dunn et al., 1994; Stoneman and Brody, 1993). Sibling strife based on social comparison (who is better? smarter? faster?) intensifies after about age 8, when children develop the cognitive skills needed to compare themselves with others (Damon, 1983). Although sibling conflict during middle childhood has not been observed to be dramatically more frequent than conflict among peers (Hartup and Laursen, 1994), by late middle childhood children themselves *feel* that it is (Buhrmester and Furman, 1990). Children also feel that sibling conflict more often results in coercive tactics and intense emotion (Hartup and Laursen, 1994). Compared with disputes between peers, many of the disagreements between siblings remain centered on possessions.

Yet intermixed with this rivalry and conflict between siblings are strong positive feelings. Younger siblings see older ones not only as controllers but also as facilitators. Older siblings often help younger ones solve a problem or perform some task. Older siblings, for their part, may resent their younger siblings, but they also feel nurturant toward them (Stillwell and Dunn, 1985). Thus, although Malcolm's older brother forbids him to look through his closet, he is also the one who teaches Malcolm how to play basketball; and although Meryl initially feels some jealousy of her baby brother, she also fusses over him as if he were one of her dolls.

The overall quality of sibling relationships varies greatly from case to case. Important factors influencing what that quality will be include closeness in age, gender composition, stress experienced by one or the other sibling, the children's personalities, and preferential treatment by parents. For example, one study that followed children into middle childhood found that a mother's preferential, more affectionate treatment of one sibling than of the other predicted competitiveness between the children (Stocker, Dunn, and Plomin, 1989). Another study found that preferential treatment by fathers was even more important than unequal treatment by mothers (Brody et al., 1992). The fact that such influences often continue over time helps to explain why the quality of sibling relationships tends to remain somewhat stable from the preschool period through middle childhood (Dunn et al., 1994).

THE IMPORTANCE OF SIBLING RELATIONS The emotional ambivalence that often characterizes sibling relations offers an important learning opportunity for children. It teaches them how to deal with anger and aggression in an ongoing relationship. When siblings fight and become angry, they cannot simply end their relationship. Unlike peers, siblings who have a major fight cannot choose to stop seeing each other (Stillwell and Dunn, 1985). Siblings who are in conflict must somehow work things out and continue to live with each other. Reconciliation is fostered by parents who constantly encourage siblings to "get along" and to treat each other as brothers and sisters "should." As a result, sib-

Sibling relationships are often tinged with strong emotion. Such emotional qualities are important because they allow children to learn that close relationships are often a mixture of positive and negative feelings and that relationships can persist despite feelings of anger.

ling relationships are an excellent way to learn that expressing anger toward someone you are close to does not necessarily threaten mutual attachment in the long run.

Sibling relationships are also important because of the mutual support they can provide. The close tie between siblings is probably what underlies reports that these relationships often help children weather parental divorce (Jenkins, 1992). Similarly, research suggests that sibling relationships may compensate somewhat for poor peer relationships (East and Rook, 1992).

Other benefits of sibling relations depend on the children's relative ages. For instance, in some cultures older siblings (generally girls) are assigned the role of caring for younger siblings (Whiting and Edwards, 1988; Zukow, 1989). We illustrated this with our story of Meryl's friend Rita, a member of the Hispanic subculture. This caregiving role helps prepare the older children for later parenting, and it increases the number of people to whom infants become attached. In dominant U.S. culture, with the growing number of families in which both parents work, care of younger siblings sometimes falls to older children by default. And even when parents are home, older children often look after their younger siblings in an informal way, making sure they don't touch forbidden objects or venture into places off-limits, and helping them learn new things. Such behaviors provide older siblings with experience in role taking, in nurturance toward others, and in the teaching of skills (Stillwell and Dunn, 1985). Adopting the role of "boss" may also help older siblings practice leadership skills and enhance their social confidence. One study found that in families in which the typical bickering between siblings occurred in a framework where the older child was definitely in charge, these older children were more competent with peers than were firstborns from families in which this role relationship was blurred (Marvinney, 1988). Interestingly, younger siblings, too, can benefit from a relationship in which the older sibling is usually the boss. In dealing with an older sibling who is bossier and more punitive than parents and more inclined to induce dependency, younger siblings learn how to negotiate with and accept help from other people (Stillwell and Dunn, 1985).

THE SCHOOL

The age of 6 is a momentous time for most American children because this is when they enter elementary school. With this initial step inside a "real" classroom, children's lives change dramatically. No longer are play and good behavior all that is expected of them. Now they must formally begin to learn the body of knowledge that adults deem important to master. For at least the next 12 years, many children will be at school 6 hours a day, 5 days a week, 9 months a year (or even more in some Asian countries). If influence is related to sheer length of exposure, school is certainly a major factor in many children's lives.

SOCIALIZATION IN THE CLASSROOM

Children learn many things in the classroom beyond the subjects that teachers specifically teach. Schools may encourage cooperation and prosocial behavior (Murphy, 1988), and they may provide opportunities for cross-ethnic contact and friendships unavailable in a child's own neighborhood. Research has shown that cross-racial friendships increase between kindergarten and third grade (Howes and Wu, 1990).

Mainstream cultural norms and values are repeatedly reinforced through the way schools organize activities and distribute rewards. When children are required to line up on hearing a bell ring, refrain from running in the hallways, walking through the bushes in the schoolyard, or talking too loudly over lunch, when they must do their assignments neatly, on time, and as the the teacher instructs, they are being taught such cultural values as hard work, achievement motivation, respect for private property, obedience to authority, punctuality, neatness, and compliance with rules. Teachers also encourage competition and social comparison in children by stressing each student's academic progress relative to that of classmates (Ruble, 1983). The school, in short, is a very powerful agent of socialization. At school, children are drilled in many of the values and behaviors that the dominant culture expects them to adopt.

We can see the school's role as an agent of socialization in the area of gender-role learning. At the simplest level, teachers reinforce gender differences by organizing activities around gender. They create boys' lines and girls' lines, for instance, or they pit boys against girls for spelling and arithmetic contests (Thorne, 1986). They may also assign classroom chores on the basis of gender. Moving a table might be a boys' job, for example, while laying out cookies for a party is a girls' job.

More disturbing are certain findings regarding boys' and girls' experiences in day-to-day classroom learning. Although girls more often than boys fit the stereotype of the "model pupil" (well-behaved, compliant, nondisruptive), there is evidence that many teachers are biased in favor of boys. In observational studies teachers have been found to interact more with boys and to give boys more positive feedback, whereas girls are more likely than boys to receive the teacher's criticism (Beal, 1994; Dweck et al., 1978; Serbin et al., 1993). Ironically, high-achieving girls may be the most criticized of all. In one study of fifth graders, the teacher gave girls who were high achievers the least praise and positive feedback and the most disparaging remarks of any group of students. Boys, too, of course, are sometimes criticized. But when they are, it is usually for misbehavior or lack of neatness rather than for lack of scholastic ability. Moreover, teachers tend to attribute poor performance by a boy merely to insufficient

Children's self-esteem can be affected by the structure of the classroom, depending on whether the emphasis is on competition and comparison or on cooperation and diversity.

effort, whereas they are more likely to view poor performance by a girl as a sign of low aptitude (Dweck et al., 1978). Thus, there is reason to believe that many American schools are subtly discouraging intellectual achievement in girls.

INFLUENCES ON SCHOOL ACHIEVEMENT AND ADJUSTMENT

An elementary school child's classroom adjustment and academic success are not just important in their own right. They are actually predictive of good mental health even in adulthood (Spivack, Marcus, and Swift, 1986). Because of its overall importance in a person's life, researchers have wondered what factors influence school success.

Michael Rutter and his colleagues tried to find out the role the school itself plays by assessing all the primary school children in one borough of London just before they entered secondary school, which in England starts at age 11 (e.g., Rutter, 1981). Rutter measured intellectual abilities and academic achievement, as well as social and emotional adjustment at home and in the classroom. He then followed the children through their secondary school careers. This part of the study included a thorough assessment of attitudes, atmosphere, and teaching practices at the particular school each child attended. The pupils were extensively surveyed, the teachers were carefully interviewed, and detailed observations were made in many of the classrooms. Rutter found strong correlations between certain school characteristics and certain outcomes in students. In particular, schools that emphasized academic achievement, that provided incentives for good performance, and that had skilled teachers who allowed students to assume responsibilities tended to turn out pupils with above-average records and few behavior problems. In contrast, children assigned to lower-quality schools faced an increased risk of performing poorly both scholastically and socially. Other research shows that noninteractive teaching strategies and required public self-evaluation of performance are related to lower performance expectations in children (Oettingen et al., 1994).

Other factors are also involved in school adjustment and achievement (Kindermann, 1993; Pianta and Steinberg, 1992; Teo et al., in press). For instance, a child's intelligence is highly predictive of academic success (as discussed in Chapter 11), and a child's level of cognitive development influences interactions with his or her teachers and classmates. Association with well-adjusted, academically motivated peers also has a positive impact. A history of nurturant support from parents and a well-organized home environment also seems to be important. These family factors strongly predict both achievement and school adjustment, and such effects hold even after IQ and earlier achievement are statistically controlled (Teo et al., in press). Finally, a child's personality or behavioral style affects school adjustment. For example, feelings of helplessness in the early grades predict low school performance later (Homan, 1990).

Parents and school staff often wonder whether starting a child in school a year later, or repeating a year in the same grade, will benefit that child's overall academic performance and school adjustment. Contrary to what many people believe, neither practice is supported by research. For example, retained children are no better off academically by late elementary school than similarly low-performing children who were not retained, and they are less well adjusted (Jimerson et al., in press).

AFTER-SCHOOL CARE

Given the prevalence of single-parent and two-career families (approximately 75 percent of American households in 1995), researchers have become interested in the after-school care of children (e.g., Posner and Vandell, 1994; Vandell and Ramanan, 1991). They are especially concerned about latchkey children, those who let themselves into the house after school and care for themselves until the parents get home. How well these children fare depends in part on their socioeconomic status. For middle- and upper-middle-class children, few drawbacks of self-care have been found, perhaps because any negative impact is offset by economic advantages or indirect parental supervision (Vandell and Ramanan, 1991). For children of poverty, however, significant amounts of time in after-school self-care are associated with both academic and behavioral problems (Galambos and Maggs, 1991; Posner and Vandell, 1994). Formal after-school programs run by the schools have been shown to be associated with better academic achievement and social adjustment for children of poverty than either mother care, informal care by others, or self-care after school (Posner and Vandell, 1994).

THE COHERENCE OF DEVELOPMENT IN MIDDLE CHILDHOOD

Development in middle childhood is coherent in several ways. First, it is coherent in that the various influences on it tend to be mutually reinforcing. As a result, these influences tend to channel development in a broadly similar direction. For example, parents, peers, and teachers all tend to promote the distinctiveness of boys' and girls' experience. Second, development in middle childhood is coherent in the sense that the various characteristics of an individual child are not randomly assembled. As in the preschool period, a child's characteristics seem to fit together in a way that makes sense. Finally, development in middle childhood is coherent in that it has continuity with the past. Although individual differences in children also reflect current influences, they tend to be predictable from preceding periods of development.

COHERENT SETS OF INFLUENCES

Family, peers, and school, the major agents of socialization in middle childhood, are not independent from one another. They are an interacting set of forces, and because they affect one another, the influences they exert on the child tend to be similar in certain ways.

By the middle childhood period, children have the capacity to develop loyal, empathic friendships. This capacity draws on a history of positive social experiences and current cognitive capabilities.

Competence with peers, for example, is a major issue in middle childhood and a barometer of the child's overall functioning. As such, it predicts other aspects of functioning, such as later achievement and adjustment at school (Teo et al., in press). Peer competence may also influence sibling and parent-child relationships (Kramer and Gottman, 1992; Vuchinich et al., 1992), and it is strongly related to the child's sense of well-being (Parker and Asher, 1993). However, peer competence itself is influenced by the other contexts of development. For example, peer problems at school have been linked to a history of low school achievement (Teo et al., in press), and competence with peers is predicted by the quality of sibling relationships (Marvinney, 1988). Parents, too, influence peer relationships. They do so directly through the encouragement, support, training, and advice they provide to children (Hartup, 1992; Lollis and Ross, 1992), as well as through the general quality of the parent-child relationship (MacKinnon-Lewis et al., 1994; Parke and Ladd, 1992; Park and Hazan, 1990; Vuchinich et al., 1992). Parents also influence peer relationships indirectly. For instance, when a parent is depressed, under a great deal of stress, or having marital problems, those factors can indirectly take a toll on how well a son or daughter interacts with other children (e.g., Parke and Ladd, 1992).

Likewise, a child's adjustment at school affects adjustment in other contexts. Poor school adjustment can be a source of family conflict and problems with peers, just as good school adjustment can have the opposite impact. At the same time, school adjustment is influenced by a host of factors outside the classroom. Children like school better if they are getting along with teachers and peers, but the attitudes and problems they bring with them to school influence others' reactions to them and are strongly related to achievement (Oettingen et al., 1994). Teachers (and frequently peers as well) like children less who have behavior problems, are very dependent, and have poor school attitudes (Nelson-LeGall and Jones, 1990). These characteristics, in turn, are influenced by the amount of stress experienced by the family and the social support available to the child (Dubow and Tisak, 1989), as well as by parental involvement with the school (Grolnick and Slowiaczek, 1994; Teo et al., in press). And so it goes, with school adjustment influencing each of the other major contexts of child development as well as being influenced by them. As a result, the child tends to be exposed to a set of interrelated influences that are similar in quality and tone.

THE COHERENCE OF INDIVIDUAL ADAPTATIONS

The distinctive characteristics of children—their individual patterns of adaptation—also are coherent. For instance, children who are effective in the peer group tend to be popular with peers, to form close, loyal friendships, to coordinate friendship and group demands, and to maintain gender boundaries

(Sroufe, Carlson, and Shulman, 1993). There are exceptions, of course. For example, some children who are not well accepted by the group nevertheless have close friends, and this makes a difference to their sense of well-being (Parker and Asher, 1993). Still, there are strong correlations between different aspects of peer competence. Likewise, individual differences in peer functioning, harmony of parent-child relationships, and adjustment to school are often closely related (Teo et al., in press).

THE COHERENCE OF DEVELOPMENT OVER TIME

Not only are individual patterns of adaptation coherent clusters of characteristics, there is also coherence to how these characteristics have developed over time. Socially competent toddlers who are securely attached to their caregivers tend to become preschoolers who are competent with peers, and they, in turn, tend to go on to be popular and well-adjusted during the elementary school years. In fact, with age, a child's current characteristics become increasingly predictable from his or her past characteristics (Sroufe et al., 1993).

This coherence of individual development over time was shown in a study of children attending a series of 4-week summer day camps. Counselors judged youngsters with a history of secure attachment (unknown to them at the time) to be more socially skilled, more inclined to form friendships, more self-confident, and less dependent. Other observers confirmed the counselors' judgments. They also found that children with secure attachment histories spent less time alone, less time with counselors, and more time with other children than did youngsters who had been anxiously attached as infants and toddlers (Elicker et al., 1992). Moreover, those with secure attachment histories spent more time in groups of same-gender peers and were more effective in these peer groups. Other researchers report that children who have been securely attached are less often ridiculed or excluded from group activities in middle childhood (Grossmann and Grossmann, 1992).

There also were differences in the nature of friendships among children with histories of secure attachment versus those who had been anxiously attached (Shulman et al., 1994). The children with secure attachment histories tended to choose each other as friends, and their friendship selections were more often reciprocal rather than one-sided. Moreover, a close friendship among secure children didn't prevent them from functioning in the larger peer group. The two friends often spent time together in groups, and their play together also included other children.

Developmentalists seek to explain why such continuity exists in patterns of adaptation over time. It is not that the quality of early attachment inevitably causes certain kinds of peer relations in middle childhood. Some anxiously attached infants are competent with peers in elementary school, so anxious attachment cannot directly cause later problems. In part it may be a matter of whether the influence of parents remains stable over time. For instance, if parents who promoted a secure attachment in their infant and toddler go on to support peer relationships when their child is in school (as many do), secure attachment becomes correlated with peer effectiveness in middle childhood.

Still, such continuity in the parents' influence is probably not the whole story. It has been shown, for example, that attachment assessments predict middle childhood behavior even after current family support has been accounted for (Sroufe et al., 1990). Undoubtedly also entering the picture are factors within

These drawings are representative of those made by 8-year-old children with different attachment histories. The drawing at top left was made by a child who had been securely attached. The figures are grounded, balanced, and well proportioned; they are complete, rich in detail, individuated. The drawing is colorful and full of life. In the drawing at top right, made by a child with a history of avoidant attachment, the self-drawing (far right) is not complete. The figures are not grounded and have an aggressive aspect. The drawing at left, made by a child with a mixed anxious attachment history, is skillfully drawn, yet has an ominous quality. The mother (lower right) was placed "under the ground" though, in reality, she is not dead. The child and his brother are shut up in the black tower.

the child—namely, the skills and experiences, the personal beliefs and social expectations formed in the context of attachment history and carried forward into middle childhood. For instance, from their relationships with caregivers, securely attached toddlers acquire positive beliefs and expectations about the self and others that help them master the challenge of social give-and-take as preschoolers, and in turn form a basis for tackling the tasks of friendship and peer group functioning in middle childhood. Feelings of self-worth, a sense of social effectiveness, and positive expectations regarding others all serve to move the child toward closer and more complex relationships. These feelings and expectations about the self and others that originate in early attachment experiences are what Bowlby (1973) referred to as *internal working models* (discussed in detail in Chapters 1 and 6).

Different internal working models of the self and others are reflected in school-age children's stories and drawings (e.g., Bretherton, 1990; Fury, 1994; McCrone et al., 1994). In stories told about pictures of peers who are interacting, children with a history of secure attachment talk about cooperation and successful negotiation of conflict. On sentence-completion tests (for example, complete the sentence: "Other kids . . .") these same children project positive attitudes ("Other kids . . . are fun to be with"). And when asked to draw a picture of their family, secure children show connections between the family members, appropriate sizing of the figures, and positive emotions being expressed (Fury, 1994). As the examples above show, such drawings are often quite different from those of children with histories of anxious attachment.

Gang violence is a serious problem in virtually every large American city, and school-age children are often involved in it. If they are not already members of gangs themselves by the age of 11 or 12, many youngsters in tough urban neighborhoods have witnessed gang violence, including sometimes fatal beatings, knifings, and shootings. Observers wonder how so much violence comes about. What causes groups of young people to attack each other so fiercely? Although the problem of intergang violence is highly complex, research suggests that one reason for it lies in competition for scarce resources (McDonald, 1988). In areas of deprivation, where poverty is all around, gangs strive to "make it" by whatever means they can and aggressively retaliate against anyone who is seen as trespassing on their territory or otherwise getting in their way.

The power of competition for scarce resources to breed intense intergroup conflict was demonstrated in a classic study by psychologists Muzafer and Carolyn Sherif (Sherif and Sherif, 1953; Sherif et al., 1961). The Sherifs recruited 22 11- and 12-year-old boys to attend a summer camp. The boys were divided into two groups, each of which was housed at a different campsite. As the members of each group worked together on special tasks that required cooperation, they developed a strong sense of group identity. Soon the boys were using group names—the Eagles and the Rattlers—and were fashioning other symbols of their "we-ness," such as group flags and banners. Thus, the act of repeatedly coordinating their activities toward mutually desirable goals transformed what were originally collections of strangers into two very cohesive groups. In much the same way, members of urban gangs develop a strong sense of "we-ness" as they work together to acquire the things they collectively want.

The Sherifs next demonstrated that conflict between groups could be provoked by putting the Eagles and the Rattlers in competition for limited resources. The researchers organized a series of games between the previously isolated groups (ball games, races, tugs of war), for which the winners received valuable prizes. At first, these competitive pressures tended to cause upheaval in each group, especially following losses. Group members would blame one another for their frustrating failures, and angry confrontations often resulted. However, this initial reaction soon faded, and each group emerged more unified than ever (often with new leadership). Group spirit reached a new high. Each group became the target for the other's hostility. Inter-

group bickering, name calling, fights, and raids rapidly became the norm. This phase of the study revealed some of the ways in which intergroup prejudices and hatreds develop.

Finally, the Sherifs decided it was time to end the intergroup warfare, but doing so proved far from easy. Requests that each group try to see the other's good side met with no success. Neither did attempts to get the groups together for friendly, shared activities such as picnics, fireworks displays, and movies. These social events inevitably dissolved into chaos as the Eagles and the Rattlers hurled food and insults at each other.

The one strategy that did work was a series of bogus emergencies. The camp truck mysteriously broke down and had to be repaired before food could be delivered to the campers. An unexplained leak in the water pipes had to be found or the entire water system would have to be shut down. Resolving these and other staged difficulties required cooperation among *all* the boys at the camp. Intergroup conflict sharply decreased, and friendships began to form across group lines. Apparently when enemies are forced to pull together for their own mutual good, they often begin to see each other in a new, more favorable light. The old prejudices and stereotypes are difficult to maintain when the person working next to you seems so much like yourself.

This lesson in reducing intergroup conflict among school-age boys has application to reducing intergang violence in our society. If gang members can be encouraged to work together on projects that benefit the community as a whole—building a playground, painting a mural, refurbishing a recreation center—hostilities between the gangs may begin to decline (*Barrio Warrior*, 1993). Even athletic events such as softball games can reduce rivalries, when teams are made up of members of both gangs, rather than pitting one gang against another.

Such cooperative efforts have ranged from the local to the national level. An example of a local effort is the "Junior Sherrifs Program" in Watsonville, California, in which rival gang members go together on patrols with officers. On a broader scale, Barrios Unitos is an effort to end violence among Latino gangs throughout the West, and the National Gang Summit of 1993, inspired by a truce between the Crips and the Bloods, marks an effort to begin putting gang energy toward economic development in urban minority communities (Barrio Warriors, 1993; Crogan, 1993).

Good illustrations of how internal working models may be related to behavior come from the study of aggressive children. Such children frequently interpret others' actions as implying hostile intent, especially when cues are ambiguous and they feel threatened (e.g., Weiss et al., 1992). This is not because these children have some cognitive deficit that makes them misinterpret. Their interpretations "fit" their history of anxious-avoidant attachment and early harsh treatment (Suess et al., 1992; Weiss et al., 1992). In other words, their perception of hostility in others seems to be based on their prior experience with hostility and rejection. These experiences, moreover, are often self-perpetuating because the children's aggressiveness, in part fueled by their social expectations and interpretations, tends to elicit angry responses from others. *Non*aggressive peers, in fact, share the expectation that others, including teachers, will be more angry at aggressive children in ambiguous situations (Tractenberg and Viken, 1994). Thus, how children think and how they behave are tied together in middle childhood and derive from their experiences.

Children certainly may change during middle childhood. A bright child who does well academically may get a boost in self-esteem along with positive feedback from teachers. And sometimes a gifted and caring teacher will be responsive to children despite their behavior problems and poor attitudes. Peers may also respond favorably to some special skill or talent a child has. Family circumstances may change, too, and children change in response to those changes (Egeland et al., 1990). Once a child's self-esteem is raised and behavior changes, feedback from others may become more positive, and the child's attitude toward school may improve.

CHAPTER SUMMARY

1. During middle childhood youngsters begin to integrate their various ideas about the self into a coherent self-concept. In contrast to the preschooler, who sees the self largely in terms of physical traits, the elementary school child has a much more psychologically based self-concept (the **psychological self**). Another advance in self-understanding that occurs during this period is development of what is called the **social self.** Elementary school children begin to define themselves in terms of the groups they belong to and in terms of their social tendencies ("I am shy," "I am friendly," "I am kind," and so forth). They also have a more elaborated sense of their gender. Closely related to these developments is the tendency to use others as a source of comparison in making self-evaluations. By about 8 years of age children begin to think of themselves as more or less capable in relation to peers. They also increasingly realize that their successes or failures depend on their own actions.

2. During middle childhood the peer group becomes an especially important developmental setting. This is due partly to the large amount of time that school-age children spend with peers. It is also due to the unique learning experiences that equal-status peer relationships provide. The peer group is especially conducive to learning firsthand about such principles as fairness, reciprocity, and equity. Because school-age children adhere so strictly to many such cultural norms and values, their peer groups are major agents of socialization. One area of socialization in which the peer group's influence stands out clearly is that of maintaining a boundary between the genders.

3. Among the changes that take place in peer interactions during middle childhood are advances in social communication skills as youngsters become much better at adopting the perspectives of other people. At the same time, children are now more likely to express hostile aggression by verbally insulting peers—another change that shows their growing ability to grasp how other people think and feel. During middle childhood friendships become much deeper and are increasingly based on mutual loyalty and support as well as on common interests. Friends also develop a sense of "we-ness," an awareness of the boundaries of their special peer relationships. An important task of middle childhood is learning to coordinate the demands of close friendships with the demands of being part of a larger group.

4. In general middle childhood brings a deeper understanding of emotions and a changing basis for emotional reactions. Children are now able to consider multiple aspects of an emotion-arousing situation, which helps them to better understand how other people feel and what emotional response is appropriate in a particular situation. Emotional advances help support an increased empathy for others, a deepening of moral concerns, and a greater understanding of moral issues.

5. The family remains an important developmental context in middle childhood. Children learn a great deal from their siblings, for example, including how to be nurturant, how to teach new skills, how to negotiate, and how to deal with anger without ending a close relationship. Parents continue to have a great impact. The styles of child-rearing they adopt are related to many of the personality characteristics youngsters display. Developmentally important factors seem to be the amount of love the parents show, how much autonomy they allow, how responsive they are to their children's viewpoints, how much conflict there is between parents and children, how much the parents rely on power-assertive techniques of discipline, and how good they are at imposing reasonable limits and monitoring their children. In order to be fairly accurate in predicting developmental outcomes from the behavior of parents, researchers must employ complex, multidimensional models of parenting.

6. The influence of marital conflict and divorce on children is another family issue that researchers have explored. It appears that conflict between parents may be a key cause of the developmental problems sometimes seen in children of divorce. These problems, especially among boys, can include increased aggression, lack of impulse control, and troubled relations with peers. Girls more commonly respond to marital conflict with anxiety, inhibition, and withdrawal. Separation from a parent can also have negative developmental outcomes. The likely effects vary greatly, depending on such factors as the child's age and sex and how he or she interprets the meaning of the parents' breakup.

7. Children learn many things in their classrooms besides the subjects teachers specifically teach. The school is a place where mainstream cultural norms and values are repeatedly reinforced. This can be seen in the area of gender-role learning. Teachers tend to stress traditional expectations regarding gender, including the expectation that academic achievement is more appropriate for boys than for girls. The quality of after-school care is another topic of current interest to developmentalists because of the large proportion of American families in which both parents work.

8. Development in middle childhood is coherent in that the various influences on it tend to be mutually reinforcing. It is also coherent in the sense that a child's individual characteristics fit together in a way that makes sense. And finally it is coherent in the sense that current development has continuity with the past.

PART FIVE
EPILOGUE

Middle Childhood

Development continues to be rapid during middle childhood, roughly ages 6 through 12, although the changes taking place may not always be as obvious as those that occurred in earlier periods. Physical growth has slowed to a few inches yearly and is no longer as dramatic as it was in infancy and toddlerhood. Now the major developmental changes are largely internal—having to do with the child's ways of thinking and feeling. Although these internal changes may not be apparent to casual observers, they are nevertheless of great importance, both in their own right and because they pave the way for the far-reaching changes that will occur in adolescence.

Like all developmental periods, middle childhood involves qualitative change—major developmental reorganizations that boost children to higher levels of social and cognitive functioning. One such major reorganization occurs between the ages of 6 and 8, as children become able to reason systematically, using more than one piece of information. By age 8 or 9, children have acquired most of the basic tools of thinking and reasoning. They come to grasp the "logic" of concrete operations carried out on objects. They understand most conservation rules with enough flexibility to effectively use measuring devices, such as rulers and measuring cups. Children age 8 and older also understand hierarchical classifications. If they are shown a group of objects that consists of toy dogs and toy cats, they know that there are fewer "dogs" than "animals" present, because they grasp that "dog" is a subclass of "animal." Similar advances occur in the area of social cognition, or understanding of people. Youngsters are now much better at taking the perspective of others. They can also coordi-

nate their knowledge of the various social categories that apply to people. For instance, a girl whose father is a doctor would now understand that she can be both a patient and a daughter to him at the same time (Watson, 1981).

The age of 8 is also a milestone in self-understanding. By this age children view the self in more psychological terms. They realize that "who they are" is partly what they think and feel, not just the physical traits they possess. At the same time, they begin to compare themselves with others in order to appraise their own abilities, and they realize that how other people respond to them can depend on their own actions.

Advances in peer relations accompany this new view of the self. By age 8 children have a more mature view of friendship than preschoolers do. They begin to recognize that the basis of friendship lies in loyalty and mutual support, not just in the sharing of toys. With this advancement, relations with peers take on much deeper meaning. In fact, the formation of close "chumships" is one of the hallmarks of this age. In their interactions with friends school-age children adhere very closely to peer group norms. Equity, fairness, and reciprocity are cardinal principles of their relationships. Because of this, peer relations in middle childhood play an important role in moral development (Damon, 1988). In addition, school-age children have a new understanding of the legitimacy of authority, including parental authority. This understanding, coupled with their greater desire to conform to norms and values, helps make the job of parenting easier than it was before. Markus and Nurius (1984) have summed up these many social advances this way: (1) school-age children acquire a relatively stable and comprehensive understanding of the self; (2) they acquire a refined understanding of how the social world works; and (3) they acquire a set of standards and expectations regarding their dealings with others.

As in other developmental periods, all these changes are intimately interconnected. For example, school-age children can solve classification problems and understand conservation in large part because they can now consider two aspects of a problem simultaneously (the height *and* the width of a glass, for instance). This same capacity underlies their ability to unify different aspects of the self and to make social comparisons—that is, to understand their own behavior and that of others at the same time. Advances in different areas of development are also mutually influencing and supportive. For example, the cognitive ability to understand different perspectives and to take on different roles help school-age children interact more maturely with peers. At the same time, interactions with peers provide experiences that foster these cognitive skills. Social development and cognitive development, in other words, always proceed together, with each helping to make possible advances in the other.

This is true despite the fact that our discussions may sometimes have implied that cognitive advances occasionally occur a little earlier than social ones. This unintended implication is partly the product of researchers' goals. Cognitive researchers often look for the first appearance of a particular skill, whereas social researchers often search for the age at which a certain ability is regularly used. Time and experience are typically needed before a new capacity is used often. Thus, in their everyday behaviors children may not always show their highest potential levels of functioning.

UNEVENNESS IN DEVELOPMENT

Repeatedly we have stressed the orderliness and coherence of human development, whether we are talking about general developmental changes or the life of an individual child. But this doesn't mean that development proceeds in a lockstep fashion, with related changes always occurring together. Sometimes there seems to be an unevenness in development, as when a change that we would expect to occur at a certain age is delayed. You saw, for instance, that children in traditional societies generally pass tests of conservation concepts later than children in Western industrialized societies do. For them there is a lag in achieving this developmental milestone, in part because their lack of formal schooling sharply reduces opportunities to learn about and practice these skills. Such unevenness in development can occur for reasons that have nothing to

do with a child's culture or subcultural group. When Meryl was a preschooler, for example, her social development lagged somewhat behind her cognitive progress. This is not unusual. In fact, even within the same domain—cognitive *or* social—closely related developmental milestones may not be reached simultaneously. Thus, a 6-year-old who grasps the concept of conservation of number may not necessarily also grasp conservation of liquid volume.

In addition to the unevenness in general developmental changes, unevenness occurs in the progress of individual lives. Individual children experience ups and downs. Life goes well for a time, but then a child appears to be struggling. You saw this pattern especially in the development of Meryl and Mikey during their school-age years. It occurs in the lives of all children and in adults as well. These ups and downs in the quality of individual adaptations are *not* incoherent and illogical. They make sense in terms of what is happening to the child at a particular time. The child may be responding to external circumstances, such as conflict in the family or a poor environment at school, or the child may be reacting to internal changes, such as illness. Pulling back and retrenching before moving forward again may even be the typical way in which children make developmental progress. Parents often notice that their children undergo a period in which they consolidate already acquired skills before tackling new ones. In fact, much of middle childhood can be viewed as a period of consolidation, a gathering of potentials to be used during adolescence. Such a view of middle childhood gives new meaning to the concept of latency that Freud attached to this period.

THREE CHILDREN IN MIDDLE CHILDHOOD

Our three children have continued to develop during middle childhood, often predictably, but sometimes taking unexpected turns. Although all have developed normally, each has encountered problems at times. These problems illustrate the continuing need of school-age children for care, understanding, and guidance from adults.

For Mikey Gordon the elementary school years are a very stressful time because of his parents' divorce. It is complicated to assess the impact of the divorce on Mikey—even to say whether it has been good or bad for him. On the one hand, things were going poorly before the separation. The conflict between Christine and Frank had become intense, and Mikey was suffering ill effects both at home and at school. Despite their best intentions, Christine and Frank could not shelter Mikey from such a troubled marriage. On the other hand, the divorce was very hard on Mikey because he loved both his parents and desperately wanted them to stay together. Even more than most children, a child like Mikey feels responsible for the breakup. Isn't he supposed to be the peacemaker, the one who keeps conflicts from getting out of control? His parents' divorce means that he has failed in this role. Fortunately, Mikey is old enough to begin to understand that the divorce is not his fault, but he will need help to come to this realization. Since both parents care deeply for Mikey, and Christine is the kind of parent who talks to him about his feelings, we can be optimistic that Mikey will ultimately pull through this developmental crisis.

In the long run, in fact, the divorce may in some ways be harder on Becky and Janie because it has shown so clearly the extent to which their father favors Mikey. They would probably feel more resentment toward Mikey if they did not have each other and were closer to Mikey's age. They cope largely by denying any interest in activities with their father and by becoming very involved with their friends. The effects on them are different from those on Mikey, but they are no easier.

It is tempting to see Frank's behavior as the cause of the Gordons' troubles. He is the one with the drinking problem, and he is also totally unsupportive of his wife's desire for a career outside the home. Ultimately, he is responsible for his violent behavior against Christine. From a systems perspective, however, causes cannot be attributed solely to one person. Any relationship is the product of two individual histories (Sroufe and Fleeson, 1986). Christine's contribution partly stems from the fact that she was raised to take care of men. Her mother's only advice when the marriage became rocky was to work harder at being a "good" wife. It is also difficult for Christine to ask that her own needs be met; she has been taught to be self-sacrificing. To cope with the mounting resentment Frank feels about her job, she strives to keep her working life separate from her home life. As Frank's self-esteem is increasingly damaged by Christine's business success and his own reduced income, Frank criticizes Christine ever more sharply. She responds by trying to mollify him. This reaction feeds the system as much as Frank's tendency to blame her does. And both of them, in their own way, put Mikey in the middle. The one thing that bodes well for the future is that through it all Frank and Christine remain devoted to Mikey. If this deep caring for their son can continue while they become disentangled from their problems, Mikey can still come out all right.

Malcolm's development during this period is nowhere near as conflict-ridden as Mikey's. Middle childhood for Malcolm seems to be a busy, productive, generally fun-filled time. But the incident in which Malcolm takes the gun to school illustrates how normal, healthy children can sometimes get into trouble and cause their parents concern. The lovable exuberance Malcolm exhibits when bounding up the stairs and his unthinking impulsiveness in taking the gun both stem from the same high-spirited energy. Malcolm hits upon the idea of carrying the gun to school in a naive effort to defend himself against a gang of older boys. We see him becoming very upset about Derek's "ratting" on him. But this is Malcolm's nature. He will not be upset for long. He knows that Derek was wrong to tell on him, and he has confidence in his own sense of right and wrong. The incident will pass, and Malcolm will be fine again. In fact, he has probably learned some important lessons from it. In the long run there may be as much reason to be concerned about Derek, who has intentionally broken a peer group norm, than there is to be concerned about Malcolm, whose infraction of a school rule was more unthinking than deliberate.

In Malcolm's life we also see the special challenges that urban children face: gangs to be dealt with going to and from school, incidents that foster interracial mistrust. Malcolm is fortunate that he does not have to deal with the additional challenge of a poor-quality school. His teacher and principal recognize his talents despite his occasional impulsive behavior and difficulty concentrating. At the same time, we once again see the benefits of Malcolm's large and constantly supportive family. Many ears listen to his reports of school achievements; many voices guide him when he gets into trouble. All this serves to encourage positive development in Malcolm.

Meryl also seems to be getting some good support at home. She has become a much more competent and self-confident child than we would have predicted from her infant and toddler periods. She takes the arrival of her baby brother in stride and even seems to blossom in the role of big sister. She is generally doing well at school and has formed the normal close friendship characteristic of middle childhood. The only times we see vestiges of the old, hesitant Meryl are under conditions of stress. Amy befriends Rita, and Meryl loses her confidence; Karen and Joe have a period of tension, and Meryl becomes withdrawn. But even during the time of family problems, Meryl works in her own way toward bolstering herself psychologically. We find her in her room drawing pictures of mother dogs caring for their puppies. As Karen and Joe resolve their difficulties, Meryl brightens once again and regains her confidence. With each developmental period she seems to be getting stronger.

PART SIX

Adolescence

PART SIX

Three Children in Adolescence

MALCOLM WILLIAMS

Malcolm could barely contain his excitement on the way home. He had just been offered an after-school job stocking shelves at Jewel's store. Now he would have money to cruise around with his buddies, buy cool-looking clothes, and—most important—take Felicia out. But Malcolm knew that he would first have to get his parents' approval. Let's see, he would start by pointing out that he was almost 16, certainly no longer a kid. By the time his daddy was 16, he'd had several jobs. Then there was the argument that jobs are good for keeping guys off the streets and out of trouble. Not that Malcolm was interested in joining one of the neighborhood gangs. He and his brother JJ were smarter than that. But it was a good point to bring up with his parents anyway. And, of course, he'd have to promise to keep his grades up. Malcolm was sure he could manage if he put his mind to it.

Leaping up the steps two at a time, Malcolm pushed open the front door. All right! His mother and father weren't home from work yet. That meant he could work on Momma Jo first, win her over, and then have her behind him when it came time to talk to his parents. Maybe Momma Jo didn't see too well anymore, but at 82 she was still one sharp lady. Everyone respected her judgment. In his eagerness to convince Momma Jo before his parents got home, Malcolm's words spilled out rapidly, his points becoming more and more jumbled. Momma Jo had trouble following what he was saying. By the time she was beginning to put it all together, DeeDee and John walked in. Oh, no, thought Malcolm. Now I have to work on all three at once.

When Malcolm had finished presenting his case, his father looked doubtful. He felt that Malcolm had been a little less serious about his schoolwork lately. Momma Jo saw John's expression. "I remember you nearly burstin' with pride when you showed me your first pay slip," she said.

"Momma, I'm not saying that a job wouldn't be good for Malcolm," John answered. "I'm just concerned about him handling all the responsibilities that go with it."

"Oh, I'll be responsible, Daddy," Malcolm assured him. I won't ever be late for work 'cause they dock your pay and—"

"Listen to me, man," John cut in sharply. "I'm not talking about being late for work. I'm talking about your responsibilities right here at home. You've got to keep your school grades up and do your chores around the house."

"Oh, I know *that*," said Malcolm quickly. "Sure, I'll do all those things. I'm not gonna goof off or mess up goin' to college. But I can do those things *and* have a job."

DeeDee had been quiet all this time. Now she finally spoke. "What do you say we let him take the job on a trial basis? If his grades slip or his chores don't get done, the job goes—no second chances."

"That sounds OK to me," John said, "as long as he holds the hours to fifteen a week—no more. And remember what your momma said, *no* second chances."

"All riiiight!" crowed Malcolm. "Y'all are cool!" He hugged his mother and Momma Jo and punched his father's arm. Then he charged out of the kitchen, heading for the phone to call the stockroom manager at Jewel's. Hallelujah, he thought. I got me a job!

The next morning Malcolm jumped out of bed, surging with energy. Appraising himself in the mirror, he noticed with satisfaction his developing muscles, the smooth sheen of his brown skin, and the facial fuzz marking the beginnings of a small mustache. I'm a man with style, he thought. Felicia, you *one* lucky lady!

When Malcolm came down to breakfast, he was ready for the affectionate teasing his family usually gave him about his clothes. This time it was his mother: "My, *my.* I'd think you were entering a fashion show!"

"You dig my threads?" Malcolm grinned, pretending to model them for his mother. "I kind of appreciate them myself." And with that he slid into his chair at the table and began to wolf down his breakfast.

"Well, if you're so handsome and sophisticated," DeeDee continued, "maybe you'd like to come along with your daddy and grandma and me this weekend to show yourself off at the church retreat."

Malcolm's spoonful of cereal froze midway to his mouth. "Oh, no!" he said with exasperation. "Here we go again. I *told* you I didn't want to go to that thing! Why would I want to spend a whole weekend hanging out with old folks? And anyway, I'll probably be working Saturday morning. Mr. Lacey and I are gonna figure out my hours today."

DeeDee shook her head in resignation. "Well I'm not about to leave you here entirely on your own," she said. "I guess I'll see if JJ can come for the weekend—at least to stay over Saturday night."

"That's cool with me," Malcolm answered, digging into his cereal again. He knew his 27-year-old brother was not about to give him any trouble as far as his plans with Felicia were concerned.

When Saturday evening rolled around, Malcolm was relieved to see his brother show up all dressed to go out and party. "Hey, man," JJ said, "it's like this. I ain't gonna daddy you or nothin' 'cause I know this is a chance that don't come along too often. But I promised Momma that you would be cool, so whatever you do don't have the neighbors callin' over here and don't let me know what you're plannin' to do. That way, when I tell Momma everything was cool, I can say it without lying. You got that?"

"Got it," agreed Malcolm. "No problem."

The two brothers slapped hands as JJ headed for the door. "And another thing, Motor Man," JJ added, turning back toward Malcolm. "Daddy asked me how much I think you know about not pickin' up any nasty germs when you're out prowlin' with the ladies. I told him you was a man with brains who knew just what to do. Am I right?"

"Hey, I ain't *dumb*," Malcolm answered. "They've been tellin' me about that in school since the seventh grade! I'm not gonna get no AIDS or nothin'. Besides, we ain't gonna do anything."

"Yeah, well, whatever," said JJ, reaching for the door-knob. "Just remember, it's either latex or later, my man. Those are your only two options." And with that he left for his own date.

As soon as the door closed, Malcolm ran to the phone and nervously began to dial Felicia's number.

The next year of Malcolm's life passed quickly. True to his word, he kept up his grades and did his chores at home despite his job at Jewel's. In fact, Malcolm seemed to thrive on the added workload. It forced him to think more about using his time wisely. Often now, if he found himself with a few spare hours, he would get a head start on some upcoming project, rather than just lounging around in front of the television. DeeDee was impressed with this new maturity. She was also impressed with Malcolm's growing interest in the world beyond girls, sports, and clothes. Especially when the family conversation turned to racial prejudice or unfair treatment of the poor, Malcolm joined in eagerly, expressing very passionate views.

One evening in March of Malcolm's junior year in high school, his father brought up the subject of a new redevelopment plan. The mayor's office was proposing a scheme that would affect much of the Williams' neighborhood. Many of the area residents had great misgivings. They feared that lower-income people would be gradually forced out as property values rose and rents spiraled. Malcolm was indignant at the thought of such a thing. How could they let people be pushed out of their homes just because a bunch of yuppies wanted to move in? "We have to *fight* this," he nearly shouted at his father.

"That's why the Community Action Committee is holding an open meeting next Tuesday night," John Williams answered. "If you feel so strongly about it, why don't you come along with me and let the mayor's staff know your views?"

"You *bet* I will," said Malcolm. "I'm not gonna let 'em get away with this!"

"But first you'd better read up on the subject," John Williams advised, passing Malcolm all the clippings and information he had accumulated.

"Right!" said Malcolm. "By Tuesday night I'll know this plan inside and out."

The following Tuesday Malcolm and his father had front-row seats at the meeting. Malcolm was fascinated by every facet of the discussion. He leaned forward in his seat, soaking up every word. Finally, toward the end of the evening, he bravely raised his hand. The chairman of the committee nodded in his direction, and Malcolm rose to his feet. "I've lived in this neighborhood all my life," he began in a strong, clear voice, "and I think that some change would be a good thing, but its got to be *fair*. That low-income project you're talking about building over on Melrose would be pushing poor people out of the center of this neighborhood. My grandma's 82, and if she had to get to the stores and back from all the way over on Melrose, I don't think she could make it. And another thing that bothers me, my father always says that diversity is what made this country great. Well, doesn't that apply to communities too? All kinds of people living together is what'll make this neighborhood a good place to live in."

Malcolm sat down abruptly and looked straight ahead. He was surprised to hear a murmur in the audience, and then a round of loud applause. John Williams placed his hand on Malcolm's shoulder and smiled proudly at him. "Good for you, son," he said softly. "You're gonna make your mark." Yeah, I am, thought Malcolm. I'm gonna be somebody. I'm gonna make a difference. With growing pride in himself as a black teenager in Chicago, Malcolm resolved to fight the odds and make an impression on the world.

MIKE GORDON

"Mikey!" Christine's voice called out for the third time. Damn it, thought Mikey, a guy can't get any privacy around here! "Coming," he yelled as he put out his cigarette and turned off his stereo. Bounding down the stairs, he headed for the kitchen. "What is it, Mom?" he asked.

"It's my car again. It doesn't start right. Would you take a look at it?"

"What do you mean, it doesn't start right?"

"Well, you know. It sounds like it's going to start but then it takes a long time to turn over."

"Do you have enough gas?"

"Of course. I've got almost a full tank."

"Does it ever make a real loud grinding kinda noise?"

"No. I haven't heard anything like that."

"Then it's probably your spark plugs or your distributor. I'll check 'em."

"Thanks, Mikey," Christine said. "I really appreciate it." Christine was truly grateful for her son's impressive talent with anything mechanical. It certainly helped to keep the cost of home repairs down.

"But, Mom, could you remember to can the Mikey stuff? I've told you a million times. The name's Mike, OK? For cripes sake, I'm almost fifteen."

"Mike. Got it," Christine answered, pointing a finger in her son's direction. "Old habits die hard, I guess."

"Well, just bury them, will ya?" Mike said, as he headed out the back door.

Christine watched the wiry adolescent in jeans and tee shirt opening the hood of her car. He certainly was growing up fast these days, and she wasn't always happy with the way he was doing it. Since he entered senior high school last September he had started hanging out with a different crowd of boys. These new friends dressed tough, talked tough, and acted tough. Christine worried that if she criticized them that might only make Mikey defensive and cement the friendships further. Christine was also unhappy that Mikey had started to smoke on the sly. She was sure he must be drinking beer at parties and had probably tried pot. Could that lead him into harder drugs like crack, or who knows what? It bothered her too that Mikey was spending so much time alone in his room. She knew he wasn't doing schoolwork. Although his math and science grades were fair, his grades in English and history were barely passing. When she mentioned these problems to Frank, he just laughed them off, telling her that he too had "sown some wild oats" at Mikey's age.

Christine wondered whether competition with Matt had anything to do with the way Mikey was acting. Matt was the son of Frank's second wife, Nancy, and he was almost Mikey's age. Mikey had hated him from the start, and Christine didn't like his smart-aleck manner much either. When Mikey visited Frank at home, he felt that Nancy was always giving Matt preferential treatment, and Mikey resented that bitterly. Then Nancy and Frank had had Nicolas four years ago, and Mikey's resentment deepened. He referred to his new stepbrother as "that obnoxious little brat" and would see his father only when Nick was left at home.

Desperate for a sympathetic man to confide in, Christine turned to her brother-in-law, Dan. Dan smiled when she told him her suspicions about what Mikey was doing behind that door with the large "PRIVATE" sign on it. He felt it was perfectly normal for a 14-year-old boy to spend time by himself listening to loud music. "If I were you," he advised, "I'd be more worried about those new friends of his. If Mikey really wants to go to college like his cousin Danny, he'd better stop hangin' out with kids who are goin' nowhere and pull his grades up. He needs a spark to set him in the right direction." Christine sighed, wondering where such a spark would come from. Mikey certainly wasn't about to listen to her or to his uncle Dan. As it turned out, the spark came in Mikey's sophomore year, and as sometimes happens, it came from an unexpected source.

"Did you know that early reptiles had large fins that soaked up solar heat and helped keep them warm?" Mike reached for a third piece of chicken and another helping of mashed potatoes. "I learned that in biology today."

Christine smiled, both with pleasure and amusement. Ever since her son had entered Mr. Yamoto's class this fall, he had become an endless source of such information. What a difference a teacher can make, she thought. Mike pored over books on animal physiology and behavior as if they were sports magazines. For the first half of his sophomore year his grade in biology was a B+. This half of the year he was well on his way to earning an A.

"Aren't you interested in learning any *human* biology?" Janie asked. She was in her first year at Community College of Rhode Island, studying to be a nurse.

"Sure I am," said Mike defensively. "Probably more than you. I bet you didn't know that if you take a human heart out of the body and put it in the right kind of fluid it'll keep beating on its own."

"Yuck! That's disgusting," answered Janie. "Leave it to you to bring up something like that at the dinner table."

The school year ended as Christine had predicted. Mike received an A in biology, and his other grades were up somewhat as well. That summer Mr. Yamoto helped Mike get a job at the marine biology station where he worked. The experience opened up a whole new world for Mike. Although he was only washing bottles and doing other clean-up chores, he felt that he was part of very important research on Narragansett Bay. Long conversations with Mr. Yamoto while driving to and from the station each day filled Mike's head with dreams of the future. *He* would end the ravages of pollution on marine life. *He* would invent new conservation-conscious methods of farming the seas. The entire world might even be saved by one of his discoveries!

On weekends that summer Mike began to confide his new ambitions to his uncle Dan. Dan was helping Christine tend a backyard garden she had planted in return for a share of the vegetables. Mike knew his uncle was interested in gardening, so maybe marine biology would interest him too. Mike broached the subject hesitantly, however, fearing that Dan might react to the idea of a career in science just as his father would. (Frank always referred to scientists as eggheads). To Mike's delight, his uncle was enthusiastic. "Gee, Mike," Dan had said as the two of them cleared out the pea patch to make room for some more spinach, "I think that sounds great! You've got the stuff to do whatever you want if you put your mind to it. You know, I got off on the wrong track when I was in high school—messin' around with a lot of losers. And I've always regretted it. I think I could have done a lot more with my life if I had buckled down and

tried to go to college. But my dad didn't think it was important, so I didn't get the push I needed. Not that I've done so bad, really. But I'd do things differently if I were your age again."

Mike was struck by the wistfulness in his uncle's voice. He had never thought that Uncle Dan would confide in him like this, and he had never imagined that he would feel so comfortable telling his uncle the things that he had. He would talk with his uncle often in the months to come.

In September Mike returned to school for his junior year, determined to "set the place on fire." Mike, Mr. Yamoto, and Mrs. Miller, the guidance counselor, worked out a plan whereby Mike would be in a position to go on to college. Because Mr. Yamoto had gone to Amherst, Mike wanted to go there too. But he knew his family could never afford it if he didn't land a big scholarship. Mike doggedly tackled the program he had set for himself. Christine was impressed with his tenacity and even more impressed with his grades: a B+ in both English and American history, an A− in advanced algebra, and an A in chemistry. These successes confirmed Mike's belief that he could go to Amherst if he really tried. He forged ahead with renewed determination, the goal of a scholarship to Amherst lodged firmly in his mind.

In order to appear well-rounded to the Amherst admissions board, Mike made time to keep up his participation in sports. That winter he went out for wrestling, much to his father's delight. ("That's a real man's sport," Frank had said with pride.) But although Mike was number one in his weight class at his own school, he often lost in competition with boys from other high schools. "Where's your killer instinct, Gordon?" the wrestling coach complained. "Yeah, yeah. I'll get 'em next time," Mike would answer. But to him, doing well at wrestling was just a means to an end. He just hoped the varsity letter he earned that year put him one step closer to Amherst.

For a varsity letter man who regularly made the honor roll, Mike dated very little. He went to parties and dances and would ask a girl out once or twice, but that was as far as he let things develop. He felt girls were trying to crowd him, wanting some kind of steady commitment, and he wasn't ready for that. "The next thing you know she'll be talkin' about getting married," Mike once remarked about a girl who seemed especially attracted to him. "And I don't want any part of that. I've got big plans for myself."

"There's a letter for you on the table," Christine said to her son as he walked through the back door late one afternoon in March of his senior year. "It's from Amherst."

"Did you open it?" Mike asked in excitement, hurrying over to the table.

"No, of course not. It's addressed to *you*. But it's thick. That's a good sign."

Mike's diligence in schoolwork had paid off this year. His grades remained in the B+ to A range. He had taken the SATs in the fall and had learned shortly before Christmas that he had gotten a 620 on the verbal part—quite a good showing—and a 740 on the math—an outstanding score. Mike had already been accepted at both of the two "backup" universities he'd applied to. Now the long-awaited news from Amherst had finally arrived. With nervous fingers, Mike tore open the thick envelope. His eyes raced across the top page, then he skimmed the page that followed. A gigantic grin spread across his face. Tossing all the pages into the air, he let out a rebel yell.

"I made it!" he shouted ecstatically. "I got a scholarship to Amherst! Mom, look! This is all we're gonna have to pay. Can we afford that? Can we?"

Christine hurried over for a look. "Fantastic!" she beamed. "Between your father and me, we can do it!"

It was a proud family that watched Mike graduate from high school in June. Christine and Janie, now a nurse at Rhode Island Hospital, had front-row seats, as did Frank, his wife Nancy, and their three sons Matt, Nick, and Tim. Becky also made the trip down from Boston, where she had just been promoted to assistant production manager at the radio station where she worked. As he walked up to the podium to receive his diploma and a special award in science, Mike Gordon's eyes looked over the audience and beyond as if toward the future. Not quite 18—barely a fourth of the way into his life—he smiled with the joy of someone who is eagerly awaiting new experiences.

MERYL POLONIUS TURNER

"Close the door," Meryl said to Amy as they hurried into Meryl's bedroom, school books clutched in their arms. "I don't want my little brother snooping. He'd tell Mom for sure."

Amy dumped her books on the bed, then went back and shut the door, locking it for good measure. "I don't know what you're so worried about. It's *your* hair. At fourteen you have a right to do what you want with it."

Meryl reached into her large canvas handbag and pulled out a small cardboard box. "Drop of Sun" the carton read in pale blue letters beneath the picture of a glamorous woman with long, light-blond hair. "Return to the natural blond you were born with," Meryl read out loud. "The golden glow of soft, healthy, natural-looking hair kissed by the sun."

"Anyway," Amy continued, "your mom's never even gonna notice. It says natural-looking, doesn't it? I mean, you're blond already, Mer. So who's gonna notice a little lighter? It'll be just like the sun did it."

"I don't know," answered Meryl. "I don't feel so brave anymore. What if it turns my hair, like, *real* platinum? Everyone will notice then. They'll stare at me like I'm a freak or something. I already get stared at because my arms are so long. Have you ever noticed how my hands hang down so low?"

"What's wrong with your arms?" asked Amy, lying back on the bed and unwrapping a piece of gum. "They match your legs. And long legs are sexy. Everyone knows *that*."

"Uh-oh!" Meryl exclaimed, jumping up and looking out the window. "There's my mom in the driveway. I'd better hide this stuff somewhere."

Ever since Meryl had turned 13 she had started to develop a new view of her mother. Suddenly her mom seemed like an obstacle blocking all the things that Meryl now wanted to do. "Sometimes my mom is *so dense!*" Meryl confided to Amy. "She just doesn't understand what it's like to be my age." This new view led to frequent arguments between Meryl and Karen, especially where boys were concerned. Take the time Meryl was asked out on her first date to the movies. Meryl had gone to many mixed-sex parties, but she had never gone out on a date alone with a boy before. "But Mom, you've just *got* to let me go," Meryl pleaded. "All my friends date. I'll be so embarrassed if you won't let me! Don't you see how unfair you're being?"

Karen searched for a compromise, suggesting that perhaps Joe could drive Meryl and her date to the movies. Meryl was horrified. "Have *Dad* drive us?" she asked in utter shock. "Don't you know *anything*, Mom?" Finally, Karen yielded to the inevitable. Meryl was a very pretty teenager. She couldn't keep protecting her from boys forever. But Karen remained strict about when Meryl could go out (never on a school night) and what time she had to be home.

"Amy's parents don't have all these dumb rules," Meryl complained. "She comes in whenever she wants. And she doesn't always have to say exactly where she's going, like she was some kind of prisoner or something."

"Well, we're not Amy's parents," Karen answered. "Dad and I do things differently."

"But Mom, I'm *fourteen*," Meryl protested.

"That's just it. You're very grown-up for fourteen, but you're still only fourteen. You're not old enough to make all your own rules yet. Teenagers can get into trouble if they're left to do anything they please."

"Just because *you* got pregnant, you think *I'm* going to!" Meryl blurted out. "It's not fair of you not to trust me because of something *you* did."

"It's not that I don't trust you, honey," Karen answered, knowing there was some truth to what her daughter said. "You handle yourself real well, and I'm proud of you for it. But I do worry. You've been seeing an awful lot of Jim lately, and I just think you have to slow things down a bit. You have your girlfriends to spend time with too."

Although Meryl often got angry during these talks with her mother, she felt better afterward. Sometimes a few hours later she would seek her mother out and begin discussing other things that happened to be on her mind. She might tell Karen about a spat between two of her girlfriends, about how "dumb" one of her teachers was, or about how she just *had* to have a new sweater to wear Saturday night. And more and more often, Meryl would turn the conversation to her "other" father. She wanted to know what he looked like, what her mother had felt about him, why he didn't want to get married, and where he might be now. Karen answered all these questions as honestly as she could, but sometimes they disturbed her. One night she asked Joe if he thought all this interest in Jeff was all right.

"Don't worry about it," Joe answered. "It's only natural. And it's no big deal to me. I know Meryl loves me, even if I am sometimes *so dense*." Karen laughed at Joe's imitation of Meryl's favorite phrase. Having him in her life to share things with made all the difference.

Karen's concerns about Meryl and Jim didn't last very long. That summer they broke up. At first Meryl was hurt and sank into what she described as the deepest state of depression ever experienced. But when she found out Jim was dating Barbie, her hurt turned to anger. "How could he go out with *her?*" she asked Amy. "Everyone knows her reputation!" By the end of the summer, Jim seemed to have been forgotten. Meryl began dating other boys and going out in mixed-sex groups. She was having more fun than ever, and her confidence was growing. The self-consciousness that had dogged her in the past seemed to be fading. Then another blow came. One afternoon when Karen asked Meryl why she hadn't seen Amy for a while, Meryl confided in her mother with much bitterness:

"She only wants to be with *Bill* these days. Bill this! Bill that! She never wants to be with *me* anymore. Even when she's not with Bill, she just stays home."

"Well, maybe something's bothering her, honey," Karen answered sympathetically. "It could be all the trouble her parents have been having. But she's still your best friend, you know. You just have to work on getting her to open up."

"But that's just it, Mom," Meryl persisted. "She doesn't act like a best friend. We used to tell each other *everything*. Now when I ask her what's wrong, she just says she doesn't want to talk about it. It's like she doesn't trust me anymore, and I don't know why. I've never blabbed secrets to anybody—not *ever*."

"Well, give her time, Meryl. She can't cut herself off from her best friend forever."

In time Meryl did find out what was the matter with Amy. She was pregnant. Her parents were insisting she have an abortion, but Amy wasn't sure. Finally she relented, but afterward she hardly seemed like the same person. The girl who had once been so full of energy and self-assurance was now apathetic and depressed. Then in the spring Amy's father was transferred and the family moved to Los Angeles. Although Meryl and Amy exchanged letters for a while, they gradually grew apart. Meryl was devastated by this loss. It was some time before she had another friend as close as Amy.

"How can you eat that lettuce?" asked 17-year-old Meryl, looking at her mother incredulously. "Don't you know about the terrible conditions of the farm workers?"

"You're right," said Karen, feeling slightly guilty. "But what's summer without salads?"

"Don't you think that's a little hypocritical, Mom?" Meryl asked. "I mean, if you think the farm workers are being exploited, you shouldn't give money to the guys who are doing the exploiting."

Karen felt trapped. On the one hand, she knew her daughter had a point and she was pleased with Meryl's convictions about injustice in the world. On the other hand, Meryl could be so dogmatic. It was frustrating! She vowed to herself not to get dragged into another argument. Last week when Meryl had attacked the "morality" of making big commissions from selling houses, Karen had been totally exasperated. Where was that sweet little girl who used to be so proud of her mother "the real estate lady"? When Karen had tried to explain that real estate agents often worked long hours on deals that never pay off, Meryl had shaken her head self-righteously and walked out of the room, sipping her diet soda.

"It's just a stage," Karen said to Joe. "It's all part of growing up—isn't it?"

"Don't ask me," Joe answered, throwing up his hands in mock despair. "I'm just that dumb city editor who persists in covering trite local news when people in Third World countries are starving to death."

Karen laughed and gave him a hug. "But you're lovable-dumb," she said.

Despite their occasional frustration over the intensity of some of Meryl's convictions, Karen and Joe had much to be proud of in their daughter. The talent for art that she had shown all through childhood had begun to blossom and mature. Her sketches and watercolors were exhibited in citywide art shows, and a few pieces had even been sold. This year Meryl was given the job of set director for the senior class play. She threw herself into the project with great enthusiasm, spending long hours painting scenery and attending to every detail. On opening night, when Meryl came out to take a shy bow at the end of the performance, Karen felt so proud that it brought tears to her eyes.

Gradually Meryl began to think about the possibility of teaching art some day. "If you want to teach," Joe suggested, "it wouldn't be a bad idea to get a little practice talking in front of a group. When I was your age I used to have a great time on the high school debating team." Meryl looked at him as if he had just told her to walk to San Francisco. "The *debating* team?" she asked in disbelief. "No *way* I'm gonna volunteer to stand up and give a speech—in front of *judges*, no less!"

Pursuing the idea of a possible teaching career, Meryl applied to Fresno State for the following fall. She thought she would major in art with a minor in education. The day she received her acceptance, the whole family celebrated. Two of Meryl's friends would be going there as well, so the three girls decided to share an apartment near campus.

"You know, honey," Karen said to Meryl a week later, when all the excitement had died down, "I've been doing some thinking about my own future lately. I'd like to take some courses in business this fall, and Fresno State's the perfect place. How would you feel about bumping into your mom on campus once in a while?"

"I think that'd be great, Mom!" Meryl said with genuine pleasure. "With all that business sense of yours, you should really go for it!"

"Thanks," said Karen, smiling and putting an arm affectionately around Meryl's shoulder. "Did I ever tell you how lucky I am to have a daughter like you?"

Chapter 13

Physical and Cognitive Development in Adolescence

Chapter 13

Physical and Cognitive Development in Adolescence

Fourteen-year-old Mike Gordon stood before the mirror, combing his hair for the third time. Tonight's party was important to him. He wanted to look good. Finished, he stood back and tried to appraise himself with an impartial eye. He was too short, that was certain. With a father who was over 6 feet tall, how could he still be only 5 feet 7? And those arms! They were so scrawny they looked like a girl's! Mike pulled his shoulders back and tried flexing his muscles. It was no use. He was still skinny. There was no getting around it. He decided to put on a long-sleeved shirt over his favorite blue tee-shirt. Of course, everyone would look at him funny for wearing a shirt like that on such a hot night, even if he did roll up the sleeves. All the kids would know he was trying to hide those scarecrow arms of his. Would the other guys give him a hard time? Ben and Doug might. As much as he wanted to be accepted by them, he had to admit they weren't like "real" friends. Real friends didn't jump at every chance to put a guy down, and Ben and Doug were always doing that. Well, it was better than still hanging out with wimps like Richie and Jeff. Mike took one last critical look in the mirror, adjusted his collar, and walked out the door.

Adolescence, the period from roughly age 12 through the late teens, is a time of dramatic and far-reaching change. It is characterized by an especially close connection between physical development and a young person's psychological world. Notice Mike's great concern about his physical appearance. In his mind he is not maturing fast enough, and this makes him feel self-conscious. Mike's behavior also illustrates **adolescent egocentrism**—teenagers' assumption that they are the focus of everyone's attention and that their experiences, thoughts, and feelings are unique. For instance, because Mike is so conscious of his thin arms, he assumes that everyone else must be too. This kind of egocentrism is partly the product of new cognitive skills. These skills are also responsible for changes in the way Mike thinks about friendship. Compared with elementary school children, he has a more psychological view of friendship; he sees friends as people who offer each other emotional support and avoid inflicting psychological discomfort. This more mature understanding of friendship goes hand in hand with increased introspection and a greater ability to conceptualize human thoughts and feelings. In this chapter we will discuss these and other changes that come with adolescence.

Adolescence acquired the status of a unique developmental period only in the late nineteenth century (Modell and Goodman, 1990). Before then, reproductive maturity marked entry into adulthood, not into a special transitional phase *between* childhood and adulthood. The view of adolescence as a special, preadult period of development was partly inspired by the work of G. Stanley Hall (1904). Hall argued that adolescence is a time when all earlier developmental issues are reworked. He also saw it as a period of inevitable storm and stress, emanating from the rapid and dramatic physical changes that occur. Many psychologists now question this conflict-ridden view of adolescence (see Chapter 14). Nevertheless, Hall made an enduring contribution by recognizing the specialness of this developmental period and the key role that biological changes play in it.

The period labeled adolescence in our society is now longer than it was in

Adolescent egocentrism: Teenagers' assumption that they are the focus of everyone's attention and that their experiences, thoughts, and feelings are unique.

Adolescence is a time of rapid change when physical, cognitive, and social development are closely related to each other.

Hall's day, partly because puberty occurs earlier than it used to and partly because people now need more years of schooling to prepare for most adult occupations. At the beginning of the twentieth century, most young people in the United States left school after the eighth grade. By the middle of the century, most adolescents received some high school education, but few went on to college. Today, nearly half of all high school graduates go directly on to college (Steinberg, 1993). These additional years spent in school have lengthened the transition between childhood and adulthood.

Because adolescence covers so many years, it makes sense to divide it into substages (Elliott and Feldman, 1990). *Early adolescence* covers the years from about age 12 to age 14, *middle adolescence* the years from 15 to 17, and *late adolescence* the years from 18 to the early 20s. In each of these substages, young people face a different set of challenges and opportunities, and their thinking and behavior differ considerably across the three substages. Early adolescence includes most of the major physical changes of adolescence and accompanying changes in relationships with parents and peers. During middle adolescence, the focus is on increasing independence and preparation for adult occupations or for further education. Many young people enter adult roles directly from middle adolescence. The rest continue their preparation for adulthood during late adolescence, usually in college or other educational settings.

Because of the impact that biological changes have on other areas of development during adolescence, we devote the first section of this chapter to them. An understanding of the physical transformations associated with adolescence sets the stage for understanding other aspects of adolescent development, both cognitive and social. From our discussion of physical development during the teenage years, we go on to explore some of the changes in thinking that adolescents experience. Finally, we look at two aspects of adolescent social cognition: the adolescent form of egocentrism and the development of moral reasoning.

The physical changes associated with puberty occur at different ages for different individuals. Differences in timing of physical maturation pose emotional challenges for both boys and girls.

BIOLOGICAL CHANGES DURING ADOLESCENCE

The dramatic biological changes that occur in adolescence are apparent to everyone. Teenagers experience an accelerated growth rate, more rapid than at any time since infancy. Accompanying this spurt in growth are changes in body shape and proportions, such as development of broader shoulders in boys and wider hips in girls. At the same time, significant changes take place in the structure and function of the brain, which may have important implications for cognitive development. The biological changes of puberty also have major impacts on social development. Partly because of changes in their physical appearance, teenagers stop thinking of themselves as children, and parents begin to expect more mature and responsible behavior from them. Increased sexual urges and the capacity for reproduction are issues that both teenagers and their families must face. Finally, variations in the age at which the physical changes of adolescence occur have a major impact on how teenagers view themselves and how they relate to others.

PUBERTY: NORMS AND INDIVIDUAL DIFFERENCES

Puberty:
The period during which a child changes from a sexually immature person to one who is capable of reproduction.

Menarche:
The onset of menstruation.

Spermarche:
The first ejaculation of mobile sperm.

Puberty is the period during which a child changes from a sexually immature person to one who is capable of reproduction. For girls, the clearest indication that this change has occurred is **menarche,** the onset of menstruation. In the United States and western Europe, the average age at which menarche occurs is about 12.5 years (Brooks-Gunn and Reiter, 1990). However, a girl has not reached true reproductive maturity until she begins to ovulate (release egg cells ready for fertilization), which usually does not occur until several months after menarche. For boys, the critical change marking puberty is **spermarche,** the first ejaculation of mobile sperm. Because this event is not as noticeable as menarche, it is hard to specify an average age at which it occurs. Tests for the presence of live sperm in the urine indicate that most boys in the United States reach spermarche by age 14 (Brooks-Gunn and Reiter, 1990).

Puberty is best thought of not as a single event, but rather as a more extended period during early adolescence when sexual organs and other sexual characteristics are developing rapidly (Kimmel and Weiner, 1985). By the time menarche or spermarche occurs, an adolescent girl's or boy's body has already been undergoing major changes for several years. Although the major noticeable changes of puberty usually occur over a span of about four years, the total duration of puberty may actually be longer than this. The very earliest hormonal changes can begin as young as age 7 or 8, and the latest phases can continue into the midteens. In most cases, puberty begins about two years earlier in girls than it does in boys (Brooks-Gunn and Reiter, 1990).

Even children of the same sex differ markedly in the timing of puberty. The onset is influenced by heredity, nutrition, level of stress, and amount of exercise, all of which vary from one individual to the next. For example, girls who are serious ballet students or competitive runners or gymnasts often experience delayed puberty compared with their peers (Warren, 1983).

Defining the "normal" range for beginning and completing puberty is really a statistical task. James Tanner, a highly respected researcher in this field, defines "normal" as the range experienced by 95 percent of the population (Tanner, 1990). According to this definition, it is normal for menstruation to begin as early as age 9 or as late as age 16, and it is normal for sperm production to start as early as age 10 or as late as age 19. However, youngsters who mature earlier or later than most of their peers, even though they fall within the normal range, may encounter special psychological issues. We will discuss these issues later in this chapter.

The average age at which puberty occurs has been decreasing for at least the last 100 years. Girls in the United States and western Europe now begin menstruating about two years earlier than their great-grandmothers did (Tanner, 1990). Boys, too, show signs of an earlier onset of puberty. This generational change is most likely due to improvements in nutrition and health care. The trend toward earlier puberty will probably not continue in countries with already high standards of living. In the United States, for instance, the average age of menarche has been relatively stable over the last few decades, suggesting that we may have reached the limits of accelerating puberty (Brooks-Gunn and Reiter, 1990).

Cross-cultural research supports the idea that improved nutrition and health care are major causes of earlier puberty. Around the world, girls in industrialized countries tend to reach menarche sooner than girls in developing countries, where malnutrition and chronic disease are more common. For example, the median age at menarche in North America, western Europe, and Japan is about 12.5 to 13.5 years; in Africa and New Guinea, it is 14 to 17 years. Similar differences are found across income levels within cultures. In such widely separated parts of the world as Hong Kong, Tunisia, South Africa, and the United States, girls from higher-income families reach menarche earlier than girls from lower-income families (Eveleth and Tanner, 1976). When groups with adequate nutrition are compared, however, there do not seem to be ethnic differences in the age at which puberty begins or the rate at which it progresses. In the United States, for example, no significant differences have been found in age at menarche for African-American, Asian-American, and European-American girls (Brooks-Gunn and Reiter, 1990).

HORMONAL CONTROL OF PUBERTY

Puberty is not a transformation that arises out of nowhere, but the final stage in a much longer process of sexual development. Remember from Chapter 3 that sexual differentiation begins soon after conception. Whether a fertilized egg becomes male or female depends on the presence or absence of a Y chromosome, which in turn governs the amount of male hormones, or *androgens,* that the embryo produces. A relative abundance of androgens triggers the development of male sex organs, whereas a relative lack of androgens allows the development of female organs. At puberty, hormones once again govern sexual changes. In boys, an increased secretion of androgens results in the production of live sperm and the development of such characteristics as facial hair and a deeper voice. Increased androgen levels also account for some pubertal changes in girls, such as the growth of underarm and pubic hair. Other changes in girls, such as menstruation and breast development, result from stepped-up secretion of female hormones called *estrogens.*

Complex feedback systems, involving various hormone-producing glands, are responsible for regulating the levels of hormones in the body. Figure 13.1 shows how these systems work. The **pituitary gland,** a small structure attached to the base of the brain, plays a central role in the feedback systems, which is why it is often referred to as the "master gland." The pituitary gland in turn is affected by hormones from a part of the brain known as the **hypothalamus.** These brain hormones, or *releasing factors,* as they are often called, turn the production of pituitary hormones on and off. Some of the pituitary hormones are called **gonadotropins** because they travel through the bloodstream and affect hor-

Pituitary gland:
A small gland at the base of the brain that plays a major role in regulating the hormonal output of other glands.

Hypothalamus:
A part of the brain that regulates many body functions, including the production of pituitary hormones.

Gonadotropins:
Pituitary hormones that affect hormone output by the gonads.

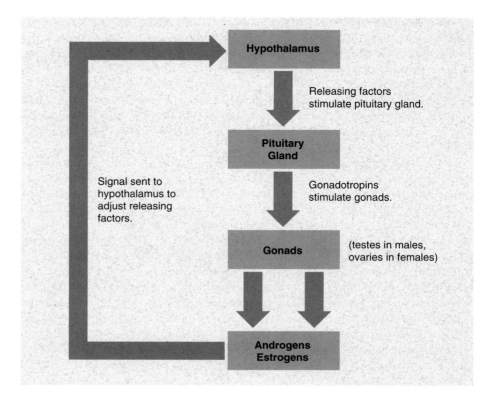

FIGURE 13.1
HORMONE FEEDBACK
LOOP
Levels of sex hormones are regulated by a feedback system composed of the hypothalamus, pituitary gland, and gonads. (Source: Adapted from Grumbach et al., 1974.)

mone output from the sex glands, or **gonads.** The gonads of men are the testes, which produce androgens. The gonads of women are the ovaries, which produce estrogens and another female hormone called *progesterone,* as well as small quantities of androgens. The levels of sex hormones in the blood provide signals to the hypothalamus, which modifies its activities accordingly and affects output from the pituitary gland. This complex control system functions even prior to birth. Through middle childhood it works to keep sex hormones at low levels (Grumbach et al., 1974).

At the end of middle childhood the brain delivers a message for the gonads to step up production of sex hormones. How the brain "knows" it is time to begin puberty is something we do not yet understand. One explanation, called the *critical weight hypothesis* (Frisch and Revelle, 1970), was based on data suggesting that menarche occurs at a relatively constant weight in girls and that the adolescent growth spurt in both sexes is also weight-related. However, menarche seems not to be controlled by weight per se, but by factors *related* to weight, such as the proportion of fat to lean tissue (Frisch, 1983). At least 17 percent of a girl's body mass must be made up of fat for menstruation to begin or continue (Petersen, 1979). This would explain the prevalence of delayed menarche in ballet dancers and certain kinds of athletes, whose intense physical training may result in a level of body fat below the critical percentage. It also explains why nutritional factors would be involved in the trend toward earlier menarche over the last few generations and in cross-cultural and social class differences in age at menarche. Some researchers now suspect that subtle changes in the body's metabolism (the chemical reactions occurring in its cells) may provide signals to the brain that trigger the stepped-up production of sex hormones (Brooks-Gunn and Reiter, 1990).

Regardless of what brings about increased output of sex hormones at the end of middle childhood, that increase starts the changes we call puberty. Rising levels of sex hormones circulate in the blood, becoming available to cells throughout the body. When the concentrations of these hormones reach a critical threshold, cells that are receptive to them change their growth patterns (Root, 1973). Note the importance of a critical threshold in the levels of sex hormones. Androgens and estrogens are present in the blood throughout childhood, but they do not trigger puberty until their concentrations rise to some critical level. Only then do the other physical changes of adolescence begin.

CHANGES IN APPEARANCE AT PUBERTY

Among the physical changes of puberty are the development of **secondary sex characteristics**—physical features that differentiate adult males from adult females but are not directly involved in reproduction. Secondary sex characteristics include new distributions of muscle and fat tissue, the growth of hair on certain parts of the body, the development of breasts in females and broadened shoulders in males, and the lowered pitch of the male voice. Major secondary sex characteristics are often used as markers for various stages of puberty. For instance, Tanner (1962) has identified five stages of puberty on the basis of the development of pubic hair and genitals in boys, and pubic hair and breasts in girls (see Table 13.1). The development of the various secondary sex characteristics does not always occur at the same rate. In fact, a person often develops faster in one area than in another. For instance, a male might be at stage 4 for genital development but only at stage 2 for the development of pubic hair.

Gonads:
The sex glands: testes in men and ovaries in women.

Secondary sex characteristics:
Physical features that differentiate adult males from adult females but are not directly involved in reproduction.

TABLE 13.1
STAGES OF PUBERTY

Stage	Pubic Hair Development	Female Breast Development	Male Genital Development
1	No pubic hair.	Elevation of papilla (nipple) only.	Penis, scrotum, and testes stay in the same proportion to body size as in early childhood.
2	First pubic hair, which is sparse, long, and slightly pigmented, appears; usually grows at base of the penis or along the labia.	Breast buds appear. The breast and papilla are elevated slightly in a small mound.	Scrotum and testes enlarge and scrotum darkens.
3	Hair darkens, becomes coarser and more curled; remains sparse but spreads over the midsection of the pubic region.	Breast and areola continue to enlarge, but there is no separation of their contours.	Penis grows, primarily in length, and scrotum and testes continue to grow.
4	Hair development is completed, but area covered is still smaller than in adults.	Areola and papilla elevate above the mound of the breast to form a secondary mound.	Growth of penis includes width and enlargement of glans; scrotum continues to grow and darken.
5	Quantity and area covered reach adult proportions.	Papilla continues to project, but areola recesses to the general contour of the breast.	Genitals attain adult size and shape.

SOURCE: Adapted from Tanner, 1962.

Most adolescents also experience noticeable changes in their skin and sweat glands. The skin becomes rougher and more oily, and acne may develop. The sweat glands enlarge and become more active, especially in the underarm and genital areas, resulting in new body odors. In our evolutionary past these body odors may have functioned as *pheromones,* chemical scents used by members of the same species to communicate a message, such as a readiness to mate. But today both body odors and acne can be sources of embarrassment for adolescents.

Another physical change that occurs near the beginning of adolescence is a marked spurt in growth. Figure 13.2 shows that increases in height slow substantially during the late preschool years and early middle childhood. Across this age range, the average height of girls and boys is virtually identical (Tanner, 1990; Tanner, Whitehouse, and Takaishi, 1966). Then the growth spurt for girls begins, at an average age of 10.5 years. For boys, the spurt starts a couple of years later, on average at age 12.5 years. The adolescent growth spurt reaches its peak about a year and a half after it begins. The peak rate of growth for boys is greater than the peak rate for girls, which partly explains why their average adult height is about 2½ inches taller.

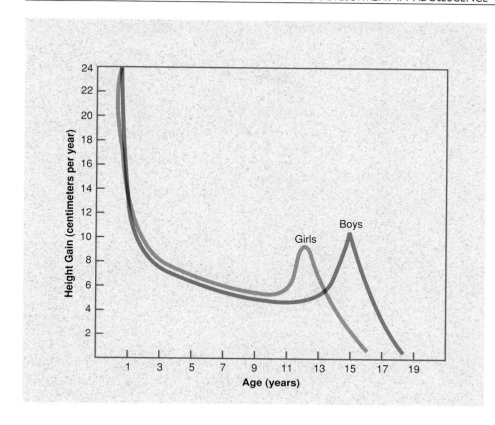

FIGURE 13.2 GROWTH RATES FOR BOYS AND GIRLS

The rate of growth, which is at its maximum in infancy, declines through childhood and is followed by a spurt in adolescence. The growth spurt for males is greater than for females, and their growth continues over a longer period of time, which is why they are usually taller. (Source: Tanner, Whitehouse, and Takaishi, 1966.)

Growth occurs near the ends of bones in rings of cartilage called *epiphyseal growth plates*. Ultimately, adolescent skeletal growth ceases when increased amounts of sex hormones cause calcification of the cartilage involved in this process. Different patterns of skeletal growth among adolescent boys and girls partially account for the gender-related differences in body shape. The classic male growth pattern leads to broader shoulders, narrower hips, and longer legs relative to torso. The classic female growth pattern leads to narrower shoulders, broader hips, and shorter legs relative to torso (see Figure 13.3). Differences in the amount and distribution of body fat also contribute to gender differences in body shape. During adolescence, girls develop fat deposits on the thighs, hips, buttocks, and upper arms. By adulthood, women normally have about twice as much body fat relative to their total body mass as men (Warren, 1983).

During the adolescent growth spurt the arms and legs grow before the torso does in both boys and girls. This growth pattern can make the limbs seem temporarily out of proportion to the rest of the body and is one source of self-consciousness among teenagers. Meryl expresses this concern to her friend Amy in the story that precedes this chapter. The torso growth that follows usually brings the whole body back into "normal" proportions.

In addition to increases in height, adolescents experience increases in weight, strength, and endurance. Part of the weight gain comes from growth in both the size and number of muscle cells. As a result, adolescents become stronger than they were as children, although males experience a greater increase in

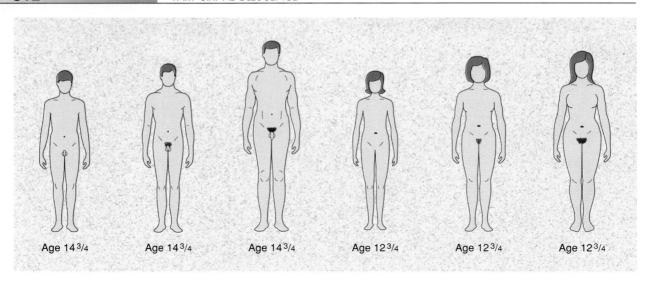

Age 14³/₄   Age 14³/₄   Age 14³/₄   Age 12³/₄   Age 12³/₄   Age 12³/₄

FIGURE 13.3

DEVELOPMENTAL DIFFERENCES IN SAME-AGE BOYS AND GIRLS

The three males in this figure are all the same age (14³/₄ years), as are the three females (12³/₄ years), but they are in different stages of development. These pictures illustrate different rates of development within gender and the different patterns of growth for males and females. (Source: Tanner, 1962.)

strength than females do (Malina, 1978). During adolescence the heart and lungs also develop in ways that contribute to increased endurance and allow for participation in more demanding competitive sports.

The growth patterns we have described are but a sampling of the physical changes that occur during puberty. They are meant to illustrate what a dramatic transformation is going on at this time. In just a few years youngsters change from looking like children to looking like young adults. In the process, they gain new capacities for strength and endurance and, perhaps most important, for sexual reproduction. All these physical changes help propel adolescents toward a new set of social roles.

IMPACTS OF PUBERTAL CHANGE

The physical changes of puberty have a powerful impact on adolescents' psychological functioning, behavior, and relationships with others. In fact, some of the behavioral changes of adolescence are tied more closely to these physical changes than to chronological age or level of cognitive development. The impact of puberty on an individual adolescent depends partly on its timing—that is, on whether it occurs early, on schedule, or late compared to the majority of his or her peers.

PUBERTY AND BODY IMAGE

Body image is strongly affected by puberty and its timing (Tobin-Richards et al., 1983; Petersen, 1987). In early adolescence, boys who are more physically mature are more likely to have a positive body image and to perceive themselves as generally attractive than are boys who are less physically mature. One reason for this is that boys who have passed puberty have an athletic advantage over boys who have not, because of the increased height and muscle development that come with puberty.

For girls, in contrast, puberty tends to have a negative effect on body image, mostly because of the increase and redistribution of body fat that occur at this time. Girls in early adolescence generally have a poorer body image than boys of the same age and tend to think of themselves as too heavy (Dornbusch et al., 1987; Richards et al., 1990). Girls who are well ahead of their peers in physical development have the most negative self-perceptions, even more so than girls who lag behind. Among early adolescent girls, those who are about *average* in physical development generally have the most positive body image and the greatest feelings of attractiveness.

Studies in both the United States and Sweden have found that early-maturing girls remain dissatisfied with their height and weight as they go through adolescence (Simmons et al., 1983, 1987; Stattin and Magnusson, 1990). These findings can be explained by the fact that early-maturing girls tend to differ from their peers in height and weight in ways that are a disadvantage at every age. In sixth grade, they are taller and heavier than most of their classmates, both male and female. By tenth grade, they are generally shorter and heavier than the late-maturing girls in their classes, who have continued to grow taller but have not yet acquired the deposits of body fat that tend to follow puberty. The early-maturing girls thus are less likely to fit the cultural ideal of the slender, long-legged woman. This difference in height and weight between early- and late-maturing girls persists into adulthood (Brooks-Gunn and Reiter, 1990).

The one physical change of puberty that seems to have a positive effect on girls' body image is breast development (Brooks-Gunn and Reiter, 1990). In sixth and seventh grade, girls who have passed menarche think they are too tall and weigh too much, but they are more satisfied with their figures than are girls who have not reached menarche. What these early maturers actually seem to be expressing satisfaction with is their relatively advanced breast development (Simmons et al., 1983, 1987). The most likely explanations for the impact that breast development has on body image are the strong sexual significance of female breasts in our culture and the fact that breast development is more obvious to other people than many of the other changes of puberty.

PUBERTY AND SOCIAL RELATIONSHIPS

Puberty is associated with increased interest in the opposite sex and an increased likelihood of dating and sexual activity. Roberta Simmons and her colleagues (1983, 1987) found that girls who had reached puberty by sixth and seventh grades considered themselves more popular with boys and were more likely to be dating than girls who had not yet reached puberty. Young adolescents of both sexes who are further along in puberty are more likely to date and talk on the telephone with members of the opposite sex (Petersen, 1987). These behaviors may be due partly to increased sexual interest as a result of higher androgen levels (Smith, 1989) and partly to increased sexual attractiveness as a result of the appearance of secondary sex characteristics. Timing of puberty also affects relationships with the opposite sex. One study of early- and late-maturing girls in Sweden found that the early-maturing girls were more likely to have a steady boyfriend and sexual experience by midadolescence and were more likely to experience an unwanted pregnancy by the end of adolescence (Stattin and Magnusson, 1990).

Puberty also affects parent-child relationships. When children reach puberty, they often experience an increase in conflicts with their mothers (Steinberg, 1989; Papini and Sebby, 1987; Stattin and Magnusson, 1990). Near the end of puberty, adolescents report increased feelings of emotional and behavioral autonomy from their parents (Steinberg, 1987; Simmons et al., 1983). The timing of puberty has some impact on these effects. Mother-son conflict is often

Interest in the opposite sex increases around the time of puberty.

greater for early-maturing boys than for late-maturing boys (Steinberg, 1987), and early-maturing girls often have an unusually prolonged period of conflict with their parents (Hill et al., 1985). Puberty is more likely to be associated with increased feelings of autonomy for late-maturing adolescents, particularly girls. This shows that parents consider chronological age as well as pubertal status in allowing their children more independence. We will discuss changes in parent-child relationships during adolescence more extensively in Chapter 14.

PUBERTY AND PROBLEM BEHAVIORS

Various problem behaviors become more common at puberty, especially in early-maturing girls. Simmons and her colleagues (1983, 1987) found increased problem behaviors at school and decreased academic performance in sixth- and seventh-grade girls who had passed menarche. In Sweden, Stattin and Magnusson (1990) found heightened rates of such problem behaviors as truancy, academic trouble, drug and alcohol use, running away, and shoplifting among early-maturing girls. A study of Finnish girls at midadolescence (Aro and Taipale, 1987) found that those who had been early maturers were more likely to consume alcohol on a regular basis than those who had been late maturers.

TIMING OF PUBERTY AND OVERALL ADJUSTMENT

As we have already seen, the age at which puberty occurs has an impact on many aspects of an adolescent's development, with girls and boys affected differently. For girls, the early maturers are at a disadvantage compared to the late maturers, at least during adolescence. For boys, in contrast, it is late maturers who are likely to experience more problems in the short term.

In addition to the various negative effects we have already mentioned, early-maturing girls tend to have lower self-esteem and are at greater risk for a variety of emotional problems than are late-maturing girls (Simmons and Blyth, 1988). It is not completely clear what the long-term effects of early maturation are for girls. One study suggests that early-maturing girls develop coping skills during adolescence that result in greater psychological flexibility in adulthood (Peskin, 1973). However, the problem behaviors that some early-maturing girls engage in can have lasting impacts. For example, Stattin and Magnusson (1990) followed their subjects into adulthood and found that the long-term effects included a tendency for early-maturing girls to have children earlier and to complete fewer years of education.

Late-maturing boys tend to be less popular and less self-confident than early maturers during adolescence; they are often regarded by their peers as childish, bossy, tense, and restless (Jones, 1957; Petersen, 1985). In adulthood they are frequently viewed as impulsive and nonconforming, but also insightful and creative. Early-maturing boys, in contrast, are often viewed as competent, poised, and successful as adolescents, but in adulthood tend to become inflexible and conventional (Livson and Peskin, 1980). The very characteristics that contributed to their social success in adolescence become less useful in adulthood.

This pattern of different effects for boys and girls makes sense if the key issue in the timing of puberty is being in step with the physical development of one's peers. Early-maturing girls, who can reach puberty as young as age 9, and late-maturing boys, who can reach puberty as late as age 19, are the *most* out of step developmentally. It is thus not surprising that these two groups seem to encounter the most negative consequences of puberty.

DIRECT AND INDIRECT EFFECTS OF PUBERTY

Obviously the causal connections between puberty and adolescent behavior are complex. Sexual maturity alone does not produce the effects we have discussed; social factors are also extremely important. Puberty produces both unseen internal and visible external physical changes in adolescents. The internal changes may directly affect adolescents' feelings and behaviors through the influences of hormones—increasing sexual desire, for example. The external changes may affect feelings and actions too, both through the impact they have on an adolescent's own body image and through the reactions they trigger in others. For example, parents may perceive physically mature teenagers as being more personally responsible, while members of the opposite sex may find them more sexually attractive. These reactions in turn can have powerful influences on the adolescent's behavior.

Of course, how the adolescent and others react to the changes of puberty depends on the meaning attached to those changes, which is partly a product of the person's particular group or culture. For example, ballet students regard late maturation and the elongated, slender body type that results as particularly advantageous (Brooks-Gunn, 1987), and the emphasis placed on weight by adolescent girls in the United States seems to vary from one community to another, even within the same ethnic group (Richards, 1990). Reactions to puberty, in other words, are not universally the same. They depend on the particular context in which these physical changes occur.

NEUROLOGICAL CHANGES AT PUBERTY

Along with all the other physical changes occurring at puberty, mounting evidence suggests that the brain undergoes substantial change too. It is not yet clear what causes these neurological changes. They may be produced partly by the hormonal changes of puberty and partly by experiences during earlier developmental periods. In any case, once adolescence is over, the brain seems to be a somewhat different organ than it was in childhood.

One change in the brain between childhood and adulthood is a decline in its **plasticity,** or the ability of various brain regions to take on new functions. Adults have more difficulty recovering from brain injuries than children do, in part because the functions previously performed by damaged parts of their brains are less readily taken over by parts that remain undamaged. Further evidence for decreased plasticity comes from the decline in language-learning abilities between childhood and adulthood. Those who start learning a second language in early childhood have the greatest chance of achieving the fluency of a native speaker. As we discussed in Chapter 7, success at second-language learning apparently begins to decline gradually somewhere in middle childhood, but drops off sharply around the time of puberty (Johnson and Newport, 1989). Both these lines of evidence suggest that the brain of a young child has a marked capacity for "reprogramming," some of which is lost around the time of puberty.

One change that may contribute to the loss of reprogramming ability is **hemispheric specialization** in the brain, a process by which certain brain functions become localized in either the right or left side of the cerebral cortex (the portion of the brain in which higher-order thinking occurs). In most adults, for example, language is primarily a function of the left hemisphere and spatial abilities are primarily a function of the right hemisphere. The process of hemispheric specialization probably begins in early childhood, but it is thought to be completed in most people around the time of puberty. Adults vary in their extent of hemispheric specialization, and one factor that may contribute to this variability is age at puberty. Several researchers have found evidence of greater hemispheric specialization among late maturers than among early maturers, but they have not found consistent differences in cognitive functioning between the two groups (Waber, 1977; Newcombe, Dubas, and Baenninger, 1989).

Another change that may contribute to the brain's loss of plasticity is a decrease in the number of connections (called *synapses*) among brain cells. One researcher has reported a sharply decreased density of synapses in certain parts of the brain between ages 10 and 15 (Huttenlocher, 1994). In keeping with this finding, electronic brain scans show that between the ages of 10 and 14 there is roughly a 50 percent drop in the energy being used in these brain regions (Graber and Petersen, 1991). Since substantial energy is needed to send messages from one brain cell to another, this decrease in energy use could arise partly from a "pruning" of brain synapses—that is, the elimination of synapses that are not needed. Research on animal brains suggests that interconnections among brain cells may at first be overproduced, with some later eliminated, depending on the type of stimulation the brain receives (Greenough, Black, and Wallace, 1987). This early overproduction has the advantage of allowing for maximum cognitive flexibility early in life. The later decrease in synapses does not represent a loss of brain function; instead, it allows for more efficient functioning of the synapses that remain.

Developmental studies of sleep patterns also support the theory that the brain changes at the time of puberty. Children between the ages of 2 and 11 spend about twice as much time as adults do in what is called *deep sleep,* a state characterized by extremely slow brain waves. Then, between the ages of 11 and 14, the amount of deep sleep declines to adult levels (Graber and Petersen,

Plasticity:
The ability of brain regions to take on new functions.

Hemispheric specialization:
The process by which certain brain functions become localized in either the right or left side of the cerebral cortex.

1991). We do not know what prompts this nighttime change in brain-wave patterns. One possibility is that deep sleep somehow helps the brain recover from its metabolic activities during the day. If the brain becomes more efficient at the time of adolescence, its amount of metabolic activity would decline, as would the need for deep sleep (Graber and Petersen, 1991; Lund, 1978).

Let's summarize the findings about changes in the brain at puberty. Apparently, during early adolescence the brain becomes more efficient at certain tasks. Greater efficiency comes at the price of a decrease in flexibility, however. After adolescence, the brain cannot adapt as readily to new demands, such as learning a new language or recovering from damage. Still, the increased efficiency in the brain's functioning may play a role in the changes in cognitive abilities that occur during adolescence.

CHANGES IN THINKING DURING ADOLESCENCE

Adolescence is a time when youngsters acquire important new cognitive skills. Some developmentalists, such as Piaget, see these new skills as marking the transition to a qualitatively different period of development. Although these researchers believe the skills of adolescence are built on those of childhood, they tend to focus on how adolescent thinking differs from thinking earlier in life. In contrast, other developmentalists tend to put more stress on continuity with the past. They see the cognitive accomplishments of adolescence as logical and steady progressions from the skills of middle childhood (Keating, 1980; Siegler, 1978). Despite these different approaches, however, all developmentalists agree that during adolescence youngsters become much more mature in their reasoning and problem-solving abilities.

One major change is that logical thinking is now applied to the possible (what *might* exist), not just to the real (what *does* exist). In one investigation of this change, children were shown poker chips of varying colors, one of which

During adolescence, young people become able to solve increasingly abstract and complex problems.

An understanding of relationships among abstract concepts is one of the cognitive advances made during adolescence.

Hypothetico-deductive reasoning:
Piaget's term for the ability to think up hypothetical solutions to a problem and to formulate a systematic plan for deducing which of these solutions is correct.

was then hidden in the experimenter's hand (Osherson and Markman, 1975). The experimenter said "Either the chip in my hand is green or it is not green." The children were then asked to decide if this statement was true or false. Youngsters in middle childhood had great difficulty answering the question correctly. They kept trying to determine whether or not the chip was green, and upon discovering that they couldn't do so, they said there was no way to answer the researcher's question. These children seemed wedded to a *contingent* notion of truth: to know if the experimenter's words are true, you must *see* what is in his hand. Adolescents, by contrast, can break free of this focus on concrete things perceived by the senses. They are able to consider the possibilities contained in the statement (the chip may be green or it may be some other color) and examine their logical implications. Using this more abstract perspective, adolescents correctly conclude that the statement involves a *necessary,* not a contingent, truth.

A second cognitive advance in adolescence is the ability to think about *relationships* among mentally constructed concepts—that is, among abstract concepts that are built up from the more concrete things we perceive. Number, for instance, is an abstract, mentally constructed concept drawn from more concrete, observable concepts: one, two, three, and so forth. Elementary school children are able to form *individual* abstract concepts, but they have trouble reasoning about the logical relationships between them. The adolescent's newfound ability to think about such relationships is evident in a variety of contexts. For instance, whereas an elementary school child might define an abstract concept such as morality by focusing on specific behaviors—not stealing, telling the truth, obeying parents—an adolescent understands that morality entails interrelations among subordinate concepts such as honesty, fairness, and kindness. Because of their ability to think in this manner, teenagers have a more mature grasp of many abstract concepts, including identity, justice, religion, society, existence, and friendship. The ability to think about relationships among abstract concepts also gives adolescents even more capacity for *metacognition*— thinking about thinking—than they had in middle childhood (Flavell, Miller, and Miller, 1993). This capacity reveals itself not only in improved memory strategies but also in teenagers' introspection and focus on their own thoughts (Elkind, 1974).

A third major advance is that adolescents' thinking becomes even more logical and systematic than it was in childhood. These improved powers of reasoning make adolescents much better than they have been previously at constructing logical arguments and at seeing fallacies in others' logic—a development that does not always endear them to their parents. Using their new abilities to think about the possible as well as the actual and to reason about relationships among abstract concepts, adolescents become able to engage in what Piaget referred to as **hypothetico-deductive reasoning.** This ability allows an adolescent to think up hypothetical solutions to a problem (ideas about what *might* be) and then formulate a logical and systematic plan for deducing which of these possible solutions is correct. Consider the car repair problem facing Mike Gordon in the story that precedes this chapter. He is able to solve this problem partly because he is knowledgeable about engines and partly because he is able to lay out the possible reasons for the malfunction his mother describes and then deduce what symptoms would differentiate one possibility from another.

Adolescents' increased skill with formal logic, as studied by Piaget, is particularly useful in scientific reasoning.

Hypothetico-deductive reasoning is also useful in situations that require thinking about possible consequences of various courses of action. Research on adolescents' competence to consent to medical treatment has revealed that by age 14 children are able to weigh the consequences of proposed treatments, consider multiple relevant factors such as treatment advantages and disadvantages, and arrive at a rational decision (Weithorn and Campbell, 1982). In contrast, younger children tend to focus on one or two particularly salient features of a proposed treatment, such as pain or duration, and to have trouble coordinating multiple factors that need to be considered.

Developmentalists are still trying to determine what underlies the cognitive changes of adolescence. One explanation is contained in Piaget's theory of formal operations. Because Piaget's ideas have had such an influence on the field, we will describe them in some detail.

PIAGET'S THEORY OF FORMAL OPERATIONS

Piaget attributed the cognitive advances of adolescents to their developing ability to use principles of propositional logic, which he called **formal operations.** Propositional logic involves combining individual statements or *propositions* to reach logical conclusions, as in the following example: "All A's are B. X is an A. Therefore, X is a B." Principles of propositional logic can be applied to statements based in reality: "All mammals are warm-blooded. Whales are mammals. Therefore, whales are warm-blooded." But they can be applied just as easily to hypothetical or fanciful statements: "All wonkets have three eyes. Cleo is a wonket. Therefore, Cleo has three eyes."

Piaget argued that formal operations allow adolescents to think more abstractly and systematically than ever before. Elementary school children can use logic to reason about concrete situations, but they have difficulty with problems based on hypothetical situations, especially situations that are contrary to fact. In contrast, adolescents are able to think about the logical implications in

Formal operations:
In Piaget's theory, a set of principles of formal logic on which the cognitive advances of adolescence are based.

a problem, whether or not it is grounded in reality. For example, adolescents would have no difficulty answering the following question: "If all dogs were green, and I had a dog, would it be green too?" (Ault, 1983). Younger children would be likely to object that dogs cannot be green. They would have trouble getting beyond the fact that the situation portrayed in the problem did not match their concrete experience.

Piaget did not believe that formal operations needed to be taught. Instead, he maintained that adolescents develop the ability to understand and apply formal operations as a result of their own reasoning and experimentation. Once this ability has developed, adolescents can use it to solve problems and expand their understanding of the world.

Piaget believed that the cognitive skills that constitute formal operations are qualitatively different from any skills the child has had in the past. Nevertheless, he saw these skills as produced by the same processes of adaptation and equilibration that produced earlier cognitive structures. Thus, cognitive structures and abilities may change, but the underlying processes of development do not.

PIAGET'S EXPERIMENTS

Piaget built his theory of formal operations on extensive research into adolescents' reasoning abilities. This research involved presenting youngsters of different ages with scientific experiments to conduct. The youngsters were given an apparatus (such as a pendulum) or a set of materials (such as chemicals capable of producing a certain reaction when combined in a particular way). Their task was to manipulate these items in any way they wished in order to determine how they "worked." Piaget found that adolescents approached and understood these tasks in markedly different ways than elementary school children did.

To give you a clearer sense of the basis for Piaget's ideas about formal operations, we'll look at three of his experiments. As you read about them, notice the general cognitive abilities that they demonstrate. The first one shows the ability to reason about relationships among abstract concepts; the second one shows the ability to isolate variables that may be having an effect on results; and the last one shows the ability to combine a number of different factors in a systematic way. Piaget believed that all these abilities resulted from adolescents' use of formal logical reasoning.

THE LAW OF FLOATING BODIES STUDY
In the law of floating bodies study, youngsters were given objects that were of different sizes and were made of different materials, along with a large container of water. Their first task was to classify the objects according to whether they thought they would float or sink. Then they were asked to explain their classification. Finally, they were given a chance to experiment with each object in the water and describe what they had learned.

At the beginning of middle childhood (ages 6 to 7) youngsters were often wrong in their hypotheses about what would float and what would not. Moreover, when given a chance to experiment and draw more accurate conclusions, their reasoning was often unsystematic, illogical, and incomplete. Here are some examples (adapted from Inhelder and Piaget, 1955/1958, pp. 26–27):

Child 1:   (explaining why a large piece of wood floats) Because this plank is bigger

Child 1: and it came back up. (Interviewer: And why does the ball come up?) Because it's smaller.

Child 2: (explaining why certain items sink) They are little things. (Interviewer: Why do the little ones go to the bottom?) Because they aren't heavy; they don't swim on top because it's too light. (Later the same child says that a metal key sinks "because it's too heavy to stay on top.")

Child 3: (explaining why a candle sinks) Because it's round. (Interviewer: And why does the wooden ball stay on top?) Because it's round too.

These examples highlight the self-contradictions in young children's explanations. The children apparently focused on an object's most obvious features (large, small, round, and so forth) regardless of the question being asked and regardless of the answers they had previously given.

Somewhat older children (7 to 10 years of age) tried to avoid self-contradictions. They frequently expressed the idea that light objects float and heavy ones sink. When reminded that some very light objects sink and some very heavy ones float, they groped for an overall explanation that would accommodate these facts. Here is how two older elementary school youngsters tackled the problem (adapted from Inhelder and Piaget, 1955/1958, pp. 29, 35):

Child 1: (explaining why the ball floats): It stays on top. It's wood. It's light. (Interviewer: And this key?) It goes down. It's iron. It's heavy. (Interviewer: Which is heavier, the key or the ball?) The ball. (Interviewer: Why does the key sink?) Because it's heavy. (Interviewer: And the nail?) It's light but it sinks anyway. It's iron and iron always goes under.

Child 2: (explaining why the wooden ball floats while the iron key sinks) Wood isn't the same as iron. It's lighter; there are holes in between. (Interviewer: And steel?) It stays under because there aren't any holes in between.

Notice that both these children were quite good at predicting what would float and what would sink. But when confronted with the fact that some light objects do sink, the first child offered an explanation that simply appealed to empirical knowledge ("iron *always* goes under"). This child was struggling toward an understanding that some things can be "heavy" and still feel relatively light. The second child, who referred to "holes in between," had moved a step further by developing an implicit notion of an object's density (weight per unit of volume). But this child was still unable to articulate the concept maturely.

More mature explanations come in adolescence. This older adolescent described the principle in very adultlike terms (adapted from Inhelder and Piaget, 1955/1958, p. 44):

Adolescent: (explaining why the key sinks despite the fact that it is relatively small and light) With the same volume the water is lighter than the key. (Interviewer: How would you prove that?) I would take some modeling clay, then I would make an exact pattern of the key and I would put water inside it. It would have the same volume of water as the key . . . and it would be lighter.

This example illustrates how the cognitive skills of adolescents are built upon those developed in middle childhood. Elementary school children have acquired the concepts of volume and weight, which is why they are able to solve conservation problems. An understanding of density is based on an understanding of the *ratio* of weight to volume. Notice how understanding a ratio involves the ability to think about relationships among mentally constructed concepts (in this case the concept of weight and the concept of volume). Kurt Fischer calls this the ability to coordinate abstract systems (Fischer et al., 1990). During adolescence, youngsters become able to see how two or more mentally constructed concepts can be related to produce a third, even more abstract concept. Thus, they grasp that the ratio of weight to volume yields the concept of density.

THE PENDULUM STUDY

The pendulum study measured the ability to investigate the effects of a single variable while holding all other factors constant (Inhelder and Piaget, 1955/1958). Here youngsters had to figure out which of four factors determines the period of a pendulum—that is, the time it takes to complete a swing from one side to the other and back. As illustrated in Figure 13.4, the four factors were the length of the pendulum's string, the weight of the pendulum, the height from which the pendulum is first released, and the force with which the pendulum is pushed when set in motion.

The solution to this problem is contrary to most adults' intuitions: the length of the string is the *only* factor that influences the period of the pendulum's swing. Because the correct answer is unlikely to be guessed, the pendulum problem provides a good way of demonstrating the new skills in experimentation and logical deduction that adolescents acquire. Elementary school children do not appropriately isolate each of the possible variables, so they draw the wrong conclusions. Adolescents, in contrast, systematically test each of the factors while holding the others constant. This approach enables them to discover the right answer.

THE ALL POSSIBLE COMBINATIONS STUDY

In another of Piaget's experiments, subjects had to try systematically all possible combinations of five different colorless liquids to determine which combinations cause a yellow color to appear (Inhelder and Piaget, 1955/1958). Four of the liquids were in large flasks numbered 1 through 4. The fifth, labeled g, was in a smaller bottle with an eye dropper in it. The experimenter first showed the youngster a flask with an unidentified liquid in it (actually a combination of liquids 1 and 3). To this he added a few drops of g, and the liquid in the flask turned yellow. The subject was then asked to reproduce the yellow color in as many ways as possible using the five liquids originally provided.

Elementary school children typically took the small bottle labeled g and placed a few drops from it in each of flasks 1 through 4. When nothing happened, they usually realized that the liquids from more than one flask must first be mixed together, but their approach to finding the right mixture or mixtures was haphazard. If they stumbled on the $1 + 3 + g$ combination through trial and error, they generally stopped their search, not thinking that some other combination might also produce yellow. (In fact, $1 + 3 + 2 + g$ produced yellow, too.)

In contrast, youngsters in midadolescence or older adopted a systematic approach and tried all possible combinations. After working through the two-liquid combinations ($1 + g$, $2 + g$, and so on), they proceeded to the three-, four-, and five-liquid ones, trying to avoid repeats while not missing any. These older subjects readily discovered the two combinations that worked.

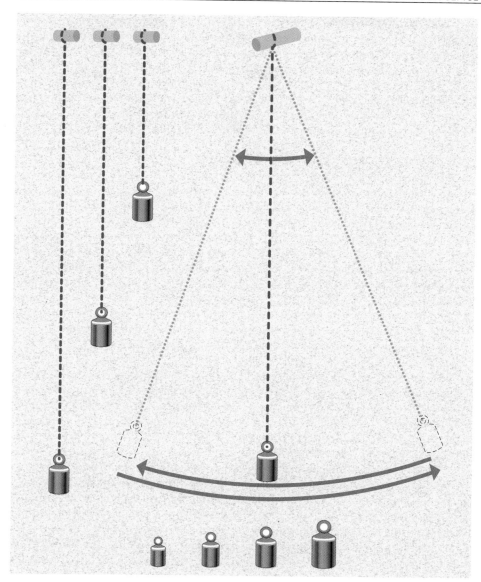

FIGURE 13.4
APPARATUS FOR PIAGET'S PENDULUM PROBLEM
The pendulum problem uses a simple apparatus consisting of a string, which can be shortened or lengthened, and a set of varying weights. Other variables to be considered are the height of the release point and the force with which the pendulum is pushed. (Source: Inhelder and Piaget, 1955/1958, p. 68.)

IS PIAGET'S VIEW CORRECT?

Piaget's *description* of adolescent reasoning abilities has proven to be quite accurate. Other researchers have found similar age-related changes in performance on the tasks that Piaget designed, as well as on other kinds of problem-solving tasks (Keating, 1980; Neimark, 1982). However, there has been criticism of Piaget's *explanation* of adolescents' new cognitive skills. Researchers have not found strong evidence to support Piaget's idea that the advances in reasoning that occur during adolescence are based on mastery of specific principles of formal logic. Various other explanations for those changes have been proposed, but we still lack consensus about how they are best explained (Keating, 1990).

Adolescents are most likely to use formal operations to solve problems in areas where they are knowledgeable and have a high level of interest.

We also lack consensus as to whether the ability to deal with propositional logic is entirely new to adolescents. For example, elementary school-age children have been found to be quite good at solving simple, relatively concrete logical problems like the following: "If Jack washes the dishes, then his father will be very pleased. If Jack's father is very pleased, then Jack gets 50 cents. Jack washes the dishes. Does Jack get 50 cents?" (Brainerd, 1978). Such findings call into question Piaget's belief that the cognitive skills of adolescence are qualitatively different from anything possessed before.

HOW PERVASIVE ARE FORMAL OPERATIONS?

Another question about Piaget's theory is how pervasive formal operations are in the thinking of adolescents. For one thing, skill at using formal operations appears to develop gradually, rather than all at once. Some researchers have suggested that a distinction should be made between the levels of expertise in formal operations that are commonly demonstrated in early adolescence and in late adolescence (Kuhn et al., 1977). In early adolescence, the capacity for formal operational thought seems to be present, but not yet fully developed or consistently applied. Young teenagers often use formal reasoning on some tasks or in some situations, but not others—a type of thinking that has been characterized as *emergent formal operations*. By middle or late adolescence, some young people show evidence of mature, consistent use of formal reasoning in their usual approach to problem solving—in other words, of *consolidated formal operations.*

However, this use of formal reasoning does not appear to be universal. A number of studies have shown that many adolescents (and even many adults) do not normally use formal operations to solve problems (Blasi and Hoeffel, 1974). On tests of the ability to use formal operations, only about one-third of adolescents and adults pass (Capon and Kuhn, 1979; Keating, 1980). In one study, for example, only 32 percent of 15-year-olds and 34 percent of 18-year-olds were even beginning to use formal operations, and only 13 and 19 percent, respectively, used them in mature ways (Epstein, 1979). Individual differences in the use of formal operations are substantial, of course. Generally speaking, the higher the scholastic ability and performance of a teenager, the more likely he or she is to use this kind of thinking (Shayer, 1980).

In addition, formal operations seem to be more culture-bound than the earlier cognitive abilities in Piaget's theory. They represent a form of reasoning that is most useful and most valued in cultures with an orientation toward science and technology. Across cultures, some secondary school education appears to be a prerequisite for the emergence of formal operations (Shea, 1985). Researchers using standard Piagetian tasks have found little evidence of formal operations in cultures that do not emphasize formal schooling, scientific thought, and technological sophistication (Dasen and Heron, 1981). However, characteristics of formal operational thought, such as hypothesis testing and logical inference, have been observed among people in nonindustrialized cultures when they are engaged in tasks that are meaningful to them, such as hunting by Kalahari Desert tribesmen (e.g., Tulkin and Konner, 1973).

Defenders of Piaget say that the lack of pervasiveness of formal operations must be viewed in light of the distinction between *cognitive competence* (or optimal ability) and *cognitive performance* (or actual behavior in a particular situation). Some psychologists argue that the gap between competence and performance captures a significant characteristic of adolescent thought; teenagers who possess the skills of formal operations may still fail to use them in many circumstances. There are a number of reasons why adolescents do not always use their optimal cognitive abilities. For instance, they may not recognize that these abilities are appropriate to a particular situation. They may lack the specific knowledge needed to use higher-level reasoning (as in the case of a teenager who knows nothing about engines trying to repair a car by aimless fiddling). They may be inattentive to the demands of a situation, they may experience an information overload, or they may be overwhelmed by emotional factors or the need to arrive at a quick solution. Piaget himself (1972) suggested that adults may use formal operational thought only when dealing with domains in which they have high interest and expertise. The cross-cultural findings raise the issue of competence versus performance in a different way. Although human beings as a species are capable of developing and using formal operations, it may not always be adaptive or necessary for them to do so. Formal operations, as Piaget measured them, are needed mainly for scientific and mathematical reasoning and are of little use in other contexts.

CAN FORMAL OPERATIONS BE TAUGHT?

As we saw in Chapter 11, Piaget was not entirely correct in his belief that the cognitive skills of a given developmental period cannot easily be taught. Researchers have had some success in teaching the concrete operation of conservation to very young elementary school children, particularly those who are in a transitional phase with regard to this skill. Similar success has been obtained in efforts to teach formal operations (Beilin, 1976, 1980; Inhelder, Sinclair, and Bovet, 1974). Most of this success has been with youngsters in later middle childhood and with adolescents who did not show formal operational reasoning on a pretest. Using the same training procedures with younger children often has no effect, except with children of above-average intelligence. In one study, for instance, bright 8-year-olds were successfully taught how to isolate variables in order to determine which factor was causing a certain result (Case, 1974). Apparently, high intelligence may be associated with early onset of formal operational skills.

Edith Neimark (1982) has argued that the reason training in formal operations is sometimes effective may be that the procedures simply encourage existing competencies to be displayed, rather than teaching brand-new skills. This view is consistent with the frequent finding that adolescents and adults fail to exhibit their highest level of reasoning because of limitations on performance rather than because of lack of skills. You can see this quite clearly in a study in which adults were presented with an experiment similar to Piaget's all possible combinations problem (Pitt, 1983). Even physical science professors performed badly when they were simply given the equipment and encouraged to forge ahead and find the solution. Both they and other subjects performed much better when asked to plan a strategy before actually beginning to gather data. Thus, studies in which the teaching of formal operations seems to be successful may tell us more about how to get people to perform at their peak ability than about the development of new competencies.

ARE FORMAL OPERATIONS RELATED TO ACADEMIC PERFORMANCE?

Another question psychologists have raised is whether formal operations are useful to academic performance. Since performance on formal operational tasks is related to measures of intelligence, and since measures of intelligence predict performance in school (as you know from Chapter 11), it is not surprising that tests of formal operations can also be used to predict school success. However, assessments of formal operations provide different insights into cognitive skills than IQ tests do. For one thing, tests of formal operations predict performance in science and math better than they predict overall academic performance (Cooper and Robbins, 1981). This finding makes sense when you consider the kinds of tasks used to assess formal operational reasoning.

Researchers have found that explicit training in formal operations can improve a student's grades in science classes. In one British study, a group of adolescents spent two years learning science from a curriculum that emphasized the use of formal operational reasoning, beginning at age 12. At the end of the 2 years, they scored no better than a control group on a science achievement test, though they did have better formal operational reasoning skills. Over time, however, these superior reasoning skills seemed to pay off; the group that had received the special curriculum did earn superior science achievement scores both 1 year and 2 years after it had ended (Adey and Shayer, 1990; Shayer and Adey, 1992, 1993).

Even simple exposure to formal operational tasks, without explicit instruction in the principles involved, may have a similar effect. In one study, 53 percent of the students in an introductory college astronomy class failed to exhibit consistent use of formal operations on an initial test. Half of these students then completed a set of laboratory exercises that required the collection and evaluation of data but included no explicit instruction in formal operational skills. The other half received only supplemental audiovisual material. The students who completed the laboratory exercises not only showed greater improvement on a post-test of formal operations, but also received higher average grades in the course (Cooper and Robbins, 1981).

OTHER APPROACHES TO ADOLESCENT COGNITION

As we mentioned earlier, Piaget's theory is not the only explanation that has been provided for the widely observed changes in adolescent cognitive abilities. Other accounts have centered mainly on adolescents' information-processing abilities, but growing attention is also being paid to the influence of cognitive socialization.

INFORMATION-PROCESSING EXPLANATIONS

Research on adolescents' information-processing abilities consistently indicates continuing improvement in attention and memory skills. Typically, major advances are seen between middle childhood and early adolescence (roughly between ages 8 and 12), with smaller further advances between early and late adolescence (Keating, 1990).

Compared to younger children, adolescents are better at both *selective attention* (focusing attention on relevant information despite distractions) and *divided attention* (paying attention to two tasks at the same time) (Higgins and Turnure, 1984; Schiff and Knopf, 1985). There is some evidence that attentional skills continue to improve through late adolescence; in one study 12-year-olds did markedly better than 8-year-olds on a divided-attention task, and 20-year-olds outperformed the 12-year-olds (Manis, Keating, and Morrison, 1980).

Improvements are also seen in both short- and long-term memory from middle childhood to adolescence. Short-term memory can be measured by the ability to recite back a string of digits read by an experimenter. As mentioned in Chapter 11, there is a slight improvement in performance on this task between age 9 and adulthood; 9-year-olds can typically recall a string of six digits, while adults can typically recall seven (Dempster, 1981). Adolescents' short-term memory skills also appear to give them an advantage over younger children on some problem-solving tasks, such as analogies (e.g., "Sun is to day as _____ is to night.") A series of studies by Robert Sternberg and his colleagues focused on the processes used by third graders, sixth graders, ninth graders, and college students to solve analogy problems. The third and sixth graders' performance was inferior to that of the ninth graders and college students, apparently because they had trouble keeping in mind all the information needed to solve the problem (Sternberg and Nigro, 1980). In the area of long-term memory, adolescents are better than younger children at intentionally memorizing material and recalling it later in situations such as school tests (Flavell, Miller, and Miller, 1993).

One question about adolescent memory improvements is to what extent they are due to increases in memory capacity and to what extent they are due to improvements in memory processes. The increased efficiency of brain functioning during early adolescence may result in a modest increase in capacity, but most researchers agree that improved memory processes probably play a larger role in adolescent memory advances (Kail and Bisanz, 1992). Increased sophistication in the use of mnemonic strategies accounts for some of the improvement in memory processes; adolescents are better than younger children at recognizing when they need to use a mnemonic strategy, at selecting an appropriate strategy, and at actually deploying it. They are also better at using external memory aids and outside sources of information to solve problems—for example, taking notes, writing themselves reminders, and remembering where to find information they need for solving a particular problem (Flavell, Miller, and Miller, 1993).

Another factor in adolescent advances in both memory and attentional processes may be an increase in available cognitive processing capacity, as proposed by Robbie Case (1985). Case attributes this increased capacity partly to **automatization** of basic cognitive processes. As adolescents become increasingly practiced at attentional and memory tasks, these processes become less effortful and more automatic. As basic cognitive processes become more automatic, adolescents have more cognitive resources available to devote to more complex cognitive tasks.

A good example of automatization is learning to drive. When you first started driving a car, chances are you devoted most of your attention to making sure each task involved in driving was done accurately and in sequence. Coordinating gas pedal, clutch, and brake, steering, checking the rearview mirror, watching oncoming traffic, and keeping track of where you were trying to go may at times have resulted in an information overload. As you gained experience and confidence as a driver, however, these tasks became increasingly automatic, until they seemed like second nature. Today you probably use the processing capacity freed up by this automatization for such additional activities as conversing with passengers, singing along with the radio, juggling fast-food containers, and thinking about what you need to do when you get to your destination.

Another factor that may help to explain adolescents' increased cognitive sophistication is their expanding knowledge base. Compared to younger children, adolescents have a larger store of general knowledge and a greater likeli-

Automatization:
The tendency for basic cognitive processes to become less effortful and more automatic with practice.

hood of extensive specialized knowledge in particular areas. As we discussed in Chapter 11, extensive knowledge in a specific domain leads to improved performance on memory tasks in that domain, even for children (Chi, 1978). During early and middle adolescence, specialized abilities and skills become increasingly prominent (Keating, 1990). The result is that teenagers' apparent level of cognitive sophistication is likely to vary, depending on what content area is being tested.

However, adolescents' knowledge base does not always have a positive impact on their cognitive functioning and education. Especially in technical and scientific areas, adolescents often have strong misconceptions that are amazingly resistant to correction (Carey, 1986; diSessa, 1988). Even within a specific domain, such as physics, their knowledge is often fragmented and not part of a coherent theory.

COGNITIVE SOCIALIZATION

Cognitive socialization refers to the influence of social environment on the development of cognitive skills. Social environment includes not only influences in the immediate environment, such as interactions with friends, family, and teachers, but also influences from the larger social, economic, and cultural contexts. Recent thinking and research in this area have been heavily influenced by the ideas of Vygotsky, as we discussed in Chapters 9 and 11. Compared to the Piagetian and information-processing approaches, relatively little research has been done on the impact of cognitive socialization on adolescents' thinking. However, there is evidence that social factors do play an important role, and the practical implications of cognitive socialization are considerable (Keating, 1990).

To begin with, it appears that individual social interaction plays a key role in the cognitive advances of adolescence. Adolescents do not simply invent principles of logical reasoning and effective approaches to problem solving on their own. Instead, especially during early adolescence, discussion with others, individually or in small groups, seems to foster the emergence of higher-order thinking skills (Newmann, 1991; Resnick, 1986). Some of this improvement occurs through direct instruction, as when a parent or teacher suggests a strategy for memorizing material for a test. But the reason for much of the impact of social interaction is that it provides a setting for trying out ideas, responding to opposing points of view, and learning to evaluate the soundness of arguments and evidence.

At the broader social level, schools are the institutions that play the most obvious role in adolescents' cognitive socialization. Much of the research into the impact of schooling on adolescent thinking has emphasized achievement-test results. This research has prompted much concern about test score declines in the United States and deficits in American teenagers' performance compared to that of adolescents in other industrialized countries (Keating, 1990; Stevenson, 1995). Unfortunately, the emphasis on improving achievement-test scores may have contributed to educational practices that work against the development of higher-order cognitive skills. For example, one of the best ways to foster critical thinking and mastery of subject matter is to provide extensive opportunities for substantive student-teacher discourse. However, in typical secondary school classrooms, less than 10 percent of instructional time is devoted to such discourse (Goodlad, 1984). (For a discussion of how schools can encourage the development of critical thinking, see the box on p. 536.)

A variety of other cultural factors are also involved in adolescents' cognitive socialization. Some researchers have argued that television has an impact on cognitive functioning, by means of both its content and the format in which it presents information (Keating, 1990). Many commercials, for example, present large amounts of information, much of it irrelevant, in a short period of time; the effect is to discourage critical thinking and reasoned decision making. The frequent shifts of topic and the rapid pace at which information is presented on television encourage a style of information processing that is in many ways the opposite of what schools typically seek to develop in their students. Experience with other media, such as computers and video games, may also have an impact on adolescents' thinking processes and, perhaps more important, on which cognitive skills they perceive to be most useful. A genuine understanding of adolescents' day-to-day cognitive skills depends in part on further study of these issues.

SOCIAL COGNITIVE CHANGES OF ADOLESCENCE

The new cognitive skills of adolescence do much more than simply allow teenagers to think more systematically and with more mature logic when solving problems in math and science. These same skills also have an impact on adolescents' reasoning in the social domain. For instance, their effects can be seen in a new kind of egocentrism that develops during adolescence, an egocentrism quite unlike that displayed by younger children. The effects of new cognitive skills can also be seen in the new ways that adolescents are able to reason about moral issues.

ADOLESCENT EGOCENTRISM

Egocentrism involves a failure to distinguish one's own point of view from a more objective conception of reality. Young infants, for example, do not realize that objects continue to exist even when they are not looking at them. Later, as children acquire object permanence, this kind of egocentrism disappears, but other kinds linger throughout the preschool years. For instance, you saw in Chapter 9 that when 4-year-olds select a gift for an adult, they act as if the adult's desires are the same as their own. The cognitive development that occurs during middle childhood frees youngsters from this and other forms of early egocentrism. Then, during adolescence, dramatic new cognitive abilities develop. Youngsters are now able to think about their own thinking and to consider abstract possibilities. These new abilities give rise to a new kind of egocentrism.

In describing adolescent egocentrism, David Elkind (1967) stresses the concept of an **imaginary audience.** By this he means teenagers' unjustified concern that they are the focus of other people's attention. Because adolescents can think about other people's thoughts, they are able to consider what others might be thinking of them. You saw an example of such self-consciousness in Meryl's certainty that the whole world was staring at her long arms. Notice how Meryl's cognitive ability to dwell on others' opinions interacted with her awareness of the physical changes of puberty. These physical changes are a major

Imaginary audience: Teenagers' unjustified concern that they are the focus of other people's attention.

The physical changes of puberty, combined with adolescents' newfound ability to imagine what others are thinking, often lead to a preoccupation with physical appearance.

source of concern for adolescents and are one reason why they turn their thoughts to others' opinions of them. This kind of egocentrism may help explain the adolescent's desire for privacy; teens who believe that others are viewing them negatively want privacy in order to escape their imaginary audiences. Oddly enough, the imaginary audience concept may also help explain why adolescents sometimes act in a loud and boorish manner, thus drawing real attention to themselves. If they think that others are already observing them critically, then behaving badly should not make any difference.

Personal fable: Teenagers' exaggerated belief in their own uniqueness.

Another aspect of adolescent egocentrism described by Elkind is the **personal fable**—teenagers' belief that they are unique and that no one has ever before had the same thoughts or feelings they are having. Elkind (1978) gives the example of the adolescent girl who says to her mother, "You just don't know how it feels to be in love!" The girl is convinced that her emotions are beyond the capacity of anyone else (especially adults) to know or understand. The personal fable can also include feelings of invulnerability to risks and physical dangers. Teenagers' belief in their own uniqueness often extends to a sense that bad things are unlikely to happen to them. For example, they may discount the likelihood that they will have an accident if they drive too fast or that they will get pregnant or catch a sexually transmitted disease if they engage in unprotected sex.

One reason adolescents develop this egocentric viewpoint is that their new cognitive skills allow them to think about concepts with which they have little actual experience, such as sex and romantic love. However, because many of these issues are quite personal, they seldom discuss them with adults. Lacking a broader perspective for viewing their new thoughts and feelings, they come to the conclusion that these thoughts and feelings are unique to them. Eventually, communication with close friends usually helps dispel personal fables. By midadolescence, when youngsters have a better understanding of the fact that many of their thoughts and feelings are shared by others, they begin to lose the sense of being different from everyone else.

Other factors besides reasoning skills may be associated with the emergence of adolescent egocentrism. Brian O'Connor and Jeannie Nikolic (1990) found that egocentrism in high school and college students was more clearly associated with the process of forming a personal identity than it was with formal operational reasoning. Perhaps the self-concerns and social demands associated with identity development heighten adolescents' sense of being at center stage and of being unique. We will discuss issues of identity development further in Chapter 14.

MORAL REASONING

Another area in the social domain in which the cognitive advances of adolescence have an impact is *moral reasoning*—the process of thinking and making judgments about the right course of action in a given situation. Piaget (1932/1965) included the development of moral reasoning within his broad theory of cognitive development. Later, Lawrence Kohlberg (1958, 1969) expanded on Piaget's approach, producing a six-stage model of how moral reasoning changes with age.

PIAGET'S MODEL

Piaget's model begins with an amoral stage, which is characteristic of children until about the age of 7. Then, during the subperiod of concrete operations, the stage of **moral realism** emerges. Children at this age treat morality as absolute and moral constraints as unalterable. They see behavior as either totally right or totally wrong, and they believe in *immanent justice,* a kind of inherent retribution. If they break a moral precept, they think that God or some other moral authority will make bad things happen to them. In addition, when asked to judge whether an action is right or wrong, children in this stage base their answer on the consequences of the action and tend to ignore the intentions of the actor.

Piaget's next stage, called **autonomous morality,** is usually attained late in childhood or early in adolescence. Now children see morality as relative to the situation. In judging whether a particular action is right or wrong, they consider intentions as well as consequences. Youngsters at this stage also recognize the possibility of diverse opinions regarding moral standards. They no longer consider moral rules to be absolute. Instead, they see them as the result of social agreement: these rules can change if people's values change.

Piaget believed that moral development is a direct consequence of both cognitive development and increased social experience. For instance, as their centration declines, elementary school children become able to consider consequences and intentions simultaneously when judging the morality of an act. Later, in adolescence, the ability to consider systematically one's own and others' opinions makes possible the recognition of different moral viewpoints and the idea that moral rules are based on social agreement.

KOHLBERG'S MODEL

Kohlberg's model of moral development is broadly similar to Piaget's, although Kohlberg divided development into more stages. Kohlberg derived his stages by presenting subjects of different ages with moral dilemmas to solve. Table 13.2 gives an example of one of these dilemmas, along with examples of responses typical of people at each of Kohlberg's six stages. Responses are assigned to stages on the basis of the reasons given for the choice that is made, not on the basis of the choice itself. At each stage, both "pro" and "con" choices are possible.

Kohlberg's first two stages are part of a broader period of **preconventional morality**—"preconventional" in the sense that the judgments children make are not based on social conventions, rules, or laws. During stage 1, "good" behavior is based on a desire to avoid punishment imposed by some external authority. Kohlberg called this the *obedience and punishment orientation.* In stage 2, "good" is whatever satisfies one's own needs (even if indirectly, as in helping another person so that he or she will help you). Actions are motivated by a desire for reward or benefit, rather than by a desire to avoid punishment. Kohlberg called this the *hedonistic and instrumental orientation,* meaning an orientation toward obtaining pleasure and getting what one wants.

As children advance into the next two stages, the period of **conventional morality,** their moral judgments are based on internalized standards that arise from concrete experience in the social world. Kohlberg called their reasoning

Moral realism:
In Piaget's theory, the stage in which children treat morality as absolute and moral constraints as unalterable.

Autonomous morality:
In Piaget's theory, the stage in which children see morality as relative to the situation.

Preconventional morality:
In Kohlberg's theory, moral reasoning based on fear of punishment or desire for reward.

Conventional morality:
In Kohlberg's theory, moral reasoning based on opinions of others or formal laws.

TABLE 13.2
KOHLBERG'S HEINZ DILEMMA AND REPRESENTATIVE RESPONSES

Dilemma

In Europe, a woman was near death from a special kind of cancer. There was one drug that the doctors thought might save her. It was a form of radium that a druggist in the same town had recently discovered. The drug was expensive to make, but the druggist was charging ten times what the drug cost him to make. He paid $200 for the radium and charged $2000 for a small dose of the drug. The sick woman's husband, Heinz, went to everyone he knew to borrow the money, but he could only get together about $1,000, which is half what it cost. He told the druggist that his wife was dying and asked him to sell it cheaper or let him pay later. But the druggist said: "No, I discovered the drug and I'm going to make money from it." So Heinz got desperate and broke into the man's store to steal the drug for his wife. Should the husband have done that?

PRECONVENTIONAL MORALITY
Stage 1—Obedience and Punishment Orientation
    Pro— "If you let your wife die, you will get in trouble. You'll be blamed for not spending the money to save her and there'll be an investigation of you and the druggist for your wife's death."
    Con—"You shouldn't steal the drug because you'll be caught and sent to jail if you do. If you do get away, your conscience would bother you thinking how the police would catch up with you at any minute."
Stage 2—Hedonistic and Instrumental Orientation
    Pro— "If you do happen to get caught, you could give the drug back and you wouldn't get much of a sentence. It wouldn't bother you much to serve a little jail term, if you have your wife when you get out."
    Con—"He may not get much of a jail term if he steals the drug, but his wife will probably die before he gets out so it won't do him much good. If his wife dies, he shouldn't blame himself; it wasn't his fault she has cancer."

CONVENTIONAL MORALITY
Stage 3—Good-Boy, Good-Girl Orientation
    Pro— "No one will think you're bad if you steal the drug, but your family will think you're an inhuman husband if you don't. If you let your wife die, you'll never be able to look anybody in the face again."
    Con—"It isn't just the druggist who will think you're a criminal; everyone else will too. After you steal it, you'll feel bad thinking how you've brought dishonor on your family and yourself; you won't be able to face anyone again."
Stage 4—Authority or Law-and-Order Orientation
    Pro— "If you have any sense of honor, you won't let your wife die because you're afraid to do the only thing that will save her. You'll always feel guilty that you caused her death if you don't do your duty to her."
    Con—"You're desperate and you may not know you're doing wrong when you steal the drug. But you'll know you did wrong after you're punished and sent to jail. You'll always feel guilt for your dishonesty and lawbreaking."

POSTCONVENTIONAL OR PRINCIPLED MORALITY
Stage 5—Social Contract Orientation
    Pro— "You'd lose other people's respect, not gain it, if you don't steal. If you let your wife die, it would be out of fear, not out of reasoning it out. So you'd just lose self-respect and probably the respect of others too."
    Con—"You would lose your standing and respect in the community and violate the law. You'd lose respect for yourself if you're carried away by emotion and forget the long-range point of view."
Stage 6—Hierarchy of Principles Orientation
    Pro—"If you don't steal the drug and let your wife die, you'd always condemn yourself for it afterward. You wouldn't be blamed and you would have lived up to the outside rule of the law, but you wouldn't have lived up to your own standards of conscience."
    Con—"If you stole the drug, you wouldn't be blamed by other people but you'd condemn yourself because you wouldn't have lived up to your own conscience and standards of honesty."

SOURCES: Kohlberg, 1969, p. 379; Rest, 1979.

According to Kohlberg, it is in adolescence that most people begin to relate moral judgments to the laws of society and concerns about harm to others.

"conventional" because it focuses either on the opinions of others or on formal laws. In stage 3, the child's goal is to act in ways that others will approve of. Actions are motivated more by a fear of disapproval than by a fear of punishment. This stage is called the *good-boy, nice-girl orientation.* In stage 4, the basis of moral judgments shifts to concern over doing one's duty as prescribed by society's laws. Concerns about possible dishonor or concrete harm to others replace concerns about other people's disapproval. Kohlberg called this the *authority or law-and-order orientation.*

The last major period in Kohlberg's model is called **postconventional or principled morality.** In this period, people transcend conventional reasoning and begin to focus on more abstract principles underlying right and wrong. In the first stage of this period, Kohlberg's stage 5, the goal is to meet one's obligation to help keep society running smoothly. Particular laws may be seen as somewhat arbitrary, but they are nevertheless deemed important because they allow people to live together in reasonable harmony. At this stage, actions are motivated by a desire to maintain self-respect and the respect of peers. Kohlberg called this the *social contract orientation.* In the sixth and final stage of moral reasoning, the goal is to make decisions on the basis of the highest relevant moral principle. At this level of thinking, the rules of society are integrated with the dictates of conscience to produce a hierarchy of moral principles. Concern shifts to avoiding self-condemnation for violating one's own principles. Kohlberg called this stage the *hierarchy of principles orientation.*

How are Kohlberg's stages of moral reasoning related to Piaget's stages of cognitive development? You might guess that children at the preoperational level in Piaget's cognitive system (ages 2 to 6) would be in Kohlberg's period of preconventional morality, that youngsters at the level of concrete operations (ages 7 to 12) would be in Kohlberg's period of conventional morality, and that adolescents at the level of formal operations (over age 12) would be in Kohlberg's period of postconventional morality. These are very reasonable guesses, but they turn out to be wrong. The actual emergence of each of Kohlberg's levels of moral reasoning seems to lag behind the cognitive skills

Postconventional or principled morality: In Kohlberg's theory, moral reasoning based on abstract principles underlying right and wrong.

needed to engage in that kind of thinking. Kohlberg (1976) concluded that preconventional morality (stages 1 and 2) is characteristic of most children until about age 9, and that most adolescents and adults are at the level of conventional morality (stages 3 and 4). One long-term longitudinal study found that stage 3 moral reasoning (concern about other people's disapproval) peaks in midadolescence and then declines, whereas stage 4 moral reasoning (concern about doing one's duty) increases dramatically in later adolescence and young adulthood (Colby et al., 1983). Probably only a minority of people ever reach the postconventional, or principled, level of moral reasoning.

CRITICISMS OF KOHLBERG'S MODEL

The most common objection to both Piaget's and Kohlberg's models of moral development is that measures of moral reasoning are often related only weakly or not at all to actual moral behavior (Krebs, 1967; Rest, 1983). Thus, adolescents may talk about doing their duty and following established rules, but when it comes to a real-life situation, they may ignore these rules. This weak relationship between thought and action has led many to wonder how meaningful it is to talk about stages of moral reasoning.

Others have objected to the idea that the form of moral reasoning can be separated from the content of moral judgments (see Rest, 1983). What matters in Kohlberg's model is not the particular solution a person offers in response to a moral dilemma, but rather the reasoning behind the solution. Critics question whether the content of a moral choice can always be ignored in assessing a person's level of moral thinking.

Kohlberg's theory of moral reasoning has also been criticized for the method used to gather the data on which it is based. Questions have been raised about the method's reliability (Kurtines and Greif, 1974). Will a child evaluated one day by a particular researcher be assessed at the same moral level a few days later when scored by someone else? This problem has been exacerbated by frequent revisions in Kohlberg's scoring system as well as in the theoretical framework used to support it (Rest, 1983). Some think that a different approach to assessment may be preferable. For instance, James Rest (1983) has developed an objectively scored test of moral reasoning that overcomes many of the limitations inherent in Kohlberg's method.

One of the most controversial challenges to Kohlberg's approach is the contention that it is biased against women. Carol Gilligan (1982) argues that women tend to respond to moral dilemmas on the basis of concepts such as caring, personal relationships, and interpersonal obligations—concepts that are likely to be scored at the stage 3 level. Men, in contrast, tend to appeal to abstract concepts, such as justice and equity—concepts that are likely to be scored at stage 5 or even stage 6. These general patterns are believed to result from the different ways in which males and females are socialized in our culture. If this is true, it doesn't seem fair to consider a woman to be at a lower level of moral reasoning because she has been taught since childhood to value compassion toward others and social obligations. In response to Gilligan's criticism, the most recent version of Kohlberg's scoring system was revised to reduce the bias against responses based on caring for others (Colby et al., 1983).

However, it is not entirely certain that Gilligan's criticism is warranted. One review of research found no consistent gender differences in the stages at which people were scored when responding to Kohlberg's dilemmas (Walker, 1984). In fact, when sex differences existed, women actually tended to score higher than men (Funk, 1986; Thoma, 1986). It is also clear that males and females

Carol Gilligan has pointed out that moral reasoning involves issues of caring for other people as well as issues of abstract justice.

consider issues related to both caring and justice in their moral reasoning (Cortese, 1989; Galotti, 1989; Walker, 1989). Nevertheless, the questions Gilligan raised have both highlighted an aspect of moral reasoning that had been neglected and broadened the issues considered in research on moral development.

A final criticism of Kohlberg's theory is that it is culture-specific, that it reflects concerns about individualism that are peculiar to middle-class groups in complex, urban societies (Snarey, 1985). As a result, members of less complex, more traditional cultures tend to give responses to Kohlberg's dilemmas that are scored at lower stages, even though their responses reflect the moral concerns of their own cultures (Edwards, 1982). For example, many traditional cultures are more *collectivist* than North American and western European cultures are. That is, the well-being of the group is assumed to be of greater importance than the well-being of any one individual. In collectivist cultures, meeting one's obligations to family and the community and submitting to the authority of elders are often considered the highest moral principles. In Kohlberg's system, however, reasoning along those lines tends to be scored at stage 3 or 4. These findings, along with Gilligan's criticisms, emphasize the need to consider socialization history and cultural context in evaluating the development of moral reasoning.

As we have seen in this chapter, physical and cognitive development are closely interrelated during adolescence. Neurological development appears to contribute to the emergence of increasingly efficient and abstract thought. This higher-order thinking makes adolescents self-reflective, painfully aware of the many changes occurring in their bodies, and at times preoccupied with how they may appear to others. As was the case throughout childhood, cognitive development is also inextricably connected with social development. Our examination of adolescent social cognition has provided some insight into the connections between cognitive and social development in adolescence. We will explore this connection further in Chapter 14.

Researchers and educators alike have expressed concern about the critical thinking skills of American adolescents. Although in theory the cognitive advances that occur during adolescence should lead to increased critical thinking, in practice this does not always happen. In a variety of subject areas, including science, math, and social studies, adolescents in the United States show distressingly low levels of critical thinking (Eylon and Linn, 1991; Newmann, 1991; Resnick, 1986). It is clear that critical thinking, like formal operations, does not *automatically* emerge in adolescence.

Critical thinking involves three key elements: (1) understanding a problem in more than a superficial way; (2) logically analyzing the problem and its possible solutions; and (3) selecting an appropriate solution based on that understanding and analysis. Adolescents' cognitive *competence*—their enhanced knowledge base, memory abilities, and logical thinking skills—should allow them to do all three of these things. However, as we have seen in this chapter's discussion of formal operations, their *performance* often does not reach the expected levels.

Adolescents may fail to think critically for a number of reasons, both cognitive and social. They may not recognize a situation as one that demands critical thinking. They may lack the specific content knowledge needed to go beyond a superficial understanding of the situation. Their grasp of the principles of logic may be incomplete. Emotional factors or social pressures may sway them to make what seem like illogical choices. Finally, they may not value critical thinking, or they may see it as something that is not valued by the people around them.

Many attempts have been made to teach critical thinking to adolescents. Usually, the focus has been on teaching specific skills, such as how to solve logic problems or how to use memory strategies. Unfortunately, evaluations of these programs have usually involved testing students' ability to solve the same kinds of problems on which they were trained. There has been little evidence that these skills generalize to other kinds of problems, to other content areas, or to settings outside the classroom (Keating, 1990).

Daniel Keating, a psychologist who studies adolescent thinking and its relationship to education, argues that critical thinking should be seen as a *disposition*—a general approach to problem solving—rather than a set of specific skills. Looked at from this perspective, the task of teaching critical thinking becomes one of encouraging students to adopt a habit of thought, a way of looking at the world, that may initially be foreign to them.

Keating suggests several ways in which parents and teachers can foster the habit of critical thinking. According to him, the process actually begins long before adolescence, when children learn basic reading and math skills and begin to acquire knowledge in core subject areas. These skills and knowledge provide a foundation on which critical thinking can be built.

Success in encouraging critical thinking in adolescents depends on four key factors. First, teaching the *process* of critical thinking should be embedded in the teaching of *content,* or expertise in particular domains. Critical thinking is an abstract ability, but it must be taught in concrete contexts. Trying to teach critical thinking skills as a separate subject, in isolation from core content areas, is ineffective and does not help students see critical thinking as a general disposition. Conversely, teaching content knowledge without reference to critical thinking fosters a tendency to accept information uncritically.

Second, adolescents must be convinced of the value of critical thinking. Teachers and parents need to show adolescents practical applications for critical thinking, talk explicitly about its value, and model its use in their own problem solving.

Third, adolescents need to be given ample opportunities to practice critical thinking. One of the best settings for such practice is extended discussions with others who can challenge adolescents' reasoning and push them to provide clarification and additional evidence for their views. Teachers and parents are usually better able to serve this function than peers are, but many adolescents have only limited opportunities for this kind of discussion with adults.

Fourth, adolescents need to be encouraged to explore subjects in depth over time. This sort of exploration fosters critical thinking by expanding students' knowledge bases and by providing additional opportunities to practice critical thinking. Unfortunately, the typical American high school curriculum is fragmented and superficial, offering few chances for this sort of extended study.

CHAPTER SUMMARY

1. Adolescence extends roughly from age 12 through the late teens. Because of the extensive changes that occur during these years, it makes sense to divide it into substages—early adolescence, middle adolescence, and late adolescence.

2. A stepped-up production of sex hormones late in middle childhood brings about the beginning of **puberty,** the transition to sexual maturity. This sexual maturation is accompanied by the development of **secondary sex characteristics** and a noticeable spurt in growth. There are substantial individual differences in the onset of puberty and the pace of its many changes. The physical changes of puberty are linked to changes in other areas of adolescents' lives, including body image, social relationships, and problem behaviors. The impact of these changes differs for boys and girls and for early- and late-maturing adolescents.

3. There is mounting evidence that the brain undergoes substantial changes during adolescence. These changes include **hemispheric specialization** and a decrease in the number of connections among brain cells. The results of these changes are decreased **plasticity** but increased efficiency in brain functioning.

4. Researchers generally agree on the broad outlines of the cognitive abilities that emerge in adolescence. First, teenagers are able to apply logical thinking skills to the possible as well as to the actual. Second, they can think about relationships among abstract concepts. Third, their thinking becomes even more logical and systematic than it was in childhood; .it now includes the ability to use **hypothetico-deductive reasoning.**

5. Piaget attributed the cognitive advances of adolescents to their developing ability to use principles of propositional logic, which he called **formal operations.** He believed that the cognitive skills involved in formal operations were qualitatively different from any skills present earlier in childhood. Piaget based his theory on studies of adolescents' reasoning as they conducted various scientific experiments, including the law of floating bodies study, the pendulum study, and the all possible combinations study.

6. Although psychologists generally agree that Piaget did a good job of describing the range of thinking skills that emerge in adolescence, they are less satisfied with his explanation of adolescent cognitive development. Formal operational thinking appears to develop more gradually and to be less pervasive among older adolescents than Piaget thought. This finding, however, may simply mean that people do not always use their highest level of cognitive competence. Formal operations also seem to be more cul-

ture-bound than the earlier stages of Piaget's theory. Contrary to Piaget's expectations, training in formal operations seems to be effective under some circumstances.

7. Other approaches to explaining adolescent cognitive development include the information-processing and cognitive socialization approaches. Research on adolescents' information-processing abilities indicates continuing improvement in attention and memory skills, especially in early adolescence. These improvements are probably due to some combination of increased capacity, improved cognitive strategies, **automatization** of basic mental processes, and expanded knowledge base. The cognitive socialization approach emphasizes the influence of social environment on cognitive development. There is evidence that individual social interaction plays a role in the emergence of higher-order thinking skills. Schools can provide a setting for this type of interaction, but often they do not. Television and other cultural influences may also have an impact on adolescents' thinking processes and on which cognitive skills they value.

8. The new cognitive skills of adolescence allow teenagers to display a new kind of egocentrism. Because adolescents can now think extensively about other people's thoughts, they are able to be self-conscious about others' possibly viewing them negatively. This feeling often promotes the sense of having an **imaginary audience,** an unjustified concern about being the focus of everyone else's attention. Young teenagers often also develop **personal fables,** based on a belief that no one else has ever before had their special thoughts and feelings.

9. The cognitive skills of adolescence also give rise to increased maturity in reasoning about moral issues. Piaget believed that during adolescence youngsters reach a stage of moral reasoning called **autonomous morality,** in which morality is seen as relative to the situation, and the possibility of diverse opinions about moral standards is recognized. Another stage theory of moral reasoning is that of Lawrence Kohlberg, which consists of three broad levels: **preconventional morality, conventional morality,** and **postconventional or principled morality.** Most adolescents have reached the stage of conventional morality, in which concerns about disapproval of others and respect for authority predominate. Stage theories of moral reasoning have been criticized because of the weak connection between moral thought and moral action, the methods used to assess moral reasoning, and possible gender and cultural biases.

Chapter 14

Social and Emotional Development in Adolescence

I just have all these feelings and things inside . . . The feelings are so strong, and my parents don't understand. They won't let me do anything. I'm afraid that by the time I'm old enough to do the things I need to do—by the time they'll let me—I won't have the feelings anymore.

These words, spoken by a 15-year-old girl during an interview with one of the authors of this book in the 1960s, illustrate how timeless the central social and emotional issues of adolescence are. Adolescence is a wonderful time of life, filled with new feelings, a higher level of self-awareness, and a sense of almost unlimited horizons to explore. But adolescence is also a very challenging period of development. The new feelings that teenagers experience are strong and imperative, demanding to be expressed. Early in adolescence the emerging inner sense of self is not yet firmly established and at times may seem so changeable that the young person wonders who he or she really is. The statement above reflects these challenges. This teenager worries that her strong feelings will disappear before she has a chance to act on them. While her parents remain important in her life, she has a sense that they are unable to understand her situation, that she cannot really share all her new thoughts and emotions with them. She also expresses frustration with the boundaries her parents continue to set for her as she moves toward greater independence.

To a large extent, this young woman is in the process of reworking many of the issues she faced in earlier developmental periods. Issues such as developing trust, establishing autonomy, increasing her feelings of competence, and expanding her sense of self are all confronting her again. This time, however, the issues are more challenging, for she has to work through them not only with her parents but also with peers who are in the throes of adolescence too. Now, though, she has cognitive and emotional resources to draw on that were not available to her when she encountered the same issues earlier in childhood. In this chapter we will explore how adolescents deal with these developmental issues in a variety of contexts—inside their own minds, in their peer relationships, in their family relationships, and in the broader worlds of school and work.

THE SOCIAL WORLD OF ADOLESCENCE: AN OVERVIEW

HOW STORMY IS ADOLESCENCE?

Many people believe that the challenges of adolescence make it an inevitably stormy and stressful period of life. Psychologists G. Stanley Hall and Anna Freud are among the developmentalists who have claimed that inner turmoil and disruption are necessary to becoming a separate, autonomous person. They argue that a difficult break with parents is essential in order to forge an identity that is independent and unique. But other psychologists believe that the struggle of adolescence has been greatly exaggerated (Hill, 1980; Steinberg, 1990). They point out that most teenagers get along well with their parents, and families that were functioning well before a child reached puberty tend to continue functioning well afterward (Block, Block, and Morrison, 1981). As with

Conflicts between parents and teenagers tend to be about everyday matters such as chores and manner of dress and grooming, not about basic values.

many controversies, both perspectives on this issue turn out to have some merit. Adolescence can be either stormy or peaceful, with the degree of turmoil varying considerably across age groups, individuals, and different domains of teenagers' lives.

Many of the studies that support the storm and stress view have investigated younger adolescents, while those that support a more harmonious view of parent-child relationships have generally looked at the later teenage years. It seems that early adolescence is a unique subphase of development during which youngsters experience more turmoil, parents more stress and dissatisfaction, and families more conflict than they have before or will in subsequent years (Collins, 1994).

There are also substantial individual differences in how conflict-ridden adolescence is. Among boys, three patterns of development have been identified (Offer and Offer, 1975). About a quarter experience *tumultuous growth,* filled with conflict and crisis; about a third show *surgent growth,* marked by periods of reasonably smooth adjustment interspersed with negative periods (anger, defiance, immaturity); and about a quarter experience *continuous growth,* characterized by self-assurance, a sense of purpose, and mutual respect between child and parents. (The remaining boys cannot be readily classified.) A similar range of individual variation occurs with girls, although early in adolescence girls may have more struggles with self-esteem than boys do (Harter, 1990). Apparently, how stormy or peaceful the teenage years are depends partly on the particular developmental history and personal characteristics of the individual involved.

High levels of stress and conflict during adolescence are often part of a generally difficult developmental pathway. Behavior and adjustment problems are most common among adolescents who have had similar problems earlier in childhood (Caspi and Moffitt, 1991). In addition, adolescents who report problems in one area of their lives, such as in their relationships with their parents, are more likely than their peers to have problems in other areas as well (Rutter et al., 1976).

Whether adolescence seems stormy or peaceful also depends on what aspects of it are considered. Teenagers do report more negative moods than younger children do, especially in early adolescence (Larson and Lampeman-Petraitis, 1989). In one study, nearly half the teenagers interviewed reported feeling unhappy (Rutter et al., 1976). But this unhappiness reflects mainly *inner* turmoil, rather than overt conflict with others. Teenagers and their parents argue most about mundane matters such as appearance, homework, phone or stereo use, and household chores (Steinberg, 1990). There is seldom much of a clash over basic values and beliefs (Collins, 1994; Montemayer and Hanson, 1985; Rutter et al., 1976). Very few teenagers (only 3 percent of females and 5 to 9 percent of males) express outright rejection of their parents (Rutter et al., 1976). Most continue to have positive feelings toward their parents, even though they may not *express* them as much as they did in childhood (Collins, 1994). The majority of teenagers continue to get along with their parents, to be influenced by them, and to respect the need for the limits they set.

Thus, although stress and conflict may occur during adolescence, they are far from the only themes of this period. The typical conflicts within the family are best thought of as arising out of normal self-assertion, not rebellion and defiance. Parents for a time may see their child as "impossible" or "lost." But this period soon gives way to a realignment in which the adolescent carves out a new place within the family, a new stance toward the world, and a new sense of self-awareness (Steinberg, 1990). Moreover, even while becoming more autonomous from parents, most teenagers remain emotionally connected to them and highly value their relationships with them (Collins, 1994).

A CROSS-CULTURAL PERSPECTIVE ON ADOLESCENCE

Even though parent-child conflict is seldom severe and prolonged in adolescence, the *inner* sense of unrest that teenagers feel can be very unsettling to them. The nature of modern Western societies may help to explain these negative inner feelings. Complex, industrialized democracies demand skilled and knowledgeable adults. Young people must therefore learn a great deal before they are given the responsibilities and privileges of adulthood. This makes for a protracted period of dependency on parents, often lasting well into the twenties. During this time, young people are also expected to delay full entry into adult sexual roles. No wonder adolescents have been called "marginal persons" (Lewin, 1951). Although they are physically no longer children, they have much more to learn and are not yet ready to be launched into the world of adults. The sense of being in a "no-man's-land" between childhood and adulthood can give rise to feelings of ambiguity, impatience, and frustration.

In nonindustrialized societies the transition to adult roles often begins much earlier than in our own. From an early age, children in these cultures are given much responsibility, such as taking care of younger siblings, making tools and utensils, or helping their parents in the fields (Whiting and Edwards, 1988). One such society is Samoa in the south Pacific. When anthropologist Margaret Mead studied its people in the 1920s, she found that adolescence was not a stressful period, but rather one of gradually maturing interests and activities (Mead, 1925/1939). Samoans not only began the transition to adulthood early, they also let it proceed gradually. Although Mead's characterization of some

In some cultures the transition from childhood to adulthood is clearly marked by formal ceremonies called rites of passage.

aspects of Samoan culture has been questioned (Freeman, 1983), her insights about the cultural basis of adolescence are still considered valid (Coté, 1992).

In other traditional societies the transition to adulthood is much more abrupt. Among the Gusii of Kenya, for example, children are given greatly expanded duties in a short period of time (Whiting and Edwards, 1988). Societies with abrupt adolescent transitions often have special ceremonies, called **puberty rites,** or **rites of passage,** to mark the entry into new adult roles. Children anticipate these rites for years in advance. There is no question in their minds about when they will be considered adults.

People in our own society are also quite abrupt in their expectation that young people "start acting like adults," but the timing of this transition to adulthood is rather ambiguous. Adolescents receive conflicting messages about their status and are allowed to take on different adult responsibilities at widely varying ages. For example, they can drive a car and work at age 16, they can vote and serve in the military at age 18, but in most states they cannot legally drink alcohol until age 21. Although many parents have in mind a certain time at which their children should "be on their own," earning a living and acting "grown-up," there is no universal agreement on when this time is. For some it is graduation from high school, for others graduation from college, and for others landing a first job. This ambiguity, which is a product of our culture and the different demands placed on people who pursue different careers, creates special challenges for both adolescents and their parents.

Puberty rite/rite of passage:
A ceremony that marks the transition from childhood to adulthood.

THE TASKS OF ADOLESCENCE

Regardless of how the transition to adulthood takes place, important tasks face every adolescent. One involves establishing a personal **identity**—a sense of an integrated, coherent, goal-directed self. Identity development is a complex process, involving an understanding of the self, of one's relationships with others, and of one's values and roles in society. Erik Erikson (1981) believed that establishing a personal identity was the central task of adolescence.

Identity:
A sense of an integrated, coherent, and goal-directed self, including an understanding of one's relationships with others, and of one's values and roles in society.

A second major task of adolescence is achieving a new level of closeness and trust with peers. Often this is accomplished first with peers of the same gender before moving on to intimate cross-gender relationships (Hartup and Laursen, 1993).

A third major task is acquiring a new status in the family. In white, middle-class families, relationships with parents generally become more equal as the child grows more independent and responsible. Family ties are not severed; connections with parents merely take a different form (Collins, 1994; Grotevant, 1992). The exact nature of the change in family roles that occurs at adolescence varies across cultural groups, however. For example, in Asian and Mexican families that have immigrated to the United States, parent-child relationships tend to remain quite formal, with children enjoying little power even after adolescence (C. Cooper, in press).

A fourth major task of adolescence is moving toward a more autonomous stance with respect to the larger world. This includes taking on more personal responsibility for schoolwork and perhaps finding a job and becoming more financially independent from parents. It also includes anticipating future adult roles and making career choices. These changes cannot be made simply by following parental wishes and plans. Instead, teenagers must make decisions themselves and actively translate them into practice.

In summary, adolescents continue the process of becoming separate individuals while remaining connected to others. They elaborate and evolve a distinctive self-system while also elaborating a social network that now includes romantic partners as well as parents and friends. In the remainder of this chapter, we will examine each of these tasks of adolescence in detail.

DEVELOPMENT OF THE SELF

THE SELF-CONCEPT DURING ADOLESCENCE

Adolescents' progress toward a personal identity involves continuing changes in their self-concepts, which have been developing since early childhood. Just as younger and older teenagers differ in how they think and reason, so do they differ in how they view themselves.

CHANGES FROM MIDDLE CHILDHOOD TO ADOLESCENCE

Studies in which adolescents are encouraged to talk about themselves or write self descriptions reveal several ways in which self-concepts change from middle childhood to adolescence (Harter, 1990; Damon and Hart, 1988; Montemayor and Eisen, 1977). First, self-concepts become more *differentiated*. Rather than seeing themselves as always having certain traits, teenagers evolve a more complex picture that takes situations into account. For instance, an adolescent might say, "I generally follow the rules, *except* when my dad is being unfair to me." At the same time, adolescents' self-concepts begin to be differentiated across various relationships, settings, and areas of competence. An adolescent's self-description might include the following assessments: "I'm pretty grouchy with my family, but I'm much more easy-going with my friends. I usually do what I'm supposed to at school, but when I go out on weekends, I know how to have a good time. I do well in my classes, but I'm not so good at sports."

Second, teenagers' self-concepts become more *individuated*, more distinct from the self-concepts of others. Whereas younger children often describe themselves in terms of similarities with peers, adolescents describe themselves more in terms of what makes them different from others. Although this tendency begins in middle childhood, it becomes more noticeable in early adolescence.

Third, teenagers' self-concepts include a particular concern with traits that "define [their] place and manner of operating in the social network" (Damon and Hart, 1988, p. 64). In middle childhood, children's self-concepts are social in the sense that they compare themselves to others. Young adolescents' self-concepts focus more on identifying their way of interacting with others. Adolescents' self descriptions are likely to include statements like the following: "I'm not very popular at school," "I like to take charge of things with my friends." "People like me because I'm friendly and outgoing."

Fourth, teenagers increasingly view themselves as *self-reflective*—as capable of thinking about and evaluating the self. Because they see themselves in this increasingly introspective manner, they believe that they are able to make their own choices about their values and behaviors.

Fifth, adolescents increasingly think of the self as a *coherent system* made up of diverse but integrated parts. They are able to put together the various aspects of a self-concept and make sense of it, in spite of any seeming contradictions. This achievement is supported by the advances in cognitive development that we described in Chapter 13. The logical powers of formal operational thought and the ability to coordinate multiple viewpoints allow adolescents to reconcile diverse aspects of the self and changing behavior in different situations. Their new capacities to reflect on the self and to consider a range of alternatives make it possible to examine the self at present, relate that self to past behavior, and project the self into the future with the many different roles it offers. As a result, the self becomes more cohesive and unified than ever before.

Changes in self-concept from middle childhood to adolescence are illustrated in Table 14.1, which shows young people's answers to questions regarding physical, social, and psychological aspects of themselves. You can see the increasing emphasis on styles of interaction with others and the decreasing emphasis on comparison with others. You can also see the youngsters becoming more introspective with age, more inclined to search for a deeper understanding of the self (Montemayor et al., 1990). While 9-year-olds list unquestioned truths about themselves ("I go to Marcy School; I have lots of friends"), adolescents often see themselves in terms of hypotheses: "Am I liberal?" "Am I conservative?" "Am I classifiable at all?" (Harter, 1990). Finally, you can see that by late adolescence self-concepts come to be guided by belief systems, plans, and ideologies. This allows the sense of self to be more coherent and lays the groundwork for a mature personal identity.

CHANGES FROM EARLY TO LATE ADOLESCENCE

Much of the research on changing self-concepts during the teenage years supports the view that there are two subphases of adolescent development. Young adolescents (ages 12 to 14) have an understanding of the self that is well advanced over that of elementary school children. However, by late adolescence (age 18 and up) there are further qualitative advances in how the self is viewed.

Evidence that older adolescents have a more complex, sophisticated self-understanding than younger adolescents do comes partly from the research of Robert Selman (1980), mentioned in Chapter 12. You may remember that Sel-

TABLE 14.1
SELF-DESCRIPTIONS IN CHILDHOOD AND ADOLESCENCE

MIDDLE CHILDHOOD
"I'm bigger than most kids."
"I like sports. . . . That's what most boys like."
"I feel proud when my parents cheer and let me know I did good."
"They can't read the hard books but I can."

EARLY ADOLESCENCE
"I wear glasses and kids make fun of me."
"I'm in terrific shape . . . everybody I meet respects me for it."
"I play sports. . . . All the kids like athletes."
"I treat people well and don't get into too many fights over stupid things. . . . I'll always have friends when I need them."
"I'm shy. . . . I don't have lots of friends, but the ones I have are good ones."
"I can understand them. Like when they have problems, they come to me to talk about it."

LATE ADOLESCENCE
"I don't have many things. . . . It's not fair to have a lot of things when some people don't have anything."
"I go to church every Sunday because I want to be a faithful Christian."
"It's good to be beautiful but only if it's real and not false."
"If more people did what we did the world would be a better place."
"I'm proud of being a good reader. . . . It helps you in learning a lot."

SOURCE: Damon and Hart, 1988.

man told subjects of different ages a story about a boy named Mike whose dog, Pepper, had run away. Two of Mike's friends were trying to decide if it was a good idea to buy him a new dog for his birthday. Selman probed each subject's conception of the self by asking questions about what he or she believed the thoughts and feelings of someone in Mike's position would be. He found that young adolescents understand that the self can sometimes manipulate inner experiences. "I can fool myself into thinking I don't want another puppy," one young teenager explained. However, it wasn't until older adolescence that youngsters started to grasp the notion of conscious and unconscious levels of experience. Here is how one older teenager described these levels in Mike:

> He might feel at some level that it would be unloyal to Pepper to just go out and replace the dog. He may feel guilty about it. He doesn't want to face these feelings, so he says no dog. (*Interviewer:* Is he aware of this?) Probably not. (p. 106)

Another aspect of self-understanding that differentiates early from late adolescence is an increased knowledge of how different aspects of the self are tied together into an integrated whole. Young teenagers make a start in this direction in their ability to link together their past and future selves when giving self-descriptions (Damon and Hart, 1988). They know, for example, that they do not always behave in the same way and that at times they act in ways they do not really feel. They recognize contradictions in the self and may have a sense of "phoniness" (Broughton, 1978). But it is only in later adolescence that youngsters are able to unify contradictory aspects of the self by explaining those con-

Older adolescents have a more integrated sense of self than younger adolescents, and a much greater understanding of the uniqueness and separateness of people.

traditions (Bernstein, 1980). For instance, a 15-year-old might say that he is talkative with his friends, but quiet with his family, and not be able to give a reason for this difference. An older teenager might offer an explanation based on situational factors: "I am really talkative with my friends because they are treating me like a person. My family doesn't listen to what I say, so I just don't like talking to hear myself speak" (Damon, 1983, p. 318).

THE DECLINING FRAGILITY OF THE SELF

Many of the changes in self-concept from early to late adolescence reflect an overall decline in the fragility of the self—that is, a decline in the degree to which the self is tentative and uncertain. As a youngster's sense of self emerges, it is at first very fragile. Like scientists who have just formulated a new theory, teenagers are unsure about the validity of the new self (Harter, 1990). Other people can easily challenge a young adolescent's self-concept. No wonder young adolescents appear to their parents to be much less open than they were as children. Teenagers feel they must be careful not to disclose too much, or else the new sense of self that is emerging might somehow be lost.

The feeling that the self is fragile is linked to several other beliefs and behaviors among young teenagers. First, it is tied to a concern that the self is transparent and readily scrutinized by others, which gives rise to the concern with an *imaginary audience* discussed in Chapter 13. Second, it partly explains the expressions of physical invulnerability that are part of the adolescent's *personal fable.* Imagining oneself to be indestructible can provide a defense against feelings of vulnerability that come with a tentative and uncertain sense of self. Third, it helps to account for the strict conformity of young teenagers in dress and hair style. Such conformity enables adolescents to hide their fragile sense of individual uniqueness, while simultaneously expressing their belonging to a distinct group. Finally, the fragility of the self underlies the young adolescent's tendency to fantasize many different roles. Just as play provided a safe haven for the preschooler to work through conflicts, so fantasies allow the adolescent to experiment with possible new dimensions of the self before actually committing to them. As grandiose as these fantasies sometimes are (Malcolm will end poverty; Mike will save the marine world), they may serve as beacons to draw the young person forward. Often they are part of a healthy adolescent idealism.

In time the uncertain, fragile sense of self that emerges in early adolescence becomes more firmly established. Through interactions with others, performance at school, and experiences in the larger world, teenagers' tentative beliefs about the self are increasingly confirmed (Harter, 1990). They now become more sure of themselves and less self-conscious. In several studies, researchers have demonstrated the teenager's declining belief that others are scrutinizing the self by asking subjects of different ages to complete the Imaginary Audience Scale. (Some of the items from this scale are shown in Table 14.2.) Self-conscious answers generally peak at age 12 or 13 and then drop off (Simmons, Rosenberg, and Rosenberg, 1973; Elkind and Bowen, 1979).

The decline in self-consciousness in later adolescence goes hand in hand with a growing ability for accurate self-appraisal, including one's personal weaknesses as well as one's strengths. Thus, twelfth graders are able to size up both their good and bad points realistically and integrate them into a coherent and stable sense of self.

TABLE 14.2
ITEMS FROM THE IMAGINARY AUDIENCE SCALE (IAS)

1. You have looked forward to the most exciting dress-up party of the year. You arrive after an hour's drive from home. Just as the party is beginning, you notice a grease spot on your trousers or skirt. (There is no way to borrow clothes from anyone.) Would you stay or go home?
   ____ Go home.
   ____ Stay, even though I'd feel uncomfortable.
   ____ Stay, because the grease spot wouldn't bother me.

2. Let's say some adult visitors came to your school and you were asked to tell them a little bit about yourself.
   ____ I would like that.
   ____ I would not like that.
   ____ I wouldn't care.

3. It is Friday afternoon and you have just had your hair cut in preparation for the wedding of a relative that weekend. The barber or hairdresser did a terrible job and your hair looks awful. To make it worse, that night is the most important basketball game of the season and you really want to see it, but there is no way you can keep your head covered without people asking questions. Would you stay home or go to the game anyway?
   ____ Go to the game and not worry about my hair.
   ____ Go to the game and sit where people won't notice me very much.
   ____ Stay home.

4. If you went to a party where you did not know most of the kids, would you wonder what they were thinking about you?
   ____ I wouldn't think about it.
   ____ I would wonder about that a lot.
   ____ I would wonder about that a little.

SOURCE: Elkind and Bowen, 1979, pp. 40–41.

THE CONCEPT OF PERSONAL IDENTITY

During late adolescence, the development of the self has advanced to the point where formation of a personal identity becomes possible. An individual's personal identity is more than just a self-concept. Forming a personal identity requires adolescents to integrate into a coherent whole their past experiences, their ongoing personal changes, and society's demands and expectations for their future (Grotevant, 1992; Sprinthall and Collins, 1995).

A personal identity includes the particular values, principles, and roles that an individual has adopted as his or her own. The process of identity formation typically includes selecting and preparing for a career, reevaluating religious and moral beliefs, working out a political ideology, and adopting social roles, including those related to sexuality, marriage, and parenthood (Harter, 1990).

James Marcia (1980) writes that identity refers to a *structure* of abilities, beliefs, and past experiences regarding the self. "The better developed this structure is, the more aware individuals appear to be of their own strengths and weaknesses. The less developed this structure is, the more confused individuals seem to be about their own distinctiveness from others and the more they have to rely on external sources to evaluate themselves" (p. 159).

Identity formation builds on the integrated self-concept that has typically developed by late adolescence. It is based in part on the cognitive abilities that emerge during adolescence, such as the ability to reason about relationships among abstract concepts. In addition, relationships with other people are essential to the process of identity formation.

The *social construction view* of identity formation, as proposed by James Youniss (1983), emphasizes the role of interpersonal relationships in the development of personal identity. According to Youniss, identity involves understanding one's own unique perspective and how it relates to the perspectives of others. Arriving at this understanding can be accomplished only through social interaction. More specifically, identity formation requires supportive relationships in which mutual criticisms can be aired and both sides can receive clarification and confirmation of their evolving roles. Both parents and peers provide the adolescent with relationships that are useful in this process, but they tend to make different kinds of contributions, as we will discuss shortly.

Erik Erikson referred to the struggle that teenagers encounter when trying to establish their personal identities as an **identity crisis.** At the time they take on this challenging task, adolescents are caught in the middle of two changing systems (Sprinthall and Collins, 1995). One is their own biological system, with its hormonal changes and resulting transformations in the body. This system is linked to new sexual urges, as well as to new ways of thinking and reasoning. The other is the social system in which the adolescent lives. Parents and other adults are making new demands on the young person but not always clearly and consistently. Often the teenager is expected to behave maturely, almost like an adult; yet many restrictions continue to be imposed as if the youngster were still a child. All these changes and contradictions push adolescents to reassess their notions about themselves and their place in the world. Despite the discomfort that this need for reassessment can create, Erikson maintained that adolescence is the ideal time for experimenting with various possible roles and identities, before adulthood requires serious commitments to a particular occupation or ideology.

Identity crisis:
In Erikson's theory, the struggle that teenagers experience when trying to establish their personal identities.

TABLE 14.3
JAMES MARCIA'S FOUR IDENTITY STATUSES

		Commitment to Adult Identity	
		No	Yes
Identity Exploration	No	Identity diffusion	Foreclosure
	Yes	Moratorium	Identity achievement

SOURCE: MARCIA, 1980.

INDIVIDUAL DIFFERENCES IN IDENTITY FORMATION

Adolescents vary in how easily they establish a personal identity. Some feel overwhelmed by the task; others retreat from it. Some get there slowly, by fits and starts, while for others it is relatively smooth sailing. By late adolescence, many young people have yet to complete the process. James Marcia (1980) has developed four categories for characterizing individuals' state of identity development, based on whether or not they have passed through a period of identity exploration and on whether or not they have made a commitment to an adult identity. Marcia's four categories are: identity diffusion (no exploration or commitment), foreclosure (commitment without exploration), moratorium (exploration without commitment), and identity achievement (exploration followed by commitment). Each of these responses represents a different **identity status** (see Table 14.3).

Adolescents in a state of **identity diffusion** are not engaged in active exploration of roles and values, and they have not made any serious commitments to an adult identity. They seem so overwhelmed by the possibilities of life that they are unable to find direction. Young people in this group have no long-range goals but live for the moment, for immediate pleasures. Their sense of self seems to have no unified core. Instead, they have what David Elkind (1967) calls a "patchwork self." Identity diffusion is normal in early adolescence, but some young people have difficulty moving beyond it.

Foreclosure involves commitment to a set of roles and values without going through a period of crisis or exploration. Teenagers in this group have not struggled to reconcile incompatible aspects of the self or to evolve their own goals and purposes. Instead, they have simply accepted the roles that others, most often their parents, have prescribed for them. For all of us, of course, *some*

Identity status:
One of the four responses to the task of identity formation described by James Marcia: identity diffusion, foreclosure, moratorium, and achievement.

Identity diffusion:
Identity status in which there has been no active exploration of roles and values and no commitment to an adult identity.

Foreclosure:
Identity status in which commitment has been made to a set of roles and values without a period of exploration.

aspects of personal identity are defined by the families and communities in which we live (Grotevant, 1992; Spencer and Markstrom-Adams, 1990). But for adolescents who take the route of identity foreclosure, their entire sense of who they are is dictated by someone else. These adolescents cannot be said to have a genuine personal identity. Their "identity" is acquired in an unquestioning manner from what others tell them they should be. As Erikson (1970) argues in his biography of Gandhi, true identity cannot be achieved without active searching and struggle.

Adolescents who are in **moratorium** are in the midst of actively exploring options for a personal identity, but have not yet committed to any of them. Moratorium is the developmentally appropriate identity status for middle adolescence, but it can become problematic if it continues into adulthood.

Identity achievement occurs when a person commits to a particular set of self-chosen roles and values following a period of active exploration. Adolescents in this group are confident about the consistency and continuity of the self, and equally confident that others see these same qualities in them. Identity achievement is seldom reached before late adolescence or early adulthood.

Across the adolescent years, there is a fairly steady increase in the percentage of young people who can be classified as identity achievers; at the same time, there is a decrease in the percentage who are in a state of identity diffusion (Harter, 1990). Keep in mind, however, that a person's identity status is not always consistent in all domains of life. College students are most likely to have reached identity achievement in the area of vocational choice, but they are often still in a state of diffusion or foreclosure regarding their religious beliefs and political ideologies (Waterman, 1985).

In studying young people in each of the four identity statuses, researchers have found some interesting correlations (Waterman, 1992). For instance, those who are identity achievers tend to have the highest levels of self-esteem. The next highest are those in the moratorium group, followed by those who adopt foreclosure, and last are those who are floundering in identity diffusion. Identity achievers are also more goal-oriented, choose more demanding college

Moratorium:
Identity status in which a person is in the midst of exploring options for a personal identity, but has not yet committed to any of them.

Identity achievement:
Identity status in which a person has committed to a set of roles and values following a period of active exploration.

Commitment to ideology is often a hallmark of the late adolescent period.

majors, show greater cognitive sophistication, and take more personal responsibility for their actions than those in other identity statuses. Although identity achievers report low levels of anxiety, anxiety is actually lowest for those in foreclosure. Self-reported anxiety is highest for those in moratorium.

According to Erikson, two sets of ingredients are needed to consolidate an "optimal" sense of personal identity. First, adolescents must carry forward from middle childhood an inner confidence about their competence and ability to master new tasks, along with a sense of basic trust, autonomy, and initiative from earlier developmental periods. Little research has been done to determine if Erikson is right in stressing these factors (Steinberg, 1990). Although studies show that a college student's identity status is often related to feelings of competence, trust, and autonomy (Harter, 1990; Hauser and Bowlds, 1990; Waterman, 1992), we do not know the *developmental* connections between these factors. We need longitudinal studies, beginning in early childhood, that explore how the resolution of issues in each developmental period is related to later identity achievement. One such study has supported Erikson's ideas (Block, 1987), but more research is needed.

The second set of ingredients that Erikson sees as critical to optimal identity formation is ample opportunity to experiment with new roles, both in fantasy and in practice, coupled with support in this effort from parents and other adults. There is some research evidence that warm, supportive parents who encourage communication and resolution of differences do foster identity formation in adolescents (Baumrind, 1989; Grotevant and Cooper, 1986).

GROUP DIFFERENCES IN IDENTITY FORMATION

Although identity formation is by definition an individual matter, there are some group differences in how the process unfolds. For instance, gay and lesbian adolescents, as a group, have social disapproval to contend with that their heterosexual peers do not. Ritch Savin-Williams (1990), who has extensively studied gay and lesbian youth, points out that negative community attitudes pose a great challenge to the identity formation and self-acceptance of these young people. Research suggests that gay and lesbian youths who are able to express their sexual orientation openly, even in the face of social stigma, show enhanced self-esteem compared with those who maintain secrecy.

Identity development also appears to proceed differently in some ways for young women and young men (Patterson, Sochting, and Marcia, 1992). During adolescence, the interpersonal domain, especially as it relates to future marriage and family roles, is more prominent in girls' identity exploration than in boys'. Girls and boys show equal concern about occupational issues, but girls show more concern than boys about how to balance career and family demands (Archer, 1985). Although Erikson believed that identity issues had to be resolved before the intimacy issues of early adulthood, there is some evidence that young women deal with identity and intimacy simultaneously rather than sequentially (Schiedel and Marcia, 1985). Because of this pattern, the process of identity formation is in some ways more complex for girls than it is for boys (Harter, 1990).

There are also distinctive challenges of identity formation faced by members of ethnic minority groups (Markstrom-Adams, 1992). Minority youth are confronted by two often conflicting sets of cultural values—those of their ethnic community and those of the larger society. Deciding which aspects of each set of values to incorporate into their own personal identities can be difficult. Identifying too closely with the values of the dominant culture may result in ostracism in their ethnic community, but identifying too closely with the values of their own community may limit opportunities for success in the larger society. As one 15-year-old girl of mixed ethnic background complained to an interviewer about one of her white friends: "She doesn't understand I have one foot in the white world and one foot in the black world, and she can't accept that I have to be solid in the black world" (Sroufe, Carlson, and Shulman, 1993). Insufficient contact with adult role models who have successfully dealt with these challenges can leave minority youth without a guide to follow. At the same time, when educational and employment opportunities are limited because of ethnic background, further obstacles arise on the road to identity achievement.

Perhaps as a result of these difficulties, minority adolescents appear more likely than white adolescents to avoid or cut short identity exploration (Markstrom-Adams, 1992). In a number of studies, researchers have found higher rates of foreclosure for African-American, Hispanic, and Native American youth than for whites (Hauser and Kasendorf, 1983; Spencer and Markstrom-Adams, 1990; Streitmatter, 1988). Foreclosure is an understandable response to the complexities of the task facing these adolescents. Adopting a set of roles and values offered by one's community is less anxiety-provoking than attempting to fashion a new set unique to oneself. Some researchers have suggested that foreclosure may even be an adaptive response to the situation. When roles are clearly defined by the community, foreclosure "may foster greater social recognition and impart a sense of well-being to the individual" (Spencer and Markstrom-Adams, 1990, p. 298).

PEER RELATIONSHIPS IN ADOLESCENCE

Peer relationships change during the adolescent years in a number of ways, and their impact on other areas of development grows. The cognitive advances of adolescence make possible a deeper, more mature understanding of others that parallels the gains taking place in self-understanding. Friendships grow deeper as teenagers acquire the cognitive potential for mutual exploration and discovery. In turn, involvement with peers becomes increasingly critical to progress in self-understanding; adolescents discover their inner feelings largely through close relationships with peers. Peer group membership also contributes to the development of personal identity. The group of friends to which an adolescent belongs helps define who he or she is, and peer groups offer chances for trying out various roles. Finally, as new types of peer groups emerge during adolescence, involvement with same-sex peers often paves the way for close relationships with members of the opposite sex.

These changes mean that peer relationships become more complex in adolescence. Youngsters must not only coordinate close friendships with same-sex peers and function in same-sex groups as they did in middle childhood, they must also coordinate same-sex friendships with opposite-sex ones and function in mixed-sex groups. How adolescents respond to these new challenges depends in part on their developmental history. Research shows that those who effectively negotiated the tasks of middle childhood peer relationships, including maintaining boundaries between the sexes, are more effective in the mixed-sex group and, in general, are better able to meet the complex challenges of adolescent peer relationships (Sroufe, Carlson, and Shulman, 1993).

ADVANCES IN UNDERSTANDING OTHERS

Understanding the self and understanding others go hand-in-hand, so it is not surprising that an adolescent's advances in self-awareness are accompanied by a growing sense of what others are like. Teenagers know that they have inner motives, and they deduce that others do too. As they come to see themselves as having coherent selves, they also recognize the coherence of others' personalities. These new understandings can be seen in adolescents' efforts to explain the behavior of others. Even younger adolescents infer that others have certain traits that prompt them to act as they do: "He's a jock," "She's sensitive" (Livesley and Bromley, 1973). By age 16 they try to reconcile inconsistent behavior in others by pointing to interrelated motives: "He's dying to be on the basketball team, but he's also worried about his grades." By this age they also give more psychological reasons for others' behavior, just as they do for their own (Selman, 1980).

Robert Selman's research shows how understanding of others is generally at the same level as self-understanding. When asked questions about Mike, his dog Pepper, and his friend Tom, adolescents in their midteens consider the feelings of both Mike and Tom in this situation, and they know that each boy will make inferences about the intentions of the other. As one 15-year-old explained it: "Mike will understand what Tom was trying to do, and even if he doesn't like the dog, he'll appreciate that Tom thought he would" (Selman, 1980, p. 106). Here we see a grasp of other people's thoughts and feelings that closely matches the youngster's depth of understanding about the self. Selman's ideas about the link between self-understanding and understanding of others are summarized in Table 14.4.

THE NATURE OF ADOLESCENT FRIENDSHIPS

CHANGES FROM MIDDLE CHILDHOOD TO ADOLESCENCE

Developmental changes in understanding the self and others underlie changes in the nature of friendship from childhood to adolescence. Compared with younger children, teenagers have a much greater capacity for true *mutual understanding* (Youniss, 1980). Elementary school children grasp the importance of give-and-take between friends, but they do not fully understand one another as persons. Adolescents, in contrast, are increasingly aware of their own unique feelings, and this goes hand in hand with a recognition that others have unique feelings too (Damon, 1983; Keller and Wood, 1989).

Partly because of this growing capacity for true mutual understanding, teenage friends want to share their inner experiences and life histories. This desire for *self-disclosure* accounts for the many hours they spend talking with each other, either on the phone or face-to-face. As three teenagers described this aspect of friendship:

> "A friend is a person you can talk to—you know, show your feelings. And he'll talk to you." "Someone you can tell your problems and she'll tell you her problems." "You can tell a friend everything." (Youniss, 1980, pp. 181–182)

When important inner feelings are shared between friends, their relationship deepens. You saw this in our story of Meryl, whose relationship with Amy has deepened over time into the type of friendship we are describing here. The dis-

TABLE 14.4
STAGES IN UNDERSTANDING SELF AND OTHERS

Level	Concept of Persons	Concept of Relations
0: Egocentric perspective taking (under 6 years)	*Undifferentiated:* Confuses internal (feelings, intentions) with external (appearance, actions) characteristics of others.	*Egocentric:* Fails to recognize that self and others have different feelings and thoughts as well as different external physical characteristics.
1: Subjective perspective taking (ages 5–9)	*Differentiated:* Distinguishes feelings and intentions from actions and appearances.	*Subjective:* Recognizes that others may feel and think differently than self—that everyone is subjective—but has limited conceptions of how these different persons may affect each other (e.g., gifts make people happy, regardless of how appropriate they are).
2: Self-reflective or reciprocal perspective taking (ages 7–12)	*Second-person:* Can reflect on own thoughts and realizes that others can do so as well (recursive thought); realizes appearances may be deceptive about true feelings.	*Reciprocal:* Puts self in others' shoes *and* realizes others may do same; thus thoughts and feelings, not merely actions, become basis for interactions; however, the two subjective perspectives are not assumed to be influencing each other.
3: Mutual perspective taking (ages 10–15)	*Third-person:* Knows that self and others act *and* reflect on effects of their action on themselves; recognizes own immediate subjective perspective and also realizes that it fits into own more general attitudes and values.	*Mutual:* Can imagine another person's perspective on oneself and one's actions, coordinates other's inferred view with own view (i.e., sees self as others see him/her); thus comes to view relationships as ongoing mutual sharing of social satisfaction or understanding.
4: In-depth and societal-symbolic perspective taking (ages 12–adult)	*In-depth:* Recognizes that persons are unique, complex combinations of their own histories; furthermore, realizes that persons may not *always* understand their own motivations (i.e., that there may be unconscious psychological processes).	*Societal-symbolic:* Individuals may form perspectives on each other at different levels, from shared superficial information or interests to common values or appreciation of very abstract moral, legal, or social notions.

SOURCE: Selman, 1980.

tress she feels when Amy no longer confides in her reflects the significance she places on mutual understanding and self-disclosure between friends.

A deep and close relationship like Meryl and Amy's is said to be characterized by *intimacy*. Intimacy includes self-disclosure, understanding of each other's feelings, and knowledge of each other's personality characteristics and preferences (Collins and Repinski, 1994). From middle childhood to middle adolescence, young people show an increased capacity and desire for intimacy with their friends (Buhrmester, 1990; Youniss, 1980). Over this age range they increasingly report that they have intimate friends (Furman and Buhrmester, 1992).

Related to the growth of intimacy is a deeper *commitment* between teenage friends. Adolescents have an increased understanding that friends share experiences and extend themselves for one another, so their friendships tend to be more loyal and faithful than those among younger children (Berndt, 1981; Buhrmester, 1990; Sprinthall and Collins, 1995). One teenager explained commitment this way:

> I think a friend is somebody that is loyal. Somebody that would stay on your side no matter what anybody—well, if somebody started a rumor and everyone believed it, somebody that wouldn't believe it. Or somebody that, if they knew you did it, they wouldn't say, "ah, you did it" just to be like everybody else. (Konopka, 1976, p. 84)

Another aspect of commitment is the ability to keep confidences, to refrain from telling something that a friend told you in private. The ability to keep confidences is very important to teenagers, as this adolescent confirms:

> Friends can keep secrets together. They can trust that you won't tell anybody else. If you tell somebody something, they won't use it to get revenge on you when you get in a fight. You talk about things you wouldn't tell other people. (Youniss, 1980, p. 181)

Throughout adolescents' descriptions of friendship, words like "trust," "faith," and "believe in" are mentioned again and again. The preciousness of inner feelings to an adolescent, who is so newly aware of them, demands absolute loyalty from friends. The highly sensitive nature of these feelings makes the teenager very vulnerable to betrayal. Mutual understanding and emotional intimacy help create the trust that is needed to make teenage friendships work. But some degree of initial trust is also needed before adolescents can share their inner experiences and build mutual understanding and closeness with a peer.

CHANGES FROM EARLY TO LATE ADOLESCENCE

The nature of friendship continues to change over the course of the teenage years. Increased intimacy with and commitment to friends appear in early to midadolescence, while during later adolescence another qualitative advance occurs. In keeping with the older teenager's ability to integrate diverse aspects of the self, older teens are able to coordinate a broader range of friends. Friendships no longer need to be so exclusive, as pairs of friends accept each other's need to establish relationships with other people and to grow through these experiences (Selman, 1980). Here is how William Damon explains this broadening of friendships:

> Friends are still seen as mutually supportive in a psychological way. Only now this support is seen on a broader scale, extending to a variety of friendship relations of differing significance and intensity (Damon, 1983, p. 256).

This broadening process is accompanied by an increased stability in friendships among older teens. Before age 15 there is only moderate stability across a 2-week period in the peers whom adolescents identify as their "best friends." By 16 to 19, however, best friends are highly stable (Hartup and Sancilio, 1986). One reason may be that adolescents are much more likely than younger children to stay together and continue interacting after conflicts (Hartup and Laursen, 1993). Here we see patterns of friendship and stability coming closer to those found among adults.

GENDER DIFFERENCES

Although teenage boys as well as girls experience the increased intimacy with and commitment to friends that we have described so far, there are some gender-related differences in the nature of friendships during adolescence (Hartup and Laursen, 1993). For instance, teenage girls report more frequent intimate interactions with same-sex friends than boys do, and they have more intimate knowledge of their friends (Collins and Repinski, 1994). However, girls also report about twice as many disagreements with friends, which often involve interpersonal issues of the "he said/she said" variety: "And Stephen said that you said that I was showing off just because I had that blouse on" (Hartup and Laursen, 1993). Girls also report that negative feelings persist following a disagreement, whereas boys do so less often. This may reflect greater intimacy in girls' relationships, or it may simply mean that boys and girls have different ideas about what disagreements mean for a friendship. Finally, boys are more likely than girls to report conflicts over friends pressuring them to do things, while girls are more likely than boys to report conflicts involving betrayal of secrets (Cooper and Cooper, 1992).

PEER INTIMACY AND IDENTITY

A question that has interested developmentalists for some time is the exact nature of the connection between establishing intimacy with others and achieving a personal identity. As we have already mentioned, Erikson believed that the identity issues of adolescence had to be resolved before true intimacy with another person was possible. In contrast, Harry Stack Sullivan (1953) argued that personal identity was an *outgrowth* of intimate relationships.

Both arguments appear to have some validity. People must have some sense of who they are before they can join others in close relationships. But at the same time peers represent a key source of social support and offer vital confirmation that one's ideas about the self are valid (Harter, 1990; Savin-Williams and Berndt, 1990). It is only through self-disclosure with close friends that we come to know that others see us as we see ourselves.

One way to reconcile Erikson's and Sullivan's apparently contradictory ideas is to recognize that the two theorists were interested in different types of intimacy. When Erikson talked about intimacy, he was referring primarily to intimacy with an opposite-sex romantic partner in adulthood. In contrast, Sullivan focused on intimacy in relationships with same-sex friends in middle childhood and early adolescence. It may be that early intimacy with same-sex friends lays the groundwork for identity development, which in turn fosters later intimacy with romantic partners. Over time, intimacy and identity may continue to influence each other in a cyclical way, with advances in identity development promoting deeper intimacy, and deeper intimacy leading to further identity consolidation. In any case, correlational research shows that identity and emotional intimacy do go hand in hand. For instance, college students with a stable sense of personal identity are more likely to have attained emotional intimacy with someone else (Fitch and Adams, 1983).

CHANGES IN THE NATURE OF PEER GROUPS

Not only does the nature of friendship change in adolescence, the nature of peer groups changes as well. The importance of being in a group increases dramatically. For younger adolescents, conformity to group norms is highly valued, and there is often antagonism to those outside one's own group (Gavin and Furman, 1989). It is also important to belong to a popular group. These behaviors and outlooks diminish markedly by late adolescence.

Two new group structures that emerge in adolescence are the *clique* and the *crowd*. A **clique** is a close-knit group of a few friends who are intimately involved with one another, going places and doing things together, having a mutual exchange of ideas, and accepting one another's different personalities (Brown, 1990). Cliques, especially those of girls, are relatively closed to newcomers (Sones and Feshbach, 1971). The mixed-gender **crowd** is larger, less exclusive, and more loosely organized than the clique. Crowds tend to be identified by the interests, abilities, attitudes, style of dress, and other personal characteristics shared by their members. In one study of 300 high school students, there were 44 cliques (composed of three to nine members each) and only 12 crowds (Dunphy, 1963). The crowds were made up of cliques, but not every clique was part of a crowd. The clique is apparently the dominant peer-group structure during adolescence. The crowd, in contrast, offers a broader range of informal contacts.

Youngsters' concepts of cliques and crowds change over time, as their cognitive abilities become more sophisticated. Sixth graders can readily describe who belongs to various cliques in their class, but they tend to label crowds on the basis of concrete characteristics, such as what they do at recess ("the jump rope group") or who their leader is ("Jessica's group"). Older adolescents, in contrast, are more likely to characterize crowds by their general dispositions or interests (Brown and Clasen, 1986; Cairns, Perrin, and Cairns, 1985).

Interestingly, teenagers' characterizations of crowds seem to be based more on *reputation* than on actual behavior (Brown, Mory, and Kinney, 1994). Most middle school and high school students can readily list the major crowds in their school (e.g., "populars," "jocks," "brains," "normals," "burnouts") and describe what people in each of these crowds are like. However, these crowd descriptions turn out not to be particularly accurate reflections of reality. For one thing, individuals who are identified by themselves or others as belonging to a particular crowd are far from uniform in dress, behavior, or attitudes. For another, when adolescents are asked to choose which characteristics on a list fit a particular crowd at their school, there is limited consensus (Brown, Lohr, and Trujillo, 1990). Adolescents also tend to exaggerate the positive characteristics of their own crowd and crowds that are socially close to theirs while emphasizing the negative characteristics of crowds that are socially distant (Mory, 1992). Crowd labels and descriptions seem to function as caricatures or shorthand characterizations of various groups. These caricatures make it easier for adolescents to understand the various social identities available to them, to predict peer behavior, and to identify potential friends and foes (Brown et al., 1994).

Interestingly, adolescents are often reluctant to assign themselves to any one crowd. In response to researchers' questions about which crowd they belong to, they often say, "I really don't belong to any one crowd," or "I have friends in several crowds" (Brown et al., 1994). In one study, one-third of the high school stu-

Clique:
A close-knit group of a few friends who are intimately involved with one another.

Crowd:
A group that is larger, less exclusive, and more loosely organized than a clique.

dents surveyed said that they belonged to two or more crowds (Youniss, McLellan, and Strouse, 1994).

During the teenage years, the importance of both cliques and crowds first increases and then declines. Membership in cliques seems to peak in early adolescence, around the eighth grade, and then fall off during high school (Crocket, Losoff, and Petersen, 1984; Shrum and Cheek, 1987). Older adolescents' social life is more likely to be organized around specific friendships and romantic relationships than around membership in a clique. Clearly identifiable crowds also appear in early adolescence, often beginning with a differentiation in middle school or junior high between the "popular" crowd and everyone else (Eder, 1985; Kinney, 1993). Through the early years of high school, crowds become more differentiated, as individuals become identified with various extracurricular activities and academic tracks. As they progress through high school, however, adolescents tend to attach decreasing importance to belonging to an identifiable crowd. By senior year, crowds typically become less prominent, and the boundaries between them often begin to break down (Brown, 1990).

These patterns are probably related to the tasks confronting youngsters in different phases of adolescence. In early adolescence, clique and crowd membership may provide teenagers with both a social identity and a reliable setting for social interaction and friendship formation. Later on, as adolescents develop a sense of individual identity and become more confident about their social skills and ability to make friends, these functions lose their importance.

The classic study of clique and crowd formation and decline was conducted by Dexter Dunphy in Australia in the 1960s (Dunphy, 1963). Table 14.5 summarizes the major stages he described. In stage 1, the precrowd stage, which occurs in early adolescence, teenagers participate only in single-sex cliques. The small size and close-knit nature of these groups allow for mutual understanding and sharing. Then, in stage 2, male and female cliques begin to interact within a loosely formed crowd. These early crowd activities allow young adolescents to have casual, nonthreatening contacts with the opposite sex. Stage 3 represents a transition during which some upper-status members of the crowd form a mixed-sex clique. The crowd is fully developed in stage 4, with several mixed-sex cliques in close association. Finally, in late adolescence, the crowd begins to disintegrate into loosely linked groups of couples (Dunphy, 1963). This progression, as you can see, has a certain logic. It allows many teenagers to move "from intimate single-sex friendships through a series of casual heterosexual contacts to a final phase of heterosexual intimacy" (Damon, 1983, p. 259).

DATING AND SEXUAL ACTIVITY

Dating and sexual activity are usually offshoots of crowd activities. Few adolescents begin dating before they participate in crowds. Whereas fewer than 10 percent of youngsters date before age 12, 90 percent are dating by age 16 (Savin-Williams and Berndt, 1990). Similarly, sexual experimentation usually does not begin until midadolescence (Brooks-Gunn and Furstenberg, 1989). And even then, mutually satisfying sexual intimacy is a long way off. Couples in midadolescence tend to operate in a "parallel" manner—together, but not mutually involved on an emotional level (Damon, 1983). It is only in later adolescence, in the eleventh grade and beyond, that intimacy with an opposite-sex

TABLE 14.5
THE PROGRESSION OF PEER GROUP RELATIONS IN ADOLESCENCE

EARLY ADOLESCENCE
Stage 1: Precrowd stage. Isolated single-sex cliques.

Stage 2: The beginning of the crowd. Single-sex cliques in group-to-group inter-action.

Stage 3: The crowd in structural transi-tion. Single-sex cliques with upper-status members forming a mixed-sex clique.

LATE ADOLESCENCE
Stage 4: The fully developed crowd. Mixed-sex cliques in close association.

Stage 5: Beginning of crowd disintegra-tion. Loosely associated groups of couples.

SOURCE: Adapted from Dunphy, 1963, p. 236.

friend becomes comparable to that occurring between same-sex friends (Shara-bany, Gershoni, and Hofman, 1981).

Commonly, the intimacy in male-female relationships surpasses that of same-sex relationships by about the twelfth grade (Buhrmester and Furman, 1987). Intimate male-female relationships may play an important role in identity formation, as we mentioned before. They may also facilitate further development of empathy and prosocial behavior, in that relating to someone different from yourself can increase sensitivity to the needs of another person (Sharabany et al., 1981). These same functions may also be served by the relationships of gay and lesbian couples (Savin-Williams and Berndt, 1990).

Sexual intimacy is another dimension of peer relations that emerges in adolescence. Adolescent sexual activity has increased in the United States in the last few decades, but the size of the increase is not entirely clear. The sensitive nature of the topic makes it difficult to get a reliable estimate of the percentage of teenagers who are sexually active. For a variety of reasons, teenagers may either overstate or understate their actual experience.

Much of the increase in adolescent sexual intercourse apparently occurred from the 1960s to the 1980s (Dreyer, 1982). During that time, the percentage of high school boys who were sexually active doubled; for girls, the percentage quadrupled. The increase in adolescent girls' sexual activity was accompanied by an increase in the pregnancy rate among unmarried teenagers, as we discussed in Chapter 2.

A nationwide longitudinal study completed in the mid-1980s indicated that the rate of sexual intercourse remains relatively low in early adolescence, but that it increases dramatically through middle and late adolescence (Hayes, 1987). At every age, boys report higher rates of intercourse than girls do. For example, at age 15, 17 percent of boys and only 6 percent of girls report that they have had sexual intercourse. By age 20, those figures have increased to 80 percent for boys and 70 percent for girls. There are also ethnic differences in rates of sexual activity, as shown in Figure 14.1. African-American teenagers, especially boys, become sexually active earlier than either white or Hispanic teenagers and continue to show higher rates of sexual activity throughout adolescence.

THE RELATIVE INFLUENCE OF PEERS

A topic of great interest to parents and researchers alike is the influence of peers on the behavior and development of adolescents. Teenagers, especially in early adolescence, adopt a style of dress and behavior that sets them apart from other age groups. Developmentalists interpret this as indicating identification with the peer group. Surveys find that while young teens are becoming more autonomous from parents, they are growing more dependent on peers (Harter, 1990; Steinberg and Silverberg, 1986). They are coming to see peers as a more important source of intimacy in their lives than parents (Collins, 1994). This increased involvement with peers may help youngsters carve out a more mature relationship with their parents. It also allows them to maintain a distance from adult roles and commitments while gaining the interpersonal experience needed to prepare them for adulthood.

The degree of conformity to the peer group changes during the years from middle childhood to late adolescence (Gavin and Furman, 1989). This was shown in a study in which youngsters of various ages were asked to decide which

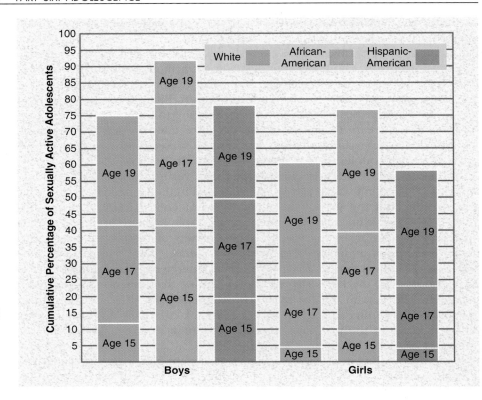

FIGURE 14.1 THE CUMULATIVE PERCENTAGE OF SEXUALLY ACTIVE ADOLESCENTS AT VARIOUS AGES, BY SEX AND ETHNICITY. *(Source: Hayes, 1987.)*

two lines in a set were the same length. Some were told that peers had chosen pairs of lines that were obviously *un*equal. As shown in Figure 14.2, 12- to 13-year-olds went along with the incorrect opinions of peers much more than 7- to 8-year-olds did. By age 16 to 17 the conformity of early adolescence had declined, and by age 19 to 21 it was no greater than it had been in middle childhood (Costanzo, 1970). Similar findings emerged from another study in which youngsters were given hypothetical situations that involved opposing pressures from parents and peers (Berndt, 1979). Young adolescents experienced the most conflict, finding it hard to decide which side to go along with. Thus, the peak period of conformity to peer behavior and beliefs seems to be in early adolescence.

This pattern makes sense when you consider that young adolescents have well-developed social-comparison skills but are still very self-conscious about what others think of them. Older adolescents, by contrast, have largely outgrown the imaginary-audience phase. They no longer feel that others are always scrutinizing them critically, so they aren't so uncomfortable about being a bit different from other people. Excessive conformity, like excessive self-consciousness, is something that most teenagers eventually outgrow.

Even during early adolescence some youngsters are more conforming than others. Teenagers who have a medium level of status with their peers are more likely to conform than are either high-status or low-status teenagers (Lansbaum and Willis, 1971). Perhaps these middle-status teens are more likely to feel they will gain in group acceptance by going along with others (Sprinthall and Collins, 1995). The source of peer influence also makes a difference in whether a particular adolescent conforms. In general, teens are more influenced by their friends, especially long-term friends, than they are by mere acquaintances (Hartup, 1992). For example, friends are more likely to behave similarly with regard to using marijuana. Even adolescents who have only recently become friends exert a noticeable influence on one another. Teenagers who become friends during a school year are more similar at the end of that year than they were at the beginning (Kandel, 1978). All this suggests that in our story Christine has good reason to be concerned when 14-year-old Mike starts hanging out with the "wrong" crowd.

Parents often view their teenager's conformity to the peer group as a sign that their own influence is waning and that the young person may be abandoning basic values taught in the home. There is little basis for this concern, however. Peer influence does not replace parental influence, which remains high even while peer influence increases (Chassin and Sherman, 1985). It is also true that parents and peers tend to influence different aspects of a teenager's life. Peers tend to have the greatest impact on superficial behaviors, such as dress and mannerisms. Parents, in contrast, retain substantial influence on adolescents' basic beliefs and values.

This pattern of dual influence was shown in a classic study in which ninth to eleventh graders were presented with hypothetical situations in which a teenager faced a dilemma (Brittain, 1963). Sometimes the subjects were told what the parents thought the teenager should do; other times they were told what peers advised doing. Each subject was then asked how the dilemma should be resolved. Many responded with their own judgments, although often the views of parents and peers were influential. Peer opinions were most influential in matters dealing with status in the peer group, whereas parental judgments were most influential in matters of important life decisions, education, and ethics. More recent studies agree with this general split in influence during the teenage years (Sprinthall and Collins, 1995).

This is not to say that peers never exert an influence on important matters.

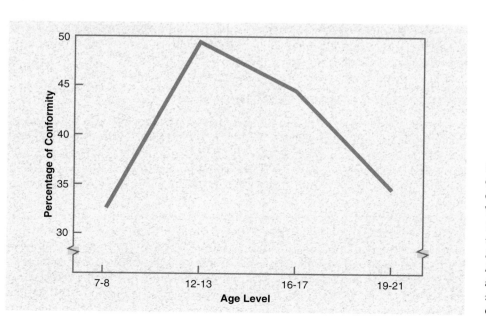

FIGURE 14.2
CHANGES IN CONFORMITY TO PEERS WITH AGE
Young people of different ages were asked to decide which lines in a set matched as to length. Some were given false information about judgments made by peers. (Source: Costanzo, 1970, p. 386.)

Sometimes they do. Friends' influence seems to outweigh that of parents in decisions about cigarette smoking and marijuana use. The influence of parents, however, seems to be greater when it comes to decisions about the use of other illicit drugs. Both peers and parents seem to have an impact on teenage choices regarding the use of alcohol (Savin-Williams and Berndt, 1990). (Adolescents' use of alcohol and other drugs is discussed in the box on pp. 574–575.) It is important to remember that peer influences generally diminish by late adolescence (Sprinthall and Collins, 1995), whereas the influence of parents usually continues into adulthood, as you will see in the next section.

FAMILY RELATIONSHIPS IN ADOLESCENCE

Despite the increasing significance of peers in teenagers' lives, the family remains a critical context for development during adolescence. For example, parents as well as peers play a key role in adolescents' identity formation. A history of experiences within the family is the foundation on which a coherent identity is built. In addition, parents can actively support identity-seeking by allowing their adolescent to explore new roles and values, by tolerating self-expression, and by discussing different views, while still providing guidelines when needed.

The parents' role in the transition from childhood to adulthood is analogous to their role in the transition from infancy to childhood. Toddlers and adolescents are not just becoming more independent of their parents, they are also becoming connected to their parents in new ways. During toddlerhood, the child's assertiveness and the parents' setting of limits lead the child to a new understanding of the boundaries between self and others. Gradually, the toddler comes to see the self not as an extension of the parent, but rather as a separate person who is linked to the parent through strong emotional ties. In a similar fashion, the adolescent's new level of self-assertion and the parents' mix of accepting and challenging this behavior promote a new level of mutual understanding. By late adolescence or early adulthood, sons and daughters have usually gained renewed respect for their parents (Collins, 1994; Steinberg, 1990). It is not the adoration of the young child, but it is a powerful connection nonetheless.

THE CHANGING FAMILY STRUCTURE

Family roles and patterns of interaction change dramatically as a child passes through adolescence, in response to the child's physical, cognitive, and social development. Far-reaching changes in family structure are needed to accommodate these developments. Thus, it is not only the adolescent who is developing but also the family (Gunnar and Collins, 1988; Powers, Hauser, and Kilner, 1989).

During adolescence, a child's changing level of understanding plays a role in bringing about changes in family relationships. The same cognitive skills that permit hypothetical thinking and exploration of inconsistencies allow teenagers to anticipate how parents will counter their arguments, to note imperfections in parents' behavior, and to conceive of other ways in which the family might function (Powers et al., 1989). Adolescents may resent an unsatisfactory family situation because they can now see what *might* be (Elkind, 1967). Teenagers also

Parents are a vital source of recognition for adolescents, despite their strong involvement with peers.

have a new understanding of parent-child relationships and parental authority. By late adolescence they see mutual tolerance and respect as the basis of interactions between themselves and their parents, and they see their power as much more nearly equal to that of their parents than it had been in childhood (Feldman and Gehring, 1988). No longer will the adolescent simply accept parental dictates without being given reasons and a chance for input. Increased size, physical maturity, and general competence also contribute to teenagers' push for greater autonomy in behavior and decision making.

This pressure from adolescents for change in the family structure was shown in a classic study of several thousand 14- to 16-year-olds. Eighty percent of them said they wanted their parents to be less restrictive and to allow them more independence (Douvan and Adelson, 1966). More recent studies of teenagers reflect the same desire for redefinition of the parent-child relationship away from unilateral parental authority toward cooperative negotiation (Steinberg, 1990).

Most parents make appropriate changes in response to these pressures from their children. For example, parents often prompt sixth graders during family discussions ("You want to invite Jenny to your birthday party, don't you?" "Wouldn't you rather have pizza for dinner than hot dogs?"). In contrast, they are much more likely to allow twelfth graders to express their own ideas without prompting (Cooper and Cooper, 1992). The emergence of a new, more symmetrical power structure in the family is clearly seen in a study in which parents and their 11- to 16-year-old sons discussed solutions to hypothetical problems, such as what to do when the son came home late. The older the sons, the greater the influence they had on the discussion, as measured by the amount of time they spent talking, the number of times they interrupted their parents, and the parents' tendency to adopt the son's point of view (Jacob, 1974).

A longitudinal study by Laurence Steinberg (1981) demonstrates more directly the process by which a more symmetrical parent-child relationship develops during adolescence. In Steinberg's study, families with sons were visited several times as the boys passed from late middle childhood through puberty. At each visit, the parents and sons were given a problem to solve jointly, such as planning a vacation together. As the boys entered puberty, the parent-child interactions during these problem-solving discussions changed considerably. Sons deferred to their mothers less. Mothers and sons interrupted each other more, responded less to each other's opinions, interacted in a more contentious and rigid manner, and offered each other fewer explanations for their views. During this period the fathers typically stepped in and asserted their opinions strongly, and the boys continued to defer to them. After the peak of puberty had passed, family interactions became more flexible again. Mothers interrupted less often and sons became more willing to justify their thinking. The sons' relative dominance in these discussions was now greater than the mothers', but still less than the fathers'. This finding does not necessarily imply that mothers have less power in the family than their older adolescent sons do. It may simply mean that because of the security of the mother-son relationship, mothers are increasingly willing to be open to their teenagers' points of view. Research does show that teenagers spend more time with their mothers than with their fathers, confide in them more, and feel more accepted by them (Collins, 1994; Collins and Russell, 1991). At the same time, mothers are more self-disclosing than fathers in conversations with their teenagers, and they encourage more closeness (Cooper and Cooper, 1992).

In any case, during adolescence there is a change in patterns of family inter- action and a recognition by both parent and child that there is now greater sym- metry in their relationship (Feldman and Gehring, 1989; Steinberg, 1990). However, the emergence of this new power structure does not always occur smoothly. Quite often it involves conflict and stress. One reason for this conflict, especially during early adolescence, is that the parents' appraisal of the child's cognitive capacities lags behind the advances the youngster is actually making (Collins, 1990; Smetana, 1988). The child may be ready to share decision mak- ing before the parents realize it. This necessitates a realignment of the parents' perceptions with the child's actual abilities (Collins, 1994). Such a realignment often comes more easily with laterborn children than with firstborns, probably because with their laterborns parents are more prepared for the changes of adolescence (Hill, 1988).

Another reason for parent-child conflict during the transition to adolescence is that many parents of adolescents are entering midlife and facing develop- mental challenges of their own (Hauser and Bowlds, 1990; Sprinthall and Collins, 1995). They may find themselves reexamining the commitments and decisions they have made, and their child's strivings toward a personal identity may intensify their turmoil and reawaken unresolved issues from their own ado- lescence (Boxer et al., 1984). However, they often feel that they are running out of time to reach their goals, and they may resent their teenager's idealism and sense of limitless horizons. Parents are most likely to experience feelings of conflict when a child of their own gender enters adolescence, and they seem to be protected somewhat from these emotions if they have a job from which they gain high satisfaction (Silverberg and Steinberg, 1990).

Fortunately, the relatively high levels of parent-child conflict seen in early adolescence generally do not persist for long. As parents and teenagers work out a new understanding of each other, the amount of conflict declines (Montemayor and Hanson, 1985; Steinberg, 1990). In keeping with this pat- tern, parental stress is generally low when children are between the ages of 10 and 12, peaks at ages 14 to 15, and then declines in late adolescence

(Hakim-Larson, Livingston, and Tron, 1985; Small, Cornelius, and Eastman, 1983). Parental satisfaction shows a similar trend: higher in the youngster's late middle childhood, low in early adolescence, and rising again at the end of the teenage years (Montemayor and Brownlee, 1986).

High parent-child conflict during early adolescence does not indicate that a family is not functioning well (Collins, 1994; Prinz et al., 1979). Conflict at this time is part of the normal family realignment process. A total *absence* of conflict between parents and a son or daughter in early adolescence is actually a more worrisome sign because it may indicate foreclosure in the adolescent's identity development (Strauss, 1979).

PARENTING PATTERNS AND ADOLESCENT DEVELOPMENT

As power relationships become more symmetrical within the family, the tasks of parenting change. Parents of adolescents must respond to their children's new ways of thinking and new strivings for autonomy, self-expression, and influence. This does not mean that the parents now let their sons and daughters do whatever they want. Adolescent development goes best when parents stay involved with their teens and continue to impose some limits on them (Baumrind, 1989; Collins, 1994; Hetherington, 1988; Patterson and Dishion, 1988). But the parents must now switch from monitoring the child to monitoring the child's own monitoring of the self (Maccoby, 1980). Guidance and feedback generally replace demands and directives, as the parents must gradually turn over more and more responsibility to the newly emerging adult.

Many of the parenting qualities that were important in earlier periods of development continue to be important now. Warmth, support, and authoritativeness are commonly found to be linked to positive outcomes (Baumrind, 1989; Bell and Bell, 1983; Sampson and Laub, 1994; Sprinthall and Collins, 1995). In particular, adolescents who receive authoritative parenting tend to be more psychologically mature, to have a stronger orientation toward achievement, and to do better in school than those from authoritarian or permissive

The adolescent, like the toddler, must evolve a new way of relating to parents that involves more separateness, but not a loss of closeness. Mothers and daughters often remain quite close.

homes (Steinberg, 1993). Likewise, consistency between the two parents in the kinds of controls they employ and their responsiveness to their children is also associated with positive development in teenagers, including higher self-esteem (Johnson, Shulman, and Collins, 1991). Erratic and harsh parental treatment is strongly correlated with aggressive behavior and delinquency in adolescents (Sampson and Laub, 1994).

A number of observational studies have explored the links between parenting practices and adolescent development (Bell and Bell, 1983; Cooper and Cooper, 1992; Grotevant and Cooper, 1986; Hauser and Bowlds, 1990; J. Sroufe, 1991). In these studies the researchers observed interactions between parents and their teenagers while they discussed dilemmas, solved problems, or planned activities. One such study (Powers et al., 1983) showed the importance of an atmosphere of warmth, support, and positive emotion in the family. The degree to which these qualities existed in the family was enough to predict a youngster's level of maturity. These same qualities also aided identity achievement. Apparently, it is not enough for parents simply to prod a teenager into exploring alternatives and questioning opinions. In order for this kind of "cognitive challenge" to encourage identity achievement, it must take place within a warm and supportive family context. Under these circumstances, such cognitive challenge comes across as a sign of the parents' interest and respect, not of their criticism.

The importance of support and responsiveness on the part of parents was also suggested in a study conducted by Hal Grotevant and Catherine Cooper (1986), who observed teenagers and their parents jointly planning a vacation. They found that when the parents responded to the teenager's feelings, accepted disagreements, and initiated compromises, the teenager was more likely to perform at a relatively high level on two key tasks involved in identity achievement: (1) exploring alternatives regarding the self; and (2) perceiving and coordinating different points of view. In a later study, the young people from these supportive families were also more successful at mutual negotiation with peers (Cooper and Cooper, 1992). Since these were correlational studies, we cannot draw conclusions about cause and effect from them. Perhaps a teenager's ability to explore alternatives and coordinate different viewpoints helps encourage parental support and responsiveness as much as the other way around. However, a recent longitudinal study shows that such differences in identity exploration are predicted by parenting patterns 3 years earlier (Williams and Sroufe, 1994). All of these findings are in keeping with the social construction view of identity formation, which stresses the importance of supportive relationships.

BIDIRECTIONAL INFLUENCES

Although parents clearly affect their children and the quality of their development, children also have an impact on their parents and the patterns of interaction that occur in the family (Cooper and Cooper, 1992). Different children seem to "bring out" different parenting responses, just as different parenting styles seem to foster different reactions in children.

One example of bidirectional influences can be seen in developmental differences between males and females. During the teenage years girls not only experience greater self-consciousness and generally lower self-esteem than boys do

Just as parents influence their children's behavior, so do children seem to elicit different responses from their parents. A good "fit" in both directions is likely to mean a more harmonious parent–child relationship during adolescence.

but also tend to seek autonomy in different ways than boys (Harter, 1990; Simmons and Blyth, 1988). For example, one study in England found that adolescent girls primarily seek recognition of their emerging uniqueness within the family, whereas adolescent boys often struggle to escape the family's confines (Coleman, 1974). In a complementary way, suggesting bidirectional influences, parents allow their sons greater freedom to be away from home than they allow their daughters, and parents have more concerns about their daughters' sexual behavior than about their sons' (Block, 1979; Hoffman and Manis, 1977). Even in the first year of college, girls continue to have more conflicts at home than boys do, and these conflicts frequently concern emotional issues that don't affect boys as often (Kinloch, 1970). Apparently, an interaction of the parents, the child, and the child's gender gives rise to significant differences in patterns of development.

THE IMPACT OF DIVORCE ON ADOLESCENTS

In Chapter 12 we discussed the impact of divorce on children. There are some very important additional findings concerning the adolescent age group. First, adolescents from both single-parent families and stepfamilies are at greater risk for behavioral problems, drug and alcohol use, and poor school performance than children in families with both natural parents, even when income level is controlled for (Allison and Furstenberg, 1989; Steinberg, 1987, 1993). Second, it appears that divorce can prompt a "sleeper" effect—a result that is not apparent at the time of the marital breakup but shows up some years later, often during adolescence (Chase-Lansdale and Hetherington, 1990; Furstenberg, 1990). Third, during adolescence we see continuing differences in the effects of divorce on males and females, just as we did during the childhood years. The consequences of divorce appear more slowly and take different forms in girls than in boys. Girls are more likely to experience academic difficulties, distress, and dissatisfaction with the family's situation, whereas boys are more likely to show problem behavior (Allison and Furstenberg, 1989). And fourth, studies of teenagers in single-parent homes show that it is not simply the absence of a father that has negative effects. The disruption caused by the death of a father, for instance, has different consequences than the disruption caused by divorce.

These conclusions were clearly illustrated in an early study by Mavis Hetherington (1972), who looked at girls ages 13 to 17, none of whom had brothers. Some of the girls came from intact families with both a mother and a father at home; others came from divorced families in which the mother had child custody and had never remarried; and still others came from mother-headed families in which the father had died. Hetherington found that girls from father-absent homes were just as sex-typed in their behavior as girls from homes in which the father was present. However, the girls with absent fathers tended to show some difficulties in their opposite-sex relations, the form of which varied greatly depending on whether the father's absence was due to death or divorce. In general, girls whose fathers had died were shy and hesitant with males, whereas daughters of divorced fathers tended to be sexually forward.

Consider the way the two groups behaved at a recreation center dance. The daughters of widows tended to stay at the "girls' end" of the hall, surrounding themselves with other girls. Two even retreated for the entire evening to the security of the restroom. In contrast, the daughters of divorcees were often found at the "stag line," initiating contact with boys. Equally revealing was their behavior later, when they were interviewed by a male psychologist. While the daughters of widows tended to sit far away from the interviewer, avoid eye contact with him, and constrict their body posture, the daughters of divorcees tended to choose a seat near the interviewer, look at him often, and position their bodies in open, even provocative ways. These tendencies were especially pronounced in girls who had lost their fathers early.

Hetherington (1988) speculates that the attitudes and behaviors of the mothers involved may largely account for these differences. Many of the divorced mothers were still hostile toward their former husbands, recalled their marriages with bitterness, and were generally dissatisfied with life. Some of their daughters may have therefore concluded that happiness greatly depends on being "successful" with men. However, because they lacked experience with males in the family, their approach to this goal was often inappropriate. In sharp contrast, the widows tended to cling to happy memories of their husbands, to the point where they may have painted idealistically perfect images of them. As a result, their daughters may have felt too awed by males to approach them. These are only hypotheses; whatever the explanation, it is clear that the *meaning* a girl attaches to the loss of her father can be a very important factor.

ADOLESCENTS IN THE BROADER WORLD

During adolescence, developmental contexts beyond the home and peer group—such as school and, for many teens, the workplace—become increasingly important. School and the workplace, of course, are often intimately tied to both family and friends. Peer relationships and family life greatly influence how well an adolescent performs in the classroom and on the job (Cairns et al., 1989; Entwisle, 1990; Lempers et al., 1989; Steinberg et al., 1989). School and work, in turn, provide opportunities for interactions with peers, and for shared pride and conflict within the family.

The school and the workplace are vital proving grounds for an adolescent's developing sense of identity. Accomplishments in the classroom and on the job not only give teenagers a feeling of competence, they also allow young people to explore and anticipate future roles. Projecting the self into the future and forming goals in life are central to Erikson's theory of identity achievement.

An internal locus of control and a sense of instrumental competence contribute to adolescent achievement in many areas. Boys are encouraged to develop these characteristics more often than girls are.

ADOLESCENTS AT SCHOOL

In some ways middle schools and high schools support adolescent development. Students are given more responsibility for mastering course material, such as completing homework assignments and doing special projects on their own. Occasionally, there are courses in which young people can explore diverse opinions on social issues through class discussion. Being exposed to peers from diverse backgrounds, as occurs especially in public schools, can also encourage adolescents to perceive different points of view.

But schools may also have some negative influences on adolescents. Typically, interracial friendships at school decline during the teenage years (DuBois and Hirsch, 1990). In addition, the peer culture at school rewards popularity and athletic performance far more than it does scholastic achievement (Entwisle, 1990). For some students, peers even encourage academic failure. Associating with potential school dropouts is one clear predictor of dropping out of school oneself (Cairns et al., 1989).

Generally speaking, grades decline during adolescence. This may be due in part to harder classes and stricter grading, but it is also tied to the process of changing from one school to another, which is often linked to loss of friends (Entwisle, 1990; Petersen, 1986). In one study, for example, young adolescents who remained in the same school from kindergarten through eighth grade received better grades than those who switched to a junior high school at the age of 12 (Simmons and Blyth, 1988). The critical variable underlying this difference was the amount of change experienced—in this case, adjustment to a new school. Other kinds of changes can also prompt a decline in academic performance. Youngsters who are in the throes of puberty or who are being affected by other sudden turns in their lives are most likely to suffer a drop in school grades.

Adolescents differ in their beliefs about what factors contribute to academic achievement (Little et al., in press; Wiener, Kun, and Benesh-Weiner, 1980). Some teenagers are convinced that success in school depends on themselves. They are said to have an **internal locus of control.** Others think that grades are largely a matter of factors outside them, such as being lucky or the teacher's favorite. These youngsters believe that nothing they do will make a difference. They are said to have an **external locus of control.** Closely related to an external locus of control is the idea that one's ability is fixed and won't be changed by effort and hard work (Henderson and Dweck, 1990). Such attitudes, not surprisingly, influence school performance.

Gender also influences achievement at school (Entwisle, 1990). Girls are often socialized away from feelings of *instrumental competence* (thinking they have the ability to accomplish things) and toward feelings of helplessness when con-

Internal locus of control: The belief that success depends on one's own efforts.

External locus of control: The belief that success depends on factors outside one's control.

fronted with a challenge (Block, 1979; Dweck, 1975). For instance, parents tend to believe that adolescent boys have more natural talent for math, and they convey this belief to their children (Parsons, Adler, and Kaczala, 1982). Girls usually have lower expectations for success at math and a variety of other tasks, despite the fact that overall they earn better grades than boys do (Entwisle, 1990; Petersen, 1986). What's more, when girls fail, they are more likely than boys to attribute that failure to something they cannot change, such as innate lack of ability (Henderson and Dweck, 1990). This prompts them to give up trying more readily than boys. In addition, success at academic tasks doesn't always give girls as much pride as it does boys. For girls, high achievement in certain areas, such as mathematics, is often associated with a negative self-image (Petersen, 1986).

In summary, many of today's teenagers, both female and male, seem to be caught in a bind (Elkind, 1978). On the one hand, they are experiencing strong pressure to succeed in what is portrayed as an increasingly competitive world. On the other hand, parents, teachers, and peers sometimes fail to give them enough support for academic achievement, and they may lack the personal outlook needed to promote their own success.

ADOLESCENTS AT WORK

Another setting in which teenagers can experience success or failure is the workplace. About 60 percent of high school sophomores and 75 percent of high school seniors have a part-time job, averaging 16 to 20 hours a week (Fine et al., 1990). Teenage girls are almost as likely to have a job as boys are, although girls continue to be paid less than boys. Adolescents from lower-income families have a lower than average rate of employment. When they do have jobs, however, they tend to work longer hours than middle-class teenagers. Adolescents from ethnic minority groups also have low employment rates. African American teenagers are about half as likely to have a job as white teenagers are, but the lowest employment rate of all (about 12 percent) has been found among some immigrants from Southeast Asia.

A job can contribute to self-esteem and a sense of personal identity by allowing adolescents to feel they are doing something useful. They often show pride in their place of work as well as in themselves as workers. Not only are they expressing the sense of industry and competence that they worked on developing in middle childhood, they are also anticipating their future economic self-sufficiency. At the same time, by taking responsibility for showing up on time and doing the tasks they are given, they confirm their emerging status as adults. The pay they earn helps make them more independent from their parents, and gives them experience with managing money. By forcing teens to budget their time, balance demands, and make choices, a part-time job can foster maturity (Fine et al., 1990; Greenberger and Steinberg, 1980).

Jobs for adolescents also have drawbacks, however. For one thing, the work that is available to teens is often routine and impersonal, with the teenagers seldom feeling close to adult coworkers (Greenberger and Steinberg, 1980). As a result, teenagers may not really enjoy their jobs and may come to feel that they are working only for the money (Fine et al., 1990). Even more important, a part-time job may cause them to neglect their schoolwork or have little time to spend with friends. High school students with jobs report fewer close relationships with peers, less involvement in school activities, less enjoyment of school, and lower grades than their nonworking peers (Fine et al., 1990).

Working per se does not seem to be the critical factor, but rather the number of hours spent working. The drawbacks seem to increase as adolescents work more hours. One large-scale survey of American high school students found that those who worked the most hours during the school year reported the worst school performance, the least investment in education, and the most psychological distress, drug and alcohol use, delinquency, and autonomy from parents (Steinberg and Dornbusch, 1991). Although earlier studies suggested that tenth graders who work more than 14 hours a week and older students who work more than 20 are the ones who suffer the most, this survey found no clear cutoff point at which the problems became suddenly severe. Negative effects were already apparent for students who worked only 11 to 15 hours weekly, and they increased from there. Interestingly, the benefits of working do not increase with the number of hours worked. They are present even for adolescents who work only a few hours a week.

THE COHERENCE OF DEVELOPMENT IN ADOLESCENCE

As in other age periods, the coherence of adolescent development takes several forms. First, the various aspects of individual development fit together in a coherent way. There are close links between the quality of parent-child relationships, peer relationships, and school functioning. For example, teens whose friendships are more intimate and supportive become increasingly involved at school, while those whose peer relationships are conflicted become less involved and exhibit more behavior problems (Berndt, Hawkins, and Hoyle, 1986).

Second, there is coherence in the course of individual development over time, with connections between how well a youngster functions in adolescence and how well he or she functioned in earlier developmental periods. Detailed longitudinal observation of children in nursery school and summer camp settings shows substantial continuity of individual functioning across childhood and adolescence. For instance, peer functioning in middle childhood predicts relationships in the teenage years, and dependency and lack of effectiveness in entering the peer group in the preschool period predict similar problems in adolescence. Even differences in the quality of attachment assessed in infancy are predictive: those who were securely attached are, as a group, dramatically less dependent, form more intimate friendships, and are more effective in the peer group as teenagers (Sroufe, Carlson, and Shulman, 1993). Such differences are not "caused" in a simple way by early attachment history. Rather, attachment history tends to set a child on a certain developmental pathway that often continues because it is supported by later circumstances.

This is not to say that the quality of a person's adjustment can't change with age. During adolescence, some young people become better adjusted than they were before, while for others the opposite is true. But such changes do not come about unexpectedly. Developmentalists see them as understandable reactions to changes in the environments in which the youngsters grow.

Despite the challenging developmental tasks encountered during adolescence, most young people pass through the teenage years relatively unscathed and emerge prepared to deal with the demands of adulthood. A minority of teenagers are overwhelmed by the demands of adolescence and develop serious problems, some of which will be discussed in Chapter 15. But for most, adolescence is a time of great change but only transitory turmoil.

Much attention has been focused on teenagers' use of alcohol and other drugs. Since 1975, researchers at the University of Michigan have been tracking teenage drug use in annual surveys of high school seniors from across the United States. These surveys indicate that drug and alcohol use increased during the 1970s, but began to decline around 1980 (see Table 14.6). Unfortunately, the 1993 data suggest that drug use is once again on the rise (Johnston, O'Malley, and Bachman, 1994).

Use of illicit drugs by high school seniors is still lower than it was when the surveys began. However, the 1993 survey showed the first increase since 1981 in the percentage of seniors who said they had tried an illicit drug (see Figure 14.3). Experimentation was up for marijuana, LSD, stimulants, and inhalants, although not for heroin and cocaine. Cigarette smoking also increased slightly in 1993 for the first time in over 10 years. Nearly 62 percent of seniors said that they had tried cigarettes, and 19 percent said that they were daily smokers.

Alcohol remains by far the most widely used drug among high school students. In 1993, 87 percent of seniors reported experience with alcohol, a percentage that has remained quite stable since 1975. However, only 51 percent said that they had consumed alcohol in the past 30 days, and this figure has declined notably since 1980. About 5 percent of seniors said that they were heavy drinkers, although 28 percent reported an episode of binge drinking (five or more drinks in a row) within the past 2 weeks.

Since 1991, the annual nationwide surveys have also included eighth and tenth graders. Alarmingly, by eighth grade a fairly high number of students have already tried one or more drugs. For example, in the 1993 survey, 67 percent of eighth graders said that they had tried alcohol, and 25 percent said that they had been drunk at least once. Forty-five percent had tried cigarettes, and 17 percent had smoked in the past month. About a third (32 percent) had tried at least one illicit drug.

The surveys reveal clear ethnic differences in drug use. Among eighth graders, Hispanic-Americans have the highest usage rates for nearly all drugs. Among high school seniors, however, it is whites who are most likely to use alcohol, cigarettes, and most illegal drugs. At this grade level, Hispanics have the highest rates only for cocaine (including crack) and heroin. This difference between eighth and twelfth grades can be explained partly by the fact that Hispanics have higher high school dropout rates than whites. Drug users are especially likely to quit high school and not be included in the twelfth grade survey. At all three grade levels studied, African-American students are less likely than whites or Hispanics to use illegal drugs, alcohol, or tobacco. In twelfth grade, for example, they are *much* less likely than whites to be daily cigarette smokers (4 percent versus 21 percent) or binge drinkers (13 percent versus 31 percent). Since the differences between whites and African-Americans are already present in eighth grade, they cannot be readily explained by high school dropout rates.

TABLE 14.6

PERCENT OF HIGH SCHOOL SENIORS REPORTING USE OF ALCOHOL, CIGARETTES, OR ILLICIT DRUGS IN THE PREVIOUS 30 DAYS, 1975–1993*

Substance	1975	1980	1985	1990	1993
Alcohol	68.3	72.0	65.9	57.1	51.0
Cigarettes	36.7	30.5	30.1	29.4	29.9
Marijuana	27.3	33.7	25.7	14.0	15.5
Stimulants	8.7	12.1	6.8	3.7	3.7
Cocaine	2.1	5.2	6.7	1.9	1.3
LSD	2.5	2.3	1.6	1.9	2.4
PCP and other psychedelics	na	2.3	1.3	0.4	1.0
Heroin	0.6	0.2	0.3	0.2	0.2

*These data are drawn from interviews of a nationally representative sample.
SOURCE: Johnston, O'Malley, and Bachman, 1994.

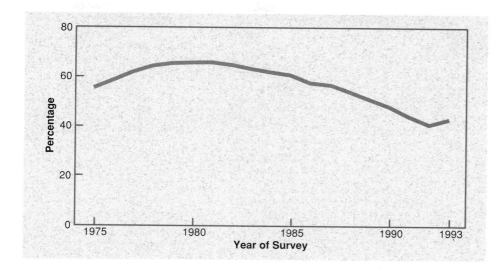

FIGURE 14.3
PERCENTAGE OF HIGH
SCHOOL SENIORS WHO
HAVE USED ANY ILLICIT
DRUG, 1975–1993
(Source: Johnston, O'Malley, and Bachman, 1994, p. 81.)

Along with the recent rise in drug use among teenagers, the annual surveys have also shown a softening in student attitudes toward drugs. Students' disapproval of drug use and their perception of its riskiness have generally declined since 1991, especially for marijuana and cocaine. Johnston and his coauthors suggest that this shift in attitudes can be explained by a shift of media attention and health education efforts away from drugs, partly because many people believe that the drug problem is no longer severe. These researchers warn that renewed attention to drug education, in schools and in the media, is needed to head off further increases in drug use.

To be effective, however, drug education programs must include more than just information about drugs and their potential risks (Millstein and Litt, 1990; Leventhal and Keeshan, 1993). Adolescents' feelings of invulnerability often lead them to downplay the chances that risky behavior will have bad consequences for them personally. Teenagers' desire to seek autonomy and to explore various personal identities can be another factor in drug use. To have much of an impact, antidrug programs must focus on changing drug-related attitudes and behaviors and must consider the social context in which these attitudes and behaviors develop. Since parents and peers both influence adolescents' decisions about drugs, including alcohol and tobacco, one way to increase the effectiveness of these programs is through parent and peer involvement. The successful campaign to reduce drunk driving among high school students is one example of this approach.

CHAPTER SUMMARY

1. Adolescence is a critical developmental stage during which major advances are made in every domain, and previous developmental issues are reworked. But adolescence is not an inevitably stormy time. The amount of turmoil varies from early to late adolescence, from one domain of an adolescent's life to another, and from one individual to another. Cultural definitions of the transition from childhood to adulthood also play a role in how difficult adolescence is. Major tasks of adolescence include establishing a personal **identity,** achieving a new level of closeness and trust with peers, acquiring a new status in the family, and gaining greater autonomy in the world outside the family.

2. Developmental changes in self-concept illustrate some of the psychological differences between early and late adolescence. Young adolescents become aware that they have inner thoughts and feelings different from those of other people, but they have trouble integrating different aspects of the self and truly understanding the perspectives of others. Older adolescents have a more integrated sense of self, can reconcile inconsistencies in themselves, and have a much greater understanding of the uniqueness and separateness of people.

3. Forming a personal identity involves integrating into a coherent whole past experiences, ongoing changes, and society's expectations for the future. The **social construction view** of identity formation emphasizes the fact that this process occurs in the context of social relationships. Erik Erikson referred to the difficulty that adolescents may encounter in establishing their identity as an **identity crisis.** James Marcia described four **identity statuses,** based on whether or not identity exploration and commitment to a particular identity had occurred: **identity diffusion** (no exploration or commitment), **foreclosure** (commitment without exploration), **moratorium** (exploration without commitment), and **identity achievement** (exploration followed by commitment). Identity development proceeds somewhat differently for males and females and for members of different ethnic groups.

4. During adolescence, peer relationships change in a number of ways, and the tasks related to peers become more complex. Compared with younger children, teenagers have a much greater capacity for true mutual understanding. This increased capacity is linked to a new desire for self-disclosure in close and intimate friendships and a new emphasis on fidelity and trust in those relationships. Two peer group structures that develop in adolescence are the **clique** and the **crowd.** Cliques, which are small groups of friends, are the context for much peer interaction, especially in early adolescence. Crowds are larger, more loosely organized groups of cliques. How adolescents perceive the members of various crowds is based more on reputation than on actual behavior. Dating and sexual activity emerge, usually in middle adolescence, in the context of the crowd.

5. During adolescence, peer influences do not replace those of parents. Instead, parental influences remain important, even while peer influences increase. However, patterns of interaction within the family must change to accommodate the emerging new adult. The adolescent, like the toddler, must evolve a new way of relating to parents, one that involves more separateness but not a loss of closeness. In the end, a much more nearly equal relationship develops between the parents and the teenager. Warm, authoritative parenting seems to foster particularly positive outcomes in adolescents' development. Parental divorce continues to affect children's development during adolescence, with some effects not being seen until well after the breakup of the marriage.

6. In addition to moving toward greater autonomy with respect to parents, adolescents must take a more autonomous stance in the larger world. This includes taking on more responsibility for schoolwork and school-related activities. Becoming more autonomous may also involve taking a part-time job. A job can boost a teenager's self-esteem, sense of identity, and feelings of financial independence from parents. However, the more hours an adolescent works per week, the more negative effects are seen.

7. Adolescence brings change in the abilities of youngsters and in the settings in which these abilities are used, but it also represents continuity with the past. All the new abilities of adolescence are built on the previous developments of childhood. There is also coherence in the quality of a youngster's adjustment over time. How well a person functions as a teenager is generally predictable from how well he or she functioned in earlier periods of development.

PART SIX

EPILOGUE

Adolescence

Adolescence can be thought of as a second revolution in human development—the first occurring during the toddler period, when a child emerges from an infant. During adolescence, a child is transformed into a young adult. Qualitative advances can be seen in all developmental areas. Among the most obvious are the physical changes. Just as toddlers lose their former babyish shape, so adolescents lose the look of children. Not only do they grow taller, heavier, and stronger, but their body proportions change and secondary sex characteristics develop. For males this includes a broadening of the shoulders, enlargement of the genitals, and growth of hair on various parts of the body. For females it includes widening of the hips, development of breasts, and the growth of pubic hair. Both sexes, of course, acquire the capacity for reproduction.

Equally important are the cognitive changes of adolescence. Teenagers are able to consider hypotheticals, to engage in "what-if" thinking about possibilities. (What if all the lakes in this country became polluted? What if I were put in charge of planning the first colony in space?) This enables them to make inferences in the absence of direct experience with something. Teenagers can also draw tentative conclusions while they gather more data to assess an idea. School-age children, in contrast, generally think that their first conclusion *must* be right, and they seldom search out additional information to make a more thorough assessment. Adolescents can also reason more systematically than younger children can. They are able to proceed step by step to logical conclusions. As a result, they can understand abstractions such as $A = 2X$ with as much certainty as they know the sun is shining. Finally, adolescents can embrace multiple viewpoints. They can take one perspective and then consider several others, examining the differences among them.

Taken together, these new abilities represent a major qualitative advancement that sets adolescents' thinking apart from that of elementary school children. Essentially, older adolescents have the cognitive capacities of adults, even though their thinking skills are still unseasoned by adult experience. Twenty years from now you will think about many things differently because of all you have learned in life, but the basic tools you use to solve problems and think about the world will be much the same as those you had acquired by late adolescence.

Along with the cognitive changes of adolescence come dramatic changes in self-understanding. Adolescents can reflect on the nature of the self—its history, its uniqueness, its complexity. They also develop much greater feelings of autonomy, which is why psychoanalytic theorists refer to adolescence as a second individuation. The first individuation occurs in toddlerhood, when children come to understand their basic separateness from parents. In adolescence, the individuation process is carried much further. Now young people come to understand that they have inner feelings that even parents can't know. Accompanying this important individuation is a de-identification with parents. Teenagers are moving toward their own ideals, goals, and values, their own unique characters. In Erik Erikson's terms, they are establishing a sense of personal identity, a knowledge of who they are as separate from their parents and of what their place in the world is.

Adolescence is especially critical in Erikson's theory because teenagers must rework all previous developmental issues—trust, autonomy, initiative, industry—in light of their newly emerging identity.

A growing sense of identity and self-awareness inevitably brings changes in an adolescent's relationships with others. Consider peer relationships. While sharing and loyalty are often seen in childhood friendships, the intimacy and self-disclosure among pairs of adolescent friends put their relationships in a different league. At first these close relationships are most often with friends of the same gender, but gradually heterosexual contact often develops. By the second phase of adolescence, most teens are not only dating but are also forming intimate relationships with members of the opposite sex. This is a marked change from the strict segregation by gender that occurred during the elementary school years.

As relationships with peers change and mature, so do relationships with parents. In mainstream American culture (although not nearly so much in traditional Asian, Latin American, or Native American families), early adolescence may be a period of new assertiveness on the youngster's part, which can produce increased conflict with parents and distancing from them (C. Cooper, in press). This new assertiveness is in some ways analogous to the contrariness of toddlers as they try to establish themselves as separate people, while still staying connected to parents in new, more mature ways. Both the toddler's behavior and that of the young teenager seem to be an important part of individuation in Western culture. Then, following each of these phases, there comes a period of realignment with parents. The 3-year-old becomes more cooperative and more self-confident. The older adolescent accepts the parents on a new level, and the relationship between them becomes more symmetrical. The parents are now advisers, counselors, and "sounding boards" more than controllers and disciplinarians. This new, more mature relationship is carried forward to young adulthood.

THREE TEENAGERS, FOUR THEMES

All the dramatic developmental changes mentioned above are apparent in our three teenagers. Malcolm, Mike, and Meryl each show advances in thinking and self-reflection. This can be seen in Meryl's discussions of her relationship with Amy and in her concerns for migrant workers, in Mike's new concern about the environment, especially the marine environment, and in Malcolm's growing political idealism and thoughts about social jus-

tice. At the same time, each displays a new self-assertiveness with parents, especially during early adolescence. Meryl tells her parents that they just don't understand, that "things are different now"; Mike insists that his mother stop calling him Mikey, a name that to him is embarrassingly babyish; and Malcolm flatly refuses to go on the church retreat, no matter how hard his parents and grandmother try to persuade him. The peer relationships of these young people also show the typical adolescent changes, although Mike seems to be getting involved in dating more slowly than the others.

Despite their typical adolescent characteristics, Malcolm, Mike, and Meryl also have distinctive personalities arising from their different temperaments, life histories, circumstances, and genders. In looking at their similarities and differences in the rest of this epilogue, we return to some of the major themes of this book. The lives of our three teenagers are useful aids in summarizing these themes.

Normative Versus Individual Development

Mike illustrates many of the normative features of adolescent development—that is, the features that most teenagers share. His desire for privacy early in adolescence, his broadening interest in the world, and the great pride he takes in his first summer job are all common among youngsters his age. Academic problems early in adolescence, like those Mike experiences, are also fairly frequent, although his were probably compounded by his parents' divorce and his father's remarriage. Mike, however, pulls himself through these difficult years. His solid early care, the continued involvement of his parents, and the special interest of his uncle and a gifted teacher all help him to turn out fine. You can think of these factors as reinforcing one another. The biology teacher is able to ignite a spark because Mike already has a positive image of his own intellectual abilities, an image fostered by years of being told by his family that he is smart and capable. The biology teacher is partly reacting to positive characteristics that he sees in Mike—characteristics that Mike's parents encouraged by their love for and interest in him.

Malcolm's movement toward independence and his growing concern for questions of right and wrong are also fairly typical of his age group. But Malcolm places his own distinctive stamp on these adolescent changes. His flamboyant nature and boundless enthusiasm are predictable from his history. We would have a hard time believing that Malcolm would ever become a socially isolated, hesitant, pessimistic teenager. For him, life is full speed ahead—getting a job, dating, spending time with friends, becoming involved in political activities. Asserting himself and embracing the future seem to pose little problem. Malcolm retains the tendency toward impulsiveness that he showed throughout childhood. But because he cares about himself and others, the impulsiveness will probably not get out of hand. He may make mistakes, as we all do, but he is likely to learn from them and work to make things right.

Meryl, too, has become a fine young person. To be sure, she still has vestiges of shyness and hesitancy in new situations. When her body first starts maturing, she feels awkward and self-conscious. Even in later adolescence she steers away from certain kinds of self-exposure, such as joining the debating team. Still, she handles relationships with peers well. Her relationship with Amy clearly illustrates the loyalty, commitment, and self-disclosure typical of adolescent friendships. When allowed to select extracurricular activities of special interest to her (doing art work, being set director for the senior class play), she shows much persistence and competence. She is growing in self-confidence day by day. She also has a plan for her future and looks forward to college. It is particularly noteworthy that Meryl breaks a two-generation pattern by not becoming pregnant as a teenager. We see the contributions of grandmother, mother, and daughter to this accomplishment—Mrs. Polonius by facing her own guilt and building a strong relationship with Karen; Karen by building a close and open relationship with Meryl; and Meryl by carving out her own identity, developing good relationships with peers, and making wise choices.

Our three teenagers, then, have much in common because of the similar issues they face. All reflect the general or normative trends in adolescent development. Yet each has an individual style of tackling developmental tasks. For instance, although they all assert their independence from their parents, they do so in distinctive ways: Mike by spending time alone behind his closed bedroom door marked PRIVATE; Malcolm by loudly announcing his plans and opinions; and Meryl by informing her mother that they are not the same people, even though she stays close to Karen through frequent conversations. Thus, Mike, Malcolm, and Meryl illustrate how general trends and individual adaptations both characterize development.

The Interaction of Social and Cognitive Development

Another theme of this book that is illustrated in the stories of our three adolescents is the continual interaction of social development and cognitive development, with each supporting the other. For instance, Malcolm's cognitive abilities to coordinate multiple perspectives, to think in terms of abstract concepts such as fairness and justice, and to contemplate the future and his place within it allow him to participate in political events in a new way. At the same time, participation in the political process stimulates Malcolm's cognitive development, encouraging him to think more deeply about social issues. This give-and-take between the social and cognitive realms of development can be seen over and over. A person's social relationships and other life experiences both influence and are influenced by cognitive advances.

STABILITY AND CHANGE IN INDIVIDUAL DEVELOPMENT

A third theme of this book concerns stability and change in individual development. The stories of our three children were constructed to illustrate both these processes because research studies document that both occur. Of the three youngsters, Malcolm has shown the most stability, the most continuity in his ways of responding from one developmental period to the next. This is largely because he has experienced the most continuity in care. For him there was no divorce, no new father, no other major stress; hence his development has made fairly continuous progress.

Meryl and Mike, in contrast, have had notable changes in their individual adaptations as their life circumstances have changed. Meryl has done better than we might have expected earlier in her life, and Mike has had more problems. Still, they continue to be in many ways the same people throughout their various developmental periods. For instance, the hesitancy Meryl showed in early childhood can still be glimpsed in her teenage years, even though she has learned to cope well with her initial shyness in new situations. We can easily picture Malcolm standing to make a speech at his first political meeting, but this is something we cannot imagine Meryl doing. For Mike, too, the past has never been completely discarded, not even during his most difficult developmental periods. His fundamental belief in himself as a competent, valuable person, a belief forged in infancy and early childhood, has served him well in disruptive and challenging times. As with Meryl, Mike's early life experiences have remained with him—transformed, to be sure, by later experiences, but never completely erased.

A final point to add in thinking about stability and change in human development is that who a person becomes is never inevitable, even given a certain general set of life circumstances. Thus, if we started Malcolm's life over in the same family, he would probably not turn out exactly as he is today. Every life has twists and turns, and complex multiple influences. We would expect that if Malcolm started over in the same family he would still end up exuberant and self-confident, but these characteristics can be expressed in many different ways. Recall the model of branching developmental pathways we talked about in Chapter 1, a model we represented by a tree. A proliferation of smaller branches lies at the end of each major branch. As a result, two pathways almost exactly alike in the beginning can lead to a diversity of possible outcomes.

The Contexts of Development

The importance of developmental contexts in shaping children's lives has been a fourth major theme of this book. One critical context is the family, which time and again has affected the fates of our three children. Without Joe and Karen finding each other and marrying, without Christine and Frank's conflict and eventual divorce, and without ongoing social support in Malcolm's family, adolescence would have been quite different for these three young people.

Broader contexts beyond the family also exert powerful influences. Relationships with peers, teachers, and others take on new significance as teenagers come to better understand themselves and establish their places in the world. Societal, cultural, and economic contexts continue to be important too. For instance, Meryl's artistic expression is influenced in part by cultural ideas about "appropriate" areas of achievement for females. Similarly, Mike's interest in marine biology is influenced by current ecological concerns in North American society, and Malcolm's interest in minority politics is in part a product of the economic and social realities of his community. The difference between the broader social context in which Malcolm is developing, and the broader social contexts of Meryl and Mike, can be seen in one of the arguments Malcolm gives in favor of a part-time job. Of our three teenagers, only he would mention avoidance of gang involvement as a reason for working after school.

Beyond these direct influences of context, there are indirect influences as well. Contextual factors often affect children through their impact on parents. The beneficial counseling that Karen received ultimately benefited Meryl. Frank Gordon's employment problems contributed to his drinking, his lowered self-esteem, and the tension in his marriage, and through these effects they influenced Mike. Mike was also influenced indirectly by the cultural factor of expanding work roles for women, because this factor encouraged his mother to pursue a career outside the home and contributed to the conflict in his parents' marriage (as well as adding to his mother's self-esteem and therefore to her confidence as a parent). Meryl, too, was indirectly influenced by this same cultural factor, but in her case it produced *less* family conflict and a positive role model of a working woman for her to emulate.

MOVING TOWARD ADULTHOOD

All three of our adolescents are reasonably well-adjusted. Because their developmental contexts have been sufficiently supportive, they have managed to handle developmental issues favorably. Each is now on the threshold of young adulthood. All have the aptitude, the means, and the motivation for higher education, and a college degree will serve them well as they make their ways in today's complex world. We can be optimistic that they will face no more than the normal struggles in coping with future challenges. None is seriously disturbed, and serious psychiatric problems do not seem likely in their futures. Could it have been otherwise if life had gone differently for them? We turn to this question in our final chapter.

PART SEVEN

Disorders
and Resiliency

CHAPTER 15

DEVELOPMENTAL PSYCHOPATHOLOGY

Chapter 15

Developmental Psychopathology

The three children we have been following—Mike, Malcolm, and Meryl—represent basically healthy patterns of development. To be sure, each child has faced difficulties, had problems, and shown vulnerabilities, as we all do. Mike has a tendency to feel more responsibility than is sometimes appropriate, especially when things go wrong in important relationships. Malcolm can at times be impulsive and others do not always appreciate his exuberant style. He also faces the challenge of being a young male in a tough urban environment. Meryl is still somewhat shy and hesitant, and she has difficulty adapting to new situations. Friends sometimes view her as unduly sensitive and lacking in self-confidence. Still, all three, now in late adolescence, are purposeful and well-directed in meeting their goals, successful in dealing with other people, and sufficiently competent at managing their own lives.

But what if they had received less nurturance and guidance from their families? Would Mike have been vulnerable to adolescent depression? Might Malcolm have been labeled "hyperactive" and had serious attention problems at school? Would Meryl have suffered a severe anxiety disorder? While it is difficult to answer these hypothetical questions, studies of people who have developed emotional problems suggest that teenagers like Mike, Malcolm, and Meryl might have turned out differently in less supportive circumstances. Such studies show that the people who succumb to emotional problems are often not qualitatively different from our three children in their initial characteristics. What tips the balance for them are life histories that are more demanding in critical ways, histories that have provided poor support for important aspects of development.

It is also interesting to ask whether other youngsters, more prone to emotional or behavioral problems, would have developed them given the *same* experiences as our three children. This question emphasizes a child's genetic or biological vulnerability. For instance, perhaps a child with a strong biological predisposition to depression would have suffered depression during adolescence if confronted with the same life challenges as those faced by Mike Gordon. Most researchers who study emotional and behavioral problems believe that such genetic factors always interact with environment. Thus, where a person falls on the continuum from emotionally healthy to unhealthy is seen as a product of both heredity and experience (Rutter, 1991).

The subfield of developmental psychology that is concerned with emotional and behavioral disorders is called **developmental psychopathology.** (The term *pathology* refers to any marked deviation from a normal, healthy state.) Developmental psychopathology is the study of the origins and course of such disorders, whenever they may occur. It includes the study of disturbed children, the developmental roots of adult disorders, and the patterns that disorders follow after they emerge (Cicchetti and Cohen, 1995; Quinton, Rutter, and Gulliver, 1990; Sroufe and Rutter, 1984). Developmental psychopathology stresses all the major themes of this book: the importance of developmental contexts, the interaction of genes and environment, the role of past development in current developmental outcomes, and the orderliness of development despite changes in a person over time.

Studying psychopathology from a developmental perspective has enriched our understanding of emotional and behavioral disorders in several ways. First,

Developmental psychopathology:
The study of the origins and course of emotional and behavioral disorders.

it has encouraged us to explore both the origins of abnormal behavior *and* the ways in which abnormal behavior changes over time. Like other aspects of development, abnormality is not static. For example, children who were hyperactive in elementary school are often no longer hyperactive as teenagers; yet they may still find it hard to concentrate on schoolwork and to control their impulses.

Second, studying psychopathology from a developmental perspective has focused attention on people who seem to be on a path to developing some disorder yet somehow manage not to develop it (Masten and Coatsworth, 1995). Such cases of *resiliency* provide clues to how to prevent or treat disorders in their early stages. If we can discover what protective factors help these individuals avoid emotional and behavioral problems, perhaps we can foster these same conditions for others who are at similar risk.

Third, using a developmental perspective to study psychopathology encourages us to explore how disorders may have their roots in the ways that certain individuals resolve (or fail to resolve) the major developmental issues that all people face (Sroufe, 1989). Developmental psychopathologists look for the precursors of disorders within the developmental challenges that are most salient at a given age (secure attachment in infancy, increased independence in the preschool period, identity formation in adolescence, and so forth). If development goes awry in these critical areas, future problems seem more likely. The key tasks are: (1) to define important developmental issues; (2) to identify normal patterns of resolving them; and (3) to describe deviations from these normal patterns. In this way, developmental psychopathology brings together the study of normal and abnormal development.

We return to these three features of the developmental perspective in the first major section of this chapter. Here we take a closer look at how developmental psychopathologists think about and analyze emotional and behavioral disorders. In the next section we look at various approaches to explaining psychopathology—first those that emphasize biological factors, then those that emphasize environmental ones. This section ends with a discussion of how the developmental perspective combines and integrates all the other views. Then, in the third major section of this chapter, we consider some of the specific developmental disorders that can arise in childhood or adolescence: early childhood autism, conduct disorders, attention deficit/hyperactivity disorder, anxiety disorders, and anorexia nervosa. Finally, in the last section, we review how the study of developmental psychopathology emphasizes all the major themes of this book.

A CLOSER LOOK AT THE
DEVELOPMENTAL PERSPECTIVE

As we've said, developmental psychopathologists seek to understand why some people who are at risk for developing an emotional or behavioral disorder do go on to develop it, while other people at similar risk do not. Put another way, developmental psychopathologists are interested in both the *risk factors* for emotional and behavioral disorders (the factors that increase the likelihood of the disorder developing) and the *protective factors* that help people avoid them. This focus is a major feature of the developmental perspective on psychopathology.

RISK FACTORS AND PROTECTIVE FACTORS

Risk factor:
Any characteristic, condition, or circumstance that increases the likelihood of some disorder.

Determining factors that place people at risk for developing an emotional or behavioral disorder is a central task for developmental researchers. A **risk factor** is any characteristic, condition, or circumstance that increases the likelihood of some disorder arising. For example, childhood risk factors for developing criminal behavior as an adult include persistent aggression, a low IQ, harsh treatment by parents, and parents who engage in criminal activity, who are poorly educated, and/or who have been hospitalized for psychiatric illness (Farrington et al., 1990). As this list suggests, a risk factor may be genetic (such as a biological parent who has a disorder with a known genetic component), familial (such as a hostile emotional climate in the home), socioeconomic (such as poverty and its associated stress), cultural (such as frequent exposure to a delinquent subculture), or developmental (such as anxious attachment in infancy or peer rejection in childhood) (Masten and Coatsworth, 1995; Sroufe, 1989). In other words, all five of the contexts of development that we discussed in Chapter 2 must be considered in assessing the risk of psychopathology. (See Table 15.1 for a summary of risk factors for psychiatric disorders in children.)

To understand the significance of risk factors, you must realize that risk is simply a statistical concept. It applies to a group of people. We cannot say that a particular child who has experienced harsh parental treatment is *destined* to become a criminal. In fact, many or even most of the people in an at-risk category will *not* develop the particular problem behavior. Consider schizophrenia, a condition that first appears in young adulthood and is characterized by extremely disordered thinking and severe social withdrawal. The rate of schizophrenia in the general population is only 1 percent. Among people with one biological parent who is schizophrenic, the rate more than triples, rising to 3.7 percent, or even somewhat higher if related disorders are taken into account (Farone and Tsuang, 1988). These are the people considered at greater risk for

TABLE 15.1
RISK FACTORS FOR CHILD PSYCHIATRIC DISORDERS

HEALTH HISTORY	ADVERSE CONDITIONS
Prematurity	Poverty
Birth complications	Neglect
Illnesses	Abuse
Accidents	Chaotic family life
	Mental illness in parent
DEMOGRAPHIC FACTORS	Alcoholism in parent
Low family income	Parental conflict
History of parental unemployment	Social isolation
Low parental education	
Minority status	**STRESSFUL LIFE EVENTS**
Unstable family structure	Serious illness or accidents involving
Large family size	immediate family
	Death of parents
	Divorce of parents
	Remarriage of parents
	Trauma (rape, witnessing violence, etc.)
	Hospitalization (repeated)
	Foster care
	Frequent moves

developing schizophrenia. But note that the vast majority of them—over 95 percent—will *not* develop schizophrenia. Being in the at-risk category in no way guarantees succumbing to the disorder. All it means is that, as a group, these people face a greater risk than does the general population.

Since risk factors don't guarantee the development of a disorder, it is generally inappropriate to assume that they are *causes*. Many risk factors may not be causal at all, but rather are simply associated with other circumstances that contribute to a disorder. Poverty, for instance, is a risk factor for emotional or behavioral problems. More children who are poor develop such problems than do children whose parents are financially secure, all other things being equal. But poverty, per se, is probably not a direct cause of disorders. Rather, it is likely that stress and other factors related to poverty are what make people who are poor more vulnerable (McLoyd, 1990; Sameroff and Fiese, 1990).

While the presence of a single risk factor often has limited predictive power, the presence of several risk factors is usually much more predictive (Masten and Coatsworth, 1995; Yoshikawa, 1994). This might be called the "multiplier effect": two or three or four risk factors occurring together predict a negative outcome far more strongly than does each factor occurring alone. For example, children with two alcoholic parents are far more likely to develop problems than are children with only one alcoholic parent (Earls et al., 1988).

Often it is the sheer number of risk factors, not the specific factors present, that predicts a negative outcome. For instance, the presence at age 8 of *any* three (or more) of the risk factors listed above for adult criminal behavior strongly predicts the development of such behavior in adulthood (Farrington et al., 1990). In fact, 75 percent of children who have three or more of these risk factors are convicted of offenses more serious than traffic violations by age 32. Similarly strong predictive power has been found for the presence of multiple risk factors regarding poor school performance and social maladjustment (Sameroff and Fiese, 1990).

The ways in which risk factors combine to encourage psychological problems can be quite complex. There is not just a single way to precipitate most disorders. The same disorder may result from different combinations of risks. Psychopathologists say that multiple causes, in varying combinations, lead to a *final common pathway* to the disorder. Conversely, the same factors may place people at risk for a number of different disorders (Robins and Price, 1991). For instance, conduct problems, harsh parental treatment, and incompetence with peers in middle childhood are risk factors for a range of negative outcomes in adulthood, including depression, alcoholism, criminal behavior, and schizophrenia (Robins and Price, 1991; Zoccolillo, 1993). Even a very specific risk factor, like having a schizophrenic biological parent, is associated with more than one disorder—in this case antisocial behavior as well as schizophrenia (Mednick, 1970). These linkages illustrate the complexity of causation and the need to consider *transformations* and branching pathways over the course of development. Problems are expressed in different ways at different stages of development, and the same pattern at one age may diverge into different outcomes over time. Thus, at a certain stage in the child's development, misconduct may elicit reactions from others that lead to the loss of self-esteem and feelings of rejection that could later contribute to depression.

Whether risk factors lead to serious emotional or behavior problems is also influenced by the presence of **protective factors**—characteristics, conditions, or circumstances that promote or maintain healthy development (Glick and Zigler, 1990). Protective factors serve as buffers, counteracting the effects of risk

Protective factor: Any characteristic, condition, or circumstance that offsets the effect of a risk factor.

factors and sometimes preventing a disorder from arising (Masten and Coatsworth, 1995; Werner and Smith, 1992). For instance, in line with other researchers, Michael Rutter (1979b) has reported that the presence of three or more common risk factors predicts a 75 percent rate of problem behavior. However, if the protective factor of a loving, dependable parent is simultaneously present, the rate of problem behavior is only 25 percent.

Thus, the route from risks to emotional and behavioral disorders is rarely direct and straight. Many twists and turns are possible along the way, including turns in a positive direction. Such an idea was presented in Bowlby's pathway model, which was discussed in Chapter 1. This web of influences underscores the need to consider the *total context* of development when assessing if or why a certain child will develop a particular problem.

ASSESSING NORMAL AND ABNORMAL

In addition to its focus on how risk factors and protective factors combine to influence development, the developmental perspective on psychopathology has other important features. One is its view that normal and abnormal behavior must be considered together because disorders often have their roots in the ways people handle the normal developmental issues we all face. Thus, developmental psychopathologists look for the origins of some problem behaviors in the ways in which people resolve the major developmental challenges we have discussed throughout this book. Challenges like developing a secure attachment in infancy and achieving greater autonomy in toddlerhood are seen as critical. When outcomes in these key areas go awry, serious problems can result.

It is not always easy to tell when a particular child's development deviates far enough from expected patterns to be considered abnormal. One way in which developmental psychologists gauge what is abnormal is by assessing how common a particular feeling or behavior is. A behavior that *seems* problematic may turn out not to be a major cause for concern when viewed in terms of how common it actually is. Many seemingly problematic behaviors are in fact fairly typical of people of a certain age and sex, and thus are not major causes for concern (Macfarlane et al., 1954).

For example, lying is common among small children, although it drops off after age 6 for girls and age 8 for boys. Temper outbursts are common throughout childhood, especially for boys. Disturbing dreams are quite common for girls when they enter school and for boys and girls just prior to adolescence. Destructiveness, however, is *not* common at any age. Such information is very important in judging the significance of a particular behavior for present and future adjustment. Problems that are common for children of a certain age and sex are usually much less cause for worry than problems that are not common. For instance, a high activity level by itself, without aggression or other symptoms, is not a major cause for concern when found in a preschool boy. In fact, about 50 percent of parents say that their preschool boys are unusually active. Similarly, food finickiness is fairly common at age 3 and is unlikely to predict anorexia (self-starvation) at age 15. Sensitivity, shyness, and specific fears—by themselves—are also not abnormal in young children and probably do not predict later pathology.

Other, less common behavior patterns, however, are strongly linked to later disorders. Conduct problems are a clear warning sign, especially a combination of aggression, lying, stealing, and defiance that persists into middle childhood. Another important warning sign is difficulty with peers—not just occasional squabbles with friends (which is relatively common), but persistent unpopularity with other children. Even though unpopularity is not generally considered pathological by itself, it is one of the strongest predictors of a range of adult disorders (Parker and Asher, 1987; Robins, 1978).

From a developmental perspective, the link between peer problems and later maladjustment is understandable. Because forming a close friendship and becoming an active member of a same-gender peer group are major tasks of middle childhood, incompetence with peers at this age represents a major adaptational failure. In addition, unsuccessful peer relations in middle childhood leave a person unprepared for close relationships later in life. Close and supportive relationships, in turn, are a major protective factor, reducing the likelihood of pathology and buffering a person against the effects of problems that do arise (Sroufe and Rutter, 1984). For instance, having family and friends who are willing and able to offer social support is associated with more rapid and complete recovery for people hospitalized with a major psychiatric disorder (Glick and Zigler, 1990). Lack of close relationships, conversely, leaves a person more vulnerable.

CHANGE AND STABILITY OVER TIME

Another feature of the developmental perspective on psychopathology is its focus on patterns of change and stability in behavior over time. Such patterns were clearly revealed in a study by Lee Robins (1966; 1978), who was able to obtain data about a large number of children who had been seen at a child guidance clinic in St. Louis. Years later, Robins studied these same people to see how well they had fared. This approach enabled her to explore such questions as: What were adult schizophrenics like as children? Did they show symptoms similar to those they showed in adulthood? What is the typical outcome for a child who is shy and withdrawn? Does such a youngster often become socially isolated in adulthood, perhaps even depressed, or are more positive outcomes likely?

Robins found that psychiatric problems in childhood were indeed related to problems in adulthood, showing continuity in development and links from past to present. For instance, 34 percent of the clinic cases had serious adult disorders, whereas only 8 percent of a control group from the same neighborhoods did. Moreover, only 20 percent of the clinic cases were free of problems as adults, compared to 57 percent of the controls.

The exact links between childhood and adult problems varied greatly, however, depending on the particular disorders involved. Sometimes the links were very predictable, with strong continuity from past to present. For example, among the clinic cases who in childhood had been classified as "sociopaths" (people who behave irresponsibly, with no concern for others and no signs of remorse for their misdeeds), 94 percent had been arrested by adulthood (versus 17 percent of the controls) and 70 percent had major adult problems such as alcoholism, criminal convictions, and psychosis. Looking at this link from the other direction, virtually *all* the diagnosed adult sociopaths had shown sociopathic behavior when they were children.

In other cases the links between childhood and adult problems were more complex and difficult to foresee. For instance, schizophrenia, a disorder often

TABLE 15.2
CLASSIFICATION
OF MODELS
OF
PSYCHOPATHOLOGY

The models used by researchers studying the development of psychopathology are divided into two categories, depending on the kind of primary cause they focus on: biological or environmental.

Biological Perspectives
Traditional medical models
Neurological models
Physiological models
Genetic models

Environmental Perspectives
Sociological models
Behavioral models
Psychodynamic models
Family models

Model:
A framework—a set of ideas and assumptions about the causes and conditions that produce a particular phenomenon.

marked by severe withdrawal and social isolation, is not generally associated with these same symptoms in childhood. Instead, adult schizophrenics often show conduct disorders as children, behaviors such as overaggressiveness or antisocial tendencies. Depression in adulthood has also been found to be linked to conduct disorders in childhood, especially among females (Robins and Price, 1991).

Finally, Robins discovered that some childhood problems were *not* so strongly linked to adult disorders. For example, children who were shy and anxious (so-called *internalizing* children) were no more likely to have problems in adulthood than were children from the control group. Thus, we might be optimistic that a child like Meryl will not go on to become a troubled adult. To summarize, although some childhood disorders show rather simple continuity with adult disorders, many do not. Some childhood problems typically disappear with time, while others evolve into quite different forms in later years. Many adult schizophrenics, for example, were not shy, withdrawn children, and many aggressive girls do not grow up to be aggressive adults. As you have seen throughout this book, development is characterized by transformations over time, rather than by simple linear continuity. Still, there are meaningful links between childhood problems and adult psychopathology.

EXPLAINING PSYCHOPATHOLOGY

Over the years, various models of psychopathology have been proposed (Lazare, 1973). A **model** is a framework for explaining why things happen. It is a set of ideas and assumptions about the *etiology* of something—its causes or the conditions that produce it. Some models of psychopathology focus mainly on the biological underpinnings of emotional and behavioral problems, while others focus mainly on environmental factors (see Table 15.2). These two approaches are not incompatible. In fact, most researchers believe that psychological disorders often involve a complex interplay of biology and environment. Researchers differ, however, in where they place their major emphasis—that is, in which factors they consider the *primary* determinants of a disorder.

BIOLOGICAL PERSPECTIVES

THE TRADITIONAL MEDICAL MODEL
The traditional medical model draws an explicit analogy between psychological disorders and physical illnesses. It holds that psychological disorders should be considered "mental illnesses," to be diagnosed and treated by doctors in an effort to bring about a cure. The medical model assumes that a psychological disturbance is caused by some underlying structural or physiological malfunction in the body, typically affecting the brain, even though the particular cause may not yet have been identified.

Certain mental disorders do fit the medical model. For instance, *general paresis,* an irreversible deterioration of all mental and physical processes, has been traced to an attack on the body's organs (the brain included) by the bacteria that cause syphilis. Similarly, early childhood *autism,* a condition characterized by a range of severe cognitive deficits and almost complete unresponsiveness to other people, also appears to be the result of biological abnormality. However, for most of the behavioral and emotional problems that children suffer, as well as for many serious adult disorders, such as depression and schizophrenia, biological factors are better viewed as contributors rather than as causes.

MODERN NEUROLOGICAL AND PHYSIOLOGICAL MODELS

Modern neurological and physiological models of psychopathology focus on these contributing biological factors, especially chemical imbalances in the brain. These imbalances involve either neurotransmitters (chemicals that govern the transfer of signals from one nerve cell to another) or other chemicals that control the activities of neurotransmitters (Cowen, 1989; Pennington and Welsh, 1995). The evidence that chemical imbalances are involved in some psychological disorders is often quite impressive. For example, researchers have found lower-than-normal levels of certain brain chemicals in people who are depressed. Drugs used to alleviate depression raise the levels of these chemicals, while substances that lower their levels cause a recurrence of depressive symptoms (Cowen, 1989).

Although it is tempting to say in this case that chemical deficiencies cause depression, determining cause is difficult because biological and environmental factors are mutually influencing. For instance, studies of young monkeys show that changes in the levels of these same brain chemicals occur following permanent separation from a parent (McKinney, 1977). The levels of these chemicals are also influenced by the quality of care the young monkey has received (Kraemer, 1992). Thus, depression and changes in brain chemistry may be a "chicken and egg" situation, in which it is impossible to say which comes first. It may be more appropriate to consider unusual brain chemistry as a correlate or "marker" of a disorder, rather than as a cause. This is true even though symptoms of depression can often be relieved by a drug that returns brain chemistry to normal. Although chemical imbalances may have come to be involved in these symptoms, faulty chemical makeup is not necessarily their initial cause. The initial cause could be environmental as well.

GENETIC MODELS

Researchers who take a genetic perspective on psychopathology assume that some people inherit a genetically based predisposition to develop emotional and behavioral problems. Since genes express themselves through activities within the cells of our bodies, genetic models of psychopathology can be thought of as a subclass of neurological and physiological models.

Virtually no modern behavior geneticist believes that there is a single gene directly causing a complex disorder such as schizophrenia (Cannon et al., 1990; Siminoff, McGuffin, and Gottesman, 1994). A single defective gene could not account for the distribution of schizophrenia found in families. If one dominant gene caused this disorder, an average of at least 75 percent of the children of two schizophrenic parents would inherit the condition too; if one recessive gene were the root of the problem, schizophrenia would occur in all youngsters with two schizophrenic parents. The actual statistics are very different. When both the mother and father have the disorder, only 25 to 35 percent of their children develop it, even though in these cases children are also dealing with very atypical environments. Such a pattern suggests that the inherited component of schizophrenia is *polygenic*—that is, arising from several genes acting together.

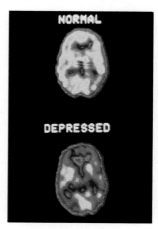

Technological advances have promoted increased interest in neurological and physiological models of psychopathology. This picture shows differences in cerebral neural activity in a depressed and a normal adult. Such differences do not really demonstrate cause and effect. How such differences originate, and whether they are consistently present in children, is yet to be established.

How do scientists know that *any* genetic component is involved in schizophrenia? Couldn't the greater incidence of schizophrenia in children born to and raised by schizophrenic parents be caused as easily by environment? To eliminate this possibility, researchers often study children born to schizophrenic women but raised by nonschizophrenic adoptive parents. Such studies show that these children have a greater chance of developing schizophrenia than do adopted children born to women who do not have the disorder (Siminoff et al., 1994). Environmental factors could still be at work here. Adopted children with a schizophrenic biological mother might have experienced more detrimental intrauterine environments, for instance, by virtue of their mothers being more anxious during pregnancy or receiving poorer nutrition. Such early environmental factors might partly account for these children's higher susceptibility to schizophrenia. Still, the preponderance of evidence from adoption studies, twin studies, and other genetic research makes a good case for a heredity factor in schizophrenia. A similar case has also been made regarding one form of depression (Harrington, 1994).

This is not to say that environmental forces do not also contribute to both schizophrenia and depression (Cannon et al., 1990; Cadoret et al., 1990). Even identical twins, with their identical genetic makeups, are only 20 to 60 percent concordant, or matched, for schizophrenia, depending on the study (Gottesman, 1991). This means that when one twin develops the disorder, there is a fair chance that the other twin will not. As a result of such findings, modern genetic models of psychopathology generally emphasize a combination of genetic and environmental influences (Rutter, 1991).

Diathesis/stress model: A model for the development of psychopathology that holds that the likelihood that a person will develop a particular disorder depends on the interaction between the level of genetic predisposition to the disorder and environmental factors.

One such view is the **diathesis/stress model** (see Figure 15.1). It holds that everyone has some degree of biological vulnerability (diathesis) for a disorder like schizophrenia; likewise, everyone encounters difficulties in life (stress). For people with a high biological predisposition, relatively little stress is needed to develop the disorder. Conversely, people with a low biological predisposition would need a great deal of cumulative stress in order to succumb (Walker et al., 1989). Thus, the likelihood of any individual developing a disorder is not fixed at birth, but depends on whether that person experiences more stress than he or she can tolerate. This idea is similar to the concept of a reaction range, which we introduced in Chapter 11 when discussing intelligence. A person does not inherit a specific IQ, but rather a range of intellectual potential. Similarly, a person does not inherit a specific probability of developing schizophrenia or depression, but rather a probability range, with the outcome depending also on environment.

ENVIRONMENTAL PERSPECTIVES

SOCIOLOGICAL MODELS

Sociological models of psychopathology stress the social context surrounding people who develop a disorder (Cadoret et al., 1990). When studying depression, for instance, a researcher who takes a sociological perspective would look at the depressed person's social situation. Has the person lost a loved one recently? Moved to a new community? Been cut off from important sources of social support? Therapy might take the form of helping the person become more involved with others (Lazare, 1973).

Many disorders besides depression have been approached from a sociological

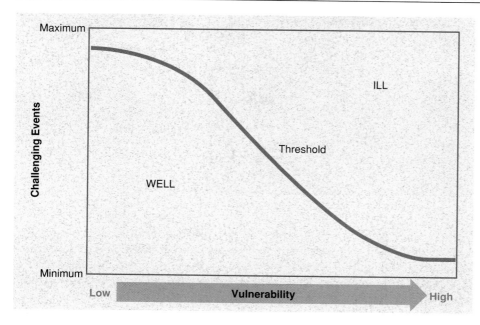

FIGURE 15.1 THE DIATHESIS/STRESS MODEL
Individuals vary both in the extent of their biological vulnerability and in the degree of stress or challenge they face. According to the diathesis/stress model, one may develop a disorder (be above the curve) either by having a high vulnerability and experiencing moderate stress or by having low vulnerability and experiencing a great deal of stress. (Source: Zubin and Spring, 1977.)

viewpoint. One is hyperactivity and attention problems. Critics of the American educational system have argued that the sedentary and regimented environment of most schools inhibits the normal development of many children, perhaps especially of boys (McGuiness, 1989). According to these critics, when a child has a problem sitting still and paying attention at school, we should look to the school situation or to the particular classroom. Notice how sharply this view contrasts with the biological perspective. Proponents of neurological and physiological models would look for some kind of brain dysfunction in a child who is persistently fidgety and inattentive at school. The sociological perspective, in contrast, assumes that constraints built into the school environment are causing the problem. Which view is right is a matter of debate and perhaps depends on the particular case.

BEHAVIORAL MODELS

Like sociological models, behavioral models focus on environmental factors; but instead of emphasizing a person's general social situation, behavioral models look at specific rewards, punishments, and modeled behaviors (Bandura, 1986). In the case of a hyperactive child, for instance, behaviorists would not assume neurological problems or concern themselves with the general school regimen. Instead, they would look at how people in the particular classroom setting (teachers, classmates) are responding to the child's behavior. The assumption is that the child's disruptive behavior persists because it is being reinforced by the outcomes it produces. For example, the child is probably getting atten-

The behavioral model focuses on changing the child's expressed behavior, regardless of whether the child is seriously disturbed or just misbehaving.

tion for "acting up" in class, and even negative attention can be rewarding to some children. The recommended treatment involves changing the environmental contingencies—that is, the connections between the child's behaviors and their consequences. The environment must be restructured so that the child is rewarded only for appropriate responses, not for disruptive ones.

This form of treatment has been found to have some limited effectiveness. When hyperactive children are rewarded for staying in their chairs, paying attention, and completing assignments (usually with points or tokens that they can exchange for desirable items such as candy), their behavior at school improves (O'Leary and O'Leary, 1977). This procedure can even be applied successfully to an entire classroom of disruptive children. Likewise, training parents to be consistent and firm in discipline leads to significant reductions in children's aggressive behavior at home (Dishion et al., 1995).

The earliest behavioral models of psychopathology assumed that a person's symptoms *are* the disorder. In other words, when a child is hyperactive and disruptive in the classroom, those negative behaviors themselves are the problem. There is no need to dig any deeper in a search for "hidden" causes within the child. According to this classic behavioral view, all the factors maintaining unwanted behavior are plainly visible in the environment to anyone who takes the time to observe contingencies carefully.

More recently, however, this classic behavioral approach has been altered to take into account internal cognitive processes, which include a person's expectations, beliefs, and ways of viewing the world (Bandura, 1986; Kendall and Lochman, 1994). Therapists who use this newer cognitive behavioral approach would try to teach hyperactive children some basic cognitive skills to help them behave appropriately in a variety of situations (Kendall and Lochman, 1994). For example, these children might be taught things they could routinely say to themselves ("Slow down, take your time") in order to encourage thinking before acting. The goal is for the results of the therapy to carry over, or *generalize*, to settings other than the one in which treatment took place.

PSYCHODYNAMIC MODELS

Psychodynamic models of psychopathology have evolved over the years from Sigmund Freud's psychoanalytic theory. Like medical models, they assume that disturbed behavior is often the manifestation of underlying causes. Psychodynamic theories, however, do not regard those causes as physical in nature. Instead, the underlying causes are thoughts and feelings—fears, anxieties, conflicts, irrational beliefs and outlooks—produced by life experiences. This is why psychodynamic therapists believe it is not enough simply to treat the behavioral symptoms of a problem. In their view, if you treated a hyperactive boy only by rewarding him for acceptable behavior, you are ignoring the core of his problem. You are leaving untouched the underlying factors—fear of abandonment, perhaps, or distress at tension between his parents—that are producing the child's negative actions. Advocates of this approach make a clear distinction between primary and secondary causes. A boy may be disruptive in the classroom because of the attention this gets him (secondary cause), but he may be seeking the attention because of conflict in the home (primary cause). Psychodynamic therapists try to address the primary causes of a disorder in treatment sessions with the child or with the child and the parents.

To understand better how a psychodynamic perspective compares with other perspectives on psychopathology, consider a woman who is deeply depressed after her husband dies (Lazare, 1973). Those who adopt a medical model would be concerned with diagnosing her problem, determining whether depression runs in her family, and assessing how she has responded to medical treatments (drugs, electric shock therapy) if she has ever suffered from depression before. Those with a sociological perspective would look at her overall social context (her current living arrangements, the number of friends she has) to see if it is adequate to meet her needs. Behaviorists would focus on the specific sources of positive reinforcement she has lost with the death of her husband, and they might help her to develop other sources of reward and satisfaction in her life.

In contrast to all these, only psychodynamic therapists would probe her inner thoughts and feelings for causes that are rooted in her history of life experiences. What was the nature of her relationship with her husband? Did it mirror any earlier relationships, such as the one she had with her father, who perhaps died when she was a teenager? Was the woman ambivalent about her father? Had she adequately mourned his loss? Does she somehow feel responsible for his death and her husband's? Is she unable to express her anger toward her husband for "leaving" her? There is some evidence that the psychodynamic approach can be helpful in understanding and treating depression (Bowlby, 1980; Harris, Brown and Bifulco, 1990).

FAMILY MODELS

Family models take yet another perspective in the effort to search the environment for the causes of psychopathology. This view holds that, while one person in a family is usually identified as having the problem, in fact that person's symptoms are a reflection of disturbance in the larger family system (S. Minuchin, 1974; P. Minuchin, 1988; Sroufe and Fleeson, 1988). In one family, for example, the hyperactive son was labeled "the problem," but a look at the entire family revealed that the problem was much broader. The boy's father devoted all his energies to caring for his dependent parents, felt burdened by the further responsibility of a wife and three children, and was totally unable to express his own needs for care and nurturance. The mother, who felt neglected by her husband, got what little satisfaction she could from the antics of her hyperactive son. The son, in turn, served as a foil for the other two children, who were models of deportment, mature beyond their years. Notice how all the behavioral "pieces" of this family fit together into an interconnected whole. The problem cannot be understood by looking at only one of the family members,

Family theorists focus on the entire family, including how each member reflects the family system, not just on the child with "symptoms."

because the behavior of each person is encouraging and supporting that of the others. In its stress on finding the deeper meanings behind people's behaviors, the family perspective on psychopathology has something in common with psychodynamic models.

Disturbed family systems are often rooted in the *family of origin*—that is, the family in which the husband or wife grew up (Boszormenyi-Nagy and Spark, 1973; Minuchin, 1974). For instance, in families where father-daughter incest occurs, it is common for both the father and mother to have experienced abuse and incest when they were children, even though they may never have admitted their pasts to each other until the current incest was discovered. In addition to the current father-daughter incest, the mother may have a seductive or "special" relationship with a son. How two such adults find each other and recreate their own histories in their children is a matter of great interest to researchers (Sroufe and Fleeson, 1986; Sroufe et al., 1985). Such cases suggest the inadequacy of labeling one member of a family "the problem" and ignoring the rest of the family system.

THE DEVELOPMENTAL PERSPECTIVE

The developmental perspective draws upon and integrates all the models we have described so far. It assumes that genetic and other biological influences, the family, socioeconomic and cultural contexts, and past developmental history all influence the development of emotional and behavioral problems just as they influence normal development (Cadoret et al., 1990; Robins and Rutter, 1990; Sroufe, 1991).

In the case of a child like Meryl, for instance, a developmental perspective would consider a wide number of possible factors contributing to her hesitancy in new situations: her biological makeup, learned cultural norms of "appropriate" female behavior, her mother's inconsistency in reinforcing more positive responses, insecurity stemming from ambivalent care experienced during infancy, and the early conflict between Karen and her mother, which encouraged Karen to develop unrealistic expectations for Meryl. A developmental perspective would also explore how Meryl's basic style of behavior changed over time in response to changes in her surroundings. As Karen's life stabilized, as she worked out problems with her mother and developed a supportive relationship with Joe, she became more confident and consistent in handling Meryl, and Meryl responded by becoming more confident and capable.

The developmental perspective has proven extremely helpful in pulling together many of the factors that contribute to far more serious emotional problems than Meryl's. For example, Remi Cadoret and his colleagues (1990) found that a number of childhood environmental factors predicted depression in a sample of adopted children followed to adulthood. These included poverty, parental illness, early deprivation of parenting, and, especially, delayed placement in a permanent adoptive home. These factors predicted adult depression even after depression in the biological parents was statistically controlled for. The researchers also demonstrated an interaction of biology and environment. A combination of biological vulnerability and delayed placement in an adoptive home predicted depression far better than either factor alone.

Evidence for the power of the developmental perspective also comes from a Finnish study of adopted children (Tienari et al., 1990). The researchers examined the quality of adoptive homes, as well as each child's genetic risk for schizophrenia (measured by whether the biological mother was schizophrenic). More children of schizophrenic mothers developed psychotic disorders, which suggests a genetic influence. Yet none of the children in supportive or "healthy" adoptive homes became psychotic, and only a few were troubled, even when they were in the genetic risk group. As Table 15.3 shows, disorders were much more likely to develop when the adoptive families functioned poorly. Thus, it appears to be a combination of genetic *and* environmental risk that leads to a psychotic disorder.

Juvenile depression is another serious disorder for which the developmental perspective has helped to integrate biological and environmental causes (Fendrich et al., 1990; Harrington, 1994; Zahn-Waxler et al., 1990). Developmental psychopathologists have noticed a marked rise in depression following puberty, which suggests that hormonal changes and other biological factors

TABLE 15.3

ADOPTIVE FAMILY RATING OF FUNCTIONING AND ADOPTEE DIAGNOSES OF PSYCHOLOGICAL DISORDERS

| Adoptee Diagnosis | TOTAL NUMBER | | ADOPTIVE FAMILY RATINGS | | | | | |
| | | | HEALTHY | | NEUROTIC | | SEVERE DYSFUNCTION | |
	At Risk*	Control†	At Risk	Control	At Risk	Control	At Risk	Control
Healthy	58	67	41	35	11	21	6	11
Neurotic	34	41	7	11	12	16	15	14
Borderline syndrome and severe personality disorder	26	17	2	1	6	8	18	8
Psychotic	8	1	0	0	3	0	5	1

*Biological mother is schizophrenic.
†No known genetic risk.
SOURCE: Tienari et al., 1990.

may be involved. At the same time, they have observed that significantly more teenage girls than boys are depressed. Perhaps this is partly due to the fact that girls in our culture are more likely to be socialized toward feelings of helplessness. Other factors contributing to juvenile depression are loss of one's mother, especially before age 11, and emotional distance from parents in early childhood (Harris, Brown, and Bifulco, 1990; Bacon, 1988). Thus, a complete explanation of depression must take into account biological factors, cultural influences, developmental history, and the youngster's immediate environment, such as home life and friends. All these factors are of concern to developmental psychopathologists.

SOME CHILDHOOD DISORDERS

Psychological disorders that usually appear first in childhood or adolescence are listed in Table 15.4 (American Psychiatric Association, 1994). In this section we will consider five of them: autism, conduct disorders, attention

TABLE 15.4
DISORDERS USUALLY FIRST EVIDENT IN CHILDHOOD OR ADOLESCENCE*

MENTAL RETARDATION Mild Moderate Profound Unspecified	**EATING DISORDERS** Anorexia nervosa Bulimia Pica Rumination disorder of infancy Atypical eating disorder
ATTENTION DEFICIT DISORDER With hyperactivity Without hyperactivity Residual type	**STEREOTYPED MOVEMENT DISORDERS** Transient tic disorder Chronic motor tic disorder Tourette's disorder Atypical tic disorder Atypical stereotyped movement disorder
CONDUCT DISORDER Undersocialized, aggressive Undersocialized, nonaggressive Socialized, aggressive Socialized, nonaggressive Atypical conduct disorder	**OTHER DISORDERS WITH PHYSICAL MANIFESTATIONS** Stuttering Functional enuresis Functional encopresis Sleepwalking disorder Sleep terror disorder
ANXIETY DISORDERS Separation anxiety disorder Avoidant disorder Overanxious disorder	
OTHER DISORDERS Reactive attachment disorder of infancy Schizoid disorder of childhood or adolescence Elective mutism Oppositional disorder Identity disorder	**PERVASIVE DEVELOPMENTAL DISORDERS** Infantile autism Childhood onset pervasive developmental disorder Atypical pervasive developmental disorder

*This list is based on the system of classification accepted by the American Psychiatric Association and described in the fourth edition of the *Diagnostic and Statistical Manual* (*DSM-IV*, 1994).
SOURCE: American Psychiatric Association, 1994.

Autistic children often resist the efforts of a therapist and require a great deal of both support and structure.

deficit/hyperactivity disorder, anxiety disorders, and anorexia nervosa. For most childhood disorders, both biological and environmental causes have been proposed, although the evidence supporting each kind of cause is not always equally compelling. Autism is the one childhood disorder about which developmentalists are in agreement that biological factors are largely to blame. The other disorders are open to a number of explanations.

EARLY CHILDHOOD AUTISM

You are touring a locked ward of a state-run psychiatric hospital. On a couch across from you an 8-year-old boy sits rhythmically rocking forward and back. Occasionally he starts to perform a strange, ritualistic flicking of his fingers in front of his face. All the while he seems oblivious of you. As you approach him, however, his rocking intensifies. When you sit on the couch a short distance from him, he hurriedly rises and goes to a corner of the room, where he again starts to rock and flick his fingers, this time furiously.

This child has been diagnosed as having **early childhood autism,** a rare disorder that affects only four children in 10,000 (Lord and Rutter, 1994). According to Leo Kanner (1943), who first identified autism, its core features are: (1) a powerful insistence on preserving sameness in the environment; (2) extreme social isolation, or autistic aloneness; and (3) severe language deficits. Autism is considered a *pervasive developmental disorder (PDD)* because it is so severe (American Psychiatric Association, 1994). Its symptoms are always apparent by the age of 3.

The first of autism's symptoms could account for the autistic child's strange, ritualistic behaviors, such as the repetitive body rocking and finger-flicking in the example above. These youngsters seem to need to maintain complete control over their environments. Any new stimulus causes them great distress. Autistic children apparently have difficulty regulating input from their senses (Lord and Rutter, 1994). As a result, they have trouble making sense of their experi-

Early childhood autism: A rare, severe developmental disorder, the core features of which are (1) a powerful insistence on preserving sameness in the environment; (2) extreme social isolation; and (3) severe language deficits.

ences and are easily overwhelmed by them. Even a small change of routine that most people would hardly notice (putting the child's chair in a different place, offering him or her milk in a different cup) can provoke a tantrum.

The second symptom, autistic aloneness, means that autistic children recoil from contact with others. As babies they do not cuddle when held by their parents. Nor do they babble, make eye contact, or engage in social smiling, imitation, or other forms of social play (Rutter, 1985). Their attachment relationships are grossly abnormal. Often they seem to form "attachments" to objects. This withdrawal from social interaction seems to be related to the sensory overload to which autistic children are prone. Apparently, interacting with others is very confusing and upsetting for a child who can't even make sense out of simple stimuli.

The third symptom, severe speech deficits, means that autistic children do not use language in spontaneous communication (Hertzig and Shapiro, 1990; Lord and Rutter, 1994). Many are mute, and most of those who do speak are *echolalic*—that is, listlessly repeating a word or phrase they have heard with no concern for its meaning. Autistic children also have great trouble learning even simple abstract concepts, such as "larger than," even though they appear to have normal memories for routine information, such as where particular toys are kept. With respect to complex, abstract thinking, such as inferring what another person is thinking or feeling, their deficits are clearly marked (Happe, 1994).

Physically, autistic children appear normal; they do not usually have any obvious brain damage. Still, most researchers agree that this disorder must have a biological cause (Lord and Rutter, 1994). There are several reasons for this conclusion. First, the behavior of autistic children is extremely atypical. Even abused and neglected youngsters do not show these dramatic symptoms. Second, the siblings of autistic children are usually normal, and the parents are typically no different from other parents. Third, autistic children often continue to have profound language and cognitive deficits even after years of treatment. And fourth, autism is statistically related to certain biological problems, such as rubella in the mother during pregnancy (see Chapter 3), and many autistic children develop signs of brain pathology (seizures, for instance) as they get older (Hertzig and Shapiro, 1990; Lord and Rutter, 1994).

Yet despite all the signs that there must be some biological basis to autism, there is little agreement as to the specific cause (Hertzig and Shapiro, 1990; Lord and Rutter, 1994). Dozens of theories have been proposed, with no resolution. Drugs have not proved effective in treating the disorder. Multidisciplinary, highly structured treatment programs are more successful (Lord and Rutter, 1994). Sometimes these programs can improve the child's functioning markedly, although certain autistic features tend to remain.

It is hard to be optimistic about the longer-term adjustment of most autistic children (Lord and Rutter, 1994). Among those who are totally unable to communicate with language and have IQ scores under 50, only a very small percentage can live outside of institutions as adults. For those who have normal nonverbal intelligence and some language skills, the outlook is better. Given extensive treatment, approximately half attain marginally adequate adjustment. But even among those who hold down jobs and are relatively independent, social behavior generally remains impaired. Few marry, for example.

CONDUCT DISORDERS

Mark is a bright, capable 11-year-old, but he also is a daredevil and a loner. A favorite activity is racing his motor bike through the woods. Younger boys are at times attracted to Mark's daring antics (such as sneaking into adult bookstores), but friendships between Mark and others are always short-lived. Mark was referred for treatment because for two years he had been ransacking and robbing houses. He is a "master of the sincere lie" and is viewed by professionals as unreachable. A routine of his, which ultimately got him caught, was to show up back at the scene of his latest robbery and offer to help put the house back in order. "His manner was one of sincere concern, and he asked for no favors in return." (Adapted from Wenar, 1990, pp. 231–232)

Mark's behavior fits a diagnosis of **conduct disorder,** a persistent pattern of repeatedly violating either the basic rights of others or age-appropriate social norms. Children who engage in drug abuse and violent acts, as well as those who chronically lie, cheat, run away from home, or show disregard for others, fall into this category. Juvenile delinquency, a legal concept that includes chronic truancy, vandalism, stealing, or otherwise breaking the law, is also subsumed under conduct disorders (Yoshikawa, 1994).

Mental health professionals distinguish among degrees of conduct disorder, from mild to severe, depending on the extent to which the child's actions harm other people (American Psychiatric Association, 1994). Mental health professionals also distinguish between a conduct disorder that involves aggressive behavior and one that does not, as well as between a child who is able to form normal bonds of friendship and affection (a "socialized" child), and one who seems to have no feelings for others (an "undersocialized" child). Although it is hard to say from such a brief description of Mark, he would likely be considered "nonaggressive, undersocialized." He ransacks the houses he robs in a destructive manner, but he does not seek physical confrontations with the owners. He does not seem to have formed any real friendships, not even with other delinquent youths. We would view his behavior with even more alarm if it included acts of deliberate interpersonal violence (such as setting fire to houses in which people were sleeping) or if his lack of feelings for others extended to members of his own family. We would be less likely to view him as emotionally disturbed if he exhibited antisocial behavior as part of peer group activities, though the behavior would still be of great concern.

Conduct disorder is one of the most frequent diagnoses given to children—especially boys—who are referred to mental-health centers (Earls 1994). These problems are also among the most persistent (Martin and Hoffman, 1990; Robins, 1966; Robins and Price, 1991; Renkin et al., 1989; Yoshikawa, 1994). Aggression and antisocial behavior are not only stable across the childhood years, but also very strong predictors of problems in adulthood.

Possible biological causes of conduct disorders have been proposed. In adult criminals, researchers have reported small differences in levels of the male hormone testosterone (Dabbs and Morris, 1990) and possible genetic differences (DiLalla and Gottesman, 1989). A genetic component has been suggested for children as well, but the link between heredity and misbehavior is tenuous and may be accounted for by differences in IQ and other factors (Earls, 1994; Plomin et al., 1990; Yoshikawa, 1994). Herbert Quay (1986) argues that there may be a biological marker of undersocialized conduct disorder: namely, a low

Conduct disorder:
A persistent pattern of behavior in which the child repeatedly violates either the basic rights of others or age-appropriate social norms.

level of dopamine-beta-hydroxylase (DBH), which converts the neurotransmitter dopamine to noradrenaline, a chemical associated with arousal. Thus, these children may have a high threshold of arousal and fear, and may engage in antisocial behavior simply to feel stimulated (Hare and Cox, 1978). This marker cannot be considered a sole cause, however. After all, there are socially acceptable sources of stimulation. At most, some children may be biologically vulnerable to conduct disorders (DiLalla and Gottesman, 1989; Yoshikawa, 1994).

A large number of studies have found a link between conduct disorders and a negative family environment, including poverty and stress, conflict between the child's parents, and the parents' hostility toward, rejection of, or abuse of the child (Caspi and Elder, 1988; Earls, 1994; Eron and Huesmann, 1990; McCord, 1988; Patterson and Dishion, 1988; Werner and Smith, 1992; Yoshikawa, 1994). Similarly, therapists working with hard-core offenders attest to their histories of early mistreatment, and large-scale interview studies further support the frequency of this relationship (Kruttschnitt, Heath, and Ward, 1986). Mark's history fits this general pattern, in that his father was extremely cold and distant toward him (Wenar, 1990). Of course, such correlational data cannot tell us for certain whether a negative family environment causes conduct disorders, but the fact that these same findings consistently appear is very suggestive. Moreover, the correlation between child aggression and parental mistreatment is greater than the correlation between child aggression and level of aggressiveness in the parents, as measured by standard psychological scales (Patterson and Dishion, 1988). This implies that how parents treat children, and not simply the genes they pass on, fosters the development of conduct disorders.

The Minnesota Parent–Child Project, which has followed a large number of children from infancy through childhood, suggests that very early parent-child problems may set the stage for a conduct disorder. While few of the preschoolers in this study had received psychiatric diagnoses, some persistently showed antisocial behavior, hostile aggression, or both. More of these children had a history of anxious-avoidant attachment during infancy (associated with parental rejection) than did nonaggressive youngsters (Sroufe, 1983). This infant attachment pattern even predicted aggression in third grade (Renkin et al., 1989). Those children who were physically abused in the preschool period were still showing high levels of aggression at age 16. Perhaps the parents' emotional rejection of their baby is linked to ongoing inadequate care, which over time encourages a conduct disorder.

Early detection and intervention may be critical to stemming the development of a conduct disorder. Once a conduct disorder has been allowed to progress to the point where a child is clearly disturbed, especially in adolescence, the problem is usually very difficult to treat (Earls, 1994; Yoshikawa, 1994). Patterson and his colleagues have had some success using behavioral approaches to break the negative cycles between parents and aggressive children (Dishion et al., 1995). Even more impressive have been efforts at early intervention and prevention with young children at high risk for a conduct disorder. Successful programs have the following characteristics in common: (1) they last at least 2 years; (2) they provide high-quality infant day-care or preschool for the child; (3) they provide emotional support and useful developmental information for the parents; and (4) they address the family's broader context, via educational and vocational counseling, for instance (Yoshikawa, 1994).

ATTENTION DEFICIT/HYPERACTIVITY DISORDER

Brad was always in trouble. His neighbors were mad at him, both because he trampled their flowers as he ran home from school and because he poured milk down the pockets of their new pool table "just to see what would happen." Brad's teachers were also upset because he was constantly whistling and generally disrupting the classroom. He couldn't seem to follow instructions or complete assignments because his attention kept wandering. Often he would fidget with objects and accidentally break them. Brad's parents were at their wits' end. They had tried everything, from bargaining to belts, but they couldn't make him "shape up." Yet he was a bright child with an IQ of 125. He was not malicious and he had a good sense of humor, along with an infectious grin. One day the lifeguard pulled him off the bottom of the community pool. It turned out he wasn't drowning; he was just trying to pull out the plug because he thought it would be funny to see all those kids in the pool with no water!

To a much greater extent than exuberantly active children like these, hyperactive children have severe difficulty managing their impulses and maintaining their arousal at a moderate level.

The term for Brad's problem is **attention deficit/hyperactivity disorder,** or **AD/HD** for short (American Psychiatric Association, 1994). Children diagnosed with this disorder are a heterogeneous group; they do not represent a single type (Barkley, 1990; Jacobvitz et al., 1990). Some are impulsive; others are not. Some are more easily distracted than others and have a harder time concentrating. All have some kind of attention-related difficulty (Douglas and Peters, 1980; Landau et al., 1992; Taylor, 1994). These children especially have trouble maintaining attention when given routine tasks. They appear careless and hurried. Their schoolwork is often sloppy, incomplete, or superficial. Many also seem restless and fidgety (Barkley, 1990). This restlessness prompts them to do things that get them in trouble, such as whistling in class. While sociable, these children also have persistent difficulties with peers (Campbell, 1990).

By definition, attention deficit/hyperactivity disorder is restricted to children of at least normal intelligence with no neurological handicaps. The condition is common, with estimates ranging from 3 to 5 percent of all children. The incidence is higher in boys. Up to 10 percent of boys referred to clinics are classified as AD/HD (Barkley, 1990) and population surveys suggest that an even larger number (14 to 17 percent) show such problems (Taylor, 1994).

It is often quite difficult to distinguish AD/HD children from those with conduct disorders. As many as half the children fitting the diagnosis of AD/HD also fit that of conduct disorders (Taylor, 1994). Such a situation is referred to as **co-morbidity** (Caron and Rutter, 1991). It may mean that the child actually has two disorders, or it may just mean that distinct psychiatric disorders are rare in childhood. Regardless, the family situation of a child showing both sets of problems is worse, as is the child's prognosis (Taylor, 1994).

Attention deficit/hyperactivity disorder (AD/HD): A behavior pattern exhibited by children of normal intelligence, with no neurological handicaps, that is characterized by extremely high activity levels coupled with attention-related difficulties.

Co-morbidity: A situation in which a person's pattern of symptoms fits more than one disorder.

CAUSES OF AD/HD

For many years biological theories of AD/HD have predominated (e.g., Shaywitz and Shaywitz, 1989). There is some evidence for a genetic influence in that identical twins show greater concordance for this disorder than fraternal twins do (Goodman and Stevenson, 1989). Yet to date, there is no solid evidence for any underlying organic problem in most cases. Most hyperactive children show no signs of brain damage (Jacobvitz et al., 1990; Taylor, 1994), and although their parents often report a difficult pregnancy or delivery and symptoms in the child since infancy, studies that actually follow youngsters from birth through childhood fail to substantiate these claims (Jacobvitz and Sroufe, 1987). When comparing hyperactive and nonhyperactive youngsters, researchers sometimes report differences in the brain's electrical activity or in levels of neurotransmitters or sugar utilization, but the results from such studies are inconsistent. So far, no biological marker has been discovered that can reliably distinguish hyperactive children from their normal peers (Taylor, 1994). Moreover, even if such a marker is found, we still won't be able to tell cause from effect. An unusual brain-wave pattern in response to a stimulus, for instance, might be the result of distractibility, not the cause of it. Similarly, although medication often reduces the symptoms of hyperactivity, this does not necessarily mean that we are dealing with an organic cause. By analogy, tranquilizers can reduce symptoms of anxiety that are totally environmental in origin.

Recent research has implicated family and other environmental factors as contributors to AD/HD, especially parental criticism and overstimulation (Taylor, 1994). In one study, researchers examined intrusiveness and overstimulating interactions, such as provoking a child who already is frustrated (Carlson et al., 1995; Jacobvitz and Sroufe, 1987). The researchers reasoned that if parents provoke and stimulate when their young children are in need of calming, the youngsters might later be unable to regulate their own arousal and so be prone to attention problems and hyperactivity. This hypothesis was borne out, with predictions of future problems being successfully made from patterns of care experienced as early as 6 months of age. The children who developed these problems had *not* been overactive or distractible as infants.

One small group, however, did show signs of motor immaturity as newborns. Interestingly, there was no overlap between these children and the larger group that experienced overstimulating care. This suggests that there may be more than one pathway to AD/HD. Another important finding of this study was that, up to the third grade, children could be deflected from the path leading to attention problems. Increased stability in the parents' lives and more supportive treatment of the child led to a reduction in symptoms. Overall, this study suggested that AD/HD is a developmental construction, rather than a biological condition.

Whatever the origins of attention deficit/hyperactivity disorder, this problem poses real challenges for parents (Barkley, 1989). We can easily imagine a cycle in which the reactions of the parents and of the child feed each other, prompting the child to become ever more difficult and the parents to become ever more exasperated.

TREATMENT AND PROGNOSIS

A common treatment for AD/HD is the use of a stimulant drug, most often Ritalin. It may strike you as strange that stimulants are given to hyperactive children. Why would doctors want to speed up their physiological processes? Some people have argued that a **paradoxical drug effect** is involved—that the stimulants are actually slowing these children down instead of speeding them up. They suggest that this effect occurs because Ritalin offsets a biochemical deficiency in the brains of hyperactive children. If there was no biochemical deficiency, they reason, how could Ritalin have any positive results? On the basis of this argument, hundreds of thousands of AD/HD children have been given stimulants (see Figure 15.2).

A thorough review of the evidence, however, reveals that this argument has at least three flaws (Jacobvitz et al., 1990; Taylor, 1994). First, there is nothing paradoxical about the effects of stimulants on AD/HD children. Stimulants do

Paradoxical drug effect: A situation in which a drug causes an effect opposite from the one it might be expected to elicit.

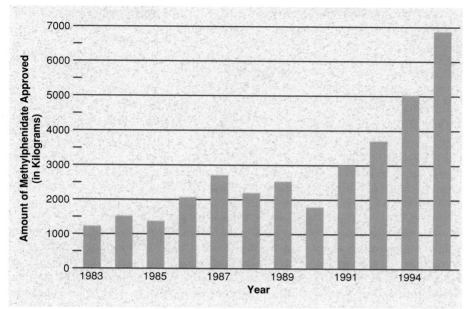

FIGURE 15.2 IS RITALIN BEING OVERPRESCRIBED? *Between 1983 and 1994 the amount of Ritalin and other brands of methylphenidate prescribed for children increased greatly. This graph shows the total amount of methylphenidate that the U.S. Drug Enforcement Agency approved for distribution each year. The figure nearly doubled between 1992 and 1994, to an amount that would be sufficient for about 700,000 children. Even assuming perfect accuracy in diagnosis and treatment, this is a very high number.*

not slow these youngsters down. To the contrary, their activity levels increase in unconstrained situations (such as a playground), their heart rates and blood pressures rise, and their general energy levels are boosted. But stimulants also enhance their abilities to concentrate, sustain attention, and persist at routine tasks. These are the same effects that stimulants have on normal children and adults (Peloquin and Klorman, 1986; Werry and Aman, 1984). Second, the fact that stimulants can improve the performance of AD/HD children does not indicate a biochemical need for them. There are no dependable neurophysiological indicators as to which children will respond best to Ritalin and similar drugs. Third, there is reason to doubt the long-term effectiveness of stimulants. Most studies that show favorable results are short-lived—only 4 to 6 weeks in duration. Long-term studies show no lasting improvement in academic achievement or peer relationships, or any reduction in problem behavior in later years (Charles and Schain, 1981; Jacobvitz et al., 1990; Weiss and Hechtman, 1986). Finally, if a child's behavior worsens when Ritalin is withdrawn, this is not an indication that the child needs the drug because of a biochemical deficiency. It could simply mean that the child has developed a dependency on stimulants, as often happens with drugs that affect the brain (Jacobvitz et al., 1990).

Behavioral therapies, which reinforce the child for appropriate behavior or teach cognitive strategies for self-control, offer alternatives to medication. These alternatives have been successful at reducing symptoms in particular settings, such as the classroom (Kendall and Lochman, 1994). Behavioral treatment with medication has been shown to be more effective than medication alone (Satterfield and Schell, 1987), and most researchers believe that medication should only be used as one part of a more comprehensive treatment program (Taylor, 1994).

You may have heard that cutting down on sugar and food additives in the diet can be beneficial to hyperactive children. This view is without scientific support, although there is some evidence that red dye in foods may contribute to hyperactivity in some children (Garfinkel, 1987). Other approaches to treatment, such as family therapy, have not been sufficiently evaluated to determine how successful they are.

It is only partly true that most AD/HD children grow out of this disorder. Recent studies show that many of them continue to have problems through adolescence, although the problems may take different forms than they did in childhood. Typical adolescent troubles among AD/HD youngsters include underachievement at school, immaturity, and work-related problems, rather than hyperactivity (Barkley, 1990; Taylor, 1994). Such problems are no less common in adolescents who have been treated over the years with stimulant drugs (Jacobvitz et al., 1990). To us this raises more doubts about the wisdom of medication, although others might say it suggests a need to continue drug treatment through the teenage years.

Before stimulants are taken for such a long period, however, it is critical to evaluate their long-term effects on the body. The suppression of growth in both weight and height (about 1 inch) that is associated with stimulant drug treatment may be due to influences on growth hormone (Jensen and Garfinkel, 1988). This fact raises concerns about sexual development in children treated during adolescence and about the long-term health consequences for kidneys and the cardiovascular system. We must also consider the damaging psychological effects on youngsters who come to think that they need a drug in order to function normally and control themselves. As one child put it: "I can't do it. I didn't have my human pill today."

ANXIETY DISORDERS

> Donny was an impeccably dressed 8-year-old who tested in the gifted range on the Stanford-Binet IQ test. His behavior mimicked his dress. He avoided dirt and messiness of any kind. He would even turn down chocolate milk because it might spill on his tie; playing with finger paint was out of the question. The play he did engage in was excessively precise and orderly. He would lay out the buildings for an airport in exact alignment. He also had an array of irrational fears. He was frightened, for example, that spiders might come out of the toilet and bite him, even though he realized that this was impossible. Not surprisingly, Donny was overtly anxious. At times he talked rapidly with pursed lips; other times he wrung his hands.

> Janice also showed anxiety, although in different ways. She was always upset when her mother dropped her off at kindergarten. She spent much of the day hovering near the teacher, hoping for attention. When the teacher tried to encourage her to play with the other children, she remained on the sidelines, never joining the activities. Her face constantly bore a worried expression and her eyes seemed perpetually filled with tears. She had chronic stomach aches, and when it came time for first grade, she refused to go to school at all.

Both of these children would probably be diagnosed as having an **anxiety disorder.** Donny would be said to suffer from **overanxious disorder,** characterized by very general and pervasive worries and fears. Janice's problem would probably be labeled **separation anxiety disorder**—excessive anxiety precipitated by separation from someone to whom the child is emotionally attached.

Anxiety disorders are less frequently seen at clinics than conduct disorders or AD/HD, yet population surveys show that they affect up to 8 percent of children (Klein, 1994). Perhaps many of these youngsters are not brought in for treatment because parents consider their problems less serious than other,

Anxiety disorder:
A disorder characterized by excessive and/or irrational worries or fears.

Overanxious disorder:
An anxiety disorder characterized by very general and pervasive fears and worries.

Separation anxiety disorder:
An anxiety disorder in which the child's excessive worries and fears are precipitated by separation from someone to whom the child is emotionally attached.

more disruptive problems of childhood. They may also assume that these children will eventually outgrow their fears and anxieties, and in this assumption they are often right. Compared with conduct disorders and hyperactivity, anxiety disorders are more likely to show **spontaneous remission**—that is, to go away without professional help. Moreover, anxiety disorders are generally not predictive of serious problems in adulthood.

Despite a great deal of speculation, there is no reason to believe that anxiety disorders in children are caused largely by biological factors (Knopf, 1984). There is, however, modest evidence to support factors in the family environment as causes (Wenar, 1994). For example, cold, distant fathers, anxiously overinvolved mothers, and high levels of family stress have been linked to anxiety disorders in boys (Hetherington and Martin, 1986; Renken et al., 1989). These children seem to have formed an inner working model of the world as unpredictable or threatening and of themselves as unable to influence events. The most frequent fear of the school-refusing child (another subcategory of anxiety disorder) is that harm will befall the mother while the child is away (Wenar, 1994). Such children have apparently learned to be worried about the caregiver's continued availability.

Anxiety disorders are generally quite responsive to a variety of treatments (Bernstein and Borchart, 1991; Wenar, 1994). Both behavioral and psychodynamic therapies are more successful than simply waiting for the problem to go away by itself. All effective treatments of school refusal involve getting the child back into the classroom as soon as possible. Focusing on the parents' anxiety also seems useful in such cases, for this seems to be a key to the problem.

It is normal for young children to cling to parents in times of threat. But if this child continues to be so preoccupied with contact, this may be a sign of anxiety disorder.

Spontaneous remission: The disappearance of a disorder without professional treatment.

ANOREXIA NERVOSA

> When Alma came in for consultation, she looked like a walking skeleton, scantily dressed in shorts and halter, with her legs sticking out like broomsticks, every rib showing, and her shoulder blades standing up like little wings. . . . Alma's arms and legs were covered with soft hair, her complexion had a yellowish tint, and her dry hair hung down in strings. Most striking was the face—hollow like that of a shriveled-up old woman with a wasting disease. . . . Alma insisted that she looked fine and there was nothing wrong with her being so skinny. (Bruch, 1979, pp. 2–3)

Alma suffers from **anorexia nervosa,** a serious eating disorder characterized by extreme reduction in food intake and loss of at least 25 percent of original body weight. No physical illness accounts for this dramatic weight loss. Anorectics deliberately starve themselves. This intentional weight loss is accompanied by a highly distorted body image. No matter how emaciated they become, anorectics are convinced that they are still overweight. The more unrealistic their belief, the more difficult the problem is to treat (Leon and Phenan, 1985). Reassurances, admonitions, even threats from concerned friends or relatives in no way weaken their resolve. Many eat almost nothing and exercise excessively. Others occasionally go on eating binges, but then induce vomiting to avoid gaining weight—a practice called **bulimia.** This self-abuse can produce very serious side effects, including physical ailments and, in some cases, death (Steinhausen, 1994).

Anorexia nervosa is primarily a disorder of adolescent girls and young adult women, and is much more common in the middle class than in the lower economic strata (Attie et al., 1990). These girls are often bright, academically successful, and viewed as perfect young ladies—neatly dressed, well-mannered, and

Anorexia nervosa: A serious eating disorder characterized by extreme reduction in food intake and loss of at least 25 percent of normal body weight.

Bulimia: A practice in which a person goes on eating binges followed by self-induced vomiting to avoid weight gain.

Treatment of anorexia nervosa can often be successful, as these before and after photographs clearly illustrate.

compliant (Wenar, 1994). In fact, a perfectionist tendency is one clue to the cause of this disorder, as we will discuss shortly.

Biological theories of anorexia include the possibility of a dysfunctional hypothalamus (the brain region that regulates hunger and affects the production of hormones), but there is little evidence to support this view (Werry, 1986). Although anorectics often suffer abnormal hormone secretions, as a result of which their menstrual cycles cease, these abnormalities seem to be more effect than cause (Steinhausen, 1994). Prisoners of war who are starved for long periods show many of the same hormonal and menstrual symptoms. Moreover, if an anorectic does gain appropriate weight, her hormonal and menstrual functioning will return to normal.

Psychological theories of anorexia have emphasized early sexual abuse (Shapiro and Rosenfeld, 1987) or overinvolved, overentangled families (Minuchin, Rosman, and Baker, 1978). The parents expect the child to be perfect and do not allow her to question the status quo or express anger. They demand absolute compliance in return for nurturance, and they repeatedly suggest that the child could be "just a little bit better." The girl comes to feel that her life, her self, even her body are not her own. Overcontrolled, she is left without a sense of autonomy (Wenar, 1994). In adolescence, she "confronts" her parents indirectly by asserting control over how much she eats. For this small victory of causing her parents worry and making them feel helpless to change her, she pays an enormous price.

You may wonder why an adolescent girl focuses on food in an effort to assert some autonomy in her life. Part of the answer is cultural (Attie et al., 1990; Steinhausen, 1994). Girls today are barraged with images of extreme thinness—on television, in music videos, in magazines and advertisements. Our culture associates extreme thinness with beauty, affluence, and success. Not surprisingly, this is the image to which a troubled girl aspires.

Anorexia nervosa is quite difficult to treat because of the person's entrenched belief that she is not too thin and perhaps should even become thinner. However, there is some evidence that behavioral therapies may be effective in the short run and that family therapy may have longer-term success with younger, less chronic patients (Russell et al., 1987). Multifaceted programs are currently advocated (Steinhausen, 1994). A first goal of any treatment is to get the anorectic eating again, but the long-term aim is to help her believe that she has a right to self-expression, including the expression of anger, and that as a person she has worth.

CHILDHOOD DISORDERS AND DEVELOPMENT

The study of developmental psychopathology calls attention to major themes of this book, including the integrated nature of development, the child as an active force in development, stability and change over time, the complexity of developmental pathways, the interaction of biology and environment, and the importance of considering the total context of development. The disorders we have reviewed underscore these themes and also shed light on normal development.

Autism, for instance, sheds light on normal development by highlighting the degree to which human beings are "social animals" who depend on emotional communication. Autistic children are striking in their lack of these fundamental human characteristics. They shun contact with others, including children, and fail to form normal attachments to adults. At the same time, autism underscores the integrated nature of development. The autistic child's profound language and cognitive handicaps are coupled with equally severe social and emotional ones. Cognitive limitations make social interaction difficult. Withdrawal from social interaction deprives autistic children of experiences that promote cognitive development, which in turn inhibits social understanding.

Conduct disorders illustrate the developmental theme of continuity over time. Signs of aggression and antisocial behavior often appear in the preschool years and may persist through middle childhood into adolescence and beyond. The most compelling explanation for this continuity is that children play active roles in their own development. Children with conduct disorders behave in ways that elicit negative, even punitive, feedback from other people, which only serves to perpetuate their problems. But just as there is continuity in the development of conduct disorders, so there is variation in the ways in which they unfold. Conduct disorders illustrate the principle of branching pathways, in that they predict a wide range of adult problems, including depression, schizophrenia, and alcoholism, as well as criminal behavior.

Attention deficit/hyperactivity disorder highlights the theme of transformations over the course of development. The condition tends to proceed from overactivity in childhood to academic failure and problems of impulse control in adolescence. AD/HD also illustrates how similar behavioral patterns may result from multiple pathways. In some cases, the origins of AD/HD seem to lie in patterns of care and other early life experiences, but in other cases they are rooted more in cultural or biological factors.

Anxiety disorders seem to result from failure to adequately negotiate the developmental issues that all children face. These disorders illustrate the usefulness of considering disturbed behavior as a deviation from normal development. Separation anxiety, for instance, is a normal part of development, and becomes pathological only when it lingers as the child grows older, preventing him or her from becoming more autonomous from parents. Specific fears are also normal in early childhood. They are pathological only when they become pervasive and interfere with functioning in many areas of the child's life. These "failures" to negotiate developmental issues are not irreversible. In fact, anxiety disorders often disappear on their own without treatment.

Anorexia nervosa is another illustration of a failure to negotiate a developmental issue that all children face. This disorder can best be seen as a delayed and self-destructive attempt to establish autonomy. Anorexia also illustrates the complexity of developmental pathways. Food finickiness in the early years does not predict anorexia in adolescence. But parental overcontrol of the child (especially overcontrol of her expressions of anger and other impulses) and parental overinvolvement (including a sexualized relationship with the father) do place girls at risk for this disorder.

Other disorders of childhood and adolescence illustrate the complex interaction of risk factors and protective factors in the development of psychopathology, both biologically based and environmental ones. For instance, when adult-like depression arises in a youngster, you might assume that the child has a genetic or physiological vulnerability to this disorder. But even in these cases, environmental factors (especially early losses, such as the death of a parent) often also play a part. Not all children with a family history of depression develop this disorder; nor do all children who have experienced early losses. For all disorders, we must consider the total context of development.

CHAPTER SUMMARY

1. The subfield of developmental psychology concerned with emotional and behavioral disorders is called **developmental psychopathology.** Researchers in this area want to understand the causes of such disorders in both children and adults. They view disorders as deviations from normal developmental patterns, and they focus on the interplay of **risk factors** and **protective factors** in making people either vulnerable or resistant to problems. In examining the role of past development in current developmental outcomes, they draw attention to the orderliness of development despite changes in a person over time.

2. In their search for causes, some psychologists focus largely on biological factors. The classic biological perspective on behavioral and emotional disorders is known as the medical model. It draws an analogy between psychological problems and physical illnesses. Most modern neurological and physiological perspectives look to chemical imbalances in the brain as important causes. Genetic models add to this a focus on the hereditary aspects of disorders— that is, on genetically transmitted predispositions toward developing them. In general, biological perspectives make their biggest contributions in helping to explain certain severe psychological disorders,

such as early childhood autism, schizophrenia, and some forms of depression.

3. In looking for the causes of behavioral and emotional disorders, other psychologists largely emphasize environmental factors. Sociological models focus on the overall social and cultural context surrounding the disturbed person. Behavioral models focus on the rewards, punishments, and modeled behaviors in the person's environment. Behavioral treatments involve changing the contingencies between the unwanted behavior and its consequences. In addition, modern cognitive behavioral approaches seek to change the disturbed person's negative thoughts and expectations. Psychodynamic models of psychopathology focus on the troubled person's fears, anxieties, and inner conflicts. Family or systems models look for the causes in troubled relationships throughout the person's family.

4. Environmental perspectives on psychological disorders are not incompatible with biological ones. Most researchers believe that many disorders involve a complex interplay of both kinds of factors. For instance, it seems likely that a genetic predisposition toward schizophrenia interacts with the environmental stress a person experiences to determine whether

or not the disorder ultimately develops. The developmental perspective on psychopathology integrates both biological and environmental factors in looking for the causes of emotional and behavioral problems.

5. Among the disorders first evident in childhood or adolescence, one of the most severe is **early childhood autism.** It is characterized by a powerful insistence on preserving sameness in the environment, extreme social isolation, and severe language deficits. Most psychologists believe that autism is caused by some as yet unidentified biological factor.

6. There is currently much debate about the extent to which **attention deficit/hyperactivity disorder (ADHD)** is biological in origin. Some investigators think it may often stem from such environmental factors as parents who persistently provoke and overstimulate a young child who is in need of calming. Those who take this view raise questions about the pervasive use of stimulant drugs to treat hyperactivity and attention problems.

7. **Conduct disorders** are behaviors in which the child repeatedly violates either the basic rights of others or age-appropriate social norms. Particularly hard to treat is the aggressive, undersocialized type of conduct disorder, in which the child both deliberately seeks to harm other people and is unable to form normal bonds of affection.

8. **Anxiety disorders,** too, involve several different subtypes, including **overanxious disorder** and **separation anxiety disorder.** The first involves very general and pervasive worries and fears, while the second is characterized by excessive anxiety over separation from a parent. Both respond quite well to treatment.

9. **Anorexia nervosa** is an eating disorder in which the person deliberately reduces food intake to the point of losing at least 25 percent of original body weight. Anorexia is primarily a disorder of bright, middle-class, academically successful adolescent girls and young women. It may be associated with parents who seek perfection and stifle their child's autonomy.

10. The study of developmental psychopathology emphasizes the major themes of this book: the integrated nature of development, continuity and change over time, the complexity of developmental pathways, the interaction of biology and environment, and the importance of considering the total context of development.

PART SEVEN

EPILOGUE

Psychopathology and Individual Lives

As a way of summarizing the material we've discussed on developmental psychopathology, let's return to the three children we have followed throughout this book and assess their degree of vulnerability to various disorders.

MALCOLM WILLIAMS

Malcolm represents an interesting case because of all the things that might have gone wrong in his development. Conduct disorders, especially the gang-socialized type, are very common among boys raised in inner cities, yet for solid reasons we portrayed Malcolm as making a positive social adjustment. He did occasionally show bad judgment, as when he brought a gun to school for "protection," but he seemed to learn from these experiences and he matured well. He also had no serious problems due to his high activity level, his exuberant style, his tendency to be impulsive, and his inclination to keep shifting his attention from one thing to another. He learned to keep these characteristics within appropriate bounds. The warmth and firm guidance from his caring family were critical factors leading him to such a good outcome (Masten and Coatsworth, 1995). Malcolm's development is quite similar to that of some well-functioning inner-city boys we have studied in the Minnesota Parent-Child Project.

But wait, you may be saying to yourself. Isn't Attention Deficit/Hyperactivity Disorder something that a child either has or doesn't have? How can we suggest that Malcolm avoided this diagnosis simply because his parents so strongly supported him? We can say this precisely because such disorders are not givens; they aren't something that children either are or are not born with. Instead, these problems are developmental constructions that depend on the interaction of internal and external factors. In Malcolm's case, firm guidance and limits provided by his family allowed him to acquire an adequate degree of self-control. Even failure at school is not something we should think of as always stemming from innate characteristics. In the Minnesota Preschool Project, being required to repeat kindergarten was not predicted by IQ or early language comprehension tests. Instead, it was predicted by social and emotional factors, such as a child's attachment history.

Another problem that *might* have arisen for Malcolm is school refusal during the period of middle childhood when he was having trouble with gang members on his way to school. But if this had happened it would have stemmed from a serious external conflict, not from anxiety over leaving home. Any form of internalizing disorder would be out of character for Malcolm, who is filled with a sense of personal ability and confidence. The overcontrol and perfectionism of the anorectic or the hopelessness and self-contempt of the depressed adolescent would not make sense in his case. Likewise, adult schizophrenia would be unlikely to develop in Malcolm. He shows none of the precursors of it. He is successful socially and academically; there is no history of family psychopathology and no disturbed pattern of family interaction. While our present state of knowledge doesn't allow us to rule out the possibility of later disorders, Malcolm seems well on his way to good adult adjustment, with only the normal ups and downs everyone has.

MERYL POLONIUS TURNER

Meryl was constructed to be in many ways the opposite of Malcolm. As is common for females in our culture, she is portrayed as being socialized toward internalizing problems. School refusal and other forms of anxiety disorder were possibilities for her. Indeed, during the early preschool years she showed signs of such problems: she had great difficulty adapting to new situations, and she tended to become greatly upset under stress. As a female, especially with her tendency to internalize stress, she might also have been at risk for anorexia nervosa or depression.

However, many factors in Meryl's life worked against her developing these disorders. When Karen met Joe and her life stabilized, Meryl's development underwent a critical turnaround. Increasingly, her parents helped her to become a self-sufficient and autonomous person. In her adolescence, Karen and Joe tolerated Meryl's normal pushing away from them—her criticisms of them, her argumentativeness, and other forms of de-identification. At the same time, they provided Meryl with a great deal of nurturance, supporting her and helping her learn to seek support when she needed it. Karen and Joe's own relationship modeled the vital role that social support can play in alleviating stress. While they had their periods of marital tension, they were able to talk about and resolve their conflicts, and Meryl was not made to feel responsible when things went wrong. All this served a child like Meryl well. We therefore described her as becoming more competent and confident in herself, thereby moving away from the path toward adult depression. Again, Meryl's developmental path parallels that of several other children, most of them girls, whom we have studied.

Given her history, the possibility of any form of adult conduct disorder would be very remote for Meryl. It would be inconceivable, for example, to see Meryl headed for a career of violent crime. Aggressive, antisocial behavior is simply not congruent with the personality or style of coping illustrated by Meryl (Robins, 1966).

Neither would adult schizophrenia be likely for someone like Meryl. Granted, for girls, there may be a link between adult schizophrenia and certain internalizing symptoms, primarily withdrawal (Watt et al., 1984). But nothing in Meryl's history is suggestive of risk for extreme disorder. Most important, she shows social competence and academic success, which together indicate that serious adult disorders are unlikely.

For a person like Meryl, however, we might expect that new situations would continue to be challenging. If confronted with a crisis, she might respond at first by becoming disorganized. But then, with effort, she is likely to cope effectively. Another area of challenge for her might be close relationships with men. We could imagine Meryl being quite demanding of the men in her life. But with her keen sensitivity to others and desire for closeness, she would also give a great deal.

MIKE GORDON

Mike was the only one of our three children who experienced prolonged parental conflict and eventual divorce. He was also the only one showing significant problems as late as adolescence. His parents burdened him with their relationship, and for a while he felt it was up to him to keep the family together. His mother leaned on him at times, and for a while he feared that his father might be turning most of his attention to his new wife and son. Such factors can be associated with conduct disorders, hyperactivity, and depression.

At one time or another Mike did show behavior congruent with some of those disorders. Still, we never intended to portray him as seriously disturbed, nor would we anticipate in him any serious adult disorders. His history of support and solid early adaptation would serve as protective factors during stressful periods (Masten and Coatsworth, 1995; Werner and Smith, 1992).

Mike at first showed more of a tendency toward internalizing symptoms than Malcolm would have done in his situation. Remember how responsible he felt for his parents' separation and how in the year following the breakup of the marriage he became less outgoing. But then, with the divorce and his father's remarriage, he began to express his pain in acting-out behaviors. This is in keeping with cultural patterns of socialization for boys. Frank Gordon's son was not going to sit around moping and having stomachaches for long. It is hard to say how likely it would have been for a teenager like Mike to continue down the path toward conduct disorders, perhaps eventually abusing drugs or alcohol. Without the strong support he received from his mother, his uncle, and his high school biology teacher, and the continuing interest shown by his father, it would have been much less likely for things to work out so well for Mike. Unfortunately, we have other cases in our research in which cumulative stress and lack of support have resulted in disorder.

Some would argue that alcoholism, conduct disorders, and schizophrenia are genetically related to one another (Wender and Klein, 1986). If so, Frank's lapse into alcoholism during the rockiest time of his first marriage, coupled with Mike's brief bouts of misconduct during early adolescence, might mean that Mike is at higher than normal risk for adult schizophrenia. But there are many factors counteracting these negative warning signs: Mike's solid developmental beginnings, his good adjustment, and his ongoing social support all work in his favor.

As for how a person like Mike will later face the roles of partner and father, we might expect him to have doubts about his ability to provide for a partner. After all, his father was unable to meet his mother's emotional needs, and Mike himself experienced a sense of failure in his efforts to fill the gap. Emotionally caring for a parent is a big task for a child. Doubts about his own caretaking abilities might also arise when Mike eventually becomes a parent. Still, he appears to have overall positive self-esteem; doubts and lack of confidence do not predominate in his general self-image. A basic commitment to family life will probably help Mike be successful as a partner and a parent. He will certainly have some vulnerabilities as he faces these adult tasks, as everyone does, but he also has particular strengths that he can bring to these challenges.

CONCLUSION: PSYCHOPATHOLOGY AND NORMAL DEVELOPMENT

Developmental psychopathology is the study of deviations from normal development, deviations that seriously impair a person's functioning and result in patterns of behavior referred to as *psychiatric syndromes*. Developmental psychopathologists seek to understand the origins and course of such deviations as well as the factors that promote the return to normal developmental pathways. As it turns out, the same principles and influences found to be important in the study of normal development are critical for understanding pathological development. These include the interplay of biology and environment, the surrounding rings of contextual influence (social support, poverty, cultural expectations, and so forth), and the person's previous developmental history.

References

The number in brackets at the end of each entry refers to the chapter of the text in which that work is cited.

Aber, J. L. (1994). Poverty, violence, and child development: Untangling family and community level effects. In C. A. Nelson, (Ed.), *Minnesota Symposia on Child Psychology,* (Vol. 27, pp. 229–272. Hillsdale, NJ: Erlbaum. [2]

Abravanel, E., and Gingold, H. (1985). Learning via observation during the second year of life. *Developmental Psychology, 21,* 614–623. [4]

Ackerman, B. (1984). Storage and processing constraints on integrating story information in children and adults. *Journal of Experimental Child Psychology, 38,* 64–92. [11]

Acredolo, L. P., and Goodwyn, S. W. (1985). Symbolic gesturing in language development: A case study. *Human Development, 28,* 40–49. [7]

Acredolo, L. P., and Goodwyn, S. W. (1988). Symbolic gesturing in normal infants. *Child Development, 59,* 450–466. [7]

Acredolo, L. P., and Goodwyn, S. W. (1990). Sign language in babies: The significance of symbolic gesturing for understanding language development. In R. Vasta (Ed.), *Annals of Child Development* (Vol. 7, pp. 1–42). London: Kingsley. [7]

Adey, P., and Shayer, M. (1990). Accelerating the development of formal thinking in middle and high school students. *Journal of Research in Science Teaching, 27,* 267–285. [13]

Ainsworth, M. (1967). *Infancy in Uganda.* Baltimore: Johns Hopkins University Press. [6]

Ainsworth, M., and Bell, S. (1974). Mother-infant interaction and the development of competence. In K. Connolly and J. Bruner (Eds.), *The growth of competence.* New York: Academic Press. [6]

Ainsworth, M., Bell, S., and Stayton, D. (1974). Infant-mother attachment and social development: Socialization as a product of reciprocal responsiveness to signals. In M. Richards (Ed.), *The integration of the child into the social world.* Cambridge, Eng.: Cambridge University Press. [1, 8]

Ainsworth, M., Blehar, M., Waters, E., and Wall, S. (1978). *Patterns of attachment.* Hillsdale, NJ: Erlbaum. [6]

Ainsworth, M., and Eichberg, C. (1991). Effects on infant-mother attachment of mother's unresolved loss of an attachment figure or other traumatic experience. In P. Morris, J. Stevenson-Hinde, and C. Parkes (Eds.), *Attachment across the life cycle* (pp. 160–183). New York: Routledge. [6]

Alberts, J. R. (1981). Ontogeny of olfaction: Reciprocal roles of sensation and behavior in the development of perception. In R. N. Aslin, J. R. Alberts, and M. R. Petersen (Eds.), *Development of perception* (Vol. 1). New York: Academic Press. [4]

Allen, D., Banks, M. S., and Norcia, A. M. (1993). Does chromatic sensitivity develop more slowly than luminance sensitivity? *Vision Research, 33,* 2553–2562. [4]

Allen, V. L. (1976). *Children as teachers.* New York: Academic Press. [11]

Allison, P., and Furstenberg, F., Jr. (1989). How marital dissolution affects children: Variations by age and sex. *Developmental Psychology, 25,* 540–549. [12, 14]

American Association of University Women. (1992). *How schools shortchange girls: A study of major findings on girls and education.* Washington, DC: AAUW Educational Foundation. [2, 11]

American Psychiatric Association. (1994). *Diagnostic and statistical manual of mental disorders* (4th ed.). Washington, DC: Author. [15]

Ames, A. (1951). Visual perception and the rotating trapezoidal window. *Psychological Monographs* (Series No. 324). [4]

Amsterdam, R. (1972). Mirror self-image reactions before age two. *Developmental Psychobiology, 5,* 297–305. [8]

Anderson, D., and Levin, S. (1976). Young children's attention to *Sesame Street. Child Development, 47,* 806–811. [9]

Andersson, B. E. (1992). Effects of daycare on cognitive and socioemotional competence of thirteen-year-old Swedish schoolchildren. *Developmental Psychology, 63,* 20–36. [6]

André-Thomas and Dargassies, Saint-Anne, S. (1952). *Études neurologiques sur le nouveau-né et le jeune nourrisson.* (Neurological studies of the newborn and the toddler.) Paris: Mason. [4]

Annunziato, P. W., and Frenkel, L. M. (1993). The epidemiology of pediatric HIV-1 infection. *Pediatric Annals, 22*(7), 401–405. [3]

Anselmi, D., Tomasello, M., and Acunzo, M. (1986). Young children's responses to neutral and specific contingent queries. *Journal of Child Language, 13,* 135–144. [7]

Antell, S. E., and Keating, D. P. (1983). Perception of numerical invariance in neonates. *Child Development, 54,* 695–706. [5]

Apgar, V., and Beck, J. (1974). *Is my baby all right?* New York: Pocket Books. [3]

617

Apgar, V., Holaday, D. A., James, L. S., Weisbrot, I. M., and Berrien, C. (1958). Evaluation of the newborn infant—second report. *Journal of the American Medical Association, 168,* 1985–1988. [3]

Appel, L. F., Cooper, R. G., McCarrell, N., Sims-Knight, J., Yussen, S. R., and Flavell, J. H. (1972). The development of the distinction between perceiving and memorizing. *Child Development, 43,* 1365–1381. [9]

Archer, S. L. (1985). Career and/or family: The identity process for adolescent girls. *Youth and Society, 16,* 289–314. [14]

Arend, R., Gove, F., and Sroufe, L. A. (1979). Continuity of individual adaptation from infancy to kindergarten: A predictive study of ego-resiliency and curiosity in preschoolers. *Child Development, 50,* 950–959. [1, 8, 10]

Arling, G., and Harlow, H. (1967). Effects of social deprivation on maternal behavior of rhesus monkeys. *Journal of Comparative and Physiological Psychology, 64,* 371–377. [6]

Aro, H., and Taipale, V. (1987). The impact of timing of puberty on psychosomatic symptoms among fourteen- to sixteen-year-old Finnish girls. *Child Development, 58,* 261–268. [13]

Arsenio, W., and Kramer, R. (1992). Victimizers and their victims: Children's conceptions of the mixed emotional consequences of moral transgressions. *Child Development, 63,* 915–927. [12]

Asher, S., and Parker, J. (1989). Significance of peer relationship problems in childhood. In B. Schneider, G. Attili, J. Nadel, and R. Weissberg (Eds.), *Social competence in developmental perspective* (pp. 5–23). Dordrecht: Kluwer. [10, 12]

Aslin, R. N. (1977). Development of binocular fixation in human infants. *Journal of Experimental Child Psychology, 23,* 133–150. [4]

Aslin, R. N. (1981). Development of smooth pursuit in human infants. In D. F. Fisher, R. A. Monty, and J. W. Senders (Eds.), *Eye movements: Cognition and visual perception.* Hillsdale, NJ: Erlbaum. [4]

Aslin, R. N., and Banks, M. S. (1978). Early visual experience in humans: Evidence for a critical period in the development of binocular vision. In H. L. Pick, Jr., H. W. Leibowitz, J. E. Singer, A. Steinschneider, and H. W. Stevenson (Eds.), *Psychology: From research to practice.* New York: Plenum Press. [4]

Aslin, R. N., Pisoni, D. B., and Jusczyk, P. W. (1983). Auditory development and speech in infancy. In P. H. Mussen (Ed.), *Handbook of child psychology* (Vol. 2, 4th ed.): M. M. Haith and J. J. Campos (Eds.), *Infancy and developmental psychobiology.* New York: Wiley. [4]

Aslin, R. N., and Salapatek, P. (1975). Saccadic localization of peripheral targets by the very young human infant. *Perception and Psychophysics, 17,* 293–302. [4]

Atkinson, J., and Braddick, O. (1989). Development of basic visual functions. In A. Slater and G. Bremner (Eds.), *Infant development.* Hove, Eng.: Erlbaum. [4]

Atkinson, R. C., and Shiffrin, R. M. (1968). Human memory: A proposed system and its control processes. In K. W. Spence and J. T. Spence (Eds.), *The psychology of learning and motivation: Advances in research and theory* (Vol. 2). New York: Academic Press. [9]

Attie, I., Brooks-Gunn, J., and Petersen, A. C. (1990). A developmental perspective on eating disorders and eating problems. In M. Lewis and S. M. Miller (Eds.), *Handbook of developmental psychopathology* (pp. 409–420). New York: Plenum Press. [15]

Ault, R. L. (1983). *Children's cognitive development* (2nd ed.). New York: Oxford University Press. [13]

Bacon, M. S. (1988). *Antecedents and correlates of depressive symptoms in middle childhood: A longitudinal perspective.* Unpublished doctoral dissertation, University of Minnesota. [15]

Bailey, J. M., Bobrow, D., Wolfe, M., and Mikach, S. (1995). Sexual orientation of adult sons of gay fathers. *Developmental Psychology, 31,* 124–129. [2]

Baillargeon, R. (1986). Representing the existence and the location of hidden objects: Object permanence in 6- and 8-month-old infants. *Cognition, 23,* 21–41. [5]

Baillargeon, R. (1987). Object permanence in 3½- and 4½-month-old infants. *Developmental Psychology, 23,* 655–664. [5]

Baillargeon, R. (1991). Reasoning about the height and location of a hidden object in 4.5- and 6.5-month-old infants. *Cognition, 38,* 13–42. [5]

Baillargeon, R., and DeVos, J. (1991). Object permanence in young infants: Further evidence. *Child Development, 62,* 1227–1246. [5]

Baillargeon, R., DeVos, J., and Graber, M. (1989). Location memory in 8-month infants in a non-search AB task: Further evidence. *Cognitive Development, 4,* 345–367. [5]

Baillargeon, R., and Hanko-Summers, S. (1990). Is the top object adequately supported by the bottom object? Young infants' understanding of support relations. *Cognitive Development, 5,* 29–53. [5]

Baillargeon, R., Spelke, E. S., and Wasserman, S. (1985). Object permanence in five-month-old infants. *Cognition, 20,* 191–208. [5]

Baird, P., Sadovnick, A., and Yee, I. (1991). Maternal age and birth defects: A population study. *Lancet, 337,* 527–530. [3]

Baker, L., and Daniels, D. (1990). Nonshared environmental influences and personality differences in adult twins. *Journal of Personality and Social Psychology, 58,* 103–110. [1]

Baldwin, A., Cole, R., and Baldwin, C. (1982). Parental pathology, family interaction, and the competence of the child in school. *Monographs of the Society for Research in Child Development, 4,* (No. 5). [12]

Bandura, A. (1977). *Social learning theory.* Englewood Cliffs, NJ: Prentice-Hall. [4]

Bandura, A. (1985). A model of causality in social learning theory. In M. Mahoney and A. Freedman (Eds.), *Cognition and therapy.* New York: Plenum Press. [1, 2]

Bandura, A. (1986). *Social foundations of thought and action: A social cognitive theory.* Englewood Cliffs, NJ: Prentice-Hall. [2, 8, 10, 15]

Banks, M. S. (1980). The development of visual accommodation. *International Ophthalmology Clinics, 20,* 205–232. [4]

Banks, M. S. (1987). Visual recalibration and the development of contrast and optic flow perception. In A. Yonas (Ed.), *Minnesota Symposia on Child Psychology.* Hillsdale, NJ: Erlbaum. [4]

Banks, M. S., and Salapatek, P. (1983). Infant and visual perception. In P. H. Mussen (Ed.), *Handbook of child psychology* (Vol. 2, 4th ed.): M. M. Haith and J. J. Campos (Eds.), *Infancy and developmental psychobiology.* New York: Wiley. [4]

Barglow, P., Vaughn, B., and Molitor, N. (1987). Effects of maternal absence due to employment on the quality of infant-mother attachment in a low-risk sample. *Child Development, 58,* 945–954. [6]

Barker, R., and Wright, H. (1955). *Midwest and its children: The psychological ecology of an American town.* Evanston, IL: Row, Peterson. [2]

Barkley, R. (1989). Hyperactive girls and boys. Stimulant drug effects on mother-child interaction. *Journal of Child Psychology and Psychiatry, 30,* 379–390. [15]

Barkley, R. A. (1990). Attention deficit disorders: History, definition, and diagnosis. In M. Lewis and S. M. Miller (Eds.), *Handbook of developmental psychopathology* (pp. 65–76). New York: Plenum Press. [15]

Barr, R., Desilets, J., and Rotman, R. (1991). The normal crying curve: Hoops and hurdles. In B. Lester (Ed.),

Biological and social aspects of infant crying. New York: Plenum Press. [4]

Barrera, M. E., and Maurer, D. (1981). Recognition of mother's photographed face by the three-month-old. *Child Development, 52,* 558–563. [4]

Barrett, M. D. (1986). Early semantic representations and early word usage. In S. A. Kuczaj and M. D. Barrett (Eds.), *The acquisition of word meaning* (pp. 39–67). New York: Springer. [7]

Barrio Warriors Magazine. (1993, Spring). Volume II (2). [12]

Bassuk, E. L., and Rosenberg, L. (1990). Psychosocial characteristics of homeless children and children with homes. *Pediatrics, 85,* 257–261. [2]

Bates, E., Bretherton, I., and Snyder, L. (1988). *From first words to grammar: Individual differences and dissociable mechanisms.* New York: Cambridge University Press. [7]

Bates, J. (1980). The concept of difficult temperament. *Merrill-Palmer Quarterly, 26,* 299–319. [4]

Bates, J. (1989). Concepts and measures of temperament. In G. Kohnstamm, J. Bates, and M. Rothbart (Eds.), *Temperament in childhood* (pp. 3–26). New York: Wiley. [6]

Bates, J., Maslin, C., and Frankel, K. (1985). Attachment security, mother-child interaction, and temperament as predictors of behavior problem ratings at age three years. In I. Bretherton and E. Waters (Eds.), *Growing points in attachment theory and research. Monographs of the Society for Research in Child Development, 50* (Whole No. 209), 167–193. [6]

Bauer, P. (1993). Memory for gender-consistent and gender-inconsistent event sequences by twenty-five-month-old children. *Child Development, 64,* 285–297. [10]

Baumeister, A. (1987, November). *The new morbidity: Poverty and handicapping conditions in America.* Paper presented at the Institute for Developmental Disabilities, University of Minnesota. [2]

Baumrind, D. (1967). Child care practices anteceding three patterns of preschool behavior. *Genetic Psychology Monographs, 75,* 43–88. [8, 10]

Baumrind, D. (1977). *Socialization determinants of personal agency.* Paper presented at the biennial meeting of the Society for Research in Child Development, New Orleans. [12]

Baumrind, D. (1989). Rearing competent children. In W. Damon (Ed.), *Child development today and tomorrow.* San Francisco: Jossey-Bass. [2, 14]

Baumrind, D. (1993). The average expectable environment is not good enough: A response to Scarr. *Child Development, 64,* 1299–1317. [11]

Baydar, N., and Brooks-Gunn, J. (1991). Effects of maternal employment and child-care arrangements on preschoolers' cognitive and behavioral outcomes: Evidence from the children of the National Longitudinal Survey of Youth. *Developmental Psychology, 27,* 932–945. [2]

Bayley, N. (1949). Consistency and variability in the growth of intelligence from birth to eighteen years. *Journal of Genetic Psychology, 75,* 165–169. [5, 11]

Beal, C. (1994). *Boys and girls: The development of gender roles.* New York: McGraw-Hill. [12]

Becker, J. (1994). Pragmatic socialization: Parental input to preschoolers. *Discourse Processes, 17,* 131–148. [7]

Becker, W. (1964). Consequences of different kinds of parental discipline. In M. Hoffman and L. Hoffman (Eds.), *Review of child development research, 1.* New York: Russell Sage. [12]

Beeghly, M., and Cicchetti, D. (1990). An organizational approach to symbolic development in children with Down syndrome. In D. Cicchetti and M. Beeghly (Eds.), *Atypical symbolic development.* San Francisco: Jossey-Bass. [3]

Behrend, D. A. (1990). Constraints and development: A reply to Nelson (1988). *Cognitive Development, 5,* 313–330. [7]

Beilin, H. (1976). Constructing cognitive operators linguistically. In H. Reese (Ed.), *Advances in child development and behavior.* New York: Academic Press. [13]

Beilin, H. (1980). Piaget's theory: Refinement, revision, or rejection? In R. Kluwe and H. Spada (Eds.), *Developmental models of thinking.* New York: Academic Press. [13]

Bell, D., and Bell, L. (1983). Parental validation and support in the development of adolescent daughters. In H. Grotevant and C. Cooper (Eds.), *Adolescent development in the family: New directions in children's development.* San Francisco: Jossey-Bass. [14]

Bell, R. (1968). A reinterpretation of the direction of effects in studies of socialization. *Psychological Review, 75,* 81–95. [2]

Belsky, J. (1980). Child maltreatment: An ecological integration. *American Psychologist, 35,* 320–335. [2]

Belsky, J. (1984). The determinants of parenting: A process model. *Child Development, 55,* 83–96. [2]

Belsky, J. (1988). Child maltreatment and the emergent family system. In K. Browne, C. Davies, and P. Strattan (Eds.), *Early prediction and prevention of child abuse* (pp. 291–302). New York: Wiley. [8]

Belsky, J. (1990). Parental and nonparental child care and children's socioemotional development: A decade in review *Journal of Marriage and the Family, 52,* 885–903. [6]

Belsky, J. (in press). Developmental risks associated with infant daycare: Attachment insecurity, non-compliance, and aggression. In S. Chehvazi (Ed.), *Balancing working and parenting.* New York: American Psychiatric Press. [6]

Belsky, J., and Braungart, J. M. (1991). Are insecure-avoidant infants with extensive day-care experience less stressed by and more independent in the strange situation? *Developmental Psychology, 62,* 567–571. [6]

Belsky, J., Fish, M., and Isabella, R. (1991). Continuity and discontinuity in infant negative and positive emotionality: Family antecedents and attachment consequences. *Developmental Psychology, 27,* 421–431. [6]

Belsky, J., and Isabella, R. A. (1987). Individual, familial, and extrafamilial determinants of attachment security: A process analysis. In J. Belskey and T. Nezworski (Eds.), *Clinical implications of attachment.* Hillsdale, NJ: Erlbaum. [2, 6, 8]

Belsky, J., and Most, R. K. (1981). From exploration to play: A cross-sectional study of infant free play behavior. *Developmental Psychology, 17,* 630–639. [7]

Belsky, J., and Rovine, M. (1987). Temperament and attachment in the strange situation: An empirical rapproachment. *Child Development. 58,* 787–795. [6]

Bem, D., and Funder, D. (1978). Predicting more of the people more of the time: Assessing the personality of situations. *Psychological Review, 85,* 485–501. [1]

Bem, S. L. (1989). Genital knowledge and gender constancy in preschool children. *Child Development, 60,* 649–662. [10]

Benenson, J. (1993). Greater preference among females than males for dyadic interaction in early childhood. *Child Development, 64*(2), 544–555. [10]

Benenson, J., and Dweck, C. (1986). The development of trait explanations and self-evaluations in the academic and social domains. *Child Development, 57,* 1179–1187. [12]

Bengtson, B., and Robertson, J. (1985). *Grandparenthood.* Beverly Hills, CA: Sage. [2]

Benn, R. (1986). Factors promoting secure attachment relationships between employed mothers and their sons. *Child Development, 57,* 1124–1231. [2]

Berg, W. K., and Berg, K. M. (1979). Psychophysiological development in infancy: State, sensory function, and attention. In J. D. Osofsky (Ed.), *Handbook of infant development.* New York: Wiley. [4]

Berg, W. K., and Berg, K. M. (1987). Psychophysiological development in infancy: State, startle, and attention. In J. D. Osofsky (Ed.), *Handbook of infant development* (2nd ed.). New York: Wiley. [4]

Berko, J. (1958). The child's learning of English morphology. *Word, 14,* 150–177. [7]

Berndt, T. (1979). Developmental changes in conformity to peers and parents. *Developmental Psychology, 15,* 608–616. [14]

Berndt, T. (1981). Effects of friendship on prosocial intentions and behavior. *Child Development, 52,* 636–643. [14]

Berndt, T., Hawkins, J., and Hoyle, S. (1986). Changes in friendship during a school year: Effects on children's and adolescents' impressions of friendship and sharing with friends. *Child Development, 57,* 1284–1297. [12, 14]

Bernstein, G., and Borchart, C. (1991). Anxiety disorders of childhood and adolescence: A critical review. *Journal of the American Academy of Child and Adolescent Psychiatry, 30,* 519–532. [15]

Bernstein, R. (1980). The development of the self system during adolescence. *Journal of Genetic Psychology, 136,* 231–245. [14]

Berzonsky, M. (1971). The role of familiarity in children's explanations of physical causality. *Child Development, 42,* 705–715. [9]

Bickhard, M. H. (1978). The nature of developmental stages. *Human Development, 21,* 217–233. [11]

Bigner, J., and Jacobsen, R. (1989). Parenting behaviors of homosexual and heterosexual fathers. *Journal of Homosexuality, 18,* 173–186. [2]

Bjork, E. L., and Cummings, E. M. (1984). Infant search errors: Stage of concept development or stage of memory development. *Memory and Cognition, 12,* 1–19. [5]

Black, B., and Hazen, N. (1990). Social status and patterns of communication in acquainted and unacquainted preschool children. *Developmental Psychology, 26,* 379–387. [10]

Blasi, A., and Hoeffel, E. C. (1974). Adolescence and formal operations. *Human Development, 17,* 344–363. [13]

Blevins, B., and Cooper, R. G. (1986). The development of transitivity of length in young children. *Journal of Genetic Psychology, 147,* 395–405. [9]

Block, J. (1987, April). *Longitudinal antecedents of ego-control and ego-resiliency in late adolescence.* Paper presented at the biennial meeting of the Society for Research in Child Development, Baltimore. [10, Pt. 4 Epilogue, 14]

Block, J. H. (1979). *Personality development in males and females: The influence of different socialization.* Master Lecture Series of the American Psychological Association, New York. [12, 14]

Block, J. H., and Block, J. (1980). The role of ego-control and ego-resiliency in the organization of behavior. In W. A. Collins (Ed.), *Minnesota Symposia on Child Psychology* (Vol. 13). Hillsdale, NJ: Erlbaum. [10]

Block, J. H., Block, J., and Gjerde, P. (1986). The personality of children prior to divorce: A prospective study. *Child Development, 57,* 827–840. [2, 12]

Block, J. H., Block, J., and Morrison, A. (1981). Parental agreement-disagreement on childrearing orientations and gender-related personality correlates in children. *Child Development, 52,* 965–974. [14]

Bloom, L. M. (1973). *One word at a time: The use of single word utterances before syntax.* The Hague: Mouton. [7]

Blos, P. (1970). *The young adolescent.* New York: Free Press. [12]

Boccia, M., and Campos, J. (1989). Maternal emotional signals, social referencing, and infants reactions to strangers. In N. Eisenberg (Ed.), *Empathy and related emotional responses. New directions for child development* (pp. 25–49). San Francisco: Jossey-Bass. [6, 8]

Bohlin, G., Hagekoll, B., Germer, M., Andersson, K. and Lindberg, L. (1990, April) *Early antecedents of attachment: Avoidant and resistant reunion behaviors as predicted by maternal interactive behavior and infant temperament.* Paper presented at the International Conference on Infant Studies, Toronto. [6]

Boller, K., and Rovee-Collier, C. (1992). Contextual coding and recoding of infants' memories. *Journal of Experimental Child Psychology, 53,* 1–23. [5]

Borja-Alvarez, T., Zarbatany, L., and Pepper, S. (1991). Contributions of male and female guests and hosts to peer group entry. *Child Development, 62,* 1079–1090. [12]

Bornstein, M. H. (1978). Chromatic vision in infancy. In H. W. Reese and L. P. Lipsitt (Eds.), *Advances in child development and behavior* (Vol. 12). New York: Academic Press. [4]

Bornstein, M. H. (1981). "Human infant color and color perception" reviewed and reassessed: A critique of Werner and Wooten (1979). *Infant Behavior and Development, 4,* 119–150. [4]

Bornstein, M. H., and Sigman, M. D. (1986). Continuity in mental development from infancy. *Child Development, 57,* 251–274. [5, 11]

Bornstein, M. H., Tamis-LeMonda, C. S., Tal, J., Ludemann, P., Toda, S., Rahn, C. W., Pecheux, M. G., Azuma, H., and Vardi, D. (1992). Maternal responsiveness to infants in three societies: The United States, France, and Japan. *Developmental Psychology, 63,* 808–821. [6]

Boszormenyi-Nagy, I., and Spark, G. (1973). *Invisible loyalties: Reciprocity in intergenerational family therapy.* New York: Harper & Row. [15]

Bouchard, T. J., and McGue, M. (1981). Familial studies of intelligence: A review. *Science, 212,* 1055–1059. [11]

Bower, B. (1990). Anxiety weighs down pregnancies and births. *Science News, 138,* 102. [3]

Bower, T. G. R. (1974). *Development in infancy.* San Francisco: Freeman. [4]

Bower, T. G. R. (1977). *A primer of infant development.* San Francisco: Freeman. [5]

Bowerman, M. (1981). Keynote address, Child Language Research Forum, Stanford University, Stanford, CA. [7]

Bowlby, J. (1969/1982). *Attachment and loss* (2nd ed.). New York: Basic Books. [6]

Bowlby, J. (1973). *Separation.* New York: Basic Books. [1, 6, 12]

Bowlby, J. (1980). *Attachment and loss: Vol. 3. Loss.* New York: Basic Books. [15]

Boxer, A., Solomon, B., Offer, D., Petersen, A., and Halprin, F. (1984). Parents' perceptions of young adolescents. In R. Cohen, B. Cohler, and S. Weissman (Eds.), *Parenthood: A psychodynamic perspective.* New York: Guilford Press. [14]

Boyer, P. J. J. (1993). HIV infection in pregnancy. *Pediatric Annals, 22*(7), 406–412. [3]

Boysson-Bardies, B., and Vihman, M. M. (1991). Adaptation to language: Evidence from babbling and first words in four languages. *Language, 67,* 297–319. [7]

Bradley, R., Caldwell, B., Rock, S., Ramey, C., Barnard, K., Gray, C., Hammond, M., Mitchell, S., Gottfried, A., Siegel, L., and Johnson, D. (1989). Home environment and cognitive development in the first 3 years of life: A collaborative study involving six sites and three ethnic groups in North America. *Developmental Psychology, 25,* 217–235. [2]

Brainerd, C. J. (1978). *Piaget's theory of intelligence.* Englewood Cliffs, NJ: Prentice-Hall. [13]

Brazelton, T. B. (1973). *Clinics in developmental medicine: No. 50. Neonatal behavioral assessment scale.* Philadelphia: Lippincott. [4]

Brazelton, T. B., and Cramer, B. (1990). *The earliest relationship.* Reading, MA: Addison-Wesley. [6]

Brazelton, T. B., Koslowski, B., and Main, M. (1974). The origins of reciprocity:

The early mother-input interaction. In M. Lewis and L. Rosenblum (Eds.), *The effect of the infant on its caregiver.* New York: Wiley. [6]

Breger, L. (1974). *From instinct to identity: The development of personality.* Englewood Cliffs, NJ: Prentice-Hall. [2, 8, 10]

Breslow, L. (1981). Reevaluation of the literature on the development of transitive inferences. *Psychological Bulletin, 89,* 325–351. [9]

Bretherton, I. (1990). Pouring new wine into old bottles: The social self as internal working model. In M. Gunnar and L. A. Sroufe (Eds.), *Minnesota Symposia on Child Psychology.* Hillsdale, NJ: Erlbaum. [10, 12]

Bridges, L., and Grolnick, W. (1995). The development of emotional self-regulation in infancy and early childhood. In N. Eisenberg (Ed.), *Social development: Review of child development research* (pp. 185–211). Thousand Lakes CA: Sage. [6, 10]

Brittain, C. (1963). Adolescent choice and parent-peer cross pressures. *American Sociological Review, 28,* 385–391. [14]

Broakroyd, A., Balkany, T. J., Geers, A., Hayes, D., McFarland, W., Muyamoto, R. T., Novak, M., and Shallop, J. K. (1986). Issues of pre- and postimplant evaluation regarding cochlear implants. *Seminars in Hearing, 7,* 349–359. [4]

Brody, G., Stoneman, Z., and McCoy, J. K. (1992). Associations of maternal and paternal direct and differential behavior with sibling relationships: Contemporaneous and longitudinal analyses. *Child Development, 63,* 82–92. [12]

Bronfenbrenner, U. (1979). *The ecology of human development.* Cambridge, MA: Harvard University Press. [2]

Bronfenbrenner, U. (1989). Ecological systems theory. *Annals of Child Development, 6,* 187–249. [2]

Bronson, G., and Pankey, W. (1977). On the distinction between fear and wariness. *Child Development, 48,* 1167–1183. [6]

Bronson, W. (1981). *Toddlers' behavior with agemates: Issues of interaction, cognition and affect.* Norwood, NJ: Ablex. [8, 10]

Brookman, K. E. (1980). *Ocular accommodation in human infants.* Unpublished doctoral dissertation, Indiana University. [4]

Brooks-Gunn, J. (1987). Pubertal processes and girls' psychological adaptation. In R. M. Lerner and T. T. Foch (Eds.), *Biological-psychosocial interactions in early adolescence* (pp. 123–153). Hillsdale, NJ: Erlbaum. [13]

Brooks-Gunn, J., Duncan, G. J., Klebanov, P. K., and Sealand, N. (1993). Do neighborhoods influence child and adolescent development? *American Journal of Sociology, 99,* 353–395. [2, 5]

Brooks-Gunn, J., and Furstenberg, F. (1989). Adolescent sexual behavior. *American Psychologist, 44,* 249–257. [14]

Brooks-Gunn, J., and Reiter, E. O. (1990). The role of pubertal processes. In S. S. Feldman and G. R. Elliott (Eds.), *At the threshold: The developing adolescent* (pp. 16–53). Cambridge, MA: Harvard University Press. [13]

Broughton, J. (1978). Development of concepts of self, mind, reality, and knowledge. *New Directions for Child Development, 1,* 75–100. [12, 14]

Brown, A. L., Bransford, J. D., Ferrara, R. A., and Campione, J. C. (1983). Learning, remembering, and understanding. In P. H. Mussen (Ed.), *Handbook of child psychology* (Vol. 3, 4th ed.): J. H. Flavell and E. M. Markman (Eds.), *Cognitive development.* New York: Wiley. [11]

Brown, B. (1990). Peer groups and peer cultures. In S. Feldman and G. Elliot (Eds.), *At the threshold: The developing adolescent* (pp. 171–196). Cambridge, MA: Harvard University Press. [14]

Brown, B. B., and Clasen, D. R. (1986, March). *Developmental changes in adolescents' conceptions of peer groups.* Paper presented at the biennial meeting of the Society for Research on Adolescence, Madison, WI. [14]

Brown, B. B., Lohr, M. J., and Trujillo, C. M. (1990). Multiple crowds and multiple lifestyles: Adolescents' perceptions of peer group characteristics. In R. E. Muuss (Ed.), *Adolescent behavior and society: A book of readings* (pp. 30–36). New York: Random House. [14]

Brown, B. B., Mory, M. S., and Kinney, D. (1994). Casting adolescent crowds in a relational perspective: Caricature, channel, and context. In R. Montemayor, G. R. Adams, and T. P. Gullotta (Eds.), *Personal relationships during adolescence* (pp. 123–167). Thousand Oaks, CA: Sage. [14]

Brown, E. R., and Zuckerman, B. (1991). The infant of the drug-abusing mother. *Pediatric Annals, 20*(10), 555–562. [3]

Brown, R. (1973). *A first language: The early stages.* Cambridge, MA: Harvard University Press. [7]

Brown, R. (1977). Introduction. In C. E. Snow and C. A. Ferguson (Eds.), *Talking to children: Language input and acquisition.* Cambridge, Eng.: Cambridge University Press. [7]

Brown, R., and Fraser, C. (1963). The acquisition of syntax. In C. N. Cofer and B. Musgrave (Eds.), *Verbal behavior and learning: Problems and processes.* New York: McGraw-Hill. [7]

Brown, R., and Hanlon, C. (1970). Derivational complexity and order of acquisition. In J. R. Hayes (Ed.), *Cognition and the development of language.* New York: Wiley. [7]

Brownell, C. A. (1990). Peer social skills in toddlers: Competencies and constraints illustrated by same-age and mixed-age interaction. *Child Development, 61,* 838–848. [8, 10]

Brownell, C., and Brown, E. (1985). *Age differences in possession negotiations during the second year.* Paper presented at the biennial meeting of the Society for Research in Child Development, Toronto. [8]

Bruch, H. (1979). *The golden cage: The enigma of anorexia nervosa.* New York: Vintage Books. [15]

Bruner, J. S. (1970). The growth and structure of skill. In K. Connolly (Ed.), *Mechanisms of motor skill development.* New York: Academic Press. [4]

Bruner, J. S. (1975). The ontogenesis of speech acts. *Journal of Child Language, 2,* 1–19. [11]

Bruner, J. S. (1981). Intention in the structure of action and interaction. *Advances in Infancy Research, 1,* 41–56. [4]

Bruner, J. S., (1983). *Child's talk.* New York: Norton. [7]

Bruner, J. S., Oliver, R. R., and Greenfield, P. M. (1966). *Studies in cognitive growth.* New York: Wiley. [9, 11]

Brunnquell, D., Crichton, L., and Egeland, B. (1981). Maternal personality and attitude in disturbances of child rearing. *American Journal of Orthopsychiatry, 51,* 680–691. [8]

Bryant, P. E., and Trabasso, T. R. (1971). Transitive inferences and memory in young children. *Nature, 232,* 456–458. [9]

Buchanan, C. M., Maccoby, E. E., and Dornbusch, S. M. (1991). Caught between parents: Adolescents' experience in divorced homes. *Child Development, 62,* 1008–1029. [2]

Bugental, D., Blue, J., and Lewis, J. (1990). Caregiver beliefs and dysphoric affect directed to difficult children. *Developmental Psychology, 26,* 631–638. [10]

Bühler, C. (1930). *The first year of life* (P. Greenberg and R. Ribin, Trans.). New York: John Day. [4]

Bukowski, W., Newcomb, A., and Hartup, W. (in press). *The company they keep: Friendships and their developmental significance.* Cambridge, Eng.: Cambridge University Press. [12]

Buhrmester, D. (1990). Intimacy of friendship, interpersonal competence, and adjustment during preadolescence and adolescence. *Child Development, 61,* 1101–1111. [14]

Buhrmester, D., and Furman, W. (1987). The development of companionship and intimacy. *Child Development, 58,* 1101–1113. [14]

Buhrmester, D., and Furman, W. (1990). Perceptions of sibling relationships during middle childhood and adolescence. *Child Development, 61,* 1387–1398. [12]

Bullock, M., and Gelman, R. (1979). Preschool children's assumptions about cause and effect: Temporal ordering. *Child Development, 50,* 89–96. [9]

Burchinal, M., Lee, M., and Ramey, C. (1989). Type of daycare and preschool intellectual development in disadvantaged children. *Child Development, 60,* 128–137. [6]

Burton, L. (in press). Development of urban African-American children: A contextual perspective. *Minnesota Symposia on Child Psychology* (Vol. 29). Hillsdale, NJ: Erlbaum. [2]

Bushnell, I. W. R. (1979). Modification of the externality effect in young infants. *Journal of Experimental Child Psychology, 28,* 211–229. [4]

Bussey, K., and Bandura, A. (1992). Self-regulatory mechanisms governing gender development. *Child Development, 63,* 1236–1250. [12]

Butler, R. (1953). Discrimination learning by rhesus monkeys to visual exploration motivation. *Journal of Comparative and Physiological Psychology, 46,* 95–98. [2]

Butler, R., and Ruzany, N. (1993). Age and socialization effects on the development of social comparison motives and normative ability assessment in kibbutz and urban children. *Child Development, 64,* 532–543. [12]

Butterworth, G. (1974). *The development of the object concept in human infants.* Unpublished doctoral dissertation, Oxford University. [5]

Butterworth, G. (1975). Object identity in infancy: The interaction of spatial location codes in determining search errors. *Child Development, 46,* 866–870. [5]

Butterworth, G. (1977). Object disappearance and error in Piaget's stage IV task. *Journal of Experimental Child Psychology, 23,* 391–401. [5]

Cadoret, R. J., Troughton, E., Merchant, L. M., and Whitters, A. (1990). Early life psychosocial events and adult affective symptoms. In L. Robins and M. Rutter (Eds.), *Straight and devious pathways from childhood to adulthood* (pp. 300–313). Cambridge, Eng.: Cambridge University Press. [1, 15]

Cairns, R. B., Cairns, B. D., and Neckerman, H. J. (1989). Early school dropout: Configurations and determinants. *Child Development, 60,* 1437–1452. [14]

Cairns, R. B., Perrin, J. E., and Cairns, B. D. (1985). Social structure and social cognition in early adolescence: Affiliative patterns. *Journal of Early Adolescence, 5,* 339–355. [14]

Caldera, Y. M., Huston, A. C., and O'Brien, M. (1989). Social interactions and play patterns of parents and toddlers with feminine, masculine, and neutral toys. *Child Development, 60,* 70–76. [10]

Campbell, F., and Ramey, C. (1994). Effects of early intervention on intellectual and academic achievement: A follow-up study of children from low income families. *Child Development, 65,* 684–698. [5]

Campbell, P. (1991). *Eureka! Participant follow up analysis.* Groton, MA: Campbell-Kibler Associates. [11]

Campbell, R. L., and Bickhard, M. H. (1986). *Knowing levels and developmental stages.* New York: Karger. [1, 11]

Campbell, S. B. (1990). The socialization and social development of hyperactive children. In M. Lewis and S. M. Miller (Eds.), *Handbook of developmental psychopathology* (pp. 77–92). New York: Plenum Press. [15]

Campos, J. J., Bertenthal, B. I., and Caplovitz, K. (1982). The interrelationship of affect and cognition in the visual cliff situation. In C. Izard, J. Kagan, and R. Zajonc (Eds.), *Emotion and cognition.* New York: Plenum Press. [4]

Campos, J. J., Hiatt, S., Ramsay, D., Henderson, C., and Svejda, M. (1978). The emergence of fear on the visual cliff. In M. Lewis and L. Rosenblum (Eds.), *The origins of affect.* New York: Wiley. [4]

Camras, L. A., Oster, H., Campos, J. J., Miyake, K., and Bradshaw, D. (1992). Japanese and American infants' responses to arm restraint. *Developmental Psychology, 28,* 578–583. [6]

Cannon, T. D., Mednick, S. A., and Parnas, J. (1990). Two pathways to schizophrenia in children at risk. In L. Robins and M. Rutter (Eds.), *Straight and devious pathways from childhood to adulthood* (pp. 328–350). Cambridge, Eng.: Cambridge University Press. [15]

Caplan, M., Vespo, J., Pedersen, J., and Hay, D. F. (1991). Conflict and its resolution in small groups of one- and two-year-olds. *Developmental Psychology, 62(6),* 1513–1524. [8]

Capon, N., and Kuhn, D. (1979). Logical reasoning in the supermarket: Adult females' use of a proportional reasoning strategy in an everyday context. *Developmental Psychology, 15,* 450–452. [13]

Carey, S. (1978). The child as word learner. In M. Halle, J. Bresnan, and G. A. Miller (Eds.), *Linguistic theory and psychological reality.* Cambridge, MA: MIT Press. [7]

Carey, S. (1986). Cognitive science and science education. *American Psychologist, 41,* 1123–1130. [13]

Carlson, E., Jacobvitz, D., and Sroufe, L. A. (1995). A developmental study of inattentiveness and hyperactivity. *Child Development, 66,* 37–54. [10, 15]

Carlson, V., Cicchetti, D., Barnett, D., and Braunwald, K. (1989). Disorganized/disoriented attachment relationships in maltreated infants. *Developmental Psychology, 25,* 525–531. [6]

Caron, A. J., Caron, R. F., and Carlson, V. R. (1979). Infant perception of the invariant shape of objects varying in slant. *Child Development, 50,* 716–721. [4]

Caron, C., and Rutter, M. (1991). Comorbidity in child psychopathology: Concepts, issues, and research strategies. *Journal of Child Psychology and Psychiatry, 32,* 1063–1079. [15]

Carr, S., Dabbs, J., and Carr, T. (1975). Mother-infant attachment: The importance of the mother's visual field. *Child Development, 46,* 331–338. [8]

Case, R. (1974). Structure and strictures: Some functional limitations on the course of cognitive growth. *Cognitive Psychology, 6,* 544–573. [13]

Case, R. (1985). *Intellectual development: Birth to adulthood.* New York: Academic Press. [5, 11, 13]

Caspi, A., and Elder, G. H. (1988). Emergent family patterns: The intergenerational construction of problem behavior and relationships. In R. Hinde and J. Stevenson-Hinde (Eds.), *Relations between relationships within families.* Oxford, Eng.: Oxford University Press. [2, 12, 15]

Caspi, A., and Moffitt, T. E. (1991). Individual differences are accentuated during periods of social change: The sample case of girls at puberty. *Journal of Personality and Social Psychology, 61,* 157–168. [14]

Cattell, R. B. (1971). *Abilities: Their structure, growth, and action.* Boston: Houghton-Mifflin. [11]

Caudill, W., and Weinstein, H. (1969). Maternal care and infant behavior in Japan and America. *Psychiatry, 32,* 12–43. [2]

Caughy, M. O., DiPietro, J. A., and Strobino, D. M. (1994). Day-care participation as a protective factor in the cognitive development of low-income children. *Child Development, 65,* 457–471. [2]

Cazden, C. (1968). The acquisition of noun and verb inflections. *Child Development, 39,* 438–443. [7]

Cazden, C. (1983). Peekaboo as an instructional model: Discourse development at school and at home. In B.

Brain (Ed.), *The sociogenesis of language and human conduct: A multidisciplinary book of readings.* New York: Plenum Press. [11]

Ceci, S. J. (in press). Cognitive and social factors in children's testimony. In B. Sales and G. VandenBos (Eds.), *APA Master Lectures: Psychology and the Law.* Washington, DC: American Psychological Association. [9]

Ceci, S. J., and Bruck, M. (1993). Child witnesses. Translating research into policy. *SRCD Social Policy Report, VII*(3). Ann Arbor, MI: Society for Research in Child Development. [9]

Ceci, S. J., Leichtman, M. D., and White, T. (in press). Interviewing preschoolers: Remembrance of things planted. In D. P. Peters (Ed.), *The child witness in context: Cognitive, social, and legal perspectives.* Dordrecht: Kluwer. [9]

Centers for Disease Control. (1993, April 23). *Morbidity and Mortality Weekly Report, 42,*(15). Atlanta,: U.S. Department of Health and Human Services. [3]

Charles, L., and Schain, R. (1981). A four year follow-up study of the effect of methylphenidate on the behavior and academic achievement of hyperactive children. *Journal of Abnormal Child Psychology, 9,* 495–505. [15]

Charlesworth, W. R. (1992). Darwin and developmental psychology. *Developmental Psychology, 28,* 5–16. [2]

Chase, W. G., and Simon, H. A. (1973). Perception in chess. *Cognitive Psychology, 4,* 55–81. [11]

Chase-Lansdale, L., and Hetherington, M. (in press). The impact of divorce on life-span development. In D. Featherman and R. Lerner (Eds.), *Life span development and behavior, 10.* [14]

Chassin, L., and Sherman, S. (1985). *Adolescents' changing relationships with parents and peers: A cohort-sequential study.* Paper presented at the biennial meeting of the Society for Research in Child Development, Toronto. [15]

Chavkin, W., Kristal, A., Seabron, C., and Guigli, P. E. (1987). The reproductive experience of women living in hotels for the homeless in New York City. *New York State Journal of Medicine, 87,* 10–13. [2]

Chervenak, F. A., Isaacson, C., and Mahoney, M. J. (1986). Advances in the diagnosis of fetal defects. *New England Journal of Medicine, 315,* 305–307. [3]

Chi, M. T. H. (1978). Knowledge structure and memory development. In R. S. Siegler (Ed.), *Children's thinking: What develops?* Hillsdale, NJ: Erlbaum. [9, 11, 13]

Chi, M. T. H., and Ceci, S. J. (1987). Content knowledge: Its role, representation, and restructuring in memory development. In H. W. Reese and L. Lipsett (Eds.), *Advances in child development and behavior.* New York: Academic Press. [9]

Children's Defense Fund (1991). *The state of America's children.* Washington, DC: Author. [6]

Chipuer, H. M., Plomin, R., Pedersen, N. L., McClearn, G. E., and Nesselroade, J. R. (1993). Genetic influences on family environment: The role of personality. *Developmental Psychology, 29,* 110–118. [2]

Chodorow, N. (1989). *Feminism and psychoanalytic theory.* New Haven: Yale University Press. [10]

Chomsky, N. (1957). *Syntactic structures.* The Hague: Mouton. [7]

Christopoulos, C., Cohn, D. A., Shaw, D. S., Joyce, S., Sullivan-Hanson, J., Kraft, S. P., and Emery, R. E. (1987). Children of abused women: I. Adjustment at time of shelter residence. *Journal of Marriage and the Family, 49*(3), 611–619. [12]

Chukovsky, K. (1941/1971). *From two to five.* (M. Morton, Trans. and Ed.). Berkeley, CA: University of California Press. [9]

Church, J. A. (1993). Clinical aspects of HIV infection in children. *Pediatric Annals, 22*(7), 417–427. [3]

Cicchetti, D., and Beeghly, M. (1990a). *The self in transition: Infancy to childhood.* Chicago: University of Chicago Press. [8]

Cicchetti, D., and Beeghly, M. (1990b). *Down syndrome: A developmental perspective.* Cambridge, Eng.: Cambridge University Press. [3, 6]

Cicchetti, D., and Carlson, V. (1989). *Child maltreatment.* New York: Cambridge University Press. [8, 12]

Cicchetti, D., and Cohen, D. (1995). Development and psychopathology. In D. Cicchetti and D. Cohen (Eds.), *Developmental processes and psychopathology* (Vol. 1). New York: Cambridge University Press. [15]

Cicchetti, D., and Olson, K. (1990). The developmental psychopathology of child maltreatment. In M. Lewis and S. Miller (Eds.), *Handbook of developmental psychopathology.* New York: Plenum Press. [8]

Cillessen, A., van Ijzendoorn, H., and van Lieshout, C. (1992). Heterogeneity among peer-rejected boys: Subtypes and stabilities. *Child Development, 63,* 893–905. [12]

Clancy, P. (1986). The acquisition of communicative style in Japanese. In B. Schieffelin and E. Ochs (Eds.), *Language socialization across cultures* (pp. 213–250). Cambridge, Eng.: Cambridge University Press. [7]

Clark, E. V. (1973). What is in a word? On the child's acquisition of semantics in his first language. In T. E. Moore (Ed.), *Cognitive development and the acquisition of language.* New York: Academic Press. [7]

Clark, E. V. (1983). Meanings and concepts. In P. H. Mussen (Ed.), *Handbook of child psychology* (Vol. 3, 4th ed.): J. H. Flavell and E. M. Markman (Eds.), *Cognitive development.* New York: Wiley. [7]

Clark, E. V. (1988). On the logic of contrast. *Journal of Child Language, 15,* 317–335. [7]

Clark, E. V. (1990). On the pragmatics of contrast. *Journal of Child Language, 17,* 417–432. [7]

Clarke-Stewart, K. A. (1973). Interactions between mothers and their young children. *Monographs of the Society for Research in Child Development, 38* (Serial No. 153). [7, 8]

Clarke-Stewart, K. A. (1977). *Child care in the family: A review of research and some propositions for policy.* New York: Academic Press. [2]

Clarke-Stewart, K. A. (1989). Infant day care: Maligned or malignant? *American Psychologist, 44,* 266–273. [6]

Clausen, J. (1968). Perspectives on childhood socialization. In J. Clausen (Ed.), *Socialization and society.* Boston: Little, Brown. [10]

Clifton, R., Muir, D. W., Ashmead, D. H., and Clarkson, M. G. (1993). Is visually guided reaching in early infancy a myth? *Child Development, 64,* 1099–1110. [4]

Clingempeel, W. G., Colyar, J. J., Brand, E., and Hetherington, E. M. (1992). Children's relationships with maternal grandparents: A longitudinal study of family structure and pubertal status effects. *Child Development, 63,* 1404–1423. [2]

Cohen, L. B., and Campos, J. (1974). Father, mother, and stranger as elicitors of attachment behaviors in infancy. *Developmental Psychology, 10,* 146–154. [2, 6]

Cohen, L. B., and Strauss, M. S. (1979). Concept acquisition in the human infant. *Child Development, 50,* 419–424. [5]

Cohen, L. B., and Younger, B. A. (1984). Infant perception of angular relations. *Infant Behavior and Development, 7,* 37–47. [5]

Cohen, S., and Beckwith, L. (1979). Preterm infant interaction with the caregiver in the first year of life and competence at age two. *Child Development, 50,* 767–776. [2]

Coie, J. (1985). Fitting social skills intervention to the target group. In B. Schneider, K. Rubin, and J. Ledingham (Eds.), *Peer relationships and social skills in childhood* (Vol. II). New York: Springer-Verlag. [10]

Coie, J., Dodge, K., Terry, R., and Wright, V. (1991). The role of aggression in peer relations: An analysis of aggression episodes in boys' play groups. *Child Development, 62,* 812–826. [12]

Colby, A., Kohlberg, L., Gibbs, J., and Lieberman, M. (1983). A longitudinal study of moral judgment. *Monographs of the Society for Research in Child Development, 48*(1–2, Serial No. 200). [13]

Cole, P. M., Caplovitz Barrett, K., and Zahn-Waxler, C. (1992). Emotional displays in two-year-olds during mishaps. *Child Development, 63,* 314–324. [8, 10]

Coleman, J. (1974). *Relationships in adolescence.* London: Routledge & Kegan Paul. [14]

Collins, P., and DePue, R. (1992). A neurobehavioral systems approach to developmental psychopathology: Implications for disorders of affect. In D. Cicchetti (Ed.), *Developmental perspectives on depression.* Rochester Symposium on Developmental Psychopathology, Vol. 4 (pp. 29–101). Rochester, NY: University of Rochester Press. [6]

Collins, W. A. (1990). Parent-child relationships in the transition to adolescence. Continuity and change in interaction, affects, and cognition. In R. Montemayor, G. Adams, and T. Gullota (Eds.), *Advances in adolescent development* (Vol. 2). Beverly Hills, CA: Sage. [1, 14]

Collins, W. A. (1994, July). *Individual development and personal relationships: Change and differentiation in relationships during adolescence.* Paper presented at the International Conference on Personal Relationships, Groningen, Netherlands. [14]

Collins, W. A., and Repinski, D. J. (1994). Relationships during adolescence: Continuity and change in interpersonal perspective. In R. Montemayor, G. R. Adams, and T. P. Gullotta (Eds.), *Personal relationships during adolescence* (pp. 7–36). Thousand Oaks, CA: Sage. [14]

Collins, W. A., and Russell, G. (1991). Mother-child and father-child relationships in middle childhood and adolescence: A developmental analysis. *Developmental Psychology, 11,* 99–136. [14]

Colombo, J. (1993). *Infant cognition: Predicting later intellectual functioning.* Newbury Park, CA: Sage. [5]

Conel, J. L. (1939–1963). *The postnatal development of the human cerebral cortex* (7 vols.). Cambridge, MA: Harvard University Press. [4]

Conger, R., Elder, G., Lorenz, F., Conger, K., Simons, R., Whitbeck, L., Huck, S., and Melby, J. (1990). Linking economic hardship to marital quality and instability. *Journal of Marriage and the Family, 52,* 643–656. [2]

Conger, R. D., Elder, G. H., Jr., Lorenz, F. O., Simons, R. L., and Whitbeck, L. B. (1994). *Families in troubled times: Adapting to change in rural America.* New York: Aldine de Gruyter. [2]

Connolly, J. A., and Doyle, A. (1984). Relation of social fantasy play to social competence in preschoolers. *Developmental Psychology, 20*(5), 797–806. [10]

Connor, E. M., Sperling, R. S., Gelber, R., Kiselev, P., Scott, G., O'Sullivan, M. J., VanDyke, R., Bey, M., Shearer, W., Jacobson, R. L., Jimenez, E., O'Neill, E., Bazin, B., Delfraissy, J.-F., Culnane, M., Coombs, R., Elkins, M., Moye, J., Stratton, P., and Balsley, J. (1994). Reduction of maternal-infant transmission of human immunodeficiency virus Type 1 with Zidovudine treatment. *New England Journal of Medicine, 331,* 1173–1180. [3]

Cooper, C. (1988). Commentary: The role of conflict in adolescent-parent relationships. In M. Gunnar and W. A. Collins (Eds.), *Minnesota Symposia on Child Psychology* (Vol. 21, pp. 181–187). Hillsdale, NJ: Erlbaum. [14]

Cooper, C. (in press). Multiple selves, multiple worlds: Cultural perspectives on individuality and connectedness in adolescent development. In A. Masten (Ed.), *Minnesota Symposia on Child Psychology* (Vol. 29). Hillsdale, NJ: Erlbaum. [10, 14, Pt. 6 Epilogue]

Cooper, C. R. (1980). Development of collaborative problem solving among preschool children. *Developmental Psychology, 16,* 433–440. [9]

Cooper, C. R., and Cooper, R. G. (1984). Peer learning discourse: What develops? In S. Kuczaj (Ed.), *Children's discourse.* New York: Springer-Verlag. [9, 11]

Cooper, C. R., and Cooper, R. G. (in press). Links between adolescents' relationships with their parents and peers: Models, evidence, and mechanisms. In R. D. Parke and G. W. Ladd (Eds.), *Family-peer relationships: Modes of linkages.* Hillsdale, NJ: Erlbaum. [11, 14]

Cooper, C., Jackson, J., Dunbar, N., Lopez, E., Cooper, R., Figueroa, J., and Cooper, D. (1995). *Linking family, school, and peers: African-American and Latino youth in university outreach programs.* Paper presented at the meeting of the Society for Research in Child Development, Indianapolis. [11]

Cooper, C. R., Marquis, A., and Edwards, D. (1986). Four perspectives on peer learning among elementary school children. In E. C. Mueller and C. R. Cooper (Eds.), *Process and outcome in peer relationships.* New York: Academic Press. [9, 11]

Cooper, R. G. (1976, April). *The role of estimators and operators in number conservation.* Paper presented at the Southwestern Psychological Association, Albuquerque. [9]

Cooper, R. G. (1984). Early number development: Discovering number space with addition and subtraction. In C. Sophian (Ed.), *Origins of cognitive skills.* Hillsdale, NJ: Erlbaum. [9]

Cooper, R. G. (1991). *The complementary roles of operator skills and strategy selection skills in early number development.* Paper presented at the Biennial Meeting of the Society for Research in Child Development, Seattle. [9]

Cooper, R. G., Leitner, E., and Moore, N. V. (1977, March). *The development of skills underlying perception, representation, and construction of series.* Paper presented at the biennial meeting of the Society for Research in Child Development, New Orleans. (ERIC Document Reproduction Service No. ED 136–952.) [9]

Cooper, R. G., and Robbins, R. R. (1981). The effect of cognitive skills on learning astronomy. *Proceedings of the 1980 Frontiers in Education Conference.* Houston, TX: Southwest Astronomy and Astrophysics Society. [13]

Coopersmith, S. (1967). *The antecedents of self-esteem.* San Francisco: Freeman. [10]

Coplan, J. (1993). New developments: Child development. *Current Problems in Pediatrics, 23*(2), 42–43. [3]

Coplan, R. J., Rubin, K. H., Fox, N. A., Calkins, S. D., and Stewart, S. L. (1994). Being alone, playing alone, and acting alone: Distinguishing among reticence and passive and active solitude in young children. *Child Development, 65*(1), 129–137. [10]

Corman, H. H., and Escalona, S. K. (1969). Stages of sensorimotor development: A replication study. *Merrill-Palmer Quarterly, 15,* 351–361. [5]

Cortese, A. J. (1989). The interpersonal approach to morality: A gender and cultural analysis. *Journal of Social Psychology, 129,* 429–442. [13]

Costanzo, P. (1970). Conformity development as a function of self-blame. *Journal of Personality and Social Psychology, 14,* 366–374. [2, 14]

Coster, W., Gersten, M., Beeghly, M., and Cicchetti, D. (1989). Communicative functioning in maltreated toddlers. *Developmental Psychology, 25,* 1020–1029. [8]

Coté, J. E. (1992). *Adolescent storm and stress: An evaluation of the Mead-Freeman controversy.* Hillsdale, NJ: Erlbaum. [14]

Cowan, C. P., and Cowan, P. A. (1992). *When partners become parents: The big life change for couples.* New York: Basic Books. [2]

Cowan, P., Cowan, C., and Heming, G. (1986). *Risks to marriage when partners become parents: Implications for family devel-*

opment. Paper presented at the annual meeting of the American Psychiatric Association, Washington, DC. [2]

Cowen, R. (1989). Receptor encounters. *Science News, 136,* 248–252. [15]

Cox, M. J., Owen, M. T., Henderson, V. K., and Margand, N. A. (1992). Prediction of infant-father and infant-mother attachment. *Developmental Psychology, 28,* 474–483. [6]

Cox, M. J., Owen, M. T., Lewis, J. M., and Henderson, V. K. (1989). Marriage, adult adjustment, and early parenting. *Child Development, 60,* 1015–1024. [6]

Craik, F. I. M., and Lockhart, R. S. (1972). Levels of processing: A framework for memory research. *Journal of Verbal Learning and Verbal Behavior, 11,* 671–684. [9]

Crane, J. (1991). The epidemic theory of ghettos and neighborhood effects on dropping out and teenage childbearing. *American Journal of Sociology, 96,* 1226–1259. [2]

Crockenberg, S. (1981). Infant irritability, mother responsiveness and social support influences on the security of infant-mother attachment. *Child Development, 52,* 857–865. [6, Pt. 4 Epilogue]

Crockenberg, S. (1986, April). *Maternal anger and the behavior of two-year-old children.* Paper presented at the International Conference on Infant Studies, Beverly Hills, CA. [8]

Crockenberg, S., and Litman, C. (1990). Autonomy as competence in 2-year-olds: Maternal correlates of child defiance, compliance, and self-assertion. *Developmental Psychology, 26,* 961–970. [8]

Crockenberg, S., and Litman, C. (1991). Effects of maternal employment on maternal and two-year-old child behavior. *Child Development, 62,* 930–953. [2]

Crocket, L., Losoff, M., and Petersen, A. C. (1984). Perceptions of the peer group and friendship in early adolescence. *Journal of Early Adolescence, 4,* 155–181. [14]

Crogan, J. (1993, April 29). Gangs looking for nationwide truce. *San Francisco Examiner.* [12]

Crouter, A. C., and McHale, S. M. (1993). Temporal rhythms in family life: Seasonal variation in the relation between parental work and family processes. *Developmental Psychology, 29,* 198–207. [2]

Crouter, A. C., Perry-Jenkins, M., Huston, T. L., and McHale, S. M. (1987). Processes underlying father involvement in dual-earner and single-earner families. *Developmental Psychology, 23,* 431–440. [2]

Crowe, K., and von Baeyer, C. (1989). Predictors of positive childbirth experience. *Birth, 16,* 59–63. [3]

Cummings, E. M., Iannotti, R. J., and Zahn-Waxler, C. (1989). Aggression between peers in early childhood: Individual continuity and developmental change. *Child Development, 60,* 887–895. [10]

Cummings, J. S., Pellegrini, D. S., Notarius, C. I., and Cummings, E. M. (1989). Children's responses to angry adult behavior as a function of marital distress and history of interparent hostility. *Child Development, 60,* 1035–1043. [10]

Cunningham, F. G., MacDonald, P. C., Grant, N. F., Leveno, K. J., and Gilstrap, L. C., III (1993). *Williams obstetrics* (19th ed.). Norwalk, CT: Appleton and Lange. [3]

Curtiss, S. (1977). *Genie: Psycholinguistic study of a modern day wild child.* New York: Academic Press. [2]

Cuvo, A. J. (1974). Incentive level influence on overt rehearsal and free recall as a function of age. *Journal of Experimental Child Psychology, 18,* 167–181. [11]

Dabbs, J., and Morris, R. (1990). Testosterone, social class, and antisocial behavior in a sample of 4,462 men. *Psychological Science, 1,* 209–211. [15]

Damon, W. (1977). *The social world of the child.* San Francisco: Jossey-Bass. [12]

Damon, W. (1983). *Social and personality development.* New York: Norton. [12, 14]

Damon, W. (1988). *The moral child.* New York: Cambridge University Press. [6, 8, 10, 12, Pt. 5 Epilogue]

Damon, W., and Hart, D. (1988). *Self-understanding in childhood and adolescence.* Cambridge, Eng.: Cambridge University Press. [12, 14]

Daniel, B. M., and Lee, D. N. (1990). Development of looking with head and eyes. *Journal of Experimental Child Psychology, 50,* 200–216. [4]

Dannemiller, J. L., and Stephens, B. R. (1988). A critical test of infant pattern preference models. *Child Development, 59,* 210–216. [4]

Dasen, P. R., and Heron, A. (1981). Cross-cultural tests of Piaget's theory. In H. Triandis and A. Heron (Eds.), *Handbook of cross-cultural psychology: Vol. 4. Developmental psychology.* Boston: Allyn & Bacon. [11, 13]

Dasen, P. R., Lavallee, M., and Retschitghi, J. (1979). Training conservation of quantity (liquids) in West African (Baoule) children. *International Journal of Psychology, 14,* 57–68. [11]

Day, R. H. (1987). Visual size constancy in infancy. In B. E. McKenzie and R. H. Day (Eds.), *Perceptual development in early infancy: Problems and issues.* Hillsdale, NJ: Erlbaum. [4]

Dayton, G. O., Jr., and Jones, M. H. (1964). Analysis of characteristics of fixation reflexes in infants by use of direct current electrooculography. *Neurology, 14,* 1152–1156. [4]

DeCasper, A. J., and Fifer, W. (1980). Of human bonding: Newborns prefer their mothers' voices. *Science, 208,* 1174–1176. [2, 4]

DeCasper, A. J., and Spence, M. J. (1986). Prenatal maternal speech influences newborn's perception of speech sounds. *Infant Behavior and Development, 9,* 133–150. [4]

DeHart, G. B. (1990). *Young children's linguistic interaction with mothers and siblings.* Unpublished doctoral dissertation, University of Minnesota. [7]

Dempster, F. N. (1981). Memory span: Sources of individual and developmental differences. *Psychological Bulletin, 89,* 63–100. [11, 13]

Denham, S., and Holt, R. (1993). Preschoolers' likability as cause or consequence of their social behavior. *Developmental Psychology, 29,* 271–277. [10]

Denham, S., Renwick, S., and Holt, R. (1991). Working and playing together: Prediction of preschool social-emotional competence from mother-child interaction. *Child Development, 62,* 242–249. [10]

Dennis, W., and Dennis, M. C. (1940). The effect of cradling practices upon the onset of walking in Hopi children. *Journal of Genetic Psychology, 56,* 77–86. [4]

de Villiers, J. G., and de Villiers, P. A. (1978). *Language acquisition.* Cambridge, MA: Harvard University Press. [7]

DeVries, R. (1969). Constancy of generic identity in the years three to six. *Monographs of the Society for Research in Child Development, 34* (Serial No. 127). [9]

Diamond, A. (1985). Development of the ability to use recall to guide action, as indicated by infants' performance on AB. *Child Development, 56,* 868–883. [5]

Diamond, A. (1988). Abilities and neural mechanisms underlying AB performance. *Child Development, 59,* 523–527. [5]

DiLalla, L., and Gottesman, I. (1989). Heterogeneity of causes for delinquency and criminality: Lifespan perspectives. *Development and Psychopathology, 1,* 339–350. [15]

DiLalla, L. F., Thompson, L. A., Plomin, R., Phillops, K., Fagan, J. F., III, Haith, M. M., Cyphers, L. H., and Fulker, D. W. (1990). Infant predictors of preschool and adult IQ: A study of infant twins and their parents. *Developmental Psychology, 26,* 759–769. [5]

DiPietro, J. A. (1981). Rough and tumble play: A function of gender. *Developmental Psychology, 17,* 50–59. [10]

DiSessa, A. A. (1988). Knowledge in pieces. In G. Forman and P. Pufall (Eds.). *Constructivism in the computer age.* Hillsdale, NJ: Erlbaum. [13]

Dishion, T., Patterson, G., Stoolmiller, M., and Skinner, M. (1991). Family, school, and behavioral antecedents to early adolescent involvement with antisocial peers. *Developmental Psychology, 27,* 172–180. [12]

Dishion, T., French, D., and Patterson, G. (1995). The development and ecology of antisocial behavior. In D. Cicchetti and D. Cohen (Eds.), *Developmental psychopathology* (Vol. 2, pp. 421–471). New York: Wiley. [15]

Dix, T., Ruble, D. N., and Zambarano, R. J. (1989). Mothers' implicit theories of discipline: Child effects, parent effects, and the attribution process. *Child Development, 60,* 1373–1391. [12]

Dodds, M. (1995). *The influence of interparental violence on children's behavior problems.* Unpublished doctoral dissertation. University of Minnesota. [8, 12]

Dodge, K., Bates, J., and Pettit, G. (1990). Mechanisms in the cycle of violence. *Science, 250,* 1678–1683. [2, 8]

Dodge, K. A., Pettit, G. S., McClaskey, C. L., and Brown, M. M. (1986). Social competence in children. *Monographs of the Society for Research in Child Development, 51* (2, Serial No. 213). [12].

Doi, T. (1981). *The structure of dependency.* New York: Kodansha International. [2]

Donaldson, M. (1978). *Children's minds.* New York: Norton. [11]

Dornbusch, S. M., Gross, R. T., Duncan, P. D., and Ritter, P. L. (1987). Stanford studies of adolescence using the National Health Examination Study. In R. M. Lerner and T. T. Foch (Eds.), *Biological-psychosocial interactions in early adolescence* (pp. 189–205). Hillsdale, NJ: Erlbaum. [13]

Dossey, J. (1990). *Women and minorities in science and engineering.* Washington, DC: National Science Foundation. [11]

Douglas, V., and Peters, K. (1980). Toward a clear definition of the attentional deficit of hyperactive children. In G. Hale and M. Lewis (Eds.), *Attention and the development of cognitive skills* (pp. 173–247). New York: Plenum Press. [15]

Douvan, E., and Adelson, J. (1966). *The adolescent experience.* New York: Wiley. [14]

Downs, M. P. (1986). The rationale for neonatal hearing screening. In E. T. Swigart (Ed.), *Neonatal hearing screening* (pp. 3–19). San Diego: College-Hill Press. [4]

Doyle, A., Bowker, A., Hayvren, M., Sherman, L., Serbin, L., and Gold, D. (1985). Developmental changes in social and solitary pretend play during middle childhood. *Research Bulletins.*

Centre for Research in Human Development, Concordia University. [12]

Dreyer, P. (1982). Sexuality during adolescence. In B. Wolman (Ed.), *Handbook of developmental psychology.* Englewood Cliffs, NJ: Prentice-Hall. [14]

Dromi, E. (1987). *Early lexical development.* Cambridge, Eng.: Cambridge University Press. [7]

Drotar, D. (1991). Children with nonorganic failure-to-thrive: A population at risk. *Child, Youth, and Family Services Newsletter, 2,* 1–3. [6]

DuBois, D. L., and Hirsch, B. J. (1990). School and neighborhood friendship patterns of blacks and whites in early adolescence. *Child Development, 61,* 524–536. [14]

Dubow, E. F., and Tisak, J. (1989). The relation between stressful life events and adjustment in elementary school children: The role of social support and social problem-solving skills. *Child Development, 60,* 1412–1423. [12]

Dubrovina, I., and Ruzska, A. (1990). *The mental development of residents in a children's home.* Moscow: Pedagogics. [6]

Duncan, G. J., Brooks-Gunn, J., and Klebanov, P. K. (1994). Economic deprivation and early childhood development. *Child Development, 65,* 296–318. [2]

Dunham, P., and Dunham, F. (1990). Effects of mother-infant social interactions on infants' subsequent contingency task performance. *Child Development, 61,* 785–793. [6]

Dunn, J. (1985). *The transition from infancy to childhood.* Address presented to the Society for Research in Child Development, Toronto. [8, 10]

Dunn, J. (1988). *The beginning of social understanding.* Cambridge, MA: Harvard University Press. [2]

Dunn, J., and Dale, N. (1984). I a Daddy: Two-year-olds' collaboration in joint pretend with sibling and with mother. In I. Bretherton (Ed.), *Symbolic play and the development of social understanding* (pp. 131–158). New York: Academic Press. [7]

Dunn, J., and Kendrick, C. (1982a). Interaction between young siblings: Association with the interaction between mother and firstborn child. *Developmental Psychology, 17,* 336–343. [2, 12]

Dunn, J., and Kendrick, C. (1982b). *Siblings.* Cambridge, MA: Harvard University Press. [7]

Dunn, J., and Kendrick, C. (1982c). The speech of two- and three-year-olds to infant siblings: "Baby talk" and the context of communication. *Journal of Child Language, 9,* 579–595. [2, 7]

Dunn, J., and Munn, P. (1986). Siblings and the development of prosocial behavior. *International Journal of Behavioral Development, 9,* 265–294. [8]

Dunn, J., and Shatz, M. (1989). Becoming a conversationalist despite (or because of) having an older sibling. *Child Development, 60,* 399–410. [10]

Dunn, J., Slomkowski, C. L. and Beardsall, L. (1994). Sibling relationships from the preschool period through middle childhood and early adolescence. *Developmental Psychology, 30,* 315–324. [12]

Dunphy, D. (1963). The social structure of urban adolescent peer groups. *Sociometry, 26,* 230–246. [14]

Dweck, C. (1975). The role of expectations and attributions in the alleviation of learned helplessness. *Journal of Personality and Social Psychology, 31,* 674–685. [14]

Dweck, C. S., Davidson, W., Nelson, S., and Erra, B. (1978). Sex differences in learned helplessness: II. The contingencies of evaluation feedback in the classroom: III. An experimental analysis. *Developmental Psychology, 14,* 268–276. [12]

Earls, F. (1994). Oppositional-defiant and conduct disorders. In M. Rutter, E. Taylor, and L. Hersov (Eds.), *Child and adolescent psychiatry* (pp. 308–329). London: Blackwell. [15]

Earls, F., Reich, W., Jung, K., and Cloninger, R. (1988). Psychopathology in children of alcoholic and antisocial parents. *Alcoholism: Clinical and Experimental Research, 12,* 481–487. [15]

East, P., and Rook, K. (1992). Compensatory patterns of support among children's peer relationships: A test using school friends, nonschool friends, and siblings. *Developmental Psychology, 28,* 163–172. [12]

Easterbrooks, M. A. (1989). Quality of attachment to mother and to father: Effects of perinatal risk status. *Child Development, 60,* 825–830. [6]

Easterbrooks, M. A., and Emde, R. N. (1988). Marital and parent-child relationships: The role of affect in the family system. In R. Hinde and J. Stevenson-Hinde (Eds.), *Towards understanding families.* Cambridge, Eng.: Cambridge University Press. [2, 8]

Eckenrode, J., Laird, M., and Doris, J. (1993). School performance and disciplinary problems among abused and neglected children. *Developmental Psychology, 29*(1), 53–62. [8]

Eckerman, C., and Stein, M. (1990). How imitation begets imitation and toddlers' generation of games. *Developmental Psychology, 26,* 370–378. [8]

Eckerman, C. O., Davis, C. C., and Didow, S. M. (1989). Toddlers' emerging ways of achieving social coordination with a peer. *Child Development, 60,* 440–453. [8]

Eder, D. (1985). The cycle of popularity: Interpersonal relations among female adolescents. *Sociology of Education, 58,* 154–165. [14]

Eder, R., and Mangelsdorf, S. (in press). The emotional basis of early personality development: Implications for the emergent self-concept. In S. Briggs, R. Hogan, and W. Jones (Eds.), *Handbook of personality psychology.* Orlando, FL: Academic Press. [10]

Edwards, C. P. (1982). Moral development in comparative cultural perspective. In D. A. Wagner and H. W. Stevenson (Eds.), *Cultural perspectives on child development* (pp. 248–279). San Francisco: Freeman. [13]

Egeland, B. (1988). The consequences of physical and emotional neglect on the development of young children. In A. Cowan (Ed.), *Child neglect.* Washington, DC: National Center on Child Abuse and Neglect. [8]

Egeland, B. (1994). Mediators of the effects of child maltreatment on developmental adaptations in adolescence. In D. Cicchetti and S. Toth (Eds.), *The effects of trauma on the developmental process* (Vol. 8). Rochester, NY: University of Rochester Press. [8, 12]

Egeland, B., Breitenbucher, M., and Rosenberg, D. (1980). Prospective study of the significance of life stress in the etiology of child abuse. *Journal of Consulting and Clinical Psychology, 48,* 195–205. [2, 6]

Egeland, B., and Brunnquell, D. (1979). An at-risk approach to the study of child abuse: Some preliminary findings. *Journal of the American Academy of Child Psychiatry, 18,* 219–225. [2]

Egeland, B., Carlson, E., and Sroufe, L. A. (1993). Resilience as process. *Development and Psychopathology, 5,* 517–528. [6]

Egeland, B., and Erickson, M. F. (1990). Rising above the past: Strategies for helping new mothers break the cycle of abuse and neglect. *Zero to Three, 11*(2), 29–35. [6]

Egeland, B., and Erickson, M. F. (1993). Attachment theory and findings: Implications for prevention and intervention. In S. Kramer and H. Parens (Eds.), *Prevention in mental health,* (pp. 21–50). Northvale, NJ: Aronson.

Egeland, B., and Farber, E. (1984). Infant-mother attachment: Factors related to its development and changes over time. *Child Development, 55,* 753–771. [6]

Egeland, B., Jacobvitz, D., and Sroufe, L. A. (1988). Breaking the cycle of abuse: Relationship predictions. *Child Development, 59,* 1080–1088. [8]

Egeland, B., Kalkoske, M., Gottesman, N., and Erickson, M. (1990). Preschool behavior problems: Stability and factors accounting for change. *Journal of Child Psychology and Psychiatry, 31,* 891–909. [Pt. 4 Epilogue, 12]

Egeland, B., and Sroufe, L. A. (1981). Developmental sequelae of maltreatment in infancy. In D. Cicchetti and R. Rizley (Eds.), *New directions in child development: Developmental approaches to child maltreatment.* San Francisco: Jossey-Bass. [2, 6, 8]

Egeland, B., Sroufe, L. A., and Erickson, M. (1983). Developmental consequences of different patterns of maltreatment. *Child Abuse and Neglect, 7,* 459–469. [8]

Eimas, P. D. (1985). The perception of speech in early infancy. *Scientific American, 204,* 66–72. [4]

Eimas, P. D., Siqueland, E. R., and Jusczyk, P. W. (1971). Speech perception in infants. *Science, 171,* 303–306. [4]

Eisenberg, N., Fabes, R. A., Bernzweig, J., Karbon, M., Poulin, R., and Hanish, L. (1993). The relations of emotionality and regulation to preschoolers' social skills and sociometric status. *Child Development, 64*(5), 1418–1438. [10]

Eisenberg, N., Fabes, R. A., Nyman, M., Bernzweig, J., and Pinuelas, A. (1994). The relations of emotionality and regulation to children's anger-related reactions. *Child Development, 65*(1), 109–128. [10]

Elder, G. H., Jr., Caspi, A., and Burton, L. M. (1987). Adolescent transitions in developmental perspective: Historical and sociological insights. In M. Gunnar (Ed.), *Minnesota Symposia on Child Psychiatry* (Vol. 21). Hillsdale, NJ: Erlbaum. [2]

Elder, G. H., Jr., Caspi, A., and Downey, G. (1986). Problem behavior and family relationships: Life-course and intergenerational themes. In A. B. Sorensen, F. E. Weinert, and L. R. Sherrod (Eds.), *Human development and the life course: Multidisciplinary perspectives.* Hillsdale, NJ: Erlbaum. [2, 8]

Elicker, J., Englund, M., and Sroufe, L. A. (1992). Predicting peer competence and peer relationships in childhood from early parent-child relationships. In R. Parke and G. Ladd (Eds.), *Family-peer relationships: Modes of linkage.* Hillsdale, NJ: Erlbaum. [8, 12]

Elkind, D. (1967). Egocentrism in adolescence. *Child Development, 38,* 1025–1034. [9, 13, 14]

Elkind, D. (1974). *Children and adolescents* (2nd ed.). New York: Oxford University Press. [13]

Elkind, D. (1978). Understanding the young adolescent. *Adolescence, 13,* 127–134. [9, 13, 14]

Elkind, D., and Bowen, R. (1979). Imaginary audience behavior in children and adolescents. *Developmental Psychology, 15,* 38–44. [14]

Elliott, G. R., and Feldman, S. S. (1990). Capturing the adolescent experience. In S. S. Feldman and G. R. Elliott

(Eds.), *At the threshold: The developing adolescent* (pp. 1–13). Cambridge, MA: Harvard University Press. [13]

Ellis, S., and Rogoff, B. (1982). The strategies and efficacy of child versus adult teachers. *Child Development, 53,* 730–735. [11]

Ellis, S., and Rogoff, B. (1986). Problem solving in children's management of instruction. In E. C. Mueller and C. R. Cooper (Eds.), *Process and outcome in peer relationships.* New York: Academic Press. [9]

Emde, R. N. (1985). The affective self: Continuities and transformations from infancy. In J. Call, E. Galenson, and R. Tyson (Eds.), *Frontiers in infant psychiatry* (Vol. II). New York: Basic Books. [6]

Emde, R. N. (1989). The infant's relationship experience: Developmental and affective aspects. In A. Sameroff and R. Emde (Eds.), *Relationship disturbances in early childhood* (pp. 33–51). New York: Basic Books. [6]

Emde, R. N. (1992). Social referencing research: Uncertainty, self, and the search for meaning. In S. Feinman (Ed.), *Social referencing and the social construction of reality in infancy* (pp. 79–92). New York: Plenum Press. [1, 8]

Emde, R. N., Biringen, Z., Clyman, R. B., and Oppenheim, D. (1991). The moral self of infancy: Affective core and procedural knowledge. *Developmental Review, 11,* 251–270. [8, 10]

Emde, R. N., and Buchsbaum, H. (1990). "Didn't you hear my mommy?" Autonomy *with* connectedness in moral self-emergence. In D. Cicchetti and M. Beeghly (Eds.), *The self in transition* (pp. 35–60). Chicago: University of Chicago Press. [10]

Emde, R. N., Gaensbauer, T., and Harmon, R. (1976). Emotional expression in infancy: A biobehavioral study. *Psychological Issues Monograph Series, 10* (Serial No. 37). [6]

Emde, R. N., Johnson, W. F., and Easterbrooks, M. A. (1985). *The do's and don'ts of early moral development: Psychoanalytic tradition and current research.* Unpublished manuscript. [Pt. 3 Epilogue]

Emde, R. N., Plomin, R., Robinson, J., Corley, R., DeFries, J., Fulker, D. W., Reznick, J. S., Campos, J., Kagan, J., and Zahn-Waxler, C. (1992). Temperament, emotion, and cognition at fourteen months: The MacArthur longitudinal twin study. *Developmental Psychology, 63,* 1437–1455. [6]

Emery, R. (1982). Marital turmoil: Interparental conflict and the children of discord and divorce. *Psychological Bulletin, 92,* 310–330. [2, 12]

Emery, R. (1988). *Marriage, divorce, and children's adjustment.* Beverly Hills, CA: Sage. [2]

Emery, R. (1989). Family violence. *American Psychologist, 44*, 321–328. [12]

Emmerich, W., Goldman, K., Kirsh, K., and Sharabany, R. (1977). Evidence for a transitional phase in the development of gender constancy. *Child Development, 48*, 930–936. [10]

Engen, T., and Lipsitt, L. P. (1965). Decrement and recovery of responses to olfactory stimuli. *Journal of Comparative and Physiological Psychology, 59*, 312–316. [4]

Engen, T. L., Lipsitt, L., and Peck, M. B. (1974). Ability of newborn infants to discriminate sapid substances. *Developmental Psychology, 10*, 741–744. [4]

Engfer, A. (1988). The interrelatedness of marriage and the mother-child relationship. In R. Hinde and J. Stevenson-Hinde (Eds.), *Relations between relationships in families.* Oxford, Eng.: Oxford University Press. [6]

Entwisle, D. (1990). Schools and the adolescent. In S. Feldman and G. Elliot (Eds.), *At the threshold: The developing adolescent* (pp. 197–224). Cambridge, MA: Harvard University Press. [14]

Entwisle, D., and Alexander, K. (1987). Long-term effects of Caesarian delivery on parents' beliefs about children's schooling. *Developmental Psychology, 23*, 676–682. [3]

Epstein, H. T. (1979). Correlated brain and intelligence development in humans. In M. E. Hahn, C. Jensen, and B. C. Dudek (Eds.), *Development and evolution of brain size: Behavioral implications.* New York: Academic Press. [13]

Erickson, M., Egeland, B., and Sroufe, L. A. (1985). The relationship between quality of attachment and behavior problems in preschool in a high risk sample. In I. Bretherton and E. Waters (Eds.), *Growing points in attachment theory and research. Monographs of the Society for Research in Child Development, 50* (1–2, Series No. 209), 147–186. [2, 6, 8, 10]

Erikson, E. H. (1963). *Childhood and society* (2nd ed.). New York: Norton. [1, 8, 10, 12]

Erikson, E. H. (1970). *Gandhi's truth.* New York: Norton. [14]

Erikson, E. H. (1981). *Youth, change, and challenge.* New York: Basic Books. [14]

Ernst, C., and Angst, J. (1983). *Birth order: Its influence on personality.* New York: Springer-Verlag. [2]

Eron, L. D., and Huesmann, L. R. (1990). The stability of aggressive behavior—even unto the third generation. In M. Lewis and S. M. Miller (Eds.), *Handbook of developmental psychopathology* (pp. 147–156). New York: Plenum Press. [15]

Evans, S., Reinhart, J., and Succop, R. (1972). Failure to thrive: A study of 45 children and their families. *Journal of the American Academy of Child Psychiatry, 79*, 209–215. [6]

Eveleth, P. B., and Tanner, J. M. (1976). *Worldwide variation in human growth.* London: Cambridge University Press. [13]

Evitar, L., Evitar, A., and Naray, I. (1974). Maturation of neurovestibular responses in infants. *Developmental Medicine and Child Neurology, 16*, 435–446. [4]

Eylon, B. and Linn, M. (1988). Learning and instruction: An explanation of four research perspectives in science education. *Review of Educational Research, 58*, 251–301. [13]

Fabes, R., Eisenberg, N., and Eisenbud, L. (1993). Behavioral and physiological correlates of children's reactions to others in distress. *Developmental Psychology, 29*, 655–663. [12]

Fabes, R., Eisenberg, N., Karbon, M., Bernzweig, J., Speer, A., and Carlo, G. (1994). Socialization of children's vicarious emotional responding and prosocial behavior. *Developmental Psychology, 30*, 44–55. [10]

Fabricius, W. V., and Cavalier, L. (1989). The role of causal theories about memory in young children's memory strategy choice. *Child Development, 60*, 298–308. [11]

Fabricius, W. V., and Hagan, J. W. (1984). The use of causal attributions about recall performance to assess metamemory and predict strategic memory behavior in young children. *Developmental Psychology, 20*, 975–987. [11]

Fagan, J. F. (1984). The relationship of novelty preferences during infancy to later intelligence and later recognition memory. *Intelligence, 8*, 339–346. [5]

Fagan, J. F., and McGrath, S. K. (1981). Infant recognition memory as a measure of intelligence. *Intelligence, 5*, 121–130. [5]

Fagan, J. F., and Singer, L. T. (1979). The role of simple features in infants' recognition of faces. *Infant Behavior and Development, 2*, 39–45. [5]

Fagot, B., and Kavanaugh, K. (1993). Parenting during the second year: Effects of children's age, sex and attachment classification. *Child Development, 64*, 258–271. [8]

Fagot, B., Leinbach, M., and O'Boyle, C. (1992). Gender labeling, gender stereotyping, and parenting behaviors. *Developmental Psychology, 28*, 225–230. [10]

Fairbanks, L. (1989). Early experience and cross-generational continuity of mother-infant contact in Vervet monkeys. *Developmental Psychobiology, 22*, 669–681. [6]

Falbo, T., and Poston, D. L. (1993). The academic, personality, and physical outcomes of only children in China. *Child Development, 64*, 18–35. [2]

Farone, S., and Tsuang, M. (1988). Familial links between schizophrenia and other disorders: Psychopathology in offspring. *Psychiatry, 51*, 37–47. [15]

Farrington, D., Loeber, R., Elliot, D., Hawkins, D., Kandel, D., Klein, M., McCord, J., Rowe, D., and Tremblay, R. (1990). Advancing knowledge about the onset of delinquency and crime. In B. Lahey and A. Kazdin (Eds.), *Advances in clinical child psychology* (Vol. 13, pp. 283–342). New York: Plenum Press. [15]

Fein, G. (1981). Pretend play in childhood: An integrative review. *Child Development, 52*, 1095–1118. [7]

Fein, G., and Fox, N. (1990). *Infant day care.* Norwood, NJ: Ablex. [2, 6]

Feldman, S., and Gehring, T. (1988). Changing perceptions of family cohesion and power across adolescence. *Child Development, 59*, 1034–1045. [14]

Fendrich, M., Warner, V., and Weissman, M. (1990). Family risk factors, parental depression, and psychopathology in offspring. *Developmental Psychology, 26*, 40–50. [15]

Ferguson, C. A. (1964). Baby talk in six languages. *American Anthropologist, 66*, 103–114. [7]

Ferguson, T., Stegge, H., and Damhuis, I. (1991). Children's understanding of guilt and shame. *Child Development, 62*, 827–839. [12]

Fernald, A. (1984). The perceptual and affective salience of mothers' speech to infants. In L. Feagans, C. Garvey, and R. Golinkoff (Eds.). *The origins and growth of communication.* Norwood, NJ: Ablex. [7]

Fernald, A. (1985). Four-month-olds prefer to listen to motherese. *Infant Behavior and Development, 8*, 181–195. [7]

Fernald, A., and Morikawa, H. (1993). Common themes and cultural variations in Japanese and American mothers' speech to infants. *Developmental Psychology, 64*, 637–656. [6]

Fernald, A., Taeschner, T., Dunn, J., Papoušek, M., de Boysson-Bardies, B., and Fukui, I. (1989). A cross-language study of prosodic modifications in mothers' and fathers' speech to preverbal infants. *Journal of Child Language, 16*, 477–501. [7]

Field, T. M., and Goldson, E. (1984). Pacifying effects of nonnutritive sucking on term and preterm neonates during heelstick procedures. *Pediatrics, 74*, 1012–1015. [4]

Fine, G., Mortimer, J., and Roberts, D. (1990). Leisure, work, and mass media. In S. Feldman and G. Elliot (Eds.), *At the threshold: The developing adolescent* (pp. 225–252). Cambridge, MA: Harvard University Press. [14]

Fischer, K. (1980). A theory of cognitive development: The control and construction of hierarchies of skills. *Psychological Review, 87*, 477–531. [5]

Fischer, K. (1987). Relations between brain and cognitive development. *Child Development, 58*, 623–632. [5]

Fischer, K., and Bullock, D. (1984). Cognitive development in school-age children. In W. A. Collins (Ed.), *Development during middle childhood*. Washington, DC: National Academy Press. [11]

Fischer, K., and Lazerson, A. (1984). *Human development: From conception through adolescence*. New York: Freeman. [5]

Fischer, K., Shaver, P., and Carnochan, P. (1990). How emotions develop and how they organize development. *Cognition and Emotion, 4*, 81–127. [10, 12, 13]

Fitch, S., and Adams, G. (1983). Ego identity and intimacy statuses: Replication and extension. *Developmental Psychology, 19*, 839–845. [14]

Flaks, D. K., Ficher, I., Masterpasqua, F., and Joseph, G. (1995). Lesbians choosing motherhood: A comparative study of lesbian and heterosexual parents and their children. *Developmental Psychology, 31*, 105–114. [2]

Flanagan, C., and Eccles, J. (1993). Changes in parents' work status and adolescent adjustment at school. *Child Development, 64*, 246–257. [2]

Flavell, J. H. (1963). *The developmental psychology of Jean Piaget*. New York: Van Nostrand. [9]

Flavell, J. H. (1985). *Cognitive development* (2nd ed.). Englewood Cliffs, NJ: Prentice-Hall. [5, 7, 9, 11]

Flavell, J. H., Beach, D. H., and Chinsky, J. M. (1966). Spontaneous verbal rehearsal in a memory task as a function of age. *Child Development, 37*, 283–299. [11]

Flavell, J. H., Botkin, P. T., Fry, C. L., Wright, J. W., and Jarvis, P. E. (1968). *The development of role-taking and communication skills in children*. New York: Wiley. [9]

Flavell, J. H., Friedrichs, A. G., and Hoyt, J. D. (1970). Developmental changes in memorization processes. *Cognitive Psychology, 1*, 324–340. [11]

Flavell, J. H., Green, F. L., and Flavell, E. R. (1986). Development of knowledge about the appearance-reality distinction. *Monographs of the Society for Research in Child Development, 51* (Serial No. 212). [9]

Flavell, J. H., Green, F. L., and Flavell, E. R. (1990). Developmental changes in young children's knowledge about the mind. *Cognitive Development, 5*, 1–27. [9]

Flavell, J. H., Miller, P. H., and Miller, S. A. (1993). *Cognitive development* (3rd ed.). Englewood Cliffs, NJ: Prentice-Hall. [9, 11, 13]

Flavell, J. H., and Wellman, H. M. (1977). Metamemory. In R. B. Kail and J. E.

Hagen (Eds.), *Perspectives on the development of memory and cognition*. Hillsdale, NJ: Erlbaum. [11]

Fogel, A. (1993). *Developing through relationships*. Chicago: University of Chicago Press. [6]

Fonagy, P., Steele, H., and Steele, M. (1991, July). *Intergenerational patterns of attachment: Maternal representations of attachment during pregnancy and subsequent infant-mother attachments*. Paper presented at the International Society for the Study of Behavior and Development, Minneapolis. [6]

Forbes, H. S., and Forbes, H. B. (1927). Fetal sense reaction: Hearing. *Journal of Comparative Psychology, 7*, 353–355. [4]

Forman, E. A. (1982). *Understanding the role of peer interaction in development: The contribution of Piaget and Vygotsky*. Paper presented at the meeting of the Jean Piaget Society, Philadelphia. [11]

Fox, N. (1989). Psychophysiological correlates of emotional reactivity during the first year of life. *Developmental Psychology, 25*, 364–372. [6]

Fox, N. A., Kimmerly, N. L., and Schafer, W. D. (1991). Attachment to mother/attachment to father: A meta-analysis. *Developmental Psychology, 62*, 210–225. [6]

Fraiberg, S., and Friedman, D. (1964). Studies in the ego development of the congenitally blind child. *Psychoanalytic Study of the Child, 19*, 113–169. [6]

Frankel, K. A., and Bates, J. E. (1990). Mother-toddler problem solving: Antecedents in attachment, home behavior, and temperament. *Child Development, 61*, 810–819. [8]

Frankenburg, W. K., and Dodds, J. B. (1967). The Denver developmental screening test. *Journal of Pediatrics, 71*, 181–185. [4]

Freeman, D. (1983) *Margaret Mead and Samoa: The making and unmaking of an anthropological myth*. Cambridge, MA: Harvard University Press. [14]

French, J. W. (1951). *The description of aptitude and achievement tests in terms of rotated factors*. Chicago: University of Chicago Press. [11]

Frey, K., and Ruble, D. (1992). Gender constancy and the "cost" of sex-typed behavior: A test of the conflict hypothesis. *Developmental Psychology, 28*, 714–721. [12]

Friedman, L. (1989). Mathematics and the gender gap: A meta-analysis of recent studies on sex differences in mathematical tasks. *Review of Educational Research, 59*, 185–213. [11]

Friend, M., and Davis, T. (1993). Appearance–reality distinction: Children's understanding of the physical and affective domains. *Developmental Psychology, 29*, 907–913. [10]

Frisch, R. E. (1983). Fatness, puberty,

and fertility: The effects of nutrition and physical training on menarche and ovulation. In J. Brooks-Gunn and A. C. Petersen (Eds.), *Girls at puberty* (pp. 29–49). New York: Plenum Press. [13]

Frisch, R. E., and Revelle, R. (1970). Height and weight at menarche and a hypothesis of critical body weights and adolescent events. *Science, 169*, 397–399. [13]

Frodi, A. (1984). When empathy fails: Aversive infant crying and child abuse. In B. Lester and Z. Boukydis (Eds.), *Infant crying: Theoretical and research perspectives*. New York: Plenum Press. [8]

Fuix, F., Keller, M., Ge, F., Edelstein, W., and Schuster, P. (1994). *Reasons for action in practical and moral reasoning*. Paper presented at the International Society for the Study of Behavior and Development, Amsterdam. [12]

Funk, J. L. (1986). *Gender differences in the moral reasoning of conventional and postconventional adults*. Unpublished doctoral dissertation, University of Texas. [13]

Furman, W., and Buhrmester, D. (1992). Age and sex differences in perceptions of networks of personal relationships. *Child Development, 63*, 103–115. [14]

Furman, W., Rahe, D., and Hartup, W. (1979). Rehabilitation of socially withdrawn preschool children through mixed age and same age socialization. *Child Development, 50*, 915–922. [10]

Furstenberg, F. (1990). Coming of age in a changing family system. In S. Feldman and G. Elliot (Eds.), *At the threshold: The developing adolescent* (pp. 147–170). Cambridge, MA: Harvard University Press. [14]

Furstenberg, F., Brooks-Gunn, J., and Chase-Lansdale, L. (1989). Teenaged pregnancy and childbearing. *American Psychologist, 44*, 313–320. [2]

Fury, G. (1994). *The relation between infant attachment history and representations of relationships in school-age family drawings*. Unpublished doctoral dissertation, University of Minnesota. [12]

Fuson, K. (1979). The development of self-regulating aspects of speech: A review. In G. Ziven (Ed.), *The development of self-regulation through private speech*. New York: Wiley. [10]

Fuson, K. C. (1988). *Children's counting and concepts of number*. New York: Springer-Verlag. [9]

Galotti, K. M. (1989). Gender differences in self-reported moral reasoning: A review and new evidence. *Journal of Youth and Adolescence, 18*, 475–488. [13]

Galambos, N., and Maggs, J. (1991). Children in self-care: Figures, facts and fiction. In J. Lerner and N. Galambos

(Eds.), *Employed mothers and their children* (pp. 131–157). New York: Garland. [12]

Gallistel, C. R., and Gelman, R. (1990). The what and how of counting. *Cognition, 34,* 197–199. [9]

Ganchrow, J. R., Steiner, J. E., and Daher, M. (1983). Neonatal facial expressions in response to different qualities and intensities of gustatory stimuli. *Infant Behavior and Development, 6,* 189–200. [4]

Gandour, M. J. (1989). Activity level as a dimension of temperament in toddlers: Its relevance for the organismic specificity hypothesis. *Child Development, 60,* 1092–1098. [8]

Ganon, E. C., and Swartz, K. B. (1980). Perception of internal elements of compound figures by one-month-olds. *Journal of Experimental Child Psychology, 30,* 159–170. [4]

Garbarino, J. (1981). An ecological approach to child maltreatment. In L. Pelton (Ed.), *The social context of child abuse and neglect.* New York:· Human Sciences Press. [2]

Garcia, J., and Koelling, R. (1966). Relation of cue to consequences in avoidance learning. *Psychonometric Science, 4,* 123–124. [4]

Garcia Coll, C. T. (1990). Developmental outcome of minority infants: A process-oriented look into our beginnings. *Child Development, 61,* 270– 289. [2]

Garcia Coll, C. T. (1994). Cultural influences on child development: Are we ready for a paradigm shift? *Minnesota Symposia on Child Psychology,* (Vol. 29). Hillsdale, NJ: Erlbaum. [2]

Gardner, H. (1983). *Frames of mind: The theory of multiple intelligences.* New York: Basic Books. [11]

Garfinkel, B. (1987, June). *Treatment strategies for ADHD.* Paper presented at the Conference on Attention-Deficit Hyperactivity Disorders in Children and Adolescence, Minneapolis. [15]

Garnica, O. (1974). *Some characteristics of prosodic input to young children.* Unpublished doctoral dissertation, Stanford University. [7]

Garvey, C. (1977). *Play.* Cambridge, MA: Harvard University Press. [8, 10]

Gavin, L., and Furman, W. (1989). Age differences in adolescents' perceptions of their peer groups. *Developmental Psychology, 25,* 827–834. [14]

Gelman, R. (1972). The nature and development of early number concepts. In H. W. Reese (Ed.), *Advances in child development and behavior* (Vol. 7). New York: Academic Press. [9]

Gelman, R. (1982). Accessing one-to-one correspondence: Still another paper on conservation. *British Journal of Psychology, 73,* 209–220. [9]

Gelman, R., and Baillargeon, R. (1983). A review of some Piagetian concepts. In P. H. Mussen (Ed.), *Handbook of child psychology* (Vol. 3, 4th ed.): J. H. Flavell and E. M. Markman (Eds.), *Cognitive development.* New York: Wiley. [5, 9]

Gelman, R., and Gallistel, C. R. (1978). *The child's understanding of number.* Cambridge, MA: Harvard University Press. [9]

Gelman, R., Meck, E., and Merkin, S. (1986). Young children's numerical competence. *Cognitive Development, 1,* 1–29. [9]

Genishi, C., and Dyson, A. H. (1984). *Language assessment in the early years.* Norwood, NJ: Ablex. [7]

George, C. (1990, July). *Fantasy play and inner working models of young children.* Presentation at the Center for Advanced Study in the Behavioral Sciences, Stanford. [10]

Gephart, M., and Pearson, R. (1988). Contemporary research on the urban under class. *Items, 42,* 1–10. New York: Social Science Research Council. [2]

Gesell, A., & Ilg, F. (1946). *The child from five to ten.* New York: Harper and Brothers. [4]

Ghiselli, E. E. (1966). *The validity of occupational aptitude tests.* New York: Wiley. [11]

Gibson, E. J., and Spelke, E. S. (1983). The development of perception. In J. H. Flavell and E. M. Markman (Eds.), P. H. Mussen (Series Ed.), *Handbook of child psychology: Vol. 3. Cognitive development* (pp. 1–70). New York: Wiley. [7]

Gibson, E. J., and Walk, R. D. (1960). The "visual cliff." *Scientific American, 202,* 64–71. [4]

Gilligan, C. (1982). *In a different voice: Psychological theory and women's development.* Cambridge, MA: Harvard University Press. [12, 13]

Gleason, J. B. (1975). Fathers and other strangers: Men's speech to young children. In D. Dato (Ed.), *Georgetown University roundtable on language and linguistics.* Washington, DC: Georgetown University Press. [7]

Gleason, J. B., Perlmann, R. Y., and Greif, E. B. (1984). What's the magic word: Learning language through routines. *Discourse Processes, 6,* 493–502. [7]

Gleason, J. B., and Weintraub, S. (1978). Input language and the acquisition of communicative competence. In K. Nelson (Ed.), *Children's language* (Vol. 1, pp. 171–222). New York: Gardiner. [7]

Gleitman, L. R., and Wanner, E. (1982). Language acquisition: The state of the state of the art. In E. Wanner and L. R. Gleitman (Eds.), *Language acquisition: The state of the art.* New York: Cambridge University Press. [7]

Glick, J. (1975). Cognitive development in cross-cultural perspective. In F. D. Horowitz (Ed.), *Review of child development research* (Vol. 4). Chicago: University of Chicago Press. [11]

Glick, J. (1992). Werner's relevance for contemporary developmental psychology. *Developmental Psychology, 28,* 558–565. [1]

Glick, M., and Zigler, E. (1990). Premorbid competence and the course and outcome of psychiatric disorders. In J. Rolf, A. Masten, D. Cicchetti, K. Neuchterlein, and S. Weintraub (Eds.), *Risk and protective factors in the development of psychopathology.* New York: Cambridge University Press. [15]

Glucksberg, S., and Krauss, R. M. (1967): What do people say after they have learned to talk? Studies of the development of referential communication. *Merrill-Palmer Quarterly, 13,* 309–316. [9]

Gnepp, J. (1989a). Children's use of personal information to understand other people's feelings. In C. Saarni and P. L. Harris (Eds.), *Children's understanding of emotion.* Cambridge, Eng.: Cambridge University Press. [9]

Gnepp, J. (1989b). Personalized inferences of emotions and appraisals: Component processes and correlations. *Developmental Psychology, 25,* 277–288. [12]

Gnepp, J., and Klayman, J. (1992). Recognition of uncertainty in emotional inferences: Reasoning about emotionally equivocal situations. *Developmental Psychology, 28,* 145–158. [12]

Gold, R. (1978). On the meaning of nonconservation. In A. M. Lesgold, J. W. Pellegrino, S. D. Fokkema, and R. Glaser (Eds.), *Cognitive psychology and instruction.* New York and London: Plenum Press. [9]

Goldberg, S., Washington, J., Morris, P., Fischer-Fay, A., and Simmons, R. J. (in press). Early diagnosed chronic illness and mother-child relationships in the first two years. *Canadian Journal of Psychiatry.* [8]

Goldfield, B., and Reznick, J. S. (1990). Early lexical acquisition: Rate, content, and the vocabulary spurt. *Journal of Child Language, 17,* 171–183. [7]

Goldfield, B. A., and Snow, C. E. (1993). Individual differences in language acquisition. In J. B. Gleason (Ed.), *The development of language* (pp. 299–324). New York: Macmillan. [7]

Goldsmith, H. (1983). Genetic influences on personality from infancy to adulthood. *Child Development, 54,* 331–355. [2]

Goldsmith, H. (1989). Behavior-genetic approaches to temperament. In G. Kohnstamm, J. Bates, and M. Rothbard (Eds.), *Temperament in childhood* (pp. 111–132). London: Wiley. [6]

Goldsmith, H., Buss, A., Plomin, R., Rothbart, M., Thomas, A., Chess, S., Hinde,

R., and McCall, R. (1987). What is temperament? Four approaches. *Child Development, 58,* 505–529. [6]

Golinkoff, R. (1986). "I beg your pardon?": The preverbal negotiation of failed communications. *Journal of Child Language, 13,* 455–476. [7]

Golinkoff, R. M., Hirsh-Pasek, K., Cauley, K. M., and Gordon, L. (1987). The eyes have it: Lexical and syntactic comprehension in a new paradigm. *Journal of Child Language, 14,* 23–45. [7]

Goodlad, J. (1984). *A place called school.* New York: McGraw-Hill. [13]

Goodman, R., and Stevenson, J. (1989). A twin study of hyperactivity: II. The etiological role of genes, family relationships and perinatal adversity. *Journal of Child Psychology and Psychiatry, 30,* 691–709. [15]

Goodnow, J. J. (1973). Compensation arguments on conservation tasks. *Developmental Psychology, 8,* 140. [9]

Goodnow, J. J. (1976). The nature of intelligent behavior: Questions raised by cross-cultural studies. In L. Resnick (Ed.), *The nature of intelligence* (pp. 169–188). Hillsdale, NJ: Erlbaum. [11]

Gopnik, A., and Meltzoff, A. N. (1987). The development of categorization in the second year and its relation to other cognitive and linguistic developments. *Child Development, 58,* 1523–1531. [7, 9]

Gordon, F. R., and Yonas, A. (1976). Sensitivity to binocular depth information in infants. *Journal of Experimental Child Psychology, 22,* 413–422. [4]

Gorman, C. (1994, June 13). Thalidomide's return. *Time,* p. 67.

Gottesmann, I. (1991). *Schizophrenia genesis.* New York: Freeman. [15]

Gottlieb, B. H. (1980). Social networks, social support, and child maltreatment. In J. Garbarino and S. H. Stocking (Eds.), *Supporting families and protecting children.* San Francisco: Jossey-Bass. [2]

Gottlieb, G. (1991). Experiential canalization of behavioral development: Theory. *Developmental Psychology, 27,* 4–13. [1, 2, 3]

Gottman, J. (1983). How children become friends. *Monographs of the Society for Research in Child Development, 48* (3, Serial No. 201). [10, 12]

Gould, S. J. (1989). *Wonderful life: The Burgess Shale and the nature of history.* New York: Norton. [1]

Gould, S. J. (1994, November 28). Curveball. *The New Yorker,* pp. 139–149. [11]

Gove, F. (1983). *Patterns and organizations of behavior and affective expression during the second year of life.* Unpublished doctoral dissertation, University of Minnesota. [8, Pt. 4 Epilogue]

Graber, J., and Petersen, A. (1991). Cognitive changes at adolescence: Biological perspectives. In K. Gibson and A. Petersen (Eds.), *Brain maturation and cognitive development* (pp. 253–280). New York: Aldine de Gruyter. [13]

Gratch, G. (1975). Recent studies based on Piaget's view of object concept development. In L. B. Cohen and P. Salapatek (Eds.), *Infant perception: From sensation to cognition.* New York: Academic Press. [5]

Gratch, G., Appel, K. J., Evans, W. F., LeCompte, G. K., and Wright, N. A. (1974). Piaget's Stage IV object concept error: Evidence of forgetting or object conception? *Child Development, 45,* 71–77. [5]

Gray, S. W., Ramsey, B. K., and Klaus, R. A. (1982). *From 3 to 20: The early training project.* Baltimore: University Park Press. [11]

Graziano, W. (1984). The development of social exchange processes. In J. C. Masters and K. Yarkin-Levin (Eds.), *Boundary areas in psychology: Social and developmental.* New York: Academic Press. [12]

Greenberg, M., and Crnic, K. (1988). Longitudinal predictors of developmental status and social interaction in premature and full-term infants at age two. *Child Development, 59,* 554–570. [2, 3]

Greenberger, E., and Steinberg, L. (1980). Part-time employment of in-school youth: A preliminary assessment of costs and benefits. In B. Linder and R. Taggart (Eds.), *A review of youth employment problems, programs, and policies: Vol. 1. The youth employment problem: Causes and dimensions.* Washington, DC: Vice-President's Task Force on Youth Employment. [14]

Greenfield, P. M. (1966). On culture and conservation. In J. S. Bruner, R. R. Oliver, and P. M. Greenfield (Eds.), *Studies in cognitive growth.* New York: Wiley. [11]

Greenough, W. T., Black, J. E., and Wallace, C. S. (1987). Experience and brain development. *Child Development, 58,* 539–559. [13]

Greif, E. B., and Gleason, J. B. (1980). Hi, thanks, and goodbye: More routine information. *Language in Society, 9,* 159–166. [7]

Grolnick, W. S., and Slowiaczek, M. (1994). Parents' involvement in children's schooling: A multidimensional conceptualization and motivational model. *Child Development, 65,* 237–252. [12]

Gross, R. (Infant Health and Development Program) (1990). Enhancing the outcomes of low-birth-weight, premature infants. *Journal of the American Medical Association, 263,* 3035–3042. [2, 6]

Gross, T. F. (1985). *Cognitive development.* Monterey, CA: Brooks/Cole. [11]

Grossmann, K., Grossmann, K. E., Spangler, G., Suess, G., and Unzer, L. (1985). Maternal sensitivity and newborn orienting responses as related to quality of attachment in Northern Germany. In I. Bretherton and E. Waters (Eds.), *Growing points of attachment theory and research. Monographs of the Society for Research in Child Development, 50,* 233–256. [6]

Grossmann, K. E., and Grossmann, K. (1992). Attachment quality as an organizer of emotional and behavioral responses. In P. Marris, J. Stevenson-Hinde, and C. Parks (Eds.), *Attachment across the life cycle.* New York: Rutledge. [12]

Grotevant, H. (1992). Assigned and chosen identity components: A process perspective on their integration. In G. Adams, R. Montemayor, and T. Gulotta (Eds.), *Advances in adolescent development* (Vol. 4). Newbury Park, CA: Sage. [14]

Grotevant, H., and Cooper, C. (1986). Individuation in family relationships. *Human Development, 29,* 82–100. [14]

Grumbach, M. M., Roth, J. C., Kaplan, S. L., and Kelch, R. P. (1974). Hypothalamic-pituitary regulation of puberty in man: Evidence and concepts derived from clinical research. In M. M. Grumbach, G. D. Grave, and F. E. Mayer (Eds.), *Control of the onset of puberty.* New York: Wiley. [13]

Grusec, J., and Goodnow, J. (1994). Summing up and looking to the future. *Developmental Psychology, 30,* 29–31. [10]

Grych, J., and Fincham, F. (1993). Children's appraisals of marital conflict: Initial investigations of the cognitive-contextual framework. *Child Development, 64,* 215–230. [12]

Guilford, J. P. (1967). *The nature of human intelligence.* New York: McGraw-Hill [11]

Gunnar, M. (1980). Contingent stimulation: A review of its role in early development. In S. Levine and H. Ursin (Eds.), *Coping and health.* New York: Plenum Press. [6]

Gunnar, M. (1991). The psychobiology of infant temperament. In J. Colombo and J. Fagan (Eds.), *Individual differences in infancy: Reliability, stability, and prediction.* Hillsdale, NJ: Erlbaum. [6]

Gunnar, M., and Collins, W. A. (1988). Development during the transition to adolescence. *Minnesota Symposia on Child Psychology* (Vol. 21). Hillsdale, NJ: Erlbaum. [14]

Gunnar, M., Mangelsdorf, S., Kestenbaum, R., Lang, S., Larson, M., and Andreas, D. (1989a). Stress and coping in early development. In D. Cicchetti (Ed.), *The emergence of a discipline: Vol. 1. Rochester Symposium on Developmental*

Psychopathology (pp. 119–138). Hillsdale, NJ: Erlbaum. [6]

Gunnar, M., Mangelsdorf, S., Larson, M., and Hertsgaard, L. (1989b). Attachment, temperament, and adrenocortical activity in infancy: A study of psychoendocrine regulation. *Developmental Psychology, 25,* 355–363. [6]

Gunnar, M., and Stone, C. (1984). The effects of positive maternal affect on infant responses to pleasant, ambiguous, and fear-provoking toys. *Child Development, 55,* 1231–1236. [8]

Haith, M. M. (1980). *Rules newborns look by.* Hillsdale, NJ: Erlbaum. [4]

Hakim-Larson, J., Livington, J., and Tron, R. (1985). *Mothers and adolescent daughters: Personal issues.* Paper presented at the biennial meeting of the Society for Research in Child Development, Toronto. [14]

Hakuta, K., and Diaz, R. (1985). The relationship between degree of bilingualism and cognitive ability: A critical discussion and some new longitudinal data. In K. E. Nelson (Ed.), *Children's language* (Vol. 5). Hillsdale, NJ: Erlbaum. [7]

Hall, E., Perlmutter, M., and Lamb, M. E. (1982). *Child psychology today.* New York: Random House. [3]

Hall, G. S. (1904). *Adolescence.* New York: Appleton. [13]

Halpern, R. (1990). Poverty and early childhood parenting: Toward a framework for intervention. *American Journal of Orthopsychiatry, 6*(1), 6–18. [2]

Halverson, H. M. (1931). An experimental study of prehension in infants by means of systematic cinema records. *Genetic Psychology Monographs, 10,* 1413–1430. [4]

Hamond, N. R., and Fivush, R. (1991). Memories of Mickey Mouse: Young children recount their trip to Disney World. *Cognitive Development, 6,* 483–448. [9]

Handler, A., Kistin, N., Davis, J., and Ferre, C. (1991). Cocaine use during pregnancy: Perinatal outcomes. *American Journal of Epidemiology, 133,* 818–825. [3]

Happe, F. (1994). Current theories of autism: The "theory of mind" account and rival theories. *Journal of Child Psychology and Psychiatry, 35,* 215–229. [15]

Hardy, D., Power, T., and Jaedicke, S. (1993). Examining the relation of parenting to children's coping with everyday stress. *Child Development, 64,* 1829–1841. [12]

Hare, R., and Cox, D. (1978). Psychological research on psychopathy. In W. Reid (Ed.), *The psychopath.* New York: Brunner/Mazel. [15]

Harkness, S. (1992). Cross-cultural research in child development: A sample of the state of the art. *Developmental Psychology, 28,* 622–625. [2]

Harlow, H. F., and Harlow, M. K. (1966). Learning to love. *American Scientist, 54,* 244–272. [1, 6]

Harrington, R. (1994). Affective disorders. In M. Rutter, E. Taylor, and L. Hersov (Eds.), *Child and adolescent psychiatry* (pp. 330–350). London: Blackwell. [15]

Harris, M., and Turner, P. (1986). Gay and lesbian parents. *Journal of Homosexuality, 12,* 101–113. [2]

Harris, P. L. (1989). Object permanence in infancy. In A. Slater and G. Bremner (Eds.), *Infant development.* Hillsdale, NJ: Erlbaum. [5]

Harris, P. L. (1983). Infant cognition. In P. H. Mussen (Ed.), *Handbook of child psychology* (Vol. 2, 4th ed.): M. M. Haith and J. J. Campos (Eds.), *Infancy and developmental psychobiology.* New York: Wiley. [4, 5]

Harris, P. L. (1994). The child's understanding of emotion: Developmental change and the family environment. *Journal of Child Psychology and Psychiatry, 35,* 3–28. [10]

Harris, T., Brown, G., and Bifulco, A. (1990). Loss of parent in childhood and adult psychiatric disorder: A tentative overall model. *Development and Psychopathology, 2,* 311–328. [15]

Harrison, A., Wilson, M., Pine, C., Chan, S., and Buriel, R. (1990). Family ecologies of ethnic minority children. *Child Development, 61,* 347–362. [2]

Harter, S. (1980). A model of intrinsic mastery motivation in children: Individual differences and developmental change. In W. A. Collins (Ed.), *Minnesota Symposia on Child Psychology* (Vol. 13). Hillsdale, NJ: Erlbaum. [2, 12]

Harter, S. (1983). Developmental perspectives on the self system. In P. H. Mussen (Ed.), *Handbook of child psychology* (Vol. 4, 4th ed.): E. M. Hetherington (Ed.), *Socialization, personality, and social development* (pp. 275–385). New York: Wiley. [12]

Harter, S. (1990). Self and identity development. In S. Feldman and G. Elliot (Eds.), *At the threshold: The developing adolescent* (pp. 352–387). Cambridge, MA: Harvard University Press. [14]

Hartup, W. (1989). Social relationships and their developmental significance. *American Psychologist, 44,* 120–126. [2]

Hartup, W. (1992). Peer relations in early and middle childhood. In V. B. VanHasselt and M. Hersen (Eds.), *Handbook of social development: A lifespan perspective.* New York: Plenum Press. [2, 10, 12]

Hartup, W., and Laursen, B. (1993). Conflict and context in peer relations. In C. Hart (Ed.), *Children on playgrounds: Research perspectives and applica-* *tions.* Ithaca: State University of New York Press. [10, 12, 14]

Hartup, W. W. (1983). Peer relations. In P. Mussen and E. M. Hetherington (Eds.), *Manual of child psychology* (4th ed.). New York: Wiley. [10, 12]

Hartup, W. W., and Sancilio, M. (1986). Children's friendships. In E. Schopler and G. Mesibov (Eds.), *Social behavior in autism.* New York: Plenum Press. [12, 14]

Hashima, P. Y., and Amato, P. R. (1994). Poverty, social support, and parental behavior. *Child Development, 65,* 394–403. [2]

Haskins, R. (1985). Public school aggression among children with varying daycare experience. *Child Development, 56,* 689–703. [6]

Hauser, S., and Bowlds, M. K. (1990). Stress, coping, and adaptation. In S. Feldman and G. Elliot (Eds.), *At the threshold: The developing adolescent* (pp. 388–413). Cambridge, MA: Harvard University Press. [14]

Hauser, S. T., and Kasendorf, E. (1983). *Black and white identity formation.* Malabar, FL: Krieger. [14]

Hawley, T. L., and Disney, E. R. (1992). Crack's children: The consequences of maternal cocaine abuse. [Social Policy Report]. *Society for Research in Child Development, 6*(4). [3]

Hay, D. (1984). Social conflict in early childhood. In G. Whitehurst (Ed.), *Annals of Child Development* (Vol. 1, pp. 1–44). Greenwich, CT: JAI. [10]

Hayes, A. (1984). Interaction, engagement, and the origins of communication: Some constructive concerns. In L. Feagans, C. Garvey, and R. Golinkoff (Eds.), *The origins and growth of communication.* Norwood, NJ: Ablex. [6]

Hayes, C. D. (Ed.). (1987). *Risking the future: Adolescent sexuality, pregnancy, and childbearing* (Vol. 1). Washington, DC: National Academy Press. [14]

Heath, S. (1989). Oral and literate traditions among Black Americans living in poverty. *American Psychologist, 44,* 367–373. [2]

Heath, S. B. (1981). Questioning at home and at school: A comparative study. In G. Spindler (Ed.), *Doing ethnography: Educational anthropology in action.* New York: Holt, Rinehart, & Winston. [11]

Heath, S. B. (1983). *Ways with words: Language, life, and work in communities and classrooms.* New York: Cambridge University Press. [11]

Hecox, K., and Deegan, D. M. (1985). Methodological issues in the study of auditory development. In G. Gottlieb and N. A. Krasnegor (Eds.), *Measurement of audition and vision in the first year of postnatal life: A methodological overview.* Norwood, NJ: Ablex. [4]

Heibeck, T. H., and Markman, E. M. (1987). Word learning in children: An examination of fast mapping. *Child Development, 58,* 1021–1034. [7]

Heinicke, C., and Westheimer, I. (1966). *Brief separations.* New York: International Universities Press. [6]

Held, R. (1978). Development of visual acuity in normal and astigmatic infants. In I. S. J. Cool and E. L. Smith (Eds.), *Frontiers in visual science.* New York: Springer-Verlag. [4]

Henderson, V., and Dweck, C. (1990). Motivation and achievement. In S. Feldman and G. Elliot (Eds.), *At the threshold: The developing adolescent* (pp. 308–329). Cambridge, MA: Harvard University Press. [14]

Herrnstein, R. J., and Murray, C. (1994). *The bell curve: Intelligence and class structure in American life.* New York: Free Press. [11]

Hertzig, M. E., and Shapiro, T. (1990). Autism and pervasive developmental disorders. In M. Lewis and S. M. Miller (Eds.), *Handbook of developmental psychopathology* (pp. 385–396). New York: Plenum Press. [15]

Hess, R., Kashiwagi, K., Azuma, H., Price, G., and Dickson, W. (1980). Maternal expectations for early mastery of developmental tasks and cognitive and social competence of preschool children in Japan and the United States. *International Journal of Psychology, 15,* 259–272. [2]

Hetherington, E. M. (1972). Effects of father absence on personality development in adolescent daughters. *Developmental Psychology, 7,* 313–326. [14]

Hetherington, E. M. (1988). Parents, children, and siblings six years after divorce. In R. Hinde and J. Stevenson-Hinde (Eds.), *Relations between relationships within families.* Oxford: Oxford University Press. [2, 12, 14]

Hetherington, E. M., and Brackbill, Y. (1963). Etiology and covariation of obstinacy, orderliness, and parsimony in young children. *Child Development, 34,* 919–943. [8]

Hetherington, E. M., and Clingempeel, W. (1992). Coping with marital transitions: A family perspective. *Monographs of the Society for Research on Child Development, 57* (2–3, Serial No. 227). [2, 12]

Hetherington, E. M., and Martin, B. (1986). Family factors and psychopathology in children. In H. Quay and J. Werry (Eds.), *Psychopathological disorders of childhood* (pp. 332–390). New York: Wiley. [15]

Hetherington, E. M., Stanley-Hagan, M., and Anderson, E. (1989). Marital transitions: A child's perspective. *American Psychologist, 44,* 303–312. [2]

Hewlett, B. S. (Ed.). (1992). *Father-child relations: Cultural and biosocial contexts.* New York: Aldine de Gruyter. [2]

Hiatt, S., Campos, J., and Emde, R. (1979). Facial patterning and infant emotional expression: Happiness, surprise, and fear. *Child Development, 50,* 1020–1035. [6]

Higgins, A., and Turnure, J. (1984). Distractibility and concentration of attention in children's development. *Child Development, 44,* 1799–1810. [13]

Hill, J. (1980). *Understanding early adolescence: A framework.* Chapel Hill, NC: Center for Early Adolescence. [14]

Hill, J. (1988). Adapting to menarche: Family control and conflict. In M. Gunnar and W. A. Collins (Eds.), *Minnesota Symposia on Child Psychology* (Vol. 21, pp. 43–77). Hillsdale, NJ: Erlbaum. [14]

Hill, J., Holmbeck, G., Marlow, L., Green, T., and Lynch, M. (1985). Menarcheal status and parent-child relations in families of seventh-grade girls. *Journal of Youth and Adolescence, 14,* 301–316. [13, 14]

Hill, R. (1970). *Family development in three generations.* Cambridge, MA: Schenkman. [2]

Hirsh-Pasek, K., Treiman, R., and Schneiderman, M. (1984). Brown and Hanlon revised: Mothers' sensitivity to ungrammatical forms. *Journal of Child Language, 11,* 81–88. [7]

Hock, E., and DeMeis, D. (1990). Depression in mothers of infants: The role of maternal employment. *Developmental Psychology, 26,* 285–291. [2]

Hofer, M. A. (1981). *The roots of human behavior: An introduction to the psychobiology of early development.* New York: Freeman. [3]

Hoff-Ginsberg, E. (1986). Function and structure in maternal speech: Their relation to the child's development of syntax. *Developmental Psychology, 22,* 155–163. [7]

Hoff-Ginsberg, E. (1990). Maternal speech and the child's development of syntax: A further look. *Journal of Child Language, 17,* 85–99. [7]

Hoff-Ginsberg, E., and Krueger, W. M. (1991). Older siblings as conversational partners. *Merrill-Palmer Quarterly, 37,* 465–481. [7]

Hoffman, L. (1984). Work, family, and the socialization of the child. In R. D. Rarke (Ed.), *Review of child development research: Vol. 7. The family.* Chicago: University of Chicago Press. [12]

Hoffman, L. (1989). Effects of maternal employment in the two-parent family. *American Psychologist, 44,* 283–292. [2]

Hoffman, L. (in press). The influence of the family environment on personality. *Psychological Bulletin.* [1]

Hoffman, L., and Manis, J. (1977, April). *Influences of children on marital interaction and parental satisfactions and dissatisfactions.* Paper presented at the Conference on Human and Family Development, Pennsylvania State University. [14]

Hoffman, M. (1979). Development of moral thought, feeling, and behavior. *American Psychologist, 34,* 958–966. [10]

Hoffman, M. (1986). Affect, cognition, and behavior. In R. M. Sorrentino and E. T. Higgins (Eds.), *Handbook of motivation and cognition.* New York: Guilford. [12]

Hoffman, M. (1994). Discipline and internalization. *Developmental Psychology, 30,* 26–28. [10]

Holden, G. W., and West, M. J. (1989). Proximate regulation by mothers: A demonstration of how differing styles affect young children's behavior. *Child Development, 60,* 64–69. [8]

Honzik, M. P. (1983). Measuring mental abilities in infancy: The value and limitations. In M. Lewis (Ed.), *Origins of intelligence in infancy and early childhood.* New York: Plenum Press. [5, 11]

Homan, K. J. (1990). *A longitudinal analysis of learned helplessness in school children.* Unpublished doctoral dissertation, University of Minnesota. [12]

Hood, B., and Willatts, P. (1986). Reaching in the dark to an object's remembered position: Evidence for object-permanence in 5-month-olds. *British Journal of Developmental Psychology, 4,* 57–66. [5]

Horn, J. L. (1982). The aging of human abilities. In B. B. Wolman (Ed.), *Handbook of developmental psychology.* Englewood Cliffs, NJ: Prentice-Hall. [11]

Howe, N. (1991). Sibling-directed internal state language, perspective taking, and affective behavior. *Child Development, 62,* 1503–1512. [2]

Howes, C. (1988). Peer interaction of young children. *Monographs of the Society for Research in Child Development, 53*(Serial No. 217), 1–78. [8, 10]

Howes, C. (1990). Can the age of entry into child care and the quality of child care predict adjustment in kindergarten? *Developmental Psychology, 26,* 292–303. [6, 10]

Howes, C., Hamilton, C. E., and Matheson, C. C. (1994). Children's relationships with peers: Differential associations with aspects of the teacher-child relationship. *Child Development, 65*(1), 253–263. [10]

Howes, C., and Matheson, C. (1992). Sequences in the development of competent play with peers: Social and social pretend play. *Developmental Psychology, 28,* 961–974. [10]

Howes, C., Unger, O., and Seidner, L. B. (1989). Social pretend play in toddlers: Parallels with social play and with solitary pretend. *Child Development, 60,* 77–84. [8]

Howes, C., and Wu, F. (1990). Peer interactions and friendships in an ethnically diverse school setting. *Child Development, 61,* 537–541. [12]

Howes, P., and Markman, H. J. (1989).

Marital quality and child functioning: A longitudinal investigation. *Child Development, 60,* 1044–1051. [6]

Hoyme, H. E. (1990). Teratogenically induced fetal anomalies. *Clinics in Perinatology, 17*(3), 547–567. [3]

Hruska, K., and Yonas, A. (1971). *Developmental changes in cardiac responses to the optical stimulus of impending collision.* Paper presented at the Meetings for Psychophysiological Research, St. Louis. [6]

Hudley, C., and Graham, S. (1993). An attributional intervention to reduce peer-directed aggression among African-American boys. *Child Development, 64,* 124–138. [12]

Husaim, J. S., and Cohen, L. B. (1982). Infant learning of ill-defined categories. *Merrill-Palmer Quarterly, 27,* 443–456. [5]

Husen, T. (1967). Analysis of hereditary and environmental factors in determining the academic success of twins. *Bulletin de Psychologie, 20,* 772–781. [11]

Huston, A. C., Carpenter, C. J., and Atwater, J. B. (1986). Gender, adult structuring of activities, and social behavior in middle childhood. *Child Development, 57,* 1200–1209. [12]

Huttenlocher, J., and Smiley, P. (1987). Early word meanings: The case of object names. *Cognitive Psychology, 19,* 63–89. [7]

Huttenlocher, P. R. (1994). Synaptogenesis, synapse elimination, and neural plasticity in the human cerebral cortex. In C. A. Nelson (Ed.), *Threats to optimal development: Integrating biological, psychological, and social risk factors. Minnesota Symposia on Child Psychology* (Vol. 27). Hillsdale, NJ: Erlbaum. [13]

Hyde, J., Fennema, E., and Lamon, S. (1990). Gender differences in mathematical performance: A meta-analysis. *Psychological Bulletin, 107,* 139–155. [11]

Hymel, S., Bowker, A., and Woody, E. (1993). Aggressive versus withdrawn unpopular children: Variations in peer and self-perceptions in multiple domains. *Child Development, 64,* 879–896. [12]

Infant Health and Development Program. (1990). Enhancing the outcomes of low-birth-weight, premature infants. *Journal of American Medical Association, 263*(22), 3035–3042. [3]

Inhelder, B., and Piaget, J. (1955/1958). *The growth of logical thinking from childhood to adolescence.* New York: Basic Books. [13]

Inhelder, B., and Piaget, J. (1964). *The early growth of logic in the child.* London: Routledge & Kegan Paul. [9, 11]

Inhelder, B., Sinclair, H., and Bovet, B.

(1974). *Learning and development of cognition.* Cambridge, MA: Harvard University Press. [13]

Institute of Medicine. (1985). *Preventing low birth-weight.* Washington, DC: National Academy Press. [3]

Isabella, R. A. (1993). Origins of attachment: Maternal interactive behavior across the first year. *Developmental Psychology, 64,* 605–621. [6]

Izard, C., and Malatesta, C. (1987). Perspectives on emotional development I: Differential emotions theory of early emotional development. In J. Osofsky (Ed.), *Handbook of infant development* (2nd ed., pp. 494–554). New York: Wiley. [6]

Jackson, J. F. (1993). Human behavioral genetics, Scarr's theory and her views on interventions: A critical review and commentary on their implications for African American children. *Child Development, 64,* 1318–1332. [11]

Jacob, T. (1974). Patterns of family conflict and dominance as a function of child age and social class. *Developmental Psychology, 10,* 1–12. [14]

Jacobs, P. I., and Vandeventer, M. (1971). The learning and transfer of double classification skills by first graders. *Child Development, 42,* 149–159. [11]

Jacobson, S. W. (1979). Matching behavior in the young infant. *Child Development, 50,* 425–430. [4]

Jacobson, S. W., and Frye, K. F. (1991). Effect of maternal social support on attachment: Experimental evidence. *Developmental Psychology, 62,* 572–582. [6]

Jacobson, S. W., Jacobson, J. L., Sokol, R. J., Martier, S. S., and Ager, J. W. (1993). Prenatal alcohol exposure and infant information processing ability. *Child Development, 64,* 1706–1721. [3]

Jacobvitz, D., and Sroufe, L. A. (1987). The early caregiver-child relationship and attention deficit disorder with hyperactivity in kindergarten. *Child Development, 58,* 1488–1495. [8, 15]

Jacobvitz, D., Sroufe, L. A., Stewart, M., and Leffert, N. (1990). Treatment of attentional and hyperactivity problems in children with sympathomimetic drugs: A comprehensive review. *Journal of the American Academy of Child Psychiatry, 29,* 677–688. [15]

Jennings, K., Stagg, V., and Connors, R. (1991). Social networks and mothers' interactions with their preschool children. *Child Development, 62,* 966–978. [10]

Jenkins, J. (1992). Sibling relationships in disharmonious homes: Potential difficulties and protective effects. In F. Boer and J. Dunn (Eds.), *Children's sib-*

ling relationships (pp. 125–138). Hillsdale, NJ: Erlbaum. [12]

Jensen, A. R. (1969). How much can we boost I.Q. and scholastic achievement? *Harvard Educational Review, 29,* 1–123. [11]

Jensen, J., and Garfinkel, B. (1988). Neuroendocrine aspects of attention deficit hyperactivity disorder. *Endocrinology and Metabolism Clinics of North America, 17,* 111–127. [15]

Jiao, S., Ji, G., and Jing, Q. (1986). Comparative study of behavioral qualities of only children and sibling children. *Child Development, 57,* 357–361. [2]

Jimerson, S., Carlson, E., Rotert, M., Egeland, B., and Sroufe, L. A. (in press). A prospective, longitudinal study of the correlates and consequences of early grade retention. *Journal of School Psychology.* [12]

Johnson, H., and Rosen, T. (1990). Mother-infant-interaction in a multi-risk population. *American Journal of Orthopsychiatry, 60,* 281–287. [6]

Johnson, B. M., Shulman, S., and Collins, W. A. (1991). Systemic patterns of parenting as reported by adolescents: Developmental differences and implications for psychosocial outcomes. *Journal of Adolescent Research, 6,* 235–252. [14]

Johnson, J. S., and Newport, E. L. (1989). Critical period effects in second language learning: The influence of maturational state on the acquisition of English as a second language. *Cognitive Psychology, 21,* 60–99. [7, 13]

Johnston, L. D., O'Malley, P. M., and Bachman, J. G. (1994). *National survey results on drug use from the Monitoring the Future Study, 1975–1993* (Vol. 1). Washington, DC: U.S. Department of Health and Human Service. [14]

Jones, M. (1957). The later careers of boys who were early or late maturing. *Child Development, 28,* 113–128. [13, 14]

Kagan, J. (1984). *The nature of the child.* New York: Basic Books. [1, 6]

Kagan, J. (1992). Yesterday's premises, tomorrow's promises. *Developmental Psychology, 28,* 990–997. [6]

Kagan, J., Kearsley, R. B., and Zelazo, P. (1978). *Infancy: Its place in human development.* Cambridge, MA: Harvard University Press. [6]

Kagan, S., and Madsen, M. (1972). Experimental analyses of cooperation and competition of Anglo-American and Mexican children. *Developmental Psychology, 6,* 49–59. [2]

Kahn, P. (1992). Children's obligatory and discretionary moral judgments. *Child Development, 63,* 416–430. [12]

Kail, R. (1990). *The development of memory in children* (3rd ed.). New York: Freeman. [5, 11]

Kail, R. (1991). Development of processing speed in childhood and adolescence. In W. Reese (Ed.), *Advances in child development and behavior.* San Diego: Academic Press. [1, 11]

Kail, R., and Bisanz, J. (1992). The information processing perspective on cognitive development in childhood and adolescence. In R. J. Sternberg and C. A. Berg (Eds.), *Intellectual development* (pp. 229–260). Cambridge, Eng.: Cambridge University Press. [13]

Kail, R., and Hagen, J. (1982). Memory in childhood. In B. B. Wolman (Ed.), *Handbook of developmental psychology.* Englewood Cliffs, NJ: Prentice-Hall. [11]

Kalnins, I. V., and Bruner, J. S. (1973). The coordination of visual observation and instrumental behavior in early infancy. *Perception, 2,* 307–314. [4]

Kandel, D. (1978). Similarity in real life adolescent friendship pairs. *Journal of Personality and Social Psychology, 36,* 306–312. [14]

Kandel, D., and Lesser, G. (1972). *Youth in two worlds: U.S. and Denmark.* San Francisco: Jossey-Bass. [14]

Kanner, L. (1943). Autistic disturbances of affective contact. *Nervous Child, 2,* 217–250. [15]

Kaplan, H., and Dove, H. (1987). Infant development among the Ache of Eastern Paraguay. *Developmental Psychology, 23,* 190–198. [4]

Karen, R. (1994). *Becoming attached.* New York: Warner. [2]

Karmiloff-Smith, A. (1991). Beyond modularity: Innate constraints and developmental change. In S. Carey & R. Gelman (Eds.), *The epigenesis of mind* (pp. 171–197). Hillsdale, NJ: Erlbaum. [1]

Katz, L., and Gottman, J. (1993). Patterns of marital conflict predict children's internalizing and externalizing behaviors. *Developmental Psychology, 29,* 940–950. [10]

Katz, P., and Ksansnak, K. (1994). Developmental aspects of gender role flexibility and traditionality in middle childhood and adolescence. *Developmental Psychology, 30,* 272–282. [12]

Kaufman, J., and Cicchetti, D. (1989). Effects of maltreatment on school-age children's socioemotional development: Assessments in a day-camp setting. *Developmental Psychology, 25,* 516–524. [12]

Kavale, K. A., and Karge, B. D. (1986). Fetal alcohol syndrome: A behavioral teratology. *Exceptional Child, 33,* 4–16. [3]

Kaye, K., and Wells, A. J. (1980). Mothers jiggling and the burst-pause pattern in neonatal feeding. *Infant Behavior and Development, 3,* 29–46. [6]

Keating, D. P. (1980). Thinking processes in adolescence. In J. Adelson (Ed.), *Handbook of adolescent psychology.* New York: Wiley. [13]

Keating, D. P. (1990). Adolescent thinking. In S. S. Feldman and G. R. Elliott (Eds.), *At the threshold: The developing adolescent* (pp. 54–89). Cambridge, MA: Harvard University Press. [13]

Keeney, T. J., Cannizzo, S. R., and Flavell, J. H. (1967). Spontaneous and induced verbal rehearsal in a recall task. *Child Development, 38,* 953–966. [11]

Keil, F. C. (1989). *Concepts, kinds, and cognitive development.* Cambridge, MA: MIT Press. [5]

Keller, A., Ford, L., and Meachum, J. (1978). Dimensions of self-concept in preschool children. *Developmental Psychology, 14,* 483–489. [12]

Keller, M., and Edelstein, W. (1993). The development of the moral self from childhood to adolescence. In G. Noam and T. Wren (Eds.), *The moral self* (pp. 310–336). Cambridge, MA: MIT Press. [12]

Keller, M., and Wood, P. (1989). Development of friendship reasoning: A study of interindividual differences in intraindividual change. *Developmental Psychology, 25,* 820–826. [14]

Kellman, P. J., and Spelke, E. S. (1983). Perception of partly occluded objects in infancy. *Cognitive Psychology, 15,* 483–524. [5]

Kellman, P. J., Spelke, E. S., and Short, K. R. (1986). Infant perception of object unity from translatory motion in depth and vertical translation. *Child Development, 57,* 72–86. [5]

Kemler-Nelson, D. G., Hirsh-Pasek, K., Jusczyk, P. W., and Cassidy, K. W. (1989). How the prosodic cues in motherese might assist language learning. *Journal of Child Language, 16,* 55–68. [7]

Kendall, P., and Lochman, J. (1994). Cognitive behavioral therapies. In M. Rutter, E. Taylor and L. Hersov (Eds.), *Child and adolescent psychiatry* (pp. 844–857). London: Blackwell. [15]

Kerns, K. (1994). Individual differences in friendship quality: Links to child-mother attachment. In W. Bukowski, A. Newcomb, and W. Hartup (Eds.), *The company they keep: Friendship in childhood and adolescence.* New York: Cambridge University Press.[10]

Kessen, W. (1965). *The child.* New York: Wiley. [2]

Kessen, W. (Ed.). (1975). *Childhood in China.* New Haven,: Yale University Press. [2]

Kestenbaum, R., Farber, E., and Sroufe, L. A. (1989). Individual differences in empathy among preschoolers: Concurrent and predictive validity. In N. Eisenberg (Ed.), *Empathy and related emotional responses: No. 44. New directions for child development* (pp. 51–56). San Francisco: Jossey-Bass. [10]

Kierkegaard, S. (1938). *Purity of heart is to will one thing.* New York: Harper & Row. [8]

Kimmel, D. C., and Weiner, I. B. (1985). *Adolescence: A developmental transition.* Hillsdale, NJ: Erlbaum. [13]

Kindermann, T. (1993). Natural peer groups as contexts for individual development: The case of children's motivation in school. *Child Development, 64,* 970–977. [12]

King, R. A. (1993). Common ocular signs and symptoms in childhood. *Pediatric Clinics of North America, 40,* 755–766. [4]

Kinloch, G. (1970). Parent-youth conflict at home: An investigation among university freshmen. *American Journal of Orthopsychiatry, 40,* 658–664. [14]

Kinney, D. A. (1993). From "nerds" to "normals": Adolescent identity recovery within a changing social system. *Sociology of Education, 66,* 21–40. [14]

Kiselevsky, B. S., and Muir, D. W. (1984). Neonatal habituation and dishabituation to tactile stimulation during sleep. *Developmental Psychology, 20,* 367–373. [5]

Kiselevsky, B. S., Muir, D. W., and Low, J. A. (1992). Maturation of human fetal responses to vibroacoustic stimulation. *Child Development, 63,* 1497–1508. [4]

Kiser, L., Bates, J., Maslin, C., and Bayles, K. (1986). Mother-infant play at six months as a predictor of attachment security at thirteen months. *Journal of the American Academy of Child Psychiatry, 25,* 68–75. [6]

Kitchener, R. F. (1983). Developmental explanations. *Review of Metaphysics, 36,* 791–817. [1]

Klaus, M., and Kennell, J. (1976). *Maternal infant bonding.* St. Louis: Mosby. [6]

Klein, R. (1994). Anxiety disorders. In M. Rutter, E. Taylor, and L. Hersov (Eds.), *Child and adolescent psychiatry* (pp. 351–374). London: Blackwell. [15]

Klein, S. B. (1987). *Learning: Principles and applications.* New York: McGraw-Hill. [5]

Kliener, K. A., and Banks, M. S. (1987). Stimulus energy does not account for 2-month-olds' face preferences. *Journal of Experimental Child Psychology, 13,* 594–600. [4]

Kline, M., Tschann, J., Johnston, J., and Wallerstein, J. (1989). Children's adjustment in joint and sole custody families. *Developmental Psychology, 25,* 1–9. [2, 12]

Knopf, I. (1984). *Childhood psychopathology* (2nd ed.). Englewood Cliffs, NJ: Prentice-Hall. [15]

Kochanska, G. (1993). Toward a synthesis of parental socialization and child temperament in early development of conscience. *Developmental Psychology,* 64(2), 325–347. [8, 10]

Kochanska, G., and Aksan, N. (in press). Mother-child mutually positive affect, the quality of child compliance to requests and prohibitions, and maternal control as correlates of early internalization. *Child Development.* [10]

Kohlberg, L. (1958). *The development of modes of moral thinking and choice in the years 10 to 16.* Unpublished doctoral dissertation, University of Chicago. [13]

Kohlberg, L. (1969). Stage and sequence: The cognitive-developmental approach to socialization. In D. A. Goslin (Ed.), *Handbook of socialization theory and research.* Chicago: Rand McNally. [13]

Kohlberg, L. (1976). Moral stages and moralization: Cognitive-developmental approach. In R. Lickona (Ed.), *Moral development and behavior: Theory, research, and social issues.* Chicago: Rand McNally. [13]

Konopka, G. (1976). *Young girls: A portrait of adolescence.* Englewood Cliffs, NJ: Prentice-Hall. [14]

Kopp, C. (1992). Emotional distress and control in young children. In N. Eisenberg and R. Fabes (Eds.), *Emotion and its regulation in early development. New Directions for Child Development* (pp. 41–56). San Francisco: Jossey-Bass. [10]

Kopp, C., and Kaler, S. (1989). Risk in infancy. *American Psychologist, 44,* 224–230. [2]

Kopp, C. B., Krakow, J. B., and Vaughn, B. E. (1983). The antecedents of self-regulation in young handicapped children. In M. Perlmutter (Ed.), *Minnesota Symposia on Child Psychology* (Vol. 17). Hillsdale, NJ: Erlbaum. [10]

Korner, A. F., Brown, B. W., Jr., Dimiceli, S., Forrest, T., Stevenson, D. K., Lane, N. M., Constantinou, J., and Thom, V. A. (1989). Stable individual differences in developmentally changing preterm infants: A replicated study. *Child Development, 60,* 502–513. [5]

Korner, A. F., Constantinou, J., Dimiceli, S., Brown, B. W., Jr., and Thom, V. A. (1991). Establishing the reliability and developmental validity of a neurobehavioral assessment for the preterm infant: A methodological process. *Developmental Psychology, 62,* 1200–1208. [6]

Korner, A. F., Hutchinson, C., Kopershi, J., Kraemer, H., and Schneider, P. (1981). Stability of individual differences of neonatal motor and crying patterns. *Child Development, 52,* 83–90. [4]

Kraemer, G. (1992). A psychobiological theory of attachment. *Behavioral and Brain Sciences, 15,* 493–511. [6, 15]

Kramer, J., Hill, K., and Cohen, L. (1975). Infants' development of object

permanence: A refined methodology and new evidence of Piaget's hypothesized ordinality. *Child Development, 46,* 149–155. [5]

Kramer, L., and Gottman, J. (1992). Becoming a sibling: "With a little help from my friends." *Developmental Psychology, 28,* 685–699. [10, 12]

Krebs, R. L. (1967). *Some relations between moral judgment, attention, and resistance to temptation.* Unpublished doctoral dissertation, University of Chicago. [13]

Kreppner, K. (1988). Changes in dyadic relationships within the family after the arrival of a second child. In R. Hinde and J. Stevenson-Hinde (Eds.), *Relationships within families* (pp. 143–167). Oxford, Eng.: Oxford Science Publications. [2]

Kreutzer, M. A., Leonard, C., and Flavell, J. H. (1975). An interview study of children's knowledge about memory. *Monographs of the Society for Research in Child Development, 40,* (1, Serial No. 159). [11]

Krugman, R., and Davidson, H. (1990). *Child abuse and neglect: Critical first steps in response to a national emergency.* Washington, DC: Department of Health and Human Services. U.S. Advisory Board on Child Abuse and Neglect. [8]

Kruttschnitt, C., Heath, L., and Ward, D. (1986). Family violence, television viewing habits, and other violent criminal behavior. *Criminology, 24,* 201–233. [15]

Kuczaj, S. (1982). Children's overextensions in comprehension and production: Support for a prototype theory of object word meaning acquisition. *First Language, 3,* 93–105. [7]

Kuczynski, L., and Kochanska, G. (1990). Development of children's noncompliance strategies from toddlerhood to age 5. *Developmental Psychology, 26,* 398–408. [10]

Kuhn, D., Langer, J., Kohlberg, L., and Haan, N. (1977). The development of formal operations in logical and moral judgment. *Genetic Psychology Monographs, 95,* 97–188. [13]

Kurtines, W., and Greif, E. G. (1974). The development of moral thought: Review and evaluation of Kohlberg's approach. *Psychological Bulletin, 81,* 453–470. [13]

Ladd, G. W. (1983). Social networks of popular, average, and rejected children in school settings. *Merrill-Palmer Quarterly, 29,* 283–308. [12]

Ladd, G. W., and Hart, C. (1992). Creating informal play opportunities: Are parents' and preschoolers' initiations related to children's competence with peers? *Developmental Psychology, 28,* 1179–1187. [10]

LaFreniere, P. (1983). *From attachment to peer relations. An analysis of individual patterns of social adaptation during the formation of a preschool peer group.* Unpublished doctoral dissertation, University of Minnesota. [10]

LaFreniere, P., and Dumas, J. (1992). A transactional analysis of early childhood anxiety and social withdrawal. *Development and Psychopathology, 4,* 385–402. [10]

Lamb, M. (1981). The development of father-infant relationships. In M. E. Lamb (Ed.), *The role of the father in child development* (2nd ed.). New York: Wiley. [2, 8]

Lamb, M. (1986). *The father's role: Cross-cultural perspectives.* Hillsdale, NJ: Erlbaum. [2]

Lamb, M., Frodi, A., Hwang, C., and Steinberg, J. (1982). Mother- and father-infant interactions involving play and holding in traditional and nontraditional Swedish families. *Developmental Psychology, 18,* 215–221. [6]

Landau, S., Lorch, E., and Milich, R. (1992). Visual attention to and comprehension of television in attention-deficit hyperactivity disordered and normal boys. *Child Development, 63,* 928–937. [15]

Langlois, J., and Downs, A. (1980). Mothers, fathers, and peers as socialization agents of sex-typed play behaviors in young children. *Child Development, 51,* 1217–1247. [2, 10]

Langlois, J. H., Roggman, L. A., Casey, R. J., Ritter, J. M., Reisser-Danner, L. A., and Jenkins, V. Y. (1987). Infant preferences for attractive faces: Rudiments of a stereotype? *Developmental Psychology, 23,* 363–369. [4]

Langlois, J. H., Roggman, L. A., and Rieser-Danner, L. A. (1990). Infants' differential social responses to attractive and unattractive faces. *Developmental Psychology, 26,* 153–159. [4]

Lansbaum, J., and Willis, R. (1971). Conformity in early and late adolescence. *Developmental Psychology, 4,* 334–337. [14]

Larsen, R., and Richards, M. (1991). Daily companionship in late childhood and early adolescence: Changing developmental contexts. *Child Development, 62,* 284–300. [12]

Larsen, W. J. (1993). *Human embryology.* New York: Churchill Livingstone. [3]

Larson, R., and Lampman-Petraitis, C. (1989). Daily emotional states as reported by children and adolescents. *Child Development, 60,* 1250–1260. [14]

Lazare, A. (1973). Hidden conceptual models in clinical psychiatry. *New England Journal of Medicine, 288,* 345–350. [15]

Lazer, I., Darlington, R. B., Murray, H., Royce, J., and Snipper, A. (1982). Lasting effects of early education. *Monographs of the Society for Research in Child Development, 47* (2–3, Serial No. 195). [11]

Lee, C. L., and Bates, J. E. (1985). Mother-child interaction at age two years and perceived difficult temperament. *Child Development, 56,* 1314–1325. [8]

Lempers, J. D., Clark-Lempers, D., and Simons, R. L. (1989). Economic hardship, parenting, and distress in adolescence. *Child Development, 60,* 25–39. [14]

Lenneberg, E. (1967). *Biological foundations of language.* New York: Wiley. [2, 7]

Leon, G., and Phenan, P. (1985). Anorexia nervosa. In B. Lahey and A. Kazdin (Eds.), *Advances in clinical child psychology* (Vol. 8, pp. 81–113). New York: Plenum Press. [15]

Lepper, M., and Gurtner, J. (1989). Children and computers. *American Psychologist, 44,* 170–178. [2]

Lester, B. M., Corwin, M. J., Sepkowski, C., Seifer, R., Peucker, M., McLaughlin, S., and Golub, H. L. (1991). Neurobehavioral syndromes in cocaine-exposed newborn infants. *Child Development, 62,* 694–705. [3]

Leventhal, H., and Keeshan, P. (1993). Promoting healthy alternatives to substance abuse. In S. G. Millstein, A. C. Petersen, and E. O. Nightingale (Eds.), *Promoting the health of adolescence* (pp. 260–284). New York: Oxford University Press. [14]

LeVine, R. A. (1988). Human parental care: Universal goals, cultural strategies, individual behavior. In R. A. LeVine, P. M. Miller, and M. M. West (Eds.), *Parental behavior in diverse societies* (pp. 3–12). San Francisco: Jossey-Bass. [2]

Levine, R., and Miller, P. (1990). Commentary. *Human Development, 33,* 73–80. [6]

Levy, G., and Carter, D. B. (1989). Gender schema, gender constancy, and gender-role knowledge: The roles of cognitive factors in preschoolers' gender-role stereotype attributions. *Development Psychology, 25,* 444–449. [10]

Lewin, K. (1951). *Field theory in social science.* New York: Harper & Row. [14]

Lewis, M. (1992). The self in self-conscious emotions. Commentary on Stipek et al. *Monographs of the Society for Research in Child Development, 57* (Serial No. 226), 85–95. [8, 10]

Lewis, M., Alessandri, S. M., and Sullivan, M. W. (1992). Differences in shame and pride as a function of children's gender and task difficulty. *Child Development, 63*(3), 630–638. [8, 10]

Lewis, M., and Brooks, J. (1978). Self-knowledge and emotional development. In M. Lewis and L. Rosenblum

(Eds.), *The development of affect.* New York: Plenum Press. [8]

Lewis, M., and Michalson, L. (1983). *Children's emotions and moods.* New York: Plenum Press. [6]

Liben, L., and Signorella, L. (1993). Gender-schematic processing in children: The role of initial interpretations of stimuli. *Developmental Psychology, 29,* 141–149. [12]

Liberman, A. M., Harris, K. S., Hoffman, H. S., and Griffith, B. C. (1957). The discrimination of speech sounds within and across phoneme boundaries. *Journal of Experimental Psychology, 54,* 358–368. [4]

Lieberman, A. F. (1977). Preschoolers' competence with a peer: Relations with attachment and peer experience. *Child Development, 48,* 1277–1287. [10]

Lieberman, A. F., Weston, D. R., and Pawl, J. H. (1991). Preventive intervention and outcome with anxiously attached dyads. *Child Development, 62,* 199–209. [6]

Lieberman, P. (1984). *The biology and evolution of language.* Cambridge, MA: Harvard University Press. [7]

Lieven, E. M. (1978). Conversations between mothers and young children: Individual differences and their possible implications for the study of language learning. In N. Waterson and C. Snow (Eds.), *The development of communication: Social and pragmatic factors in language acquisition.* New York: Wiley. [7]

Lillard, A. S. (1993). Pretend play skills and the child's theory of mind. *Child Development, 64*(2), 348–371. [10]

Linney, J., and Seidman, E. (1989). The future of schooling. *American Psychologist, 44,* 336–340. [2]

Lipsitt, L. P. (1990). Learning and memory in infants. *Merrill-Palmer Quarterly, 36,* 53–66. [4]

Little, B., Snell, L., Rosenfeld, C., Gilstrap, L., and Gant, N. (1990). Failure to recognize fetal alcohol syndrome in newborn infants. *American Journal of Diseases of Children, 144,* 1142–1146. [3]

Lively, W. J., and Bromley, O. B. (1973). *Person perception in childhood and adolescence.* London: Wiley. [14]

Livson, N., and Peskin, H. (1980). Perspectives on adolescence from longitudinal research. In J. Adelson (Ed.), *Handbook of adolescent psychology* (pp. 47–98). New York: Wiley. [13]

Lobel, M., Dunkel-Schetter, C., and Scrimshaw, S. (1990). *Emotional distress and anxiety during pregnancy: Consequences for prematurity and birth weight.* Paper presented at the Annual Meeting of the American Psychological Association, Boston. [3]

Lobel, T., and Menashri, J. (1993). Rela-

tions of conceptions of gender-role transgressions and gender constancy to gender-typed toy preferences. *Developmental Psychology, 29,* 150–155. [10]

Lock, A., Young, A., Service, V., and Chandler, P. (1990). Some observations on the origins of the pointing gesture. In V. Volterra and C. J. Erting (Eds.), *From gesture to language in hearing and deaf children* (pp. 42–55). New York: Springer. [7]

Locke, J. L. (1983). *Phonological acquisition and change.* New York: Academic Press. [7]

Loed, G. E. (1989). Neural prosthetic strategies for young children. In E. Owens and D. Kessler (Eds.), *Cochlear implants in young deaf children* (pp. 137–152). Boston: Little, Brown. [4]

Loehlin, J., Willerman, L., and Horn, J. (1982). Personality resemblances between unwed mothers and their adopted-away offspring. *Journal of Personality and Social Psychology, 42,* 1089–1099. [6]

Lollis, S. (1990). Maternal influence on children's separation behavior. *Child Development, 61,* 99–103. [8]

Lollis, S., and Ross, H. (1992). Parents' regulation of their children's peer interactions: Influence of direct intervention. In R. Parke and G. Ladd (Eds.), *Family-peer relationships: Modes of linkage.* Hillsdale, NJ: Erlbaum. [12]

Londerville, S., and Main, M. (1981). Security of attachment, compliance, and maternal training methods in the second year of life. *Developmental Psychology, 17,* 289–299. [2, 8]

Lord, C., and Rutter, M. (1994). Autism and pervasive developmental disorders. In M. Rutter, E. Taylor, and L. Hersov (Eds.), *Child and adolescent psychiatry* (pp. 569–593). Oxford, Eng.: Blackwell. [15]

Lozoff, B. (1989). Nutrition and behavior. *American Psychologist, 44,* 231–236. [2]

Lund, R. D. (1978). *Development and plasticity of the brain: An introduction.* Oxford, Eng.: Oxford University Press. [13]

Luria, A. R. (1961). *The role of speech in the regulation of normal and abnormal behavior.* New York: Pergamon Press. [10]

Lynn, R. (1982). IQ in Japan and the United States shows a growing disparity. *Nature, 297,* 222–223. [11]

Lyons-Ruth, K., Connell, D. B., Grunebaum, H. U., and Botein, S. (1990). Infants at social risk: Maternal depression and family support services as mediators of infant development and security of attachment. *Child Development, 61,* 85–98. [6]

Maccoby, E. E. (1980). *Social development.* New York: Harcourt Brace Jovanovich. [Pt. 3 Epilogue, 10, 12, 14]

Maccoby, E. (1990). Gender and relationships. *American Psychologist, 45,* 513–520. [10, 12]

Maccoby, E. E. (1992). The role of parents in the socialization of children: An historical overview. *Developmental Psychology, 28,*(6), 1006–1017. [8]

Maccoby, E. G., and Jacklin, C. N. (1974). *The psychology of sex differences.* Stanford, CA: Stanford University Press. [11]

Maccoby, E. E., and Martin, J. A. (1983). Socialization in the context of the family. In E. M. Hetherington (Ed.), *Handbook of child psychology: Socialization personality and social development* (Vol. 4). New York: Wiley. [12]

MacFarlane, A. (1975). Olfaction in the development of social preferences in the human neonate. *Parent-infant interaction.* Amsterdam: CIBA Foundation Symposium 33, ASP. [4]

MacFarlane, J., Allen, L., and Honzik, M. (1954). *A developmental study of the behavior problems of normal children.* Berkeley, CA: University of California Press. [15]

Mackinnon-Lewis, C., Volling, B., Lamb, M., Dechman, K., Rabiner, D., and Curtner, M. (1994). A cross-contextual analysis of boys' social competence: From family to school. *Developmental Psychology, 30,* 325–333. [12]

Madsen, M. (1971). Development and cross-cultural differences in cooperative and competitive behavior of young children. *Journal of Cross-Cultural Psychology, 2,* 365–371. [2]

Mahler, M., Pine, R., and Bergman, A. (1975). *The psychological birth of the human infant.* New York: Basic Books. [8]

Main, M. (1990). Cross-cultural studies of attachment organization: Recent studies, changing methodologies, and the concept of conditional strategies. *Human Development, 33,* 48–61. [6]

Main, M. (1994). Discourse, prediction, and studies in attachment: Implications for psychoanalysis. In T. Shapiro & R. Emde (Eds.), *Some empirical issues in psychoanalysis. Journal of the American Psychoanalytic Association.* [6]

Main, M. (in press). Metacognitive knowledge, metacognitive monitoring, and singular (coherent) vs. multiple (incoherent) models of attachment: Findings and directions for future research. In P. Marris, J. Stevenson-Hinde, and C. Parkes (Eds.), *Attachment across the life cycle.* New York: Routledge. [6, 10]

Main, M., and Hesse, E. (1990). Parents' unresolved traumatic experiences are related to infant disorganized attachment status: Is frightened and/or frightening parental behavior the linking mechanism? In M. T. Greenberg, D. Cicchetti, and E. M. Cummings (Eds.), *Attachment in the preschool years* (pp. 161–182). Chicago: University of Chicago Press. [6, 10]

Main, M., and Weston, D. (1981). The quality of the toddler's relationship to mother and to father as related to conflict behavior and readiness to establish new relationships. *Child Development, 52,* 932–940. [6]

Malina, R. M. (1978). Growth of muscle tissue and muscle mass. In F. Falkner and J. M. Tanner (Eds.), *Human growth: Vol. 2. Postnatal growth.* New York: Plenum Press. [13]

Mandler, J. M. (1990). A new perspective on cognitive development in infancy. *American Scientist, 78,* 236–243. [5]

Mangelsdorf, S., Gunnar, M., Kestenbaum, R., Lang, S., and Andreas, D. (1990). Infant proneness-to-distress temperament, maternal personality, and mother-infant attachment: Associations and goodness of fit. *Child Development 61,* 820–831. [6]

Mangelsdorf, S., Watkins, S., and Lehn, L. (1991, April). *The role of control in the infant's appraisal of strangers.* Paper presented at the biennial meeting of the Society for Research in Child Development, Seattle. [6]

Manis, F. R., Keating, D. P., and Morrison, F. J. (1980). Developmental differences in the allocation of processing capacity. *Journal of Experimental Child Psychology, 29,* 156–169. [13]

Mannle, S., and Tomasello, M. (1987). Fathers, siblings, and the Bridge Hypothesis. In K. E. Nelson and A. van Kleek (Eds.), *Children's language* (Vol. 6, pp. 23–41). Hillsdale, NJ: Erlbaum. [7]

Mans, L., Cicchetti, D., and Sroufe, L. A. (1978). Mirror reactions of Down syndrome infants and toddlers: Cognitive underpinnings of self-recognition. *Child Development, 49,* 1247–1250. [1, 8]

Marcia, J. (1980). Identity in adolescence. In J. Adelson (Ed.), *Handbook of adolescent psychology* (pp. 159–187). New York: Wiley. [14]

Marcus, G. F., Pinker, S., Ullman, M., Hollander, M., Rosen, T. J., and Xu, F. (1992). Overregularization in language acquisition. *Monographs of the Society for Research in Child Development, 57* (4, Serial No. 228). [7]

Margolis, L. (1982). Help wanted. *Pediatrics, 69,* 816–818. [2]

Markman, E. M. (1979). Classes and collections: Conceptual organization and numerical abilities. *Cognitive Psychology, 11,* 395–411. [11]

Markman, E. M. (1987). How children constrain the possible meanings of words. In U. Neisser (Ed.), *Concepts and conceptual development: Ecological and intellectual factors in categorization* (pp. 255–287). Cambridge, Eng.: Cambridge University Press. [7]

Markman, E. M., and Hutchinson, J. (1984). Children's sensitivity to constraints on word meaning: Taxonomic vs. thematic relations. *Cognitive Psychology, 16,* 1–27. [7]

Markman, E. M., and Siebert, J. (1976). Classes and collections: Principles of organization in the learning of hierarchical relations. *Cognitions, 8,* 227–241. [11]

Markstrom-Adams, C. (1992). A consideration of intervening factors in adolescent identity formation. In G. Adams, T. Gullotta, and R. Montemayor (Eds.), *Adolescent identity formation* (pp. 173–192). Newbury Park, CA: Sage. [14]

Markus, H., and Nurius, P. (1984). Self-understanding and self-regulation in middle childhood. In W. A. Collins (Ed.), *Development in middle childhood.* Washington, DC: National Academy Press. [Pt. 5 Epilogue]

Martin, B., and Hoffman, J. A. (1990). Conduct disorders. In M. Lewis and S. M. Miller (Eds.), *Handbook of developmental psychopathology* (pp. 109–118). New York: Plenum Press. [15]

Martin, C., and Halverson, C. (1983). Gender constancy: A methodological and theoretical analysis. *Sex Roles, 9,* 775–790. [10]

Marvin, R., and Pianta, R. (1992). Relationship-based approaches to assessment of children with motor impairments. *Infants and Young Children, 4,* 33–45. [6]

Marvinney, D. (1988). *Sibling relationships in middle childhood: Implications for social-emotional development.* Unpublished doctoral dissertation, University of Minnesota, Minneapolis. [12]

Masten, A. S., and Coatsworth, D. (1995). Competence, resilience, and psychopathology. In D. Cicchetti and D. Cohen (Eds.), *Developmental processes and psychopathology* (Vol. 1). New York: Cambridge University Press. [15]

Masten, A. S., Miliotis, D., Graham-Bermann, S. A., Ramirez, M., and Neemann, J. (1993). Children in homeless families: Risks to mental health and development. *Journal of Consulting and Clinical Psychology, 61,* 335–343. [2]

Masten, A., Morison, P., Pellegrini, D., and Tellegen, A. (1990). Competence under stress: Risk and protective factors. In J. Rolf, A. Masten, D. Cicchetti, K. Neuchterlein, and S. Weintraub (Eds.), *Risk and protective factors in the development of psychopathology.* Cambridge, Eng.: Cambridge University Press. [2]

Masur, E. F. (1990). Gestural development, dual-directional signaling, and the transition to words. In V. Volterra and C. J. Erting (Eds.), *From gesture to language in hearing and deaf children* (pp. 18–30). New York: Springer. [7]

Masur, E., and Gleason, J. B. (1980). Parent-child interaction and the acquisition of lexical information during play. *Developmental Psychology, 16,* 404–409. [7]

Matas, L., Arend, R., and Sroufe, L. A. (1978). Continuity of adaptation in the second year: The relationship between quality of attachment and later competence. *Child Development, 49,* 547–556. [2, 8]

Matheny, A. (1989). Children's behavioral inhibition over age and across situations: Genetic similarity for a trait change. *Journal of Personality, 57,* 215–235. [6, 8]

Matheny, A., Riese, M., and Wilson, R. (1985). Rudiments of infant temperament: Newborn to 9 months. *Developmental Psychology, 21,* 486–494. [6]

Matias, R., and Conn, J. (1993). Are max-specified infant facial expressions during face to face interaction consistent with differential emotions theory? *Developmental Psychology, 29,* 524–531. [6]

Maurer, D., and Maurer, C. (1988). *The world of the newborn.* New York: Basic Books. [4]

Maurer, D., and Salapatek, P. (1976). Developmental changes in the scanning of faces by young infants. *Child Development, 47,* 523–527. [1, 4]

McAninch, C., Manolis, M., Milich, R., and Harris, M. (1993). Impression formation in children: Influence of gender and expectancy. *Child Development, 64,* 1492–1506. [12]

McCall, R. (1981). Nature-nurture and the two realms of development: A proposed integration with respect to mental development. *Child Development, 52,* 1–12. [2]

McCall, R. B. (1977). Childhood IQs as predictors of adult educational and occupational status. *Science, 197,* 482–483. [11]

McCall, R. B. (1979). Qualitative transitions of behavioral development in the first years of life. In M. H. Bornstein and W. Kessen (Eds.), *Psychological development from infancy.* Hillsdale, NJ: Erlbaum. [5]

McCall, R. B., and Carriger, M. S. (1993). A meta-analysis of infant habituation and recognition memory performance as predictors of later IQ. *Child Development, 64,* 57–79. [5]

McCall, R. B., Eichorn, D. H., and Hogarty, P. S. (1977). Transitions in early mental development. *Monographs of the Society for Research in Child Development, 42.* [5]

McClelland, D. C. (1973). Testing for competence rather than for intelli-

gence. *American Psychologist, 28,* 1–14. [11]

McCord, J. (1988). Parental behavior in the cycle of aggression. *Psychiatry, 51,* 14–23. [2, 12, 15]

McCrone, E., Egeland, B., Kalkoske, M., and Carlson, E. (1994). Relations between early maltreatment and mental representations of relationships assessed with projective story telling in middle childhood. *Development and Psychopathology, 6,* 99–120. [12]

McCune-Nicolich, L. (1981). Toward symbolic functioning: Structure of early pretend games and potential parallels with language. *Child Development, 52,* 785–797. [7]

McDonald, K. (1988). *Sociobiological perspectives on human development.* New York: Springer-Verlag, Inc. [2, 12]

McGhee, P. E. (1976). Children's appreciation of humor: A test of the cognitive congruency principle. *Child Development, 47,* 420–426. [11]

McGuinness, D. (1989). Attention deficit disorder: The emperor's new clothes, animal "pharm," and other fiction. In S. Fisher and R. Greenberg (Eds.), *The limits of biological treatments for psychological distress* (pp. 151–187). [15]

McKenzie, B. E., Skouteris, H., Day, R. H., Hartman, B., and Yonas, A. (1993). Effective action by infants to contact objects by reaching and leaning. *Child Development, 64,* 415–429. [4]

McKinney, W. (1977). Animal behavioral/biological models relevant to depression and affective disorders in humans. In J. Schulterbrandt and A. Raskin (Eds.), *Depression in childhood.* New York: Raven Press. [15]

McLoyd, V. (1989). Socialization and development in a changing economy. *American Psychologist, 44,* 293–302. [2]

McLoyd, V. (1990). The impact of economic hardship on black families and children: Psychological distress, parenting, and socioemotional development. *Child Development, 61,* 311–346. [2, 15]

Mead, G. H. (1934). *Mind, self, and society.* Chicago: University of Chicago Press. [8]

Mead, M. (1925/1939). *Coming of age in Samoa.* New York: William Morrow. [8, 14]

Mednick, S. (1970). Breakdown in individuals at high-risk for schizophrenia: Possible predispositional factors. *Mental Hygiene, 54,* 50–63. [15]

Melson, G. F., Ladd, G. W., and Hsu, H. (1993). Maternal support networks, maternal cognitions, and young children's social and cognitive development. *Child Development, 64*(5), 1401–1417. [10]

Meltzoff, A. N. (1988a). Infant imitation after a 1-week delay: Long-term mem-

ory for novel acts and multiple stimuli. *Developmental Psychology, 24,* 470–476. [5]

Meltzoff, A. N. (1988b). Infant imitation and memory: Nine-month-olds in immediate and deferred tests. *Child Development, 59,* 217–225. [5] Hillsdale, NJ: Erlbaum.

Meltzoff, A., and Moore, M. (1977). Imitation of facial and manual gestures by human neonates. *Science, 198,* 75–78. [4]

Meltzoff, A. N., and Moore, M. K. (1989). Imitation in newborn infants: Exploring the range of gestures imitated and the underlying mechanisms. *Developmental Psychology, 25*(6), 954–962. [6]

Mendelson, M. J. (1990). *Becoming a brother: A child learns about life, family, and self.* Cambridge, MA: MIT Press. [2]

Menig-Peterson, C. L. (1975). The modification of communicative behavior in preschool-aged children as a function of the listener's perspective. *Child Development, 46,* 1015–1018. [9]

Menn, L., and Stoel-Gammon, C. (1993). Phonological development: Learning sounds and sound patterns. In J. B. Gleason (Ed.), *The development of language* (pp. 65–113). New York: Macmillan. [7]

Merriman, W. E. (1986). Some reasons for the occurrence and eventual correction of children's naming errors. *Child Development, 57,* 942–952. [7]

Milewski, A. E. (1978). Young infants' visual processing of internal and adjacent shapes. *Infant Behavior and Development, 1,* 359–371. [4]

Miller, G. A. (1981). *Language and speech.* San Francisco: Freeman. [7]

Miller, K. (1984). Child as the measure of all things: Measurement procedures and the development of quantitative concepts. In C. Sophian (Ed.), *Origins of cognitive skills.* Hillsdale, NJ: Erlbaum. [9]

Miller, K., and Stigler, J. W. (1987). Counting in Chinese: Cultural variation in a basic cognitive skill. *Cognitive Development, 2,* 297–305. [9]

Miller, P., and Eisenberg, N. (1988). The relation of empathy to aggressive and externalizing/antisocial behavior. *Psychological Bulletin, 103,* 324–344. [10]

Miller, P. H. (1985). Metacognition and attention. In D. L. Forest, M. Pressley, G. E. MacKinnon, and T. G. Waller (Eds.), *Metacognition, cognition, and human performance* (Vol. 2). New York: Academic Press. [9]

Miller, P. H. (1990). The development of strategies of selective attention. In D. F. Bjorklund (Ed.), *Children's strategies: Contemporary views of cognitive development.* Hillsdale, NJ: Erlbaum. [7]

Miller, P. H., and Harris, Y. R. (1990). Preschoolers' strategies of attention on a same-different task. *Developmental Psychology, 24,* 628–633. [9]

Miller, S. A., Shelton, J., and Flavell, J. H. (1970). A test of Luria's hypothesis concerning the development of self-regulation. *Child Development, 41,* 651–665. [10]

Miller-Jones, D. (1989). Culture and testing. *American Psychologist, 44,* 360–366. [11]

Millstein, S. G., and Litt, I. F. (1990). Adolescent health. In S. S. Feldman and G. R. Elliott (Eds.), *At the threshold: The developing adolescent* (pp. 431–456). Cambridge, MA: Harvard University Press. [14]

Minuchin, P. (1985). Families and individual development: Provocations from the field of family therapy. *Child Development, 56,* 289–302. [2]

Minuchin, P. (1988). Relationships within the family: A systems perspective on development. In Robert A. Hinde and J. Stevenson-Hinde (Eds.), *Relationships within families* (pp. 7–26). Oxford, Eng.: Oxford University Press. [Pt. 4 Epilogue, 15]

Minuchin, S. (1974). *Families and family therapy.* Cambridge, MA: Harvard University Press. [15]

Minuchin, S., Rosman, B., and Baker, L. (1978). *Psychosomatic anorexia nervosa in context.* Cambridge, MA: Harvard University Press. [15]

Mira, M., and Cairns, G. (1981). Intervention in the interaction of a mother and child with nonorganic failure to thrive. *Pediatric Nursing, 7,* 41–45. [6]

Mischel, H., and Mischel, W. (1983). The development of children's knowledge of self-control strategies. *Child Development, 54,* 603–619. [8]

Mischel, W., Shoda, Y., and Rodriguez, M. (1989). Delay of gratification in children. *Science, 244,* 933–937. [10, Pt. 4 Epilogue, 12]

Mize, J., and Ladd, G. (1990). A cognitive-social learning approach to social skill training with low-status preschool children. *Developmental Psychology, 26,* 388–398. [10]

Modell, J., and Goodman, M. (1990). Historical perspectives. In S. S. Feldman and G. R. Elliott (Eds.), *At the threshold: The developing adolescent* (pp. 93–122). Cambridge, MA: Harvard University Press. [13]

Moely, B. E., Olson, F. A., Halwes, T. G., and Flavell, J. H. (1969). Production deficiency in young children's clustered recall. *Developmental Psychology, 1,* 26–34. [11]

Moffitt, A. (1971). Consonant cue perception by twenty- to twenty-four-week-old infants. *Child Development, 42,* 717–782. [6]

Moffitt, A. R. (1973). Intensity discrimination and cardiac reaction in young infants. *Developmental Psychology, 8,* 357–359. [4]

Molfese, D. L., Molfese, V. J., and Carrell, P. L. (1982). Early language development. In B. B. Wolman (Ed.), *Handbook of developmental psychology.* Englewood Cliffs, NJ: Prentice-Hall. [7]

Molitor, N., Joffe, L., Barglow, P., Benveniste, R., and Vaughn, B. (1984, April). *Biochemical and psychological antecedents of newborn performance on the Neonatal Behavioral Assessment Scale.* Paper presented at the International Conference on Infant Studies, New York. [3, 6]

Money, J. (1975). Alblatiopenis: Normal male infant sex-reassigned as a girl. *Archives of Sexual Behavior, 4,* 65–72. [10]

Money, J., and Ehrhardt, A. A. (1972). *Man and woman, boy and girl.* Baltimore: Johns Hopkins University Press. [3]

Montemayor, R., Adams, G., and Gullotta, T. (Eds.). (1990). *From childhood to adolescence.* Newbury Park, CA: Sage. [14]

Montemayor, R., and Brownlee, J. (1986). *The mother-adolescent relationship in early and middle adolescence: Differences in maternal satisfaction.* Paper presented at the Society for Research on Adolescence, Madison, WI. [14]

Montemayor, R., and Eisen, M. (1977). The development of self-conceptions from childhood to adolescence. *Developmental Psychology, 13,* 314–319. [14]

Montemayor, R., and Hanson, E. (1985). A naturalistic view of conflict between adolescents and their parents and siblings. *Journal of Early Adolescence, 5,* 23–30. [14]

Montgomery, D. E. (1991). *Young children's understanding of interpretational diversity between different-aged listeners.* Paper presented at the meeting of the Society for Research in Child Development, Seattle. [9]

Moore, J. (1989). Is there an Hispanic underclass? *Journal of Social Science Quarterly, 70,* 265–284. [12]

Moore, K. L. (1974). *Before we are born.* Philadelphia: Saunders. [3]

Morelli, G. A., Rogoff, B., Oppenheim, D., and Goldsmith, D. (1992). Cultural variation in infants' sleeping arrangements: Questions of independence. *Developmental Psychology, 28,* 604–613. [2, 6]

Morgan, J. L. (1986). *From simple input to complex grammar.* Cambridge, MA: MIT Press. [7]

Morgan, J. L., and Travis, L. L. (1989). Limits on negative information in language input. *Journal of Child Language, 16,* 531–552. [7]

Morrison, P., and Masten, A. (1991). Peer reputation in middle childhood as a predictor of adaptation in adolescence: A seven-year follow-up. *Child Development, 62,* 991–1007. [12]

Morrongiello, B. A., and Fenwick, K. D. (1991). Infant's coordination of auditory and visual depth information. *Journal of Experimental Child Psychology, 52,* 277–296. [4]

Morrongiello, B. A., and Rocca, P. T. (1990). Infants' localization of sounds within hemifields: estimates of minimum audible angle. *Child Development, 61,* 1258–1270. [4]

Mory, M. S. (1992, March). *"Love the ones you're with": Conflict and consensus in adolescent peer group stereotypes.* Paper presented at the biennial meeting of the Society for Research on Adolescence, Washington, DC. [14]

Moses, L. J., and Flavell, J. H. (1990). Inferring false beliefs from actions and reactions. *Child Development, 61,* 929–945. [9]

Mosher, F. A., and Hornsby, J. R. (1966). On asking questions. In J. S. Bruner, R. Olver, and P. M. Greenfield (Eds.), *Studies in cognitive growth.* New York: Wiley. [11]

Moshman, D., and Timmons, M. (1982). The construction of logical necessity. *Human Development, 25,* 309–323. [11]

Motti, E. (1986). *Patterns of behaviors of preschool teachers with children of varying developmental history.* Unpublished predoctoral dissertation, University of Minnesota. [10]

Mueller, E., and Cooper, C. (1986). *Process and outcome in peer relationships.* New York: Academic Press. [8]

Mueller, E., and Lucas, T. (1975). A developmental analysis of peer interaction among toddlers. In M. Lewis and L. A. Rosenblum (Eds.), *Friendship and peer relations.* New York: Wiley. [10]

Mugny, G., Perret-Clermont, A. N., and Doise, W. (1981). Interpersonal coordinations and sociological differences in the construction of the intellect. In G. M. Stephenson and J. M. Davis (Eds.), *Progress in applied social psychology* (Vol. 1). New York: Wiley. [11]

Mullis, I., Owens, E., Phillips, G., and Jenkins, L. (1991). *The state of mathematics achievement: NAEP's 1990 assessment of the nation and the trial assessment of the states.* Princeton, NJ: Educational Testing Service. [11]

Munroe, R. L., and Munroe, R. H. (1975). *Cross-cultural human development.* Monterey, CA: Brooks/Cole. [2]

Murphy, L. (1988). *Working together,* No. 17. San Ramon: The Child Development Project. [12]

Murray, F. B. (1972). The acquisition of conservation through social interaction. *Developmental Psychology, 6,* 1–6. [11]

Murray, F. B. (1981). The conservation

paradigm. In D. Brodzinsky, I. Sigel, and R. Golinkoff (Eds.), *New direction in Piagetian research and theory.* Hillsdale, NJ: Erlbaum. [11]

Musick, J. S. (1993). *Young, poor, and pregnant: The psychology of teenage motherhood.* New Haven: Yale University Press. [2]

Musick, J. S. (1994). Capturing the child-rearing context. *SRCD Newsletter,* Fall, *1,* 6–7. [2]

Myers, N. A., Clifton, R. K., and Clarkson, M. G. (1987). When they were very young: Almost threes remember two years ago. *Infant Behavior and Development, 10,* 123–132. [5]

Myles-Worsley, M., Cromer, C. C., and Dodd, D. H. (1986). Children's preschool script construction: Reliance on general knowledge as memory fades. *Developmental Psychology, 22,* 22–30. [9]

Nakagawa, M., Teti, D., and Lamb, M. (1992). An ecological study of child-mother attachments among Japanese sojourners in the United States. *Developmental Psychology, 28,* 584–592. [2, 10]

National Research Council. (1993). *Understanding child abuse and neglect.* Washington, DC: National Academy Press. [8]

Neimark, E. D. (1982). Adolescent thought: Transition to formal operations. In B. B. Wolman and G. Strickler (Eds.), *Handbook of developmental psychology.* Englewood Cliffs, NJ: Prentice-Hall. [13]

Neisser, U. (1976). General, academic, and artificial intelligence. In L. Resnick (Ed.), *The nature of intelligence* (pp. 135–144). Hillsdale, NJ: Erlbaum. [11]

Nelson, C. (1994). The neural bases of infant temperament. In J. Bates and T. Wachs (Eds.), *Temperament: Individual differences at the interface of biology and behavior.* Washington DC: American Psychological Association Press. [6]

Nelson, K. (1973). Structure and strategy in learning to talk. *Monographs of the Society for Research in Child Development, 38.* [7]

Nelson, K. (1981). Experimental gambits in the service of language acquisition theory. In S. Kuczaj (Ed.), *Language development: Syntax and semantics.* Hillsdale, NJ: Erlbaum. [7]

Nelson, K. (1983). The derivation of concepts and categories from event representations. In E. Scholnick (Ed.), *New trends in conceptual representation* (pp. 129–156). Hillsdale, NJ: Erlbaum. [7]

Nelson, K. (1985). *Making sense: The acquisition of shared meaning.* New York: Academic Press. [7]

Nelson, K., and Gruendel, J. (1979). At morning it's lunchtime: A scriptal view of children's dialogues. *Discourse Processes, 2,* 73–94. [9]

Nelson-LeGall, S., and Jones, E. (1990). Cognitive-motivational influences on the task-related, help-seeking behavior of black children. *Child Development, 61,* 581–589. [12]

New, R. S. (1988). Parental goals and Italian infant care. In R. A. LeVine, P. M. Miller, and M. M. West (Eds.), *Parental behavior in diverse societies. New Directions for Child Development* (No. 40, pp. 51–63). [7]

Newberger, C., Melnicoe, L., and Newberger, E. (1986). The American family in crisis: Implications for children. *Current Problems in Pediatrics, 16,* 674–721. [2]

Newcomb, A., Brady, J., and Hartup, W. (1979). Friendship and incentive condition as determinants of children's task-oriented social behavior. *Child Development, 50,* 878–881. [12]

Newcombe, N., Dubas, J. S., and Baenninger, M. (1989). Associations of timing of puberty, spatial ability, and lateralization in adult women. *Child Development, 60,* 246–254. [13]

Newman, C. G. H. (1986). The thalidomide syndrome: Risks of exposure and spectrum of malformations. *Clinics in Perinatology, 13,* 555–573. [3]

Newmann, F. M. (1991). Higher order thinking in the teaching of social studies: Connections between theory and practice. In D. Perkins, J. Segal, and J. Voss (Eds.), *Informal reasoning and education.* Hillsdale, NJ: Erlbaum. [13]

Newport, E. H., Gleitman, H., and Gleitman, L. R. (1977). Mother, I'd rather do it myself: Some effects and noneffects of maternal speech style. In C. E. Snow and C. A. Furguson (Eds.), *Talking to children: Language input and acquisition.* Cambridge, Eng.: Cambridge University Press. [7]

Newport, E. L. (1982). Task specificity in language learning? Evidence from speech perception and American Sign Language. In E. Wanner and L. R. Gleitman (Eds.), *Language acquisition: The state of the art* (pp. 450–486). Cambridge, Eng.: Cambridge University Press. [7]

Newport, E. L. (1988). Constraints on learning and their role in language acquisition. *Language Sciences, 10,* 147–172. [7]

Newsom, J., and Newsom, E. (1974). *Cultural aspects of child-rearing in the English-speaking world.* Cambridge, Eng.: Cambridge University Press. [2]

Norcia, A. M., and Tyler, C. W. (1985). Spatial frequency sweep VEP: Visual acuity during the first year of life. *Vision Research, 25,* 1399–1408. [4]

Nordhaus, B., and Solnit, A. (1990). Adoption, 1990. *Zero to three. National Center for Clinical Infant Programs, 10,* No. 5, 1–4. [2, 6]

Norton, A. J., and Glick, P. C. (1986). One parent families: A social and economic profile. *Family Relations, 35,* 9–18. [2]

Novak, M., O'Neill, P., Beckley, S., and Suomi, S. (1992). Naturalistic environments for captive primates. In E. Gibbons, E. Wyers, and E. Waters (Eds.), *Naturalistic habitats in captivity.* New York: Academic Press. [6]

Nyitii, R. M. (1982). The validity of "cultural differences explanations" for cross-cultural variation in the rate of Piagetian cognitive development. In D. A. Wagner and H. W. Stevenson (Eds.), *Cultural perspectives on child development* (pp. 146–165). San Francisco: Freeman. [11]

Oakes, L. M., and Cohen, L. B. (1990). Infant perception of a causal event. *Cognitive Development, 5,* 193–207. [5]

O'Connor, B. P., and Nikolic, J. (1990). Identity development and formal operations as sources of adolescent egocentrism. *Journal of Youth and Adolescence, 19,* 149–158. [13]

Oettingen, G., Little, T., Lindenberger, U., and Baltes, P. (1994). Causality, agency, and control beliefs in East versus West Berlin children: A natural experiment of the role of context. *Journal of Personality and Social Psychology, 66,* 579–595. [12]

Offer, D., and Offer, J. (1975). *From teenage to young manhood.* New York: Basic Books. [14]

Olds, D. L., Henderson, C. R., Jr., Chamberlain, R., and Tatelbaum, R. (1986). Preventing child abuse and neglect: A randomized trial of nurse home visitation. *Pediatrics, 78,* 65–78. [6]

Olds, D. L., Henderson, C., and Tatelbaum, R. (1994). Intellectual impairment in children of women who smoke cigarettes during pregnancy. *Pediatrics, 93,* 221–227. [3]

O'Leary, K. D., and O'Leary, S. (1977). *Classroom management: The successful use of behavior modification* (2nd ed.). New York: Pergamon Press. [15]

Oller, D. K., and Eilers, R. (1988). The role of audition in babbling. *Child Development, 59,* 441–449. [7]

Olsen-Fulero, L. (1982). Style and stability in mother conversational behavior: A study of individual differences. *Journal of Child Language, 9,* 543–564. [7]

Olsho, L. W., Schoon, C., Sakai, R., Turpin, R., and Sperduto, V. (1982). Preliminary data on frequency discrimination in infancy. *Journal of the Acoustical Society of America, 71,* 509–511. [4]

Olson, G., and Sherman, T. (1983). Attention, learning, and memory in infants. In P. H. Mussen (Ed.), *Handbook of child psychology* (Vol. 3, 4th ed.): M. M. Haith and J. J. Campos (Eds.), *Infancy and developmental psychobiology.* New York: Wiley. [4, 5]

Ornstein, P. A., Naus, M. J., and Stone, B. P. (1977). Rehearsal training and developmental differences in memory. *Developmental Psychology, 13,* 15–24. [11]

Osherson, D. N., and Markman, E. M. (1975). Language and the ability to evaluate contradictions and tautologies. *Cognition, 2,* 213–226. [13]

Oski, F. A., DeAngelis, C. D., Feigin, R. D., McMillan, J. A., and Warshaw, J. B. (Eds.). (1994). *Principles and practice of pediatrics* (2nd ed.). Philadelphia: Lippincott. [3]

Oster, H., Hegley, D., and Nagel, L. (1992). Adult judgments and fine-grained analyses of infant facial expressions: Testing the validity of *a priori* coding formulas. *Developmental Psychology, 28,* 1115–1131. [6]

Palermo, D. S. (1978). *Psychology of language.* Glenview, IL: Scott, Foresman [7]

Pancake, V. R. (1988). *Quality of attachment in infancy as a predictor of hostility and emotional distance in preschool peer relationships.* Unpublished doctoral dissertation, University of Minnesota, Minneapolis. [10]

Papini, D., and Sebby, R. (1987). Adolescent pubertal status and affective family relationships: A multi-variate assessment. *Journal of Youth and Adolescence, 16,* 1–15. [13]

Papoušek, H. (1959). A method of studying conditioned food reflexes in young children up to the age of six months. *Pavlov Journal of Higher Nervous Activities, 9,* 136–140. [5]

Papoušek, H. (1967a). Conditioning during early postnatal development. In Y. Brackbill and G. G. Thompson (Eds.), *Behavior in infancy and early childhood.* New York: Free Press. [5]

Papoušek, H. (1967b). Experimental studies of appetitional behavior in human newborns and infants. In H. W. Stevenson, E. H. Hess, and H. L. Rheingold (Eds.), *Early behavior.* New York: Wiley. [4]

Papoušek, H. (1969). Individual variability in learned responses in human infants. In R. J. Robinson (Ed.), *Brain and early behavior.* New York: Academic Press. [2]

Papoušek, H., Papoušek, M., and

Koester, L. (1986). Sharing emotionality and sharing knowledge: A microanalytic approach to parent-infant communication. In C. Izard and P. Read (Eds.), *Measuring emotion in infants and young children* (pp. 93–122). New York: Cambridge University Press. [6]

Papoušek, M., Papoušek, H., and Bornstein, M. H. (1985). The naturalistic vocal environment of young infants: On the significance of homogeneity and variability in parental speech. In T. Field and N. Fox (Eds.), *Social perception in infants.* Norwood, NJ: Ablex. [7]

Paris, S. G. (1975). Integration and inference in children's comprehension and memory. In F. Restle, R. Shiffrin, J. Castellan, H. Lindman, and D. Pisoni (Eds.), *Cognitive theory* (Vol. 1). Hillsdale, NJ: Erlbaum. [11]

Paris, S. G., and Upton, L. (1976). Children's memory for inferential comprehension. *Child Development, 47,* 660–668. [11]

Park, K., and Hazan, C. (1990, July). *Correlates of attachment security and self-worth in middle childhood.* Paper presented at the International Conference on Personal Relationships, Oxford, England. [12]

Parke, R. D., Cassidy, J., Burks, V. M., Carson, J. L., and Boyum, L. (1992). Familial contribution to peer competence among young children: The role of interactive and affective processes. In R. D. Parke and G. W. Ladd (Eds.), *Family-peer relationships: Modes of linkage* (pp. 107–134). Hillsdale, NJ: Erlbaum. [2]

Parke, R. and Ladd, G. (1992). *Family-peer relationships: Modes of linkage.* Hillsdale, NJ: Erlbaum. [12]

Parke, R., and Stearns, P. (1993). Fathers and child rearing: A historical analysis. In G. Elder, Jr., J. Modell, and R. D. Parke (Eds.), *Children in time and place: Developmental and historical insights.* New York: Cambridge University Press. [2,8]

Parker, J., and Asher, S. (1987). Peer relations and later social adjustment. *Psychological Bulletin, 102,* 357–389. [15]

Parker, J., and Asher, S. (1993). Friendship and friendship quality in middle childhood: Links with peer group acceptance and feelings of loneliness and social dissatisfaction. *Developmental Psychology, 29,* 611–621. [12]

Parritz, R. H. (1989). *An examination of toddler coping in three challenging situations.* Unpublished doctoral dissertation, University of Minnesota, Minneapolis. [8]

Parsons, J., Adler, T., and Kaczala, C. (1982). Socialization of achievement attitudes and beliefs: Parental influences. *Child Development, 53,* 310–321. [11, 14]

Parsons, T., and Bales, R. (1955). *Family socialization and interaction process.* London: Free Press. [2]

Pascual-Leone, J. (1970). A mathematical model for the transition rule in Piaget's developmental stages. *Acta Psychologica, 32,* 301–345. [5]

Pascual-Leone, J. (1970). A mathematical model for the transition rule in Piaget's developmental stages. *Acta Psychologica, 32,* 301–345. [5]

Patterson, C. J. (in press). Lesbian mothers, gay fathers, and their children. In A. R. D'Augelli and C. J. Patterson (Eds.), *Lesbian, gay, and bisexual identities across the lifespan: Psychological perspectives.* New York: Oxford University Press. [2]

Patterson, G., and Capaldi, D. (1991). Antisocial parents: Unskilled and vulnerable. In P. Cowan and E. M. Hetherington (Eds.), *Family transitions* (pp. 195–218). Hillsdale, NJ: Erlbaum. [12]

Patterson, G. R., and Dishion, T. J. (1988). A mechanism for transmitting the antisocial trait across generations. In R. Hinde and J. Stevenson-Hinde (Eds.), *Relations between relationships within families.* Oxford, Eng.: Oxford University Press. [2, 8, 14, 15]

Patterson, S. J., Sochting, I., and Marcia, J. E. (1992). The inner space and beyond: Women and identity. In G. R. Adams, T. P. Gullotta, and R. Montemayor (Eds.), *Adolescent identity formation* (pp. 9–24). Newbury Park, CA: Sage. [14]

Peal, E., and Lambert, W. E. (1962). The relation of bilingualism to intelligence. *Psychological Monographs, 76,* 1–23. [7]

Pearson, J., and Thoennes, N. (1990). Custody after divorce: Demographic and attitudinal patterns. *American Journal of Orthopsychiatry, 60,* 233–249. [12]

Pearson, J. L., Hunter, A. G., Ensminger, M. E., and Kellam, S. G. (1990). Black grandmothers in multigenerational households: Diversity in family structure and parenting involvement in the Woodlawn community. *Child Development, 61,* 434–442. [2]

Pederson, F., Anderson, B., and Cain, R. (1977). *An approach to understanding linkages between the parent, infant, and spouse relationships.* Paper presented at the Society for Research in Child Development, New Orleans. [Pt. 4 Epilogue]

Peill, E. J. (1975). *Invention and the discovery of reality.* New York: Wiley. [9]

Peloquin, L., and Klorman, R. (1986). Effects and methylphenidate on normal children's mood, event-related potentials, and performance in memory scanning and vigilance. *Journal of Abnormal Psychology, 95,* 88–98. [15]

Pennington, B., and Welsh, M. (1995).

Neuropsychology and developmental psychopathology. In D. Cicchetti and D. Cohen (Eds.), *Developmental processes and psychopathology* (Vol. 1). New York: Cambridge University Press. [15]

Perlmutter, M., and Myers, N. A. (1979). Development of recall in 2- to 4-year-old children. *Developmental Psychology, 15*, 73–83. [9]

Peskin, H. (1973). Influence of the developmental schedule of puberty on learning and ego functioning. *Journal of Youth and Adolescence, 2*, 273–290. [13]

Peters, A. M. (1985). Language segmentation: Operating principles for the perception and analysis of language. In D. I. Slobin (Ed.), *The crosslinguistic study of language acquisition: Vol. 2. Theoretical issues* (pp. 1029–1064). Hillsdale, NJ: Erlbaum. [7]

Petersen, A. (1979, May). Can puberty come any earlier? *Psychology Today,* pp. 45–47. [13]

Petersen, A. (1985). Pubertal development as a cause of disturbance: Myths, realities, and unanswered questions. *Genetic, Social, and General Psychology Monographs, 111*, 205–232. [13]

Petersen, A. (1986, April). *Early adolescence: A critical developmental transition?* Paper presented at the annual meeting of the American Educational Research Association, San Francisco. [14]

Petersen, A. C. (1987). The nature of biological-psychosocial interactions: The sample case of early adolescence. In R. M. Lerner and T. T. Foch (Eds.), *Biological-psychosocial interactions in early adolescence* (pp. 35–61). Hillsdale, NJ: Erlbaum. [13]

Petitto, L. (1991). Modularity and constraints in early lexical acquisition. In M. Gunnar and M. Maratsos (Eds.), *Minnesota Symposium on Child Psychology* (Vol. 25). Hillsdale, NJ: Erlbaum. [2, 7]

Petitto, L. (1992). Modularity and constraints in early lexical acquisition: Evidence from children's early language and gesture. In M. R. Gunnar and M. Maratsos (Eds.), *Modularity and constraints in language and cognition. The Minnesota Symposia on Child Psychology* (Vol. 25, pp. 25–58). Hillsdale, NJ: Erlbaum. [7]

Pezdek, K. (1980). Life-span differences in semantic integration of pictures and sentences in memory. *Child Development, 51*, 720–729. [11]

Pezdek, K., and Miceli, L. (1982). Life-span differences in memory integration as a function of processing time. *Developmental Psychology, 18*, 485–490. [11]

Phillips, S. U. (1983). *The invisible culture: Communication in classroom and community on the Warm Springs Indian Reservation.* New York: Longman. [11]

Piaget, J. (1930/1969). *The child's conception of physical causality.* Totowa, NJ: Littlefield, Adams [9]

Piaget, J. (1932/1965). *The moral judgment of the child.* New York: Free Press. [13]

Piaget, J. (1952). *The child's conception of number.* New York: Humanities Press. [4, 6, 7, 9]

Piaget, J. (1962). *Play, dreams, and imitation in childhood.* New York: Norton. [4, 5]

Piaget, J. (1970). Piaget's theory. In P. H. Mussen (Ed.), *Carmichael's manual of child psychology.* New York: Wiley. [9]

Piaget, J. (1972). Intellectual evolution from adolescence to adulthood. *Human Development, 15*, 1–12. [13]

Piaget, J., and Inhelder, B. (1973). *Memory and intelligence.* New York: Basic Books. [11]

Pianta, R., Egeland, B., and Erickson, M. (1989). The effects of maltreatment on the development of young children. In D. Cicchetti and V. Carlson (Eds.), *Child maltreatment.* New York: Cambridge University Press. [8, 10]

Pianta, R., Egeland, B., and Sroufe, L. A. (1990). Maternal stress and children's development: Prediction of school outcomes and identification of protective factors. In J. Rolf, A. Masten, D. Cicchetti, K. Neuchterlein, and S. Weintraub (Eds.), *Risk and protective factors in the development of psychopathology.* New York: Cambridge University Press. [2]

Pianta, R. C., Sroufe, L. A., and Egeland, B. (1989). Continuity and discontinuity in maternal sensitivity at 6, 24, and 42 months in a high-risk sample. *Child Development, 60*, 481–487. [8]

Pianta, R., and Steinberg, M. (1992). Teacher-child relationships and the process of adjusting to school. In R. Pianta (Ed.), *Beyond the parent: The role of other adults in children's lives. New directions for child development* (pp. 61–80). San Francisco: Jossey-Bass. [10, 12]

Piers, M. (1978). *Infanticide.* New York: Norton. [2]

Pinker, S. (1987). The bootstrapping problem in language acquisition. In B. MacWhinney (Ed.), *Mechanisms of language acquisition* (pp. 399–441). Hillsdale, NJ: Erlbaum. [7]

Pitt, R. B. (1983). Development of a general problem-solving schema in adolescence and early adulthood. *Journal of Experimental Psychology—General, 112*, 547–584. [13]

Plomin, R. (1989). Environment and genes. *American Psychologist, 44*, 105–111. [1, 2]

Plomin, R. (1990). Nature and nurture: An introduction to human behavioral genetics. Pacific Grove, CA: Brooks/Cole. [3]

Plomin, R., and Daniels, D. (1987). Why are children in the same family so different from one another? *Behavioral and Brain Sciences, 10*, 1–59. [1]

Plomin, R., Emde, R., Braungart, J., Campos, J., Corley, R., Fulker, D., Kagan, J., Reznick, J. S., Robinson, J., Zahn-Waxler, C., and DeFries, J. (1993). Genetic change and continuity from fourteen to twenty months: The MacArthur Longitudinal Twin Study. *Child Development, 64*, 1354–1376. [6]

Plomin, R., Nitz, K., and Rowe, D. C. (1990). Behavioral genetics and aggressive behavior in childhood. In M. Lewis and S. M. Miller (Eds.), *Handbook of developmental psychopathology* (pp. 119–134). New York: Plenum Press. [15]

Plunkett, J., Meisels, S., Stiefel, G., Pasicke, P., and Roloff, D. (1986). Patterns of attachment among preterm infants of varying biological risk. *Journal of the American Academy of Child Psychiatry, 25*, 794–800. [6, 8]

Posner, J., and Vandell, D. (1994). Low-income children's after-school care: Are there beneficial effects of after-school programs? *Child Development, 65*, 440–456. [12]

Power, T., and Chapieski, M. (1986). Childrearing and impulse control in toddlers: A naturalistic investigation. *Developmental Psychology, 22*, 271–275. [8]

Power, T., and Manire, S. (1992). Child rearing and internalization: A developmental perspective. In J. Janssen and J. Gerris (Eds.): Influences on *Child rearing and moral prosocial development.* Amsterdam: Swets and Zeitlinger. [10]

Powers, S., Hauser, S., and Kilner, L. (1989). Adolescent mental health. *American Psychologist, 44*, 220–208. [14]

Powers, S., Hauser, S., Schwartz, J., Noam, G., and Jacobson, A. (1983). Adolescent ego development and family interaction. In H. Grotevant and C. Cooper (Eds.), *Adolescent development in the family.* San Francisco: Jossey-Bass. [14]

Pratt, C., and Bryant, P. (1990). Young children understand that looking leads to knowing (so long as they are looking in a single barrel). *Child Development, 61*, 973–982. [9]

Prechtl, H., and Beintema, D. (1964). *Clinics in developmental medicine: No. 12. The neurological examination of the full-term newborn infant.* London, Eng.: Heinemann. [4]

Premack, D. (1986). *Gavagai! or the future history of the animal language controversy.* Cambridge, MA: MIT Press. [7]

Prinz, R., Foster, S., Kent, R., and O'Leary, K. D. (1979). Multivariate assessment of conflict in distressed and nondistressed mother-adolescent dyads. *Journal of Applied Behavioral Analysis, 12,* 691–700. [14]

Provence, S. (1989). Infants in institutions revisited. *Zero to Three, 9,* 1–4. [2, 6]

Quay, H. (1986). Conduct disorders. In H. Quay and J. Werry (Eds.), *Psychopathological disorders of childhood* (3rd ed.). New York: Wiley (pp. 35–72). [15]

Quinton, D., Rutter, M., and Gulliver, L. (1990). Continuities in psychiatric disorders from childhood to adulthood in the children of psychiatric patients. In L. Robins and M. Rutter (Eds.), *Straight and devious pathways from childhood to adulthood* (pp. 259–278). Cambridge, Eng.: Cambridge University Press. [15]

Quinton, D., Rutter, M., and Liddle, C. (1984). Institutional rearing, parenting difficulties, and marital support. *Psychological Medicine, 14,* 107–124. [2]

Rabiner, D., and Coie, J. (1989). Effect of expectancy inductions on rejected children's acceptance by unfamiliar peers. *Developmental Psychology, 25,* 450–457. [12]

Radke-Yarrow, M., Richters, J., and Wilson, W. E. (1988). Child development in a network of relationships. In R. Hinde and J. Stevenson-Hinde (Eds.), *Relations between relationships within families.* Oxford, Eng.: Oxford University Press. [2, 12]

Radke-Yarrow, M., and Zahn-Waxler, C. (1984). Roots, motives, and patterns in children's pro-social behavior. In E. Staub, D. Bartal, J. Karylowski, and J. Reykowski (Eds.), *The development and maintenance of pro-social behaviors.* New York: Plenum Press. [10]

Ramey, C. T., and Campbell, F. A. (1979). Compensatory education for disadvantaged children. *School Review, 87,* 171–289. [11]

Ramey, C. T., and Haskins, R. (1981). The modification of intelligence through early experience. *Intelligence, 5,* 5–19. [11]

Ramey, C. T., Starr, R., Pallas, J., Whitten, C., and Reed, V. (1979). Nutrition, response-contingent stimulation, and the maternal-deprivation syndrome: Results of an early intervention program. *Merrill-Palmer Quarterly, 21,* 45–53. [6]

Ratner, N. B. (1985). *Cues which mark clause boundaries in mother–child speech.* Paper presented at the meeting of the American Speech-Language Hearing Association, Washington, DC. [7]

Reich, P. A. (1976). The early acquisition

of word meaning. *Journal of Child Language, 3,* 117–123. [7]

Renkin, B., Egeland, B., Marvinney, D., Sroufe, L. A., and Mangelsdorf, S. (1989). Early childhood antecedents of aggression and passive-withdrawal in early elementary school. *Journal of Personality, 57*(2), 257–281. [2, 15]

Renshaw, P., and Brown, P. (1993). Loneliness in middle childhood: Concurrent and longitudinal predictors. *Child Development, 64,* 1271–1284. [12]

Resnick, L. B. (1986). *Education and learning to think.* Washington, DC: National Research Council. [13]

Resnick, L. B. (1993). *Inventing arithmetic: Making children's intuition work in school.* Paper presented at the 28th Minnesota Symposium on Child Psychology, Minneapolis. [11]

Resnick, L. B., Siegel, S. W., and Kresh, E. (1971). Transfer and sequence in learning double-classification skills. *Journal of Experimental Child Psychology, 11,* 139–149. [11]

Rest, J. (1979). *Development in judging moral issues.* Minneapolis: University of Minnesota Press. [13]

Rest, J. (1983). Morality. In P. H. Mussen (Ed.), *Handbook of child psychology* (Vol. 3, 4th ed.): J. H. Flavell and E. M. Markman (Eds.), *Cognitive development.* New York: Wiley. [13]

Rheingold, H. (1956). The modification of social responsiveness in institutional babies. *Monographs of the Society for Research in Child Development, 21* (Serial No. 63). [6]

Rheingold, H. (1983, May). *Two-year-olds chart an optimistic future.* Paper presented at the Harvard Medical School Conference on Affective Development in Infancy, Boston. [8]

Rheingold, H. L., and Eckerman, C. O. (1971). Departures from the mother. In H. R. Schaffer (Ed.), *The origins of human social relations.* New York: Academic Press. [8]

Richards, M., Boxer, A., Petersen, A., and Albrecht, R. (1990). Relation of weight to body image in pubertal girls and boys from two communities. *Developmental Psychology, 26,* 313–321. [13]

Richman, A. M., Miller, P. M., and LeVine, R. A. (1992). Cultural and educational variations in maternal responsiveness. *Developmental Psychology, 28,* 614–621. [6]

Ricks, M. (1985). The social transmission of parental behavior: Attachment across generations. In I. Bretherton and E. Waters (Eds.), *Growing points in attachment theory and research. Monographs of the Society for Research in Child Development, 50* (Serial No. 209), 211–227. [6]

Riley, C. A., and Trabasso, T. (1974). Comparatives, logical structures, and

encoding in a transitive inference task. *Journal of Experimental Child Psychology, 45,* 972–977. [9]

Robb, M., and Mangelsdorf, S. (1987). *Sibling relationships in school-age children. Differences in play as a function of sex composition and maternal behavior.* Paper presented at the biennial meeting of the Society for Research in Child Development, Baltimore. [2]

Robins, L. (1966). *Deviant children grown up.* Baltimore: Williams and Wilkins. [15, Pt. 7 Epilogue]

Robins, L. (1978). Sturdy childhood predictors of adult antisocial behavior: Replications from longitudinal studies. *Psychological Medicine, 8,* 611–622. [15]

Robins, L., and Price, R. (1991). Adult disorders predicted by childhood conduct problems: Results from the NIMH epidemiologic catchment area project. *Psychiatry, 54,* 116–132. [15]

Robins, L., and Rutter, M. (1990). *Straight and devious pathways from childhood to adulthood.* Cambridge, Eng.: Cambridge University Press. [15]

Robinson, J. L., Kagan, J., Reznick, S. J., and Corley, R. (1992). The heritability of inhibited and uninhibited behavior: A twin study. *Developmental Psychology, 28*(6), 1030–1037. [8]

Rode, S., Chang, P., Fisch, R., and Sroufe, L. A. (1981). Attachment patterns of infants separated at birth. *Developmental Psychology, 17,* 188–191. [6]

Rodning, C., Beckwith, L., and Howard, J. (1989). Characteristics of attachment organization and play organization in prenatally drug-exposed toddlers. *Development and Psychopathology, 1,* 227–289. [3, 6, 8]

Roffwarg, H. P., Muzio, J. N., and Dement, W. C. (1966). Ontogenetic development of the human sleep-dream cycle. *Science, 152,* 604–619. [4]

Rogoff, B. (1990). *Apprenticeship in thinking: Cognitive development in social context.* New York: Oxford University Press. [5, 8, 11]

Rogoff, B., Mistry, J., Goncu, A., and Moiser, C. (1993). Guided participation in cultural activity by toddlers and caregivers. *Monographs of the Society for Research in Child Development, 58* (Serial No. 236). [8]

Rogoff, B., and Morelli, G. (1989). Perspectives on children's development from cultural psychology. *American Psychologist, 44,* 343–348. [2]

Rogosch, F. A., and Newcomb, A. F. (1989). Children's perceptions of peer reputations and their social reputations among peers. *Child Development, 60,* 597–610. [12]

Rohwer, W. D., Jr. (1973). Elaboration and learning in childhood and adolescence. In H. W. Reese (Ed.), *Advances in child development and behavior* (Vol. 8). New York: Academic Press. [11]

Root, A. W. (1973). Endocrinology of puberty: Normal sexual maturation. *Journal of Pediatrics, 83*, 187–200. [13]

Rose, S. A., and Wallace, I. F. (1985). Visual recognition memory: A predictor of later cognitive functioning in preterms. *Child Development, 56*, 843–852. [5]

Rosen, W. D., Adamson, L. B., and Bakeman, R. (1992). An experimental investigation of infant social referencing: Mothers' messages and gender differences. *Developmental Psychology, 28*(6), 1172–1178. [8]

Rosenberg, D. M. (1984). *The quality and content of preschool fantasy play: Correlates in concurrent social-personality function and early mother-child attachment relationships.* Unpublished doctoral dissertation, University of Minnesota. [10]

Rosenblith, J., and Sims-Knight, J. (1985). *In the beginning: Development in the first two years.* Belmont, CA: Brooks/Cole. [5]

Rosser, R. (1994). *Cognitive development: Psychological and biological perspectives.* Boston: Allyn & Bacon. [9, 11]

Rothbart, M. (1986). Longitudinal observation of infant temperament. *Developmental Psychology, 22*, 356–365. [8]

Rothbart, M. (1989). Temperament in childhood: A framework. In G. Kohnstamm, J. Bates, and M. Rothbart (Eds.), *Temperament in childhood* (pp. 59–73). New York: Wiley. [6, 8]

Rovee-Collier, C. (1979). *Reactivation of infant memory.* Paper presented at the biennial meeting of the Society for Research in Child Development, San Francisco. [5]

Rovee-Collier, C. (1989). The joy of kicking: Memories, motives, and mobiles. In P. R. Solomon, G. R. Goethals, C. M. Kelley, and B. R. Stephens (Eds.), *Memory: Interdisciplinary approaches.* New York: Springer-Verlag. [5]

Rovee-Collier, C. (1993). The capacity for long-term memory in infancy. *Current Directions in Psychological Science, 2*(4), 130–135. [4, 5]

Rovee-Collier, C., and Gekoski, M. J. (1979). The economics of infancy: A review of conjugate reinforcement. In H. W. Reese and L. P. Lipsitt (Eds.), *Advances in child development and behavior* (Vol. 13). New York: Academic Press. [4]

Rovee-Collier, C., and Hayne, H. (1987). Reactivation of infant memory: Implications for cognitive development. In H. W. Reese (Ed.), *Advances in child development and behavior* (Vol. 20). New York: Academic Press. [5]

Rovee-Collier, C., Sullivan, M. W., Enright, M., Lucas, D., and Fagan, J.

W. (1980). Reactivation of infant memory. *Science, 208*, 1159–1161. [5]

Ruben, S. E., and Nelson, L. B. (1993). Amblyopia diagnosis and management. *Pediatric Clinics of North America, 40*, 727–735. [4]

Rubin, K., Chin, X., and Hymel, S. (1993). Socioemotional characteristics of withdrawn and aggressive children. *Merrill-Palmer Quarterly, 39*, 518–534. [12]

Rubin, K., LeMare, L., and Lollis, S. (1990). Social withdrawal in childhood: Developmental pathways to peer rejection. In S. Asher and J. Coie (Eds.), *Peer rejection in childhood* (pp. 217–249). Cambridge, Eng.: Cambridge University Press. [10]

Rubin, Z. (1980). *Children's friendships.* Cambridge, MA: Harvard University Press. [12]

Ruble, D. (1983). The development of social comparison processes and their role in achievement-related self-socialization. In T. Higgins, D. Ruble and W. Hartup (Eds.), *Social cognitive development.* Cambridge, Eng.: Cambridge University Press. [10, 12]

Ruble, D. (1988). Sex role development. In M. Bornstein and M. Lamb (Eds.), *Developmental psychology: An advanced textbook* (2nd ed., pp. 411–460). Hillsdale, NJ: Erlbaum. [10]

Ruch, J., and Shirley, J. (1985, March). *"Genie" as an adult.* Presentation at the Center for Advanced Study in the Behavioral Sciences, Stanford, Calif. [2]

Ruff, H. A., Lawson, K. R., Parrinello, R., and Weissberg, R. (1990). Long-term stability of individual differences in sustained attention in the early years. *child Development, 61*, 60–75. [8]

Rush, D., and Callahan, K. R. (1989). Exposure to passive cigarette smoking and child development: A critical review. *Annals of the New York Academy of Sciences, 562*, 74–100. [3]

Russell, G., Szmukler, G., Dare, C., and Eisler, I. (1987). An evaluation of family therapy in anorexia nervosa and bulimia nervosa. *Archives of General Psychiatry, 44*, 1047–1056. [15]

Russell, J. (1981). Children's memory for the premises in a transitive measurement task assessed by elicited and spontaneous justification. *Journal of Experimental Child Psychology, 31*, 300–309. [9]

Rutter, M. (1979a). Maternal deprivation 1972–1978: New findings, new concepts, new approaches. *Child Development, 50*, 283–305. [15]

Rutter, M. (1979b). Protective factors in children's responses to stress and disadvantage. In M. Kent and J. Rolf (Eds.), *Primary prevention of psychopathology: Vol. III. Social competence in*

children. Hanover, NH: University Press of New England. [15]

Rutter, M. (1981). Epidemiological-longitudinal approaches to the study of development. In W. A. Collins (Ed.), *Minnesota Symposia on Child Psychology,* (Vol. 15). Hillsdale, NJ: Erlbaum. [12]

Rutter, M. (1983a). School effects on pupil progress: Research findings and policy implications. *Child Development, 54*, 1–29. [2]

Rutter, M. (1983b). The developmental psychopathology of depression: Issues and perspectives. In M. Rutter, C. Izard, and P. Read (Eds.), *Depression in childhood.* New York: Guilford Press. [15]

Rutter, M. (1985). Infantile autism. In D. Schaffer, A. Ehrhardt, and L. Greenhill (Eds.), *The clinical guide to child psychiatry* (pp. 49–78). New York: Free Press. [15]

Rutter, M. (1988). Functions and consequences of relationships: Some psychopathological considerations. In R. Hinde and J. Stevenson-Hinde (Eds.), *Towards understanding families.* Oxford, Eng.: Oxford University Press. [2, 6]

Rutter, M. (1991). Nature, nurture, and psychopathology: A new look at an old topic. *Development and Psychopathology, 3*, 125–136. [15]

Rutter, M., Grahan, P., Chadwick, O., and Yule, W. (1976). Adolescent turmoil: Fact or fiction? *Journal of Child Psychology and Psychiatry, 17*, 35–56. [14]

Rutter, M., Quinton, D., and Hill, J. (1990). Adult outcome of institution-reared children: Males and females compared. In L. Robins and M. Rutter (Eds.), *Straight and devious pathways from childhood to adulthood* (pp. 135–157). Cambridge, Eng.: Cambridge University Press. [6]

Rymer, R. (1993). *Genie: An abused child's flight from silence.* New York: HarperCollins. [2]

Sackett, G. P. (1968). Abnormal behavior in laboratory research rhesus monkeys. In M. Fox (Ed.), *Abnormal behavior in animals.* Philadelphia: Saunders. [6]

Sadker, M., and Sadker, D. (1984). *Final report: Promoting effectiveness in classroom instruction.* Washington, DC: National Institute of Education. [11]

Sadker, M., and Sadker, D. (1994). *Failing at fairness: How America's schools cheat girls.* New York: Scribner's. [2]

Sagi, A., van IJzendoorn, M., Aviezer, O., Donnell, F., and Mayseless, O. (1994). Sleeping out of home in a kibbutz communal arrangement. *Child Development, 65*. [6]

Salapatek, P., and Banks, M. (1967). Infant sensory assessment: Vision. In F. Minifie and L. Lloyd (Eds.), *Commu-*

nicative and cognitive abilities—Early behavioral assessment. Baltimore: University Park Press. [6]

Salapatek, P., and Kessen, W. (1966). Visual scannings of triangles by the human newborn. *Journal of Experimental Child Psychology, 3,* 155–167. [4]

Salzinger, S., Kaplan, S., and Artemyeff, C. (1983). Mothers' personal social networks and child maltreatment. *Journal of Abnormal Psychology, 92,* 68–76. [2]

Sameroff, A. J., and Chandler, M. (1975). Reproductive risk and the continuum of caretaking casualty. In F. D. Horowitz (Ed.), *Child development research* (Vol. 4). Chicago: University of Chicago Press. [2, 8]

Sameroff, A., and Fiese, B. (1989). Transactional regulation and early intervention. In S. J. Meisels and J. Shonkoff (Eds.), *Early intervention: A handbook of theory, practice, and analysis.* New York: Cambridge University Press. [2, 15]

Sampson, R., and Laub, J. (1994). Urban poverty and the family context of delinquency: A new look at structure and process in a classic study. *Child Development, 65,* 523–540. [14]

Samuels, C. A., and Ewy, R. (1985). Aesthetic perception of faces during infancy. *British Journal of Developmental Psychology, 3,* 221–228. [4]

Sander, L. W. (1975). Infant and caretaking environment. In E. J. Anthony (Ed.), *Explorations in child psychiatry.* New York: Plenum Press. [6, 8, 10]

Sandven, K., and Resnick, M. (1990). Informal adoption among black adolescent mothers. *American Journal of Orthopsychiatry, 60,* 210–224. [2]

Satterfield, J., and Schell, A. (1987). Therapeutic interventions to prevent delinquency in hyperactive boys. *Journal of the American Academy of Child and Adolescent Psychiatry, 26,* 56–64. [15]

Sauer, M. (1993, August 29). Decade of accusations. *San Diego Union Tribune,* pp. D1–D3. [9]

Savage-Rumbaugh, E. S., Murphy, J., Sevcik, R. A., Brakke, K. E., Williams, S. L., and Rumbaugh, D. M. (1993). Language comprehension in ape and child. *Monographs of the Society for Research in Child Development, 58* (3–4, Serial No. 233). [7]

Savin-Williams, R. (1990). *Gay and lesbian youth.* New York: Hemisphere. [14]

Savin-Williams, R., and Berndt, T. (1990). Peer relations during adolescence. In S. S. Feldman and G. R. Elliott (Eds.), *At the threshold: The developing adolescent.* Cambridge, MA: Harvard University Press. [14]

Saxe, G. B. (1982). Developing forms of arithmetic operations among the Oksapmin of Papua New Guinea. *Developmental Psychology, 18*(4), 583–594. [9]

Saywitz, K. J., Goodman, G. S., Nicholas, E., and Moan, S. F. (1991). Children's memories of a physical examination involving genital touch: Implications for reports of child sexual abuse. *Journal of Consulting and Clinical Psychology, 59,* 682–691. [9]

Scanlon-Jones, S., and Raag, T. (1989). Smile production in older infants: The importance of a social recipient for the facial signal. *Child Development, 60,* 811–818. [8]

Scarr, S. (1992). Developmental theories for the 1990s: Development and individual differences. *Child Development, 63,* 1–19. [8, 11]

Scarr, S., and McCartney, K. (1983). How people make their own environments: A theory of genotype-environment effects. *Child Development, 54,* 425–435. [1, 2]

Scarr, S., Phillips, D., and McCartney, K. (1990). Facts, fantasies and the future of child care in the United States. *American Psychological Society 1*(1), 26–35. [6]

Scarr, S., and Weinberg, R. A. (1983). The Minnesota adoption studies: Malleability and genetic differences. *Child Development, 34,* 260–267. [11]

Schaffer, H. R., and Callender, M. (1959). Psychological effects of hospitalization in infancy. *Pediatrics, 24,* 528–539. [6]

Schank, R. C., and Abelson, R. (1977). *Scripts, plans, goals, and understanding.* Hillsdale, NJ: Erlbaum. [9]

Schiedel, D. G., and Marcia, J. E. (1985). Ego identity, intimacy, sex role orientation, and gender. *Developmental Psychology, 18,* 149–160. [14]

Schieffelin, B. B. (1990). *The give and take of everyday life: Language socialization of Kaluli children.* New York: Cambridge University Press. [7]

Schiff, A., and Knopf, I. (1985). The effects of task demands on attention allocation in children of different ages. *Child Development, 56,* 621–630. [13]

Schleidt, M., and Genzel, C. (1990). The significance of mother's perfume for infants in the first weeks of their life. *Ethology and Sociobiology, 11,* 145–154. [4]

Schneider, W., and Pressley, M. (1989). *Memory development between 2 and 20.* New York: Springer-Verlag. [11]

Schneider-Rosen, K., and Wenz-Gross, M. (1990). Patterns of compliance from eighteen to thirty months of age. *Child Development, 61,* 104–112. [8]

Schore, A. N. (1994). *Affect regulation and the origin of the self: The neurobiology of emotional development.* Hillsdale, NJ: Erlbaum. [1, 2, 4, 6, 8, Pt. 3 Epilogue]

Schulman-Galambos, C., and Galambos, R. (1979). Brainstem-evoked response

audiometry in newborn hearing screening. *Archives of Otolaryngology, 105,* 86–90. [4]

Schwartz, A., Campos, J., and Baisel, E. (1973). The visual cliff: Cardiac and behavioral correlates on the deep and shallow sides at 5 and 9 months of age. *Journal of Experimental Child Psychology, 15,* 85–99. [6]

Schwartz, D., Dodge, K., and Coie, J. (1993). The emergence of chronic peer victimization in boy's play groups. *Child Development, 64,* 1755–1772. [10, 12]

Schwartz, P. (1983). Length of day-care attendance and attachment behavior in eighteen-month-old infants. *Child Development, 54,* 1073–1078. [6]

Schweinhart, L. J., and Weikart, D. P. (1993, November). Success by empowerment: The High/Scope Perry Preschool Study through age 27. *Young Children,* pp. 54–58. [10]

Schweinhart, L. J., Weikart, D. P., and Larner, M. (1986). Consequences of three preschool curriculum models through age 15. *Early Childhood Research Quarterly, 1,* 15–45. [10]

Scribner, S. (1986). Thinking in action: Some characteristics of practical thought. In R. K. Wagner and R. J. Sternberg (Eds.), *Practical intelligence* (pp. 13–30). New York: Cambridge University Press. [11]

Sears, R. R., Maccoby, E. E., and Levin, H. (1957). *Patterns of child rearing.* Evanston, IL: Row, Peterson. [10]

Segal, J., and Yahres, H. (1978, November). Bringing up mother. *Psychology Today,* pp. 92–96. [8]

Seitz, V., and Provence, S. (1990). Caregiver-focused models of early intervention. In S. Meisels and J. Shonkoff (Eds.), *Handbook of early childhood intervention* (pp. 400–427). Cambridge, Eng.: Cambridge University Press. [6]

Select Committee on Children, Youth and Families, U. S. House of Representatives (1989). *U.S. children and their families: Current conditions.* Washington, DC: U.S. Government Printing Office. [2]

Seligman, M. E. P. (1970). On the generality of the laws of learning. *Psychological Review, 77,* 406–418. [4]

Selman, R. (1980). *The growth of interpersonal understanding.* New York: Academic Press. [12, 14]

Serbin, L. A., Powlishta, K. K., and Gulko, J. (1993). The development of sex typing in middle childhood. *Monographs of the Society for Research in Child Development, 58*(2, Serial No. 232). [10, 12]

Shaffer, D. R. (1985). *Developmental psychology: Theory, research, and applications.* Monterey, CA: Brooks/Cole. [3]

Shannon, R. (1989). Detection of gaps in

sinusoeds and pulse trains by patients with cochlear implants. *Journal of the Acoustical Society of America, 85,* 2587–2592. [4]

Shantz, C. U. (1975). The development of social cognition. In E. M. Hetherington (Ed.), *Review of child development research* (Vol. 3). Chicago: University of Chicago Press. [9]

Shantz, C., and Hobart, C. (1989). Social conflict and development: Peers and siblings. In T. Berndt and G. Ladd (Eds.), *Peer relationships and child development* (pp. 71–94). New York: Wiley. [10]

Shapiro, E. G., and Rosenfeld, A. (1987). *The somatizing child: Diagnosis and treatment of conversion and somatization disorders.* New York: Springer-Verlag. [15]

Sharabany, R., Gershoni, R., and Hofman, J. (1981). Girlfriend, boyfriend: Age and sex differences in intimate friendship. *Developmental Psychology, 17,* 800–808. [14]

Shatz, M. (1978). The relation between cognitive processes and the development of communication skills. In C. B. Keasy (Ed.), *Nebraska Symposium on Motivation, 1977.* Lincoln: University of Nebraska Press. [5, 9]

Shatz, M., and Gelman, R. (1973). The development of communication skills: Modifications in the speech of young children as a function of listening. *Monographs of the Society for Research in Child Development, 38* (5, Serial No. 152). [7, 9]

Shatz, M., and O'Reilly, A. W. (1990). Conversational or communicative skill? A reassessment of two-year-olds' behaviour in miscommunication episodes. *Journal of Child Language, 17,* 131–146. [7]

Shayer, M. (1980). Piaget and science education. In S. Modgil and C. Modgil (Eds.), *Towards a theory of psychological development.* Windsor, Can.: NFER Publishing Co. [13]

Shayer, M., and Adey, P. (1992). Accelerating the development of formal thinking in middle and high school students III: Testing the permanency of effects. *Journal of Research in Science Teaching, 29,* 1101–1115. [13]

Shayer, M., and Adey, P. (1993). Accelerating the development of formal thinking in middle and high school students IV: Three years after a two-year intervention. *Journal of Research in Science Teaching, 30,* 351–366. [13]

Shaywitz, B., and Shaywitz, S. (1989). Learning disabilities and attention disorders. In K. Swaiman (Ed.), *Pediatric neurology* (Vol. 2, pp. 857–894). St. Louis: Mosby. [15]

Shea, J. D. (1985). Studies of cognitive development in Papua New Guinea. *International Journal of Psychology, 20,* 33–61. [13]

Sherif, M., Harvey, O., White, B., Hood, W., and Sherif, C. (1961). *Intergroup conflict and cooperation: The Robbers Cave experiment.* Norman: University of Oklahoma Press. [12]

Sherif, M., and Sherif, C. (1953). *Groups in harmony and tension.* New York: Harper & Row. [12]

Shore, C. (1986). Combinatorial play, conceptual development, and early multi-word speech. *Developmental Psychology, 22,* 184–190. [7]

Shrum, W., and Cheek, N. H. (1987). Social structure during the school years: Onset of the degrouping process. *American Sociological Review, 52,* 218–223. [14]

Shrum, W., Cheek, N. H., and Hunter, R. C. (1988). Friendship in the school: Gender and racial homophily. *Sociology of Education, 61,* 227–239. [11]

Shulman, L. P., Elias, S., Phillips, O. P., Grevengood, C., Dungan, J. S., and Simpson, J. L. (1994). Amniocentesis performed at 14 weeks' gestation or earlier: Comparison with first-trimester transabdominal chorionic villus sampling. *Obstetrics and Gynecology, 83*(4), 543–548. [3]

Shulman, S., Elicker, J., and Sroufe, L. A. (1994). Stages of friendship growth in preadolescence as related to attachment history. *Journal of Social and Personal Relationships, 11,* 341–361. [12]

Shultz, T. R., and Zigler, E. (1970). Emotional concomitants of visual mastery in infants: The effects of stimulus movement on smiling and vocalizing. *Journal of Experimental Child Psychology, 10,* 390–402. [6]

Shweder, R. (in press). Reflections on culture, development, and the 29th Minnesota Symposium. *Minnesota Symposia on Child Psychology* (Vol. 29). Hillsdale, NJ: Erlbaum. [2]

Siegel, M., and Share, D. (1990). Contamination sensitivity in young children. *Developmental Psychology, 26,* 455–458. [9]

Siegler, R. S. (1978). The origins of scientific reasoning. In R. S. Siegler (Ed.), *Children's thinking: What develops?* Hillsdale, NJ: Erlbaum. [13]

Siegler, R. S. (1981). Developmental sequences within and between concepts. *Monographs of the Society for Research in Child Development, 46* (2, Serial No. 189). [11]

Siegler, R. S. (1986). *Children's thinking* (2nd ed.). Englewood Cliffs, NJ: Prentice-Hall. [1, 5]

Siegler, R. S. (1991). *Children's thinking* (3rd ed.). Englewood Cliffs, NJ: Prentice-Hall. [9]

Siegler, R. S., and Robinson, M. (1982). The development of numerical understandings. In H. W. Reese and L. P. Lipsett (Eds.), *Advances in child develop-*

ment and behavior (Vol. 16). New York: Academic Press. [11]

Silverberg, S. B., and Steinberg, L. (1990). Psychological well-being of parents with early adolescent children. *Developmental Psychology, 26,* 658–666. [14]

Silverman, I., and Ragusa, D. (1990). Child and maternal correlates of impulse control in 24-month-old children. *Genetic Psychology Monographs, 116,* 435–473. [8]

Siminoff, E., McGuffin, P., and Gottesman, I. (1994). Genetic influences on normal and abnormal development. In M. Rutter, E. Taylor, and L. Hersov (Eds.), *Child and adolescent psychiatry* (pp. 129–151). London: Blackwell. [3]

Simmons, R., and Blyth, D. (1988). *Moving into adolescence: The impact of pubertal change and school context.* New York: Aldine/Hawthorne. [13, 14]

Simmons, R. G., Blyth, D. A., and McKinney, K. L. (1983). The social and psychological effects of puberty on white females. In J. Brooks-Gunn and A. C. Petersen (Eds.), *Girls at puberty* (pp. 229–272). New York: Plenum Press. [13]

Simmons, R. G., Carlton-Ford, S. L., and Blyth, D. A. (1987). Predicting how a child will cope with the transition to junior high school. In R. M. Lerner and T. T. Foch (Eds.), *Biological-psychosocial interactions in early adolescence* (pp. 325–375). Hillsdale, NJ: Erlbaum. [13]

Simmons, R., Rosenberg, F., and Rosenberg, M. (1973). Disturbance in the self-image at adolescence. *American Sociological Review, 38,* 553–568. [14]

Simons, R. L., Lorenz, F. O., Conger, R. D., and Wu, C. (1992). Support from spouse as mediator and moderator of the disruptive influence of economic strain on parenting. *Child Development, 63,* 1282–1301. [2]

Simons, R. L., Whitbeck, L. B., Conger, R. D., and Wu, C. (1991). Intergenerational transmission of harsh parenting. *Developmental Psychology, 27,* 159–171. [2]

Singer, L., Brodzinsky, D., Ramsay, D., Steir, M., and Waters, E. (1985). Mother-infant attachment in adoptive families. *Child Development, 56,* 1543–1551. [6]

Sinnott, J. M., Pisoni, D. B., and Aslin, R. N. (1984). A comparison of pure tone auditory thresholds in human infants and adults. *Infant Behavior and Development, 6,* 3–17. [4]

Skinner, B. F. (1957). *Verbal behavior.* New York: Appleton-Century-Crofts. [7]

Skinner, E. A. (1990). Development and perceived control: A dynamic model of action in context. *Minnesota Symposia on Child Psychology* (Vol. 23, pp. 167–216). Hillsdale, NJ: Erlbaum. [12]

Skodak, M., and Skeels, H. M. (1949). A final follow-up study of one-hundred adopted children. *Journal of Genetic Psychology, 75,* 85–125. [11]

Skuse, D. (1985). Nonorganic failure to thrive: A reappraisal. *Archives of Disease in Childhood, 60,* 173–178. [6]

Slater, A. (1989). Visual memory and perception in early infancy. In A. Slater and G. Bremner (Eds.), *Infant development.* Hillsdale, NJ: Erlbaum. [4]

Slater, A., Morrison, V., and Rose, D. (1984). Habituation in the newborn. *Infant Behavior and Development, 7,* 183–200. [5]

Slater, A., Morison, V., Somers, M., Mattock, A., Brown, E., and Taylor, D. (1990). Newborn and older infants' perception of partly occluded objects. *Infant Behavior and Development, 13,* 33–49. [5]

Slaughter-Defoe, D. T., Nakagawa, K., Takanishi, R., and Johnson, D. (1990). Toward cultural/ecological perspectives on schooling and achievement in African- and Asian-American children. *Child Development, 61,* 363–383. [11]

Slavin, R. E. (1987). Developmental and motivational perspectives on cooperative learning: A reconciliation. *Child Development, 58,* 1161–1167. [2]

Slavin, R. E. (1990). Comprehensive cooperative learning models: Embedding cooperative learning in the curriculum and school. In S. Shlomo (Ed.), *Cooperative learning: Theory and research.* New York: Praeger. [11]

Sleek, S. (1994, April). Bilingualism enhances student growth. *Monitor of the American Psychological Association,* pp. 48–49. [7]

Slobin, D. I. (1970). Universals of grammatical development in children. In G. B. Flores d'Arcais and W. J. Levelt (Eds.), *Advances in psycholinguistics* (pp. 178–179). Amsterdam: North-Holland. [7]

Slobin, D. I. (1982). Universal and particular in the acquisition of language. In E. Wanner and L. R. Gleitman (Eds.), *Language acquisition: The state of the art* (pp. 128–170). Cambridge, Eng.: Cambridge University Press. [7]

Slobin, D. I. (1985). *The crosslinguistic study of language acquisition: Vol. 2. Theoretical issues.* Hillsdale, NJ: Erlbaum. [7]

Small, S., Cornelius, S., and Eastman, G. (1983). *Parenting adolescent children: A period of storm and stress?* Paper presented at the annual meeting of the American Psychological Association, Anaheim, CA. [14]

Smeeding, T. M., and Torrey, B. B. (1988). Poor children in rich countries. *Science, 242,* 873–877. [2]

Smetana, J. (1988). Concepts of self and social convention: Adolescents' and parents' reasoning about hypothetical and actual family conflicts. In M. Gunnar and W. A. Collins (Eds.), *Minnesota Symposia on Child Psychology* (Vol. 21, pp. 79–122). Hillsdale, NJ: Erlbaum. [14]

Smetana, J. G. (1989). Toddlers' social interactions in the context of moral and conventional transgressions in the home. *Developmental Psychology, 25*(4), 499–508. [8]

Smetana, J., Killen, M., and Turiel, E. (1991). Children's reasoning about interpersonal and moral conflicts. *Child Development, 62,* 629–644. [12]

Smetana, J. G., Schlagman, N., and Adams, P. W. (1993). Preschool children's judgments about hypothetical and actual transgressions. *Child Development, 64*(1), 202–214. [10]

Smirnova, Y. (1990). Personal communication. [6]

Smith, D. W., and Wilson, A. A. (1973). *The child with Down syndrome (mongolism).* Philadelphia: Saunders. [3]

Smith, E. A. (1989). A biosocial model of adolescent sexual behavior. In G. R. Adams, R. Montemayor, and T. P. Gullotta (Eds.), *Biology of adolescent behavior and development* (pp. 143–167). Newbury Park, CA: Sage. [13]

Smith, M. E. (1926). An investigation of the development of the sentence and the extent of vocabulary in young children. *University of Iowa Studies in Child Welfare, 3*(5). [7]

Snarey, J. R. (1985). Cross-cultural universality of social-moral development: A critical review of Kohlbergian research. *Psychological Bulletin, 97,* 202–232. [13]

Snow, C. E. (1972). Mother's speech to children learning language. *Child Development, 43,* 549–565. [7]

Snow, C. E. (1977). The development of conversation between mothers and babies. *Journal of Child Language, 4,* 1–22. [7]

Snow, C. E. (1993). Bilingualism and second language acquisition. In J. B. Gleason and N. B. Ratner (Eds.), *Psycholinguistics* (pp. 392–416). Ft. Worth: Harcourt Brace Jovanovich. [7]

Solomon, F. (1988). *Homelessness, health and human needs.* Washington, DC: National Academy Press. [2]

Sommer, K., et al. (1993). Cognitive readiness and adolescent parenting. *Developmental Psychology, 29,* 389–398. [2]

Sones, G., and Feshbach, N. (1971). Sex differences in adolescent reactions toward newcomers. *Developmental Psychology, 4,* 381–386. [14]

Sorce, J., Emde, R., and Klinnert, M. (1981). *Maternal emotional signaling: Its effect on the visual cliff behavior of one-year-olds.* Paper read at the meeting of the Society for Research in Child Development, Boston. [8]

Sostek, A. M., and Anders, T. F. (1981). The biosocial importance and environmental sensitivity of infant sleep-wake behaviors. In K. Bloom (Ed.), *Prospective issues in infancy research.* Hillsdale, NJ: Erlbaum. [4]

Spangler, G., and Grossmann, K. (1993). Biobehavioral organization in securely and insecurely attached infants. *Child Development, 64,* 1439–1450. [6]

Spearman, C. (1927). *The abilities of man.* New York: Macmillan. [11]

Speidel, G. E., and Nelson, K. E. (1989). *The many faces of imitation in language learning.* New York: Springer. [7]

Spelke, E. S. (1985). Perception of unit, persistence, and identity: Thoughts on infants' conceptions of objects. In J. Mehler and R. Fox (Eds.), *Neonate Cognition.* Hillsdale, NJ: Erlbaum. [5]

Spelke, E. S. (1988). The origins of physical knowledge. In L. Weiskrantz (Ed.), *Thought without language.* New York: Clarendon Press. [5]

Spencer, M. B., and Markstrom-Adams, C. (1990). Identity processes among racial and ethnic minority children in America. *Child Development, 61,* 290–310. [14]

Spiker, D., Ferguson, J., and Brooks-Gunn, J. (1993). Enhancing maternal interactive behavior and child social competence in low birth weight, premature infants. *Developmental Psychology, 64,* 754–768. [5, 6, 8]

Spitz, R. A. (1945). Hospitalism: An inquiry into the genesis of psychiatric conditions in early childhood. *Psychoanalytic Study of the Child, 1,* 53–74. [2]

Spitz, R., Emde, R., and Metcalf, D. (1970). Further prototypes of ego formation. *Psychoanalytic Study of the Child, 25,* 417–444. [4]

Spivack, G., Marcus, J., and Swift, M. (1986). Early classroom behaviors and later misconduct. *Developmental Psychology, 22,* 123–131. [12]

Sprinthall, N., and Collins, W. A. (1988). *Adolescent psychology* (2nd ed.). New York: Addison-Wesley. [2]

Sprinthall, N. A., and Collins, W. A. (1995). *Adolescent psychology: A developmental view* (3rd ed.). New York: McGraw-Hill. [14]

Sroufe, J. (1991). Assessment of parent-adolescent relationships: Implications for adolescent development. *Journal of Family Psychology, 5,* 21–45. [14]

Sroufe, L. A. (1977). Wariness of strangers and the study of infant development. *Child Development, 48,* 731–746. [6]

Sroufe, L. A. (1979a). Socioemotional development. In J. Osofsky (Ed.), *Handbook of infant development.* New York: Wiley. [Pt. 3 Epilogue]

Sroufe, L. A. (1979b). The coherence of individual development. *American Psychologist, 34*, 834–841. [6, Pt. 4 Epilogue]

Sroufe, L. A. (1983). Infant-caregiving attachment and patterns of adaptation and competence. In M. Perlmutter (Ed.), *Minnesota Symposia on Child Psychology* (Vol. 16). Hillsdale, NJ: Erlbaum. [10, 15]

Sroufe, L. A. (1985). Attachment classification from the perspective of infant-caregiver relationships and infant temperament. *Child Development, 56*, 1–14. [6]

Sroufe, L. A. (1988). The role of infant-caregiver attachment in development. In J. Belsky and T. Nezworski (Eds.), *Clinical implications of attachment*. Hillsdale, NJ: Erlbaum. [6, 10, Pt. 4 Epilogue]

Sroufe, L. A. (1989). Pathways to adaptation and maladaptation: Psychopathology as developmental deviation. In D. Cicchetti (Ed.), *Rochester Symposia on Developmental Psychopathology* (Vol. 1, pp. 13–40). Hillsdale, NJ: Erlbaum. [15]

Sroufe, L. A. (1990). A developmental perspective on day care. In N. Fox and G. G. Fein (Eds.), *Infant day care: The current debate* (pp. 51–59). Norwood, NJ: Ablex. [6, 10]

Sroufe, L. A. (1991). Considering normal and abnormal together: The essence of developmental psychopathology. *Development and Psychopathology, 2* (pp. 335–347). Cambridge, Eng.: Cambridge University Press. [6, 15]

Sroufe, L. A. (1995). *Emotional development: The organization of emotional life in the early years*. New York: Cambridge University Press. [6, 8, 10]

Sroufe, L. A., Bennett, C., Englund, M., Urban, J., and Shulman, S. (1993). The significance of gender boundaries in preadolescence: Contemporary correlates and antecedents of boundary violation and maintenance. *Child Development, 64*(2), 455–466. [12]

Sroufe, L. A., Carlson, E., and Shulman, S. (1993). The development of individuals in relationships: From infancy through adolescence. In D. C. Funder, R. Parke, C. Tomlinson-Keesey, and K. Widaman (Eds.), *Studying lives through time: Approaches to personality and development* (pp. 315–342). Washington, DC: American Psychological Association. [10, 12, 14]

Sroufe, L. A., Egeland, B., and Kreutzer, T. (1990). The fate of early experience following developmental change: Longitudinal approaches to individual adaptation in childhood. *Child Development, 61*, 1363–1373. [1, 12]

Sroufe, L. A., and Fleeson, J. (1986). Attachment and the construction of relationships. In W. Hartup and Z. Rubin (Eds.), *Relationships and development*. Hillsdale, NJ: Erlbaum. [2, 12, Pt. 5 Epilogue, 15]

Sroufe, L. A., and Fleeson, J. (1988). The coherence of family relationships. In R. A. Hinde and J. Stevenson-Hinde (Eds.), *Relationships within families: Mutual influences* (pp. 27–47). Oxford, Eng.: Oxford University Press. [2, 8, 10, 12, 15]

Sroufe, L. A., Fox, N., and Pancake, V. (1983). Attachment and dependency in developmental perspective. *Child Development, 54*, 1615–1627. [8, 10]

Sroufe, L. A., Jacobvitz, D., Mangelsdorf, S., DeAngelo, E., and Ward, M. J. (1985). Generational boundary dissolution between mothers and their preschool children: A relationship systems approach. *Child Development, 56*, 317–325. [2]

Sroufe, L. A., and Rutter, M. (1984). The domain of developmental psychology. *Child Development, 55*, 17–29. [15]

Sroufe, L. A., Schork, E., Motti, F., Lawroski, N., and LaFreniere, P. (1984). The role of affect in social competence. In C. Izard, J. Kagan, and R. Zajonc (Eds.), *Emotions, cognition, and behavior*. Oxford, Eng.: Oxford University Press. [10]

Sroufe, L. A., and Ward, M. J. (1984). The importance of early care. In D. Quarm, K. Borman, and S. Gideonse (Eds.), *Women in the workplace: The effects on families*. Norwood, NJ: Ablex. [6]

Sroufe, L. A., and Waters, E. (1977). Attachment as an organizational construct. *Child Development, 48*, 1184–1199. [8]

Sroufe, L. A., Waters, E., and Matas, L. (1974). Contextual determinants of infant affective response. In M. Lewis and L. Rosenblum (Eds.), *The origins of fear*. New York: Wiley. [6]

St. James-Roberts, I., and Wolke, D. (1988). Convergence and discrepancies among mothers' and professionals' assessments of difficult neonatal behavior. *Journal of Child Psychology and Psychiatry, 29*, 21–42. [6]

Starkey, P. (1987). Early arithmetic competencies. In A. Klein and P. Starkey (Co-organizers), *Continuities and discontinuities in the development of early numerical cognition*. Symposium conducted at the meeting of the Society for Research in Child Development, Baltimore. [9]

Starkey, P., and Cooper, R. G. (1980). Perception of number by human infants. *Science, 210*, 1033–1035. [5]

Starkey, P., and Gelman, R. (1982). The development of addition and subtraction abilities prior to formal schooling in arithmetic. In T. Carpenter, J. J. Noser, and T. Romberg (Eds.), *Addition and subtraction: A cognitive perspective*. Hillsdale, NJ: Erlbaum. [9]

Starkey, P., Spelke, E. S., and Gelman, R. (1983). Detection of one-to-one correspondence by human infants. *Science, 222*, 179–181. [5]

Stattin, H., and Klackenberg-Larson, I. (1991). The short- and long-term implications for parent–child relations of parents' prenatal preferences for their child's gender. *Developmental Psychology, 27*, 141–147. [2]

Stattin, H., and Magnusson, D. (1990). *Pubertal maturation in female development*. Hillsdale, NJ: Erlbaum. [13]

Steele, S. (1986). Nonorganic failure to thrive: A pediatric social illness. *Issues of Comprehensive Pediatric Nursing, 9*, 47–58. [6]

Stein, A. H., Susser, M., Saenger, G., and Marolla, F. (1975). *Famine and human development: The Dutch hunger winter of 1944/45*. New York: Oxford University Press. [3]

Steinberg, L. (1981). Transformations in family relations at puberty. *Developmental Psychology, 17*, 883–850. [14]

Steinberg, L. (1987). Single parents, step parents and the susceptibility of adolescents to antisocial peer pressure. *Child Development, 58*, 269–275. [13, 14]

Steinberg, L. (1989). Pubertal maturation and parent-adolescent distance: An evolutionary perspective. In G. R. Adams, R. Montemayor, and T. P. Gullotta (Eds.), *Biology of adolescent behavior and development* (pp. 71–97). Newbury Park, CA: Sage. [13]

Steinberg, L. (1990). Autonomy, conflict, and harmony in the family relationship. In S. Feldman and G. Elliot (Eds.), *At the threshold: The developing adolescent* (pp. 255–276). Cambridge, MA: Harvard University Press. [14]

Steinberg, L. (1993). *Adolescence* (3rd ed.). New York: McGraw-Hill. [13, 14]

Steinberg, L., and Dornbusch, S. (1991). Negative correlates of part-time employment during adolescence: Replication and elaboration. *Developmental Psychology, 27*, 304–313. [14]

Steinberg, L., Elmen, J. D., and Mounts, N. S. (1989). Authoritative parenting, psychosocial maturity, and academic success among adolescents. *Child Development, 60*, 1424–1436. [14]

Steinberg, L., and Silverberg, S. (1986). The vicissitudes of autonomy in early adolescence. *Child Development, 57*, 841–851. [14]

Steiner, J. E. (1977). Facial expressions of the neonate infant indicating the hedonics of food-related chemical stimuli. In J. M. Weiffenbach (Ed.), *Taste and development: The genesis of sweet preference*. Washington, DC: U. S. Government Printing Office. [4]

Steinhausen, H. (1994). Anorexia and

bulimia nervosa. In M. Rutter, E. Taylor, and L. Hersov (Eds.), *Child and adolescent psychiatry* (pp. 425–440). London: Blackwell. [15]

Stern, D. N. (1985). *The interpersonal world of the infant.* New York: Basic Books. [6]

Stern, D. N., Spieker, S., and MacKain, K. (1982). Intonation contours as signals in maternal speech to prelinguistic infants. *Developmental Psychology, 18,* 727–735. [7]

Sternberg, R. J. (1985). *Beyond IQ: A triarchic theory of human intelligence.* New York: Cambridge University Press. [11]

Sternberg, R. J., and Nigro, G. (1980). Developmental patterns in the solution of verbal analogies. *Child Development, 51,* 27–38. [13]

Stevenson, H. W. (1990). *Making the grade in mathematics: Elementary school mathematics in the United States, Taiwan, and Japan.* Reston, VA: National Council of Teachers of Mathematics. [2]

Stevenson, H. W. (1993). *Learning from culture.* Paper presented at the 28th Minnesota Symposium on Child Psychology, Minneapolis. [11]

Stevenson, H. W. (1995). Mathematics achievement of American students: First in the world by the year 2000? In C. A. Nelson (Ed.), *Basic and applied perspectives on learning, cognition, and development. Minnesota Symposia on Child Psychology* (Vol. 28). Hillsdale, NJ: Erlbaum. [13]

Stevenson, H. W., Azuma, H., and Hakuta, K. (1986). *Child development and education in Japan.* New York: Freeman. [2]

Stevenson, H. W., and Lee, S. (1990). Contexts of achievement. *Monographs of the Society for Research in Child Development, 55* (1–2, Serial No. 181). [2]

Stevenson, H. W., Lee, S., Chen, C., and Stigler, J. W. (1990). Contexts of achievement: A study of American, Chinese, and Japanese children. *Monographs of the Society for Research in Child Development, 55,* 1–123. [11]

Stevenson, H. W., Lee, S., and Stigler, J. (1986). Achievement in mathematics. In H. W. Stevenson, H. Azuma, and K. Hakuta (Eds.), *Child development and education in Japan.* New York: Freeman. [11]

Stevenson, H. W., Stigler, J. W., and Lee, S. (1986). Achievement in mathematics. In H. W. Stevenson, H. Azuma, and K. Hakuta (Eds.), *Child development and education in Japan* (pp. 201–216). New York: Freeman. [11]

Stevenson, H. W., Stigler, J. W., Lee, S., Lucker, G. W., Kitamura, S., and Hsu, C. (1985). Cognitive performance and academic achievement of Japanese, Chinese, and American children. *Child Development, 56,* 718–734. [11]

Stevenson-Hinde, J. (1990). Temperament and attachment: An eclectic approach. In P. Bateman and P. Marler (Eds.), *Development and integration of behavior.* Cambridge, Eng.: Cambridge University Press. [6]

Stigler, J. W., and Perry, M. (1990). Mathematics learning in Japanese, Chinese, and American classrooms. In J. W. Stigler, R. A. Shweder, and G. Herdt (Eds.), *Cultural psychology* (pp. 328–353). New York: Cambridge University Press. [11]

Stillwell, R., and Dunn, J. (1985). Continuities in sibling relationships: Patterns of aggression and friendliness. *Journal of Child Psychology and Psychiatry, 26,* 627–637. [12]

Stipek, D., Recchia, S., and McClintic, S. (1992). Self-evaluation in young children. *Monographs of the Society for Research in Child Development, 57* (Serial No. 226). [8, 10]

Stocker, C., Dunn, J., and Plomin, R. (1989). Sibling relationships: Links with child temperament, maternal behavior, and family structure. *Child Development, 60,* 715–727. [12]

Stolnick, A. (1981). Married lives: Longitudinal perspectives on marriage. In D. Eichorn, J. Clausen, N. Haan, M. Honzik, and P. Mussen (Eds.), *Present and past in middle life* (pp. 243–265). New York: Academic Press. [2]

Stoneman, Z., and Brody, G. (1993). Sibling temperaments, conflict, warmth, and role asymmetry. *Child Development, 64,* 1786–1800. [12]

Strassberg, Z., Dodge, K., Pettit, G., and Bates, J. (1994). Spanking in the home and children's subsequent aggression toward kindergarten peers. *Development and Psychopathology, 6,* 445–462. [8]

Strauss, M. (1979). Measuring intra-family conflict and violence: The conflict tactics scale. *Journal of Marriage and the Family, 41,* 75–95. [14]

Strayer, J. (1993). Children's concordant emotions and cognitions in response to observed emotions. *Child Development, 64,* 188–201. [12]

Strayer, J., and Schroeder, M. (1989). Children's helping strategies: Influences of emotion, empathy, and age. In N. Eisenberg (Ed.), *Empathy and related emotional responses. New Directions for Child Development* (pp. 85–106). San Francisco: Jossey-Bass. [10]

Streissguth, A. P., Sampson, P. D., and Barr, H. M. (1989). Neurobehavioral dose-response effects of prenatal alcohol exposure in humans from infancy to adulthood. *Annals of the New York Academy of Sciences, 562,* 145–158. [3]

Streitmatter, J. L. (1988). Ethnicity as a mediating variable of early adolescent identity development. *Journal of Adolescence, 11,* 335–346. [14]

Strupp, H., and Binder, J. (1984). *Psychotherapy in a new key: A guide to time limited psychotherapy.* New York: Basic Books. [15]

Suess, G. J., Grossmann, K. E., and Sroufe, L. A. (1992). Effects of infant attachment to mother and father on quality of adaptation in preschool: From dyadic to individual organization of self. *International Journal of Behavioral Development, 15*(1), 43–66. [12]

Sullivan, H. S. (1953). *The interpersonal theory of psychiatry.* New York: Norton. [12, 14]

Sullivan, M. W., Rovee-Collier, C. K., and Tynes, D. M. (1979). A conditioning analysis of infant long-term memory. *Child Development, 50,* 152–162. [5]

Suomi, S. J. (1977). Development of attachment and other social behaviors in rhesus monkeys. In T. Alloway, P. Pliner, and L. Krames (Eds.), *Advances in the study of communication and affect: Vol. 3. Attachment behavior.* New York: Plenum Press. [2, 6]

Suomi, S. J., and Harlow, H. F. (1971). Abnormal social behavior in young monkeys. In J. Helmuth (Ed.), *Exceptional infant* (Vol. 2). New York: Brunner/Mazel. [6]

Suomi, S. J., Harlow, H., and McKinney, W. (1972). Monkey psychiatrists. *American Journal of Psychiatry, 128,* 41–46. [6]

Super, C. M., and Harkness, S. (1972). The infants's niche in rural Kenya and metropolitan America. In L. Adler (Ed.), *Issues in cross-cultural research.* New York: Academic Press. [4]

Susman, A., Waldman, I., Kalkoske, M., and Egeland, B. (1993). *Maternal sensitivity and infant temperament as predictors of attachment classification.* Paper presented at the biennial meeting of the society for Research on Child Development, New Orleans.

Takahashi, K. (1986). Examining the strange situation procedure with Japanese mothers and 12-month-old infants. *Developmental Psychology, 22,* 265–270. [2, 6]

Taeschner, T. (1983). *The sun is feminine: A study on language acquisition in bilingual children.* Berlin: Springer-Verlag. [7]

Tanner, J. M. (1962). *Growth at adolescence.* New York: Lippincott. [13]

Tanner, J. M. (1990). *Foetus into man: Physical growth from conception to maturity.* Cambridge, MA: Harvard University Press. [13]

Tanner, J. M., Whitehouse, R. H., and Takaishi, M. (1966). Standards from birth to maturity for height, weight, height velocity, and weight velocity: British children, 1965. *Archives of Disease in Childhood, 41,* 613–635. [13]

Taussig, H. B. (1962). A study of the German outbreak of phocomelia: The thalidomide syndrome. *Journal of the American Medical Association, 180,* 1106–1114. [3]

Taylor, E. (1994). Syndromes of attention deficit and overactivity. In M. Rutter, E. Taylor, and L. Hersov (Eds.), *Child and adolescent psychiatry* (pp. 285–307). London: Blackwell. [15]

Taylor, M., and Hart, B. (1990). Can children be trained in making the distinction between appearance and reality? *Cognitive Development, 5,* 89–99. [9]

Teller, D. Y., and Bornstein, M. H. (1987). Infant color vision and color perception. In P. Salapatek and L. B. Cohen (Eds.), *Handbook of infant perception* (pp. 185–232). New York: Academic Press. [4]

Tennes, K., Emde, R., Kisley, A., and Metcalf, D. (1972). The stimulus barrier in early infancy: An exploration of some formulations of John Benjamin. In R. Holt and E. Peterfreund (Eds.), *Psychoanalysis and contemporary sciences.* New York: Macmillan. [6]

Teo, A., Carlson, E., Mathieu, P., Egeland, B., and Sroufe, L. A. (in press). A prospective longitudinal study of psychosocial influence on achievement. *Journal of School Psychology.* [10, 12]

Teti, D. M., and Gelfand, D. M. (1991). Behavioral competence among mothers of infants in the first year: The mediational role of maternal self-efficacy. *Developmental Psychology, 62,* 918–929. [6]

Tharp, R. (1989). Psychocultural variables and constants: Effects on teaching and learning. *American Psychologist, 44,* 349–359. [2, 11]

Thelen, E. (1981). Rhythmical behavior in infancy: An ethological perspective. *Developmental Psychology, 17,* 237–257. [4]

Thelen, E. (1986). Treadmill-elicited stepping in seven-month-old infants. *Child Development, 57,* 1498–1506. [4]

Thelen, E., Corbetta, D., Kamm, K., Spencer, J. P., Schneider, K., and Zernicke, R. F. (1993). The transition to reaching: Mapping intention and intrinsic dynamic. *Child Development, 64,* 1058–1098. [4]

Thoma, S. J. (1986). Estimating gender differences in the comprehension and preference of moral issues. *Developmental Review, 6,* 165–180. [13]

Thoman, E. B., and Whitney, M. P. (1989). Sleep states of infants monitored in the home: Individual differences, developmental trends, and origins of cyclicity. *Infant Behavior and Development, 12,* 59–75. [4]

Thomas, A., and Chess, S. (1977). *Temperament and development.* New York: Brunner/Mazel. [2, 6, Pt. 3 Epilogue]

Thomas, A., and Chess, S. (1982). Infant bonding: Mystique and reality. *American Journal of Orthopsychiatry, 52,* 213–222. [2]

Thompson, M. W., McInnes, R. R., and Huntington, F. W. (1991). *Genetics in medicine* (5th ed.). Philadelphia: Saunders. [3]

Thorne, B. (1986). Girls and boys together . . . but mostly apart: Gender arrangements in elementary schools. In W. Hartup and Z. Rubin (Eds.), *Relationships and development.* Hillsdale, NJ: Erlbaum. [12]

Thurstone, L. L. (1938). *Primary mental abilities.* Chicago: University of Chicago Press. [11]

Tienari, P. L., Lahti, I., Sorri, A., Naarala, M., Moring, J., Kaleva, M., Wahlberg, K-E., and Wynne, L. (1990). Adopted away offspring of schizophrenics and controls. In L. Robins and M. Rutter (Eds.), *Straight and devious pathways from childhood to adulthood.* Cambridge, Eng.: Cambridge University Press. [15]

Tobin, J. J., Wu, D. Y. H., and Davidson, D. H. (1989). Preschool in three cultures. New Haven: Yale University Press. [2]

Tobin-Richards, M., Boxer, A., and Petersen, A. (1983). The psychological significance of pubertal change: Sex differences in perceptions of self during early adolescence. In J. Brooks-Gunn and A. Petersen (Eds.), *Girls at puberty: Biological and psychological perspectives* (pp. 127–154). New York: Plenum Press. [13]

Tomasello, M., Conti-Ramsden, G., and Ewert, B. (1990). Young children's conversations with their mothers and fathers: Differences in breakdown and repair. *Journal of Child Language, 17,* 115–130. [7]

Tomasello, M., and Mannle, S. (1985). Pragmatics of sibling speech to one-year-olds. *Child Development, 56,* 911–917. [7]

Tractenberg, S., and Viken, R. (1994). Aggressive boys in the classroom: Biased attributions or shared perceptions. *Child Development, 65,* 829–835. [12]

Tracy, R. L., Lamb, M. E., and Ainsworth, M. D. (1976). Infant approach behavior as related to attachment. *Child Development, 47,* 571–578. [6]

Trevarthan, C. (1977). Descriptive analyses of infant communicative behavior. In H. R. Schaffer (Ed.), *Studies in mother-infant interaction.* New York: Academic Press. [6]

Trickett, P. K., Aber, J. L., Carlson, V., and Cicchetti, D. (1991). Relationship of socioeconomic status to the etiology and developmental sequelae of physical child abuse. *Developmental Psychology, 27*(1), 148–158. [8]

Tronick, E. (1989). Emotions and emotional communication in infants. *American Psychologist, 44,* 112–119. [6]

Tronick, E. Z., Morelli, G. A., and Ivey, P. K. (1992). The Efe forager infant and toddler's pattern of social relationships: Multiple and simultaneous. *Developmental Psychology, 28,* 568–577. [2, 6, 8]

Troy, M., and Sroufe, L. A. (1987). Victimization among preschoolers: Role of attachment relationship history. *Journal of the American Academy of Child and Adolescent Psychiatry, 26,* 166–172. [10]

Truby-King, F. (1937). *Feeding and care of baby* (rev. ed.). Oxford, Eng.: Oxford University Press. [2]

Tulkin, S. R., and Konner, M. J. (1973). Alternative conceptions of intellectual functioning. *Human Development, 16,* 33–52. [13]

Umbel, V. M., Pearson, B. Z., Fernandez, M. C., and Oller, D. K. (1992). Measuring bilingual children's receptive vocabularies. *Child Development, 63,* 1012–1020. [7]

Underwood, M., Coie, J., and Herbsman, C. (1992). Display rules for anger and aggression in school-age children. *Child Development, 63,* 366–380. [12]

Ungerer, J., Brody, L. R., and Zelazo, P. R. (1978). Long-term memory for speech in 2- to 4-week-old infants. *Infant Behavior and Development, 1,* 127–140. [5]

Ungerer, J., Zelazo, P., Kearsley, R., and O'Leary, K. (1981). Developmental changes in the representation of objects in symbolic play from 18 to 34 months of age. *Child Development, 52,* 186–195. [8]

U. S. Bureau of the Census (1994). *Statistical abstract of the United States* (114th ed.). Washington, DC: U.S. Government Printing Office. [2, 7]

Uzgiris, I. C. (1972). Patterns of vocal and gestural imitation in infants. In F. Monks, W. Hartup, and J. de Wit (Eds.), *Determinants of behavioral development.* New York: Academic Press. [4]

Uzgiris, I. C., and Hunt, J. M. (1975). *Assessment in infancy: Ordinal scales of psychological development.* Champaign: University of Illinois Press. [4, 5]

vandenBoom, D. (1989). Neonatal irritability and the development of attachment. In G. Kohnstamm, J. Bates, and M. Rothbart (Eds.), *Temperament in childhood* (pp. 299–318). New York: Wiley. [6]

Van Leishout, C. F. M. (1975). Young children's reactions to barriers placed by their mothers. *Child Development, 46,* 879–886. [10]

Vandell, D. (in press). Child care and the family: Complex contributors to child development. In K. McCarney (Ed.), *New directions in child development*. San Francisco: Jossey-Bass. [6]

Vandell, D., and Ramanan, J. (1991). Children of the National Longitudinal Survey of Youth: Choices in after-school care and child development. *Developmental Psychology, 27,* 637–643. [12]

Vaughn, B. (1978). *The development of greeting behavior in infants from six-to-twelve months of age*. Unpublished doctoral dissertation, University of Minnesota. [6]

Vaughn, B., Bradley, C., Joffe, L., Seifer, R., and Barglow, P. (1987). Maternal characteristics measured prenatally are predictive of ratings of temperamental "difficulty" on the Carey Infant Temperament Questionnaire. *Developmental Psychology, 23,* 152–161. [6]

Vaughn, B., Egeland, B., Waters, E., and Sroufe, L. A. (1979). Individual differences in infant-mother attachment at 12 and 18 months: Stability and change in families under stress. *Child Development, 50,* 971–975. [6, 8, Pt. 4 Epilogue]

Vaughn, B., Gove, F., and Egeland, B. (1980). The relationship between out-of-home care and the quality of infant-mother attachment in an economically deprived population. *Child Development, 51,* 1203–1214. [6]

Vaughn, B. E., Lefever, G. B., Seifer, R., and Barglow, P. (1989). Attachment behavior, attachment security, and temperament during infancy. *Child Development, 60,* 728–737. [6]

Vaughn, B. E., Stevenson-Hinde, J., Waters, E., Kotsaftis, A., Lefever, G. B., Shouldice, A., Trudel, M., and Belsky, J. (1992). Attachment security and temperament in infancy and early childhood: Some conceptual clarifications. *Developmental Psychology, 28,* 463–473. [6]

Vaughn, B. E., and Waters, E. (1980). Social organization among preschool peers: Dominance, attention, and sociometric correlates. In D. Omark, F. Strayer, and D. Freedman (Eds.), *Dominance relations: An ethological view of human conflict and social interaction*. New York: Garland. [10]

Vaughn, B. E., and Waters, E. (1990). Attachment behavior at home and in the laboratory: Q-sort observations and strange situation classifications of one-year-olds. *Child Development, 61,* 1965–1973. [6]

Volterra, V. (1981). Gestures, signs, and words at two years: When does communication become language? *Sign Language Studies, 33,* 351–362. [7]

Volterra, V., and Erting, C. J. (Eds.). (1990). *From gesture to language in hearing and deaf children*. New York: Springer. [7]

Von Hofsten, C. (1977). Binocular convergence as a determinant of reaching behavior in infancy. *Perception, 6,* 139–144. [4]

Vuchinich, S., Bank, L., and Patterson, G. (1992). Parenting, peers, and the stability of antisocial behavior in preadolescent boys. *Developmental Psychology, 28,* 510–521. [12]

Vurpillot, E. (1968). The development of scanning strategies and their relation to visual differentiation. *Journal of Experimental Child Psychology, 6,* 632–650. [9]

Vygotsky, L. S. (1978). *Mind and society*. Cambridge, MA: Harvard University Press. [9]

Waber, D. P. (1977). Sex differences in mental abilities, hemispheric lateralization, and rate of physical growth at adolescence. *Developmental Psychology, 13,* 290–38. [13]

Wachs, T. (1991). Environmental considerations in studies of non-extreme groups. In T. Wachs and R. Plomin (Eds.), *Conceptualization and measurement of organism-environment interaction* (pp. 44–67). Washington; DC: American Psychological Association. [1]

Wachs, T., Bishry, Z., Sobhy, A., McCabe, G., Galal, O., and Shaheen, F. (1993). Relation of rearing environment to adaptive behavior in Egyptian toddlers. *Child Development, 64,* 586–604. [8]

Wachs, T., and Plomin, R. (in press). Organism-environment interaction. Washington, DC: American Psychological Association. [1]

Wachs, T. D., and Gruen, G. (1982). *Early experience and human development*. New York: Plenum Press. [8]

Waddington, C. H. (1957). *The strategy of the genes*. London: Allen and Unwin. [1]

Waddington, C. H. (1966). *Principles of development and differentiation*. New York: Macmillan. [2]

Wagner, R. K., and Sternberg, R. J. (1986). Tacit knowledge and intelligence in the everyday world. In R. K., Wagner and R. J. Sternberg (Eds.), *Practical intelligence* (pp. 51–83). New York: Cambridge University Press. [11]

Walker, E., Downey, G., and Bergman, A. (1989). The effects of parental psychopathology and maltreatment on child behavior: A test of the diathesis-stress model. *Child Development, 61,* 15–24. [15]

Walker, L. (1989). A longitudinal study of moral reasoning. *Child Development, 60,* 157–166. [12, 13]

Walker, L., and Taylor, J. (1991). Family interactions and the development of moral reasoning. *Child Development, 62,* 264–283. [12]

Walker, L. J. (1984). Sex differences in the development of moral reasoning: A critical review. *Child Development, 55,* 677–691. [13]

Waller, N., Kojetin, B., Bouchard, T., Lykken, D., and Tellegen, A. (1990). Attitudes and values: A study of twins reared apart and together. *Psychological Science, 1,* 138–142. [1]

Wallerstein, J. S., and Kelly, J. B. (1982). *Surviving the breakup: How children and parents cope with divorce*. New York: Basic Books. [10]

Walters, J. M., and Gardner, H. (1986). The theory of multiple intelligences: Some issues and answers. In R. K. Wagner and R. J. Sternberg (Eds.), *Practical intelligence* (pp. 163–182). New York: Cambridge University Press. [11]

Wara, D. W., Luzuriaga, K., Martin, N. L., Sullivan, J. L., and Bryson, Y. J. (1993). Maternal transmission and diagnosis of human immunodeficiency virus infection in the United States. *Annals of the New York Academy of Sciences, 693,* 14–19. [3]

Ward, M., and Carlson, E. (1995). Associations among adult attachment representations, maternal sensitivity, and infant-mother attachment in a sample of adolescent mothers. *Child Development, 66,* 69–79. [6]

Warren, A. R., and McCloskey, L. A. (1993). Pragmatics: Language in social contexts. In J. B. Gleason (Ed.), *The development of language* (pp. 195–237). New York: Macmillan. [7]

Warren, M. P. (1983). Physical and biological aspects of puberty. In J. Brooks-Gunn and A. C. Petersen (Eds.), *Girls at puberty* (pp. 3–28). New York: Plenum Press. [13]

Warren-Leubecker, A., and Bohannon, J. N. (1983). The effects of verbal feedback and listener type on the speech of preschool children. *Journal of Experimental Child Psychology, 35,* 540–548. [9]

Warton, P. M., and Goodnow, J. J. (1991). The nature of responsibility: Children's understanding of "your job." *Child Development, 62,* 156–165. [12]

Wasz-Hockert, O., Lind, J., Vuorenkoski, V., Partanen, T., and Valanne, E. (1968). *A spectrographic and auditory analysis*. Suffolk, Eng.: Lavenham Press. [4]

Waterman, A. S. (Ed.) (1985). *Identity in adolescence: Processes and contents. New directions for child development* (Vol. 30). San Francisco: Jossey-Bass. [14]

Waterman, A. S. (1992). Identity as an aspect of optimal psychological functioning. In G. R. Adams, T. P. Gullotta, and R. Montemayor (Eds.), *Adolescent identity formation* (pp. 50–72). Newbury Park, CA: Sage. [14]

Waters, E. (1978). The stability of individual differences in infant-mother attachment. *Child Development, 49,* 483–494. [6]

Waters, E., Kondo-Ikemura, K., and Richters, J. (1990). Learning to love: Milestones and mechanisms in attachment, identity and identification. In M. Gunnar and L. A. Sroufe (Eds.), *Minnesota Symposia in Child Psychology: Vol. 23. Self processes in development.* Hillsdale, NJ: Erlbaum. [8, 10]

Waters, E., Matas, L., and Sroufe, L. A. (1975). Infants' reactions to an approaching stranger: Description, validation, and functional significance of wariness. *Child Development, 46,* 348–356. [6]

Waters, E., and Sroufe, L. A. (1983). A developmental perspective on competence. *Developmental Review, 3,* 79–97. [1]

Waters, E., Wippman, J., and Sroufe, L. A. (1979). Attachment, positive affect, and competence in the peer group: Two studies in construct validation. *Child Development, 50,* 821–829. [8, 10]

Waters, H. S., and Adreassen, C. (1983). Children's use of memory strategies under instructions. In M. Pressley and J. R. Levin (Eds.), *Cognitive strategies: Developmental, educational, and treatment-related issues.* New York: Springer-Verlag. [9, 11]

Watson, J. B. (1928). *Psychological care of infant and child.* New York: Norton. [1, 2, 4]

Watson, J. S., Hayes, L. A., and Vietze, P. (1979). Bidimensional sorting in preschoolers with an instrumental learning task. *Child Development, 50,* 1178–1183. [9]

Watson, M. (1981). Development of social roles: A sequence of social-cognitive development. In K. Fischer (Ed.), *New directions for child development: No. 12. Cognitive development.* San Francisco: Jossey-Bass. [Pt. 5 Epilogue]

Watt, N., Anthony, E. J., Wynne, L., and Rolf, J. (1984). *Children at risk for schizophrenia: A longitudinal perspective.* Cambridge, Eng.: Cambridge University Press. [Pt. 7 Epilogue]

Weinberg, R. A. (1989). Intelligence and IQ: Landmark issues and great debates. *American Psychologist, 44,* 98–104. [11]

Weiner, B., Kun, A., and Benesh-Wiener, M. (1983). The development of mastery, emotion, and morality from an attributional perspective. In W. A. Collins (Ed.), *Minnesota Symposia on Child Psychology* (Vol. 13). Hillsdale, NJ: Erlbaum. [14]

Weiss, B., Dodge, K., Bates, J., and Pettit, G. (1992). Some consequences of early harsh discipline: Child aggression and

a maladaptive social information processing style. *Child Development, 63,* 1321–1335. [12]

Weiss, G., and Hechtman, L. (1986). *Hyperactive children grown up.* New York: Guilford Press. [15]

Weithorn, L. A., and Campbell, S. B. (1982). The competency of children and adolescents to make informed treatment decisions. *Child Development, 53,* 1589–1598. [13]

Wellman, H. M. (1983). Metamemory revisited. In M. T. H. Chi (Ed.), *Trends in memory development.* Basel, Switzerland: Karger. [11]

Wellman, H. M. (1986). A child's theory of mind: The development of conceptions of cognition. In S. R. Yussen (Ed.), *The growth of reflection.* New York: Academic Press. [11]

Wellman, H. M., Cross, D., and Bartsch, K. (1986). A meta-analysis of research on stage 4 object permanence: The A-not-B error. *Society for Research in Child Development Monographs, 51* (3, Serial No. 214). [5]

Wellman, H. M., and Gelman, S. A. (1992) Cognitive development: Foundational theories of core domains. In M. R. Rosenzweig and L. W. Porter (Eds.), *Annual review of psychology.* Palo Alto, CA: Annual Reviews. [9]

Wellman, H. M., Ritter, K., and Flavell, J. H. (1975). Deliberate memory behavior in the delayed reactions of very young children. *Developmental Psychology, 11,* 780–787. [9]

Wellman, H. M., Sommerville, S. C., and Haake, R. J. (1979). Development of search procedures in real-life spatial environments. *Developmental Psychology, 15,* 530–542. [9]

Wenar, C. (1976). Executive competence in toddlers: A prospective, observational study. *Genetic Psychology Monographs, 93,* 189–285. [8]

Wenar, C. (1990). *Developmental psychopathology* (2nd ed.). New York: McGraw-Hill. [15]

Wenar, C. (1994). *Developmental psychopathology* (3rd ed.). New York: McGraw-Hill. [15]

Wender, P., and Klein, D. (1986). *Mind, mood, and medicine: A guide to the new psychobiology.* New York: Farrar, Straus & Giroux. [10, 15]

Werner, E., and Smith, R. S. (1989). *Vulnerable but invisible: A longitudinal study of resilient children and youth.* New York: Adams, Bannister & Cox. [2]

Werner, E., and Smith, R. (1992). *Overcoming the odds: High risk children from birth to adulthood.* Ithaca, NY: Cornell University Press. [6, 15]

Werry, J. (1986). Biological factors. In H. Quay and J. Werry (Eds.), *Psychopathological disorders in childhood* (3rd ed., pp. 294–332). New York: Wiley. [15]

Werry, J., and Aman, M. (1984). Methylphenidate in hyperactive and enuretic children. In B. Shopin and L. Greenhill (Eds.), *The psychobiology of childhood* (pp. 183–195). Jamaica, NJ: Spectrum. [15]

White, B. L., Castle, P., and Held, R. (1964). Observations on the development of visually directed reaching. *Child Development, 35,* 349–364. [4]

White, K., and Kistner, J. (1992). The influence of teacher feedback on young children's peer preferences and perceptions. *Developmental Psychology, 28,* 933–940. [10]

White, R. (1959). Motivation reconsidered: The concept of competence. *Psychological Review, 66,* 297–333. [2, 10]

White, S. (1965). Evidence for a hierarchical arrangement of learning processes. In L. Lipsitt and C. Spiker (Eds.), *Advances in child development and behavior.* New York: Academic Press. [2]

Whitehurst, G. J. (1982). Language development. In B. B. Wolman (Ed.), *Handbook of developmental psychology.* Englewood Cliffs, NJ: Prentice-Hall. [7]

Whiting, B. B., and Edwards, C. P. (1988). *Children of different worlds.* Cambridge, MA: Harvard University Press. [2, 8, 10, 12, 14]

Whiting, B., and Whiting, J. (1975). *Children of six cultures: A psycho-cultural analysis.* Cambridge, MA: Harvard University Press. [2]

Wickens, D. D., and Wickens, C. A. (1940). A study of conditioning in the neonate. *Journal of Experimental Psychology, 26,* 94–102. [4]

Wiesenfeld, A., Malatesta, C., and DeLoach, L. (1981). Differential parental response to familiar and unfamiliar infant distress signals. *Infant Behavior and Development, 4,* 281–295. [4]

Wigdor, A. K., and Garner, W. R. (Eds.). (1982). *Ability testing: Uses, consequences, and controversies.* Washington, DC: National Academy Press. [11]

Wilson, M. (1989). Child development in the context of the Black extended family. *American Psychologist, 44,* 380–385. [2]

Wimmer, H., and Perner, J. (1983). Beliefs about beliefs: Representation and constraining function of wrong beliefs in young children's understanding of deception. *Cognition, 13,* 102–128. [9]

Winick, M. (1975). Effects of malnutrition on the maturing central nervous system. In W. J. Friedlander (Ed.), *Advances in neurology* (Vol. 13). New York: Raven Press. [3]

Winnicott, D. W. (1965). *The maturational processes and the facilitating environment.*

New York: International Universities Press. [6]

Wittmer, D., and Honig, A. (1988). Teacher re-creation of negative interactions with toddlers. *Early Child Development and Care, 33,* 77–88. [8]

Wolf, D. (1982). Understanding others: A longitudinal case study of the concept of independent agency. In G. Furman (Ed.), *Action and thought.* New York: Academic Press. [8]

Wolf, D. (1990). Being of several minds: Voices and versions of the self in early childhood. In D. Cicchetti and M. Beeghly (Eds.), *The self in transition.* Chicago: University of Chicago Press. [10, 12]

Wolff, P. H. (1969). The natural history of crying and other vocalization in early infancy. In B. M. Foss (Ed.), *Determinants of infant behavior* (Vol. IV). London, Eng.: Methuen. [4]

Wolff, P. H. (1987). *The development of behavioral states and the expression of emotions in early infancy: New proposals for investigation.* Chicago: University of Chicago Press. [4]

Wolkind, S., and Rutter, M. (1985). Sociocultural factors. In M. Rutter and L. Hersov (Eds.), *Child and adolescent psychiatry.* Oxford, Eng.: Blackwell. [2]

Wolley, J. D. (1991). Origin and truth: Young children's understanding of the relation between mental states and the physical world. Paper presented at the meeting of the Society for Research in Child Development, Seattle. [9]

Woollacott, M. H. (1987). Children's development of posture and balance control: Changes in motor coordination and sensory integration. In D. Gould and M. Weiss (Eds.), *Advances in pediatric sport sciences: Behavioral issues.* Champaign, IL: Human Kinetics Publishers. [4]

Woolley, J. D., and Wellman, H. M. (1990). Young children's understanding of realities, nonrealities, and appearances. *Child Development, 61,* 946–961. [9]

Worobey, J., and Blajda, V. (1989). Temperament ratings at 2 weeks, 2 months, and 1 year: Differential stability of activity and emotionality. *Developmental Psychology, 25,* 257–263. [6]

Worobey, J., and Lewis, M. (1989). Individual differences in the activity of young infants. *Developmental Psychology, 25,* 663–667. [6]

Wortman, C., and Loftus, E. (1992). *Psychology* (4th ed.). New York: McGraw-Hill. [7]

Wright, J. D. (1990). Homelessness is not healthy for children and other living things. *Child and Youth Services, 14,* 65–88. [2]

Wynn, K. (1990). Children's understanding of counting. *Cognition, 36,* 104–143. [9]

Yarrow, M. R., Scott, P., de Leeuw, L., and Heinig, C. (1962). Childrearing in families of working and nonworking mothers. *Sociometry, 25,* 122–140. [2]

Yates, P. D. (1987). A case of mistaken identity: Interethnic images in multicultural England. In G. Spindler and L. Spindler (Eds.), *Interpretative ethnography of education: At home and abroad* (pp. 195–218). Hillsdale, NJ: Erlbaum. [11]

Yonas, A., Cleaves, W., and Pettersen, L. (1978). Development of sensitivity to pictorial depth. *Science, 200,* 77–79. [4]

Yonas, A., and Granrud, C. E. (1985). Development of visual space perception in young infants. In J. Mehler and R. Fox (Eds.), *Neonate cognition: Beyond the blooming, buzzing confusion.* Hillsdale, NJ: Erlbaum. [4]

Yonas, A., and Hartman, B. (1993). Perceiving the affordance of contact in four- and five-month-old infants. *Child Development, 64,* 298–308. [4]

Yonas, A., and Owlsley, C. (1987). Development of visual space perception. In P. Salapatek and L. Cohen (Eds.), *Handbook of infant perception* (pp. 80–122). New York: Academic Press. [4]

Yonas, A., Petterson, L., Lockman, J. J., and Eisenberg, P. (1980, April). *The perception of impending collision in 3-month-old infants.* Paper presented at the International Conference on Infant Studies, New Haven. [4]

Yoshikawa, H. (1994). Prevention as cumulative protection: Effects of early family support and education on chronic delinquency and its risks. *Psychological Bulletin, 115,* 28–54. [15]

Younger, B. A. (1985). The segregation of items into categories by ten-month-old infants. *Child Development, 56,* 1574–1583. [5]

Younger, B. A. (1992). Developmental changes in infant categorization: The perception of correlations among facial features. *Child Development, 63,* 1526–1535. [5]

Younger, B. A., and Cohen, L. B. (1986). Developmental change in infants' perception of correlations among attributes. *Child Development, 57,* 803–815. [5]

Younger, B. A., and Gotlieb, S. (1988). Development of categorization skills: Changes in the nature or structure of infant form categories. *Developmental Psychology, 24,* 611–619. [5]

Youngblade, L., and Belsky, J. (1992). Parent-child antecedents of 5-year-olds' close friendships: A longitudinal analysis. *Developmental Psychology, 28,* 700–713. [10]

Youniss, J. (1980). *Parents and peers in social development: A Sullivan-Piaget perspective.* Chicago: University of Chicago Press. [12, 14]

Youniss, J. (1983). Social construction of adolescence by adolescents and parents. In H. Grotevant and C. Cooper (Eds.), *New directions for child development: Adolescent development in the family.* San Francisco: Jossey-Bass. [14]

Youniss, J., McLellan, J. A., and Strouse, D. (1994). "We're popular, but we're not snobs": Adolescents describe their crowds. In R. Montemayor, G. R. Adams, and T. P. Gullotta (Eds.), *Personal relationships during adolescence* (pp. 101–122). Thousand Oaks, CA: Sage. [14]

Zahn-Waxler, C., Kochanska, G., Krupnick, J., and McKnew, D. (1990). Patterns of guilt in children of depressed and well mothers. *Developmental Psychology, 26,* 51–59. [15]

Zahn-Waxler, C., Radke-Yarrow, M., Wagner, E., and Chapman, M. (1992). Development of concern for others. *Developmental Psychology, 28,* 126–136. [8, 10]

Zajonc, R., and Markus, G. (1975). Birth order and intellectual development. *Psychological Review, 82,* 74–88. [2]

Zaporozhets, A. V. (1965). The development of perception in the preschool child. *Monographs of the Society for Research in Child Development, 30* (Serial No. 100). [4]

Zaslow, M. J. (1989). Sex differences in children's response to parental divorce: 2. Samples, variables, ages, and sources. *American Journal of Orthopsychiatry, 59,* 118–141. [12]

Zeanah, C. H., Keener, M. A., Thomas, F., and Viera-Baher, C. C. (1987). Adolescent mother's perceptions of their infants before and after birth. *American Journal of Orthopsychiatry, 57,* 351–360. [6]

Zelazo, P. R. (1972). Smiling and vocalizing: A cognitive emphasis. *Merrill-Palmer Quarterly, 18,* 349–365. [6]

Zelazo, P. R. (1983). The development of walking: New findings and old assumptions. *Journal of Motor Behavior, 15,* 99–137. [4]

Zinsmeister, K. (1990, June). Growing up scared. *Atlantic,* pp. 49–66. [2]

Zoccolillo, M. (1993). Gender and the development of conduct disorder. *Development and Psychopathology, 5,* 65–78. [15]

Zukow, P. (1989). *Sibling interaction across cultures.* New York: Springer-Verlag. [12]

Zuckerman, B., and Bresnahan, K. (1991). Developmental and behavioral consequences of prenatal drug and alcohol exposure. *Pediatric Clinics of North America, 38*(6), 1387–1406. [3]

Acknowledgments

CHAPTER 1

Fig. 1.1: Waddington, C. H. (1957). *The strategy of the genes* (London: Allen & Unwin). In Bowlby, J. (1973). *Attachment & loss, volume II: Separation: Anxiety & anger.* Copyright © 1973 by The Tavistock Institute of Human Relations. Adapted by permission of BasicBooks, a division of HarperCollins Publishers, Inc.

CHAPTER 3

Figure 3.2: Adapted in part from Hall, E., Perlmutter, M., and Lamb, M. E. (1982). *Child psychology today.* Used by permission of McGraw-Hill, Inc. Adapted in part from Larsen, W. J. (1993). *Human embryology,* 6. © Churchill Livingstone, New York, 1993. Used by permission.

Figures 3.3 and 3.5: Shaffer, D. R. (1985). *Developmental psychology: Childhood and adolescence,* 2nd edition, 81, 84. Copyright © 1989, 1985 by Brooks/Cole Publishing Company, a division of Thomson Publishing, Inc., Pacific Grove, CA 93950. Adapted by permission of the publisher.

Figure 3.4: Hall, E., Perlmutter, M., and Lamb, M. E. (1982). *Child psychology today,* 80. Copyright 1982. Used by permission of McGraw-Hill, Inc.

Figure 3.6: Adapted from Moore, K. L., and Persand, T. V. N. (1989). *Before we are born,* 4th edition, 96. Used by permission of W. B. Saunders Company, Philadelphia and the authors.

Table 3.1: Rosenblith, J., and Sims-Knight, J. (1985). *In the beginning,* 24. Copyright ©1989, 1985 by Sage Publications, Inc. Used by permission.

Table 3.3: Apgar, V., Holaday, D. A., James, L. S., Weisbrot, I. M., and Berrien, C. (1958). Evaluation of the newborn infant – second report. *Journal of the American Medical Association, 168,* 1985–1988. Copyright 1958, American Medical Association. Used by permission.

CHAPTER 4

Figure 4.2: Sostek, A. M., and Anders, T. F. (1981). The biosocial importance and environmental sensitivity of infant sleepwake behaviors. In K. Bloom (ed.), *Prospective issues in infancy research.* Used by permission of Lawrence Erlbaum Associates, Inc., Publishers and the authors.

Figure 4.3: Adapted in part from Frankenburg, W. K., Dodds, J. Archer, P., Bresnick, B., et al. (1992). *Denver II training manual 1992.* Denver Developmental Materials, Denver, CO. Adapted in part from Shirley, M. M. (1933). *The first two years.* Institute of Child Welfare Monograph No. 7. Copyright 1933, renewed 1961. Reprinted by permission of University of Minnesota Press.

Figure 4.9: Maurer, D., and Salapatek, P. (1976). Developmental changes in the scanning of faces by young infants. *Child Development, 47,* 523–527. © The Society for Research in Child Development, Inc. Used by permission.

CHAPTER 5

Figure 5.2: Kellman, P. J., and Spelke, E. S. (1983). Perception of partly occluded objects in infancy. *Cognitive Psychology, 15,* 483–524. Used by permission of Academic Press and the authors.

Figure 5.3: Baillargeon, R. (1986). Representing the existence and the location of hidden objects: Object permanence in 6- and 8-month-old infants. *Cognition, 23,* 21–43. Used by permission of *Cognition* and Elsevier Science, Lausanne, Switzerland.

Figure 5.4: Cohen, L. B., and Younger, B. A. (1984). Infant perception of angular relations. *Infant Behavior and Development, 7,* 37–47. Used by permission of Ablex Publishing Corporation.

Figure 5.5: Starkey, P., and Cooper, R. G. (1980). Perception of number by human infants. *Science, 210,* (November), 1033–1035. Copyright 1980 American Association for the Advancement of Science. Used by permission of the American Association for the Advancement of Science and the authors.

Table 5.2: Bayley, N. (1969). Bayley scales of infant development. Copyright ©1969 by the Psychological Corporation. Reproduced by permission. All rights reserved.

Page 169: Piaget, J. (1962). *Plays, dreams, and imitation in childhood*, 63. Copyright © 1962 by W. W. Norton & Company, Inc. Used by permission.

CHAPTER 6

Figure 6.1: Brazelton, T. B., Koslowski, B., and Main, M. (1974). The origins of reciprocity: The early mother-input interaction. In M. Lewis and L. Rosenblum (eds.), *The effect of the infant on its caregiver* (New York: John Wiley & Sons). Used by permission of Michael Lewis and Leonard Rosenblum.

Figure 6.3: Emde, R., Gaensbauer, T., and Harmon, R. (1976). *Emotional expression in infancy.* Psychological Issues Monograph Series, *10*(2, Serial no. 37), 112. Copyright 1976 by International Universities Press, Inc. Used by permission.

Figure 6.4: Waters, E., Matas, L., and Sroufe, L. A. (1975). Infants' reactions to an approaching stranger: Description, validation, and functional significance of wariness. *Child Development, 46*, 348–356. © The Society for Research in Child Development, Inc. Used by permission.

Table 6.1: Ainsworth, M., Blehar, M., Waters, E., and Wall, S. (1978). *Patterns of attachment.* Adapted by permission of Lawrence Erlbaum Associates, Inc., Publishers, and Mary Ainsworth.

CHAPTER 7

Table 7.1: Brown, R. (1973). *A first language: The early stages.* Used by permission of Harvard University Press.

Page 280: Piaget, J. (1962). *Play, dreams, and imitation in childhood.* Translated by C. Gattegno and F. M. Hodgson. Used by permission of W. W. Norton & Company, Inc.

CHAPTER 8

Figure 8.A: Strassberg, Z., Dodge, K. A., Pettit, G. G., and Bates, J. E. (1994). Spanking in the home and children's subsequent aggression toward kindergarten peers. *Development and psychopathology, 6*, 445–461. Copyright © 1994 Cambridge University Press. Used by permission.

Table 8.1: Adapted in part from Belsky, J. (1988). Child maltreatment and the emergent family system. In K. Browne, C. Davies, and P. Stratton (eds.), *Early prediction and prevention of child abuse*, 291–302. Copyright © 1988 by John Wiley and Sons, Ltd. Used by permission of John Wiley and Sons, Ltd. Adapted in part from Cichetti, D., and Olson, K. (1990). The developmental psychopathology of child maltreatment. In M. Lewis and S. Miller (eds.), *Handbook of developmental psychopathology.* Adapted by permission of Plenum Publishing Corporation and the authors.

Page 302: Kierkegaard, S. (1938). From *Purity of heart* translated by Douglas V. Steere. Copyright 1938 by Harper & Brothers, renewed © 1966 by Douglas V. Steere. Used by permission of HarperCollins Publishers, Inc.

CHAPTER 9

Figure 9.4: Atkinson, R. C., and Shiffrin, R. M. (1968). Human memory: A proposed system and its control processes. In K. W. Spence and J. T. Spence (eds.), *The psychology of learning and motivation: Advances in research and theory*, Vol. 2. Used by permission of Academic Press and the authors.

Figure 9.5: Vurpillot, E. (1976). *The visual world of the child*, translated by W. E. C. Gilfram. Originally published in 1972. Reprinted by permission of International Universities Press.

Figure 9.6: Glucksberg, S. and Krauss, R. M. (1967). What do people say after they have learned how to talk? Studies of the development of referential communication. *Merrill-Palmer Quarterly, 13*, No. 4, 309–316. Used by permission of the Wayne State University Press and the authors.

Pages 328, 332: Chukovsky, K. (1941/1971). *From two to five*, translated and edited by M. Morton. Copyright © 1963 The Regents of the University of California. Used by permission.

Page 361: Ceci, S. J., and Bruck, M. (1993). Child witnesses: Translating research into policy. *Society for research in child development social policy report*, Vol. VII, no. 3. Used by permission of the Society for Research in Child Development.

CHAPTER 10

Figures 10A & 10B: Schweinhart, L. J., and Weikart, D. P. (1993). *Success by empowerment: The High/Scope Perry preschool study through age 27.* © High/Scope Educational Research Foundation, Ypsilanti, MI. Used by permission.

Table 10.1: Ruble, T. (1983). Sex stereotypes: Issue of change in the 1970's. *Sex Roles, 9*, 397–402. Used by permission of Plenum Publishing Corporation and the author.

Table 10.2: Clausen, J. (1968). Perspectives on childhood socialization. In J. Clausen (ed.), *Socialization and society* (Boston: Little, Brown & Company). Adapted by permission of the author.

Page 377: Mueller, E. and Lucas, T. (1975). A developmental analysis of peer interaction among toddlers. In M. Lewis and L. A. Rosenblum (eds.), *Friendship and peer relations* (New York: John Wiley & Sons). Used by permission of Michael Lewis and Leonard A. Rosenblum.

CHAPTER 11

Figure 11.3: Leary, W. E. (1988, June 22). Survey finds sharp drop in tooth decay. *New York Times*, A1. Copyright © 1988 by The New York Times Company. Used by permission.

Figure 11.5: Bruner, J. S., Olver, R. R., and Greenfield, P. M. (1966). *Studies in Cognitive Growth.* Copyright © 1966 by John Wiley & Sons, Inc. Used by permission of J. S. Bruner.

Figure 11.6: Bloom, B. S. (1964). *Stability and change in human characteristics.* Copyright © 1964. Published by John Wiley & Sons, Inc. Used by permission of the author.

Table 11.1: Gross, T. F. (1985). *Cognitive development.* Copyright © 1985 Brooks/Cole Publishing Company, a division of International Thomson Publishing Inc., Pacific Grove, CA 93950. Adapted by permission of the publisher.

Table 11.2: Flavell, J. H., Friedrichs, A. G., and Hoyt, J. D. (1970). Developmental changes in memorization processes. *Cognitive Psychology, 1*, 324–340. Used by permission of Academic Press and the authors.

Table 11.3: Bouchard, T. J., and McGue, M. (1981). Familial studies of intelligence: A review. *Science, 212*, 1055–1059. Copyright 1981 American Association for the Advancement of Science. Used by permission of the American Association for the Advancement of Science and the authors.

Page 414: McGhee, P. E. (1976). Children's appreciation of humor: A test of the cognitive congruency principle. *Child Development, 47*, 420–426. © The Society for Research in Child Development, Inc. Used by permission.

Pages 428–429: Paris, S. G. (1975). Integration and inference in children's comprehension and memory. In F. Restle, R. Shiffrin, J. Castellan, H. Lindman, and D. Pisoni (eds.), *Cog-

nitive theory, vol. 1. Used by permission of Lawrence Erlbaum Associates, Inc., Publishers and Scott Paris.

Page 439: Walters, J. M., and Gardner, H. (1986). The theory of multiple intelligences: Some issues and answers. In R. K. Wagner and R. J. Sternberg (eds.), *Practical intelligence.* Copyright 1986 by Cambridge University Press. Used by permission.

CHAPTER 12

Figure 12.1: Selman, R. (1980). *The growth of interpersonal understanding.* Adapted by permission of Academic Press and the author.

Figure 12.2: Dodge, K. A., Petit, G. S., McClaskey, C. L., and Brown, M. M. (1986). *Social competence in children.* Monographs of the Society for Research in Child Development, *51* (2, Serial no. 213). © The Society for Research in Child Development, Inc. Used by permission.

Table 12.1: Sroufe, A. L., Bennett, C., et al. (1993). The significance of gender boundaries in preadolescence: contemporary correlates and antecedents of boundary violation and maintenance. *Child Development, 64*(2), 455–466. © The Society for Research in Child Development. Used by permission.

Pages 456, 457: Selman, R. (1980). *The growth of interpersonal understanding,* 95, 175. Used by permission of Academic Press and the author.

CHAPTER 13

Figure 13.1: Grumbach, M. M., Grave, G. D., and Mayer, F. E. (1974). *Control of the Onset of Puberty.* Copyright © 1974 John Wiley & Sons, Inc.

Figures 13.2 & 13.3: Tanner, J. M. (1962). Growth at adolescence. Published by Charles C. Thomas, Publisher, Springfield, IL. Used by permission of Blackwell Scientific Publications Ltd.

Figure 13.4: Piaget, J., & Inhelder, B. (1958). *The growth of logical thinking: From childhood to adolescence.* Copyright © 1958 by Basic Books, Inc. Reprinted by permission of BasicBooks, a division of HarperCollins Publishers, Inc., and Routledge Kegan Paul Ltd.

Table 13.1: Tanner, J. M. (1962). *Growth at adolescence.* Adapted by permission of Blackwell Scientific Publications.

Table 13.2: Kohlberg, L. (1969). Stage and sequence: The cognitive-developmental approach to socialization. In D. A. Goslin (ed.), *Handbook of socialization theory and research.* Adapted by permission of David A. Goslin.

Pages 521: Inhelder, B. and Piaget, J. (1955/1958). *The growth of logical thinking: From childhood to adolescence.* Copyright © 1958 by Basic Books, Inc., a division of HarperCollins Publishers. Used by permission.

CHAPTER 14

Figure 14.1: Hayes, C. *Risking the future: Adolescent sexuality, pregnancy and childbearing,* Vol. 1. Copyright 1987 by the National Academy of Sciences. Adapted by permission of the National Academy Press, Washington, DC.

Figure 14.2: Costanzo, P. (1970). Conformity development as a function of self-blame. *Journal of Personality and Social Psychology, 14,* 368. Copyright © 1970 by the American Psychological Association. Used by permission.

Table 14.1: Damon, W. and Hart, D. (1988). *Self-understanding in childhood and adolescence.* Used by permission of Cambridge University Press and William Damon.

Table 14.2: Elkind, D. and Bowen, R. (1979). Imaginary audience behavior in children and adolescents. *Developmental Psychology, 15,* 40–41. Copyright © 1979 by the American Psychological Association. Used by permission of the American Psychological Association and the authors.

Table 14.3: Marcia, J. (1980). Identity in adolescence. In J. Adelson (ed.), *Handbook of adolescent psychology,* 159–187. Copyright © 1980. Used by permission of John Wiley & Sons, Inc.

Table 14.4: Selman, R. (1980). *The growth of interpersonal understanding.* Adapted by permission of Academic Press and the author.

Table 14.5: Dunphy, D. (1963). The social structure of urban adolescent peer groups. *Sociometry, 26,* 236. Adapted by permission of Beacon House, Inc.

Pages 546, 554: Selman, R. (1980). *The growth of interpersonal understanding,* 106. Used by permission of Academic Press and the author.

Page 549: Marcia, J. (1980). Identity in adolescence. In J. Adelson (ed.), *Handbook of adolescent psychology,* 159–187. Copyright © 1980. Used by permission of John Wiley & Sons, Inc.

CHAPTER 15

Figure 15.1: Zubin, J., and Spring, B. (1977). Vulnerability: A new view of schizophrenia. *Journal of Abnormal Psychology, 86,* 103–126. Copyright © 1977 by the American Psychological Association. Used by permission of the American Psychological Association and B. Spring.

Table 15.3: Tienari, P. L., Lahti, I., Sorri, A., Naarala, M., Moring, J., Kaleva, M., Wahlberg, K. E., and Wynne, L. (1990). Adopted away offspring of schizophrenics and controls. In L. Robins and M. Rutter (eds.), *Straight and devious pathways from childhood to adulthood.* Used by permission of Cambridge University Press and L. Robins.

Table 15.4: American Psychiatric Association (1994). *Diagnostic and statistical manual of mental disorders,* 4th edition. Adapted by permission of the American Psychiatric Association, Washington, DC.

Page 601: Wenar, C. (1990). *Developmental psychopathology,* 2nd edition. Copyright 1990. Adapted by permission of McGraw-Hill, Inc.

Page 607: Bruch, H. (1979). *The golden cage: The enigma of anorexia nervosa.* Copyright © 1978 by the President and Fellows of Harvard College. Used by permission of the Harvard University Press, Cambridge, MA.

PHOTO CREDITS

CHAPTER 1

Page 2, Philip Jon Bailey/Stock, Boston; p. 5: D. LaSota; p. 7, Suzanne Arms/The Image Works; p. 9, American Museum of Natural History; p. 10, *(left)* G. Ziesler/Peter Arnold, Inc.; *(center)* Stan Wayman/Photo Researchers; *(right)* C. Allan Morgan/Peter Arnold, Inc.; p. 11, Jacques Jangoux/Peter Arnold, Inc.; p. 12, Joe McNally; p. 15, *(left)* Jerry Howard/Stock, Boston; *(right)* Bob Daemmrich/The Image Works; p. 17, Anderson/Monkmeyer; p. 19, National Library of Medicine; p. 20, AP/Wide World; p. 23, Erik Hesse; p. 27, Hank Morgan/Rainbow; p. 29, Cliff Haac/Frank Porter Graham Child Development Center.

CHAPTER 2

Page 40, Owen Franken/Stock, Boston; p. 43, Culver Pictures; p. 44, Karen Kasmauski/Woodfin Camp & Assoc.; p. 46, Harlow Primate Laboratory/University of Wisconsin p. 48, Bob Busby/Photo Researchers; p. 49, Anthony Jalandoni/Monkmeyer; p. 51, Erika Stone; p. 53, Steve Starr/Stock, Boston; p. 54, Bob Daemmrich/The Image Works; p. 56, Byron/Monkmeyer; p. 65, Zinsmeister, 1990, The Atlantic Monthly; p. 62, Mimi Forsyth/Monkmeyer; p. 68, *(left)* Bruno J. Zehnder/Peter Arnold, Inc.; *(right)* Joseph Schuyler/Stock, Boston; p. 69, Lippman/UNICEF; p. 71, Paul Conklin/PhotoEdit.

CHAPTER 3

Page 76, C. Edelmann/La Villette/Photo Researchers; p. 78, David M. Grossman/Photo Researchers; p. 80, Joel Gordon; p. 88, Petit Format/Nestle/Science Scource/Photo Researchers; p. 90, *(above left)* Petit Format/Science Source/Photo Researchers; *(above right)* Petit Format/Nestle/Science Source/Photo Researchers; *(below left)* Petit Format/Nestle/Science Source/Photo Researchers; *(below right)* S. J. Allen/Daily Telegraph Colour Library/International Stock Photo; p. 94, David Hundley/The Stock Market; p. 96, *(above left)* John Maier/J. B. Pictures; p. 96, *(below)* National Clearinghouse for Alcohol Information; p. 99, Guy Gillette/Photo Researchers; p. 100, Joel Gordon; p. 102, Andrew Brilliant/The Picture Cube; p. 104, Paul Conklin/PhotoEdit; p. 106, Mimi Cotter/International Stock Photo; p. 108, William Thompson/The Picture Cube.

CHAPTER 4

Page 120, Laura Dwight/Peter Arnold, Inc.; p. 123, Tony Mendoza/The Picture Cube; p. 129, Elizabeth Crews; p. 130, Elizabeth Crews, p. 132, Sarah Putnam/The Picture Cube; p. 137, Terry E. Eiler/Stock, Boston; p. 138, From *Sensation and Perception*, 2nd edition, by E. Bruce Goldstein © 1984 by Wadsworth Inc. Used by permission of the publisher. p. 139, Julie O'Neil/The Picture Cube; p. 142, *(above)* Joseph Nettis/ Photo Researchers; *(below)* Ida Wyman/International Stock Photo; p. 151, Linda Albrizio/The Stock Market; p. 155, Elizabeth Crews.

CHAPTER 5

Page 160, Gabe Palmer/The Stock Market; p. 163, *(left)* G. W. Piccolo; p. 163, *(right)* Elizabeth Crews/Stock, Boston; p. 166, Suzanne Szasz/Photo Researchers; p. 169, Laura Dwight/Peter Arnold, Inc.; p. 170, Doug Goodman/Monkmeyer; p. 177, Carolyn Rovee-Collier/Rutgers University; p. 180, Dr. Joseph Fagan; p. 184, Rita Nannini/Photo Researchers; p. 185, L. Rourke/The Image Works; p. 189, Melissa Hayes English/Photo Researchers.

CHAPTER 6

Page 198, Michael Dwyer/Stock, Boston; p. 201, *(above)* M. Siluk/The Image Works; p. 201, *(below)* Erika Stone; p. 203, Elizabeth Crews/Stock, Boston, p. 207, Andrew Brilliant/The Picture Cube; p. 209, Jane Vaicunas; p. 211, Erika Stone/Peter Arnold, Inc.; p. 215, Innervisions; p. 217, Bruce Plotkin/The Image Works; p. 221, Erika Stone; p. 224, Burt Glinn/Magnum Photos; p. 228, Erika Stone; p. 230, Harlow Primate Laboratory/University of Wisconsin, Madison; p. 232, Ed Kashi; p. 234, Elizabeth Crews.

CHAPTER 7

Page 252, Scolney/Monkmeyer; p. 255, *(left)* Linda Benedict-Jones/The Picture Cube; *(right)* Elizabeth Hathon/The Stock Market; p. 256, Carolyn McKeone/Photo Researchers; p. 259, George Goodwin/Monkmeyer; p. 262, Tom Dunham; p. 263, Tom Dunham; p. 264, Sybil Shackman/Monkmeyer; p. 272, Carl Purcell/Photo Researchers; p. 276, Peter Glass/Monkmeyer; p. 278, Michal Heron/Monkmeyer; p. 281, Alan Carey/The Image Work; p. 282 Elizabeth Crews.

CHAPTER 8

Page 286, Bob Daemmrich/The Image Works; p. 289, Elizabeth Crews; p. 291, Elizabeth Crews/The Image Works; p. 292, J. Kramer/The Image Works; p. 294, Elizabeth Crews; p. 295, Shirley Zeiberg; p. 297, David Young-Wolff/PhotoEdit; p. 298, Elizabeth Crews; p. 299, Robert A. Isaacs/Photo Researchers; p. 301, Ellen B. Senisi; p. 302, Elizabeth Crews; p. 304, Dr. Mary J. Ward/Cornell University Medical College; p. 305, Dorothea Mooshake/Peter Arnold, Inc.; p. 307, Michal Heron/Woodfin Camp & Assoc.

CHAPTER 9

Page 326, Sonya Jacobs/The Stock Market; p. 328, Patrick Grace/Photo Researchers; p. 332, Herb Snitzer/Stock, Boston; p. 339, Laura Dwight; p. 343, Erika Stone; p. 344, Joseph Schuyler/Stock, Boston; p. 350, Steve Liss/Time Magazine; p. 355, Tony Freeman/PhotoEdit p. 358, Erika Stone; p. 360, Tom McCarthy/The Picture Cube.

CHAPTER 10

Page 364, Bob Daemmrich/Stock, Boston; p. 367, Frank Siteman/The Picture Cube; p. 369, Jeffry W. Myers/The Stock Market; p. 372, *(left)* George Goodwin/Monkmeyer; *(right)* Ken Karp; p. 374, Alan Carey/The Image Works; p. 378, Rameshwar Das/Monkmeyer; p. 380, Elizabeth Crews; p. 382, Erika Stone; p. 383, George Goodwin/Monkmeyer; p. 385, Elizabeth Crews; p. 388, Alice Kandell/Photo Researchers; p. 390, Spencer Grant/The Picture Cube; p. 391, Martha Cooper/Peter Arnold, Inc.; p. 392, Frank Siteman/The Picture Cube; p. 397, Tony Freeman/PhotoEdit.

CHAPTER 11

Page 412, Bob Daemmrich/Stock, Boston; p. 414, Lynn Johnson/Black Star; p. 416, George Goodwin/Monkmeyer; p. 420 Nancy Sheehan/The Picture Cube; p. 428, Elizabeth Crews; p. 430, Charles Gupton/Stock, Boston; p. 433, Sven Martson/Comstock; p. 435, Elizabeth Crews; p. 438, Maureen Fennelli/Comstock; p. 443, Bob Daemmrich/The Image Works.

CHAPTER 12

Page 452, Erika Stone/Peter Arnold, Inc.; p. 454, Naoki Okamoto/Black Star; p. 458, *(above)* Spencer Grant/The Picture Cube; *(below)* Erika Stone; p. 460, Nancy Sheehan/The Picture Cube; p. 462, *(left)* Grantpix/Monkmeyer; *(right)* Elizabeth Zuckerman/PhotoEdit; p. 463, Barbara Rios/ Photo Researchers; p. 466, *(left)* Michael Newman/PhotoEdit; *(right)* Catherine Karnow/Woodfin Camp & Assoc.; p. 467, Elizabeth Crews; p. 473, M. Nichols/The Picture Cube; p. 475, Mike Kagan/Monkmeyer; p. 479, Tony Freeman/PhotoEdit; p. 481, Milton Feinberg/The Picture Cube; p. 483, Elizabeth Crews; p. 485, Courtesy of L. Alan Sroufe.

CHAPTER 13

Page 502, Tony Freeman/PhotoEdit; p. 505, Bob Daemmrich/The Image Works; p. 506 Alice Kandell/Photo Researchers; p. 514, Richard Hutchings/Photo Researchers; p. 517, Rafael Macia/Photo Researchers; p. 518, The Bettmann Archive; p. 519, Michelle Bridwell/PhotoEdit; p. 524, J.H. Sullivan/Photo Researchers; p. 529, Jeffry W. Myers/Stock, Boston; p. 533, Paul Conklin/Monkmeyer; p. 535, Joel Gordon.

CHAPTER 14

Page 538, Bob Daemmrich/Stock, Boston; p. 541, Karin Rosenthal/Stock, Boston; p. 543, Martin Etter/AnthroPhoto; p. 547, Louis Fernandez/Black Star; p. 551, Joel Gordon; p. 560, top to bottom: Grant LeDuc/Monkmeyer; Momatiuk-Eastcott/Woodfin Camp & Assoc.; Renate Hiller/ Monkmeyer; Paul Conklin/Monkmeyer; Peter Vandermark/Stock, Boston; Rick Kopstein/Monkmeyer; p. 565, Peter Russell Clemens/International Stock Photo; p. 567 Billy E. Barnes/Stock, Boston; p. 569, Peter Arnold/Peter Arnold, Inc.; p. 571, Mimi Forsyth/Monkmeyer.

CHAPTER 15

Page 582, Bob Daemmrich/The Image Works; p. 591, NIH/Science Scource/Photo Researchers; p. 594, Mimi Forsyth/Monkmeyer; p. 596, Innervisions; p. 599, Mimi Forsyth/Monkmeyer; p. 603, George Zimbel/Monkmeyer; p. 607, Joel Gordon; p. 608, William Thompson/The Picture Cube.

Name Index

Subject Index